Thailand

China Williams

Aaron Anderson, Brett Atkinson, Tim Bewer,
Becca Blond, Virginia Jealous, Lisa Steer

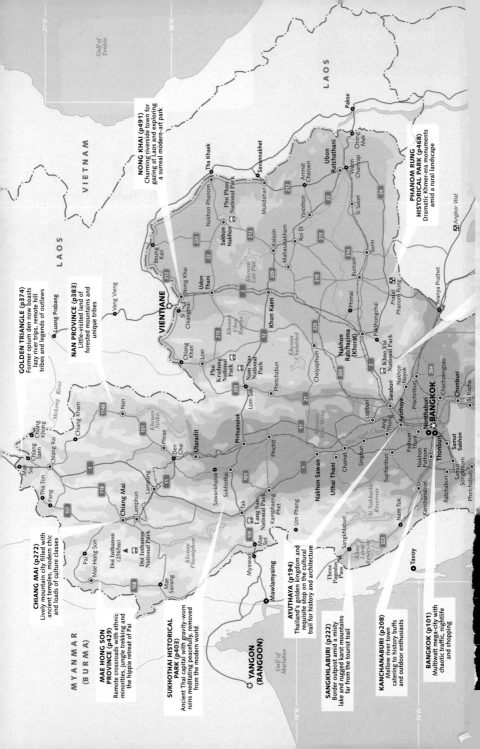

MYANMAR (BURMA)

LAOS

VIETNAM

Gulf of Tonkin

MAE HONG SON PROVINCE (p429)
Remote crossroads with ethnic minorities, jungle trekking and the hippie retreat of Pai

CHIANG MAI (p272)
Lively mountain city filled with ancient temples, modern chic and loads of culture classes

GOLDEN TRIANGLE (p374)
Former opium den now boasts lazy river trips, remote hill tribes and legends of outlaws

NAN PROVINCE (p383)
Little-visited land of forested mountains and unique tribes

NONG KHAI (p491)
Charming riverside town for gazing at Laos and exploring a surreal modern-art park

SUKHOTHAI HISTORICAL PARK (p403)
Ancient Thai capital with gravity-worn ruins meditating peacefully, removed from the modern world

SANGKHLABURI (p222)
Border outpost amid a misty lake and rugged karst mountains far from the tourist trail

AYUTHAYA (p194)
Thailand's golden kingdom and requisite stop on the cultural trail for history and architecture

KANCHANABURI (p208)
Mellow river town catering to history buffs and outdoor enthusiasts

BANGKOK (p101)
Multiwatt mega-city with chaotic traffic, nightlife and shopping

PHANOM RUNG HISTORICAL PARK (p468)
Dramatic Khmer-era monuments amid a rural landscape

☆ **YANGON (RANGOON)**

VIENTIANE

Gulf of Martaban

Anakor Wat

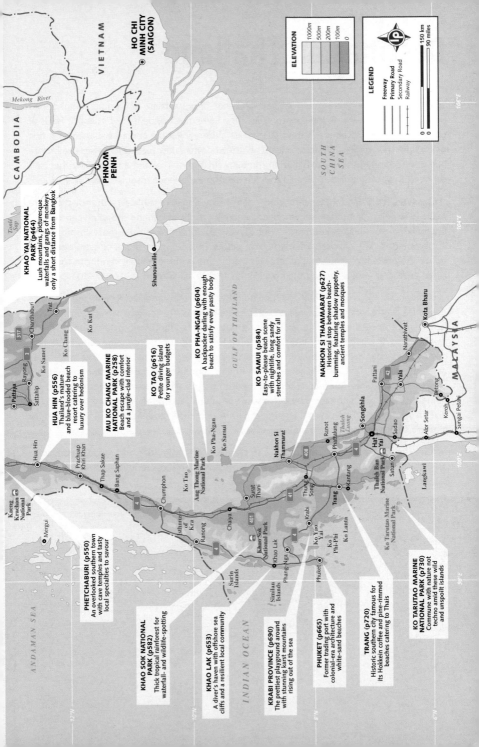

KHAO YAI NATIONAL PARK (p464)
Lush mountains, picturesque waterfalls and gangs of monkeys only a short distance from Bangkok

HUA HIN (p556)
Thailand's mature and blue-blooded beach resort catering to luxury over hedonism

MU KO CHANG MARINE NATIONAL PARK (p258)
Beach escape with comfort and a jungle-clad interior

KO TAO (p616)
Petite diving island for younger budgets

KO PHA-NGAN (p604)
A backpacker darling with enough beach to satisfy every pasty body

KO SAMUI (p584)
Easy-to-please beach scene with nightlife, long sandy stretches and comfort for all

NAKHON SI THAMMARAT (p627)
Historical stop between beach-bumming featuring shadow puppetry, ancient temples and mosques

PHETCHABURI (p550)
An overlooked southern town with cave temples and tasty local specialties to savour

KHAO SOK NATIONAL PARK (p582)
Thick tropical rainforest for waterfall- and wildlife-spotting

KHAO LAK (p653)
A diver's haven with offshore sea cliffs and a resilient local community

KRABI PROVINCE (p690)
The prettiest playground around with stunning karst mountains rising out of the sea

PHUKET (p665)
Former trading port with colonial-era architecture and white-sand beaches

TRANG (p720)
Historic southern city famous for its Hokkien coffee and pine-rimmed beaches catering to Thais

KO TARUTAO MARINE NATIONAL PARK (p730)
Commune with nature not techno amid these wild and unspoilt islands

LEGEND

Freeway
Primary Road
Secondary Road
Railway

0 ─── 150 km
0 ─── 90 miles

ELEVATION

1000m
500m
200m
100m
0

Destination Thailand

Thailand is often referred to as a golden land, not because there is precious metal buried underground but because the country gives off a certain lustre, be it the fertile rice fields of the central plains or the warm hospitality of its citizenry. People come here as miners: first perhaps for the uniquely Western concept of R&R. And while they toast themselves to a bronze hue on the sandy beaches, they find in the daily rhythm of Thailand a tranquillity that isn't confined to vacation time. Welcome to a life-altering experience disguised as a holiday.

This is an exotic land that is surprisingly convenient and accessible. First introductions are made in Bangkok, a modern behemoth of screaming traffic, gleaming shopping centres and international sensibilities interwoven with devout Buddhism. Even the most cosmopolitan Thais wouldn't dare choose a marriage date without consulting a monk or astrologer. And notice the protective amulets that all Thais – from the humble noodle vendor to the privileged aristocrat – wear around their necks: this is holy fashion.

Sitting upon the crown of the kingdom are misty mountains and Chiang Mai, the country's bohemian centre, where the unique and precise elements of Thai culture become a classroom, for cooking courses and language lessons, for curious visitors. Climbing into the mountain range are the stupa-studded peaks of Mae Hong Son and villages of post–Stone Age cultures. Sliding down the coastal tail are evergreen limestone islands filled with tall palms that angle over pearlescent sand. Thailand's beaches are stunning, hedonistic and mythic among residents of northern latitudes. But few visitors trudge into the northeast, a region better suited for homestays and teaching gigs than quick souvenir snapshots. In this scrappy region you can dive deep into the Thai psyche, emerging with a tolerance for searingly spicy food and a mastery of this strange tonal language.

Always eager to please, Thailand is a thick maze of ambiguities and incongruities with an irresistible combination of natural beauty, historic temples, renowned hospitality and robust cuisine.

JERRY ALEXANDER

Thailand's Cuisine

Fresh seafood served hot and tangy is just one of Thailand's culinary delights (p75)

Fire up your tastebuds at Bangkok's markets (p177)

A banana leaf filled with *klûay thâwt* (fried bananas; p78) makes a tasty streetside snack

Urban Scene

Discover Bangkok's growing contemporary art scene (p136)

VW-bars selling cocktails fuel the party scene on Th Khao San (p167), Bangkok

Shop till you drop with Bangkok's hip and wealthy at the Emporium Shopping Centre (p175)

Explore the labyrinth of handicrafts at Chiang Mai's Sunday Walking Street (p284)

DENNIS JOHNSON

Catch the cool river breezes from the back of the Chao Phraya Express (p140), Bangkok

RICHARD I'ANSON

Hone your bargaining skills at Bangkok's Chatuchak Weekend Market (p178)

Rock out at Bangkok's cool clubs and cosy beer halls (p169)

MICK ELMORE

Historic Architecture

Atop an extinct volcano, the Angkor-era temple complex of Phanom Rung (p468) is breathtaking

Angkorean ruins, steep cliffs and dreamy views are highlights of the Prasat Khao Phra Wihan National Park (p545)

The sacred Wat Phra That Doi Suthep (p325), near Chiang Mai

MANFRED GOTTSCHALK

Cycling around Sukhothai (p403) and Si Satchanalai-Chaliang (p408) Historical Parks is the perfect way to explore the ruins of Thailand's 'golden age' – including the impressive Wat Chang Lom (above; p409)

JULIET COOMBE

A serene Buddha figure sits among the ruins of Wat Mahathat, Sukhothai (p404)

TOM COCKREM

Traces of ancient cultures meld at Prang Sam Yot, Lopburi (p205)

Islands & Beaches

KAREN TRIST

Laze away days under a coconut palm on Ko Phi Phi's (p705) white-sand beaches

NOBORU KOMINE

Snorkel the sparkling waters of Ang Thong Marine National Park (p589), Ko Samui

RICH PROHASKA

Scale limestone cliffs above emerald green seas in Railay (p700)

Don your bathers and explore the turquoise wonders of Phuket's legendary coast (p660)

JULIET COOMBE

BRETT SHEARER

The beaches of Laem Hat Rin are home to Ko Pha-Ngan's legendary Full Moon parties (p615)

Cruise the crystal-clear waters of the Andaman Coast (p642) in a traditional long-tail boat

IZZET KERIBAR

Beachside dining lights up Hat Chaweng Noi, Ko Samui (p584)

ANDREW LUBRAN

National Parks

JOHN ELK III

Khao Yai National Park (p464) teems with rainforest giants and wildlife

OTHER HIGHLIGHTS

- Soak up the breathtaking views from the top of Thailand's highest peak, Doi Inthanon (p337).
- Find pure solitude in the rolling sandstone hills of Nam Nao National Park (p481).
- Explore one of Thailand's remotest corners, Phu Chong Nayoi National Park (p540).

JOE CUMMINGS

Savour the ancient rainforest and rugged mountains of Khao Sok National Park (p582)

See the sunrise over the coastal wilderness of Laem Son National Park (p649)

ROB BLAKERS

Contents

Regional Map Contents

Northern Chiang Mai p326

Southern Chiang Mai p335

Northern Thailand p341

Northeastern Thailand p453

Central Thailand p193

Bangkok pp114–15

Southeastern Thailand pp228–9

Upper Southern Gulf p549

Lower Southern Gulf p577

Andaman Coast p644

The Authors

CHINA WILLIAMS Coordinating Author, Bangkok & Central Thailand

China grew up in South Carolina, where the hot summers and casual chitchat prepared her well for a Thailand encounter. She first arrived in the kingdom as an English teacher in the small provincial capital of Surin and made periodic trips to Bangkok for visa business, navigating the city by public bus long before the Skytrain was anything more than a stalled eyesore. China now lives in the US, skipping across the Pacific twice a year to Thailand to update various guidebooks. Home is most recently in Montana with her husband, Matt, and baby son, Felix.

My Favourite Trip

I thought I had explored every corner of Thailand until I waved down that orange bus and trundled northwest of Kanchanaburi to Thong Pha Phum and then to Sangkhlaburi – delightful rain-soaked towns surrounded by shaggy green mountains. I climbed to a hilltop temple just in time to get stuck in a rain storm. Later I hopped aboard a sǎwngthǎew that shuttles between Thailand and Myanmar past simple bamboo huts and a mix of ethnicities that only a border can cultivate. The villages were poor, the clothes hand-me-downs inherited from the mountains beyond. I ate at a food shop on the Burmese side of Three Pagodas Pass, where the owner asked in broken English if I had a brother, meaning why was I travelling alone. All the motorcycle taxis wanted to take me somewhere, where I'm not sure, but I was the only potential customer and thus a minor celebrity.

O Three Pagodas Pass
O Sangkhlaburi
O Thong Pha Phum
O Kanchanaburi

AARON ANDERSON & BECCA BLOND Andaman Coast & Lower Southern Gulf

Despite arriving in the midst of a coup and leaving in a flood, Becca and Aaron managed to have a spectacular time exploring southern Thailand's islands, beaches and national parks for this guide. Between interviewing tsunami victims for Lonely Planet TV in Khao Lak and learning to surf in Phuket, the engaged couple, and author team, never had a dull moment. This was Becca's third trip to Thailand and the second time she's come to research this title; it was Aaron's first trip to Asia. Becca and Aaron spend most of the year traversing the globe for Lonely Planet.

LONELY PLANET AUTHORS

Why is our travel information the best in the world? It's simple: our authors are independent, dedicated travellers. They don't research using just the internet or phone, and they don't take freebies in exchange for positive coverage. They travel widely, to all the popular spots and off the beaten track. They personally visit thousands of hotels, restaurants, cafés, bars, galleries, palaces, museums and more – and they take pride in getting all the details right, and telling it how it is. Think you can do it? Find out how at lonelyplanet.com.

BRETT ATKINSON   Southeastern Thailand & Upper Southern Gulf

Brett first travelled to Thailand in 1991 and since then has returned several times to explore the country using the world's most diverse and idiosyncratic network of public transport. He's learnt the hard way to keep his knees tucked in when crossing Bangkok on a motorcycle taxi during rush hour, met loads of friendly locals on crowded săwngthăew, and overcome the transportation challenge of exploring Ko Chang's outer islands during the wet season. When he's not working for Lonely Planet, Brett writes about travel, sport, and the media, and shares a house in Auckland with Carol and a crazy Siamese cat called Havoc.

TIM BEWER   Northeastern Thailand

While growing up, Tim didn't travel much except for the obligatory pilgrimage to Disney World and an annual summer week at the lake. He's spent most of his adult life making up for this, and has since visited over 50 countries, including most in Southeast Asia. When Lonely Planet asked him to return to Thailand, he said 'Isan, please', as this is, in his opinion, far and away the most fascinating part of the country; his most recent visit only reinforced this belief. When not shouldering a backpack, he lives in Minneapolis, Minnesota. Someday, if he can ever find the time, he will finish his novel.

VIRGINIA JEALOUS   Surin & Similan Islands

Virginia has travelled through, lived in, worked in and written about national parks in Australia and Southeast Asia since the 1980s. Various roles as tour guide, tour-guide trainer, bushwalker, supporter of locally owned tourism projects and drinker-of-sunset-cocktails-in-lovely-places have given her strong opinions about tourism in protected areas. A birder from way back, Virginia was thrilled to visit the Surin and Similan Islands and to finally tick off her life-list the eccentric-looking Nicobar pigeon, a bird that eluded her on the Indian side of the Andaman Sea.

LISA STEER   Chiang Mai & Northern Provinces

Realising early on that making motor parts in a London workshop wasn't the life for her, Lisa headed to Southeast Asia hoping for an epiphany. Getting so hooked on all things Thai and Indonesian she went back to university to study their cultures, religions, politics and languages. Returning to the region for a few years, she wrote a couple of dissertations, did a stint as a UN election observer and finally became a travel-guide writer. Romance led her to Paris, and work to London, where she had a glam time at *Elle Decoration* magazine. But high heels were traded in for monsoon-season welly boots when Thailand beckoned again.

CONTRIBUTING AUTHORS

Dr Trish Batchelor wrote the Health chapter. She is a general practitioner and travel medicine specialist who is currently the Medical Director of the Travel Doctor clinic in Canberra, as well as a Medical Advisor to the Travel Doctor New Zealand clinics. She previously worked at the CIWEC Clinic in Nepal and has a special interest in the impact of tourism on host countries. She has travelled extensively throughout Southeast and East Asia.

Joe Cummings was born in New Orleans and developed an attraction to seedy, tropical ports at a young age. An interest in Buddhism and Southeast Asian politics led him to Bangkok, where he took up residence in an old wooden house on a canal and began exploring the provinces in his spare time. He later delved more deeply into the country as Lonely Planet's *Thailand* and *Bangkok* author through the 1980s, '90s and '00s. When he's not testing mattresses and slurping *tôm yam kûng* for Lonely Planet, Joe dabbles in Thai and foreign film production as a location consultant, script reader/translator and occasional actor.

Joel Gershon applied for a newspaper job in Bangkok on a whim and got it. Joel, a life-long Brooklynite, quickly packed up his life after he was told to arrive within one week. He has been living and working as a print and broadcast journalist there ever since. He also teaches journalism at a top university and has experienced many Asian adventures. Visit www.joelgershon.com for more info.

Getting Started

Most people find travel in Thailand to be relatively easy and economical. Of course, a little preparation will go a long way towards making your trip hassle-free and fun.

WHEN TO GO

The best time to visit most of Thailand is between November and February, primarily because it rains the least and is not too hot during these months. This period is also Thailand's main season for both national and regional festivals.

If you plan to focus on the mountains of the northern provinces, the hot season (March to May) and early rainy season (June to July) are not bad either, as temperatures are moderate at higher elevations. Haze from the burning-off of agricultural fields during these months, however, does obscure visibility in the north. Northeastern and central Thailand, on the other hand, are best avoided from March to May, when temperatures may climb over 40°C during the day and aren't much lower at night. Because temperatures are more even year-round in the south (because it's closer to the equator), the beaches and islands of southern Thailand are a good choice for respite when the rest of Thailand is miserably hot.

Thailand's peak – and we mean peak – tourist season runs from November to late March, with secondary peaks in July and August. If your main objective is to avoid crowds and to take advantage of discounted rooms and low-season rates, you should consider travelling during the least crowded months (typically April to June, September and October).

See Climate Charts (pp739–40) for more information.

COSTS & MONEY

Thailand is an inexpensive country to visit by almost any standards. Those on a budget should be able to get by on about 500B per day outside Bangkok and the major beach towns and islands. This amount covers basic food, guesthouse accommodation and local transport but excludes all-night beer binges, tours, long-distance transport or vehicle hire. Travellers with more money to spend will find that for around 600B to 1000B per day, life can be quite comfortable.

In Bangkok there's almost no limit to the amount you *could* spend. Because there are so many hotel options, Bangkok is a good place to splurge for recovery from a long flight or as a reward for reentering 'civilisation'. For under US$100 you can get a river-view room with all the starred trimmings; try finding that in London or New York. In the provinces, guesthouses tend to be better value than the midrange hotels (which are rarely well maintained). Guesthouses also have a built-in community of travellers and lots of tale swapping.

ATMs are widespread and are the easiest ways to get Thai baht. Have a supply of US dollars in cash on hand, just in case. Credit cards are accepted in big cities and resort hotels but not in family-run guesthouses or restaurants.

HOW MUCH?

1st-class bus, Bangkok to Surat Thani 450B

Beach bungalow on Ko Pha-Ngan 300B

One-day Thai cooking course, Chiang Mai 800–990B

National park admission 400B

Dinner for two at a mid-range restaurant 300B

See also Lonely Planet Index, inside front cover.

TRAVEL LITERATURE

Beyond the girlie-bar genre of literature, pickings are slim for English readers looking for travelling paperbacks. Here are a few standouts.

Sightseeing (2005) is a debut collection of short stories by Rattawut Lapcharoensap that hops between Thai households and tourist cafés. The stories give visitors a 'sightseeing' tour of Thai life and coming-of-age moments.

TOP 10 THAILAND

TOP TENS

One of the best ways to get ready for a Thailand tour is to start dreaming about this faraway land, and here are a few memorable (and unstereotypical) highlights:

SCENERY

1 Bangkok's skyscrapers viewed from a rooftop bar
2 Monks making their morning alms route
3 Karst mountains of Ao Phang-Nga
4 Jewel-coloured waters of Ko Phi-Phi
5 A temple fair
6 Thais swimming fully clothed in the ocean

7 A water buffalo and farmer ploughing a field
8 A motorcycle carrying a family of four and groceries
9 Construction workers wrapped up like mummies
10 Freshly powdered babies wearing small amulets

SOUNDS

1 Ice-cream jingle – a repetitive, tinny tune played by the ice-cream sǎamláws
2 Amplifiers – as a culture that disapproves of speaking loudly, Thailand blasts noise from karaoke machines through official loud-speakers
3 Roosters – it is a myth that these creatures only announce the dawn
4 *Túk-kae* and *jîng-jòk*– these reptiles make up the nightly serenade of rural Thailand
5 Cell-phone ring tones – pop hits, cat's meow; even proper Thai grandmas have hip ring tones

6 Car Horns – used like a blinker with frequency and enthusiasm
7 Bob Marley tunes – a beach bar is incomplete without 'No Woman No Cry'
8 *Sôm-tam* music – the rhythmic pounding of the mortar and pestle mixing the ingredients together
9 Two-stroke engines – the most ubiquitous and talkative machine on the road
10 'Hey you' – the favourite tourist pitch of hawkers and touts

SMELLS

1 Rice cooking in the morning
2 Jasmine garlands for sale at the temples and shrines
3 Frangipani trees
4 Fish sauce
5 Chilli-laden smoke from a street-stall wok

6 *Kài yâang* (grilled chicken)
7 Burning joss sticks
8 Diesel fuel
9 Sewer stench
10 Your sweat-stained clothes

DON'T LEAVE HOME WITHOUT...

Pack light wash-and-wear clothes, plus a sweater (pullover) or light jacket for chilly evenings and mornings in northern Thailand or air-con places. Slip-on shoes or sandals are better than lace-up boots. Laundry is cheap in Thailand, so don't lug your whole wardrobe around the country.

You can buy toothpaste, soap and most other toiletries cheaply almost anywhere in Thailand. Tampons can be difficult to find outside of a few expat-oriented shops in Bangkok. Thai deodorants aren't as potent at fighting sweaty stink as antiperspirants from home. See p772 for a list of recommended medical items.

Other handy items include: a small torch (flashlight), sarong (dries better than a towel), waterproof money/passport container (for swimming outings) and sunscreen (high SPFs are not widely available outside of big cities).

Be sure to check government travel advisories for Thailand before you leave. See p741 for general security issues.

Canadian poet Karen Connelly realistically yet poetically chronicles a year of small-town living in northern Thailand in *The Dream of a Thousand Lives: A Sojourn in Thailand* (2001).

Thailand Confidential (2005), by ex–*Rolling Stone* correspondent Jerry Hopkins, weaves an exposé of everything expats and visitors love about Thailand and much they don't, and thus makes an excellent read for newcomers.

On the surface, *Bangkok 8* (2004), by John Burdett, is a page-turning whodunnit, but the lead character, a Thai-Westerner cop, provides an excellent conduit towards understanding Thailand's interpretation of Buddhism.

Very Thai (2005), by Philip Cornwel-Smith, is a pop-culture encyclopaedia, filled with colourful essays about everyday Thailand, from the country's fascination with uniforms to household shrines. As a hardcover, it isn't very portable but it does answer a lot of those first-arrival questions.

INTERNET RESOURCES

Lonely Planet (www.lonelyplanet.com) Country-specific information as well as reader information exchange on the Thorn Tree forum.

Thai Students Online (www.thaistudents.com) Sriwittayapaknam School in Samut Prakan maintains the country's largest and most informative website.

Thailand Blogs (www.thai-blogs.com) Stories about culture, language and small-town travel are posted by various expat and Thai contributors.

Thailand Daily (www.thailanddaily.com) Part of World News Network, offering a thorough digest of Thailand-related news in English.

ThaiVisa.com (www.thaivisa.com) Aside from the extensive, impartial info on visas for Thailand, you'll find plenty of travel-related material, news alerts and a helpful forum for both visitors and expats.

Tourism Authority of Thailand (www.tourismthailand.org) Contains a province guide, press releases, Thai Authority of Thailand (TAT) contact information and planning hints.

Itineraries
CLASSIC ROUTES

JUST THE HIGHLIGHTS
Two Weeks / Bangkok to Bangkok

Even if you're only doing a Thailand 'pop-in', you've still got lots of sightseeing choices thanks to the affordability of domestic flights. Start off in **Bangkok** (p101) and then head off to the tropical sea breezes of either **Ko Samui** (p578) or **Phuket** (p660). If you need a more bohemian setting, hop over to **Ko Pha-Ngan** (p604) from Samui or **Ko Yao** (p689) from Phuket. Thailand's popular beach destinations are quieter, and some say better, during the low season but the near-constant rain can be a vacation damper. In general, the Andaman gets more rain than the Gulf coast, so be prepared to hop across the peninsula. If a multiday soaker is in the works, check out the beaches of **Ko Samet** (p243) or **Ko Chang** (p257) on the Southeastern Gulf, which tends to get less rain than the peninsula.

Once you've tired of sand between your toes, fly up to **Chiang Mai** (p272) for a Thai cooking class and temple wanderings. Hike up to the top of **Doi Suthep** (p325) to a popular religious pilgrimage site. Rent a car or motorcycle to explore the mountains and villages around Chiang Mai, including **Chiang Dao** (p328) and **Doi Ang Khang** (p330).

Before buzzing back to Bangkok to spend your last baht, stop at **Sukhothai** (p402), a former ancient capital with picturesque temple ruins.

Bangkok to Ko Samui or Phuket by plane. Ferry to Ko Pha-Ngan or Ko Yao. Fly, train or bus to Chiang Mai. Bus to Doi Suthep, Chiang Dao and Doi Ang Khang. Bus to Sukhothai.

Doi Ang Khang

Chiang Dao

Doi Suthep

Chiang Mai

Sukhothai

BANGKOK

Ko Samet
Ko Chang

Ko Pha-Ngan
Ko Samui

Phuket
Ko Yao

GRAND CIRCUIT
One Month / Bangkok to Bangkok

If you've got a month to 'do' Thailand, spend a few days in **Bangkok** (p101; or leave it till last), then take a slow ride north with a stop in the former ancient capital of **Ayuthaya** (p194) and the monkey capital **Lopburi** (p203). Visit more historic temple ruins in **Sukhothai** (p402) and then continue to **Chiang Mai** (p274), the cultural capital of the north. For more intensive immersion in the north, see the Remote North trip (p25).

You'll need to do an overnight, long-haul bus ride to dip your toes into the northeast region known as Isan. **Nakhon Ratchasima** (Khorat; p455) is a good landing point with easy access to **Phimai** (p461), which has one of Thailand's most impressive Angkor-period temple complexes, and **Khao Yai National Park** (p464), a forest filled with waterfalls, monkeys and, if you're lucky, a python.

Slide down the Thai-Malay Peninsula to spend the last week of your trip kicking back on Thailand's famous islands. The classic stops include the gulf coast islands of upscale **Ko Samui** (p584), low-key **Ko Pha-Ngan** (p604) or the budget dive scene of **Ko Tao** (p578).

Hop over to the Andaman coast to see those postcard limestone mountains jutting out of the tropical ocean. **Phuket** (p660) and **Ko Phi-Phi** (p705) compete for the bulk of high-end tourists, while **Krabi** (p691) is a favourite for rock climbers.

Train from Bangkok to Ayuthaya, Lopburi and Sukhothai. Bus to Chiang Mai. Bus to Nakhon Ratchasima and Phimai. Train to Surat Thani, jumping-off point for the Ko Samui archipelago, or fly direct to Ko Samui or Phuket. Bus across the peninsula to Krabi. Ferry to Ko Phi-Phi. Bus back to Bangkok.

BEACH BUMMING

Three Weeks / Surat Thani to Khao Lak

Southern Thailand has culture that has been spiced by ancient traders from China, India and Arabia. It makes a perfect stop for mixing up your beach fun. Hop down to the port town of **Surat Thani** (p578), the launching point to the string of Gulf islands: **Ko Samui** (p584), **Ko Pha-Ngan** (p604) and **Ko Tao** (p578). Or make a side trip west to **Khao Sok National Park** (p582), one of Thailand's most important rainforests.

Further down the Thai-Malay Peninsula, visit **Nakhon Si Thammarat** (p627), the cultural capital of the deep south. Head to **Songkhla** (p631) for seafood and Thai-style beachcombing. Saunter across the peninsula to **Satun** (p726), the departure point for boats to the **Ko Tarutao Marine National Park** (p730).

The Andaman celebrities of **Krabi** (p691), **Ko Phi-Phi** (p705) and **Phuket** (p660) are lined up in a row. But if you need more solitude, check out **Ko Lanta** (p714) or **Ko Yao** (p660).

Pay your respects to the tsunami-recovering beach at **Khao Lak/Lamru National Park** (p653), where whale-sized boulders decorate a turquoise bay. Then hop over to the **Similan Islands Marine National Park** (p655) for some of Thailand's best diving.

Train from Bangkok to Surat Thani. Boat to the islands. Bus to Khao Sok. Bus to Nakhon Si Thammarat, Songkhla and Satun. Boat to Ko Tarutao Marine National Park. Bus to Krabi. Boat to the islands. Bus to Phuket and Khao Lak. Boat to Similan Islands. Bus back to Bangkok.

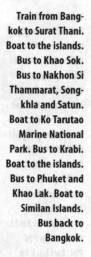

ROADS LESS TRAVELLED

REMOTE NORTH
Two Weeks / Chiang Mai to Nong Khai

Misty mountains and a mix of ethnic hill-tribe villages continue to attract trekkers and ethno-tourists to the northern apex of Thailand. From **Chiang Mai** (p274) wander outside of the city to **Chiang Dao** (p328) for a spooky cave walk or hike through the jungle. Then hop over to **Chiang Rai** (p350), where ecotreks visit hill-tribe villages. Catch a ride to **Mae Salong** (p361), a Yunnanese mountaintop settlement. From Mae Salong you can follow a network of roads high along narrow mountain ridges all the way to **Doi Tung** (p368), in the infamous Golden Triangle area where opium poppy was once grown, and then on to **Mae Sai** (p365), a border town with Myanmar. Follow the border to **Chiang Saen** (p371), where boats navigate the Mekong River all the way to China. You can head downstream to **Chiang Khong** (p375) and loop back to Chiang Rai. Catch an overnight bus to **Nan** (p383), a remote provincial capital surrounded by hill-tribe villages not found in other parts of northern Thailand.

Drop south to **Phitsanulok** (p393), a charming market town and transfer point to **Thung Salaeng Luang National Park** (p401). Keep heading east to **Loei Province** (p501) to catch the spirit festival at **Dan Sai** (p505). Continue northeast to **Chiang Khan** (p507), a mellow riverside village, and the Mekong darling of **Nong Khai** (p491), a gateway to Laos, and take an overnight train ride back to Bangkok. You can also connect this route with Mekong River trip (p27).

Bus from Chiang Mai to Chiang Dao and Chiang Rai. Bus to Mae Salong, Doi Tung, Mae Sai and Chiang Saen. Boat to Chiang Khong. Bus to Chiang Rai, Nan and Phitsanulok. Bus to Thung Salaeng Luang on to Loei and then to Dan Sai. Bus to Chiang Khan to Nong Khai. Train to Bangkok.

TAILORED TRIPS

MOUNTAIN SCRAMBLE

Climb into the bosom of lush mountains and ethnic minority villages that cling to the border between Thailand and Myanmar. Because these areas are fairly remote, they offer many of the same outdoor activities as Chiang Mai and Chiang Rai but with fewer visitors. Due west of Bangkok is **Kanchanaburi** (p207), a popular base for soft adventures into the jungle and the sight of the WWII 'Bridge over the River Kwai'. Continue to remote **Sangkhlaburi** (p222), with its Mon community, and **Three Pagodas Pass** (p224), where you can visit Myanmar for a day at a busy border market.

Continue north to **Um Phang** (p424), famous for its pristine waterfalls, white-water rapids and trekking adventures to Karen villages rarely visited by foreigners. You can do a multiday hike between Um Phang and Sangkhlaburi or bus from Kanchanaburi to Um Phang.

Take the high and winding 'Death Highway' north to **Mae Sot** (p417), a cross-pollinated town of Karen, Burmese and Thai residents. Because of violence on the Myanmar border, Mae Sot and surrounding villages provide refugee camps to displaced Burmese nationals. Follow the backroads to the trekking towns of **Mae Sariang** (p429) and **Mae Hong Son** (p429). Next up is **Pai** (p445), a hippie outpost with lots of live music and rural strolls. Descend out of the winding mountain route into urban Chiang Mai. From here you can tack on the Remote North trip (see p25).

ANCIENT ARCHITECTURE

This trip takes in several former royal capitals and one-time outposts of the Angkor empire, many of which are designated UNESCO World Heritage Sites. Start at the former ancient capital of **Ayuthaya** (p194) and then continue to **Lopburi** (p203), one of Thailand's oldest towns and former Angkor centre and later an Ayuthayan capital in exile. Continue north to **Sukhothai** (p402), which is considered the first Thai kingdom. Nearby Sukhothai-era ruins can be found in **Kamphaeng Phet** (p411), an historic walled city, and **Si Satchanalai-Chaliang** (p408), an ancient pottery-making centre.

Take an overnight bus to **Nakhon Ratchasima** (Khorat; p456), a good launching point to the Angkor-era ruins at **Phimai** (p461). Follow the Angkor trail east to Buriram Province where an extinct volcano is topped by **Prasat Hin Khao Phanom Rung** (p468), the most important and visually impressive Angkorean temple site in Thailand. It's a short jaunt to **Prasat Meuang Tam** (p470) – known for its L-shaped lily ponds – and smaller Angkorean sites.

Further south visit **Khao Phra Wihan** (p545), dramatically perched on a 600m-high cliff, over the Cambodian border from Surin Province.

MEKONG RIVER

The Mekong River, the lifeblood of Southeast Asia, defines the northern and northeastern border of the country. Alongside the fertile river, villages and towns exchange cultures and peoples with Laos. This is most pronounced in the northeastern region known as Isan.

Start in the charming riverside town of **Nong Khai** (p491), a rock-skipping throw from Laos. This is one of the most popular border-crossing points into Laos. If the pace here is too fast, backtrack along the river road to little-visited **Sangkhom** (p499). Then pick up the river road heading east as it curves around the tip of Thailand to tidy **Nakhon Phanom** (p510) and sleepy **That Phanom** (p513), both sporting vestiges of Lao-French architecture. Foreigners are few in these parts, making for a perfect tourist-trail buster. **Mukdahan** (p528) is another gateway to Laos and entertains visitors with an Indochinese market. For a little urban Isan, check out **Ubon Ratchathani** (p532), which puts you on the train route back to Bangkok or positions you for the Ancient Architecture trip (opposite) in reverse. At this point the river dives into the southern tip of Laos, through Cambodia and Vietnam to empty into the South China Sea.

Sangkhom ○   ○ Nong Khai
○ Nakhon Phanom
○ That Phanom
○ Mukdahan
Ubon Ratchathani ○

THAILAND FOR KIDS

This circuit is designed to offer children plenty to see and do without the need for marathon travel. Bangkok is as hyperactive as your average toddler and has enough attractions to last kids a week. Get your requisite animal watching at **Dusit Zoo** (p145) and **Queen Saovabha Memorial Institute** (p137), where deadly snakes are milked daily to make antivenom. On the outskirts of Bangkok you'll find culture and history bundled into a walkable, climbable form at **Muang Boran** (p190) in nearby Samut Prakan.

A half-day's train ride will deliver you to **Lopburi** (p203), Thailand's monkey capital and an extraordinary annual festival in which the town provides a banquet feast for the creatures. Further northeast, **Surin** celebrates an annual elephant round-up with parades, mock battles and lots of photo opportunities.

If your visit doesn't coincide with these festivals, take the train to **Kanchanaburi** (p207), a centre for jungle elephant rides as well as historic attractions. Outside of town take the tykes along the scenic trails following the seven-tiered waterfall at **Erawan National Park** (p217) or pet the tigers at the **Tiger Temple** (p218).

End the trip with a relaxing stay at the beachside resort of **Hua Hin** (p556), whose advantages include relatively calm waters, plenty of restaurant variety and pony rides on the beach.

Erawan National Park 🔲   ○ Lopburi   ○ Surin
Kanchanaburi ○   ○ Bangkok &
   Samut Prakan
   ○ Hua Hin

Snapshot

Since the bloodless, 'smooth as silk' military coup d'etat on 19 September 2006, the political situation in Thailand has been most intriguing. After assuming power, the leaders of the coup promptly handed power to an interim government, approved of by King Bhumibol Adulyadej. The new leaders have pledged to leave in early 2008 after a new constitution is drawn up and democratic elections take place.

This stunning turn of political events started brewing after the former ruling political party, Thai Rak Thai, won by a huge margin in the February 2005 elections. Then prime minister, Thaksin Shinawatra, arrogantly wielded his mandate and personal agenda against anyone standing in his way – the press, political opponents, and, many have speculated, the king. A period of protest followed, particularly in Bangkok, as influential people in politics, academia and the press began to hit back, creating visible, though peaceful, unrest in the streets.

Rumours of a coup flew around for months before it happened, so it wasn't a huge surprise. After some initial fears of chaos, Thais soon embraced the new government with relief and a sense of humour. This was far from the societal collapse many foreigners had assumed would happen. The interim government has been cautious in its approach and has pledged to clean up the rampant corruption and restore national unity. But some of these unelected leaders, not used to the political game, have made some embarrassing stumbles along the way. Meanwhile Thaksin, in self-exile, has continued to give interviews with high-profile news organisations, and many in the public wonder whether he is plotting a return to power.

A series of random attacks by anonymous Muslims in the three southernmost provinces, Yala, Narathiwat and Pattani, have become recognised as a serious ongoing threat. Since 2004, more than 1800 people have been murdered in the deep south, and because the insurgents haven't listed specific demands and have no known leader, the violence has been difficult to stop. After more than two years of Thaksin's strong-armed policies and harsh tactics in the region in which innocent Muslims were arrested and even killed, it became clear that the efforts were counterproductive and were fuelling even more violence. But the interim government, after trying a conciliatory approach, has not had any more success, as daily bombs and killings have continued.

On New Years Eve 2006, Bangkok itself suffered through a series of bomb attacks in high-profile places throughout the city – the first of its kind in the capital – killing three people and injuring dozens. Most ruled out Muslim involvement and have instead blamed Thaksin loyalists. Since that incident, higher security measures have been introduced in Bangkok, such as bag searches at mall entrances and at Skytrain and subway stations.

Thailand has mostly recovered from the tragic December 2004 tsunami, which left an estimated 8000 people dead. Thousands of dedicated Thai and foreign volunteers made this heroic recovery possible. But while popular tourist areas were quickly cleaned up and restored to pre-tsunami standards, those in many poorer fishing villages are still struggling to overcome the deaths of family members and the loss of livelihoods.

In 2006 Thais jubilantly celebrated the king's 60th year on the throne with great fanfare (he's currently the longest-serving monarch in the world) and continue to look to him for inspiration during these somewhat turbulent times. Despite everything, things have held together nicely as the economy is steady and tourism is as robust as eve:. Visitors won't notice anything amiss and Thais haven't stopped smiling.

FAST FACTS:

Area: 514,000 sq km

Border countries: Cambodia, Laos, Malaysia, Myanmar (Burma)

Population: 64,632,000

Inflation: 5.1%

GDP per capita: US$9100

Religion: 95% Buddhist

Literacy: 92.6%

Original name: Siam

Number of coups d'etat since 1932: 18

Number of 7-Elevens: currently 3800

Highest Point: Doi Inthanon 2565m

Rice exports: 7.4 million tonnes in 2006 (number one rice exporter in the world)

History

PREHISTORY

Modern linguistic theory and archaeological evidence suggest that the first true agriculturists in the world, perhaps also the first metal workers, spoke an early form of Thai and lived in what we know today as Thailand. The Mekong River valley and Khorat Plateau in particular were inhabited as far back as 10,000 years ago, and rice was grown in the Ban Chiang and Ban Prasat areas of northeastern Thailand as early as 4000 BC (China, by contrast, was growing and consuming millet at the time). The Ban Chiang culture began bronze metallurgy before 3000 BC; the Middle East's Bronze Age arrived around 2800 BC, China's a thousand years later. Ban Chiang bronze works were stronger than their Mesopotamian or Chinese counterparts, mainly due to Ban Chiang's access to the abundant tin resources of the Thai-Malay Peninsula.

> The US Library of Congress maintains a Thailand Studies page (http://countrystudies .us/Thailand) that covers history and societal structure.

Early Thais, often classified with the broader Austro-Thai group, were nomadic and their original homeland a matter of academic debate. While most scholars favour a region vaguely stretching from Guangxi in southern China to Dien Bien Phu in northern Vietnam, a more radical theory says the Thais descended from an ocean-based civilisation in the western Pacific. The oceanic proponents trace the development of symbols and myths in Thai art and culture to arrive at their conclusions.

This vast, non-unified zone of Austro-Thai influence spread all over Southeast Asia at various times. In Thailand, these Austro-Thai groups belonged to the Thai-Kadai and Mon-Khmer language families.

> Thailand is 543 years ahead of the West, at least according to their calendar, which measures the beginning of the modern era from the birth of Buddha instead of Christ.

The Thai-Kadai is the most significant ethno-linguistic group in all of Southeast Asia, with 72 million speakers extending from the Brahmaputra River in India's Assam state to the Gulf of Tonkin and China's Hainan Island. To the north, there are Thai-Kadai speakers well into the Chinese provinces of Yunnan and Guangxi, and to the south they are found as far as the northern Malaysian state of Kedah. In Thailand and Laos they are the majority populations, and in China, Vietnam and Myanmar (Burma) they are the largest minorities. The predominant Thai half of the Thai-Kadai group includes the Ahom (Assam), the Siamese (Thailand), the Black Thai or Thai Dam (Laos and Vietnam), the Thai Yai or Shan (Myanmar and Thailand), the Thai Neua (Laos, Thailand and China), the Thai Lü (Laos, Thailand and China) and the Yuan (Laos and Thailand). The less numerous Kadai groups (under a million) include such comparatively obscure languages in southern China as Kelao, Lati, Laha, Laqua and Li.

A linguistic map of southern China, northeastern India and Southeast Asia clearly shows that the preferred zones of occupation by the Thai peoples have been river valleys, from the Red (Hong) River in the south of China and Vietnam to the Brahmaputra River in Assam, India. At one time there were two terminals for movement into what is now Thailand. The 'northern terminal' was in the Yuan Jiang and other river areas in China's modern-day Yunnan and Guangxi provinces, and the 'southern terminal' along central Thailand's Mae Nam Chao Phraya (Chao Phraya River). The human populations remain quite concentrated in these areas today, while

TIMELINE 4000–3000 BC	6th–10th centuries
Ban Chiang in Northeastern Thailand pioneers rice cultivation and bronze metallurgy	Theravada Buddhism establishes itself among Mon communities in central Thailand

Thailand: A Short History (2003), by David Wyatt, offers a succinct overview from the early Thai era to the turn of the millennium.

areas between the two were merely intermediate relay points and have always been less populated.

The Mekong River valley between Thailand and Laos was one such intermediate zone, as were river valleys along the Nan, Ping, Kok, Yom and Wang Rivers in northern Thailand, plus various river areas in Laos and also in the Shan State of Myanmar. As far as historians have been able to piece together, significant numbers of Austro-Thai peoples in southern China or northern Vietnam probably began migrating southward and westward in small groups as early as the 8th century AD – most certainly by the 10th century.

These migrant Thais established local polities along traditional social schemata according to *meuang* (roughly 'principality' or 'city-state'), under the rule of chieftains or sovereigns *(jâo meuang)*. Each *meuang* was based in a river valley or section of a valley and some were loosely collected under one *jâo meuang* or an alliance of several.

Wherever Thais met indigenous populations of Tibeto-Burmans and Mon-Khmers in the move south and westward (into what is now Myanmar, Thailand and Laos), they were somehow able to displace, assimilate or co-opt them without force. The most probable explanation for this relatively smooth assimilation is that there were already Thai peoples indigenous to the area.

EARLY KINGDOMS

With no written records or chronologies it is difficult to say with certainty what kind of cultures existed in Thailand before the middle of the first millennium AD. However, by the 6th century an important network of agricultural communities was thriving as far south as modern-day Pattani and Yala, and as far north and northeast as Lamphun and Muang Fa Daet (near Khon Kaen).

Theravada Buddhism was flourishing and may have entered the region during India's Ashoka period, in the 3rd or 2nd century BC, when Indian missionaries are said to have been sent to a land called Suvannabhumi (Land of Gold). Suvannabhumi most likely corresponds to a remarkably fertile area stretching from southern Myanmar, across central Thailand, to eastern Cambodia. Two different cities in Thailand's central river basin have long been called Suphanburi (City of Gold) and U Thong (Cradle of Gold).

Dvaravati

Nakhon Pathom in central Thailand seems to have been the centre of Dvaravati culture. The main ethnicity of the Dvaravati peoples was Mon, whose culture quickly declined in the 11th century under the political domination of the invading Khmers, who made their regional headquarters in Lopburi. A Mon kingdom – Hariphunchai – in today's Lamphun Province, held out until the late 12th or early 13th century, when it was annexed by northern Thais.

Dvaravati is a Sanskrit name meaning Place of Gates, referring to the city of Krishna in the Indian epic poem *Mahabharata*. The French art historian Georges Coedès discovered the name on some coins that were excavated in the Nakhon Pathom area. The Dvaravati culture is known for its art work, including Buddha images (showing Indian Gupta influence), stucco reliefs on temple walls and in caves, architecture, exquisite terracotta heads, votive tablets and various sculptures.

8th–10th centuries	9th–13th centuries
Thai-Kadai peoples from northern Vietnam and southern China begin migrating into the Mekong River valley	Angkor extends control across central Thailand

Dvaravati may have also been a cultural relay point for the Funan and Chenla cultures of ancient Laos and Cambodia to the northeast and east. The Chinese, through the travels of the famous pilgrim Xuan Zang, knew the area as Tuoluo-bodi, between Sriksetra (Myanmar) and Isanapura (Laos-Cambodia).

Khmer & Srivijaya

The Khmer kingdom, with its capital in present-day Cambodia, expanded westward into a large swath of present-day Thailand between the 9th to 11th centuries. Much of Thailand made up the Khmer frontier with administrative capitals in Lopburi, Sukhothai and Phimai. Roads and temples were built linking these centres to the capital at Angkor. As a highly developed society, Khmer culture infused the border regions with its art, language, religion and court structure. Monuments from this period located in Kanchanaburi, Lopburi and many northeastern towns were constructed in the Khmer style, most notably found in Angkor.

Elements of the Khmer religions – Brahmanism, Theravada Buddhism and Mahayana Buddhism – were intermixed as Lopburi became a religious centre, and some elements of each Buddhist school – along with Brahmanism – remain in Thai religious and court ceremonies today.

A number of Thais became mercenaries for the Khmer armies in the early 12th century, as depicted on the walls of Angkor Wat. The Khmers called the Thais 'Syam', and this was how the Thai kingdom eventually came to be called Syam, or Sayam. In Myanmar and northwestern Thailand the pronunciation of Syam became 'Shan'.

Meanwhile southern Thailand – the upper Malay Peninsula – was under the control of the Srivijaya empire, the headquarters of which is believed to have been located in Palembang, Sumatra, between the 8th and 13th centuries. The regional centre for Srivijaya was Chaiya, near modern Surat Thani. Remains of Srivijaya art can still be seen in Chaiya and its environs.

Sukhothai & Lan Na Thai

Several Thai principalities in the Mekong River valley united in the 13th and 14th centuries, when Thai princes wrested the lower north from the declining Khmer empire to create Sukhothai (Rising of Happiness). They

---

FISH IN THE WATER, RICE IN THE FIELDS

Many Thais today have a sentimental view of the Sukhothai period, seeing it as a 'golden age' of Thai politics, religion and culture – an egalitarian, noble period when all the people had enough to eat and the kingdom was unconquerable. Among other accomplishments, the third Sukhothai king, Ramkhamhaeng, encouraged the use of a fledgling Thai writing system, which became the basis for modern Thai; he also codified the Thai form of Theravada Buddhism, as borrowed from the Sinhalese.

A famous passage from Sukhothai's Ramkhamhaeng inscription reads:
This land of Sukhothai is thriving. There is fish in the water and rice in the fields…The King has hung a bell in the opening of the gate over there; if any commoner has a grievance which sickens his belly and grips his heart, he goes and strikes the bell; King Ramkhamhaeng questions the man, examines the case and decides it justly for him.

Several Thai principalities resist Khmer suzerainty and unite to form Sukhothai, considered to be the first Thai kingdom

Ayuthaya in central Thailand rivals and later annexes Sukhothai as the primary Thai kingdom and conquers former Khmer territory

later took the capital Hariphunchai from the Mon to form Lan Na Thai (Million Thai Rice Fields).

In 1238 the Sukhothai kingdom declared its independence under King Si Intharathit and quickly expanded its sphere of influence, taking advantage not only of the declining Khmer power but the weakening Srivijaya domain in the south. Sukhothai is considered by the Thais to be the first true Thai kingdom. Under King Ramkhamhaeng, the Sukhothai kingdom extended from Nakhon Si Thammarat in the south to the upper Mekong River valley (Laos) and to Bago (Myanmar). For a short time (1448–86) the Sukhothai capital was moved to Phitsanulok. It was annexed by Ayuthaya in 1376, by which time a national identity of sorts had been forged.

The Legend of Suriyothai (2002), a Francis Ford Coppola re-edit of the royally financed, four-hour original (Suriyothai), recounts a famous 1548 battle between Bago (part of Burma) and Siam.

Ramkhamhaeng also supported two northern Thai *jâo meuang* – Phaya Mengrai of Chiang Mai and Phaya Ngam Meuang of Phayao – in the 1296 founding of Lan Na Thai (or Lanna). Lanna extended across northern Thailand to include Wiang Chan along the middle reaches of the Mekong River. In the 14th century Wiang Chan was taken from Lanna by Chao Fa Ngum of Luang Prabang, who made it part of his Lan Xang (Million Elephants) kingdom. Wiang Chan later flourished as an independent kingdom for a short time during the mid-16th century and eventually became the capital of Laos in its royal, French and now socialist incarnations. During the French era it got its more popular international spelling 'Vientiane'. After a period of dynastic decline, Lanna fell to the Burmese in 1558.

Ayuthaya

The Thai kings of Ayuthaya grew very powerful in the 14th and 15th centuries, taking over U Thong and Lopburi, former Khmer strongholds, and moving east in their conquests until Angkor was defeated in 1431. Even though the Khmers were their adversaries in battle, the Ayuthaya kings adopted large portions of Khmer court customs and language. One result of this acculturation was that the Thai monarch gained more absolute authority during the Ayuthaya period and assumed the title *devaraja* (god-king; *thewárâat* in Thai) as opposed to the *dhammaraja* (dharma-king; *thammárâat*) title used in Sukhothai.

Ayuthaya was one of the greatest and wealthiest cities in Asia at the time, a thriving seaport that entertained emissaries and traders from Europe, China and beyond. In 1690 Londoner Engelbert Campfer proclaimed, 'Among the Asian nations, the Kingdom of Siam is the greatest. The magnificence of the Ayuthaya Court is incomparable'. It has been said that London, at the time, was a mere village in comparison. The kingdom

THE FALCON OF SIAM

An exceptional episode unfolded in Ayuthaya when Constantine Phaulkon, a Greek, became a high official in Siam under King Narai, from 1675 to 1688. Wisely courting royal favour by fending off would-be colonisation by the Dutch and the English, he nevertheless allowed the French to station 600 soldiers in the kingdom. Eventually the Thais, fearing a takeover, expelled the French and executed Phaulkon. Siam sealed itself off from the West for 150 years following this experience with the *faràng* (a Westerner or foreigner of European descent; from *faràngsèt*, meaning 'French').

1511	1765
The Portuguese establish the first European mission in Ayuthaya, soon to be followed by the Dutch, English, Danish and French	Ayuthaya's wealth attracts the attention of the Burmese, whose siege reduces the city to a devastated shell

sustained an unbroken 400-year monarchical succession through 34 reigns, from King U Thong (r 1350–69) to King Ekathat (r 1758–67).

In the mid-16th century Ayuthaya and the independent kingdom of Lanna came under the control of the Burmese, but the Thais regained rule of both by the end of the century. Later attempts by the Burmese were successful in invading Ayuthaya in 1765 and the capital fell after two years of fighting. This time the invaders destroyed everything sacred to the Thais, including manuscripts, temples and religious sculpture. But the Burmese were unable to maintain a foothold in the kingdom, and the military leader Phraya Taksin, a half-Chinese, half-Thai general, re-established order in the kingdom, claimed the vacated monarchy for himself in 1769, and began ruling from the new capital of Thonburi on the banks of the Mae Nam Chao Phraya, opposite Bangkok. Taksin eventually came to regard himself as the next Buddha; his ministers, who did not approve of his religious fantasies, deposed and then executed him.

EARLY BANGKOK ERA
Founding of the Chakri Dynasty

One of Taksin's key generals, Chao Phraya Chakri, came to power and was crowned in 1782 as Phra Yot Fa. He moved the royal capital across the river to Bangkok and ruled as the first king of the Chakri dynasty. In 1809 his son, Loet La, took the throne and reigned until 1824. Both monarchs assumed the task of restoring the culture, which had been severely damaged by the Burmese decades earlier.

The third Chakri king, Phra Nang Klao (r 1824–51), went beyond reviving tradition and developed trade with China, while increasing domestic agricultural production. He also established a new royal title system, posthumously conferring 'Rama I' and 'Rama II' upon his two predecessors and taking the title 'Rama III' for himself. During Nang Klao's reign, American missionary James Low brought the first printing press to Siam and produced the country's first printed document in Thai script. Missionary Dan Bradley published the first Thai newspaper, the monthly *Bangkok Recorder,* from 1844 to 1845.

The Golden Jubilee Network (http://kan chanapisek.or.th) is the official website of the royal family.

Modernisation

Commonly known as King Mongkut (Phra Chom Klao to the Thais), Rama IV was a colourful and innovative Chakri king. He originally missed out on the throne in deference to his half-brother, Rama III, and lived as a Buddhist monk for 27 years. During his long monastic term he became adept in Sanskrit, Pali, Latin and English, studied Western sciences and adopted the strict discipline of local Mon monks. He kept an eye on the outside world and, when he took the throne in 1851, immediately courted diplomatic relations with a few European nations, taking care to evade colonisation.

In addition, he attempted to demythologise Thai religion by aligning Buddhist cosmology with modern science, and founded the Thammayut monastic sect, based on the strict discipline he had followed as a monk.

King Mongkut loosened Thai trade restrictions and many Western powers signed trade agreements with the monarch. He also sponsored Siam's second printing press and instituted educational reforms, developing a school system along European lines. Although the king courted the West, he did so with caution and warned his subjects, 'Whatever they have invented or done

which we should know of and do, we can imitate and learn from them, but do not wholeheartedly believe in them'. Mongkut was the first monarch to show his face to Thai commoners in public.

Mongkut's son King Chulalongkorn (known to the Thais as Rama V or Chula Chom Klao; r 1868–1910) continued his father's tradition of reform, especially in the legal and administrative realms. Educated by European tutors, Rama V abolished prostration before the king as well as slavery and corvée (state labour). Siam further benefited from relations with European nations and the USA: railways were built, a civil service was established and the legal code restructured. Although Siam still managed to avoid European colonisation, the king was compelled to concede territory to French Indochina (Laos in 1893 and Cambodia in 1907) and British Burma (three Malayan states in 1909) during his reign.

Rama V's son King Vajiravudh (Mongkut Klao or Rama VI; r 1910–25), was educated in Britain and during his reign he introduced educational reforms, including compulsory education. He further 'Westernised' the nation by conforming the Thai calendar to Western models. His reign was clouded by a top-down push for Thai nationalism that resulted in strong anti-Chinese sentiment.

Before Vajiravudh's reign Thai parents gave each of their children a single, original name, with no surname to identify family origins. In 1909 a royal decree required the adoption of Thai surnames for all Thai citizens – a move designed to parallel the European system of family surnames and to weed out Chinese names.

In 1912 a group of Thai military officers unsuccessfully attempted to overthrow the monarchy, the first in a series of coup attempts that have plagued Thai history. As a show of support for the Allies in WWI, Vajiravudh sent 1300 Thai troops to France in 1918.

THE 20TH CENTURY
1932 Revolution

While Vajiravudh's brother King Prajadhipok (Pokklao or Rama VII; r 1925–35) ruled, a group of Thai students living in Paris became so enamoured of democratic ideology that in 1932 they mounted a successful coup d'état against absolute monarchy in Siam. This bloodless revolution led to the development of a constitutional monarchy along British lines, with a mixed military-civilian group in power (see box text opposite).

A royalist revolt in 1933 sought to reinstate absolute monarchy, but it failed and left Prajadhipok isolated from the royalist revolutionaries and the constitution-minded ministers. One of the king's last official acts was to outlaw polygamy in 1934, leaving behind the cultural underpinnings that now support Thai prostitution.

In 1935 the king abdicated without naming a successor and retired to Britain. The cabinet promoted his nephew 10-year-old Ananda Mahidol, to the throne as Rama VIII, although Ananda didn't return from school in Switzerland until 1945. Phibul Songkhram, a key military leader in the 1932 coup, maintained an effective position of power from 1938 until the end of WWII.

Under the influence of Phibul's government, the country's English name was officially changed in 1939 from Siam to Thailand (*pràthêt thai* in Thai).

Under Thailand's *lese majeste* laws, criticising the king carries with it a seven-year prison sentence, applicable to both Thais and foreigners. A major critic of the law is Sulak Sivaraksa, a respected Buddhist scholar and self-described monarchist.

The King Never Smiles: A Biography of Thailand's Bhumibol Adulyadej, by Paul M Handley, is the latest examination of how Thailand's democratic revolution was successfully undermined by royalists and the current king; it is banned in Thailand.

1851	1902
King Mongkut (Rama V) ascends the Chakra throne, instituting a period of reform and opening diplomatic relations with Europe	Siam annexes Yala, Pattani and Narathiwat from the former sultanate of Pattani

'Thai' is considered to have the connotation of 'free', although in actual usage it refers to the Thai, Tai or T'ai peoples.

Ananda Mahidol came back to Thailand in 1945 but was shot dead in his bedroom under mysterious circumstances in 1946. Although there was apparently no physical evidence to suggest assassination, three of Ananda's attendants were arrested two years after his death and executed in 1954. No public charges were ever filed, and the consensus among historians today is that the attendants were 'sacrificed' to settle a karmic debt for allowing the king to die during their watch. His brother, Bhumibol Adulyadej, succeeded him as Rama IX. Nowadays no-one ever speaks or writes publicly about Ananda's death – whether it was a simple gun accident or a regicidal plot remains unclear.

In 2006 King Bhumibol Adulyadej celebrated 60 years on the throne and is the longest reigning monarch in the world.

Militarisation

During the Japanese invasion of Southeast Asia in 1941, the Phibul government sided with Japan and Phibul declared war on the USA and Britain in 1942. But Seni Pramoj, the Thai ambassador in Washington, refused to deliver the declaration. Phibul resigned in 1944 under pressure from the Thai underground resistance (known as Thai Seri), and after V-J Day in 1945, Seni became premier. Seni changed the English name of the country back to 'Siam' but kept 'Prathet Thai' as the official Thai name.

In 1946 Seni was unseated in a general election and a democratic civilian group took power under Pridi Phanomyong, a law professor who had been instrumental in the 1932 revolution. Pridi's civilian government survived long enough to create the 1946 Constitution of the Thai Kingdom, only to be overthrown by Phibul, then a field marshal, in 1947.

Phibul suspended the constitution and reinstated 'Thailand' as the country's official English name in 1949. He took an extreme anticommunist stance, refusing to recognise the newly declared People's Republic of China, and also became a loyal supporter of French and US foreign policy in Southeast Asia. Pridi, meanwhile, took up exile in China.

In 1951 power was wrested from Phibul by General Sarit Thanarat, who continued the tradition of military dictatorship. However, Phibul retained the actual title of premier until 1957 when Sarit finally had him exiled. Elections that same year forced Sarit to resign and go abroad for 'medical treatment'; he returned in 1958 to launch another coup. This time he abolished

---

CAFÉ-BREWED COUP

As Bangkok prospered in the early 20th century, many wealthy merchant families sent their children to study abroad in Europe. Students of humbler socioeconomic status who excelled in school had access to government scholarships for overseas study as well. In 1924 a handful of Thai students in Paris formed the Promoters of Political Change, a group that met in Paris cafés to discuss ideas for a future Siamese government patterned after democratic Western models.

After completing studies in Paris and returning to Bangkok, three of the 'Promoters' – attorney Pridi Phanomyong and military officers Phibul Songkhram and Prayoon Phamonmontri – organised an underground 'People's Party' dedicated to the overthrow of the Siamese system of government. The People's Party found a willing moral accomplice in Rama VII, and a bloodless revolution in 1932 transformed Thailand from an absolute monarchy into a constitutional one.

1932	1934
Following a bloodless coup, Rama VII presides over a change from absolute monarchy to a constitutional monarchy	Polygamy, a Thai tradition, is outlawed

the constitution, dissolved the parliament and banned all political parties, maintaining effective power until he died of cirrhosis in 1963.

From 1964 to 1973 the Thai nation was ruled by the army officers Thanom Kittikachorn and Praphat Charusathien. During this time Thailand allowed the USA to establish several military bases within its borders in support of the US campaign in Vietnam.

Reacting to the political repression, 10,000 Thai students publicly demanded a real constitution in June 1973. On 14 October of the same year the military brutally suppressed a large demonstration at Thammasat University in Bangkok, but King Bhumibol and General Krit Sivara, who sympathised with the students, refused to support further bloodshed, forcing Thanom and Praphat to leave Thailand. Oxford-educated Kukrit Pramoj took charge of a 14-party coalition government and steered a leftist agenda past a conservative parliament.

Among Kukrit's lasting achievements were a national minimum wage, the repeal of anticommunist laws and the ejection of US military forces from Thailand. Kukrit's elected constitutional government ruled until 6 October 1976, when students demonstrated again, this time protesting against Thanom's return to Thailand as a monk. Thammasat University again became a battlefield as border-patrol police and right-wing paramilitary civilian groups assaulted a group of 2000 students holding a sit-in. It is estimated that hundreds of students were killed and injured in the fracas, and more than a thousand were arrested. Using public disorder as an excuse, the military stepped in and installed a new right-wing government with Thanin Kraivichien as premier.

This bloody incident disillusioned many Thai students and older intellectuals not directly involved with the demonstrations. Numerous idealists 'dropped out' of Thai society and joined the People's Liberation Army of Thailand (PLAT), a group of armed communist insurgents based in the hills who had been active since the 1930s.

In October 1977 the military replaced Thanin with the more moderate General Kriangsak Chomanand in an effort to conciliate antigovernment factions. When this failed, the military-backed position changed hands again in 1980, leaving Prem Tinsulanonda at the helm. By this time PLAT had peaked with around 10,000 members. A 1981 coup attempt by the 'Young Turks' (a group of army officers who had graduated together from the Chulachomklao Royal Military Academy and styled themselves after a 1908 military movement at the heart of the Ottoman Empire) failed when Prem fled Bangkok for Khorat in the company of the royal family.

Stabilisation

Now in his 80s, General Prem Tinsulanonda serves as privy council (or chief advisor) to the king and is believed to have orchestrated the 2006 coup. He also has his own website (www.general prem.com).

Prem served as prime minister until 1988 and is credited with the political and economic stabilisation of Thailand in the post-Vietnam War years (only one coup attempt in the 1980s!). The major success of the Prem years was a complete dismantling of the Communist Party of Thailand (CPT) and PLAT through an effective combination of amnesty programmes (which brought the students back from the forests) and military action. His administration is also considered to have been responsible for a gradual democratisation of Thailand that culminated in the 1988 election of his successor, retired general and businessman Chatichai Choonhavan. Prem

1939	1941–45
Siam changes its name to 'Thailand'	Japanese forces occupy parts of Thailand until they're defeated at the close of WWII

continues to serve as a privy councillor and is a *rátthàbùrùt* (elder states-man) of the country.

It may be difficult for later arrivals to Thailand to appreciate the political distance Thailand covered in the 1980s. Under Prem, for example, a long-standing 1am curfew in Bangkok was lifted, and dissenting opinions were heard again in public.

Ever since 1932 every leading political figure in Thailand has needed the support of the Thai military to survive. Considering Thailand's geographic position during the Cold War years, it's not difficult to understand their influence. But as the threat of communist takeover (either from within or from nearby Indochinese states) diminished, the military gradually began loosening its hold on national politics.

Under Chatichai Thailand enjoyed a brief period of unprecedented popular participation in government. Around 60% of Chatichai's cabinet members were former business executives rather than the ex-military officers in the previous cabinet. Thailand entered a new era in which the country's dou-ble-digit economic boom ran concurrently with democratisation. Critics praised the political maturation of Thailand, even if they also grumbled that corruption seemed as rife as it ever was. By the end of the 1980s, however, certain high-ranking military officers had become increasingly dissatisfied, complaining that Thailand was being run by a plutocracy.

The Return of the Military

On 23 February 1991 the military overthrew the Chatichai administration in a bloodless coup and handed power to the newly formed National Peace-Keep-ing Council (NPKC), headed by General Suchinda Kraprayoon. Although it was Thailand's 19th attempted coup and one of 10 successful coups since 1932, it was only the second coup to overthrow a democratically elected civil-ian government. The NPKC abolished the 1978 constitution and dissolved the parliament, charging Chatichai's civilian government with corruption and vote buying. Rights of public assembly were curtailed but the press was only closed down for one day.

Following the coup, the NPKC appointed a handpicked civilian prime minister, Anand Panyarachun, former ambassador to the USA, Germany, Canada and the UN, to dispel public fears that the junta was planning a return to 100% military rule. Anand claimed to be his own man, but like his predecessors – elected or not – he was allowed the freedom to make his own decisions only insofar as they didn't affect the military. In spite of obvious constraints, many observers felt Anand's temporary premiership and cabinet were the best Thailand has ever had, either before or since.

In December 1991 Thailand's national assembly passed a new constitu-tion that guaranteed a NPKC-biased parliament – 270 appointed senators in the upper house stacked against 360 elected representatives. Under this constitution, regardless of who was chosen as the next prime minister or which political parties filled the lower house, the government would remain largely in the hands of the military.

A general election in March 1992 ushered in a five-party coalition govern-ment with Narong Wongwan, whose Samakkhitham (Justice Unity) Party received the most votes, as premier. But amid US allegations that Narong was involved in Thailand's drug trade, the military exercised its constitutional

'Ever since 1932 every leading po-litical figure in Thailand has needed the support of the Thai military to survive'

1946	1973
The present king, Rama IX, ascends the throne; Thailand's first democratically elected government comes to power	Thai students, workers and farmers unite to repel military dictatorship and install a democratic government

prerogative and replaced Narong with (surprise, surprise) General Suchinda in April 1992.

In May 1992 several huge demonstrations demanding Suchinda's resignation – led by the charismatic Bangkok governor, Chamlong Srimuang – rocked Bangkok and larger provincial capitals. Chamlong won the 1992 Magsaysay Award (a humanitarian service award issued by a foundation in the Philippines) for his role in galvanising the public to reject Suchinda. After street confrontations between the protesters and the military near Bangkok's Democracy Monument resulted in nearly 50 deaths and hundreds of injuries, Suchinda resigned, having been premier for less than six weeks. Anand Panyarachun was reinstated as interim premier, winning praise for his fair and efficient administration.

'Asia was borrowing billions more than it could afford on the basis of optimistic predictions of future growth'

Musical Chairs & a New Constitution

The September 1992 elections squeezed in veteran Democrat Party leader Chuan Leekpai, who helmed a four-party coalition government. A food vendor's son and native of Trang Province instead of a general, tycoon or academic, the new premier didn't fit the usual mould. Although well regarded for his honesty and high morals, Chuan accomplished little in the areas of concern to the majority of Thais, most pointedly Bangkok traffic, national infrastructure and the undemocratic NPKC constitution.

After Chuan was unseated in a vote of no confidence, a new general election ushered in a seven-party coalition led by the Chart Thai (Thai Nationality) Party. At the helm was billionaire Banharn Silapa-archa, whom the press called a 'walking ATM'; they immediately attacked his tendency to appoint from a reservoir of rural politicians known to favour big business over social welfare. In September 1996 the Banharn government collapsed amid a spate of corruption scandals and a crisis of confidence.

The November 1996 national election, marked by electoral violence and accusations of vote buying, saw the former deputy prime minister and army commander Chavalit Yongchaiyudh, of the New Aspiration Party, secure premiership with a dubious mix of coalition partners.

In July 1997, following several months of warning signs that almost everyone in Thailand and in the international community chose to ignore, the Thai currency fell into a deflationary tailspin and the national economy crashed and screeched to a virtual halt. Along with Indonesia, Malaysia, the Philippines and South Korea, Thailand had huge current-account deficits, massive external debt and low foreign-exchange reserves. Asia was borrowing billions more than it could afford on the basis of optimistic predictions of future growth.

On 27 September 1997 the Thai parliament voted in a new constitution, Thailand's 16th since 1932 and the first to be decreed by a civilian government. Known as *rátthàthamanun pràchaachon* (people's constitution) it put new mechanisms in place to monitor the conduct of elected officials and political candidates and to protect civil rights, achieving many of the aims of the prodemocracy movement.

Hope faded as Chavalit, living up to everyone's low expectations, failed to deal effectively with the economy and was forced to resign in November 1997. An election brought Chuan Leekpai back into office, where he did a reasonably decent job as an international public-relations man for the crisis.

1982	1991–92
A general amnesty reduces the ranks of the armed insurgency to a handful; the communist movement is vanquished; martial law ends	A military coup lands General Suchinda in power and when protestors are shot, King Rama IX intervenes and democracy is restored

THE NEW MILLENNIUM
The Rise of Thaksin

Self-made billionaire and former police colonel Thaksin Shinawatra capitalised on the country's rising nationalism after the Asian currency crisis by forming the Thai Rak Thai (Thais Love Thais; TRT) political party in 1998. He was named prime minister in 2001 after winning a landslide victory in compulsory nationwide elections – the first in Thailand to be held under strict guidelines established by the 1997 constitution – on a platform of eliminating corruption, investing in impoverished villages and instituting affordable health care.

The working class adored his Western-style accessibility – he shook hands, listened to constituents and responded to opinion polls. He was also rich (having established the country's largest telecommunication empire), a factor that carries a lot of political weight in Thailand. But his supporters were more impressed that he delivered on his campaign promises, a marked departure from old-fashioned Thai politics. Ambitious and charismatic, Thaksin was also intolerant of the press and demonstrated little appreciation for democratic civil liberties, earning him many enemies among the urban intelligentsia. To avoid charges of conflict of interest, Thaksin took the nominal steps of transferring ownership of Shin Corp to his family and domestic employees, an ominous gesture according to his critics.

In 2003 Thaksin announced a 'war on drugs' intended to rid the country of illicit drug use within 90 days. Lists of drug dealers and users were compiled in every province and the police were given arrest quotas to fulfil or else lose their jobs. Within two months over 2000 Thais on the government blacklist had been killed. The Thaksin administration denied accusations by the UN, the US State Department, Amnesty International and Thailand's own human rights commission that the deaths were extrajudicial killings by Thai police. Independent observers claim that the 'war on drugs' has succeeded in increased prices but not reduced drug use.

On 26 December 2004 a magnitude 9.3 earthquake – the second-largest quake in recorded history – erupted on the floor of the Indian Ocean off the northwest coast of Sumatra. Along Thailand's Andaman coast the tsunami waves struck six provinces, reaching as high as 10m in the worst-hit areas. Thailand's tsunami toll reached 5000 confirmed dead. Relief and reconstruction efforts moved quickly and aggressively to restore normal living conditions. Prime Minister Thaksin's speedy handling of the tsunami disaster, along with yet more promises of rural development, brought the TRT a landslide victory in the general election of February 2005.

'the tsunami waves struck six provinces, reaching as high as 10m in the worst-hit areas'

Muslim Insurgency

In the south during 2001–02, a decades-old Muslim nationalist movement, perhaps responding to the Thaksin administration's authoritarianism, began reheating. Sporadic attacks were staged on police stations, schools, military installations and other government institutions. Discontent in the south picked up momentum after the storming of the Krue Se Mosque, in which police gunned down 112 Muslim militants inside an historic mosque in Pattani. Then in October 2004 police broke up a large demonstration in Tak Bai, and while they were transporting around 1300 arrestees in overcrowded trucks, at least 78 died of suffocation or from being crushed under the weight of other arrestees.

1997	2001
After a decade of energetic economic growth, the Thai economy crashes and the national currency suffers precipitous deflation	Thaksin Shinawatra, the richest man in Thailand, is elected prime minister on a populist platform

By 2005 the region was declared an emergency zone as attacks increased and became more sophisticated, suggesting involvement from outside militant groups, such as Jemaah Islamiyah (JI). In mid-2006 simultaneous explosions at 22 banks in Yala and later timed explosions in Hat Yai did more to convince the government that the insurgency was maturing than the previous bloodshed had. Sonthi Boonyaratglin, a Muslim army commander assigned to the region, criticised the Thaksin administration for refusing to negotiate with the insurgents, but to this date the government has not identified a leading group responsible for the attacks. There are six known separatist groups that may be acting in the region and it is believed that they are acting in competition with each other rather than in concert.

Following the ouster of Thaksin it was hoped that peace negotiations in the south would gain strength, but after a brief break, violence continued. In late 2006 schools were forced to close in Pattani, Yala and Narathiwat after arson fires, shootings of teachers and threatening phone calls.

Global Terrorism Analysis (www.jamestown .org/terrorism) publishes online articles about the southern Thai insurgency as well as other international hot spots.

2006 Coup

But the violence in the south would not be Thaksin's downfall; he would ultimately lose at the public-relations campaign, his usual forte. At the beginning of 2006 a series of lawsuits filed against his critics spawned a popular anti-Thaksin campaign. The movement gained more support when the Thaksin family sold all shares of Shin Corporation to the Singaporean government for a profit of 73 billion baht (US$1.88 billion), tax-free thanks to new telecommunications legislation that exempted individuals from capital gains tax. But what stuck most with urban Thais was Thaksin's perceived ambitions for the monarchy. He presided over a ceremony traditionally reserved for the monarch, attempted to place allies in key military positions loyal to the crown and, according to online rumours, enlisted the help of Khmer witch doctors. The upper-class royalists feared that Thaksin's consolidation of political power would unseat an ageing king with an heir apparent of marginal popularity.

Thaksin responded to the growing discontent by first dissolving the parliament, calling for re-elections to occur one month later and announcing massive populist measures aimed directly at the rural poor. The opposition chose to boycott the election. When all the ballots were tallied, Thaksin proclaimed victory for one momentous day, but after a private council with the king, he announced that he would not accept the prime minister position. The constitutional court decided that new elections would take place later in the year, a vote that many assumed Thaksin would win handily.

Some five months later on 19 September 2006, a military coup led by army chief Sonthi Boonyaratglin took control of the government and blocked Thaksin's return from a UN general assembly session in New York. This was the 18th coup in Thailand's modern history but the first in 15 years. The coup leadership threw out the 1997 constitution, dissolved the parliament and suspended activity of political parties. But Bangkok citizens and Thaksin critics were overjoyed and soldiers guarding government buildings were presented with flowers and gifts. An interim government was appointed and general elections set for October 2007; the military leadership assured the public that they had no intention to rule the country but rather wanted to ensure 'national unity' by removing a divisive figure.

Monitor current events by visiting Asia Times (www.atimes.com) and 2Bangkok.com (www.2bangkok.com).

2004	2006
Devastating tsunami hits Thailand's Andaman Coast, killing 5000 and temporarily paralysing tourist and fishing industries	Thailand's democratically elected government is dismantled by a military coup, and Prime Minister Thaksin is forced into exile

Thailand & You Making the most of your trip

RESPONSIBLE TRAVEL

Thailand is an easy country to love: the pace of life is unhurried, the people are generally friendly and the pressures on the short-term visitor are relatively few. A smile goes a long way here, chitchat is more important than a to-do list and doling out compliments is a national sport.

That doesn't mean that every Thai is a cheery Pollyanna. So many foreigners pass through the country completely oblivious of the culture and customs that many Thais, especially in the tourist industry, suffer from 'foreigner fatigue'. They have used up their patience on penny-pinchers, neocolonialists and paranoiacs.

Keep in mind that the demographics of this country are just as complex as those of your own, plus you're handicapped by language and culture from being able to spot the genuine sweethearts from the shysters. By and large, the tourist industry has a thick veneer of fast operators, but step outside of the trail and you'll meet a gentler sort. Emanate a sense of warmth and happiness and the Thais will instinctively respond in kind. Know how to behave politely in public and you'll coax a smile from the schoolmarm types. Learn some of the language and you'll become a fast friend with everyone from the noodle vendor to the taxi driver.

THE CULTURE

Thais are generally tolerant of most kinds of behaviour and assume that the majority foreigners know nothing about their country. When you do exhibit the slightest bit of etiquette mastery, Thais will beam with gratitude. For information on how to understand Thai culture as a whole, see p49.

www.responsible-travel
.org offers common-sense
advice on how to travel
with a conscience.

Monarchy Etiquette

If you do nothing else, remember to treat the monarchy and the religion with extreme deference. Thais regard any image of the king and the royal family

---

STOPPING CHILD-SEX TOURISM IN THAILAND *ECPAT and Child Wise Australia*

Sadly, Thailand has become a destination for a significant number of foreigners seeking to sexually exploit local children. A range of socioeconomic factors renders many children vulnerable to such abuse, and some depraved individuals seem intent to prey upon this vulnerability.

The sexual abuse and exploitation of children has serious, lifelong and even life-threatening consequences. Child-sex tourism is a crime and an intolerable violation of the rights of a child. Strong laws exist in Thailand to prosecute offenders. Many countries also have extraterritorial legislation that allows nationals to be prosecuted in their own country for such crimes.

Responsible travellers can help to stop the scourge of child-sex tourism by reporting suspicious behaviour. Don't ignore it! Your actions may be critical in helping to protect children from future abuse and exploitation.

In Thailand, travellers can report on a dedicated hotline number: ☎ 1300.

If you know the nationality of the individual, you can report them directly to their embassy.

ECPAT (End Child Prostitution & Trafficking; ☎ 0 2215 3388 in Bangkok; www.ecpat.net) is a global network focusing on these issues with more than 70 affiliate organisations around the world. Its head office is located in Bangkok. ECPAT is actively working to combat child-sex tourism in Thailand and around the world.

Child Wise (www.childwise.net) is the Australian member of ECPAT. Child Wise has been involved in providing training to the tourism industry in Thailand to counter child-sex tourism.

Culture Shock: Thailand, by Robert and Nanthapa Cooper, explains Thailand's quirky, curious and practical customs.

with religious devotion. This means that postage stamps bearing the king's image are never licked for adhesion to letters; use the provided sponge or glue station. Money, which also bears images of the king, is never stepped on (in the case of a dropped bill) or kept in one's shoe.

In addition avoid criticising or disparaging the royal family. Thais are very guarded about discussing negative aspects of the monarchy for fear of offending someone or worse, being charged for lese-majesty, which carries a punishment of seven years' imprisonment.

It's also considered a grave insult to Thai nationhood, and to the monarchy, not to stand when you hear the national or royal anthems. Radio and TV stations in Thailand broadcast the national anthem daily at 8am and 6pm; in towns and villages this can be heard over public loudspeakers in the streets or in bus and train stations. In Bangkok, the national anthem is played in Skytrain and subway stations. The Thais stop whatever they're doing to stand during the anthem and visitors are expected to do likewise. The royal anthem is played just before films are shown in public cinemas; again, the audience always stands until it's over.

Temple Etiquette

When visiting a temple, it is very important to dress neatly and to take your shoes off when you enter any building that contains a Buddha image. Buddha images are sacred objects, so don't pose in front of them for pictures and definitely do not clamber upon them. When sitting in a religious edifice, keep your feet pointed away from any Buddha images. The usual way to do this is to sit in the 'mermaid' pose in which your legs are folded to the side, with your feet pointing backwards.

Shorts or sleeveless shirts are considered improper dress for both men and women when visiting temples. At some temples, there will be trousers or long sarongs for rent so that tourists dressed in shorts may enter the compound.

Monks are not supposed to touch or be touched by women. If a woman wants to hand something to a monk, the object should be placed within reach of the monk or on the monk's 'receiving cloth' and not handed directly to him.

Since most temples are maintained from the donations received, when you visit a temple please remember to make a contribution.

Social Conventions

The traditional Thai greeting is with a prayer-like palms-together gesture known as a *wâi*. If someone shows you a *wâi*, you should return the gesture, unless the greeting comes from a child or a service person. Overusing the *wâi* or placing your hands too low in respect to your face trivialises a very intricate and respected custom.

A smile and a cheery *sàwàt-dii khráp* if you're male or *sàwàt-dii khâ* if you're female (the all-purpose Thai greeting) goes a long way towards calming the initial trepidation that locals may feel upon seeing a foreigner, whether in the city or the countryside.

Payap University in Chiang Mai (p293) offers a well-regarded academic programme in Thai culture and language.

In the more traditional parts of the country, it is not proper for members of the opposite sex to touch one another, either as lovers or as friends. Hand-holding is not acceptable behaviour outside of the major cities such as Bangkok or the prostitute cities such as Pattaya. But same-sex touching is quite common and is typically a sign of friendship, not sexual attraction. Older Thai men might grab a younger man's thigh in the same way that buddies slap each other on the back. Thai women are especially affectionate with female friends, often sitting close to one another or linking arms.

When hailing a bus or a taxi, Thais extend their arms slightly, with their hand below their waists and wave downward. The same hand gesture – the palm facing downward with a slight wave – is used to call a person. Turning the palm upward, as is common in Western cultures, is only used on animals.

When handing an object to another person or receiving something, the ultimate in polite behaviour is to extend the right hand out while the left hand gently grips the right elbow.

Dress & Hygiene

Thailand is a very modest country. Shorts above the knee, sleeveless shirts, tank tops (singlets) and other beach-style attire are not appropriate when you're not at the beach or sporting events, or when you're outside Bangkok. First-time visitors can't believe that we would make such a controversial fashion stand, especially in a tropical country but we really do mean it. If you insist on wearing less, do it in Bangkok where international standards of skin exhibition are more accepted. And don't exempt yourself because of the humid climate. Covering up with light, loose fabric offers protection from the sun, and frequent showers act as better natural air-conditioning than spaghetti-strap tops.

The importance of modesty extends to the beach as well. Except for urban Bangkokians, most Thais swim fully clothed. For this reason, sunbathing nude or topless is not acceptable and in some cases is even illegal. Baring private parts helps promote the misconception that Western women and men are advertising themselves for sex.

Thais are fastidious in their personal appearance and even in the hottest weather rarely sweat, whereas new arrivals are in a constant state of perspiration and body odour. One way to avoid the continual drip is to bathe often. Talcum powder is another antidote to moisture and stink, and helps prevent prickly heat.

Sandals or slip-on shoes are perfectly acceptable for almost any but the most formal occasions.

Head & Feet Taboos

From practical and spiritual viewpoints, Thais regard the head as the highest and most sacred part of the body and the feet as the dirtiest and

Thai for Beginners, by Benjawan Poomsan Becker, is a good primer for learning the basics of spoken and written Thai.

Green Leaf Foundation (www.greenleafthai .org) has established environmental operating standards for the hotel industry in Thailand; search the online directory for qualifying hotels.

BANGKOK'S STREET WALKERS

The heat, the hawkers, the hookers – Bangkok is already a zoo at night, and then you'll spot a baby elephant plodding down the road with a flashing light tied to its tail. And its skinny mahout will thrust a bunch of bananas in your hands to feed to the animal in exchange for a fistful of baht. Surreal, indeed. Heartbreaking, most certainly.

Thailand has a pachyderm crisis. Throughout Thai history, these animals were revered for their strength, endurance and intelligence. And then the modern world invaded and promptly made the elephant redundant.

The elephants and their dependent mahouts came to the big city, like the rest of the country's economic refugees, in search of work. And what can an elephant do in the time of planes, trains and automobiles? One option is to roam the streets like a beggar. This isn't an example of ignorant cruelty, but of economic desperation.

A promising alternative to street walking is the elephant rescue preserves that support themselves through volunteer tourism. Guests learn how to bathe, feed and train the elephant in the tradition of a mahout. Pattaya's Eco Explorer (p236) and Lampang's Thai Elephant Conservation Center (p348) are two possibilities.

VISITING HILL-TRIBE VILLAGES

It is especially important to 'tread lightly' in hill-tribe villages as many of these places had little or no interaction with mainstream society before being yanked abruptly into the modern era. While these communities may appreciate the revenue source brought by trekkers, the pressures of ill-informed visitors who are invariably more affluent than the average villager introduces many social strains beyond polite and impolite behaviour. Talk to your guide about village taboos and carefully observe protocol before acting. Here is a rough sketch of the general precautions you should take when visiting a hill-tribe village:

▪ Always ask for permission before taking any photos of tribespeople, especially at private moments inside their dwellings. Many traditional belief systems view photography with suspicion.

▪ Show respect for religious symbols and rituals. Don't touch totems at village entrances or other sacred items. Don't participate in ceremonies unless invited to join.

▪ Avoid cultivating a tradition of begging, especially among children. Definitely avoid handing out candy unless you can also arrange for modern dentistry. Talk to your guide about donating to a local school instead.

▪ Set a good example by not using drugs.

▪ Don't litter while trekking or staying in villages.

▪ Speak quietly, and smile at villagers even if they stare at you.

lowest part of the body. Many of the taboos associated with the feet are also directly related to a consideration of cleanliness. Traditionally Thais ate, slept and entertained on the floor of their homes with little in the way of furniture.

To keep their homes and eating surfaces clean, the feet (and shoes) contracted a variety of rules. All feet and head taboos in Thailand come with certain qualifiers and exceptions that will make more sense the more familiar you are with the culture. In the meantime, err on the side of caution with the following tips.

One of the most considerate things you can do in Thailand is to remember to take off your shoes inside private homes or some guesthouses and businesses. (When entering temple buildings, removing your shoes is an absolute must.) Not every establishment asks for shoe removal, but a good sign that this is required is a pile of shoes left at or near the entrance. Several Thais have confided in us that they can't believe how oblivious some foreigners seem to be of this simple and obvious custom. To them wearing shoes indoors is just plain disgusting and rude.

Don't prop your feet on chairs or tables while sitting, especially at a restaurant or in a guesthouse. This is an obvious one as you wouldn't treat a public place back home like your living room, so why start now in a culture that is footphobic? On some buses and 3rd-class trains, you'll see Thais prop up their feet; while this isn't the height of propriety, do notice that they always remove their shoes before doing so. Thais also take off their shoes if they need to climb up onto a chair or seat.

Never step over someone or their personal belongings, even on a crowded 3rd-class train; instead squeeze around them or ask them to move. The same holds for food that might be served on a mat or on the floor, as is commonly seen in rural areas or at temple fairs. When sitting with a group of Thais, remember to use the mermaid pose, with your feet tucked behind you to one side so that the bottoms of your feet aren't pointed at sacred images or people of high status.

Also avoid tying your shoes to the outside of your backpack where they might accidentally brush against someone (like, totally gross) or worse touch someone's head (shame on you).

Westerners often use their feet informally as secondary hands: we might close the refrigerator door with our feet, stop something from blowing away with our feet or point at something with our feet. These are all no-nos in Thailand and will cause gasps from onlookers. If you need to move, motion or touch something, do it with your hands. With enough consideration, all of this will become second nature and you'll soon feel embarrassed when you see these conventions broken.

Now for the head taboos: don't touch Thais on the head or ruffle their hair. This is perceived as an insult, not a sign of affection. Occasionally you'll see young people touching each other's head, which is akin to a 'tittie-twist', a teasing gesture between friends. Don't sit on pillows meant as headrests, as this represents a variant of the taboo against head touching.

To be superpolite, lower your head slightly when passing between two people having a conversation or when passing near a monk.

> Thais are more likely to yield a seat on a crowded bus to a child than an elderly person.

LOCAL COMMUNITIES

Hair-raising adventures and postcard snapshots make great souvenirs from a trip, but the travel experiences that become lifelong companions are the moments when you stop being an invading alien and connect with someone who may not speak your language or share your culture. A conversation at a bus stop or an invitation to join a family picnic – these are all open doors for 'snapshot' friendships, a temporary connection between strangers that teaches appreciation or shares a good joke. These unscripted interactions aren't available in the midst of a tourist ghetto. You must first place yourself in local communities where people have the time and the curiosity to befriend a stranger.

Community immersion can range from a solo foray into a town or an area of town off the tourist circuit, or better yet you can temporarily adopt a Thai address while giving something back through a volunteer programme.

Volunteering

If you speak a little bit of the language, invariably Thais will ask if you are a teacher, a profession that carries a great amount of respect. Some will even assume the case and will be on their 'Sunday-best' behaviour. Taking on a teaching position in Thailand not only elevates your status from forgettable tourist to honourable guest, but it gives you insight and access into a community pleased to have you.

> Thai Tribal Crafts (www .ttcrafts.co.th) is a fair-trade outlet for hill-tribe handicrafts.

Finding a teaching job is fairly easy, as native English speakers are always in demand. But finding an experience that suits your interests takes some research. If you want more of a cultural challenge than just a job overseas, look into programmes in rural areas where English is limited and foreigners are few. In these situations, you'll learn Thai more quickly and observe a way of life with deeper connections to the past. The following organisations provide volunteers with jobs and accommodation for a modest weekly or monthly fee:

The **Mirror Art Foundation** (☎ 0 5373 7412; www.mirrorartgroup.org) is a nongovernmental organisation working in Chiang Rai Province in the Mae Yao hill-tribe villages. Because many villagers here are not recognised as Thai citizens, their children do not have access to public education. This foundation provides basic education in Thai and English languages and places volunteers directly within the community. Mirror Art also offers trekking opportunities (p354).

Volunthai (www.volunthai.com; 1739 Soi Mookmontree 13, Nakhon Ratchasima) is a homy operation that places volunteers in teaching positions at local schools with homestay accommodation. No previous teaching experience is necessary and the programme is best suited for cultural chameleons who want to experience a radically different way of life in a nontouristed part of the county. The programme is based in the northeast (the poorest part of Thailand) and offers a fascinating glimpse into the country's agricultural heart.

Travel to Teach (☎ 0 8424 60351; www.travel-to-teach.org; 1161/2 Soi Chitta Panya, Nong Khai) offers flexible volunteering positions from two weeks to six months in schools, English camps or in temples teaching monks. Many volunteers end up in this programme after travelling around Thailand and deciding that they just aren't ready to go home yet. Volunteers receive training so that they are equipped to assume responsibility in a classroom where English may be very limited. There are also homestay options and placements in the charming tourist towns of Nong Khai, Pai and Ko Chang.

Open Mind Projects (☎ 0 4241 3578; www.openmindprojects.org; 1039/3 Th Keawworawut, Nong Khai) offers a lengthy list of volunteering options, including English-teaching and IT/computer-teaching positions in schools, temples and orphanages throughout the country.

Homestays

You can still travel independently without isolating yourself from the culture by staying at one of Thailand's quickly expanding networks of local homestays. More popular with domestic tourists, these homestays differ from guesthouses in that visitors are temporarily 'adopted' by a host family, who provides lodging, meals and sometimes sightseeing or cultural activities for a flat daily fee. Accommodation can range from a mat on the floor to a private room, and cultural activities often highlight a region's traditional way of life, from rice farming to silk weaving. English fluency varies, so homestays are also an excellent way to exercise your spoken Thai.

Every regional Tourist Authority of Thailand (TAT) office has a list of registered homestays; however, do note that the term 'homestay' is sometimes loosely applied to generic guesthouses rather than cultural immersions. The majority of genuine homestays are in the northeast, including the award-winning Ban Prasat programme (p463) outside Khorat. The homestay programme on Ko Yao Noi (p690), a Muslim fishing island, has also been recognised as a sustainable alternative to beach-style tourism, or you could work up a sweat helping out an ethnic Akha family in northern Thailand through the Akha Association for Education and Culture in Thailand (p354), a hybrid programme that combines aspects of volunteering and a homestay.

> A great ice-breaker is to find out how different cultures reproduce the sounds of everyday animals, such as cats, dogs and cows. The website www.hilltribe.org has an audio guide to a rooster's crow in different mountain languages.

BUYING LOCAL

Cottage industries are widespread in Thailand. To provide supplemental income, a housewife might open up a snack shop in her living room or set up a vendor stall on a busy corner. Tourist centres are especially big draws for these scrappy entrepreneurs who, with minimal overheads, crank out business selling fresh-squeezed orange juice, cold water, pad Thai and even dreadlocks. But these little businesses are vulnerable to pressures from the trends of modern economics: larger corporations. The first on the endangered species list is the corner sundry shop, where neighbourhood kids typically load up on after-school snacks and drinks. As 7-Elevens and other air-conditioned convenience stores become more prolific, mom-and-pop shops close down because they can't compete with the prices or variety. Keep this in mind the next time you pass through the chiming 7-Eleven door: is there a local shop nearby where you could buy water? The prices might be a little higher, but perhaps it is worth it.

RESPONSIBLE DIVING TIPS

The popularity of Thailand's diving industry places immense pressure on fragile dive sites. To help preserve the ecology, adhere to these simple rules:

- Avoid touching living marine organisms, standing on coral or dragging equipment (such as fins) across the reef. Coral polyps can be damaged by even the gentlest contact.
- When treading water in shallow reef areas, be careful not to kick up clouds of sand, which can easily smother the delicate reef organisms.
- Take great care in underwater caves where your air bubbles can be caught within the roof and leave previously submerged organisms high and dry.
- Take home all your rubbish and any litter you may find as well. Plastics are a particularly serious threat to marine life.
- Resist the temptation to feed fish.
- Avoid collecting or buying corals or shells.
- Encourage dive operators not to use anchors on the reef or ground boats on coral.

THE ENVIRONMENT

Along the Thai coastline, the oceans and the beaches are postcard perfect. But wake up before the vendors have had time to clean the beach and you'll see all the litter left behind by high tide. And those streams that feed into the open water: this is the island's sewage system. Although Thailand has made great headway in outlawing coral dynamiting and limiting the fishing industry, the country has not yet begun to address the damaging effects of coastal development on its greatest tourist draw: the coastal and marine environment. Also, the environmental and conservation movement in Thailand is often undermined by larger economic forces and a rush to modernise. See p85 for more information on Thailand's natural environment.

The conscientious visitor might hope for do-it-yourself measures to reduce the impact of tourism, but the solution requires a more powerful agent: the widespread enforcement of environmental controls such as proper sewage treatment and the adoption of smart-growth principles. In short, the Thai government has to seriously limit either development or tourism – both are unlikely.

The individual's greenest option is a holiday downer: avoid the islands where you'll be yet another trash-maker, freshwater-user or gas-guzzler. Even more radical is the argument that the next paradise is not worth discovering because of the environmental impact. Phuket, Phi-Phi, Samui and Samet are better equipped to deal with tourism than the islands that aren't on the tourist map, but many islandhoppers love the thrill of conquering virgin territory. Typically these emerging tourism islands have very fragile ecosystems and very little infrastructure. Sewage and garbage is either dumped into the ocean or a fire pit, and vital mangrove forests are ripped out if the landowners can make more money with new bungalows. Before you know it the sleepy fishing village is yet another resource-swallowing resort. Travellers call this the Lonely Planet syndrome, but it is often unregulated market forces.

There is no easy formula for the overused term of ecotourism. But we do suggest visiting the well-known beaches where the infrastructure exists to accommodate visitors. While on the developed beaches, practise common-sense conservation: use public transport (if possible) to cut down on road traffic and petrol consumption, reduce your generation of trash and opt for a cold shower. If you must visit the less-developed islands, do so with a volunteer programme so that you are giving back environmental awareness as well as economic development.

Tending to the emotional scars of the 2004 tsunami, Insight Out! organises photography and storytelling workshops for affected children. View its online gallery at www.insight out-project.org.

Planes, trains and automobiles generate CO_2 emissions that contribute to global climate change. To determine the 'carbon footprint' generated by your flight to Thailand, click on the CO_2 calculator at www.co2balance.com.

REDUCING THE IMPACT ON THE ENVIRONMENT. HOW?

■ Don't buy coral or sea shells – it's illegal in Thailand to buy or sell either.

■ Avoid all restaurants serving 'exotic' wildlife species.

■ When using hired boats near coral reefs, insist that boat operators don't lower anchor onto coral formations.

■ Refrain from purchasing or accepting drinking water offered in plastic bottles wherever possible. When there's a choice, request glass water bottles, which are recyclable in Thailand. The deposit is refundable when you return the bottle to any vendor who sells drinking water in glass bottles.

■ In outdoor areas where rubbish has accumulated, consider organising an impromptu cleanup crew to collect plastic, Styrofoam and other nonbiodegradables for delivery to a regular rubbish pick-up point.

■ Volunteer to collect (and later dispose of) rubbish when trekking or boating.

In the larger cities, you can abide by many of your at-home ecomeasures: forgo plastic bags at shops, rent a bicycle rather than a motorcycle for touring and team up with other travellers for chartered transport. The rural areas of northern Thailand are in many ways as fragile as the undeveloped beaches of the south. In some cases, sticking to the well-worn path is more considerate towards the threatened environment than forging into virgin territory. When trekking in the north, be a hospitable guest of the natural environment by keeping your distance from wild animals, staying on trails and taking out what you brought in.

Volunteering

The following programmes offer conservation, animal rescue or community-building work along Thailand's famed coastline.

Wild Animal Rescue Foundation (WAR; www.warthai.org), a Thai NGO, operates the Phuket Gibbon Rehabilitation Project (p671) and a sea-turtle conservation project in Ranong Province on the Andaman Coast. Volunteers at the gibbon sanctuary help care for the animals that are being rehabilitated for life in the wild, while sea-turtle volunteers help count and monitor nests.

Wildlife Friends of Thailand Rescue Centre (p560) puts volunteers to work caring for sun bears, macaques and gibbons who have been rescued from animal shows or abusive owners.

Starfish Ventures (☎ 44 800 1974817; www.starfishventures.co.uk; PO Box 9061, Epping, CM16 7WU, UK) arranges for volunteers to assist in the Turtle Conservation Centre (p243), a Thai-run, sea-turtle conservation programme on a protected island off the coast of Rayong on the Upper Southern Gulf.

Naucrates (www.naucrates.org) is an Italian NGO that works on a sea-turtle conservation project on Ko Phra Thong, an offshore Andaman island in Phang Nga province. Volunteers help in collecting scientific data that is used in the protection of three different marine turtle species (leatherback, olive ridley and green). The island is fairly undeveloped with one resort and several fishing villages.

Tsunami Volunteer Project (☎ 0 9882 8840; www.tsunamivolunteer.net; 26/61 Moo 7, Tambon Khuk Khak Takuapa, Phang Nga) is a Thai-led NGO based in Khao Lak, a coastal area that was severely affected by the 2004 tsunami. The organisation works primarily on rebuilding the affected communities through English education, construction projects, small business development and other community-based initiatives. Homestays with local villagers are also available.

The Culture

THE NATIONAL PSYCHE
Traditional Culture

Thais don't have a word that corresponds with the English term 'culture'. The nearest equivalent, *wáthánátham*, emphasises fine arts and ceremonies. Ask Thais to define their culture and they'll often talk about architecture, food, dance and festivals. Religion – a big Western influence on culture – is considered more or less separate from *wáthánátham*.

When outsiders speak of 'Thai culture' they're referring to behavioural modes rooted in the history of Tai migration throughout Southeast Asia, with commonalities shared by the Lao people of neighbouring Laos, the Shan of northeastern Myanmar (Burma) and the numerous tribal Tais found in isolated pockets from Dien Bien Phu (Vietnam) all the way to Assam (India). These modes are most prevalent in Thailand, the largest of the Tai homelands.

In the most 'modernised' of the existing Tai societies, the cultural underpinnings are evident in virtually every facet of life. 'Westernised' aspects (eg the wearing of trousers instead of a *phâakhamáa* or sarong, the presence of automobiles, cinemas and 7-Eleven stores) show how Thailand has adopted and adapted elements from other cultures. Nevertheless there are certain aspects of Thai society that virtually everyone recognises as 'Thai'.

SÀNÙK

The Thai word *sànùk* means 'fun' and anything worth doing – even work – should have an element of *sànùk*, otherwise it automatically becomes drudgery. This doesn't mean Thais don't want to work, just that they approach tasks with a sense of playfulness. Nothing condemns an activity more than *mâi sànùk* – 'not fun'. While you're in Thailand, sit down beside a rice field and watch workers planting, transplanting or harvesting rice. That it's backbreaking labour is obvious, but there's generally lots of *sànùk* – flirtation between the sexes, singing, trading insults and cracking jokes. The famous Thai smile comes partially out of this desire to make *sànùk*.

SAVING FACE

Thais believe strongly in the concept of saving face, ie avoiding confrontation and endeavouring not to embarrass yourself or other people (except when it's *sànùk* to do so). The ideal face-saver doesn't bring up negative topics in conversation, and when they notice stress in another's life, they usually won't say anything unless that person asks for help. Laughing at minor accidents – such as when someone trips and falls down – may seem callous but it's really just an attempt to save face on behalf of the person undergoing the mishap. This is another source of the Thai smile – it's the best possible face for almost any situation.

Talking loudly is perceived as rude by cultured Thais, whatever the situation. When encounters take a turn for the worse, try to refrain from getting angry – it won't help matters, since losing your temper means a loss of face for everyone present.

STATUS & OBLIGATION

All relationships in traditional Thai society – and those in the modern Thai milieu as well – are governed by connections between *phûu yài* ('big person' or senior) and *phûu náwy* ('little person' or junior). *Phûu náwy* defer to *phûu*

Very Thai (2005), by Philip Cornwell-Smith, is an exhaustive effort to uncover every mystery and explain all the quirks in Thailand that you ever wondered about, accompanied by evocative photos shot by John Goss.

www.thaivisa.com is where to look if you want to live/work in Thailand, with answers to question you might have along with numerous colourful posts.

www.faqs.org/faqs /thai/culture is the newsgroup's informative digest on Thai culture.

yài following simple lines of social rank defined by age, wealth, status, and personal and political power. Some examples of 'automatic' *phûu yài* status include adults (versus children), bosses (versus employees), elder classmates (versus younger classmates), elder siblings (versus younger siblings), teachers (versus pupils), members of the military (versus civilians), Thais (versus non-Thais) and so on.

Although this tendency towards social ranking is to some degree shared by many societies around the world, the Thai twist lies in the set of mutual obligations linking *phûu yài* to *phûu náwy*. *Phûu náwy* are supposed to show a degree of obedience and respect (together these concepts are covered by the single Thai term *kreng jai*) towards *phûu yài*, but in return *phûu yài* are obligated to care for or 'sponsor' the *phûu náwy* they have frequent contact with. In such relationships *phûu náwy* can, for example, ask *phûu yài* for favours involving money or job access. *Phûu yài* reaffirm their rank by granting requests when possible; to refuse would be to risk a loss of face and status.

Age is a large determinant where other factors are absent or weak. In such cases the terms *phîi* (elder sibling) and *náwng* (younger sibling) apply more than *phûu yài* and *phûu náwy*, although the intertwined obligations remain the same. Even people unrelated by blood quickly establish who's *phîi* and who's *náwng*. This is why one of the first questions Thais ask new acquaintances is 'How old are you?'.

When dining, touring or entertaining, the *phûu yài* always picks up the tab; if a group is involved, the person with the most social rank pays the bill for everyone, even if it empties his or her wallet. For a *phûu náwy* to try and pay would risk loss of face.

Money plays a large role in defining *phûu yài* status in most situations. A person who turned out to be successful in his or her post-school career would never think of allowing an ex-classmate of lesser success (even if they were once on an equal social footing) to pay the bill. Likewise a young, successful executive will pay an older person's way in spite of the age difference.

The implication is that whatever wealth you come into is to be shared, at least partially, with those less fortunate. This doesn't apply to strangers, but always comes into play with friends and relatives.

Check out www.thai-blogs.com to peek into the lives of various Thais and expats and link to sites translating Thai music or offering free Thai cooking video downloads.

www.thaiworldview.com/culture/htm is a useful website, with photos covering everything from housing to Thai TV and cinema.

LIFESTYLE

Tune in to any Thai TV channel around 8pm and let soap opera plots draw a rough outline of the Thai story. Most series are set in the capital and although they are hardly realistic – the men are always handsome, the women beautiful, their automobiles are spotless – the plotlines are propped up by Thai realities. A young Thai Isan girl from the northeastern countryside takes a cleaning job in a wealthy Bangkok household, and the resulting weekly culture clashes keep Thai viewers glued to the screen. In another, a college student argues with his father, a *khâa râatchákaan* (government civil servant), over whether he should spend a Saturday afternoon at a fashionable shopping area notorious for tattoo parlours, punk hair salons and the abundance of unaccompanied girls in revealing spaghetti-strap tops.

Individual lifestyles vary tremendously according to family background and income. If you could sneak a peek at what Thais eat for breakfast, you'd have a fighting chance at guessing both. *Khâo tôm phúi*, an array of small dishes of dried fish, peanuts and pickled vegetables eaten with hot rice soup, indicates probable Chinese ancestry. Add a plate of pricey sweet cured sausage and they're middle-class Chinese Thai. Spot a bowl of steaming *kaeng khĭaw-wăan* (sweet-green curry) or *kaeng phèt* (Thai red curry) over rice and it's likely your diner comes from mostly Thai genes, and prefers a basic,

economic diet. The same Thai choosing ham, eggs and toast, accompanied by espresso, has money and has probably travelled abroad. Meanwhile a *thai pàk tâi* in southern Thailand might be digging into *khâo yam*, a spicy salad of rice, shaved lemongrass, toasted coconut and tamarind sauce.

Walk the streets early in the morning and you'll catch the flash of shaved heads bobbing above bright ochre robes, as monks engage in *bindabàat*, the daily house-to-house alms food gathering. Thai men are expected to shave their heads and don monastic robes at least once in their lives. Some enter the monkhood twice, first as 10-vow novices in their pre-teen years and again as fully ordained, 227-vow monks after the age of 20.

Green-hued onion domes looming over lower rooftops belong to mosques and mark the neighbourhood as Muslim, while brightly painted and ornately carved cement spires indicate a Hindu temple. A handful of steepled Christian churches, including a few historic ones, have taken root over the centuries in Chanthaburi and other places near the borders of former French Indochina – Cambodia and Laos – as well as in Bangkok. In urban centres, large round doorways topped with heavily inscribed Chinese characters and flanked by red paper lanterns mark the location of *săan jâo*, Chinese temples dedicated to the worship of Buddhist, Taoist and Confucian deities.

Thai royal ceremonies remain almost exclusively the domain of one of the most ancient religious traditions still functioning in the kingdom, Brahmanism. White-robed, top-knotted priests of Indian descent keep alive an arcane collection of rituals that, it is believed, must be performed regularly to sustain the three pillars of Thai nationhood, namely sovereignty, religion and the monarchy. Such rituals are performed regularly at a complex of shrines near Wat Suthat in Bangkok.

Animism predated the arrival of all other religions in Thailand and still plays an important role in the everyday life of most residents who believe that *phrá phuum* (guardian spirits) inhabit rivers, canals, trees and other natural features. The Thais build shrines to house the displaced spirits. These dollhouse-like structures perch on wood or cement pillars next to their homes and receive daily offerings of rice, fruit, flowers and water. Peek inside the smaller, more modest spirit homes and you'll typically see a collection of ceramic or plastic figurines representing the property's guardian spirits.

Larger, more elaborate spirit shrines stand alongside hotels and office buildings and may contain bronze images of Brahma or Shiva. Day and night you'll see Thais kneeling before such shrines to offer flowers, incense and candles, and to pray for favours from these Indian 'spirit kings' (see p58).

One in 10 citizens lives and works in Bangkok and some 60% of the country's wealth is concentrated here. The legal minimum daily wage in Bangkok and the adjacent provinces of Samut Prakan, Samut Sakhon, Pathum Thani, Nonthaburi and Nakhon Pathom amounted to 170B (US$4.50) in 2004, roughly 35B higher than the rest of Thailand.

A typical civil servant at an entry-level government job earns around 7000B per month, but with promotions and extra job training may earn up to 15,000B. In the private sector an office worker starts at about the same level but will receive quicker pay rises.

In rural areas, female members of a family typically inherit the land and throughout Thailand women tend to control the family finances. Women constitute 55% of all enrolments in secondary and tertiary schools and about half of the workforce, outranking many countries in both categories. In economics, academia and health services, women hold most of the administrative positions – 80% of all Thai dentists are female.

Visit www.thaifolk.com /Doc/culture2_e.htm for details on Thai festivals, folk rituals and common Buddhist ceremonies.

Thailand has a penchant for Guinness World Records, including: man with longest hair, largest aerobics workout, largest mass scuba dive, biggest hamburger, and most linked skydivers.

Fun Bar Karaoke (1997) – this cinematic satire of Bangkok life received critical acclaim for its realistic depiction of modern urban living mixed with sage humour.

So much for the good news. Although women generally fare well in education, the labour force and in rural land inheritance, their cultural standing is less than that of men. An oft-repeated Thai saying reminds us that men form the front legs of the elephant, women the hind legs (at least they're pulling equal weight). Parts of some Buddhist temples may be off limits to women, and when hanging laundry, the custom is always to place female underwear lower than men's!

www.bangkokrecorder
.com is your up-to-the-
minute guide to Bangkok
activities and nightlife,
with cheeky bar and
restaurant reviews and
photo galleries of the
coolest parties.

Thailand's commercial sex industry actually caters far more to the local market (about 95%) than to foreign visitors. The infamous red-light districts that have perpetually captivated Western media attention are limited to a few areas of Bangkok, Pattaya and Phuket.

Tolerance towards sex extends to homosexuality, and Thailand has a relatively open and liberal attitude towards gay orientations, compared to most other nations.

POPULATION

Estimated at 65 million the population of Thailand is currently growing at just under 1% per annum, because of a vigorous nationwide family-planning campaign.

Over one-third of all Thais live in urban areas. Bangkok is by far the largest city with around six million people in the city proper, or eight million including the adjacent provinces.

Ranking the nation's other cities by population depends on whether you look at the rather limited municipal districts *(thêtsàbaan)* or more realistic metropolitan districts *(meuang)*. Using the *meuang* measure, after Bangkok, the five most-populated cities in descending order (not counting the densely populated 'suburb' provinces of Samut Prakan and Nonthaburi, which rank second and third if considered separately from Bangkok) are: Udon Thani (population 244,000), Chonburi (221,000), Nakhon Ratchasima (210,000), Chiang Mai (196,000) and Hat Yai (191,000). Most other towns have populations below 100,000.

On the 2002 UN Human Development Index, Thailand received an overall ranking of 76, falling in the upper half of the UN-designated 'medium human development' range. The average life expectancy is 70 years, the highest in mainland Southeast Asia. It has a relatively youthful population; only about 12% are older than 50 years and 6% are aged over 65.

*Child of the North-East
(Luk Isan)*, by Wichit
Khunawut, follows the
ups and downs of a
farming family living in
drought-ridden Isan; it
became one of the first
films to offer urban Thais
an understanding of the
hardships endured in the
country.

The Thai Majority

Some 75% of citizens are ethnic Thais, who can be divided into four groups: Central Thais, or Siamese, of the Chao Phraya Delta (the most densely populated region of the country); Thai Lao of northeastern Thailand; Thai Pak Tai of southern Thailand; and northern Thais. Each group speaks its own dialect and to a certain extent practises customs unique to its region. Politically and economically the Central Thais are the dominant group, although they barely outnumber the Thai Lao.

Small minority groups who speak Thai dialects include the Lao Song (Phetchaburi and Ratchaburi); the Phuan (Chaiyaphum, Phetchaburi, Prachinburi); the Phu Thai (Sakon Nakhon, Nakhon Phanom, Mukdahan); the Shan (Mae Hong Son), the Thai Khorat or Suay (Khorat); the Thai Lü (Nan, Chiang Rai); the Thai-Malay (Satun, Trang, Krabi); and the Yaw (Nakhon Phanom, Sakon Nakhon).

The Chinese

People of Chinese ancestry – second- or third-generation Hakka, Chao Zhou, Hainanese or Cantonese – make up 11% of the population. In northern

Thailand there is also a substantial number of Hui-Chinese Muslims who emigrated from Yunnan in the late 19th century to avoid religious and ethnic persecution during the Qing dynasty.

Ethnic Chinese in Thailand probably enjoy better relations with the majority of the population than they do in any other country in Southeast Asia – although there was a brief spell of anti-Chinese sentiment during the reign of Rama VI (1910–25; see p34). Wealthy Chinese also introduced their daughters to the royal court as consorts, developing royal connections and adding a Chinese bloodline that extends to the current king.

Other Minorities

The second-largest ethnic minority are the Malays (3.5%), most of whom reside in the provinces of Songkhla, Yala, Pattani, Satun and Narathiwat. The remaining 10.5% of the population is divided among smaller non-Thai-speaking groups like the Vietnamese, Khmer, Mon, Semang (Sakai), Moken (*chao leh* or 'sea gypsies'), Htin, Mabri, Khamu and a variety of hill tribes.

A small number of Europeans and other non-Asians reside in Bangkok and the provinces.

Hill Tribes

Ethnic minorities in the mountainous regions of northern Thailand are often called 'hill tribes', or in Thai vernacular, *chao khǎo* (mountain people). Each hill tribe has its own language, customs, mode of dress and spiritual beliefs.

Most are of seminomadic origin, having come from Tibet, Myanmar, China and Laos during the past 200 years or so. They are 'fourth world' people in that they belong neither to the main aligned powers nor to the developing nations. Rather, they have crossed and continue to cross national borders, often fleeing oppression by other cultures, without regard for recent nationhood.

Language and culture constitute the borders of their world. Some groups are caught between the 6th and 21st centuries, while others are gradually being assimilated into modern life. Many tribes people are also moving into lowland areas as montane lands become deforested by both traditional swidden (slash-and-burn) cultivation and illegal logging.

The Tribal Research Institute in Chiang Mai recognises 10 different hill tribes but there may be up to 20. The institute estimates the total hill-tribe population to be around 550,000.

The tribes most likely to be encountered by visitors fall into three main linguistic groups: the Tibeto-Burman (Lisu, Lahu, Akha), the Karenic (Karen, Kayah) and the Austro-Thai (Hmong, Mien). Within each group there may also be several subgroups, eg Blue Hmong, White Hmong; these names usually refer to predominant elements of clothing that vary between the subgroups.

Hill tribes tend to have among the lowest standards of living. Although it's tempting to correlate this with traditional lifestyles, their situation is compounded, in most cases, by a lack of Thai citizenship. Without the latter, they don't have the right to own land or even to receive the minimum wage, plus they may be denied access to health care and schooling. In the last couple of decades efforts to integrate hill tribes into Thai society via free education and the issuing of Thai identity cards may have improved the lot of a minority of tribes people. Of course, the irony is that further Thai assimilation will threaten their cultural identities.

The Shan (Thai Yai, meaning 'large Thai') are not included in the following descriptions as they are not a hill-tribe group per se – they have permanent habitations and speak a language similar to Thai. The Shan are considered by

www.hilltribe.org teaches you about the hill tribes of northern Thailand and how to behave yourself in hill-tribe villages.

Thai scholars to have been the original inhabitants of the area. Nevertheless, Shan villages are often common stops on hill-tribe treks.

The following comments on dress refer mostly to the females as hill-tribe men tend to dress like rural Thais. The population figures are taken from the most recent estimates.

AKHA (I-KAW)
Population: 48,500
Origin: Tibet
Present locations: Thailand, Laos, Myanmar, Yunnan
Economy: rice, corn, opium
Belief system: animism, with an emphasis on ancestor worship
Cultural characteristics: Headdress of beads, feathers and dangling silver ornaments are common adornments. Villages are along mountain ridges or on steep slopes 1000m to 1400m in altitude. The well-known Akha Swing Ceremony takes place from mid-August to mid-September, between planting and harvest. The Akha are among the poorest of Thailand's ethnic minorities and tend to resist assimilation into the Thai mainstream. Like the Lahu, they often cultivate opium for their own use.

Akha houses are constructed of wood and bamboo, usually atop short wooden stilts and roofed with thick grass. At the entrance of every traditional Akha village stands a simple wooden gateway consisting of two vertical struts joined by a lintel. Akha shamans affix various charms made from bamboo strips to the gateway to prevent malevolent spirits from entering. Standing next to the gateway are crude wooden figures of a man and a woman, each bearing exaggerated sexual organs, in the belief that human sexuality is abhorrent to the spirit world.

LAHU (MUSOE)
Population: 73,200
Origin: Tibet
Present locations: south China, Thailand, Myanmar
Economy: rice, corn, opium
Belief system: theistic animism (supreme deity is Geusha); some groups are Christian
Cultural characteristics: Black-and-red jackets with narrow skirts are worn by women, bright green or blue-green baggy trousers are worn by men. The Lahu tend to live at about 1000m altitude. There are five main groups – Red Lahu, Black Lahu, White Lahu, Yellow Lahu and Lahu Sheleh. Known to be excellent hunters, the Thai term for this tribe, *musoe*, is derived from a Burmese word meaning 'hunter'.

Houses are built of wood, bamboo and grass, and usually stand on short wooden posts. Intricately woven Lahu shoulder bags (*yâam*) are prized by collectors. Lahu food is probably the spiciest of all the cuisines.

LISU (LISAW)
Population: 28,000
Origin: Tibet
Present locations: Thailand, Yunnan
Economy: rice, corn, opium, livestock
Belief system: animism with ancestor worship and spirit possession
Cultural characteristics: The women wear long multicoloured tunics over trousers and sometimes black turbans with tassels. Men wear baggy green or blue pants pegged in at the ankles. Premarital sex is said to be common (although some observers dispute this), along with freedom in choosing

'Akha shamans affix various charms made from bamboo strips to the gateway to prevent malevolent spirits from entering'

marital partners. Patrilineal clans have pan-tribal jurisdiction, which makes the Lisu unique among hill-tribe groups (most of which have power centred with either a shaman or a village headman). Lisu villages are usually in the mountains at about 1000m. Homes are built on the ground and consist mostly of bamboo and grass. Older homes – today quite rare – may be made from mud brick or mud-and-bamboo thatch.

MIEN (YAO)
Population: 40,300
Origin: central China
Present locations: Thailand, south China, Laos, Myanmar, Vietnam
Economy: rice, corn, opium
Belief system: animism with ancestor worship and Taoism
Cultural characteristics: Women wear trousers and black jackets with intricately embroidered patches and red furlike collars, along with large dark-blue or black turbans. The Mien are heavily influenced by Chinese traditions and they use Chinese characters to write their language. They settle near mountain springs at between 1000m and 1200m. Kinship is patrilineal and marriage is polygamous. They are highly skilled at crafts such as embroidery and silver-smithing. Houses are built at ground level, out of wood or bamboo thatch.

'The Mien are heavily influenced by Chinese traditions and use Chinese characters to write their language'

HMONG (MONG OR MAEW)
Population: 124,000
Origin: south China
Present locations: south China, Thailand, Laos, Vietnam
Economy: rice, corn, opium
Belief system: animism
Cultural characteristics: Tribespeople wear simple black jackets and indigo or black baggy trousers (White Hmong) with striped borders or indigo skirts (Blue Hmong) and silver jewellery. Sashes may be worn around the waist, and embroidered aprons draped front and back. Most women wear their hair in a large bun. They usually live on mountain peaks or plateaus above 1000m. Houses, made of wood or thatch, sit on the ground. Kinship is patrilineal and polygamy is permitted. The Hmong are Thailand's second-largest hill-tribe group and are especially numerous in Chiang Mai Province.

KAREN (YANG OR KARIANG)
Population: 322,000
Origin: Myanmar
Present locations: Thailand, Myanmar
Economy: rice, vegetables, livestock
Belief system: animism, Buddhism, Christianity, depending on the group
Cultural characteristics: Thickly woven V-neck tunics of various colours (unmarried women wear white) are typically worn. Kinship is matrilineal and marriage is monogamous. They tend to live in lowland valleys and practise crop rotation rather than swidden agriculture. Karen homes are built on low stilts or posts, with the roofs swooping quite low. There are four distinct Karen groups – the Skaw (White) Karen, Pwo Karen, Pa-O (Black) Karen and Kayah (Red) Karen. These groups number about half of all hill-tribe people.

EDUCATION
At 92.6%, Thailand's literacy rate is one of the highest in Southeast Asia. Free public schooling is compulsory for nine years. Although high value is placed on education as a way to achieve material success, at most levels the system itself tends to favour rote learning over independent thinking.

Check out www.thailand
life.com – created by a
Thai student, this site is
one of the most compre-
hensive online collections
of Thai cultural vignettes.

Thailand's public school system is organised around six years at the *pràthŏm* (primary) level, beginning at the age of six, followed by either three or six years of *mátháyom* (secondary) education. The three-year course is for those planning to follow school with three to five years of *wí-chaa-chîip* (trade school), while the *mátháyom* (six-year course) is for students planning to continue at the *ùdom* (tertiary) level ie university. Less than nine years of formal education is the national norm.

Private and international schools for the foreign and local elite are found in Bangkok and Chiang Mai, and in the other large provincial cities. The country boasts over 30 public and five private universities, as well as numerous trade schools and technical colleges.

A teaching certificate may be obtained after attending a two-year, post-secondary programme at one of the many teachers' colleges. Two of Thailand's universities, Thammasat and Chulalongkorn, are considered to be among the top 50 in Asia.

SPORT
Muay Thai

The energy boosting
beverage Red Bull has its
origins in Thailand and
was originally called Krating Daeng, or Red Gaur (a
type of ox).

Almost anything goes in this martial sport, both in the ring and in the stands. If you don't mind the violence (in the ring), a *muay thai* (Thai boxing) match is worth attending for the pure spectacle – the wild musical accompaniment, the ceremonial beginning of each match and the frenzied betting throughout the stadium.

All surfaces of the body are considered fair targets and any part of the body, except the head, may be used to strike an opponent. Common blows include high kicks to the neck, elbow thrusts to the face and head, knee hooks to the ribs and low crescent kicks to the calf. Punching is considered the weakest of all blows and kicking merely a way to 'soften up' one's opponent; knee and elbow strikes are decisive in most matches.

A *ram muay* (boxing dance) precedes every match. This ceremony usually lasts about five minutes and expresses obeisance to the fighter's guru *(khruu)*, as well as to the guardian spirit of Thai boxing. The complex series of gestures and movements is performed to the ringside musical accompaniment of Thai *pìi* (oboe) and percussion.

Ong Bak: Muay Thai
Warrior (2003; Prachya
Pinkaew) is a film that
harkens back to early
Jackie Chan. A sacred
Buddha is stolen from
a Thai village, and one
of the villagers uses his
incredible muay thai skills
to retrieve the image
from mafioso in Bangkok.

Fighters wear sacred headbands and armbands into the ring for good luck and divine protection. The headband is removed after the *ram muay*, but the armband, which contains a small Buddha image, is worn throughout the match.

With around 60,000 full-time boxers in Thailand, matches are staged at provincial rings and temple fairs all over the country. The most competitive are fought at two Bangkok stadiums, Ratchadamnoen and Lumphini.

For more on *muay thai* courses, see p740.

Kràbìi-Kràbawng

Another traditional martial art still practised in Thailand is *kràbìi-kràbawng*. It focuses on hand-held weapons, in particular the *kràbìi* (sword), *phlawng* (quarter-staff), *ngáo* (halberd), *dàap sǎwng meu* (a pair of swords held in each hand) and *mái sun-sàwk* (a pair of clubs). Although for most Thais *kràbìi-kràbawng* is a ritual to be displayed during festivals or at tourist venues, the art is still solemnly taught according to a 400-year-old tradition handed down from Ayuthaya's Wat Phutthaisawan. The king's elite bodyguards are trained in *kràbìi-kràbawng*; many Thai cultural observers perceive it as a 'purer' tradition than *muay thai*.

Modern matches are held within a marked circle, beginning with a *wâi khruu* ceremony and accompanied throughout by a musical ensemble. Thai-

---

SIAMESE FOOTBALL

Football (soccer) is very popular throughout Thailand as both a spectator and participatory sport. In 2004 Prime Minister Thaksin Shinawatra tried to buy a majority share in Liverpool Football Club, but public aversion to the idea persuaded him not to follow through on the purchase.

---

boxing techniques and judo-like throws are employed in conjunction with weapons techniques. Although sharpened weapons are used, the contestants refrain from striking their opponents – the winner is decided on the basis of stamina and the technical skill displayed.

Tàkrâw

Sometimes called Siamese football in old English texts, *tàkrâw* refers to games in which a woven rattan ball about 12cm in diameter is kicked around. The rattan (or sometimes plastic) ball itself is called a *lûuk tàkrâw*. Popular in several neighbouring countries, *tàkrâw* was introduced to the Southeast Asian Games by Thailand, and international championships tend to alternate between the Thais and Malaysians. In Thailand the traditional way to play is for players to stand in a circle (the size depends on the number of players) and simply try to keep the ball airborne by kicking it soccer-style. Points are scored for style, difficulty and variety of kicking manoeuvres.

A popular variation on *tàkrâw* – and the one used in intramural or international competitions – is played like volleyball, with a net, but with only the feet and head permitted to touch the ball. It's amazing to see the players perform aerial pirouettes, spiking the ball over the net with their feet. Another variation has players kicking the ball into a hoop 4.5m above the ground – basketball with feet, and no backboard!

'It's amazing to see the players perform aerial pirouettes, spiking the ball over the net with their feet'

MEDIA

Thailand's 1997 constitution guarantees freedom of the press, although the Royal Police Department reserves the power to suspend publishing licences for national security reasons. Newspaper editors nevertheless exercise self-censorship in certain realms, particularly with regard to the monarchy.

Thai press freedom reached its high watermark in the mid-1990s, while Chuan Leekpai's Democrat Party was in power. After the 1997 economic downturn and the ascension of Thaksin Shinawatra's Thai Rak Thai (TRT) Party, Thailand's media have found themselves increasingly subject to interference by political and financial interests.

Before the 2001 general election, Shin Corp, a telecommunications conglomerate owned by former prime minister Thaksin's family, bought a controlling interest in iTV, Thailand's only independent TV station. Shortly thereafter the new board sacked 23 iTV journalists who complained that the station was presenting biased coverage of the election to favour Thaksin and TRT. Almost overnight, the station transformed from an independent, indepth news channel to an entertainment channel with flimsy, pro-Thaksin news coverage.

The country's international reputation for press freedom took another serious dent in 2002 when two Western journalists were nearly expelled for reporting on a public address presented by the Thai king on his birthday, a portion of which was highly critical of then-prime minister Thaksin. In 2004 Veera Prateepchaikul, editor-in-chief of the *Bangkok Post*, lost his job due to direct pressure from board members with ties to Thaksin and TRT. Allegedly the latter were upset with *Post* criticism of the way in which Thaksin handled the 2003–04 bird flu crisis.

Observers agree that Thai press freedom has reached it lowest ebb since the 1970s era of Thai military dictatorship, and will probably remain there as long as TRT are in power.

During office, Thaksin's disdain for criticism, along with his vast riches, led him and TRT to file a litany of 'defamation' lawsuits against critical individuals, publications and media groups who printed embarrassing revelations about his regime.

The interim regime after the 2006 coup didn't start off so well either, as they strongly advocated that news outlets should go easy on them, and the government even blocked Thai cable from transmitting a CNN interview Thaksin gave months after the coup.

RELIGION
Buddhism

Approximately 95% of Thai people are Theravada Buddhists. Scholars sometimes refer to the religion as Lankavamsa (Sinhalese lineage) Buddhism because this form of Buddhism came from Sri Lanka during the Sukhothai period. Prior to the arrival of Sinhalese monks in the 13th century, an Indian form of Theravada existed at the kingdom of Dvaravati (6th to 10th centuries), while Mahayana Buddhism of the Tantric variety was known in pockets of the northeast under Khmer control in the 10th and 11th centuries. One of the most complete selections of material on Theravada Buddhism available on the web can be found at www.access toinsight.org.

Since the Sukhothai period (13th to 15th centuries), Thailand alone has maintained an unbroken canonical tradition and 'pure' ordination lineage. Ironically, when the ordination lineage in Sri Lanka broke down during the 18th century under Dutch persecution, it was Thailand that restored the *sangha* (Buddhist monastic community) there.

Theravada doctrine stresses the three principal aspects of existence: *dukkha* (stress, unsatisfactoriness, disease), *anicca* (impermanence, transience of all things) and *anatta* (insubstantiality or nonessentiality of reality – no permanent 'soul'). These three concepts, when 'discovered' by Siddhartha Gautama in the 6th century BC, were in direct contrast to the Hindu belief in *paramatman*, an eternal, blissful self. Hence Buddhism was originally a 'heresy' against India's Brahmanic religion. Gautama, an Indian prince-turned-ascetic, subjected himself to many years of severe austerity before he realised that this was not the way to reach the end of suffering. He became known as Buddha, 'the enlightened' or 'the awakened' and as Gautama Buddha he spoke of four noble truths that had the power to liberate any human being who could realise them.

The ultimate end of Theravada Buddhism is *nibbana* ('nirvana' in Sanskrit), which literally means the 'blowing out' or extinction of all grasping and thus of all suffering (*dukkha*). Effectively, *nibbana* is also an end to the cycle of rebirths (both moment-to-moment and life-to-life) that is existence.

In reality, most Thai Buddhists aim for rebirth in a 'better' existence rather than the supramundane goal of *nibbana*. By feeding monks, giving donations to temples and performing regular worship at the local wat they hope to improve their lot, acquiring enough merit (*puñña* in Pali; *bun* in Thai) to prevent or at least reduce their number of rebirths. The concept of rebirth is almost universally accepted in Thailand, even by non-Buddhists, and the Buddhist theory of karma is well expressed in the Thai proverb *tham dii, dâi dii; tham chûa, dâi chûa* (good actions bring good results; bad actions bring bad results).

Being Dharma: The Essence of the Buddha's Teachings (2001) is an inspiring and informative collection of talks on Buddhist practice given by the late Thai forest monk Ajahn Chan.

The novel *Bangkok 8* (2003), by John Burdett, is a thriller told in the first person by a half-*faràng* (half-Westerner), half-Thai police officer, whose mind is paradoxically divided between Buddhism and the dangerous Bangkok underworld.

All the Tiratana (Triple Gems) revered by Thai Buddhists – the Buddha, the *dhamma* (the teachings) and the *sangha* (the Buddhist community) – are quite visible in Thailand. The Buddha, in his myriad sculptural forms, is found on a high shelf in the lowliest roadside restaurants as well as in the lounges of expensive Bangkok hotels. The *dhamma* is chanted morning and evening in every wat and taught to every Thai citizen in primary school. The *sangha* is seen everywhere in the presence of orange-robed monks, especially in the early morning hours when they perform their alms rounds.

Thai Buddhism has no particular 'Sabbath' or day of the week when Thais are supposed to make temple visits. Instead, Thai Buddhists visit the wat whenever they feel like it, most often on *wan phrá* (excellent days), which occur every 7th or 8th day depending on phases of the moon. On such visits typical activities include: the traditional offering of lotus buds, incense and candles at various altars, and bone reliquaries around the wat compound; the offering of food to the temple *sangha* (monks always eat first); meditating (individually or in groups); listening to monks chanting *suttas* or Buddhist discourse; and attending a *thêt* or *dhamma* talk by the abbot or some other respected teacher.

OK Baytong (2003), by Nonzee Nimibutr, is set in the Thai-Malaysian border town of Betong, Yala, and follows a man who leaves the Buddhist monkhood to care for his niece after his sister dies; it's full of insights into southern Thai ways of life and the Thai Muslim nationalist movement.

MONKS & NUNS

Socially, every Thai male is expected to become a monk (*bhikkhu* in Pali; *phrá* or *phrá phíksù* in Thai) for a short period in his life, optimally between the time he finishes school and the time he starts a career or marries. Men or boys under 20 years of age may enter the *sangha* as novices (*samanera* in Pali; *naen* in Thai) – this is not unusual since a family earns great merit when one of its sons 'takes robe and bowl'. Traditionally, the length of time spent in the wat is three months, during the *phansăa* (Buddhist lent), which begins in July and coincides with the rainy season. However, nowadays men may spend as little as a week to accrue merit as monks. There are about 32,000 monasteries in Thailand and 460,000 monks; many of these monks are ordained for a lifetime.

Monks who live in the city usually emphasise study of the Buddhist scriptures, while those living in the forest tend to emphasise meditation.

At one time India had a separate Buddhist monastic lineage for females. The fully ordained nuns were called *bhikkhuni* and observed more vows than monks did – 311 precepts as opposed to the 227 followed by monks. The *bhikkhuni sangha* travelled from its birthplace in India to Sri Lanka around two centuries after the Buddha's lifetime, taken there by the daughter of King Ashoka, Sanghamitta Theri. However, the tradition died out there following the Hindu Chola invasion in the 13th century. Monks from Siam later travelled to Sri Lanka to restore the male *sangha*, but because there were no ordained *bhikkhuni* in Thailand at the time, Sri Lanka's *bhikkhuni sangha* wasn't restored until recent years.

In Thailand, the modern equivalent is the *mâe chii* (mother priest) – women who live the monastic life as *atthasila* (eight-precept) nuns. They are largely outnumbered by male monastics (by 46 to one). Thai nuns shave their heads, wear white robes and take vows in an ordination procedure similar to that of the monks. Generally speaking, *mâe chii* nunhood in Thailand isn't considered as 'prestigious' as monkhood. The average Thai Buddhist makes a great show of offering new robes and household items to the monks at the local wat but pays much less attention to the nuns. This is mainly due to the fact that nuns generally don't perform ceremonies on behalf of lay people, so there is often less incentive for people to make offerings to them. Furthermore, many Thais equate the number of precepts observed with

Thai Buddhist nun Chatsumarn Kabilsingh writes about what it means to be Thai, female and Buddhist in *Thai Women in Buddhism* (1991).

THAILAND'S FIRST FEMALE ORDINATION

In February 2002 Mae Chee Varangghana Vanavichayen underwent a *samanera* (novice Buddhist nun) ordination at Wat Songthamkalayanee in Nakhon Pathom. The ordination was conducted in the Sinhalese style by eight *bhikkhuni* (fully ordained nuns) hailing from Sri Lanka, Indonesia and Taiwan. Four years earlier, two Thai women had been ordained in Sri Lanka but this was the first female ordination ever to take place on Thai soil. The tradition was revived in Sri Lanka via ordination from Mahayana Buddhist nuns.

Thailand's clerical leaders publicly criticised the ordination as contrary to tradition, but did nothing to obstruct the ceremony or annul the ordination afterwards, leading many to believe that the hierarchy views the new lineage as inevitable.

---

the total merit achieved; hence nunhood is seen as less 'meritorious' than monkhood because *mâe chii* keep only eight precepts.

A movement to ordain *bhikkhuni* in Sri Lanka, however, has provided new opportunities, and in 2002 a Thai woman was fully ordained in Thailand for the first time.

FURTHER INFORMATION

Wat Bowonniwet A Buddhist bookshop across the street from the north entrance to this temple (p132) in Bangkok sells a variety of English-language books on Buddhism.

World Fellowship of Buddhists (☎ 0 2661 1284-87; www.wfb-hq.org; 616 Soi 24, Th Sukhumvit, Bangkok). Senior *faràng* (Westerner) monks hold English-language *dhamma*/meditation classes here on the first Sunday of each month from noon to 6pm.

Other Religions

A small percentage of Thais, and most of the Malays in the south (which amounts to about 4% of the total population), are followers of Islam. Half a per cent of the population – primarily missionised hill tribes and Vietnamese immigrants – profess Christian beliefs, while the remaining 0.5% are Confucianists, Taoists, Mahayana Buddhists and Hindus. Mosques (in the south) and Chinese temples are common enough that you will probably come across some while travelling throughout Thailand. Before entering any temple, sanctuary or mosque you must always remove your shoes, and in a mosque your head must be covered.

Arts

Thailand's emphasis on artistic beauty infuses the audacious temples, the humble traditional houses, the religious offerings and the high arts developed for the royal court. Many of the country's ancient handicrafts and traditions reflect some of Asia's dominant cultures – Khmer, Indian and Chinese – that passed through Thailand. The global exchange continues today with a maturing world of modern Thai artists adapting outside techniques and themes on canvas and in multimedia.

The Arts of Thailand (1999), by Steven Van Beek, is a thorough account of artistic movements in Thailand from the Bronze Age to the Ratanakosin era.

ARCHITECTURE
Traditional Residential Architecture

A harmonious blend of function and style, traditional Thai homes accommodated the weather and the family. A typical home would consist of a wooden single-room house raised on stilts; more elaborate homes might link a series of single rooms by elevated walkways. Since many Thai villages were built near rivers, the elevation provided protection for the home from the flooding during the annual monsoon. During the dry season the space beneath the house was used as a hideaway from the heat of the day, an outdoor kitchen or as a barn for farm animals. Later this all-purpose space would shelter bicycles and motorcycles. Once plentiful in Thai forests, teak was always the material of choice for wooden structures and typically indicates that a house is at least 50 years old.

Rooflines in central, northern and southern Thailand are steeply pitched and often decorated at the corners or along the gables with motifs related to the *naga*, a mythical sea serpent long believed to be a spiritual protector of Thai-speaking cultures throughout Asia. In southern Thailand bamboo and palm thatch have always been more common building materials than wood, and even today these renewable plant sources remain important construction elements.

In Thailand's four southernmost provinces it's not unusual to come upon houses of entirely Malay design, in which high masonry pediments or foundations, rather than wood stilts, lift the living areas well above the ground. Roofs of tile or thatch tend to be less steeply pitched, and hipped gables – almost entirely absent in traditional Thai architecture – can be found further north.

Temple Architecture

Most striking of Thailand's architectural heritage is the Buddhist temple that dazzles in the tropical sun with wild colours and soaring lines.

Thai temples (wat) are a compound of different buildings serving specific religious functions. The most important structures include the *uposatha* (*bòt* in central Thai, *sǐm* in northern and northeastern Thai), which is a conse-

---

HOUSES OF THE HOLY

Every building or working space in Thailand has an associated 'spirit house', built to provide a home for the *phrá phuum* (earth spirits) that reside at that location. These spirits ensure good fortune, but they must be persuaded to stay in the spirit houses through daily offerings of food, flowers and incense. If the house is enlarged the spirit house must also be enlarged, so the spirits do not feel slighted. Spirit houses must be consecrated by a Brahman priest, dating the tradition back to the Khmer period, when the region was predominantly Hindu. However, the idea of guardian spirits is probably older still – a leftover from the original animist faith of the region.

crated chapel where monastic ordinations are held, and a *wíhǎan*, where important Buddha images are housed.

The architectural symbolism of these temple buildings relies heavily on Hindu-Buddhist iconography: naga, the mythical serpent that guarded Buddha during meditation, is depicted in the temple roofline where the green and gold tiles are said to represent the serpent's scales and the soaring eaves that of its diamond-shaped head. On the tip of the roof is the silhouette of the *châwfáh*: often bird-shaped decorations the colour of gold. Rooflines are usually tiered into three levels, representing the triple gems of Buddhism: the Buddha, the *dhamma* (Buddhist philosophy) and the *sangha* (the Buddhist community).

Another classic component of temple architecture is the presence of one or more stupa (*chedi* in Thai), a solid mountain-shaped monument that pays tribute to the enduring stability of Buddhism. Stupas come in a myriad of styles, from simple inverted bowl-shaped designs imported from Sri Lanka to the more elaborate multisided stupas of northern Thailand that are influenced by the great Thai-Lao kingdoms of Lan Na and Lan Xang. Many stupas are believed to contain 'relics' (pieces of bone) belonging to the historical Buddha. In northern and northeastern Thailand such stupas are known as *thâat*. A variation of the stupa inherited from the Angkor kingdom is the corn cob-shaped *prang*, a feature in the ancient Thai temples of Sukhothai and Ayuthaya.

> 'naga, the mythical serpent that guarded Buddha during meditation, is depicted temple rooflines'

Other structures typically found in wat compounds include one or more *sǎalaa* (open-sided shelters) that are used for community meetings and *dhamma* lectures; a number of *kùtì* (monastic quarters); a *hǎw trai* (Tripitaka library), where Buddhist scriptures are stored; a *hǎw klawng* (drum tower), sometimes with a *hǎw rákhang* (bell tower); various stupas, including the smaller squarish ones known as *thâat kràdùuk* (bone reliquaries), where the ashes of deceased worshippers are interred; plus various ancillary buildings, such as schools or clinics.

Contemporary Architecture

Thailand's modern cities aren't its artistic selling point as postmodern concrete construction often blots out the stylishly functional aspects of traditional architecture. There are, however, a few inspirational exceptions that fuse together Thai, Chinese and Western techniques.

Thais began mixing traditional Thai with European forms in the late 19th and early 20th centuries, as exemplified by Bangkok's Vimanmek Teak Mansion (p133), the Author's Wing of the Oriental Hotel (p155) and certain buildings of the Grand Palace (p108).

The port cities of Thailand, including Bangkok and Phuket, acquired fine examples of Sino-Portuguese architecture – buildings of stuccoed brick

---

LOTUS LANGUAGE

For 600 years after the death of the Buddha, artists used only nonhuman symbols to depict the Buddha. These included the lotus bud, the bodhi tree, the Buddha footprint and the Wheel of Law, which contains eight spokes representing the eight-fold path to truth. The lotus symbol survived the switch to human images and carries with it a shorthand reminder of the tenets of Buddhism. The lotus plant can create a dramatic flower in the most rancid pond. This natural phenomenon becomes a parable for religious perfection and symbolises a cooling effect on the fires of passion that bring about suffering. The lotus motif is used atop the veranda columns of many temple buildings or the spires of Sukhothai-era *chedi* (stupa), and images of the Buddha, the enlightened one, is often depicted meditating in the cup of a lotus blossom. The lotus flowers are used solely for merit-making in Thailand not as secular decorations.

decorated with an ornate façade – a style that followed the sea traders during the colonial era. In Bangkok this style is often referred to as 'old Bangkok' or 'Ratanakosin'.

Buildings of mixed heritage in the north and northeast exhibit French and English influences, while those in the south typically show Portuguese influence. Shophouses *(hâwng thǎew)* throughout the country, whether 100 years or 100 days old, share the basic Chinese shophouse design, where the ground floor is reserved for trading purposes while the upper floors contain offices or residences.

In the 1960s and '70s the trend in modern Thai architecture, inspired by the European Bauhaus movement, moved towards a boring functionalism – the average building looked like a giant egg carton turned on its side. The Thai aesthetic, so vibrant in the pre-WWII era, almost entirely disappeared in this characterless style of architecture.

When Thai architects finally began experimenting again during the building boom of the mid-1980s, the result was hitech designs such as ML Sumet Jumsai's famous 'Robot Building' on Th Sathon Tai in Bangkok that formerly housed the Bank of Asia. Rangsan Torsuwan, a graduate of Massachusetts Institute of Technology (MIT), introduced the neoclassic (or neo-Thai) style; the best example is the Grand Hyatt Erawan (p153) in Bangkok. Another architect using traditional Thai architecture in modern functions is Pinyo Suwankiri, who has designed a number of Bangkok's government buildings.

PAINTING & SCULPTURE
Traditional Art
While Westerners go to museums to admire the masters, Thais goes to temple, where ornate and stylised murals depict Hindu-Buddhist mythology and religious sermons. Always instructional in intent, such painted images ranged from the depiction of the *jataka* (stories of the Buddha's past lives) and scenes from the Indian Hindu epic *Ramayana,* to elaborate scenes detailing daily life in Thailand.

Reading the murals requires both knowledge of these religious tales and an understanding of the murals spatial relationship to chronology. Most murals are divided into scenes, in which the main theme is depicted in the centre with resulting events taking place above and below the central action. Usually in the corner of a dramatic episode between the story's characters are independent scenes of Thai village life: women carrying food in bamboo baskets, men fishing or a happy communal get-together; all of these simple village folk wear the ubiquitous Thai smile of contentment.

Lacking the durability of other art forms, pre-20th century religious painting is limited to very few surviving examples. The earliest surviving temple examples are found at Ayuthaya's Wat Ratburana (1424; p197), Wat Chong Nonsi in Bangkok (1657–1707; p139) and Phetchaburi's Wat Yai Suwannaram (late 17th century).

Nineteenth-century religious painting has fared better. Ratanakosin-style temple art is, in fact, more highly esteemed for painting than for sculpture or architecture. Typical temple murals feature rich colours and lively detail. Some of the finest are found at Bangkok's National Museum (p111) in the Wihan Buddhaisawan, and at Thonburi's Wat Suwannaram (p140).

However, the study and application of mural painting techniques have been kept alive, and often use improved techniques and paints that promise to hold fast much longer than the temple murals of old.

Temple murals have regained the interest of a privileged few who receive handsome sums for painting the interior walls of well-endowed ordination halls. Chakrabhand Posayakrit's postmodern murals at Wat Tritosathep

Clay and terracotta engravings found on cave walls and on votive tablets date as far back as the 6th century in Thailand, but the bronze culture of Ban Chiang sculptural endeavours began at least 4000 years ago.

Mahawarawihan in Banglamphu, Bangkok, only half completed, are being hailed as a masterwork of Thai Buddhist art of any era. Continued renovation of older murals also encourages the study of these ancient techniques in young art students.

In the sacred temple spaces alongside the brilliant murals are revered Buddha images that depict Thailand's most famous contribution to the world of religious art. The country's sculptural legacy encapsulates the Thai artistic traditions of serenity and grace. Like other Buddhist cultures, Thailand borrowed and adapted the iconography and symbolism that first developed in India. Based on rules defined by Indian artists, the Buddha is depicted in various poses (mudra), which are symbolic gestures based on a significant period in his life or certain religious precepts. The most common poses found in Thai art include the following:

Dispelling fear Typically a standing Buddha with one or both hands raised with palms facing forward and fingers pointed upwards.

Meditation Buddha sitting in the lotus position with hands folded and palms facing upwards.

Subduing Mara Buddha sitting in the lotus position with his right hand pointing towards the earth. (During meditation the Buddha resisted the temptations of Mara by pointing his fingers to the ground and calling on the earth goddess Mae Thorani.)

'The country's sculptural legacy encapsulates the Thai artistic traditions of serenity and grace'

Contemporary Art

Adapting traditional themes and aesthetics to the secular canvas began around the turn of the 20th century as Western influence in the region became more powerful. In general, Thai painting favours abstract over realism and continues to preserve the one-dimensional perspective of traditional mural paintings. There are two major trends in Thai art: the updating of religious themes and tongue-in-cheek social commentary. With some of the younger artists the two trends often overlap.

Italian artist Corrado Feroci is often credited as the father of modern Thai art. He was first invited to Thailand by Rama VI in 1924 and built the Bangkok's Democracy Monument and Western-classical statues, such as the bronze statue of Rama I that stands at the entry to Memorial Bridge. Feroci founded the country's first fine arts institute in 1933, a school that eventually developed into Silpakorn University, Thailand's premier training ground for artists. In gratitude, the Thai government made Feroci a Thai citizen, with the Thai name Silpa Bhirasri.

In the 1970s Thai artists began to tackle the modernisation of Buddhist themes through abstract expressionism. Leading works in this genre include the colourful surrealism of Pichai Nirand, the mystical pen-and-ink drawings of Thawan Duchanee, and the fluid naturalist oil and watercolours of Pratuang Emjaroen. Receiving more exposure overseas than at home, Montien Boonma used the ingredients of Buddhist merit-making, like gold leaf, bells and candle wax, to create abstract temple spaces within museum galleries. Other recognised names include Songdej Thipthong and his spare mandalas, Surasit Saokong and his realist paintings of rural temples, and Monchai Kaosamang and his ephemeral watercolours. Jitr (Prakit) Buabusaya painted in the French impressionist style but is most remembered as an art teacher.

Politically motivated artwork defines a parallel movement in Thai contemporary art. As a quickly industrialising society, many artists have watched as the rice fields became factories, the forests became asphalt and the spoils went to the politically connected. During the student activist days of the 1970s, the Art for Life Movement was the banner under which creative discontents – including musicians, intellectuals and painters – rallied against the military dictatorship and embraced certain aspects of communism and

workers' rights. Sompote Upa-In and Chang Saetang are two important artists from that period.

During and after the boom times of the 1980s, a punk-style, anti-authority attitude emerged in the work of the artists known as the 'Fireball' school. Manit Sirwanichpoom is best known for his 'Pink Man On Tour' series, in which he depicted artist Sompong Thawee in a pink suit and a shopping cart amid Thailand's most iconic attractions. Less famous are Manit's evocative black-and-white photographic pieces denouncing capitalism and consumerism, typically identified as unwelcome Western imports. Vasan Sitthiket is more blatantly controversial and uses mixed-media installations to condemn the players he views as corrupt. His works have been banned in Thailand and widely criticised as 'anti-Thai'.

Less cynical and more pop are the works of Thaweesak Srithongdee. He paints flamboyantly cartoonish human figures with an element of traditional Thai handicrafts or imagery. Jirapat Tasanasomboon pits traditional Thai figures in comic book-style fights or sensua embraces with Western icons.

Flavours – Thai Contemporary Art (2003), by Steven Pettifor, focuses on the work of some of Thailand's most prominent contemporary artists.

ART IN-SITU

The development of Thai religious art is broken into different periods or schools typically defined by the patronage of the ruling capital. Today the greatest collection of religious sculpture is contained at Bangkok's National Museum (p111). As you travel around the country, you can visit the important ùtháyaan pràwàttìsàat (historical parks), temples and museums for an appreciation of the geographic setting of these artistic periods. Below are the key periods and their relevant sites:

Dvaravati Period (7th–11th centuries) Borrowing heavily from the Indian periods of Amaravati and Gupta, the distinctive sculptural characteristics of this period include large hair curls on the Buddha's head, eyebrows arched to represent a flying bird, protruding eyes, thick lips and a flat nose. Examples can be seen at Phra Pathom Chedi (p186).

Srivijaya Period (7th–13th centuries) Depictions of Buddha and bodhisattvas were closely linked to Indian forms, and were more sensual and stylised than central and northern Thai art. Examples can be found in Chaiya's Wat Phra Boromathat and Nakhon Si Thammarat's Wat Mahathat.

Khmer Period (9th–11th centuries) Generally, the signature characteristics of this period include images of Buddha meditating under the canopy of the seven-headed naga or on a lotus pedestal. In the U-Thong style, the Buddha is frequently depicted in the pose of subduing Mara. The signature temple feature of the Khmer style is a central corncob-shaped stupa (called a *prang*); it represents Mt Meru in the Buddhist cosmology.

Chiang Saen-Lanna Period (11th–13th centuries) The northern Thai kingdom drew inspiration from its Lao, Shan and Burmese neighbours in depicting Buddha, who appears with a plump figure and round, smiling face. Standing Buddhas were often in the pose of dispelling fear or giving instruction. Lanna-style temples are typically made of teak and the *chedi* often resembles a tiered pagoda. Examples can be found in and around Chiang Mai (p284) and at Chiang Saen National Museum (p287).

Sukhothai Period (13th–15th centuries) One of the first Thai capitals, Sukhothai set forth the underlying aesthetic of successive Thai art. Buddha images were depicted with serenity and grace but without anatomical human detail. The intention was to highlight the Buddha's spiritual qualities rather than his human status. The pose of the walking Buddha is a signature Sukhothai style and best viewed at Sukhothai Historical Park (p403). Glazed ceramics, known as *sǎnghálôhk*, were important during this time in nearby Si Satchanalai–Chaliang Historical Park (p408).

Ayuthaya Period (14th–18th centuries) Incorporating elements inherited from the Khmer and Sukhothai kingdoms, important departures included Buddha images that depicted a king wearing a gem-studded crown and regalia, instead of an austere monk's robe, and the bell-shaped *chedi*. Ayuthaya Historical Park (p195) offers an introduction to this period.

Bangkok-Ratanakosin Period (19th century–) The religious artwork of the modern capital is noted for merging traditional Thai styles with Western influences. Wat Phra Kaew and the Grand Palace (p108) is a good starting point.

In *Hanuman is Upset!*, the monkey king chews up the geometric lines of Mondrian's famous gridlike painting.

Kritsana Chaikitwattana is considered an up-and-coming artist working in moody paint-and-collage abstracts, including a series of self-portraits inspired during his years as a Buddhist monk. Jaruwat Boonwaedlom explores modern realism, a genre not well populated by Thai artists, with her prismlike paintings of Bangkok street scenes.

Although lacking in commercial attention, Thai sculpture is often considered to be the strongest of the contemporary arts, not surprising considering the country's long involvement in Buddha figures. Moving into nonreligious arenas, Khien Yimsiri is the classic master of the modern era creating elegant human and mythical forms out of bronze. Sakarin Krue-On is often applauded for adapting sculpture and installation. His work *Phawang Si Leuang* (Yellow Simple) fashioned a huge, hollow Buddha head from a mixture of clay, mud, papier-mâché and turmeric. Manop Suwanpinta similarly moulds the human anatomy into fantastic shapes that often intersect with technological features, such as hinged faces that open to reveal inanimate content.

To view Thailand's contemporary art scene, visit the Bangkok modern museums (p136) and commercial galleries (p176).

MUSIC

Throughout Thailand you'll find a diversity of musical genres and styles, from the serene court music that accompanies classical dance-drama to the chest-thumping house music played at dance clubs.

Traditional Music

Classical *phleng thai doem* (central-Thai music) features a dazzling array of textures and subtleties, hair-raising tempos and pastoral melodies. The classical orchestra is called the *pìi-phâat* and can include as few as five players or more than 20. Among the more common instruments is the *pìi*, a woodwind instrument that has a reed mouthpiece; it is heard prominently at Thai-boxing matches. The four-stringed *phin*, plucked like a guitar, lends subtle counterpoint, while the *ránâat èhk*, a bamboo-keyed percussion instrument resembling the xylophone, carries the main melodies. The slender *saw*, a bowed instrument with a coconut-shell soundbox, provides soaring embellishments, as does the *khlùi* (wooden Thai flute).

One of the more attention-drawing *pìi-phâat* instruments, the *kháwng wong yài*, consists of tuned gongs arranged in a semicircle and played in simple rhythmic lines to provide a song's underlying fabric. Several types of drums carry the beat, often through multiple tempo changes in a single song. The most important is the *tà-phon* (*thon*), a double-headed hand-drum that sets the tempo for the entire ensemble. Prior to a performance the players offer incense and flowers to the *tà-phon*, considered to be the 'conductor' of the music's spiritual content.

The standard Thai scale divides the eight-note octave into seven full-tone intervals, with no semitones. Thai scales were first transcribed by the Thai-German composer Peter Feit (also known by his Thai name, Phra Chen Duriyanga), who composed Thailand's national anthem in 1932.

The *pìi-phâat* ensemble was originally developed to accompany classical dance-drama and shadow theatre, but can be heard these days in straightforward performances at temple fairs and concerts.

Classical Thai music has not been forgotten in the dusty annals of history, but has been fused with international jazz elements. Fong Nam, a Thai orchestra led by American composer Bruce Gaston, performs an inspiring blend of Western and Thai classical motifs that have become a favourite choice

Rama IX Art Museum (www.rama9.org) is an online reference focusing on top Thai contemporary artists, galleries and collections.

The Overture (2004), by Ittisoontorn Vichailak, is a melodrama inspired by the life of composer Luang Pradit Phairao, a *ránâat èhk* artist who protects Thai classical music from the influx of European music.

PI BIRD

You are unlikely to become a devotee, but you've got to give kudos to Thongchai 'Bird' Macintyre (also known as Pi Bird) for pop longevity. His first album hit in 1986 and he has followed up with an album almost every year since. He has Madonna's staying power coupled with the nice-guy factor, which appeals to a broad audience from kids in nappies to toothless grannies. Backed by GMM Grammy Entertainment, Thailand's leading music producer, Bird fast-tracks into every emerging pop trend ensuring radio and disco airtime.

for movie soundtracks, TV commercials and tourism promotion. Another leading exponent of this genre is the composer and instrumentalist Tewan Sapsanyakorn (also known as Tong Tewan), who plays soprano and alto sax, violin and *khlùi* with equal virtuosity. Tewan's compositions are often based on Thai melodies, but the improvisations and rhythms are drawn from such diverse jazz sources such as Sonny Rollins and Jean-Luc Ponty.

Lûuk Thûng & Mǎw Lam

The bestselling of all modern musical genres in Thailand remains *lûuk thûng* (literally 'children of the fields'), which dates back to the 1940s. Analogous to country-and-western music in the USA, it's a genre that tends to appeal most to working-class Thais. Subject matter almost always cleaves to tales of lost love, tragic early death, and the dire circumstances of farmers who work day in and day out and at the end of the year are still in debt.

There are two basic styles: the original Suphanburi style, with lyrics in standard Thai; and an Ubon style sung in Isan dialect.

Thailand's most famous *lûuk thûng* singer, Pumpuang Duangjan, rated a royally sponsored cremation when she died in 1992, and a major shrine at Suphanburi's Wat Thapkradan receives a steady stream of worshippers. When she died many feared that the genre passed with her, but gravely voiced Siriporn Amphaipong helped carry the tradition and is one of the most beloved *lûuk thûng* superstars. Other big names include ex-soap opera star Got Chakraband, and Monsit Khamsoi, whose trademark silky – almost sleazy – vocal style has proved enormously popular.

If *lûuk thûng* is Thailand's country-and-western, then *mǎw lam* is the blues. *Mǎw lam* is a folk tradition firmly rooted in the northeast of Thailand and based on the songs played on the Lao-Isan *khaen* (a wind instrument devised of a double row of bamboolike reeds fitted into a hardwood soundbox). The oldest style is most likely heard at a village gathering or parade and it has a simple but very insistent bass beat topped by plaintive vocal melodies. Unlike Thai classical music, *mǎw lam* has jumped the generational fence and now has an electrified pop version.

Jintara Poonlap and Chalermphol Malaikham are the current reigning queen and king of *mǎw lam*. These singers and others also perform *lûuk thûng prá-yúk*, a blend of *lûuk thûng* and *mǎw lam* that's emerging as *mǎw lam* loses its 'country bumpkin' image. Purists, however, eschew the latter in favour of rootsier, funkier *mǎw lam* artists such as Rumpan Saosanon. Sommainoi Duangcharoen goes in a completely different direction, mixing a bit of jazz and even rap into his *mǎw lam*. Tune into Bangkok radio station Luk Thung FM (FM95.0) for large doses of both *lûuk thûng* and *mǎw lam*. For more information about *mǎw lam*, see the Northeastern Thailand chapter (p492).

'If *lûuk thûng* is Thailand's country-and-western, then *mǎw lam* is the blues'

Thai Rock & Pop

The 1970s ushered in a new style inspired by the politically conscious folk rock of the USA and Europe, which the Thais dubbed *phleng phêua chii-wít*

RECOMMENDED THAI POP CDS

■ *That Song* (Modern Dog) – Latest album from Thailand's grunge gurus containing the hit song 'Tar Sawang' (Clear Eyes).

■ *Khaw Du Jai Kawn* (Banyen Raggan) – A good introduction to *mǎw lam*.

■ *Made in Thailand* (Carabao) – Carabao's most classic and internationally popular album.

■ *Khon Kap Khwai* (Caravan) – The album that kicked off the *phleng phêua chii-wít* movement.

■ *The Nang Hong Suite* (Fong Nam) – Brilliant Thai funeral music, but think New Orleans second-line cheer rather than dirge.

■ *Sorry I'm Happy* (Joey Boy) – Thailand's hip-hop bad-boy Joey Boy delivers dance and ska-rap.

■ *The Best of Loso* (Loso) – Thai anthems of teen angst.

■ *Best* (Pumpuang Duangjan) – Compilation of the late *lûuk thûng* diva's most famous tunes.

(music for life). Most identified with the Thai band Caravan, this style remains the most major musical shift in Thailand since *lûuk thûng* arose in the 1940s. Songs of this nature have political and environmental topics rather than the usual love themes. During the authoritarian dictatorships of the '70s many of Caravan's songs were officially banned. Another durable example of this style, Carabao, took *phleng phêua chii-wít*, fused it with *lûuk thûng*, rock and heavy metal, and spawned a whole generation of imitators as well as a chain of barnlike performance venues seating a thousand or more.

Thailand also has a thriving teen-pop industry – sometimes referred to as T-Pop – centred on artists who have been chosen for their good looks and then mated with syrupy song arrangements. Singers who are *lûuk khrêung* – half-Thai, half-*faràng* (Westerner) – and sport English names have been dancing across the top 10 charts since the mid-1980s. Thongchai 'Bird' Macintyre is the undisputed yet ageing pop king. Once sending conservative Thais into fits of outrage, Tata Young and her sexy dance moves have made a jump across the pond in the hopes of landing on the US pop charts. Teen-girl pop singers Palmy and Mint are top-selling darlings, while Bie The Star holds up the boy-band end of the market. The latest pop craze has been for hip-hop, more accurately classified as radio rap, and best epitomised by Thaitanium and Joey Boy.

Among the disc-buying public, karaoke CDs and VCDs comprise a huge share of the market. Many major Thai artists – even alternative rock groups – release VCDs specially formatted for karaoke-style sing-alongs.

The 1990s saw an emergence of an alternative pop scene – known as *klawng sěhrii* (free drum) or *phleng tâi din* (underground music) in Thailand. The independent record label Bakery Music, which has since been absorbed by a larger corporation, helped promote the 'indie' scene and found a successful conduit in Modern Dog, a Brit-pop inspired band of four Chulalongkorn University graduates, now one of the leading alternative bands in Thailand. Bakery label's founding members also took to the stage in the band Pru, which upstaged the pop aristocracy of Grammy music at the 2002 MTV Asia awards.

Crowd-pleasers Loso (from 'low society' as opposed to the Bangkok clique of 'hi-so' or high-society) updated Carabao's affinity for Thai folk melodies and rhythms with indie guitar rock. Their songs have anthem status – every young Thai can sing 'Som Sarn' (Hesitant) and others by heart. Other indies that lead the pack include Photo Sticker Machine, Day Tripper, punk-metal Ebola and electronica/underground Futon.

Listen to and buy popular Thai songs (with English and Thai lyrics) at www .ethaimusic.com.

In 2006 many of Bakery Music's alumni plus other leading Thai musicians went to New York City to stage an ambitious rock-opera adaptation

of the *Ramakian*, which slightly confused an audience unfamiliar with Bangkok rock.

For the latest indie Thai hits, tune into Fat Radio, FM104.5.

THEATRE & DANCE

Traditional Thai theatre consists of six dramatic forms: *khŏhn* (formal masked dance-drama depicting scenes from the *Ramakian* – the Thai version of India's *Ramayana*); *lákhon* (a general term covering several types of dance-drama); *lí-keh* (a partly improvised, often bawdy folk play featuring dancing, comedy, melodrama and music); *mánohraa* (the southern Thai equivalent of *lí-keh*, but based on a 2000-year-old Indian story); *năng* (shadow plays limited to southern Thailand); *lákhon lék* or *hùn lŭang* (puppet theatre); and *lákhon phûut* (contemporary spoken theatre).

Khŏhn

In all *khŏhn* performances, four types of characters are represented – male humans, female humans, monkeys and demons. Monkey and demon figures are always masked with the elaborate head coverings often seen in tourist promotional material. Behind the masks and make-up, all actors are male. Traditional *khŏhn* is a very expensive production – Ravana's retinue alone (Ravana is the *Ramakian*'s principal villain) consists of over 100 demons, each with a distinctive mask.

Perhaps because it was once limited to royal venues and hence never gained a popular following, the *khŏhn* or *Ramakian* dance-drama tradition nearly died out in Thailand. Bangkok's National Theatre (p172) was once the only place where *khŏhn* was regularly performed for the public, but now the renovated Chalermkrung Royal Theatre (p172) hosts occasional performances.

> '**Monkey and demon figures are always masked with elaborate head coverings**'

Scenes performed in traditional *khŏhn* (and *lákhon* performances) come from the 'epic journey' tale of the *Ramayana*, known as the *Ramakian* in Thai. The central story revolves around Prince Rama's search for his beloved Princess Sita, who has been abducted by the evil 10-headed demon Ravana and taken to the island of Lanka.

Lákhon

The more formal *lákhon nai* ('inner' *lákhon*, performed inside the palace) was originally performed for lower nobility by all-female ensembles. Today it's a dying art, even more so than royal *khŏhn*. In addition to scenes from the *Ramakian*, *lákhon nai* performances may include traditional Thai folk tales; whatever the story, text is always sung. *Lákhon nâwk* ('outer' *lákhon*, performed outside the palace) deals exclusively with folk tales and features a mix of sung and spoken text, sometimes with improvisation. Both male and female performers are permitted. Like *khŏhn* and *lákhon nai*, performances are becoming increasingly rare.

Much more common these days is the less-refined *lákhon chaatrii*, a fast-paced, costumed dance-drama usually performed at upcountry temple festivals or at shrines (commissioned by a shrine devotee whose wish was granted by the shrine deity). *Chaatrii* stories have been influenced by the older *mánohraa* theatre of southern Thailand.

A variation on *chaatrii* that has evolved specifically for shrine worship, *lákhon kâe bon* involves an ensemble of around 20 members, including musicians. At an important shrine like Bangkok's Lak Meuang, four different *kâe bon* troupes may alternate performances, each for a week at a time, as each performance lasts from 9am till 3pm and there is usually a long list of worshippers waiting to hire them.

Lí-Keh

In outlying working-class neighbourhoods in Bangkok you may be lucky enough to come across the gaudy, raucous *lí-keh*. This theatrical art form is thought to have descended from drama rituals brought to southern Thailand by Arab and Malay traders. The first native public performance in central Thailand came about when a group of Thai Muslims staged a *lí-keh* for Rama V in Bangkok during the funeral commemoration of Queen Sunantha. *Lí-keh* grew very popular under Rama VI, peaked in the early 20th century and has been fading slowly since the 1960s.

Most often performed at Buddhist festivals by troupes of travelling performers, *lí-keh* presents a colourful mixture of folk and classical music, outrageous costumes, melodrama, slapstick comedy, sexual innuendo, and up-to-date commentary on Thai politics and society. Foreigners – even those who speak fluent Thai – are often left behind by the highly idiomatic, culture-specific language and gestures.

'*lí-keh* presents a colourful mixture of folk and classical music, outrageous costumes, melodrama, slapstick comedy and sexual innuendo'

Marionettes

Lákhon lék (little theatre), also known as *hùn lǔang* (royal puppets), like *khǒhn*, was once reserved for court performances. Metre-high marionettes made of *khòi* paper and wire, wearing elaborate costumes modelled on those of the *khǒhn*, are used to convey similar themes, music and dance movements.

Two to three puppetmasters are required to manipulate each *hùn lǔang* by means of wires attached to long poles. Stories are drawn from Thai folk tales, particularly *Phra Aphaimani*, and occasionally from the *Ramakian*. The *hùn lǔang* puppets themselves are highly collectable; the Bangkok National Museum has only one example in its collection. A smaller, 30cm court version called *hùn lék* (little puppets) are occasionally used in live performances.

Another Thai puppet theatre, *hùn kràbàwk* (cylinder puppets) is based on popular Hainanese puppet shows. It uses 30cm hand puppets carved from wood. The best place to see *lákhon lék* is at the Natayasala (Joe Louis Puppet Theater; p172) in Bangkok.

Nǎng

Shadow-puppet theatre – in which two-dimensional figures are manipulated between a cloth screen and a light source at night-time performances – has been a Southeast Asian tradition for perhaps five centuries. Originally brought to the Malay Peninsula by Middle Eastern traders, the technique eventually spread to all parts of mainland and peninsular Southeast Asia; in Thailand it is mostly found in the south. As in Malaysia and Indonesia, shadow puppets in Thailand are carved from dried buffalo or cow hides (*nǎng*).

Two distinct shadow-play traditions survive in Thailand. The most common, *nǎng tàlung*, is named after Phattalung Province, where it developed around Malay models. Like their Malay-Indonesian counterparts, Thai shadow puppets represent an array of characters from classical and folk drama, principally the *Ramakian* and *Phra Aphaimani* in Thailand. A single puppetmaster manipulates the cut-outs, which are bound to the ends of buffalo-horn handles. *Nǎng tàlung* is still occasionally seen at temple festivals in the south, mostly in Songkhla and Nakhon Si Thammarat Provinces. Performances are also held periodically for tour groups or visiting dignitaries from Bangkok.

The second tradition, *nǎng yài* (big hide), uses much larger cut-outs, each bound to two wooden poles held by a puppetmaster; several masters may

participate in a single performance. *Năng yài* is rarely performed nowadays because of the lack of trained *năng* masters and the expense of the shadow puppets. Most *năng yài* that are made today are sold to interior designers or tourists; a well-crafted hide puppet may cost as much as 5000B.

In addition to the occasional performance in Nakhon Si Thammasat or Bangkok, *năng yài* can be seen at Wat Khanon in Amphoe Photharam, Ratchaburi Province, where *năng yài* master Khru Chalat is passing the art along to younger men. There's usually a performance at the wat from 10am to 11am Saturday.

CINEMA

When it comes to Thai cinema, there are usually two concurrent streams: the movies that are financially successful and the movies that are considered cinematically meritorious; only occasionally do these overlap.

Popular Thai cinema ballooned in the 1960s and '70s, especially during the period when the government levied a tax on Hollywood imports thus spawning a home-grown industry. The majority were cheap action flicks that were often dubbed '*nám nâo*' (stinking water); but the fantastic, even nonsensical, plots and rich colours left a lasting impression on modern-day Thai filmmakers, who have inserted these elements with distinctive measure.

The leading couple of the action genre was Mit Chaibancha and Petchara Chaowaraj, a duo who starred in some 75 films together. One of their last films was *Insee Thong* (Golden Eagle), in which Mit, playing the film's hero, was inadvertently killed during the filming of a helicopter stunt. Another beloved film of the era was *Mon Rak Luk Thung*, a musical rhapsodising Thai rural life. Isan musicals were a theatre darling during this era and re-emerged in 2001 with *Monpleng Luk Thung FM* (Hoedown Showdown) and Pen-Ek Ratanaruang's *Monrak Transistor*, which paid tribute to the music of Suraphol Sombatcharoen. In 2005 comedian-actor-director Petchtai Wongkamlao wrote, directed and starred in *Yam Yasothon*, a colourful homage to the 1970s musicals.

For a country renowned for its sense of fun, comedy will always be a guaranteed local money maker, and the classic flick of the 1960s was *Ngern Ngern Ngern* (Money, Money, Money), starring comedian Lor Tork. The modern comedies invariably feature *kàthoey* (transvestites and transsexuals), always a comic element in Thai humour. The 2000 film *Satree Lek* (Iron Ladies) dramatised the real-life exploits of a Lampang volleyball team made up almost entirely of *kàthoey*. At home, this Yongyoot Thongkongtoon–directed film became Thai cinema's second-largest grossing effort to date.

> 'For a country renowned for its sense of fun, comedy will always be a guaranteed local money maker'

More important as an artiste than as an entrepreneur, the director Rattana Pestonji is often credited as the father of Thai new wave. His 1957 movie *Rong Raem Nark* (Country Hotel) is a dark comedy set in a Bangkok bar and guesthouse and filmed using only one camera.

Although sad endings rarely attract Thai moviegoers, Vichit Kounavudhi carved a niche for himself as one of the first socially conscious filmmakers. His 1983 movie *Luk Isan* (Child of the North-East), based on a Thai novel of the same name, followed the ups and downs of a farming family living in drought-ridden Isan and became one of the first popular films to offer urban Thais an understanding of the hardships of the impoverished farmers.

The current era boasts a new generation of seriously good Thai directors, several of whom studied film abroad during Thailand's '80s and early '90s boom period. Nonzee Nimibutr is regarded as the most mainstream (and profitable) of the new crop. His 1998 release of *Nang Nak* was a retelling of a famous Thai spirit tale that had seen no fewer than 20 previous cinematic renderings. The film became the largest-grossing film in Thai history,

out-earning even *Titanic*, and earned awards for best director, best art director and best sound at the 1999 Asia-Pacific Film Festival.

A popular player in the foreign-film circuit is the director Pen-Ek Ratanaruang. His films are gritty and satirical, and garner fans of film not just fans of Thailand. His debut film was *Fun Bar Karaoke*, a 1997 satire of Bangkok life in which the main characters are an ageing Thai playboy and his daughter. But it will be his 2003 *Ruang Rak Noi Nid Mahasan* (Last Life in the Universe), written by Prabda Yoon, that will secure him a position in the vault of cinema classics.

One of Thai cinema's proudest moments arrived when Cannes 2002 chose *Sut Sanaeha* (Blissfully Yours) for the coveted Un Certain Regard (Of Special Consideration) screening. Helmed by Apichatpong Weerasethakul, the film dramatises a romance between a Thai woman and an illegal Burmese immigrant. Just two years later Apichatpong's dreamlike *Sut Pralat* (Tropical Malady) won the Cannes Jury Prize, although his avant-garde films have generated little interest in Thailand.

'Colourful tales that merge myth and reality are vital parts of the Thai imagination'

Colourful tales that merge myth and reality are vital parts of the Thai imagination and this theme appears in both popular and indie movies. *Fah Talai Jone* (Tears of the Black Tiger; 2000), directed by Wisit Sasanatieng, bridged the gap between new wave and the 1960s action genre with a campy homage. Jira Malikul's *Mekhong Sipha Kham Deuan Sip-et* (Full Moon Party; 2002) juxtaposes folk beliefs about mysterious 'dragon lights' emanating from Mekong River with the scepticism of Bangkok scientists.

Back in the box-office world of Thai cinema, Prachya Pinkaew's *Ong Bak* (2004) and his follow-up *Tom-Yum-Goong* (2005) created a *muay thai* hero in Tony Jaa. Otherwise, horror flicks are eating up the majority of moviewatchers' budgets in Thailand, averaging three or four per year with a wealth of ghost stories and occult arts to mine for material. A few recent frightfests include *Shutter* (2004), about the aftermath of a hit-and-run, and the *Art of the Devil* series (2005) by the Ronin Team, a collection of Thai filmmakers specialising in ghouls and suspense. A little artier than the usual fare, Wisit Sasanatieng's most recent film, *The Unseeable* (2006), is a ghost story set in the 1930s, written by one of the members of the Ronin Team.

LITERATURE

The written word has a long history in Thailand, dating back to the 11th or 12th century when the first Thai script was fashioned from an older Mon alphabet. The first known work of literature to be written in Thai is thought to have been composed by Sukhothai's Phaya Lithai in 1345. This was *Traiphum Phra Ruang*, a treatise that described the three realms of existence according to a Hindu-Buddhist cosmology. According to contemporary scholars, this work and its symbolism was, and continues to be, of considerable influence on Thailand's artistic and cultural universe.

Classical

The 30,000-line *Phra Aphaimani*, composed by poet Sunthorn Phu in the late 18th century, is Thailand's most famous classical literary work. Like many of its epic predecessors around the world, it tells the story of an exiled prince who must complete an odyssey of love and war before returning to his kingdom in victory.

But of all classical Thai literature, *Ramakian* is the most pervasive and influential in Thai culture. The Indian source, *Ramayana*, came to Thailand with the Khmers 900 years ago, first appearing as stone reliefs on Prasat Hin Phimai and other Angkor temples in the northeast. Eventually, however, the Thais developed their own version of the epic, which was first written down

during the reign of Rama I. This version contained 60,000 stanzas and was a quarter longer than the Sanskrit original.

Although the main theme remains the same, the Thais embroidered the *Ramayana* by providing much more biographical detail on arch-villain Ravana (Dasakantha, called Thotsakan, or '10-necked' in the *Ramakian*) and his wife Montho. Hanuman, the monkey-god, differs substantially in the Thai version in his flirtatious nature (in the Hindu version he follows a strict vow of chastity). One of the classic *Ramakian* reliefs at Bangkok's Wat Pho depicts Hanuman clasping a maiden's bared breast as if it were an apple.

Also passed on from Indian tradition are the many *jataka*: life stories of the Buddha (*chaa-dòk* in Thai). Of the 547 *jataka* in the Pali *Tipitaka* (Buddhist canon), each one chronicling a different past life, most appear in Thailand almost word for word as they were first written down in Sri Lanka.

A group of 50 'extra' stories, based on Thai folk tales of the time, were added by Pali scholars in Chiang Mai 300 to 400 years ago. The most popular *jataka* in Thailand is one of the Pali originals known as the *Mahajati* or *Mahavessantara*, the story of the Buddha's penultimate life. Interior murals in the ordination chapels of Thai wat typically depict this *jataka* and nine others: Temiya, Mahajanaka, Suvannasama, Nemiraja, Mahosatha, Bhuridatta, Candakumara, Narada and Vidhura.

Poetry

During the Ayuthaya period, Thailand developed a classical poetic tradition based on five types of verse – *chan, kàap, khlong, klawn* and *râi*. Each of these forms uses a set of complex, strict rules to regulate metre, rhyming patterns and number of syllables. Although all of these poetic systems use the Thai language, *chan* and *kàap* are derived from Sanskrit verse forms from India, while *khlong, klawn* and *râi* are native forms. The Indian forms have all but disappeared from 21st-century use.

During the political upheavals that characterised the 1970s, several Thai newspaper editors, most notably Kukrit Pramoj, composed lightly disguised political commentary in *klawn* verse. Modern Thai poets seldom use the classical forms, preferring to compose in blank verse or with song-style rhyming.

Contemporary

The first Thai-language novel appeared only around 70 years ago, in direct imitation of Western models. Unfortunately much of Thai fiction, both past and present, has not been translated into English. The following are a few exceptions.

Considered the first Thai novel of substance, *The Circus of Life* (Thai 1929; English 1994), by Arkartdamkeung Rapheephat, follows a young, upper-class Thai as he travels the world in the 1920s. The fact that the author, himself a Thai prince, took his own life at the age of 26 has added to the mystique surrounding this work.

The late Kukrit Pramoj, former ambassador and Thai prime minister, novelised Bangkok court life from the late 19th century through to the 1940s in *Four Reigns* (Thai 1935; English 1981), the longest novel ever published in Thai. *The Story of Jan Darra* (Thai 1966; English 1994), by journalist and short-story writer Utsana Phleungtham, traces the sexual obsessions of a Thai aristocrat. Praphatsorn Seiwikun's well-tuned, rapid-paced *Time in a Bottle* (Thai 1984; English 1996) turned the life dilemmas of a fictional middle-class Bangkok family into a bestseller.

Writing under the pen name Siburapha, a common conceit with Thai writers, Kulap Saipradit spun romantic tales, including the novel *Behind the*

Buy English translations of Thai literature from DCO Thai (www.dcothai .com).

COMIC CULTURE

When it comes to reading, Thailand claims a high literacy rate, but don't expect to find folks buried in books. Comic books, mainly from Japan, account for a larger market share than paperbacks and the average provincial 'bookstore' is really a comic-book trading post. Of the few home-grown series, *Cartoon Maha Sanuk* (Super Fun Cartoon) introduced readers to the character Noo Hin, the Amelia Bedelia of Thailand. She's a country girl from Isan who's best intentions result in chaos. In the later series *Noo Hin Inter*, the trouble-making heroine goes to Bangkok to work as a maid for a refined family. In the manga genre, Suttichart Sarapaiwanich has attracted the attention of Nike advertisers with his crime-solving octopus character named Joe. Even the ousted Prime Minister Thaksin Shinawatra has been the subject of a 212-page graphic novel in which Thaksin returns to finish his mission of helping the poor; the comic was published by a citizen supporter shortly after the coup. But Thaksin's exploits have sold very little compared to the king's own comic book about Tongdaeng (meaning copper), a stray dog the palace adopted.

Painting, about a student who falls in love with a married aristocrat during the postwar era.

For a look at rural life in Thailand, the books of Pira Sudham are unparalleled. Sudham was born into a poor family in northeastern Thailand and has written *The Force of Karma, Monsoon Country, People of Esarn* and his latest, *Shadowed Country*. These books are not translations – Sudham writes in English in order to reach a worldwide audience.

Thai wunderkind SP Somtow has written and published more titles in English than any other Thai writer. Born in Bangkok, he was educated at Eton and Cambridge. The most accessible Somtow novel, and the one most evocative of Thai culture, is *Jasmine Nights*, a coming-of-age novel set in 1960 Bangkok.

Chart Korbjitti is a two-time winner of the Southeast Asian Writers Award (Seawrite), in 1982 for *The Judgement*, about a young village man wrongly accused by his nosy neighbours; and in 1994 for *Time*. The writer Sri Daoruang adapted the *Ramakian* into modern-day Bangkok in *Married to the Demon King*. Other short stories by modern Thai women writers appear in the collection *A Lioness in Bloom*, translated by Susan Kepner. *Of Time & Tide*, by Atsiri Thammachoat, chronicles the lives of inhabitants of a coastal community dealing with changing times.

The leading postmodern writer is Prabda Yoon, whose short story 'Probability' won the 2002 SEA Write award. Although his works have yet to be translated, he wrote the screenplay for the movie the *Last Life in the Universe* and other Pen-ek Ratanaruang-directed films. Ngarmpun Vejjajiva and her first novel, *The Happiness of Kati*, is another SEA Write award winner and follows the story of a young girl growing up on the banks of the Mae Nam Chao Phraya.

Food & Drink

Thai food is currently the pin-up model of international cuisine with outpost kitchens in little towns across the globe. A culinary pilgrimage to the mother country will expand your appreciation of the cuisine's versatility, simplicity and communal traditions. Food is everywhere in Thailand and you will quickly discover that eating is one of the country's great preoccupations. The average Thai takes time out to eat, not three times per day, but four or five. Sitting down at a roadside *rót khěn* (vendor cart) after an evening of cinema or nightclubbing, a Thai may barely have finished one steaming bowl of noodles before ordering a second round, just to revel in the experience a little longer. At the market stalls across Thailand, you'll witness first-hand the interbreeding of numerous foreign contributions from India, China and Asian Oceania, and how Thailand has adapted these cooking techniques and ingredients.

STAPLES & SPECIALITIES
Rice

Rice is so central to Thai food culture that the most common term for 'eat' is *kin khâo* (literally, 'consume rice') and one of the most common greetings is *'Kin khâo láew rěu yang?'* ('Have you consumed rice yet?'). To eat is to eat rice, and to many traditionalists a meal is not acceptable without this staple. You may even detect a hint of pity from an older Thai who thinks Westerners have to survive without rice in their daily diet.

There are many varieties of rice in Thailand and the country has been among the world leaders in rice exports since the 1960s. The highest grade is *khâo hǎwm málí* (jasmine rice), a fragrant long grain that is so coveted by neighbouring countries that there is allegedly a steady underground business in smuggling out fresh supplies.

Rice is customarily served alongside main dishes, like curries, stir-fries or soups typically classified as *kàp khâo* (with rice).

If you're eating with Thai friends, leaving a little rice on your plate will indicate that you are full. A clean plate means you're ready for another helping.

Noodles

Although Thai culture admires conformity, Thais are rugged individualists when it comes to food choices, a trait best observed in the noodle department. Descendent from China, noodles come in four basic varieties. The most popular is referred to as *kǔaytǐaw*, which is made from pure rice flour mixed with water to form a paste that is then steamed to form wide, flat sheets. These are then folded and sliced into noodles of varying widths – for example, *sên lék* (thin) and *sên yài* (broad). Already you've got two choices to make. Now on to the type of noodle dish you're after.

The simplest and most ubiquitous is *kǔaytǐaw náam,* a bowl of noodles served with chicken or beef stock along with bits of meat and various vegetables, including a garnish of *phàk chii* (coriander leaf). This dish is eaten round the clock as a quick snack before work, after shopping, post-clubbing or in between the real meal. *Kǔaytǐaw phàt* involves the quick stir-frying of the noodles in a wok with sliced meat, *phàk kha-náa* (Chinese kale), soy sauce and various seasonings. Chilli-heads must give *kǔaytǐaw phàt khîi mao* (drunkard's fried noodles) a try. A favourite lunch or late-night snack, this spicy stir-fry consists of wide rice noodles, fresh basil leaves, chicken or pork, seasonings and a healthy dose of fresh sliced chillies.

It Rains Fishes: Legends, Traditions and the Joys of Thai Cooking, by Kasma Loha-Unchit, is both a cookbook and a cultural exposé on Thai food.

The most famous *kŭaytĭaw* dish among foreigners is *phàt thai*, a plate of thin rice noodles stir-fried with dried or fresh shrimp, bean sprouts, fried tofu, egg and seasonings. On the edge of the plate the cook usually places little piles of ground peanuts and ground dried chilli, along with lime halves and a few stalks of spring onion, for self-seasoning.

Another kind of noodle, *khànŏm jiin*, is produced by pushing rice-flour paste through a sieve into boiling water, much the way Italian-style pasta is made. *Khànŏm jiin* is a popular morning market meal that is eaten doused with various spicy curries and loaded up with a self-selection of fresh and pickled vegetables.

'fresh ingredients are pounded in a stone mortar and pestle to form a thick, aromatic and extremely pungent paste'

The third genre of noodle, *bà-mìi*, is made from wheat flour and sometimes egg. It's yellowish in colour and round in shape. *Bà-mìi* is typically an alternative option in noodle soups and is a good companion with duck or red pork.

Finally there's *wún-sên*, an almost clear noodle made from mung-bean starch and water. *Wún-sên* (literally, 'jelly thread') is used for only three dishes in Thailand: *yam wún-sên*, a hot and tangy salad made with lime juice, fresh sliced *phrík khîi nŭu* (mouse-dropping peppers), mushrooms, dried or fresh shrimp, ground pork and various seasonings; *wún-sên òp puu*, bean thread noodles baked in a lidded clay pot with crab and seasonings; and *kaeng jèut*, a bland, Chinese-influenced soup with ground pork, soft tofu and a few vegetables. All of these dishes are most easily found in simple restaurants and sometimes at night markets. If you're ordering a Thai meal, *wún-sên* dishes are treated a lot like an appetiser.

Curries & Soups

Green, red, panang, matsaman – the average traveller arrives on Thai shores with a menu's worth of Thai curry knowledge. And just wait till you try the real McCoy, a curry that is made from fresh, handmade curry paste, a light dab of coconut milk, and a pretty assortment of chillies, aubergines and meat.

A Thai curry is usually light and fresh in flavour with more heat than sweet. The Thai word for curry is *kaeng* (it rhymes with the English 'gang') and is used much more broadly than the English translation to describe any dish with a lot of liquid. What foreigners know as red curry is *kaeng phèt* (literally, 'spicy curry') and derives its colour from the paste's primary ingredient of red chillies. Green curry *(kaeng khĭaw wăan)* uses green chillies instead and is a kiss sweeter than red; many green curries prepared for Westerners tend to exaggerate the sugar flavour at the expense of the subtle interplay of sour and salty notes.

All chilli-based *kaeng* start as fresh – not powdered – ingredients that are smashed, pounded and ground in a stone mortar and pestle to form a thick, aromatic and extremely pungent paste. Typical ingredients include dried chilli, galangal (also known as Thai ginger), lemongrass, kaffir lime (peel, leaves, or both), shallots, garlic, shrimp paste and salt.

During cooking, most *kaeng* are blended in a heated pan with coconut cream, to which the chef adds the rest of the ingredients along with coconut

---

MASTER YOUR NOODLES

Sit down to a bowl of noodle soup and you'll be presented with the four fundamentals of Thai flavours: spicy, sweet, sour and salty. Every Thai dish displays this interplay using different ingredients to achieve the balance. In the case of *kŭaytĭaw náam*, the diner is the mixologist sprinkling a little bit of the chillies, sugar, vinegar and fish sauce to reach an individual standard of perfection. Omit one of the seasonings – such as sugar – based on food misconceptions and you'll never join the noodle cult. Employ each seasoning option at your own discretion and be your own master, if only for one meal.

milk to thin and flavour the *kaeng*. Some recipes omit coconut milk entirely to produce a particularly fiery *kaeng* known as *kaeng pàa* (forest curry).

Kaeng jèut (literally, 'bland soup'), in contrast, is a soothing broth seasoned with little more than soya or fish sauce and black pepper. It is rarely eaten on its own, but is a nice counterpoint to a large meal or accompaniment to a simple lunch of fried fish. Although the number of variations on *kaeng jèut* are seemingly endless, common ingredients include *wún-sên* (mung-bean starch noodles), *tâo hûu* (tofu), *hǔa chai tháo* (Chinese radish) and *mǔu sàp* (ground pork).

Another food celebrity that falls into the soupy category is *tôm yam* – a spicy and sour soup made with seafood or chicken. Although it looks like an ordinary soup, *tôm yam* is actually a *faux amie* in that it is filled with ingredients (like lemongrass, galangal and kaffir lime peel) intended only for flavouring not ingestion. The convention of eating *tôm yam* also differs from what its appearance would suggest. *Tôm yam* is typically served in a large metal bowl heated by a small sterno flame underneath. The most polite way to tackle this contraption is to spoon the edible bits (meat or seafood and mushrooms) along with some broth into a small bowl. Diners can then sip the broth and spoon the chewables on to a plate of rice. It might seem like a lot of wasted steps to feed yourself, but a classic Thai dish like *tôm yam* is often adorned with ritualistic pageantry. Eating *tôm yam* with rice also helps quell the fiery flavours from fresh *phrík khîi nǔu* or *náam phrík phǎo* (a paste of dried chillies roasted with shrimp paste).

'a classic Thai dish like *tôm yam* is often adorned with ritualistic pageantry'

Hot & Tangy Salads

Less well-known outside of the country, the dish commonly translated as 'salad' *(yam)* is a combination of lime, chilli, fresh herbs and a choice of seafood, noodles or meat. Thais prize *yam* dishes so much that they are often eaten on their own like an appetiser without rice, or as snack food to accompany a night of boozing.

This is the closest that you'll come to raw or lightly cooked vegetables in Thailand. Aromatic herbs like mint, lemongrass, kaffir lime leaves and Chinese celery give *yam* a dynamic flavour that will make an ordinary lettuce and tomato salad look pale and predictable. And then there is the chilli factor. It is a common trick in Thailand to offset the burn of chillies with fresh vegetables; this technique is used in the assembly of *yam*, often in dare-devil proportions. The spiciest of the genre is *yam phrík chíi fáa* (spur-chilli *yam*), while a more mild incarnation is *yam wún-sên* (bean-thread noodles tossed with shrimp, ground pork, coriander leaf, lime juice and fresh sliced chillies).

Stir-fries & Deep-Fries

To really appreciate Thai food, you need to develop a rapport with the vendor stalls, many of whom can whip up a handful of stir-fry standards. There is also an undeniable entertainment factor in the visual spectacle of a stir-fry cook clanging the ingredients around the wok, teasing with the open flame and moving on to the next order in rapid succession. In a matter of minutes the plate is set before you along with a ceramic bowl of *phrík náam plaa* (fish sauce with sliced chillies), which is used as a condiment much like soy sauce is used in Chinese cuisine.

Ordering a stir-fry dish is a lot like making a radio request: the name-your-dish routine is based on whatever ingredients the vendor has on hand, not a pre-set menu. The vegetable and meat options are usually displayed in a plastic case beside the wok – it is your job as the eater to name a tasty combination. A no-fail option is *khâo phàt* (fried rice), which, when done well, is better than any version you've encountered back home.

DOUGH BOY

The macho staple of the West has been reduced to a prissy dessert in Thailand. Forget about finding Indochinese baguettes or even a chewy multigrain, Thais like bread to be sweet and airy and it is often served toasted with sweetened condensed milk. Even the Thai word for bread – *khànŏm* (meaning 'sweet pastry or dessert') *bang* – reveals its status in the food end.

Many of the techniques for Thai stir-fries *(phàt)* were imported by the Chinese, who are famous for being able to prepare a whole banquet in a single wok. There is also a sub-set of Thai stir-fries that are often classified as Thai-Chinese and served in simple open-air restaurants run by families of Chinese descent. Such dishes include *néua phàt náam-man hăwy* (beef in oyster sauce) or *kài phàt mét mámûang hìmáphaan* (sliced chicken stir-fried in dried chillies and cashews).

Thailand wouldn't be able to cultivate a global cuisine fan base without a well-developed repertoire of fried foods. Usually prepared by street vendors, deep-fried snacks include *klûay thâwt* (fried bananas) or *pàw-pía* (fried spring rolls). You'll never step foot in a KFC after trying Thailand's *kài thâwt* (fried chicken), typically served with a spicy dipping sauce and sticky rice.

Fruits & Sweets

Being a tropical country, Thailand excels in the fruit department with exceptionally delicious *sàppàrót* (pineapple), *málákaw* (papaya) and *taeng moh* (watermelon) sold from ubiquitous vendor carts, often accompanied by a dipping mix of salt, sugar and ground chilli. You'll find more exotic fruits sold in produce markets. The king of fruits is the spiky-shelled *thúrian* (durian), an acridly pungent delicacy in Southeast Asia. The fruit smells so strong that it is banned from airlines, air-conditioned buses and some hotels. Other seasonal fruits that you deserve to meet include creamy *náwy náa* (custard apple), the Velcro tennis-ball shaped *ngáw* (rambutan), the purplish skinned *mang-khút* (mangosteen), and the grape-shaped *lámút* (sapodilla) and *lam yai* (longan).

Mámûang (mangoes) come in a dozen varieties that are eaten at different stages of ripeness. Some are served green and crisp and taste like apples, while others are ripe and luscious and served in the intoxicating dessert *khâo nĭaw mámûang* (mangoes and sticky rice).

Khăwng wăan (Thai desserts) stay true to their literal translation as 'sweet things'. The typical ingredients might appear to be savoury components – like rice flour, tapioca and corn kernels – but are arranged in such a sugary nest that no one could blur the line between meal and dessert. Most of the traditional desserts are ancient and elaborate recipes, like *făwy thawng*, which imitates the appearance of golden threads with an egg-yolk batter.

DRINKS
Coffee, Tea & Fruit Drinks

Thais are big coffee drinkers, and good-quality arabica and robusta are cultivated in the hilly areas of northern and southern Thailand. The traditional filtering system is nothing more than a narrow cloth bag attached to a steel handle. The bag is filled with ground coffee, and hot water poured through producing *kaafae thŭng* (bag coffee) or *kaafae boh-raan* (traditional coffee). The usual *kaafae thŭng* is served in a glass, mixed with sugar and sweetened with condensed milk – if you don't want either, be sure to specify *kaafae dam* (black coffee) followed with *mâi sài náam taan* (without sugar).

Black tea, both local and imported, is available at the same places that serve real coffee. *Chaa thai* derives its characteristic orange-red colour from ground

> 'The king of fruits is the spiky-shelled *thúrian* (durian), an acridly pungent delicacy in Southeast Asia'

tamarind seed added after curing. *Chaa ráwn* (hot tea) and *chaa yen* (iced tea) will almost always be sweetened with condensed milk and sugar.

Fruit drinks appear all over Thailand and are an excellent way to rehydrate after water becomes unpalatable. Most *náam phŏn-lá-mái* (fruit juices) are served with a touch of sugar and salt and a whole lot of ice. Many foreigners object to the salt, but it serves a metabolic role in helping the body to cope with tropical temperatures.

Beer & Spirits

Advertised with such slogans as *pràthêht rao, bia rao* (Our Land, Our Beer), the Singha label is considered the quintessential 'Thai' beer and is a strong-tasting pilsner. Pronounced sing (not 'sing-ha'), it claims about half the domestic market, and has an alcohol content of 6%. Beer Chang matches the hoppy taste of Singha but pumps the alcohol content up to 7%. There are other varieties of beer, like Leo, that offer more alcohol for the baht. Dutch-licensed but Thailand-brewed Heineken and Singapore's Tiger brand are also popular selections. Beer Lao is now available in some cities and Phuket Beer is one of Thailand's only microbrews.

When in the company of Thais, beer is rarely consumed directly from the bottle but instead enjoys yet another communal ritual. Each drinker gets a glass, filled with ice, into which the elixir is poured. A toast goes round and the younger member of the group is usually in charge of keeping everyone's glass filled with ice and beer. The ice helps keep the beverage cool in a hot climate and combats the dehydrating effects of a hangover.

Rice whisky is a favourite of the working class, struggling students and family gatherings as it's more affordable than beer. Most rice whiskies are mixed with distilled sugarcane spirits and thus have a sharp, sweet taste not unlike rum. The most famous brands are Mekong and Sang Som, which are typically sold in a large bottle *(klom)* or a flask-sized bottle *(baen)*, and are mixed with ice, soda water and a splash of Coke.

News and views about Southeast Asia's leading brews can be found at www.beerasia.blogspot.com.

Once spending money becomes a priority, Thais prefer to upgrade to the whiskies produced from barley. Johnnie Walker is of course an immediate status symbol, but for more modest means there are the Thai versions branded as Blue Eagle, 100 Pipers and Spey Royal.

CELEBRATIONS

Food plays an important part in many Thai religious festivals and merit-making occasions. Before dawn the Buddhist monks travel the streets barefoot collecting alms from the devout. Housewives wait by their front doors to dispense fresh-cooked rice and curries for the temple's meals. The spiritual world requires daily feeding as well. Every morning business owners set out small offerings of food – such as rice, fruit and water or tea – in hopes that their day will be prosperous. When gaining merit at important temples or shrines, there are a variety of important offertory foods such as roasted pig's head, pomelo, or liquor.

Thailand has a burgeoning wine industry centred around the cool hills of Khao Yai where *chenin blanc* grapes prosper.

During important landmark events, like weddings, house blessings or ordinations, certain auspicious foods are used to invite good fortune on the participants. The long and chewy texture of *khànŏm jiin* will encourage the longevity of a marriage. The complicated dish of *hàw mòk* bundles together many disparate ingredients, such as fish and herbs, into a creamy coconut custard wrapped in a banana leaf, and signifies a loving and cooperative family. The egg yolk–based desserts that look like gold are always invited to the celebratory table because of their association with wealth.

Community festivals of food often centre around an agricultural region's principal crop: eastern provinces of Chanthaburi, Rayong and Trat celebrate

TRAVEL YOUR TASTEBUDS

Need to break out of the *phàt thai* rut? Try these quintessential Thai dishes that don't always register on the tourist radar:

- **kaeng phèt kài nàw mái** – chicken and bamboo-shoot curry, a working-class mainstay usually pre-made at rice-and-curry shops.
- **kǔaytǐaw plaa** – rice noodles with fish balls (boiled ground-fish balls) available at most noodle shops or stalls.
- **tôm yam pó tàek** – when you tire of *tôm yam kûng*, try *pó tàek* (broken fish trap), which has a similar broth with the addition of basil and assorted seafood; available at some restaurants.
- **mîang kham** – tiny chunks of lime, ginger and shallot, toasted grated coconut, roasted peanuts, fresh sliced chillies and dried shrimp, all wrapped up in a wild-tea leaf with sweet-sour tamarind sauce; available at some restaurants.
- **náam phrík plaa thuu** – chilli dip made with shrimp paste and served with steamed mackerel and parboiled vegetables; available at vendor carts and restaurants.
- **plaa dàet diaw** – 'once-sunned fish', a whole fish split down the middle, sundried for half a day, then deep-fried and served with a mango-peanut sauce; usually available from day markets as a takeaway dish.
- **sangkhayǎa fák thâwng** – creamy egg-and-palm-sugar custard baked inside a Thai pumpkin; usually available from day markets.
- **yam hua plii** – spicy banana-flower salad; available at restaurants.
- **yam phrík chíi fáa** – hot and tangy salad centred on fresh *phrík chíi fáa* (very spicy 'sky-pointing' chillies); available at restaurants.

the durian, mangosteen, rambutan and pomelo harvest; Chiang Mai trumpets the mango season; and Nan marks the ripening of its signature citrus, the golden orange.

The most famous food festival in Thailand is tied with the beliefs of the Chinese Buddhists. The annual Vegetarian Festival (late September or early October; see p746) is hosted throughout the country with abstinence from meat, and a proliferation of street stalls selling vegetarian food. But Phuket moves the festival beyond a dietary shift to religious frenzy with a street procession that involves ritualistic self-mutilation.

Visit www.realthai.blog spot.com for profiles of local mom-and-pop restaurants in Bangkok and beyond.

WHERE TO EAT & DRINK

For a culture that eats almost every meal outside the home, dining is incredibly informal, at least in terms of setting.

The majority of meals in Thailand come from the *rót khěn* (vendor cart), which specialises in a particular type of dish and if done well cultivates a local following. These vendors can be found clustered together at the day markets as energy builders for grocery-shopping housewives, or the carts make up the main event at night markets. The changing landscape of the vendor carts provides a sun-dial service for judging the time of day. In the mornings stalls selling coffee and Chinese-style doughnuts spring up along busy commuter corridors. At lunchtime, midday eaters might grab a plastic chair at yet another stall for a simple stir-fry or plate of noodles. In most small towns, night markets are the provincial equivalent of a restaurant row. These hawker centres set up in the middle of town with a cluster of vendors, metal tables and chairs, and some shopping as an after-dinner mint.

Fresh fruits, vegetables and meat are still sold from the old-fashioned open-air warehouse markets *(tàlàat)*, despite the influx of Western-style

supermarkets. For many of Thailand's working mothers, the markets are also a stand-in cook, selling a variety of wholesome dishes that are spooned into takeaway plastic bags and shuttled off to hungry mouths at home.

There are, of course, restaurants *(ráan aahǎan)* in Thailand that range from simple food stops to formal affairs. Lunchtime is the right time to point and eat at the *ráan khâo kaeng* (rice-and-curry shop), which sells a selection of pre-made dishes. The more generic *ráan aahǎan taam sàng* (food-to-order shop) can often be recognised by one or more tall refrigerated cabinets with clear glass windows at the front of the shop. These will be filled with many of the raw ingredients – Chinese kale, tomatoes, chopped pork, fresh or dried fish, noodles, eggplant, spring onions – for a standard repertoire of Thai and Chinese dishes. As the name implies, the cooks attempt to prepare any dish you can name, including any kind of rice or noodle dish as well as more complex multidish meals.

All standard restaurants, large and small, typically have a simple collection of utilitarian tables and chairs lined up along the walls. Decoration may be limited to a few Singha or Sang Som posters, or something more incongruous, such as a faded picture of the Swiss Alps. Fluorescent lighting – cheap and cool – is the norm. Such restaurants typically specialise in a single cuisine, whether local or regional. Ambience and entertainment is provided by the diners, not by the setting.

For many years, Thais celebrated special occasions with a meal at a Chinese banquet restaurant, a cuisine viewed as more refined than their own, or Chinese-style seafood restaurant. Depending on the region, there are semi-formal Thai restaurants that might have a waterfront setting or a flashy lounge singer who takes requests from the crowd. Rarely do Thais refer to a menu, preferring instead to order their favourite dishes from memory. Bangkok, Chiang Mai and other internationally influenced cities tend to have more of a Western-style restaurant scene with hip décor and nouveau or imported cuisine.

Thai Hawker Food, by Kenny Yee and Catherine Gordon, is an illustrated guide to recognising and ordering street food in Thailand.

VEGETARIANS & VEGANS

Vegetarianism isn't a widespread trend in Thailand, but many of the tourist-oriented restaurants cater to vegetarians. That doesn't mean that all Thais are monogamous carnivores; there are, however, home-grown practices of vegetarianism and veganism rooted in a strict interpretation of Buddhism made popular by Bangkok's ex-Governor Chamlong Srimuang. Now there are several nonprofit *ráan aahǎan mangsàwírát* (vegetarian restaurants) in Bangkok and several provincial capitals where the food is served buffet-style and is very inexpensive. Dishes are almost always 100% vegan (ie no meat, poultry, fish or fish sauce, dairy or egg products).

During the Vegetarian Festival, celebrated by Chinese Buddhists, many restaurants and street stalls in Bangkok, Phuket and in the Chinese business districts of most Thai towns go meatless for one month. Other easy, though less common, venues for vegetarian meals include Indian restaurants, which usually feature a vegetarian section on the menu.

Find vegetarian restaurants across Thailand at www.happycow.net.

USING THE RIGHT TOOL FOR THE JOB

If you're not offered chopsticks, don't ask for them. Thais only use chopsticks to eat noodle soups or other dishes inherited from China. Most rice dishes are eaten with a fork and spoon. When it comes to certain northern and northeastern Thai dishes, the fingers are a diner's best friend. You can go *sans* utensils with *khâo nǐaw* (sticky rice), rolling it into a ball and dipping it into a chilli sauce. Do note that the fingers or a utensil is used to eat fried or grilled chicken, unlike the Western style of meeting mouth to flesh.

The phrase 'I'm vegetarian' in Thai is *phŏm kin jeh* (for men) or *dì-chăn kin jeh* (for women). Loosely translated this means 'I eat only vegetarian food', which includes no eggs and no dairy products – in other words, total vegan.

HABITS & CUSTOMS

Like most of Thai culture, eating conventions appear relaxed and informal but are orchestrated by many implied rules. Dining is considered an important social occasion not only to chat with friends but to enjoy many different dishes, which is made easier if there are more mouths interested in sampling. Solo diners are more common at Thailand's original version of 'fast-food' restaurants: places that serve one-plate dishes.

Whether at home or in a restaurant, Thai meals are always served 'family-style', that is from common serving platters, and the plates appear in whatever order the kitchen can prepare them. This tends to frustrate Western diners unaware that the kitchen presumes the party will share whatever dish arrives first. Another factor in a Thai meal is achieving a balance of flavours and textures. Traditionally, the party orders a curry, a steamed or fried fish, a stir-fried vegetable dish and a soup, taking care to balance cool and hot, sour and sweet, salty and plain. Thais tend to over-order at social occasions – the more food is left, the more generous the host appears.

When eating Thai family–style, all the dishes are arranged on the table and everyone digs in rather than passing the plates to each diner. Reaching over someone to a plate is customary, but picking up a plate to serve yourself is considered rude. If you can't reach the platter at all, it's best to hand your plate to someone near the serving platter, who can then place some food on your plate. Most Thais will do this automatically if they notice you're out of platter range. In fact, Thais are very conscientious of fellow diners and will pass the best part of the fish to the honoured guest or the clueless *faràng*.

In most cases, the elder or honoured guest is the first to reach toward the communal dishes to commence the meal. When serving yourself from a common platter, put no more than one spoonful onto your plate at a time. Heaping your plate with all the options will look greedy to Thais unfamiliar with Western conventions. It's also customary at the start of a shared meal to eat a spoonful of plain rice first – a gesture that recognises rice as the most important part of the meal.

Getting the food from your individual plate to your mouth requires more specific instructions. For dishes served over rice, like curries and stir-fries, the locals use a fork and spoon, but not in the way you think. Thais use a fork like we use a knife, to push food on to the spoon, which then enters the mouth. From the Thai standpoint, sticking a fork in the mouth is just plain strange.

EAT YOUR WORDS

While some restaurants in Thailand may have English-language menus, most will not. So you'll need to have some stock phrases on hand to tell *phàt thai* from *khâo phàt*. For pronunciation guidelines, see p781.

You could learn the secrets of a Thai kitchen through a cooking course. Formal and informal classes are widespread in Bangkok, Chiang Mai and other tourist centres.

SCHOOLS IN SESSION

Do you spend more time hanging around the markets than the temples? Are you packing in three or more meals a day? Then you are a good candidate for a cooking course, which can range from formal, equipment-oriented instructions to simple chop-and-talk introductions. Bangkok, Chiang Mai and the popular tourist islands offer different types of cooking classes, most of which include a market tour. See the respective destination chapters for more information.

Useful Phrases
EATING OUT

I'd like...	*khǎw...*
Not too spicy please.	*khǎw mâi phèt mâak*
glass	*kâew*
cup	*thûay*
fork	*sâwm*
spoon	*cháwn*
plate	*jaan plào*
napkin	*kràdàat chét pàak*
Thank you, that was delicious.	*khàwp khun mâak, aràwy mâak*
Bring the bill, please.	*khǎw bin*

VEGETARIAN & SPECIAL MEALS

Does this dish have meat?	*aahǎan jaan níi sài néua sàt mǎi*
I'm allergic to...	*phǒm/dì-chǎn pháe ...*
I don't eat ...	*phǒm/dì-chǎn kin ... mâi dâi*
meat	*néua sàt*
chicken	*kài*
fish	*plaa*
seafood	*aahǎan thálch*
pork	*mǔu*
Please don't use fish sauce.	*karúnaa mâi sài náam plaa*
Please don't use MSG.	*karúnaa mâi sài phǒng-chuu-rót*
Don't add salt.	*mâi sài kleua*

Food Glossary
STAPLES

ah-hǎan thá-leh	อาหาร ทะเล	seafood
jóhk	โจ๊ก	thick rice soup or congee
kài	ไก่	chicken
khài	ไข่	egg
khànǒm	ขนม	sweet pastries or desserts
khâo jâo	ข้าวเจ้า	white rice
khâo klâwng	ข้าวกล้อง	brown rice
khâo phàt	ข้าวผัด	fried rice
khâo plào	ข้าวเปล่า	plain rice
khâo	ข้าว	rice
kǔaytǐaw	ก๋วยเตี๋ยว	rice noodles
kûng	กุ้ง	variety of shrimp, prawn and lobster
mǔu	หมู	pork
néua	เนื้อ	beef, meat
pèt	เป็ด	duck
plaa	ปลา	fish
plaa mèuk	ปลาหมึก	squid; cuttlefish (generic)
puu	ปู	crab

VEGETABLES

phàk	ผัก	vegetables
hèt	เห็ด	mushrooms
mákhěua	มะเขือ	eggplant/aubergine
mákhěua-thêht	มะเขือเทศ	tomatoes
man faràng	มันฝรั่ง	potatoes
tâo-hûu	เต้าหู้	tofu
thùa fàk yao	ถั่วฝักยาว	long bean, yard bean, green bean

thùa lěuang	ถั่วเหลือง	soybean
thùa ngâwk	ถั่วงอก	mung bean sprouts
thùa pòn	ถั่วป่น	ground peanuts
thùa thâwt	ถั่วทอด	fried peanuts

CONDIMENTS & SEASONINGS

khǐng	ขิง	ginger
kleua	เกลือ	salt
náam jîm	น้ำจิ้ม	dipping sauces
náam plaa	น้ำปลา	fish sauce
náam sii-íw	น้ำซีอิ๊ว	soy sauce
náam sôm sǎi chuu	น้ำส้มสายชู	vinegar
náamtaan	น้ำตาล	sugar
phàk chii	ผักชี	coriander leaf
phǒng-chuu-rót	ผงชูรส	monosodium glutamate (MSG)
phrík	พริก	chilli
sàránàe	สะระแหน่	mint

FRUIT

phǒn-lá-mái	ผลไม้	fruit
faràng	ฝรั่ง	guava
klûay	กล้วย	banana
mákhǎam	มะขาม	tamarind
málákaw	มะละกอ	papaya
mámûang	มะม่วง	mango
mánao	มะนาว	lime
mang-khút	มังคุด	mangosteen
máphráo	มะพร้าว	coconut
ngáw	เงาะ	rambutan
taeng moh	แตงโม	watermelon

DRINKS

bia	เบียร์	beer
chaa	ชา	tea
kaafae	กาแฟ	coffee
khrêuang dèum	เครื่องดื่ม	beverages
náam	น้ำ	water or juice
náam âwy	น้ำอ้อย	raw, lumpy cane sugar/sugar-cane juice
náam dèum	น้ำดื่ม	drinking water
náam khǎeng	น้ำแข็ง	ice
náam sôm	น้ำส้ม	orange juice
náam tâo-hûu	น้ำเต้าหู้	soy milk
nom jèut	นมจืด	milk

METHODS OF PREPARATION

dìp	ดิบ	raw
nêung	นึ่ง	steamed
phǎo	เผา	grilled (chillies, vegetables, fish and shrimp only)
phàt	ผัด	stir-fried
tôm	ต้ม	boiled
thâwt	ทอด	deep fried
yâang	ย่าง	grilled or roasted

Thailand's Natural Wonders

THE LAND

The land lying to the east of India was poetically referred to as Suvarnab-humi, a Sanskrit term meaning 'Land of Gold', before it was carved up into independent states and strung together as the geographic region of Southeast Asia. Although Thailand is not known for the namesake element, the country has woven much of the majesty and prestige associated with gold into its cultural and geographic identity.

The shape of the country is often likened to two important national themes: sometimes described as a golden axe or as the head of an elephant with the shaft or the trunk represented by the Malay Peninsula. More practically, the Thai boundary encompasses 514,000 sq km, making it about the size of France. The capital of Thailand, Bangkok, sits at about 14° latitude north – level with Madras, Manila, Guatemala City and Khartoum. Needless to say, the golden land of Thailand is tropical and fecund, stretching from lush mountains in the north to an endless coastline in the south.

In the north of the country, the Tibet Plateau has planted a petite off-shoot of its heaven-poking mountains into a more benevolent climate, the southernmost occurrence of this mighty Himalayan range. The topography mellows into the central region's rice basket, which is fed by rivers that are as revered as the national monarchy. Thailand's most exalted river is the Mae Nam Chao Phraya. The country's early kingdoms emerged around the Chao Phraya basin, still the seat of the monarchy today. The river delta spends most of the year in cultivation – from muddy plots of land to emerald green fields of youthful rice shoots, to the golden bows of the mature plant. Shore birds from the not-too-distant coast break the irregular paddy patterns with their elegant white profiles, hunting for fish that live among the flooded fields.

A Land on Fire: The Environmental Consequences of the Southeast Asian Boom (2003), by James David Fahn, reports on the environmental outcome of Thailand and Southeast Asia's conversion into modern, tourist-oriented areas.

Giant karst formations tower over emerald waters along the coast of Krabi Province (p690)

SARA-JANE CLELAND

FOR BEACHES & CORAL GARDENS: THAILAND'S BEST NATIONAL PARKS

- Similan Islands (p655): a well-protected preserve famed for snorkelling and diving; it is best visited from November to May

- Ko Tarutao (p730): a series of islands ranging from deserted to developed for back-to-naturists, coral exploration and hiking; best visited from November to May

- Khao Lak/Lamru (p653): coastal park with blonde beaches, crystal-clear water for snorkelling, and rainforest hikes; it is best visited from January to May

- Ko Lanta (p714): a low-key island combining rainforest hiking with beach-bum activities

- Khao Sam Roi Yot (p564): a coastal mangrove forest filled with birdlife

---

Opposite page: The underwater world of the Similan Islands Marine National Park (p655)

MICHAEL AW

The golden sands of Hat Khao Lak border the stunning Khao Lak/Lamru National Park (p653)

JOE CUMMINGS

Outlining the contours of Thailand's northern and northeastern border is another celebrated river: the Mekong River. The artery of Southeast Asia, the Mekong both physically separates and culturally fuses Thailand with its neighbours. It is a workhorse river that has been dammed for hydroelectric power, and swells and contracts based on the seasonal rains. In the dry season, riverside farmers plant vegetables in the muddy floodplain, harvesting the fruits of their labour before the river reclaims it territory.

Thailand's northeastern border sits on an arid plateau rising some 300m above the central plain. This is a hardscrabble land where the rains are meagre, the soil anaemic and the red dust stains as stubbornly as betel nuts chewed by ageing grandmothers.

The kingdom's rivers dump their odd assortment of mountain minerals and upstream fresh water into the Gulf of Thailand, a shallow basin distinct from the neighbouring South China Sea. The warm, gentle waters of the gulf are an ideal cultivation ground for brilliantly coloured coral reefs that further temper the rollicking tendencies of the open ocean.

The southernmost stretch of Thailand is the upper portion of the Malay Peninsula, bordered on the east by the Gulf of Thailand and on the west by the Andaman Sea, a watery subdistrict of the vast Indian Ocean. Limestone-

Khao Yai National Park
(p464) protects one of
mainland Asia's largest
tracts of monsoon forest

CASEY MAHANEY

encrusted islands dot the Andaman coast, adding drama to the jewel colours of the tropical sea. On the mainland, the Malay Peninsula is dominated by remaining stands of rainforests and cultivated tracts of rubber and palm-oil plantations. Thailand's Andaman Sea and Gulf of Thailand coastlines form 2710km of beaches, hard shores and wetlands. Hundreds of oceanic and continental islands lie offshore on both sides. Thailand's coral-reef system, including the Andaman coast from Ranong to northern Phuket and the Surin and Similan Islands, is one of the world's most diverse.

WILDLIFE

Unique in the region because its north–south axis extends some 1800km from mainland to peninsular Southeast Asia, Thailand's remaining stands of undeveloped land provide habitats for an astounding variety of flora and fauna.

Thai Birding (www
.thaibirding.com) is a
great online resource for
bird spottings and trip
reports.

Animals

In the northern half of Thailand, most of the indigenous species are classified zoologically as Indochinese, referring to fauna originating from mainland Southeast Asia, while that of the south is generally Sundaic, typical of peninsular Malaysia, Sumatra, Borneo and Java. A large overlap between the two zoogeographical and vegetative zones starts around Prachuap Khiri Khan on the southern peninsula, and extends north to Uthai Thani, providing habitat for plants and animals from both zones.

*Guide to the Birds of Thai-
land* (1991), by Boonsong
Lekagul et al, remains
the classic field guide for
birders in Thailand.

Thailand is particularly rich in birdlife, with more than 1000 recorded resident and migrating species – approximately 10% of the world's bird species. The cool mountains of northern Thailand are populated by montane species and migrants, especially flycatchers and thrushes. The forests of Khao Yai National Park in northeastern Thailand are a favourite for hornbills. Marshland birds prefer the wetlands of the central region, while Sundaic species such as Gurney's Pitta flock to the wetter climate of southern Thailand.

SWEATY HIKES & GREAT VIEWS: THAILAND'S BEST NATIONAL PARKS

- Doi Inthanon (p337): tall granite mountains, views of misty valleys and lots of birdlife; it is best visited from November to May
- Doi Phu Kha (p391): a steep mountain summit overlooking misty valleys, karst caves and silvery waterfalls; it is best visited from November to May
- Um Phang Wildlife Sanctuary (p425): Thailand's biggest, most beautiful waterfall
- Thung Salaeng Luang (p401): massive grasslands are home to carpets of flowers (after the rainy season) and varied wild animals and birdlife
- Khao Yai (p464): a dense monsoon forest famed for its waterfalls and bird and monkey populations; it is best visited from November to April
- Phu Kradung (p504): a popular mountain hike rewards trekkers with sunset views and lots of camping camaraderie; it is best visited from January to May
- Kaeng Krachan (p553): an energy-sapping 6km hike delivers you to the summit of Phanoen Tung for breathtaking views of misty morning valleys
- Khao Sok (p582): a pristine southern rainforest, well-suited for jungle safaris and kayak trips; monkeys and hornbills are commonly spotted and if you time your trip just right you might also see the *Rafflesia*; it is best visited from February to May

Insect species in the kingdom number some 6000 and the country's marine environment counts tens of thousands of species.

More so than any other famous mammal, it is the monkey that visitors are more likely to spot in the country's national parks. Thailand is home to five species of macaque, four species of the smaller leaf-monkey and three species of gibbon. Although they face the same habitat loss as other native species, monkeys in Thailand live in varying states of domestication with humans. But Thais' relationship with monkeys seesaws between generosity and cruelty: food is often given to resident monkey troops as an act of Buddhist merit-making, but it isn't unusual to see a monkey kept in a small cage as an ignored pet.

Other species found in the kingdom's parks and sanctuaries include gaur (Indian bison), banteng (wild cattle), serow (an Asiatic goat-antelope), sambar deer, barking deer, mouse deer and tapir – to name a few.

Left: The renowned foraging skills of macaques are sometimes used in harvesting coconuts on plantations

JAMES MARSHALL

Right: Dusky langurs are some of the resident creatures you might spot in Thailand's national parks

TOM COCKREM

Thailand has several venomous varieties of snake, including the cobra

CAROL WILEY

Opposite page: Once the backbone of the logging industry, many of Thailand's domesticated elephants now carry tourists, not timber

MICK ELMORE

The oceans on both sides of the Malay peninsula are home to abundant fish life and coral

MICHAEL AW

They are not as numerous as decades past, but lizards and snakes also claim a Thai address. Thailand has six of the venomous variety: the common cobra, king cobra, banded krait, green viper, Malayan viper and Russell's pit viper. Although the relatively rare king cobra can reach up to 6m in length, the nation's largest snake is the reticulated python, which can reach a whopping 10m. The country's many lizard species include two commonly seen in homes – *túk-kae*, a reclusive and somewhat homely gecko that is heard in the early evening coughing its name; and *jîng-jòk*, a spirited house lizard that is usually spotted chasing after bugs on ceilings and walls. The black jungle monitor, which looks like a miniature dinosaur, lives in some of the southern forests.

The oceans on either side of the Malay Peninsula are home to hundreds of species of coral, and the reefs created by these tiny creatures provide the perfect living conditions for hundreds of species of fish, crustaceans and tiny invertebrates. The oceans are alive with prehistoric beasts and aquarium-style quick sprinters. You can find the world's smallest fish (a 10mm-long goby) and the largest (the 18m-long whale shark), plus reef denizens such as clownfish, parrotfish, wrasse, angelfish, triggerfish and lionfish. Deeper waters are home to larger species such as grouper, barracuda, sharks, manta rays, marlin and tuna. You might also encounter turtles, whales and dolphins.

Thailand's most famous animals are also its most endangered. The Asian elephant, a smaller cousin to the African elephant, once roamed the

There's an estimated population of around 2000 wild elephants in Thailand, such as this pair in Khao Yai National Park (p464)

ANDERS BLOMQVIST

The Elephant Keeper (1987; directed by Prince Chatrichalerm Yukol) tells the story of an honest forestry chief who tries to protect the wilderness from illegal logging interests; he is assisted by a courageous mahout and his faithful elephant.

unclaimed forests of Indochina in great herds. The elephant's massive size and intelligence made it a reliable beast of burden, often corralled during important cultural festivals for the purposes of domestication. The elephant is still a national symbol and has served many roles in Thailand's history: war machine, timber logger, royal transport and godlike character in the Hindu-inherited myths. But both the wild and domesticated elephants face extinction and displacement as Thailand's human population increases and modernises. The population of wild elephants in Thailand is estimated at about 2000. The few remaining stands of elephant habitat often border agricultural villages; this results in ongoing battles between farmers and wild elephants who are prone to raiding crops instead of foraging in the forest. Despite the animals' protected status, retaliation or poaching is often seen by struggling farmers as the only solution to this threat to their livelihood.

The domesticated elephant has suffered more indignity than its wild counterpart as it is now obsolete in modern society. No longer employable in the timber industry or honoured in ceremonial processions, the domesticated elephant and its mahout often wander the streets of the kingdom's major cities reduced to beggars and sideshows. See p43 for information about elephant-sanctuary programmes.

Reclusive wild tigers stalk the hinterland between Thailand and Myanmar but in ever decreasing numbers. It is difficult to obtain an accurate count of surviving tigers, but most experts theorise that around 200 to 300 wild tigers remain in Thailand. Although tiger hunting and trapping is illegal, poachers continue to kill the cats for the lucrative overseas wildlife trade.

Roughly 250 animal and plant species in Thailand are on the International Union for Conservation of Nature (IUCN) list of endangered or vulnerable species, with fish, bird and plants species being the most affected.

Plants

The days of Thailand as a vast jungle country are long gone. The cultivating hand of the farmer and more recently the industrialist has moulded the canopy into field and city. In the remaining protected areas, there are two types of primary forest: monsoon (with a distinct dry season of three months or more) and rainforest (where rain falls more than nine months per year). The most heavily forested provinces are Chiang Mai and Kanchanaburi.

Most of the northern and central forests are made up of the deciduous trees of a monsoon forest, which become green and lush during the rainy season, and dusty and naked during the dry season in order to conserve water. Teak is one of the most famous monsoon timbers and still survives in limited quantities in Thailand's forests.

In southern Thailand, where the rainfall is more plentiful, the forests are classified as rainforests with a few zones of mixed monsoon and rainforest vegetation. One remarkable species found in some southern forests is *Rafflesia kerrii*, Thailand's largest flower (which reaches 80cm across); you can see it at Khao Sok National Park (p582) near Surat Thani.

Along the coastal areas are the wetland mangroves that proved to be a helpful buffer during the 2004 tsunami. These mangrove forests were once considered wastelands and have been heavily depleted by urban development and commercial farming, despite the forests' role as a protective incubator for many coastal fish and animal species.

Flourishing in every backyard large enough to claim sunshine is an incredible array of fruit trees (mango, banana, papaya, jackfruit and occasionally durian). Common in the forests are bamboo (more species than any other country outside China), tropical hardwoods and more than 27,000 flowering species, including Thailand's national floral symbol, the orchid. Commercial plantings in the south include coconut, palm oil, cashew and rubber. In the denuded northeast, eucalyptus is often planted to prevent erosion and as a cheap and quick timber source.

Left: The orchid is Thailand's national floral symbol

MARGARET JUNG

Right: Bananas are one of Thailand's staple tropical fruits

FRANK CARTER

Ko Kham (p265), one of the dazzling islands of the Mu Ko Chang National Marine Park

WOODS WHEATCROFT

NATIONAL PARKS & PROTECTED AREAS

With 15% of the kingdom's land and sea designated as park or sanctuary, Thailand has one of the highest percentages of protected areas of any nation in Asia. There are more than 100 national parks, plus more than 1000 'nonhunting areas', wildlife sanctuaries, forest reserves, botanic gardens and arboretums. Twenty-six of the national parks are marine parks that protect coastal, insular and open-sea areas. Thailand began its conservation efforts in 1960 with the creation of a national system of wildlife sanctuaries under the Wild Animals Reservation and Protection Act, followed by the National Parks Act of 1961. Khao Yai National Park was

Seahorses are just one of the underwater delights of Thailand's marine kingdom

ROBERT HALSTEAD

Opposite page: The protected mountainous interior of Ko Chang (p257) is home to dense jungle and tumbling waterfalls

ANDREW LEANNE WALKER

the first wild area to receive this new status. In 2005, Khao Yai along with four other neighbouring parks and sanctuaries was designated a Unesco World Heritage site because of the protected areas' 200km coverage of major rainforest habitat. The parks are administrated by the **National Park, Wildlife & Plant Conservation Department** (DNP; www.dnp.go.th).

Marine national parks along the Andaman coast experienced varying amounts of damage from the 2004 tsunami. Roughly 5% to 13% of the coral in reef systems associated with these parks is estimated to have been heavily damaged by the waves or by debris brought by the waves. None of the damage was extensive enough to interfere with park activities in the long run, and all of the parks are open as usual.

ENVIRONMENTAL ISSUES
Deforestation, Flooding & Species Loss

Typical of countries with high population densities, Thailand has put enormous pressure on its ecosystems. The natural forest cover makes up about 28% of the kingdom's land area as compared to 70% some 50 years ago. The rapid depletion of the country's forests coincides with the modern era's industrialisation, urbanisation and commercial logging. Although these statistics are alarming, forest loss has slowed since 1990 and now equals about a 0.7% per year loss, according to statistics published by the World Bank.

In response to environmental degradation, the Thai government has created a large number of protected areas since the 1970s and has enacted legislation to protect specific plant and animal species. The government hopes to raise the total forest cover to 40% by the middle of this century, but satellite imaging shows that many areas designated as forest cover have been denuded or are so significantly fragmented that they cannot support wildlife populations. In 1989 all logging was banned in Thailand following a disaster the year before in which hundreds of tonnes of cut timber washed down deforested slopes in Surat Thani Province, burying a number of villages and killing more than 100 people. It is now illegal to sell timber felled in Thailand, and all imported timber is theoretically accounted for before going on the market.

Seasonal flooding is a common natural disaster in Thailand, but 2006 was an exceptionally destructive year, especially in Nan Province, which experienced its worst occurrence in 40 years after days of incessant rains. Monsoonal rains during this period caused flooding in 46 provinces in northern and central Thailand. Many environmental experts suspect human alteration of natural flood barriers and watercourses is responsible for increased occurrences of severe flooding. Increased incidents of flooding along the Mekong River are often linked to upstream infrastructure projects, such as dams and removal of rapids for easier navigation, and increased riverside populations. Deforestation and destruction of wetlands and river margins are some of the many compounding factors. Increased seasonal

Ecology Asia (www .ecologyasia.com) has an econews section that follows green headlines in Thailand.

Doi Inthanon (2565m) is Thailand's tallest mountain.

Deforestation places enormous pressure on Thailand's fragile ecosystems

DENNIS JOHNSON

YOU CALL THIS A PARK?

Why do some Thai national parks look more like tourist resorts? To be perfectly honest, the government's commitment to enforcement of environmental protection is firmer on paper than in practice. Back when forests were natural resources not natural treasures, the Royal Forest Division (RFD) managed the profitable teak concessions. How does a government replace a money-making venture like logging with a money-losing venture like conservation? A sizeable enforcement budget would have been a good start, but rarely did the necessary funds materialise to bar moneyed interests from operating surreptitiously in public lands. The conflict between paper legislation and economic realities became most acute in the late 1990s after the Asian currency crisis crippled the RFD's enforcement budget.

Another loophole arises around land ownership and land use: many of Thailand's parks contain local communities, in some cases marginalised ethnic minorities, subsistence farmers or fisherfolk, whose presence predates the area's park status. Villagers are often disrespectful of forest-protection rules that conflict with traditional practices like slash-and-burn agriculture or firewood collection; some even augment incomes through illegal poaching. More obvious, though, are the southern marine parks where coastal villagers have turned their fishing shacks into bungalows for the emerging tourism industry. In the case of Ko Chang, for example, commercial development of the park was orchestrated by business interests connected to the Thaksin government. The island was once a rural community with a few basic guesthouses and intermittent electricity, but during the Thaksin era the island was given a special economic status and touted as an ecotourism model. The end result was a sizeable profit for politically connected land buyers and a mini-Samui.

It is easy to judge Thailand for mismanaging its natural endowments when the West has, in many cases, squandered and auctioned off its own, but the Thai government is undoubtedly conflicted in its commitment to environmental protection. This is a habit that can be traced back to the creation of the park system and one that is further encouraged with a new revenue source: tourism.

---

rains, possibly an indication of broader climate changes, overload an otherwise healthy ecosystem.

Thailand is a signatory to the UN Convention on International Trade in Endangered Species (CITES). Although Thailand has a better record than most of its neighbours, corruption hinders government attempts to shelter 'exotic' species from the illicit global wildlife trade, which is the third-largest black-market activity after drugs and arms dealing. Between the border of Thailand and Myanmar it is quite easy for poachers and illegal loggers to move contraband from the unregulated forests of Myanmar into the markets of Thailand and beyond. Southeast Asia is a poaching hotspot due to the region's biodiversity and because of inconsistent enforcement of wildlife protection laws.

In any case, wildlife experts agree that the greatest danger faced by Thai fauna is neither hunting nor the illegal wildlife trade but rather habitat loss – as is true worldwide. Species that have become notably extinct in Thailand include the kouprey (a type of wild cattle), Schomburgk's deer and the Javan rhino.

Coastal Development & Overfishing

Coastal development has put serious pressures on Thailand's diverse coral reef system and marine environment. It is estimated that about 25% of Thailand's coral reefs have died and that the annual loss of healthy reefs will continue at a rate of 20% a year. Coral's biggest threat is sedimentation from coastal development, such as new condominiums, hotels, roads and houses. Other common problems include pollution from anchored tour

EnviroSEA (www.envirosea.com) is an online news outlet covering environmental issues of coastal Thailand.

Large-scale fishing places pressure on the region's marine environment

PAUL BEINSSEN

boats, rubbish and sewage dumped directly into the sea and agricultural and industrial runoff. Coastal development and the attendant light pollution also threaten the breeding cycles of the marine turtles who rely on a dark night sky lit by the moon.

The overall health of the ocean is deteriorating because of Thailand and its neighbours' large-scale fishing industries. Fish catches have declined by up to 33% since the 1980s in the Asia-Pacific region and the upper portion of the Gulf of Thailand is no longer as fertile as it once was. Most of the commercial catches are sent to overseas markets and rarely see a Thai dinner table. The seafood sold in Thailand is typically from fish farms, another large coastal industry for the country.

Air & Water Pollution

Step off the plane in Bangkok and take a deep breath to experience one of Thailand's most pressing environmental problems: poor urban air quality. Bangkok is one of the world's most polluted cities and at least a million Bangkok residents suffer from respiratory problems or allergies triggered by the levels of air pollution. The WHO estimates that particulate matter

There are 2.6 million registered cars in Bangkok

JOHN ELK III

in Bangkok is 2.5 times higher than acceptable standards. The primary culprits are emissions from vehicles, mainly diesel vehicles, which comprise less than 10% of the cars in the metropolitan area but contribute approximately 89% of emissions of particulate matter. Even the cleaner cars play a role as the sheer numbers of vehicles on the road in the city each day creates a critical mass of emissions.

However, in the past 10 years, Bangkok has reduced lead, dust and carbon monoxide levels, due to the government's emphasis on phasing out leaded petrol and improving diesel quality. But there are still fleets of old trucks and buses

---

**TRAVEL WIDELY, TREAD LIGHTLY, GIVE SUSTAINABLY –
THE LONELY PLANET FOUNDATION**

The Lonely Planet Foundation proudly supports nimble nonprofit institutions working for change in the world. Each year the foundation donates 5% of Lonely Planet company profits to projects selected by staff and authors. Our partners range from Kabissa, which provides small nonprofits across Africa with access to technology, to the Foundation for Developing Cambodian Orphans, which supports girls at risk of falling victim to sex traffickers.

Our nonprofit partners are linked by a grass-roots approach to the areas of health, education or sustainable tourism. Many – such as Louis Sarno who works with BaAka (Pygmy) children in the forested areas of Central African Republic – choose to focus on women and children as one of the most effective ways to support the whole community. Louis is determined to give options to children who are discriminated against by the majority Bantu population.

Sometimes foundation assistance is as simple as restoring a local ruin like the Minaret of Jam in Afghanistan; this incredible monument now draws intrepid tourists to the area and its restoration has greatly improved options for local people.

Just as travel is often about learning to see with new eyes, so many of the groups we work with aim to change the way people see themselves and the future for their children and communities.

---

on the road, including the city's bus transit system, which cough up clouds of asphyxiating black smoke and also shower the city with fine dust particles.

Chiang Mai, Thailand's second-largest city, also suffers from air pollution due to traffic pressures, and the problem is further augmented by agricultural burning and household rubbish fires. Industrial and chemical pollution from factory activities also adversely affect air quality. Petrochemical pollutants are particularly high in Rayong Province, which is home to Map Ta Phut Industrial Estate, the country's biggest industrial port.

Water pollution varies according to region but is, as would be expected, most acute in the Bangkok metropolitan area because of the relatively high concentration of factories, particularly east of the city. Chemical runoff from agribusiness, coastal shrimp farming and untreated sewage also pollute groundwater and coastal areas. Offshore oil and gas exploration in the Gulf of Thailand has also increased marine pollution.

ENVIRONMENTAL ORGANISATIONS

Chiang Mai has a large concentration of NGOs working on rural- and forest-related issues, especially environmental justice regarding minority hill tribes. International funding, research and policy organisations typically base their headquarters in the capital, Bangkok. Along the Gulf and Andaman coasts are informal village associations that regard the ocean as their backyard and periodically orchestrate beach cleanups or animal rescues. The following activist or research organisations work on environmental and conservation issues in Thailand. For information

Feel like hanging with a gibbon? Then lend a hand at the Phuket Gibbon Rehabilitation Centre (p671).

ANDERS BLOMQVIST

on environmental volunteering opportunities, see the Thailand & You chapter (p41).

Bird Conservation Society of Thailand (☎ 0 2691 4816; www.bcst.or.th; 43 Soi 29/Chok Chai Ruam Mit, Th Vipahvadee-Rangsit, Dindaeng, Bangkok 10320) Works to preserve birding sites through public and government outreach.

Friends of Asian Elephant (☎ 0 2945 7124; www.elephant.or.th; 350 Mu 8, Soi 61, Th Ramindra, Bangkhen, Bangkok 10230) This Thai NGO operates an animal hospital in Mae Yao National Park in Lampung Province, and specialises in treating abused and injured elephants.

Southeast Asia Rivers Network (Searin; ☎ 0 5327 8334; www.searin.org/indexE.htm; 78 Mu 10, Th Suthep, Chiang Mai 50200) An activist group working to maintain local communities' access to rivers and waterways and to oppose the development of large-scale damming projects. Its projects focus on the Mekong, Mun and Salween rivers.

Thailand Environment Institute (TEI; ☎ 0 2503 3333; www.tei.or.th; 16/151 Muang Thong Thani, Th Bond, Bangpood, Pakkred, Nonthaburi 11120) A nonprofit research institute devoted to sustainable human development and promoting green business models.

Wild Animal Rescue Foundation of Thailand (WAR; ☎ 0 2712 9515; www.warthai.org; 65/1 Soi 55, Th Sukhumvit 55, Bangkok 10110) One of Thailand's leading conservation NGOs working to protect native species through rehabilitation programmes and conservation projects.

World Wide Fund for Nature (WWF; ☎ 0 2524 6128; www.panda.org; 104 Outreach Bldg, Asian Institute of Technology, PO Box 4, Klong Luang, Pathum Thani 12120) WWF has a Thailand-based office working on reducing human-wild elephant conflicts and protecting the ecosystem of the Mekong River and marine environment.

Bangkok

In recent years, Bangkok has broken away from its old image as a messy third-world capital to be voted by numerous metro-watchers as a top-tier global city. The sprawl and tropical humidity are still the city's signature ambassadors, but so are gleaming shopping centres and an infectious energy of commerce and restrained mayhem. The veneer is an ultramodern backdrop of skyscraper canyons containing an untamed universe of diversions and excesses. The city is justly famous for debauchery, boasting at least four major red-light districts, as well as a club scene that has been revived post-coup. Meanwhile the urban populous is as cosmopolitan as any Western capital – guided by fashion, music and text messaging.

But beside the 21st-century façade is a traditional village as devout and sacred as any remote corner of the country. This is the seat of Thai Buddhism and the monarchy, with the attendant splendid temples. Even the modern shopping centres adhere to the old folk ways with attached spirit shrines that receive daily devotions.

Bangkok will cater to every indulgence, from all-night binges to shopping sprees, but it can also transport you into the old-fashioned world of Siam. Rise with daybreak to watch the monks on their alms route, hop aboard a long-tail boat into the canals that once fused the city, or forage for your meals from the numerous and lauded food stalls.

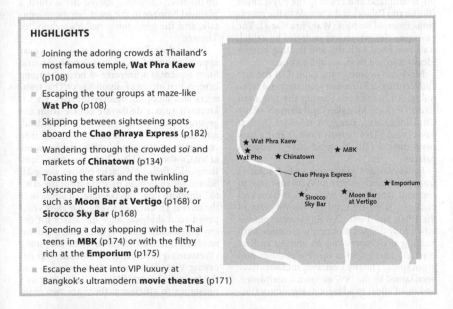

HIGHLIGHTS

- Joining the adoring crowds at Thailand's most famous temple, **Wat Phra Kaew** (p108)

- Escaping the tour groups at maze-like **Wat Pho** (p108)

- Skipping between sightseeing spots aboard the **Chao Phraya Express** (p182)

- Wandering through the crowded *soi* and markets of **Chinatown** (p134)

- Toasting the stars and the twinkling skyscraper lights atop a rooftop bar, such as **Moon Bar at Vertigo** (p168) or **Sirocco Sky Bar** (p168)

- Spending a day shopping with the Thai teens in **MBK** (p174) or with the filthy rich at the **Emporium** (p175)

- Escape the heat into VIP luxury at Bangkok's ultramodern **movie theatres** (p171)

★ Wat Phra Kaew
★
Wat Pho   ★ Chinatown   ★ MBK

— Chao Phraya Express

                                    ★ Emporium
              ★ Sirocco   ★ Moon Bar
                Sky Bar   at Vertigo

BANGKOK

FAST FACTS

- **Best Time to Visit** November to February
- **Population** 7.5 million

HISTORY

The centre of government and culture in Thailand today, Bangkok was a historical miracle during a time of turmoil. Following the fall of Ayuthaya in 1767, the kingdom fractured into competing forces, from which General Taksin emerged as a decisive unifier. He established his base in Thonburi, on the western bank of Mae Nam Chao Phraya (Chao Phraya River), a convenient location for sea trade from the Gulf of Thailand. Taksin proved more of a military strategist than a popular ruler. He was later deposed by another important military general, Chao Phraya Chakri, who moved the capital across the river in 1782 to a more defensible location in anticipation of a Burmese attack. The succession of his son in 1809 established the present-day dynasty, and Chao Phraya Chakri is referred to as Rama I.

Court officials envisioned the new capital as a resurrected Ayuthaya, complete with an island district (Ko Ratanakosin) carved out of the swampland and cradling the royal court (the Grand Palace) and a temple to the auspicious Emerald Buddha (Wat Phra Kaew). The emerging city, which was encircled by a thick wall, was filled with stilt and floating houses ideally adapted to seasonal flooding.

Modernity came to the capital in the late 19th century as European aesthetics and technologies filtered east. During the reigns of Rama IV (King Mongkut) and Rama V (King Chulalongkorn), Bangkok received its first paved road (Th Charoen Krung) and a new royal district (Dusit) styled after European palaces.

Bangkok was a gangly town when soldiers from the American war in Vietnam came to rest and relax in the city's go-go bars and brothels. It wasn't until the boom years of the 1980s and 1990s that Bangkok exploded into a fully fledged metropolis crowded with hulking skyscrapers and an endless spill of concrete that gobbled up rice paddies and green space. The city's extravagant tastes have been tamed by the 1997 economic meltdown, and in an effort to address its legendary traf-

fic, Bangkok now boasts an elevated lightrail system (Skytrain) and an underground subway (Metro).

The turn of the millennium has seen the return of many foreign-educated Thai nationals, infusing the city with a cultured and cosmopolitan poise. Multinational businesses continue to see Bangkok as a stable regional investment, helping move Thailand toward internationalism. Today the maturing metropolis holds a common footing with other regional centres, such as Singapore and Hong Kong.

ORIENTATION

Occupying the east side of Mae Nam Chao Phraya, Bangkok proper can be divided in two by the main north–south railway terminating at Hualamphong train station.

The portion between the serpentine river and the railway is old Bangkok, a district of holy temples, crowded markets and family-owned shophouses. Swarming either side of the train station is the dense neighbourhood of Chinatown, a frenzy of red, gold and neon. Chinatown's chaos is subdued by Ko Ratanakosin, the former royal-palace district and Bangkok's most popular tourist district. Charming Banglamphu and the backpacker strip of Th Khao San (Khao San Rd) are north up the river. Crowning the old city is Dusit, a planned homage to the great European capitals, and the easy-going neighbourhood of Thewet.

East of the railway is new Bangkok – a near approximation of a sci-fi megalopolis. Around Siam Square is a universe of boxy shopping centres that attracts fashion-savvy Thai teenagers and shopping holiday tourists. Th Sukhumvit runs a deliberate course from the geographic city centre to the Gulf of Thailand, and has limblike tributaries reaching into corporate-expat cocoons and the girl-bar scene at Soi Cowboy and Nana Entertainment Plaza. Bangkok's financial district centres along Th Silom, which cuts an incision from the river to Lumphini Park. Intersecting Th Silom near the river is Th Charoen Krung; Bangkok's first paved road that was once the artery for the city's mercantile shipping interests. Its narrow *sois* (lanes) branch off through the old *faràng* (Western) quarters that are littered with decaying Victorian monuments, churches and the famous Oriental Hotel. True to the city's resistance to efficiency, there are two main

embassy districts: Th Withayu (Wireless Rd) and Th Sathon.

On the opposite (west) side of the river is Thonburi, which was Thailand's capital for 15 years, before Bangkok was founded. *Fàng thon* (Thonburi Bank), as it's often called by Thais, seems more akin to the provincial capitals than Bangkok's glittering high-rises.

Bangkok Addresses

Any city as large and unplanned as Bangkok can be tough to get around. Street names are often unpronounceable to begin with, and the problem is compounded by the inconsistency of Romanised spellings as well as a mystifying array of winding streets that never lead where a map dares to propose.

Building numbers are equally confounding; the string of numbers divided by slashes and dashes (eg 48/3-5 Soi 1, Th Sukhumvit) indicate lot disbursements rather than sequential geography. The number before the slash refers to the original lot number; the numbers following the slash indicate buildings (or entrances to buildings) constructed within that lot. The preslash numbers appear in the order in which they were added to city plans, while the postslash numbers are arbitrarily assigned by developers.

STREET ALIASES

As there is no standardisation for transliterating Thai into the Roman alphabet, Bangkok's streets operate under many aliases. Here are some common variants:

- Rajadamri and Ratchadamri are often abbreviated as Rat'damri

- Phetburi, Phetchaburi, and the eastern extension become Phetburi Tat Mai (often appearing as its English translation: New Phetburi)

- Phra Ram (I-VI) is sometimes Rama (I-VI)

The Thai word *thànŏn* (Th) means road, street or avenue. Hence Ratchadamnoen Rd (sometimes called Ratchadamnoen Ave) is always Th Ratchadamnoen in Thai.

A *soi* is a small street or lane that runs off a larger street. So, the address referred to as 48/3-5 Soi 1, Th Sukhumvit, will be located off Th Sukhumvit on Soi 1. Alternative ways of writing the same address include 48/3-5 Th Sukhumvit Soi 1 or even just 48/3-5 Sukhumvit 1. Some Bangkok *sois* have become so large that they can be referred to both as *thànŏn* and *soi*, eg Soi Sarasin/Th Sarasin and Soi

---

BANGKOK IN...

Tackling Bangkok is simple if you avoid rush hour and dehydration. Try mixing and matching these suggestions for a short fling or a long affair.

One Day

Make an early-morning visit to **Wat Phra Kaew** and the **Grand Palace** (p108), quirky **Wat Pho** (p108) and the crowded **Amulet Market** (p109). Charter a long-tail boat to ride through Thonburi's **canals** (p147) to **Wat Arun** (p110).

For dinner, head to **Ton Pho** (p159) or **Harmonique** (p163). Then go-go to the red-light district in **Patpong** (p171).

Three Days

Do as the Thais do – go **shopping** (p174). Zip to and fro aboard the ultramodern **Skytrain** (p184). Glimpse old-style Bangkok with a trip to **Jim Thompson's House** (p135) and wrap up the daylight hours with a traditional **Thai massage** (p139). Then work off those rice calories at the dance clubs of **RCA** (p170).

One Week

Now that you're accustomed to the noise, pollution and traffic, you're ready for **Chinatown** (p134) and its congested markets. On the weekend, take the Skytrain to **Chatuchak Weekend Market** (p178) for intensive souvenir hunting. For a little R&R, take a river ferry to **Ko Kret** (p138), a car-less island north of central Bangkok.

Asoke/Th Asoke. Smaller than a *soi* is a *trok*, sometimes spelt *tràwk* (alleyway).

Maps

A map is essential for finding your way around Bangkok. The long-running and oft-imitated *Nancy Chandler's Map of Bangkok* is a schematic guide to the city, with listings of out-of-the-way places, beloved restaurants, and colourful anecdotes about neighbourhoods and markets. It is an entertaining visual guide but should be complimented by a more hard-nosed navigator, such as Think Net's *Bangkok* bilingual map with accompanying mapping software. To master the city's bus system, purchase Roadway's *Bangkok Bus Map*. For visitors who consider eating to be sightseeing, check out Ideal Map's *Good Eats* series, which has mapped mom-and-pop restaurants in three of Bangkok's noshing neighbourhoods. For nightcrawlers, Groovy Map's *Bangkok Map 'n' Guide* series makes a good drinking companion.

If travelling to districts outside central Bangkok, invest in *Bangkok & Vicinity A to Z Atlas*, which covers the expressways and surrounding suburbs.

INFORMATION

Bookshops

Dasa Book Café (Map pp122-3; ☎ 0 2661 2993; 710/4 Th Sukhumvit, btwn Soi 26 & 28; Skytrain Phrom Phong) Multilingual used bookstore.

Kinokuniya Siam Paragon (Map pp128-9; ☎ 0 2610 9500; 3rd fl, Th Phra Ram I; Skytrain Siam) Emporium (Map pp122-3; ☎ 0 2664 8554; 3rd fl, Th Sukhumvit; Skytrain Phrom Phong) Multilanguage selections, magazines, children's books.

Mahamakuta Buddhist Bookshop (Map pp120-1; ☎ 0 2281 1085; 241 Th Phra Sumen; ⏰ 8.30am-5pm Mon-Fri, 9am-3pm Sat & Sun; air-con bus 511) Has a handful of Buddhist titles in English.

Rim Khob Fah Bookstore (Map pp120-1; ☎ 0 2622 3510; 78/1 Th Ratchadamnoen, Democracy Monument; bus 511, 512, khlong taxi to Tha Phan Fah) Small selection of booklets on culture and history.

Suksit Siam (☎ 0 2222 5698; 113-115 Th Fuang Nakhon; ⏰ 9am-6pm Mon-Fri, 9am-5pm Sat; bus 507, 508) Political works by social critic Sulak Sivaraksa and the progressive Santi Pracha Dhamma Institute. Located south of Mae Thorani Shrine

Cultural Centres

Various international culture centres in Bangkok organise film festivals, lectures, language classes and other educational liaisons.

Alliance Française (Map p127; ☎ 0 2670 4200; www .alliance-francaise.or.th; 29 Th Sathon Tai; bus 17, 22, 62)

British Council (Map pp128-9; ☎ 0 2652 5480; www .britishcouncil.or.th; Siam Square, Th Phra Ram I, 254 Soi Chulalongkorn 64; Skytrain Siam)

Foreign Correspondents Club of Thailand (FCCT; Map pp128-9; ☎ 0 2652 0580; www.fccthai.com; Penthouse, Maneeya Center, 518/5 Th Ploenchit; Skytrain Chitlom)

Goethe Institut (Map p127; ☎ 0 2287 0942; www .goethe.de; 18/1 Soi Goethe, btwn Th Sathon Tai & Soi Ngam Duphli; subway Lumphini)

Japan Foundation (Map pp122-3; ☎ 0 2260 8560; Serm-mit Tower, Th Sukhumvit, 159 Soi Asoke; bus 136, 206)

Emergency

If you have a medical emergency and need an ambulance, contact the English-speaking hospitals listed on opposite. In case of a police

---

CITY OF ANGELS

Krungthep mahanakhon amonratanakosin mahintara ayuthaya mahadilok popnopparat ratchathani burirom udomratchaniwet mahasathan amonpiman avatansathit sakkathattiya witsanukamprasit.

A real tongue twister, Bangkok's official name was conveniently truncated to Krung Thep (City of Angels) for everyday usage. The breathtaking 43 syllables were transformed into a hypnotic pop tune by Asanee-Wasan in 1989 and its recitation by memory is always a winning bar game. The bombastic title translates roughly as 'Great City of Angels, Repository of Divine Gems, Great Land Unconquerable, Grand and Prominent Realm, Royal and Delightful Capital City Full of Nine Noble Gems, Highest Royal Dwelling and Grand Palace, Divine Shelter and Living Place of Reincarnated Spirits'.

But why does the rest of the world call it 'Bangkok'? Turns out the royal capital was founded on a little village named Bang Makok (Place of Olive Plums) and stubborn foreign traders never bothered to adjust the appellation.

or safety issue, contact the city hotlines for the following emergency services:

Fire ☎ 199
Police/Emergency ☎ 191
Tourist police (☎ 1155; ⊙ 24hr) An English-speaking unit that investigates criminal activity involving tourists, including gem scams. It can also act as a bilingual liaison with the regular police.

Internet Access

There is no shortage of internet cafés in Bangkok competing against each other to offer the cheapest and fastest connection. Rates vary depending on the concentration and affluence of net-heads – Banglamphu is infinitely cheaper than Sukhumvit or Silom, with rates as low as 30B per hour. Many internet shops are adding Skype and headsets to their machines so that an international call can be made for the price of surfing the web.

Internet Resources

2Bangkok (www.2bangkok.com) News sleuth and history buff follows the city headlines from today and yesterday.
Asia-Hotels (www.asia-hotels.com) Handy rundown on hotels, their amenities and comments from former guests.
Bangkok Recorder (www.bangkokrecorder.com) Nightlife site following hot club nights, visiting DJs, music trends and other vexing capital questions.
Khao San Road (www.khaosanroad.com) News, reviews and profiles of Bangkok's famous tourist ghetto.
Mango Sauce (www.mangosauce.com) Bangkok's news of the weird for sexpats who need a breather.
Real Thai (www.realthai.blogspot.com) Local Bangkok foodie takes a bite out of the Big Mango.

Libraries

Besides offering an abundance of reading material, Bangkok's libraries make a peaceful escape from the heat and noise.

British Club's Neilson Hays Library & Rotunda Gallery (Map pp124-5; ☎ 0 2233 1731; 195 Th Surawong; family membership 2800B; ⊙ 9.30am-5pm Tue-Sun; Skytrain Chong Nonsi) The oldest English-language library in Thailand, with many children's books and titles on Thailand.
National Library (Map pp116-17; ☎ 0 2281 5212; Th Samsen; admission free; ⊙ 9am-7.30pm; river ferry Tha Thewet) A few foreign-language resources, but the library's strength is in its astrological books and star charts, as well as recordings by the king and sacred palm-leaf writings and ancient maps.
Siam Society (Map pp122-3; ☎ 0 2661 6470; Th Sukhumvit, 131 Soi Asoke; ⊙ 9am-5.30pm Mon-Sat; Skytrain Asoke, subway Sukhumvit) Royal patronage society with a public-access library on academic subjects.

Media

Daily newspapers are sold in 7-Eleven stores as well as streetside newsagents. Monthly magazines are available in most bookstores.

Bangkok 101 A monthly city primer with photo essays and reviews of sights, restaurants and entertainment.
Bangkok Post No-nonsense English-language daily with Friday and weekend supplements covering city events.
BK Magazine Free monthly for the young and hip.
Gavroche French-language magazine with news and views.
Metro: Magazine Glossy monthly targeted at the city's bilinguals.
Nation English-language daily with more style and flair than the *Bangkok Post*.
Untamed Travel Going where the guidebooks don't go anymore, the old *Faràng* magazine finally bought a bus ticket from Th Khao San to other exotic destinations, including bars in other Bangkok neighbourhoods.

Medical Services

Thanks to its high standard of hospital care, Bangkok is fast becoming a destination for medical tourists shopping for more affordable dental checkups, elective surgery and cosmetic procedures. Pharmacists (chemists) throughout the city can diagnose and treat most minor ailments (Bangkok belly, sinus and skin infections etc). The following hospitals offer 24-hour emergency services, and the numbers below should be contacted if you need an ambulance or immediate medical attention. Most hospitals also have daily clinics with English-speaking staff.

Bangkok Adventist (Mission) Hospital (Map pp116-17; ☎ 0 2282 1100; 430 Th Phitsanulok; bus 16, 23, 99)
BNH (Map pp124-5; ☎ 0 2632 0550; 9 Th Convent, off Th Silom; Skytrain Sala Daeng)
Bumrungrad Hospital (Map pp122-3; ☎ 0 2667 1000; Th Sukhumvit, 33 Soi 3; Skytrain Ploenchit & Nana)
Phayathai Hospital 1 (Map pp116-17; ☎ 0 2245 2620; 364/1 Th Si Ayuthaya; bus 503)

GUIDEBOOKS

Lonely Planet's *Bangkok* is ideal for those spending a month or more in the capital city. Weekenders should consider picking up a copy of Lonely Planet's *Bangkok Encounter*.

Samitivej Hospital (Map pp122-3; ☎ 0 2392 0011; Th Sukhumvit, 133 Soi 49)

St Louis Hospital (Map pp124-5; ☎ 0 2675 9300; 215 Th Sathon Tai; Skytrain Surasak)

Rutnin Eye Hospital (Map pp122-3; ☎ 0 2258 0442; 80/1 Soi 21/Asoke) Contact this hospital for urgent eye care.

Money

Regular bank hours in Bangkok are 10am to 4pm, and ATMs are common in all areas of the city. Many Thai banks also have currency-exchange bureaus; there are also exchange desks within the Skytrain stations and within eyeshot of most tourist areas. Go to 7-Eleven shops or other reputable places to break 1000B bills; don't expect a vendor or taxi to able to make change on a bill 500B or larger.

Post

Main post office (Map pp124-5; Th Charoen Krung; ☯ 8am-8pm Mon-Fri, 8am-1pm Sat & Sun; Chao Phraya Express Tha Si Phraya) Services include poste restante and packaging within the main building. Do not send money or valuables via regular mail. Branch post offices throughout the city also offer poste restante and parcel services.

Telephone & Fax

Bangkok's city code (☎ 02) is incorporated into all telephone numbers dialled locally or from outside the city. Public phones for both domestic and international calls are well distributed throughout the city, but it is tricky to find one that is quiet enough to have a conversation. Try the shopping centres for noiseless comfort.

Communications Authority of Thailand (CAT; Map pp124-5; ☎ 0 2573 0099; Th Charoen Krung; ☯ 24hr; river ferry Tha Si Phraya) Next door to the main post office; offers Home Country Direct service, fax transmittal and phone-card services.

Telephone Organization of Thailand (TOT; Map pp128-9; ☎ 0 2251 1111; Th Ploenchit; Skytrain Chitlom) Long-distance calling services and an English version of Bangkok's *Yellow Pages*.

Tourist Information

Official tourist offices distribute maps, brochures and advice on sights and activities. Don't confuse these free services with the licensed travel agents that book tours and transport on a commission basis. Often, travel agencies incorporate elements of the official national tourism organisation name (Tourism Authority of Thailand; TAT) into their own to purposefully confuse tourists.

Bangkok Tourism Division (Map pp120-1; ☎ 0 2225 7612-5; www.bangkoktourist.com; 17/1 Th Phra Athit; ☯ 9am-7pm; river ferry Tha Phra Athit) City-specific tourism office provides maps, brochures and directions; yellow information booths staffed by student volunteers are located throughout the city.

TAT main office (Map pp116-17; ☎ 0 2250 5500/1672; www.tourismthailand.org; ground fl, 1600 Th Petchaburi Tat Mai; ☯ 8.30am-4.30pm; Skytrain Asoke) City and country travel information.

Tourist police (Map pp116-17; ☎ 1155; Bangkok Tower, Th Petchaburi Tat Mai; ☯ 24hr) Handles matters involving theft and crimes against tourists.

Travel Agencies

Bangkok is packed with travel agencies where you can book bus and air tickets. Some are reliable, while others are fly-by-night scams issuing bogus tickets or promises of (undelivered) services. Ask for recommendations from fellow travellers before making a major purchase from a travel agent. The following are some long-running agencies:

Diethelm Travel (Map p127; ☎ 0 2255 9150; www .diethelm-travel.com; 140/1 Th Withayu, Kian Gwan Bldg; bus 13, 17, 62)

STA Travel (Map pp124-5; ☎ 0 2236 0262; www.sta travel.com; 14th fl, Wall Street Tower, 33/70 Th Surawong; Skytrain Sala Daeng)

Vieng Travel (Map pp120-1; ☎ 0 2280 3537; www .viengtravel.com; Trang Hotel, 99/8 Th Wisut Kasat; bus 49)

DANGERS & ANNOYANCES

You are more likely to be charmed rather than coerced out of your money in Bangkok. Practised con artists capitalise on Thailand's famous friendliness and a revolving door of clueless tourists. The tourist police can be effective in dealing with some of the 'unethical' business practices and crime. But in general you should enter into every monetary transaction with the understanding that you have no consumer protection or recourse.

Bangkok's most heavily touristed areas – Wat Phra Kaew, Jim Thompson's House, Th Khao San, Siam Square – are favourite hunting grounds. The most typical scenario involves a well-dressed, professional-acting person who appears to come to your aid when an attraction is 'closed'. They will then graciously arrange an affordable túk-túk ride to an undiscovered wat or authentic market,

which is usually a guise for taking you and your wallet for the proverbial 'ride'. Don't believe anyone on the street who tells you that a popular attraction is closed; check for yourself. And don't engage in any sort of purchase – gems, tailors or jewellery – to which you've been referred by a helpful stranger.

More obvious are the túk-túk drivers who are out to make a commission by dragging you to a local silkstore, tailor or jewellery shop, even though you've requested an entirely different destination. Even if you're in the market for a tailor, avoid the hidden commissions by patronising businesses who don't engage in this practice.

Then there is the long-running and quite infamous gem scam, in which you act as an agent for selling bulk quantities of gems in your home country. It is only after you cough up the quoted wholesale price of the gems that you will discover your unexpected windfall comprises a collection of worthless pieces of glass.

The card-game scam has resurfaced after a brief hiatus. Perhaps it is the recent rise of online gambling and celebrity poker that has made average card players consider themselves in the league of sharks. After you've been invited to a Thai person's home, the card game usually starts off as an innocent way to pass the time and then money is added for the fun of it, and the rest is well documented in the classic movie *The Hustler*.

Uncharacteristically aggressive robberies have been perpetrated by groups of *kàthoey* (lady boys), typically around the lower Sukhumvit bar area. Lone, and generally drunk, foreign men have reportedly been approached by a solo *kàthoey* ('Hello, where you go, handsome?') who then creates a diversion while a partner swipes the victim's wallet.

Even though Thai children are taught to toss their garbage out of windows, foreigners should avoid following suit. This includes cigarette butts, too. An underpaid police officer will be more than happy to enforce the law (however broadly interpreted) on a foreigner who might possibly have the 1000B fine that an average Thai might not be able to afford.

See p741 for more information on countrywide scams.

SIGHTS
Ko Ratanakosin & Thonburi
เกาะรัตนโกสินทร์/ธนบุรี

Ko Ratanakosin is the ancient royal district, housing Bangkok's most famous attractions. These sights are within walking distance of each other and are best visited early in the morning before the day comes to a boil. Ignore anyone who approaches you in this area as most are touts commissioned to steer tourists to gem or tailor shops. Even guards or other official-looking people may be acting as agents for commission-paying businesses.

Directly across the river is Thonburi, which served a brief tenure as the Thai capital after

---

PRELUDES TO A RIP-OFF

Want to know the key to a great Thailand visit? Commit these warnings to memory and join us in our ongoing crusade to outsmart Bangkok's crafty scam artists.

■ Remember your mother's advice: don't talk to strangers. In this self-absorbed city, the only people interested in chatting you up are usually interested in your wallet, not cultural exchange. You should be doubly suspicious if they are professionally dressed but aren't busy at a real job somewhere.

■ If you ignore your mother's advice and talk to said stranger, your suspicion-meter should register if the stranger says (a) that wherever you're going is closed, (b) that he or she knows someone who is studying/working in your home country, or (c) there is a great one-day sale on jewellery, gems or silk. For a good laugh, you can always ask to see their TAT licence, which isn't a sign of legitimacy but does make their blood pressure visibly rise.

■ A túk-túk driver offers a sightseeing tour for 10B to 20B. Do the maths: petrol and time will get paid by you thanks to a commission from whatever tailor or furniture store the driver 'happens' to know about.

■ A metered taxi quotes a flat price for your fare. Any quoted price is usually three times higher than using the meter. Most in-town destinations are around 50B to 80B.

DRESS FOR THE OCCASION

Temples are sacred places and visitors should dress and behave appropriately. Wear shirts with sleeves, long pants or skirts and close-toed shoes (for some reason Thais are exempt from this latter rule). Sarongs and baggy pants are available on loan at the entry area for Wat Phra Kaew. Shoes should be removed before entering the main *bòt* (chapel) or *wíhaan* (sanctuaries). When sitting in front of a Buddha image, tuck your feet behind you to avoid the highly offensive pose of pointing your feet towards a revered figure.

Remember to leave a donation when you visit temples; your contributions help with upkeep.

---

the fall of Ayuthaya. Today the area along the river is easily accessed from Bangkok's cross-river ferries, and there are museums and temples here that are historical complements to those in Ko Ratanakosin.

WAT PHRA KAEW & GRAND PALACE
วัดพระแก้ว/พระบรมมหาราชวัง

Also known as the Temple of the Emerald Buddha, **Wat Phra Kaew** (Map p130; ☎ 0 2224 1833; admission 250B; ◷ 8.30am-3.30pm; bus 508, 512, river ferry Tha Chang) is an architectural wonder and home to the venerable Emerald Buddha. Adjoining the temple is the former residence of the monarch, the Grand Palace.

This ground was consecrated in 1782, the first year of Bangkok rule, and is today a pilgrimage destination for devout Buddhists and nationalists. The 94.5-hectare grounds encompass more than 100 buildings that represent 200 years of royal history and architectural experimentation. Most of the architecture, royal or sacred, can be classified as Ratanakosin (or old-Bangkok style).

Housed in a fantastically decorated *bòt* and guarded by pairs of *yaksha* (mythical giants), the **Emerald Buddha** is the temple's primary attraction. It sits atop an elevated altar, barely visible amid the gilded decorations. The diminutive figure is always cloaked in royal robes, one for each season (hot, cool and rainy). In a solemn ceremony, the king himself changes the garments at the beginning of each season.

Extensive **murals of the Ramakian** (the Thai version of the Indian epic *Ramayana*) line the in-

side walls of the compound. Originally painted during the reign of Rama I (1782–1809) and continually restored, the murals illustrate the epic in its entirety, beginning at the north gate and moving clockwise around the compound.

Except for an anteroom here and there, the buildings of the **Grand Palace** (Phra Borom Maharatchawong) are now put to use by the king only for certain ceremonial occasions, such as Coronation Day (the king's current residence is Chitlada Palace in the northern part of the city). The exteriors of the four buildings are worth a swift perusal for their royal bombast. The intrigue and rituals that occurred within the walls of this once-cloistered community are relatively silent to the modern visitor. A fictionalised version is told in the trilogy *Four Reigns*, by Kukrit Pramoj.

Borombhiman Hall (eastern end), a French-inspired structure that served as a residence for Rama VI, is occasionally used to house visiting foreign dignitaries. In April 1981 General San Chitpatima used it as headquarters for an attempted coup. The building to the west is **Amarindra Hall**, originally a hall of justice but used today for coronation ceremonies.

The largest of the palace buildings is the **Chakri Mahaprasat**, the Grand Palace Hall. Built in 1882 by British architects using Thai labour, the exterior shows a peculiar blend of Italian Renaissance and traditional Thai architecture. This is a style often referred to as *faràng sài chádaa* (Westerner in a Thai crown) because each wing is topped by a *mondòp* – a heavily ornamented spire representing a Thai adaptation of the Hindu *mandapa* (shrine). The tallest of the *mondòp*, in the centre, contains the ashes of Chakri kings; the flanking *mondòp* enshrine the ashes of Chakri princes. Thai kings traditionally housed their huge harems in the inner palace area, which was guarded by combat-trained female sentries.

Last, from east to west, is the Ratanakosin-style **Dusit Hall**, which initially served as a venue for royal audiences and later as a royal funerary hall.

The admission charge for the complex includes entrance to **Dusit Park** (p132), which includes Vimanmek Teak Mansion and Abhisek Dusit Throne Hall.

WAT PHO
วัดโพธิ์(วัดพระเชตุพน)

The modest hero of Bangkok's holy temples, **Wat Pho** (Map p130; Wat Phra Chetuphon; ☎ 0 2221 9911;

Th Sanamchai; admission 50B; ✆ 8am-5pm; bus 508, 512, Chao Phraya Express Tha Tien) features a host of superlatives: the largest reclining Buddha, the largest collection of Buddha images in Thailand and the country's earliest centre for public education.

Almost too big for its shelter, the tremendous **reclining Buddha**, 46m long and 15m high, illustrates the passing of the Buddha into nirvana (ie the Buddha's death). The figure is modelled out of plaster around a brick core and finished in gold leaf. Mother-of-pearl inlay ornaments the feet, displaying 108 different auspicious *láksànà* (characteristics of a Buddha).

The **Buddha images** on display in the other four *wíhǎan* are worth a nod. Particularly beautiful are the Phra Chinnarat and Phra Chinnachai Buddhas, both from Sukhothai, in the west and south chapels. The galleries extending between the four chapels feature no less than 394 gilded Buddha images, many of which display Ayuthaya or Sukhothai features. The remains of Rama I are interred in the base of the presiding Buddha image in the *bòt*.

A small collection of tiled stupas commemorates the first three of the Chakri kings (Rama III has two stupas) and there are 91 smaller stupas. Note the square bell shape with distinct corners, a signature of Ratanakosin style.

Wat Pho is also the national headquarters for the teaching and preservation of traditional Thai medicine, including Thai massage, a mandate legislated by Rama III when the tradition was in danger of extinction. The famous massage school has two massage pavilions without air-con located within the temple area and air-con rooms within the training facility outside the temple (p139). Nearby stone inscriptions showing yoga and massage techniques still remain in the temple grounds, serving their original purpose as visual aids.

The rambling grounds of Wat Pho cover eight hectares, with the major tourist sites occupying the northern side of Th Chetuphon and the monastic facilities on the southern side.

WAT MAHATHAT
วัดมหาธาตุ

Sightseeing is not the reason to wander through the whitewashed gates of **Wat Mahathat** (Map p130; ✆ 0 2221 5999; 3 Th Maharat; ✆ 9am-5pm; bus 47, 53, 503, 508, 512, river ferry Tha Phra Chan or Tha Maharat). But prospective students of Buddhist meditation will find a warm reception from the English-speaking director of the temple's **International Buddhist Meditation Centre** (which is located in Section 5), where classes in sitting and walking meditation are held three times daily.

Founded in the 1700s, Wat Mahathat is the national centre for the Mahanikai monastic sect and headquarters for the renowned Maha Chulalongkorn Rajavidyalaya, one of Bangkok's two Buddhist universities. Religious scholarship is extended to visiting foreigners with twice-monthly lectures in English on different aspects of *dhamma* (Buddhist philosophy). Stop by Section 5 for lecture topics and room assignment.

AMULET MARKET
ตลาดพระเครื่องวัดมหาธาตุ

Just outside the theological solitude of Wat Mahathat is a more vibrant application of

---

TRAVELS OF THE EMERALD BUDDHA

The Emerald Buddha (Phra Kaew Morakot) holds a prominent position in Thai Buddhism in spite of its size (a mere 75cm) and original material (probably jasper quartz or nephrite jade rather than emerald). In fact, the Emerald Buddha was just another ordinary image, with no illustrious pedigree, until its monumental 'coming out' in 15th-century Chiang Rai. During a fall, the image revealed its luminescent interior, which had been covered with plaster (a common practice to safeguard valuable Buddhas from being stolen). After a few successful stints in various temples throughout northern Thailand, the image was stolen by Laotian invaders in the mid-16th century.

The Emerald Buddha achieved another promotion in the cult of Buddha images some 200 years later when Thailand's King Taksin waged war against Laos, retrieving the image and mounting it in Thonburi. Later, when the capital moved to Bangkok and General Chakri took the crown, the Emerald Buddha was honoured with one of the country's most magnificent monuments, Wat Phra Kaew.

Thailand's diverse spirituality. A **tàlàat phrá khrêuang** (holy amulet market; Map p130; Th Maharat; ☉ 9am-5pm) claims sidewalk space and rabbit-warren *sois* near Tha Phra Chan, displaying a wide variety of small talismans carefully scrutinised by collectors. Monks, taxi drivers and people in dangerous professions are the most common customers well versed in the different powers of the images. Also along this strip are handsome shophouses overflowing with family-run herbal-medicine and traditional-massage shops. In the cool season, vendors sell aromatic herbal soups that ward off colds and sinus infections.

WAT ARUN
วัดอรุณฯ

Striking **Wat Arun** (Map p130; ☎ 0 2891 1149; Th Arun Amarin, Thonburi; admission 20B; ☉ 9am-5pm; cross-river ferry from Tha Tien) commands a martial pose as the third point in the holy triumvirate (along with Wat Phra Kaew and Wat Pho) of Bangkok's early history. After the fall of Ayuthaya, King Taksin ceremoniously clinched control here on the site of a local shrine (formerly known as Wat Jaeng) and established a royal palace and a temple to house the Emerald Buddha. The temple was renamed after the Indian god of dawn (Aruna) and in honour of the literal and symbolic founding of a new Ayuthaya.

It wasn't until the capital and the Emerald Buddha were moved to Bangkok that Wat Arun received its most prominent characteristic: the 82m-high *prang* (Khmer-style tower). The tower's construction was started during the first half of the 19th century by Rama II and later completed by Rama III. Rebuilding was necessary because the porous mud initially used was an inferior base. Not apparent from a distance are the ornate floral mosaics made from broken, multihued Chinese porcelain, a common temple ornamentation in the early Ratanakosin period, when Chinese ships calling at the port of Bangkok used tonnes of old porcelain as ballast.

Also worth an inspection is the interior of the *bòt*. The main Buddha image is said to have been designed by Rama II himself. The murals date from the reign of Rama V; particularly impressive is one that depicts Prince Siddhartha encountering examples of birth, old age, sickness and death outside his palace walls, an experience that led him to abandon the worldly life. The ashes of Rama II are interred in the base of the presiding Buddha image.

LAK MEUANG (CITY PILLAR)
ศาลหลักเมือง

Serving as the spiritual keystone of Bangkok, **Lak Meuang** (Map p130; cnr Th Ratchadamnoen Nai & Th Lak Meuang; admission free; ☉ 8.30am-5.30pm; bus 506, 507, river ferry Tha Chang) is a phallus-shaped wooden pillar erected by Rama I during the founding of the new capital city in 1782. Today the structure shimmers with gold leaf and is housed in a white cruciform sanctuary. Part of an animistic tradition, the pillar embodies the city's guardian spirit (Phra Sayam Thewathirat) and also lends a practical purpose as a marker of the town's crossroads and measuring point for distances between towns.

The pillar was once of a pair. Its taller counterpart, which was carved from *chaiyá-préuk* (tree of victory; laburnum wood), was cut down in effigy following the Burmese sacking of Ayuthaya during 1767. Through a series of Buddhist-animist rituals, it is believed that the felling of the tree empowered the Thais to defeat the Burmese in battle. Thus it was considered an especially talismanic choice to mark the founding of the new royal capital. Two metres of the pillar's 4.7m total length are buried in the ground.

If you happen to wander through and hear the whine of traditional instruments, investigate the source as a *lákhon kâe bon* (commissioned dance) may be in progress. Brilliantly costumed dancers measure out subtle movements as thanks to the guardian spirit for granting a worshipper's wish.

SANAM LUANG
สนามหลวง

The royal district's green area is **Sanam Luang** (Map p130; Royal Field; bordered by Th Na Phra That, Th Na Phra Lan, Th Ratchadamnoen Nai, Th Somdet Phra Pin Klao; admission free; ☉ 6am-8pm; bus 30, 32, 47, 53, river ferry Tha Chang), which introduces itself to most visitors as a dusty impediment to Wat Phra Kaew and other attractions. The park's more appealing attributes are expressed during its duties as a site for royal cremations and for the annual Ploughing Ceremony, in which the king officially initiates the rice-growing season. The most recent ceremonial cremation took place here in March 1996, when the king presided over funeral rites for his mother. Before that, the most recent Sanam Luang cremations

were held in 1976, without official sanction, for Thai students killed in the demonstrations of that year. A large kite competition is also held here during the kite-flying season (mid-February to April).

A statue of **Mae Thorani**, the earth goddess (borrowed from Hindu mythology's Dharani), stands in a white pavilion at the northern end of the field. Erected in the late 19th century by Rama V (King Chulalongkorn), the statue was originally attached to a well that provided drinking water to the public.

NATIONAL MUSEUM
พิพิธภัณฑสถานแห่งชาติ

Often touted as Southeast Asia's biggest museum, the **National Museum** (Map p130; ☎ 0 2224 1402; 1 Th Na Phra That; admission 40B; ⊗ 9am-3.30pm Wed-Sun; bus 503, 506, 507, 53, river ferry Tha Mahathat) is home to an impressive collection of religious sculpture – from Dvaravati to Ratanakosin periods – best appreciated on one the museums weekly **tours** (⊗ 9.30am Wed; in English, German & French).

In addition to the cluttered art and artefacts building, the restored **Buddhaisawan (Phutthaisawan) Chapel** provides a welcome relief from the curatorial hotchpotch. Inside the chapel (built in 1795) are some well-preserved original murals and one of the country's most revered Buddha images, Phra Phut Sihing. Legend says the image came from Sri Lanka, but art historians attribute it to 13th-century Sukhothai.

The recently renovated **history wing** has made impressive bounds towards mainstream curatorial aesthetics with a succinct chronology of prehistoric, Sukhothai-, Ayuthaya- and Bangkok-era events and figures. Despite the hokey dioramas, there are some real treasures here: look for King Ramakamhaeng's inscribed stone pillar, the oldest record of Thai writing; King Taksin's throne; the Rama V section; and the screening of King Prajadhipok's movie *The Magic Ring*.

Perhaps part of the charm, though, is wandering through a veritable attic of Thai art and handicrafts. For the free-form culturalist, peruse the scatterbrained collections in the **central exhibit hall**, which cover every possible handicraft: traditional musical instruments, ceramics, clothing and textiles, woodcarving, regalia and weaponry.

Most of the museum buildings were built in 1782 as the palace of Rama I's viceroy, Prince Wang Na. Rama V turned it into a museum in 1884. The ticketing office provides free maps of the grounds.

ROYAL BARGES NATIONAL MUSEUM
เรือพระที่นั่ง

The royal barges are slender, fantastically ornamented vessels used in ceremonial processions along the river. The tradition dates back to the Ayuthaya era, when most travel (for commoners and royalty) was by boat. Today the royal barge procession is an infrequent occurrence, most recently performed in 2006 in honour of the 60th anniversary of the king's ascension to the throne.

When not in use, the barges are on display at this Thonburi **museum** (Map p130; ☎ 0 2424 0004; Khlong Bangkok Noi, Thonburi; admission 30B, photo permit 100B; ⊗ 9am-5pm; tourist shuttle boat from Tha Phra Athit). At the time of writing, the museum was temporarily closed for restoration work on the elderly boats. Check with the Chao Phraya Express desk at Tha Phra Athit for the current situation.

Suphannahong, the king's personal barge, is the most important of the boats. Made from a single piece of timber, it's the largest dugout in the world. The name means 'Golden Swan', and a huge swan head has been carved into the bow. Lesser barges feature bows that are carved into other Hindu-Buddhist mythological shapes such as *naga* (mythical sea serpent) and *garuda* (Vishnu's bird mount). Historic photos help envision the grand processions in which the largest of the barges would require a rowing crew of 50 men, plus seven umbrella bearers, two helmsmen and two navigators, as well as a flagman, rhythm-keeper and chanter.

The easiest way to get to the museum is by the tourist boat from Tha Phra Athit (20B). You can also walk from the Bangkok Noi train station (accessible by ferrying to Tha Rot Fai), but the walk is unpleasant and you'll encounter uninvited guides who will charge for their service. The museum is also a stop on long-tail boat trips through Thonburi's canals.

NATIONAL GALLERY
หอศิลปแห่งชาติ

The humble **National Gallery** (Map p130; ☎ 0 2282 2639; Th Chao Fa; admission 30B; ⊗ 9am-4pm Wed-Sun; river ferry Tha Phra Athit) belies the country's impressive tradition of fine arts. Decorating the walls of this early Ratanakosin-era building are works

of traditional and contemporary art, mostly by artists who receive government support. The general consensus is that it's not Thailand's best – in fact, some of the art snobs criticise it as a 'dead zone' – but the gallery is worth a visit if you need an escape from the crowds.

SILPAKORN UNIVERSITY
มหาวิทยาลัยศิลปากร

Thailand's first **art university** (Map p130; ☎ 0 2221 1422; Th Na Phra Lan; ⏰ 8am-7pm Mon-Fri, 8am-4pm Sat & Sun; bus 12, 44, 503, 506, 508, river ferry Tha Chang), opposite the Grand Palace, originally trained civil servants in traditional painting techniques. It then led the nation's transition into European and contemporary art, thanks to the contributions of Professor Silpa Bhirasri (Corrado Feroci), an Italian artist who designed the Democracy Monument. A student and faculty art gallery is open to the public.

Banglamphu
บางลำพู

Banglamphu is Bangkok's most charming neighbourhood and offers easy access to the river and lots of unfettered wandering. It is also home to Th Khao San, a decompression zone for backpackers transiting in and out of the country. Khao San's long tourist-trap-

ping tentacles – internet cafés, Western-style restaurants, silver shops, beer stalls – sprawl throughout neighbouring streets but quickly disappear as you move away from the river. In the Thai parts of the area there is a work-day streetscape – safari-uniformed civil servants and lottery-ticket dealers with their wooden portfolio boxes. Bus is the primary public transport option for inland destinations. The *khlong* (canal) taxi along Khlong Saen Saeb is another convenient option for hopping over to Siam Square or Sukhumvit. The closest Skytrain station is Ratchathewi.

DEMOCRACY MONUMENT
อนุสาวรีย์ประชาธิปไตย

One of the first striking landmarks you'll notice on your way into Banglamphu is this large, Art Deco **monument** (Map pp120-1; Th Ratchadamnoen Klang, Th Din So; river ferry Tha Phra Athit, bus 44, 511, 512) occupying the avenue's traffic circle. It was erected in 1932 to commemorate Thailand's momentous transformation from absolute to constitutional monarchy. Italian artist Corrado Feroci designed the monument and buried 75 cannon balls in its base to signify the year Buddhist Era (BE) 2475 (AD 1932). Before immigrating to Thailand to become the nation's 'father of modern

---

SO REAL THAILAND

You've wandered up and down Th Khao San five times now and just can't believe how touristy Bangkok has become. The obvious answer is to get on a bus and go to another tourist ghetto and curse Lonely Planet for being lazy. Or you could realise that Khao San is for tourists and any Thais who once lived here have long since moved away because they couldn't come and go easily for all the half-naked 'ghosts' milling about. If you take a left off Th Khao San on to Th Tanao and then another left or right on Th Phra Sumen, BAM!, there's a Thai neighbourhood. No internet shops, no beer stalls, just some shops selling dusty mosquito coils and book satchels.

There are plenty of places like this all over the city, where nobody cares where you're going, what you want to eat or where you're from. Here are our favourite spots for blessed anonymity and Thai people-watching:

Victory Monument (Map pp116–17; Skytrain Victory Monument) Exit the Skytrain station to the elevated walkway that encircles a monument honouring a very minor Thai victory over the French. After sunset, the elevated walkway becomes a city park with students filling the empty spaces for flirting and chilling.

MBK (Map pp128–9; Skytrain National Stadium) On the weekends, this is where Bangkok hangs out. Bands and fashion shows perform in front of the shopping centre. On one visit, we saw a fully choreographed dance routine staged in front of idling cars during a long red traffic light. Sure you'll see some foreigners and big extended Arab families haggling over beaded sandals but you'll also see average Thai folk.

Nonthaburi (Chao Phraya Express Tha Nonthaburi) North of central Bangkok, this quiet suburb still has săamláw and a multiblock market of hairbrushes, batteries, polyester clothes and other general-store goods.

art', Feroci designed monuments for Italian dictator Benito Mussolini. In recent years the 'Demo' has become a symbolic spot for public demonstrations, most notably during the antimilitary, pro-democratic protests of 1992.

OCTOBER 14 MEMORIAL
อนุสาวรีย์14ตุลาคม

This peaceful **amphitheatre** (Map pp120–1; Khok Wua intersection, Th Ratchadamnoen Klang; bus 2, 82, 511, 512) commemorates the civilian demonstrators who were killed on 14 October 1973 (remembered in Thai as 'sip-see tula', the date of the event) by the military during a pro-democracy rally. More than 200,000 people assembled at the Democracy Monument and along Th Ratchadamnoen to protest the arrest of political campaigners and to express their discontent over the continued military dictatorship; more than 70 demonstrators were killed when the tanks met the crowd. The complex is an interesting adaptation of Thai temple architecture for a secular and political purpose. A central *chedi* (stupa) is dedicated to the fallen, and a gallery of historic photographs lines the interior walls.

WAT SAKET & GOLDEN MOUNT
วัดสระเกศ

Even if you're wat-ed out, you should take a brisk walk to **Wat Saket** (Map pp120–1; ☎ 0 2223 4561; btwn Th Wora Chak & Th Boriphat; admission to Golden Mount 10B; ⏰ 8am-5pm; bus 508, 511, khlong taxi to Tha Phan Fah). Like all worthy summits, the temple's Golden Mount (Phu Khao Thong), which is visible from Th Ratchadamnoen, plays a good game of optical illusion, appearing closer than its real location. Serpentine steps wind through an artificial hill shaded by gnarled trees, some of which are signed in English, and past graves and pictures of wealthy benefactors.

This artificial hill was created when a large stupa, under construction by Rama III, collapsed because the soft soil beneath would not support it. The resulting mud-and-brick hill was left to sprout weeds until Rama IV built a small stupa on its crest. Rama V later added to the structure and housed a Buddha relic from India (given to him by the British government) in the stupa. The concrete walls were added during WWII to prevent the hill from eroding. Every year in November there is a big festival on the grounds of Wat Saket,

which includes a candle-lit procession up the Golden Mount.

At the peak, you'll find a breezy 360-degree view of Bangkok's most photogenic side.

WAT RAJANADDA
วัดราชนัดดา

Across Th Maha Chai from Wat Saket, **Wat Rajanadda** (Ratchanatda; Map pp120–1; ☎ 0 2224 8807; cnr Th Ratchadamnoen Klang & Th Mahachai; ⏰ 9am-5pm; bus 56, 505, khlong taxi to Tha Phan Fah) dates from the mid-19th century. It was built under Rama III and is an unusual specimen, possibly influenced by Burmese models. The wat has a well-known market selling Buddhist *phrá phim* (magical charm amulets) in all sizes, shapes and styles. The amulets not only feature images of the Buddha, but also famous Thai monks and Indian deities. Full Buddha images are also for sale. Wat Rajanadda is an expensive place to purchase a charm, but a good place to look.

BAN BAHT (MONK'S BOWL VILLAGE)
บ้านบาตร

Just when you start to lament the adverse effects of tourism, pay a visit to this **handicraft village** (Map pp120–1; Soi Ban Baht, Th Bamrung Meuang; ⏰ 10am-6pm; bus 508, khlong taxi to Tha Pan Fah), within walking distance of Th Khao San. This is the only surviving village established by Rama I to make the *bàat* (rounded bowls) that the monks carry to receive food alms from faithful Buddhists every morning. Today the average monk relies on a bowl mass produced in China, but the traditional technique survives in Ban Baht thanks to patronage by tourists.

About half a dozen families still hammer the bowls together from eight separate pieces of steel representing, they say, the eight spokes of the Wheel of Dharma (which symbolise Buddhism's Eightfold Path). The joints are fused in a wood fire with bits of copper, and the bowl is polished and coated with several layers of black lacquer. A typical output is one bowl per day. If you purchase a bowl, the craftsperson will show you the equipment and process used. To find the village from Tha Pan Fah (khlong taxi pier), head south along Th Boriphat, past Th Bamrung Meuang, then turn left into Soi Ban Baht.

(Continued on page 132)

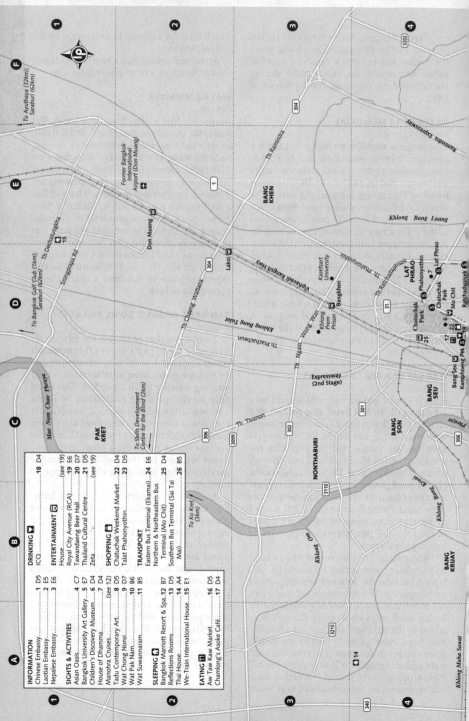

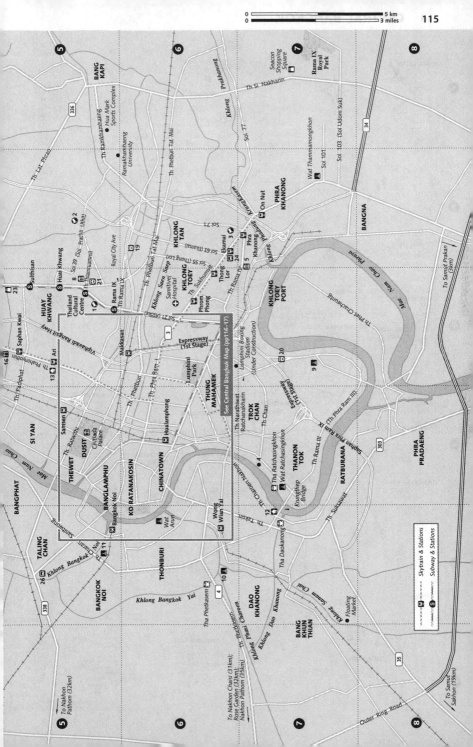

0 — 5 km
0 — 3 miles

Seacon Shopping Square

Rama IX Royal Park

BANG KAPI

Th Si Nakharin

Th Rankhamhaeng · Hua Mark Sports Complex

Ramkhamhaeng University

Th Phetburi Tat Mai

Prakhanong

Khlong

336

Th Lat Phrao

Sol 77

Th 101 (Sol Udom Suk)

Wat Thammamongkhon

34

2

Sol 39 (Sol Pracha-Uthit)

Royal City Ave

Th Phetburi Tat Mai

19

Sulthisan 23

Huai Khwang 8

Th Thiamruamit

Th Rama IX

KHLONG TAN

Sol 71

Ekamai 3

On Nut

PHRA KHANONG

BANGNA

Khlong

Mae Nam Chao Phraya

HUAY KHWANG

Sol 55 (Thong Lor)

Sol 63 (Ekamai)

Phra Khanong

5 24

Th Phetburi Tat Mai

Thailand Cultural Centre

Rama IX

1

Khlong Saen Saep

Samitivej Hospital

KHLONG TOEY

Phrom Phong

Sol 21 (Asok)

Sol 71

Thong Lor

KHLONG TOEY PORT

13

Ari

Main Nam Chao Phraya

Th Phra Ram III

Th Phet Chaoebung

Saphan Khwai

Th Phahonyothin

Th Padiphat

Th Samsen

Th Ratwithi

16

Expressway (1st Stage)

See Central Bangkok Map (pp116-17)

Makkasan

3

Th Phetburi

Th Phra Ram I

Th Rama IV

Lumphini Park

THUNG MAHAMEK

Th Naradhiwat Ratchanakharin

Lumphini Boxing Stadium (Under Construction)

20

Expressway (1st Stage)

9

SI YAN

THEWET

DUSIT

Chitlada Palace

Hualamphong

BANGLAMPHU

CHINATOWN

Th Phra Ram IV

TROK CHAN

Th Chan

Th Phra Ram IX

RATBURANA

PHRA PRADAENG

KO RATANAKOSIN

Bangkok Noi

Wat Arun

Wong Wian Yai

Tha Ratchasingkhon

Wat Ratchasingkhon

4

Th Ratchadaphisek

Th Charoen Nakhon

Krungthep Bridge

Saphan Phra Ram IX

Th Suksawat

303

Mae Nam Chao Phraya

BANGPHAT

TALING CHAN

Sathonwong

26

Khlong Bangkok Noi

THONBURI

BANGKOK NOI

11

Khlong Bangkok Yai

4

10

DAO KHANONG

Tha Daokanong

Th Taksin

Th Phetkasem

Tha Phetkasem

338

Khlong Dao Khanong

Khlong Phasi Charoen

BANG KHUN THIAN

Sanam Chai

Floating Market

Khlong

35

Outer Ring Road

To Nakhon Chaisi (31km); Rose Garden (32km); Nakhon Pathom (35km)

To Nakhon Pathom (32km)

To Samut Prakan (3km)

To Samut Sakhon (19km)

Skytrain & Stations
Subway & Stations

5 6 7 8

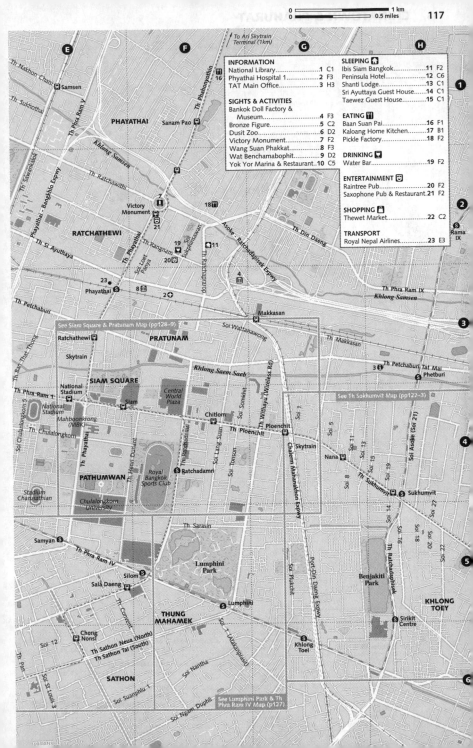

0 | 1 km
0 | 0.5 miles

INFORMATION
National Library.............................1 C1
Phyathai Hospital 1........................2 F3
TAT Main Office.............................3 H3

SIGHTS & ACTIVITIES
Bankok Doll Factory &
   Museum.....................................4 F3
Bronze Figure................................5 C2
Dusit Zoo.......................................6 D2
Victory Monument..........................7 F2
Wang Suan Phakkat.......................8 F3
Wat Benchamabophit......................9 D2
Yok Yor Marina & Restaurant......10 C5

SLEEPING 🏠
Ibis Siam Bangkok.........................11 F2
Peninsula Hotel.............................12 C6
Shanti Lodge.................................13 C1
Sri Ayuttaya Guest House..............14 C1
Taewez Guest House......................15 C1

EATING 🍴
Baan Suan Pai...............................16 F1
Kaloang Home Kitchen...................17 B1
Pickle Factory...............................18 F2

DRINKING 🍷
Water Bar......................................19 F2

ENTERTAINMENT 🎭
Raintree Pub.................................20 F2
Saxophone Pub & Restaurant.21 F2

SHOPPING 🛍
Thewet Market..............................22 C2

TRANSPORT
Royal Nepal Airlines......................23 E3

To Ari Skytrain
Terminal (1km)

Th Nakhon Chaisi

Samsen

Th Sukhothai

Th Phra Ram V

PHAYATHAI

Sanam Pao

Th Phahonyothin

Khlong Samsen

Th Ratchawithi

Phayathai - Bangkho Expwy

Th Savankalok

Victory Monument

RATCHATHEWI

Th Si Ayutthaya

Th Phayathai

Soi Rangnam

Asoke - Ratchadaphisek Expwy

Th Din Daeng

Th Ratchaprarop

Th Rangnam

Soi Sutphinsawan

Soi Loet Panya

23

Phayathai

8

2

Th Petchaburi

Makkasan

Soi Wattanawong

Th Phra Ram IX

Khlong Samsen

Rama IX

See Siam Square & Pratunam Map (pp128–9)

Ratchathewi

Skytrain

PRATUNAM

Th Makkasan

Th Petchaburi Tat Mai

Phetburi

SIAM SQUARE

Khlong Saem Saeh

National Stadium

Central World Plaza

Siam

Chitlom

Th Ploenchit

Ploenchit

Th Withayu (Wireless Rd)

Soi Somkit

Chalerm Mahanakhon Expwy

See Th Sukhumvit Map (pp122–3)

Th Phra Ram 1

National Stadium

Mahboonkrong (MBK)

Th Chulalongkorn

Soi Chulalongkorn 5

Th Henri Dunant

Ratchadamri

Th Lang Suan

Soi Tonson

Skytrain

Nana

Soi 5

Soi 11

Soi 13

Soi 15

Soi 19

Sukhumvit

Th Sukhumvit

Soi Asoke (Soi 21)

PATHUMWAN

Royal Bangkok Sports Club

Ratchadamri

Chulalongkorn University

Stadium Chanusathian

Soi 8

Soi 14

Soi 16

Soi 18

Soi 20

Soi 22

Th Ratchadaphisek

Th Sarasin

Samyan

Th Phra Ram IV

Lumphini Park

Benjakiti Park

KHLONG TOEY

Silom

Sala Daeng

Th Convent

Lumphini

Soi Phiphat

Soi Phulochit

Port-Din Daeng Expwy

Sirikit Centre

Chong Nonsi

Soi 12

THUNG MAHAMEK

Khlong Toei

SATHON

Th Sathon Neua (North)

Th Sathon Tai (South)

Th St Louis 3

Th Pan

Soi Nantha

Soi Anukpiosat

Soi Suanphlu

Soi Ngam Duphli

See Lumphini Park & Th
Phra Ram IV Map (p127)

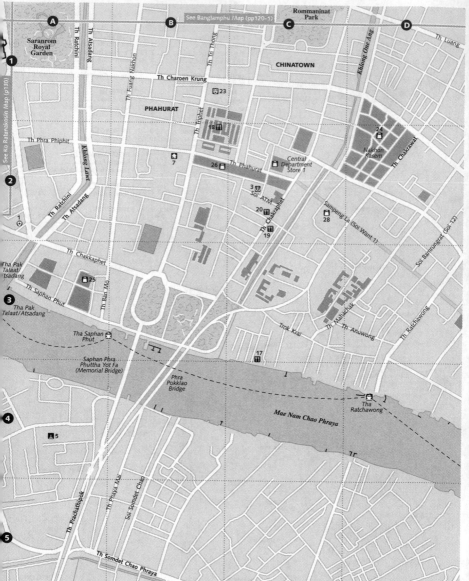

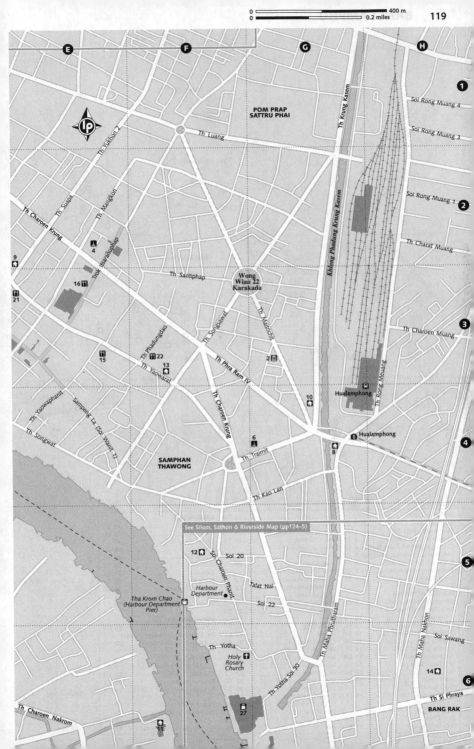

0   400 m
0   0.2 miles

E   **F**   **G**   **H**

Soi Rong Muang 4

**POM PRAP
SATTRU PHAI**

Th Luang

Soi Rong Muang 3

Th Krung Kasem

Soi Rong Muang 1

Th Charat Muang

Th Charoen Krung

Th Suapa

Th Yukhon 2

Th Mangkon

4

Th Santiphap

Wong
Wian 22
Karakada

Trok Itsaranuphap

9

16

21

15

Th Phadungdao

22

13

Th Yaowarat

Th Songwat

Th Yaowaphanit

Sampeng La (Soi Wanit 1)

Th Songwat

Th Maitrichit

Th Songsawat

Th Phra Ram IV

2

Th Charoen Muang

Khlong Phadung Krung Kasem

Hualamphong

Th Rong Meuang

Th Charoen Krung

10

6

**SAMPHAN
THAWONG**

Th Traimit

Th Kao Lan

Hualamphong

S

8

See Silom, Sathon & Riverside Map (pp124–5)

12

Soi Charoen Phanit

Soi 20

Talat Nai

Soi 22

Harbour
Department

Tha Krom Chao
(Harbour Department
Pier)

Th Yotha

Holy
Rosary
Church

Th Yotha Soi 30

Th Maha Phrutharam

Th Maha Nakhon

Soi Sawang

14

Th Charoen Nakrom

11

27

Th Si Phraya

BANG RAK

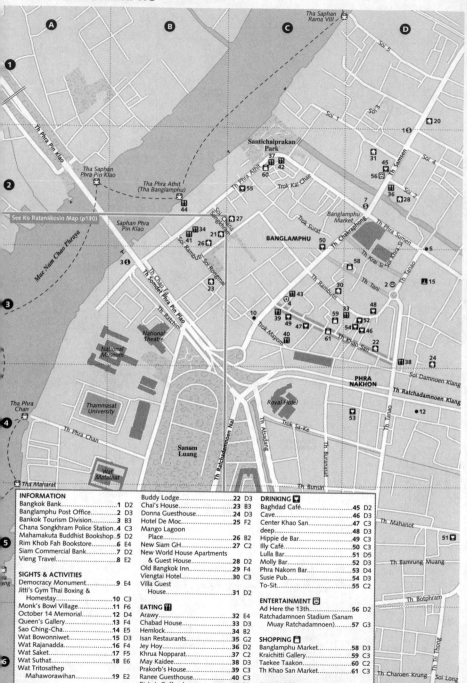

See Ko Ratanakosin Map (p130)

INFORMATION
Bangkok Bank	**1** D2
Banglamphu Post Office	**2** D3
Bankok Tourism Division	**3** B3
Chana Songkhram Police Station	**4** C3
Mahamakuta Buddhist Bookshop	**5** D2
Rim Khob Fah Bookstore	**6** E4
Siam Commercial Bank	**7** E2
Vieng Travel	**8** E2

SIGHTS & ACTIVITIES
Democracy Monument	**9** E4
Jitti's Gym Thai Boxing & Homestay	**10** C3
Monk's Bowl Village	**11** F6
October 14 Memorial	**12** D4
Queen's Gallery	**13** E5
Sao Ching-Cha	**14** E5
Wat Bowonniwet	**15** D3
Wat Rajanadda	**16** F4
Wat Saket	**17** F5
Wat Suthat	**18** E6
Wat Tritosathep Mahaworawihan	**19** E2

SLEEPING
Baan Chantra	**20** D1
Bella Bella House	**21** B2
Buddy Lodge	**22** D3
Chai's House	**23** B3
Donna Guesthouse	**24** D3
Hotel De Moc	**25** F2
Mango Lagoon Place	**26** B2
New Siam GH	**27** C2
New World House Apartments & Guest House	**28** D2
Old Bangkok Inn	**29** F4
Viengtai Hotel	**30** C3
Villa Guest House	**31** D2

EATING
Arawy	**32** E4
Chabad House	**33** C2
Hemlock	**34** B2
Isan Restaurants	**35** G2
Jey Hoy	**36** D2
Khrua Nopparat	**37** C2
May Kaidee	**38** D3
Prakorb's House	**39** C3
Ranee Guesthouse	**40** C3
Ricky's Coffeeshop	**41** C3
Roti-Mataba	**42** C2
Shoshana	**43** C3
Ton Pho	**44** B2

DRINKING
Baghdad Café	**45** D2
Cave	**46** D3
Center Khao San	**47** C3
deep	**48** D3
Hippie de Bar	**49** C3
Illy Café	**50** C3
Lulla Bar	**51** D5
Molly Bar	**52** D3
Phra Nakorn Bar	**53** D4
Susie Pub	**54** C3
To-Sit	**55** C2

ENTERTAINMENT
Ad Here the 13th	**56** D2
Ratchadamnoen Stadium (Sanam Muay Ratchadamnoen)	**57** G3

SHOPPING
Banglamphu Market	**58** D3
Kraichitti Gallery	**59** C3
Taekee Taakon	**60** C2
Th Khao San Market	**61** C3

TRANSPORT
Tha Phan Fah (Khlong taxis)	**62** F4
Thai Airways International	**63** F4

0 ————————— 400 m
0 ————————— 0.2 miles

E 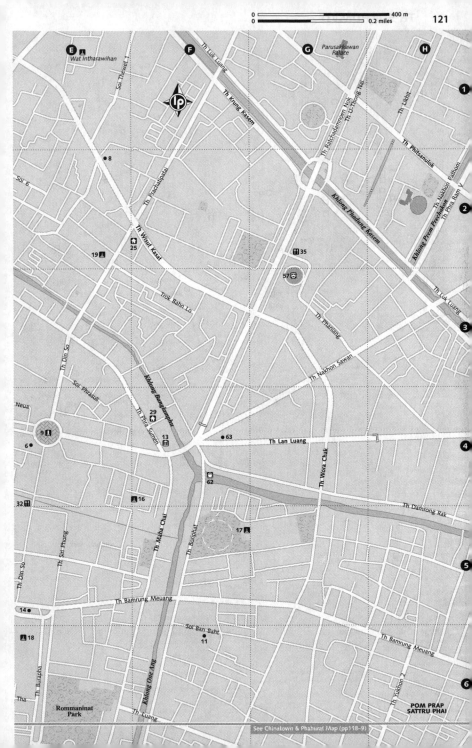 Wat Intharawihan
F Th Luk Luang
G Parusakkawan Palace
H

Th Ratchadamnoen Nok
Th U-Thong Nai
Th Phitsanulok
Th Likhit
Th Nakhon Pathom
Th Phra Ram V

Th Krung Kasem

Khlong Phadung Kasem

Khlong Prem Prachakon

Th Luk Luang

● 8

Soi Thevet I

Th Pradiphatai

Soi 6

Th Wisut Kasat
25
19

Trok Bahn Lo

35
57

Th Phanang

Th Din So

Khlong Banglamphu

Th Nakhon Sawan

Soi Phrasuli

Neua

Th Phra Sumen

29

9
6 ●

13
● 63
Th Lan Luang

Th Wora Chak

62

32
16

Th Maha Chai

17

Th Damrong Rak

Th Sri Phong

Th Boriphat

Th Din So

Th Bamrung Meuang

14 ●

18

Soi Ban Baht
11

Th Bamrung Meuang

Th Burapha

Tha

Rommaninat Park

Khlong Ong Ang

Th Luang

Th Yakhon 2

POM PRAP SATTRU PHAI

See Chinatown & Phahurat Map (pp118–9)

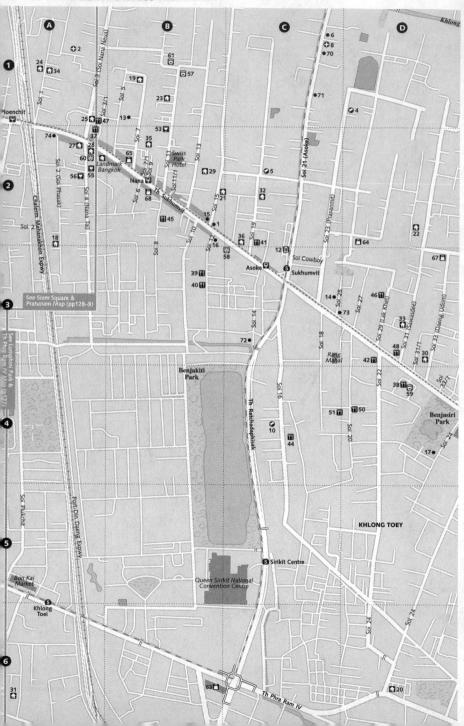

0 400 m
0 0.2 miles

INFORMATION
Asia Books	1 B2
Asia Books	(see 62)
Bumrungrad Hospital	2 A1
Dasa Book Café	3 E4
Indian Embassy	4 D1
Israeli Embassy	5 C1
Japan Foundation	6 C1
Kinokuniya	(see 62)
Philippine Embassy	7 E5
Rutnin Eye Hospital	8 C1
Samitivej Hospital	9 F3
Siam Society	(see 12)
Spanish Embassy	10 C4

SIGHTS & ACTIVITIES
ABC Amazing Bangkok Cyclists	11 E4
Ban Kamthieng	12 C3
Buathip Thai Massage	13 B1
Divana Spa	14 C3
Marble House	15 B2
Play Gallery	(see 66)
Pro Language	16 B2
Thailand Creative & Design Center	(see 62)
World Fellowship of Buddhists	17 D4

SLEEPING
Atlanta	18 A3
Bel-Aire Princess	19 B1
Davis	20 D6
Dream Bangkok	21 B2
Eugenia	22 D2
Federal Hotel	23 B1
Golden Palace Hotel	24 A1
Grace Hotel	25 A1
HI-Sukhumvit	26 G6
JW Marriott Hotel	27 A2
Majestic Suites	28 A2
Miami Hotel	29 B2
Novotel Lotus Bangkok	30 D3
Sala Thai Daily Mansion	31 A6
Sam's Lodge	32 C2
Seven	33 D3
Soi 1 Guesthouse	34 A1
Suk 11	35 B2
Westin Grande Sukhumvit	36 C2

EATING
Al Hussain	37 A2
Atlanta Coffeeshop	(see 18)
Bourbon St Bar & Restaurant	38 D4
Cabbages & Condoms	39 B3
Crepes & Co	40 B3
Dosa King	41 C2
Govinda	42 D3
Great American Rib Company	43 F5
Greyhound Café	(see 62)
Kuppa	44 C4
Le Banyan	45 B2
Maha Naga	46 D3
Nasir al-Masri Restaurant & Shishah	47 A1
Pizzeria Bella Napoli	48 D3
Soi 38 Night Market	49 G5
Tamarind Café	50 D4
Thong Lee	51 D4
Vientiane Kitchen	52 F5

DRINKING
Cheap Charlie's	53 B2
Face Bangkok	54 G6
Jool's	55 A2
Sin Bar	56 A2

ENTERTAINMENT
Bed Supperclub	57 B1
Living Room	58 C3
Mambo Cabaret	59 D4
Nana Entertainment Plaza	60 A2
Q Bar	61 B1
SFX Cinema	(see 62)

SHOPPING
Emporium Shopping Centre	62 E4
Gallery F-Stop	(see 50)
Greyhound	(see 62)
Khlong Toey Market	63 B6
Nandakwang	64 D2
Phu Fa	65 B2
Playground!	66 H2
Propaganda	(see 62)
Rasi Sayam	67 D3
Th Sukhumvit Market	68 B2

TRANSPORT
Eastern Bus Terminal (Ekamai)	69 H6
Lufthansa Airlines	70 C1
Myanmar Airways International	71 C1
One-Two-Go	72 C3
Orient Thai	(see 72)
Scandinavian Airlines	73 C3
Vietnam Airlines	74 A2

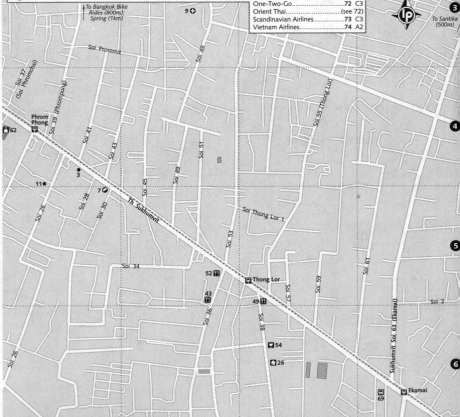

A B C D

1

Th Charoen Krung

Soi Charoen Phani
Soi 20
Talat Nai
Soi 22

Tha Krom Chao (Harbour Department Pier)

Th Maha Phrutharam

Th Maha Nakhon

Soi Sawang

Th Kaeo Fa

Th Si Phraya

2

Th Yotha

Th Yotha Soi 30

River City Complex

Th Naret

See Chinatown & Phahurat Map (pp118–9)

Tha Si Phraya

21

65

Soi 32

Soi 43 (Soi Saphan Yao)

3

34

Soi 34

Th Charoen Krung

4

2

27

Soi 35

Th Mahesak

39

BANG RAK

Th Surawong
9
58

Soi 20 (Soi Pradit)

Soi 22

Neilson Hays Library Rotunda Gallery

Th Surawong

Tha Meuang Khae

18

28

Soi 18

4

3

29

Soi 36
53
38

20

Soi 38 (Soi Oriental)

Central Department Store

Soi 26

Soi 30

36

55

14

Tha Oriental

Soi 40

Soi 42

Th Silom

57

59

Soi 17

Soi 15

5

Shangri-La Hotel

43

23

Soi Si Wiang

Th Pramuan

Saphan Taksin

Soi Wat Suan Phlu

Th Charat Wiang

Th Surasak

Th Pan

Tha Sathon (Central Pier)

Mae Nam Chao Phraya

Saphan Taksin

Surasak

6

24

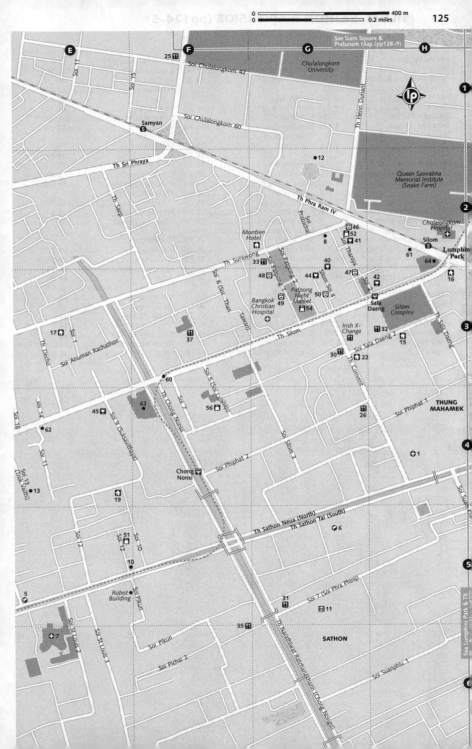

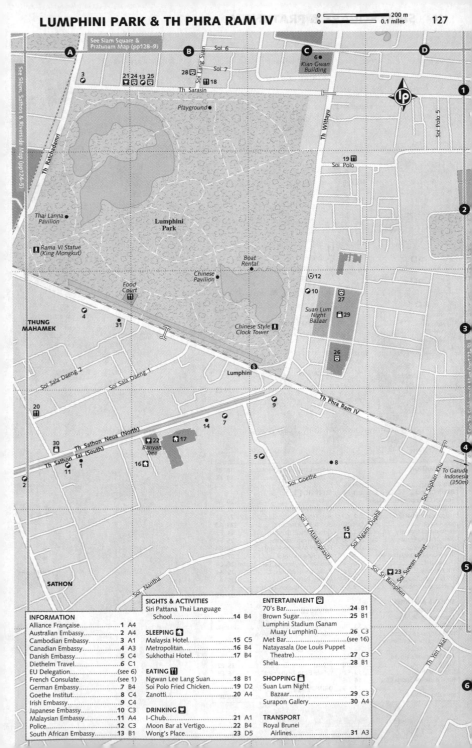

0 — 200 m
0 — 0.1 miles

See Siam Square &
Pratunam Map (pp128–9)

Soi 6

Soi 7

Kian Gwan
Building

28

18

Th Sarasin

Playground

Th Ratchadamri

Th Wittayu

Soi Polo 5

Soi Polo

Thai Lanna
Pavilion

Lumphini
Park

Rama VI Statue
(King Mongkut)

Food
Court

Chinese
Pavilion

Boat
Rental

Suan Lum
Night
Bazaar

THUNG
MAHAMEK

Chinese Style
Clock Tower

Soi Sala Daeng 2

Soi Sala Daeng 1

Lumphini

Th Phra Ram IV

Th Sathon Neua (North)

Th Sathon Tai (South)

Banyan
Tree

Soi Goethe

To Garuda
Indonesia
(350m)

Soi Saphan Khu

SATHON

Soi Nantha

Soi I (Akanprasit)

Soi Ngam Duphli

Soi Sri Bamphen

Soi Suan Sawat

Th Yen Akat

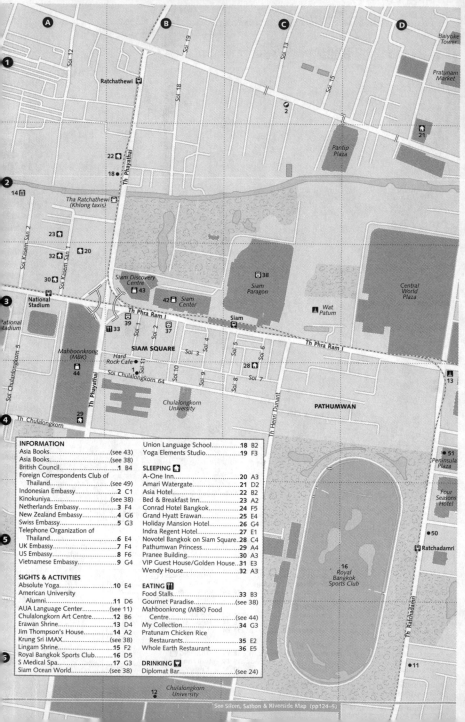

INFORMATION
Asia Books.............................(see 43)
Asia Books.............................(see 38)
British Council............................**1** B4
Foreign Correspondents Club of
   Thailand...........................(see 49)
Indonesian Embassy...................**2** C1
Kinokuniya.............................(see 38)
Netherlands Embassy..................**3** F4
New Zealand Embassy.................**4** G6
Swiss Embassy............................**5** G3
Telephone Organization of
   Thailand..............................**6** E4
UK Embassy................................**7** F6
US Embassy................................**8** F6
Vietnamese Embassy....................**9** G4

SIGHTS & ACTIVITIES
Absolute Yoga...........................**10** E4
American University
   Alumni..............................**11** D6
AUA Language Center............(see 11)
Chulalongkorn Art Centre..........**12** B6
Erawan Shrine...........................**13** D4
Jim Thompson's House...............**14** A2
Krung Sri IMAX.......................(see 38)
Lingam Shrine...........................**15** F2
Royal Bangkok Sports Club.........**16** D5
S Medical Spa...........................**17** G3
Siam Ocean World..................(see 38)

SLEEPING
A-One Inn................................**20** A3
Amari Watergate.......................**21** D2
Asia Hotel................................**22** B2
Bed & Breakfast Inn..................**23** A2
Conrad Hotel Bangkok...............**24** F5
Grand Hyatt Erawan..................**25** E4
Holiday Mansion Hotel...............**26** G4
Indra Regent Hotel....................**27** E1
Novotel Bangkok on Siam Square.**28** C4
Pathumwan Princess...................**29** A4
Pranee Building.........................**30** A3
VIP Guest House/Golden House..**31** E3
Wendy House............................**32** A3

EATING
Food Stalls...............................**33** B3
Gourmet Paradise...................(see 38)
Mahboonkrong (MBK) Food
   Centre.............................(see 44)
My Collection...........................**34** G3
Pratunam Chicken Rice
   Restaurants.......................**35** E2
Whole Earth Restaurant.............**36** E5

DRINKING
Diplomat Bar.........................(see 24)

Union Language School...............**18** B2
Yoga Elements Studio.................**19** F3

See Silom, Sathon & Riverside Map (pp124–5)

ENTERTAINMENT
Calypso Cabaret	(see 22)	
EGV Grand	(see 43)	
Lido Cinema	**37**	B3
Paragon Cineplex	**38**	C3
SF Cinema City	(see 44)	
Scala Cinema	**39**	B3

SHOPPING
100 Tonson Gallery	**40**	F5
Fly Now	**41**	E3
Jaspal	**42**	B3
Mae Fah Luang	**43**	B3
Mahboonkrong (MBK)	**44**	A4
Narayana Phand	**45**	E3
Pratunam Market	**46**	E1

TRANSPORT
American Airlines	(see 48)	
Avis	**47**	G4
Cathay Pacific Airways	**48**	F4
China Airlines	(see 51)	
Gulf Air	**49**	E4
Japan Airlines	**50**	D5
KLM-Royal Dutch Airlines	(see 51)	
Malaysia Airlines	(see 48)	
Northwest Airlines	**51**	D4
United Airlines	**52**	F6

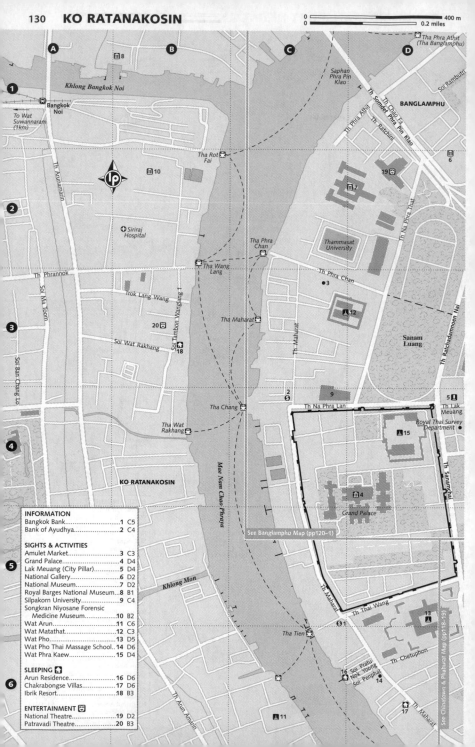

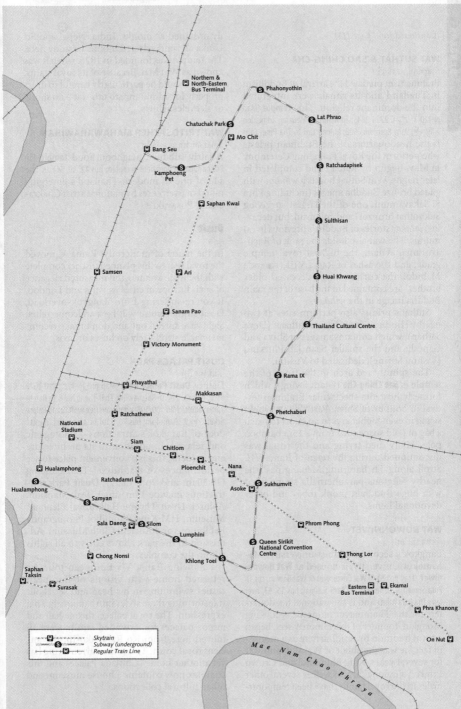

Northern &
North-Eastern
Bus Terminal

Ⓢ Phahonyothin

Ⓢ Lat Phrao

Chatuchak Park Ⓢ

🚉 Mo Chit

🚉 Bang Seu

Ⓢ Ratchadapisek

Ⓢ
Kamphoeng
Pet

🚉 Saphan Kwai

Ⓢ Sulthisan

🚉 Samsen   🚉 Ari

Ⓢ Huai Khwang

🚉 Sanam Pao

Ⓢ Thailand Cultural Centre

🚉 Victory Monument

Ⓢ Rama IX

🚉 Phayathai

Makkasan
🚉

Ⓢ Phetchaburi

🚉 Ratchathewi

National
Stadium
🚉

Siam
🚉   Chitlom
🚉   🚉
Ploenchit   Nana
🚉

🚉 Hualamphong   Ⓢ Sukhumvit
Ⓢ   Ratchadamri 🚉   Asoke Ⓢ
Hualamphong
Ⓢ Samyan   🚉 Phrom Phong

Sala Daeng 🚉 Ⓢ Silom
Ⓢ Lumphini
🚉 Chong Nonsi   🚉 Thong Lor
Khlong Toei Ⓢ
Saphan   Ⓢ Queen Sirikit
Taksin   National Convention
🚉   🚉 Surasak   Centre
Eastern 🚉 🚉 Ekamai
Bus Terminal
🚉 Phra Khanong

On Nut 🚉

M a e   N a m   C h a o   P h r a y a

```
⌐💀⌐~~~~~~~~~~   Skytrain
————Ⓢ————      Subway (underground)
—+—🚉—+—       Regular Train Line
```

(Continued from page 113)

WAT SUTHAT & SAO CHING-CHA

วัดสุทัศน์/เสาชิงช้า

Brahmanism predated the arrival of Buddhism in Thailand and its rituals were integrated into the dominant religion. This **temple** (Map pp120-1; ☎ 0 2224 9845; Th Bamrung Meuang; admission 20B; ☉ 9am-8pm; bus 508, khlong taxi to Tha Phan Fah) is the headquarters of the Brahman priests who perform the Royal Ploughing Ceremony in May. Begun by Rama I and completed in later reigns, Wat Suthat boasts a *wíhăan* with gilded bronze Buddha images (including Phra Si Sakayamuni, one of the largest surviving Sukhothai bronzes) and colourful, but decaying, *jataka* (stories of Buddha's previous lives) murals. The wat also holds the rank of Rachavoramahavihan, the highest royal-temple grade; and the ashes of Rama VIII (Ananda Mahidol, the current king's deceased older brother) are contained in the base of the main Buddha image in the *wíhăan*.

Suthat's priests also perform rites at two nearby Hindu shrines: Thewa Sathaan (Deva Sathan), which contains images of Shiva and Ganesh; and the smaller Saan Jao Phitsanu (Vishnu Shrine), dedicated to Vishnu.

The spindly red arch in the front of the temple is **Sao Ching-Cha** (Giant Swing), which formerly hosted a spectacular Brahman festival in honour of Shiva. Participants would swing in ever-higher arcs in an effort to reach a bag of gold suspended from a 15m bamboo pole. Many died trying and the ritual was discontinued during the reign of Rama VII. Stroll along Th Bamrung Meuang past the nearby religious-paraphernalia shops filled with huge Buddhas, monk robes and other devotional items.

WAT BOWONNIWET

วัดบวรนิเวศ

Bangkok's second Buddhist university, Mahamakut University, is housed at **Wat Bowonniwet** (Map pp120-1; Wat Bovornives or Wat Bowon; cnr Th Phra Sumen & Th Tanao; ☉ 8am-5.30pm; bus 15, 53, river ferry Tha Phra Athit) and is the national headquarters for the Thammayut monastic sect. King Mongkut, founder of this minority sect, began a royal tradition by residing here as a monk – in fact, he was the abbot of Wat Bowonniwet for several years. King Bhumibol and Crown Prince Vajiralongkorn, as well as several other males in the royal family, have been temporar-

ily ordained as monks. India, Nepal and Sri Lanka all send selected monks to study here. The temple was founded in 1826, when it was known as Wat Mai. Because of its royal status, visitors should be particularly careful to dress properly for admittance to this wat – no shorts or sleeveless shirts.

WAT TRITOSATHEP MAHAWARAWIHAN

วัดตรีทศเทพวรมหาวิหาร

A fairly subdued neighbourhood **temple** (Th Prachathipatai; donations accepted; bus 12, 19, 56) is the site of one of modern Thailand's emerging mural masterpieces by national artist Chakrabhand Posayakrit.

Dusit

ดุสิต

In the name of modernity, Rama V moved the royal seat to this planned district complete with the wide avenues and measured elegance of such European cities as Paris and London. If you're suffering from Bangkok-overload, Dusit's quiet poise will be a welcome relief. Sights are spread out and don't make recommendable strolls; rely on buses or taxis.

DUSIT PALACE PARK

วังสวนดุสิต

Dainty **Dusit Palace Park** (Map pp116-17; ☎ 0 2628 6300; bounded by Th Ratchawithi, Th U-Thong Nai & Th Ratchasima; adult/child 100/50B, admission free with Grand Palace ticket; ☉ 9.30am-4pm; bus 70, 510) is the girl-next-door of Bangkok's attractions – photogenic and relaxed. In addition to its architecture and gardens, this is a convenient place to see performances of traditional Thai dancing (10.30am and 2pm daily). Dusit Park's attractions include Vimanmek Teak Mansion, Abhisek Dusit Throne Hall, Royal Elephant Museum, HM King Bhumibol Photography Exhibitions and Ancient Cloth Museum. Admission to the park allows entry to all sights within the complex.

Following Rama V's European tour, he returned home with visions of European castles swimming in his head and set about transforming these styles into a uniquely Thai expression. The royal palace, throne hall and minor palaces for extended family were all moved here from Ko Ratanakosin, the ancient royal court. Today the current King has yet another home (Chitlada Palace) and this complex now contains a house museum and other cultural collections.

Because this is royal property, visitors should wear long pants (no capri pants) or long skirts and shirts with sleeves.

Vimanmek Teak Mansion

Originally constructed on Ko Si Chang in 1868 and moved to the present site in 1910, this beautiful L-shaped, three-storey mansion contains 81 rooms, halls and anterooms, and is said to be the world's largest golden-teak building. The staircases, octagonal rooms and lattice work are nothing short of magnificent, but in spite of this, the mansion retains a surprisingly serene and intimate atmosphere.

Vimanmek was the first permanent building on the Dusit Palace grounds. It served as Rama V's residence in the early 1900s. The interior of the mansion contains various personal effects of the king and a treasure-trove of early Ratanakosin art objects and antiques.

Compulsory English-language tours last an hour. Don't expect to learn a lot on the tours as the guide's English is quite laboured and tours tend to overlap with one another.

Abhisek Dusit Throne Hall

Originally built as a throne hall for Rama V in 1904, the smaller Abhisek Dusit Throne Hall is typical of the finer architecture of the era. Victorian-influenced gingerbread architecture and Moorish porticoes blend to create a striking and distinctly Thai exterior. The hall houses an excellent display of regional handiwork crafted by members of the Promotion of Supplementary Occupations & Related Techniques (SUPPORT) foundation, an organisation sponsored by Queen Sirikit. Among the exhibits are cotton and silk, *málaeng tháp* (collages made from metallic, multicoloured beetle wings), damascene and nielloware, and basketry.

Royal Elephant Museum

Near the Th U-Thong Nai entrance, two large stables that once housed three white elephants – animals whose auspicious albinism automatically made them crown property – are now a museum. One of the structures contains artefacts and photos outlining the importance of elephants in Thai history and explaining their various rankings according to physical characteristics. The second stable holds a sculptural representation of a living royal white elephant (now kept at the Chitlada Palace, home to the current Thai king).

Draped in royal vestments, the statue is more or less treated as a shrine by the visiting Thai public.

Ananta Samakhom Throne Hall

The domed neoclassical building at the foot of Royal Plaza is Ananta Samakhom Throne Hall, which was built in the early 1900s by Italian architects in the style of European government houses. Used today for ceremonial purposes, the throne hall also hosted the first meeting of the Thai parliament until their meeting place was moved to a facility nearby. Visitors can explore the architecture of the building and view rotating exhibits.

HM King Bhumibol Photography Exhibitions

Near the Th Ratwithi entrance, two residence halls display a collection of photographs and paintings by the present monarch. Among the many loving photos of his wife and children are also historic pictures of the king playing clarinet with Benny Goodman and Louis Armstrong in 1960.

WAT BENCHAMABOPHIT
วัดเบญจมบพิตร(วัดเบญจะ)

Made of white Carrara marble, **Wat Benchamabophit** (Marble Temple; Map pp116–17; cnr Th Si Ayuthaya & Th Phra Ram V; admission 20B; ✆ 8am–5.30pm; bus 72, 503) was built in the late 19th century under Rama V. The large cruciform *bòt* is a prime example of modern Thai wat architecture. The base of the central Buddha image, a copy of Phitsanulok's Phra Phuttha Chinnarat, contains the ashes of Rama V. The courtyard behind the *bòt* exhibits 53 Buddha images (33 originals and 20 copies) representing famous figures and styles from all over Thailand and other Buddhist countries.

Rama V Memorial
พระบรมรูปทรงม้า

A bronze **figure** (Map pp116–17; Royal Plaza, Th U-Thong Nai) of a military-garbed leader may seem like an unlikely shrine, but Bangkokians are flexible in their expression of religious devotion. Most importantly, the figure is no forgotten general – this is Rama V (King Chulalongkorn; 1868–1910), who is widely credited for steering the country into the modern age and for preserving Thailand's independence from European colonialism. He is also considered a champion of the common person for his

abolition of slavery and corvée (the requirement that every citizen be available for state labour when called). His accomplishments are so revered, especially by the middle class, that his statue attracts worshippers who make offerings of candles, flowers (predominantly pink roses), incense and bottles of whisky, and is the site of a huge celebration during the anniversary of the monarch's death.

Chinatown

เยาวราช(สำเพ็ง)

Bangkok's Chinatown (called 'Yaowarat' after its main thoroughfare, Th Yaowarat) comprises a confusing and crowded array of commerce organised into guildlike districts – rubber-bath-plug stores in one block, bulk plastic bags in another, handmade signs, hand guns and even used-vinyl-record stores can be found. The district was born in 1782 when Bangkok's Chinese population, many of them labourers who came to build the new capital, were moved here from today's Ko Ratanakosin area by the royal government.

The neighbourhood's energy is exhausting and exhilarating. There are endless pedestrian wanderings, especially in the tiny *sois* along the river, but getting in and out of Chinatown is hindered by continuous traffic. The Chao Phraya Express connects the neighbourhood to Ko Ratanakosin, Banglamphu and Silom, but slow-moving buses are needed to get to inland Siam Square and Sukhumvit.

WAT MANGKON KAMALAWAT

วัดมังกรกมลาวาส

Explore the labyrinthine passageways of this busy Chinese-style **temple** (Neng Noi Yee; Map pp118-19; Th Charoen Krung; 9am-6pm; bus 73, 501, 507, river ferry Tha Ratchawong) to find Buddhist, Taoist and Confucian shrines. During the annual Vege-

tarian Festival, religious and culinary activities are centred here. But almost any time of day or night, this temple is packed with worshippers lighting incense, filling the ever-burning altar lamps with oil and making offerings to their ancestors. The Thai name means Dragon Lotus Temple.

WAT TRAIMIT

วัดไตรมิตร

The attraction at **Wat Traimit** (Temple of the Golden Buddha; Map pp118-19; 0 2225 9775; cnr Th Yaowarat & Th Charoen Krung; admission 20B; 9am-5pm; subway Hualamphong, bus 53) is undoubtedly the impressive 3m-tall, 5.5-tonne, solid-gold Buddha image, which gleams like, well, gold. Sculpted in the graceful Sukhothai style, the image was 'discovered' some 40 years ago beneath a stucco or plaster exterior, when it fell from a crane while being moved to a new building within the temple compound. It has been theorised that the covering was added to protect it from marauding hordes, either during the late Sukhothai period or later in the Ayuthaya period when the city was under siege by the Burmese. The temple itself is said to date from the early 13th century.

PHAHURAT

พาหุรัด

At the western edge of Chinatown is a small but thriving Indian district, generally called **Phahurat** (Map pp118-19; around intersection of Th Phahurat & Th Chakraphet). Here, dozens of Indian-owned shops sell all kinds of fabric and clothes. Behind the more obvious shopfronts along these streets, in the bowels of the blocks, is **Phahurat Market** (Map pp118-19; Th Phahurat & Th Chakraphet; bus 73, river ferry Tha Saphan Phut), an endless bazaar selling flamboyant Bollywood fabric and other necessities.

ON THE AIRWAVES

In a city as gridlocked as Bangkok, many drivers' best friend is the radio, broadcasting stations that are always at the ready to entertain and inform. The taxi drivers typically listen to the stations that play *lûuk thûng*, the Thai equivalent of country music in which the lyrics often feature a poor family having to send a devoted child to Bangkok to work after their buffalo dies – the personal story of many cabbies. Ruam Duay Chuuay Kan (Helping Each Other) is a call-in show where people report accidents, breakdowns and other odd sights. Political talk shows are also popular and the former prime minister Thaksin Shinawatra used to hold weekly state of the nation broadcasts. During the peak of Thaksin's unpopularity, a Thai satirical newspaper column called 'Poojadkuan', the Thai version of the *Onion* (US parody newspaper), quoted a grocer who wished to save energy by turning off his radio during the prime minister's weekly address.

In an alley off Th Chakraphet is **Sri Gurusingh Sabha** (Map pp118-19; Th Phahurat; ◷ 9am-5pm; bus 53, 73, river ferry Tha Saphan Phut), a large Sikh temple reminiscent of a mosque interior, devoted to the worship of the *Guru Granth Sahib*, the 16th-century Sikh holy book, which is itself considered to be a 'living' guru and the last of the religion's 10 great teachers. Reportedly the temple is the second-largest Sikh temple outside India. Visitors are welcome, but they must remove their shoes.

Siam Square & Pratunam
ปทุมวัน/ประตูน้ำ

Boxy shopping centres dominate the landscape of Siam Square's teeming commercial zone. Back behind the modern façade is the former lifeblood of the neighbourhood: soot-coloured Khlong Saen Saeb, lined with rickety wooden shacks and drying laundry. Skytrain and the *khlong* taxis provide easy access to most attractions here.

JIM THOMPSON'S HOUSE
บ้านจิมทอมป์สัน

A pretty place to pass some time, **Jim Thompson's House** (Map pp128-9; ☎ 0 2216 7368, 0 2215 0122; Th Phra Ram I, Soi Kasem San 2; adult/child 100/50B; ◷ 9am-5pm; compulsory tours (English & French) every 10min; Skytrain National Stadium, bus 73, 508, khlong taxi to Ratchathewi) is also a museum-quality preservation of Thai residential architecture and Southeast Asian art. Another hook is the home's former owner, Jim Thompson, a compelling character who created an international appetite for Thai silk.

Born in Delaware in 1906, Thompson was a New York architect who briefly served in the Office of Strategic Services (forerunner of the CIA) in Thailand during WWII. Following the war he found New York too tame and returned to Bangkok. His neighbours' handmade silk caught his eye and piqued his business sense; he sent samples to fashion houses in Milan, London and Paris, gradually building a steady worldwide clientele.

A tireless promoter of traditional Thai arts and culture, Thompson also collected parts of various derelict Thai homes in central Thailand and had them reassembled in their current location in 1959. One striking departure from tradition is the way each wall has its exterior side facing the house's interior, thus exposing the wall's bracing system. His small but splendid Asian art collection and

his personal belongings are also on display in the main house.

Thompson's story doesn't end with his informal reign as Bangkok's best-adapted foreigner. While out for an afternoon walk in the Cameron Highlands of western Malaysia in 1967, Thompson mysteriously disappeared. That same year his sister was murdered in the USA, fuelling various conspiracy theories. Was it communist spies? Business rivals? Or a man-eating tiger? The most recent theory – for which there is apparently some hard evidence – has it that the silk magnate was accidentally run over by a Malaysian truck driver who hid his remains. *Jim Thompson The Unsolved Mystery*, by William Warren, is an excellent book on Thompson, his career, residence and subsequent intriguing disappearance.

ERAWAN SHRINE
ศาลพระพรหม

A seamless merging of commerce and religion occurs at all hours of the day at this bustling **shrine** (San Phra Phrom; Map pp128-9; cnr Th Ratchadamri & Th Ploenchit; admission free; ◷ 8am-7pm; Skytrain Chitlom). Claiming a spare corner of the Grand Hyatt Erawan hotel, the four-headed deity Brahma (Phra Phrom) represents the Hindu god of creation and was originally built to ward off bad luck during the construction of the first Erawan Hotel (torn down to make way for the current structure). Apparently the developers of the original Erawan (named after Airvata,

---

FORTUNE'S FOLLOWERS

Some people travel to Thailand because they want a tan or an adventure, but others know that fortune is fond of the Land of Smiles and come for a slice of luck. Of the many auspicious outposts, Lak Muang (City Pillar; p110) has an impressive reputation for wiping away misfortune and strengthening the powers of merit-making. Cheaper than a financial consultant, Wat Arun and Wat Phra Kaew (p108) have granted many requests for wealth and prosperity. Some even joke that the Emerald Buddha likes *sôm-tam* (papaya salad) because of his brief exile in Laos. The trouble with merit-making is that fortune is often slow and subtle, but the Erawan Shrine has a reputation for fast action, regardless of the request.

Indra's three-headed elephant mount) first erected a typical Thai spirit house but decided to replace it with the more impressive Brahman shrine after several serious mishaps delayed the hotel construction. The shrine was later adopted by the lay community as it gained a reputation for granting wishes. Worshippers who have had a wish granted may return to the shrine to commission the musicians and dancers, who are always on hand for an impromptu performance.

Silom & Lumphini

สีลม/ลุมพินี

Forming the artery of Bangkok's financial district, Th Silom has only a few daytime tourist attractions scattered among its corporate hotels, office towers and wining-and-dining restaurants. As Th Silom approaches Th Charoen Krung, the area becomes spiced with the sights and smells of its Indian and Muslim residents. The sliver of land that buffers Th

Charoen Krung from the river was the international mercantile district during Bangkok's shipping heyday. Crumbling Victorian buildings and luxury hotels now occupy this neighbourhood of tributary *sois*.

Silom's most famous attraction is Patpong, a raunchy circus of go-go bars and an oddly complementary market of pirated goods. Traffic is notorious in this part of town, but the Skytrain, subway and Chao Phraya Express provide some transport relief.

SRI MARIAMMAN TEMPLE

วัดพระศรีมหาอุมาเทวี(วัดแขกสีลม)

As flourishing as it is flamboyant, this **Hindu temple** (Wat Phra Si Maha Umathewi; Map pp124-5; cnr Th Silom & Th Pan; donations accepted; 🕑 6am-8pm; Skytrain Chong Nonsi) visually leaps off the block. Built in the 1860s by Tamil immigrants in the centre of a still thriving ethnic enclave, the main temple is a stacked façade of intertwined, full-colour Hindu deities, topped by a gold-plated cop-

---

BANGKOK'S EXHIBITIONISTS

After surveying Thailand's artistic traditions of temple murals and religious sculpture, fast forward into the present time to see how these inherited techniques are being adapted to the contemporary language of modern art. The noncommercial galleries and exhibition spaces listed here range from conventional to avant-garde and display a wide range of media. Rotating exhibits are advertised in the English-language press and online at www.rama9.org. For a list of commercial galleries, see the boxed text on p176.

About Studio/About Café (Map pp118-19; ☎ 0 2623 1742; 418 Th Maitrichit; subway Hualamphong) Cutting-edge Thai artists working in alternative and experimental media.

Bangkok Sculpture Center (☎ 0 2559 0505; www.bangkoksculpturecenter.org; PM Center Co, Soi Nuanchan, Th Ramindra; 🕑 by appointment 10am-4pm 2nd/4th Sat of each month) Many art critics believe that Thai sculpture, not its canvases, hold the true promise of Thai modern art. This private collection is one of the few venues to admire the graceful lines of 3-D art.

Bangkok University Art Gallery (Map pp114-15; ☎ 0 2350 3626, 0 2671 7526; 3rd fl, Bldg 9, Kluay Nam Thai Campus, Th Rama IV; 🕑 9am-7pm) This art university excels in mixed-media exhibits.

Chulalongkorn Art Centre (Map pp128-9; ☎ 0 2218 2964; 7th fl, Library Bldg, Chulalongkorn University, Th Phayathai; 🕑 9am-7pm Mon-Fri, 9am-4pm Sat; Skytrain Siam) Major names in the modern-art scene, as well as international artists.

Play Gallery (Map pp122-3; ☎ 0 2714 7888; Playground!, 2nd fl, Soi 55, Th Sukhumvit; 🕑 10am-11pm; Skytrain Thonglor to red soi bus) Urban art, including manga and graffiti, gets an artistic salute at this exhibition space within a concept mall.

Queen's Gallery (Map pp120-1; ☎ 0 2281 5360; www.queengallery.org; 101 Th Ratchadamnoen Klang; 🕑 10am-7pm Thu-Tue; bus 2, 511, 512, khlong taxi to Tha Phan Fah) Modern painters receiving royal patronage are displayed at this new and tidy museum, walking distance from Th Khao San.

Silpakorn University Art Gallery (Map p130; ☎ 0 2623 6120; 31 Th Na Phra Lan; 🕑 9am-4pm; Chao Phraya Express Tha Chang) Known as the primary university for painting, this campus gallery displays student and faculty work.

Tadu Contemporary Art (Map pp114-15; ☎ 0 2645 2473; www.tadu.net; 7th fl, Barcelona Motors Bldg, 99/2 Th Tiamruammit; 🕑 10am-6pm Mon-Sat; subway Thailand Cultural Centre) Major centre for experimental art, culture and conversation.

per dome. In the centre of the main shrine is Jao Mae Maha Umathewi (Uma Devi, also known as Shakti, Shiva's consort); her son Phra Khanthakuman (Subramaniam) is on the right; on the left is her other son, elephant-headed Phra Phikkhanet (Ganesh). Along the left interior wall sit rows of Shiva, Vishnu and other Hindu deities, as well as a few Buddhas, so that just about any non-Muslim, non-Judaeo-Christian Asian can worship here – Thai and Chinese devotees come to pray and offer bright-yellow marigold garlands alongside the Indian residents.

Thais call this temple Wat Khaek – *khàek* is a colloquial expression for people of Indian descent. The literal translation is 'guest', an obvious euphemism for a group of people you don't particularly want as permanent residents; hence most Indians living permanently in Thailand don't appreciate the term.

LUMPHINI PARK
สวนลุมพินี
Named after the Buddha's place of birth in Nepal, **Lumphini Park** (Map p127; Th Phra Ram IV, btwn Th Withayu & Th Ratchadamri; admission free; ☽ 5am-8pm; bus 13, 505, Skytrain Sala Daeng, subway Lumphini) is the best way to escape Bangkok without leaving town. Shady paths, a large artificial lake and swept lawns temporarily blot out the roaring traffic and hulking concrete towers.

One of the best times to visit the park is before 7am when the air is fresh (well, relatively so for Bangkok) and legions of Thai-Chinese are practising *taijiquan* (t'ai chi). Also in the

morning, vendors set up tables to dispense fresh snake blood and bile, considered health tonics. The park reawakens with the evening's cooler temperatures – aerobics classes collectively sweat to a techno soundtrack.

SNAKE FARM
สถานเสาวภา
Snake farms tend to gravitate towards carnivalesque rather than humanitarian, except at **Queen Saovabha Memorial Institute** (Map pp124-5; ☎ 0 2252 0161; cnr Th Phra Ram IV & Th Henri Dunant; admission 70B; ☽ 8.30am-4.30pm Mon-Fri, 8.30am-noon Sat & Sun; Skytrain Sala Daeng, subway Samyan & Silom). Founded in 1923, the snake farm prepares antivenin from venomous snakes – common cobra, king cobra, banded krait, Malayan pit viper, green pit viper and Russell's viper. This facility was only the second of its kind in the world (the first was in Brazil).

Tourists are welcome to view the **milkings** (11am & 2.30pm Mon-Fri, 11am Sat & Sun) or to stroll the small garden where the snakes are kept in escape-proof cages. The snakes tend to be camera-shy during nonperformance times.

M R KUKRIT PRAMOJ HOUSE
บ้านหม่อมราชวงศ์คึกฤทธิ์ปราโมช
Author and statesman Mom Ratchawong Kukrit Pramoj once resided in this charming Thai house now open to the public as a **museum** (Map pp124-5; ☎ 0 2286 8185; Soi 7/Phra Phinij, Th Narathiwat Rachananakharin; admission 50B; ☽ 10am-5pm Sat & Sun; Skytrain Chong Nonsi). European-educated but devoutly Thai, M R Kukrit surrounded

himself with the best of both worlds: five traditional teak buildings, Thai art, Western books and lots of heady conversations. A guided tour is recommended for a more intimate introduction to the former resident, who authored more than 150 books and served as prime minister of Thailand.

Sukhumvit
สุขุมวิท

Executive-strength expat neighbourhoods branch off this marathon-running street. More time will be spent here eating, drinking and perhaps sleeping (as there is a high concentration of hotels here) than sightseeing. The Skytrain is the primary public-transport option.

BAN KAMTHIENG
บ้านคำเที่ยง

An engaging **house museum** (Map pp122-3; ☎ 0 2661 6470; Siam Society, 131 Soi Asoke/Asoke, Th Sukhumvit; adult/child 100/50B; ☒ 9am-5pm Mon-Sat; Skytrain Asoke), Ban Kamthieng transports visitors to a northern Thai village complete with informative displays of daily rituals, folk beliefs and everyday household chores, all within the setting of a traditional wooden house. This museum is operated by and shares space with the Siam Society, the publisher of the renowned *Journal*

of the Siam Society and a valiant preserver of traditional Thai culture. A reference library is open to visitors and contains titles on anything you'd want to know about Thailand (outside the political sphere, since the society is sponsored by the royal family).

THAILAND CREATIVE & DESIGN CENTER

Modern design is all the rage in Bangkok and this new **museum** (Map pp122-3; ☎ 0 2664 8448; www .tcdc.or.th; 6th fl, Emporium Shopping Center, Th Sukhumvit; free admission; ☒ 10.30am-10pm Tue-Sun; Skytrain Phrom Phong) invites retrospectives of international designers to educate burgeoning Thai creatives. Rotating exhibits have included costume displays by former punk-queen Vivienne Westwood and profiles of regional handicrafts.

Greater Bangkok
WANG SUAN PHAKKAT
วังสวนผักกาด

An overlooked treasure, **Lettuce Farm Palace** (Map pp116-17; ☎ 0 2245 4934; Th Sri Ayuthaya, near Th Ratchaprarop; admission 100B; ☒ 9am-4pm; Skytrain Phayathai, bus 63, 504) is a collection of five traditional wooden Thai houses that was once the residence of Princess Chumbon of Nakhon Sawan and before that a lettuce farm – hence the name. Within the stilt buildings

---

BANGKOK'S ISLAND GETAWAY

Soothe your nerves with a half-day getaway to **Ko Kret**, a car-free island in the middle of Mae Nam Chao Phraya, at Bangkok's northern edge. It is home to one of Thailand's oldest settlements of Mon people, who were the dominant culture in central Thailand between the 6th and 10th centuries AD. The Mon are also skilled potters, and Ko Kret continues the culture's ancient tradition of hand-thrown earthenware, made from local Ko Kret clay. Along the narrow footpaths that circumnavigate the island are small pottery shops behind which the potters work with relaxed precision in open-air studios.

Beside the long-tail boat pier, a Mon Buddhist temple called **Wat Paramai Yikawat**, also known simply as 'Wat Mon', contains a Mon-style marble Buddha. A leisurely stroll around the island provides a fascinating contrast to the Big Mango's streetlife – Ko Kret's rush hour may consist of two motorcycles, and the counterparts to those fierce soi dogs are now lazy creatures too content to scratch themselves. That is, if you visit during the week. On weekdays Ko Kret is a popular Thai outing with lots of food vendors, tacky souvenir stalls and even traditional dance performances.

Current transport options from Bangkok include hiring a long-tail boat from the Tha Nonthaburi (accessible via Chao Phraya Express boat heading north). You can also take bus 33 from Sanam Luang to Pak Kret and board the cross-river ferry to Ko Kret.

Alternatively, you can join one of the long-tail tours that depart from Tha Nonthaburi (100B per person; three hours); these outings spend 1½ hours on the island and the remaining time visiting nearby dessert-making shops. The Sunday tours operated by **Chao Phraya Express** (☎ 0 2623 6001; fax 0 2225 3002; adult/child 500/250B; ☒ 9am-3.30pm) depart from Tha Maharat.

are displays of art, antiques and furnishings, and the landscaped grounds are a peaceful oasis complete with ducks, swans and a semi-enclosed garden.

The diminutive **Lacquer Pavilion**, at the back of the complex, dates from the Ayuthaya period and features gold-leaf *jataka* and *Ramayana* murals, as well as scenes from daily Ayuthaya life. The building originally sat in a monastery compound on Mae Nam Chao Phraya, just south of Ayuthaya. Larger residential structures at the front of the complex contain displays of Khmer-style Hindu and Buddhist art, Ban Chiang ceramics and a very interesting collection of historic Buddhas, including a beautiful late U Thong–style image.

WAT CHONG NONSI
วัดช่องนนทรีย์
Close to the Bangkok side of the river, this **temple** (Map pp114–15; Th Nonsi, off Th Phra Ram III; 8.30am-6pm) contains some notable *jataka* murals painted between 1657 and 1707. It is the only surviving Ayuthaya-era temple in which both the murals and architecture are of the same period with no renovations. As a single, 'pure' architectural and painting unit, it's considered quite important for the study of late Ayuthaya art.

ACTIVITIES
Traditional Massage
Bangkokians regard traditional massage as a vital part of preventative health care and they frequent massage parlours more regularly than gyms. You'll have no trouble finding a massage shop (rather, they'll find you), but after a few visits to the backpacker hangars, you may want a more focused, professional experience. A good sign is a small shop off the main path, but don't be deterred by a petite masseuse – many of them have vice-grip strength.

Depending on the neighbourhood, prices for massages tend to stay fixed: about 250B for a foot massage and 500B for a full body massage.

The primary training ground for the masseuses who are deployed across the country is **Wat Pho Thai Massage School** (Map p130; 0 2221 3686; Soi Penphat, Th Sanamchai; 8am-5pm; bus 12, 53, 503, 508, 512, Chao Phraya Express Tha Tien); there are also massage pavilions inside the temple complex.

Don't worry that **Marble House** (Map pp122-3; 0 2651 0905, 3rd fl, Ruamchit Plaza, 199 Th Sukhumvit at Soi 15; 10am-midnight) is in the middle of the sleazy Sukhumvit girlie scene. The work of its traditional masseurs doesn't reflect the neighbouring 'friendly' services.

Other tried-and-true practitioners can be found at **Buathip Thai Massage** (Map pp122-3; 0 2251 2627; 4/13 Soi 5, Th Sukhumvit; 10am-midnight; Skytrain Nana), which is on a small sub-*soi* behind the Amari Boulevard Hotel.

Skills Development Centre for the Blind (suun pháthánaa sàmàtthàphâap khon taa bàwt; 0 2583 7327; Pak Kret, north of central Bangkok) is a government outreach programme that trains the blind in Thai massage, creating what many people consider to be expert masseuses because of their sensitive sense of touch. While a massage might be memorable, getting here is the primary adventure. Take bus 33 from Sanam Luang to Pak Kret and hire a motorcycle taxi from there. You'll need a little Thai to pull this off, but Pak Kret villagers are pretty easy-going and willing to listen to foreigners massacre their language.

Spas
Bangkok isn't the prettiest city in the world, but its residents outshine the architectural shortcomings. Keeping up with these flawless beauties means your humidified look is going to need professional assistance. To undo the stresses of Bangkok pollution or just to treat yourself like royalty, consider a spa splurge complete with body rubs, floral baths and age-defying treatments. For true luxe, the spas in the Oriental Hotel and the Shangri-La are the city's reigning retreats, but for more local tastes, try out these options:

Offering international beauty and well-being therapies, **Divana Spa** (Map pp122-3; 0 2261 6784; www.divanaspa.com; 7 Soi 25, Th Sukhumvit; spa package from 2500B; Skytrain Asoke) retains a unique Thai touch with a private and soothing setting in a garden house.

More down-to-earth than your average Bangkok spa, **Health Land** (Map pp124-5; 0 2637 8883; 120 Th Sathon Neua; spa treatments from 750B; Skytrain Chong Nonsi) started its career as an all-purpose health centre selling organic vegetables, promoting meditation and providing basic massage treatments. Now the winning formula of affordable prices and expert treatments has created a small empire of Health Land centres throughout the city.

BANGKOK

Need to lose weight, erase wrinkle lines, clear-up persistent acne, or flush out the lymphatic system? Then head to **S Medical Spa** (Map pp128-9; ☎ 0 2253 1010; www.smedspa.com; Th Withayu; treatments from 1000B; Skytrain Ploenchit), part of the new generation of Bangkok spas merging alternative medicine with relaxation techniques and cosmetic surgery. The centre has a textbook menu of possible treatments from acupuncture, hydrotherapy, nutritional counselling, face lifts and exercise programmes.

River & Canal Trips

Glimpses of Bangkok's past as the 'Venice of the East' are still evident today, even though the motor vehicle has long since become the city's conveyance of choice. Along the river and the canals is a motley fleet of watercraft, from paddled canoes to rice barges. In these areas many homes, trading houses and temples remain oriented towards life on the water and provide a fascinating glimpse into the past, when Thais still considered themselves *jâo náam* (water lords).

An exploration of the Mae Nam Chao Phraya is a journey through Thailand's watery artery. Hulking barges transport sand to points upriver, or long-tail boats ricochet from one bank to another, kicking up the muddy water into a boil. At each pier, the boat hands plead to the crowd to keep a 'cool heart' *(jai yen)* and allow the gap between dock and boat to close before disembarking or boarding.

The best way to commute between riverside attractions is the **Chao Phraya Express** (Map p183; ☎ 0 2623 6001; tickets 10-27B). The terminus for most northbound boats is Tha Nonthaburi and for most southbound boats is Tha Sathon (also called Central Pier), near the Saphan Taksin Skytrain station, although some boats run as far south as Wat Ratchasingkhon. See p182 for more information about boat travel.

Across the river in Thonburi are several functional canals, including **Khlong Bangkok Noi** and **Khlong Bangkok Yai**, both of which offer lovely leafy scenery.

Along Khlong Bangkok Noi, **Wat Suwannaram** (Map pp114-15; ☎ 0 2434 7790; 33 Soi 32, Th Charoen Sanitwong, Khlong Bangkok Noi; 5am-9pm) contains 19th-century *jataka* murals painted by two of early Bangkok's foremost religious muralists. Art historians consider these the best surviving temple paintings in Bangkok.

Along Khlong Bangkok Yai, Wat Intharam is the home to a stupa that contains the ashes of King Taksin, the Thai general who re-established order in the kingdom after the fall of Ayuthaya. He was assassinated in 1782. Fine gold-and-black lacquerwork adorning the main *bòt* doors depicts the mythical *naari-iphon* tree, which bears fruits that are shaped like beautiful maidens.

Khlong Mon, between Bangkok Noi and Bangkok Yai, offers more typical canal scenery, including orchid farms.

Mit Chao Paya (Tha Chang) arranges long-tail boat tours along the river to sights such as the Royal Barges National Museum, Wat Arun and into the Thonburi canals. It usually costs 700B for the entire boat for one hour, excluding admission and various mooring fees. There are other similar services at every boat pier and most operators have set tour routes, but if you have a specific destination in mind you can request it. Some operators quote rates for chartering the boat and others per person.

Sports Facilities

If you're dedicated to the cause of athletics in this energy-sucking climate, you need access to an air-conditioned facility. Most membership gyms and top-end hotels have fitness centres and swimming pools. Some hotels offer day-use fees but these policies vary per establishment.

British Club (Map pp124-5; ☎ 0 2234 0247; www .britishclubbangkok.org; 189 Th Surawong; fitness centre 6am-10pm Mon-Fri, 6am-9pm Sat & Sun) maintains a membership gym open to citizens of Australia, Canada, New Zealand and the UK, or to other nationalities through a waiting

---

RIVER SURGERY

Mae Nam Chao Phraya experiences a diurnal tide that is felt as far as 180km upriver, a phenomenon that enabled ocean-going sailing ships to trade with Ayuthaya. One tricky bend in the river, from the present-day sights of Wat Arun to Thammasat University, required the digging of a shortcut to aid nonmotorised vessels. The original course of the river has been demoted to Khlong Bangkok Noi, which is not a canal at all.

list. Among the sports facilities are a pool, golf driving range, and squash and tennis courts.

Clark Hatch Physical Fitness Centers (www .clarkhatchthailand.com) is a top-class operation with more than 14 locations throughout the city. All branches have weight machines, aerobics classes, pool, sauna and massage.

Other commercial gyms include **California Wow** (www.californiawowx.com; 13 branches) and **Fitness First** (www.fitnessfirst.co.th; 7 branches).

These days Bangkok has every imaginable fitness trend: Pilates, kickboxing and even salsa dancing. Most exercise options are centred around the business district on Th Ploenchit or Th Sukhumvit, but there are also studios directly on Th Khao San.

Yoga Elements Studio (Map pp128-9; ☎ 0 2655 5671; www.yogaelements.com; 23rd fl, 29 Vanissa Bldg, Soi Chitlom; Skytrain Chitlom) teaches classes in Vinyasa and Ashtanga and offers attractive introductory rates.

Absolute Yoga (Map pp128-9; ☎ 0 2252 4400; www .absoluteyogabangkok.com; 4th fl, Amarin Plaza, Th Ploenchit; Skytrain Chitlom) offers yoga for the gym rat, not the spiritualist, with classes in hot yoga, Pilates and Vinyasa.

One of Bangkok's longest-running sports groups is the **Hash House Harriers** (www.bangkokhhh .com), who pride themselves both on their dedication to running and their ability to subdue dehydration with massive amounts of beer. If you've got commitment issues with either pursuit, start with a simple jog at a local park, like Lumphini or Sanam Luang. Every imaginable hometown sport – be it softball, football, rugby or biking – attracts a loyal group of expat participants. Most clubs have websites with more information.

WALKING TOUR
Ko Ratanakosin

On this action-packed walking tour, you can efficiently tick off Bangkok's 'must-sees' in just one morning. The city's highlights reside in compact Ko Ratanakosin, the former royal district filled with gleaming temples and bustling markets. It is best to start early to beat the heat and before the hordes have descended. Remember to dress modestly (long pants and skirts, shirts with sleeves and close-toed shoes) in order to gain entry to the temples. Also ignore any strangers who approach you offering advice on sightseeing or shopping.

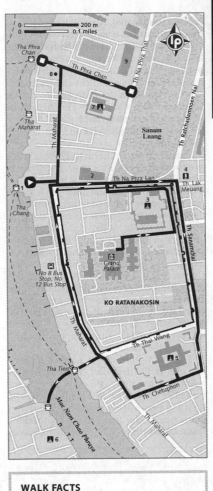

WALK FACTS

Start Tha Chang
Finish Thammasat University
Distance 2.1km
Duration 1–2 hours
Fuel Stop Food stall off Th Maharat

Start at **Tha Chang (1)** and follow Th Na Phra Lan east with a quick diversion to **Silpakorn University** (**2**; Th Na Phra Lan), Thailand's premier fine-arts university. Originally founded as the School of Fine Arts by Italian artist Corrado Feroci, the university campus includes part of an old palace built for Rama I. Continue east to the third gate into the **Wat Phra Kaew &**

BANGKOK

Grand Palace (3; p108), two of Bangkok's most famous attractions.

Cross Th Sanamchai to the home of Bangkok's city spirit, **Lak Meuang** (4; p110), which is generally alive with the spectacle of devotion – including burning joss sticks and traditional dancing. Go south down Th Sanamchai for 500m and turn right onto Th Chetuphon, where you'll enter **Wat Pho** (5; p108), home of the giant reclining Buddha and lots of quiet nooks and crannies.

Take Th Mahathat north to Th Thai Wang and turn left to catch the cross-river ferry to Khmer-influenced **Wat Arun** (6; p110).

Return to Bangkok and head up Th Maharat and stop for a spot of lunch from one of the food stalls or air-con restaurants along the way. North of Th Na Phra Lan, Th Maharat becomes an informal healing centre of herbal apothecaries and sidewalk amulet sellers, catering to the health of one's body and spirit. On your right is **Wat Mahathat** (7; p109), one of Thailand's respected Buddhist universities. Take a left into the narrow alley immediately after Trok Mahathat to discover the cramped **amulet market** (8; p109). Follow the alley all the way towards the river to appreciate how extensive the amulet trade is.

If you've worked up yet another appetite, hop over to the next alley, Trok Nakhon, to a dim alternate world of food vendors; some even offer a river view. The graduation-gown stalls and swarm of white-and-black uniforms is an obvious clue that you are approaching **Thammasat University** (9; Th Phra Chan), known

for its law and political-science departments. The campus was also the site of the bloody October 1976 prodemocracy demonstrations, when hundreds of Thai students were killed or wounded by the military.

If you've made it this far, feel free to call it a day; hang a left on Th Phra Chan towards Sanam Luang to return home by bus. Alternatively you could take a cross-river ferry from Tha Phra Chan to Tha Wang Lang, where you can pick up Chao Phraya express boats in either direction.

Chinatown

Busy and chaotic, Chinatown is the walking-tour version of an obstacle course: you'll be dodging street vendors, traffic and other shoppers.

Start at **Tha Ratchawong (1)**. Walk along Th Ratchawong to **Sampeng Lane (2**; p134); you won't see a street sign here, but you'll know it by the queue of people slowly shuffling into the alley. You have now entered the shopping fun house, where the sky is completely obscured and bargains lie in wholesale ambush – 500 Hello Kitty pens, a tonne of stuffed ani-

---

WALK FACTS

Start Tha Ratchawong
Finish Th Charoen Krung
Distance 1.5km
Duration 1 hour
Fuel Stop Hong Kong Noodles

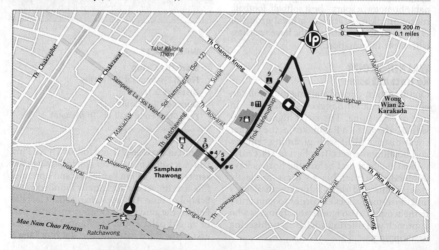

mals and books of stickers. Sampeng was originally a trading centre built in 1782 near the river for goods bound for the international markets.

After about 100m, Sampeng Lane crosses Th Mangkon. On either side of the intersection are two of Bangkok's oldest commercial buildings, a **Bangkok Bank (3)** and the venerable **Tang To Kang (4)** gold shop, which are both more than 100 years old and are classic examples of early Ratanakosin architecture.

Continue walking another 60m or so to **Trok Itsaranuphap (5)**, where you'll take a left on to a wider lane past rows of vendors selling huge bags of fried pork skins, dried fish and other delicacies. Down the lane on your right is **Talat Kao (6)**, Chinatown's two-centuries-old market. The real action runs from 4am to 11am, any later and you'll only find slick sidewalks and piles of rubbish.

From Trok Itsaranuphap, continue to Th Yaowarat, Chinatown's main thoroughfare, lined with gold shops. Cross the road to **Talat Leng-Buai-la (7)**, the new market where you'll find all manner and size of freshwater and saltwater fish and shellfish, alive or filleted – or, as is sometimes the case, half alive and half filleted. If uncooked food makes the belly grumble, stop in at **Hong Kong Noodles (8**; p161), on the left side of the alley.

Cross the next major intersection, Th Charoen Krung, and turn left. Continue for 20m to **Wat Mangkon Kamalawat (9**; Leng Noi Yee), one of Chinatown's largest and liveliest temples. Along this stretch of Th Charoen Krung, shops sell fruit, cakes, incense and ritual burning paper for offering at the temple. Work your way back to Trok Itsaranuphap and continue past funerary stalls to the termination of the *soi* at Th Yommarat Sukhum. Turn right on to Th Phla Phla Chai and follow the bend in the road to return to Th Charoen Krung. About midblock, this tour ends fittingly beside a coffin shop.

COURSES

Culture and cooking courses dominate Bangkok's continuing education syllabus.

Cooking

One of the best ways to crack Thailand's lengthy menu is to take a cooking course. Bangkok has several different types of programmes aimed at backpackers, expat housewives or wannabe master chefs.

Blue Elephant Thai Cooking School (Map pp124-5; ☎ 0 2673 9353; www.blueelephant.com; Thai Chine Bldg, 233 Th Sathon Tai; class 3300B; Skytrain Surasak) is considered the most gourmet of the cooking schools. The half-day sessions introduce students to Thai cooking techniques and ingredients. The morning session includes a trip to the market.

Oriental Hotel Cooking School (Map pp124-5; ☎ 0 2659 9000; Oriental Hotel, Soi 38/ Oriental, Th Charoen Krung; course US$120) features cooking demonstrations, lectures and hands-on work under the direction of well-known chefs. The intimate setting in a traditional Thai-style house adds to the charm, but to get your money's worth pick a menu that covers more complex dishes than basic *phàt thai*.

Thai House (Map pp114-5; ☎ 0 2903 9611; www .thaihouse.co.th; Bang Yai, Nonthaburi; class 3500B) is held in a homey teak house about 40 minutes north of Bangkok by boat. You can choose between one- to three-day programmes, which include preparing Thai standards (*tôm yam*, *phàt thai* and various curries). There are also cooking and lodging packages available. There are public boats that run from Tha Chang to Bang Yai but their schedule is pegged to commuter hours and is not always reliable.

May Kaidee (Map pp120-1; ☎ 0 9137 3173; Soi Damnoen Klang; class 1000B) is Khao San's favourite vegetarian restaurant and also offers cooking courses. There are two half-day sessions that include a visit to the market and preparation of a whopping 10 dishes. The menu differs between the morning and afternoon classes.

Silom Thai Cooking School (Map pp124-5; ☎ 0 4726 5669; 31/11 Soi 13, Th Silom; class 1000B), run out of a private home, is an introduction to both homecooking and ordinary Thai life. The setting is rustic (and not entirely hygienic) but it is completely hands-on: you'll sit cross-legged on the floor to chop shallots, pound chillies into paste and fry it all up in the pan. Includes a market tour and five dishes.

Meditation

Although at times Bangkok may seem like the most un-Buddhist place on earth, there are several places where foreigners can practise Theravada Buddhist meditation.

Wat Mahathat (Map p130; ☎ 0 2222 6011; 3 Th Maharat; ⏰ 9am-5pm; bus 47, 53, 503, 508, 512, river ferry Tha Phra Chan or Tha Maharat) provides three daily meditation sessions (7am, 1pm and 6pm) based on the Mahasi Sayadaw system of developing the

satipatthana (foundations of mindfulness). Accommodation for long-term meditation is also available; just stop by and fill out an application. Phra Suphe, the monk who runs the centre, speaks flawless English, and there are often Western monks or long-term residents available to interpret. Within the temple complex is the International Buddhist Meditation Centre, which hosts twice-monthly lectures on various aspects of Buddhism.

Wat Pak Nam (Map pp114-15; ☎ 0 2467 0811; Th Thoet Thai, Phasi Charoen, Thonburi; bus 103, 504, 509), where hundreds of monks and nuns reside during *phansǎa* (Buddhist Lent), has hosted many foreigners over the years. Meditation classes are held twice a day (8.30am and 6pm). The teacher usually speaks some English and there are often people around who can interpret. The emphasis is on developing concentration through *nimitta* (acquired mental images) in order to attain *jhana* (state of 'absorption'). If interested in residing at the temple, you can talk to the head monk or nun for permission. The wat can also be reached by chartered long-tail boat.

Baan Dvara Prateep (☎ 0 1845 5445; www.baandvara prateep.com; 53/3 Mu 5, Ko Kret) is a perfect solution for the moderately mindful. This meditation and cultural retreat is more relaxed than the strict temple environment and is often used as a meeting centre for corporate team-building. Meditation classes focus on relieving stress and achieving peace, and culture classes connect visitors to Thai handicrafts.

House of Dhamma (Map pp114-15; ☎ 0 2511 0439; www.houseofdhamma.com; 26/9 Soi 15, Th Lat Prao; Skytrain Mo Chit) is a meditation centre in the northern suburbs of Bangkok. The centre hosts monthly introduction courses to vipassana meditation as well as weekend retreats in co-operation with the Young Buddhists Association of Thailand.

For more information about meditation centres or teachers with English skills in Bangkok and beyond, contact the **World Fellowship of Buddhists** (WFB; Map pp122-3; ☎ 0 2661 1284; www .wfb-hq.org; Soi 24, Th Sukhumvit, beside Benjasiri Park), which sells a guide to mediation centres and hosts meditation classes on the first Sunday of every month. Also visit the online guide to Thai meditation centres at www.dhammathai. org for details such as instructions on applications, size of monastery and proficiency of English (of the monks and meditation instructors).

For background information on Buddhism, see p58; for temple etiquette, see p42.

Muay Thai

Training in *muay thai* (Thai boxing) for foreigners has increased in popularity in the past five years and many camps all over the country are tailoring their programmes for English-speaking fighters. The following camps provide instruction in English and accept men and women. Food and accommodation are usually provided at *muay thai* camps for an extra charge. The website www .muaythai.com contains loads of information on training camps.

Fairtex Muay Thai (☎ 0 2757 5147; www.fairtexbkk .com; 99/5 Mu 3, Soi Buthamanuson, Th Thaeparak, Bangpli, Samut Prakan; tuition per day 400B) is a popular, long-running camp south of Bangkok.

Jitti's Gym Thai Boxing & Homestay (Sor Vorapin; Map pp120-1; ☎ 0 2282 3551; 13 Soi Krasab, Th Chakraphong; tuition per day/month 400/8000B) specialises in training foreign students of both genders; the gym is sweating distance from Th Khao San.

Muay Thai Institute (Map p187; ☎ 0 2992 0096; www .muaythai-institute.net; Rangsit Muay Thai Stadium, 336/932 Th Prachatipat, Pathum Thani; tuition for 1st level 6400B) is associated with the respected World Muay Thai Council. The institute offers a fundamental course (consisting of three levels of expertise), which can be completed in 120 days, as well as courses for instructors, referees and judges. If you're interested, make an appointment to visit the facility, which is north of Bangkok International Airport, and watch the teachers and students at work.

Thai Language & Culture
American University Alumni Language Centre (AUA; Map pp128-9; ☎ 0 2252 8170; www.auathai.com; 179 Th Ratchadamri; tuition per hr 102B; Skytrain Ratchadamri) is run by the American University Alumni and is one of the largest English-language teaching institutes in the world. There are 10 levels consisting of 200 hours worth of class time that can be completed within a sliding timescale. The teaching method is based on the natural language acquisition of children, first focusing on listening and comprehension and then advancing to speaking and reading.

Chulalongkorn University's Intensive Thai Office (Map pp128-9; ☎ 0 2218 4640; www.inter.chula.ac.th; Faculty of Arts, Chulalongkorn University, Th Phayathai; Skytrain Siam) offers three different levels (basic, intermediate and advanced) of Thai-language

coursework with each level lasting five weeks (100 hours of study). At the intermediate level, the classes focus on specialised vocabulary, such as environment, tourism, culture, religion, economics and news reading. The programme is best suited for academics or business professionals. Contact the department for tuition, enrolment and accommodation queries.

Chulalongkorn's Thai Studies Center (Map p128-9; ☎ 0 2218 4862; www.inter.chula.ac.th; Faculty of Arts, Chulalongkorn University, Th Phayathai; Skytrain Siam) offers MA and PhD degrees in Thai studies, an English-language programme that covers aspects of Thai culture, including folklore, theatre, ecology and urbanisation. The PhD programme includes additional years of supervised doctoral research. Depending on class availability, the centre also accepts students who are not enrolled in the full MA programme. Contact the department for tuition, enrolment and accommodation queries.

Siri Pattana Thai Language School (Map p127; ☎ 0 2677 3150; siri_pattanathai@hotmail.com; Bangkok Insurance Bldg, 13 Th Sathon Tai; tuition from 7500B), located in front of the YWCA building, offers Thai-language courses that cover 30 hours broken into one- or two-hour classes per day, as well as preparation for the *paw hòk* (teaching proficiency exam).

Pro Language (Map pp122-3; ☎ 0 2250 0072; www .prolanguage.co.th; 10th fl, Times Square Bldg, Th Sukhumvit; Skytrain Nana) is a favourite of expat professionals. Pro Language starts with the basics and increases in difficulty to the advanced level, which involves studying examples of Thai literature. Classes are thematically designed: asking questions, giving opinions, business Thai, and the like.

Union Language School (Map pp128-9; ☎ 0 2214 6033; www.unionlanguage.com; 7th fl, 328 CCT Office Bldg, Th Phayathai; tuition from 6000B; Skytrain Ratchathewi) is generally recognised as having the best and most rigorous courses (many missionaries study here). Union employs a balance of structure- and communication-oriented methodologies in 80-hour, four-week modules.

Thai Massage

Wat Pho Thai Massage School (Map p130; ☎ 0 2221 3686; www.watpomassage.com; 392/25-28 Soi Phenphat 1, Th Maharat; tuition from 6500B; 8am-4pm; river ferry Tha Tien) offers basic and advanced courses in traditional massage; each course comprises 30 hours available in five- to 10-day increments.

There are two basic level courses: general massage and foot massage. The advanced level covers therapeutic and healing massage or oil and aromatherapy. Some knowledge of Thai will ease the communication barrier in all of these courses. The school is outside the temple compound in a restored Bangkok shophouse.

BANGKOK FOR CHILDREN

Want to ingratiate yourself into Thai culture? Bring your children along as passports. The family is so revered in Thailand that even the most aloof taxi driver will warm to a fat *faràng* baby. Blonde-headed children will get even more attention, and children of all ages will be showered with affection and treats.

Bangkok Doll Factory & Museum (Map pp116-17; ☎ 0 2245 3008; 85 Soi Ratchataphan/Mo Leng; admission free; 8am-5pm Mon-Sat) houses a colourful selection of traditional Thai dolls, both new and antique. This museum is really hard to find: approach via Th Si Ayuthaya heading east. Cross under the expressway past the intersection with Th Ratchaprarop and take the *soi* to the right of the post office. Follow this windy street until you start seeing signs.

Children's Discovery Museum (Map pp114-15; ☎ 0 2615 7333; Chatuchak Park, Th Kamphaeng Phet 4; adult/child 70/50B; 9am-5pm Tue-Fri, 10am-6pm Sat & Sun; Skytrain Mo Chit, subway Chatuchak Park) disguises learning as kid's play. Most activities are geared to early elementary–aged children. There is also a toddler-aged playground at the back of the main building. Opposite Chatuchak Weekend Market

Dusit Zoo (Map pp116-17; ☎ 0 2281 2000; Th Phra Ram V, btwn Th Ratwithi & Th Sri Ayuthaya; adult/child 100/50B; 8am-5pm; bus 18, 510) covers 19 hectares with caged exhibits of more than 300 mammals, 200 reptiles and 800 birds, including relatively rare indigenous species such as banteng, gaur, serow and some rhinoceros. The facilities are a bit tired, but if nothing else, the zoo is a nice place to get away from the noise of the city and observe how Thai people amuse themselves – mainly by eating. There are shady grounds plus a lake in the centre with paddle boats for hire. There's also a small children's playground.

Siam Ocean World (Map pp128-9; ☎ 0 2687 2000; www.siamoceanworld.co.th; basement, Siam Paragon, Th Phra Ram I; adult/child 450/280B; 9am-10pm; Skytrain Siam) A massive underwater world has been re-created at this shopping-centre aquarium. Gaze into

BIZARRE BANGKOK

If you've joined the routine of the lotus-eaters and have stopped noticing the taxi-cab shrines, the groundskeepers sweeping the lawns, the children bathing in the filthy canals, or mangy soi dogs, then you need to wake up and smell the fish sauce. Or spend the day experiencing Bangkok's freakier side.

Horse Races

Bangkok's bluebloods and accomplished nouveau riche enjoy the status, privilege and…oh yeah, sports facilities at the exclusive **Royal Bangkok Sports Club** (RBSC; Map pp128-9; ☎ 0 2251 0181-86; btwn Th Henri Dunant & Th Ratchadamri; bus 16 & 21). Commoners can gain a glimpse of greener pastures during public horse-racing events held twice a month.

Kàthoey Cabaret

Thailand's third gender (*kàthoey*; lady boys) pushes gender-bending well into gender-illusion, in turn fooling many unsuspecting foreign visitors. While night stalkers will no doubt encounter lady-boys at go-go bars, the more straight-laced visitor can witness the magic of sequinned costumes, big hair and natural hour-glass figures at the city's *kàthoey* cabarets. **Calypso Cabaret** (Map pp128-9; ☎ 0 2653 3960; www.calypsocabaret.com; Asia Hotel, 296 Th Phayathai; tickets 1000B; ☺ showtimes 8.15pm & 9.45pm) and **Mambo Cabaret** (Map pp122-3; ☎ 0 2259 5128; Washington Theatre, Th Sukhumvit, btwn Soi 22 & 24; tickets 800B; ☺ showtimes 8.30pm & 10pm) host choreographed stage shows featuring Broadway high kicks and lip-synched pop tunes.

Lingam Shrine at Nai Lert Park

Clusters of carved stone and wooden phalli surround a spirit house and **shrine** (Saan Jao Mae Thap Thim; Map pp128-9; Nai Lert Park Hotel, Th Withayu; Skytrain Ploenchit, khlong taxi Tha Withayu) built by millionaire businessman Nai Lert to honour Jao Mae Thap Thim, a female deity thought to reside in the old banyan tree on the site. Someone who made an offering shortly thereafter had a baby, and the shrine has received a steady stream of worshippers – mostly young women seeking fertility – ever since. To get here if facing the entrance of the Raffles hotel follow the small concrete pathway to the right which winds down into the bowels of the building beside the car park. The shrine will be at the end of the building next to the *khlong*.

Songkran Niyosane Forensic Medicine Museum

Holy gun-shot wound, Batman! This grisly **museum** (Map p130; ☎ 0 2419 7000; 2nd fl, Forensic Pathology Bldg, Siriraj Hospital, Th Phrannok, Thonburi; admission 40B; ☺ 8.30am-4.30pm Mon-Fri; river ferry Tha Rot Fai) will efficiently separate the aspiring doctors from the reluctant patients. One of seven medical museums on the hospital premises, this one's claim to fame is the leathery cadaver of Si Ouey, an infamous Thai serial killer, and other appendages and remnants of famous murders, including the bloodied T-shirt from a victim who was stabbed to death with a dildo.

From Tha Rot Fai, follow the road to the second entrance into the Siriraj Hospital campus. The museum building will be on your left.

the glass-enclosed deep reef zone or view the daily feedings of penguins and sharks.

Lumphini Park (Map p127; Th Phra Ram IV, btwn Th Withayu & Th Ratchadamri; admission free; ☺ 5am-8pm; bus 13, 505, Skytrain Sala Daeng, subway Lumphini) is a trusty ally in the cool hours of the morning and evening for kite-flying (in season) as well as stretching of the legs and lungs. View lethal snakes become reluctant altruists at the anti-venin-producing **Snake Farm** (p137).

Join the novice monks and other children as they sprinkle tiny pellets of fish food (which are sold on the pier) into the river at **Tha Thewet** (Map pp116-17; Th Samsen; ☺ 7am-7pm), transforming the muddy river into a brisk boil of flapping bodies.

Near the old Portuguese quarter in Thonburi, **Wat Prayoon** (Map pp118-19; 24 Th Prachadhipok cnr Thetsaban Soi 1; admission free; ☺ 8am-6pm; cross-river ferry from Tha Pak Talaad/Atsadang) is an ar-

tificial hill cluttered with miniature shrines and a winding path encircling a turtle pond. Vendors sell cut fruit for feeding to the resident turtles. It's near Memorial Bridge.

MBK (p174) and Siam Paragon (p175) both have bowling alleys to keep the older ones occupied. **Krung Sri IMAX** (Map pp128-9; ☎ 0 2511 5555; Siam Paragon, Th Phra Ram I; admission adult/child 600/250B) screens special-effects versions of Hollywood action flicks and nature features.

TOURS
Dinner Cruises
Perfect for romancing couples or subdued families, dinner cruises swim along the Mae Nam Chao Phraya basking in the twinkling city lights at night, far away from the heat and noise of town. Cruises range from downhome to sophisticated and several even sail underneath Saphan Phra Ram IX, the longest single-span cable-suspension bridge in the world. The food, of course, runs a distant second to the ambiance.

Yok Yor Marina & Restaurant (Map pp116-17; ☎ 0 2863 0565; www.yokyor.co.th; 885 Soi Somdet Chao Phraya 17, Thonburi; adult/child 120/60B plus meal costs; ☒ 8-10pm) is a favourite among Thai friends celebrating birthdays with rousing renditions of 'Happy Bert-day'.

Wan Fah Cruises (Map pp118-19; ☎ 0 2639 0704; River City Shopping Complex; dinner cruise 680-780B; ☒ 7-9pm) runs a buxom wooden boat that floats in style with accompanying Thai music and traditional dance. Dinner options include a standard or seafood set menu.

Manohra Cruises (Map pp114-15; ☎ 0 2476 0022; www.manohracruises.com; Bangkok Marriott Resort & Spa, Thonburi; cocktail/dinner cruise 500/1700B; ☒ 6-7pm & 7.30-10pm) commands a fleet of converted teak rice barges that part the waters with regal flair. Boats depart from the Marriott Resort, accessible via a free river shuttle that operates between Tha Sathon (near Saphan Taksin Skytrain station).

Bang Pa-In & Ayuthaya Cruises
A little faster than the days of sailing ships, river cruises from Bangkok north to the ruins of the former royal capital of Ayuthaya (p194) take in all the romance of the river. Most trips include a guided tour of Ayuthaya's ruins with a stop at the summer palace of Bang Pa-In (p202). To ruin-weary travellers, the river journey might broaden the historical centre's appeal. Normally only one leg of the

journey between Bangkok and Ayuthaya is aboard a boat, while the return or departing trip is by bus.

Asian Oasis (Map pp114-15; ☎ 0 2651 9101; www.mekhalacruise.com; Menam Riverside Hotel; 2-day trip US$289-$347 depending on season) sails the waters aboard a fleet of restored rice barges with old-world charm and modern conveniences. Trips include either an upstream or downstream journey to/from Ayuthaya with bus transfer in the opposite direction. Lodging and a candlelit dinner are provided on the boat. Offering food alms to the monks at Ayuthaya is an optional activity.

Manohra Cruises (Map pp114-15; ☎ 0 2477 0770; www.manohracruises.com; Bangkok Marriott Resort & Spa, Thonburi; 3-day trip US$1265) operates the *Mekhala 2*, the nautical equivalent of the *Eastern & Oriental Express* train. This is a restored teak rice barge decorated with antiques, Persian carpets and four luxury sleeping berths. The trip is a three-day, two-night excursion to Ayuthaya, and the package price is all-inclusive except for tax and service. In the evening the boat anchors at a temple, where a candlelit dinner is served. The next morning passengers offer food to the monks from the wat before the barge moves on to Bang Pa-In. Private charter is also available.

Bicycle & Segway Tours
Just beyond all of Bangkok's concrete is a lush, undeveloped district known as Phra Phradeang, where narrow walkways crisscross irrigation canals that feed small-scale fruit plantations and simple villages. Cycling is a great way to explore the area.

ABC Amazing Bangkok Cyclists (Map pp122-3; ☎ 0 2665 6364; www.realasia.net; 10/5-7 Soi 26, Th Sukhumvit; tours from 1000B; ☒ daily tours depart at 10am or 1pm) offers one of the longest-running two-wheeled adventures to this area. Seasoned cyclists start from crowded Th Sukhumvit stopping at Khlong Toey produce market and transferring to Phra Phradeang via long-tail boat.

Bangkok Bike Rides (Map pp122-3; ☎ 0 2712 5305; www.bangkokbikerides.com; 14/1-B Soi Phromsi 2, off Soi 39, Th Sukhumvit; tours from 2000B), a division of the tour company Spice Roads, also conducts bike tours to outlying agricultural areas, to Ko Kret and Damnoen Saduak floating market and beyond.

Not into tropical exertion? Then climb aboard a Segway, the nonmotorised scooter that any monkey, except George Bush, can ride without effort. **Thailand Segway Tours** (☎ 0 2255 8463;

BANGKOK

www.thailandsegwaytours.com; 90-min tours from 1900B) offers several tours through Bangkok's parks, and to the Ancient City in Samut Prakan (p186).

FESTIVALS & EVENTS

In addition to the national holidays, there's always something going on in Bangkok. Check the website of TAT (www.tourismthailand.org) or the **Bangkok Tourism Division** (www.bangkoktourist.com) for exact dates. The cultural centres also host various international festivals.

January

Bangkok International Film Festival (www.bangkok film.org) Home-grown talent and overseas indies arrive on the silver screens. If you haven't heard, Bangkok is fast becoming a Bollywood and Hong Kong movie hybrid. Held in mid-January.

February/March

Chinese New Year Thai-Chinese celebrate the lunar New Year with a week of housecleaning, lion dances and fireworks. Most festivities centre around Chinatown. Dates vary.

March

Kite-Flying Season During the windy season, colourful kites battle it out over the skies of Sanam Luang and Lumphini Park.

April

Songkran The celebration of the Thai New Year has morphed into a water war with high-powered water guns and water balloons being launched at suspecting and unsuspecting participants. The most intense water battles take place on Th Khao San. Held in mid-April.

May

Royal Ploughing Ceremony His Majesty the King commences rice-planting season with a ceremony at Sanam Luang. Dates vary.

Miss Jumbo Queen Contest (early May) With fat-trends creeping across the globe, Thailand hosts a beauty pageant for extra-large women (over 80kg) who display the grace of an elephant at Nakhon Pathom's Samphran Elephant Park.

June

International Festival of Music & Dance An extravaganza of arts and culture sponsored by the Thailand Cultural Centre. Held twice a year in June and September.

August

Queen's Birthday The queen's birthday is recognised as Mother's Day throughout the country. In Bangkok, festivities centre around Th Ratchadamnoen and the Grand Palace. Held on 12 August.

September/October

Vegetarian Festival A 10-day Chinese-Buddhist festival wheels out yellow-bannered streetside vendors serving meatless meals. The greatest concentration of vendors is found in Chinatown. Dates vary.

October/November

King Chulalongkorn Day Rama V is honoured on the anniversary of his death at the Royal Plaza in Dusit. Crowds of devotees come to make merit with incense and flower garlands. Held on 23 October.

November

Loi Kràthong A beautiful festival where, on the night of the full moon, small lotus-shaped boats made of banana leaf and containing a lit candle are set adrift on the Mae Nam Chao Phraya. Held in early November.

Fat Festival Sponsored by FAT 104.5FM radio, Bangkok's indie-est indie bands gather for an annual fest. Held in early November.

Bangkok Pride (www.utopia-asia.com) A week-long festival of parades, parties and awards is organised by the city's gay businesses and organisations. Held in mid-November.

December

King's Birthday Locals celebrate their monarch's birthday with lots of parades and fireworks. Held on 5 December.

SLEEPING

Accommodation in Bangkok ranges from the threadbare to ultraluxurious, and there are seemingly thousands of choices, true to the Thai commercial philosophy of 'more is better'. Because of the wide distribution of places and budget types, you might first narrow your choices by neighbourhood and then by budget range.

For close to two decades, Banglamphu and its tourist ghetto of Th Khao San have reigned as the most likely crashpad for a recent Bangkok arrival. Fast becoming a rival, Chinatown is less touristy and is stealing many of the independent-minded travellers from Banglamphu. Both neighbourhoods offer a variety of affordable options and are less urbanised than other areas, meaning that shophouses far outnumber skyscrapers. Ko Ratanakosin, the former royal district, is beginning to sprout a few beautiful boutique options, if you're looking for something romantic and unique.

WHAT TO EXPECT IN BANGKOK

We list high-season rack rates. For midrange and top-end hotels, search online booking agencies or individual hotel websites for promotional rates. Some of the top-end hotels quote rates in US dollars, a holdover from the Asian currency crisis.

- Budget (less than 700B) – Don't expect much in the low end of this price range. From 100B to 300B, you'll get a bed and four walls. You'll share a bathroom (no hot water), and a rickety fan will chase the hot air around the room. Once you step up to the 400B range, you should start to expect air-con, private bathroom with hot-water shower and walls thick enough to block out noise.

- Midrange (700B to 3999B) – The biggest mixed bag of all, the midrange level starts out with the high-quality guesthouses, then moves into a grey area of mediocrity. Above 1000B, the hotels have all the appearance of a hotel back home – a bellboy, uniformed desk clerks and a well-polished lobby – but without the predictability. Swimming pools and complimentary breakfasts are noted in the review. Some hotels also charge a 7% tax.

- Top end (more than 4000B) – These hotels will maintain international standards and have at least one pool either tropically landscaped or with city views, fitness and business centres, and sometimes a spa. Rooms typically have data ports, IDD international phones, international cable channels, minibar, safety-deposit boxes etc. New-trend boutique hotels have a lot of style, but rooms can be tiny. Rates usually include breakfast. Special perks are listed in the individual reviews. The hotels in this category will add a 10% service charge plus 7% tax to hotel bills.

The Siam Square area is centrally located between old and new Bangkok and is on both Skytrain lines. High-rise hotels and low-rise guesthouses offer the variety of budget choices within striking distance to shopping-centre nirvana.

Th Sukhumvit and Th Silom are major business areas with corporate hotel chains and package-tour specials. The Sukhumvit area tends to attract sex tourists visiting the nearby go-go bars.

The most famous hotels, however, are along the riverside near Th Silom. The river views are scenic and the experience is a comfortable and sanitised version of a country that can be a little rough on the edges.

Banglamphu

Banglamphu, the neighbourhood that includes the backpacker street of Th Khao San, is a well-padded landing zone for jet-lagged travellers. As a rule you can arrive anytime at night and find a place to crash. And services abound: you can't swing a túk-túk driver without hitting an internet shop, travel agent or beer stall.

If you're hanging out in the low end of the budget range, just show up and start hunting, as most cheapies don't take reservations. The cheapest options start at 180B (shared bath-

room); look for long-running guesthouses such as Lek, Chada House and Nat on Th Khao San, or other spots in the alleys behind Th Khao San or across Th Tanao.

More and more, the neighbourhood is gravitating towards the multistorey, upper-budget phenomenon with in-room décor (truly a revolution compared to the former flophouse aesthetic of dried projectile vomit) and comfort (air-con, sturdier beds, private bathrooms). New hotels are always opening up, accompanied by attractive promotional rates. Savvy travellers should shop on Th Khao San, Th Rambutri, Soi Rambutri and Th Kraisi.

Most of the year, it pays to visit several guesthouses before making a decision, but in the high season (December to February), take the first vacant bed you come across. The best time of day to find a vacancy is around check-out time; 10am or 11am.

The following are only a cross section of the accommodation options. We trust you to be savvy enough to find the best fit for you and your wallet.

BUDGET

Chai's House (Map pp120-1; ☎ 0 2281 4901; 49/4-8 Soi Rongma; s/d 165/275B; bus 53, 506, river ferry Tha Phra Athit) This family-run guesthouse has shared

---

LATE-NIGHT TOUCHDOWN

A lot of nail-biting anxiety is expended on the international flights arriving in Bangkok around midnight. Will there be taxis into town, will there be available rooms, will my family ever hear from me again? Soothe those nagging voices with the knowledge that most international flights arrive late and that Bangkok is an accommodating place. Yes, there are taxis and even an airport bus service (see p181). And if you haven't made hotel reservations, go straight to Th Khao San, which stays up late, is full of hotels and guesthouses, and sees a near-continuous supply of 'fresh-off-the-birds' just like you. But do keep in mind that jet lag, noise and lack of cleanliness may all hinder a restful night if you opt for a budget cheapie. On the other hand, Th Khao San has plenty of watering holes to smooth the path to slumberland.

---

bathrooms. It's a quiet and secure spot that enforces a 1am curfew.

Donna Guesthouse (Map pp120-1; ☎ 0 2281 9374; subsoi off Soi Damnoen Klangnella, Th Ratchadamnoen; d 250-350B; bus 53, 506, river ferry Tha Phra Athit; ❄) Dear Donna, we are so happy to have found you. The sign pointing down a little sub-*soi* was followed on a whim, and tucked back in there was a clean and quiet nest with big twin beds, new comforters and large shared bathrooms. Not all rooms have windows.

New Siam GH (Map pp120-1; ☎ 0 2282 4554; www .newsiam.net; 21 Soi Chana Songkhram, Th Phra Athit; s 290B, d 320-490B; river ferry Tha Phra Athit, bus 53, 506; ❄ ◙) Long-running New Siam is a smart spot to park your backpack. It passed the schoolmarm's cleanliness inspection (shower curtains are mould-free). Singles share bathrooms, while some doubles have private facilities. There are also small, self-accessible lockers for safekeeping valuables. Guests can use the pool at the affiliated guesthouse New Siam II for a day-use fee.

Bella Bella House (Map pp120-1; ☎ 0 2629 3090; 74 Soi Rambutri, Th Chakraphong; s 250B, d 420-500B; bus 53, 506, river ferry Tha Phra Athit; ❄) Just past Soi Chana Songkhram, Bella Bella has great views into the tiled roofs of the neighbouring temple. Rooms are spartan and clean with rickety beds, and the bathrooms are new and shiny. Singles have shared bathrooms. As with most guesthouses, the desk staff tends to be the usual cast of grumpy teenagers.

Villa Guest House (Map pp120-1; ☎ 0 2281 7009; 230 Soi 1, Th Samsen; s/d 250/500B; bus 30, 53, 506, river ferry Tha Phra Athit & Tha Saphan Ram VIII) Just over the *khlong* is a great residential neighbourhood of bicycle-riding children and chatting housewives. This old teak house occupies a womblike garden amid the village noises of crowing roosters and the smells of mesquite cooking fires. With only 10 fan rooms (all with shared bathrooms), Villa is often full and reservations are recommended.

Mango Lagoon Place (Map pp120-1; ☎ 0 2281 4783; Soi Rambutri, Th Chakraphong; r from 650B; bus 53, 506, river ferry Tha Phra Athit; ❄) Sunny, lemon-yellow complex has rooms that look surprisingly like a real hotel: bed and box spring, wall-to-wall carpet (a bad idea in the tropics), big TVs and art on the wall. The pretty garden at the front is a nice noise buffer.

MIDRANGE
New World House Apartments & Guest House (Map pp120-1; ☎ 0 2281 5596; www.newworldlodge.com; Soi 2, Th Samsen; r from 1300B; bus 30, 53, 506, river ferry Tha Phra Athit & Tha Saphan Ram VIII; ❄) It is surprising to find such a big hotel in a residential neighbourhood; in fact, it is easy to walk right by and never notice it. You'll be glad you did, if you score a room on the 4th or 5th floor, which boast terraces overlooking Khlong Banglamphu.

Hotel De Moc (Map pp120-1; ☎ 0 2629 2100; fax 0 2280 1299; 78 Th Prachathipatai; r from 1500B; bus 12, 56; ❄ ◙) Recently adopted by the Buddy Lodge group and rechristened, the former Thai Hotel is expecting a grand makeover. In the meantime, the rooms are large and charmingly outdated.

Viengtai Hotel (Map pp120-1; ☎ 0 2805 4345; www .viengtai.co.th; 42 Th Rambutri; d 1600-2000B; bus 53, 506, ferry Tha Phra Athit; ❄ ◙) Before Th Khao San was 'discovered', this was an ordinary Chinese-style hotel in a quiet neighbourhood. It now sits comfortably in the midrange with reliable but unstylish rooms. Make advance bookings for cheaper rates.

Buddy Lodge (Map pp120-1; ☎ 0 2629 4477; www .buddylodge.com; 265 Th Khao San; r from 2200B; bus 53, 506, river ferry Tha Phra Athit; ❄ ◙) This splashy bou-

tique hotel has lead Th Khao San's gentrification. Rooms are evocative of a breezy tropical manor house and outfitted with traditional Thai designs. And then at your doorstep is the continuous freak show of Th Khao San.

our pick **Baan Chantra** (Map p120-1; ☎ 0 2628 6988; www.baanchantra.com; 120 Th Samsen; d from 2200B; ❊) Promoted as a boutique hotel, Baan Chantra is much too big and casually dressed to be pinned with such a title. Akin to its residential neighbourhood, this converted house is without pretensions, preferring to be comfortable and roomy than fashionable and pinched. Many of the house's original teak details remain, and the deluxe room boasts a sunny patio. Free wi-fi.

Old Bangkok Inn (Map pp120-1; ☎ 0 2629 1785; www.oldbangkokinn.com; 609 Th Phra Sumen; d incl breakfast from 3100B; bus 2, 82, 511, 512, khlong taxi Tha Phan Fah; ❊ 💻) This atmospheric shophouse has been transformed into a cottage-cosy boutique hotel with romantically decorated, if slightly cramped, rooms. Shop at its website for rate promotions.

Ko Ratanakosin & Thonburi

The most touristed area of Bangkok was until recently utterly devoid of lodging options. But with the advent of the Bangkok boutique hotels, the riverside warehouses are being transformed into charming tourists nests.

our pick **Arun Residence** (Map p130; ☎ 0 2221 9158; www.arunresidence.com; 36-38 Soi Pratu Nok Yoong, Th Maharat; r from 2950B; river ferry Tha Tien; ❊) A simple wooden house on the river has been polished and coaxed into a comfortable and airy boutique hotel. Most rooms are lofts, but the best is the top floor with its own balcony and view of Wat Arun.

Ibrik Resort (Map p130; ☎ 0 2848 9220; www.ibrikresort.com; 256 Soi Wat Rakang, Th Arunamrin, Thonburi; d incl breakfast 4000B; Thonburi; river ferry Tha Wang Lang; ❊) Only three rooms big, this itty-bitty hotel offers style and privacy for the average professional. The rooms are minimal cool and cosy with a morning wake-up view of the busy river.

Chakrabongse Villas (Map p130; ☎ 0 2622 3356; www.thaivillas.com; 396 Th Maharat; r from US$140; river ferry Tha Tien; ❊) Members of royalty were the usual residents of this converted minor palace, just a brief stroll from the historic sites of Ko Ratanakosin. But today, you can usurp the royal birthright in one of three luxury retreats surrounded by a lush garden and a river view.

Thewet

Thewet, the district north of Banglamphu near the National Library, is another backpackers enclave, especially popular with families and the over-30 crowd. It is a lovely leafy area, but during the rainy season it is prone to flooding.

Taewez Guest House (Map pp116-17; ☎ 0 2280 8856; 23/12 Soi Thewet, Th Si Ayuthaya; s/d 182/328B; bus 30, 503, river ferry Tha Thewet; ❊) At the end of the block, Taewez's no-frills concrete rooms vary greatly in quality, but the spot ranks highly with travellers because of the buddy mood that flourishes in the common spaces. Singles share a bathroom.

Sri Ayuttaya Guest House (Map pp116-17; ☎ 0 2282 5942; Soi Thewet, Th Si Ayuthaya; d 350-500B; bus 30, 503, river ferry Tha Thewet; ❊) Sri Ayuttaya has romantic rooms with pretty hardwood floors, exposed brick and other stylish touches.

Shanti Lodge (Map pp116-17; ☎ 0 2281 2497; 37 Soi Thewet, Th Si Ayuthaya; d 350-600B; bus 30, 503, river ferry Tha Thewet; ❊) The omphalos of the street's family-owned (all by the same family) guesthouses, Shanti masters a yogalike atmosphere. The cheaper bamboo-walled rooms don't do a good job of blocking out the neighbours, but more expensive rooms are creative and sealed.

Chinatown

Crowded and chaotic, Chinatown is the traditional host of mainland Chinese tourists and Indian import-exporters. Lately, Western backpackers have started to slip into the neighbourhood with little fanfare – a distinctly anonymous experience than the usual walking-ATM treatment you'll get elsewhere. The hotels in the heart of Chinatown are high-rise numbers with basic midrange amenities and relatively easy-going rates; accommodation around the Hualamphong area can provide simple shelter before making a train escape.

This area is central but difficult to get in and out of (unless travelling by boat) because of a steady supply of traffic.

TT Guest House (Map pp118-19; ☎ 0 2236 2946; fax 0 2236 3054; 516-518 Soi Sawang, Th Maha Nakhon; d 250-280B) In a low-key neighbourhood, this family-run guesthouse is an easy walk to the train station. Step through the gate into a shaded courtyard perfect for sipping coffee and reading a newspaper. The rooms, which share bathrooms, are clean, with a few touches to stave off blandness. To get here, follow Th Maha Nakhon

underneath the expressway, turn left onto Soi Sawang and follow it all the way to the end of the block past the machine shops and deep-fry woks.

238 Guesthouse (Map pp118-19; ☎ 0 2623 9287; 238 Th Phahurat; d 400-600B; bus 73, Chao Phraya Express Tha Tien; ☒) A popular option for Wat Pho massage students, this converted shophouse has generous rooms with all the basics. The guesthouse is within walking distance of the temple on the edge of Chinatown.

River View Guest House (Map pp118-19; ☎ 0 2234 5429; fax 0 2237 5428; 768 Soi Phanurangsi, Th Songwat; d 450-690B; river ferry Tha Si Phraya; ☒) The River View has a great hidden location amid machine shops and streamlike *soi*, just north of River City Complex, and a river-view restaurant on the top floor. But the rooms aren't on speaking terms with mops or brooms. If you want to see for yourself, you'll need these directions: heading north from Th Si Phraya along Charoen Krung, take a left into Th Songwat (before the Chinatown Arch), then the second left onto Soi Phanurangsi. You'll start to see signs at this point.

Krung Kasem Srikung Hotel (Map pp118-19; ☎ 0 2225 0132; fax 0 2225 4705; 1860 Th Krung Kasem; d 650-700B; subway Hualamphong, bus 25, 35, 53; ☒) West of the train station, this high-rise is the tweener version of a grown-up hotel: more comfort than a guesthouse but still a little rough around the edges.

Bangkok Centre Hotel (Map pp118-19; ☎ 0 238 4980; www.bangkokcentrehotel.com; 328 Th Phra Ram IV; r from 1400B; subway Hualamphong; ☒ 🖳 ☒) From this hotel tower, you can see your train pull into the station. It has all the usual midrange amenities: large frumpy rooms with a crew of túk-túk drivers working the entrance.

Grand China Princess (Map pp118-19; ☎ 0 2224 9977; www.grandchina.com; 215 Th Yaowarat; s/d 2000/2200B; river ferry Tha Ratchawong, bus 73, 507; ☒) Literally in the heart of Chinatown, this multistorey matron has acceptable rooms buoyed by great views of Banglamphu. The top floor has a panoramic rotating restaurant to fulfil your dreams of gaudy Asia.

Shanghai Inn (Map pp118-19; ☎ 0 2221 2121; www .shanghai-inn.com; 479 Th Yaowarat; r from 2500B; ☒) Nouveau-Shanghai style has arrived in worn-down Chinatown. Pink and purple lanterns, bamboo floors and imperial-style furniture crowd the rooms creating a 1920s cigarette girls boudoir in colonial Shanghai.

Siam Square & Pratunam

Siam Square and the area around it are centrally located on both Skytrain lines and smack dab in the middle of the city's shopping orgy. The area is also perfect for those who have been away from civilisation for awhile and are starved for bookshops, cinemas and Western fast food (psst, we won't tell anyone). The only drawback is that nightlife is nonexistent, but you're a short taxi ride to nightspots in Silom or Sukhumvit.

Found in the shadow of Mahboonkrong (MBK; p174), a low-key backpacker community bunks down on Soi Kasem San 1, intermixed with a local community of lunching shop girls and commuting office workers. The foreign crowd is an early-to-bed, early-to-rise troupe dedicated to do-it-yourself itineraries. Taxi drivers have a terrible time understanding foreigners trying to pronounce this street. To bridge the language barrier, try telling them that Soi Kasem San 1 (pronounce

---

WHERE YOU GO?

Getting around Bangkok has always been a challenge, even way back in the 18th century as canals were ceding to roads, and human-drawn *rót chék* (rickshaws) were the era's taxis. During the early 20th century, the rickshaw gave way to the squeaky *săamláw* (three-wheeled pedicab), which better suited Bangkok's flat terrain. At certain arched bridges, however, the incline was too steep and passengers would have to walk across themselves. Once cars and trucks dominated the roadways, the *săamláw* was replaced by its motorised counterpart: the three-wheeled, onomatopoeic túk-túk. These wily go-carts fly around corners, kicking up a cloud of blue smoke and coughing like asthmatic power saws. Even though most short-term visitors will get ripped-off by unscrupulous túk-túk drivers, few can resist the call 'Hey you, where you go?'. If you can withstand this siren's song, you should not apologise for your disinterest. It is not considered rude in Thailand to ignore a hawker; in fact, a polite 'no thank you', a requisite in Western cultures, is considered an invitation for a stronger sales pitch in Thailand. It might feel disrespectful but the silent treatment delivers untold sums of sanity.

'Kasem' with a 'g' instead of 'k') is across from the National Stadium (*trong khâam sanaam kii-laa hàeng châat*).

BUDGET

Pranee Building (Map pp128-9; ☎ 0 2216 3181; 931/12 Soi Kasem San 1, Th Phra Ram I; r 450B; Skytrain National Stadium, khlong taxi Tha Ratchathewi; 🐱) One of the cheapest options on the street, Pranee isn't fancy but the rooms are large with air-con and hot water; the bathrooms are a tad decrepit.

Bed & Breakfast Inn (Map pp128-9; ☎ 0 2215 3004; Soi Kasem San 1, Th Phra Ram I; s/d incl breakfast 400/500B; Skytrain National Stadium, khlong taxi Tha Ratchathewi; 🐱) This maze-like guesthouse has standard, recently remodelled rooms.

A-One Inn (Map pp128-9; ☎ 0 2215 3029; www .aoneinn.com; 25/13-15 Soi Kasem San 1, Th Pha Ram I; d from 600B; Skytrain National Stadium, khlong taxi Tha Ratchathewi; 🐱) Well-proportioned rooms don't have a lot of bells and whistles but are just plain good value. A-One sees a lot of return business.

MIDRANGE

Wendy House (Map pp128-9; ☎ 0 2216 2436; fax 0 2216 8053; Soi Kasem San 1, Th Phra Ram I; d incl breakfast from 1000B; Skytrain National Stadium, khlong taxi Tha Ratchathewi; 🐱) Wendy House is as professional as they come with a genuine Thai-style concern for its guests. The rooms are on the small side, though.

VIP Guest House/Golden House (Map pp128-9; ☎ 0 2252 9535; fax 0 2252 9538; 1025/5-9 Th Ploenchit; d incl breakfast 2000B; Skytrain Chitlom; 🐱) Shiny lobby of this small inn leads to rooms with mammoth-sized beds and parquet floors. Bathrooms, however, don't have tubs, only showers. VIP is down a little alley near Telephone Organization of Thailand.

Holiday Mansion Hotel (Map pp128-9; ☎ 0 2255 0099; fax 0 2253 0130; 53 Th Withayu; d incl breakfast 2500B; Skytrain Ploenchit; 🐱 🈂) A solid midrange option, the Mansion is a poster child of provincial sophistication. There is a pleasant interior courtyard pool, marble lobby and a dusty grandfather clock (the standard uniform for hotels of this calibre). The generous-sized rooms are entering the sunset years of their career, but the whole package becomes utterly charming when promotions give your credit card a holiday.

Indra Regent Hotel (Map pp128-9; ☎ 0 2208 0022-33; www.indrahotel.com; 120/126 Th Ratchaprarop, d from 2800B; Skytrain Chitlom, khlong taxi Tha Pratunam; 🐱 🈂) This soot-stained box doesn't look like much from

the outside, but the interior offers one of the better-value stays in this price range. Junior suites are touted as the best buys.

Asia Hotel (Map pp128-9; ☎ 0 2215 0808; www .asiahotel.co.th; 296 Th Phayathai; d from 2900B; Skytrain Ratchathewi, khlong taxi Tha Ratchathewi; 🐱 🈂) A favourite with ageing backpackers who have creaky joints and more fat around their wallets, this huge place has a good location and large rooms with generous-sized bathrooms. A walkway from the Skytrain is another plus, sparing visitors the barrage of 'whereyougos' from the taxis and túk-túk that park outside.

Novotel Bangkok on Siam Square (Map pp128-9; ☎ 0 2255 6888; www.accorhotels-asia.com; Soi 6, Siam Square; d from 3500B; Skytrain Siam; 🐱 🈂) For business or leisure, Novotel Siam is conveniently located near the Skytrain and shopping. Rooms are spitting images of corporate class back home, but the deluxe ones are better suited for business purposes.

Pathumwan Princess (Map pp116-17; ☎ 0 2216 3700; www.pprincess.com; 444 Th Phyathai; r from 3700B; Skytrain Siam; 🐱 🈂) Families rave about this hotel because it is connected to MBK shopping centre and the Skytrain. The deluxe rooms have a work desk and huge bathrooms with separate shower and tub, and the suites boast two TVs and fabulous views (your choice between pool or city views). The sky-high swimming pool is another plus.

TOP END

Amari Watergate (Map pp128-9; ☎ 0 2653 9000; www .amari.com; 847 Th Petchaburi; s/d from US$125; Skytrain Chitlom, khlong taxi Tha Pratunam; 🐱 🈂) This 34-storey hotel is right in the centre of Bangkok's Pratunam district and its crowded street market. The large rooms receive a stylish blending of Thai and European details, and the large fitness centre keeps off those extra pounds graciously added by too many Thai sweets. The 8th-storey pool catches breezes and views unimaginable from street level.

Grand Hyatt Erawan (Map pp128-9; ☎ 0 2254 1234; www.bangkok.hyatt.com; cnr Th Ratchadamri & Th Ploenchit; d from US$150; Skytrain Chitlom; 🐱 🈂) Just an elevated walkway away from shopping bliss, the Erawan provides one of Bangkok's most prestigious postcommerce slumbers. Rooms are sleek and modern with fully functional European-style tubs and tall shower heads. Rooms at the rear of the hotel overlook the Royal Bangkok Sports Club racetrack.

Conrad Hotel Bangkok (Map pp128-9; ☎ 0 2690 9999; www.conradhotels.com; 87 Th Withayu; d from US$165; Skytrain Ploenchit; ✷ ☒) Bangkok's legendary luxury hotels can be a tad musty for the 30-something jet-setters. But this business-district option delivers enough nouveau style and attitude to keep the media-weened from being fussy. The rooms are decorated with Thai silks and rich earth tones, and the bathrooms transform washing into spa-ing with deep-soak tubs and overhead 'rain' shower heads.

Silom, Lumphini & Sathon

The city's financial district along Th Silom is not the most charming area of town, but it is convenient to nightspots and to the Skytrain for quick access to modern parts of Bangkok. Traffic can be thick, and getting to older, more historic parts of town can be time-consuming.

If you were hitting the Asian hippie trail back in the 1970s, you would have laid your love beads at a guesthouse in Soi Ngam Duphli, off Th Phra Ram IV, near Lumphini Park. Some shoestringers still filter into this traffic-clogged area to get business done at the nearby embassies or to trade the postbeach scene on Khao San with a 'busted-flat-in-Bangkok' seediness.

Along Th Sathon are several top-end hotels that counterbalance Soi Ngam Duphli's proletariat aesthetic. The hotels are stylish but the location is severed from the Skytrain by a shadeless megaroad.

BUDGET & MIDRANGE

Sala Thai Daily Mansion (Map p127; ☎ 0 2287 1436; 15 Soi Si Bamphen, off Soi Ngam Duphli; d 200-400B; subway Lumphini, bus 74, 109, 116, 507) At the end of a narrow cul-de-sac, this family-run guesthouse is more akin to the lodging options in the provinces than bright-lights Bangkok. All rooms are standard issue – four walls, bed and a light, with shared bathroom. To get here, take a left off Soi Ngam Duphli at the 7-Eleven, then take the second left and the first right.

Niagara Hotel (Map pp124-5; ☎ 0 2233 5783; 26 Soi 9/Suksavitthaya, Th Silom; d 700B; Skytrain Chong Nonsi; ☒) From the outside, Niagara looks like just another crummy no-tell motel, but inside reveals one of the best bargains in Silom. The rooms are immaculate, almost sterile, and the rock-hard bed is graced with a plush comforter.

Malaysia Hotel (Map p127; ☎ 0 2286 3582; fax 0 2287 1457; 54 Soi Ngam Duphli, Th Phra Ram IV; s/d from

700B/800B; subway Lumphini, bus 74, 109, 116, 507; ☒ ☒) The Malaysia was once Bangkok's most famous budget lodge and even gave shelter to Maureen and Tony Wheeler on their maiden shoestring trip through Southeast Asia. Nowadays it is an HQ for gay sex tourists, but the well-maintained rooms and trim prices make it a good spot for those who are amused by the hormone scene.

our pick La Résidence Hotel (Map pp124-5; ☎ 0 2233 3301, fax 0 2237 9322; 173/8-9 Th Surawong; d 1200-1500B, ste 2700B; Skytrain Chong Nonsi; ☒) La Résidence is a boutique inn with playfully and individually decorated rooms. A standard room is very small and fittingly decorated like a child's bedroom. The next size up is more mature and voluptuous with blood-red walls and modern Thai motifs.

Bangkok Christian Guest House (Map pp124-5; ☎ 0 2233 2206; www.bcgh.org; 123 Soi Sala Daeng 2, Th Convent; s/d 1100/1540B; Skytrain Sala Daeng; ☒) Puritan austerity reigns at this boarding house originally serving Protestant missionaries after WWII. Today all are welcome – as long as you aren't accompanied by durian or alcohol. A 2nd-floor children's play area and lots of tourist information are also available.

TOP END

Swiss Lodge (Map pp124-5; ☎ 0 2233 5345; www.swisslodge.com; 3 Th Convent; d 3880-4150B; Skytrain Sala Daeng; ✷ ☒) The small inn with big-guy muscles prides itself on its personal touches – handwritten welcome notes to return guests or predawn breakfasts for early-morning departures. Its central location is padded against exterior noise by soundproofed rooms, which are a tad tight. It's also green; rooftop panels help supply 90% of the hotel's hot-water needs.

Dusit Thani (Map pp124-5; ☎ 0 2200 9000; www.dusit.com; 946 Th Phra Ram IV; d US$210-300; Skytrain Sala Daeng, subway Silom; ✷ ☐ ☒) Much to everyone's shock, this conservative old gal has gone under the knife of the global Zen design trend. Despite the identity crisis, this venerable hotel has an impressive tiered lobby, a central location and a train-station excitement as Thais in their finest arrive and depart for wedding banquets or conferences.

Metropolitan (Map p127; ☎ 0 2625 3333; www.metropolitan.como.bz; 27 Th Sathon Tai, d from US$240; ✷ ☒) This London-hotel boutique is ground zero for Bangkok's minimalism fascination. The rooms are spare and severe, but ultracosmo-

politans are still enamoured of the hotel's naked coolness.

our pick **Sukhothai Hotel** (Map p127; ☎ 0 2344 8888; www.sukhothai.com; 13/3 Th Sathon Tai; d from 11,900B; 🔲 🔁) Stylishly unique, the Sukhothai mines the temple monuments of its namesake, Thailand's ancient capital, for design inspiration. White colonnaded antechambers look out at exterior pools with floating stupas or serene Buddha figures. The rooms are exquisitely decorated and have hardwood floors and war-room-sized bathrooms.

Riverside

When people swoon about Bangkok, they've typically lodged along the river at one of the luxury hotels.

New Road Guesthouse (Map p124-5; ☎ 0 2237 1094, fax 0 2237 1102; 1216/1 Th Charoen Krung; d 600-700B; river ferry Tha Si Phraya; 🔲) Sandwiched between the luxe hotels is New Road, a friendly cheapie with clean, tiled rooms with compact bathrooms. A comfortable downstairs sitting area collects all the guests in front of the communal TV.

Royal Orchid Sheraton (Map pp124-5; ☎ 0 2266 0123; www.starwoodhotels.com; Soi 30, Th Charoen Krung; d from US$150; 🔲 🔲 🔁) More down-to-earth and affordable than its other riverside neighbours, the Royal Sheraton has high-end service and picture-postcard views without

a lot of style or sophistication to hike up the room rates.

Millennium Hilton (Map pp118-19; ☎ 0 2442 2000; www.bangkok.hilton.com; 123 Th Charoen Nakorn, Thonburi; r from US$150; 🔲 🔁) Reviving a long-abandoned ghost tower on the river, the Hilton delivers a riverside eyrie without bankrupting the piggy bank. Because of the building's oblong design, most rooms claim a riverside view, with the standard rooms possessing better feng shui. There are lots of design toys: a soaring atrium, an infinity pool through which a glass-enclosed elevator does a perfect nose-dive and the attached beach (real sand included). The only trouble is that its Thonburi location makes late nights in Bangkok a long taxi ride away.

Peninsula Hotel (Map pp116-17; ☎ 0 2861 2888; www.peninsula.com; 333 Th Charoen Nakhon, Thonburi; d from US$200; private pier near Tha Oriental; 🔲 🔁) Across the river in Thonburi, the Peninsula Hotel is one of the highest-ranking luxury hotels in the world. The lobby exudes a hushed sense of privilege and pedigree with polished marble and squat, squared hallways. Rooms have breathtaking views of Bangkok's high-rises. The Peninsula is also known for its affiliated golf course.

Oriental Hotel (Map pp124-5; ☎ 0 2659 9000; www .mandarinoriental.com; 48 Soi Oriental/Soi 38, Th Charoen Krung; d US$300; river ferry Tha Oriental; 🔲 🔁) While

---

BANGKOK'S GRANDE DAME

The Oriental Hotel started out as a roughshod boarding house for European seafarers in the late 19th century, but was transformed into an aristocratic magnet by Hans Niels Anderson, the founder of the formidable East Asiatic Company (which operated between Bangkok and Copenhagen). He hired an Italian designer to build what is now known as the Authors' Wing, which was the city's most elaborate secular building; all other grand architecture at the time was commissioned by the king.

With a dramatic setting beside Mae Nam Chao Phraya, the hotel has gained its reputation from its famous guests. A Polish-born sailor named Joseph Conrad stayed here in between nautical jobs in 1888. W Somerset Maugham stumbled into the hotel with an advanced case of malaria contracted during his overland journey from Burma. In his feverish state, he heard the German manager arguing with the doctor about how a death in the hotel would hurt business. Maugham's recovery and completion of *Gentleman in the Parlour: A Record of a Journey from Rangoon to Haiphong* contributed to the long-lasting literary appeal of the hotel. Other notable guests have included Noël Coward, Graham Greene, John le Carré, James Michener, Gore Vidal and Barbara Cartland. Some modern-day writers even claim that a stay in the Oriental will overcome writer's block.

To soak up the ambiance of old seafaring Bangkok, stop by for a cocktail at the Bamboo bar or toast the 'swift river' as Noël Coward did from the riverside terrace. For teatotallers, an afternoon brew is served in a frilly Victorian lounge filled with black-and-white photographs of Rama V. To ensure its aristocratic leanings in a less formal age, the hotel enforces a dress code (no shorts, sleeveless shirts or sandals allowed).

the rest of the city jumps overboard for the new Zen trend, the classic Oriental stays rooted in its Victorian past. It is consistently rated as one of the best hotels in the world and prides itself on personalised service. For the full bygone immersion, there is the original Authors' Wing rooms named after famous writers who have bedded here. But new generations might prefer the simply decorated new wing that drinks in full draughts of a river view.

Sukhumvit

Staying in this area puts you in the newest part of Bangkok. Th Sukhumvit can clearly be divided into two personalities. West of Soi Asoke (Soi 21) is the sex-tourist sector ruled by girlie bars and the quintessential Nana couple (an overweight, older *faràng* man with a young Thai girl). If you're not wowed or amused by it, stay elsewhere. East of Soi Asoke, every imaginable nationality calls Bangkok home, forming a motley, yet well-paid, expat community.

Because visitors with larger budgets stay in Sukhumvit, tourist services are more expensive here than in Banglamphu. Although traffic is horrendous because of the one-way streets, the Skytrain has opened up vast frontiers from the start of Th Sukhumvit at Th Ploenchit to well beyond the Eastern bus terminal.

BUDGET

Soi 1 Guesthouse (Map pp122-3; ☎ 0 2655 0604; www .soi1guesthouse.com; 220/7 Soi 1, Th Sukhumvit; dm from 250-300B; 🔀 🖳) Basic accommodation within hobbling distance of Bumrumgrad Hospital, Soi 1 Guesthouse has six and eight-bed dorms and a few private-room options (shared bathrooms). The owners are well travelled and give all new arrivals a quick introduction on how to avoid scams and hassles.

Atlanta (Map pp122-3; ☎ 0 2252 1650, 0 2252 6069; fax 0 2656 8123; 78 Soi 2, Th Sukhumvit; d from 400B; Skytrain Ploenchit; 🔀 🖳) You half expect Humphrey Bogart to trot down the stairs in the perfectly preserved, mid-century lobby. The rooms are skeletal compared to the lobby, complete with old-fashioned letter-writing desks (remember, before email), and a jungle-landscaped swimming pool. Another plus is that the Atlanta is also the only hotel in the area that openly forbids sex tourists.

Suk 11 (Map pp122-3; ☎ 0 2253 5927; www.suk11 .com; dm/s/d 250/550/750B; Skytrain Nana; 🔀) A garden

village has been re-created amid Sukhumvit's traffic at this budget-friendly spot. Mood music along with toast-and-jam breakfasts are enjoyed in the shady common space. Advance reservations required.

HI-Sukhumvit (Map pp122-3; ☎ 0 2391 9338; www .Hisukhvmit.com; 23 Soi 38, Th Sukhumvit; dm 300B, s 550-600B; d 800-850B; Skytrain Thong Lor) This friendly multistorey dorm (floors segregated by sex) is within walking distance of Ekamai (Eastern) bus terminal and the Skytrain. There is lots of tourist information, a rooftop deck, laundry and kitchen. The hostel is open 7am to 11am and 4pm to 1am.

MIDRANGE

Miami Hotel (Map pp122-3; ☎ 0 2253 0369; 2 Soi 13, Th Sukhumvit; s/d 650/750B; Skytrain Nana; 🔀 🖳) Bearing the mark of the GI days in more ways than its name, the Miami has a strange down-and-out charm. The *kàthoey* desk clerk, poolside lizards and lumpy beds have all the makings of a greenhorn-does-Bangkok novel.

Golden Palace Hotel (Map pp122-3; ☎ 0 2252 5115; www.goldenpalacehotel.com; 15 Soi 1, Th Sukhumvit; r 950B; Skytrain Ploenchit; 🔀 🖳) A contender in the featherweight midrange division, Golden Palace is an institutional vision in aquamarine. The rooms are functional and affordable but not stylish.

Sam's Lodge (Map pp122-3; ☎ 0 2253 2993; www .samslodge.com; 28-28/1 Soi 19, Th Sukhumvit; d 1000B; Skytrain Asoke; 🔀) Above a tailor shop, this guesthouse has touches of Japanese minimalism and a cosy roof terrace. All rooms share bathrooms (an oversight considering the price) and some don't have windows. According to the desk clerk, the place also discourages prostitutes and bad manners.

Federal Hotel (Map pp122-3; ☎ 0 2253 0175; federalhotel@hotmail.com; 27 Soi 11, Th Sukhumvit; d from 1100B; Skytrain Nana; 🔀 🖳) Since its freewheelin' days as an R&R stop for American GIs, the Federal has gone upmarket, sort of, and now enjoys the affectionate nickname of 'Club Fed' from its sexpat fans. The upstairs rooms are comfortably decorated with rattan furniture and generous beds. The ground-level rooms, however, should be avoided. The real draw is the frangipani-lined pool and time-warped American-style coffee shop.

Majestic Suites (Map pp122-3; ☎ 0 2656 8220; www .majesticsuites.com; 110-110/1 Th Sukhumvit, btwn Soi 4 & 6; s/d 1160/1500B; Skytrain Nana; 🔀) Small and friendly, Majestic has hermetically sealed rooms that

deliver privacy and quiet even with screaming Sukhumvit right outside. Front rooms have a bird's-eye view of the street's traffic-snarled grandeur. The petite among us will find the rooms cosy, while others may argue for the term 'cramped'.

Novotel Lotus Bangkok (Map pp122-3; ☎ 0 2261 0111; www.accorhotels-asia.com; 1 Soi 33, Th Sukhumvit; d from 3000B; Skytrain Phrom Phong; ✸ ✭) Another in the Accor brand is this well-designed modern creation complete with a soothing lotus pond in the centre of the lobby. Rooms are plush and private. There are also suites on a semiprivate floor with a terrace.

Davis (Map pp122-3; ☎ 0 2260 8000; www.davisbangkok.net; Soi 24, Th Sukhumvit; d from 3000B; ✸ ✭) Close to Th Phra Ram IV, the Davis is a peach of a place with cool sophistication and rooms decorated like a Raj's palace, a Kyoto hermitage or a Burmese plantation. Freshen up in the big marble bathrooms after a dreamy slumber in the fluffy beds. Straight from the pages of *Architectural Digest*, the detached Thai villas are polished to a burnished golden wood with deep sleigh beds and big sunny windows arranged around a private lap pool and garden.

Bel-Aire Princess (Map pp122-3; ☎ 0 2253 4300; www.bel-aireprincess.com; 16 Soi 5, Th Sukhumvit; d from 3500B; Skytrain Nana; ✸ ✭) This hotel is all dolled up with a stylish lobby and rooms that are being upgraded to match.

TOP END

Seven (Map pp122-3; ☎ 0 2662 0951; www.sleepatseven.com; 3/15 Soi 31, Th Sukhumvit; d from 4000B; Skytrain Phrom Phong; ✸) Did you know that in Thailand the days of the week are associated with the Hindu Gods and their symbolic colours? This new boutique hotel has incorporated this cultural hook into its conversion of a Sukhumvit apartment building. Each room is decorated to match the colour associated with a particular day of the week. The décor is evocative of Thai mural painting in modern and elegant hues. To further the theme, pick the room that represents the day of the week you were born – an important component of Thai astrology.

Eugenia (Map pp122-3; ☎ 0 2259 9011; www.theeugenia.com; 267 Soi 31, Th Sukhumvit; r from 5800B; Skytrain Phrom Phong; ✸ ✭) Colonial manor houses aren't an indigenous legacy in Thailand but this anachronistic hotel polishes the anomaly to reflect a refined Victorian lady. Here in the most modern part of town, Eugenia looked into the history books for inspiration, decorating 12 guest rooms with canopy beds, old-fashioned light fixtures and other clean yet feminine touches.

Dream Bangkok (Map pp122-3; ☎ 0 2254 8500; 10 Soi 15, Th Sukhumvit; Skytrain Asoke or Nana; r from US$136; ✸ ▢ ✭) If heart-shaped beds and champagne-glass tubs were given a modern makeover, you'd have Dream Bangkok, another conquest by New York hotelier and socialite Vikram Chatwal. The clubby blue-lit décor is unintentionally kitsch, making it a match made in dreamland for the City of Angels and a welcome addition to beer-belly Nana.

Westin Grande Sukhumvit (Map pp122-3; ☎ 0 2207 8000; www.westin.com/bangkok; 259 Th Sukhumvit, Soi 19;

SPEAKING BANGKOK

You might not learn Thai during your stay in Bangkok, but plenty of Thai phrases and hybrid words infuse the city's unique bilingual dictionary. Here are a few:

▪ *Hi-so* – There are three criteria for being *hi-so*: young, rich and beautiful. Most are bilingual Thais or *lûuk khrêung* (half Thai-*faràng*) with VIP credentials and serious shopping addictions satisfied at the Emporium Shopping Centre. Don't expect to sit next to a *hi-so* on the Skytrain, they have chauffeured cars. Oddly, the English word 'hipster' has been coopted by the *hi-so* crowd to refer to things that are fabulous.

▪ *Khunying* – An aristocratic title, this term is sometimes used more broadly to refer to Bangkok's ruling matrons. With their Imelda Marcos–helmet hairdos, jewel-toned Thai silks and thick pancake makeup, *khunyings* can usually be found at official ceremonies or heading an entourage of merit-makers.

▪ *Dek Neaw* – Supercool teenagers who hang out in Siam Square showing off urban fashion and meticulously styled bed-head hairdos.

▪ Freelancer – Careful when you use this all-purpose word to refer to a contract worker. In Bangkok, it means you are a prostitute who doesn't belong to a brothel.

r from US$140; Skytrain Asoke; ✷ ▣) Central and professional, the Westin boasts efficient staff and roomy rooms outfitted with the trade-marked 'Heavenly' beds, as soft and cosy as an eternal reward should be. Bathrooms have separate tub and shower with a shower head that is *faràng*-sized.

Greater Bangkok

We-Train International House (Map pp114–15; ☎ 0 2967 8550-4; www.we-train.co.th; 501/1 Mu 3, Th Dechatungkha, Don Muang, dm/r 200/740D; ✷ ▣) This basic hotel is operated by a nonprofit women's group with proceeds going to fund emergency shelters for abused women and children. Its location near Don Muang, the old airport, was the second-ary selling point, but now that the airport has moved, lodgers should come solely for good deeds not flight layovers.

Thai House (Map pp114–15; ☎ 0 2903 9611; www .thaihouse.co.th; 32/4 Mu 8, Bang Yai, Nonthaburi; d from 1200B) North of central Bangkok in Nonthaburi is this traditional Thai home surrounded by fruit trees, which has been converted into a guesthouse. Contact the proprietors for trans-port details. The guesthouse also conducts cooking courses open to guests and nonguests (see p143).

Ibis Siam Bangkok (Map pp116–17; ☎ 0 2209 3888; www.accorhotels.com/asia; 97 Th Ratchaprarop; r 2300B; Sky-train Victory Monument, bus 513) Part of a new line-up of business-friendly hotels for modest budgets, Ibis Siam delivers comfort and convenience without a corporate expense account. Shop the website for plumper discounts.

Reflections Rooms (Map pp114–15; ☎ 0 2270 3344; 0 2270 3359; www.reflections-thai.com; 81-83 Soi 7/Ari, Th Phahonyothin; d 2850-3450B; Skytrain Ari; ✷ ▣ ▣) All dressed up in fun arty colours, Reflections is the best thing Bangkok has cooked up since lunch. Local designers were assigned a room (30 in all) and went to town with brushes of whimsy, urbanity and straight-up cool. They use Starbucks sizing for their rooms: small is really big and large is really large.

Novotel Suvarnabhumi Airport Hotel (☎ 0 2131 1111; www.accorhotels-asia.com; Th Ratchathewi, Samut Prakan; d from 3600B; ✷ ▣ ▣) The closest lodging option to the new Suvarnabhumi International Airport, which is just a 300m stroll away.

Bangkok Marriott Resort & Spa (Map pp114–15; ☎ 0 2476 0022, fax 0 2476 1120; 257/1-3 Th Charoen Nakhon; d from US$180; hotel shuttle boat from Tha Sathon & Tha Oriental; ✷ ▣ ▣) Set amid lush landscaped gardens by the river, the Marriott really is a place where you can get away from it all. Because it's downriver from the main action, it gives you the perfect excuse not to leave the pool.

EATING

No matter where you go in Bangkok, food is always available. There is so much variety just at street level that days can go by with-out stepping inside a restaurant. Enacting the modern equivalent of hunter-gatherers, many visitors skip from stall to stall sampling *kŭaytiaw* (noodles), plates of *râat khâo* (rice and curry) or *mùat phàt* (stir-fries) for 25B to 40B.

When the need comes for a restaurant, Bangkok's best are the décor-less mom-and-pop shops that concentrate only on the food; most of these restaurants hover around 60B to 100B for a main dish. As the prices increase, so does the ambience – more servers, traditional Thai antiques, white tablecloths or ultramod-ern outfits. Be careful treading in these waters, as dining in Bangkok's fashionable or touristy restaurants is sometimes more for show than for flavour.

While Thai food may be sufficiently ex-otic, Bangkok offers an international menu prepared by its many immigrant communi-ties. Chinatown is naturally a good area for Chinese food. In the crowded bazaarlike area of Little Arabia, just off Th Sukhumvit, there is Middle Eastern cuisine. All of Europe and America have their culinary embassies that

---

WHAT'S FOR DINNER?

The wealth of dining choices can cripple you with indecision. We've taken the liberty here of providing a cross section of Bang-kok's culinary landscape.

▪ **Best Thai Restaurants** – Vientiane Kitchen (p165), Reflections (p166), Hemlock (p161), Ton Pho (opposite)

▪ **Best Snapshots of Bangkok's Expat & Immigrant Communities** – Nasir al-Masri Restaurant & Shishah (p165), Dosa King (p165), Eat Me (p164)

▪ **Best Restaurants to Brag about in Backpacker Circles** – Shoshana (p161), Pickle Factory (p166), Th Phadungdao Seafood Stalls (p162), hotel buffets (p163)

prepare the tastes of home in the *haute* fashion for power players or as pub grub to cure homesickness.

Banglamphu

This area near the river is one of the best for cheap Thai eats. Open-air restaurants and street vendors claim the majority of grazing options. Because of the backpacker presence, Western and vegetarian food are well represented. Duck into the maze of *soi* for more authentic street-side eating than what you'll find along Th Khao San.

THAI

Arawy (Alloy; Map pp120-1; 152 Th Din So; dishes 35B; breakfast & lunch; bus 10, 19, 42, khlong taxi to Tha Phan Fah) Opposite the Municipal Hall and a few doors down from a 7-Eleven store, this matron of meatless is one of the best Thai vegetarian restaurants in the city. A selection of prepared dishes makes it user-friendly, and the chef brings out the flavour of the veggies without the tasteless oil spill. The restaurant was inspired by the strict vegetarianism of Chamlong Srimuang, the ex-governor of Bangkok.

May Kaidee's (Map pp120-1; subsoi off Soi Damnoen Klang; dishes 50B; lunch & dinner; bus 56, 506, river ferry Tha Phra Athit) For an all-veggie menu at meatless prices, follow Th Khao San to Th Tanao and jog right to the small *soi* beside the Burger King (yup, Khao San has gone corporate) and then another left to a string of vegetarian shops.

Roti-Mataba (Map pp120-1; cnr Th Phra Athit & Th Phra Sumen; dishes 60-80B; lunch & dinner Tue-Sun; river ferry Tha Phra Athit) A Bangkok legend, Roti-Mataba does a whirlwind business of *kaeng mátsàmàn* (Thai Muslim curry) served with *rotii* (fried flatbread), and chicken or vegetable *mátàbà* (a stuffed *rotii*).

Khrua Nopparat (Map pp120-1; Th Phra Athit; dishes 60-100B; lunch & dinner Mon-Sat; river ferry Tha Phra Athit) With as much charm as a school cafeteria, the Nopparat's kitchen devotes all of its resources to the menu. The dishes are a little small, so don't shy away from the Thai tradition of overordering. Winners include the deep-fried shrimp or *phàt phàk kha-náa* (stir-fried Chinese greens).

Ton Pho (Map pp120-1; ☎ 0 2280 0452; Th Phra Athit; dishes 80-100B; lunch & dinner; river ferry Tha Phra Athit) Right beside Tha Phra Athit is this converted floating dock that does all the staples with the expertise of a Thai grandmother. Do the litmus test here: the lack of décor inversely matches the strength of the food.

Ranee Guesthouse (Map pp120-1; 77 Trok Mayom; dishes 70-120B; breakfast, lunch & dinner; bus 56, 506, river

---

VEGGING OUT IN BANGKOK

Although most Thais regard vegetarianism as antithetical to good sense, there are several strong currents of meatless philosophies represented in Bangkok's restaurant scene.

Banglamphu has the greatest concentration of vegetarian-friendly restaurants thanks to the nonmeat-eating *faràng*; these are typically low-scale stir-fry shops that do something akin to what your hippie roommates have cooking in their kitchens. A few standouts include **May Kaidee's** (above) and **Ranee Guesthouse** (above).

An indigenous vegetarian movement can be found in the food centres operated by the Santi Asoke community, an ascetic Buddhist sect that practises self-sufficiency through agriculture and strict vegetarian diets. The food centres are operated in conjunction with Bangkok's former governor Chamlong Srimuang, who popularised both the sect and vegetarianism during his corruption-reducing tenure in the 1980s and '90s. **Baan Suan Pai** (p166), **Chamlong's Asoke Café** (p166) and **Arawy** (above) are all affiliated centres.

Indian, Chinese and Muslim restaurants are also veggie-friendly. **Dosa King** (p165) and **Yogi** (p164) are both solely vegetarian. During the vegetarian festival in October, the whole city goes mad for tofu, and stalls and restaurants indicate their nonmeat menu with yellow banners; Chinatown has the highest concentration of stalls. **MBK Food Centre** (p162) has a vegetarian stall that requires mastery of the Asian queue in order to sneak in an order.

A more modern trend in vegetarianism is the health-conscious gourmet treatment that is well-established overseas. Stylish spots, such as **Govinda** (p166) and **Tamarind Café** (p166), deliver date settings for vegetarian epicures, tired of suffering with the meatless afterthoughts on most menus.

STREET EATS

Surely you've heard the rumours about what type of food in Bangkok to avoid, right? It goes: avoid ground meat, crushed ice, something borrowed, something blue – no that's not quite it. Just to be on the safe side, take that mental list and toss it in the first stinky *khlong* (canal) you see. By and large, most street food is not only hygienic but delicious. Granted you'll get Bangkok belly, which is often a result of personal intolerance to chillies or Beer Chang, rather than a tainted plate of *khâo phàt* (fried rice). At least with the street vendors you can see all the action, whereas you don't know the state of affairs in the supposedly 'safe' guesthouse kitchen.

If you're thoroughly convinced that streetside eating is a healthy pursuit, here is a profile of each neighbourhood's general grazing options.

Banglamphu

As you'll quickly discover, Th Khao San (Map pp120–1) is great for late-night snacking: fresh fruit, spring rolls, shwarma sandwiches and stand-and-gulp *phàt thai*. Near the 7-Eleven on Th Rambutri, postimbibing Thais fend off a hangover with a bowl of *jóhk* (rice porridge), which is also a good antidote to Bangkok belly. Soi Rambutri does a brisk business of grilled fish, chicken and cold beer. Night-time stalls on Th Samsen, between Soi 2 and 8, serve *sôm-tam* (papaya salad), *kǔaytǐaw*, and *râat nâa* (noodles with gravy).

A few Muslim vendors occupy Trok Surat, between the shoe stores on the western side of Th Chakraphong between Th Tani and Th Rambutri.

Siam Square

If you're staying on or nearby Soi Kasem San 1, you don't have to suck motorcycle fumes crossing Th Phra Ram I and Th Phayathai to find something to eat. A row of vendors on the *soi* caters mainly to lunching Thais but they have mastered international sign language.

Go to the right of Siam Square's Scala cinema and plunge into the alley that curves behind the Th Phayathai shops (Map pp128–9) to find a row of cheap food stalls (closed weekends). If approaching this alley from Th Phayathai, look for the sign that reads 'food centre'. Behind the Sindhorn Building on Th Withayu, a village of umbrella-shaded vendors caters to lunchtime crowds.

Silom

Just off Th Silom at Soi Pradit (Soi 20), a market (Map pp124–5) assembles in front of the Masjid Mirasuddeen mosque every day. Daytime vendors sell fresh fruit, takeaway meals and spicy *khànom jiin* (stark, white-rice noodles served with curry sauce). There are also a few duck noodle vendors (just look for signs with an image of a duck). **Talat ITF** (Soi 10) has a string of food stalls purveying pots of curry and miles of noodles. Lunch stalls can also be found on Soi Sala Daeng 2 and on Soi 7. A midday vendor ekes out a small business selling *khâo mòk kài* (chicken briyani) in front of the Irish X-Change on Th Convent.

Sukhumvit

Soi 38 Night Market (Map pp122-3; Soi 38, Th Sukhumvit; dishes 30-50B; ✆ 8am-3am) offers gourmet night-noshing, and stays open late for the bleary-eyed clubbers. Try a busy bowl of *kǔaytǐaw* or Chinese-style spring rolls.

ferry Tha Phra Athit) Quantity-loving vegetarians will appreciate this guesthouse kitchen, which serves large portions of vegetable-adoring dishes. Stir-fries are cooked to perfection and can be enjoyed in a quiet garden courtyard where the owner's children play pretend dinner party. Specify if you want brown rice.

Jeh Hoy (Map pp120-1; cnr Th Samsen & Soi 2; dishes 50-150B; ✆ dinner; bus 53, 506, river ferry Tha Phra Athit) If it is feeding time, this open-air restaurant has the best ad campaign around – an ice tray laden with seafood and the hypnotic manoeuvrings of the wok cook. Try the Hokkien special *puu phàt phŏng kàrìi* (crab stir-fried

with curry powder and egg). If it is too busy, skip down the *soi* to other similar outfits.

Hemlock (Map pp120-1; ☎ 0 2282 7507; 56 Th Phra Athit; dishes 80-200B; ☼ dinner; river ferry Tha Phra Athit) Living-room-sized restaurants line Th Phra Athit and form a social gathering point for Banglamphu's bohemians (writers, artists and intellectuals). This cosy gem has an eclectic menu inspired by ancient literary works; try the flavourful *mîang kham* (tea leaves wrapped with ginger, shallots, peanuts, lime and coconut flakes) or *náam phrík khàa* (spicy dipping sauce served with vegetables and herbs), both items that don't usually pop up on menus.

INTERNATIONAL

Prakorb's House (Map pp120-1; ☎ 0 2281 1345; 52 Th Khao San; dishes 50-100B; ☼ breakfast, lunch & dinner; bus 56, 506, river ferry Tha Phra Athit) Good old Prakorb's does exceptionally good guesthouse fare. A huge menu covers all Southeast Asia's interpretations of Western breakfasts, but the real winner is the chewy cup of hot coffee.

Ricky's Coffeeshop (Map pp120-1; 22 Th Phra Athit; dishes 80-150B; ☼ 9am-7pm; river ferry Tha Phra Athit) Why Thais prefer the Wonder variety of bread is a great mystery. But you can gnaw your way to carbo bliss with Ricky's crusty baguettes. Plus, the marble tabletops and wooden gallery will make you feel like a grown-up in perpetually adolescent Th Khao San.

Shoshana (Map pp120-1; unnamed soi off Th Chakraphong; dishes 100-150B; ☼ lunch & dinner; bus 56, 506, river ferry Tha Phra Athit) One of Khao San's longest-running Israeli restaurants, tucked away in an almost secret alley beside the petrol station, Shoshana serves gut-filling falafel-and-hummus plates, but don't overlook the tasty *baba ghanoush* (Middle Eastern eggplant dish).

Chabad House (Map pp120-1; Th Rambutri; dishes 100-200B; ☼ lunch & dinner Sun-Fri; bus 56, 506, river ferry Tha Phra Athit) One plus to sharing the beaten path with Israeli travellers is the opportunity to sample the Mediterranean's comfort food. This well-scrubbed café serves Israeli kosher food directly underneath a Jewish worship centre.

Chinatown & Phahurat

When you mention Chinatown, Bangkokians begin dreaming of noodles, usually prepared by street vendors lining Th Yaowarat, near Trok Itsaranuphap, after dark. During the annual Vegetarian Festival (which is in September/October and centred around Wat Mangkon Kamalawat on Th Charoen Krung), the neighbourhood explodes with street stalls and vendors.

On the western side of the neighbourhood is the Indian fabric district of Phahurat, filled with small restaurants tucked into the *soi* off Th Chakraphet. The soi next to the old ATM building shelters a popular samosa push-cart vendor.

Hong Kong Noodles (Map pp118-19; 136 Trok Itsaranuphap, Th Charoen Krung; dishes 30B; ☼ lunch & dinner; bus 53,

---

CHINATOWN STREET EATS

Even if you've mastered the street stalls in other parts of town, little of that savvy can be applied to the variations that appear in the night markets in Chinatown. Here is a quick introduction to the street vendors and the dishes worth noting. Once you've met and befriended these dishes, you'll spot them in other neighbourhoods too.

- *kuay jáp* – This steamy soup consists of tubular noodles, pork offal and *mǔu krâwp* in a broth spiced with star anise. Try it at the vendor who sets up in the lobby of the old movie theatre at 404 Th Yaowarat.

- *hǎwy jaw* and *hàe kěun* – Usually sold together, these blistered sausages are wrapped in tofu and stuffed with either crab (*hǎwy jaw*; whitish in colour and formed into segments) or shrimp (*hàe kěun*; orange-coloured tubes).

- *hǎwy thâwt* – Fried mussels in batter are prepared in wide flat-bottomed skillets; a well-known vendor sets up near the Th Phadungdao and Th Yaowarat intersection.

- herbal drinks – Huge ice coolers spill over with small plastic bottles of oddly coloured liquid all along Th Yaowarat. In keeping with the Chinese observances of food as medicine, these drinks are made from various herbal teas renowned for their health benefits. The yellow ones are chrysanthemum; brown, *náam râak bua* (lotus root); and the green, *náam bai bua bòk* (a water plant).

73, 507, river ferry Tha Ratchawong) Deep in the heart of a fresh-meat market, this busy shop does a bustling trade in steaming bowls of roast duck noodles.

Bà-mìi Hong Kong (Map pp118-19; cnr Th Yaowarat & Soi Yaowiphanit; dishes 50B; Ⓨ dinner; bus 53, 73, 507 river ferry Tha Ratchawong) Look for a big red sign with Chinese characters near the gold shop and you will have found a noodle adventure. The noodles are in great demand and there is an endless combination of choices, so you'll need a little Thai to accomplish an order, we've found the *bà mìi náam mǔu daeng kíaw* (egg noodles with red pork and wontons) to be a reliable choice.

Th Phadungdao Seafood Stalls (Map pp118-19; cnr Th Phadungdao & Th Yaowarat; dishes 160-300B; Ⓨ 6-10pm; bus 53, 73, 507, river ferry Tha Ratchawong) After sunset, this street sprouts outdoor barbecues, iced seafood trays and sidewalk seating. Servers dash every which way, cars plough through narrow openings, and before you know it you're tearing into a plate of grilled prawns like a starved alley cat.

Shangarila Restaurant (Map pp118-19; ☎ 0 2235 7493; 206 Th Yaowarat; dishes 100-500B; Ⓨ lunch & dinner; bus 73, river ferry Tha Ratchawong) Near the corner of Th Ratchawong, this venerable old gal stays in the restaurant race with a wide selection of dim sum and lunchtime dishes.

Royal India (Map pp118-19; ☎ 0 2221 6565; 392/1 Th Chakraphet; dishes under 100B; Ⓨ lunch & dinner; bus 25, 508, 507, river ferry Tha Saphan Phut) Over in Phahurat, the Indian fabric district, Royal India is a long-running favourite because of its North Indian cuisine, heavily influenced by Moghul or Persian flavours and spices. Follow the signs off Th Chakraphet into a concrete alley.

Old Siam Plaza (Map pp118-19; ground fl, Old Siam Plaza, cnr Th Phahurat & Th Triphet; dishes 50-100B; Ⓨ lunch; bus 25, 508, 507, river ferry Tha Saphan Phut) The Thai version of Willy Wonka's factory occupies the ground floor of this shopping centre. Seemingly savoury ingredients, such as beans, corn and rice, are turned into syrupy sweet desserts right before your eyes. Such transformations include *lûuk chúp* (miniature fruits made of beans), *tàkôh* (coconut pudding in banana leaves) and *khànǒm bêuang* (taco-shaped pancakes filled with shredded coconut and sweetened egg yolks).

Siam Square & Pratunam

When in Shop-landia, you must pay homage to the mall food courts, which are a subset of the market-vendor cult. You'll also find every imaginable Western and Japanese fast-food chain, including a *wâi*-ing Ronald McDonald.

Pratunam Chicken Rice Restaurants (Map pp128-9; cnr Th Phetchaburi & Th Ratchaprarop; dishes 30-50B; Ⓨ 7pm-4am) At the Pratunam intersection are two competing *khâo man kài* (chicken rice) restaurants known by every taxi driver in the city (just say 'Midnight Kai Ton' to get here). Folks argue about which one is better, but we vote for the shop further from the corner.

MBK Food Centre (Map pp128-9; 6th fl, MBK, cnr Th Phayathai & Th Phra Ram I; dishes 40-60B; Ⓨ lunch & dinner; Skytrain National Stadium) Consider MBK's food centre to be a food boot camp – Thai and English signage accompanies an array of typical street eats. After a few sessions here, you'll be equipped for outdoor reconnaissance. Buy coupons from the ticket desk and cash in whatever you don't spend.

Gourmet Paradise (Map pp128-9; ☎ 0 2610 8000; ground fl, Siam Paragon, Th Phra Ram I; dishes 60-250B; Ⓨ lunch & dinner; Skytrain Siam) One entire floor is dedicated to food and eating in Siam Paragon's ubermall universe. The feudal divisions of Thai society are in full effect on weekends. The aristocrats file into the branches of successful white-linen restaurants, while the working class hustles through the food court with trays of noodles and stir-fries.

Whole Earth Restaurant (Map pp128-9; ☎ 0 2252 5574; 93/3 Soi Lang Suan; dishes 100-200B; Ⓨ lunch & dinner) This family-friendly restaurant will put your vegetarian conscience and your belly at ease, but your taste buds might feel left out. The Thai dishes are all extremely fresh but lacking in flair, an obvious shortcoming considering the fetching prices.

My Collection (Map pp128-9; ☎ 0 2655 7502; 2/10 Th Withayu; dishes 250-320B; Ⓨ lunch daily, dinner Fri & Sat) Moonlighting as an antique store, this family-run bistro is filled with pretty things – antique linen, teak furniture and bone China – when floral prints not funeral colours defined sophistication. The ambiance is delicate and intimate, everything that Bangkok's fine-dining scene is lacking. The menu is firmly international and the bistro does a brisk weekday-lunch business for the nearby embassies.

Silom

Come lunchtime, the financial district goes into a feeding frenzy at the shanty villages of

street vendors or the buffets at the English-Irish pubs. Dinner offerings include more gourmet choices, with a handful of elegant restaurants preparing international fusion and royal-Thai cuisine. Simple, family-run Indian restaurants proliferate towards the western end of Th Silom and Th Surawong.

THAI

Chulalongkorn University Canteen (Map pp124–5; Soi Chulalongkorn 42, Th Phayathai, Chulalongkorn Campus; dishes 20B; ☺ lunch; subway Samyan) You might be the only one here not in uniform, but who could say no to an innocent noodle craving? The university's canteen does a delicious sesame-seed-encrusted *kài thâwt* (fried chicken) that is served solo or atop a steaming bowl of noodles. You can also get the noodles spiked with a lip-tingling *tôm yam* broth. A little Thai is needed to order, but no conversation is required to gulp it down beside the uni students copying each others' homework.

Harmonique (Map pp124–5; ☎ 0 2237 8175; Soi 34, Th Charoen Krung; dishes 70–150B; ☺ lunch & dinner) Earning more points for ambience than cuisine, Harmonique is a rambling oasis anchored by a banyan-tree courtyard. With twinkling fairy lights and marble-topped tables, you might not notice (or be troubled by) the shortcomings of the bland dishes.

Ban Chiang (Map pp124–5; ☎ 0 2236 7045; 14 Soi Si Wiang, Th Surasak; dishes 100–180B; ☺ lunch & dinner; Skytrain Surasak) A barely tamed garden girthed by a wooden fence marks the entrance to Ban Chiang, which delivers the fiery cuisine of the northeast. This restaurant is a favourite of undiscerning tour groups and sometimes tip-toes too close to mediocre (avoid the *tôm yam kûng*). Luckily the *yam plaa duk foo* (salad of fried shredded catfish) swoops in to rescue any sagging opinions.

Sara-Jane's (Map pp124–5; ☎ 0 2676 3338; 55/21 Th Narathiwat Ratchanakharin; dishes 100–200B; ☺ lunch & dinner) One of Bangkok's most famous *faràng* (who is married to a Thai) has built a small food empire from the fusion of Isan and Italian food. There is another branch on Th Withayu, but this location puts more passion into the otherwise incongruous food traditions.

Tongue Thai (Map pp124–5; ☎ 0 2630 9918; 18–20 Soi 38, Th Charoen Krung; dishes 150–250B; ☺ lunch & dinner) When you need to be pleased, Tongue Thai is at your service. The dining room is filled with teak furnishings and oh-so Thai décor. The menu is equally accommodating with a few Western ingredients added to traditional Thai recipes in an effort for familiarity.

Le Lys (Map pp124–5; ☎ 0 2287 1898; 104 Soi 7, Th Narathiwat Ratchanakharin; dishes 100–250B; ☺ lunch & dinner; Skytrain Chong Nonsi) Foreign-friendly Thai dishes and a homey setting make Le Lys a trustworthy dinner companion for the city's expats. Some diners snack and drink in between sets of *pétanque* (French lawn bowling) in the restaurant's backyard.

Blue Elephant (Map pp124–5; ☎ 0 2673 9353; 233 Th Sathon Tai; dishes 250–500B; ☺ lunch & dinner; Skytrain Surasak) Set in a refurbished Sino-Thai colonial building with service fit for royalty, the Blue Elephant balances the once-secret recipes of the monarchy with international fusion. The setting and service is impeccable, but the dishes are merely pedestrian.

INDIAN & MUSLIM

Sallim Restaurant (Map pp124–5; Soi 32, Th Charoen Krung; dishes 50–70B; ☺ lunch & dinner; river ferry Tha Meuang Khae) This open-air restaurant could easily win the

---

BEEFING UP AT THE HOTEL BUFFETS

If you're a feast or famine eater, then the hotel buffets are your trough. The huge, all-you-can-eat spread offers a one-stop introduction to Thai food, a raw fish bar, continental specialities or dim-sum exploration. Most hotel buffets are offered for lunch, dinner or Sunday brunch. Reservations are recommended (call for prices, as these vary); business-casual attire is appropriate.

Sukhothai Hotel (Map p127; ☎ 0 2344 8888; 13/3 Th Sathon) offers one of the city's most decadent Sunday brunches. **Royal Orchid Sheraton** (Map pp124–5; ☎ 0 2266 0123; Soi 30, Th Charoen Krung) is geared towards the kiddies with games and finger food. **JW Marriott Hotel** (Map pp122–3; ☎ 0 2656 7700; 4 Th Sukhumvit, Soi 4) is known for its American-style abundance. The riverside hotels, such as the **Oriental** (Map pp124–5; ☎ 0 2659 9000; 48 Soi Oriental/Soi 38, Th Charoen Krung) and the **Peninsula** (Map pp116–17; ☎ 0 2861 2888; 333 Th Charoen Nakhon, Thonburi) add an additional element of elegance to the gorging. Various hotel restaurants will also host seasonal promotions or feature a prominent visiting chef; watch the English-language press for these culinary events.

challenging award for the dirtiest restaurant in Thailand, but the food is fabulous. Dig into one of the southern Thai-Muslim curries – *kaeng kài* (chicken), *néua* (beef) or *plaa* (fish) – served with your choice of rice or *rotii* (two loaves should be enough). The restaurant is the last option along the right-hand block.

Yogi (Map pp124-5; Soi Phuttha Osot, Th Mahesak; dishes 70-100B; lunch & dinner Mon-Sat; river ferry Tha Oriental) Practically sawed in half by the nearby expressway, this New York City–sized restaurant whips up all-vegetarian South Indian meals in a small kitchen. Wash up at the outdoor sink before eating.

Islamic Restaurant (Map pp124-5; ☎ 0 2234 7911; 196-198 Soi 36, Th Charoen Krung; dishes 80-180B; lunch Mon-Sat, dinner daily) Around the corner from the French embassy, this neighbourhood spot is a site for sore feet: the low-key dining area is blissfully air-conditioned and the outdoor patio attempts a café-culture setting. Dishes draw from the Muslim traditions that proliferate on the Malay peninsula and include a turmeric-spiked *khâo mòk kài*.

Indian Hut (Map pp124-5; ☎ 0 2237 8812; Th Surawong; dishes 100-250B; lunch & dinner; river ferry Tha Oriental) Opposite the Manohra Hotel, Indian Hut proudly displays a slightly altered Pizza Hut logo (so much for pesky copyright laws), and specialises in Nawabi (Lucknow) cuisine for a well-scrubbed business set. The vegetarian samosa, fresh prawns cooked with ginger and homemade *paneer* (soft Indian cheese) are all must nibbles.

INTERNATIONAL

Mizu's Kitchen (Map pp124-5; ☎ 0 2233 6447; Soi Patpong 1, Th Silom; dishes 80-150B; noon-1am; Skytrain Sala Daeng, subway Silom) Relive the grubby days of Bangkok's R&R era at this Patpong institution. Old-style Japanese-Western dishes (such as macaroni and cheese, steak and vegetable hotplate) are the most recent decorations amid chequered tablecloths and fading girlie calendars. All the dishes are warm and salty, and a perfect companion for a slurred-speech night.

La Boulange (Map pp124-5; ☎ 0 2631 0355; 2-2/1 Th Convent; dishes 160-240B; breakfast, lunch & dinner) Should you need a breather from the working grind in Silom, stop by this European-style café with marble-topped tables facing all the street action.

Eat Me (Map pp124-5; ☎ 0 2238 0931; Soi Phiphat 2, off Th Convent; dishes 200-400B; dinner; Skytrain Sala

Daeng) A little bit of cosmo Sydney has blossomed here off Th Silom. Chic, minimalist décor is accessorised by rotating art exhibits, supplied by H Gallery, a nearby contemporary gallery. And lest we forget, the food is creative, modern, and spans the globe; from pumpkin risotto to tuna tartare.

Lumphini

Soi Polo Fried Chicken (Map p127; ☎ 0 2655 8489; 137/1-2 Soi Polo, Th Withayu; dishes 160B; lunch & dinner; Skytrain Ploenchit, subway Lumphini) Golden and crispy on the outside, moist and meaty inside and sprinkled with fried garlic bits – it is easy to see why this is a beloved *kài thâwt* (fried chicken) restaurant. One half-serve will generously feed two, but don't forget about ordering sticky rice for the spicy dipping sauces.

Ngwan Lee Lang Suan (Map p127; ☎ 0 2250 0936; cnr Soi Lang Suan & Th Sarasin; dishes 150-300B; dinner; Skytrain Chitlom) Hardly more than a mess hall, this sweaty open-air place specialises in Chinese-style seafood and *kài lâo daeng* (chicken steamed in Chinese herbs).

Zanotti (Map p127; ☎ 0 2636 0002; 211 1st fl, Sala Daeng Colonnade, Soi Sala Daeng 1, Th Silom; dishes 350-550B; lunch & dinner) Never a surly word is uttered about this Italian restaurant. The dining room is intimate; the menu has been airlifted from the Piedmont and Tuscany regions; and premeal nibblers are rewarded with a huge selection of antipasto plates. Many meals become late-nighters.

BREAKFAST OF CHAMPIONS

What's for breakfast in the City of Angels? Well, judging by the platoon of túk-túk drivers parked outside your hotel, Thailand's morning mainstay is an M150 energy drink and a cigarette. Too nutritious, you say? In addition to the name-only guesthouse pancakes, the Western breakfast tradition is charmingly pantomimed at the **Atlanta Coffeeshop** (opposite) and the coffee shop of the **Federal Hotel** (p156), both appealing for their flashback in time. Expats who have forgotten what a toaster looks like go to **Bourbon St Bar & Restaurant** (p166). Yuppy Thais who claim international upbringings prefer the gourmet chic of **Kuppa** (p166). And anyone who has the Gaul to do so, savour the crepes at **Crepes & Co** (opposite).

Sukhumvit

This avenue, stretching east all the way to the city limits, is the communal dining room of most of Bangkok's expat communities, from Italian to Arabic. While a recent arrival might not be craving the tastes of home, many of these satellite stations are good observation points on the city's many microcosms. Sukhumvit's restaurants also provide an interesting looking glass through which to view a universal occurrence – locals embracing 'exotic' cuisines.

THAI

Thong Lee (Map pp122-3; ☎ 0 2258 1983; Soi 20, Th Sukhumvit; mains 60-100B; ❤ 9am-8pm, closed 3rd Sun of the month; Skytrain Asoke) In any other neighbourhood, Thong Lee would be nearly indistinguishable from all the other shopfront wok shops, but Sukhumvit sometimes forgets that it is in Thailand. Instead of being transformed into a massage parlour or visa-wedding service, Thonglee offers a more nutritious service: lovingly made rice and curries.

Atlanta Coffeeshop (Map pp122-3; ☎ 0 2252 6069; Atlanta Hotel, 78 Soi 2, Th Sukhumvit; dishes 60-150B; ❤ breakfast, lunch & dinner; Skytrain Ploenchit) Preserving the era of pillbox hats and white gloves, the Atlanta is the most grounded fashion idol in Bangkok. The subdued diner features a heavily annotated menu, and scratchy recordings of Thai, classical and jazz (including an hour of King Bhumibol's compositions beginning at noon). Vegetarian, standard Thai and Western breakfasts are all exemplary selections.

Cabbages & Condoms (Map pp122-3; ☎ 0 2229 4611; Soi 12, Th Sukhumvit; dishes 150-200B; ❤ lunch & dinner; Skytrain Asoke) If you haven't cottoned onto the rustic aspects of Thai food, then Cabbages & Condoms is a perfect 'wading' pool; plus, all proceeds go towards sex-education and AIDS-prevention programmes in Thailand through the Population & Community Development Association (PDA), headquartered next door. A reminder of the restaurant's community outreach appears in the form of a packaged condom, a clever alternative to the traditional after-dinner mint.

Vientiane Kitchen (Map pp122-3; ☎ 0 2258 6171; 8 Soi 36, Th Sukhumvit; dishes 150-220B; ❤ dinner; Skytrain Thong Lor) Vientiane Kitchen is a cultural display for the reluctant tourist. In a big barnlike structure, *măw lam* (traditional northeastern Thai music) bands play all the rollicking tunes of the Isan countryside, while the fiery *tôm yam kûng*, *lâap mǔu* (minced pork salad), *kài yâang* (grilled marinated chicken) will give you a bee-stung pout without collagen injections.

INDIAN & MUSLIM

Nasir al-Masri Restaurant & Shishah (Map pp122-3; ☎ 0 2253 5582; 4/6 Soi 3/1, Th Sukhumvit; dishes 80-120B; ❤ breakfast, lunch & dinner; Skytrain Nana) You can't miss this blinding silver temple to Egyptian food. The fruity perfume from the nearby *shishah* (waterpipe) smokers scents the predinner atmosphere, until the sensory banquet arrives. Worth crowding the table is the sesame-freckled flatbread, creamy hummus and flawlessly fried falafels. Open until 4am.

Dosa King (Map pp122-3; ☎ 0 2651 1651; 265/1 Soi 19, Th Sukhumvit; dishes 120-240B; ❤ lunch & dinner; Skytrain Asoke) Nosh alongside the sari-wrapped mamas or clubbing teenagers at this Punjabi vegetarian favourite. The regional speciality, *dosa* (a thin, stuffed crepe), adorns most tables like ancient parchment scrolls. (If you don't know, you eat these with your hands, using the wrapper as a spoon.)

Al Hussain (Map pp122-3; 75/7 Soi 3/1; dishes 150-250B; ❤ lunch & dinner; Skytrain Nana) Just off Th Sukhumvit near Soi 3 (Soi Nana Neua), there is a winding maze of cramped sublanes known as Little Arabia. At the crossroads is this open-air café displaying a steam table of vegetarian and meat curries, along with *dahl* (curried lentils), *aloo gobi* (spicy potatoes and cauliflower), *naan* (bread) and rice.

INTERNATIONAL

Crepes & Co (Map pp122-3; ☎ 0 2653 3990; 18/1 Soi 12, Th Sukhumvit; dishes 150-280B, ❤ breakfast, lunch & dinner; Skytrain Asoke) This cottage oasis creates delicate, platter-sized crepes stuffed with smoky bacon and woodsy mushrooms, as well as mud-thick coffee. Servers, striped in the colours of the French flag, sail these piping hot dishes to the garden-view tables, which are packed during weekend brunch.

Greyhound Cafe (Map pp122-3; ☎ 0 2664 8663; 2nd fl, Emporium, btwn Soi 22 & 24, Th Sukhumvit; dishes 100-250B; ❤ lunch & dinner; Skytrain Phrom Phong) Oh, the follies of fashion. This trendy café continues the lifestyle branding efforts of Thailand's hottest design label, Greyhound. Like the clientele, the hybrid menu on offer here emphasises updated Thai cuisine after a sojourn in southern Europe. Of late, the branch at J Avenue (Soi

Thong Lor, Th Sukhumvit) has been everyone's darling.

Tamarind Café (Map pp122-3; ☎ 0 2663 7421; 27 Soi 20, Th Sukhumvit; dishes 200-250B; ⏱ lunch & dinner; Skytrain Asoke) Pacific Rim cuisine goes vegetarian at this sleek eatery. Imaginative fresh juice concoctions will stave off a cold or transport you to a long-forgotten beach vacation. Tamarind shares space with Gallery F-Stop (p176), which hosts rotating photography exhibits.

Govinda (Map pp122-3; ☎ 0 2663 4970; Soi 22, Th Sukhumvit; mains 150-300B; ⏱ dinner Wed-Mon; Skytrain Phrom Phong) Pizzas and pastas get a soya-based makeover at this all-Italian, all-vegetarian restaurant.

Bourbon St Bar & Restaurant (Map pp122-3; ☎ 0 2259 0328; Soi 22; dishes 150-300B; ⏱ breakfast, lunch & dinner; Skytrain Asoke & Phrom Phong) Near Mambo Cabaret, this New Orleans–style restaurant fills the bellies of all-day breakfast cravers. Mexican concoctions score with their home-made salsa and the riddle of chicken-fried steak continues to defy common sense.

Kuppa (Map pp122-3; ☎ 0 2663 0450; 39 Soi 16, Th Sukhumvit; dishes 200-400B; ⏱ Tue-Sat; Skytrain Asoke) A popular brunch date, Kuppa administers Western replacement therapy: a modern but comfortable dining room with spot-on white sauces and real salads.

Pizzeria Bella Napoli (Map pp122-3; ☎ 0 2259 0405; 3/3 Soi 31, Th Sukhumvit; dishes 200-500B; ⏱ dinner Mon-Fri, lunch Sat & Sun; Skytrain Phrom Phong) In Bangkok's Little Italy, an eclectic and boisterous crowd gulps down glasses of blood-red wine and gooey, garlicky wood-fired pizzas in this Neapolitan outpost. Prepare to be jealous when the table next to you orders the prosciutto-bridge pizza.

Spring (Map pp122-3; ☎ 0 2392 2747; 199 Soi 2/Soi Promsri, btwn Soi 39 & Soi 49, Th Sukhumvit; dishes 200-350B; ⏱ lunch & dinner; taxi) In the dry season, this fashion restaurant spreads its guests out on the lawn for alfresco wining and dining. To soak up a garden ambiance in urban Bangkok is as luxurious as the chocolate desserts.

Great American Rib Company (Map pp122-3; ☎ 0 2661 3891; 32 Soi 36, Th Sukhumvit; mains 165-400B; ⏱ 11.30am-11.30pm; Skytrain Thong Lor) Big plates of slow-cooked meat create an edible map of the American South: pulled pork from the Carolinas, Memphis-style ribs and slathered Texas-style chicken. The menu may be American but the setting and the clientele is totally Thai with outdoor picnic tables, chilli-laced sauces and lots of happy birthday celebrations.

Maha Naga (Map pp122-3; ☎ 0 2662 3060; Soi 29/Lak Khet, Th Sukhumvit; dishes 300-700B; ⏱ 11.30am-2.30pm & 5pm-1am; Skytrain Phrom Phong) Upscale Maha Naga, named after the mythical sea serpent, has a setting to die for: a pan-Asian fantasy of winking candles, Moorish courtyards and Balinese carvings. So the East-meets-West flavours fall short of competent, but these are the sacrifices you have to make for beauty in Bangkok.

Le Banyan (Map pp122-3; ☎ 0 2253 5556; 59 Soi 8, Th Sukhumvit; dishes 400-900B; ⏱ dinner Mon-Sat; Skytrain Nana) In a charming Ratanakosin-style house surrounded by a lush garden, this is the landed gentry of French restaurants in a city enamoured with upstarts. The French-managed kitchen is best known for its pressed duck.

Greater Bangkok

Chamlong's Asoke Café (Map pp114-15; ☎ 0 2272 4282; 580-592 Th Phahon Yothin, Chatuchak; dishes 20-30B; ⏱ lunch Sat & Sun; subway Chatuchak Park) Operated by the Asoke Foundation, the vegetarian restaurant near the Chatuchak Weekend Market is one of Bangkok's oldest. Take the footbridge across Th Kamphaeng Phet, away from the market, and towards the southern end of Th Phahonyothin. Turn right onto the first through street and walk past bars into the car park. Behind a block of buildings selling bulk food stuff is the restaurant. Like Baan Suan Pai, you buy tickets at the front desk.

Baan Suan Pai (Bamboo Garden House; Map pp116-17; ☎ 0 2615 2454; Th Phahonyothin; dishes 25B; ⏱ lunch & dinner; Skytrain Ari) This vegetarian food centre offers a garden's bounty of diversity. Buy coupons from the woman at the desk by the door. (Some coupons are printed with Thai numbers only, but the denominations are colour-coded: green, 5B; purple, 10B; blue, 20B; and red, 25B). Everything is strictly vegetarian, there's even no fish sauce. Don't miss the handmade ice cream of such exotic flavours as passionfruit, lemongrass and lotus root.

Pickle Factory (Map pp116-17; ☎ 0 2246 3036; 55 Soi 2, Th Ratchawithi; dishes 150-200B; ⏱ dinner; Skytrain Victory Monument) Occupying a 1970s Thai house, the Pickle Factory creates a dinner-party mood with indoor sofa seating and outdoor tables around a pool – in short, the perfect place to kick back for an evening with friends. The menu includes creative pizza toppings, such as Chiang Mai sausage and basil paste with wing beans.

Aw Taw Kaw Market (Map pp114-15; Th Kampangphet; dishes 30-40B; ⏱ lunch; Skytrain Mo Chit,

---

THE WATER DIET

Despite the heat and the chaos, Bangkok's quintessential eating experiences are always outdoors. Nibble away an entire evening at an outdoor food market or at one of the rustic riverside restaurants. Riverside dining comes in all shapes and sizes, but a good rule of thumb is a converted pier with zero ambience except what nature intended: cool evening breezes and views of the city lights. Because the river is the primary draw, the food tends to run a distant second, but the following restaurants have either surprised us flavourwise or have been affordable enough for us not to care.

Ton Pho (p159), **Kaloang Home Kitchen** (Map pp116–17; ☎ 0 2281 9228; Soi Wat Thewet; dishes 70–280B; ☙ lunch & dinner) and **Nang Nual Riverside Pub** (Map pp118–19; Trok Krai, Th Mahachak; dishes 90–170B; ☙ dinner) are all incredibly low-key and serve standard Thai dishes. For a little more fuss, consider a dinner cruise (p147).

---

subway Chatuchak Park) Across the street from Chatuchak Weekend Market, Aw Taw Kaw is one of Bangkok's biggest fruit and produce markets, and next door are food stalls that earn equal veneration for duck curries and other street treats.

DRINKING

Where can you get a drink in this town? The original R&R capital will water your gullet just about anywhere. Banglamphu has a dressed-down vibe in an otherwise fashion-status city. Th Silom and Sukhumvit represent the stock-and-trade of Bangkok bars: English-Irish-style pubs and yuppie clubs, while Royal City Ave (RCA; p169) has become an official entertainment zone for everyone old enough to drink.

Bangkok has gone through a mandatory detox thanks to the Thaksin administration's social-order policy, which enforced closing times (1am for bars, 2am for clubs). But the political crisis that followed the flawed elections in April 2006 pushed Bangkok back into its all-night boozing ways. Once a new government is instated, it is unclear if the police will once again enforce the curfew or continue to turn a blind eye.

Banglamphu

The tourist strip of Th Khao San (Map pp120–1) is one big, mutlicultural party with every imaginable outlet for swilling and socialising, and the party extends to the surrounding streets of Th Rambutri and Soi Rambutri. Backpackers drain away bottles of Beer Chang at outdoor stalls. Mixed Thai-*faràng* couples sip sweet cocktails at bars converted from VW buses. Thai teenagers flex their rebellious streak among this anything-goes circus. Even

moneyed Thais have joined the street parade at chic wine-sipping bars.

Beyond the pull of Khao San's packed party zone are more low-key options along Th Phra Athit and beyond.

To-Sit (Map pp120–1; Ran Kin Duem; ☎ 0 2629 1199; 24 Th Phra Athit) One of several art bars in the wooden shophouses along Th Phra Athit. Less crowded than the Khao San bars, this bar-restaurant usually hosts a solo singer and a squeaky guitar.

Illy Café (Ran Siri Poom; Map pp120–1; Th Chakraphong; bus 53, river ferry Tha Phra Athit) Eclectic and funky, Illy Café is a restaurant by day and a 30-something bar at night. The vintage décor captures Banglamphu's bohemian aesthetic and egalitarian spirit.

Phra Nakorn Bar (Map pp120–1; ☎ 0 2222 0282; 58/2 Soi Damnoen Klang Tai; ☙ 6pm-midnight; river ferry Tha Phra Athit, bus 2, 82, 511, 512) A well-kept secret that Lonely Planet has finally sniffed out, Phra Nakorn is just steps away from Th Khao San but a world removed. Students and arty types make this a home away from hovel with eclectic décor, gallery exhibits and, the real draw, a rooftop terrace for a view of the Golden Mount.

Lulla Bar (Map pp120–1; ☎ 0 2622 2585; Th Mahanot) This off-campus hang-out of a rotating cast of Thai students has been transformed into a makeshift bar. Hardly anybody who isn't a friend bothers to cross the threshold, making the odd foreigner who finds the place a barfly conquistador. The food is fantastic, the beers are cold, and the soundtrack skips through classics from the Beatles and the Cure.

Baghdad Café (Map pp120–1; Soi 2, Th Samsen) Just over the Khlong Banglamphu is this sardine-tight *shishah* bar for puffing pungent fruit tobacco on Arabic water pipes and chatting

---

SMOKING IN THE CAPITAL

Bangkok gives the gift of a smoker's cough after only a few days of sucking in the city's toxic stew. If your lungs have Olympic prowess and can still suck on a cigarette, then be aware of the following smoking restrictions.

Most budget guesthouses discourage smoking in rooms as a fire-prevention measure; midrange hotels could care less where you light up, and top enders provide nonsmoking and smoking rooms on request.

Air-conditioned restaurants don't permit smoking, but air-conditioned bars do despite an unenforced city ban. Don't smoke in the Skytrain or subway stations. And don't throw your butts on the ground – the police love to pop foreigners with a hefty littering fine.

---

with your neighbours about distant lands. A divergence from the Arabic tradition is that alcohol is sold right alongside.

Bars tend to segregate into foreigner and Thai factions, but you can always reverse that trend. Here are few popular options:

Cave (Th Khao San) A Thai 'kitchen' club hosting folk and pop bands and an indoor climbing wall.

Center Khao San (Th Khao San) One of many front-row views of the human parade on Th Khao San; the upstairs bar hosts late-night bands.

deep (329/1-2 Th Rambutri) Stylish young Thai crowd and live bands.

Hippie de Bar (Th Khao San) Retro décor, pool tables and chill DJs.

Molly Bar (Th Rambutri) Packed on weekends for Thai local bands; more mellow on weekdays with outdoor seating.

Susie Pub (108/5-9 alley, btwn Th Khao San & Th Rambutri) Thai pop and pool tables.

Silom, Lumphini & Sathon

Barbican Bar (Map pp124-5; ☎ 0 2234 3590; 9 Soi Thaniya, Th Silom) Surrounded by massage parlours with teenage prom queens cat-calling at Japanese businessmen, this is a straight-laced yuppie bar where office crews come for some happy-hour drinks and stay until closing time.

O'Reilly's Irish Pub (Map pp124-5; ☎ 0 2632 7515; 62/1-2 Th Silom) At the entrance to Soi Thaniya, O'Reilly's needs to be on everyone's map for its wallet-friendly, happy-hour specials and

proximity as a warm-up spot to Silom's dance clubs (see p170).

Tower Inn Sky Garden (Map pp124-5; ☎ 0 2237 8300; Soi 9, Th Silom; ⏲ 6pm-midnight; Skytrain Chong Nonsi) Finding a sky-top bar in this city is easy. Finding one where you can afford to be is another matter. Luckily there is the poor-man's beer garden on the 19th floor of the Tower Inn. The view isn't as breathtaking as in some other places, but for down-to-earth beer cheerleaders this spot is lovable kitsch.

Sirocco Sky Bar (Map pp124-5; ☎ 0 2624 9555; The Dome, 1055 Th Silom) Descend the sweeping stairs like a Hollywood golden girl to the precipice bar of this rooftop restaurant. A dress code is enforced and drinks are impressively priced, but so is the view.

Moon Bar at Vertigo (Map p127; ☎ 0 2679 1200; Banyan Tree Hotel, 21/100 Th Sathon Tai) This sky-high, open-air bar will literally take your breath away. From ground level, the elevator delivers you to the 59th floor where you weave your way through dimly lit hallways to the roar of Bangkok traffic far below. Come at sunset and grab a coveted seat to the right of the bar for more impressive views.

Wong's Place (Map p127; 27/3 Soi Sri Bumphen, off Soi Ngam Duphli, Th Phra Ram I; subway Lumphini) A time warp into the backpacker world of the early 1980s, Wong's Place resuscitated a Soi Ngam Duphli institution. No-one shows up until after midnight, when they're too drunk to realise that they really need to go home. Never mind – Wong's is like home, except with a bar and a music library.

Diplomat Bar (Map pp128-9; ☎ 0 2690 9999; Conrad Hotel, 87 Th Withayu) Young sophisticates toast their good fortune and good looks at one of Bangkok's leading hotel bars. The bubbly and the grapey spirits are raised in grand toasts while the diva-led lounge band serenades.

Sukhumvit

Cheap Charlie's (Map pp122-3; Soi 11, Th Sukhumvit; ⏲ Mon-Sat) Claiming the noble honour of serving the cheapest beer on the block, this wooden stall festooned with junk-yard decorations is a favourite happy-hour spot for the neighbourhood's wage-slave *faràng*. Turn a sharp left before the Federal Hotel at the 'Sabai Sabai Massage' sign to join the collective milling and swilling.

Jool's (Map pp122-3; ☎ 0 2252 6413; Soi 4/Nana Tai, Th Sukhumvit) A few doors down from the Nana Entertainment Plaza, Jool's is a sink-

ing ship of a dive bar navigating through the district's commercial 'friendliness'. The horseshoe-shaped bar encourages entertaining exhibitionism and spinning of tall tales. With a ring of the captain's bell, indicating a free round, the mood shifts to a good-times drinking club.

Sin Bar (Map pp122-3; ☎ 0 9501 6735; 18 Soi 4/Nana Tai, Th Sukhumvit) Technically an 'entertainment' complex, Sin Bar is Nana's alter ego: three floors divided into a pool hall, dance club and rooftop bar all noticeably lacking in the soi's namesake industry (prostitutes), and reliably sneaking past the curfew restrictions. Working girls might come in with their dates but so do other crowds more interested in carousing.

Face Bangkok (Map pp122-3; ☎ 0 2713 6048; 29 Soi 38, Th Sukhumvit) When you no longer need cheap and grungy, Face has a classy cocktail lounge attached to its affiliated Indian and Thai restaurants. The crowd and the décor are pretty and the soundtrack is conversation audible, if ranked on the Asian volume scale.

Central Bangkok

Water Bar (Map pp116-17; ☎ 0 2642 7699; 107/3-4 Th Rangnam) Every new arrival should learn the whisky-set routine, a drinking tradition integral to Thai family gatherings. At this misnomered bar, the Sang Som set (Thai whisky with Coke, soda and ice) still reigns as the tipple of choice. The attentive waitress will keep your glass filled to the right proportions (two fingers whisky, a splash of coke, the rest soda). You should offer up a toast after each refill.

ENTERTAINMENT

Bangkok's entertainment scene goes well beyond its naughty-nightlife image. Today Bangkok's nightscape looks a lot like that of New York or London, only with thinner bartenders and louder sound systems. Even if you're usually in bed by 9pm, Bangkok still offers interesting postdinner diversions, from flash cinemas to traditional cultural performances.

Live Music

Since Bangkok is the capital of Thailand's music industry, the city is always host to big-name performers and small-time garage bands. Of late, Th Khao San has become a music venue for Thai indie bands playing

street concerts or shows at various Khao San clubs (see p167). Also check out the music calendar at **Thai Poppers** (www.thaipoppers.com/live/) for appearances by top-10 bands. Nightly lineups at smaller venues can be found online at **Bangkok Gig Guide** (www.bangkokgigguide.com).

Ad Here the 13th (Map pp120-1; 13 Th Samsen) Beside Khlong Banglamphu, Ad Here is everything a neighbourhood joint should be – lots of regulars, cold beer and heartwarming tunes delivered by a masterful house band starting at 10pm. Everyone knows each other, so don't be shy about mingling.

Living Room (Map pp122-3; ☎ 0 2653 0333; Sheraton Grande Sukhumvit, 250 Th Sukhumvit, btwn Soi 12 & 14) With studio-style perfection, the well-scrubbed jazz bands of international calibre put a sizzle into the men's-club aesthetic of this hotel bar. Order yourself a Johnny on the rocks and revel in being a first-class internationalist.

Radio City (Map pp124-5; ☎ 0 2266 4567; Soi Patpong 1) Wet your whistle and shake your tail feathers at this Patpong favourite after a bargaining crusade at the nearby night market. The masters of ceremonies include a Thai Elvis and a Tom Jones impersonator. Come late with a sufficient amount of social lubrication to enjoy the vacation-land cheesiness.

Bamboo Bar (Map pp124-5; ☎ 0 2236 0400; Oriental Hotel, Soi 38/Oriental, Th Charoen Krung) The Oriental's Bamboo Bar is famous for its live lounge jazz, which holds court inside a colonial-era cabin of lazy fans, broad-leafed palms and rattan décor.

Brown Sugar (Map p127; ☎ 0 2250 1825; 231/20 Th Sarasin, opposite Lumphini Park) Crescent City would be proud of this cluttered jazz space of odd angles and smoking chops. Brown Sugar whips up inspired performances that lean more towards bebop than brass.

Saxophone Pub & Restaurant (Map pp116-17; ☎ 0 2246 5472; 3/8 Th Phayathai) A Bangkok institution, Saxophone is reminiscent of a German beer cellar, with brilliant acoustics and up-close views of the nightly bands. Reggae, rhythm and blues, jazz and rock will bridge any troubling language barriers.

Tawandaeng Beer Hall (Map pp114-15; ☎ 0 2678 1114; 462/61 Th Narathiwat Ratchanakharin, cnr Th Phra Ram III) You'll find half of Bangkok in this huge, village-sized brewhouse sipping German-style microbrews and singing with stage pop shows. Between sets, choruses of 'Happy Birthday' erupt from overcrowded tables. Another draw is the Wednesday night performance by Fong

Nam, a fusion band of Western and Thai classical music.

Raintree Pub (Map pp116-17; ☎ 0 2245 7230; 116/63-64 Soi Rangnam, Th Phahon Yothin) Decorated like a country-and-western bar with driftwood and the signature buffalo horns, Raintree is a relic in Bangkok's music scene. The nightly bands carry on the 'songs for life' tradition, one of Thailand's most unique adaptations of rock music, that has now passed from current to classic.

Dance Clubs

All the big-city trends are here: clubs featuring international DJs, hip-hop and various electronica. The trick in doing Bangkok is to catch the right spot on the right night. Bangkok's discos burn strong and bright on certain weekends or during hot 'theme' nights, but then fall into comatose slumbers on off nights.

Dude Sweet (www.dudesweet.org) does monthly party roundups at various clubs, and **Bangkok Recorder** (www.bangkokrecorder.com) documents the rotating theme nights and visiting DJ celebs.

Cover charges for clubs and discos range from 500B to 600B and usually include a drink. Don't even think about showing up before 11pm, and always bring ID. Most clubs close at 2am. You'll see more Thais out on the town at the beginning of the month (pay day) than other times.

Lucifer (Map pp124-5; ☎ 0 2234 6902; 2nd fl above Radio City, Soi Patpong 1, Th Silom) The keystone of Bangkok's dance halls, the Lord of the Underworld has chosen a consistently tripped-out techno-rave soundtrack. The modest cover charge also ensures that warm bodies pack the floor when other clubs are empty.

Tapas (Map pp124-5; Soi 4, Th Silom) The ambassador of Soi 4's dead-end cruise, Tapas is a

---

GAY & LESBIAN BANGKOK

With out-and-open nightspots and annual pride events, Bangkok's homosexual community enjoys an unprecedented amount of tolerance considering attitudes in the rest of the region.

Utopia (www.utopia-asia.com) is an online resource for the Southeast Asian gay community, listing Bangkok entertainment venues, news and views, and providing travel services. **Dreaded Ned** (www.dreadedned.com) also does a rundown on gay nightlife in Bangkok and Pattaya. The city's lesbian community keeps a quieter profile than their more flamboyant counterparts, but there are a few hang-outs to tap into the community. The **Lesbian Guide to Bangkok** (www.bangkoklesbian .com) is one of the only English-language trackers of the scene.

Bangkok's pink triangle is formed on one side by Th Silom and the other by Th Sarasin, where cruising limits reach highway speeds. All of Soi 2 on Th Silom is lined with dance clubs, such as **DJ Station** (Map pp124-5; ☎ 0 2266 4029; 8/6-8 Soi 2, Th Silom; cover 300B), where the crowd is a mix of Thai guppies (gay professionals), money boys and a few Westerners. Just a half soi over is **Freeman** (Map pp124-5; ☎ 0 2632 8032; small soi btwn Soi 2 & Soi Thaniya, Th Silom), which reputedly does the best (and seediest) kàthoey cabaret in town. Traipse on over to Soi 4 to find the old-timer conversation bars, such as **Balcony** (Map pp124-5; ☎ 0 2235 5891; 8/6-8 Soi 4, Th Silom) and **Telephone** (Map pp124-5; ☎ 0 2234 3279; 114/11-13 Soi 4, Th Silom). The gay men's equivalent of Patpong's go-go bars can be found on nearby Soi Thaniya and Soi Anuman Ratchathon.

If you prefer to dine before you imbibe, check out Eat Me (p164), a gay-owned restaurant with class and cuisine.

Th Sarasin, behind Lumphini Park, is lined with more loungey options, such as **70s Bar** (Map p127; ☎ 0 2253 4433; 231/16 Th Sarasin), a small dance club that resuscitates the era of disco, and **I-Chub** (Map p127; ☎ 0 1208 5069; 2nd fl, 297 Th Sarasin), a karaoke bar for the shy and big-boned.

Further out of town is a more local scene where a little Thai will make you feel more welcome. The bars around Chatuchak, including **ICQ** (Map pp114-15; ☎ 0 2272 4775; Th Kamphaengphet, Chatuchak; Skytrain Mo Chit, subway Chatuchak Park), are favourites for loud and lushy behaviour.

Bangkok has just started to develop a lesbian-only nightclub scene with two newcomers: **Shela** (Map p127; Soi Lang Suan, Th Ploenchit) and **Zeta** (Map pp114-15; ☎ 0 2203 0994; 29/67 Block S, RCA, Th Phra Ram IX). Both are easy-going clubs for the girls with a nightly band doing Thai and Western covers. The night-hopping tom-dees tend to start out at Shela's and then make the trek out to Zeta's as the night gets later. The restaurant Hemlock (p161) and other art bars along Th Phra Athit are neighbourhood hang-outs for an intellectual and artistic crowd of lesbians and gays.

rendezvous point for the paired and the pair-able. In its Moroccan-inspired spaces, small samplers fit every taste: from the outdoor peo-ple-watching tables to the upstairs dance floor of soulful sounds and sweaty bodies.

Met Bar (Map p127; ☎ 0 2625 3333; Metropolitan Hotel, Th Sathon) Cosy and fashionable, the Met Bar started its career as a members-only club but has re-laxed its policy to include everyone dressed to impress. The Friday night theme nights get the most attention, but the Met's social standing is a precarious one in this fickle city.

Q Bar (Map pp122-3; ☎ 0 2252 3274; Soi 11, Th Sukhumvit; Skytrain Nana) Much debate rages over this long-running club. New York–style industrial chic is merged with groovy beats and competent cocktails (including absinthe and 40 kinds of vodka), but dissenters charge that the beautiful crowd has migrated elsewhere and has been replaced by too many working girls.

Bed Supperclub (Map pp122-3; ☎ 0 2651 3537; 26 Soi 11, Th Sukhumvit; Skytrain Nana) Inside this futuristic building is an all-white interior reminiscent of the set from *2001: A Space Odyssey*. As the name suggests, there are beds for lounging with your friends, and supper is served in a separate restaurant. It is a fixture on the theme-night calendar.

Santika (Map pp122-3; ☎ 0 2711 5886; 235/11 Soi 63/ Ekkamai, Th Sukhumvit) That weekend traffic jam on Ekkamai is feeding into supersized Santika, a *hi-so* Thai favourite. Shove yourself into the main dance hall for live bands, or squirm into the hip-hop room. If all else fails, grab an outdoor table with the grown-ups.

Royal City Avenue (RCA; Map pp114-15; Royal City Avenue, Th Phra Ram IX) is a suburban block of nightclubs that has graduated from teenage binge drinking to good times for all kinds. Starting at the begin-ning of the block, you'll find the following:

Club Astra (☎ 0 2255 8476; www.club-astra.com) This place coaxes a funkier crowd with electronica DJs and indie bands.

Flix/Slim (☎ 0 2203 0377) The poshest choice on the strip with big thumping house beats and a more club-jaded clientele.

Old Leng (☎ 0 2203 0972) Expect an easier-listening soundtrack for more sensitive eardrums.

Route 66 (☎ 0 1440 9666; www.route66club.com) It rocks to a younger beat with hip-hop and R&B to the 'east' and varying shades of house to the 'west'.

Go-Go Bars

You might have heard that Bangkok is happy-hooker land. The rumours are true –

whole neighbourhoods are dedicated to sex tourism, from massage parlours to go-go bars, and tales about these places comprise the majority of English-language literature about the city. In fact, the courtship habits of the hairless mammal are so pronounced in Bangkok that any moral revulsion toward the flesh trade eventually mellows into am-bivalent absurdity. One of the more palatable documenters of Bangkok's sexy underbelly is **Stickman's Guide to Bangkok** (www.stickmanbangkok .com), which offers tips and perspectives on 'doing' Bangkok.

Patpong (Map pp124-5; Soi Patpong 1 & 2, Th Silom) Bangkok's most famous red-light district dates back to the beginning of the West's fas-cination with Asian prostitutes. Patpong has become more of an all-purpose circus than a flesh market. A major diluter is the popu-lar souvenir market on Soi Patpong 1, which draws in families and conservative couples. The remaining go-go bars still put on erotica shows that are visited by gawkers for a good laugh rather than a hard-on.

Soi Cowboy (Map pp122-3; btwn Soi 21 & Soi 23, Th Sukhumvit) This single-lane strip of 25 to 30 bars claims direct lineage to the post–Vietnam War R&R era. A real flesh trade functions amid the flashing neon. For a fly-on-the-wall perspective, stop in at the nearby internet cafés to see groups of bar girls writing love-letter emails to their new sugar daddies; the well-worn piece of paper in front of them is something of a 'master' copy.

Nana Entertainment Plaza (Map pp122-3; Soi 4/ Nana Tai, Th Sukhumvit) This three-storey complex forms a nucleus of strip clubs that comes complete with its own hotel, used almost exclusively by female bar workers for illicit assignations.

Grace Hotel (Map pp122-3; ☎ 0 2253 0651; 12 Soi 3/Nana Nua, Th Sukhumvit) Across Th Sukhumvit is this legendary skin scene that specialises in the tastes of Arab men. All the cultural elements are in place: the Thai 'freelancers' tend to be a little chunky and the men hud-dle together in groups as if at a high-school dance.

Cinemas

Get out of the smog and heat at one of the city's hi-tech cinemas. For the royal treat-ment, opt for the VIP section with reclining seats and table service. All movies screened in Thai cinemas are preceded by the Thai royal

CELLULOID ENCOUNTERS

The Land of Smiles used to be the Land of Sappy Movies until a new breed of film-makers started bringing visual storytelling to the silver screen. Spotlighted at the annual Bangkok International Film Festival (p148) and at art-house theatres such as Scala, Lido and House, locally made movies have cultivated a devoted fan base of bohemians and intellectuals, both domestic and international, although commercial success still eludes the artier flicks. Keep an eye out for new releases from the feel-good king Nonzee Nimibutr; art-freaky Apichatpong Weerasethakul; and hip Pen-Ek Ratanaruang. For a historical snapshot of Thailand's cinematic new wave, see p71.

But if you are more of a cinematic populist, then you can gorge on a rotating diet of locally made horror flicks that headlines the mainstream cinemas. The genre is so prolific that the Ronin Team, a group of Thai film-makers, and their bloody and ancient-curse-filled film *Art of the Devil 2* won the People's Choice award at the 2006 Bangkok International Film Festival.

anthem and everyone is expected to stand respectfully for its duration.

All of Hollywood's big releases plus a steady diet of locally bred comedies and horror flicks hit Bangkok's cinemas in a timely fashion. The foreign films are often altered by Thailand's film censors before distribution; this usually involves obscuring nude sequences, although gun fights are sometimes edited out, too. Film buffs may prefer the offerings at Bangkok's foreign cultural centres. For contact details, see p104.

At the following cinemas, English movies are shown with Thai subtitles rather than being dubbed. The shopping-centre cinemas have plush VIP options, while Lido and Scala are older and artier. House is Bangkok's first 'art-house' theatre. Visit **Movie Seer** (www.movie seer.com) for show times.

EGV Grand (Map pp128-9; ☎ 0 2515 5555; Siam Discovery Center, Th Phra Ram; Skytrain Siam)

House (Map pp114-15; ☎ 0 2641 5177; www.house rama.com; UMG Bldg, RCA, near Th Petchaburi; subway Phetburi)

Lido Cinema (Map pp128-9; ☎ 0 2252 6498; Siam Square, Th Phra Ram I; Skytrain Siam)

Paragon Cineplex (Map pp128-9; ☎ 0 2515 5555; Siam Paragon, Th Phra Ram I Siam; Skytrain Siam)

Scala Cinema (Map pp128-9; ☎ 0 2251 2861; Siam Square, Soi 1, Th Phra Ram I; Skytrain Siam)

SF Cinema City (Map pp128-9; ☎ 0 2268 8888; 7th fl, MBK, cnr Th Phra Ram I & Th Phayathai; Skytrain National Stadium)

SFX Cinema (Map pp122-3; ☎ 0 2268 8888; 6th fl, Emporium, Th Sukhumvit, btwn Soi 22 & 24; Skytrain Phrom Phong)

Traditional Arts Performances

As Thailand's cultural repository, Bangkok offers an array of dance and theatre perform-

ances. For background information about these ancient traditions, see p66 and p69.

Chalermkrung Royal Theatre (Sala Chaloem Krung; Map pp118-19; ☎ 0 2222 0434; www.salachalermkrung.com; cnr Th Charoen Krung & Th Triphet; bus 507, 508) In a Thai Art Deco building at the edge of the Chinatown-Phahurat district, this theatre provides a striking venue for *khohn* (masked dance-drama based on stories from the *Ramakian*). When it opened in 1933, the royally funded Chalermkrung was the largest and most modern theatre in Asia. Mom Chao Samaichalem Kridakara, a former student of the École des Beaux-Arts in Paris, designed the hexagonal building.

Khohn performances last about two hours plus intermission; call for the schedule. The theatre requests that patrons dress respectfully, which means no shorts, tank tops or sandals. Bring along a wrap or long-sleeved shirt in case the air-con is running full blast.

Natayasala (Joe Louis Puppet Theatre; Map p127; ☎ 0 2252 9683, www.thaipuppet.com; Suan Lum Night Bazaar, cnr Th Phra Ram IV & Th Withayu; tickets 900B; ☾ show 7.30pm) The ancient art of Thai puppetry was heroically rescued by Sakorn Yangkeawsot, more popularly known as Joe Louis, in 1985. Today his children carry on the tradition of reenacting the *Ramakian* by using knee-high puppets requiring three puppeteers to strike humanlike poses. The present home of the theatre, Suan Lum Night Bazaar, is set for redevelopment in 2007, but a new location for the theatre was not certain at the time of research.

National Theatre (Map p130; ☎ 0 2224 1352; Th Na Phra That; admission 50-100B) Near Saphan Phra Pin Klao, the National Theatre hosts monthly performance of the royal dance traditions of *lákhon* (a play) and *khohn*. Unfortunately, the advertisements for these events are printed

only in Thai on placards outside the gates of the theatre. Occasionally the Bangkok Tourist Division (p106) can provide an English-language calendar.

Patravadi Theatre (Map p130; ☎ 0 2412 7287; www .patravaditheatre.com; 69/1 Soi Tambon Wenglang 1; tickets 500B; ☺ performances vary) Next to the Supatra River House in Thonburi, this open-air theatre is Bangkok's leading promoter of avantgarde dance and drama. Led by Patravadi Mejudhon, who is a famous Thai actress, the troupe's performances blend traditional Thai arts and folk tales with modern choreography, music and costumes. A free river shuttle picks up patrons at Tha Mahathat, near Silpakorn University; reservations for performances are recommended.

Sala Rim Nam (Map pp124-5; ☎ 0 2437 3080; Oriental Hotel, Soi 38/Oriental, Th Charoen Krung; tickets 1850B; ☺ 7-10pm) The Oriental Hotel's affiliated dinner theatre is a Thai-style teak pavilion. Readers rave about the hour-long classical dance performance, but give the food a mediocre rating, a common trait of many dinner theatres; reservations are recommended.

Thailand Cultural Centre (Map pp114-15; ☎ 0 2247 0028; www.thaiculturalcenter.com; Th Ratchadaphisek btwn Th Thiam Ruammit & Th Din Daeng; subway Thailand Cultural Centre) Occasionally, classical dance performances are held at this venue featuring a concert hall, art gallery and outdoor studios. International dance and theatre groups are also profiled, especially during the International Festival of Dance & Music (p148). Call for upcoming events as the website doesn't carry an up-to-date schedule.

Dusit Palace Park (p132) also hosts daily classical dance performances.

Muay Thai

Thai boxing's best of the best fight it out at Bangkok's two boxing stadiums: **Lumphini**

Stadium (Sanam Muay Lumphini; Map p127; ☎ 0 2251 4303; Th Phra Ram IV; subway Lumphini) and **Ratchadamnoen Stadium** (Sanam Muay Ratchadamnoen; Map pp120-1; ☎ 0 2281 4205; Th Ratchadamnoen Nok; bus 70, 503, 509). For the past two years there has been much talk about plans to move the Lumphini Stadium to a new location south of central Bangkok, but a date for the move has yet to be set.

Tickets at both stadiums cost 1000/1500/2000B for 3rd class/2nd class/ringside; advance reservations are needed for ringside seats. Be forewarned that these admission prices are exponentially more than what Thais pay, and the inflated price offers no special service or seating. In fact, at Ratchadamnoen Stadium, foreigners are sometimes corralled into an area with an obstructed view. As long as you are mentally prepared for the financial jabs from the promoters, you'll be better prepared to enjoy the real fight.

Ringside puts you right up on the central action but amid a fairly subdued crowd where gambling is prohibited. Second-class seats are filled with backpackers and numbers runners who take the bets from the crowd. Like being in the pit of a stock exchange, hand signals fly between the 2nd- and 3rd-class areas communicating bets and odds. The 3rd-class area is the rowdiest section. Fenced off from the rest of the stadium, most of the die-hard fans follow the match (or their bets) too closely to sit down. If you're lukewarm on watching two men punch and kick each other, then 3rd-class offers the diversion of the crowd.

Fights are held throughout the week, alternating between the two stadiums. Ratchadamnoen hosts the matches on Monday, Wednesday and Thursday at 6pm and on Sunday at 5pm. Lumphini hosts matches on Tuesday, Friday and Saturday at 6pm.

SHRINE DANCING

Stumbling across the minor-chord cacophony of a *lákhon kâe bon* (commissioned shrine dance) can be an unexpected visual and cultural treat and a release from the ever-present self-consciousness of being a tourist. At **Lak Meuang** (p110) and **Erawan Shrine** (p135) worshippers whose wishes have been granted hire dance troupes in gratitude. Although many of the dance movements are the same as those seen in *lákhon,* these relatively crude performances are specially choreographed for ritual purposes, and don't represent true classical dance forms. But it is colourful – the dancers wear full costume and are accompanied by live music.

Also keep an eye out in the newspaper for announcements of temple fairs, where folk dance performances such as *lí-keh* (folk dance) and *lam tàt* (drama), are performed.

Aficionados say the best-matched bouts are reserved for Tuesday nights at Lumphini and Thursday nights at Ratchadamnoen. There is a total of eight to 10 fights of five rounds a piece. The stadiums don't usually fill up until the main events, which usually start around 8pm or 9pm.

There are English-speaking 'staff' standing outside the stadium who will practically tackle you upon arrival. Although there have been a few reports of scamming, most of these assistants help steer visitors to the foreigner ticket windows and hand out a fight roster; they can also be helpful in telling you which fights are the best match-ups between contestants. (Some say that welterweights, between 135lb and 147lb, are the best). To keep everyone honest, though, remember to purchase tickets from the ticket window not from a person outside the stadium.

As a prematch warm-up, catch a plate of *kài yâang* (grilled chicken) and other northeastern dishes from the restaurants surrounding the Ratchadamnoen Stadium.

SHOPPING

Bangkok excels in one major category when it comes to shopping: cheap stuff, not luxury goods. The tradition of bargaining and Thailand's well-honed sense of fun is elevated to elation in the markets where a simple purchase can be all smiles and compliments.

The difficulty is finding your way around since the city's intense urban tangle sometimes makes orientation difficult. A good shopping companion is *Nancy Chandler's Map of Bangkok*, with annotations on all sorts of small and out-of-the-way shopping venues and *tàlàat* (markets).

Antiques

Real Thai antiques are rare and costly. Most Bangkok antique shops keep a few authentic pieces for collectors, along with lots of pseudo-antiques or traditionally crafted items that look like antiques. The majority of shop

---

BIG FAT WARNING!

Be sure to read about the pitfalls of shopping in Bangkok (p750) before setting out on a spree. Amid all the bargains are a number of cleverly disguised rip-off schemes – caveat emptor!

---

operators are quite candid about what's really old and what isn't.

River City Complex (Map pp118-19; Th Yotha, off Th Charoen Krung; many stores close Sun; river ferry Tha Si Phraya) Near the Royal Orchid Sheraton Hotel, this multistorey shopping centre is an all-in-one stop for old-world Asiana. Several high-quality art and antique shops occupy the 3rd and 4th floors. Old Maps & Prints offers one-of-a-kind rare maps and illustrations, with a focus on Asia. Although the quality is high, the prices are too, as many wealthy tourists filter in and out.

Oriental Place (Map pp124-5; Soi 38, Th Charoen Krung) Near the Oriental Hotel, this subdued shopping centre is well stocked for discriminating collectors knowledgeable about Southeast Asian antiques.

Department Stores & Shopping Centres

Bangkok may be crowded and polluted, but its department stores are modern oases of order. By no accident, the Skytrain stations often have shaded walkways delivering passengers directly into nearby stores without ever having to set foot on ground level.

One pesky tradition is that shop assistants follow you around the store from rack to rack like the lonely new girl at school. This is the definition of Thai 'service' rather than an indication that they've sniffed you out as a shoplifter. Be sure you're satisfied with an item as returns are an unimported phenomenon.

Most shopping centres are open from 10am or 11am to 9pm or 10pm.

Mahboonkrong (MBK; Map pp128-9; 0 2217 9111; cnr Th Phra Ram I & Th Phayathai; Skytrain National Stadium) Capturing the spirit of Thailand's outdoor markets into comfy air-con, MBK is a Bangkok teen's home away from home. On any given weekend, half the city can be found here combing through an inexhaustible range of small stalls and shops or shuffling (sometimes tentatively) up and down the escalators. This is the cheapest place to buy contact lenses, mobile (cell) phones and accessories, and name-brand knock-offs.

Playground! (Map pp122-3; 0 2714 7888; www .playgroundstore.co.th; 818 Soi 55/Thong Lor, Th Sukhumvit; Skytrain Thong Lor to red soi bus) This concept mall is street-smart cool in a neighbourhood that's not alternative enough to get it. Graffiti art, J-pop vinyl dolls, manga: Bangkok has fully embraced street art. The hulking building balances commerce on the periphery with

large central spaces dedicated to alternative art exhibits or performance spaces.

Siam Center & Siam Discovery Center (Map pp128–9; cnr Th Phra Ram I & Th Phayathai; Skytrain National Stadium & Siam) These linked sister centres feel almost monastic in their hushed hallways compared to frenetic MBK, just across the street. Siam Discovery Center excels in home décor with the whole 3rd floor devoted to Asian-minimalist styles and jewel-toned fabrics. Attached Siam Center, Thailand's first shopping centre built in 1976, has recently gone under the redesign knife for a younger, hipper look. Youth fashion is its new focus, with weekend fashion shows occupying the central atrium.

Siam Paragon (Map pp128–9; ☎ 0 2610 8000; Th Phra Ram I; Skytrain Siam) The biggest, newest and glitziest of Bangkok's shopping malls, Siam Paragon is more of an urban park than shopping centre. Astronomically luxe brands occupy most floors, while the majority of shoppers hang out in the reflecting pool atrium or basement-level food court.

Central World Plaza (Map pp128–9; ☎ 0 2635 1111; Th Ratchadamri & Th Phra Ram I; Skytrain Chitlom) After being left behind in the mall race, this behemoth box has gutted itself and transformed from ho-hum shopping mall to extrahuge 'lifestyle' scene. The new above-ground walkway to the shopping centre helps to funnel in heat-stroked pedestrians.

Gaysorn Plaza (Map pp128–9; cnr Th Ploenchit & Th Ratchadamri; Skytrain Chitlom) A *haute couture* catwalk, Gaysorn's spiralling staircases and all-white halls preserve all of fashion's beloved designers under museum-curatorship style. Thai fashion leaders occupy the 2nd floor, while the top floor is a stroll through chic home décor.

Central Department Store (Map pp128–9; ☎ 0 2655 1444; 1027 Th Ploenchit; Skytrain Chitlom) Generally regarded as the all-round best for quality and selection, Central has 13 branches in Bangkok in addition to this chi-chi flagship. If you're curious about local hooks, look for Thai designers such as Tube and the Thai cosmetic brand Erb.

Emporium Shopping Centre (Map pp122–3; 622 Th Sukhumvit, cnr Soi 24; Skytrain Phrom Phong) You might not have access to the beautiful people's nightlife scene, but you can observe their spending rituals at this temple to red hot and classic cool. Robust expat salaries and trust funds dwindle amid Prada, Miu Miu, Chanel

and Thai brands such as Greyhound and Propaganda.

Pantip Plaza (Map pp128–9; 604 Th Phetchaburi; Skytrain Ratchathewi) North of Siam Square, this is five storeys of computer and software stores ranging from legit to flea market. Many locals come here to buy 'pirated' software and computer peripherals.

Fashion & Textiles

Bangkok is a fashion-conscious and fashion-generating city. Local designers have cultivated a high-fashion scene that can compete on the international catwalk. More affordable looks are exhibitioned by the city's trendy teens who strut their distinctive 'Bangkok' look in the various shopping areas.

Siam Square (Map pp128–9; btwn Th Phra Ram I & Th Phayathai) This low-slung commercial universe is a network of some 12 *soi* lined with trendy teenage boutiques, many of which are the first ventures of young designers. Soi 3 and 4 are the primary shopping areas for cute flouncey dresses. The varying weekend product promotions are usually filled with giddy 'model girls' and breakdancers.

Mae Fah Luang (Map pp128–9; ☎ 0 2658 0424; www .doitung.org; 4th fl, Siam Discovery Center, cnr Th Phayathai & Th Phra Ram I; Skytrain Siam) For a royally funded project, Mae Fah Luang ventures into impressive fashionable realms with its feminine cotton suits and skirts. The handmade cotton and linen come from villages formerly involved with poppy production.

Fly Now (Map pp128–9; ☎ 0 2656 1359; 2nd fl, Gaysorn Plaza, cnr Th Ploenchit & Th Ratchadamri; Skytrain Chitlom) A long-standing leader in Bangkok's

---

FLOWERING TROUBLE

Forming floating carpets where birds alight and garbage collects, water hyacinths are the *femme fatale* of Bangkok's river environments. This invasive species was imported to Thailand by Rama V's wife after a visit to Indonesia. The plant was originally intended as a decorative flower for the palace ponds but soon escaped to the river frontier, where it clogs waterways and spreads into virgin territory. One promising industry for this aquatic weed is to dry the stalks and weave them into furniture and rugs, which are sold in furniture stores and shopping centres throughout the city.

home-grown fashion scene, Fly Now creates feminine couture that has caught the eyes of several international shows.

Jaspal (Map pp128–9; ☎ 0 2658 1000-19; Siam Center, cnr Th Phayathai & Th Phra Ram I; Skytrain Siam) Cute snappy basics define this home-grown label that is slowly maturing beyond its Thai shores. There is also a branch at the Emporium Shopping Centre (Map pp122–3).

Greyhound (Map pp122–3; ☎ 0 2261 7121; www .greyhound.co.th; 2nd fl, Emporium, Th Sukhumvit, btwn Soi 22 & 24; ☒ 10.30am-10pm; Skytrain Phrom Phong) Streetwear for people who have drivers and dual citizenship, Greyhound is a local lifestyle brand that includes the spin-offs Playhound and Grey, as well as Greyhound Cafe (p165). There is also a branch in Siam Center (Map pp128–9).

Jim Thompson (Map pp124–5; ☎ 0 2632 8100; www .jimthompson.com; 9 Th Surawong; ☒ 9am-9pm; Skytrain Sala Daeng, subway Silom) The company credited with creating an international market for Thai silk is now solidly positioned with the tastes of the middle-aged mamas. Bolts of fabric, silk scarves and neckties, and table accessories are all of the highest quality. Beware of touts hanging around this store trying to divert customers to another shop that pays commissions.

Handicrafts & Décor

The tourist markets have tonnes of factory-made pieces that pop up all along the tourist route. The shopping centres sell products with a little better quality at proportionally higher prices, but the independent shops sell the best items all round.

Silom Village Trade Centre (Map pp124–5; Soi 24, Th Silom) Behind the Silom Village Inn, this arcade of compact shops sells souvenir-quality reproductions, including teak carvings, textiles, *khohn* masks and ceramics. The pace is relaxed and rarely crowded.

Narayana Phand (Map pp128–9; ☎ 0 2252 4670; Th Ratchadamri; Skytrain Chitlom, khlong taxi to Tha Pratunam) A bit on the touristy side, this huge warehouse is a government-operated enterprise funnelling run-of-the-mill knick-knacks to the masses. No haggling is necessary at this place.

Suan Lum Night Bazaar (Map p127; cnr Th Withayu & Th Phra Ram IV; ☒ 6pm-midnight; bus 13, 17, 76, 106, subway Lumphini) This government-backed bonanza is a great night-time activity for shoppers, families, groups, teenagers, you name

---

SOUVENIRS THAT LAST

Looking for something that will have a longer shelf life than the average street-stall souvenir or a shoddily tailored suit? It will cost you a bit more but Thai contemporary art is inexpensive for the art world, with typical prices between US$3000 and US$5000. And if art collectors continue to look East, canvases from Southeast Asia will soon join the exhibition halls alongside China and India, turning relatively unknown names into famous acquisitions. But for the average art buyer in Thailand, most look for what they like. Here are a few commercial galleries to start:

100 Tonson Gallery (Map pp128–9; ☎ 0 2684 1527; www.100tonsongallery.com; 100 Soi Tonson, Th Ploenchit; Skytrain Chitlom) Atmospheric gallery focusing on painting, sculpture and mixed media.

Gallery F-Stop (Map pp122–3; ☎ 0 2663 7421; www.galleryfstop.com; Tamarind Café, 27 Soi 20, Th Sukhumvit; ☒ 11am-11pm; Skytrain Asoke) Southeast Asian–themed photography with approachable prices.

H Gallery (Map pp124–5; ☎ 0 1310 4428; www.hgallerybkk.com; 201 Soi 12, Th Sathon, beside Bangkok Bible College; ☒ noon-6pm Wed-Sat; Skytrain Chong Nonsi) Leading commercial gallery for emerging Thai abstract painters.

Jamjuree Art Gallery (☎ 0 2218 3708; Jamjuree Bldg, Chulalongkorn University, Th Phayathai; ☒ 10am-7pm Mon-Fri, noon-6pm Sat & Sun; Skytrain Siam) Modern spiritual themes and brilliantly coloured abstracts from emerging student artists.

Kraichitti Gallery (Map pp120–1; ☎ 0 1623 8284; Sunset Street Complex, Th Khao San; ☒ 3-11pm; bus 53, 511, river ferry Tha Phra Athit) An ambitious intersection of photography and entertainment in an elegant 100-year-old home smack dab on Th Khao San.

Thavibu Gallery (Map pp124–5; ☎ 0 2266 5454; www.thavibu.com; 3rd fl, Silom Galleria, 91 9/1 Th Silom; ☒ 11am-7pm Tue-Sat, noon-6pm Sun; Skytrain Chong Nonsi) Paintings by artists from Cambodia, Thailand and Myanmar; much of the gallery's business is done online.

Surapon Gallery (Map p127; ☎ 0 2638 0033; Tisco Tower, 1st fl, Th Sathon Neua; Skytrain Sala Daeng) Unique contemporary Thai art.

it. At the time of writing, Suan Lum Night Bazaar was slated for closure and the land set for redevelopment. Due to several court battles and the popularity of the market, some suspect that the eviction notice given to night bazaar vendors may go unheeded. We aren't sure when the bazaar will be completely dismantled (and secretly hope that this stellar attraction remains intact).

Rasi Sayam (Map pp122-3; ☎ 0 2262 0729; 82 Soi 33/Daeng Udom, Th Sukhumvit; ⏱ 9am-5.30pm Mon-Sat; Skytrain Asoke) Rasi Sayam sells charming wall hangings, *benjarong* (Thai ceramics), basketry and pottery that are made exclusively for this shop by handicraft villagers.

Nandakwang (Map pp122-3; ☎ 0 2258 1962; 108/3 Soi 23, Th Sukhumvit; Skytrain Nana) A branch of a factory shop from northern Thailand, Nandakwang specialises in high-quality folksy woven-cotton handbags, totes and table linens. There are also some cute stuffed animals. There is also another branch in Siam Discovery Center (Map pp128-9).

Taekee Taekon (Map pp120-1; ☎ 0 2629 1473; 118 Th Phra Athit; ⏱ 10am-5pm; river ferry Tha Phra Athit) Representing Thailand's main silk-producing regions, this charming store has a beautiful selection of table runners and wall hangings. Alongside silk products, you will also find small examples of celadon pottery and blue-and-white china.

Propaganda (Map pp122-3; ☎ 0 2664 8574; 4th fl, Emporium, btwn Sois 22 & 24, Th Sukhumvit; Skytrain Phrom Phong) This nouveau design shop proves that toilet humour is universal. The signature character, Mr P, who appears on drinking glasses, ashtrays and table lamps is a 3-D cartoon character who pokes fun at all the things our mothers' told us were impolite. There is another branch in Siam Discovery Center (Map pp128-9).

Phu Fa (Map pp122-3; ☎ 0 2650 3311; cnr Th Sukhumvit & Soi 7; Skytrain Nana) This new outlet sells products from HRH Princess Srindhorn's economic development programme for rural villagers. The Thai-made products are mainly kid-friendly: notebooks, change purses and hand-woven Karen textiles.

Gems & Jewellery

Although it is common wisdom that Thailand is a bonanza for gems and jewellery, the risk of a rip-off is much greater than finding bargain bling and spotting a fake is nearly impossible without sophisticated training and equipment. Many visitors arrive with visions of gemstones and leave with coloured glass. Be sceptical of recommendations from túk-túk drivers, hotel staff, strangers on the street and even from fellow travellers (who might be in denial about being ripped off). If you don't buy expensive jewellery at home, then don't start a collection in Thailand. Stick to the bangles if you need a souvenir adornment.

Markets

Quintessential Thailand and all its do-it-yourself entrepreneurial spirit can be found among the city's markets, occupying unused alleys or treacherous sidewalks. Most vendors are women who raise their children alongside a stall packed with an odd assortment of plastic toys, household goods and polyester clothes mixed with knock-off designer watches and bags. Even more interesting are the food markets where Thais forage for brightly coloured tapioca desserts, spicy curries and fruits that look like medieval torture devices.

THE WAR ON THE GEM SCAM

We're begging you, if you aren't a gem trader, then don't buy unset stones in Thailand – period. Countless tourists are sucked into the prolific and well-rehearsed gem scam in which they are taken to a store by a helpful stranger and are tricked into buying bulk gems that can supposedly be resold in their home country for 100% profit. The expert con artists (part of a well-organised cartel) seem trustworthy and convince tourists that they need a citizen of the country to circumvent tricky customs regulations. Guess what, the gem world doesn't work like that, and what most tourists end up with are worthless pieces of glass. By the time you sort all this out, the store has closed, changed names and the police can do little to help. Want to know more or want to report a scam? Visit www.2bangkok.com and navigate to the 'Gem Scam' page for five years' worth of tracking the phenomenon, or go to **Thai Gems Scam Group** (www.geocities .com/thaigemscamgroup) for photos of touts who troll the temples for victims. The tourist police can also help to resolve some purchase disputes but don't expect miracles.

BANGKOK

ALL-PURPOSE MARKETS

Chatuchak Weekend Market (Talat Nat Jatujak; Map pp114-15; ✆ 8am-6pm Sat & Sun; Skytrain Mo Chit, subway Chatuchak Park) This is it, the big one you've heard about. The behemoth of Thai markets where everything imaginable is for sale – from handmade silks from the provinces, extras-mall fashion for the art-school fashionistas, fighting cocks and fighting fish, fluffy puppies and every imaginable souvenir. Although variety is its claim to fame, the market's speciality is clothing. Don't forget to try out your bargaining skills.

Plan to spend a full day, as there's plenty to see, do and buy. But come early to beat the crowds and the heat. If everything starts to inexplicably suck, then you are suffering from dehydration and need a pitstop at one of the many food stalls. There is an information centre and a bank with ATMs and foreign-exchange booths at the Chatuchak Park offices, near the northern end of the market's Soi 1, Soi 2 and Soi 3. Schematic maps and toilets are conveniently located throughout the market.

There are a few vendors out on weekday mornings, and a daily vegetable, plant and flower market opposite the market's southern side. One section of the latter, known as the Aw Taw Kaw Market, sells organically grown fruit and vegetables, and is a good spot for tasty duck curry.

Sampeng Lane (Map pp118-19; Sampeng Lane/Soi Wanit 1, Chinatown; river ferry Tha Ratchawong) This wholesale market runs roughly parallel to Th Yaowarat, bisecting the two districts of Chinatown and Phahurat. Pick up the narrow artery from Th Ratchawong and follow it through its many manifestations – handbags, homewares, hair decorations, stickers, Japanese-animation gear, plastic beeping keychains. As the lane cuts across into Phahurat, fabric shops, many operated by Indian (mostly Sikh) merchants, start to dominate. Unless you're shopping for a grassroots import-export group, Sampeng is more for entertainment than for purchases.

Nakhon Kasem (Map pp118-19; Th Yaowarat & Th Chakrawat; river ferry Tha Saphan Phut) Also known as the Thieves Market because this area used to specialise in stolen goods, Nakhon Kasem has gone legit with industrial-sized cooking equipment, spare electronic parts and other bits you didn't even know could be resold. For the budding entrepreneur, all the portable street-stall gear for frying bananas, making *phàt thai* or grinding coconuts is sold here.

Phahurat Market (Map pp118-19; Th Phahurat & Th Triphet, across from Old Siam Plaza; river ferry Tha Saphan Phut) The Indian-fabric district prefers boisterous colours, faux fur, neon sparkles and everything you'll need for a Halloween costume or a traditional Thai dance drama. Deeper into the market are cute clothes for kids and good deals on traditional Thai textiles.

Pratunam Market (Map pp128-9; cnr Th Petchaburi & Th Ratchaprarop; ✆ 8am-6pm; khlong taxi to Tha Pratunam) Considered the in-town version of Chatuchak, Pratunam is a tight warren of stalls trickling deep into the block. Cheap clothes, luggage, bulk toiletries, market-lady sarongs and souvenirs are just a few options.

Banglamphu Market (Map pp120-1; Th Chakraphong, Th Tanao & Th Tani; ✆ 9am-6pm; river ferry Tha Phra Athit) Spread out over several blocks, the Banglamphu market attracts a no-nonsense crew of street vendors selling snacks, handbags, brassieres, pyjamas, household items and *phuang malai* (Thai flower garlands). You may never come here on purpose, but passing through invariably leads to a purchase.

Soi Lalaisap (Map pp124-5; Soi 5, Th Silom; ✆ 8am-6pm; Skytrain Chong Nonsi) The 'money-melting' street has a number of vendors selling all sorts of cheap clothing, watches and homewares during the day. Regular perusers say that imperfections from name-brand factories often appear in the stacks.

Khlong Toey Market (Map pp122-3; cnr Th Phra Ram IV & Th Narong) Beside Bangkok's port, this market is the cheapest all-purpose choice proffering regional food stuff, fresh meat and kitchen supplies.

FLOWER & PLANT MARKETS

Pak Khlong Market (Map pp118-19; Th Chakkaphet & Th Atsadang; ✆ 8am-6pm; river ferry Tha Saphan Phut) Near the river and the mouth of Khlong Lawt, Pak Khlong is the city's largest wholesale flower source. The colourful displays of baby roses and delicate orchids are endless and so inexpensive that even a cement-cell dweller on Th Khao San could afford a bouquet. Pak Khlong is also a big market for vegetables.

Thewet Market (Map pp116-17; Th Krung Kasem, off Th Samsen) You'll find a good selection of tropical flowers and plants available at this low-key market creating a temporary garden near Tha Thewet.

Talat Phahonyothin (Phahonyothin Market; Map pp114-15; Th Kamphaengphet; Skytrain Mo Chit, subway Chatuchak Park) The city's largest plant market is opposite the southern side of Chatuchak Market.

TOURIST MARKETS

The souvenir sellers have an amazing knack for sniffing out what new arrivals want to haul back home – perennial favourites include raunchy T-shirts, *mon khwan* (traditional Thai wedge-shaped pillow), CDs and synthetic sarongs. Not all tourist markets are created equal: porn is hard to come by on Th Khao San but plentiful on Th Sukhumvit; and hemp clothing is noticeably absent from Patpong.

Th Sukhumvit Market (Map pp122-3; Th Sukhumvit btwn Soi 2 & 12, 3 & 15; ☽ 11am-10.30pm; Skytrain Nana) Knock-offs bags and watches, stacks of skin-flick DVDs, Chinese throwing stars, penis-shaped lighters and other questionable gifts for your high-school-aged brother dominate at this market peddling to package and sex tourists.

Th Khao San Market (Map pp120-1; Th Khao San; ☽ 11am-11pm; river ferry Tha Phra Athit) The main guesthouse strip in Banglamphu is a day-and-night shopping bazaar for the serious baht pinchers. Cheap T-shirts, 'bootleg' CDs, wooden elephants, hemp clothing, *mon khwan*, fisherman pants and other goods that make backpackers go ga-ga. Ask around to find out which of the vendors sell the best-quality CDs.

Patpong Night Market (Map pp124-5; Patpong Soi 1 & 2, Th Silom; ☽ 6pm-midnight; Skytrain Sala Daeng) Drawing more crowds than the ping-pong shows, this market continues the street's illicit leanings with a deluge of pirated goods. Bargain with intensity as first-quoted prices tend to be astronomically high.

Tailors

Although Bangkok's diplomatic corps provides a steady clientele for the city's established tailors, the continuous supply of tourists provides a lot of 'fresh meat' for the less-scrupulous businesses. Common scams usually involve those wily túk-túk drivers who deliver customers to shops that pay commissions, thus driving the cost of the work far beyond its normal value. Other reported problems involve shoddy workmanship and inferior fabrics.

But often the real problem is that the customers don't know enough about formal attire to be savvy shoppers; many see the price tag and think it is about time to get a suit makeover. This is the ideal formula for getting less than what you paid for. If you don't normally wear suits at home, then Thailand is no place to learn. Instead stick to fun accessories – a silk robe, a Chinese-style dress – items that will remind you of your trip but don't require fine fabric or craftsmanship.

If you've flown to Thailand wearing a suit, then you're a good candidate for sartorial circles. Spend time courting a tailor, as it is one of those old-world relationships not well suited for the modern stopwatch. Before you engage a tailor on a big custom job, assess their workmanship by looking at pieces in progress or commissioning them to copy a small item of clothing. Wear the piece for awhile to make sure it can withstand wear and tear before returning with business.

Once you find a tailor you trust, the next hurdle is selecting quality fabric. Be especially wary of claims of 100% cotton, which is usually a blend of the real stuff and a synthetic. Most wools are imported from Italy and England, but the stocks at many tailor shops are synthetic blends from factories outside Bangkok. Good-quality silk, on the other hand, is plentiful. If the tailoring shop doesn't offer fabrics to your liking, you can supply your own material from another source.

Shirts and trousers can be turned around in 48 hours or less with only one fitting. But no matter what a tailor may tell you, it takes more than one or two fittings to create a good suit, and most reputable tailors will ask for two to five sittings.

GETTING THERE & AWAY
Air

Bangkok is a major centre for international flights throughout Asia as well as being Thailand's domestic hub.

Suvarnabhumi International Airport (Map p187; ☎ 0 2723 0000; www.bangkokairportonline.com), the much anticipated new and improved airport, 30km east of Bangkok in Nong Ngu Hao (Cobra Lake) area of Samut Prakan Province, began commercial international and domestic service in September 2006 after several years of delay. The airport is designed to handle 45 million passengers a year with expansion plans to accommodate up to 100

million passengers. Once the airport is up to full capacity, it will be the largest in Asia and able to handle Airbus A380s (555 seaters). The airport name is pronounced 'soo-wan-na-poom', and it inherited the airport code (BKK) previously used by the old airport at Don Muang.

After September 2006 Bangkok's former international and domestic **Don Muang airport** (☎ 0 2535 1111; www.airportthai.co.th), 25km north of central Bangkok, was retired from commercial service, only to be partially reopened five months later to handle overflow from Suvarnabhumi. As of March 2007, Don Muang began servicing some domestic carriers and at the time of writing was being used by the following carriers: One-To-Go, Nok Air and PB Air, as well as the domestic services of Thai Airways International (THAI). At the time of writing it was unclear if Don Muang would fulfil this role permanently or only until construction and safety problems at Suvarnabhumi were resolved. Be advised that his situation could change prior to or after publication.

For a list of domestic and international airlines serving Thailand, see the Transport chapter (p756).

AIRLINES

The following are carriers that service domestic destinations; a few also fly routes to international destinations. For a list of international carriers, see p755.

Air Asia (☎ 0 2515 9999; www.airasia.com; Suvarnabhumi airport) Bangkok to Chiang Mai, Chiang Rai, Hat Yai, Phuket, Surat Thani, Narathiwat, Udon Ratchathani and Udon Thani.

Bangkok Airways (☎ 0 2132 0342; www.bangkokair .com; Suvarnabhumi airport) Bangkok to Chiang Mai, Phuket, Ko Samui, Sukhothai, Trat and Trang.

Nok Air (☎ 1318; www.nokair.co.th; Suvarnabhumi Airport) Bangkok to Chiang Mai, Nakhon Si Thammarat, Hat Yai, Udon Thani and Phuket.

One-Two-Go (Map pp122-3; ☎ 0 2229 4260, call centre 1126; www.fly12go.com; 18 Th Ratchadaphisek) Domestic arm of Orient Thai; flies from Bangkok to Surat Thani, Phuket, Chiang Rai, Chiang Mai, Phuket, Hat Yai and Krabi.

PB Air (☎ 0 2261 0220; www.pbair.com; Suvarnabhumi airport) Bangkok to Chiang Mai, Mae Hong Son, Lampang, Nan, Sukhothai, Nakhon Phanom, Roi-Et, Buriram and Nakhon Si Thammarat.

THAI (www.thaiair.com) Silom (Map pp124-5; ☎ 0 2232 8000; 485 Th Silom); Banglamphu (Map pp120-1; ☎ 0 6

1111; 6 Th Lan Luang) Operates domestic air services to many provincial capitals.

Bus

Bangkok is the centre for bus services that fan out all over the kingdom. For long-distance journeys to popular tourist destinations, it is advisable to buy tickets directly from the bus companies located at the bus stations, rather than through travel agents in tourist centres, such as Th Khao San. See Bus Safety (p763) for tips on common transport scams.

BUS STATIONS

There are three main public bus terminals. Allow an hour to reach all terminals from central Bangkok.

Northern & Northeastern bus terminal (Map pp114-15; ☎ for northern routes 0 2936 2852 ext 311/442, for northeastern routes 0 2936 2852 ext 611/448; Th Kamphaeng Phet) is just north of Chatuchak Park. It's also commonly called sàthaanii maw chít (Mo Chit station). Buses depart from here for northern and northeastern destinations such as Chiang Mai, Nakhon Ratchasima (Khorat), Ayuthaya and Lopburi. Buses to Aranya Prathet also leave from here, not from the Eastern bus terminal as you might expect. To reach the bus station, take Skytrain to Mo Chit and transfer onto city bus 3, 49, 77 or 512.

Eastern bus terminal (Map pp114-15; ☎ 0 2391 2504; Soi 40/Ekamai, Th Sukhumvit; Skytrain Ekamai) is the departure point for buses to Pattaya, Rayong, Chanthaburi and other points east. Most people call it sàthaanii èkkà mai (Ekamai station).

Southern bus terminal (Map pp114-15; ☎ 0 2435 1200; Hwy 338/Th Nakhon Chaisi & Th Phra Pinkao, Thonburi) handles buses south to Phuket, Surat Thani and closer centres to the west, such as Nakhon Pathom and Kanchanaburi. This station is known as sàthaanii saai tâai mài (Sai Tai Mai) and is in Thonburi. To reach the station, take bus 30 (for Banglamphu), 516 (for Thewet), 507 and 511 (for Pak Nam), and 170 and 127 (for Mo Chit). Although there are plans to move the terminal further out of town, there is still no official word on when this will happen.

Train

Bangkok is the terminus for the main rail services to the south, north, northeast and east. See p768 for information about train classes and services.

Hualamphong station (Map pp118-19; ☎ 0 2220 4334, general information & advance booking 1690; Th Phra Ram IV) handles services to the north, north-east, east and south. Bookings can be made in person at the advance booking office (just follow the signs; open from 8.30am to 4pm). The other ticket windows are for same-day purchases, mostly 3rd class. From 5am to 8.30am and 4pm to 11pm, advance bookings can also be made at windows 2 to 11. You can obtain a train timetable from the information window.

Hualamphong has the following services: shower room, mailing centre, luggage storage, cafés and food courts.

Smiling 'information' staff will try to direct all arrivals to a travel agency in the mezzanine level, which will arrange transport on a commission basis. To skip the charge, make all arrangements at ticketing windows on the ground floor.

To get to the station from Sukhumvit take the subway to the Hualamphong stop. From western points (Banglamphu, Thewet) take bus 53.

Bangkok Noi station (Map p130; next to Siriraj Hospital, Thonburi) handles services to Nakhon Pathom, Kanchanaburi and Nam Tok. The station can be reached by river ferry to Tha Rot Fai. Tickets can be bought at the station.

GETTING AROUND

The main obstacle to getting around Bangkok is the traffic, which introduces a 45-minute delay to most daytime outings. This

---

TAXI TO NOWHERE

In most large cities, the taxi drivers are usually seasoned navigators familiar with every out-of-the-way neighbourhood. This is not the case in Bangkok where many a displaced farmer finds himself ploughing the city streets in a metered taxi after a failed rice crop. Further complicating matters is the language barrier: most street names are multisyllabic requiring acrobatic tone variations that if mispronounced will induce confused head scratching. Even borrowed words from English have their own peculiar Thai pronunciation. To ensure that you'll be able to return home, grab your hotel's business card, which will have directions in Thai.

---

means advance planning is a must when you are attending scheduled events or arranging appointments.

If you can travel by river, canal or Skytrain from one point to another (ie avoid the roads), it's always the best choice.

To/From the Airport

The following ground transport options are allowed to leave directly from the airport terminal to in-town destinations: metered taxis, hotel limousines, the airport express bus, private vehicles and private buses. If there are no metered taxis available curbside or if the line is too long, you can take the airport shuttle to the taxi stand at the public transport centre.

The public transport centre is 3km from the airport terminal and includes a public bus terminal, metered taxi stand, car rental and long-term parking. A free airport shuttle running both an ordinary and express route connects the transport centre with the passenger terminals.

Metered taxis are available curbside from the Suvarnabhumi airport terminals and from the taxi stand at the public transport centre. Typical metered fares from the airport: 200B to 250B to Th Sukhumvit, 250B to 300B to Th Khao San, and 500B to Mo Chit. Toll charges (paid by the passenger) vary between 20B to 60B. Do note that there is also a 50B surcharge that is added to all fares departing from the airport, payable to the driver. You can hail a taxi directly from the street for airport trips, or you can arrange one through the hotels or by calling ☎ 1681 (which charges a 20B dispatch surcharge). A taxi trip from the Don Muang airport into the middle of Bangkok should cost you around 200B to 300B, plus tolls (40B to 80B) and a 50B airport fee. Don't be shy in telling the driver to put the meter on.

The airport express bus operates along four routes between central Bangkok and the airport between 5am to midnight. The cost is 150B. Route AE1 travels to Silom, AE2 to Banglamphu/Th Khao San, AE3 to Th Sukhumvit and Th Withayu (Wireless Rd), and AE4 to Hualamphong train station. For a more detailed route description, visit www.bangkokairportonline.com/node/55.

Public buses serving the airport's transport centre include six Bangkok routes and three provincial routes. Buses to Bangkok travel to the following destinations and cost around 35B: Minburi (549), Happy Land (550),

Victory Monument (551), On Nut Skytrain station (552), Samut Prakan (553) and Don Muang (554). From these points, you can continue on public transport or taxi to your hotel. If your hotel is in Banglamphu, the Victory Monument bus will be the closest option; for Siam Square, Sukhumvit or Silom, use the On Nut bus.

If you are bypassing Bangkok entirely, you have three direct options from the airport. Public buses travel to Pattaya (106B, two hours); Talat Rong Kleua (187B, five hours), which is in the town of Aranya Prathet (p270) and is walking distance from the Cambodian border town of Poipet; and Nong Khai (454B, eight hours; p491), a border-crossing point into Laos.

Tentatively scheduled for completion in 2008, the Airport Train Link will provide service from the airport to central Bangkok at Makkasan (corner Th Petchaburi and Th Ratchadaphisek, with access to Petchaburi subway station) and Phayathai (corner of Th Phayathai and Phra Ram VI, with access to the Phayathai Skytrain station). According to initial planning, the express train service will take about 15 minutes to reach the airport. The line will also be used for commuter services, with stops at eight stations between the airport and the central terminus. The airport train link began with great gusto two years ago but has since lagged behind the progress of the new airport, making the 2008 opening date an optimistic one.

Trains from Don Muang station are accessible via an elevated walkway from the international terminal and travel to Bangkok's Hualamphong station. Regular trains run to Bangkok roughly every hour or 1½ hours from 4am to 11.30am and then again every hour from 2pm to 9.30pm (3rd class ordinary/express 5/10B, one hour)

Boat

Once the city's dominant form of transport, public boats still survive along the mighty Mae Nam Chao Phraya and on a few interior *khlong.*

RIVER ROUTES
Chao Phraya Express (☎ 0 2623 6001; www.chaophraya boat.co.th) provides one of Bangkok's most scenic transport options, running ferries along the Mae Nam Chao Phraya to many popular riverside tourist attractions. The company

operates express (indicated by an orange, yellow or blue flag), local (without a flag) and Tourist Boat (larger boat) services. See the Map p183 for routes and piers. Hold on to your ticket as proof of purchase (an occasional formality).

Chao Phraya Express company operates the following lines:

Local (⊗ 6-8.40am & 3-6pm Mon-Fri; 10-27B) The local line serves all company piers between Wat Ratchasingkhon, in south-central Bangkok, north to Nonthaburi.

Tourist (⊗ 9.30am-4pm; 18B) The more expensive tourist boat accommodates the reduction in service of the local line; it operates from Tha Sathon to 10 major sightseeing piers (including Tha Chang, Tha Phra Athit, among others).

Express (Orange; ⊗ 5.50am-6.40pm Mon-Fri, 6am-6.40pm Sat & Sun; 18-27B) The orange express boats operate between Wat Ratchasingkhon and Nonthaburi with stops at major piers.

Express (Blue; ⊗ 7-7.45am & 3-4.20pm Mon-Fri; 18-27B) The blue express line operates between Tha Sathon and Nonthaburi with stops at major piers.

Express (Yellow; ⊗ 6-8.40am & 4.30-6.20pm Mon-Fri; 18-32B)The yellow express line operates between Ratburana to Nonthaburi with stops at major piers.

There are also flat-bottomed cross-river ferries that connect Thonburi and Bangkok. These piers are usually next door to the Chao Phraya Express piers and cost 3B per crossing.

There are additional piers further south to Samut Prakan and there has been talk of expanding service, but concessions have yet to be decided.

CANAL ROUTES
Over the years boat services along Bangkok and Thonburi's *khlong* have diminished, but with mounting traffic woes there may be plans to revive these water networks. There are a few Bangkok khlong taxis, operated by the Bangkok Metropolitan Authority, that traverse Khlong Saen Saep from Banglamphu to Ramakamhaeng. The canal service is the quickest option for travelling across town during rush hour between Banglamphu and points east. A few useful stops include: Tha Withayu (Map pp128–9) for the Nai Lert Hotel; Tha Pratunam (Map pp128–9) for Pratunam market; Tha Ratchathewi (Map pp128–9) for Asia Hotel; and Tha Phan Fah (Map pp120–1) for Wat Saket. Fares cost 8B to 16B and service runs from 6am to 7pm. Be warned, though, that this is extreme Bangkok. The canal is seriously polluted and passengers

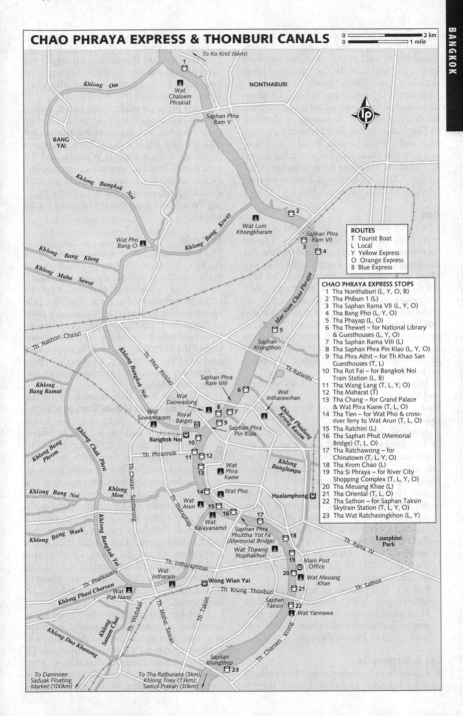

CHAO PHRAYA EXPRESS & THONBURI CANALS

ROUTES
T Tourist Boat
L Local
Y Yellow Express
O Orange Express
B Blue Express

CHAO PHRAYA EXPRESS STOPS
1 Tha Nonthaburi (L, Y, O, B)
2 Tha Phibun 1 (L)
3 Tha Saphan Rama VII (L, Y, O)
4 Tha Bang Pho (L, Y, O)
5 Tha Phayap (L, O)
6 Tha Thewet – for National Library & Guesthouses (L, Y, O)
7 Tha Saphan Rama VIII (L)
8 Tha Saphan Phra Pin Klao (L, Y, O)
9 Tha Phra Athit – for Th Khao San Guesthouses (T, L)
10 Tha Rot Fai – for Bangkok Noi Train Station (L, B)
11 Tha Wang Lang (T, L, Y, O)
12 Tha Maharat (T)
13 Tha Chang – for Grand Palace & Wat Phra Kaew (T, L, O)
14 Tha Tien – for Wat Pho & cross-river ferry to Wat Arun (T, L, O)
15 Tha Ratchini (L)
16 Tha Saphan Phut (Memorial Bridge) (T, L, O)
17 Tha Ratchawong – for Chinatown (T, L, Y, O)
18 Tha Krom Chao (L)
19 Tha Si Phraya – for River City Shopping Complex (T, L, Y, O)
20 Tha Meuang Khae (L)
21 Tha Oriental (T, L, O)
22 Tha Sathon – for Saphan Taksin Skytrain Station (T, L, Y, O)
23 Tha Wat Ratchasingkhon (L, Y)

typically hold newspapers over their faces to prevent being splashed by the stinky water. Climbing in and out of the boats can be a little tricky and shouldn't be attempted when decked out in heels and pearls.

Two new *khlong* services between Thonburi and Bangkok have been added for commuters. Boats travel between Daokanong in Thonburi to Tha Sathon in Bangkok between 6.20am to 8am and 3.45pm to 6pm Monday to Friday and cost 15B. Boats travel between Phetkasem in Thonburi to Saphan Phut in Bangkok between 7.30am to 8am and 3.45pm to 6pm Monday to Friday and cost 15B.

Bus

The city's public-bus system, which is operated by Bangkok Metropolitan Transit Authority (BMTA), is the best option for reaching Chinatown, Banglamphu, Thewet, Dusit and other areas not serviced by Skytrain. The buses are also a lot cheaper than the newer public transport options, but are also subject to the hassles of traffic. Air-con bus fares typically start at 10B or 12B and increase by increments of 2B, depending on the distance. Fares for ordinary (fan) buses start at 7B or 8B. Smaller 'baht buses' ply major *soi* and cost 5B.

Most of the bus lines run between 5am and 10pm or 11pm, except for the 'all-night' buses, which run from 3am or 4am to midmorning.

Bangkok Bus Map by Roadway, available at Asia Books (p104), is the most up-to-date route map available. The following bus lines are useful for tourists travelling between Banglamphu and Siam Square area:

- Bus 15: Tha Phra to Sanam Luang with stops at MBK, Th Ratchadamnoen Klang (accessible to Th Khao San) and Sanam Luang (accessible to Wat Phra Kaew).
- Bus 47: Khlong Toei Port to Department of Lands with stops along Th Phra Ram IV, MBK, Th Ratchadamnoen and Sanam Luang.
- Bus 73: Huay Khwang to Saphan Phut with stops at MBK (connect to Skytrain), Hualamphong (connect to train or subway), Chinatown and Saphan Phut (connect to Chao Phraya Express).

Car & Motorcycle

For short-term visitors, you will find parking and driving a car in Bangkok more trouble than it is worth. Even long-term expats typically opt for a chauffeured car rather than battling the Buddhist approach to driving. If you need private transport, consider hiring a car and driver through your hotel or hire a taxi driver that you find trustworthy.

If you're not dissuaded, cars and motorcycles can be rented throughout town, including such international chains as **Avis** (Map pp128-9; ☎ 0 2255 5300; 2/12 Th Withayu). There are more rental agencies along Th Withayu and Th Petchaburi Tat Mai. Some also rent motorcycles. Rates start at around 2000B per day, excluding insurance. An International Driving Permit and passport are required for all rentals.

Skytrain

The most comfortable option for travelling in 'new' Bangkok (Silom, Sukhumvit and Siam Square) is the *rót fai fáa* (Skytrain), an elevated rail network that sails over the city's notorious traffic jams. The Skytrain has revolutionised travel in the modern parts of Bangkok. Trips that would have taken an hour now take 15 minutes. Another advantage of the Skytrain is that it offers a pleasant bird's-eye view of the city, allowing glimpses of greenery and historic architecture not visible at street level.

So far two lines have been built by the **Bangkok Mass Transit System Skytrain** (BTS; ☎ 0 2617 7300; www.bts.co.th) – Sukhumvit and Silom lines. There were ambitious plans to extend the system but these got tied up in political infighting between Bangkok's municipal government and the Thaksin administration. With the new government have come renewed pledges to undertake the extensions.

The Sukhumvit line terminates in the north of the city at the Mo Chit station, next to Chatuchak Park, and follows Th Phayathai south to Siam interchange station at Th Rama I and then swings east along Th Ploenchit and Th Sukhumvit to terminate at the On Nut station, near Soi 81. There are plans to extend this line 5km southeast to Soi 107, Th Sukhumvit.

The Silom line runs from the National Stadium station, near Siam Square, and soon after makes an abrupt turn to the southwest, continuing above Th Ratchadamri, down Th Silom to Th Narathiwat Ratchanakharin, then out Th Sathon until it terminates next to the foot of Saphan Taksin on the banks of Mae

Nam Chao Phraya. There are plans to extend this line a further 4.5km over the river into Thonburi.

Trains run frequently from 6am to midnight along both the lines. Fares vary from 10B to 40B, depending on your destination. Ticket machines at each station accept 5B and 10B coins only, but change is available from the information booths. The staffed booths are also where you buy value-stored tickets. Brochures available at the information booths detail the various commuter and tourist passes.

Once through the ticket gates, follow the signs for the desired line and terminus. You can change between the two lines at the double-height Siam station, in front of Siam Square and Siam Center. Free maps of the system are available at all Skytrain station ticket booths. All trains are air-conditioned, often heavily so.

Subway

Bangkok's first subway line opened in 2004 and is operated by the **Metropolitan Rapid Transit Authority** (MRTA; ☎ 0 2624 5200; www.mrta.co.th). Thais call the subway *rót fai tâi din* or 'Metro'.

The blue line connects the minor train station of Bang Seu, in the northern part of the city, with Chatuchak (with access to the Mo Chit Skytrain station), Thailand Cultural Centre, Sukhumvit (with access to Asoke Skytrain station), Queen Sirikit National Convention Centre, Lumphini Park, Silom (with access to Sala Daeng Skytrain station) and terminates at Hualamphong train station. There are plans to extend this line from Bang Seu across Mae Nam Chao Phraya into the Bang Yai district. Future extensions will connect Hualamphong to Chinatown and Thonburi.

Trains operate 6am to midnight and cost 15B to 39B, depending on distance. To pass through the fare gates, buy a magnetised coin from the ticket window or automated dispenser. At the end of the journey, the coin is inserted into the gate slot for exiting.

One main advantage with the subway is that it has made the train stations (Hualamphong and Bang Sue) more accessible from eastern city points. If travelling south into Bangkok by rail, many passengers shave an hour off the trip into Hualamphong by disembarking at Bang Sue and catching the subway to their final in-town destination.

Taxi & Motorcycle Taxi

Tháeksii miitôe (metered taxis) were introduced in Bangkok in 1993 and have signs on top reading 'Taxi Meter'. The set price is 35B at flag fall for the first 2km, then 4.50B for the next 10km, 5B for 13km to 20km, and 5.50B for any distance over 20km, but only when the taxi travels at 6km/h or more; at speeds under 6km/h, a surcharge of 1.25B per minute kicks in. Freeway tolls – 30B to 40B depending where you start – must be paid by the passenger. Fares to most places within central Bangkok cost 60B to 80B.

A 24-hour **phone-a-taxi** (☎ 1681) is available for an extra 20B. Taxis are usually plentiful except during peak commute hours, when bars are closing (1am to 2am), or when it is raining and your destination requires sitting in too much traffic.

Taxis that hang around tourist centres typically refuse to use the meter and will quote an exorbitantly high rate. You are more likely to find an honest driver if you walk out to a main thoroughfare.

At the mouth of the *soi*, motorcycle taxis camp out to deliver passengers the last few kilometres home; a *soi* trip is usually 10B. Motorcycle taxis can also be hired for longer journeys as a time-saving antidote to gridlock; fares in these instances are about the same as túk-túk, except during heavy traffic, when they may cost a bit more.

Riding on the back of a speeding motorcycle taxi is a close approximation to an extreme sport. Keep your legs tucked in – the drivers are used to carrying passengers with shorter legs than those of the average Westerner and they pass perilously close to other vehicles while weaving in and out of traffic. Women wearing skirts should sit side-saddle and gather any extra cloth to avoid it catching in the wheel or drive chain.

Túk-Túk

Good luck getting a fair shake from a túk-túk if you're new in town. These drivers have a knack for smelling crisp bills and will take you and your wallet far beyond your desired destination. Beware of túk-túk drivers who offer to take you on a sightseeing tour for 10B or 20B – it's a touting scheme designed to pressure you into purchasing overpriced goods Despite the pitfalls, túk-túk rides are still beloved by new arrivals. Surviving the hassles, the hairpin turns, and the suffocating exhaust are all part

of a quintessential Bangkok experience that keeps the city from becoming an adult-sized Disneyland with no hard edges.

Although it seems unlikely, túk-túk do serve a very useful purpose besides hassling tourists. Locals use the three-wheelers when their destination is closer and cheaper than a metered-taxi flag fall or when gridlock requires a more nimble vehicle. Unfortunately the recent rise in petrol prices means that túk-túk quotes often start at 100B, sometimes even 200B, making it difficult to negotiate a fair price.

AROUND BANGKOK

If you're itching to get out of the capital city, but don't have a lot of time, consider a day trip to some of the neighbouring towns. At Bangkok's doorstep are all of Thailand's provincial charms – you don't have to go far to find ancient religious monuments, floating markets, architectural treasures and laid-back fishing villages.

NAKHON PATHOM

นครปฐม

pop 120,657

Nakhon Pathom is a typical provincial Thai city, with Phra Pathom Chedi as a visible link to Nakhon Pathom's claim as the country's oldest city. The town also proudly wears its first-born status within its name, which derives from the Pali 'Nagara Pathama' meaning 'First City'. At one time Nakhon Pathom functioned as the centre of the Dvaravati kingdom, a loose collection of Mon city states that flourished between the 6th and 11th centuries AD in Mae Nam Chao Phraya valley. Some historians speculate that the area may have been inhabited before India's Asokan period (3rd century BC), as there is a theory that Buddhist missionaries from India visited Nakhon Pathom at that time.

Although the town is quite sleepy, it is an easy destination to see everyday Thai ways and practise your newly acquired language skills on a community genuinely appreciative of such efforts.

Sights

In the centre of town, **Phra Pathom Chedi**, rising to 127m, is the tallest Buddhist monument in the world. The original stupa, which is buried

within the massive orange-glazed dome, was erected in the early 6th century by Theravada Buddhists of Dvaravati (possibly at the same time as Myanmar's famous Shwedagon stupa). But, in the early 11th century the Khmer king, Suriyavarman I of Angkor, conquered the city and built a Brahman *prang* (Hindi/Khmer-style stupa) over the sanctuary. The Burmese of Bagan, under King Anawrahta, sacked the city in 1057 and the *prang* lay in ruins until Rama IV (King Mongkut) had it restored in 1860. The temple is best visited on weekends when local families come to make merit.

On the eastern side of the monument, in the *bòt*, is a Dvaravati-style Buddha seated in a European pose similar to the one in Wat Phra Meru in Ayuthaya. It may, in fact, have come from there.

Also of interest are the many examples of Chinese sculpture carved from a greenish stone that came to Thailand as ballast in the bottom of some 19th-century Chinese junks. Opposite the *bòt* is a **museum** (admission by donation; ⏰ 9am-4pm Wed-Sun), which contains some interesting Dvaravati sculpture and lots of old junk. Within the chedi complex is **Lablae Cave**, a manmade tunnel containing the shrine of several Buddha figures.

The wat surrounding the stupa enjoys the kingdom's highest temple rank, Rachavoramahavihan; it's one of only six temples so honoured in Thailand. King Rama VI's ashes are interred in the base of the Sukhothai-era Phra Ruang Rochanarit, a large standing Buddha image in the wat's northern *wíhăan*.

Southeast of the city stands **Phra Phuttha-monthon**, a Sukhothai-style standing Buddha designed by Corrado Feroci. At 15.8m, it is reportedly the world's tallest, and it's surrounded by a 400-hectare landscaped park that contains sculptures representing the major stages in the Buddha's life (eg a 6m-high dharma wheel, carved from a single slab of granite). All Bangkok–Nakhon Pathom buses pass the access road to the park at Phra Phutthamonthon Sai 4; from there you can walk, hitch or flag a săwngthăew into the park itself. From Nakhon Pathom you can also take a white-and-purple Salaya bus; the stop is on Th Tesa across from the post office.

Thai Human Imagery Museum (☎ 0 3433 2607; admission 250B; ⏰ 9am-5.30pm Mon-Fri, 8.30am-6pm Sat & Sun) contains an exhibition of lifelike resin sculptures. A group of Thai artists report-

edly spent 10 years studying their subjects and creating the figures, which fall into four categories: famous Buddhist monks of Thailand, former kings of the Chakri dynasty, Thai lifestyles and chess playing. The museum is outside town at the Km 31 marker on Th Pinklao–Nakhon Chaisi (the highway to Bangkok). Any Nakhon Pathom–Bangkok or Salaya bus can drop you off here.

Eating

Nakhon Pathom has an excellent market along the road between the train station and Phra Pathom Chedi; its *khâo lǎam* (sticky rice and coconut steamed in a length of bamboo) is reputed to be the best in Thailand. There are many good, inexpensive food vendors and restaurants in this area.

Getting There & Away

Nakhon Pathom is 56km west of Bangkok. The city doesn't have a central bus station, but most transport arrives and departs from near the market and train station.

Air-con buses 83 and 997 leave from the Southern bus terminal (in Thonburi) for Nakhon Pathom (41B, one hour, frequent departures). To return to Bangkok, catch one of the idling buses on Th Phayaphan, a block from the train station. Buses to Damnoen Saduak floating market (bus 78, 30 minutes) leave from the same stop, departing every 30 minutes. You can also wave down Samut Sakhon–bound buses (bus 402, 30B, 45 minutes) at this stop.

Nakhon Pathom is on the spur rail line that runs from Thonburi's Bangkok Noi station to Kanchanaburi's Nam Tok station. Until recently, it was a minor commuter line, but because a portion of the line is part of the historic 'Death Railway', built by WWII prisoners of war during Japanese occupation, rates for foreigners have increased under a tourism-promotion scheme. Ordinary trains (3rd class) leave Thonburi (Bangkok Noi) for Nakhon Pathom at 7.40am and 1.45pm (100B, approximately 1¼ hours) en route to Kanchanaburi and Nam Tok. The return train leaves Nakhon Pathom at 8.55am and 4.20pm.

There are also more frequent (and affordable) trains from Bangkok's Hualamphong

station (from 35B, two hours) throughout the day.

FLOATING MARKETS
ตลาดน้ำ

The photographs of Thailand's floating markets – wooden canoes laden with multicoloured fruits and vegetables, paddled by women wearing indigo-hued clothes and wide-brimmed straw hats – has become an iconic and alluring image for the kingdom. It is also a sentimental piece of history. In the past 20 years, Thailand has modernised, replacing canals with roads, and boats with motorcycles and cars. The floating markets, which were once lively trading posts for produce farmers and local housewives, have crawled ashore, an evolutionary step shared with humans.

The most heavily promoted floating market is **Damnoen Saduak** (⊙ 7am-4pm Sat & Sun), little more than a souvenir market catering to tourists. But it is one of the most accessible markets from Bangkok and is ideal for those who haven't yet filled their suitcases with touristy gifts. Damnoen Saduak is 104km southwest of Bangkok between Nakhon Pathom and Samut Songkhram. Air-con buses 78 and 996 go direct from the Southern bus terminal in Thonburi to Damnoen Saduak (82B, two hours, every 40 minutes from 6am to 9pm). Most buses will drop tourists off directly at the piers that line Th Sukhaphiban 1, which is the land route to the floating market area. The going rate for boat hire is about 300B per person per hour. A yellow săwngthăew (5B) does a frequent loop between the floating market and the bus stop in town.

A closer descendant of the original floating markets, **Taling Chan** (⊙ 7am-4pm Sat & Sun) offers less of a sales pitch than Damnoen Saduak. On the access road to Khlong Bangkok Noi, Taling Chan looks like any other fresh market busy with produce vendors from nearby farms. But the twist emerges at the canal where several floating docks serve as informal dining rooms, and the kitchens are dugout canoes tethered to the docks. Many local Thai families come to feast on grilled shrimp, noodles and river fish all produced aboard a bobbing boat. Taling Chan is in Thonburi and can be reached from Bangkok's Th Ratchadamnoen Klang or Th Ratchaprasong via air-con bus 79 (16B, 25 minutes). Long-tail boats from any Bangkok

pier can also be hired for a trip to Taling Chan and the nearby Khlong Chak Phra.

Another riverside market, atmospheric **Talaat Ban Mai** (⊙ 7am-6pm Sat & Sun) originated 100 years ago as a bustling trading centre in Chachoengsao Province. Today the old-fashioned wooden shophouses teetering on the river bank are mainly a weekend attraction for local Thais prowling for good eats. Many of the businesses are owned by the second and third generation of ethnic Teochew Chinese who had originally migrated to Thailand's central plains in search of work. The story of these immigrants is a classic success tale: many arrived with only a suitcase and a few coins in their pocket, but laboured on the farms and factories with enough diligence to secure a merchant future for their children and a university education for their grandchildren. The market's Chinese heritage is continued in the foods on offer, such as *kŭay chai* (Chinese dumplings stuffed with green vegetables) and *galorchi* (sweet tapioca patties deep fried and patted in sugar).

The market can be reached by túk-túk from Chachoengsao bus or train station. A more scenic venture is via a **boat tour** (☎ 0 3851 4333; adult 100B; hourly from 9am-3pm Sat & Sun) along Mae Nam Bang Pakong, which begins from Wat Sothon Waram Worawihan in Chachoengsao town. From November to February, this brackish river is full of striped catfish that entice hungry dolphins from the Gulf of Thailand. Chachoengsao is 80km east of Bangkok and accessible by train from Hualamphong station (15B to 40B, two hours, hourly departures). Buses from Bangkok's Ekamai bus station leave for Chachoengsao (90B, 1½ hours, frequent departures).

SAMUT SAKHON
สมุทรสาคร
pop 68,398

Samut Sakhon is popularly known as Mahachai because it straddles the confluence of Mae Nam Tha Chin and Khlong Mahachai. Just a few kilometres from the Gulf of Thailand, this busy port features a lively market area and a pleasant breezy park around the crumbling walls of **Wichian Chodok Fort** (Hwy 35). A few rusty cannons pointing towards the river testify to the fort's original purpose of guarding the mouth of Mae Nam Tha Chin from foreign invaders. Before the arrival of European traders in the 17th century, the

town was known as Tha Jin (Chinese pier) because of the large number of Chinese junks that called here.

A few kilometres west of Samut Sakhon, along Hwy 35, is the Ayuthaya-period **Wat Yai Chom Prasat**, which is known for the finely carved wooden doors on its *bòt*. You can easily identify the wat by the tall Buddha figure standing at the front. To get here from Samut Sakhon, take an orange westbound bus (15B) heading towards Samut Songkhram from the bus station; the wat is only a 10-minute ride from the edge of town.

Getting There & Away

Samut Sakhon is located 28km southwest of Bangkok.

Air-con bus 976 (79B, 1½ hours) from the Southern bus terminal in Thonburi leaves for Samut Sakhon throughout the day. Buses also frequently run between Samut Sakhon and Samut Songkhram (ordinary/air-con 20/27B, one hour).

Samut Sakhon is nearly midway along the 3rd-class Mahachai Shortline train route that runs between Thonburi's Wong Wian Yai

station (see boxed text, below). The fare costs 10B and there are roughly hourly departures and returns from 5.30am to 7pm.

SAMUT SONGKHRAM
สมุทรสงคราม
pop 34,949

Commonly known as Mae Klong, this provincial capital lies along a sharp bend in Mae Nam Mae Klong and just a few kilometres from the Gulf of Thailand. Due to the flat topography and abundant water sources, the area surrounding the city is well suited to the steady irrigation needed to grow guavas, lychees and grapes. Along the highway from Thonburi, visitors will pass a string of artificial sea lakes used in the production of salt. A profusion of coconut palms makes the area look unusually lush, considering its proximity to Bangkok.

Samut Songkhram is a fairly modern city with a large market area between the train and bus stations. The sizeable **Wat Phet Samut Worawihan**, in the centre of town near the train station and river, contains a renowned Buddha image called Luang Phaw Wat Ban Laem.

MAHACHAI SHORTLINE

Sometimes it is all about the journey, rather than the destination. This is certainly the case for taking the Mahachai Shortline to the string of gulf-side towns southwest of Bangkok. The adventure begins when you take a stab into Thonburi looking for the **Wong Wian Yai train station** (Map pp116-17; Th Taksin; bus 37). Just past the traffic circle is a fairly ordinary food market, which camouflages the unceremonious end of this commuter line.

Only 15 minutes out of the station and the city density yields to palm trees, small rice fields and marshes filled with giant elephant ears and canna lilies. There's lots of peaking into homes and shops where locals go to pick up odds and ends or a shot of rice whisky for the morning commute.

The wilderness and backwater farms evaporate quickly as you enter Samut Sakhon (Mahachai). This is the end of the first segment, so work your way along the road that runs parallel to the train tracks through a dense market of fishermen's boots and trays of tentacled seafood to the harbour pier. The harbour is clogged with water hyacinth, which forms floating islands for fish-hunting cranes and bug-chasing birds. Just beyond are the big wooden fishing boats, pregnant with the day's catch and draped like a veiled widow with fishing nets. Boarding the ferry, you have to jockey for space with the motorcycles, which are driven by school teachers and errand-running housewives.

Once on the other side, take a right at the first intersection, follow it all the way through the temple and past the drying fish racks to the train tracks and turn right to reach the station. This is Ban Laem, from where trains continue on to Samut Songkhram (Mae Klong).

Ban Laem is a sleepy little station that keeps up a convincing charade that no one has ever come or gone from here. Along the route to Samut Songkhram, the wilderness is so dense that it seems the surrounding greenery might gobble up the train tracks, so that the middle of nowhere stays that way. You'll be surprised once you reach the bustling city of Samut Songkhram by this back-door entrance.

At the mouth of Mae Nam Mae Klong, not far from town, is the province's most famous tourist attraction, a bank of fossilised shells known as **Don Hoi Lot**. The type of shells embedded in the bank come from *hăwy làwt* (clams with a tube-like shell). The shell bank is best seen late in the dry season (typically April and May) when the river has receded to its lowest level. To get to Don Hoi Lot you can hop on a blue sǎwngthǎew (15B, 15 minutes) in front of Somdet Phra Phuttalertla Hospital at the intersection of Th Prasitwatthana and Th Thamnimit. Or you can charter a boat from Tha Talat Mae Klong, a scenic journey that takes about 45 minutes.

Wat Satthatham, 500m along the road to Don Hoi Lot, is notable for its *bòt* constructed of golden teak and decorated with 60 million baht worth of mother-of-pearl inlay. The inlay covers the temple's interior and depicts scenes from *jataka* in murals above the windows and the *Ramakian* below.

King Buddhalertla Naphalai Memorial Park (museum admission 20B; ☼ park 9am-6pm, museum 9am-4pm Wed-Sun) is dedicated to King Rama II, who was a native of Amphoe Amphawa. The museum is housed in traditional central-Thai houses set over two hectares, and contains a library of rare Thai books, antiques from early-19th-century Siam and an exhibition of dolls depicting four of Rama II's theatrical works (*Inao, Mani Phichai*, a version of the *Ramakian* and *Sang Thong*). Behind the houses is a lush botanic garden and beyond that, a drama school. To get to the park take an Amphawa-bound blue bus (12B) to Talat Nam Amphawa, then walk over the bridge and follow the road that goes through the gardens of Wat Amphawan Chetiyaram.

Getting There & Away

Samut Songkhram is Thailand's smallest province and is 74km southwest of Bangkok. Buses from Bangkok's Southern bus terminal to Damnoen Saduak also stop in Samut Songkhram (68B, 1½ hours, frequent) near the train station and down the street from the Siam Commercial Bank. There are also daily buses to Samut Sakhon (ordinary/air-con 20/27B, one hour, frequent). Taxis and local buses park at the intersection of Th Ratchayat Raksa and Th Prasitphatthana.

Samut Songkhram is the southernmost terminus of the Mahachai Shortline. There are four departures to Samut Songkhram (10B, one hour, approximately 7.30am 10.10am, 1.30pm, 4.40pm) and four return trips (6.20am, 9am, 11.30am, 3.30pm). See the boxed text (p189) for more information. The train station is located on Th Kasem Sukhum where it terminates at Th Prasitphatthana, near the river.

SAMUT PRAKAN

สมุทรปราการ

pop 378,694

At the mouth of Mae Nam Chao Phraya, where it empties into the Gulf of Thailand, Samut Prakan (sometimes referred to as Meuang Pak Nam) smells fishier than the ocean. Most residents' lives revolve around fishing; motorcycle taxi drivers mend fishing nets while waiting for a fare or vendors shoo flies from crates of iced ocean dwellers.

The city's name means Ocean Wall, a reference to **Phra Chula Jawm Klao Fort**, built around 1893, 7km south of the provincial hall.

Erawan Museum

พิพิธภัณฑ์เอราวัณ

Both an architectural and religious attraction, the **Erawan Museum** (☎ 0 2371 3135; www.erawan -museum.com; Soi 119 Th Sukhumvit; adult/child 150/50B; ☼ 8am-3pm) is a five-storey-high sculpture of Erawan, Indra's three-headed elephant mount from Hindu mythology, built by Khun Lek Viriyapant, the same benefactor and cultural preserver who built the Ancient City (below). The sculpture comprises three levels symbolic of the underworld, the earth, and Mt Sumeru and the heavens. Inside the building is a collection of sacred antiques that attract many merit makers.

The museum is 8km from Bangkok's Ekamai bus station and any Samut Prakan–bound bus can drop you off; just tell the driver your destination (Chang Sam Sian).

Ancient City

เมืองโบราณ

Billed as the largest open-air museum in the world, **Muang Boran** (☎ 0 2323 9253; www .ancientcity.com; adult/child 300/200B; ☼ 8am-5pm) covers more than 80 hectares of peaceful countryside and is littered with 109 scaled-down facsimiles of many of the kingdom's most famous monuments. The grounds have been shaped to replicate Thailand's general

geographical outline, with the monuments placed accordingly.

Visions of Las Vegas and its corny replicas of world treasures may spring to mind, but the Ancient City is architecturally sophisticated – a preservation site for classical buildings and art forms. It's also a good place for undistracted bicycle rides (daily rental 50B), as it is usually quiet and never crowded.

The Ancient City is outside of central Samut Prakan on the Old Sukhumvit Hwy. From the bus station cross the main road and catch a white or red sǎwngthǎew (7B).

Getting There & Away

Ordinary bus 25 (5B) and air-con buses 507, 508 and 511 (16B to 18B) ply regular routes between central Bangkok and Pak Nam (central Samut Prakan). The trip can take up to two hours, depending on traffic. If the traffic is horrendous, consider catching the Skytrain's Sukhumvit line to On Nut station and then taking the aforementioned buses on the road heading out of Bangkok.

Samut Prakan's bus station is a few kilometres outside town on the Old Sukhumvit Hwy.

Central Thailand

CENTRAL THAILAND

Buffering Bangkok from the sea and the hinterlands, this fertile river plain is Thailand's cultural heartland. It has birthed rice crops without coaxing, and cultivated a distinct Thai culture centred around the seasonal patterns of the region's 'mother waters'. The rivers brought rich mineral deposits from the northern mountains and sea traders from the oceans. Many of the ancient Southeast Asian kingdoms, like the Dvaravati and the Khmers, reached across the once undivided continent into modern-day central Thailand to plant their own cultural traditions in this earthly womb.

Due north of Bangkok is Ayuthaya, the former Thai capital. Touring the ruined temples on bicycle and learning the names of the illustrious kings will put you close to the Thai psyche. Further north is the little town of Lopburi, a pit-stop for journeys to Chiang Mai. The downtown nurses many crumbling ruins and a resident tribe of monkeys.

Heading northwest from Bangkok leads to the mountain range that climbs into Myanmar. In the wet season, rain feeds foaming waterfalls and keeps the dragon-scaled peaks lush. Kanchanaburi is the base town for organised expeditions into the surrounding wilderness; it also played an unlikely role in WWII when occupying Japanese forces used POW labour to build a railway through the demanding terrain.

Penetrating deeper into the mountain passes, Thong Pha Phum and Sangkhlaburi are two outpost towns, nearly forgotten by the outside world and blissfully undeveloped. This is the end of the line, an attraction in itself, as the Myanmar (Burma) border limits crossings to day-trips only. The cultural story continues beyond these political conventions, but you'll have to save that trip for another time.

HIGHLIGHTS

- Visiting the ruins of **Ayuthaya** (p194), Unesco World Heritage site and former capital of Siam
- Cycling to the WWII memorials in easy-going **Kanchanaburi** (p208)
- Climbing the turquoise waterfall at **Erawan National Park** (p217)
- Snapping pictures of the mischievous **monkey gangs** (p203) in Lopburi
- Escaping the crowds with a weekday trip to sleepy **Thong Pha Phum** (p220)
- Being an 'end-of-the-road' traveller with a trip through rustic **Sangkhlaburi** (p222) and beyond to **Three Pagodas Pass** (p224)

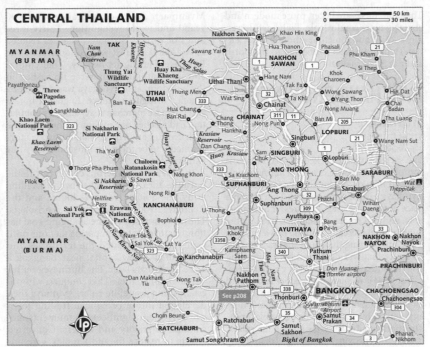

CENTRAL THAILAND

Climate

Central Thailand experiences the country's three seasons in distinct measure; it can dump rain in Sangkhlaburi for days while Kanchanaburi only sees sun. It is hot from February to June, rainy from June to roughly October, and cool (relatively speaking) from October to January: one constant is the humidity. Within the region there are some variations. During the rainy season, Sangkhlaburi is inundated with rain, days and days of it, while Kanchanaburi might only see a few afternoon sprinkles. Because of altitude, it can be significantly cooler in Sangkhlaburi than in other parts of the region. Ayuthaya and Lopburi sit in a wide-open plain that receives similar amounts of rain and heat as Bangkok.

National Parks

Kanchanaburi Province is the wildest of the region and its mountain range once acted as a natural barrier to Myanmar to the west. Within the province there are five national parks: popular Erawan and Sai Yok, and lesser visited Si Nakharin, Chaloem Ratanakosin and Khao Laem.

Language

The people of central Thailand share a common dialect that is considered 'standard' Thai simply because Bangkok, the seat of power, happens to be in the region. High concentrations of Chinese are found in the cities of the central provinces since this is where a large number of Chinese immigrants started out as farmers and labourers and then later as merchants. Significant numbers of Mon and Karen live in Kanchanaburi Province. Pockets of Lao and Phuan – the descendents of war captives who were forcibly resettled following Thai raids into Laos over the centuries – can be found in all three provinces.

Getting There & Away

Most people will leave Bangkok on a bus or train headed to destinations in central

---

FAST FACTS

■ **Best Time to Visit** October to December

■ **Population** 3.1 million

Thailand. Buses are faster, more modern and arguably more comfortable. Trains are slower, more scenic and sometimes more social. Central Thailand is also connected to the north and northeast via train.

AYUTHAYA PROVINCE

AYUTHAYA

พระนครศรีอยุธยา

pop 90,500

The sacred city, the sacked city, Ayuthaya is complexly intertwined with Thai nationalism and religion. As the former royal capital, Ayuthaya earned the emerging Thai nation a place among the great empires of Southeast Asia, and placement on the map used by the international merchants sailing between India and China during the era of the trade winds. As a city that was destroyed by an invading army, Ayuthaya is eulogised like a slain hero.

But what is recounted in history and legend is not easily recognisable today. The ancient monuments retain little of their bygone majesty, with only a handful in recognisable forms. The modern city that grew among the rubble is busy and provincial, adding a distracting element of chaos to the meditative mood of crumbled kingdoms.

Still, the city is a necessary stop on the culture trail, because of its position in the historical hierarchy and because its story as a kingdom is more approachable and better recorded than Thailand's other ancient capital, Sukhothai. Ayuthaya's proximity to Bangkok also makes it an alternative base for recent arrivals who find the modern capital just plain crummy.

History

Ayuthaya was the Siamese royal capital from 1350 to 1767. Prior to the emergence of the Ayuthaya kingdom, the town was a Khmer outpost. The city was named after Ayodhya (Sanskrit for 'unassailable' or 'undefeatable'), the home of Rama in the Indian epic *Ramayana*. Its full Thai name is Phra Nakhon Si Ayuthaya (Sacred City of Ayuthaya).

Although the Sukhothai period is often referred to as the 'golden age' of Thailand, in many ways the Ayuthaya era was the kingdom's true historical apex – at least in terms of sovereignty (which extended well into present-day Laos, Cambodia and Myanmar), dynastic endurance (over 400 years) and world recognition. Thirty-three kings of various Siamese dynasties reigned in Ayuthaya until it was conquered by the Burmese. During its heyday, Thai culture and international commerce flourished in the kingdom, and Ayuthaya was courted by Dutch, Portuguese, French, English, Chinese and Japanese merchants. Ayuthaya's population had reached one million by the end of the 17th century and virtually all foreign visitors claimed it to be the most illustrious city they had ever seen.

In 1767, after numerous conflicts with the Burmese, the city was sacked by the invading army, the golden treasures looted and the Ayuthaya royals were carted off as prisoners. The nervous system of the emerging Thai nation fractured into competing factions until General Taksin united the territories and established a new capital near Bangkok a mere three years later. The Burmese eventually abandoned their Thai conquest without establishing a satellite ruler. Ayuthaya then developed into a provincial trading town while its once magnificent monuments succumbed to gravity and looters. Concerted efforts to restore the old temples were undertaken by various Bangkok kings and then more formally by the Fine Arts Department starting in the 1950s. In 1991 the ancient city was designated a Unesco World Heritage site.

Today the city sees a steady supply of cultural tourists ranging from independent couples cycling between ruins to busloads of escorted package tourists. Despite these visitors, the city is surprisingly untouristy and still very rough around the edges. The surrounding area is transitioning from agricultural to manufacturing and new factories are replacing old rice paddies.

Orientation

Central Ayuthaya is surrounded on all sides by water, having been built at the confluence of three rivers (Mae Nam Chao Phraya, Mae Nam Pa Sak and the smaller Mae Nam Lopburi). A wide canal links them, encircling the town. The town's historic sites are often classified as being 'on the island' (within the boundaries of the rivers) or 'off the island' (on the opposite river banks). The most prominent sites are on the island, except for a few temples accessible via ferry. Accom-

modation and some transport options are located within central Ayuthaya, while the train station and the long-distance bus station are located off the island in the eastern part of town.

Information

EMERGENCY
Tourist Police (☎ emergency 1155; Th Si Sanphet)

INTERNET ACCESS
The ever-changing internet shops clustered on and around Soi 1, Th Naresuan offer decent connects for 30B per hour.

MEDICAL SERVICES
Ayuthaya Hospital (☎ 0 3524 1446; cnr Th U Thong & Th Si Sanphet) Has an emergency centre and several English-speaking doctors.

MONEY
ATMs are abundant in the city, especially along Th Naresuan near the Amporn Shopping Centre.
Bank of Ayuthaya (Th U Thong near Th Naresuan)
Kasikorn Bank (Th Naresuan)
Siam City Bank (Th U Thong)
Siam Commercial Bank (Th Naresuan)

POST
Main post office (Th U Thong; ☽ 8.30am-4.30pm Mon-Fri, 9am-noon Sat) Has an international telephone service, open 8am to 8pm, upstairs.

TOURIST INFORMATION
Tourist Authority of Thailand (TAT; ☎ 0 3524 6076, 0 3524 1672; 108/22 Th Si Sanphet; ☽ 8.30am-4.30pm) Tourist information is available from the large white municipal building, which is located beside the traditional Thai-style houses also labelled as TAT (these are administrative buildings). The free interactive display upstairs offers a comprehensive introduction to the history of Ayuthaya.

Dangers & Annoyances
If you're on a bike, motorised or otherwise, watch out for unpredictable traffic, uneven roads and bag-snatchers. Daypacks in unprotected front baskets are easy to grab at traffic stop lights.

Also, be wary of the local dog packs. They won't take notice of you unless you cross into their territory, which will trigger a shrill chorus of barking, exposed fangs and even biting. One dog-avoidance trick is to not catch their eye.

Sights
Over 400 temples were constructed in the ancient city of Ayuthaya. The largest concentration is referred to as the Ayuthaya Historical Park, which was later designated a Unesco World Heritage site. Very little remains of the once monumental temples, but the rows of roofless columns and sagging steps create an ambience of great imaginative wandering. Even fewer Buddha images

VISUALISING THE PAST

Like the famous Angkor monuments in present-day Cambodia, Ayuthaya and its temple ruins were an earthly re-creation of the Hindu-Buddhist cosmology. Based on ancient texts, these religious traditions visualised a universe composed of different vertical and horizontal planes roughly corresponding to heaven, earth and hell. In the centre of the universe was Mt Sumeru (or Mt Meru in Hindu texts), where Brahma and other important deities resided and around which the sun and moon orbited.

True to the architectural traditions of the region, Ayuthaya as a whole reflected this sacred geography due to its island location, an intentional invocation of Mt Sumeru. Each of Ayuthaya's ancient temple complexes were a smaller mandala of this microcosm. Mt Sumeru was symbolised by the central *chedi* (conical-shaped Buddhist monument) or *prang* (tall corn-cob shaped tower indicative of the Khmer style), and the minor *chedi* placed at the cardinal directions of surrounding verandas that represented minor peaks and oceans encircling Sumeru.

The architectural representation of Mt Sumeru changed throughout the monument-building career of Ayuthaya to reflect different external influences. The earliest representations (best found at Wat Ratburana) employed the artistic style of a *prang*. After the fall of Sukhothai, the Ayuthaya kings developed the bell-shaped *chedi* (best viewed at Wat Phra Si Sanphet). Around the 17th century until the fall of the city, the Khmer style was again revitalised, most stunningly at Wat Chai Wattanaram (p199).

CENTRAL THAILAND

CENTRAL THAILAND

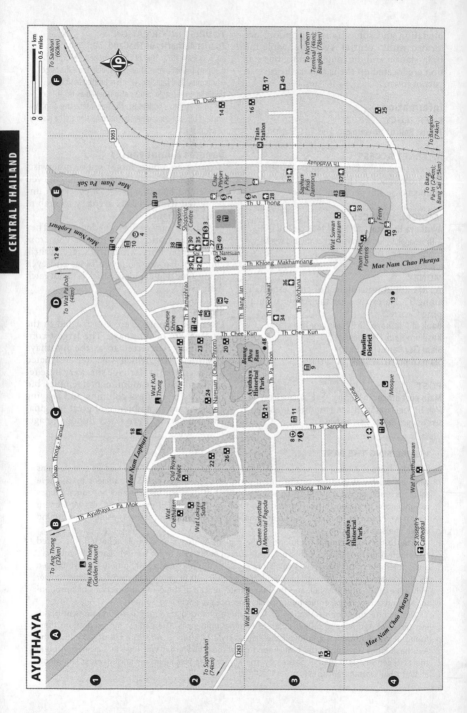

AYUTHAYA

remain intact: according to some sources, most were beheaded by looters for overseas antique collectors. The histories of the temples have also decayed and mingled with local legend, making for inexact reconstructions of the past.

For easier navigation, we've divided up the sites into 'on the island' and 'off the island' sections. Avoiding the searing heat of the day will make your visit more enjoyable. Also consider hiring a guide (available through TAT) for historical context and architectural insights.

Most temples are open from 8am to 4pm; the more famous sites charge an entrance fee.

ON THE ISLAND
The following sites are located in central Ayuthaya, within the boundaries of the river and can be visited over a day or three.

Wat Phra Si Sanphet
วัดพระศรีสรรเพชญ์
One of the most photographed temples in Ayuthaya, **Wat Phra Si Sanphet** (admission 30B) attracts the shutterbugs for its elegant queue of three bell-shaped *chedi* (stupas), which epitomise the quintessential Ayuthaya architectural style. Built in the late-14th century, the compound was originally used for important royal ceremonies and once contained a towering 16m-high standing Buddha (Phra Si Sanphet) covered with 250kg of gold, which was melted down by the Burmese conquerors.

Wihaan Mongkhon Bophit
วิหารมงคลบพิตร
Next door to Wat Phra Si Sanphet, this sanctuary hall was reconstructed at different points between 1930 and 1957, and provides an interesting counterpoint between modern and ancient temple architecture. Step inside to view one of Thailand's largest Buddha images, a 15th-century bronze casting.

Wat Phra Mahathat
วัดพระมหาธาตุ
The centre of the old sacred city, **Wat Phra Mahathat** (admission 30B) was built during the reign of King Borom Rachathirat I in the 14th century. But it is the handiwork of the encroaching forest that has created the temple's most visited image: the Buddha head embedded in twisted tree roots. The intertwining of a sacred image with nature is extremely auspicious in Thai Buddhism and the site often receives merit-makers. The structure in the centre of the complex was a Khmer-style tower, of which only the base remains, surrounded by more intact satellite *chedi*.

Wat Ratburana
วัดราชบูรณะ
Across Th Naresuan from Wat Phra Mahathat, this **temple** (Ratcha-burana; admission 30B) retains one of the best preserved *prang* on the island. It was built in the 15th century by King Borom Rachathirat II on the cremation site for his two brothers who had died battling each other in hopes of assuming the throne. Monument building in Ayuthaya was often done as an act

CENTRAL THAILAND

CENTRAL THAILAND

RUIN THE DARK

If you think the remains of an ancient era are amazing by day, you should see them at night. Some of Ayuthaya's most impressive ruins take on an other-worldly glow after dark when they are dramatically illuminated. Wat Ratburana, Wat Chai Wattanaram, Wat Phra Ram and Wat Mahathat are all lit up from 7pm to 9pm. The grounds are not open, but it is still worth it to walk by or enjoy dinner at a nearby restaurant.

---

of merit for a deceased royal elder rather than for glorification of the present ruler.

Wat Thammikarat
วัดธรรมิกราช

To the west of Wat Ratburana, this temple sees fewer visitors and is a pleasant place to sit among the ruins. The most prominent feature is a central *chedi* surrounded by *singha* (guardian lion) sculptures. It is believed by the local people that the temple pre-dated the Ayuthaya period, a claim unsupported by architectural evidence.

Wat Phra Ram
วัดพระราม

Displaying a sturdy *prang*, **Wat Phra Ram** (admission 30B) has a complicated lineage, indicative of much of Ayuthaya's chronicled structures. Claims of construction are often attributed to numerous kings throughout a 300-year period. Some accounts state that this was the cremation site of King U Thong (the founder of the Ayuthaya kingdom).

Ayuthaya Historical Study Centre
ศูนย์ศึกษาประวัติศาสตร์อยุธยา

Although the city's temples are in ruins, it is the history of the relatively modern kingdom that engages cultural visitors. One of the best places to begin digesting the ancient city's role in international commerce and in domination of the neighbouring city-states is at the **Ayuthaya Historical Study Centre** (☎ 0 3524 5124; Th Rotchana; admission adult/student 100/50B; 9am-4.30pm Mon-Fri, to 5pm Sat & Sun). Funded by the Japanese government, the centre is filled with modern and interesting models, and displays outlining city development, port, administration, lifestyles and traditions. This is a good place to start before a solo exploration of the temple ruins.

Chao Sam Phraya National Museum
พิพิธภัณฑสถานแห่งชาติเจ้าสามพระยา

Like the Egyptian pyramids, the temple's *chedi* were royal tombs, containing the ashes of the deceased (a departure from the Egyptian tradition) and important golden treasures. Very little of the ceremonial jewellery and ornaments traditionally buried with the ashes of the kings survived into the present day due to rampant thievery, but what was salvageable from the temples was put on display at this **museum** (admission 30B; 9am-4pm Wed-Sun). Exhibitions include gold treasures that were originally kept in the *chedi* of Wat Phra Mahathat and Wat Ratburana. There are also displays of Buddhist sculpture, from varying artistic styles, including many distinctive Ayuthaya-style pieces. Don't miss the traditional teak house on the western edge of the property.

Chantharakasem National Museum
พิพิธภัณฑสถานแห่งชาติจันทรเกษม

This national **museum** (Th U Thong; admission 30B; 9am-4pm Wed-Sun) houses a collection of Ayuthaya artefacts and devotional items. The physical home of the museum is the greater draw; it is located in Wang Chan Kasem (Chan Kasem Palace), a former palace built for King Naresuan by his father in 1577. During the Bangkok period, King Rama IV had this palace rebuilt and established as a museum in 1936.

OFF THE ISLAND

On the opposite side of the river-like moat that surrounds central Ayuthaya are several famous temples, as well as ethnic communities that defined the former kingdom's international prestige. You can reach some of the sites easily on a good bicycle, but others will require a motorbike. Evening boat tours around the island are another alternative for visiting the highlights.

Wat Phanan Choeng
วัดพนัญเชิง

One of the major Ayuthaya highlights, this busy and modern-looking **temple** (admission 20B) is a popular pilgrimage destination for weekenders from Bangkok. Although the original temple allegedly pre-dates the Ayuthaya era, many Thai-Chinese regard this temple with special reverence because of its later benefactor Sam Po Kong (Zheng He),

a Chinese explorer who visited Ayuthaya in 1407. As an emissary of the Chinese imperial court, Sam Po established diplomatic and trading relations all along his sea voyage, which extended as far west as Africa. For many local worshippers, the famous Buddha image (Luang Por Phanan Choeng or Phra Phanan Choeng) is often directly associated with the explorer himself. From an artistic perspective, the 19m-high sitting Buddha image displays many facial characteristics of the U-Thong style (characterised by double lips). A gallery of 84,000 Buddha images sit in crevices that line the walls of the *wíhǎan* (large hall), directly behind the large Buddha. There is also a smaller Chinese temple on the grounds.

In the ordination hall are three Buddha images (showing a central U-Thong image flanked by two Sukhothai images). The mural directly behind the altar depicts the Buddhist version of heaven, earth and hell. On the opposite wall from the altar another mural depicts the legend of Mae Thorani, the earth goddess, who helped dispel temptations during Buddha's journey to enlightenment. She did so by wringing out a flood from her long hair and washing away the demons and tempters.

The primary activity for the entire temple is merit making rather than architectural surveying, and the road leading to the temple is busy with vendors selling bags of fish that are ritualistically released into the river.

The easiest way to get to Wat Phanan Choeng from central Ayuthaya is by ferry (5B) from the pier near Phom Phet Fortress. You can take a bicycle with you on the boat.

Foreigner Quarter

Due south of the island is the historical district of the kingdom's former diplomatic entourages, many of whom arrived during the reign of King Narai. Japanese, Chinese, Dutch, Portuguese and other foreign representatives came to the Ayuthaya court to encourage trade, serve as advisors or assist in defending the city. One of the eeriest remnants of the foreigners' footprint is the cemetery at the **Portuguese Settlement**. An open pit displays the petrified skeletons of Portuguese residents, many of whom died of small pox. The traditional Thai spirit house on the grounds contains figures of St Joseph and St Paul. To the west of the Portuguese Settlement is

Ayuthaya's **Muslim district**, a community that dates back to ancient times when many Muslim traders called at the Ayuthaya port.

Wat Chai Wattanaram

วัดไชยวัฒนาราม

Everyone's favourite sunset shot, **Wat Chai Wattanaram** (admission 30B) is one of Ayuthaya's most impressive homages to the Angkor/Khmer style. A central *prang* is flanked by minor *prang* arranged in each cardinal direction, in a prime riverside setting. The temple is said to have been built in the 17th century by King Prasat Thong in honour of his mother and was extensively restored in the 1980s. These ruins can be reached by boat or by bicycle via a nearby bridge.

Phu Khao Thong

เจดีย์ภูเขาทอง

Northwest of town, this landscape-dominating *chedi*, translated as Golden Mount, was originally built during a 15-year occupation of Ayuthaya by the Burmese (prior to the 1767 invasion and collapse). The statue in front of the *chedi* depicts King Naresuan, the great Ayuthaya liberator, surrounded by almost comical statues of fighting cocks. According to common lore, Naresuan had been taken to Burma as a hostage where he proved his mettle in a cockfight match with one of the Burmese princes. He later returned to Ayuthaya and kicked out the occupying forces.

Wat Na Phra Meru

วัดหน้าพระเมรุ

This **temple** (Phra Mehn; admission 30B) escaped destruction during the Burmese attack in 1767 because it was used as the invading army's headquarters. It was also the site where the Burmese king was fatally injured after firing a defective cannon. His death ended the sacking of Ayuthaya.

Restoration of the temple, which was originally built in 1546, took place during the reign of King Rama III of the Bangkok era. The primary draw here is the main *bòt* (central sanctuary), which contains an amazing carved wooden ceiling depicting the Buddhist heavens, with Mt Sumeru in the centre. There is also a splendid Ayuthaya-era Buddha image sitting 6m high. The unique characteristics of the Ayuthaya artistic style was to depict Buddha as a king; also note how detailed and

human-like the facial features are, another departure from traditional Buddha images. Inside a smaller *wíhǎan* (large hall) behind the *bòt* is a green-stone Buddha from Sri Lanka; it's in a European pose (sitting in a chair), and is said to be 1300 years old. The walls of the *wíhǎan* show traces of 18th- or 19th-century murals.

Elephant Kraal
เพนียดคล้องช้าง

In olden times Thais resupplied their stocks of elephants with an annual roundup, in which wild herds were chased into captivity for use as beasts of burden or as war machines. This restored stockade (known in Thai as a *kraal*) is an example of the enclosed structures once used as the final destination of the roundups. A huge fence of teak logs planted at 45-degree angles keep the elephants in; the king had a special raised pavilion from which to observe the thrilling event. The last elephant roundup staged here occurred in 1903.

The *kraal* is about 4km from the centre of town, so you can either ride a bicycle here or hire a túk-túk (motorised three-wheeled pedicab) for 50B.

Baan Th Dusit
บ้านถนนดุสิต

East of the island and just beyond the train station is another collection of ruins in a more pastoral setting than central Ayuthaya. Tourist groups are rare out here and most of the grounds are kept trimmed by local farmers' livestock.

Wat Maheyong is an operational temple with a popular weekend meditation retreat held in a leafy courtyard beside the temple ruins. The historic portion of the temple was built in 1438. The outstanding *chedi* is bell shaped and was once surrounded by a ring of carved elephants statues, a unique feature in Ayuthaya. A brick walkway connects the ruins to nearby Khlong Maheyong; the middle way was reserved for the king.

Wat Kudi Dao is charmingly ruined with grasses sprouting between the roofless structures. Looking closer at the windows and gates you'll see an impressive amount of surviving details, often described as French architectural influences. Continue past the graveyard of spirit houses to **Wat Ayuthaya**, which has a bell-shaped *chedi* on a square pedestal, an early Ayuthaya characteristic.

Wat Yai Chai Mongkhon
วัดใหญ่ชัยมงคล

Built by King U Thong in 1357, **Wat Yai** is a quiet old place that was once a famous meditation wat. According to some legends, the monks at this temple were consulted by conspirators for an auspicious time to stage a royal coup. Most impressive, though, is the large 7m-long reclining Buddha, obviously enjoying the sunshine. The temple is southeast of the town proper and is best reached by motorised transport

Tours

Informal boat tours (from 200B per hour) can be arranged at the pier near the night market or at various guesthouses. Several guesthouses offer night tours of the ruins (100B per person). These tours can be cancelled at the last minute if not enough people sign up.

If you'd like more indepth coverage of Ayuthaya history, talk to TAT (p195) about hiring a guide.

Sleeping

Most of Ayuthaya's budget options are clustered around the mini-backpacker ghetto of Soi 1, Th Naresuan, and are simple lodgings in converted private homes.

There isn't a lot of value in Ayuthaya's midrange and top-end places. The majority of clientele in this range are package tourists who aren't independently shopping for accommodation, so there is little incentive to keep quarters spiffy. The following prices in this range are typical rack-rates. Some top-end places offer huge discounts (up to 50%) during the low season (April to November). Few budget or midrange places offer discounts.

BUDGET

PU Guest House (☎ 0 3525 1213; 20/1 Soi Thaw Kaw Saw; s/d from 200/300B; ✗ 🖳) Just off the main drag, this clean and friendly place offers a low-key social atmosphere and comfortable rooms. Those with air-con, TV and mini-bar are particularly good value.

Sherwood Guest House (☎ 0 666 0813; 21/25 Th Dechawat; r 280-380B; ✗ 🖳 🖳) Run by an expat, who has become a defacto expert, Sherwood's café has become a second home for other resident foreigners in town. Rooms are ordinary, with shared bathroom, and the pool

is available to nonguests for a day-use fee (adult/child 45/30B).

Baan Lotus Guest House (☎ 0 3525 1988; 20 Th Pamaphrao; r 500B) Hands-down this is the best value for the bookish sort. Everything from the hostesses to the linen is nicer at this beautifully restored teak home. Get a room overlooking the lotus-covered pond and let the frogs and birds drown out the distant traffic.

Tony's Place (☎ 0 3525 2578; 12/18 Soi 1, Th Naresuan; r 200-500B; ﹩) It's the party atmosphere that keeps this place packed (the rooms aren't bad either).

Chantana Guest House (☎ 0 3532 3200; 12/22 Soi 1, Th Naresuan; r 350-500B; ﹩) A breezy house with sweet staff makes Chantana a safe choice. The 2nd-storey rooms with balconies are extra nice.

Wieng Fa Hotel (☎ 0 3524 3252; 1/8 Th Rotchana; r 400-500B; ﹩) With helpful and professional staff, this motel-style place has a pleasant outdoor patio. Rooms are spacious but worn.

Baan Khun Phra (☎ 0 3524 1978; 48/2 Th U Thong; s/d 300/600B) This rambling 80-year-old teak house is the most atmospheric place in town. Unfortunately the prices aren't as enjoyable. The best rooms overlook the river, but most are very simple in décor.

MIDRANGE & TOP END

There isn't a lot of value in Ayuthaya's non-budget places. The majority of clientele in this range are package tourists who aren't independently shopping for accommodation, so there is little incentive to keep quarters spiffy.

Woraburi Hotel (☎ 0 3524 9600; 89 Th Watkluay; r from 1800B; ﹩ ▯ ﹩) Ayuthaya's latest newcomer has eight floors of rooms with a touch of Bangkok sophistication. Most rooms get a bear-hug view of the river.

River View Place Hotel (☎ 0 3524 1444; 35/5 Th U Thong; r from 2000B; ﹩ ▯ ﹩) A little removed from the action, River View has decent rooms with river views and all the amenities to separate you from those impoverished backpacker days.

Krungsri River Hotel (☎ 0 3524 4333; www.krungsri river.com; 27/2 Th Rotchana; r from 2350; ﹩ ﹩) This nine-storey hotel has a nice location on the river and is one of the better so-called upscale options.

Ayothaya Hotel (☎ 0 3523 2855; fax 0 3525 1018; 12 Soi 2, Th Naresuan; r 1200-3500B; ﹩ ▯ ﹩) Although it's

a bit dated, the Ayothaya is a nice option for the wheelie-cart luggage set, with a doorman, English-speaking staff and spacious rooms.

Eating

The backpacker street of Soi 1 is filled with several friendly open-air cafés should you be too tired to venture far. The stalls at the **Chao Phrom Market** (Th Naresuan) offer a good variety of Thai-Chinese and Muslim dishes during the day.

our pick Hua Raw Night Market (Th U Thong) is the centre of nightlife in Ayuthaya, with stalls preparing Thai and Muslim dishes.

Roti Sai Mai Stalls (Th U Thong; ⊙ 10am-8pm) Ayuthaya's food specialty is the Muslim dessert known as *roti sai mai*. A row of stalls across from the Ayuthaya Hospital sells this sweet concoction that is made on the premises. The vendors stretch melted palm sugar into a thread-like consistency, which is then wrapped in a flaky roti. It is probably one of the only desserts that will give you muscles – that is if you make it yourself.

Baan Khun Phra (☎ 0 3524 1978; 48/2 Th U Thong; 40-80B) Behind the guesthouse of the same name, this restaurant serves good nibblers with an intimate riverside atmosphere.

Malakor (Th Chee Kun; dishes 50-100B; ⊙ 9.30am-midnight) This charming, two-storey wooden house has an incredible view of Wat Rat-burana, which is most stunning after dark when it's all lit up.

29 Steak (Th Pamaphrao; dishes 50-100B; ⊙ 3.30-11pm) Yep, the focus here is steak. But there are plenty of Western-style salads and other veggie options, plus many Thai favourites. It's popular with a casual local crowd.

Tony's Place (Soi 1, Th Naresuan; dishes 50-100B) This guesthouse restaurant buzzes with visitors and the food gets a heaping dose of concern.

Chainam (☎ 0 3525 2013; 36/2 Th U Thong; dishes 40-120B) Pleasantly situated overlooking the river, Chainam has long attracted foreigners with its extensive bilingual menu, but don't expect too much authenticity fron the dishes.

Phae Krung Kao (dishes 60-200B; ⊙ 11am-11pm) One of several floating riverside restaurants on Mae Nam Pa Sak. The English menu is limited, but the ambience is still serene.

Drinking

Ayuthaya is a sleepy town and most backpackers don't bother to venture off Soi 1, Th Naresuan for a little night-time tipple. The

local university students tend to hangout at the nightclub at the **Ayuthaya Grand Hotel** (☎ 0 3533 5483; 55/5 Th Rotchana).

Getting There & Away

BOAT

There are no passenger boat services operating between Bangkok and Ayuthaya, but there are several tour companies that make the river journey north from the capital; see p147.

BUS

Ayuthaya has two bus terminals. The long-distance terminal is 5km east of central Ayuthaya and serves destinations north of the city; most locals refer to it as the Asia Highway station. The provincial bus stop is on Th Naresuan, a short walk from the guesthouse area. Buses from Bangkok arrive two blocks away from the provincial stop.

Ayuthaya-bound buses leave from Bangkok's Northern and Northeastern bus terminal (45B, 1½ hours, frequent) and pass by the old Don Muang airport on their way out of town. The old airport used to provide an ideal getaway for visitors who wanted to skip Bangkok in favour of Ayuthaya, but now that the airport has moved to Bangkok's eastern suburbs the trip is more involved. You must take a bus from the new airport to Don Muang and then catch an Ayuthaya-bound bus from the stop near the Don Muang train station.

There are also minivans to Bangkok's Victory Monument (60B, two hours, every 20 minutes from 5am to 5pm), leaving from Th Naresuan, east of the main bus terminal.

Buses to Lopburi (45B, two hours) leave frequently from the provincial terminal on Th Naresuan. Oversized såwngthåew (small pick-up trucks) to/from Bang Pa-In (20B, one hour) also leave from this stop.

The long-distance bus station has services to most major northern towns, including Sukhothai (216B to 300B, six hours, hourly departures), Chiang Mai (605B to 805B, nine hours, three evening departures) and Nan (500B to 800B, eight hours, three nightly departures).

TRAIN

The train station is east of central Ayuthaya and is accessible by a quick cross-river ferry (3B).

Trains to Ayuthaya leave Bangkok's Hualamphong station (15B to 20B, 1½ hours)

throughout the day with more departures between 6am to 10am and from 3pm to 11pm. Train schedules are available from the information booth at Hualamphong station. To save transit time, consider using Bangkok's subway system to go to Bang Sue station, which intersects with the state railway line at the station of the same name.

You can also use the train to go north to Chiang Mai (586B to 1298B, depending on class, three departures a day) or northeast to Pak Chong (130B, numerous departures), the jumping-off point for Khao Yai National Park.

Getting Around

Såamláw (three-wheeled pedicabs) and shared túk-túk ply the main city roads (5B to 10B per person), but good luck hopping aboard as most see a foreigner and immediately switch into 'charter' mode. A túk-túk from the train station to any point in old Ayuthaya should cost around 40B; on the island itself figure no more than 20B per trip.

For touring the ruins, the most economical and ecological option is to rent a bicycle from one of the guesthouses (30B to 50B per day). Motorcycles (150B) are also available for rent. Elephant 'taxis' (500B) are also available for touring Wat Mahathat; inquire about a ride at the elephant kraal in town on Th Pa Thon.

See p200 for information on hiring a long-tail boat for trips around the island.

AROUND AYUTHAYA
Bang Pa-In
บางปะอิน

Europeans teethed on royal palaces may find that **Bang Pa-In** (☎ 0 3526 1548; admission 100B; ⌚ 8am-3.30pm), a complex of European and Chinese-style palace buildings, creates geographic dislocation. But if this photogenic site is put into historic perspective, its brains and beauty become more apparent. It wasn't until the era of Bangkok's Rama V (King Chulalongkorn, 1868–1910) that the Thai kings began to build monuments to themselves. Known as the great moderniser, King Chula introduced many Western traditions into Thai society to avoid being completely swallowed up by those technologically advanced, and quickly advancing, nations. King Chula could also be described as a Europhile having made a grand tour of the continent and returned with even grander ideas for his own

kingdom. Architecture in particular captured his imagination and he set to work building residences fit for a king, in the most European sense of the word.

The result was the refurbishment of Bang Pa-In, 24km south of Ayuthaya and long used as a royal summer palace, into an homage to every style that had ever caught the king's fancy. Amid the peaceful grounds is a scenic reflecting pool crossed by a neoclassical bridge, giving photographers a well-documented vantage point. Across the pool is a classical **Thai pavilion**, the Chinese-style **Wehat Chamrun Palace** and the **Withun Thatsana** (a fanciful Victorian tower). The rest of the buildings are colonial-style royal residences. The gardens include an interesting topiary garden where the bushes have been trimmed into the shape of a small herd of elephants.

Wat Niwet Thamaprawat, across the river but within the Bang Pa-In complex, could easily be mistaken as a Gothic church, complete with stained-glass window and a Christian-style altar minus the pews. You can reach the wat by crossing the river in a small trolley-like cable car. The crossing is free.

During November the **Loi Krathong festival** (p746) is celebrated here, with much traditional ceremony and touristic outreach.

Bang Pa-In can be reached from Ayuthaya by public sǎwngthǎew (20B, one hour), which departs from the provincial bus stop on Th Naresuan. The sǎwngthǎew stops at the Bang Pa-In bus station, which is 4km from the palace. A motorcycle to the palace should cost 15B. The train service from Ayuthaya (3rd class 3B, 30 minutes) is more scenic but a little more expensive as you'll need to hire a sǎwngthǎew from the train station to the palace and quoted rates are never Westerner-friendly (around 40B).

LOPBURI PROVINCE

LOPBURI
ลพบุรี
pop 62,812
Walkable and amiable, Lopburi is a pleasant small town for tiptoeing off the tourist trail. Ancient ruins amid modern shophouses attest to Lopburi's role in the central region's shifting empires – the Dvaravati, Khmers, Sukhothai and Ayuthaya all established administrative centres here.

Today the rulers of the ruins are a resident troop of monkeys who add mischief and mayhem to these retired places. Meanwhile, a

CENTRAL THAILAND

MONKEY TROUBLE

Tight-rope artists, fence-post sitters and general troublemakers: Lopburi's resident monkeys (a type of macaque) inhabit the city with acrobatic bravado. The ruins of **San Phra Kan** (Kala Shrine; Th Wichayan) are their usual daytime hang-out, but once the sun begins to set they cross the railroad tracks to roost in the halls of **Prang Sam Yot** (Th Wichayan).

But their range isn't limited to the ruins. There are just too many tempting places to crawl and fiddle for these dexterous creatures. Up above the usual reach of a human are the telephone and electricity wires that act as monkey roadways to TV antennas that need uninvited adjustment. The train station is also nearby and wanderlust monkeys have been known to hitch a ride for a weekend outing – or so say tall-tale spinning locals.

Like Thailand's legions of stray dogs, Lopburi's monkey population survives in part due to Buddhist discouragement of killing animals. Moreover, many locals say that Lopburi's monkeys are the 'children' of the Hindu god Kala and that to harm one would bring on misfortune. For the most part, however, the inhabitants of Lopburi seem to agree that the monkeys' delinquent behaviour is outweighed by the tourist dollars that they bring in. In late November Lopburi holds a feast for the monkeys at Prang Sam Yot to thank them for their contribution to the prosperity of Lopburi. Buffet tables are meticulously laid out with peanuts, cabbage, watermelon, bananas, pumpkin, pineapple, boiled eggs and cucumbers; the latter two items are monkey favourites, causing plenty of spats. Thousands of Thais turn out to watch the spectacle.

While monkeys frolicking on stone temples make for great photo opportunities, visitors to Lopburi should keep in mind that these are wild animals whose natural fear of humans has diminished over time. Monkeys have been known to attack humans, especially would-be photographers who use food to lure monkeys within the range of their camera lenses.

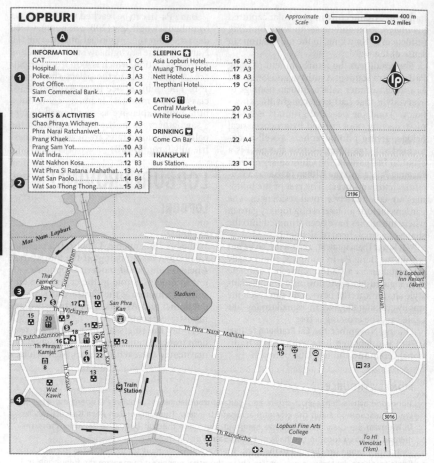

CENTRAL THAILAND

low-key town filled with motorcycle shops and ice-cream parlours has grown like a weed, providing an engaging vantage point for Thai provincial life as well as a historical retrospective.

Most of Lopburi's highlights can be seen and appreciated in one or two days en route north from Ayuthaya.

History

Lopburi is considered to be one of Thailand's oldest cities, dating from the Dvaravati period (6th to 11th centuries) when Lopburi was called Lavo. When the Khmer kingdom expanded into present-day Thailand in the 10th century, Lavo became a frontier hub for the empire and was filled with the Khmer's

signature architectural monuments, including Prang Khaek (Shiva Shrine), San Phra Kan (Kala Shrine), Prang Sam Yot (Three Spired Shrine) and the tower at Wat Phra Si Ratana Mahathat – many of which remain in various states today.

Power over Lopburi was wrested from the Khmers in the 13th century as the Sukhothai kingdom to the north grew stronger, but the Khmer cultural influence remained to some extent throughout the Ayuthaya period. King Narai fortified Lopburi in the mid-17th century to serve as a second capital when the kingdom of Ayuthaya was threatened by a Dutch naval blockade. His palace in Lopburi was constructed in 1665 and he died there in 1688.

Orientation

Lopburi is distinctly split into two: the old town sandwiched between the western side of the railroad tracks and the river, and the new town that sprawls east of the city. The old part of town is massively more charming, with all the historical sites within walking distance. The train station is also easily reached from the old town on foot.

Information

There are several banks in the old part of Lopburi.

Communications Authority of Thailand (CAT; Th Phra Narai Maharat; ☺ 8.30am-4pm)

Hospital (☎ 0 3662 1537-45; Th Ramdecho)

Police (☎ 0 3642 4515; Th Na Phra Kan)

Post Office (Th Phra Narai Maharat)

TAT (☎ 0 3642 2768-9; Th Phraya Kamjat; ☺ 8.30am-4.30pm) Has helpful maps and brochures.

Sights

PHRA NARAI RATCHANIWET
พระนารายณ์ราชนิเวศน์

Start your tour of Lopburi at this **former royal palace** (entrance Th Sorasak; admission 30B; ☺ gallery 9am-4pm Wed-Sun, palace grounds 7am-5.30pm), which is a combination of palace ruins and artefact galleries.

During the reign of Ayuthaya's King Narai, Lopburi was used as a second capital. The king chose this site for his palace, which took 12 years to build between 1665 and 1677. At the time, the Ayuthaya kingdom hosted many Western envoys, and French architects contributed to the design. Interestingly, Khmer architectural influence was still strong in central Thailand so the palace exhibits an unusual blend of Khmer and European styles. Upon the king's death in 1688, the palace was used only by King Phetracha (King Narai's successor) for his coronation ceremony and was then abandoned until King Mongkut (Rama IV of Bangkok's Chakri dynasty) ordered restoration in the mid-19th century.

The main gate into the palace, **Pratu Phayakkha**, is off Th Sorasak. The grounds are well kept, planted with trees and shrubbery, and serve as a kind of town park for local children and young lovers.

Immediately on the left as you enter are the remains of former storage buildings and the palace reservoir. In the quadrangle to the left is the royal reception hall, often used for foreign dignitaries, and the **Phra Chao Hao**, which most likely served as a *wíhaan* for a valued

Buddha image. Continuing to the southwest quadrangle of the complex are the ruins of the elephant stables and the **Suttha Sawan** pavilion, a former royal residence.

In the northwest quadrangle are buildings that were used during the king's reign as audience halls and residential quarters for the king's harem, but today have been renovated and house the **Lopburi Museum** (or more officially known as Somdet Phra Narai National Museum). The museum's collection is divided into three separate buildings. The most important building is the Phiman Mongkut Pavilion, which contains a fine collection of Lopburi-period sculpture as well as a variety of Khmer, Dvaravati, U Thong and Ayuthaya art. The Chantara Phisan Pavilion is a memorial to King Narai and ecclesiastical artefacts. The Phra Pratiab Building has a few minor displays of traditional tools (hand looms, and fishing and farming equipment) and shadow play carvings.

WAT PHRA SI RATANA MAHATHAT
วัดพระศรีรัตนมหาธาตุ

The Fine Arts Department has restored this large 12th-century Khmer **wat** (Th Na Phra Kan; admission 30B; ☺ 7am-5pm), considered one of the city's oldest. During Lopburi's heyday, it was the town's largest monastery, a fact clearly shown on a map drawn by French cartographers in 1687. A tall laterite tower still stands and features a few intact lintels and some ornate stucco. There is also a large *wíhaan* added by King Narai. Several *chedi* and smaller towers dot the grounds.

CHAO PHRAYA WICHAYEN
บ้านวิชาเยนทร์

King Narai built this Thai-European **palace** (Th Wichayen; admission 30B; ☺ 9am-4pm) as a residence for foreign ambassadors, of whom the Greek Constantine Phaulkon was the most famous. Phaulkon became one of King Narai's advisers and was eventually a royal minister. He was also implicated in an attempted coup and in 1688, as Narai lay dying, Phaulkon was assassinated by Luang Sorasak, who wanted power for himself. The palace is across the street and northeast of Wat Sao Thong Thong.

PRANG SAM YOT
ปรางค์สามยอด

Opposite San Phra Kan, this **shrine** (Th Wichayen; admission 30B; ☺ 8am-6pm) represents classic

Khmer-Lopburi style and is Lopburi's most photographed Hindu-turned-Buddhist temple. Originally, the three towers symbolised the Hindu Trimurti of Shiva, Vishnu and Brahma. Now two of them contain ruined Lopburi-style Buddha images. Some Khmer lintels can still be made out, and some appear unfinished.

An U Thong–Ayuthaya imitation Buddha image sits in the brick sanctuary in front of the linked towers. At the back are a couple of crudely restored images, probably once Lopburi style. The grounds allotted to Prang Sam Yot are quite small and virtually surrounded by modern buildings. The best view of the monument is probably from one of the upper floors of the Muang Thong Hotel. The monument is lit up at night and is constantly crawling with monkeys.

PRANG KHAEK
ปรางค์แขก

Situated on a triangular slice of land bordered by Th Wichayen to the north, Prang Khaek features towers with Khmer-style brickwork. The structure is thought to have originally been a temple to the Hindu god Shiva and dates back to the 11th century.

OTHER RUINS

Built by the Khmers in the 12th century, **Wat Nakhon Kosa** (Th Na Phra Kan) may originally have been a Hindu shrine. The U Thong and Lopburi images found at the temple are thought to have been added later. There's not much left of this wat, but the foliage growing on the brick ruins is an interesting sight. A notably larger base below the monument was uncovered several years ago.

A partial brick and stucco tower is all that's left of **Wat San Paolo** (Th Ramdecho), a Jesuit church founded by the Portuguese during King Narai's reign. A contingent of a dozen French priests came to run the church in 1687. An octagonal, three-storey celestial observatory was also erected here, though it is unclear under which direction it was built.

Northwest of the palace centre, **Wat Sao Thong Thong** (Th Wichayen) is in pretty poor shape. The wíhǎan and large seated Buddha are from the Ayuthaya period; King Narai restored the wíhǎan (changing its windows to an incongruous but intriguing Gothic style) so it could be used as a Christian chapel. Niches along the inside walls contain Lopburi-style Buddhas with naga (serpent) protectors.

Practically nothing is known about the history of **Wat Indra** (Th Ratchadamnoen), which is now merely a sizable brick foundation, the curse of a forgetful history.

Festivals & Events

In mid-February the Phra Narai Ratchaniwet is the focus of the three-day **King Narai Festival** (www.thailandgrandfestival.com), which includes lákhon ling (traditional drama performed by monkeys) and the exhibit and sale of locally woven textiles. Visit the website for exact dates.

Blessed be the simians on the last week of November when Lopburi celebrates its annual **Monkey Festival**; the monkeys get a banquet feast while Thais and tourists watch the gorgefest with fear and delight.

Sleeping

Lopburi doesn't have a guesthouse scene, so most of the lodging options are the usual stock of worn-out Thai-Chinese hotels complete with a spittoon and outdated 1960s stylings. The old city has the most convenient options for walkers. There are some equally run-down midrange options in the new part of town but you'll need your own transport for sightseeing.

BUDGET

Lopburi's budget hotels are quite adequate, if cheap, basic and worn.

Muang Thong Hotel (☎ 0 3641 1036; 1/1-11 Th Prang Sam Yot; r 160B) Great location overlooking Prang Sam Yot, but dumpy, squat-toilet rooms.

Asia Lopburi Hotel (☎ 0 3661 8894; cnr Th Sorasak & Th Phraya Kamjat; s/d from 220/250B; 🖭) More of the same: basic rooms ranging from spiffy to depressing. Look at more than one before settling in.

Nett Hotel (☎ 0 3641 1738; 17/1-2 Th Ratchadamnoen; r from 200-350B; 🖭) Clean and friendly option, the Nett has newly tiled air-con rooms.

HI Vimolrat (Lopburi Youth Hostel; ☎ 0 3661 3731; www.tyha.org/LopburiYH.html; 5/19 Mu 3, Th Naresuan; dm/d/q 140/340/370B; 🖭) Inconveniently located southeast of the town, this hostel is a good place to meet young Thais and other travellers. The train station and old town ruins are an 80B túk-túk ride away.

MIDRANGE & TOP END

Thepthani Hotel (☎ 0 3641 1029; Th Phra Narai Maharat; r 400B; 🖭) Run by the Rajabhat university's tourism and hospitality department, Thep-

thani is a respectable midrange option. Rooms are spacious with cable TV and central hot water. Blue buses travelling between the old and new town will drop you here for 8B.

Lopburi Inn Resort (☎ 0 3642 0777; www.lopburiinn resort.com; 144 Tambon Tha Sala; r 1000-1200B; ❄ ⚊) You might need a sense of humour to appreciate the extensive monkey theme at this resort. It may not be sophisticated or contemporary, but it is the nicest place in town.

Eating & Drinking

Lopburi has the usual assortment of street stalls serving tasty food, which congregate in front of the Nett Hotel and on Th Na Phra Kan in the evenings. For air-con comfort, try the ice-cream parlours around town that offer student snack foods and Western-style breakfasts.

White House (Th Phraya Kamjat; dishes 60-120B; ❄ 5pm-10pm) Across the street from the TAT office, this pleasant little spot offers a range of Thai-Chinese specialties and vegetarian options.

Central Market (off Th Ratchadamnoen & Th Surasongkhram; ❄ 8am-2pm) Just north of the palace, this day market is a great place to pick up *kài thâwt* (fried chicken) or *kài yâang* (roast chicken) with sticky rice; *hàw mòk* (soufflé-like fish and coconut curry steamed in banana leaves); *klûay khàek* (Indian-style fried bananas); and a wide selection of fruit, satays, *khâo krìap* (crispy rice cakes), *thâwt man plaa* (fried fish cakes) and other delights. In the centre of the market is a vegetarian pavilion.

A sleepy town like Lopburi doesn't see much nightly action beyond the night market, but the **Come On Bar** (Th Phraya Kamjat) is an exception with a solid Western soundtrack, as well tourist information.

Getting There & Away

BUS

Lopburi's **bus station** (Th Naresuan) is almost 2km outside of the old district. The following destinations are served: Ayuthaya (47B, two hours, every 20 minutes) and Bangkok's Northern and Northeastern bus terminal (130B, 3½ hours, every 20 minutes).

Lopburi can also be reached from the west via Suphanburi (55B, three hours, every hour). From Supanburi you can catch another local bus to Kanchanaburi (40B, one hour, every 20 minutes). Other nearby cities that can serve as hopscotch points west include Singburi or Ang Thong, across the river from Lopburi. There are frequent local buses between the

cities, and the Singburi bus (15B, one hour) makes a stop in front of Prang Sam Yot in old Lopburi.

Lopburi can also be reached from the northeast via Khorat (Nakhon Ratchasima) on air-con buses for 120B.

TRAIN

Most people arrive in Lopburi via the train coming north from Ayuthaya or south from Phitsanulok. The **train station** (Th Na Phra Kan) is within walking distance to historic sites and lodging. The station also has baggage storage if you are only stopping in Lopburi for a few hours.

Trains heading south toward Ayuthaya (ordinary/rapid/express 13/120/140B) and Bangkok's Hualamphong station (ordinary/rapid/express 28/125/170B) leave throughout the day with six daytime departures, roughly every hour from 5am to 9pm, and several afternoon and late-night departures. Rapid and express trains take about three hours, ordinary trains about 4½ hours. If headed to Bangkok, you can shave some time off your trip by disembarking at Bangkok's Bang Sue station and taking the nearby subway to points within central Bangkok.

Trains heading north from Lopburi stop at Phitsanulok (ordinary/rapid/express 150/223/390B). There are numerous services with roughly hourly departures between 8am and 3pm and again from 8pm to 11pm.

Getting Around

Săwngthăew and city buses run along Th Wichayen and Th Phra Narai Maharat between the old and new towns for 8B per passenger; *saamláw* will go anywhere in the old town for 30B.

KANCHANABURI PROVINCE

This frontier province stretches from the fertile sugar-cane fields of the namesake provincial capital all the way to the sparsely inhabited western border with Myanmar. It is home to some of Thailand's largest tracts of preserved land, gushing waterfalls in the rainy season and several declining populations of reclusive but celebrity animal species. Its mountains form a natural boundary with

CENTRAL THAILAND

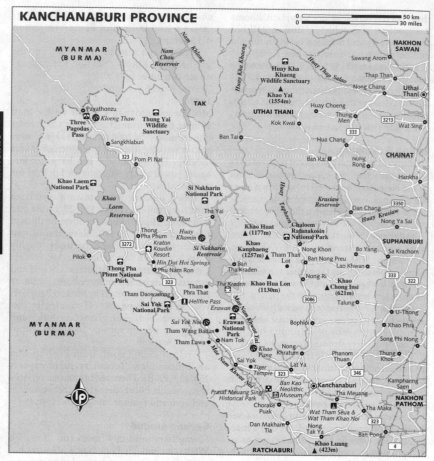

KANCHANABURI PROVINCE

Myanmar, discouraging major population growth and preserving a wilder way of life. These mountains also provide a slightly cooler climate than Bangkok, especially in the evenings. Most visitors check into Kanchanaburi, do a few days of organised activities and then rush on to Chiang Mai or to the south. But following the highway northwest to the outbound towns provides an immersion into nature and culture that the traveller grapevine claims only exists in Laos.

KANCHANABURI
กาญจนบุรี
pop 64,300
With field, forest and stream, Kanchanaburi has become a catch basin for new arrivals overwhelmed by Bangkok (a mere 130km east) and a closer alternative than Chiang Mai for Thailand's soft version of 'trekking' (elephant rides, short hikes and bamboo rafting). The town sits in a fertile valley where sugar-cane fields bow in the breeze, measuring out an easy pace.

In addition to outdoor appreciation, the limestone hills surrounding Kanchanaburi are famous for their temple caves, an underground communion of animistic spirit worship and traditional Buddhism. Winding arteries burrow into the guts of the caves past bulbous calcium deposits and altars for Buddha images, surrounded by offerings from pilgrims.

Crawling out of the mountains to the sea, the surrounding rivers (Mae Nam Khwae Noi and Mae Nam Mae Klong) define much of the

lazy character of the town, except on weekends and holidays when Bangkok Thais come by the busloads to pound the night into light aboard floating discos and karaoke barges. That such tranquillity attracts such mayhem is a true test in appreciating cultural differences.

This quiet provincial capital also played an unlikely role during WWII. Here, occupying Japanese forces used captured Allied prisoners of war (POWs) and conscripted Southeast Asians to build a demanding, deadly rail route to present-day Myanmar. You might have heard of this minor war story thanks to Pierre Boulle's *The Bridge on the River Kwai* and the movie of the same name. The bridge, several museums and cemeteries have respectfully preserved the history and memorialised the dead.

History

Kanchanaburi was originally established by Rama I as a first line of defence against the Burmese along an old invasion route through the Three Pagodas Pass on the Thailand–Myanmar border.

During WWII the Japanese used Allied prisoners of war to build the infamous 'Death Railway' along this same invasion route, from Mae Nam Khwae Noi to the pass. Thousands of prisoners died as a result of brutal treatment by their captors.

Orientation

Kanchanaburi has a mini-Th Khao San concentrated along Th Mae Nam Khwae, within walking distance of the train station. Most accommodation is built beside the river. The commercial strip of the town follows Th Saengchuto. The in-town attractions are spread out enough to be too far on foot, so you'll want a bicycle or motorcycle to get around.

Information

EMERGENCY
Tourist Police (☎ 0 3451 2668, 0 3451 2795; Th Saengchuto)

INTERNET ACCESS
Internet cafés change names and locations often, but there are always several connections available somewhere along Th Mae Nam Khwae. Prices vary from 20B to 30B per hour.

WHY BRIDGE THE RIVER KWAI?

Monumental engineering projects are often the modern measure of a sophisticated and superior society. And the railway now known as the 'Death Railway' is one of the most obvious examples of this fascination with mechanised domination. The railway was built during the WWII-era Japanese occupation of Thailand (1942-43) and its strategic objective was to link 415km of rugged terrain between Thailand and Burma (Myanmar) in order to secure an alternative supply route for the Japanese conquest of India. It was an ambitious goal that was accomplished with limited equipment, brutal treatment of forced labour and engineering creativity.

Construction of the railway began on 16 September 1942 at existing stations at Thanbyuzayat in Myanmar and Nong Pladuk (Ban Pong) in Thailand. Japanese engineers at the time estimated that it would take five years to link Thailand and Burma by rail. In actuality, the Japanese army forced the POWs to complete the 1m-gauge railway in only 16 months. Most of the work was done by hand with simple tools, building high bridges and carving cuttings into the sides of the mountains. The rails were finally joined 37km south of Three Pagodas Pass; a Japanese brothel train inaugurated the line.

The bridge that spans the River Kwai near Kanchanaburi (dubbed the 'Death Railway Bridge'; see p211) was in use for 20 months before the Allies bombed it in 1945. Rather than a supply line, the route had quickly become an escape for Japanese troops. After the war the British took control of the railway on the Burmese side of the border and ripped up 4km of the tracks leading to Three Pagodas Pass for fear of the route being used by Karen separatists.

On the Thai side, the State Railway of Thailand (SRT) assumed control and continues to operate trains on 130km of the original path between Nong Pladuk, south of Kanchanaburi, to Nam Tok. See Getting There & Away (p216) for information about riding this historic route.

Approximately 40km of the railway is now submerged under the Khao Laem Dam, while the remaining track on either side of the dam was dismantled. Hellfire Pass (Konyu Cutting), one of the most demanding construction points, is still visible today at the Hellfire Pass Memorial (p218).

CENTRAL THAILAND

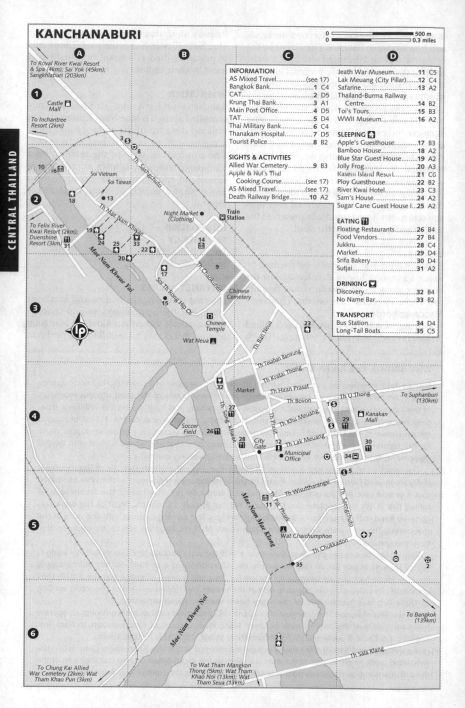

KANCHANABURI

0 — 500 m
0 — 0.3 miles

INFORMATION
AS Mixed Travel.....................(see 17)
Bangkok Bank...........................1 C4
CAT...2 D5
Krung Thai Bank.......................3 A1
Main Post Office......................4 D5
TAT..5 D4
Thai Military Bank....................6 C4
Thanakarn Hospital...................7 D5
Tourist Police..........................8 B2

SIGHTS & ACTIVITIES
Allied War Cemetery.................9 B3
Apple & Noi's Thai
    Cooking Course............(see 17)
AS Mixed Travel.................(see 17)
Death Railway Bridge.............10 A2

Jeath War Museum..................11 C5
Lak Meuang (City Pillar)..........12 C4
Safarine................................13 A2
Thailand-Burma Railway
    Centre.............................14 B2
Toi's Tours.............................15 B3
WWII Museum........................16 A2

SLEEPING
Apple's Guesthouse................17 B3
Bamboo House.......................18 A2
Blue Star Guest House.............19 A2
Jolly Frog.............................20 A3
Kasem Island Resort...............21 C6
Ploy Guesthouse....................22 B2
River Kwai Hotel.....................23 C3
Sam's House..........................24 A2
Sugar Cane Guest House I.......25 A2

EATING
Floating Restaurants...............26 B4
Food Vendors........................27 B4
Jukkru..................................28 C4
Market..................................29 D4
Srifa Bakery...........................30 D4
Sutjai...................................31 A2

DRINKING
Discovery...............................32 B4
No Name Bar.........................33 B2

TRANSPORT
Bus Station............................34 D4
Long-Tail Boats......................35 C5

Connections and processing strength varies, so shop around.

MEDICAL SERVICES
Thanakarn Hospital (☎ 0 3462 2359; Th Saengchuto) Near the junction of Th Chukkadon, this hospital is best equipped for foreign visitors.

MONEY
Several major Thai banks can be found on Th Saengchuto near the market and the bus terminal.
AS Mixed Travel (☎ 0 3451 2017; Apple's Guesthouse, 52 Soi Rong Hip Oi) Foreign-exchange service available outside of bank hours.
Bangkok Bank (Th U-Thong) Located near the market.
Krung Thai Bank (Th Saengchuto) Near River Kwai Bridge.
Thai Military Bank (Th Saengchuto) Near the bus station.

POST
Main post office (Th Saengchuto; ☉ 8.30am-4.30pm Mon-Fri, 9am-12pm Sat & Sun)

TELEPHONE
There are numerous private shops along Th Mae Nam Khwae offering long-distance calls.
CAT (☉ 7am-10pm) This office has an international telephone service.

TOURIST INFORMATION
TAT (☎ 0 3451 1200, 0 3451 2500; Th Saengchuto; ☉ 8.30am-4.30pm) Has free maps of the town and province. It also has comprehensive information on accommodation, activities and transport.

Sights
There is a lot to see in Kanchanaburi town and the countryside to the northwest, so much that many visitors get overwhelmed and just sign up for a tour to erase the guesswork. This is a shame because Kanchanaburi is so laid-back that you'll surely encounter all sorts of lovely stories if you step outside the tourist incubator and flag down a local bus.

Most attractions in town – the WWII historic sites and Kanchanaburi's cave temples – can be tackled in one or two days aboard a bicycle or motorcycle. Another two days can be used to visit the out-of-town destinations aboard a public bus.

THAILAND-BURMA RAILWAY CENTRE
ศูนย์รถไฟไทย–พม่า
This well-designed **museum** (☎ 0 3451 0067; www .tbrconline.com; 73 Th Chaokanen; admission 80B; ☉ 9am-

5pm) is the best place to start your exploration of Kanchanaburi's role in WWII. The museum succeeds in its aim to offer a nonpartisan explanation of the Japanese occupation of Thailand, the reasons for building the Thailand–Burma railway, the technological impediments to its construction, the harsh working conditions and the state of the railway since the end of the war. Each of the nine galleries is packed with interesting facts presented in a dynamic way. There are also video interviews with POWs and Japanese officials who worked on the railway, adding a necessary element of human drama to historical events. The models of the landscape and the faithful reproductions of the Japanese designs show why building the railway was such a treacherous challenge.

ALLIED WAR CEMETERY
สุสานทหารสัมพันธมิตรดอนรัก
Directly across the street from the museum is the **Allied War Cemetery** (Th Saengchuto; ☉ 8am-6pm), a fitting memorial to the POWs who died building the railway. The lovingly tended grounds is the final resting place of only a small portion of the total number of prisoners who died during the construction of the railway. It is estimated that more than 100,000 men died, 16,000 of whom were Western POWs, mainly from Britain and Holland. Conscripted labourers, many from Japanese-occupied Southeast Asian countries, suffered even higher causalities; it is estimated that 90,000 to 100,000 labourers died in the area.

DEATH RAILWAY BRIDGE (BRIDGE OVER THE RIVER KWAI)
สะพานข้ามแม่น้ำแคว
This little railway **bridge** (Th Mae Nam Khwae) is not nearly as impressive in person as the dramatic story that made it famous. The materials for the bridge were brought from Java by the Imperial Japanese Army during its 1942–43 occupation of Thailand. The first version of the bridge, completed in February 1943, was all wood. In April of the same year a second bridge of steel was constructed. In 1945 the bridge was bombed several times by Allied planes and was only rebuilt after the war – the curved portions of the bridge are original.

Train enthusiasts should not miss the old locomotives used during WWII that are parked on display near the bridge. During the last week of November and first week of

December there is a nightly sound-and-light show at the bridge, commemorating the Allied attack on the Death Railway in 1945. It's a big scene, with the sounds of bombers and explosions, fantastic bursts of light and more. The town gets a lot of Thai tourists during this week, so book early if you want to witness this spectacle.

The bridge spans Mae Nam Khwae Yai, which is 2.5km from the centre of Kanchanaburi. The most enjoyable way to get to the bridge from town is to rent a bicycle or motorcycle. You can also catch a northbound săwngthăew (10B) along Th Saengchuto.

WWII MUSEUM
พิพิธภัณฑ์สงครามโลกครั้งที่สอง

Despite what the sign out front says, this **museum** (admission 30B; ⏱ 9am-6pm), unlike the Jeath War Museum, is a monument to kitsch, with a random and almost ridiculous collection of stuff inside.

The larger, more lavish of the two buildings contains Burmese-style alabaster Buddhas and a *phrá khrêuang* (sacred amulets) display. Upper floors exhibit Thai weaponry from the Ayuthaya period, ceramics and brightly painted portraits of all the kings in Thai history. On the 5th and uppermost floor – above the royal portraits (flirting with lese-majesty) – is the history of the Chinese family who built the museum.

A smaller building opposite holds WWII relics, including photos and sketches made during the POW period, and a display of Japanese and Allied weapons. Along the front of this building stand life-size sculptures of historical figures associated with the war, including Churchill, MacArthur, Hitler, Einstein, de Gaulle and Hirohito. The English captions are sometimes unintentionally amusing or disturbing – a reference to the atomic bomb dropped on Hiroshima, for example, reads 'Almost the entire city was destroyed in a jiffy'. Even more odd is a diorama of the famous bridge being bombed. More lighthearted is the collection of Miss Thailand clothing on the 2nd floor.

The museum is just south of the Death Railway Bridge and is an amusing tourist spot, but not essential for a history buff.

JEATH WAR MUSEUM
พิพิธภัณฑ์สงคราม

This worn but heart-felt **museum** (Th Wisuttharangsi; admission 30B; ⏱ 8.30am-6pm), on the grounds of Wat Chaichumphon (Wat Tai), is worth visiting just to sit on the cool banks of Mae Nam Mae Klong and to witness the genuine concern modern-day Thais feel toward the suffering that occurred on their soil. The museum is a replica of the bamboo-*atap* huts used to house Allied POWs during the occupation. The long huts contain various photographs taken during the war, drawings and paintings by POWs, maps, weapons and other war memorabilia. The acronym Jeath represents the meeting of Japan, England, Australia/America, Thailand and Holland at Kanchanaburi during WWII.

The war museum is at the west end of Th Wisuttharangsi (Visutrangsi), not far from the TAT office. The common Thai name for this museum is *phíphítháphan songkhraam wát tâi*.

LAK MEUANG (CITY PILLAR)
ศาลหลักเมือง

Like many older Thai cities, Kanchanaburi has a **city pillar** (làk meuang; Th Lak Meuang) denoting the original town centre and providing shelter for the city spirit. The bulbous-tipped pillar is covered with gold leaf and is much worshipped. Within sight of the pillar, towards the river, stands Kanchanaburi's original city gate.

CHUNG KAI ALLIED WAR CEMETERY
สุสานสัมพันธมิตรช่องไก่

This former POW camp is now a memorial cemetery that sees fewer visitors than the more central Allied War Cemetery. The burial plaques at this cemetery carry names, military insignia, and short epitaphs for Dutch, British, French and Australian soldiers.

The cemetery is approximately 4km south of central Kanchanaburi across the Mae Nam Khwae Noi and is best reached by bicycle or motorcycle. The route here is very scenic, passing by sugar-cane fields and village life.

WAT THAM KHAO PUN
วัดถ้ำเขาปูน

Another kilometre beyond Chung Kai Allied War Cemetery is this quiet cave **temple** (admission by donation; ⏱ 7am-4pm), filled with shrines to the Buddha, Hindu deities and Thai kings, that attracts a trickle of pilgrims from around Thailand. The cave complex is fairly extensive and more interesting to explore

than similar caves at Wat Tham Seua. During WWII the cave complex was used by the Japanese to store weapons and equipment, and some of the smaller chambers are said to have been used to imprison and torture POWs. The caves were the site of another tragedy in 1995 when a British tourist was murdered by a drug-addicted monk living at the wat. Kanchanaburi residents, like the rest of Thailand, were mortified by the crime, and many now refer to the cave as 'Johanne's Cave' in memory of the victim. The monk was defrocked and sentenced to death (commuted to life imprisonment without parole by the king in 1996).

WAT THAM MANGKON THONG
วัดถ้ำมังกรทอง
The 'Cave Temple of the Golden Dragon' has long been an attraction because of the 'floating nun' – a *mâe chii* (Thai Buddhist nun) who meditated while floating on her back in a pool of water. The original nun passed away, but a disciple continues the tradition – sort of. The current floating nun does not meditate but instead she strikes Buddha-like poses based upon traditional *mudra* (ritual hand movements). Shows do not have a set schedule but instead are timed for the arrival of tour groups.

Most Western visitors prefer to visit the temple cave instead of the swimming antics. A long, steep series of steps with dragon-sculpted handrails leads up the craggy mountainside behind the main *bòt* to a complex of limestone caves. Follow the string of light bulbs through the front cave and you'll find a view of the valley and mountains beyond. One section of the cave requires crawling or duck-walking, so wear appropriate clothing and shoes – the cave floor can be slippery.

The temple is 7km south of town and accessible via bicycle or motorbike.

WAT THAM SEUA & WAT THAM KHAO NOI
วัดถ้ำเสือ/วัดถ้ำเขาน้อย
Built on a ridge overlooking a patchwork of fields and forests, these adjacent hilltop monasteries are important local pilgrimage spots, especially for Chinese Buddhists, and are just high enough above the ground to put the faithful closer to heaven.

Wat Tham Khao Noi (Little Hill Cave Monastery) has crowned its side of the shared hillside with a fanciful Chinese-style pagoda, similar in size and style to Penang's Kek Lok Si. Next door, Wat Tham Seua (Tiger Cave Monastery) boasts a Thai-style *chedi* framing a huge 18m-tall Buddha facing Mae Nam Khwae Noi.

You can ascend the hill either on an inclined cable car or climb a set of *naga* stairs. To the right of the hill-top landing is a cave filled with the usual assortment of Buddha images and shrines.

The temples are about 15km southeast of Kanchanaburi in Tha Meuang district. By public transport, you can take a bus (10B) to the Tha Meuang Hospital and then a motorcycle taxi (50B) directly to the temples. If you're on a motorbike, take the right fork of the highway when you reach Tha Meuang, turn right across the Kheuan Meuang (City Dam) and right again on the other side of the river. By bicycle, you can avoid taking the highway by using back roads along the river. Follow Th Pak Phraek in Kanchanaburi southeast and cross the bridge towards Wat Tham Mangkon Thong, then turn left on the other side and follow the road parallel to the river. After about 14km, you'll see the Kheuan Meuang up ahead – at this point you should start looking for the hill-top pagodas on your right.

Activities
THAI COOKING
Although Kanchanaburi's main highlights are the outdoors, **Apple & Noi's Thai Cooking Course** (Apple's Guesthouse, Th Saengchuto; course 950B) poses a formidable indoor rival. Their full-day Thai cooking course is held in a specially designed kitchen and includes a morning trip to the market. To reserve an apron, contact Apple or Noi at their guesthouse.

TREKKING & KAYAKING
The 'treks' offered by tour agencies of Kanchanaburi are far from being strenuous adventures into the wilderness. Most offer a one-day, greatest-hits tour of Kanchanaburi's sites: ride an elephant, see the Erawan Waterfall, visit the Death Railway Bridge or Hellfire Pass, or some combination of these that requires a lot of crawling in and out of minivans. Most of these day-tour sites can be visited independently aboard public transport and we strongly encourage those who have a guidebook to actually use it.

CENTRAL THAILAND

The tours are better options if you're interested in doing either an elephant or an overnight trek that usually includes a visit to a Karen village and a short river journey on a bamboo raft. But don't expect Indiana Jones – this is Thailand, a country that loves photo ops over swashbuckling.

Be careful when choosing a trek as many companies will cancel at the last minute if not enough people sign up. New companies pop up every season, so ask around for recommendations. The following agencies are reputable:

AS Mixed Travel (☎ 0 3451 2017; www.applenoi -kanchanaburi.com; Apple's Guesthouse) A locally owned and well-organised company with longevity. Overnight tours go to Chaloem Ratanakosin National Park.

Toi's Tours (☎ 0 3451 4209; 45/3 Soi Th Rong Hip Oi) If you need a French-speaking guide, this is a good option. There's a second office on Th Tha Makam.

Whether or not you're an experienced paddler, river kayaking is a great way to explore Kanchanaburi. The French-managed **Safarine** (☎ 0 3462 4140; www.safarine.com; 4 Soi Taiwan; ◷ Mon-Sat) is a complete tour company that specialises in river-based trips and will design custom tours for groups.

Sleeping

Along the mini-Th Khao San strip of Th Mae Nam Khwae are numerous guesthouses with cheap interior rooms and more expensive riverside bungalows or floating rafts. Many

---

SLEEP TIGHT, DON'T LET THE KARAOKE BITE

During the day Kanchanaburi is so peaceful that those floating raft rooms right on the river look the perfect place to be cradled to sleep. And then just when the crickets and frogs might switch on, karaoke dominates the airwaves. It seems that urban Thais define fun as leaving noisy Bangkok and going to quiet Kanchanaburi for all-night amplification. On weekdays most of the ruckus booms out of the karaoke restaurants and piers along Th Song Khwae, making the older guesthouses along Soi Rong Hip Oi uninhabitable. Then on the weekends, the floating disco barges lumber up and down the river chasing the sandman away for good.

---

budget guesthouses now offer rooms with air-con and hot-water showers that straddle budget and midrange options. The old backpacker area of Soi Th Rong Hip Oi is a fine spot until nightfall when the thumping karaoke starts to raise the dead; for this reason we have not listed these options here, but feel free to decide for yourself.

Many traditional midrange hotels are located on Th Saengchuto, but we've found the rooms to be lacking in ambience and quality compared to the upper-budget river guesthouses. Several resorts located outside of the city centre are visited by families with their own transport; check out **Kanchanaburi Info** (www.kanchanaburi-info.com) for more resort options.

BUDGET

There are many, many more options than these, so explore on your own if nothing here suits. The following are listed geographically from south to north.

Sugar Cane Guest House I (☎ 0 3462 4520; 22 Soi Pakistan, Th Mae Nam Khwae; s/d from 150/250B; ✦) Sugar Cane has the cleanest interior fan rooms in town. Its river-raft rooms share a wide veranda but don't stand out against the competition. There is a second location closer to the bridge.

Jolly Frog (☎ 0 3451 4579; 28 Soi China; s 70B, d 150-290B; ✦) A favourite with young backpackers, Jolly Frog is a happening spot with a social café and riverfront lawn. Rooms aren't the cleanest but neither are the guests.

Bamboo House (☎ 0 3462 4470; 3-5 Soi Vietnam, Th Mae Nam Khwae; r 200-500B; ✦) Serene, well-kept Bamboo House is close to the bridge, and far from all the hubbub in town.

Sam's House (☎ 0 3451 5956; www.samsguesthouse .com; Th Mae Nam Khwae; d 150-600B; ✦) Just one of Sam's empire outposts, this spot has a mix of options, the best being the fan-cooled, wooden rooms overlooking the river.

Blue Star Guest House (☎ 0 3451 2161; 241 Th Mae Nam Khwae; r 200-600B; ✦) Budget rooms here are ordinary and adequate, but the more expensive A-frame bungalows overlooking the river are extraordinary. They are creatively constructed with naturally twisted wood, reminiscent of a fantasy tree house.

Apple's Guesthouse (☎ 0 3451 2017; www.apple noi-kanchanaburi.com; 52 Soi Th Rong Hip Oi; r 300-600B) Apple's is a homey place with comfortable outdoor seating areas for socialising and

simple interior rooms for sound sleeping. The on-site restaurant and one-day Thai cooking courses (see p213) both get rave reviews.

MIDRANGE

Many midrange places offer discounts during the low season (April to November), but reservations should be made in advance.

Kasem Island Resort (☎ 0 3451 3359, in Bangkok 0 2255 3604; r from 800B; 🖭 🖳) On an island in the middle of Mae Nam Mae Klong, this long-running resort may be in the sunset of its years, but its still got a golden location. The pricier rooms are more soundproofed against the floating discos and have a lovely view of the surrounding mountains. From Th Chukkadon, you can arrange for a free shuttle boat to the island.

Ploy Guesthouse (☎ 0 3451 5804; www.ploygh .com; 79/2 Th Mae Nam Kwai; r 600-800B; 🖭) With gracious staff and remarkable rooms, Ploy Guesthouse has comfort and contemporary design smack dab in backpacker-land. The clientele tends to be older wanderers. The ground-floor rooms have a bath that opens up into an atrium garden. Don't miss the view from the elevated restaurant-bar and the rooftop terrace.

Inchantree Resort (☎ 0 3462 4914; www.inchant reeresort.com; Th Mae Nam Khwae; r from 950-1500B; 🖭 🖳) North of the bridge, this boutique resort has set stylish Balinese-style bungalows with open-air showers in among Kanchanaburi's usual assortment of stuffy hotels.

TOP END

Although the following places fall into the top-end category, they do vary in quality and amenities. Most resorts are north of the bridge on either side of the river. Shop the online booking services for discounts.

Duenshine Resort (☎ 0 3465 3369; www.duenshine .com; Th Thamakham; r from 1500; 🖭 🖳) Across the river near Felix River Kwai Resort, this family resort has clean and comfortable rooms that aren't especially stylish; the balconies and porches overlooking the lush gardens make up for the dowdy interiors.

River Kwai Hotel (☎ 0 3451 3348; www.riverkwai .co.th; 284/3-16 Th Saengchuto; r from 1500B; 🖭 🖳) Big and anonymous in-town hotel with modern and spacious rooms that are lacking in character. The on-site disco and bar are a mainstay in the Kanchanaburi nightscene.

Royal River Kwai Resort & Spa (☎ 0 3465 3297; 88 Kanchanaburi-Saiyok Rd; d/ste 1500/2900B; 🖭 🖳) Stylishly Zen, the rooms could be featured in an interior-design magazine. The riverside, wood-decked pool is the real highlight.

Felix River Kwai Resort (☎ 0 3451 5061; www .felixhotels.com/riverkwai; r from 3500B; 🖭 🖳) One of Kanchanaburi's longest-running resorts, Felix has the perfect riverside location with manicured grounds and all the resort amenities. Its heyday has come and gone but it hasn't yet been unseated by any other competition.

Eating

Kanchanaburi is a festive, prosperous town and people eat out a lot. Th Saengchuto near the River Kwai Hotel is packed with inexpensive restaurants catering mostly to a local clientele. Don't miss the **night market** (Th Saeng-hchuto), near the bus station, which has the best *hǎwy thâwt* (fried mussels in an egg batter) in Thailand.

There are also **food vendors** (Th Song Khwae) on both sides of the road, along the river where you can buy inexpensive takeaways and picnic on mats along the riverbank. In the evenings the floating restaurants along this street are set ablaze with Thais and package tourists. The food quality varies, but it's hard not to enjoy the atmosphere.

Th Mae Nam Khwae is lined with Western tourist-driven restaurants; we trust you and your stomach to make a good choice.

Jukkru (no Roman-script sign; dishes 50-160B) This restaurant is in a tasty spot on the row opposite the floating restaurants – look for the blue tables and chairs.

Sutjai (dishes 60-180B) A garden-style place on the western bank of the river next to the one-lane bridge. It has a bilingual menu, but little English is spoken. It's a little out of the way, though better than the other riverside restaurants in town.

Srifa Bakery, located on the west side of the bus station, handles most of the pastry and bread business in town. It's a modern place that has bakes up everything from Singapore-style curry puffs to French-style pastries.

Drinking

A crop of bars, complete with videos, pool tables and even prostitutes, has sprouted up along Th Mae Nam Khwae. Along the interior

side of Th Song Khwae are another cluster of bars and discos for weekending Thais.

No Name Bar (Th Mae Nam Khwae) With a slogan that goes 'Get shitfaced on a shoestring', who could resist this brash backpacker hang-out. Besides coming here for suds, there's a range of Western snacks, satellite TV for football games and BBC.

Discovery (Th Song Khwae) Loud and flashy, this riverside disco fills to the gills on weekends with locals and Bangkok Thais who don't need karaoke to have a good time.

Getting There & Away

BUS

Kanchanaburi's bus station is at the southern end of town, near the TAT office on Th Saengchuto. The following destinations are served: Bangkok's Southern bus terminal (100B, three hours, every 20 minutes between 4am and 8pm); Bangkok's Northern and Northeastern bus terminal (2nd/1st class 100/122B, three hours, every hour between 6.30am and 5pm); Nakhon Pathom (70B, two hours, every 15 minutes between 4am and 7pm); Sangkhlaburi (ordinary/air-con 110/200B, five hours, every hour); and Suphanburi (42B, 1½ hours, every 20 minutes), where you can connect to Ayuthaya.

You can bypass Bangkok if you're heading south by going to Ratchaburi (47B, two hours, frequent) and picking up a Hua Hin- or Phetchaburi-bound bus. If you're heading north to Chiang Mai or around, your best bet is to backtrack to Bangkok's Northern and Northeastern terminal in time to pick up a Chiang Mai–bound bus.

TRAIN

Kanchanaburi's train station is 2km northwest of the bus station and is within walking distance to the guesthouse area. Kanchanaburi is on the Bangkok Noi–Nam Tok rail line, which includes a portion of the historic Death Railway built by WWII POWs during the Japanese occupation of Thailand. Although the modern usage of the line used to be a low-key commuter route, SRT has decided to promote it as a historic line and hike the rates for foreigners to 100B between any station, regardless of distance. If you're travelling from Bangkok Noi station (located in Thonburi, across the river from Bangkok), this flat fare represents reasonable value, considering the scenery and

subtracting the discomfort of an ordinary (non-airconditioned) cabin.

The most historic part of the journey begins north of Kanchanaburi as the train crosses the Death Railway Bridge and terminates at Nam Tok station. For some the flat rate of 100B will seem negligible; others will feel slightly stung considering a bus costs half the amount and we won't even bother telling you what Thais pay.

Ordinary trains leave Thonburi's Bangkok Noi station at 7.45am and 1.30pm for Kanchanaburi. Trains return to Bangkok Noi from Kanchanaburi at 7.15am, 2.45pm and 5.40pm. The journey takes about four hours.

Trains along the historic portion of the rail line leave Kanchanaburi heading north to Nam Tok at 5.50am, 10.20am and 4.20pm. Return trains depart from Nam Tok at 5.20am, 12.50pm and 3.15pm. The trip takes about two hours. The Nam Tok train station is within walking distance to Sai Yok Noi waterfall and beside the highway; if you miss the return train, you can always flag down one of the frequent Sangkhlaburi-Kanchanaburi buses.

The SRT operates a special **tourist train** (☎ 0 3451 1285) on weekends and holidays that leaves Kanchanaburi around 10.30am for Nam Tok (300B).

Getting Around

Trips from the bus station to the guesthouse area should cost 30B to 40B on a *saamláw* and 20B on a motorcycle taxi. Public *săwngthǎew* run up and down Th Saengchuto for 10B per passenger and are an alternative for shuttling between the bus station and the guesthouse area (hop off once you see the cemetery). The train station is within walking distance of the guesthouse area.

Motorcycles can be rented at guesthouses and shops along Th Mae Nam Khwae for 150B a day. Bicycle rentals cost 50B.

The river ferry that crosses Mae Nam Mae Klong costs 8B per person. Sometimes there's an extra few baht charge for bikes (motor or push), although usually it's included.

One way to see the river and Kanchanaburi's sights is to hire a long-tail boat. To travel between the Jeath War Museum and the Death Railway Bridge costs approximately 250B for up to six people one way. For a two-hour roundtrip tour to three riverside attractions, rates start at 700B. Boats can be hired

from the boat pier off Th Chukkadon or at the Jeath War Museum.

AROUND KANCHANABURI

It isn't obvious how stunning the Kanchanaburi countryside is until you travel northwest of the town into a barely tamed landscape of dragon-scaled mountains and crystalline waterfalls. The peaks and valleys are lush thanks to the bountiful rains and are preserved from concrete by a series of protected forests, the largest such complex in Thailand. Many visitors only skim the surface of this natural world on speedy one-day tours, but real explorers can hit all the highlights on their own and then continue northwest to sleepy Thong Pha Phum, Sangkhlaburi and even peak over the Myanmar border.

The following sites are organised geographically along the major access highways to make it easier to visit via public transport.

The waterfalls outside of Kanchanaburi are best visited during the rainy season from June to October or in November and December, the cool season, when the water levels are most impressive.

Erawan National Park

อุทยานแห่งชาติเอราวัณ

Best known for its stunning seven-tiered waterfall, this 550-sq-km park (☎ 0 3457 4222; www .dnp.go.th; admission 400B; ☼ 8am-4.30pm) is easily accessed by public bus from Kanchanaburi.

The cascading and pooling waterfall feeds into Mae Nam Khwae Yai, and it's a 2km hike to the top pool. The uppermost fall is said to resemble Erawan, the three-headed elephant of Hindu mythology.

The trail can be steep, slippery and nonexistent from place to place, so wear good walking shoes or sneakers. Also bring a bathing suit as several of the pools are great for swimming.

On weekends and holidays, the falls are very crowded, and are a favourite destination during Songkran (Thai New Year).

The rest of the park is not as popular, especially for people without their own transport. If you have your own transport, check out **Tham Phra That** (off Hwy 323, 12km northwest of the turn-off to the park) and **Tham Wang Badan** (off Hwy 32, 30km northwest of the turn-off to the park).

Park bungalows (☎ 0 3457 4222, in Bangkok 0 2562 0760; bungalows 800-4000B) sleep between two and 50 people. Camping is also available for 90B to 150B; park offices rent out camping equipment. Advance reservations are necessary.

There are run-down hotels outside of the park entrance, but options near Kanchanaburi are better. There are food stalls near the bus station, which is 800m from the falls. To cut down on rubbish, food is not allowed beyond this point.

Buses run from Kanchanaburi all the way to the entrance of the Erawan waterfall (40B, 1½ hours, every hour from 8am to 5.20pm). The last bus back to Kanchanaburi is at 4pm. Within the park, you can rent bicycles for 20B per day and a pick-up truck for 500B for one hour.

Prasat Meuang Singh Historical Park

อุทยานประวัติศาสตร์ปราสาทเมืองสิงห์

One of the most southwestern corners of the Angkor kingdom, this **historical park** (☎ 0 3459 1122; admission 40B; ☼ 8am-5pm) preserves the remains of a 13th-century Khmer outpost that might have been used as a relay point for trade along Mae Nam Khwae Noi. The restored ruins cover 73.6 hectares and were declared a historical park under the administration of the Fine Arts Department in 1987.

All the park's shrines are constructed of laterite bricks and are situated in a huge grassy compound surrounded by layers of laterite ramparts. Sections of the ramparts show seven additional layers of earthen walls, suggesting cosmological symbolism in the city plan. Evidence of a sophisticated water system has also been discovered amid the ramparts and moats.

The town encompasses four groups of ruins, although only two groups have been excavated and are visible. In the centre of the complex is the principal shrine **Prasat Meuang Singh**, which faces east (the cardinal direction of most Angkor temples). Walls surrounding the shrine have gates in each of the cardinal directions. A reproduction of a sculpture of Avalokitesvara stands on the inside of the northern wall and establishes Meuang Singh as a Mahayana Buddhist centre. The original is in the National Museum in Bangkok. Inside the main *prang* is a reproduction of a sculpture of Prajnaparamita, another Mahayana Buddhist deity.

To the northeast of the main temple are the remains of a smaller **shrine** whose original

contents and purpose are unknown. Near the main entrance to the complex at the north gate is a small **exhibition hall** that contains various sculptures of Mahayana Buddhist deities and stucco decorations, most of which are reproductions.

Prasat Meuang Singh is approximately 43km west of Kanchanaburi and is most easily reached by private transport. The train heading north of Kanchanaburi to Nam Tok stops 1.5km away at Ban Kao/Tha Kilen stop (100B; see p216 for train departure times). There might be motorcycle taxis available at the train station if you don't want to walk. Bicycles can be rented at the park for 20B per day.

Ban Kao Neolithic Museum
พิพิธภัณฑ์บ้านเก่ายุคหิน

You really need an archaeology degree to appreciate this **museum** (admission 30B; ☆ 9am-4pm Wed-Sun), displaying 3000- to 4000-year-old artefacts from the excavation of the Ban Kao neolithic site. During the construction of the Death Railway along Mae Nam Khwae Noi, a Dutch POW named Van Heekeren uncovered Neolithic remains in the village of Ban Kao (Old Village), about 7km southeast of Meuang Singh. After WWII a Thai-Danish team retraced Van Heekeren's discovery, concluding that Ban Kao is a major Neolithic burial site. Archaeological evidence suggests it may have been inhabited 10,000 years ago.

Ban Kao is best reached by private transport. The train heading north of Kanchanaburi to Nam Tok stops 6km away at Ban Kao/Tha Kilen stop (100B; see p216 for train departure times). There might be motorcycle taxis available at the train station for the remaining trip to the museum.

Tiger Temple (Wat Luang Ta Bua Yanna Sampanno)
วัดหลวงตาบัวญาณสัมปันโน

What quite possibly be one of the worst tourist traps in history is actually an incredible photo opportunity. This **forest monastery** (☎ 0 3453 1557; admission 300B; ☆ 3.30-6pm) is a petting zoo for the big boys, tigers that is. Fulfilling its mission as a refuge for all life, this temple adopted its first tiger cub in 1999 after its mother was killed by poachers. Word spread that the temple could care for orphaned tigers and soon others were brought in for adoption. Now 10 tigers reside with the monks.

In the afternoons (between 1pm and 5pm), the tigers are taken out of their cages to an enclosed canyon for exercise and community outreach. Visitors are allowed under supervision to be photographed up close with the beasts. Some of the tigers clearly love to pose, while others get agitated easily. The temple requests that visitors avoid wearing 'hot' colours (red, pink and orange) that would excite the animals.

The obvious question is why the king of the jungle can be approached like a house cat. Some speculate that it is pure monk magic, probably coupled with the docile daytime behaviour of a nocturnal creature, and their familiarity with humans. But a healthy respect of the tigers' power is important, just ask Siegfried and Roy.

Many locals complain that the admission price is too high and whisper about the money being used on superfluous toys for the monks. The temple claims that the entrance fee is being used to build a natural 'island' enclosure so that the tigers can be released from their cages. At this point, it is impossible to predict the outcome.

The temple is 38km from Kanchanaburi on Hwy 323. You could take the Kanchanaburi–Sangkhlaburi public bus to the turn-off, but the temple is another 8km from the main road. An easier alternative is to signup for one of the guesthouse-arranged afternoon tours to the temple.

Sai Yok Noi Waterfall
น้ำตกไทรโยค

Part of Sai Yok National Park (opposite), this roadside waterfall is a popular local attraction, best visited for observing Thais in nature instead of appreciating nature. The waterfall is 60km northwest from Kanchanaburi on Hwy 323 and easily reached by the Sangkhlaburi–Kanchanaburi bus (40B, one hour, frequent departures); just let the driver know your destination is '*náam tok sai yok noi*'. The last bus back is at 4.30pm. Alternatively Nam Tok train station is 2km away (100B; see p216 for train departure times).

Hellfire Pass Memorial
ช่องเขาขาด

To round out your exploration of the Death Railway historical sites, this **museum** (www.dva .gov.au/commem/oawg/thailand.htm; admission by donation; ☆ 9am-4pm) contains informative background

on the railway and a 4km-long walking trail (which takes four hours roundtrip) along the original railbed. The trail passes seven mountain cuttings that were carved with minimal equipment by POW labour.

The most famous cutting is the 110m **Hellfire Pass** (also known as Konyu Cutting), which is 300m from the museum entrance. The ominous nickname was earned during the 'speedo' period of construction when crews worked around the clock in 16- to 18-hour shifts for 12 weeks. At night the eerie glow of torch light casting shadows of the workers' emaciated frames were reminiscent of the fires of hell. During this period the original crew of 400 Australian POWs was later augmented with 600 additional Australian and British prisoners. By the time the cuttings were finished, 70% of the POW crew had died and were buried in the nearby Konyu Cemetery.

Northwest of the Konyu Cutting, the **Pack of Cards bridge** was so named by prisoners because it collapsed three times during construction.

The museum is operated by the Australian-Thai Chamber of Commerce to honour the Allied POWs and Asian conscripts who died while constructing some of the most difficult stretches of the Thailand–Burma Death Railway. A walking trail map is available at the museum information desk.

The museum and walking trail is 80km northwest of Kanchanaburi on Hwy 323. It is easily accessed by Sangkhlaburi–Kanchanaburi bus (45B, 1½ hours, frequent departures). Tell the driver that your destination is *châwng khao kháat* (Hellfire Pass). The last bus back to Kanchanaburi passes here around 4pm.

Sai Yok National Park
อุทยานแห่งชาติไทรโยค

The 500-sq-km **Sai Yok National Park** (☎ 0 3451 6163; www.dnp.go.th; admission 400B) is not as well developed as other national parks but it is Kanchanaburi's most accessible wilderness. Within the main entrance of the park, you'll find limestone caves, remains of a bridge on the Death Railway and Japanese cooking stoves (actually little more than piles of brick). There's also a network of clear streams that bubble up from springs in the park, and a cave where people go to watch clouds of bats stream out at dusk. Unfortunately, the park does not produce detailed hiking maps or much in the way of visitors information for English speakers.

Near the visitors centre is the misnomer Nam Tok Sai Yok Yai (Sai Yok Yai waterfall), which is better described as being a small cascading creek than a big waterfall. It empties into Mae Nam Khwae Noi near the suspension bridge. It was at this park that the famous Russian-roulette scenes in the 1978 movie *The Deer Hunter* were filmed.

Notable wildlife in the park includes Kitti's hog-nosed bats (the world's smallest mammal), regal crabs, barking deer, blue pittas, wreathed hornbills, gibbons, Malayan porcupines, slow loris and serow. There are also wild elephants that occasionally cross over from Myanmar.

Forestry department **bungalows** (☎ 0 2562 0760; bungalows 800-2100B) are available at Sai Yok National Park; they sleep up to six. Incredibly scenic are the raft guesthouses near the suspension bridge that are totally deserted on weekdays during the rainy season – just you and the river. One of the prettiest ones is **Saiyok View Raft** (☎ 0 3451 4194; r 700B), which has rooms with private bathrooms that look out on to the river. Ask when making reservations about arranging meals, as food options are limited.

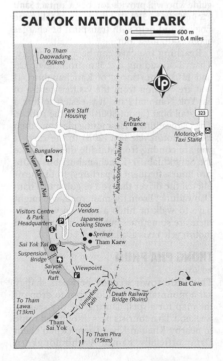

SAI YOK NATIONAL PARK

CENTRAL THAILAND

There are a row of permanent food stalls near the visitors centre.

The entrance to the park is about 100km northwest of Kanchanaburi and 5km from Hwy 323. You can take the Sangkhlaburi-Kanchanaburi bus (50B, two hours, frequent departures) to the turn-off and hire a motorcycle taxi from the main road to the entrance. Tell the driver that you want 'náam tok sai yok yai'. The last bus back to Kanchanaburi passes at about 3.30pm.

From the raft guesthouses near the suspension bridge, you can rent long-tail boats for sightseeing along the river and to the caves **Tham Daowadung** (below) or Tham Lawa. Chartering a long-tail costs about 400B per hour, but rates are negotiable.

Tham Daowadung
ถ้ำดาวดึงส์

The eight-room **Tham Daowadung** (Daowadung Cave) is one of Thailand's prettiest limestone caves. The cave is best visited once the rainy season has ended when the paths are less slippery and the mosquito population less thriving. Park rangers recommend that you hire a guide who will provide torches. Contact **Santi** (☎ 0 6167 6855, 0 9151 4357), who can speak some English and help with transport; he charges about 200B for a tour.

Reaching the cave can be a little tricky. Tham Daowadung is 2.5km from Hwy 323 and 110km northwest of Kanchanaburi. If you are coming from the visitors centre of Sai Yok National Park, it is easiest to hire a long-tail boat (about 800B) from the park to Tha Daowadung (Daowadung pier) and then take a motorcycle taxi (20B) to the cave. If you are coming from outside the park, take the Sangkhlaburi–Kanchanaburi bus (50B, two hours, frequent departures) to the turn-off; tell the driver that you're going to Tham Daowadung. From the main road, you might have to walk or hitch a ride; on weekends there are sometimes public sǎwngthǎew and motorcycle taxis available.

THONG PHA PHUM
ทอง ผาภูมิ

This little town wedged between shaggy karst mountains is an ideal spot to drop off the map for a spell. During the dry season, weekend Thai tourists pass through en route to nearby Kheuan Khao Laem (Khao Laem Dam; officially named Vachiralongkorn Dam), but otherwise the major comings and goings are shipments of produce and a few rickety buses. Many of its inhabitants are ethnic Mon or Burmese who originally congregated here to work on the construction of the dam. During the rainy season, life becomes slower, albeit wetter – much wetter.

The town of Thong Pha Phum isn't much, with all of its businesses (including one ATM) along one street. Mae Nam Khwae Noi runs along the east side of town.

If you arrive without transport, you can entertain yourself with a walk to the hill-top **temple** on the opposite side of the river. Follow the riverfront road in the direction of the main highway to a footbridge. On the opposite bank of the river, you can scale the steps to the hill top or wander the length of the road through forests and small villages.

South of Thong Pha Phum town is **Hin Dat Hot Springs** (admission 20B; ☼ 6am-10pm), a pleasant place to wrinkle your skin and turn a lobster's shade of red. Protected by trees, two geothermal pools sit beside a fast-moving stream, creating three temperature options for contrasting soakers. Foreigners arrive hardly dressed, while Thai women come fully clothed. The *bàw náam ráwn* (hot springs) is accessible via the Sangkhlaburi–Kanchanaburi bus on Hwy 323 (Km 105 marker) and is about 1km from the main road.

On the same road as the hot springs is **Nam Tok Pha That**, a low-key waterfall. Every foreigner that finds it feels satisfied with their inherent intrepidness.

The southern entrance to **Kheuan Khao Laem** is about 10km northwest of town. Several rustic lakeside resorts, with thatched bungalows and raft houses, become a weekend home-away-from-dorm for Thai college students who pack the rooms with as many friends as they can SMS, and stay up all night for guitar and whiskey sessions. The lake is a huge draw for these students.

All of the places to stay in Thong Pha Phum town cater to Thai tourists. On the main street between the market and the highway, **Som Jainuk Hotel** (☎ 0 3459 982; 29/10 Mu 1; r 200-500B; ❄) has a range of options from basic boarding rooms to more comfortable air-con bungalows set around a shaded courtyard.

So Boonyong Hotel (☎ 0 3459 9441; 27 Mu 1; r 200-400B; ❄), just beyond the market, is a multistorey hotel with large modern rooms. The

THAILAND'S GREEN BELT

In a country where more concrete means more success, the western portion of Kanchanaburi Province is a surprising retreat into the wilderness. Save for a few minor towns and villages, most of the landscape is dominated by national parks that have developed little in the way of Thailand's signature hybridisation of resorts and reserves. These are fairly far-flung outings that don't normally appear on a tourist's two-week itinerary and have little in the way of amenities.

The entrance fee to all national parks is 400B; park-run **accommodations** (☎ bookings 0 2562 0760; www.dnp.go.th/parkreserve; bungalows from 1200-1800B) are also available. The following parks are best accessed by private transport.

Si Nakharin National Park (☎ 0 3451 6667; Tha Kradan district) is best known for Huay Khamin (Turmeric Stream), one of the provinces most powerful waterfalls. This area is also the headwaters of Mae Nam Khwae Yai. The park can be accessed on Hwy 3199 north of Erawan National Park, but the 42km stretch of road is quite rough. Continue to Tha Kradan (Kradan Pier), near Si Nakharin Dam, to take a ferry across the reservoir to the waterfall trail. Camping is available near the falls. There are plans to improve access to this area but road construction has been suspended pending an environmental impact study.

Chaloem Ratanakosin National Park (☎ 0 3451 9606; Nong Preu district) is a 59-sq-km park that attracts spelunkers because of two caves: Tham Than Lot Yai and Tham Than Lot Noi. There are also waterfalls within hiking distance of park bungalows and the forest area is the watershed of Mae Nam Mae Klong. The park is 97km north of Kanchanaburi. Buses from Kanchanaburi to Ban Nong Preu (55B, two to three hours) leave every 20 minutes between 6.15am and 6.30pm. Once in Ban Nong Preu, you can hire transport to the park entrance, but most visitors arrive by private transport via Hwy 3086.

Thong Pha Phum National Park (☎ 0 1382 0359; Thong Pha Phum district) is a 1120-sq-km green belt that connects Khao Laem and Sai Yok national parks to encourage the migration of the provinces' threatened animal species. Waterfalls, caves and a lush tropical climate are the park's main attributes. Nearby in the town of Pilok is a reclusive but charming guesthouse-homestay called **Forest Glade** (☎ 0 1325 9471; r 1200-1400B); the locals know it and can provide directions. The park is about 60km west of Thong Pha Phum and is accessible by private transport via Hwy 3272 off Hwy 323.

Khao Laem National Park (☎ 0 3453 2099; Thong Pha Phum district), measuring in at 3200-sq-km, is Thailand's largest protected land parcel. Popular attractions include Nam Tok Takien Thong, where pools are suitable for swimming nearly year-round. Tham Sukho is a large limestone cave shrine just off the highway at the Km 42 marker. The park is 34km south of Sangkhlaburi between the Km 39 and Km 40 markers; you'll find a turn-off on the east side of the highway.

Thung Yai & Huay Kha Khaeng Wildlife Sanctuary was designated a Unesco World Heritage site in 1991 and it adjoins Um Phang Wildlife Sanctuary to the north and Khao Laem National Park to the west, forming one of the largest protected areas in the region. The area preserves grassland and dry tropical forest, claiming a diverse ecosystem of flora and fauna. The sanctuary is also one of the last natural habitats in Thailand for the tiger. The **Western Forest Conservation Club** (WFCC; www.thungyai.org), along with other groups, works with the Thai government to track, count and protect the tigers that roam in this area. Bordering Myanmar, the reserve is also home to many displaced Karen and Hmong communities that introduce many potential threats to the forest integrity. Poaching as well as illegal logging and farming have contributed to the decline of natural habitat, including the tiger population. Infrastructure within the park is limited; the Uthai Thani–based company **Thai Country Trails** (www.thaicountrytrails.com) can arrange tours or provide additional information.

manager speaks English and can give you sightseeing advice.

Hardly a step above camping, the **Kraton Koudin Resort** (☎ 0 1362 8857; r 300-600B) is a collection of rustic, wooden bungalows (all with shared bathrooms), planted beside a cascading stream that slices the property in half so that guests can sleep to the sounds of rushing water. The owners can arrange transport from the main road as well as outings to nearby

waterfalls and the hot springs. It's south of Thong Pha Phum – to get here, take the Sangkhlaburi–Kanchanaburi bus to Baan Saphan Lao. The 'resort' is 7km from the Km 110 marker on Hwy 323 .

In typical Mon style, vendors on the main street near the highway proffer curry in long rows of pots; instead of two or three curry choices more typical of Thai vendors, the Mon vendors lay out eight or more – all delicious. A small night market convenes near the centre of town each evening with the usual rice and noodle dishes.

Getting There & Away

All buses arrive and depart from Thong Pha Phum's market. Ordinary buses depart from Kanchanaburi (70B, three hours, every 30 minutes between 6am and 6.30pm) and minivans to Sangkhlaburi also stop in Thong Pha Phum (60B, two hours, three times daily). There is also a new air-con bus service to Bangkok's Northern and Northeastern bus terminal (150B, five hours, four departures daily).

SANGKHLABURI
สังขละบุรี

pop 10,800

Geopolitical borders guillotine one nation from another but rarely succeed in severing the body ethnic identity. Sangkhlaburi is an excellent example of a border town's ethnic spectrum, populated by Burmese, Karen, Mon, Thai and a small group of Lao. Each group holds fast to their mother tongue; in some cases because it is the only language they know, in other cases as a farewell gesture to an abandoned homeland. To the immigrants from Myanmar, Sangkhlaburi must represent a beginning, but from any other direction this is the end of the road with all of its attendant remoteness.

Sangkhlaburi sits at the edge of the huge Kheuan Khao Laem (Khao Laem Dam); the town was created after the dam flooded out an older village near the confluence of the three rivers that now feed the reservoir. There's not much to do in town except wander the traffic-less streets and watch the fishing boats putter across the lake. The town has become a popular recreation spot for jungle tours and elephant treks. The town comes alive on **Mon National Day**, celebrated during the last week of July.

Information

For foreign-exchange services head to Siam Commercial Bank (ATM), in the city centre near the market. Internet access has arrived in town, but the exact location is always changing; it's typically within eye-shot of the market. There is an international phone in front of the post office (located on the main street).

Sights & Activities

WANG KHA
วังคา

On the opposite bank of the lake from Sangkhlaburi is a **Mon settlement** (Wang Kha). The village was relocated to this spot after the dam's construction flooded the original village that developed in Thailand during Burma's post-independence civil wars. The persistent conflicts across the border swelled the population with displaced people who sustained Wang Kha's connection with its ethnic Mon character. Just 15 years ago the settlement looked more like an isolated Burmese village than a run-of-the-mill Thai neighbourhood. Assimilation and development has taken its natural course and the geographic dislocation of years past is not as pronounced. But the quiet lanes are still worth a look; you'll see squatty wooden houses and bike-riding kids, and some of the older women still wearing the Burmese-style face powder and gnawing on a cheroot.

To get to the settlement follow the **wooden bridge** (Saphan Mon), said to be Thailand's longest, across the lake from town.

A **day market** in the centre of the village is a good spot to sample pots of rich Mon curry and peruse the daily shopping needs.

North of the market is **Wat Wang Wiwekaram** (Wat Mon), which is regarded as the spiritual centre of the Mon people in Thailand. The temple occupies two complexes that are approximately 3km apart. To the right of the T-junction is the multiroofed *wíhaan* with stainless-steel-plated pillars, heavy, carved wooden doors, and marble banisters. To the left of the T-junction (near the shores of the lake) is the landscape-dominating Chedi Luang Phaw Uttama. Constructed in the style of the Mahabodhi *chedi* in Bodhgaya, India, it is topped by about 6kg of gold.

A 300- to 400-year-old disintegrating *chedi* is located about 50m south of Chedi Luang Phaw Uttama. From the edge of the *chedi* grounds is a view of the tremendous lake and

WHO ARE THE MON?

The Mon ethnic group is one of Southeast Asia's oldest peoples, whose historic kingdom of Dvaravati flourished in the 6th to 11th centuries, covering parts of Burma and the central plains of modern-day Thailand. The Mon and their cultural traditions intermarried extensively with ethnic groups in the central plains, and much of what is associated with 'Thai' culture today derives from this union.

Eventually the Mon territory shrank to a distinct section of Burma where they struggled against the more dominant ethnic Burmese. The British capitalised on this long-standing rivalry during its colonisation campaign, promising the Mon independence in exchange for support. After Burma's independence in 1948, the Mon resisted the consolidation of power under the ethnic Burmese-led military and struggled for self-determination. A semi-autonomous Mon state was created in 1974, but armed clashes continued until the late 1990s when a ceasefire was negotiated.

During surges in violence, Mon villagers escaped fighting by crossing the border into western Thailand, mainly around Sangkhlaburi. The greatest influx of refugees occurred between the mid-1980s until 1997. They were often given temporary asylum in refugee camps, but periodically forced to return to Myanmar. Like other ethnic refugees, Mon who remained in Thailand have no political status, can't work legally in the country or send their children to Thai public schools. One major improvement in their limbo state came in 2006 when the Thai government granted citizenship to some 2000 Mon children living in Sangkhlaburi who were born in the country.

Although displacement of Mon people from Myanmar has decreased, Thailand still receives ongoing waves of economic migrants as well as other ethnic asylum seekers from its unstable neighbour. Of the two refugee camps on the border near Sangkhlaburi, Karen make up the majority with a minority of Burmese nationals of varying ethnic backgrounds who have been caught working illegally in Thailand.

the three rivers that feed into it. A Burmese handicrafts market convenes at the *chedi* daily from mid-morning until sunset.

For such a remote temple, Wat Wang Wiwekaram claims a nationally revered monk, Luang Phaw Uttama. He was born in Burma in 1910 and fled to Thailand in 1949 to escape civil war; he was instrumental in the spiritual and educational life of the Mon community and helped secure this area after the Mon village's previous location was submerged by the construction of the dam. He died at the age of 97 at Bangkok's Srirat Hospital in 2006 and his medical bills were covered by the queen.

KHAO LAEM RESERVOIR
เขื่อนเขาแหลม

This huge lake was formed when the Vachiralongkorn Dam (locally known as Khao Laem Dam) was constructed across Mae Nam Khwae Noi near Thong Pha Phum in 1983. The lake submerged an entire village at the confluence of the Khwae Noi, Ranti and Sangkhalia Rivers. The spires of the village's **Wat Sam Prasop** (Three Junction Temple) can be seen protruding from the lake in the dry season.

Canoes can be rented for exploring the lake, or for longer trips you can hire a long-tail boat and pilot. **Lake boating** is a tranquil pastime, best early in the morning with mist and bird life; early evening is also good for bird-watching.

Guesthouses in Sangkhlaburi arrange all sorts of activities on the water, including bamboo rafting and sightseeing boat tours.

For those interested in practising forest meditation, the Sunyataram Forest Monastery, 42km south of Sangkhlaburi, also operates a meditation centre on an island in the middle of the lake called **Ko Kaew Sunyataram** (Sunyataram Jewel Isle). Permission to visit the meditation island must be obtained from Sunyataram Forest Monastery beforehand; see **Dhamma Thai** (www.dhammathai.org) for more information.

Volunteering

At the end of the main road through town is **Baan Unrak** (House of Joy; www.baanunrak.org), founded in 1991 to care for orphaned children. Several years later the centre expanded to include a weaving centre to provide supplemental income to local women struggling to support their families, a shelter for abused or destitute women, and a primary school. The need for such outreach is great in

Sangkhlaburi because of the refugee population and other non-Thai citizen groups who suffer from poverty, HIV/AIDs and/or substance abuse.

Access to medical care is another pressing concern for the impoverished community, many of whom do not qualify for Thailand's national health-care plan. The foundation offers natural medicines, underwrites some medical procedures and partners with **Unite For Sight** (www.uniteforsight.org), an international medical volunteer organisation. Volunteers are welcome to donate their time to the orphanage or the school and typically reside at the complex following the rules of the foundation's neo-humanist philosophy, an Indian tradition of universal love, daily meditation and a vegetarian lifestyle.

Sleeping

Burmese Inn (☎ 0 3459 5146; www.sangkhlaburi.com; 52/3 Mu 3; r from 80-500B; 🔁) It isn't the cleanest in town, but it is the cheapest. The flimsy huts are hammered into a hillside overlooking the wooden bridge. The Austrian co-owner is knowledgeable about the area.

P Guest House (☎ 0 3459 5061; www.pguesthouse .com; 8/1 Mu 1; r from 200-700B) Well worth the 1.2km walk from the bus stop, P Guest House has spacious, stone bungalows with verandas along a slope overlooking the lake. Cheaper rooms share a remarkably clean bathroom. P also organises elephant treks, and rents canoes and kayaks.

Ponnatee Resort (☎ 0 3459 5134; 84 Mu 1; r 800-1200B; 🔁) Trickling down the hillside overlooking the lake, this maze-like hotel has modern but drab rooms, some with stunning views.

Eating

Don't leave town without trying the local Burmese curry. There are a couple of places around the market that serve a delicious assortment of curries (20B). Many of the guesthouses do a thriving dinner business because of their waterfront locations.

Baan Unrak Bakery (☎ 0 3459 5428; snacks 10-30B) One of the few non-guesthouse restaurants in town, this simple café has a rotating selection of baked goods and vegetarian options. It is affiliated with the Baan Unrak organisation that operates an orphanage and school in Sangkhlaburi (p223); many volunteers spend their free time at the café.

Shopping

Visitors interested in acquiring some Karen weaving should check out the small store at the Baan Unrak Bakery; the products are made by the Baan Unrak women's cooperative.

Getting There & Away

Sangkhlaburi's buses haphazardly assemble either at the informal bus station across from the market or at ticket counters nearby. If you're looking for a particular bus, go and ask the motorcycle taxi drivers – they know everything.

Ordinary bus 8203 leaves Sangkhlaburi for Kanchanaburi (110B) at 6.45am, 8.15am, 10.15am and 1.15pm, and takes five to six hours, depending on how many mishaps occur on the Thong Pha Phum to Sangkhlaburi road. An air-con bus (200B) leaves every hour from 6.30am to 3.30pm and takes four hours. An air-con bus also trundles to Bangkok's Northern and Northeastern bus terminal (Mo Chit, 2nd/1st class 228/295B, four times daily).

The distance between Kanchanaburi and Sangkhlaburi is about 230km. From Thong Pha Phum to Sangkhlaburi it's 74km. The road between Thong Pha Phum and Sangkhlaburi is quite rough but it is one of the most beautiful in Thailand. It winds through mountains of limestone and through a major teak reforestation project.

THREE PAGODAS PASS

ด่านเจดีย์สามองค์

Thailand's western border town with Myanmar is named for three rather small pagodas (Chedi Sam Ong). But these forgettable landmarks are not the reason for a visit. Instead travellers come to peak into Myanmar without a full commitment. This is not an official border crossing, but foreigners are allowed a day pass into the Myanmar town of **Payathonzu** and its souvenir market.

A true frontier town, Payathonzu has around a half-dozen Burmese **teahouses** (a couple of them with *nam-bya* – the Burmese equivalent to Indian naan bread); several **mercantile shops** with Burmese *longyi* (sarongs), cheroots and clothes; and a few general souvenir shops with Mon-Karen-Burmese handicrafts. It is necessary to bargain; traders speak some English and also some Thai.

A Buddhist temple, **Wat Suwankhiri**, can be seen on a bluff near the town. A Myanmar

military checkpoint at the edge of town usually bars all visitors from leaving the town limits.

Three Pagodas Pass hosts a **Songkran Festival** during April, complete with cockfights; hemp-fisted, Thai-Burmese kickboxing; and Karen, Thai, Burmese and Mon folk dancing.

Not readily apparent to the daytripper, this remote crossing once vacillated between the Karen National Union and the Mon Liberation Front, since Three Pagodas was one of the only passable routes through hundreds of miles of rugged mountains. This 'toll gate' was used by the ethnic armies to collect tax on smuggled goods. The funds were often used to finance armed resistance against the Myanmar government.

The Myanmar government wrested control of the town in 1989 from both the Karen and Mon and has been firmly established here ever since. It renamed the town Paya-thonzu (Three Pagodas) and filled it with shops catering to an odd mix of troops and tourists. Teak furniture shops on either side of the border are one of the most dominant cottage industries, but recent reports suggest that these businesses are declining because of scarcer sources of timber or excessive logging taxes levied by the Myanmar government or ethnic groups.

Foreigners are allowed to enter Myanmar on a day pass and all immigration formalities can be arranged at the border. This crossing does not issue visa extensions. You will need to temporarily surrender your passport, along with a passport photo, to the Thai immigration office before crossing the border. At the Myanmar immigration office, you must submit a copy of the photo page of your passport and a passport photo, in addition to 500B or US$10. Upon your return into Thailand, you will receive your passport back. There is a small photocopy shop near the Thai immigration office where you can arrange border documentation.

Occasionally this border is closed, especially during conflicts between ethnic armies and the central Myanmar government, but these incidents are less frequent now than in years past.

Getting There & Away

Săwngthăew leave Sangkhlaburi's bus station (30B) every half-hour from 6am to 4pm. Along the way you'll pass little bamboo-hut villages inhabited by Mon or Karen people. The last săwngthăew back to Sangkhlaburi leaves Three Pagodas Pass at around 4pm.

The border is only a short walk from the săwngthăew stop in Three Pagodas Pass.

Southeastern Thailand

Welcome to the past, present and future of tourism in Thailand. Pulsating and brazen, Pattaya is where the Thai tourism miracle began a few short decades ago, and legions of visitors continue to be lured by its addictive grab-bag of sun-drenched hedonism and tacky twilight. The island getaways of Ko Samet and Ko Chang showcase the present, as their humble backpacker origins are overlaid with a glossy patina of flashier resorts: on busy weekends and public holidays, local travellers join Bangkok expats to commandeer the sunlight and the limelight. Just a zippy speedboat ride from rugged Ko Chang, tiny islands like Ko Wai and Ko Mak flag the future, as pioneering travellers join Thai tourists who've known about these pristine getaways for years.

And the change is ongoing. Sultry Pattaya is trying to reinvent itself with a family-friendly face. Development proceeds on Ko Chang, but amid the new luxury spas and poolside bars, it remains a breeze to escape to the island's rugged jungle interior and reassert your sense of adventure.

Beyond the coastal and island extremes of Southeastern Thailand, other less-visited treasures often struggle to be heard above Pattaya's nocturnal preening and the buzzing banana boats of Ko Samet. The spirit of old Siam lingers in the quiet backstreets of Trat and on Sri Racha's ramshackle piers, and Chanthaburi's intriguing history is as precious as the sapphires and rubies traded at its weekly gem market.

And while the region's national parks (including Khao Chamao/Khao Wong and Khao Khitchakut) are among Thailand's smallest, there's more than enough hush and diversity on offer to counter the part paradise/part pandemonium contrast of elsewhere in the region.

HIGHLIGHTS

- Discovering the other side of Thai island life amid the fishing village atmosphere of **Ko Si Chang** (p230)
- Diving into the risqué delights of **Pattaya's** nightlife (p240), then relaxing on the beach before doing it all again the next night
- Losing the crowds and losing yourself in a book on the quieter beaches of **Ko Samet's** (p243) southeastern coast
- Taking your foot off the travel accelerator with a few days doing nothing, soaking up the old-Siam ambience of **Trat** (p253)
- Working up an island-sized thirst and appetite during a jungle trek on rugged **Ko Chang** (p260)

FAST FACTS

- **Best Time to Visit** November to May
- **Population** 3.6 million

Climate

Southeastern Thailand experiences a three-season, monsoonal climate: a relatively cool dry season in November and December is followed by a hot dry season stretching from January to May. A hot wet season follows from June to October.

During the wet season, Ko Samet stays unusually dry and is the region's most 'monsoon-proof' island.

National Parks

The islands of Ko Samet (p243) and Ko Chang (p257) both fall within national parks (the Khao Laem Ya/Mu Ko Samet National Park and Mu Ko Chang Marine National Park, respectively) and are the region's biggest draw cards after Pattaya. Ko Chang is covered in dense, unspoilt forest, and while the island's coastline is developing fast, the interior is rugged and untouched.

Khao Chamao/Khao Wong (p243), Khao Khitchakut (p252) and Nam Tok Phlio (p252) National Parks hold fewer surprises, but are worth a visit for a break from the coastal buzz.

Getting There & Away

For the majority of travellers, a trip into, and then through, southeastern Thailand is an eastward progression from Bangkok to Hat Lek on the Cambodian border. Air-con buses link the capital with all major towns, and there are flights from Phuket and Ko Samui to Pattaya, and from Bangkok to Trat. A once-daily train service links Bangkok with Pattaya.

If you are coming from northeast Thailand, regular air-con bus services travel to Rayong and Pattaya from Khorat and Ubon Ratchathani.

Getting Around

Getting around southeastern Thailand is straightforward, with good bus links between all main attractions. Hourly ferries run to the region's main islands throughout the year, although services to the outlying islands of

the Ko Chang archipelago are significantly reduced during the wet season. Tourist minibuses also provide convenient direct links between main attractions, but are usually more expensive than public transport.

CHONBURI PROVINCE

SRI RACHA

ศรีราชา

pop 151,000

Look closely and you can still see Sri Racha's fishing village roots in the labyrinth of rickety piers and pontoons affixed to its waterfront. While modern Thailand encroaches with a jumble of billboards and traffic lights, down on the seafront glimpses of old Siam linger in the restaurants, simple hotels and markets perched above the tide. Hell-for-leather buses are replaced by puttering fishing boats, and locals sit on their decks mending fishing nets in a tropical twilight. Ships waiting to dock at Sri Racha's modern port stud the near horizon, but they're far enough away not to spoil the illusion of days gone by.

Sri Racha is home to the famous *náam phrík sii raachaa* (spicy sauce), a perfect complement to the town's excellent seafood.

Information

CafBarNet (80 Th Sri Racha Nakorn 3; 🕙 9am-9pm) Coffee (30B) and internet (per minute 1B).

Krung Thai Bank (cnr Th Surasakdi 1 & Th Jermjompol)

Post office (Th Jermjompol) A few blocks north of the Krung Thai Bank.

Sights

Other than the shambling ambience of the waterfront piers, Sri Racha's sole attraction is **Ko Loi**, a small rocky island connected to the mainland by a long jetty at the northern end of Sri Racha's waterfront. There is a **Thai-Chinese Buddhist temple** (🕙 daylight), a low-key festival atmosphere with food stalls and a couple of giant ponds with turtles of every size, from tiny hatchlings to seen-it-all-before seniors.

Sleeping

Sri Racha is more of a transit point than an overnight stop. The most authentic (read basic) places to stay are the wooden hotels on the piers. There's one flashier spot near the water, but Sri Racha's best hotel is situated further inland.

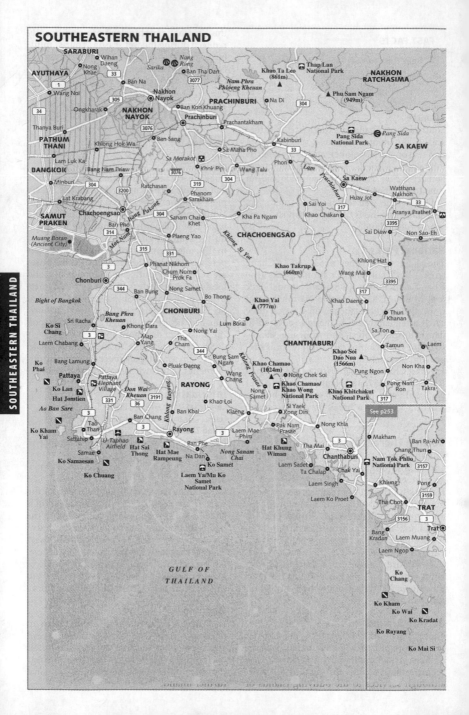

SOUTHEASTERN THAILAND

SOUTHEASTERN THAILAND

SARABURI
AYUTHAYA
Nong Khae
Wihan Daeng
Nang Rong
Sarika
Ban Tha Dan
Khao Ta Leo (861m)
Thap Lan National Park
NAKHON RATCHASIMA
Ban Na
Nam Phra Phloeng Kheuan
Na Di
Phu Sam Ngam (949m)
Wang Noi
Nakhon Nayok
PRACHINBURI
Ongkharak
NAKHON NAYOK
Ban Kon Khuang
Prachinburi
Pang Sida
Pang Sida National Park
Thanya Buri
Prachantakham
Kabinburi
SA KAEW
PATHUM THANI
Khlong Hok Wa
Ban Sang
Sa Maha Pho
Phon
Sa Kaew
Lam Prachinburi
BANGKOK
Sa Morakot
Khok Pip
Wang Talu
Watthana Nakhon
Minburi
Ratchasan
Phanom Sarakham
Sai Yoi
Huay Jot
Aranya Prathet
Lat Krabang
SAMUT PRAKEN
Chachoengsao
Ban Pho
Sanam Chai Khet
Kha Pa Ngam
Khao Chakan
Sai Diaw
Non Sao-Eh
Muang Boran (Ancient City)
Plaeng Yao
CHACHOENGSAO
Khlong Si Yot
Khlong Hat
Phanat Nikhom
Khao Takrup (660m)
Wang Mai
Bight of Bangkok
Chonburi
Chum Nom Prok Fa
Nong Samet
Bo Thong
Khao Yai (777m)
Khao Daeng
Thun Khanan
Sri Racha
Ban Bung
CHONBURI
Lum Borai
CHANTHABURI
Sa Ton
Tamun
Laem
Ko Si Chang
Khong Dara
Nong Yai
Khao Soi Dao Nua (1566m)
Non Kha
Laem Chabang
Map Yang
Tha Cham
Bung Sam Ngam
Khao Chamao (1024m)
Nong Chek Soi
Pung Ngon
Pong Nam Ron
Takra
Ko Phai
Bang Lamung
Pluak Daeng
Wang Chang
Khao Chamao/ Khao Wong National Park
Khao Khitchakut National Park
Pattaya
Pattaya Elephant Village
RAYONG
Nong Samet
Si Yaek Kong Din
Ko Lan
Don Wai Kheuan
Khao Loi
Hat Jomtien
Ban Chang
Ban Khai
Klaeng
Pak Nam Prasae
Nong Khla
Ao Ban Sare
Tao Than
Rayong
Ban Phe
Laem Mae Phim
Tha Mai
See p253
Ko Kham Yai
Sattahip
U-Taphao Airfield
Ban Phe
Hat Khung Wiman
Nong Sanam Chai
Chanthaburi
Makham
Ban Pa-Ah
Samae
Hat Sai Thong
Hat Mae Rampeung
Na Dan
Laem Sadet
Nam Tok Phliu National Park
Chang Thun
Ko Samaesan
Ko Samet
Ta Chalap
Chak Yai
Khlung
Pong
Ko Chuang
Laem Ya/Mu Ko Samet National Park
Laem Singh
Laem Ko Proet
Tha Chot
TRAT
Bang Kradan
Laem Muang
Trat
Laem Ngop
GULF OF THAILAND
Ko Chang
Ko Kham
Ko Wai
Ko Kradat
Ko Rayang
Ko Mai Si

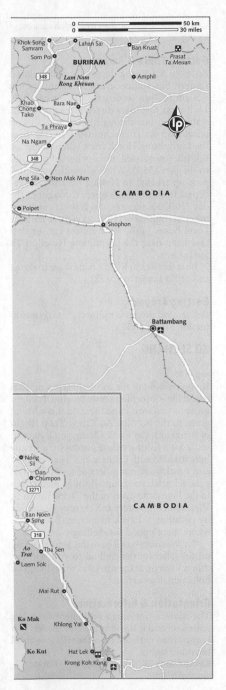

SOUTHEASTERN THAILAND

Siriwatana Hotel (☎ 0 3831 1037; 35 Th Jermjompol; s/d 160/200B) Fulfil your dreams of old Siam in this wooden hotel above the sea. The staff move as slowly as their motley array of dogs, but the basic rooms are cheap. Try not to look through the floorboards at the debris washed up by the tide.

Samchai (☎ 0 3831 1800; Soi 10; r 260-480B; 🐾) Going up in the world, the Samchai has similar ambience with some air-con rooms. There are cheaper fan rooms for 260B, and a store at reception selling everything from fishing supplies to Ovaltine.

Seaview Sri Racha Hotel (☎ 0 3831 9000; fax 0 3832 7706; 50-54 Th Jermjompol; r 950B; 🐾 🖥) You'll pay slightly more for a sea view at this spot near the water with spacious and comfortable rooms. Rooms facing the street can be a tad noisy, but Sri Racha's not Times Square, and a gentle hush settles relatively early.

City Hotel (☎ 0 3832 2700; www.citysriracha.com; 6/126 Th Sukhumvit; r 1695B; 🐾 🖥 🏊) The super chilled air-con in reception takes your breath away, but a range of creature comforts including wi-fi internet, a swimming pool and a gym brings it back. Service is slick but friendly, and the slightly austere rooms are softened with a veneer of classy Asian décor.

Eating & Drinking

Sri Racha is famous for seafood, and a sprawling night market kicks off around 5pm on Th Sri Racha Nakorn 3.

Picha Bakery (☎ 0 3832 4796; cnr Th Jermjompol & Th Surasakdi 1; coffee 30B, snacks 20-40B; 🕑 breakfast, lunch & dinner) Baked goodies, excellent coffee and spotless air-con surroundings make this a convenient haven from Sri Racha's busy streets. The iced coffee is especially good.

The Summer (☎ 08 6844 3238; Th Jermjompol 100; coffee 20-40B, breakfast 60B; 🕑 breakfast, lunch & dinner) A cooked breakfast and a robust espresso will kick start your day in this coffee'n'cake place with retro beachy décor. There's loads of Thai travel magazines to give you inspiration.

Grand Seaside Restaurant (☎ 0 3832 3851; Soi 18; dishes 60-200B; 🕑 lunch & dinner) Refurbished in a colonial style with modern accents, this overwater pavilion is a top spot to enjoy seafood with a relaxing soundtrack of retro lounge music.

The Pop (Th Jermjompol; dishes 60-220B; 🕑 5-11pm) More like 'The Rock', this raucous beer hall meets music club boasts a menu ranging from

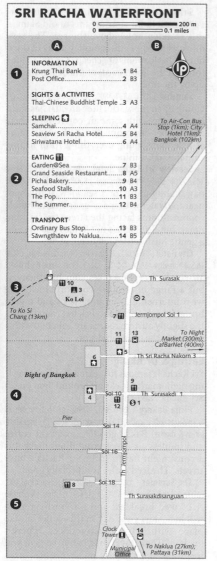

SRI RACHA WATERFRONT

INFORMATION	
Krung Thai Bank	1 B4
Post Office	2 B3

SIGHTS & ACTIVITIES	
Thai-Chinese Buddhist Temple	3 A3

SLEEPING	
Samchai	4 A4
Seaview Sri Racha Hotel	5 B4
Siriwatana Hotel	6 A4

EATING	
Garden@Sea	7 B3
Grand Seaside Restaurant	8 A5
Picha Bakery	9 B4
Seafood Stalls	10 A3
The Pop	11 B3
The Summer	12 B4

TRANSPORT	
Ordinary Bus Stop	13 B3
Săwngthăew to Naklua	14 B5

specialise in fresh seafood. There is no English menu but it's all good.

Getting There & Away

Buses to Sri Racha depart from Bangkok's Eastern bus station every 30 minutes from 5.30am to 7pm (ordinary 73B; air-con 94B; 1¾ hours). Ordinary direct buses stop on the waterfront, but through buses and air-con buses stop on Th Sukhumvit (Hwy 3), near the Laemthong Hotel, from where there are túk-túk (motorised, three-wheeled pedicab) to the pier (35B). White săwngthăew (small pick-up trucks) to Naklua (north Pattaya) depart from the clock tower throughout the day (30B, 30 minutes). In Naklua catch another săwngthăew (10B) to central Pattaya. Local buses (40B, 30 minutes) run to Pattaya from near the Laemthong Hotel on Th Sukhumvit.

Boat services to Ko Si Chang leave from the end of Ko Loi jetty, (p232).

Getting Around

Get around town via motorcycle taxi or túk-túk for 30B to 40B.

KO SI CHANG

เกาะสีชัง

pop 4100

If you're looking for the archetypes of Thai island life – sweeping sandy beaches, coconut groves – you won't find them on this sliver of green in the big blue Ao Krung Thep (Bight of Bangkok). On Ko Si Chang you'll have to settle for a fishing village atmosphere; gentle hills studded with Chinese and Thai temples; and beachfront reminders of a stately royal palace. Enrich your mind through meditation in the limestone caves of the Tham Yai Phrik Vipassana Monastery and exercise your body by paddling a kayak to nearby Bat Island, where there's good snorkelling.

On weekdays you'll have this gentle footfall on the Thai tourist trail all to yourself, but things liven up at the weekend when Bangkok holidaymakers arrive.

Orientation & Information

The island's one small settlement faces the mainland and is the terminus for the ferry. A bumpy road network links the village with all the other sights.

Kasikornbank (99/12 Th Atsadang) Has an ATM and exchange facilities.

drinking snacks to full meals. Sunglasses are mandatory for all band members.

Other recommendations:

Garden@Sea (Th Jermjompol; drinks 25-50B; ☻ 6am-8pm) A cosy parkside kiosk for drinks and ice cream with pleasant outdoor seating. Try the refreshing green-tea frappé.

Seafood stalls (Ko Loi jetty; dishes 40-160B; ☻ lunch & dinner) Perched on the Ko Loi jetty, these humble spots

Post office (Th Atsadang) A further 30m past the Tourist Services Centre.

Tourist Services Centre (☎ 0 3821 6201; Th Atsadang; ☽ 9am-4.30pm Mon-Fri) Opposite the Sichang Palace on the main road to the right as you walk up from the pier. Ask for the *Island Welcome* brochure.

www.koh-sichang.com An excellent source of local information.

Sights & Activities

The Buddhist **Tham Yai Phrik Vipassana Monastery** (☎ 0 3821 6104; ☽ dawn to dusk) is built around several meditation caves running into the island's central limestone ridge, and offers fine views from its hilltop *chedi* (stupa). Monks and *mâe chii* (nuns) from across Thailand come to take advantage of the caves' peaceful environment, and foreigners wishing to sample monastic life are also welcomed. Studying at the monastery is free of charge (phone ahead to make sure there's room and bring your passport), but you'll be expected to follow the monastery's strict code of conduct. Whether you visit for an hour, or stay a month, leave an appropriate donation (roughly equivalent to basic food and lodging if staying a few days) with the monk or nun who shows you around.

The western side of the island has some OK swimming spots. **Hat Tham Phang** (Fallen Cave Beach) in the southwest has simple facilities with deckchair and umbrella rental. A beach area along the coast by Hat Tha Wang Palace (below) is popular with locals, and the island's best swimming is at **Hat Sai Kaew** to the south.

At the western end of the island (2km from the pier), you can visit **Hat Tha Wang Palace** (Th Chakra Pong; admission free; ☽ 9am-5pm). The carefully managed lawns are a prime picnic spot for visitors from Bangkok, who share the gardens with foraging white squirrels. The palace was once used by Rama V (Chulalongkorn) over the summer months, but was abandoned when the French briefly occupied the island in 1893. The main throne hall – a magnificent golden teak structure called Vimanmek – was moved to Bangkok in 1910 (p133). The Fine Arts Department has since restored the remaining palace buildings.

Overlooking Hat Tha Wang is a large white stupa that holds **Wat Atsadangnimit** (☽ daylight), a small, consecrated chamber where Rama V used to meditate. The unique Buddha image inside was fashioned more than 50 years ago by a local monk. Nearby is a stone outcrop wrapped in holy cloth, called Bell Rock because it rings like a bell when struck.

Near Wat Atsadangnimit a large limestone cave, **Tham Saowapha** (admission free; ☽ daylight), plunges deep into the island. Have a nosy if you've got a torch.

The most imposing sight is the ornate **San Jao Phaw Khao Yai Chinese Temple** (☽ daylight). During Chinese New Year in February, the island is overrun with Chinese visitors from the mainland. This is one of Thailand's most interesting Chinese temples, with shrine caves, multiple levels and a good view of the ocean. It's east of the town, high on a hill overlooking the sea.

Several locals run **snorkelling trips** to Koh Khaang Khao (Bat Island) on Ko Si Chang's southern tip. A boat for 10 people will cost

---

WHAT TO EXPECT IN SOUTHEASTERN THAILAND

We list high-season rates (November to May). Rates for locations near Bangkok (eg Pattaya and Ko Samet) do not vary much on a seasonal basis, but during the week you can expect to negotiate significant discounts. If you're visiting on a busy holiday weekend don't be surprised to be quoted significantly higher rates – in some cases up to 100% more – than the rates quoted here.

■ Budget (less than 700B) – In Pattaya, competition keeps prices low and for this price you can expect air-con and private facilities with hot water. Rates are sneaking up on the islands and you may have to make do with a beach bungalow and cold showers.

■ Midrange (700B to 1700B) – In Pattaya throughout the year, and on Ko Chang and Ko Samet out of the peak season, the lower end of this range will secure air-con, private facilities, and maybe even a pool and cable TV. At the upper end, expect all mod cons, especially if you shop around.

■ Top End (over 1700B) – You can expect a better standard of design and décor. The size of the rooms and the range of facilities will be similar to the higher end of the Midrange category, but expect better service and a more private stay.

around 2500B. Ask at Pan & David Restaurant (below) or the Tiewpai-Park Resort (below).

Sea kayaks are available for rent (400B per day) on Hat Tham Phang. A nice paddle is down the coast to Koh Khaang Khao, where there is good snorkelling. Recharge at the **Si Chang Healing House** (☎ 0 3821 6467; 167 Mu 3 Th Makhaam Thaew; � 8am-6pm, Thu-Tue), which offers massage and beauty treatments (400B to 800B) in a garden labyrinth opposite Pan & David Restaurant.

Sleeping

Rim Talay (☎ 0 3821 6237; 38/3 Mu 2 Th Devavongse; r 500-800B, 'houseboats' 1500B; ☒) Behind the Pan & David Restaurant, this waterside spot has simple but clean air-con rooms, and a selection of colourful Thai fishing boats that have been transformed into mini-apartments sleeping up to five people. The bow of each 'houseboat' is a chill-out area with comfy couches.

Sichang View Resort (☎ 0 3821 6210; r 890B; ☒ ☐) You'll need transport to make this your island base, but the spacious rooms and expansive gardens provide a relaxing getaway. Sunset is special. To get there, follow the road up the hill past the Chinese temple. After 1.5km Sichang View Resort is on your right.

Sichang Palace (☎ 0 3821 6276; Th Atsadang 81; r 1050B; ☒ ☒) The lobby features an ostentatious display of wooden furniture and carvings, but the modern rooms are not as over the top. You'll pay an extra 200B for a sea view, and nonguests can use the hotel pool for 50B.

Other recommendations:

Jeff's Bungalows (☎ 0 3821 6615; r 600B; ☒) Up the hill just past Pan & David Restaurant, these cosy bungalows feature hot showers, cable TV and DVD players.

Tiewpai-Park Resort (☎ 0 3821 6084; tom_tiewpai@ hotmail.com; Th Atsadang; r 400-850B; ☒) Spread throughout a quiet glade, this central option with a range of rooms is showing its age a little, but is still good for local information and snorkelling trips.

Eating

The town has several small restaurants, with simply prepared seafood your best bet. For all restaurants phoning ahead on weekdays is recommended. The restaurant at **Sichang View Resort** features a cliff-top setting and excellent seafood from 180B to 300B. The resort's **Malee Blue Hut Café** does great coffee all day and excellent sundowners.

Pan & David Restaurant (☎ 0 3821 6629; 167 Mu 3 Th Makhaam Thaew; mains 40-260B; � breakfast, lunch & dinner, Wed-Mon) Former adman David and wife Pan are sociable hosts at the island's best restaurant. You shouldn't get bored by David's Asian anecdotes, but if you do the menu includes Thai food, pasta and burgers, and a tidy little wine list. Finish with homemade ice cream and you'll go to bed a contented traveller.

Getting There & Away

Boats to Ko Si Chang leave hourly from the Ko Loi jetty in Sri Racha. The fare is 40B each way; the first boat leaves at 7am and the last at 8pm. From Ko Si Chang boats shuttle back hourly from 6am to 6pm. Boats leave promptly. A túk-túk to the ferry from Sri Racha's waterfront hotels is 20B.

Getting Around

Ko Si Chang has some of Thailand's biggest motorcycle taxis and they'll take you anywhere for 30B to 40B. Island tours are available for around 250B: be prepared to haggle. Motorbikes are available to rent from Tiewpai-Park Resort for 250B per day.

PATTAYA

พัทยา

pop 85,000

A heavy-breathing and testosterone-fuelled testament to holiday hedonism, Pattaya has lured tourists for almost four decades, and it's showing no sign of slowing down. And as past visitors move on to more genteel Thai resorts, first-time travellers from Russia and Eastern Europe now air their new passports with a fling in Asia's first and foremost Sin City. Anyone for Pattayagrad?

The cast may be evolving, but the scenery and soundtrack remain the same. The gorgeous half-moon of Pattaya Bay swoops around the headland to (slightly) more refined Hat Jomtien, and delicate sea-breezes whip up a heady cocktail of suntan lotion, fast food, and motorcycle and jet-ski fumes. Wide-eyed package tourists jostle with Indian tailors, ruddy-faced middle-aged Western men, and beachfront fruit and seafood vendors. Thumping beats, cruising 'baht buses' and the commercial hubbub provide an irresistible symphony. And after dark the tourists' eyes open even wider with a stroll past Pattaya's infamous go-go bars amid the sex tourism hub of Walking St.

Pattaya's a stay up late kind of town, but wake up earlier than most and there are ac-

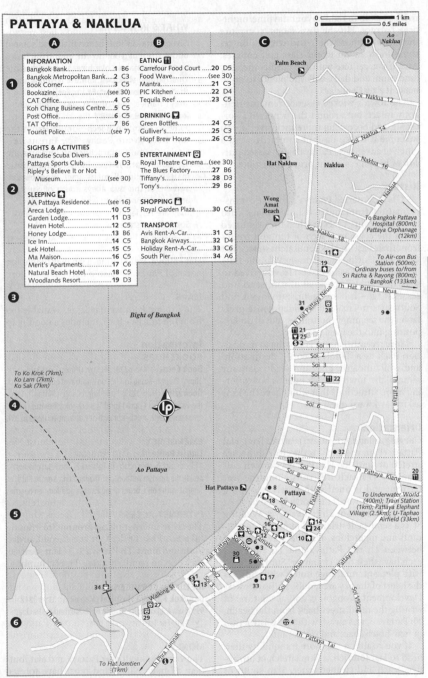

PATTAYA & NAKLUA

INFORMATION
Bangkok Bank.........................1 B6
Bangkok Metropolitan Bank....2 C3
Book Corner.........................3 C5
Bookazine........................(see 30)
CAT Office..........................4 C6
Koh Chang Business Centre....5 C5
Post Office..........................6 C5
TAT Office..........................7 B6
Tourist Police....................(see 7)

SIGHTS & ACTIVITIES
Paradise Scuba Divers............8 C5
Pattaya Sports Club................9 D3
Ripley's Believe It or Not
   Museum.......................(see 30)

SLEEPING
AA Pattaya Residence..........(see 16)
Areca Lodge........................10 C5
Garden Lodge.....................11 D3
Haven Hotel.......................12 C5
Honey Lodge......................13 B6
Ice Inn.............................14 C5
Lek Hotel..........................15 C5
Ma Maison........................16 C5
Merit's Apartments..............17 C6
Natural Beach Hotel.............18 C5
Woodlands Resort...............19 D3

EATING
Carrefour Food Court 20 D5
Food Wave..................(see 30)
Mantra..........................21 C3
PIC Kitchen 22 D4
Tequila Reef 23 C5

DRINKING
Green Bottles..................24 C5
Gulliver's.......................25 C3
Hopf Brew House............26 C5

ENTERTAINMENT
Royal Theatre Cinema...(see 30)
The Blues Factory...........27 B6
Tiffany's........................28 D3
Tony's...........................29 B6

SHOPPING
Royal Garden Plaza.........30 C5

TRANSPORT
Avis Rent-A-Car..............31 C3
Bangkok Airways............32 D4
Holiday Rent-A-Car.........33 C6
South Pier.....................34 A6

Ao Naklua

Palm Beach

Soi Naklua 12

Soi Naklua 14

Hat Naklua   Naklua

Soi Naklua 16

Th Naklua

Wong Amat Beach

Soi Naklua 18

To Bangkok Pattaya
Hospital (800m);
Pattaya Orphanage
(12km)

To Air-con Bus
Station (500m);
Ordinary buses to/from
Sri Racha & Rayong (800m);
Bangkok (133km)

Th Hat Pattaya Neua

Bight of Bangkok

Soi 1
Soi 2
Soi 3
Soi 4
Soi 5

Th Pattaya 3

To Ko Krok (7km);
Ko Larn (7km);
Ko Sak (7km)

Ao Pattaya

Hat Pattaya

Soi 6

Th Pattaya Klang

To Underwater World
(400m); Train Station
(1km); Pattaya Elephant
Village (2.5km); U-Taphao
Airfield (33km)

Soi 7
Soi 8
Soi 9
Pattaya

Th Pattaya 2

Soi 10
Soi 11
Soi 12
Soi Yamato

Th Pattaya 3

Th Hat Pattaya Tai

Soi Post Office

Th Bua Khao

Soi Viking

Walking Street

Th Cliff

Th Phra Tamnak

Th Pattaya Tai

To Hat Jomtien
(1km)

0   1 km
0   0.5 miles

SOUTHEASTERN THAILAND

tivities galore to redress your daytime/night-time balance. Hit the dive shops to explore the city's offshore reefs and wrecks, or get some fresh air on world-class golf courses. And if you're here with the family, the kids (and mum and dad), will find plenty to do to make it a real holiday.

The town's wicked essence remains defiantly intact, but around the fringes it's softening and becoming more inclusive. If you welcome it with a dash of confidence and a pinch of adventure, Pattaya's sun-kissed pursuit of happiness might prove irresistible.

History

US GIs kick-started Pattaya's dramatic transformation from quiet fishing village into throbbing tourist mecca when they ventured down the coast in search of fun and frolics from their base in Nakhon Ratchasima. That was 1959. During the Vietnam War, the flow become a flood as troops on leave arrived to soak up Pattaya's cocktail of sun, sand and sex. Package – and sex – tourists followed, and Southeastern Thailand's golden goose grew fat on the seemingly bottomless pot of dollars pouring into the local economy.

More recently Pattaya is striving to re-position itself as a 'family-friendly' destination, and while the grit, glitz and seedy glamour remain, the 'town that sex built' is now offering more attractions that won't have the kids asking awkward questions.

Orientation

Curving around Ao Pattaya (Pattaya Bay), Hat Pattaya (Pattaya Beach) is the city's showcase stretch of sand. Th Hat Pattaya (known colloquially as Beach Rd) runs along the waterfront and is lined with hotels, shopping centres and, towards the north, go-go bars. At the southern end of Th Hat Pattaya, 'Walking St' is a semi-pedestrianised jumble of restaurants and nightclubs. The alleyways running between Th Hat Pattaya and Th Pattaya 2 each have their own character: Soi 13 is filled with pleasant, midrange hotels while Soi 3 is the heart of the gay area, dubbed 'Boyztown'. Development is ongoing, and at the time of writing the third street back from the beach, Th Pattaya 3, was awash with the construction of new hotels, bars and restaurants.

If you're after a tad more tranquillity then head to Hat Jomtien, a 6km stretch of attractive beach and cleaner water, 5km south of

WHAT'S IN A NAME?

Given Pattaya's international appeal, some of the streets are known by both their Thai and English names. We have stuck with the Thai names, although some city maps use the English equivalent. Examples of the Thai street names, with the English equivalent include: Th Hat Pattaya (Beach Rd), Th Hat Jomtien (Jomtien Beach Rd), Th Hat Pattaya Neua (North Pattaya Rd), Th Pattaya Klang (Central Pattaya Rd) and Th Pattaya Tai (South Pattaya Rd). To further confuse matters, while all maps (including ours) agree that the two alleys south of Soi 13 are called Soi Yamato and Soi Post Office, they are respectively labelled Soi 13/1 and Soi 13/2 on street signs.

Hat Pattaya. Hat Naklua, a smaller beach 1km north of Pattaya, is also quiet.

MAPS

The *Explore Pattaya* magazine, available free from the tourist office, includes a good map.

Information

BOOKSHOPS

Book Corner (Map p233; Soi Post Office; ☺ 10am-10pm) English-language fiction and travel guides.

Bookazine (Map p233; 1st fl, Royal Garden Plaza, Th Hat Pattaya; ☺ 11am-11pm) Travel books, literature and magazines, with another branch at Hat Jomtien (Map p235).

EMERGENCY

Tourist Police (Map p233; ☎ 0 3842 9371, emergency 1155; tourist@police.go.th; Th Pattaya 2) The head office is beside the Tourism Authority of Thailand office on Th Phra Tamnak with police boxes along Pattaya and Jomtien beaches.

INTERNET ACCESS

There are internet places around Soi Praisani (aka Soi Post Office), at the Royal Garden Plaza and along Th Pattaya 2. At Hat Jomtien, they pop up regularly along Th Hat Jomtien.

MEDICAL SERVICES

Bangkok Pattaya Hospital (Map p233; ☎ 0 3842 9999; www.bph.co.th; 301 Mu 6, Th Sukhumvit, Naklua; ☺ 24hr) For 1st-class health care.

MONEY

There are banks all over Pattaya and Hat Jomtien; all have ATMs and most have foreign

exchange booths that stay open late (usually 8pm).

Bangkok Bank (Map p233; Th Hat Pattaya)
Bangkok Metropolitan Bank (Map p233; Th Hat Pattaya)

MEDIA
Explore Pattaya, a free fortnightly magazine, contains information on events and attractions as well as hotel and restaurant listings. *What's On Pattaya* is a similar monthly publication. *Pattaya Mail* (www.pattayamail .com), a weekly newspaper, covers Pattaya's famed social ills while *Pattaya People* (www .pattayapeople.com), another weekly, is an even racier read.

POST
Post office (Map p233; Soi 13/2)

TELEPHONE
There are many private long-distance phone offices, charging 12B per minute to the USA, Australia and Europe. Most internet cafés offer Skype.

Communications Authority of Thailand (CAT; Map p233; ☎ 0 3842 5301; cnr Th Pattaya Tai & Th Pattaya 3;

⊙ 8.30am-4.30pm Mon-Fri, 9am-noon Sat) Southeast of central Pattaya.

TOURIST INFORMATION
Tourism Authority of Thailand (TAT; Map p233; ☎ 0 3842 8750; tatchon@tat.or.th; 609 Muu 10, Th Phra Tamnak; ⊙ 8.30am-4.30pm) Located at the northwestern edge of Rama IX Park. The helpful staff have many brochures, including the excellent *Bigmap Pattaya*.

TRAVEL AGENCIES
Travel agencies all over town offer activities and accommodation around Thailand.

Ko Chang Business Centre (Map p233; ☎ 0 3871 0145; Soi Post Office; ⊙ 9am-midnight) Specialises in trips to Ko Chang and Ko Samet.

Dangers & Annoyances
Remember sex tourism is a booming industry in Pattaya and large sections of the city are chock full of go-go bars and strip clubs. This seedier side of Pattaya is hard to avoid, especially at night, and if you are travelling with young children prepare yourself for some awkward questions.

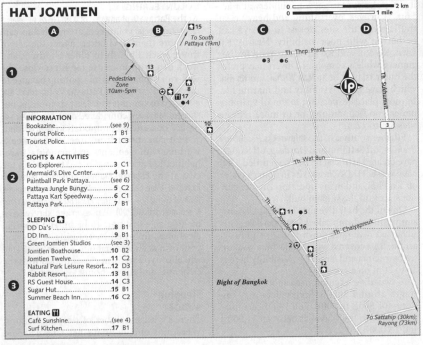

SOUTHEASTERN THAILAND

SOUTHEASTERN THAILAND

Sights & Activities
BEACHES
Hat Pattaya is the city's showcase stretch of sand, sporting sunbathers, souvenir sellers, and buzzing jet skis and speedboats. The sand is reasonably clean and the water is calm. If you get bored there's good shopping over the road.

Hat Jomtien, about 1km south of Pattaya, stretches for 6km and is quieter than its northern neighbour. You're relatively removed from Pattaya's sex scene at this beach. At the northern end of the beach, **Hat Dongtan** is a hub for gay travellers.

Hat Naklua, a smaller beach north of Pattaya, is quiet and a good choice for families.

The islands of **Ko Larn**, **Ko Krok** and **Ko Sak** are around 7km offshore and have some popular beaches – especially **Hat Ta Waen** on Ko Larn. Boats leave Pattaya's **South Pier** (Map p233) every two hours between 8am and 4.30pm (20B). The last boat back from Ko Larn is at 5pm. A daytrip including viewing from a glass bottom boat costs 150B.

WATERSPORTS
Though not home to Thailand's best dive sites, Pattaya's proximity to Bangkok makes it a popular spot to get some underwater action. However, overfishing and heavy boat traffic mean the sites closest to Pattaya can be barren with poor visibility. Nearby Ko Larn, Ko Sak and Ko Krok are good for beginners, while accomplished divers may prefer the outer islands of **Ko Man Wichai** and **Ko Rin**, which have better visibility and marine life. In most places expect 3m to 9m of visibility under good conditions, or in more remote sites 5m to 12m.

Further southeast, the **shipwrecks** *Petchburi Bremen,* off Sattahip and *Hardeep,* off Samae, have created artificial reefs. The scuttled Thai navy vessel HMS *Khram* sits in 30m of water off Ko Phai, and many operators offer excursions around the sunken hulk.

One of the best dive sites is an old US navy ammunition dump called **Samaesan Hole**. This advanced dive goes down to 87m and has a gentle slope covered with coral where you can see barracuda and large rays. Visibility here is up to 20m on a good day.

A two-dive excursion to most sites averages around 3000B. Snorkellers may tag along for 500B to 800B. Full PADI certification (three to four days), is between 11,000B and 15,000B.

The following established dive shops are popular.

Mermaid's Dive Center (Map p235; ☎ 0 3823 2219; www.mermaiddive.com; Soi White House, Hat Jomtien)

Paradise Scuba Divers (Map p233; ☎ 0 3871 0567; www.tauchenthailand.de; Siam Bayview Resort, Th Hat Pattaya)

Pattaya and Jomtien have some of the best water-sports facilities in Thailand with **water-skiing** for 1200B per hour; **parasailing** 250B to 300B (about 10 to 15 minutes); and **windsurfing** for 500B an hour. **Game fishing** is also possible, with the rental rates for boats, fishing guides and tackle all reasonable. Hat Jomtien is the best for windsurfing because you're less likely to run into parasailors or jet skis.

SPORTS
Pattaya offers many sports including **bowling**, **snooker**, **archery**, **target-shooting**, **softball**, **horse-riding** and **tennis**. Most are available at the **Pattaya Sports Club** (Map p233; ☎ 0 3836 1167; www.pattayasports.org; 3/197 Th Pattaya 3) or can be organised by hotels. **Golf** packages can be booked through **East Coast Travel & Golf Organisation** (☎ 0 3830 0927; www.pattayagolfpackage.com).

VOLUNTEERING
At the **Pattaya Orphanage** (☎ 0 3871 6628; volunteer@redemptorists.or.th) volunteers are needed to care for more than 50 children under the age of three; teach English to older children; and work in a drop-in centre for street kids. The well-run orphanage is an uplifting balance to the Sin City streets of Pattaya. Volunteers are expected to commit to at least six months, but shorter stays are considered on a case-by-case basis. Food and accommodation is provided.

You can spend from one to four weeks working with elephants and mahouts, in rehabilitation after being forced to work in the city, at the **Elephant Mahout Project** run by **Eco Explorer** (Map p235; ☎ 0 3830 3941; www.ecoexplorer thailand.com; 217/7 Soi 15 Thep Prasit Rd; per week incl food & accommodation £300). An average day might include an early start to bathe and feed the elephants, followed by training to develop your own skills as a mahout. A four-week stay will allow you to form closer bonds with the elephants and the mahouts.

Sleeping
BUDGET
There's a huge number of sleeping options. Weekends and holidays get crowded and

PATTAYA FOR CHILDREN

Ripley's Believe It or Not Museum (Map p233; ☎ 0 3871 0294; 2nd fl, Royal Garden Plaza, Th Pattaya 2; adult/child 370/270B; ☾ 11am-11pm), puts a Disneyesque spin on the world's oddities and includes high-tech theme rides.

Budding Michael Schumachers (and petrolhead dads) should head to **Pattaya Kart Speedway** (Map p235; www.karting-thailand.com; ☎ 0 3842 2004; 248/2 Th Thep Prasit Soi 9; ☾ 9am-6pm), where you can race go-karts around an impressive 800m loop. Prices start at 300B for 10 minutes in a 10HP kart. There's a down'n'dirty off-road circuit and the littlest ones will enjoy the 'baby karts' on a 400m beginners' track.

At nearby **Paintball Park Pattaya** (Map p235; ☎ 0 3830 0608; 248/10 Muu 12, Th Thep Prasit; 50 bullets starting at 450B; ☾ 9am-6pm), older kids can vent their frustration at being on holiday with their uncool parents. If the kids don't behave then threaten them with the 50m jump at **Pattaya Jungle Bungy** (Map p235; ☎ 08 6378 3880; www.thaibungy.com; Soi 14, Th Hat Jomtien; jumps 1500B; ☾ 9am-6pm).

Pattaya Park's (Map p235; ☎ 0 3836 4129; www.pattayapark.com; 345 Th Hat Jomtien; adult/child 100/50B; ☾ 8.30am-6pm) bustling Water Park has three different ways to exit its 55-storey tower. Once the kids (and Mum and Dad) have recovered, get them all excited again on the roller coaster and dodgems at Pattaya Park's Funnyland Amusement Park.

Escape the heat and sun at **Underwater World** (☎ 0 3875 6879; Th Sukhumvit; adult/child 360/180B; ☾ 9am-6pm) with acrylic tunnels making up a walk-through aquarium. It's 200m south of the Tesco-Lotus shopping centre on the main road south.

The **Pattaya Elephant Village** (☎ 0 3824 9818; www.elephant-village-pattaya.com) is a nonprofit sanctuary for former working elephants. There's a 2.30pm elephant show (adult/child 500/400B) which demonstrates training techniques, and one-hour (adult/child 900/700B) and 3½-hour (adult/child 1900/1300B) elephant treks. The elephant village is 7km off Th Sukhumvit.

many budget options fill up, but on quieter weekdays, many hotels and guesthouses offer discounts.

Pattaya

The cheapest guesthouses are in south Pattaya, along Th Pattaya 2, the street parallel to Th Hat Pattaya. Most are clustered near Soi 6, 10, 11 and 12. Expect better value if you splash out a little more on a midrange place though.

Ice Inn (Map p233; ☎ 0 3872 0671; www.pattayacity. com/iceinn; 528/2-3 Th Pattaya 2; r 250-650B; ☷ ⌨) Ice Inn is the best value in town. Upstairs the rooms are clean and modern, and come with air-con or fan; downstairs things get funkier with an internet café and a gallery full of contemporary art and Asian antiques.

Honey Lodge (Map p233; ☎ 0 3842 9133; fax 0 3871 0185; 597/8 Muu 10 Th Pattaya 2; r 550B; ☷ ⌨) Somehow they manage to squeeze in cable TV, air-con, *and* a swimming pool for the budget traveller. Ask for an upstairs room as the downstairs rooms are a bit dark.

Merit's Apartments (Map p233; ☎ 0 3842 6258; fax 0 3842 6258; 215/47-50 Th Pattaya 2; r 800B; ☷) Good value air-con rooms in a quiet lane just off bustling Th Pattaya 2.

Hat Jomtien

Explore the area around Soi 3 and 4 for good value budget guesthouses.

RS Guest House (Map p235; ☎ 0 3823 1867; Th Hat Jomtien; r 500B; ☷) With small but clean rooms at the quieter southern end of the beach, RS Guest House is a good value haven away from the bright lights.

DD Inn (Map p235; ☎ 0 3823 2995; ddinn@hotmail.com; 410/50 Muu 12, Th Hat Jomtien; r 550-600B; ☷) At the northern end of the beach, this spot bedecked with Aussie paraphernalia sits in an arcade filled with travellers cafés and bars. Rooms are simple and clean, but all you'll need after a night on the town.

DD Da's (Map p235; ☎ 0 3823 3585; d.d.dahouse02@ hotmail.com; 406/357 Muu 12 Thaphraya Rd; r 600B; ☷) Slightly away from the beach, but with clean rooms and a restaurant downstairs, DD Da's is a good value option near Jomtien's nightlife.

MIDRANGE

Pattaya has many midrange hotels, with competition keeping standards high and prices (relatively) low. Hotels tend to age fast in Pattaya, so watch out for the latest openings which may be offering special deals. At the

time of writing several new hotels were being built on Th Pattaya 3, the third road back from the beach.

Pattaya

Natural Beach Hotel (Map p233; ☎ 0 3842 9239; naturalbeach@excite.com; 216 Muu 10, Soi 11; r 750-950B; ⚇ ⚛) Infused with a low-key relaxed ambience that's nicely at odds with the surrounding hubbub of Pattaya, the Natural Beach delivers a pretty garden, a shady swimming pool and tidy rooms with an unintentional 1970s retro feel.

Lek Hotel (Map p233; ☎ 0 3842 5552; lek_hotel@hotmail .com; 284/5 Th Pattaya 2; r 850-1200B; ⚇ ⚛) The Lek is popular with return visitors, who come back for the central location, bigger than normal rooms, and good value breakfast (110B) and dinner (60B) buffets. The doormen are a great source of local information. Ask for a quieter room away from the street.

Areca Lodge (Map p233; ☎ 0 3841 0123; www.areca lodge.com; 198/23 Muu 9, Soi Diana Inn, Tha Pattaya 2; r incl breakfast 1090B; ⚇ ▢ ⚛) With stylish rooms, two pools and a Jacuzzi, this place almost gatecrashes into the top-end category. No-one's told the owners though, and for 10 months of the year rooms start at an affordable 1090B. Expect increases of around 50% in December and January.

Ma Maison (Map p233; ☎ 0 3871 0433; www.ma maisonhotel.com; Soi 13; r 1100B; ⚇ ▢ ⚛) Sip your *pastis* around *la piscine* (swimming pool) at this very French low-rise oasis. The French management can be a bit snooty to non-French speakers, but just wear your Inspector Clouseau disguise and you should be OK. You can hitch your laptop to its wi-fi network.

Haven Hotel (Map p233; ☎ 0 3871 0988; www.the haven-hotel.com; 185 Soi 13; r 1100B; ⚇ ⚛) Just over the road from Ma Maison, this stylish midranger has 15 rooms around a pretty pool. All rooms have DVD players and stereos, so it's a handy spot to try out the bootleg movies and CDs you were lured into buying the night before.

AA Pattaya Residence (Map p233; ☎ 0 3842 3403; aaresidence@yahoo.com; 109/20 10 Soi 13; r 1350B; ⚇) Near Ma Maison, the rooms in this newish high-rise border on flash. You'll pay a little more than other nearby midrange accommodation, but the increase in standards is significant. Use the skills you've perfected buying bootleg DVDs to bargain them down to a midweek or off season rate of 900B.

Naklua

Garden Lodge (Map p233; Th Naklua; ☎ 0 3842 9109; fax 0 3842 1221; r 1100B; ⚇ Ⓟ) Escape the hype and hustle of Pattaya in one of town's best value midrange options. There's no skimping on the garden atmosphere with fishponds and leafy pavilions, and the tour desk at reception offers a raft of day trips.

Hat Jomtien

Head to the southern end of the beach for a quieter and more family-friendly atmosphere. It's popular with Thai tourists, who come for fresh seafood on weekends.

Summer Beach Inn (Map p235; ☎ 0 3823 1777; fax 0 3823 1778; Th Hat Jomtien; r 750B; ⚇) Popular with holidaying Thais, this slightly ageing spot with Miami Beach Art-Deco styling offers good value rooms a short distance from the beach.

Green Jomtien Studios (Map p235; ☎ 0 3830 3941; www.ecoexplorerthailand.com; 217/7 Soi 15 Thep Prassit Rd; r incl breakfast 850B; ⚇) Attached to the Elephant Mahout Project (p236), this place about 1km from the beach also offers spotless rooms in a quiet residential neighbourhood. Booking ahead is recommended as volunteers at the project also stay here.

Jomtien Boathouse (Map p235; ☎ 0 3875 6143; www .jomtien-boathouse.com; 380/5-6 Th Hat Jomtien; r 1050B; ⚇) You're only metres from the beach, but you might find it hard to leave the cosy downstairs pub with interesting antique maps. Upstairs a nautical theme drifts into the comfortable rooms, some with balconies and sea views.

Jomtien Twelve (Map p235; ☎ 0 3875 6865; jomtientwelve@gmail.com; 240/13 Soi 12 Th Hat Jomtien; r 800-1250B; ⚇) The lobby promises urbane designer delights, but the rooms are slightly less impressive. It's popular with weekending Bangkok yuppies. Next door there is an elegant café/restaurant.

Natural Park Leisure Resort (Map p235; ☎ 0 3823 1561; www.naturalparkresort.com; 412 Th Hat Jomtien; r 1800B, bungalow 5000B; ⚇ ▢ ⚛) At the quieter southern end of the beach, Natural Park has leafy grounds filled with birdsong, a Mediterranean-style resort building and lovely (but more expensive) Thai-style family bungalows.

TOP END

Pattaya is popular with package tourists and convention goers, so there are plenty of top-end options. Rooms are often cheaper when booked through a Bangkok travel agency, or via the internet. There are plenty of standard

high-rise resorts, but the following three offer something different.

Naklua

Woodlands Resort (Map p233; ☎ 0 3842 1707; www .woodland-resort.com; 164/1 Th Naklua; r incl breakfast 2900-3900B; ⚒ 🖳 🖳) Low key but sophisticated, Woodlands Resort is set around tropical gardens with two swimming pools, and is good for families. The rooms are light and airy with teak furniture, and include high speed internet, and CD and DVD players.

Hat Jomtien

Rabbit Resort (Map p235; ☎ 0 3830 3303; www.rab bitresort.com; Dongtan Beach, Hat Jomtien; r 4600-5900B; villas (up to four people) 9900-10,600B; ⚒ 🖳) Rabbit Resort has stunning bungalows and villas set in beachfront forest at the northern end of Jomtien. Furnishings showcase Thai design and art, with wooden floors and handmade, rustic textiles. Bathrooms are especially stylish with accents of riverstone and granite.

Sugar Hut (Map p235; ☎ 0 3825 1686; www.sugar -hut.com; 391/18 Muu 10, Th Thapraya; 1-/2-room villa 7000/11,700B; ⚒ 🖳) Amid overgrown jungle-like grounds, the Sugar Hut's Thai-style villas and bungalows are gathered around shaded fish ponds and winding paths patrolled by peacocks and rabbits. Décor is a delicious combo of Asian chic and rustic seclusion. If you grow weary of your romantic hideaway, there are three swimming pools, a spa and sauna, and an atmospheric restaurant.

Eating

Western food rules the roost in Pattaya, and while there are plenty of Thai restaurants, the taste of authentic Thailand is sometimes lacking. Whether you want schnitzel, samosas or smorgasbord, you'll find it amid the many eateries. Head to south Pattaya around Walking St for the best selection of seafood restaurants.

Carrefour Food Court (Map p233; Th Pattaya Klang; ⏲ 11am-10pm) In the absence of a decent night market, head to the food court under the Carrefour supermarket. The Thai food is authentically spicy and dishes start from 30B.

Food Wave (Map p233 ; Th Hat Pattaya; dishes 40-120B; ⏲ 11am-11pm) Atop the Royal Garden Plaza shopping mall, this expands the food court concept with a wider range of cuisines, including Japanese, Vietnamese and Italian. There's also Starbucks if you, like, really, really need an organic soy latte. You'll find other fast food chains you didn't know you were missing downstairs.

Surf Kitchen (Map p235; ☎ 0 3823 1710; Th Hat Jomtien; dishes 80-260B; ⏲ breakfast, lunch & dinner) A cosmopolitan team combines with very good chefs to keep Surf Kitchen at the top of relaxed dining options on Jomtien Beach. The Thai food is authentic in all the right places and the talented kitchen staff are skilled at Western food as well.

PIC Kitchen (Map p233; ☎ 0 3842 8374; 10 Soi 5, Th Pattaya 2; dishes 110-290B; ⏲ lunch & dinner) This teak-lined place has an intimate atmosphere with open-sided rooms, cushions and low wooden tables. Excellent Thai food is the main draw, and live jazz bubbles away upstairs every night from 8pm at the Jazz Pit.

Café Sunshine (Map p235; Th Hat Jomtien; dishes 100-300B; ⏲ breakfast, lunch & dinner) With its shady garden, Café Sunshine is a haven from the tropical heat. It's especially recommended for breakfast, and if you time it right you'll still be there when happy hour kicks off at a ridiculously early 10am.

Tequila Reef (Map p233; ☎ 0 3841 4035; Soi 7, Th Hat Pattaya; dishes 220-310B; ⏲ lunch & dinner) Mexican cantina meets Californian surf shack in this buzzy restaurant that dispenses Pattaya's best margaritas. It's popular with the lads from the United States navy who probably know a thing or two about a good burrito.

Mantra (Map p233; ☎ 0 3842 9591; Th Hat Pattaya; dishes 240-800B; ⏲ dinner Mon-Sat, brunch & dinner Sun; ⚒) Cool like a chic Shanghai bordello, Mantra's terrific bar is swathed in raw silk and the expansive dining room is draped in dark wood. The menu combines Japanese, Thai and Indian flavours, and there's a big cocktail list and more than 20 wines by the glass. Even if you don't eat there, it's worth popping in for a classy drink.

Drinking

Despite the profusion of noisy, identikit beer bars, go-go bars and nightclubs (p240), there are still some good places for a no-strings-attached drink.

Hopf Brew House (Map p233; ☎ 0 3871 0650; Th Hat Pattaya 219; ⏲ 3pm-1am Sun-Fri, 4pm-2am Sat; ⚒) Moodily authentic in dark wood, the Hopf Brew House is a haven for middle-aged beer aficionados and splurging Scandinavian backpackers. A very drinkable pilsener and wheat beer are brewed on site, and both are cheaper before 8pm when the live music starts. Huge wood-fired pizzas and only slightly smaller

schnitzels are recommended to soak up the liquid hospitality.

Gulliver's (Map p233; ☎ 0 3871 0641; Th Hat Pattaya; ⏰ 11.30am-2am; 🚼 💻) At the northern end of Pattaya, Gulliver's has pool tables, free wi-fi internet, and a big Thai and Western menu. Before 7pm, take advantage of happy hour with discounted beer and cocktails. Outside the action spills onto tables around an ornamental pool. Don't get too close if you've had an extended happy hour.

Green Bottles (Map p233; ☎ 0 3842 9675; 216/6-20 Th Pattaya 2; ⏰ 11am-2am; 🚼) Charmingly cosy and retro (you can even request your favourite songs from the band), Green Bottles has been on the scene since 1988 and is one of Pattaya's more traditional pubs. The dim lights mean it's good for easing into another night's carousing with an early evening hair of the dog.

Entertainment

Merry-making in Pattaya, aside from the sex scene, means everything from hanging out in a video bar to dancing all night in a south Pattaya disco. The best place to start is Th Hat Pattaya. At its southern end, this main drag becomes 'Walking St' a semi-pedestrianised area with bars and clubs for every predilection. Nearby, 'Pattaya Land' encompasses Soi 1, 2 and 3 and is packed with go-go bars. The many gay bars on Soi 3 are announced by a sign reading 'Boyztown'. Around Hat Dong-

tan at the northern end of Hat Jomtien there is another burgeoning gay scene.

CLUBS & CABARETS

Tony's (Map p233; ☎ 0 3842 5795; www.tonydisco.com; 139/15 Walking St; admission free; ⏰ 8.30pm-2.30am; 🚼) You'll either love or hate this supernova monument to nocturnal nirvana. A pumping neon-saturated disco, magic shows, karaoke and pool tables blend seamlessly with good value buffet food, strong cocktails and Tony's own beer. The following day you can even repent at Tony's own gym.

Tiffany's (Map p233; ☎ 0 3842 1700; www.tiffany-show .co.th; 464 Mu 9, Th Pattaya 2; admission 500-800B; ⏰ from 6pm; 🚼) Established in 1974, Pattaya's leading transvestite cabaret is a remarkably chaste affair, oozing old-school showbiz charm and covering the globe in a fast-paced show lasting 75 minutes. The absolutely fabulous parade of sequins, satin and surprises begins at 6pm, 7.30pm and 9pm.

The Blues Factory (Map p233; ☎ 0 3830 0180; www .thebluesfactorypattaya.com; Soi Lucky Star; admission free; ⏰ from 8.30pm; 🚼) Off Walking St, Pattaya's best venue for no-nonsense live music features at least two bands every night, and a hassle-free atmosphere just metres from the heavier hype of Walking St.

CINEMAS

Royal Theatre Cinema (Map p233; ☎ 0 3842 8057; shop C30, 2nd fl, Royal Garden Plaza, Th Pattaya 2; admission 120B)

PATTAYA VICE

Pattaya's notoriety for sex tourism revolves around the agglomeration of discos, outdoor 'beer bars' and go-go clubs making up Pattaya's red-light district at the southern end of the beach. Known as 'the village', the area attracts a large number of prostitutes, including *kàthoey* (transvestites), who pose as female hookers and ply their trade among the droves of *faràng* (Western) sex tourists. There is also a prominent gay sex-for-sale scene in Pattaya, especially at nearby Hat Dongtan. This activity is obvious to any visitor, but less overt is the shadowy and sickening child sex trade, and sadly it is not uncommon to see Western men walking with young Thai boys and girls: see also p41.

Traditionally the sex scene was focussed around 'Walking St' at the southern end of the beach, but every year a batch of new beer bars opens, especially along Sois 7, 8 and 9 to the north. A sign at the entrance to Walking St proclaims 'International Meeting Place', and they're not kidding. White prostitutes come from Romania and Moldova (favourites with male Asian sex tourists), and black male prostitutes from Nigeria (primarily servicing female sex tourists from Japan) can all be had in Pattaya. Globalisation is all too evident too with the growing influence of organised crime cartels from as far away as Russia.

Of course, prostitution is just as illegal here as elsewhere in Thailand. But with millions of baht swilling around from money laundering, drug trafficking and diamond trading, let's just say enforcement of the laws against it is cyclic at best.

Get away from the stall holders selling fake designer gear by escaping into the latest make-believe offering from Hollywood.

Shopping

Thanon Hat Pattaya is lined with stalls selling everything from dodgy DVDs and counterfeit CDs to T-shirts and jewellery. For more serious shopping, head to the **Royal Garden Plaza** (Map p233; Th Pattaya 2; ◷ 11am-11pm).

Getting There & Away

AIR

Bangkok Airways (Map p233; ☎ 0 3841 2382; www.bang kokair.com; 75/8 Mu 9, Th Pattaya 2; ◷ 8.30am-4.30pm Mon-Fri, to noon Sat) links **U-Taphao airfield** (☎ 0 3824 5599) about 33km south of Pattaya, with Ko Samui (one way 3125B, daily) and Phuket (one way 3845B, daily).

BUS

There are air-con buses to Pattaya from Bangkok's Eastern and Northern bus terminals (124B, two hours, every half-hour from 6am to 9pm). In Pattaya the air-con bus stop is on Th Hat Pattaya Neua, near the intersection with Th Sukhumvit. Once you reach the main Pattaya bus terminal, waiting red săwngthăew will take you to the main beach road for 30B per person. Several hotels and travel agencies run minibuses to addresses within Bangkok, or east to Ko Samet and Ko Chang – the fares start at about 200B. Try **Ko Chang Business Centre** (p235) or ask at your hotel. At the time of writing a direct bus service had commenced from Bangkok's newly opened Suvarnabhumi airport and Pattaya (106B, two hours).

From Sri Racha, you can grab a public bus on Th Sukhumvit to Pattaya (30B, 30 minutes) – in Pattaya, they stop near the corner of Th Sukhumvit and Th Pattaya Neua. From here, you can flag down buses to Rayong (ordinary/air-con 60/93B, 1½ hours). The air-con buses are worth the extra cost.

TRAIN

One train per day travels between Pattaya and Bangkok's Hualamphong station (third class 31B, 3¾ hours). It leaves Bangkok at 6.55am only on Monday to Friday. The return train departs from Pattaya at 2.20pm. Schedules for this service are subject to change, so check times at **Pattaya train station** (Map p233; ☎ 0 3842 9285) before travelling.

Getting Around

CAR & MOTORCYCLE

Avis Rent-A-Car (Map p233; ☎ 0 3836 1628; www.avisthai land.com; Th Hat Pattaya Neua; ◷ 9am-5pm) has offices at the Dusit Resort.

Holiday Rent-A-Car (Map p233; ☎ 0 3842 6203; www .pattayacar-rent.com; Th Pattaya 2; ◷ 9am-5pm), located opposite Royal Garden Plaza, is a cheaper local company and also offers full insurance. Prices for a 1500cc Toyota Vios start at 1150B per day. Discounts are offered for longer periods.

Local travel agents offer Suzuki jeeps from around 1000B per day, but expect to pay through the nose if you have an accident.

Motorcycles cost 150B to 250B per day for a 100cc machine; a 125cc to 150cc will cost around 300B, and you'll see 750cc to 1000cc machines for hire for 500B to 1000B. There are motorcycle hire places along Th Hat Pattaya and Th Pattaya 2.

SĂWNGTHĂEW

Locally known as 'baht buses', săwngthăew cruise Th Hat Pattaya and Th Pattaya 2 frequently – just hop on, and when you get out pay 10B anywhere between Naklua and south Pattaya, or 30B for as far as Jomtien. Price lists posted in the vehicles state the maximum drivers can charge for any given journey.

Readers have complained about having taken the 10B săwngthăew with local passengers and then having been charged a higher 'charter' price of 20B to 50B. Establish the correct fare in advance. Also don't board a săwngthăew that is waiting empty at the side of the road, as the driver may insist you have 'chartered' the entire vehicle.

At the time of writing a system of 'tourist' minibuses was being trialled in Pattaya on three different routes. One-way tickets are 30B, with one-day passes (90B) and three days passes (180B) also available.

RAYONG PROVINCE

PATTAYA TO KO SAMET

From Pattaya, most travellers fast-forward down the coast to the day-time calm and occasional night-time chaos of Ko Samet. The little port of Ban Phe is the jumping-off point for the island, but a brief stop in Rayong is usually on the cards for a change of buses. If you're definitely bound for Samet, it doesn't make much sense to hang around the mainland

beaches, but if you do venture to the other strips of sand and small islands in the vicinity, you'll probably be the only Western face.

For information about travelling to and from Rayong and Ban Phe, see p249.

Rayong

ระยอง

pop 49,000

For the traveller, the dusty strip of banks, markets and motorcycle dealerships that makes up Rayong holds few surprises. You're most likely to be here taking advantage of its location as a major transport interchange, but if you do arrive too late to secure an onward connection for a boat to Koh Samet, there are a couple of OK hotels.

INFORMATION

Krung Thai Bank (Th Sukhumvit 144/53-55) One of several banks along Rayong's main drag, Th Sukhumvit, with exchange services and ATMs.

Rayong President Hotel (☎ 0 3861 1307; Th Sukhumvit) Has internet access (per 10 minutes 5B).

TAT (☎ 0 3865 5420; tatyong@tat.or.th; 153/4 Th Sukhumvit; ☒ 8.30am-4.30pm) Located 7km east of Rayong on Hwy 3; a worthwhile stop if you have your own transport.

SLEEPING & EATING

For cheap food, head to the market near the Thetsabanteung cinema or the restaurants and noodle shops along Th Taksin Maharat, just south of Wat Lum Mahachaichumphon. There's food stalls around the bus station.

Rayong President Hotel (☎ 0 3861 1307; Th Sukhumvit; r incl breakfast 700B; ☒ 🖳) There's not much English spoken, but the welcome is friendly and it's quiet at night. From the bus station, cross to the other side of Th Sukhumvit, turn right and after three minutes' walk you'll see a sign pointing down a side street.

Star Hotel Rayong (☎ 0 3861 4901; www.starhotel .th.com; 109 Th Rayong Trade Center; r incl breakfast 1500B; ☒ 🖳) Rayong's ritziest spot is a favourite with business and government honchos who demand a swanky four stars. The rooms are huge, and there is a bowling alley and two swimming pools. From the bus station, walk away from Th Sukhumvit, turn left at the top of the square and the hotel is on your right.

Ban Phe

บ้านเพ

The little port of Ban Phe is only on the map thanks to its role as a launch pad for nearby

Ko Samet. However, the busy seafood markets near the ferry terminal are worth a peek, and there's a few beaches nearby that are blissfully quiet during the week and make a nice detour before or after a spell on the island.

Check email and make international calls at **Tan Tan Café** (☎ 08 1925 6713; Soi 2; per min 1B; ☒ 7.30am-7pm), down a lane opposite the ferry terminal. There's an ATM outside the 7-Eleven store opposite Christies Guesthouse. Opposite the pier, **Blue Sky Books** (☎ 0 3865 1885; Soi 1; ☒ 10am-7pm) has a good range of English language titles, arranged by genre by a true bibliophile. The array of old Lonely Planet titles is positively archaeological.

SLEEPING

There are several hotels in Ban Phe in proximity to the pier.

Hotel Diamond (☎ 0 3865 1826; fax 0 3865 1757; 286/12 Mu 2; r 350-500B; ☒) The combined efforts of all three sisters will be needed before they understand you, but the welcome is friendly and the rooms clean, if a little dark. Turn left out of the ferry terminal and walk 150m down the main road. It's fine for one night if you miss the last ferry.

Christie's Guesthouse (☎ 0 3865 1976; fax 0 3865 2103; 280/92 Soi 1; d/tr 500/700B; ☒ ☒) With refurbished rooms and a good restaurant/bar downstairs, Christie's is the most comfortable place near the pier. With a good pizzeria and second-hand bookshop next door you might find yourself missing the ferry on purpose. Breakfast is an additional 100B and it's definitely worth it.

You can also rent one of two tidy air-con rooms at **Tan Tan Café** (☎ 08 1925 6713; Soi 2; 600B).

EATING

Christie's Bar & Restaurant (☎ 0 3865 1976; 280/92 Soi 1; ☒ breakfast, lunch & dinner) With funky tunes and friendly staff, Christie's is where you'll meet other travellers waiting for the ferry. Buy a takeaway baguette sandwich before you board the boat. At night, the bar becomes the regular drinking hole for expats in town teaching English.

Phe Pizza (☎ 0 3865 1885; Soi 1; pizza 180-280B; ☒ lunch & dinner) Generous toppings and authentic stringy mozzarella help to compensate for the high(ish) prices. While your pizza is being cooked, see if you can find a good mob thriller in Blue Sky Books next door.

Around Rayong & Ban Phe

KHAO CHAMAO/KHAO WONG NATIONAL PARK

อุทยานแห่งชาติเขาชะเมา–เขาวง

Although less than 85 sq km, **Khao Chamao/ Khao Wong National Park** (☎ 0 3889 4378; reserve@dnp .go.th; admission 400B; ✆ 8.30am-4.30pm) is famous for limestone mountains, high cliffs, caves, dense forest and waterfalls. Secreted in the rugged landscape are tigers, wild elephants and bears. It is inland from Ban Phe, 17km north of the Km 274 marker off Hwy 3. To get to the park, take a săwngthăew from Ban Phe to the marker for 40B, and another săwngthăew (20B) to the park.

You can stay at a camp site (per person 50B) or rent a 2-person bungalow (600B to 800B). To book, email reserve@dnp.go.th, or phone ☎ 0 2562 0760.

ISLANDS & BEACHES

Ko Man Klang and **Ko Man Nok**, along with **Ko Man Nai** to the west, are part of Laem Ya/Mu Ko Samet National Park. This official status hasn't kept away all development, only moderated it. Ko Man Nai is home to the Rayong **Turtle Conservation Centre** (☎ 0 3861 6096; ✆ 9am-4pm), which is a breeding place for endangered sea turtles and has a small visitors centre that describes their life cycle. Ask at Christie's Bar & Restaurant (opposite) about visiting from Ban Phe, or join a boat tour from Ko Samet (p245).

You can also volunteer to work at the centre by contacting **Starfish Ventures** (www.star fishventures.co.uk; 2 weeks incl accommodation from £595). Activities include monitoring the progress of the turtles, releasing young turtles into the ocean and explaining the project to tourists on day trips from Ko Samet. Accommodation is in a fishing village, and every day you'll go to work in a speedboat across to Ko Man Mai. It's pretty leisurely – you'll be expected to work two to three hours per day for four days a week – and in your downtime there are good beaches nearby to explore and relax on.

Ko Saket, a small island near Rayong, is a 20-minute boat ride from the beach of Hat Sai Thong (turn south off Hwy 3 at the Km 208 marker).

Suan Son (Pine Park), 5km further down the highway from Ban Phe, is a popular place for Thai picnickers.

Suan Wang Kaew is 11km east of Ban Phe and has more beaches, and **Ko Thalu**, across from Suan Wang Kaew, has good diving.

Other resort areas along the Rayong coast include **Laem Mae Phim** and **Hat Sai Thong**. **Hat Mae Rampeung**, a 10km strip of sand between Ban Taphong and Ban Kon Ao (11km east of Rayong), is also part of Laem Ya/Mu Ko Samet National Park. There are relatively frequent săwngthăew to all these beaches, leaving from the eastern edge of Ban Phe. At the weekend, they are busy with weekending Thais, but during the week you'll have them to yourself. Laem Mae Phim has the best range of options for eating and sleeping.

SLEEPING

Ko Man Klang and Ko Man Nok offer up-market accommodation packages that include boat transport from the mainland and all meals. These can only be arranged by phone in advance through Bangkok reservation numbers.

Ko Nok Island Resort (Bangkok office ☎ 0 2860 3025 www.munnorkislandresort.com; packages per person 3590-4190B; ✖) On Ko Man Nok, this classy resort has one-night, two-day packages in a variety of villas. The island is 15km off Pak Nam Prasae (53km east of Ban Phe).

Raya Island Resort (Bangkok office ☎ 0 2316 6717; 1-night, 2-day package per person 1400B; ✖ ✉) This comfortable place has 15 bungalows and plenty of hush. It is eight kilometres off Laem Mae Phim (27km east of Ban Phe), on Ko Man Klang.

GETTING THERE & AWAY

Public transport to the pier departure points for Ko Man Klang and Ko Man Nok can be arranged in Ban Phe. On weekends and holidays there may be săwngthăew out to the piers; otherwise charter a vehicle from the market for around 100B one way – arrange a pick-up for your return.

KO SAMET

เกาะเสม็ด

What happens when an island blessed with 14 white-sand beaches is just half a day's travel from a Southeast Asian super city? If it's pretty Ko Samet it becomes a weekend and holiday getaway for the good people of Bangkok – locals and expats alike. Toss in the fact that the island is unusually dry (it misses the worst impact of the monsoons) and you've got the geographic equivalent of Miss Popularity. Arrive on a weekend and you may be hit with rate hikes of up to 100%, and you could be

SOUTHEASTERN THAILAND

SOUTHEASTERN THAILAND

KO SAMET

ducking for cover from volleyballs and banana boats on certain beaches.

Ostensibly Ko Samet is a national park, but along the developed northeast coast it's hard to see where your 400B park entrance fee is being invested. The island's ecosystem is overtaxed and it is vital visitors play their part by conserving water and being mindful of rubbish.

If you're willing to venture further south, there are some undeniably gorgeous bays where development is still low-key and come with a relaxed traveller vibe. Ko Samet was originally a backpacker idyll, but accommodation is inching up the price chain, and many simple beach bungalows are being reborn as midrange or even luxury operations.

Weekends and holidays are undeniably fun, with Bangkok students fuelling the nightlife, and you're bound to leave with a whole swag of email addresses from your new Thai friends. Come on a relaxed weekday and the atmosphere will be less frantic, and you're more likely to discover what attracted the original backpackers a few short decades ago.

History

Ko Samet won a place in Thai literature when classical Thai poet Sunthorn Phu set part of his epic *Phra Aphaimani* on its shores. The story follows the travails of a prince exiled to an undersea kingdom ruled by a lovesick female giant. A mermaid aids the prince in his escape to Ko Samet, where he defeats the giant by playing a magic flute. Formerly Ko Kaew Phitsadan or 'Vast Jewel Isle' – a reference to the abundant white sand – this island became known as Ko Samet or 'Cajeput Isle' after the cajuput tree that grows in abundance here and is highly valued as firewood throughout Southeast Asia. Locally, the *samet* tree has also been used in boat building.

Orientation

Ko Samet is a T-shaped island. The best beaches and most development are located on the island's eastern shore. A few upmarket hotels are on the west coast, clustered around pretty Ao Prao bay. Na Dan, the island's biggest village and the terminus for the Ban Phe ferry, is on the north coast, facing the mainland. A few low-key sleeping options are on the north coast; it's nice and quiet but the beaches are not that flash.

Information

Ko Samet is a national park and the entrance fee (adult/child 400/200B) is collected at the main National Parks office – retain your ticket for inspection. .

There are three ATMs on Ko Samet, all attached to 7-Elevens. One is at the pier and the other two are near the National Parks office.

There are internet cafés on the road from Na Dan to Hat Sai Kaew; the best is Miss You Café (p248).

Around the island you can check your email at Jep's Bungalows (p246) and Naga's Bungalows (p246) in Ao Hin Hok, and at an unnamed spot at the southern end of Ao Tub Tim. All charge a steep 2B per minute.

A satellite phone for making international calls is located outside the National Parks office visitor centre.

Ko Samet Health Centre (☎ 0 3861 2999; ☒ 8.30am-8pm Mon-Fri, to 4.30pm Sat & Sun) On the main road between Na Dan and Hat Sai Kaew.

National Parks main office (between Na Dan and Hat Sai Kaew) Has another office on Ao Wong Doan.

Police station (☎ 1155) On the main road between Na Dan and Hat Sai Kaew.

Post office Naga's Bungalows in Ao Hin Khok acts as the island's post office; it also has a small range of secondhand books.

Samed Booking Center (☎ 0 3864 4247; ☒ 8.30am-5pm Mon-Fri, until noon Sat) Opposite the ferry terminal; makes transport and accommodation bookings.

Silver Sand (Ao Phai) Has an OK range of new books in the small, attached minimart.

Dangers & Annoyances

Ko Samet has been malarial in the past, and while the health centre now claims to have the problem under control, the island is infested with mosquitoes. Cover up and use buckets of repellent.

Ko Samet has a big collection of stray dogs. The crusty curs can be annoying when they park themselves nearby and stare longingly at your food.

Take care on the road leading away from the beach past Sea Breeze Bungalows in Ao Phai, as travellers have reported being robbed in this area.

Activities

Sailboards, boogie boards, inner tubes and snorkelling equipment can all be rented on the beaches at Hat Sai Kaew, Ao Hin Khok and Ao Phai. Dive operators run trips to nearby

sites; the best diving is at Hin Pholeung, halfway between Ko Samet and Ko Chang. This isolated spot is well away from destructive boat traffic and has two towering underwater rock pinnacles with excellent visibility (up to 30m). Here you can spot large pelagics like manta rays, barracuda, sharks and, if you're lucky, whale sharks.

Two reputable dive operations on the island are **Ploy Scuba Diving** in Hat Sai Kaew, and **Ao Prao Divers** (☎ 0 3864 4100-3; aopraodivers@hotmail .com), based at the Ao Prao Resort and Saikaew Villa.

Tours
Jimmy's Tours (☎ 08 9832 1627) runs tours around Ko Samet and the neighbouring islands. A six-hour boat tour (10am to 4pm) of the neighbouring islets, including the Turtle Conservation Centre (p243) on Ko Man Nai costs 1000B per person (minimum group size of 10 people).

Sleeping
Ko Samet is evolving. Luxury resorts are being built, simple bungalows are being redeveloped and prices are creeping up. Apart from the flash resorts on Ao Prao and Ao Kiu Na Nok (which charge around 15,000B for a villa), most places are around 350B for a simple bamboo hut and 2000B for an air-con bungalow.

We quote standard weekday rates, which *may* (it's all about supply and demand) as much as double in price during weekends and holidays. If you do turn up at the weekend, make sure you ask for the reduced weekly rate on the Monday – this reduction is often conveniently forgotten. If you come during the week, always ask for a discount. Most bungalows now provide 24-hour electricity and running water.

In the past many places did not take forward bookings, but that is changing and more places now have websites and email addresses. Note that for some of the more simple places, even if they have phones, they still may not take – or honour – bookings. Be prepared to be flexible, because your chosen accommodation may still operate on a first-come-first-served basis. There are offices and touts offering reservations in Ban Phe, but prices are inflated.

EAST COAST
The two most developed beaches are Hat Sai Kaew and Ao Wong Deuan. Most other beaches are still *relatively* quiet, but more resorts were under construction at the time of writing. Accommodation is listed from north to south.

Hat Sai Kaew
Known as 'Diamond Sand', this is the island's biggest and busiest beach. The sand here is white and relatively clean, but the seafront is lined with hotels, bars and restaurants. It's a favourite for Thais from Bangkok, and at the weekends expect a cacophony of jet skis and karaoke. Accommodation is solid but can be a tad functional.

Saikaew Villa (☎ 0 3864 4144; r 700-2550B; 🆒) Big rooms or small rooms, fan or air-con, Saikaew Villa conjures up a wide range of accommodation options amid a manicured space that (almost) goes too far with the holiday-camp atmosphere. Don't expect much privacy, but do expect food, drinks and activities all on tap.

Tonsak Resort (☎ 0 3864 4212; www.tonsak.com; r 2000-3000B; 🆒) At first the faux Wild West log-cabin styling seems odd, but inside the bungalows feel nice'n'natural, with comfy beds and stylish bathrooms. Just metres from the beach, the bar and restaurant is the perfect spot to get your Geronimojo back with a few cocktails.

Samed Grand View (☎ 0 3864 4220; www.grandview group.net; bungalow 2000-4000B; 🆒) You're paying more for being right on the island's most popular beach, but the white bungalows in a pretty garden are clean and undeniably central. There are also fan rooms from 600 to 800B, so you can save money and spend more time terrorising the beach on a banana boat.

Ao Hin Khok
At the south end of Hat Sai Kaew, statues of the prince and the mermaid from Sunthorn Phu's epic (see p245) gaze lovingly into each other's eyes. Ao Hin Khok begins here: a pretty stretch of sand, lined with trees and boulders. This is the island's traditional backpacker hub, and while the ambience is slowly moving upmarket, there's still loads of energy from independent travellers to make it a fun spot – especially after dark.

Naga's Bungalows (☎ 0 3864 4035; r 350-600B; 💻) Nowhere are Ao Hin Khok's backpacker creds more intact than at Naga's, with a range of fan rooms set into a forested hillside. Before or after a few drinks in the bar, the brave and/or

foolhardy can venture into Naga's own kick-boxing ring.

Tok's (☎ 0 3864 4072; r 300-800B; 🌐) Same, same, but different (there are some air-con rooms at Tok's). You'll need a torch after dark to negotiate the steep hillside to the simple bungalows – especially if you've been taking part in Tok's regular drinking games.

Jep's Bungalows (☎ 0 3864 4112; www.jepbungalow .com; r 600B-2600; 🌐 🖳) Spearheading the evolution of Ao Hin Khok, the long established Jep's offers rooms ranging from fan bungalows to air-con rooms with satellite TV. Despite the changes, a backpacker spirit lingers with nightly movies, and barbecues in the sea-front restaurant.

Ao Phai

Around the next headland Ao Phai is another shallow bay with a wide beach, but it can get crowded during the day. After dark, there's fun aplenty.

Silver Sand (☎ 08 6530 2147; www.silversandresort.com; s 300-800B, d 1200-2000B; 🌐) The white picket fences and manicured gardens look like a collision between *Desperate Housewives* and Disneyland, but the bungalows are clean and comfortable. Thankfully, the after-hours action in the Silver Sands bar can be a tad more disorderly.

Samed Villa (☎ 0 3864 4094; www.samedvilla.com; r 1800-2300B; 🌐) Exceedingly pleasant bungalows are cached within a riot of tropical vegetation offering a fair degree of seclusion. Unlike some other Thai resorts, the architects allocated a substantial budget to make the inside of some of the rooms as flash as the outside.

Ao Phutsa

Also known as Ao Tub Tim, this small and secluded beach is popular with return travellers and Bangkok expats.

Pudsa Bungalow (☎ 0 3864 4030; r 600-800B; 🌐) The nicer bungalows near the beach are trimmed with funky driftwood, but unfortunately are right beside the main footpath from Ao Phai to Ao Phutsa. You might have to put up with overhearing inane alcohol-fuelled conversations late at night. An OK backup if Tubtim is full.

Tubtim Resort (☎ 0 3864 4025; www.tubtimresort .com; r 900-1600B; 🌐) A range of bungalows, (air-con or cheaper ones with fans), fill a garden that's edging slowly towards jungle status. The restaurant is a good spot to dine with sand between your toes.

Ao Nuan

This tiny beach is the most secluded place to stay without having to go to the far south of the island.

Ao Nuan (r 500-700B) Simple wooden bungalows are concealed among vegetation on a rocky headland, and a funky gazebo/bar/restaurant is packed with books, board games and after dark beats. There's no phone and it doesn't take reservations. Bring along your mozzie repellent.

Ao Cho

A five-minute walk from Ao Nuan, Ao Cho is undergoing a minor renaissance with the opening of a new resort.

Ao Cho Grand View (☎ 0 3864 4219; www.grand viewgroup.net; d 2800B; 🌐 🖳) It's a bit prim and proper and the garden is overly manicured, but there's lots of friendly smiles from the helpful staff to soften the edges and make you feel at home.

Ao Wong Deuan

This crescent shaped bay has good nightlife with a chilled after-dark vibe, but your daytime soundtrack may be jet skis and speedboats. Ferries (70B each way) run to and from Ban Phe, with increased services at the weekend.

Blue Sky (☎ 08 1509 0547; r 600-800B; 🌐) One of the last budget spots on Ao Wong Deuan, Blue Sky has simple bungalows set on a rocky headland. The restaurant does tasty things with seafood, and there are a few tables for romantic seaside dining.

Samed Cabana (☎ 08 2260 3592; pariya@hotmail .com; r 2000B) At the quieter northern end of the beach, this has chic Asian stylings, with modern accents including polished concrete floors. With private decks under well-established trees, there's seclusion here from the bar hoppers at the other end of the bay.

Vongduern Villa (☎ 0 3865 2300; www.vongduernvilla .com; r 1200-2500B; 🌐) Sprawling along the bay's southern edge are bungalows, either near the beach or higher on the clifftop for better views. The Beach Front Bar is a sociable spot for sundowner cocktails, but romantic couples may prefer the subdued ambience of the Rock Front Restaurant.

Vongdeuan Resort (☎ 0 3865 1777; www.vongdeuan .com; r 2000-3500B; 🌐) The prettiest (and most expensive) options are Thai-style teak houses near the beach, but the concrete bungalows

further back are comfortable, and still allow you to partake of the lush gardens. Unfortunately the staff can be a bit surly.

Ao Thian

Better known by its English name, Candlelight Beach, Ao Thian has stretches of sand with rocky outcrops. To get here, catch a ferry to Ao Wong Deuan and walk south over the headland.

Candlelight Beach (☎ 08 9914 5585; bungalow 900-1200B; ✗) On the beach, these fan and air-con bungalows have a natural, woody ambience.

Lung Dam Apache (☎ 08 1659 8056; bungalow 900-1200B; ✗) These quirky bungalows look like they've been thrown together from marine debris. With a laid-back atmosphere, you may wish to become marooned for a few days yourself.

Sang Thian Beach Resort (☎ 0 3865 3210; www .sangthian.com; r 1500- 1800B; ✗) There's hill-top views from these up-scale bungalows, and a cosy bar/restaurant stands sentinel above a secluded cove. Larger groups will appreciate the bigger houses – 3500B for up to six people and 4000B for up to eight people.

Baan Thai Sang Thian Samed (☎ 08 1305 9408; r 1800-2500B; ✗) This new place, featuring traditional Thai architecture, represents the evolution of quiet Candlelight Beach away from its backpacker origins. Rooms are resplendent in natural wood and there's a proud heritage feel.

Ao Wai

The southern reaches of the island are still practically untouched, with only a couple of hotels spread over as many kilometres of coastline. Lovely Ao Wai is about 1km from Ao Thian, but can be reached from Ban Phe by chartered speedboat (300B).

Samet Ville Resort (☎ 0 3865 1682; www.sametville resort.com; r 980-3780B; ✗) Under a forest canopy, it's a case of 'spot the sky' at the very secluded Samet Ville. It's a romantic spot, but if you do have a fight with your loved one, take advantage of the water sports on offer and cool off in separate kayaks for the day. At dusk, patch things up over cocktails and subdued beats in the beachfront bar. There is a huge range of different fan and air-con rooms for all budgets.

Ao Kiu Na Nok

Further south, Ao Kiu Na Nok has the island's most upmarket accommodation.

Paradee Resort & Spa (☎ 0 2438 9771; www.samed resorts.com; villa 15,000B; ✗ ▢ ▣) The price tag is high, but you do get your own self-contained, beachfront villa on probably Ko Samet's best beach. There's gorgeous Thai furniture, a personal swimming pool/Jacuzzi, DVD player, espresso maker – even your own butler. A speedboat from Ban Phe can be arranged – don't even think about catching the ferry. Paradee is promoted as a 'couples only' resort.

AO PRAO

West-facing Ao Prao gets fabulous sunsets, and offers a smattering of chic hotels for the posh set. Speedboat transfers from the mainland are included (of course).

Ao Prao Resort (☎ 0 2438 9771; www.samedresorts .com; r from 5720B; ✗ ▢) This resort opened in the 1990s as the island's first luxury accommodation. It's holding its age well, with private bungalows cascading down a hill to the gorgeous beach. High ceilings create a spacious ambience and there is an excellent restaurant.

Ao Noi Na

Northwest of Na Dan, the beach at Ao Noi Na is only average, but there is a refreshing solitude with a couple of good places to stay.

Samed Resort (☎ 08 5871 1362; www.samed-resort .com; bungalow 600-800B, camping per person 250B) Has comfy fan bungalows and a fairly raucous bar doing its best to kick start an after-hours scene away from the bright lights of the east coast.

Baan Puu Paan (☎ 0 3864 4095; r 1000B; ✗) This English-run spot has a couple of stand-alone huts above the ocean at the end of a pier. Bring a big book – it's a good place to get away.

Eating & Drinking

Most places to stay have restaurants that moonlight as bars at sunset. The food won't blow you away, but it's OK value, with Thai and Western favourites for around 80B to 130B. Most choice is on Hat Sai Kaew, Ao Hin Khok, Ao Pha and Ao Wong Deuan, but hotels on the remote stretches make sure you won't go to bed hungry. Look for nightly beach barbecues, particularly along Ao Hin Khok and Ao Phai.

Drinking-wise, many places offer nightly 'toss-a-coin' promotions. Basically heads or tails decides if you end up paying for your drink or not. Another favourite is a shared

cocktail bucket of Sangsom rum or Mekhong whiskey. Ao Wong Deuan is slightly more upmarket, but not much.

For seriously cheap eats, check out the food stalls which set up in the late afternoon on the road between Na Dan and Hat Sai Kaew.

Safari Noodle Stand (noodles 35B; ☯ lunch & dinner) This mobile noodle stand plies the road between Na Dan and Ao Phai, serving up delicious meals.

Miss You Café (coffee 40-90B; ☯ breakfast, lunch & dinner; ☒ ▢) Located beside the National Parks main office, this spot has 13 different kinds of coffee, and almost as many variations on cake and ice cream. Have a latté as you hitch your laptop to its wi-fi network.

Rabeang Bar (Na Dan; dishes 30-100B; ☯ breakfast, lunch & dinner) Right by the ferry terminal, this over the water spot has good waiting-for-the-next-boat-to-the-mainland kind of food.

Jep's (☎ 0 3864 4112; Ao Hin Khok; dishes 40-150B; ☯ breakfast, lunch & dinner) With Thai, Indian, Mexican and European food, you should find something you like at this sand-between-the-toes spot that also does regular beach barbecues. If not, there are always the drinks specials that may have you imitating the scurrying squirrels in the palm trees above.

Naga's Bar (☎ 0 3864 4035; Ao Hin Khok; dishes 60-150B) Next door to Tok's, and same, same but slightly different, with the addition of kick-boxing bouts in its own ring.

Tok's Little Bar (☎ 0 3864 4072; Ao Hin Khok; dishes 60-150B) With sticks'n'straw décor, a few locals who fancy themselves as ladykillers, and nightly drinking games, you won't mistake this place for a sophisticated cocktail bar.

Silver Sand Bar (☎ 0 6530 2417; Ao Phai; dishes 60-180B; ☯ breakfast, lunch & dinner) As well as a regular menu, Silver Sand offers fresh crepes (sweet and savoury), a juice bar and nightly movies. Once the movies end, the action progresses (regresses?) to cocktail buckets, and reluctant dancing to all those '80s classics you're ashamed to know the words to. There is even a burger bar to appease the midnight munchies.

Baywatch Bar (☎ 08 1826 7834; Ao Wong Deuan; kebabs 190-290B; ☯ breakfast, lunch & dinner) With chill-out platforms and Asian umbrellas, this place deserves a visit from the 'Hoff' himself. There's Thai and Western food, including huge kebabs. After a couple of the robust cocktails, overcome the urge to run in slow motion down the beach. At the time of writing, Baywatch was planning to offer European cheeses, fresh bread and freshly brewed coffee for breakfast.

Getting There & Away
BOAT
To Ko Samet

Ferries (one way/return 50/100B, 40 minutes) depart throughout the day from Ban Phe's Saphan Nuan Tip pier – opposite the 7-Eleven, where the buses and săwngthăew stop. Tickets can be bought from a small **tourist information center** (☎ 0 3889 6155; ☯ 7am-5pm) on the pier itself.

From Ban Phe, three scheduled ferries (9.30am, 1.30pm, 5pm) also make the run to Ao Wong Deuan (one way/return 70/110B, one hour). In the high season boats run to other bays if enough people show an interest. Ignore the touts that congregate around the ferry terminal, as they charge inflated prices for boat tickets and will hassle you into pre-booking expensive accommodation – just go straight to the ticket office.

Alternatively, you can charter a speedboat to any of the island's beaches. They are quite expensive (1200B to Na Dan or 1600B to Ao Wai), but they take up to 10 passengers for this price, so it's worthwhile if you're travelling in a group.

From Ko Samet

Ferries (one way/return 50/100B) return to Ban Phe from the pier in Na Dan hourly from 7am to 5pm – buy your ticket at the pier. There are also three scheduled ferries per day from Ao Wong Deuan (one way/return 70/110B; 8.30am, midday, 4pm).

To get off Ko Samet in a hurry, charter a speedboat. Ask at your hotel, or call **Jimmy's Tours** (☎ 08 9832 1627). Prices start at 1200B from Na Dan.

BUS

Air-con buses to Rayong (146B, 2½ hours, every 30 minutes) leave Bangkok's Eastern (Ekmai) bus terminal from 4am to 10pm. Air-con buses direct to Ban Phe (167B, three hours, hourly) leave Ekmai hourly from 5am to 8.30pm and return from 4am to 6.30pm. Buses to Chanthaburi from Rayong bus station cost 90B and take about 2½ hours. From Pattaya to Rayong, flag down a southbound bus near the corner of Th Sukhumvit and Th Pattaya Neua (ordinary/air-con 60/93B, 1½

SOUTHEASTERN THAILAND

hours). Săwngthăew from Rayong bus station to Ban Phe cost 20B.

Slightly more straightforward, but also more expensive, are the tourist minivans that run to/from Ban Phe and other traveller destinations: Pattaya (200B per person); Th Khao San in Bangkok (250B per person); and the Laem Ngop pier, the departure point for Ko Chang (300B per person). These can be booked through guesthouses on Ko Samet, the travel agencies near the 7-Eleven opposite the ferry terminal in Ban Phe, or through travel agencies in Pattaya.

Getting Around

Ko Samet's small size makes it a great place to explore on foot. A network of dirt roads connects the western beach and most of the southern bays, while walking trails snake over the boulders and headlands that separate beaches all the way to the southernmost tip.

It's only a 15-minute walk from Na Dan to Hat Sai Kaew, but if you are carting luggage or want to go further, săwngthăew meet arriving boats at the pier and provide drop-offs down the island. Set fares for transport from Na Dan are posted on a tree in front of Na Dan harbour. Nobody takes them that seriously, but you shouldn't have to pay much more than 20B to 50B. If drivers don't have enough people to fill the vehicle, they either won't go or they will charge passengers 200B to 500B to charter the whole vehicle. There is another săwngthăew stop behind the beach on Ao Wong Deuan.

Motorcycles can be rented in Na Dan and at most bungalows on Hat Sai Kaew, Ao Phai and Ao Phrao. Expect to pay about 300B per day or an hourly rate of 100B. The dirt roads are rough and quite hilly – you may want to walk or rent a mountain bike (50B per hour) instead.

CHANTHABURI PROVINCE

CHANTHABURI

จันทบุรี

pop 147,000

The so-called 'City of the Moon' is proof that all that glitters is not gold. Here, gemstones do the sparkling, and if traders get the deal right, the glimmer infuses their pockets with healthy profits. Buyers from across Southeast Asia come to Chanthaburi to deal in sapphires and rubies, and from Friday to Sunday the city is bustling and cosmopolitan. On other days the city breathes out, and a diverse history including French, Chinese and Vietnamese influences echoes around the quiet riverside lanes to provide a calming remedy to the push and shove of its more mercantile face.

History

The city's Vietnamese community began arriving in the 19th century, when Christian refugees escaped religious and political persecution in Cochin China (southern Vietnam). A second wave followed in the 1920s and 1940s, fleeing French rule, and a third arrived after the 1975 communist takeover of southern Vietnam. From 1893 to 1905, while negotiating with the Siamese over the borders for Laos and Cambodia, the French occupied Chanthaburi, stamping their own identity on the town as well.

Orientation

Th Si Chan, running parallel to the river, is Chanthaburi's commercial heart and famed gem shops can be around this thoroughfare. The bus station and King Taksin Park are about 800m west.

Information

Banks with change facilities and ATMs can be found across town.

Bank of Ayudhya (Th Khwang)

Chanthaburi Hospital (☎ 0 3932 1378; Th Saritidet; ⏱ 6am-9pm)

Internet & Game (134 Th Si Chan; per hr 20B; ⏱ 9am-10pm)

Sights & Activities

Peering through magnifying glasses and peddling their wares from stalls along Th Si Chan and Th Thetsaban 4, the city's **gem dealers** are Chanthaburi's living, breathing highlight. All day Friday and Saturday, and on Sunday mornings, the surrounding streets are overflowing with the banter and intrigue of the hard sell. You'll be offered the 'deal of a lifetime', but walk away unless you really know what you're doing. This is strictly a spectator sport, and they probably saw you coming when you first arrived at the bus station. Great deals can be clinched by the savvy, but amateurs are likely to go home with a bagful of worthless rocks. You're better off filling up at the food stalls surrounding the commercial bustle; there'll be more guarantee of satisfaction. If you re-

ally feel the urge to buy, plenty of air-con gem shops offer pricier but less risky deals.

The Vietnamese and French have left an indelible stamp on Chanthaburi. Creaking **shop houses** run alongside the river on Th Rim Nam and garish **Chinese temples** punctuate the town. The French-style **cathedral** (daylight), across a footbridge from Th Rim Nam, is the architectural highlight. A small missionary chapel was built here in 1711, but after undergoing four reconstructions between 1712 and 1906 (the last by the French), the structure is now the largest building of its kind in Thailand.

King Taksin Park (24hr) is the town's main oasis and is filled with picnicking families. Judging by some of the expressions on show, that includes a few who have lost out on the gem market. It's a pleasant spot for a quiet, thoughtful stroll.

Four kilometres north of town off Rte 3249 is **Khao Phloi Waen** (Sapphire-Ring Mountain; admission free; daylight hr), which is only 150m high but features a Sri Lankan-style *chedi* on top, built during the reign of Rama IV. Tunnels dug into the side of the hill were once gem-mining shafts.

Wat Khao Sukim (daylight) doubles as a local meditation centre and is 16km north of Chanthaburi, off Rte 3322. The **museum** (donation appreciated; daylight) on the wat (temple) grounds contains valuable items donated to the temple, such as jade carvings, ceramics and antique furniture, as well as resin figures of some of Thailand's most revered monks.

Festivals

During early December every year there is a **gem festival**, when Chanthaburi gets very crowded. Highlights of the festival include jewellery shows and a gem-design competition. In the first week of June each year, Chanthaburi's annual fruit festival is a good opportunity to sample the region's superb produce.

Sleeping

Accommodation can get busy. Try and book ahead, especially from Friday to Sunday when the gem traders are in town.

River Guest House (0 3932 8211; Th Si Chan 3/5-8; r 150-350B;) Chanthaburi's real gems are the friendly team who run this relaxed place

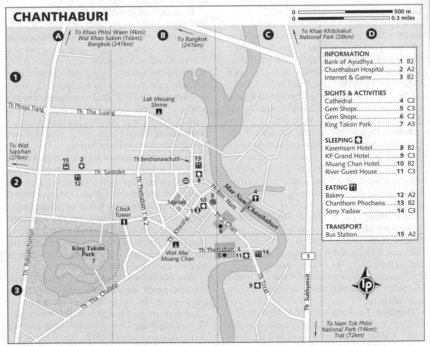

CHANTHABURI

INFORMATION	
Bank of Ayudhya	1 B2
Chanthaburi Hospital	2 A2
Internet & Game	3 B2

SIGHTS & ACTIVITIES	
Cathedral	4 C2
Gem Shops	5 C3
Gem Shops	6 C2
King Taksin Park	7 A3

SLEEPING	
Kasemsarn Hotel	8 B2
KP Grand Hotel	9 C3
Muang Chan Hotel	10 B2
River Guest House	11 C3

EATING	
Bakery	12 A2
Chanthorn Phochana	13 B2
Sony Yadaw	14 C3

TRANSPORT	
Bus Station	15 A2

To Khao Phloi Waen (4km); Wat Khao Sukim (16km); Bangkok (241km)

To Bangkok (241km)

To Khao Khitchakut National Park (28km)

0   500 m
0   0.3 miles

Th Phraya Trang

Lak Meuang Shrine

Th Tha Luang

To Wat Sapchan (27km)

Th Benchamarachutit

Th Santidet

Th Thetsaban 1 & 2

Market

Clock Tower

Mae Nam Chanthaburi

Th Rim Nam

Th Si Chan

Th Khwang

King Taksin Park 7

Wat Mai Muang Chan

Th Thetsaban 4

Th Tha Chalaep

Th Raksakchamun

Th Tirat

Th Sukhumvit

To Nam Tok Phlio National Park (14km); Trat (72km)

beside the river. The air-con rooms at the front are a bit noisy, so if you're happy with a fan ask for a room at the back. Downstairs is a good restaurant which does it best to overcome its proximity to the town's busiest bridge.

Muang Chan Hotel (☎ 0 3932 1073; fax 0 3932 7244; Th Si Chan 257-259; r 230-600B; 🗙) Grey and labyrinthine from the outside, but relatively clean and quiet inside, this is an OK backup if River Guest House is full.

KP Grand Hotel (☎ 0 3932 3201; www.kpgrandhotel .com; 35/200-201 Th Trirat; r incl breakfast 1200B; 🗙 ☐ ☎) In reception the air-con is cranked up to cryogenic levels, and there are enough faux chandeliers to seriously challenge the bling bartering the town's known for. Rooms are spacious and comfortable; proof your baht goes further off the tourist trail.

Kasemsarn Hotel (☎ 0 3931 1100; kasemsarnhotel@ yahoo.com; Th Benchamarachutit 98/1; r 1300-1500B; 🗙) This renovated hotel in the town centre drips designer Asian cool in reception, but the rooms are more functional. With discounts of up to 45% during the week it's still good value – even if you lose your shirt in a dodgy gem deal.

Eating

To try the famous Chanthaburi *kŭaytĭaw sên jan* (noodles), head for the Chinese–Vietnamese part of town along Mae Nam Chanthaburi where you'll see variations on the basic rice-noodle theme, including delicious crab with fried noodles. You'll find food stalls around the gem trading area. Fruit harvested locally is famous throughout Thailand. Get to the market early for the best selection.

Bakery (33-35 Th Saritidet; coffee 30B, snacks 15-30B; 🕑 breakfast, lunch & dinner) This popular spot up the road from the bus station is especially good for breakfast. Combine an iced coffee with a coconut bun filled with creamy sweet corn. Trust us – it's a winning combination of sweet and savoury.

Sony Yadaw (Th Si Chan; dishes 30-100B; 🕑 breakfast, lunch & dinner) Many Indian and Sri Lankan gem dealers come to Chanthaburi to trade, and this tiny hole-in-the-wall vegetarian restaurant is their home away from home. Luckily the friendly Indian owner will also sell you a Heineken, so you don't have to be too healthy and righteous.

Chanthorn Phochana (☎ 0 3931 2339; Th Benchamarachutit 102/5-8; dishes 30-120B; 🕑 breakfast, lunch & dinner) A dazzling array of Thai and Chinese

meals includes such specialities as stir-fried papaya and local mangosteen wine. Try the Vietnamese spring rolls, and buy a bag of a local durian chips (tastier than you think) for your next bus ride.

Getting There & Away

Buses operate between Chanthaburi and Bangkok's Eastern bus terminal (187B, 4½ hours) every half hour throughout the day and less frequently at night. Buses also travel to Rayong (90B, 2½ hours, five daily) and Trat (70B, 1½ hours, hourly).

If you have your own set of wheels, take Rte 317 north to Sa Kaew, then along Hwy 33 west to Kabinburi and Rte 304 north to Khorat. From Sa Kaew you can head eastwards and reach Aranya Prathet on the Thailand–Cambodia border after 46km. From this border crossing you can take a share taxi from Poipet on the Cambodian side of the border to Siem Reap (near Angkor Wat).

AROUND CHANTHABURI

Two small national parks are within an hour's drive of Chanthaburi. Both are malarial, so take the usual precautions.

Khao Khitchakut National Park (☎ 0 3945 2074; reserve@dnp.go.th; admission 400B; 🕑 8.30am-4.30pm) is 28km northeast of town off Rte 3249 and is known for Nam Tok Krathing waterfall. It's one of Thailand's smallest national parks (59 sq km) although the unprotected forest surrounding the park is much larger and is said to harbour herds of wild elephants. There's a series of trails to the falls nearest the park headquarters, but visitors are discouraged from going deeper into the forest without being accompanied by a ranger.

Park **accommodation** (reserve@dnp.go.th; ☎ 0 2562 0760) is available in a camp site (50B per person) or in a 2-person bungalow (600B per room). Phone or email ahead for bookings.

To get to Khao Khitchakut by public transport, take a săwngthăew from the northern side of the market in Chanthaburi (40B, 45 minutes). The săwngthăew stops 1.5km from the park headquarters on Rte 3249, from which point you'll have to walk.

Nam Tok Phlio National Park (☎ 0 3943 4528; reserve@dnp.go.th; admission 400B; 🕑 8.30am-4.30pm), off Hwy 3, is 14km to the southeast of Chanthaburi and features many waterfalls, Phra Nang Ruar Lom stupa (c 1876) and the Along Khon *chedi* (c 1881).

Accommodation is available in a camp site (site 10B, plus 50B per person) or in a 6-person bungalow (1800B per room). Phone or email **park reservations** (reserve@dnp.go.th; ☎ 0 2562 0760) for bookings.

To get to the park, catch a săwngthăew from the northern side of the market in Chanthaburi to the park entrance (30B, 30 minutes).

The River Guest House (p251) is a good source of up-to-date information on the two border crossings.

TRAT PROVINCE

In Trat Province, gem trading is a favoured method of putting rice on the table – unsurprisingly, *tàlàat phloi* (gem markets) abound. A by-product of this gem mining has been the destruction of vast tracts of land, as the topsoil is stripped away, leaving hectares of red-orange mud.

But there's plenty more to fire your imagination. Before you head to the beaches of rugged Ko Chang or its more delicate and subdued island neighbours, linger in the traditional riverside ambience of Trat. If you're in no hurry to travel west to Cambodia, then relax on the expansive beaches that run lazily down the coast to the border. Hat Sai Si Ngoen, Hat Sai Kaew, Hat Thap Thim and Hat Ban Cheun are all worth a look.

At the Km 70 marker, off Rte 318, is Jut Chom Wiw (Lookout Point), where you can survey the surrounding area, including Cambodia. Trat Province's southeasternmost point is Hat Lek, the transit point for trips along the Cambodian coast.

TRAT

ตราด

pop 23,000

For too many travellers, all they see of Trat is the shiny new bus station before they are shunted onto a săwngthăew to the Ko Chang ferry, or a minibus west to the Cambodian border at Hat Lek.

But if you linger for at least a night, the town's relaxed appeal takes hold. Meandering pedestrian alleys are lined with century-old teak houses filled with traveller friendly guesthouses and restaurants, and you'll spend longer than you realise at the bustling markets.

If you're heading to Ko Chang, ignore the touts at the bus station advising you to hurry to catch the 'last ferry' to the island. If you do catch the last ferry, then expect the cost of your săwngthăew from the pier in Ko Chang to be inflated. With Trat's guesthouses such good value, you're better off staying at least one night (don't miss the night market) and continuing your journey in the morning.

Orientation & Information

Across the lane from Tratosphere Books is Wan Laundry, if you need to get spruced up before heading to Ko Chang. It can turn a load around in three hours for 30B per kilo.

Trat's new bus station is around 1.5km north of the centre of town. A săwngthăew or motorbike taxi to the guesthouse area will cost around 20B.

Bangkok Trat Hospital (☎ 0 3953 2735; Th Sukhumvit; ☼ 24hr) Best health care in the region. It's 400m north of the town centre.

Koh Chang New Travel Agency (☎ 0 3953 1135; Th Sukhumvit; ☼ 8am-5pm)

Krung Thai Bank (Th Sukhumvit) Has an ATM and currency-exchange facilities.

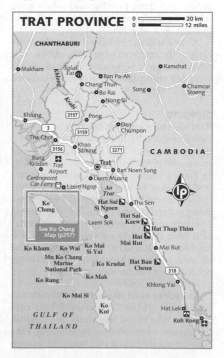

TRAT PROVINCE

0 —— 20 km
0 —— 12 miles

CHANTHABURI

Makham • Salak Tai • Ban Pa-Ah • Kamchat
Chang Thun • Song • Chamcar Stoeng
Bo Rai • Nong Si
Khlung • 3157 • Pong • Dan Chumpon
3 • 3159
Tha Chot • 3156 • Khao Saming • 3271 • CAMBODIA
Bang Kradan • Trat Airport • Trat • Ban Noen Sung
Centrepoint Car Ferry • Laem Ngop • Laem Muang • Ao Trat
Ko Chang • Hat Sai Si Ngoen • Tha Sen
Laem Sok • Hat Sai Kaew
See Ko Chang Map (p257) • Hat Thap Thim
Ko Kham • Ko Wai • Ko Mai Si Yai • Hat Mai Rut • Mai Rut
Mu Ko Chang Marine National Park • Ko Kradat • Hat Ban Cheun • 318
Ko Rang • Ko Mak • Khlong Yai
Ko Mai Si
GULF OF THAILAND • Ko Kut • Hat Lek • Koh Kong

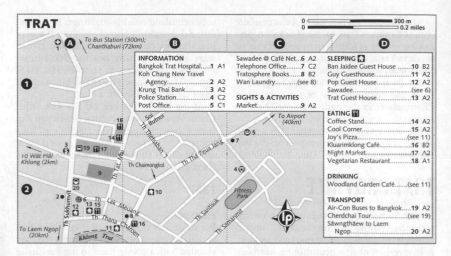

TRAT

Police station (☎ 1155; cnr Th Santisuk & Th Wiwatthana) Located a short walk from Trat's centre.

Post office (Th Tha Reua Jang) East of Trat's commercial centre.

Sawadee @ Café Net (☎ 0 3952 0075; Th Lak Meuang; per min 1B; ☼ 10am-10pm) Internet & Skype are both available.

Telephone office (Th Tha Reua Jang) Located near the post office.

Tratosphere Books (Rimklong Soi 23; ☼ 8am-10pm) Has second-hand English-language titles. Owner Serge is a good source of information about Ko Kut, Ko Wai and Ko Mak, and can book island accommodation for you.

Sights

Wat Plai Khlong (Wat Bupharam; ☼ 9am-5pm) offers a quiet (during the week) retreat from the bustle of central Trat. Several of the wooden buildings date to the late-Ayuthaya period, including the *wíhaan* (large hall), bell tower and *kùtì* (monks' quarters). The *wíhaan* contains sacred relics and Buddha images dating from the Ayuthaya period and earlier. It is 2km west of the centre.

Trat is overpopulated with **markets**. The day market beneath the municipal shopping centre off Th Sukhumvit, the old day market off Th Tat Mai, and another nearby day market are all worth a look. The latter becomes an excellent night market in the evening.

Trat is famous for *náam-man lěuang* (yellow oil) a herb-infused liquid touted as a remedy for everything from arthritis to stomach upsets. It's produced by a resident, Mae Ang-Ki (Somthawin Pasananon), using a secret

pharmaceutical recipe that has been handed down through her Chinese-Thai family for generations. It's said if you leave Trat without a couple of bottles of *náam-man lěuang*, then you really haven't been to Trat. This stuff really works! Put a couple of drops on your palms, rub them together and take a good whiff. It's also great for aches and pains, and is available at pharmacies across town.

A new **walkway** has been erected on the river at the southern edge of the old town. It provides a good perspective of life along the river, but unfortunately has been constructed in ugly concrete.

Sleeping

Trat has many cheap hotels housed in traditional wooden buildings on and around Th Thana Charoen. You'll find it hard to spend more even if you want to. Guesthouse owners in Trat are becoming increasingly competitive and you may be met by a scrum at the bus station. There have been reports of travellers being offered air-con rooms, but then having to accept cheaper, more budget accommodation once they were delivered to the guesthouse. Ask the touts to ring their guesthouse for you, and try and speak to reception to get an assurance that the room type being offered is actually available.

Ban Jaidee Guest House (☎ 0 3952 0678; 6 Th Chaimongkol; r 120-150B) This relaxed Thai-style home is one of the best deals in Thailand. The simple rooms share a bathroom and the whole place is finished with beautiful wooden

objects (handmade by one of the artistically inclined owners), green foliage and moody lighting. It's very popular and booking ahead is essential.

Guy Guest House (☎ 0 3952 3389; guy.gh2001@gmail .com; Th Thana Charoen 82/86; r 100-400B; 🖭 🖵) Guy Guest House is your next best bet if you really need air-con. Some rooms could be a tad cleaner, but there's a friendly traveller vibe and the owners can book transport for your onward journey. Cheaper fan rooms are also available.

Pop Guest House (☎ 0 3951 2392; popson1958@hotmail .com; Th Thana Charoen 1/1; r 100-500B; 🖭 🖵) The forever expanding Pop operation is testament to the satisfaction of past travellers at this friendly spot, with lots of rooms at different prices. The best rooms are beside the river, but bring your mozzie repellent. You'll be made to feel at home in the attached restaurant and beer garden. Good luck in getting the owner's kids to switch from Animal Planet on the restaurant's TV though.

Other recommendations:

Sawadee (☎ 0 3952 0075; sawadee_Trat@yahoo.com; 90 Th Lak Meuang; r 100-3000B) Simple, but fastidiously clean, fan rooms with shared bathroom.

Trat Guest House (☎ 0 3951 1152; 4 Soi Khunpoka, Th Lak Meuang; r 80-120B) Super-simple and super-friendly accommodation in an old teak house with interesting nooks and crannies.

Eating & Drinking

With all the markets in Trat, you're usually just metres from something tasty. The **indoor market** beneath the shopping centre has a food section, with cheap noodle and rice dishes from early morning to early evening. Grab a cheap breakfast at the ancient **coffee stand** in the old day market on Th Tat Mai.

In the evenings, visit the **night market** (advertised confidently as 'Food Safety Street') or a **vegetarian restaurant** (dishes 20B; 🕑 6am-11am) down a nearby lane, offering tasty veggie food at knockdown prices from the crack of dawn. It closes as soon as the food is gone – usually well before midday.

Joy's Pizza (☎ 0 3952 2551; 49-51 Th Thana Charoen; pizzas 115-150B; 🕑 lunch & dinner) When he's not turning out pizzas, Dutch owner Alex keeps himself busy dispensing essential travellers information, and maintaining just maybe Southeast Asia's biggest collection of music MP3s. The restaurant doubles as a gallery for the quirky installations and paintings created by Joy, his Thai wife.

Kluarimklong Café (☎ 0 3952 4919; Soi Rimklong; dishes 70-90B; 🕑 breakfast, lunch & dinner; 🖭) The winning combination here is delicious Thai food served in modern surroundings that could (almost) be New York. It's popular with local bigwigs so if you see a couple of flash cars outside and a few bouncers at the door, it's probably closed for a 'private function'. Hey, there's always the night market – one of Thailand's best.

Other recommendations:

Cool Corner (☎ 08 6156 4129; Th Thana Charoen; dishes 50-150B; 🕑 breakfast, lunch & dinner) Traveller central with mellow beats, English-language magazines, fruit shakes & huge cooked breakfasts – ideally all at the same time.

Woodland Garden Café (53 Th Thana Charoen; 🕑 6pm-midnight) Your best bet for cocktails and cold beers. Food is dangerously restricted to ice-cream sundaes, and most nights you'll find Trat's band of expats in good form.

Getting There & Away
BANGKOK

Bangkok Airways (☎ in Bangkok 0 2265 5555, Trat Airport 0 3952 5767; www.bangkokair.com) flies three times a day to/from Trat and Bangkok (one way/return 2550/5100B). The airport is 40km from town; minibuses and taxis meet all flights. In the high season booking ahead is highly recommended. At the time of writing there were rumours of a new route linking Trat with Ko Samui. Check the website for details.

Cherdchai Tour (☎ 0 3951 1062; Th Sukhumvit; 🕑 7am-11pm) runs hourly from Trat's bus station to Bangkok's Eastern bus terminal (Ekmai) and Northern bus terminal (Mo Chit), both 5½ hours, with fares 223B to 257B. Buses from Bangkok to Trat depart with the same frequency. Cherdchai provides a free shuttle from its office to the Trat bus station. Note that most Mo Chit buses also stop at Bangkok's Suvarnabhumi Airport, so if you're leaving Thailand you don't need to double back to Bangkok. At the bus station, **Suparat Tour** (☎ 3951 1481) also offer services to Ekmai and Mo Chit.

Ordinary government buses make the run to/from Bangkok's Eastern bus terminal for 188B, departing on an hourly basis.

CHANTHABURI

Cherdchai and Suparat's air-con Bangkok bus services also stop in Chanthaburi (70B, 1¼ hours).

HAT LEK & LAEM NGOP

Direct minibuses from Trat to Hat Lek (110B, one hour) leave every 45 minutes from the bus station. Săwngthăew (50B) also trundle from the bus station to Hat Lek, but you will have to wait for enough people to show up.

Săwngthăew for Laem Ngop and Centrepoint Pier (40B to 60B) leave Trat from a stand on Th Sukhumvit, next to the municipal shopping centre market, and also from the bus station. They depart regularly throughout the day, but after dark you will have to charter one (250B).

Getting Around

Săamláw (three-wheeled pedicabs) around town should cost 15B per person.

AROUND TRAT

Beaches

The sliver of Trat Province that extends southeast along the Cambodian border is fringed by several Gulf of Thailand beaches. **Hat Sai Si Ngoen** (Silver Sand Beach) lies just north of the Km 41 marker off Hwy 3. Nearby, at the Km 42 marker, is **Hat Sai Kaew** (Crystal Sand Beach) and at the Km 48 marker, **Hat Thap Thim** (also known as Hat Lan); they're OK to walk along the water's edge or picnic in the shade of casuarina and eucalyptus trees. The only place for accommodation here is the **Sun Sapha Kachat Thai** (Thai Red Cross; ☎ 0 3950 1015; r 800B), which has comfortable bungalows with all the usual amenities and a restaurant.

There is accommodation at **Hat Ban Cheun**, a long stretch of clean sand near the Km 63 marker. The 6km road that leads to the beach passes a defunct Cambodian refugee camp. There are casuarina and eucalyptus trees, a small restaurant and basic bungalows (300B) set on swampy land behind the beach.

Laem Ngop

แหลมงอบ

Laem Ngop is the jumping-off point for Ko Chang (see p267). **TAT** (☎ 0 3959 7259; tattrat@tat .or.th; 100 Mu 1, Th Trat-Laem Ngop; ☉ 8.30am-4.30pm) has an information office right near the pier. Further north on the road to Trat there is an **immigration office** (☎ 0 3959 7261; Th Trat-Laem Ngop; ☉ 8.30am-noon & 1-4.30pm Mon-Fri), where you can apply for visa extensions.

Between the two, **Kasikornbank** (Th Trat-Laem Ngop) has an exchange counter.

SLEEPING & EATING

There's usually no reason to stay here, as there are regular boats to Ko Chang during the day and Trat is only 20km away. If you do get stuck, try **Laem Ngop Inn** (☎ 0 3959 7044; s/d 300/600B; ❷), with a choice of simple air-con and fan rooms. It's a five- to seven- minute walk on the road to Trat.

Near the pier in Laem Ngop are several seafood **eateries** with views of the sea and islands.

GETTING THERE & AWAY

Săwngthăew for Laem Ngop and Centrepoint Pier (40B to 60B) leave Trat from a stand on Th Sukhumvit next to the municipal shopping centre market, and also from the bus station. They depart regularly throughout the day, but after dark you will have to charter one (around 250B). From Bangkok there are two buses per day at 7.30am and 9.30am from Bangkok's Eastern bus terminal direct to the Centrepoint Pier (250B, six hours). Many travel agencies in Bangkok also advertise VIP buses (480B, 5½ hours) direct to the pier which have the (expensive) advantage of more legroom and a pick-up from your accommodation in the capital. Travel agents at Tha Laem Ngop arrange a daily 11am minibus to Th Khao San in Bangkok (250B to 300B, 5½ hours), a 1pm minibus to Pattaya (350B, four hours) and 11am and 1pm minibuses to Ban Phe for Ko Samet (300B, 2½ hours).

HAT LEK TO CAMBODIA

The small Thai border outpost of **Hat Lek** is the southernmost part on the Trat mainland. There's not much here apart from a small market just before the border crossing, and loads of touts to guide you through border protocols.

Motorcycle and automobile taxis are available from Hat Lek into Cambodia for 50B. There is accommodation on the island of Krong Koh Kong in Cambodia, but little to keep you there. If you plan to continue further, you can embark on a four-hour boat ride (US$15) to Sihanoukville. There is only one boat per day to Sihanoukville and it leaves at 8am, so if you don't get across the border early you'll have to spend a night on Koh Kong. Basically, if you want to get from Trat to Sihanoukville in one day on the boat, you should be on the 6am minibus to Hat Lek and at the border with passport in hand as soon as it opens at 7am. From Koh Kong, there are

also minibuses that go to Sihanoukville (550B) and Phnom Penh (650B); both leave at 9am.

Cambodian tourist visas (1200B) are available at the border (bring a passport photo), but you should check with the Cambodian embassy in Bangkok before heading out there. Despite Cambodian tourist visas costing US$20 at other borders, payment is only accepted in baht (1200B) at this border. If you try and debate the issue, be prepared for a frustrating time.

If you are going into Cambodia for a day trip, you may need a valid Thai visa to return to Thailand. Nowadays Thailand grants most nationalities a one-month visa on arrival. If your nationality is not on the instant-visa list, you will find yourself stuck in Cambodia. This border crossing closes at 8pm.

See p255 for transport information to Hat Lek.

KO CHANG & AROUND
อุทยานแห่งชาติเกาะช้าง

Rising like a rugged, verdant leviathan from the waters near Cambodia, Ko Chang is fast becoming an essential stop on the Thai tourist trail. Earmarked as the 'next Phuket' a few short years ago, development has transformed swathes of the island's west coast and expansion is now beginning to stud other more isolated areas of Thailand's second largest island. But escape to Ko Chang's mountainous interior and you'll find a lost world of rugged waterfalls and impenetrable jungle filled with a Noah's ark of wildlife, including stump-tailed

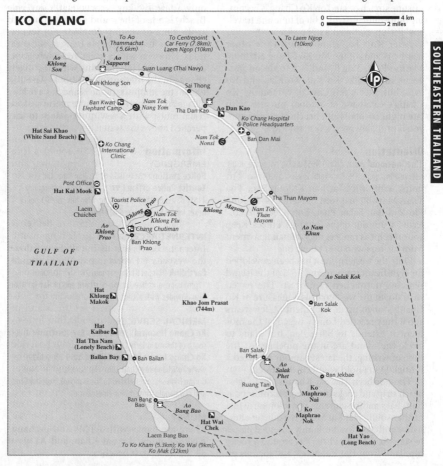

KO CHANG

macaques, small Indian civets and reticulated pythons. Emerge from the forest and you'll reach isolated lookouts which gaze down on beaches just made for wannabe Crusoes. And if your time on other Thai islands has included just a few too many days laying on the beach, on Ko Chang you can get nicely active and brush off any holiday cobwebs.

After all that honest exercise, recharge in an increasingly cosmopolitan range of bars and restaurants, and relax in accommodation that stretches from basic beach bungalows to luxury five-star resorts. Each of Ko Chang's beaches has a different style, from the family-friendly ambience of Hat Sai Khao and Hat Kai Mook, to the perfect party vibe of Lonely Beach (Hat Tha Nam). And while it's true that finding a pristine stretch of sand on Ko Chang is becoming more difficult, with a bit of time and travellers' get-up-and-go it's still possible.

After Ko Chang, move on to the other nearby islands of the Mu Ko Chang National Marine Park. You'll find less to do on gorgeous islands like Ko Kut, Ko Mak and Ko Wai, but after a few days of combining Ko Chang's catalogue of outdoor pursuits with late night cocktails and beachside barbecues, you'll probably need a rest anyway.

Orientation

The **national park** (☎ 0 3955 5080; entry fee 400B; reserve@dnp.go.th; ☼ 8am-5pm) is divided into four units, with offices at Ban Khlong Son, Tha Than Mayom, just west of Nam Tok Khlong Plu and Ban Salak Phet. Entry fees are collected at any one of the four park offices. Keep your receipt as rangers may demand payment from visitors who don't have one.

Only the western coast has been developed for significant tourism and 75% of the island remains untouched rainforest. The paved road down the west coast is a measure of Ko Chang's ongoing development. A few years ago it only reached Lonely Beach; at the moment it extends to Bang Bao, but plans to circle the island are in the pipeline. At the time of writing, the latest rumour involved a tunnel. Don't hold your breath though.

The northern Hat Sai Khao is the longest beach strip and packs in the most accommodation, bars and restaurants per kilometre. Just further south, Hat Kai Mook is a quieter alternative with good-value, family-oriented places to stay. Ao Khlong Phrao sits around a rocky headland from Hat Kai Mook and focuses on more up-market digs, while Hat Kaibae, further south, is transitioning between a laid-back beach setting and a bustling tourist centre.

The fast developing Lonely Beach needs a new English name, and is the island's centre for nightlife for younger travellers. However, there are still quieter bays with relatively deserted beaches just north and south of Lonely Beach's nocturnal fun. Bang Bao is a small fishing settlement in the far south with several places to stay, good seafood restaurants and a busy pier with dive shops, boat transport companies and souvenir shops. Development is impending and, at the time of writing, a luxury condominium and golf complex were planned for near Bang Bao.

The east coast is largely undeveloped with only a few low-key resorts. Hat Yao (Long Beach) is one of the island's best beaches and at the time of writing development was restricted to just two simple bungalow operations. However with a paved road now going all the way to Hat Yao, this will most likely change in the lifetime of this book. Ao Salak Phet in the southeast of the island has a fishing village atmosphere and features good seafood restaurants, with a few quiet places to stay perched above the water.

Information

EMERGENCY

Police station (☎ 0 3958 6191; Ban Dan Mai)
Tourist Police office (☎ 0 3957 7255, emergency 1155) Based in Ban Khlong Prao. Also has smaller police boxes in Hat Sai Khao and Hat Kaibae.

INTERNET ACCESS

Internet access is easy to find all the way down the west coast. Expect to pay 2B per minute.
Earthlink (Hat Sai Khao; per min 2B; ☼ 10.30am-11pm) For cool coffees at the northern end of Hat Sai Khao. Also provides wi-fi access.

MEDICAL SERVICES

Ko Chang Hospital (☎ 0 3952 1657; Ban Dan Mai) Just south of the main ferry terminal.
Ko Chang International Clinic (☎ 0 1863 3609; www.kohchanginterclinic.com; Hat Sai Khao; ☼ 24hr during high season) Related to the Bangkok Hospital Group and can handle most minor emergencies.

MONEY

There are banks with ATMs and exchange facilities along Hat Sai Khao, and ATMs at all the west coast beaches.

POST
Ko Chang post office (☎ 0 3955 1240; Hat Sai Khao)
At the far southern end of Hat Sai Khao.

TOURIST INFORMATION
The nearest tourist office is in Laem Ngop (p256). The free magazine *Koh Chang, Trat & The Eastern Islands* (www.whitesandsthai land.com), which comes out quarterly, is widely available on the island and is packed with useful listings and tips. Its website is an excellent resource for pre-trip planning. It also publishes a Koh Chang Restaurants & Bars guide.

A comprehensive website for booking accommodation is www.koh-chang.com, while www.iamkohchang.com is a labour of love from an irreverent Brit living on the island. His 'KC Essentials A-Z' section is jam-packed with opinion and information.

Dangers & Annoyances
The western beaches are often posted with warnings about dangerous riptides and undercurrents during the monsoon (May to September). If a beach has such a warning, don't go in above your knees. Lonely Beach, Hat Sai Khao and Ao Khlong Phrao have suffered several fatalities in recent years.

The police conduct regular drug raids on the island's accommodation. If you get caught with narcotics, you could face heavy fines or imprisonment.

Although the island's ring road is now paved, roads are very steep with several hairpin turns. Don't ride a motorbike unless you're experienced.

Activities
COURSES
The **Koh Chang Thai Cookery School** (☎ 08 1940 0649; www.kohchangcookery.com; Ao Khlong Prao) at the Blue Lagoon Resort (p262) offers fun cookery courses for those wanting to re-create their favourite tastes once they get home. Five-hour courses cost 1000B and you can expect to learn four recipes per visit. Book ahead.

COVER UP ON KO CHANG

Nudity and topless sunbathing are forbidden by law in Mu Ko Chang Marine National Park; this includes all beaches on Ko Chang, Ko Kut, Ko Mak, Ko Kradat etc.

Jungle Way (p262; www.jungleway.com) offers tuition in the subtle art of reiki (Japanese healing). Week-long courses held in a relaxed forest setting cost 4500B. At the time of writing Jungle Way were also planning courses in Thai massage.

If you wish to learn a new discipline in a lagoon-side setting, head to **Baan Zen** (☎ 08 6530 9354; www.explorakohchang.com/Baan_Zen_Yoga/index. html; Ao Khlong Prao) on the lagoon at Ao Khlong Prao. In a breezy pavilion beside the water, courses are held in yoga and natural healing techniques (weekend course 4000B, three-day course 5500B).

If learning a new skill isn't a priority, both Jungle Way and Baa Zen also offer regular sessions in yoga, massage and natural healing.

DIVING & SNORKELLING
The seamounts off the southern tip of the island stretch between Ko Chang and Ko Kut, offering a new frontier of diving opportunities in Thailand. **Hin Luk Bat** and **Hin Lap**, rocky, coral-encrusted seamounts with depths of around 18m to 20m, are havens for schooling fish. Both **Hin Phrai Nam** and **Hin Gadeng** (between Ko Wai and Ko Rang) are formed by spectacular rock pinnacles and have coral visible to around 28m. Southwest of Ao Salak Phet, reef-fringed **Ko Wai** features a good variety of colourful hard and soft corals at depths of 6m to 15m.

But by far the best diving is around **Ko Rang**. Protected from fishing by its marine park status, this place has some of the most pristine coral in Thailand. Visibility here is much better than near Ko Chang and averages between 10m and 20m. In the area, **Ko Yak** and **Ko Laun** are both shallow dives perfect for beginners and advanced divers. These two small rocky islands can be circumnavigated and have lots of coral, schooling fish, puffer fish, morays, barracuda, rays and the occasional turtle. **Hin Kuak Maa** (also known as Three Finger Reef) is probably the top dive and is home to a coral-encrusted wall sloping from 2m to 14m and attracting swarms of marine life.

Fun diving trips typically include two dives with all guiding, transport, equipment and food, and cost around 3500B. PADI Open Water certification costs 11,500B per person. Many dive shops close during the off season as visibility and sea conditions can be poor. The following are some of the more popular dive shops:

SOUTHEASTERN THAILAND

BB Divers (☎ 0 3955 8040; www.bbdivers.com) Based at Tha Ban Bang Bao.

Ploy Scuba Diving (☎ 08 1451 1387; www.ployscuba .com) Has a shop on all the major west coast beaches and also on Ko Wai, Ko Mak and Ko Kut; the main office is at Tha Ban Bang Bao.

ELEPHANT TREKKING

There are several elephant camps on Ko Chang where you can get up close and personal with former working elephants. Of these, **Ban Kwan Elephant Camp** (☎ 08 1919 3995; changtone@yahoo.com; ⏰ 8.30am-5pm), near Ban Khlong Son, is the best. In a beautiful setting the owner stresses the importance of seeing elephants in the wild, and he delivers informative and educational programmes. A 1½-hour 'experience', involving feeding, bathing and an elephant ride, costs 900B; a 40-minute ride costs 500B.

Chang Chutiman (☎ 08 9939 6676; Ban Khlong Prao; ⏰ 8am-5pm) offers a similar deal in a less dramatic setting. A one-hour ride costs 500B; two hours cost 900B. Kids under five ride free. It's in Ban Khlong Prao, opposite Blue Lagoon Resort (p262).

Transfers are included in these prices, but make sure you book in advance. Most places to stay can arrange these treks with a day's notice.

HIKING

A combination of steep terrain and year-round streams creates scenic waterfalls. A series of three falls along the stream of Khlong Mayom in the interior of the island, **Nam Tok Than Mayom** (park fee 400B; ⏰ 8am-5pm) can be reached via Tha Than Mayom or Ban Dan Mai on the east coast. The view from the top is superb and nearby there are inscribed stones bearing the initials of Rama V, Rama VI and Rama VII.

Nam Tok Khlong Plu (park fee 400B; ⏰ 8am-5pm), another impressive fall, is easily accessible from Ao Khlong Phrao on the western coast. Set amid striking jungle scenery, the fall is quickly reached by walking 600m along a well-marked, lush, jungle path. There's a pool to cool off in after your mini-adventure.

At the southeastern end of Ao Bang Bao, around the headland that leads to Ao Salak Phet, is a beautiful and secluded beach, **Hat Wai Chek**. Don't try hiking all the way from Bang Bao to Ao Salak Phet unless you're an experienced tropical hiker with moderate orienteering skills – there are a lot of hills and many interconnecting, unmarked trails.

If you don't get lost, this rewarding hike will take four to six hours. Should you decide to attempt it, carry enough food and water for an overnight stay. If you do get lost, climb the nearest hill and try to locate the sea or a stream to get your bearings. Following any stream will usually take you either to a village or to the sea. Then you can follow the coast or ask directions.

The ranger stations around the island aren't very useful for solo trekkers, but you can arrange guides at **Evolution Tour** (☎ 0 3955 7078; www.evolutiontour.com; Khlong Prao). Lek from **Jungle Way** (p262) runs one-day (800B) and two-day (950B) treks into the island's interior. The one-day Chang Noi peninsula trek in the island's north is recommended if you're after some serious exercise. Mr Rahit from **Kongoi Trekking** (☎ 08 9763 0832) runs treks (six hours, 500B) in the rugged and largely untouched south of the island. Birdwatchers should contact the **Trekkers of Koh Chang** (☎ 08 1578 7513) who run one-day and two-day trips (1200B to 2000B) into the national park.

KAYAKING

The **Salak Kok Kayak Station** (☎ 08 1919 3995; Ban Salak Kok), in a traditional stilt village in the island's southeast, hires kayaks for viewing the mangrove-forested bay. Kayak rental for one hour costs 100B and a 90-minute guided tour is 200B. It also runs a three-hour 'dinner cruise' (1200B per person) where you're guided through the mangroves at sunset while dining on home-cooked food.

Nearby a raised concrete walkway wends its way through the mangroves. It's not the most attractive construction, but it does immerse you in this fascinating ecosystem.

OTHER ACTIVITIES

Some of the guesthouses at Hat Sai Khao, Hat Kai Mook and Hat Kaibae rent out kayaks, sailboards, masks and snorkels, and boogie boards. Mountain bikes can be rented for 150B per day at several places on the island, most of which are located at Hat Sai Khao and Hat Kaibae. You can also organise day trips (200B to 1000B) and overnight trips (1500B to 2000B) to nearby islands from most accommodation places.

Bailan Herbal Sauna (☎ 08 6252 4744; Bailan Beach; ⏰ 4-9pm) has a round adobe sauna set amid lush greenery where you can get healthy with different herbal concoctions for 100B. Bailan

also offers massage (300B) and facial treatments (40B to 60B). Cool down afterwards in the juice bar.

VOLUNTEERING

You'll probably notice fewer stray animals on Ko Chang compared to other places in Thailand. This is due to the efforts of the **Koh Chang Animal Foundation** (☎ 08 9042 2347; www. kohchanganimalfoundation.org; Ban Khlong Son), established in 2000 by American Lisa McAlonie. The foundation is funded entirely by donations, offers free-of-charge vet services to the people of Ko Chang, and provides refuge and treatment for stray animals around the island. Volunteer visits by travelling vets and veterinarian nurses are particularly appreciated, but the foundation also welcomes day visits from anyone who loves animals and wants to donate a bit of TLC to help bathe and socialise abused animals. As well as furry cuddles on tap, you'll also get lunch.

Sleeping

As developers continue to have Ko Chang in their sights, you're likely to see more snazzy sleeping options opening up in the years to come. Indeed, when we visited many new resorts were being built. Rustic backpacker bungalows are far from gone, however, and the resulting mix of accommodation should please all tastes. Most development has been limited to the west coast, where you will find nearly all the sleeping and eating facilities. Beaches further south tend to be quieter and are generally more popular with those looking for the laid-back life. Ko Chang is also seeing a growth in package tourists from Europe, and remains very popular with Thai visitors on weekends and public holidays.

A few places close down during the wet season (April to October), during which time boats will usually go only as far as Ao Sapparot and Tha Dan Kao. Note that the surf further south along the east coast can be impassable during heavy rains.

The following are high season prices; expect discounts of up to 40% from April to October. Traditionally it has been difficult to book accommodation in advance, but many places now offer websites and email addresses. During peak season (November to March), weekends and major holidays, booking ahead is recommended as the island fills up quickly.

Accommodation is listed from north to south.

Ban Khlong Son

At the northern tip of the island is the largest village, Ban Khlong Son, which has a network of piers at the mouth of the *khlawng* (canal; also spelt *khlong*), a wat, a school, several noodle shops, a health clinic and an ATM.

Jungle Way (☎ 08 9223 4795; www.jungleway.com; bungalow 250-400B) Four bungalows and a funky restaurant with a wildlife viewing platform are tucked into the jungle near the Ban Kwan Chang Elephant Camp. You're nowhere near the beach, but there's trekking on offer (opposite), and you can also take part in healing and massage classes (p259).

Hat Sai Khao

The long beach at Hat Sai Khao is not the island's best, but a wide range of eating and sleeping options, and a lively nightlife keep it popular. Over the last few years, more package tourists are staying here, keeping the prices of accommodation higher than elsewhere on the island.

Tantawan (☎ 0 3955 1168; r 500B) The red-brick bungalows are a bit garish, but with Jack's Tattooing on site, and nightly performances from the Sticky Rice Blues Band, Tantawan lives and breathes its friendly backpacker vibe.

Top Resort (☎ 0 3955 1364; www.topresort-koh-chang .com; r incl breakfast 1440B; ☒) Atop the cliff at the southern end of the beach, this German-run spot has spotless rooms, and a quirky garden with fish ponds and bird cages. For families there are good value, larger stand-alone bungalows (2960B) with kitchen and laundry facilities.

Logan's Place (☎ 0 3955 1451; www.logansthailand .com; r 1800B; ☒) Cool and crisp Scandinavian décor and service features in this Swedish-run boutique hotel across the road from the beach. While you feel like you're sitting in an IKEA catalogue, you can grab a bite to eat at Heli's Kitchen downstairs.

Cookies Hotel (☎ 0 3955 1056; www.fly.to/cookiesho tel; Hat Sai Khao; r 1800-2800B; ☒ ☒) In Ko Chang's backpacker days, Cookies offered simple beachside huts. Now they've progressed to two grand buildings straddling the main beach road. You'll pay about half as much again on the beach side, but the rooms in the low-slung building are nicer than across the road. On the beachside is a new pool and bar.

KC Grande Resort (☎ 0 3955 1199; www.kcresortkoh chang.com; r 500-3600B; 🕱 🖵 🔁) Gradually this long established place at the northern end of Hat Sai Khao is moving upmarket. The cheapest bungalows now cost 500B, and a pool has been added. Unfortunately, the original rustic charm of this spot has been diluted and the atmosphere is now a bit like a holiday camp. Still, if you're attracted to the nearby nightlife it's a very handy location and there is a big range of rooms.

Next door to the Tantawan, **Sang Arun Resort** and **Bamboo Resort** offer similar ambience at a similar cost, but with fewer red bricks.

Hat Kai Mook

Laid-back Hat Kai Mook (Pearl Beach) is a quieter alternative to Hat Sai Khao and features mostly midrange accommodation. Most places are on the small, rocky beach and away from the busy main road.

Paradise Palms (☎ 08 9094 6023; www.paradise palmsresort.net; bungalow 1299B; 🕱 🖵) The first place on Hat Kai Mook (the beach is actually named after the owners' daughter Muksuda), the Thai/British owned Paradise Palms has spotless bungalows with air-con and satellite TV. There's good snorkelling off the rocks and it even throws in free use of a motorbike for their guests.

Penny's Bungalow Resort (☎ 08 1595 9750; www .penny-thailand.com; r incl breakfast 1500B; 🕱 🔁) To make room for the pool, the bungalows are a bit close together, but this is still a well run and quiet option a short ride from the brighter lights of Hat Sai Khao. Families will get good value from the larger four-person bungalow (2600B).

Saffron on the Sea (☎ 0 3955 1253; Hat Kai Mook; r 1500-1800B; 🕱) Owned by an arty escapee from the hectic streets of Bangkok, this friendly boutique guesthouse has a deliciously bohemian ambience. After a few relaxing hours in the hammocks and gazebos, you'll be phoning work to tell them you won't be coming in next month (or maybe even next year). Bathrooms are especially funky.

Remark Cottages (☎ 0 3955 1261; www.remarkcot tage.com; bungalow 2000-3300B; 🕱) A wonderfully overgrown garden conceals 15 Balinese-style bungalows which look simple at first, but are actually accented with interesting design details. Relax in the wooden spa pool or treat yourself with a course of shower spray therapy. File under green and serene.

Ao Khlong Prao

About 4km south of Hat Sai Khao, Ao Khlong Prao is developing as the island's luxury hub, but a few affordable places remain.

Blue Lagoon Resort (☎ 08 1940 0649; www.koh changcookery.com; Ao Khlong Prao; r 600-1000B; 🕱) Simple wooden bungalows with private decks sit right above the water, and further back air-con concrete bungalows lie in a shady grove. A wooden walkway leads to the beach. The other reason to come here is to attend a Thai cooking class (p259), so you can be sure the restaurant's food will be great.

Aana (☎ 0 3955 1539; www.aanarsort.com; r 3500-7000B; 🕱 🖵 🔁) With interesting angles and crisp whitewashed décor, the Aana throws away the rule book for tropical resort design, and comes up with something fresh and unique. The rooms are effortlessly romantic with spacious bathrooms, top-class bed linen and softly spinning ceiling fans. With a secluded location overlooking the Khlong Prao river, two swimming pools and personal Jacuzzis, this is one of the island's best.

Tropicana (☎ 0 3955 7122; www.kochangtropicana .com; r 5200-7200; 🕱 🖵 🔁) More traditional in design than the Aana Resort (but no less flash) the Tropicana fits 77 individual bungalows into grounds criss-crossed by lush gardens, bridges and fish ponds. The pool is a beachside stunner, and the spacious rooms maintain a natural feel with high ceilings, wooden floors and 'stay-in-the-shower-all-day' outdoor bathrooms.

Hat Kaibae

South of the lagoon, Hat Kaibae is a rapidly expanding scene of midrange places and former backpacker spots moving upmarket. In the high season there are bad traffic jams (especially at weekends) as traffic squeezes through the narrow main road. At the time of writing, there were plans to build a much-needed bypass road.

Kaibae Beach (☎ 0 3955 7132; www.kaibaebeach.com; r 700-1800B; 🕱) Choose between simple wooden fan bungalows or concrete (but well designed) air-con ones. A sea view costs an extra 300B, but we reckon you should save your money and spend up large in the open-air restaurant. Nightly barbecues are a good place to start.

Garden Resort (☎ 0 3955 7260; www.gardenre sortkohchang.com; r 1200-2100B; 🕱 🖵 🔁) In a quiet location off the busy main road, Garden Resort has individually decorated bungalows,

in-room internet access and the biggest big screen TV you'll ever see in reception. When we visited, the hole that was to become its new swimming pool was filling gently with the monsoon rains. We're pretty sure it will be finished by the time you read this.

KB Resort (☎ 0 1862 8103; www.kbresort.com; r 1150-2600B; ☒) Another backpacker fave that is creeping upmarket, KB Bungalows has re-launched as KB Resort with higher prices, a wider range of rooms and nightly barbecues at the over-water restaurant. Décor and design are very nice, but everything is a tad over-priced. Welcome to the future of Ko Chang.

Lonely Beach (Hat Tha Nam) & Bailan Bay

South from Hat Kaibae is Hat Tha Nam – more commonly known as Lonely Beach. It's fast becoming Not-So-Lonely Beach, with flashier resorts moving in and a pumping nightlife scene in the tiny village. If you're looking for peace and quiet you're in the wrong place. Just slightly south, Bailan Bay is still nicely low-key.

Siam Beach Resort (☎ 08 9161 6664; www.siam beachkohchang.com; Hat Tha Nam; bungalow 600-800B, r 2500B; ☒ ☐ ☒) Here's the past, present and future of Ko Chang. Fan and air-con bungalows cluster on the beach and the hillside, and there are also new 'deluxe' air-con rooms right on the water. If you're really counting your baht, the same outfit runs **Siam Huts** just down the coast with simple, but slightly tatty, huts (250B to 350B), complete with a retinue of friendly cats and noisy dogs.

Nature Beach Resort (☎ 0 3955 8027; Hat Tha Nam; bungalow 300-600B) Seemingly getting bigger every year, Nature Beach is a mix of seclusion and socialising. Daylight hours are quiet amid the well-spaced bungalows, but most nights there are parties and fire shows. Spend your nights in party mode, and then cruise the on-site book shop and internet café when you (finally) get up.

P & Nico Guest House (☎ 08 6111 9349; Hat Tha Nam; bungalow 800B) Tastefully decorated in summertime blue and yellow, these new bungalows come with a welcome in Thai, French or English. You're away from the beach but well placed for bars and restaurants.

The Magic Garden (☎ 0 3955 8027; www.magicgar denthailand.com; Hat Tha Nam; bungalow 500-700B; ☐) Mix up Thai island style with an Ibiza groove and add a touch of the Burning Man festival. The Magic Garden's not for everyone, but this

is perfect for sociable 21st-century neo-hippies. All bungalows face The Power Lounge, a central bar/chillout area that delivers house, trance and world music from noon to the wee small hours. Look forward to seriously altering your sleep patterns.

The Mangrove (☎ 08 1949 7888; Bailan Bay; bungalow 1000B) Here's proof that not all bungalows are created equal. Cascading down a hill to a private beach and an architecturally designed restaurant, the bungalows here are spacious, private and pretty damn stylish.

Bailan Family Bungalows (☎ 08 9051 2701; www .bailanfamilybungalow.com; Bailan Bay; huts 450B, bungalow 900B; ☒) While the young 'uns party up the coast on Lonely Beach, this spot has simple, but well-designed, fan-cooled huts amid a subdued family ambience. A private beach is one minute away and there's a larger air-con bungalow if you're splashing out.

Bang Bao

Floating on stilts above the ocean, the picturesque fishing village of Bang Bao features charming accommodation on the pier, and interesting places to stay nearby. The pier is rapidly becoming a roll call of dive shops, souvenir shops and cafés, but is still a magical place in the late afternoon sun when the day trippers have retreated north.

Elephant Garden (☎ 08 7143 2286; bungalow 250B) You're a fair hike from the beach, but there's a relaxed bohemian atmosphere at this rambling spot run by a proud Scotsman. At its hub is a laid-back restaurant serving tasty vegetarian curries. If you get too laid-back, boost your adrenaline by watching a DVD or jumping onto PlayStation for a session or three.

Remark Puzi (☎ 0 3955 8116; www.remarkpuzi.com; bungalow 350-600B) Simple wood and bamboo bungalows are given a lift with funky bed linen, and hammocks are interspersed in a leafy, beachy glade. Unfortunately a new concrete wharf has been built right out front, but this is still a relaxing place to stay at the quieter end of Ko Chang.

Ocean Blue (☎ 08 1889 2348; www.oceanbluethailand .com; r 700B) Simple fan rooms line this traditional house at the end of a quiet pier. The young crew running the place are quirky and funny, and the combination of a shady hammock, a good book and a cold Singha adds up to a hell of a way to spend an afternoon.

Bang Bao Sea Hut (☎ 08 1285 0570; www.bangbao seahut.com; r 2000B; ☒) With individual bungalows

extending into Bang Bao harbour, this is one of Ko Chang's more enchanting places to stay. Each thatched roof 'hut' (actually much flasher than it sounds) is surrounded by a private deck, with wooden shutters opening to the sea breeze. Be sure to pack a loved one for a romantic escape.

Nirvana (☎ 0 3955 8061; www.nirvana-kohchang.com; Bang Bao; r 4620-9240B; 🅇) Ko Chang's premium resort is hidden away on a quiet peninsula, and almost impossible to spot among rambling vegetation. 'Balinese' was the initial design brief, but each bungalow is furnished slightly differently in muted earth tones with subtle Asian accents. Make sure you bring along your airline's phone number because there's every chance you'll be phoning them to catch a later flight.

East Coast

This part of the island can feel isolated with most resorts catering to Thai customers. A few stand-out options do exist though. At the time of writing transport was limited to this area.

A road now runs from just south of Judo Resort to Hat Yao (Long Beach), a quiet, pristine slice of sand with minimal development. However, with the road now complete, don't be surprised to see other resorts pop up. Keep your eyes peeled.

Treehouse Lodge (☎ 08 1847 8215; www.tree-house .org; Hat Yao; bungalow 300B) Pristine stretch of sand – check. Simple but funky bungalows – check. Hippy, drippy boho ambience – check. Yep, the operators of the original (and legendary) Treehouse Lodge on Hat Yao have done a good job of recreating the original set-up on isolated Hat Yao. Plan on staying a while – most travellers do. During the peak season, transport (100B) leaves Lonely Beach at 10am going to Hat Yao.

Island View Resort (☎ 08 9155 2669; www.erleb nisreisen-thailand.de; Ao Salak Phet; r 900B; 🅇 🖳) Sea breezes and secluded island views are standard at this unique spot perched at the end of a private pier in quiet Ao Salak Phet. The spacious air-con rooms are excellent value, and the friendly German-Thai owners arrange kayaking and sailing trips around the quiet bay. Don't leave without trying the sublime fried fish with mango. Host Dieter can pick you up at the ferry.

Judo Resort (☎ 08 9925 4122; Ban Jekbae; r 500-1500B; 🅇 🅇) Newish air-con rooms cater to the flashpacker set, while spacious tent arrangements fulfil the budget crowd. Grab a kayak and paddle to the nearby beach if you want real peace and quiet, but the whole set-up is nicely secluded anyway.

Funky Hut Resort (☎ 0 3958 6177; www.funkyhut -thailand.com; Ao Dan Kao; r 650-1950B; 🅇 🖳 🅇) While everyone else turns right from the ferry, turn left and head to this friendly spot on quiet Ao Dan Kao. There's virtually no nightlife in close proximity, and that's just the way the owners and guests like it. Choose from air-con poolside rooms or cheaper fan bungalows. Englishman Chris and his Thai wife Oh are especially proud of their burgers, but all the food is great. Rates increase from mid-December to the end of January.

Eating & Drinking

Virtually all of the island's accommodation options have attached restaurants, but a few specialist restaurant scenes are also developing.

Hat Sai Khao

Hat Sai Khao has the highest concentration of eateries.

Thor's Palace (☎ 08 1927 2502; Hat Sai Khao; 🕑 breakfast, lunch & dinner) The deliciously camp Thor serves up excellent food and terrific beats amid gorgeous surroundings dotted with mementos of his globetrotting. This shrine to Thor's innate good taste is only open in the high season.

Tonsai (☎ 08 9895 7229; Hat Sai Khao; mains 40-150B; 🕑 lunch & dinner) Settle down on the funky cushions in this treehouse/restaurant built in a sturdy banyan tree (*tonsai* in Thai). There's a good selection of Thai and Western eats amid a nicely relaxed ambience. Make an afternoon of it.

Invito (☎ 0 3955 1326; Hat Sai Khao; mains 200-250B; 🕑 lunch & dinner) Authentic wood-fired pizzas and hand-made pasta are the signature dishes at this classy space with excellent service. It's at the southern end of Hat Sai Khao. Invito also delivers its pizzas.

Invito Delicatessen (☎ 0 3955 1460; Hat Sai Khao; 🕑 9am-2pm, 5-8pm) Just up the road from Invito, this place has a terrific selection of cheese, salami and the island's best bread to assemble the island's best DIY picnics.

Oodie's Place (☎ 0 3955 1193; Hat Sai Khao; pizza 170-260B; 🕑 lunch & dinner) Local musician Oodie runs a nicely diverse operation with excellent French food, tasty Thai specialities, movies

at 7.30pm and live music from 10pm. Make a night of it. And yes, they do play *Knocking on Heaven's Door*.

Hat Kaibae

Hat Kaibae is also developing a good bar and restaurant scene. At the time of writing, the always-evolving area included a French restaurant, a Muslim vegetarian eatery and a good Indian curry house. See what else you can discover.

Kharma (☎ 08 1663 3286; Hat Kaibae; ☽ breakfast, lunch & dinner) Eclectic music, a wide-ranging menu featuring Thai, Mexican and vegetarian food, and a few inflated blowfish are all good reasons to head to this gay-friendly spot. The cocktails aren't to be sneezed at either.

Ban Bang Bao

A handful of excellent seafood restaurants lie along the pier in Ban Bang Bao.

Bang Bao Delight (☎ 08 1844 1434; Bang Bao; doughnut 20B, coffee 40B; ☽ breakfast, lunch & dinner) Good coffee and fresh juices are served on low tables and cushions at this top spot for breakfast on Bang Bao's pier. Later in the day treat yourself to a freshly baked sugar doughnut or raisin roll. It's OK – you're on holiday.

The Bay (☎ 08 1773 4860; Bang Bao; mains 80–220B; ☽ lunch & dinner) Fresher-than-fresh seafood goes down very well with one of the island's best cocktail lists at this breezy over-water restaurant with a sophisticated ambience.

Near The Bay, **Chow Talay** and **Ruan Thai** offer similar food in more rustic surroundings.

Surrounding Islands

There are some dazzling smaller islands in Mu Ko Chang National Marine Park, some uninhabited but many starting to welcome tourists with open arms to postcard-perfect beaches. Getting to these islands is still expensive, but becoming more straightforward every year. Costs for transport, food and accommodation remain relatively high compared to Ko Chang and Ko Samet.

On **Ko Kut** you'll find beaches mostly along the western side at Hat Taphao, Hat Khlong Chao and Hat Khlong Yai Ki. The water along these beaches is a gorgeous shade of aquamarine. A sealed road links Ban Khlong Hin Dam, the island's main village on the west coast, with Ao Klong Chao further south, and with Bang Ao Salat on the northeastern shore. Just south from Ao Klong Chao the road disintegrates

into a bumpy dirt track, eventually petering out into a single track only suitable for motorcycles. Other villages on the island include Ban Ta Poi, Ban Laem Kluai and Ban Lak Uan. Nam Tok Tan Sanuk and Khlong Chao offer inland water diversions including hiking and kayaking to nearby waterfalls. Ko Kut can be reached from Tha Laem Ngop on the mainland or from Ko Chang and Ko Mak.

Ko Mak, the smallest of the three main islands, has a scenic beach along the northwest bay. Rainforest covers 30% of the island while coconut plantations take up another 60%. A few tractors and jeeps travel along the single paved road that leads from the pier to the main village. It is possible to rent motorcycles and organise diving trips from the resorts on the island. The nearby small islands of **Ko Rang** and **Ko Rayang** have good coral.

Ko Wai has some of the best coral and is excellent for snorkelling and diving. There are also a couple of bungalow operations.

Ko Kham is also recommended for underwater explorations; accommodation is available. Note also that in the high season many daytrippers from Ko Chang head to Ko Wai and Ko Kham for a spot of snorkelling.

SLEEPING

Ko Kut, Ko Mak, Ko Rayang, Ko Kham and Ko Wai are quieter and more secluded than popular Ko Chang. Transport to the islands has traditionally been a bit hit and miss, but boat connections are becoming more regular as people discover these hidden gems.

Visiting the islands is really only an option in the high season, and during the May to September low season most boats stop running and many bungalow operations wind down. On weekends and holidays during the high season, vacationing Thais fill the resorts on Ko Kut, Ko Wai and Ko Mak, but during the week the ambience is very laid-back.

In Trat, Serge at Tratosphere Books (p254) is a reliable source for up-to-date information on accommodation on the islands, and can make bookings for you before you leave the mainland.

Ko Kut

Traditionally the domain of prepaid package tourists, it is now possible to visit the island independently, though transport infrastructure, restaurants and self-catering facilities are thin on the ground. The following all take

SOUTHEASTERN THAILAND

walk-in bookings, but you'd be wise to phone ahead. Most speedboat operators will drop you at your accommodation if you have pre-booked.

KohKood-Ngamkho Resort (☎ 08 1825 7076; www .kohkood-ngamkho.com; Ao Ngam Kho; hut/bungalow 350/650B) 'Uncle Joe' runs a great spot that's the best budget option on pretty Ao Ngam Kho. Choose from simple huts or flashier fan bungalows. Campers can pitch a tent for 200B, and there's guaranteed sea views from every hammock.

Dusita (☎ 08 1523 7369; Ao Ngam Kho; bungalow 700-1200B; 🞰) With a sandy beach, leafy surroundings, and pavilions and restaurants open to the sea breezes, the fan and air-con bungalows at Dusita are good value. Weekends are especially busy in the high season.

Siam Beach (☎ 08 1945 5789; http://siambeachkoh kood.6te.net; Ao Bang Bao; r 500-1500B; 🞰 🖳) Simple fan huts and more expensive air-con bungalows sit on a wonderfully private beach. Kayaks and snorkelling are on offer, and in the evening the restaurant serves up close relatives of the fish you eyeballed earlier in the day.

The Beach Natural Resort (☎ 08 6999 9420, Bangkok 0 2222 9969; www.thebeachkokhood.com; Ao Bang Bao; bungalow incl breakfast 1200-2600B; 🞰 🖳) Balinese-style bungalows sit among loads of vegetation on a private beach that's great for kayaking. Thais pack this place for karaoke-fuelled fun at the weekend, so try and come on a weekday. 'Beckham' the golden retriever will greet you with his 'special stone'. Correct protocol is to throw it off the wharf so he can dive in after it. Try not to lose it as we almost did.

Bai Kood Shambala (☎ 0 3592 4193; www.baikood shambala.com; Ao Klong Chao; bungalow incl breakfast 1100-3550B; 🞰 🖳) Sitting on a quiet bay opposite a delicate sandpit, relaxing comes easily at Shambala. Rooms are decorated with designer touches, and service in the bar and excellent restaurant is relaxed but professional. When you're done taking it easy jump in a kayak and negotiate the pretty 3km river estuary to the Klong Chao waterfall. Ask for a weekday discount.

Shantaa (☎ 08 1817 9648; www.shantaakohkood .com; Ao Yai Kee; bungalow incl breakfast 3500B; 🞰) The surroundings at this clifftop spot are a tad exposed, but the gorgeous bungalows more than compensate. The open-air bathrooms with herbal toiletries could be Thailand's best, and acres of polished wood, sea views, personal stereos and private gardens come as standard.

Ko Mak

Like Ko Kut, several 'resorts' on Ko Mak paved the way by attracting package tourists to the island in large numbers. It is still difficult to get accommodation at these places without being on an all-inclusive package tour.

The saving grace here is that there are also some charming non-resorts that rent rooms the old-fashioned way and offer a glimpse of slow-paced, Thai-island life. We have listed high season prices – expect discounts of up to 50% in the low season at the places that remain open.

Ko Mak is very small, and the whole island, including all the accommodation operators, shows up to meet the daily boat from the mainland. Don't worry, they'll find you.

At the Ao Nid pier (where most boats arrive from the mainland or from Ko Kut), the **Ball Café** (☎ 08 1925 6591) has internet access (1B per minute) and can arrange accommodation bookings across the island.

Island Time (☎ 08 7139 5537; huts 250B) Colourful huts, over-water swings and lazy hammocks give this simple spot a funky feel, and the welcome from the friendly family is legendary. Expect excellent food.

TK Huts (☎ 08 7134 8435 1631; www.tk-hut.com; bungalow 400-800B) Spartan in design, but set amid shady trees, and run by a friendly German guy who encourages a social vibe.

Baan Koh Maak (☎ 0 3952 4028; www.baan-koh -mak.com; bungalow 850-1000B; 🞰) A well-run and friendly spot, the simple bungalows here have stylish interiors, but the white picket fences can make it feel like a holiday camp. Thankfully a good restaurant with great cocktails easily compensates for the slightly twee ambience. Next door it's opened **Koh Mak Cottages** with simple fan bungalows (450B).

Monkey Island (☎ 08 9501 6030; www.monkeyisland kohmak.com; bungalow 400-3000B; 🞰) Depending on your budget, Baboon Huts, Chimpanzee Huts and Gorilla Huts are all on offer here in nicely natural beachfront surroundings. Tasty design touches include open-air bathrooms and spacious decks, and a friendly laid-back air infuses everything and everyone.

Good Time Resort (☎ 08 3118 0011; www.goodtime -resort.com; villa 2500-3000B; 🞰) Sixteen gorgeous two- to three-bedroom Thai-style villas are nestled in an expansive tropical garden. Relax by the pool, enjoy the spa services or journey to the owner's private island. Good value and easily Ko Mak's best.

Ko Mak Coco-Cape (☎ 08 1937 9024; www.kohmak cococape.com; r 500-4500; 🏊) Owned by a couple of Bangkok architects (and it shows) this sprawling place is kinda Ko Med with lots of crisply whitewashed walls in the flashier bungalows and villas. There are cheaper options with a bamboo feel, starting at 500B for a shared bath fan bungalow, and a compact swimming beach is just minutes away. The restaurant serves good food, but it's somewhat overpriced.

Call ahead, as some of these places close during the rainy season.

Ko Kham
Ko Kham Resort (☎ 08 1393 1229; bungalow 400-1800B) Just off Ko Mak, this tiny island has one simple, but overpriced, resort. Expect lots of gawking and snorkelling daytrippers during the high season. From November to May there is a daily boat from Laem Ngop, or you could kayak across from Ao Suan Yai on Koh Mak. Speedboats (70B) zip across from Ko Mak Resort.

Ko Rayang
Rayang Island Resort (☎ 08 3118 0011; www.rayang -island.com; bungalow 1700-2800B) Another tiny island off Ko Mak and another tiny resort. The Rayang Island Resort has fifteen refurbished one- and two-bedroom bungalows. There are no daytrippers, so it's wonderfully quiet. If you do want to be noisy, you can rent the whole island for €500 per day. It's owned by the same family who have the Good Time Resort on Ko Mak.

Ko Wai
Ko Wai Paradise (r 300B) This welcoming spot has simple wooden bungalows on the beach. Readers have praised the restaurant as the island's best.

Ko Wai Pakarang (☎ 08 4113 8946; www.kohwaipa karang.com; bungalow 700-1000B) The fan bungalows at Pakarang are as flash as it gets on Ko Wai. There are better beaches on the island, but the friendly staff whips up a range of daytrips and activities. Most nights movies offset the delicious ennui of island life.

Getting There & Away
Services to Ko Chang are year-round; boats to other islands become irregular, or even disappear completely, in the May to September rainy season.

At the time of writing this was a summary of available services, but each year sees an increase in the range and frequency of boats during the high season. Especially keep an eye out for improved services to the outer islands.

KO CHANG
There are now three piers in Laem Ngop serving Ko Chang: the main one, at the end of the road from Trat, is called Tha Laem Ngop; another 4km northwest of Laem Ngop is Tha Ko Chang Centrepoint; and the new pier, called Tha Thammachat, is located at Ao Thammachat, further west of Laem Ngop.

During the high season, Tha Laem Ngop is the main pier to many of the Ko Chang Marine Park islands. There is a passenger (backpacker) ferry which runs to Ko Chang hourly (80B, one hour), but this rusty fishing boat often gets overcrowded and it's not the safest option.

From Tha Ko Chang Centrepoint, there are hourly ferries to and from Ko Chang's Tha Dan Kao from 6am until 7pm daily (one-way/return 100/200B, 45 minutes). This is also a vehicle ferry – cars and motorbikes can ride this ferry free with every paying passenger. This is a faster, cheaper and safer option than the backpacker ferry and will drop you off closer to the main beaches. A săwngthăew from Trat to Tha Ko Chang Centrepoint costs around 60B per person.

Another way to get to Ko Chang is via the hourly vehicle ferry from Tha Thammachat. This ferry arrives at Ao Sapparot on Ko Chang (per person/car 100/150B, 30 minutes) and may be the only boat running during rough seas.

KO MAK & KO KUT
Year round there is a daily 3pm boat to Ko Mak, via Ko Wai, leaving from Tha Laem Ngop (300B, three hours). This boat returns from Ko Mak at 8am and can drop you off at Ko Chang's Long Beach (for Tree House Lodge) on request.

Ko Kut Seatrans (☎ 0 3959 7646; Laem Ngop) has boats leaving from Laem Ngop for Ko Mak (300B, 1½ hours) and Ko Kut (500B, 2½ hours) on Tuesday, Saturday and Sunday at 9am, departing for the return journey on Thursday, Friday and Sunday at 12.30pm from Ko Kut and 1.30pm from Ko Mak.

Due to the increasing popularity of the outlying islands, several fast craft make extra

SOUTHEASTERN THAILAND

trips in the high season. **Ko Mak Express** (☎ 0 1863 9400; Laem Ngop) speeds to Ko Mak from Laem Ngop on Friday, Saturday and Sunday at 12pm (400B, 1½ hours) and returns on the same day at 1.30pm.

Departing from Tha Dan Kao, 5km east of Trat (not to be confused with Ko Chang's Tha Dan Kao), **Speedboat Dan Kao** (Dan Kao) leaves at 9am for Ko Mak (300B, one hour) and onto Ko Kut (550B, two hours) on Monday, Wednesday, Friday and Saturday. This boat returns from Ko Kut at 9.30am and Ko Mak at 10.30am on Tuesday, Thursday, Friday and Sunday. Transfers to and from Trat are included in your ticket, or you can catch a såwngthåew to Dan Kao for 40B.

Siriwite Speedboat (☎ 08 6126 7860; Laem Sok) also services these two islands and departs from Tha Laem Sok, 22km (approximately 45 minutes) southeast of Trat. It has daily departures at 9am and 1pm for Ko Mak (400B, 40 minutes) that go onto Ko Kut (500B, 1¼ hours). In the reverse direction, boats leave Ko Kut at 10am and 2pm and Ko Mak at 10.30am and 2.30pm. A share taxi from Trat to Laem Sok should cost about 60B per person.

From October to May, you can also reach Ko Mak and Ko Kut from Ban Bang Bao on Ko Chang. **Island Hopper** (☎ 08 1865 0610; www.is landhopper-kochang.com) ferries leave from the Bang Bao pier at 8am and noon daily, returning from Ko Mak at noon, and from Ko Kut at 10am and 3pm. From Ko Chang to Ko Mak costs 350B each way, and from Ko Chang to Ko Kut is 600B each way. Island Hopper boats also call in at Ko Kham and Ko Wai during their twice-daily runs. **Bang Bao Boats** (☎ 08 7054 4300) operates a similar service. You'll see them both widely advertised on Ko Chang.

KO WAI & KO KHAM

From Ko Mak to Ko Kham it's a short hop from the pier at Ko Mak Resort; boats leave several times a day (around 70B).

A boat leaving Tha Laem Ngop daily at 3pm stops at Ko Wai (250B) before continuing on to Ko Mak. Island Hopper boats (see above) stop at Ko Wai (250B) at 9am and 1pm daily, and at Ko Kham (350B) every day at 10am and 2pm.

Getting Around
BOAT
Charter trips to nearby islands cost around 600B to 900B for a half day, or 1200B to 2000B

for a full day. Make sure that the charter includes all 'user fees' for the islands – sometimes boat operators demand 200B on top of the charter fee for 'using' the beach.

At the southern end of Ko Chang, you can charter a long-tail boat or fishing boat between Hat Kaibae and Ao Bang Bao for 1000B, or around 150B per person if you can manage to fill a boat. Similar charters are also available between Ao Bang Bao and Ao Salak Phet.

Boat rides up Khlong Phrao to the falls cost 50B per person and can be arranged through most bungalows.

CAR & MOTORCYCLE
Bungalow operations along the west coast charge 200B per day for motorbike hire. Elsewhere on the island, rental bikes are scarce. Ko Chang's hilly and winding roads are quite dangerous and are best left to relatively experienced riders, as there have been a number of fatal accidents involving Western tourists. Jeeps can be hired for around 2000B per day in the high season. **Mr Phol** (☎ 08 1887 9515) is reliable and can arrange all sorts of transport with two or four wheels.

SÅWNGTHÅEW
The såwngthåew meeting the boats at Tha Dan Kao and Ao Sapparot charge 40B per person to Hat Sai Khao, 50B to Ban Khlong Phrao, 60B to Hat Kaibae and 80B to Lonely Beach along the west coast. At the time of writing there were irregular såwngthåew to Bang Bao, but as the number of daytrippers increases frequency will no doubt increase. Between Tha Dan Kao and Ao Salak Phet, the local price is 50B per person, although tourists may be charged more.

PRACHINBURI & SA KAEW PROVINCES

The town of Prachinburi is worth a look for its interesting hospital, and the area is a good base to explore the Khao Yai National Park (p464). Near the quieter, southern border of the park, the village of Ban Kon Khuang on Rte 33 includes some good accommodation, and it is much closer to Bangkok than the main park entrance at Pak Chong in Nakhon Ratchasima Province.

The rural areas of Prachinburi and Sa Kaew provinces are peppered with many

small Dvaravati and Khmer ruins. Sa Kaew means 'Jewel Pool', a reference to various Mon-Khmer reservoirs in the area. Little more than loose collections of laterite blocks, most are of little interest to the casual visitor. Keep going east on Rte 33 and cross the border at Aranya Prathet to Cambodia and the real deal at Angkor Wat.

Further west on Rte 33, the town of Nakhon Nayok (in Central Thailand) is a popular getaway for Thais from Bangkok keen on outdoor adventure, especially year-round rafting. Try to come on a weekend as it's often difficult to find companies running weekday trips. It's a good area to explore with your own transport.

National Parks

To the north of Prachinburi, Rte 3077 leads to Khao Yai National Park (p464). North and northeast of Kabinburi, the length of the southern escarpment of the Khorat Plateau, are the contiguous Thap Lan and Pang Sida National Parks.

At 2235 sq km, the **Thap Lan National Park** (☎ 0 3721 9408; reserve@dnp.go.th; 400B; ⏰ 8am-5pm) is Thailand's second-largest national park. Well known as a habitat for the abundant *tôn laan* (talipot palm; see below), the park is also home to elephants, tigers, gaur, sambar, barking deer, palm civets, hornbills and gibbons. It is hoped that the kouprey, a rare species of primitive cattle, still lives here, though it has been more than 30 years since the last official sighting. Illegal logging has damaged the park, but tree-planting programmes are redressing the imbalance.

Facilities are minimal;. To explore the interior contact the rangers at **park headquarters**

(☎ 0 3721 9408) in Thap Lan village. They can arrange a tour of the park and provide camping permits (50B per person). There are three six-bed bungalows (1500B) – book through the Thap Lan National Park email address.

There is no public transport to the park entrance, which is 32km north of Kabinburi via Rte 304 (the road to Nakhon Ratchasima).

Approximately 30km southeast of Thap Lan close to Sa Kaew, **Pang Sida National Park** (☎ 0 3724 6100; reserve@dnp.co.th; 400B; ⏰ 8am-5pm) is smaller but hillier than Thap Lan. There are several scenic waterfalls, including Nam Tok Pang Sida and Nam Tok Na Pha Yai near the park headquarters, and the more difficult to reach Suan Man Suan Thong and Nam Tok Daeng Makha.

Sights & Activities

In Prachinburi the **Chao Phraya Abhaibhubejhr Hospital** (☎ 0 3721 3610; www.adhaiherb.com; 32/7 Moo 12, Th Prachin-Ahuson) is renowned across Thailand for using traditional medicine to develop herbal remedies. The hospital's shop (open 8.30am to 8.30pm) sells interesting health and beauty products. The soaps, including galangal and mangosteen variants, are excellent and the safflower herbal tea is recommended for lowering cholesterol. Buy these authentic products before your local Body Shop or Starbucks launches the mass-market versions.

Attached to the hospital is a serene massage room (massage per hour 160B) where masseuses take your blood pressure before they begin. Next door is a gorgeous baroque building built by the hospital's founder, Siamese governor Chao Phraya Abhaibhubejhr. The building is now a museum of herbal medicine.

SOUTHEASTERN THAILAND

A GIANT OF A PALM

Look out for the spectacular talipot palm *(Corypha umbraculifera)*, one of the largest palms in the world. Native to southern India and Sri Lanka, it is now found throughout Southeast Asia and further north into Yunnan Province in China. The talipot grows to a height of 25m, and is topped with a graceful umbrella of leaves up to 5m in diameter. This tree is all about being showy, and when the talipot finally blooms (after 30 to 80 years), 10 million tiny flowers only 3mm wide emerge simultaneously in a spectacular display at the top of the tree. Marble-sized fruits develop, fall gently to the ground and the spectacular talipot begins a rapid decline. The umbrella-like leaves wilt, having fulfilled their sole purpose of collecting moisture to allow the tree to bloom, and the talipot dies a few months after flowering. Traditionally the gracefully arced leaves were used for manuscripts, and many important Buddhist scriptures were recorded with iron styli on the giant canvases. The leaves are also used for thatching and the trunks are tapped to make palm wine. Unfortunately, development is threatening the talipot, and it is considered an endangered species.

Labels are in Thai, but you'll work most things out. A túk-túk to the hospital from Prachinburi's bus station is 40B, and from the train station is 60B. Palm Garden Lodge (below) will also run you into town for 100B each way.

In **Ban Kon Khuang**, Palm Garden Lodge runs daytrips (1300B per person) to the Khao Yai National Park. The night safari (300B extra) is not worth it, but the waterfall-laden day trips are good value.

Southeast of Prachinburi via Rtes 319 and 3070, in the village of Ban Sa Khoi (between Khok Pip and Sa Maha Pho on Rte 3070), is the Angkor-period **Sa Morakot** (Emerald Pool; admission free; ☽ daylight). This was an important Khmer reservoir during the reign of Angkor's Jayavarman VII. Original laterite-block sluices next to the dam, along with assorted *sěmaa* (boundary stones), *naga* (a mythical serpent-like being with magical powers) sculptures, pedestals and a sandstone lingam can still be seen here. Water from this reservoir is considered sacred and has been used in Thai coronation ceremonies.

Sa Kaew (Jewel Pool; admission free; ☽ daylight), another historic reservoir site, is just south of Khok Pip off Rte 3070. This one features a Dvaravati-period laterite quarry with some bas-relief surviving on the walls. There are a number of other Dvaravati and Angkor laterite foundations in the area. You'll need private transport to get to Sa Morakot and Sa Kaew.

Sarika Adventure Point (☎ 0 3732 8432), in **Nakhon Nayok**, runs combination trips featuring rafting on the nearby Tha Dan dam and mountain biking (one day 1000B, two days 1900B). There's also abseiling on offer (one day 1500B). Sarika is 11km from town near the intersection of Rte 3049 and Rte 3050.

Sleeping

Accommodation in Nakhon Nayok is pretty grim and you're better off staying in one of the family-run bungalows along Soi Suan Lung Nai off Rte 3029. Thai tourists pack these places on weekends, but on weekdays it's very quiet. There are misty views of nearby mountains and a network of pretty streams. Most places hire mountain bikes and kayaks. Don't expect much English to be spoken. There's no public transport but a taxi from the Nakhon Nayok bus station is around 200B.

Palm Garden Lodge (☎ 08 9989 4470; www.palmgalgo .com; Moo 10, Ban Kon Khuang, Prachinburi; r 400-650B, bungalow 1200B; ⊠) Set in a leafy garden and featur-

ing fan and air-con rooms, the friendly family who run Palm Garden Lodge are a national treasure. The food's exceptional and they've got loads of ideas for seeing the area. Motorcycles can be hired (250B per day) and they can arrange transport (100B) to Prachinburi's excellent night market and the Chao Phraya Abhaibhubejhr hospital.

Tha Dan Homestay (☎ 0 3738 5015; Nakhon Nayok; s from 100B) Expect friendly cats, good food and simple (fan plus mattress on the floor) rooms with shared bathrooms. There's no English spoken so book through the Tourism Authority of Thailand office (☎ 0 3731 2284) in Nakhon Nayok.

Blue Diamond Resort & Spa (☎ 0 3738 5262; Nakhon Nayok; bungalow 1200-1400B, f 2000B; ⊠ ⊠) Pleasant bungalows sit in shady surroundings. There are also some larger rooms sleeping up to 10. Massages (400B per 90 minutes) are available.

Getting There & Away

Frequent buses run to Nakhon Nayok (90B) and Prachinburi (110B) from Bangkok's Northern bus terminal (Mo Chit). Four trains a day (two to three hours; 42B to 110B) travel from Bangkok's Hualamphong station to Prachinburi. Buses along Rte 33 to Aranya Prathet from Bangkok's Northern bus terminal stop in Ban Kon Khuang on request. **Palm Garden Lodge** (www.palmgalo.com) have transport instructions on its website.

Getting Around

Motorcycles can be hired (250B per day) from Palm Garden Lodge (left). The area has excellent roads and is good to explore with a private car.

ARANYA PRATHET

อรัญประเทศ

pop 60,000

The dusty border town of Aranya Prathet (aka Aran) has long been a magnet for refugees fleeing the turbulent chapters of Cambodia's roller-coaster 20th century. Displaced Cambodians flooded into the area after the Khmer Rouge takeover of 1975 and the subsequent Vietnamese invasion of 1979. Random skirmishes between Khmer Rouge guerrillas and the Phnom Penh government continued until 1998, but now the area is safe and is the most used border crossing for trips between Thailand and Angkor Wat in Cambodia.

A crackdown on gambling in Phnom Penh has caused a glut of casinos to be built in Poipet. Most cater to Thais from Bangkok, and the contrast between visiting Thais and poor Khmers pushing rudimentary handcarts is startling.

Parts of this area are still heavily mined – do not stray from marked roads and paths.

Sights

The large border market of **Talat Rong Kleua**, at the northern edge of town, attracts a rag-tag crowd of Cambodians who cross the border to trade with the more affluent Thais. Gems, handicrafts and textiles were traditionally sold but the emphasis is now on second-hand gear from developed countries. It's mainly thrift-store tat, but if you're after a pair of knockoff Converse, a retro Japanese baseball shirt or taekwando gear formerly used by the South Korean national team, it's definitely worth a browse. Hire a bike (20B) to explore the maze of over 3000 shops. If you're not buying, it's still fascinating to observe the steady stream of Cambodians crossing the border with huge hand-pulled carts piled high with market goods.

Sleeping & Eating

Simple **rooms for rent** (r 200–300B) are available near the turn-off to the market just before the border. Look for the Pepsi sign in Thai.

Market Hotel (☎ 0 3723 2302; 105/30-32 Th Rat Uthit; r 250-400B; ❖ ☒) It gets mighty dusty around Aranya Prathet so having a pool and air-con is a wise investment to recharge before the long journey to Siem Reap.

Aran Mermed Hotel (☎ 0 3722 3655; fax 0 3722 3666; 33 Th Tanawithi; r/ste 1200/2500B; ❖) With air-con that goes all the way to 11, and spacious and comfy rooms in a shiny high-rise, you almost forget you're in a Thai border town. The Aran Mermed is tucked right behind the bus station.

Little House (☎ 0 3723 1546; 67 Th Chaoprayabirdin; ❖ breakfast, lunch & dinner) The owners may be Chinese, but their culinary skills extend to surprisingly good pizza and burgers.

Niza Restaurant (Talat Rong Kleua; ❖ breakfast, lunch & dinner) Break your shopping marathon at this friendly eatery on the western edge of the market.

Around the market there are many cheap food stalls.

Getting There & Away

Ordinary buses from Bangkok's Northern and Northeastern bus station to Aranya Prathet (118B, five hours) leave on an hourly basis from 5.30am to 4.30pm; air-con buses (207B, 4¼ hours) leave hourly from 5.30am to 10.30am, and from noon to 5pm. If you're travelling to Northeastern Thailand there are regular buses from Aranya Prathet to Khorat (200B, five hours). At the time of writing a direct bus service had commenced from Bangkok's newly opened Suvarnabhumi airport to the border with Cambodia (210B, four hours).

Two trains per day (5.55am and 1.05pm) depart Bangkok's Hualamphong station for Aranya Prathet (third-class only, 48B, six hours).

Getting Around

From the bus station, a local bus (15B) goes to Talat Rong Kleua, from where you can walk to the border. The train station is near the bus station and a túk-túk from either the border or the market is 80B.

Border Crossing (Cambodia)

The border to Cambodia is open daily from 7am to 8pm. First proceed through the Thai immigration office and then cross the border by foot to the Cambodian immigration office. You'll need a photo and 1000B (or US$25). You can also pre-arrange a Cambodian visa in Bangkok at the Cambodian embassy. A tourist shuttle bus outside the Cambodian immigration office delivers passengers free of charge to Poipet's taxi stand, where onward transport can be arranged. At the time of writing the road from Poipet had *still* not been sealed. In the dry season, it's a four-hour trip but considerably longer in the wet season. See Lonely Planet's *Cambodia* guidebook for more information.

Note that this border gets very busy at weekends when Thais are crossing to the casinos in Poipet. Border officials suggest you get there early to avoid delays.

Chiang Mai Province

CHIANG MAI PROVINCE

Chiang Mai Province straddles the most important historical crossroads of northern Southeast Asia, a fertile region of mountains, valleys and rivers where peoples from China, Laos, Myanmar (Burma) and Thailand have long traded goods and ideas in a fusion of cultures. This blend has been further enlivened by the presence of tribal societies – such as the Hmong-Mien – whose ethnic heritage knows no fixed political boundaries.

In past centuries Chiang Mai served as an entrepôt for a flourishing caravan trade in opium, silks and timber. Today it is Thailand's second-largest city and the north's principal hub for tourism, transport, education and cross-border commerce. In a period of rapid development, Chiang Mai – crowned to the west by Doi Suthep mountain and its sacred temple, and centred on a moated old town – has managed to retain its charm and laid-back feel. Find ancient *chedi* (stupas) side by side with modern architecture, a delicious and distinctive cuisine, accommodation ranging from back-packing digs to boutique hotels, as well as great shopping, pampering spas and a myriad of courses to try out.

Outside of the provincial capital, Chiang Mai Province boasts more natural forest cover than any other province in the north. In addition, two of Thailand's highest mountain peaks are in Chiang Mai Province: Doi Inthanon (2565m) and Doi Chiang Dao (2195m). Cycling, hiking, elephant trekking, bird-watching and river rafting attract those interested in Chiang Mai Province's natural surrounds, while visitors keen on learning more about the region's fascinating ethnic minorities can visit semi-remote villages on mountain slopes.

HIGHLIGHTS

- People-watching or shopping till you drop on Chiang Mai's bustling **Sunday Walking Street** (p284)
- Enjoying an invigorating **traditional Thai massage** (p292) or enrolling in a **course** (p293) to become a thumb master yourself
- Experiencing serenity in the brick-lined meditation tunnels of **Wat U Mong** (p286)
- Taking in the far-reaching views at **Wat Phra That Doi Suthep** (p325) and exploring the surrounding **Doi Suthep-Pui National Park** (p325) by motorbike
- Checking out the impressive caves, taking a challenging hike and bird-watching around **Chiang Dao** (p328)

Chiang Dao ★

Wat Phra That
Doi Suthep ★

Wat U Mong ★★ Chiang Mai

FAST FACTS

- **Best Time to Visit** November to February
- **Population** 1.7 million

Climate

Chiang Mai Province has much the same climate as adjacent provinces in the north. Most visitors will find the weather is most enjoyable from November to mid-February, when temperatures are mild and rain is scarce.

During the cool season (December to February), temperatures can warrant a jacket or pullover at night, particularly at higher elevations.

From February until the monsoon season begins in June, a thick haze often forms over the city, a combination of dust and smoke from the burning off of rice fields near the city. The hot season (March to May) can be brutal in Chiang Mai, although temperatures don't burst the thermometer as much as they do in Lampang or in northeastern Thailand. You'll find some relief from the heat (and to a lesser extent, the smoke) at the cooler elevations of Chiang Dao and Doi Inthanon, or anywhere else where you can get above the Mae Ping plains.

The annual monsoons are generally lighter in Chiang Mai than in central or southern Thailand, lasting from June to October, and rarely into November. Chiang Mai city can flood when rains are unusually heavy.

Language

Around 80% of the people living in Chiang Mai Province are native to the area, belonging to an ethnic group once known as Yuan or Yün, or less frequently Phayap. Nowadays many Chiang Mai residents consider these to be pejorative names and they prefer the term *khon meuang* (meaning people of the Tai principality).

Most non-hill-tribe people speak Northern Thai as their first language. Northern Thai – or *kham meuang* (speech of the Tai principality) – is very similar to Central (or 'Standard') Thai, as spoken in central Thailand, and with a mutual intelligibility rated at greater than 70%.

Central Thai is taught in local schools and is the official language of all government agencies. Thus most educated Chiang Mai residents can speak Central Thai, and will usually do so automatically with anyone from outside the region.

Northern Thai has its own script, based on a half-millennium-old Mon script that was originally used only for Buddhist scripture. The script became so popular during the Lanna period that it was exported for use by the Thai Lü in China, the Khün in the eastern Shan State and other Thai–Kadai-speaking groups living between Lanna and China. Although few northerners nowadays can read the Northern Thai script – often referred to as 'Lanna script' – it is occasionally used in signage to add a Northern Thai cultural flavour. The script is especially common for use on signs at the entrance gates of Chiang Mai monasteries, although the name of the wat (temple) will also be written in Thai (and occasionally Roman) script.

Very few outsiders bother to learn Northern Thai, since Central Thai is so widely spoken. Unless you have a very keen interest in learning the Northern dialect, it's best to stick to Central Thai, as many northerners seem to take offence when outsiders try speaking *kham meuang* to them. This attitude dates back to a time, perhaps no more than 25 or 30 years ago, when central Thais considered northerners to be very backward, and thus made fun of their language.

The Language chapter (p781) covers only the Central Thai dialect. If you're interested in learning *kham meuang,* the only generally available book is *Lanna Language* by Kobkan Thangpijaigul. All materials are written out in Lanna script, International Phonetic Alphabet (IPA), English translation and Thai translation. It's mostly intended for people who are already fluent, or very familiar with, Central Thai. An optional 90-minute cassette tape is also available to go with the text.

Getting There & Away

Chiang Mai International Airport fields dozens of daily flights from Bangkok, as well as various other cities in Thailand. There are also international connections with cities in Myanmar, China and Laos.

Chiang Mai serves the main road transport hub for all of northern Thailand, with virtually every town and village linked to the city by bus or *sǎwngthǎew* (small pick-up trucks). Most buses to other provinces in the north (as well as elsewhere in Thailand) arrive at and

depart from the Chiang Mai Arcade (New) bus terminal.

The State Railway of Thailand's (SRT) northern line terminates in Chiang Mai, and many travellers arrive by overnight train from Bangkok.

Getting Around

Buses and sǎwngthǎew run frequently to towns and villages around Chiang Mai Province from Chiang Mai's Chang Pheuak bus terminal. Cars, 4WD vehicles, pick-up trucks and motorcycles are easily rented in Chiang Mai for excursions around the province.

CHIANG MAI

เชียงใหม่

pop 204,000

One of the many questions Thais may ask a foreigner visiting Thailand is 'Have you been to Chiang Mai yet?', underscoring the feeling that Chiang Mai is a keystone of any journey to Thailand. Along with Sukhothai further south, it was the first Southeast Asian state to make the historic transition from domination by Mon and Khmer cultures to a new era ruled by Thais.

Located more than 700km northwest of Bangkok, Chiang Mai has in excess of 300 temples (121 within the *thêtsàbaan* or municipal limits) – almost as many as are in Bangkok – a circumstance that makes the old city centre visually striking. Thais idealise their beloved northern capital as a quaint, moated and walled city surrounded by mountains with legendary, mystical attributes. In reality, Chiang Mai is a dynamic and modern city, which has successfully managed to combine its rich history and traditions with its increasingly modern side. However, a result of this rapid development has been the rise in traffic and pollution. Environmentalists are also voicing concerns about development of the verdant and auspicious Doi Suthep mountain (1676m), located to the west of the city, and sometimes referred to as Chiang Mai's lungs.

Chiang Mai has always had many feathers to its bow with its cultural riches, relative peacefulness, fantastic handicraft shopping, delicious food and proximity to many natural treasures. Changes are afoot however, with the city becoming somewhere to watch

in the style stakes. Chic, Thai-style boutique hotels are popping up everywhere, and one look at the trendsetters setting up shop (and bars and restaurants), particularly in the Th Nimmanhaemin area, shows that the city's identity is changing. Yet, the northern capital still manages to retain the relaxed, temple-sprinkled, cultural capital atmosphere of yore, alongside these new hip happenings. With its many and varied attractions, the days of Chiang Mai just being a quick stop off point before heading to the hills are long gone.

HISTORY

Thai king Phaya Mengrai (also spelt Mangrai), originally from the Mekong riverside principality of Ngoen Yang (present-day Chiang Saen), established Nopburi Si Nakhon Ping Chiang Mai in 1296 after conquering the Mon kingdom of Hariphunchai (modern Lamphun). Traces of the original 1296 earthen ramparts can still be seen today along Th Kamphaeng Din in Chiang Mai.

Later, in an alliance with Sukhothai in the 14th and 15th centuries, Chiang Mai (New Walled City) became a part of the larger kingdom of Lan Na Thai (Million Thai Rice Fields), which extended as far south as Kamphaeng Phet and as far north as Luang Prabang in Laos. During this period Chiang Mai became an important religious and cultural centre – the eighth world synod of Theravada Buddhism was held here in 1477.

The Burmese capture of the city in 1556 was the second time the Burmese had control of Chiang Mai Province. Before Phaya Mengrai's reign, King Anawrahta of Pagan (present-day Bagan) had ruled Chiang Mai Province in the 11th century. This time around, the Burmese ruled Chiang Mai for more than 200 years.

In 1775 Chiang Mai was recaptured by the Thais under Phaya Taksin, who appointed Chao Kavila, a *jâo meuang* (chieftain) from nearby Lampang principality, as viceroy of northern Thailand. In 1800 Kavila built the monumental brick walls around the inner city, and expanded the city in southerly and easterly directions, establishing a river port at the end of what is today Th Tha Phae (*thâa phae* means 'raft pier').

Under Kavila, Chiang Mai became an important regional trade centre. Many of the later Shan- and Burmese-style temples seen around the city were built by wealthy teak merchants

who emigrated from Burma during the late 19th century. Not all the Shan residents were merchants, however. In 1902 several hundred labourers, most of them Shan, protested against the practice of corvée (involuntary service to the state) by refusing to construct roads or otherwise follow government orders. The ensuing skirmishes between *corvée* labourers and Chiang Mai troops – dubbed the 'Shan Rebellion' by historians – didn't

CARAVANS OF NORTHERN THAILAND

Dating from at least the 15th century, Chinese-Muslim caravans from Yunnan Province (China) used Chiang Mai as a 'back door' for commodities transported between China and the Indian Ocean port of Mawlamyaing (Moulmein) in Myanmar (Burma) for international seagoing trade.

British merchant Ralph Fitch, the first person to leave an English-language chronicle of Southeast Asian travel, wrote of his 1583 to 1591 journey through Thailand: 'To the town of Jamahey (Chiang Mai) come many merchants out of China, and bring a great store of Muske, Gold, Silver, and many other things of China worke.'

The principal means of transport for the Yunnanese caravaneers were ponies and mules, beasts of burden that were in contrast with the Southeast Asian preference for oxen, water buffalo and elephants. The Chinese Muslims who dominated the caravan traffic owed their preferred mode of conveyance, as well as their religious orientation, to mass conversions effected during the Mongol invasions of Yunnan in the 13th century. The equestrian nature of the caravans led the Thais to call the Yunnanese *jiin haw* (galloping Chinese).

Three main routes emanated from the predominantly Thai Xishuangbanna (Sipsongpanna) region in southern Yunnan into northern Thailand, and onward to the Gulf of Martaban via Mawlamyaing. The western route proceeded southwest from Simao to Chiang Rung (now known as Jinghong), then went on through Chiang Tung (Kengtung) to Fang or Chiang Rai.

The middle route went south to Mengla near the border of China and Laos, crossed Laos via Luang Nam Tha, and entered Thailand at Chiang Khong (which was an independent principality at the time) on the Mekong River. At this point the middle route merged with the western route at Chiang Rai Province, and formed a single route through Chiang Mai to Mae Sariang, a line that continued along the Salawin River to Mawlamyaing in present-day Myanmar.

The third route went from Simao to Phongsali in northern Laos then via Luang Prabang (Laos), crossing the Mekong River to Nan and Phrae before curving northwestward via Lampang and Lamphun to Chiang Mai.

Principal southward exports along these routes included silk, opium, tea, dried fruit, lacquerware, musk, ponies and mules, while northward the caravans brought gold, copper, cotton, edible birds' nests, betel nut, tobacco and ivory. By the end of the 19th century many artisans from China, northern Burma and Laos had settled in the area to produce crafts for the steady flow of regional trade. The city's original transhipment point for such trade movements was a market district known as Ban Haw, just a stone's throw from today's Night Bazaar (p317) in Chiang Mai.

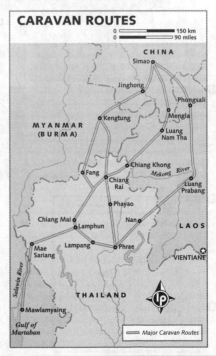

CARAVAN ROUTES

0 ═══ 150 km
0 ═══ 90 miles

CHINA
Simao
Jinghong
Phongsali
Kengtung
Mengla
MYANMAR (BURMA)
Luang Nam Tha
Fang
Chiang Khong
Chiang Rai
Mekong River
Luang Prabang
Phayao
Chiang Mai
Lamphun
Nan
LAOS
Mae Sariang
Lampang
Phrae
VIENTIANE
Salawin River
THAILAND
Mawlamyaing
Gulf of Martaban
═══ Major Caravan Routes

CHIANG MAI PROVINCE

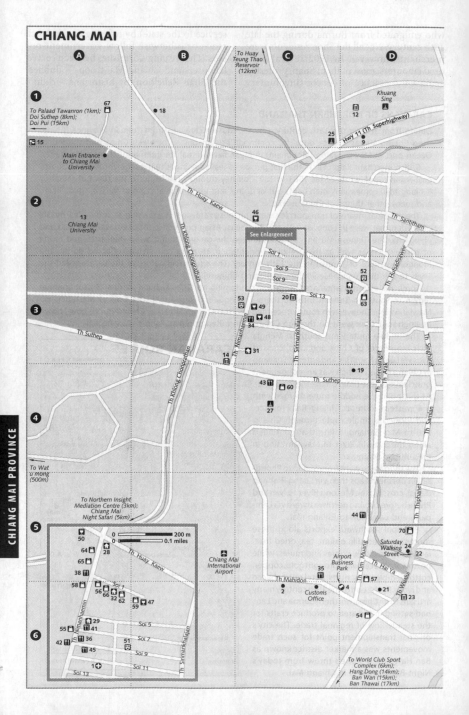

CHIANG MAI

CHIANG MAI PROVINCE

To Huay
Teung Thao
Reservoir
(12km)

Khuang
Sing
12

To Palaad Tawanron (1km);
Doi Suthep (8km);
Doi Pui (15km)

67
18
15
25
9

Hwy 11 (Th Superhighway)

Main Entrance
to Chiang Mai
University

Th Huay Kaew

13
Chiang Mai
University

Th Santitham

46

See Enlargement

Soi 1
Soi 5
Soi 9

Th Suthep

Th Khong Choitpathan

53
49
48
34
20
Soi 13
30
63
52

Th Nimmanhaemin

Th Srimankhalajan

Th Hutsadisawee

31
14

Th Bunreuangrit
Th Arak

Th Samlan

19
Th Suthep
43
60
27

To Wat
u'mong
(500m)

To Northern Insight
Mediation Centre (3km);
Chiang Mai
Night Safari (5km)

44

Th Thiphanet

70
Saturday
Walking
Street
24
22

50
64
28
65
38
58
66
32
62
59
47

Th Huay Kaew

200 m
0.1 miles

Chiang Mai
International
Airport

Th Mahidon

Airport
Business
Park

35
Th Om Muang

Th Hai Ya

57
21
23

2
Customs
Office

4

Soi 1

Soi 5

29
41
55
36
42
45
51
1

Th Nimmanhaemin

Soi 7

Soi 9

Soi 11

Soi 13

Th Srimankhalajan

54

To World Club Sport
Complex (6km);
Hang Dong (14km);
Ban Wan (15km);
Ban Thawai (17km)

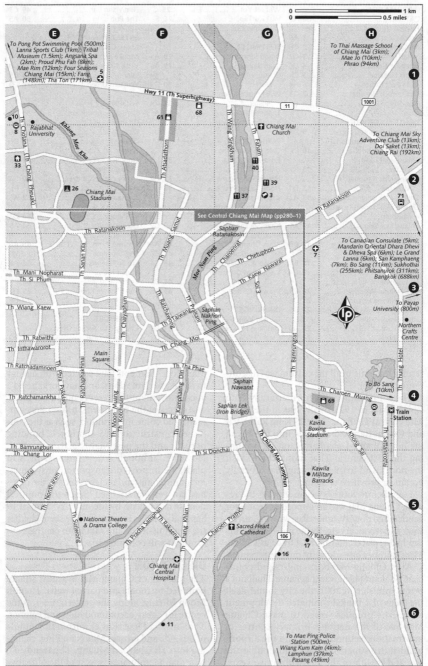

resolve the issue until the custom was discontinued in 1924.

The completion of the northern railway to Chiang Mai in 1921 finally linked the north with central Thailand. In 1927 King Rama VII and Queen Rambaibani rode into the city at the head of an 84-elephant caravan, becoming the first central Thai monarchs to visit the north, and in 1933 Chiang Mai officially became a province of Siam.

Long before tourists began visiting the region, Chiang Mai was an important centre for handcrafted pottery, umbrellas, weaving, silverwork and woodcarving. By the mid-1960s tourism had replaced commercial trade as Chiang Mai's number one source of outside revenue.

After Chiang Mai born-and-raised politician Thaksin Shinawatra became Thailand's prime minister in 2001, the city found itself the focus of a Thaksin-initiated development drive. The premier vowed to make Chiang Mai one of the nation's primary centres of information technology, expand the airport, build more superhighways and double the size and wealth of the city within five years.

Many local residents have reacted with dismay to these proclamations, and have organised a vocal movement to preserve quality of life.

Aspects of the proposed Thaksin developments did come into fruition, such as the continued construction of 5-star hotels, building of roads and the new Night Safari (see p289). However, although a new bus system is in place, the improved transportation system – including trams and metered taxis in the city – has not yet materialised. Since the political demise of Thaksin by the military coup of 19 September 2006, it remains to be seen whether the funding of Chiang Mai from central government will continue apace.

ORIENTATION

The old city of Chiang Mai is a neat square bounded by moats and partial walls. Thanon Moon Muang, along the eastern moat, is the centre for cheap accommodation and eateries. Thanon Tha Phae runs east from the middle of this side and crosses Mae Nam Ping, changing into Th Charoen Muang. The trendy Th Nimmanhaemin area is west of the old city.

The train station and the main post office are further down Th Charoen Muang, a fair distance from the city centre. There are two intercity bus terminals in Chiang Mai, one near Pratu Chang Pheuak (White Elephant Gate; Map pp280–1) and a larger one called Chiang Mai Arcade (Map pp276–7).

Several of Chiang Mai's important temples are within the moat area, but there are others to the north and west. Doi Suthep rises up to the west of the city and from its temples you get a fine view over the city.

Maps

Navigating around Chiang Mai is pretty simple, although a copy of Nancy Chandler's *Map of Chiang Mai*, available in bookshops, is a worthwhile 160B investment. It shows the main points of interest, shopping venues and oddities that you would be most unlikely to stumble upon by yourself. *Groovy Map Chiang Mai Map'n'Guide*, also in bookshops, adds Thai script and more nightspots.

The Tourism Authority of Thailand (TAT) puts out a sketchy city map that is free and available from the TAT office on Th Chiang Mai-Lamphun. Several other ad-laden giveaway maps are also available in tourist shops and restaurants.

INFORMATION
Bookshops

Book Zone (Map pp280-1; ☎ 0 5325 2418; Th Tha Phae) Directly opposite Wat Mahawan; offers new travel guides and travel literature, plus contemporary fiction.
Gecko Books (Map pp280-1; ☎ 0 5387 4066; Th Ratchamankha) A large selection of used & new books. There's also a shop on Th Chiang Moi Kao.
Lost Book Shop (Map pp280-1; ☎ 0 5320 6656; 34/3 Th Ratchamankha) Primarily used books, with a wide choice, and cheaper than Gecko Books.
Suriwong Book Centre (Map pp280-1; ☎ 0 5328 1052; 54 Th Si Donchai) Chiang Mai's best new-book selection, especially strong in nonfiction about Thailand and Southeast Asia.

Cultural Centres

Several foreign cultural centres in Chiang Mai host film, music, dance and theatre, as well as other cultural events.
Alliance Française (Map pp280-1; ☎ 0 5327 5277; chiangmai@alliance-francaise.or.th; 138 Th Charoen Prathet) French films (subtitled in English) are screened at 4.30pm every Tuesday and at 8pm on Friday; admission is free to members, 30B to general public.

American University Alumni (AUA; Map pp280-1; ☎ 0 5327 8407, 0 5321 1377; 73 Th Ratchadamnoen) Offers English and Thai language courses (see p293).
British Council (Map pp280-1; ☎ 0 5324 2103; 198 Th Bamrungrat) Features a small English-language library and offers the services of an honorary consul.

Dentists

Thailand has a very good reputation for its dental care, and it is cheaper than at home. Most offer cosmetic dentistry too. The following have been recommended.
Dental 4U (Map pp280-1; ☻ 0 5387 4149; www.dental 4uchiangmai.com; 382-384 Th Tha Phae)
Grace Dental Care (Map pp276-7; ☻ 0 5389 4568; www.gracedentalclinic.com; 45 Soi 11 Th Nimmanhaemin)

Digital Photos

Most internet cafés will download digital camera pictures onto CDs or DVDs for around 80/200B respectively.

Emergency

Tourist police (Map pp280-1; ☎ 0 5324 8130, 0 5324 8974, 24hr emergency 1155; Th Chiang Mai-Lamphun; ☻ 6am-midnight)

Internet Access

You'll find plenty of internet centres along the following streets: Tha Phae, Moon Muang, Ratchadamnoen, Ratchamankha, Ratchadamri, Nimmanhaeman, Huay Kaew, Chang Khlan and Suthep.

Internet Resources

www.chiangmai-online.com Basic information about Chiang Mai, along with comprehensive accommodation listings.
www.chiangmainews.com Posts a variety of articles on local events, culture and art, along with current news developments.

Media

Chiangmai Mail Weekly newspaper; good source of local news.
City Life Oriented as much towards residents as tourists, with articles on local culture, politics and people.
City Now Published by *City Life* magazine, *City Now* is a fortnightly pamphlet listing events and workshops.

Medical Services

At most hospitals in Chiang Mai, many of the doctors speak English.
Chiang Mai Ram Hospital (Map pp280-1; ☎ 0 5322 4861; www.chiangmairam.com; 8 Th Bunreuangrit)

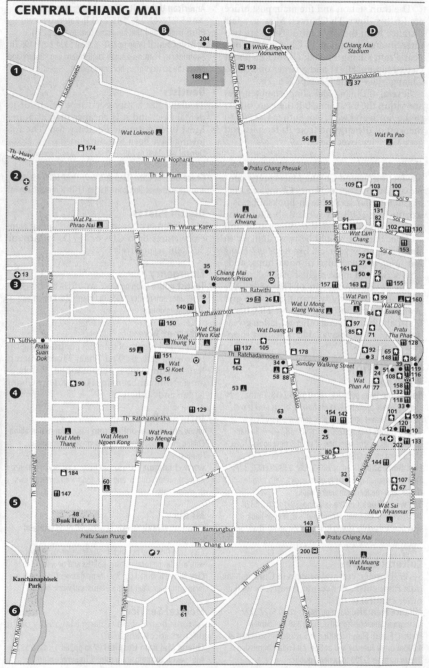

CENTRAL CHIANG MAI

CHIANG MAI PROVINCE

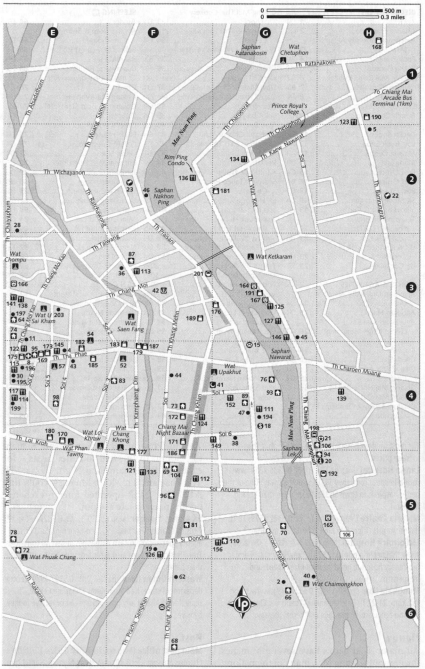

CHIANG MAI PROVINCE

The most modern hospital in town, with higher-than-average prices.

Lanna Hospital (Map pp276-7; ☎ 0 5335 7234; www.lanna-hospital.com; Hwy 11/Th Superhighway) One of the better hospitals in town and less expensive than Chiang Mai Ram.

Malaria Centre (Map pp280-1; ☎ 0 5322 1529; 18 Th Bunreuangrit) Offers free blood checks for malaria.

McCormick Hospital (Map pp276-7; ☎ 0 5326 2200; www.thai.net/mccormick; 133 Th Kaew Nawarat) Former missionary hospital; good for minor treatment, and inexpensive.

Mungkala (Map pp280-1; ☎ 0 5327 8494; www.mungkala.com; 21-27 Th Ratchamankha) Traditional Chinese clinic offering acupuncture, massage and herbal therapy.

Money

All major Thai banks have several branches throughout Chiang Mai, many of them along Th Tha Phae; most are open from 8.30am to 3.30pm. In the well-touristed areas – for example, the Chiang Mai Night Bazaar, Th Tha Phae and Th Moon Muang – you'll find ATMs and bank-operated foreign-exchange booths open as late as 8pm.

SK Moneychanger (Map pp280-1; ☎ 0 5327 1864; 73/8 Th Charoen Prathet; ☾ 8am-6pm Mon-Sat) Private agency specialising in cash exchanges in several currencies. Travellers cheques are also accepted, usually at better rates than banks.

Western Union (Map pp276-7; ☎ 0 5322 4979; Central department store, Kad Suan Kaew Shopping Centre, Th Huay Kaew) Also at any post office; send or receive money by wire.

Post

Main post office (Map pp276-7; ☎ 0 5324 1070; Th Charoen Muang; ☾ 8.30am-4.30pm Mon-Fri, 9am-12pm

Sat & Sun) Other useful branch post offices are at Th Singarat/Samlan, Th Mahidon at Chiang Mai International Airport, Th Charoen Prathet, Th Phra Pokklao, Th Chotana and Chiang Mai University.

Telephone

Many internet cafés are able to arrange inexpensive internet phone hook-ups. There are also numerous yellow phone-card booths in shops and bars around town.

Communications Authority of Thailand (CAT; Map pp276-7; ☎ 0 5324 1070; Th Charoen Muang; ⏱ 24hr) Out of the way, by the main post office.

Home Country Direct Phones 7-Eleven (Th Moon Muang); Chiang Mai International Airport (Map pp276-7); Main post office (Map pp276-7; Th Charoen Muang); TAT (Map pp280-1; Th Chiang Mai-Lamphun) Easy one-button connection to foreign operators in a number of countries around the world.

Tourist Information

TAT (Map pp280-1; ☎ 0 5324 8607; Th Chiang Mai- Lamphun; ⏱ 8am-4.30pm) Friendly English-speaking staff can answer questions, and there are racks filled with free maps and brochures.

DANGERS & ANNOYANCES

Upon arrival in Chiang Mai by bus or train, most waiting săwngthăew and túk-túk (motorised pedicab) drivers will try to get you to a particular hotel or guesthouse so that they can collect a commission. Since the better guesthouses refuse to pay any commissions, this means if you follow the driver's lead you may end up at a place with less appealing conditions or an out-of-the-way location. A handful of guesthouses now maintain their own free shuttle services from the train station. At any rate, if you call a guesthouse from

the bus or train station, staff will be delighted to arrange a ride to avoid paying such exorbitant commissions.

Beware of bus or minivan services from Th Khao San in Bangkok, which often advertise a free night's accommodation in Chiang Mai if you buy a Bangkok–Chiang Mai ticket. What usually happens on arrival is that the 'free' guesthouse demands you sign up for one of the hill treks immediately; if you don't, the guesthouse is suddenly 'full'. Sometimes they levy a charge for electricity or hot water. The better guesthouses don't play this game.

Theft is also more of a risk on the Th Khao San buses than on legitimate buses that leave from Bangkok's Moh Chit terminal.

Many less expensive guesthouses in Chiang Mai will evict guests who don't engage trekking or tour services through the guesthouse, or who don't eat meals regularly at the guesthouse. We've tried to avoid listing guesthouses where this practice is known to happen, but if in doubt, be sure to ask before checking in whether it's OK to take a room only.

Take care in the unlit backstreets around the Night Bazaar. We have had a few reports of women being attacked and robbed.

SIGHTS
Walking Streets

A more chilled out shopping experience than the Night Bazaar, Chiang Mai's **Sunday Walking Street** (pp280-1; Th Ratchadamnoen; ☺ 4pm-midnight Sun) has become more and more popular with Thais and tourists alike. Stretching from Tha Pae Gate square and along most of Th Ratchadamnoen, the area is blocked off to traffic from late Sunday afternoon to midnight. The whole of Th Ratchadamnoen, and the wats along its length, are filled with colourful stalls selling wares ranging from hill-tribe crafts and blinking lights, to wooden bangles and tasty morsels. There is a great atmosphere helped along by buskers playing down the street. When tired of the shopping, it is fun to sit at one of the bars or restaurants along the strip and watch the hubbub.

The newer and not yet as popular **Saturday Walking Street** (pp280-1; Th Wualai; ☺ 4pm-midnight Sat), happens in the south of the city on Th Wualai. There are similar stalls to the Sunday Walking Street but the point of interest here is the historic silver shops. Thai Khün silversmiths from Kengtung in Myanmar's Shan State migrated to Chiang Mai a century

or two ago and established several silverwork shops in this street. The descendents of those silversmiths have shops and stalls here still. There is also a beautiful textile museum further down the street (p288).

Wat Phra Singh
วัดพระสิงห์

Chiang Mai's most visited Buddhist temple, **Wat Phra Singh** (Map pp280-1; ☎ 0 5381 4164; Th Singarat) owes its fame to the fact that it houses the city's most revered Buddha image, Phra Singh (Lion Buddha). Started by King Pa Yo in 1345, the wíhǎan (large hall) that houses the Phra Singh image was completed between 1385 and 1400. Architecturally it's a perfect example of the classic northern Thai or Lanna style followed during this period from Chiang Mai to Luang Prabang. The Phra Singh Buddha supposedly comes from Sri Lanka, but is not particularly Sinhalese in style. As it is identical to two images in Nakhon Si Thammarat and Bangkok, and has quite a travel history (Sukhothai, Ayuthaya, Chiang Rai, Luang Prabang – the usual itinerary for a travelling Buddha image, involving much royal trickery), no-one really knows which image is the real one, nor can anyone document its place of origin. The sǐm (central sanctuary) was finished in about 1600.

Wat Phra Singh's main chedi displays classic Lanna style with its octagonal base. Wihan Lai Kham, a small chapel next to the chedi, features sumptuous laai kham (gold pattern) stencilling on its interior back wall. The wíhǎan is also well known for the narrative mural paintings which run along its main walls and date back to c 1870. The scene on the south wall depicts the popular northern Thai story of a divine golden swan, Phra Suwannahong.

Paintings on the north wall, executed by an ethnic Chinese thought to have trained in Bangkok, display a much higher level of skill. A small figure above one of the windows is thought to be a self-portrait of the artist.

Wat Chedi Luang
วัดเจดีย์หลวง

This **temple complex** (Map pp280-1; ☎ 0 5327 8595; main entrance Th Phra Pokklao) encloses a very large and venerable Lanna-style chedi dating from 1441. Now in partial ruins, stories say it was damaged by either a 16th-century earthquake or the cannon fire of King Taksin in 1775

during the recapture of Chiang Mai from the Burmese.

The Phra Kaew ('Emerald' Buddha), now held in Bangkok's Wat Phra Kaew, sat in the eastern niche here in 1475. Today there is a jade replica of the original Phra Kaew sitting in its place, financed by the Thai king and carved in 1995 to celebrate the 600th anniversary of the *chedi* (according to some reckonings), and the 700th anniversary of the city.

A restoration of the great *chedi* of the wat, financed by Unesco and the Japanese government, stopped short of creating a new spire, since no-one knows for sure how the original superstructure looked. New Buddha images have been placed in three of the four directional niches.

New porticoes and *naga* (mythical serpent) guardians for the *chedi* lack the finesse of the originals. On the southern side of the monument, six elephant sculptures in the pediment can be seen. Five are cement restorations; only the one on the far right – without ears and trunk – is original brick and stucco.

The *làk meuang* (guardian deity post) for the city can be seen in a small building to the left of the compound's main entrance.

Have a chat to the monks while you are here. They sit at the tables on the right side of the *chedi* as you walk in (see the boxed text, p295).

Wat Chiang Man

วัดเชียงมั่น

A stone slab inscription, engraved in 1581 and erected at **Wat Chiang Man** (Map pp280-1; ☎ 0 5337 5368; Th Ratchaphakhinai), bears the earliest known reference to the city's 1296 founding. It is thus thought to be the oldest wat in the city, and founded by Phaya Mengrai. The wat features typical northern Thai temple architecture, with massive teak columns inside the *bòt* (central sanctuary; *sĭm* in Northern Thai).

Two important Buddha images are kept in a glass cabinet inside the smaller sanctuary, to the right of the *sĭm*. The Phra Sila, a marble bas-relief Buddha that stands 20cm to 30cm high, is supposed to have come from Sri Lanka or India 2500 years ago, but since no Buddha images were produced anywhere before around 2000 years ago, it must have arrived later. The well-known Phra Satang Man, a crystal seated-Buddha image, was shuttled back and forth between Thailand and Laos like the Emerald Buddha. It's thought to have come from Lavo (Lopburi) 1800 years ago and stands just 10cm high.

Red-and-gold stencilled murals on the walls of the *sĭm*, which were completed in 1996 to celebrate the 700th anniversary of the founding of the city, depict scenes from the life of Chiang Mai's founding father, Phaya Mengrai.

The chapel housing the venerated images is open between 9am and 5pm. Wat Chiang Man is off Th Ratchaphakhinai in the northeastern corner of the old city.

Wat Jet Yot

วัดเจ็ดยอด

Out of town on the northern highway loop near the National Museum, **Wat Jet Yot** (Map pp276-7; ☎ 0 5321 9483; Hwy 11/Th Superhighway) was built in the mid-15th century to host the eighth World Buddhist Council in 1477. Based on the design of the Mahabodhi Temple in Bodhgaya, India, the proportions for the Chiang Mai version are quite different from the Indian original; it was probably modelled from a small votive tablet depicting the Mahabodhi in distorted perspective. The *jèt yâwt* (seven spires) represent the seven weeks Buddha was supposed to have spent in Bodhgaya after his enlightenment.

Some of the original stucco relief, depicting Bodhisattva (Buddhist saints, usually associated with Mahayana Buddhism) remains on the outer walls of the old *wíhăan*. There's an adjacent *chedi* of undetermined age and a very glossy *wíhăan*. The entire area is surrounded by well-kept lawns. It's a pleasant, relaxing temple to visit, but a bit too far from the city centre to reach on foot; by bicycle it's easy, or you can take a red *săwngthăew*.

CHIANG MAI PROVINCE

WAT'S NOT TO MISS

- Wat Phra Singh (opposite), with its impressive Lanna architecture
- Wat Chedi Luang (opposite), for a relaxed atmosphere and monk chats
- Wat Chiang Ma (left), the oldest temple in Chiang Mai
- Wat U Mong (p286), a beautiful, atmospheric forest wat
- Wat Phra That Doi Suthep (p325), a jewel on the mountain

Wat Phan Tao
วัดพันเถา

Diagonally adjacent to Wat Chedi Luang, **Wat Phan Tao** (Map pp280-1; ☎ 0 5381 4689; Th Phra Pokklao) contains a large, old teak *wíhǎan* that is one of the unsung treasures of Chiang Mai. Constructed of moulded wooden teak panels fitted together and supported by 28 gargantuan teak pillars, the *wíhǎan* features *naga* bargeboards inset with coloured mirror mosaic. On display inside are old temple bells, some ceramics, a few old northern-style gilded wooden Buddhas, and antique cabinets stacked with old palm-leaf manuscripts. Also in the compound are some old monastic quarters.

Wat U Mong
วัดอุโมงค์

This **forest wat** (☎ 0 5327 3990; Soi Wat U Mong) was first used during Phaya Mengrai's rule in the 14th century. Brick-lined tunnels through a large, flat-topped hill were allegedly fashioned around 1380 for the clairvoyant monk Thera Jan. The monastery was abandoned at a later date and wasn't reactivated until a local Thai prince sponsored a restoration in the late 1940s. The since-deceased Ajahn Buddhadasa, a well-known monk and teacher at southern Thailand's Wat Suanmok, sent a number of monks to re-establish a monastic community at U Mong in the 1960s.

One building contains modern artwork by various monks who have resided at U Mong, including several foreigners. A marvellously grisly image of the fasting Buddha – ribs, veins and all – can be seen in the grounds on top of the tunnel hill, along with a very large and highly venerated *chedi*. Also on the grounds is a small artificial lake, surrounded by *kùtì* (monastic cottages).

A small library/museum with English-language books on Buddhism can be found on the premises. Resident foreign monks give talks in English on Sunday afternoon at 3pm by the lake.

To get to Wat U Mong, travel west on Th Suthep for about 2km, then take a left and follow the signs for another kilometre to Wat U Mong.

Note that there is another temple named Wat U Mong in Chiang Mai, a smaller urban version found in the old city. To make sure a săwngthăew or túk-túk driver understands you want the original, ask for 'Wat U Mong Thera Jan'.

Wat Suan Dok
วัดสวนดอก

Phaya Keu Na, the sixth Lanna king, built this **temple** (Map pp276-7; ☎ 0 5327 8967; Th Suthep) in a forest grove in 1373 as a place where the visiting Phra Sumana Thera, who was a teaching monk from Sukhothai, could spend in retreat. The large, open *wíhǎan* was rebuilt in 1932. The *bòt* contains a 500-year-old bronze Buddha image and vivid *jataka* (Buddha's past-life stories) murals. Amulets and Buddhist literature printed in English and Thai can be purchased inexpensively in the *wíhǎan*.

On the grounds stands a group of striking whitewashed Lanna *chedi*, framed by Doi Suthep when viewed from the east. The large central *chedi* contains a Buddha relic that, according to legend, miraculously duplicated itself in the 14th century. The duplicate relic was mounted on the back of a white elephant (commemorated by Chiang Mai's Pratu Chang Pheuak), which was allowed to wander until it 'chose' a site on which a wat could be built to enshrine it. The elephant stopped and died at a spot on Doi Suthep, 13km west of Chiang Mai, where Chiang Mai residents built Wat Phra That Doi Suthep.

Today Wat Suan Dok is home to a large population of resident monks and novices, many of them students at the monastery's Mahachulalongkorn Buddhist University. See p295 for details on how visitors may interact with monastic students at Wat Suan Dok.

Wat Ku Tao
วัดกู่เต้า

North of the moat, near Chiang Mai Stadium, **Wat Ku Tao** (Map pp276-7; ☎ 0 5321 1842) dates from 1613 and has a unique *chedi* that looks like a pile of diminishing spheres, a Thai Lü design common in Yunnan, China. The *chedi* is said to contain the ashes of Tharawadi Min, a son of the Burmese king Bayinnaung, ruler of Lanna from 1578 to 1607.

Wat Chiang Yeun
วัดเชียงยืน

Another unique local temple is the 16th-century **Wat Chiang Yeun** (Map pp280-1; Th Mani Nopharat) outside the northeastern corner of the old city, east of Pratu Chang Pheuak. Besides the large northern-style *chedi* here, the main attraction is an old Burmese colonial-style gate and pavilion on the eastern side of the school grounds attached to the wat.

CHIANG MAI PROVINCE

Catering to Shan and Burmese temple-goers, a few shops and street vendors in the vicinity of Wat Chiang Yeun sell Burmese-style pickled tea (*miang* in Thai) and Shan-style noodles.

Wat Chetawan, Wat Mahawan & Wat Bupparam

วัดเชตวัน/วัดมหาวัน/วัดบุปผาราม

These three wats along Th Tha Phae feature highly ornate *wíhǎan* and *chedi* designed by Shan and Burmese artisans. Financed by Burmese teak merchants who immigrated to Chiang Mai a century or more ago, evidence of Shan/Burmese influence is easily seen in the abundant peacock symbol (a solar symbol common in Burmese and Shan temple architecture) and the Mandalay-style standing Buddhas found in wall niches.

At **Wat Mahawan** (Map pp280-1; ☎ 0 5384 0189) and **Wat Bupparam** (Map pp280-1; ☎ 0 5327 6771), no two guardian deity sculptures are alike; the whimsical forms include animals playing and various mythical creatures. Wat Bupparam contains a charming little *bòt* constructed of teak and decorated in pure Lanna style.

Wat Sisuphan

วัดศรีสุพรรณ

This **wat** (Map pp280-1; ☎ 0 5320 0332; Th Wualai), south of the moat, was founded in 1502, but little remains of the original structures except for some teak pillars and roof beams in the *wíhǎan*. The murals inside show an interesting mix of Taoist, Zen and Theravada Buddhist elements. Wat Sisuphan is one of the few wats in Chiang Mai where you can see the Poy Luang (also known as Poy Sang Long) Festival, a Shan-style group ordination of young boys as Buddhist novices, in late March.

Wat Phuak Hong

วัดพวกหงส์

Located behind Suan Buak Hat (Buak Hat Park), this **wat** (☎ 0 5327 8864; Th Samlan) contains the locally revered Chedi Si Pheuak. The *chedi* is more than 100 years old and features the 'stacked spheres' style seen only here and at Wat Ku Tao, and most likely influenced by Thai Lü *chedi* in China's Xishuangbanna district, Yunnan.

Chiang Mai City Arts & Cultural Centre

หอศิลปวัฒนธรรมเชียงใหม่

Chiang Mai's former Provincial Hall, originally built in 1924 and a masterpiece of post-colonial Thai architecture, has been converted into a cultural space with interesting, interactive exhibits, music, historical displays and more, spread across 15 rooms. There are also temporary art exhibitions, monthly workshops and a library.

The **Chiang Mai City Arts & Cultural Centre** (Map pp280-1; ☎ 0 5321 7793; www.chiangmaicitymuseum.org; Th Phra Pokklao; adult/child 90/40B; ⏰ 8.30am-5pm Tue-Sun) was awarded a Royal Society of Siamese Architects award in 1999 for its faithful architectural restoration.

Chiang Mai National Museum

พิพิธภัณฑสถานแห่งชาติเชียงใหม่

Established in 1954 with a lone curator overseeing a small collection of Lanna Buddhas and potsherd (fragments of pottery), **Chiang Mai National Museum** (Map pp276-7; ☎ 0 5322 1308; www.thailandmuseum.com; off Hwy 11/Th Superhighway; admission 30B; ⏰ 9am-4pm Wed-Sun) has grown to having a full-time staff of 20 cataloguing and caring for up to a million artefacts. These items are shared among four important national museums in Chiang Mai, Lamphun, Chiang Saen and Nan, all under the auspices of the Chiang Mai National Museum. The museum displays a very good selection of Buddha images in all styles, including a huge bronze Buddha downstairs. Pottery is also displayed downstairs, while upstairs there are household and agricultural tools, along with historic weaponry.

The museum is close to Wat Jet Yot on Hwy 11 (also known as 'the Superhighway'), which curves around the city.

Tribal Museum

พิพิธภัณฑ์ชาวเขา

Overlooking a lake in Suan Ratchamangkhala on the northern outskirts of the city, this octagonal **museum** (☎ 0 5321 0872; admission free; ⏰ 9am-4pm Mon-Fri) houses a collection of handicrafts, costumes, jewellery, ornaments, household utensils, agricultural tools, musical instruments and ceremonial paraphernalia. There are also informative displays showing the cultural features and background of each of the major hill tribes in Thailand; an exhibition on activities carried out by the Thai royal family on behalf of the hill tribes; and various bits of research and development sponsored by governmental and non-governmental agencies. Video shows run from 10am to 2pm (20B to 50B). The museum is closed on public holidays.

Sbun-Nga Textile Museum

The three-year-old **Sbun-Nga Textile Museum** (Map pp276-7; ☎ 0 5320 0655; www.sbun-nga.com; 185/20 Th Wualai; admission 100B; ◑ 10.30am-6.30pm Thu-Tue) displays a stunning collection of northern Thai textiles set in five adjoining Lanna teak buildings. The result of 20 years of collecting by the owner Akarat Nakkabunlung, the museum showcases different ethnic textiles with old photographs, accessories and furniture.

Tai Lue, Tai Lao, Tai Kaun, Tai Yai and *Tai Yuan* textiles are on display, with explanations of the geographical areas they come from, and the designs they are most famous for. Textiles range from everyday sarongs to opulent royal garments, and include the Lanna-and-Burmese-patterned dress of Princess Dararasmi (consort of King Rama V) and the bejewelled coronation costume of a *Thai Yai* prince.

Anusawari Sam Kasat (Three Kings Monument)

อนุสาวรีย์สามกษัตริย์

Next to the Chiang Mai City Arts & Cultural Centre, these three **bronze sculptures** (Map pp280-1; Th Phra Pokklao) portray men standing in 14th-century royal costume. They represent Phaya Ngam Meuang, Phaya Mengrai and Phaya Khun Ramkhamhaeng, the three northern Thai-Lao kings most associated with Lanna history. The statuary has become a shrine to local residents, who regularly leave offerings of flowers, incense and candles at the bronze feet in return for (hoped for) blessings from the powerful spirits of the three kings.

Chiang Mai Zoo

สวนสัตว์/แหล่งเพาะพันธุ์ไม้ป่าเขตร้อนเชียงใหม่

At the foot of Doi Suthep, the modern Chiang Mai Zoo (☎ 0 5335 8116; www.chiangmaizoo.com; Th Huay Kaew; adult/child 100/50B, Twilight Zone adult/child 200/100B, motorcycle & bicycle 10B, car & truck 50B; ◑ 8am-6pm, Twilight Zone 6pm-9pm) is set in a lush location, with waterfalls, forests and lakes on the grounds. Open-sided buses take you around the site, which houses a walk-through aviary with over 5000 birds, an aquarium, a children's zoo and a penguin house. It's also home to large African and Asian mammals, including tigers and giraffes. There are also giant pandas (adult/child extra 100/50B) and koalas.

Come here in the evening for the 'Twilight Zone', which gives an alternative (and cooler) view. The price includes a visit to the pandas, animal feeding and zoo transport. It costs around 30B to 40B by săwngthăew to Chiang Mai Zoo from town.

Chiang Mai University (CMU)

มหาวิทยาลัยเชียงใหม่

The city's principal public **university** (Map pp276-7; ☎ 0 5384 4821; Th Huay Kaew), established in 1964, was the first Thai university to be established outside of Bangkok. Today the 14-sq-km university boasts more than 18,000 students and 2000 lecturers divided among 107 departments.

Although scholastically CMU doesn't compare overall to such notable Bangkok universities as Silpakorn, Chulalongkorn or Thammasat, the CMU has earned special respect for its faculties of engineering and medical technology.

The main campus lies 2km west of the city centre in a 2.9-sq-km wedge of land between Th Suthep and Th Huay Kaew; there are entrances to the campus along both roadways. Students live in more than 20 dormitories on campus, as well as in off-campus housing.

Chiang Mai University Art Museum (Map pp276-7; ☎ 0 5394 4833; cnr Th Suthep & Th Nimmanhaemin; ◑ 9am-5pm, Tue-Sun) has temporary exhibitions set in a slick modern building, showcasing contemporary Thai and international art.

The abundant green areas between the faculty buildings and student residences, along with the tree-shaded, tranquil Ang Kaew reservoir, are pleasant places for strolling. For more vigorous movement, the campus offers a fitness park and sports track, both open to the public at no charge, as well as a public swimming pool with a small usage fee. Other facilities on the main campus include restaurants, banks, a post office, a bookshop and grocery store.

Mosques

Of the 12 mosques in Chiang Mai, the oldest and most interesting is **Matsayit Chiang Mai** (Chiang Mai Mosque; Map pp280-1; Th Charoen Prathet, Soi 1), also known as Ban Haw Mosque. Founded by *jiin haw* more than 100 years ago, it still primarily caters to this unique ethnic group; you'll hear Yunnanese spoken as often as Thai within the compound. It's located between Th Chang Khlan and Th Charoen Prathet, not far from the Chiang Mai Night Bazaar.

Along this *soi* (lane) are several Yunnanese Muslim restaurants that serve *khâo sawy kài* (curried chicken and noodles).

Hindu & Sikh Temples

The most colourful of Chiang Mai's two Hindu temples is the brightly painted *mandir* (traditional shrine room) and the *sikhara* (tower) of **Devi Mandir Chiang Mai** (Map pp280-1; Th Ratanakosin), opposite Chiang Mai Stadium.

Namdhari Sikh Temple (Map pp280-1; Th Ratchawong), between Th Chang Moi and Th Tha Phae, is the place of worship for the Namdhari sect of Sikhism.

Suan Buak Hat (Buak Hat Park)

สวนบวกหาด

This well-maintained public **park** (Map pp280-1; ⏰ 8am-5pm), wedged into the southwestern corner of the old city quadrangle, is Chiang Mai's miniature counterpart to Bangkok's Lumphini Park (p137), with pleasant expanses of grass, fountains and palms; many people jog in this area.

Wiang Kum Kam

เวียงกุมกาม

These **excavated ruins** (☎ 0 5332 1523; ⏰ 8am-5pm) are tucked away near the banks of Mae Nam Ping, 5km south of the city via Hwy 106 (also known as Th Chiang Mai-Lamphun). The earliest historical settlement in the Chiang Mai area, it was established by the Mon in the 11th or 12th century as a satellite town for the Hariphunchai kingdom. The city was abandoned in the early 18th century due to massive flooding, and visible architectural remains are few – only the four-sided Mon-style *chedi* of Wat Chedi Si Liam and the layered brick pediments of Wat Kan Thom (its Mon name; in Thai the temple was known as Wat Chang Kham) are left. Chedi Si Liam is said to have been inspired by the similar *chedi* at Wat Kukut in Lamphun.

Over 1300 inscribed stone slabs, bricks, bells and *chedi* have been excavated at the site. The most important archaeological discovery has been a four-piece inscribed stone slab, now on display in the Chiang Mai National Museum. The early-11th-century inscriptions on this slab indicate that the Thai script predates King Ramkhamhaeng's famous Sukhothai inscription (introduced in 1293) by 100 or more years.

An ideal way to reach Wiang Kum Kam is to hire a bicycle; follow Th Chiang Mai-Lamphun southeast for approximately 3km and look for a sign to the ruins on the right. From this junction it's another 2km. You could also hire a túk-túk or red sǎwngthǎew to take you there for around 90B (one way). The site is around 3 sq km, so if you're not on a bicycle, you can rent a horse and cart (200B) to see the main sites.

Once you've finished looking around you can walk back to Th Chiang Mai-Lamphun and catch a sǎwngthǎew or a blue Chiang Mai–Lamphun bus back into the city.

Chiang Mai Night Safari

One of former Prime Minister Thaksin Shinawatra's projects, the slick **Night Safari** (☎ 0 5399 9050; www.chiangmainightsafari.com; Moo12, Tambon Nong-Kwali; adult/child day 100/50B, adult/child night 500/300B; ⏰ 1pm-4pm Mon-Fri, 10am-4pm Sat & Sun, 6pm-midnight daily) has obviously had a lot of money spent on it. It's caused much controversy throughout its creation – primary of which is its location on 1.3 million sq km of Doi Suthep National Park land, and the consequential (and as yet unassessed) environmental impact it may have.

In the evening, you can go through the parkland on an open-sided bus on either the 'Savannah Safari' (wildebeests, giraffes, white rhinoceroses, zebras etc) or the 'Predator Prowl' (tigers, lions, Asiatic black bears, crocodiles etc). The more dangerous animals are separated from the bus by deep trenches; other animals sometimes come right up close. Afterwards an impressive water show, accompanied by the King's Jazz, is held at the 'Swan Lake'.

During the day, the Jaguar Trail around the same lake is a pleasant 1.2km walk where the 50 species (ranging from rabbits to orangutans) are generally not in cages. The breeding of animals has been a success here, with the recent addition of two black leopards and four lion cubs. It costs 30B by sǎwngthǎew to get to the Night Safari from town.

ACTIVITIES

Flying

Chiang Mai Sky Adventure Club (☎ 0 5386 8460; www.skyadventures.info; 143 Mu 6, Tambon Choeng Doi, Amphoe Doi Saket; per person 15/30min 1700/2900B) offers 15- and 30-minute microlight flights over the Doi Saket area. Prices include transport from your hotel to the airfield.

If you're looking for an early morning hot-air balloon flight over the Chiang Mai countryside, contact **Oriental Balloon Flights** (☎ 08 5040 2001; www.orientalballoonflights.com; 1hr flight per

person 8800B; ☺ Nov–Feb). The rate includes transport to/from your hotel or guesthouse, and a champagne breakfast.

Horse Riding

At **Chiang Mai Horse Riding** (Map pp280-1; ☎ 0 5387 4091; http://horseriding.chiangmaiinfo.com; Travel Shop, 2/2 Th Chaiyaphum; per person 2200B) instructors lead horse and pony trails, with a maximum of five people, in the Mae Rim area. The price includes three hours riding, and transport to and from your hotel.

Motorcycle & Mountain Bike Tours

Contact Travel (Map pp280-1; ☎ 0 5381 2444; www .activethailand.com; 73/7 Th Charoen Prathet; per trip including meals, bike & accommodation from 4800B) arranges mountain-bike trips with guides and escort vehicles. Itineraries include two- to four-day trips from Chiang Mai, through Chiang Dao to Chiang Rai, as well as into Laos and Cambodia.

Velocity (Map pp280-1; ☎ 0 5341 0665; velocity@ thaimail.com; 177 Th Chang Pheuak) also offers cycling tours and hires out mountain bikes.

Stephen from **Tony's Big Bikes** (Map pp280-1; ☎ 08 6730 1088; cookyboy9@yahoo.com; 17 Th Rachamanka; 1-day tour incl 400cc bike 1700B) runs motorcycle tours around northern Thailand. Options range from one-day trips around Doi Suthep, to four- to five-day trips doing the Mae Hong Son loop.

Check out the **Golden Triangle Rider** (www.gt -rider.com) website for excellent information on motorcycle touring in northern Thailand.

River Cruises

Operating from a small pier behind Wat Chaimongkhon, **Mae Ping River Cruises** (Map pp280-1; ☎ 0 5327 4822; www.maepingrivercruise.com; Th Charoen Prathet; per person 400B) offers two-hour daytime cruises in roofed long-tail boats. After cruising through countryside, the boats stop at a small fruit and flower farm (about 40 minutes away) where fruit can be sampled and a beverage is provided. Hotel pick-up is included in the price and tours run between 8.30am and 5pm. The Thai dinner cruise offers a set menu (500B; alcoholic drinks extra) and goes from 7pm to 9pm.

With a boat landing 200m north of Nakhon Ping bridge, **Scorpion Tailed River Cruise** (Map pp280-1; ☎ 08 1960 9308; www.scorpiontailed.com; Th Charoen Prathet; per person 400B; ☺ 9am-5pm) focuses more on the history of the river. It also

stops at a fruit farm for free tastings. Call for a pick-up.

Riverside Bar & Restaurant has dinner cruises; see p305.

Rock Climbing

Rock-climbing and caving courses by experienced instructors are offered at **Chiang Mai Rock Climbing Adventures** (Map pp280-1; ☎ 0 6911 1470; www.thailandclimbing.com; 55/3 Th Ratchaphakhinai; 1-day top-rope climbing course 1800B, 3-day intensive course 6600B). It offers climbing and caving trips to Crazy Horse Buttress, an impressive set of limestone cliffs located behind Tham Meuang On (about 20km east of Chiang Mai). Rates include two guides trained in first aid and CPR, transport, food, drinking water, equipment rental, insurance and a T-shirt. The office on Th Ratchaphakhinai has gear sales and rental, a partner-finding service and a bouldering wall for practice sessions.

The Peak (Map pp280-1; ☎ 0 5382 0777, 08 1716 4032; 28/2 Th Chang Khlan; climbing wall per hr from 150B, 1-day climbing course 2500B; ☺ 5pm-midnight) also offers a variety of climbing courses at Crazy House Buttress. Its climbing wall at Th Chang Khlan is 15m high and 16m wide – one of the largest rock-climbing walls in Southeast Asia. Non-climbers can watch the action from several adjacent bars and restaurants.

Swimming

Landlocked Chiang Mai can get very hot, particularly from March to July. Fortunately, local opportunities for a refreshing swim abound.

There are several swimming pools open to the public. Fees can range from 20B to 100B per day (public pools are cheaper than hotel or private pools), while annual memberships start at around 300B. Some recommended pools:

Anodard Hotel (Map pp280-1; ☎ 0 5327 0755; 57-59 Th Ratchamankha)

Chiang Mai University (☎ 0 5322 1699; Faculty of Education, Th Huay Kaew) 300B membership, then daily fee.

Maharaj Hospital (Map pp276-7; ☎ 0 5322 1310; Faculty of Medicine, Th Suthep)

Pong Pot Swimming Pool (Map pp276-7; ☎ 0 5321 2812; 73/22 Soi 4, Th Chotana)

SK House (Map pp280-1; ☎ 0 5341 8396; www .sk-riverview.com; Th Moon Muang, 30 Soi 9)

Top North Guest House (Map pp280-1; ☎ 0 5327 8900; Th Moon Muang, 15 Soi 2)

Top North Hotel (Map pp280-1; ☎ 0 5327 9623; www
.topnorthgroup.com; 41 Th Moon Muang)
World Club Sport Complex (☎ 0 5343 1501; 178/832
Mu 7, Nong Khwai, Th Hang Dong)

Tennis

Located opposite Chiang Mai National Museum, the **Anantasiri Tennis Courts** (Map pp276-7;
☎ 0 5322 2210; off Hwy 11/Superhighway; court hire day/
night 70/130B; 6am-8pm daily) is the best public
tennis facility in Chiang Mai. The six courts
are lit at night, and you can hire a 'knocker'
(tennis opponent) for a 30B/hour in addition
to the regular court fee.

Other recommended tennis courts in
Chiang Mai:
Chiang Mai Land Village (☎ 0 5327 2821; Th Chiang
Mai Land) South of the city.
Gymkhana Club (Map pp276-7; ☎ 0 5324 1035; Th
Ratuthit)
Lanna Sports Club (off Map pp276-7; ☎ 0 5322 1911;
Th Chotana) North of the city.

Thai Boxing Matches

Thapae Boxing Stadium (Map pp280-1; ☎ 08 6187 7655;
Th Ratchaphakhinai; admission 400B; 9pm Mon) has
Thai boxing matches every Monday, complete
with a cabaret.

WALKING TOUR
Old City Temple Tour

Within the walls of the old city, this tour takes
you through the most historic parts of Chiang
Mai. It includes a stop at the Chiang Mai City
Arts & Culture Centre and a look at some
interesting temples. There is some massage
along the way too.

Starting at **Wat Chiang Man** (**1**; p285), the
oldest wat in the city, head south down Th
Ratchaphakhinai until you hit Th Ratwithi.
Turn right and walk for about 500m until you
see the **Anusawari Sam Kasat** (**2**; p288) on the left;
you may see residents leaving offerings at the
bronze statues of these famous Lanna kings.
Next door is the impressive post-colonial Thai
building, now home to the **Chiang Mai City Arts &
Cultural Centre** (**3**; p287). Head in here to learn
about the history of the old city you're walking around.

If your feet are aching, carry on along Th
Ratwithi until you reach Chiang Mai Wom-
en's Prison, where you'll find a **spa** (**4**; p295).
Don't attempt to enter the prison itself (unless you have something to confess!) but go
to the building on the right with the 'Prison

Shop' sign. Inside, inmates offer very good
massage, the earnings of which are saved for
when they're released.

When your massage is finished, head back
down Th Ratwithi until you hit the Anusawari Sam Kasat again. Go south on Th Phra
Pokklao until you reach **Wat Phan Tao** (**5**; p286)
on your right. This intricate teak temple is
an unsung treasure of Chiang Mai. Adjacent
to Wat Phan Tao, further south on Th Phra
Pokklao, is the charming **Wat Chedi Luang** (**6**;
p284). If you're starting to wonder what Buddhism is all about, go and have a chat with
the monks at the north side of the *chedi*. Or
you can pay your respects to the relics inside
by filling a can with some blessed water and,
with a pulley, pouring it over the top of the
chedi.

As you leave Wat Chedi Luang, turn left
on Th Ratchadamnoen until you come to the
Writer's Club and Wine Bar (**7**; p306). Stop here
for some food, a drink and a scribble. Keep
heading to the end of Th Ratchadamnoen,
where you'll find the entrance to **Wat Phra Singh**
(**8**; p284), one of the most impressive temples
in Chiang Mai and home to the city's most
revered Buddha image.

WALK FACTS

Start Wat Chiang Man
Finish Wat Phra Singh
Distance 3.5km
Duration Two to three hours

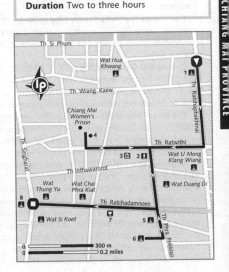

CHIANG MAI PROVINCE

For those who just want to flop and be pampered, turn right out of Wat Phra Singh, and on the corner is the **Oasis spa** (below) – perfect for a bit of accessible Nirvana.

However, if you feel inspired by all the temples you've just seen, jump aboard a săwngthăew and head to **Wat Suan Dok** (opposite) for a short meditation retreat. Alternatively, if it's a Sunday afternoon and you feel like being a consumer, go back up Th Ratchadamnoen and shop on the **Sunday Walking Street** (p284).

PUMMELLING & PAMPERING

In Thailand, *nûat phăen boraan* (traditional massage) is seen as a health essential rather than a pampering treat. Traditional massage places are all over Chiang Mai, with seats even lined up in markets for reviving foot massages. Sometimes dubbed 'yoga massage', *nûat phăen boraan* is done while you're fully clothed. It often feels like yoga is being performed on you, with postures that stretch the muscles; strong acupressure is also used. It tends to be a social activity, so in most *nûat phăen boraan* places don't be surprised to hear the gossip of the day rather than plinky-plonky New Age music.

For years, a different kind of massage culture has been emerging in Chiang Mai, with spas becoming big business. This new style tends to combine traditional Thai techniques with the quiet, retreat like atmosphere associated with Western spas. Most have Thai massage, herbal compress massage (local herbs steamed in a muslin compress then applied hot to the body) and reflexology, as well as the newer additions of oil massage, aromatherapy, body wraps, scrubs, facials and whole day pampering packages.

All of the massage schools (opposite) offer extremely good massage, usually for around 200B per hour. For some added pampering the following have been recommended:

Heaven Hut (Map pp280–1; ☎ 0 5327 6205; Th Charoen Prathet, Soi 6; 1hr treatment from 200B) In the midst of the Night Bazaar, Heaven Hut is perfectly placed for shopping fatigue. Flop in a chair for an excellent foot massage or go the whole hog with one of the spa packages on offer.

Let's Relax (Map pp280–1; ☎ 0 5381 8498; www.bloomingspa.com; 2nd fl, Chiang Mai Pavilion, 145/27 Th Chang Khlan; 1hr treatment from 400B) Another spot in the heart of Night Bazaar land, this place offers full-body massage, as well as half-hour back, shoulder and foot massages for those who don't want to lose precious shopping time.

Spa de Siam (Map pp280–1; ☎ 0 5382 0312; 62/3 Th Charoen Prathet; 1hr treatment from 500B) This simple, relaxing place has very good and well-priced massages, scrubs and facials. Call for free transport.

RarinJinda Wellness Center (Map pp280–1; ☎ 0 5324 7000; www.rarinjinda.com; 14 Th Charoenrat; 1hr treatment from 1000B) This smart, tastefully decorated new spa opposite the Riverside Restaurant has herbal steam rooms, hot stone massage, the usual facials and massage treatments, plus day packages.

Chiang Mai Oasis Spa (Map pp280–1; ☎ 0 5381 5000; www.chiangmaioasis.com; 4 Th Samlan; 1hr treatment from 1200B) This spa features individual, thatched wooden huts for single or couples treatments, set in calming grounds of decked walkways lined with small fountains. Signature treatments include four hands massage and herbal hot oil massage.

The Chedi (Map pp280–1; ☎ 0 5325 3333; www.ghmhotels.com; 123 Th Charoen Prathet; 1hr treatment from 1800B) The new Chedi's spa is all understated contemporary chic with 10 private rooms. Try a Thai herbal clay bath or a couples' 'love bath' with essential oils, petals and champagne. A variety of massages, wraps and facials are also on offer.

Angsana Spa (☎ 0 5329 7716; www.greenviewresort.com; 183/1 Chotana Rd; 1hr treatment from 2600B) Part of the Chiang Mai Green Valley Country Club, Angsana Spa is a luxurious space offering treatments from a variety of massage techniques to body scrubs, wraps and facials. The treatment rooms have views of the club's landscaped gardens.

Dheva Spa (☎ 0 5388 8888; www.mandarinoriental.com/hotel; Dhara Dhevi Chiang Mai, 51/4 Th Chiang Mai-San Kamphaeng; 1hr treatments from 3400B) Chiang Mai's grandest spa (3100 sq metre) is part of the Mandarin Oriental Dhara Dhevi resort, east of the city. Treatments range from relaxation massage to prescribed Ayurvedic programmes.

COURSES
Buddhist Meditation
International Buddhism Center (IBC; ☎ 0 5329 5012; www.fivethousandyears.org; admission free, donations appreciated) Located at Wat Phra That Doi Suthep, 16km northwest of Chiang Mai, the centre offers informal chats and discussion (1pm to 3pm) as well as chanting (6pm). It's also possible to do a three-day meditation retreat; see p325.

Northern Insight Meditation Centre (☎ 0 5327 8620; www.palikanon.com/vipassana/tapotaram/tapota ram.htm; donation) Located at Wat Ram Poenghe, where 10- to 26-day individual intensive courses in Vipassana are taught by a Thai monk or nun, with Western students or bilingual Thais acting as interpreters. Days start at 4am and meals are in silence. The formal name for Wat Ram Poeng is Wat Tapotaram.

Wat Suan Dok (Map pp276-7; ☎ 0 5380 8411 ext 114; www.monkchat.net; Th Suthep; retreats/courses free) Wat Suan Dok has a two-night/three-day meditation retreat at the end of each month. It also offers a meditation course every Tuesday (2.15pm) to Wednesday (1.30pm), with an overnight stay. You meet at Wat Suan Dok before being taken to its new meditation centre 15km northeast of Chiang Mai. It's worth booking online for the three-day retreat.

Cooking
THAI
Courses in Thai cuisine are another staple of Chiang Mai's vacation learning scene. Nowadays at least a dozen independent schools, as well as virtually every guesthouse in Chiang Mai, offer cooking classes from 800B to 990B a day. Some courses offer a choice of city or countryside based classes.

Classes typically include an introduction to Thailand's herbs and spices, a local market tour, cooking instructions and a recipe booklet. Of course, you get to eat the delicious Thai food as well – everything from Chiang Mai-style chicken curry to steamed banana cake. These courses have been recommended:

Baan Thai (Map pp280-1; ☎ 0 5335 7339; www .baanthaicookery.com; Th Ratchadamnoen, 11 Soi 5)

Chiang Mai Thai Cookery School (Map pp280-1; ☎ 0 5320 6388; www.thaicookeryschool.com; 47/2 Th Moon Muang) The most established cooking school, it has classes at The Wok restaurant, and also in a rural setting outside of Chiang Mai.

Gap's Thai Culinary Art School (Map pp280-1; ☎ 0 5327 8140; www.gaps-house.com; Gap's House, Th Ratchadamnoen, 3 Soi 4)

Thai Farm Cooking School (Map pp280-1; ☎ 08 7174 9285; www.thaifarmcooking.com; Th Ratchadamnoen, 2/2 Soi 5) Learn to cook at this organic farm.

INDIAN
Indian Restaurant Vegetarian Food (Map pp280-1; ☎ 0 5322 3396; Soi 9, Th Moon Muang) offers inexpensive cooking lessons; see p303.

Jewellery-making
From creating a silver ring or pendant to setting stones, **Nova Artlab** (Map pp280-1; ☎ 0 5327 3058; www.nova-collection.com; Th Tha Phae, 16/1 Soi 4; 1-/5-day course 1100/5500B) teaches the fundamentals of jewellery craft in workshops lasting from one to five days. Materials cost extra.

Language & Culture
American University Alumni (AUA; Map pp280-1; ☎ 0 5327 8407, 0 5321 1377; www.auathailand. org/chiangmai; 73 Th Ratchadamnoen; 1hr private lesson 270B, 60hr course 3900B) The AUA Thai course consists of three levels, with daily two-hour lessons (Mon-Fri). Private tutoring is also available.

Chiang Mai Thai Language Center (Map pp280-1; ☎ 0 5327 7810; www.chiangmai-adventure-tour.com /thai-language.html; 131 Th Ratchadamnoen; 1hr private lesson 230B, 30hr course from 2200B) Offers courses for beginners to advanced learners, as well as private lessons. As part of the course it is possible to stay in a village homestay just north of Chiang Mai.

Payap University (☎ 0 5330 4805 ext 250-1; http:// thaistudies.payap.ac.th; Th Kaew Nawarat; 60/120hr course 7000/14,000B) Intensive 60- and 120-hour Thai language courses at beginner, intermediate and advanced levels. These focus on conversational skills, as well as elementary reading and writing, and Thai culture. Payap also offers a Thai Studies Certificate Program, which involves two semesters of classroom lectures and field trips.

Thai Boxing
Lanna Muay Thai Boxing Camp (Kiatbusaba; ☎ 0 5389 2102; www.lannamuaythai.com; 64/1 Soi Chiang Khian; fees per day/month 250/7000B) offers authentic *muay thai* (Thai boxing) instruction to foreigners as well as Thais. Several Lanna students have won stadium bouts, including the famous transvestite boxer Parinya Kiatbusaba. According to the camp director, foreign boxers are much sought after, and match-ups with local boxers is offered. Simple camp accommodation is available (2600B to 3600B per month).

Traditional Massage
More visitors learn to pummel bodies the Thai way in Chiang Mai than anywhere else in Thailand. We've received good reports about the following courses:

Ban Nit (Map pp280-1; Th Chaiyaphum, Soi 2) A unique, one-on-one course available from Khun Nit, an older woman who is a specialist in deep-tissue, nerve and herbal massages. Length of study and payment for Nit's tutelage is up to the individual – according to what you can afford. Most students live in and eat meals with Nit and her family.

Chetawan Thai Traditional Massage School (Map pp276-7; ☎ 0 5341 0360; www.watpomassage .com/map_chiangmai_en.html; Th Pracha Uthit, 7/1-2 Soi Samud Lanna; foot massage/Thai massage 30hrs 5500/7000B) Off Th Chotana, this highly recommended massage school is affiliated with the Wat Pho massage school in Bangkok. Foot and Thai traditional massage courses are available over 5 days (6hrs per day).

Lek Chaiya (Map pp280-1; ☎ 0 5327 8325; www .nervetouch.com; 25 Th Ratchadamnoen; 5-day course 4000B) Khun Lek, a Thai woman who has been massaging and teaching for more than 40 years, specialises in *jàp sên* (similar to acupressure) and the use of medicinal herbs.

Old Medicine Hospital (OMH; Map pp276-7; ☎ 0 5327 5085; www.thaimassageschool.ac.th; Th Wualai, 78/1 Soi Siwaka Komarat; 2-day foot massage course 2000B, 10-day course 4000B) The OMH curriculum is very traditional, with a northern-Thai slant. There are two massage courses a month year-round (except for the first two weeks of April), as well as weekend foot-massage courses. Classes tend to be large from December to February, but smaller the rest of the year.

Thai Massage School of Chiang Mai (TMC; ☎ 0 5385 4330; www.tmcschool.com; Th Chiang Mai-Mae Jo; 30hr/5 day foundation course 5300B, 2-day reflexology course 3200B) Northeast of town, TMC has a solid, government-licensed massage curriculum. Different levels are offered, from foundation course to teacher training. Transport to the school is included.

Yoga

Yoga Sense Discovery of Life (Map pp280-1; ☎ 08 1021 6566; caymeeto@yahoo.co.uk; 191/15 Chang Klan Plaza, Th Chang Klan; classes 129B)

Yoga Studio (Map pp280-1; ☎ 08 4698 1982; www .yoga-chiangmai.com; 90/1 Th Ratchamankha; classes 200-250B) In a convenient location, Yoga Studio offers 1½hr morning & evening classes.

FESTIVALS & EVENTS

During the week-long **Winter Fair** (*thêtsàkaan ngaan reuduu nǎo*) in late December and early January, the area around Pratu Tha Phae assumes a country-fair atmosphere, with an abundance of rustic booths purveying northern Thai culinary delicacies, handicrafts, local designer clothing and just about anything else that can be traded.

Perhaps Chiang Mai's most colourful festival is the **Flower Festival** (*thêtsàkaan mái dàwk mái pràdàp*), also called the Flower Carnival, held annually in February (dates vary from year to year). Events occur over a three-day period and include displays of flower arrangements, a parade of floats decorated with hundreds of thousands of flowers, folk music, cultural performances and the Queen of the Flower Festival contest. Most activities are centred at Buak Hat Park near the southwestern corner of the city moat. People from all over the country turn out for this occasion, so book early if you want a room in town.

In mid-April the **Songkran Water Festival** is celebrated with an enthusiasm bordering on pure pandemonium. Thousands of revellers line up along all sides of the moat, and temporary pumps are installed so that water can be sucked from the moats and sprayed about with liberal abandon. It is virtually impossible to stay dry during the five days of this festival.

In May the **Intakin Festival** (*ngaan tham bun sǎo inthákin*), held at Wat Chedi Luang and centred around the *làk meuang* (city pillar), propitiates the city's guardian deity to ensure that the annual monsoon will arrive on time. Also in May – when the mango crop is ripe – a **Mango Fair** (*thêtsàkaan mámûang*) is celebrated in Suan Buak Hat, with lots of mango eating and the coronation of the Mango Queen.

During the festival of **Loi Krathong**, usually celebrated in late October or early November, Chiang Mai's river banks are alive with people floating the small lotus-shaped boats that mark this occasion. In Chiang Mai this festival is also known as Yi Peng, and some *khon meuang* (people of northern Thailand) celebrate by launching cylindrical hot-air balloons, lighting up the night skies with hundreds of pinpoints of light.

SLEEPING
Budget

Inexpensive guesthouses are clustered in several areas, primarily along the streets and lanes off Th Moon Muang and along several lanes running south off Th Tha Phae. You'll also find a few along Th Charoen Prathet, parallel to and west of Mae Nam Ping.

There are basically two kinds of budget guesthouse accommodation – old family homes

QUIRKY CHIANG MAI

Chiang Mai's Prison Spa

'Spa' and 'prison' are not two words you usually use together, but at **Chiang Mai Women's Prison** (Map pp280-1; ☎ 08 1706 1041; 100 Th Ratwithi; ⏰ 8.30-4.30pm) you'll find just that. A small spa at the women's prison offers traditional Thai full-body massage (150B), foot massage (120B), herbal massage (180B) and a sauna. The money earned from these treatments goes directly to the prisoners to save for when they are released. The atmosphere here is nice and the massages are great. And don't worry: you're not going to be massaged by a hardened crim – and those working in the massage centre are due for release within six months. Other rehabilitation initiatives include teaching sewing and cake baking to prisoners – the results of which you'll find in the same building. It's located in the 'Prison Shop' building.

Museum of World Insects & Natural Wonders

พิพิธภัณฑ์แมลงโลก

If the idea of face-to-face encounters with prehistoric flying superinsects, giant iridescent scarabs or long-tailed scorpions excites, then visit this private **museum** (Map pp276-7; ☎ 0 5321 1891; insects_museum@hotmail.com; Th Sirimangkhalajan by Soi 13; adult/child 300/100B; ⏰ 9am-5pm). Aside from perusing a detailed, well-labelled collection of preserved insects, you'll learn about the habits and habitats of Thailand's 436 mosquito species – 22 of which were named by the owner, renowned entomologist Manop Rattanarithikul. There are also fantastic fossil samples and pieces of petrified wood, some of which are humorously labelled. A true eccentric, Manop is passionate about his collection, and is as much a reason to visit this museum as the insects themselves.

Monk Chat

มราวาสสนทนาวัดสวนดอก

A room at **Wat Suan Dok** (Map pp276-7; ☎ 0 5327 3149; Th Suthep; admission free; ⏰ 5-7pm Mon, Wed & Fri) is set aside for foreigners to meet and chat with resident monks and novices. It is a chance for the monastic students to practise their English, and for foreigners to learn about Buddhism and Thai life. To find the room, enter the wat from the main entrance and walk straight past the large *wíhǎan* to a smaller building 100m or so into the temple grounds. Turn right at this smaller temple and watch for the 'Monk Chat' signs. The monastery asks that visitors dress modestly – covered shoulders, no shorts or short skirts – and that women visitors take care not to make physical contact with the monks.

Wat Chedi Luang (Map pp280-1; ☎ 0 5327 8595; main entrance Th Phra Pokklao; ⏰ 1-6pm, not Buddhist holidays) also gives an opportunity to chat to the monks. As you enter the wat head to the right side of the *chedi* and you'll see some tables set up outside with a 'Monk Chat' sign.

Foreign Cemetery

สุสานต่างชาติ

For spooky atmosphere, head out to this historic **cemetery** (Map pp276-7; Th Chiang Mai-Lamphun) near the Gymkhana Club. Century-old headstones bearing American, English and European names mark the remains of traders, missionaries, failed entrepreneurs and numerous other expats who have died in Chiang Mai. A bronze statue of Queen Victoria, imported from Calcutta, India, during the Raj era, stands sentinel.

converted into guest rooms (these usually have the best atmosphere, but the least privacy), and hotel- or apartment-style places with rows of cell-like rooms. In both, the furnishings are basic – a bed and a few sticks of furniture. You can assume that rooms under 150B won't have a private bathroom but will probably have a fan.

The cheaper guesthouses make most of their money from food service and hill-tribe trekking rather than from room charges, hence you may be pressured to eat and to sign up for a trek. Places that charge 200B or more usually don't hassle guests in this way.

Many of the guesthouses can arrange bicycle and motorcycle rental. If you phone a

CHIANG MAI PROVINCE

WHAT TO EXPECT IN CHIANG MAI

■ Budget (under 600B)

■ Midrange (600B to 2500B; 1500B in provinces)

■ Top end (over 2500B; 1500B in provinces)

---

guesthouse, most will collect you from the train or bus terminal for free if they have a room available (this saves them having to pay a commission to a driver).

INNER MOAT AREA

Lamchang House (Map pp280-1; ☎ 0 5321 0586; Soi 7, Th Moon Muang; r 90-170B) Run by a Thai family, this wooden Thai-style house is a great budget choice and has plenty of character. Rooms have some Thai decorations and fresh flowers, and there's a small garden restaurant. The downside is that all the bathrooms are shared.

ourpick Julie Guesthouse (Map pp280-1; ☎ 0 5327 4355; www.julieguesthouse.com; Th Phra Pokklao, 7 Soi 5; dm 60B, r 90-300B) This funky place has a colourful range of rooms and is a great place to meet other travellers. There are lots of areas to hang out, like the covered roof terrace with hammocks and the garden café with a pool table. There is a travel agency on site.

Supreme House (Map pp280-1; ☎ 0 5322 2480; 44/1 Soi 9, Th Moon Muang; s/d/tr 150/175/250B) This nondescript three-storey, hotel-like building attracts mainly long-termers. The atmosphere is relaxed, the rooms are large, the roof has hammocks and there's a library on the ground floor.

Montra House (Home; Map pp280-1; ☎ 0 5341 8658; Th Ratchadamnoen, Soi 5; r 200B; 🖳) Opposite Chiang Mai White House, this place has good-value, basic but spotless digs. Some rooms are in a wooden house with shared bathrooms, others are concrete rooms behind the wooden house, each with bathroom; all rooms cost the same.

Safe House Court (Map pp280-1; ☎ 0 5341 8955; 178 Th Ratchaphakhinai; r 200-350B; 🔀) This friendly budget choice features basic rooms with large bathrooms in an apartment-court feel.

Baan Manee (Map pp280-1; ☎ 0 5320 7133; nanthakwang@hotmail.com; Th Moon Muang, 31 Soi 2; r 250-350B; 🔀) Next door to Top North Guest House, this new place has well-equipped,

super clean rooms with cable TV. If you fancy a swim, you can use Top North's pool (100B per day).

Siri Guesthouse (Map pp280-1; ☎ 0 5332 6550; www.siri.gh@hotmail.com; Th Moon Muang, Soi 5; r 300-350B) This new place offers fantastic value rooms, stylishly decorated with dark wood furniture and some Thai touches. There's a pretty fishpond out front.

Eagle House 2 (Map pp280-1; ☎ 0 5321 0620; www.eaglehouse.com; Th Ratwithi, 26 Soi 2; dm 80B, r 200-360B; 🔀) This three-storey, modern building has basic rooms with a jarring yellow, green and red décor. There's a pleasant garden sitting area. It's fairly quiet except when the bars around Th Ratwithi get going from 9pm to midnight.

RCN Court (Map pp280-1; ☎ 0 5341 8280-2, 0 5322 4619; fax 0 5321 1969; Th Moon Muang, 35 Soi 7; r 300-450B; 🔀 🖳) This welcoming place has well-equipped, large and light rooms with cable TV, fridge and safety box. Facilities include a small fitness room, 24-hour internet, laundry service and a kitchen. Monthly rates are available.

Chiang Mai White House (Map pp280-1; ☎ 0 5335 7130; www.chiangmaiwhitehouse.com; Th Ratchadamnoen, 12 Soi 5; r 250-400B; 🔀) This guesthouse features clean, quiet, air-con rooms with cable TV.

Jonadda Guest House (Map pp280-1; ☎ 0 5322 7281; Th Ratwithi, 23/1 Soi 2; s/d/tr 250/350/450B) Run by an Aussie-Thai couple, this place has spotless but bland rooms. There is a pleasant café attached and it's convenient to the pub crawl area off Th Ratwithi.

Rendezvous Guest House (Map pp280-1; ☎ 0 5321 3763; rendezvouschiangmai@hotmail.com; Th Ratchadamnoen, 3/1 Soi 5; r 300-450B; 🔀) All the rooms in this three-storey guesthouse have TV, safety box and fridge. Ask for the slightly more expensive 'new rooms' – these are much better value. There is a pleasant restaurant with red banquettes.

Top North Guest House (Map pp280-1; ☎ 0 5327 8900; Th Moon Muang, 15 Soi 2; r 300-500B; 🔀 🖳) Same location as the Top North Hotel – come here for the pool but don't expect great shakes from the rooms. There's also a small spa and sauna.

ourpick Tri Gong Residence (Map pp280-1; ☎ 0 5321 4754; www.trigong.com; Th Sribhum, 8 Soi 1; r 600B; 🔀 🖳) Located at the end of Th Moon Muang's *soi* 9, Tri Gong has a courtyard surrounded by stylish rooms. The large rooms feature smart rattan and teak furniture, big

bathrooms, cable TV, fridges and free wireless internet. There are cheaper fortnightly rates, a kitchen, plus free internet on computers at reception.

Smile House 1 (Map pp280-1; ☎ 0 5320 8661; www .smileguesthouse.com; Th Ratchamankha, 5 Soi 2; r 200-600B; 🔀 🔊) This place offers plain rooms in an old Thai house surrounded by a row of newer rooms. The small pool is a plus but the communal area is shabby. This house once served as the 'safe house' of the infamous Shan-Chinese opium warlord Khun Sa whenever he came to Chiang Mai.

ourpick SK House (Map pp280-1; ☎ 0 5341 8396; www.sk-riverview.com; Th Moon Muang, 30 Soi 9; r 300-600B; 🔀 🖳 🔊) Rooms here have traditional Thai scenes painted on the door, tasteful furnishings and a cosy feel. Air-con rooms have cable TV. Extras include a large swimming pool, an atmospheric communal area full of antiques, a restaurant and TV, and an internet room.

Awana Sleep and Swim Guesthouse (Map pp280-1; ☎ 0 5341 9005; www.awanahouse.com; Th Ratchadamnoen, Soi 1; dm 120B, r 450-700B; 🔀 🖳 🔊) Down a quiet *soi*, yet right by Thae Pae Gate, Awana is a good deal with its large, neat and light rooms with balconies, TV and fridge. The tiny pool is good for a plunge but not for sunbathing. Dorm beds with mozzie nets are available on the covered roof terrace; there's also a pool table.

Gap's House (Map pp280-1; ☎ 0 5327 8140; www .gaps-house.com; Th Ratchadamnoen, 3 Soi 4; r 350-750B; 🔀) Gap's wooden rooms have some lovely antiquey furnishings but the walls are thin. The cheaper, sturdier concrete rooms are more basic. All rooms surround a lush garden and breakfast area, filled with cabinets of trinkets. A cookery course (p293) and tours are offered, as well as a popular nightly vegetarian buffet upstairs.

PRATU THA PHAE TO THE RIVER

Daret's House (Map pp280-1; ☎ 0 5323 5440; 4/5 Th Chaiyaphum; r 180B) A long-time backpackers' fave with stacks of basic, well-worn rooms. The large sidewalk café at the front is popular.

Sarah Guest House (Map pp280-1; ☎ 0 5320 8271; www.sarahguesthouse.com; Th Tha Phae, 20 Soi 4; r 250-400B; 🔀) Run by an English woman, the rooms have chunky wood furniture and large bathrooms, with the option of fan or air-con. In a pretty garden setting, this is a quiet place with a café attached.

New Mitrapap Hotel (Map pp280-1; ☎ 0 5323 5436; fax 0 5325 1260; 94-98 Th Ratchawong; r/suite incl breakfast 330-430/700B; 🔀) This is a classic Thai-Chinese spot on Chiang Mai's small Chinatown, between the east moat and Mae Nam Ping. A major renovation was near completion at the time of writing. The rooms are good value but feel quite child-like with the outside of the doors painted in different pastel and primaries, and matching paint work inside. It's close to several inexpensive Chinese restaurants, as well as the Talat Warorot (p318).

ourpick Riverside House (Map pp280-1; ☎ 0 5324 1860; www.riversidehousechiangmai.com; 101 Th Chiang Mai-Lamphun; r 350-600B; 🔀) Next door to TAT, this quiet and friendly place is set back from the road. The rooms are large, pristine, well-furnished and great value. Arranged around a pretty garden, all have cable TV and include breakfast. There is an adjoining travel agency, coffee shop and internet service.

Roong Ruang Hotel (Roong Raeng; Map pp280-1; ☎ 0 5323 4746; fax 0 5325 2409; 398 Th Tha Phae; 350-800B; 🔀) With a prime location near Pratu Tha Phae, on the eastern side of the city moat, all of the well-furnished rooms with cable TV have pleasant sitting areas out the front. The more expensive rooms have air-con and are in the new building. This is a good place to stay for the Flower Festival in February as the Saturday parade passes right by the entrance, but for the same reason it's probably not the best choice for the raucous Songkran and Loi Krathong festivals.

TH NIMMANHAEMIN AREA

ourpick Thanasiri House (Map pp276-7; ☎ 0 5321 5949; oulan51@yahoo.com; Th Nimmanhaemin, Soi 1; r incl breakfast 400-500B; 🔀) The simple yet stylish rooms here are a good-value base for the area. Rooms have cable TV, and a small desk and chair.

Midrange

In this range you can expect daily room cleaning, the option of air-con, cable TV and additional (and usually, more stylish) furniture. Prices at midrange go from 600B to around 2500B.

INNER MOAT AREA

Montri Hotel (Map pp280-1; ☎ 0 5321 1069/70; www .norththaihotel.com/montri.html; 2-6 Th Ratchadamnoen; r 750B; 🔀) This conveniently located five-storey hotel is on the busy corner of Th Moon Muang and Th Ratchadamnoen. The rooms

have no character but are well equipped with safety deposit box, cable TV and fridge. A renovation was in process at the time of writing. Avoid the noisy street-facing rooms.

Top North Hotel (Map pp280-1; ☎ 0 5327 9623; www .topnorthgroup.com; 41 Th Moon Muang; r 600-800B; ☒ ☒) This high-rise, close to Pratu Tha Phae, is in a good location and has a great pool. Unfortunately, the rather dark rooms look grubby and are in need of a major revamp.

Mini Cost (Map pp280-1; ☎ 0 5341 8787; www .minicostcm.com; Th Ratchadamnoen, Soi 1; s/d 500/750-850B; ☒ ☒) This new guesthouse has contemporary styled rooms with easy chairs, calming colours and modern Thai prints. The larger rooms are better value as the single rooms are a bit cramped. All are nonsmoking and have TV. Shame the boss is rather gruff.

ourpick Sri Pat Guest House (Map pp280-1; ☎ 0 5321 8716; www.sri-patguesthouse.com; Th Moon Muang, 16 Soi 7; r 900B; ☒) This stylish 17-room guesthouse is decorated in a chic Thai modern style. The rooms have rustic looking tiles in the bathrooms, plenty of rattan furniture and lots of Thai touches. All rooms have a terrace, cable TV, minibar and hairdryer.

Parasol Inn (Map pp280-1; ☎ 0 5381 4011; www.para solinn.com; 105/1 Th Phra Pokklao; r 1000-1500B; ☒ ☒) Just off the Sunday Walking Street, this new hotel has large, well-equipped rooms decorated in a modern Thai style. Some rooms at the back have views of Wat Chedi Luang. Big discounts can be had in low season.

PRATU THA PHAE TO THE RIVER

Baan Kaew Guest House (Map pp280-1; ☎ 0 5327 1606; www.baankaew-guesthouse.com; 142 Th Charoen Prathet; r 700B; ☒) Opposite Wat Chaimongkhon and two doors south of the Alliance Française, Baan Kaew is set back off the road, so it's very quiet. Well-furnished and maintained, the rooms, although rather bland, have fridges, safety deposit boxes and outdoor seating areas. Meals are available in a small outdoor dining area.

Lai-Thai Guesthouse (Map pp280-1; ☎ 0 5327 1725; www.laithai.com; 111/4-5 Th Kotchasarn; r 750B; ☒ ☒) Northern Thai décor is the bonus to what is otherwise just another three-storey hotel court. The rooms, with cable TV and minibar, feel cramped as too much furniture is squashed in.

Chiangmai Gold Star Hotel (Map pp280-1; ☎ 0 5323 2492; 53 Th Si Donchai; r 350-750B; ☒) This friendly 29-room hotel is a little old fashioned but has

character. The large rooms are decorated with ornate Burmese furniture and Thai pictures. There is a restaurant on site.

Viangbua Mansion (Map pp276-7; ☎ 0 5341 1202; www.viangbua.com; 3/1 Th Viangbua; r from 900B; ☒ ☒) North of Pratu Chang Pheuak and opposite the Rajabhat University, this new hotel has smart, contemporary, Thai-styled rooms. Designed for the longer-term guest, rooms have wardrobes, shelving, a large fridge, small lounge, cable TV and wireless internet; some also have a kitchen. A gym, restaurant and coffee shop are on the premises, and weekly rates are available.

Galare Guest House (Map pp280-1; ☎ 0 5381 8887; www.galare.com; Th Charoen Prathet, 7/1 Soi 2; r 1100B; ☒) Set in an old style Thai house, this well-managed and friendly guesthouse has spacious rooms with some charm. The Galare is popular with repeat visitors for its Mae Nam Ping location and proximity to the Chiang Mai Night Bazaar. The traffic over nearby Saphan Nawarat can be a bit noisy.

Buarawong Residence (Map pp280-1; ☎ 0 5327 3283; www.buarawong.com; 129/9 Th Rakaeng; r/ste incl breakfast 600-800/1500B; ☒ ☒) This well-looked-after high-rise has good value, well-furnished large rooms with wood floors and cable TV. Avoid the rooms by the main road as they can get noisy.

Pornping Tower Hotel (Map pp280-1; ☎ 0 5327 0099; www.pornpinghotelchiangmai.com; 46-48 Th Charoen Prathet; r from 1800B; ☒ ☒) This large, 324-room high-rise looming over the back of the Chiang Mai Night Bazaar has standard, comfortable rooms. The Pornping is most famous for Bubbles, a popular disco in town, but there are also two restaurants (one of them open 24 hours), a lobby bar, karaoke lounge, live music club, fitness centre and massage service. Discounts are usual in low season.

Royal Princess (Map pp280-1; ☎ 0 5328 1033; www.royalprincess.com; 112 Th Chang Khlan; r from 1950B; ☒ ☒ ☒) In the middle of the Chiang Mai Night Bazaar, facilities at this hotel include international, Chinese and Japanese restaurants and a lobby bar. Rooms have a contemporary bent.

ourpick River View Lodge (Map pp280-1; ☎ 0 5327 1109; www.riverviewlodgch.com; 25 Soi 2, Th Charoen Prathet; r 1450-2200B; ☒ ☒) The River View Lodge has got an edge on charm, with cabinets stuffed full of objects, a two-level garden overlooking Mae Nam Ping and a good-size pool. The rooms by contrast are rather plain. In the

dry season you'll find the owner's collection of classic cars in the parking lot.

Suriwongse Hotel (Map pp280-1; ☎ 0 5327 0051; www.suriwongsehotels.com; 110 Th Changklan; r incl breakfast 1500-3000B; ⊠ ⬜ ⬛) Close to the Night Bazaar, the rooms here are spick-and-span but slightly old fashioned. The staff are friendly, and facilities include a massage centre, restaurant, coffee shop and business centre.

TH NIMMANHAEMIN AREA & CHIANG MAI UNIVERSITY (CMU)

CMU International Center Hostel (Map pp276-7; ☎ 0 5394 2881; www.ic.cmu.ac.th; 239 Th Nimmanhaemin; r 690-790B; ⊠ ⬜) Housed in CMU's busy International Center, this cosy hostel offers 88 rooms, all with TV and fridge. Rates include breakfast and monthly rates are available. Downstairs there's Doi Wawi café and Lemongrass restaurant.

our pick **Baan Say-La** (Map pp276-7; ☎ 08 6911 1184; aimaschana@gmail.com; Th Nimmanhaemin, Soi 5; r 450-950B; ⊠) This chic and contemporary new addition has rooms with four-poster beds, rattan furnishing and cable TV. Black-and-white photography decorates the walls, and the shared seating areas have large easy chairs, sofas and hammocks. The 450B rooms have shared, well-equipped bathrooms. Downside is that it is behind the 'Fine Thanks' live music bar, so some rooms may be noisy.

Top End

In general, hotel rates for luxury hotels are lower in Chiang Mai than in Bangkok. You can expect to pay anywhere from 2600B to around 20,000B and beyond for large, well-maintained rooms with air-con, TV and International Direct Dial (IDD) telephone in hotels with a restaurant (usually more than one), swimming pool and fitness centre. Booking through a travel agency or via the internet almost always means lower rates, or try asking for a hotel's 'corporate' discount.

Since 2004, the city has seen a sudden boom in five-star hotels. Some are chains, but the more interesting ones are the smaller 'boutique' hotels that tend to marry Lanna styles with a modern edge and a more intimate setting. In addition to some of our favourites listed here, hammers and drills are busy assembling more top-end offerings.

IN TOWN

our pick **D2hotel** (Map pp280-1; ☎ 0 5399 9999; www .d2hotels.com; 100 Th Chang Khlan; r US$154-513;

⊠ ⬜ ⬛) Chiang Mai's ultimate flashpacker digs, D2 attracts hip international and Thai visitors. The rooms manage to be minimalist and cosy at the same time with orange, brown and cream lux fabrics, understated abstract art and slinky white bathrooms. The Moxie restaurant and Mix Bar are chic places to hang out. There's also a fitness centre, business club lounge and spa.

Amora (Map pp280-1; ☎ 0 5325 1531; www.amora group.com; 22 Th Chiayapoom; r from 2584B; ⊠ ⬜ ⬛) The most central top-end option, the Amora is right near Thae Pae Gate. The rooms are light and fresh looking with all the amenities you'd expect at this price range.

Imperial Mae Ping Hotel (Map pp280-1; ☎ 0 5328 3900; www.imperialhotels.com; 153 Th Si Donchai; r from 3000B; ⊠ ⬜ ⬛) This sprawling hotel near the Chiang Mai Night Bazaar has well-outfitted standard rooms with some Thai touches. There's also a pool and fitness centre on the premises.

Central Duangtawan Hotel (Map pp280-1; ☎ 0 5328 3900; www.imperialhotels.com; 132 Th Loi Kroh; r incl breakfast 2696-6217B; ⊠ ⬜ ⬛) Located by Chiang Mai Night Bazaar this 24-floor, 500-room hotel has smart, modern, although rather bland rooms, with good views of Chiang Mai. There's a 4th floor pool, fitness centre, conference facilities and restaurant. Better deals can be had online.

Yaang Come Village (Map pp280-1; ☎ 0 5323 7222; www.yaangcome.com; 90/3 Th Si Donchai; r 4800-9800B; ⊠ ⬜ ⬛) This new addition is Tai Lue in architecture and style. Rooms are tastefully decorated with murals, intricate textiles and beautiful teak furniture. Winding paths and a manicured garden lead to the impressive pool and a romantic restaurant.

Tea Vanna (Map pp280-1; ☎ 0 5330 2805; www .tea-vanna.com; 75 Th Chiang Mai-Lamphun; r 2700-10,000B; ⊠ ⬛) Tea Vanna is a funky new 30-room hotel with a contemporary Chinese feel. The well-designed, chic rooms are named after different teas and surround a pool decorated with a kitschy lotus mural. Some have fun '60s inspired bubble-shaped furniture, others are all sleek lines and Chinese motifs. A spa and stylish looking restaurant were being built at the time of writing.

Tamarind Village (Map pp280-1; ☎ 0 5341 8898; www.tamarindvillage.com; 50/1 Th Ratchadamnoen; r 5000-10,000B; ⊠ ⬛) A fusion of Thai and Mediterranean architectural styles, this quiet spread with 40 rooms on the grounds of an

old tamarind orchard features a pool, bar, modest restaurant and, like its more upscale sister the Rachamankha, easy access to old city sights.

our pick The Chedi (Map pp280-1; ☎ 0 5325 3333; www.ghmhotels.com; 123 Th Charoen Prathet; r 10,400-15,600B; ❄ 🖳 🖭) Located on the Mae Ping river, The Chedi mixes minimalist design with Lanna style. The hotel is centred around the beautiful, colonial style, ex-British Consulate, now functioning as the breakfast area, restaurant and bar. With floor to ceiling windows, the contemporary style rooms are all understated luxury and sleek lines. A spa, fitness centre and pool are on site. Definitely one of the most stylish hotels in the city.

Manathai (Map pp280-1; ☎ 0 5328 1666; www.manathai.com; Th Tha Phae, 39/9 Soi 3; r 7000-16,000B; ❄ 🖳 🖭) This new boutique hotel is conveniently located in a quiet *soi* off Th Tha Phae. Manathai has a colonial feel with two-storey buildings surrounding a pool. Rooms are stylishly decked out with teak furniture, black-and-white photographs and contemporary touches. The intimate atmosphere makes it a nice place for a romantic stay. Online rates are cheaper.

Rachamankha (Map pp280-1; ☎ 0 5390 4111; www.rachamankha.com; 6 Th Ratchamankha; r 6900-18,000B; ❄ 🖳 🖭) Walking into this architect-owned hotel is like walking into the compound of a 16th-century Lanna temple built for royalty. The 24 tastefully decorated, supremely serene guest rooms are a mix of Lanna and Chinese styles. The Rachamankha also has a gourmet dining room (see p302), small bar, and impressive library, all filled with exquisite Lanna antiques and artworks.

TH NIMMANHAEMIN AREA

Chiang Mai Orchid Hotel (Map pp276-7; ☎ 0 5322 2091; www.chiangmaiorchid.com; 23 Th Huay Kaew; r from 2800B; ❄ 🖳 🖭) A 266-room hotel next to Kad Suan Kaew shopping centre, the Chiang Mai Orchid is oriented towards business travellers and upscale package tourists. The rooms have some Thai styling, and there's a fitness centre, business centre, pool and beauty salon.

Amari Rincome Hotel (Map pp276-7; ☎ 0 5322 1130, 0 5322 1044; www.amari.com; 1 Th Nimmanhaemin; r 2700-6200B; ❄ 🖳 🖭) Very reliable business hotel. Amenities include a lovely pool area, a tennis court, Italian restaurant, coffee shop, lobby bar, conference facilities and nail salon. The

deluxe rooms have recently been revamped with a more contemporary look.

OUT OF TOWN

North of the city in the Mae Rim/Mae Sa area are a few plush countryside resorts. Most of these establishments have free shuttle vans to/from the city.

Four Seasons Chiang Mai (☎ 0 5329 8181; www.fourseasons.com; Th Mae Rim-Samoeng Kao; r US$450; ❄ 🖳 🖭) Located north of the city, this is one of Chiang Mai's premier resorts, featuring 64 vaulted pavilion suites (each around 75 sq metres), plus two- and three-bedroom residences spread amid eight hectares of landscaped gardens and rice terraces worked by water buffalo. On the premises are a state-of-the-art, semi-outdoor cooking school, two full-service restaurants, a bar, a health club, two swimming pools and two illuminated tennis courts. The resort's Lanna Spa has earned much acclaim.

Mandarin Oriental Dhara Dhevi (☎ 0 5388 8888; www.mandarinoriental.com; 51/4 Th Chiang Mai-San Kamphaeng; r US$429-1100; ❄ 🖳 🖭) Almost a kingdom unto itself, the new Dhara Dhevi has taken 52 partially wooded acres just east of the city limits and filled them with architecture inspired by Greater Lanna (including neighbouring Shan State, northern Laos and Sipsongpanna/Xishuangbanna in southern China) at its 15th- to 17th-century peak. The 310-sq-metre spa is the largest in northern Thailand.

Proud Phu Fah (☎ 0 5387 9389; www.proudphufah.com; Km 17, Th Mae Rim-Samoeng; r 4000-6500B; ❄ 🖳 🖭) This new, well signposted place has a very relaxed and romantic setting. It offers modern bungalows with four-poster beds, all-white interiors, huge windows and individual decked terraces over the river. The infinity pool and restaurant make the most of the panoramic mountain views. Mountain bikes are available to rent.

EATING

You won't lack for variety in Chiang Mai as the city has arguably the best assortment of restaurants of any city in Thailand outside of Bangkok. Chiang Mai's guesthouses serve a typical menu of Western food along with a few pseudo-Thai dishes. If you're interested in authentic Thai cuisine, you'll do well to leave the guesthouse behind for the most part.

Thai

Sailomyoy (Map pp280-1; Th Ratchadamnoen; dishes 20-50; ✆ 9am-11pm) By Pratu Tha Phae, this simple, cheap place serves good Thai noodles, rice, curries and soups. Breakfast is available; try the mango and sticky rice pudding.

Si Phen Restaurant (Map pp280-1; ☎ 0 5331 5328; 103 Th Inthawarorot; dishes 40-80B; ✆ 9am-5pm) This inexpensive stopover near Wat Phra Singh specialises in both northern- and northeastern-style dishes. The kitchen prepares some of the best *sôm-tam* (spicy papaya salad) in the city, including a variation made with pomelo fruit.

Ratana's Kitchen (Map pp280-1; ☎ 0 5387 4173; 320-322 Th Tha Phae; dishes 30-90B; ✆ 9am-11pm) An aircon spot owned by an English-Thai couple, Ratana's is situated in a prime Th Tha Phae location near Book Zone. The inexpensive menu offers Thai dishes from several regions, as well as a few *faràng* items.

Aroon (Rai) Restaurant (Map pp280-1; ☎ 0 5327 6947; 45 Th Kotchasarn; dishes 40-90B; ✆ 8am-10pm) Look for Chiang Mai specialities such as *kaeng hang-leh*, *kaeng awm* and *kaeng khae*. The latter two dishes are more like stews than curries, and rely on local roots and herbs for their distinctive, bitter-hot flavours. The spacious open-air dining area upstairs is favoured by night-time clientele, and in hot weather it's cooler than downstairs.

Sila-aat (Map pp280-1; ☎ 0 5381 4552; 3/6-7 Th Samlan; dishes 30-100B; ✆ 8am-8pm) Opposite the entrance to Wat Phra Singh, this is a good place to refuel after temple exploring. Sila-aat offers generous portions of Thai and Chinese dishes. Their *pad thai* (rice noodle dish) is particularly delicious and has lots of salad on the side.

ourpick Hong Tauw Inn (Map pp276-7; ☎ 0 5322 8333; 95/17-18 Nantawan Arcade, Th Nimmanhaemin; dishes 30-120B; set menu 400-470B; ✆ 11am-11pm) This intimate, charming place has got an old-fashioned feel, with 1940s pendulum clocks, scattered antiques and traditional tablecloths. Particularly good are the northern Thai dishes, like the intense *phanaeng* curry and the yummy banana flower salad. The set menu is for two people and includes seven dishes.

Heuan Phen (Map pp280-1; ☎ 0 5327 7103; 112 Th Ratchamankha; dishes 50-140B; ✆ 8.30am-3pm & 5-10pm) Highly regarded for its northern Thai food, the house specialities include *khâo sawy* (egg noodles in a curried broth), *lâap khûa* (northern-style minced-meat salad), *náam phrík*

nùm (a chilli dip made with roasted peppers) and *kaeng hang-leh* (very rich Burmese-style pork curry). Daytime meals are served in a large dining room out the front, while evening meals are served in an atmospheric antique-decorated house at the back.

Heuan Soontharee (no Roman-script sign; Map pp276-7; ☎ 0 5325 2445; 46/2 Th Wang Singkham; dishes 40-150B; ✆ 5pm-1am) Rustic dining areas built on several levels open onto the west bank of the river. The owner, famous northern Thai singer Soontaree Vechanont, performs at the restaurant on weekends; other local musicians perform during the week. The menu is a pleasant blend of northern, northeastern and central Thai specialities.

The Wok (Map pp280-1; ☎ 0 5320 8287; 44 Th Ratchamankha; dishes 60-150B; ✆ 3pm-10pm) Run by the Chiang Mai Cookery School, this popular place is set in a covered outside eating area with pretty lanterns. It serves a selection of veggie dishes and is especially good on northern Thai cuisine. If you are thinking of doing its cookery course, come here first to get an idea of the kind of dishes you'll be making.

Cafe de Nimman (Map pp276-7; Room, Th Nimmanhaemin; dishes 55-160B; ✆ 10am-11pm) Located at the front of the 'Room – boutique mall' (an open-air walkway with a row of shops and bars). Sit in the pleasant outside seating area or the small air-con section and choose from a large menu of Thai rice dishes, spicy salads and curries.

Antique House (Map pp280-1; ☎ 0 5327 6810; 71 Th Charoen Prathet; dishes 80-160B; ✆ 11am-11pm) Set in a two-storey teak house filled with interesting antiques, the food here is beautifully presented and predominately northern Thai. There is also a garden seating area. There is no smoking allowed in the house.

Dalaabaa Bar and Restaurant (Map pp280-1; ☎ 0 5324 2491; 113 Th Bamrungrat; dishes 100-200B; ✆ 6pm-midnight Mon-Sat) This trendy eatery, with subdued lighting washing over orange and red silks, brings a Bangkok-style sophistication to Chiang Mai dining with a clever Thai fusion menu.

Whole Earth Restaurant (Map pp280-1; ☎ 0 5328 2463; 88 Th Si Donchai; dishes 120-300B) Set in a teak house, there is the option to sit outside on the 2nd-floor terrace, or inside with air-con. The food here is well presented Thai and Indian (both vegetarian and nonvegetarian). The atmosphere is suitably mellow, as are the toned-down flavours.

ourpick **Palaad Tawanron** (☎ 0 5321 6039; Th Suthep; dishes 90-350B; ⌚ 11.30am-midnight) Set by a waterfall, this buzzing new restaurant draws in Thais and foreigners alike for the fantastic Thai food and the spectacular views over twinkly Chiang Mai. Try the fiery *tôm yam* (spicy and sour soup) or any of the delicious fish dishes. Entry is via the rear gate to Chiang Mai Zoo; go to the end of Th Suthep, then at the zoo follow the signs.

Le Grand Lanna (☎ 0 5385 0111; Mandarin Oriental Dhara Dhevi Hotel, 51/4 Th Chiang Mai-San Kamphaeng; dishes 150-350B) Part of the Mandarin Oriental Dhara Dhevi complex, Le Grand Lanna is a 4000-sq-metre complex of restored northern Thai buildings filled with antique furniture, high-end art and handicrafts. The cuisine can be wonderful, especially the upmarket versions of northern Thai specialities.

Rachamankha (Map pp280-1; ☎ 0 5390 4111; 6 Th Ratchamankha; dishes 220-1100B) Tucked away behind Wat Phra Singh, in the sumptuous grounds of the boutique hotel of the same name, one dines at the Rachamankha to enjoy the antique-laden atmosphere as much as the food. The menu is Thai-centred, with hints of Myanmar, Yunnan and Europe floating at the periphery. On Friday to Sunday evening (7pm to 9pm) there's traditional Thai music.

Chinese & Japanese

Yok Fa (Map pp280-1; Th Ratchaphakhinai; dishes 25-30B; ⌚ 8am-8pm) Opposite the Red Cross Building, this simple but popular place cooks up fresh food in the massive woks upfront. Try *pat see lew* (fried wide noodles with pork, soybean sauce, morning glory and egg) or the suckling pig and rice.

Mitmai Restaurant (Map pp280-1; ☎ 0 5327 5033; 42/2 Th Ratchamankha; dishes 50-120B; ⌚ 9am-9pm) A clean, simple and spacious Yunnanese place specialising in delicious vegetable soups made with pumpkin, taro, snowpeas, mushrooms or other vegetables. Try the *tôm sôm plaa yâwt máphráo* (hot-and-sour fish soup with coconut shoots). The bilingual menu also includes *yam* (tangy, Thai-style salad) made with Chinese vegetables, as well as Yunnanese steamed ham and many vegetarian dishes. No MSG is used in the cooking.

Dai-Kichi (Map pp276-7; ☎ 0 5322 3873; 40/2-3 Moda Place, Th Nimmanhaemin; set menus 90-250B, set menu 129-169B; ⌚ 10am-10pm) Just past *soi* 7, this new, highly recommended place on the main road offers reasonably priced sushi and sashimi, plus a variety of nine-dish set menus.

Chiang Mai's small **Chinatown** (Map pp280-1; Th Ratchawong) is located on Th Ratchawong, north of Th Chang Moi. Here you'll find a whole string of inexpensive Chinese rice and noodle shops, most of them offering variations on Tae Jiu (Chao Zhou) and Yunnanese cooking. Recommended is **Aomngurn** (Map pp280-1; ☎ 0 5323 3675; Th Ratchawong; dishes 20-90B), next to the New Mitrapap Hotel. This funky looking place with blackboard signs outside serves fantastic grilled chicken and various Chinese/Thai dishes. There are English menus.

Noodles

Khâo sawy – a Shan-Yunnanese concoction of chicken (or, less commonly, beef), spicy curried broth and flat, squiggly, wheat noodles – is one of the most characteristic of Chiang Mai's noodle dishes. It's served with small saucers of shallot wedges, sweet-spicy pickled cabbage and a thick red chilli sauce.

Khao Soi Prince (Map pp280-1; Th Kaew Nawarat; dishes 20-35B; ⌚ 9am-3pm) Near Prince Royal's College, this is regarded by many locals as their favourite spot for authentic *khâo sawy*. The *khâo mòk kài* (Thai-style chicken briyani) is also well worth trying.

Rot Sawoei (Map pp280-1; Th Arak; dishes 25-35B) Around the corner from Buak Hat Park, this unassuming open-air spot is famous for its delectable *kŭaytĭaw kài tŭn yaa jiin* (rice noodles with Chinese herb-steamed chicken) that practically melts off the bone. A normal bowl costs 25B, while a *phísèht* (special) order with extra chicken costs 35B.

Kuaytiaw Kai Tun Coke (Map pp280-1; Th Kamphaeng Din; dishes 40B) A small food stall directly opposite the main entrance to the Imperial Mae Ping Hotel prepares a simpler version of *kŭaytĭaw kài tŭn yaa jiin* but substitutes Coca-Cola for the Chinese herbs. Here the chicken is marinated in cola and spices overnight, then steamed and served with rice noodles. It's actually quite good and has become famous as far away as Bangkok.

Khao Soi Lam Duan (Map pp276-7; Th Faham; dishes 30-55B) This place serves large bowls of beef, pork or chicken *khâo sawy*. Also on the menu are *kao-lăo* (soup without noodles), *mŭu sà-té* (grilled spiced pork on bamboo skewers) and *khànŏm rang phêung* (literally beehive pastry – a coconut-flavoured waffle).

Just Khao Soi (Map pp280-1; ☎ 0 5381 8641; 108/2 Th Charoen Prathet; dishes 100B; ⊗ lunch & dinner) This is the gourmet version of *khâo sawy*. Served on a wooden artist's palette you can create your own noodle broth with several condiments, including coconut milk, to thicken it at will. Two different noodle shapes are offered: Chiang Mai style and Mae Salong style.

Two other good *khâo sawy* places along Th Faham are **Khao Soi Samoe Jai** (Map pp276-7; Th Faham) and **Khao Soi Ban Faham** (Map pp276-7; Th Faham).

Indian, Muslim & Middle Eastern

Along Soi 1, Th Charoen Prathet, between Th Chang Khlan and Th Charoen Prathet and near Matsayit Chiang Mai, are a number of simple restaurants and alley vendors selling inexpensive but tasty Thai Muslim curries and *khâo sawy*. *Néua òp hǎwm* ('fragrant' Yunnanese Muslim-style dried beef), a speciality of Chiang Mai, is also sold along the lane. A food vendor, also on this lane, does delicious *rotii* (Indian flat bread) as well as chicken murtabak (*mátàbà kài; rotii* stuffed with chicken). Burmese food stalls set up along here on Friday mornings.

Sophia (Map pp280-1; Th Charoen Prathet, Soi 1; dishes 30-50B; ⊗ 8am-7pm Sat-Thu) Sophia serves good curries and *khâo mòk kài* (Thai-Muslim version of chicken briyani).

Indian Restaurant Vegetarian Food (Map pp280-1; ☎ 0 5322 3396; Th Moon Muang, Soi 9; dishes 30-70B; ⊗ 8am-11pm) A very friendly, family-owned place that serves up cheap and adequate vegetarian thalis as well as individual Indian dishes. The owners also offer Indian cooking lessons.

Arabia (Map pp280-1; ☎ 0 5381 8850; Anusan Night Market; dishes 30-90B) This small restaurant does north Indian-Pakistani-Arab–style cuisine very well, perhaps better than any of the others in terms of the freshness of the flavours. Don't let the fact that it's often empty throw you off the trail; it has a steady and discerning, if small, clientele.

Shere Shiraz (Map pp280-1; ☎ 0 5327 6132; Th Charoen Prathet, Soi 6; dishes 50-120B) Serves mostly north Indian food, with a few south Indian dishes. The extensive menu includes many vegetarian options.

our pick Jerusalem Falafel (Map pp280-1; ☎ 0 5327 0208; 35/3 Th Moon Muang; dishes 60-160B; ⊗ 9am-11pm Sat-Thu) This brightly coloured restaurant serves a selection Middle Eastern food, as well as salads and sandwiches. Choose from a list of side dishes like falafels, shashlik, hummus and tabbouleh, or have mains like beef kebab and moussaka. The meze for two or four people is a good deal. Yogurt, haloumi and feta cheese are homemade here.

Italian

La Gondola (Map pp280-1; ☎ 0 5330 6483; dishes 60-120B) Fresh pasta, salads and vegetarian dishes are offered in an atmospheric, under-the-stars setting on a grassy area by the river.

La Villa Pizzeria (Map pp280-1; ☎ 0 5327 7403; 145 Th Ratchadamnoen; dishes 60-140B) Set in and around a large, old Thai house, La Villa serves pizza baked in a wood-fired oven, and the rest of the Italian food on the menu is tops.

Pum Pui Italian Restaurant (Map pp280-1; ☎ 0 5327 8209; 24 Soi 2, Th Moon Muang; dishes 60-150B; ⊗ 11am-11pm) This casual place features a low-key garden setting and moderate prices. The menu includes olive pâté and other antipasti, along with salads, lots of vegetarian options, ice cream, breakfast, Italian wines and espressos.

Da Stefano (Map pp280-1; ☎ 0 5387 4189; 2/1-2 Th Chang Moi Kao; dishes 70-160B) An intimate, well-decorated, air-con place, Da Stefano focuses on fresh Italian cuisine, with one of the better wine lists in town.

Giorgio Italian Restaurant (Map pp280-1; ☎ 0 5381 8236; 2/6 Th Pracha Samphan; dishes 100-250B) Chiang Mai's most ambitious, and some say best, Italian eatery features a full range of pasta, some of it homemade. The salads are particularly good, while the décor is classy and retro.

International Food

our pick Café Souvannaphoum (Map pp280-1; ☎ 0 5390 3781; 20/1 Th Ratchamankha; dishes 60-100B; ⊗ 8am-12pm) Next to Lost Book Shop, this new, Swiss-Thai run, hip looking café and wine bar stands out in this budget backpacker area. Real coffee, good breakfast, sandwiches and salads are served in a chic décor of rattan-and-cream easy chairs. Wine is a big focus of this place, with regular wine-tastings. Expect a bigger menu by the time this guide is published.

Art Café (Map pp280-1; ☎ /fax 0 5320 6365; cnr Th Tha Phae & Th Kotchasarn; dishes 50-110B; ⊗ 10am-10pm) Facing Pratu Tha Phae, this popular place has a huge menu including Thai, Italian, Mexican and American food. It is particularly good for breakfasts and there are lots of vegetarian options. This is a non-smoking restaurant.

CHIANG MAI PROVINCE

Mike's Burgers (Map pp280-1; cnr Th Chaiyaphum & Th Chang Moi; dishes 40-115B; ☺ 6pm-3am) Grab a stool for a dose of après-clubbing handmade burgers and chilli fries. Considered the best burgers outside the US by expats, there is also a branch on Th Nimmanhaemin.

Bierstube (Map pp280-1; ☎ 0 5327 8869; 33/6 Th Moon Muang; dishes 50-130B; ☺ 7am-midnight) This cosy place, decorated with black-and-white photos of Thailand, has wooden benches and a bar. It's popular with German expatriates and visitors, and the menu is mainly German/European with some Thai. It's near Pratu Tha Phae.

ourpick Herb Garden (Map pp280-1; ☎ 0 5341 8991; Th Ratchadamnoen, Soi 1; dishes 40-150B; ☺ 8am-11pm) This small and friendly place, run by a Thai-English couple, is one of those rare places where the Western food and Thai food are equally good. Thai dishes like *néua deh dio* (beef salad with sesame seeds and basil) are delicious. For something very English, choose the bangers and mash (with proper pork sausages) and the treacle tart. Breakfast is good here too.

Zest (Map pp276-7; ☎ 0 5390 4364; 41/3 Th Moon Muang; 50-170B; ☺ 6am-midnight) Sitting in a pukka position in front of the Top North Hotel, this funky alfresco café has the usual Thai and European menu. It's a good place to watch the world of Chiang Mai go by.

UN Irish Pub (Map pp280-1; ☎ 0 5321 4554; 24/1 Th Ratwithi; dishes 40-200B; ☺ 9am-midnight) This 'pub' offers comfort food like jacket potatoes, fresh bread and good coffee. There is beer on tap, and fruit and vegetable juices. The homey indoor section is decorated with Irish kitsch and there's pleasant garden seating out the back.

Chez John (Map pp276-7; ☎ 0 5320 1551; 18/1 Th Mahidon; dishes 90-250B) Near the airport and opposite the customs office, Chez John prepares moderately priced French cuisine and has a large selection of wines.

Chiangmai Saloon (Map pp280-1; ☎ 0 6161 0690; 80/1 Th Loi Kroh; dishes 80-300B) Ignore the ersatz Wild West décor, and head straight for the huge steaks and Tex-Mex.

Moxie (Map pp280-1; ☎ 0 5399 9999; D2 Hotel, 100 Th Chang Klan; dishes 90-460B; ☺ 10.30am-1am) This achingly hip restaurant has a sleek and ultra-modern décor in orange, cream and dark wood. The interesting lunch and dinner menu offers Thai, Japanese and Italian choices.

ourpick House (Map pp280-1; ☎ 0 5341 9011; 199 Th Moon Muang; tapas 50-110B, mains 200-790B; ☺ 6pm-11pm) This ambitious restaurant occupies a mid-20th-century house that once belonged to an exiled Burmese prince. The menu successfully fuses Thai and European elements, complemented by an excellent wine list and attentive service. For a more relaxed setting, lounge in the separate and sumptuous, Morrocanesque area for delicious tapas and drinks.

The main fast-food district in Chiang Mai runs along Th Chang Khlan, in the Chiang Mai Night Bazaar area (Map pp280-1). This strip features the usual Western fast-food outlets, most of which are clustered within the Pavilion building. Similar franchise-style places can be found in the Kad Suan Kaew shopping centre (Map pp276-7) on Th Huay Kaew and at Central Airport Plaza (Map pp276-7) near the airport.

Coffee, Juice & Sandwich shops

ourpick Juicy 4U (Map pp280-1; ☎ 0 5327 8715; 5 Th Ratchamankha; dishes 50-135B; ☺ 8.30am-5.30pm) This cute café serves fantastic organic breakfasts, sandwiches, salads, juices and smoothies. Choose your own sandwich fillings and bread type from a list, and they will rustle up your concoction. The Thai owner studies nutrition and can advise on the best juices for ailments ranging from a killer hangover to insomnia.

Black Canyon Coffee (Map pp280-1; ☎ 0 5327 0793; 1-3 Th Ratchadamnoen; dishes 50-115B; ☺ 8am-10.30pm) Right at Pratu Tha Phae, this contemporary styled place is great for people watching, especially on Sundays, when the Walking Street is on. Delicious ice coffee and teas, plus the usual Thai and Western food suspects are on offer here.

ourpick Wawee Coffee (Map pp276-7; ☎ 0 5326 0125; Th Nimmanhaemin, Soi 9; coffee 40-75B; ☺ 7am-10pm) Want to go where the hip Thais go? Head to *soi* 9 in the trendy Nimmanhaemin area and drink coffee among the fashionable, laptop tapping locals. There's a pretty outside area with a fountain, while inside it's contemporary and air-conditioned. Don't get this one mixed up with Wawee Coffee on the main road.

Smoothie Blues (Map pp276-7; Th Nimmanhaemin; dishes 50-120B; ☺ 7.30am-9pm) Great for breakfast and lunch, Smoothie Blues does fantastic muffins, bagels, waffles and muesli, as well as sandwiches and baguettes. Its smooth-

ies are to die for – try Berry Berry Booster packed with raspberries, and blue, red and black berries.

Libernard Café (Map pp280-1; ☎ 0 5323 4877; 295-299 Th Chang Moi; dishes 50-110B; ☺ 7.30am-5pm) Libernard serves fresh Arabica coffee grown in Thailand and roasted daily on the premises. The array of pancakes and other breakfast specialities also deserve acclaim, and Thai food is available as well. This is a good place to buy coffee to take home.

Love at First Bite (Map pp280-1; ☎ 0 5324 2731; 28 Soi 1, Th Chiang Mai-Lamphun; pastries 40-80B; ☺ 10.30am-6pm) It's almost too good to be true: the cheesecakes, layer cakes, pies and blintzes stocked in the glass-fronted refrigerators taste as delicious as they look. There are tables where you can sit and drink coffee or tea while sampling the fruits of the Thai owners' 27-year sojourn in the USA.

Bake & Bite (Map pp280-1; ☎ 0 5328 5185; Th Kotchasan, 6 Soi 1; dishes 40-160B; ☺ 7am-6pm Mon-Fri, 7am-4pm Sat & Sun) Bake & Bite prepares delicious European- and American-style pastries, pies and sandwiches on your choice of bread. It also offers more vegetarian options than most for breakfast, and has good chocolate cake. There's another branch at 183/8–9 Th Chang Klan.

Vegetarian

Chiang Mai is blessed with more than 25 vegetarian restaurants, most of them very inexpensive. All of the Indian restaurants mentioned earlier in this section feature short vegetarian sections in their menus.

Mangsawirat Kangreuanjam (Map pp280-1; Th Inthawararot, Soi 1; dishes 10-30B; ☺ 8am-early afternoon) Look for the difficult-to-see English sign that reads 'Vegetarian Food'. The cooks put out 15 to 20 pots of fresh, 100% Thai vegetarian dishes daily. The dishes feature lots of tofu, squash, peas, pineapple, sprouts and potato, and the desserts are good.

Suandok Vegetarian (Map pp276-7; Th Suthep; dishes 10-30B; ☺ 7am-2pm) This tiny stall just west of the entrance to Wat Suan Dok offers a simple array of inexpensive, wholesome Thai vegetarian dishes and brown rice.

Vegetarian Centre of Chiang Mai (Map pp276-7; ☎ 0 5327 1262; 14 Th Om Muang; dishes 15-30B; ☺ 6am-2pm Mon-Fri) Sponsored by the Asoke Foundation, an ascetically minded Buddhist movement, the long-running Vegetarian Centre serves extremely inexpensive but very good cafeteria-

style veg – you push a tray along a rack and point out what you want.

our pick **Khun Churn** (Map pp276-7; ☎ 0 5322 4124; Th Nimmanhaemin, Soi 7; dishes 35-80B; ☺ 9am-2pm & 5pm-10pm) This new place, in a pleasant covered outdoor setting, has more interesting vegetable choices than most. Start with crispy rice with coconut dip or try the pomelo salad with deep fried coconut, limejuice and chilli. Lots of tofu and fresh veg are used. It's closed on the 16th of each month.

AUM Vegetarian Food (Map pp280-1; ☎ 0 5327 8315; 66 Th Moon Muang; dishes 40-100B; ☺ 8am-2pm & 5-9pm) Near Pratu Tha Phae, AUM at first appears to be a second-hand book shop. Go inside though and the all-veggie menu features a varied list of traditional Thai and Chinese dishes prepared without meat or eggs. There is an upstairs eating area with cushions on the floor and low tables.

On the River

our pick **Riverside Bar and Restaurant** (Map pp280-1; ☎ 0 5324 3239; Th Charoenrat; dishes 75-200B; ☺ 10am-1am) This rambling set of wooden buildings has been the most consistently popular riverside place for over 20 years. The food – Thai, Western and vegetarian – is always good, and it's as popular with Thais as with *faràng*. The atmosphere is convivial and there's live music nightly. Choose from the indoor and outdoor dining areas or pay 70B for a seat (extra for food) on the nightly 8pm river cruise.

Good View (Map pp280-1; ☎ 0 5324 1866; 13 Th Charoenrat; dishes 80-200B; ☺ 10am-1am) Next door to the Riverside, Good View also offers open-air areas in a more contemporary setting. The huge menu covers everything Thai, and there's a Japanese sushi stand at the back. There's also live music.

Gallery (Map pp280-1; ☎ 0 5324 8601; 25-29 Th Charoenrat; dishes 70-300B; ☺ 11am-midnight) This elegant eatery, in a converted 100-year-old teak Chinese shophouse that's half gallery/shop, half restaurant, has a colonial feel. The quality of the food and service goes up and down, but the setting remains the primary attraction.

On the west bank of the river, Heuan Soontharee (p301) serves a mix of northern, northeastern and central Thai dishes.

Night Markets

Chiang Mai is full of interesting day and night markets stocked with inexpensive and tasty foods.

our pick Anusan Night Market (Map pp280-1; btwn Th Chang Khlan & Th Charoen Prathet; 6pm-midnight) In Chiang Mai Night Bazaar, this buzzing food market is best known for its seafood and its lively atmosphere. Stalls surround a large cluster of tables where each 'restaurant' has a section allocated with its own waiters – head to the parts that look most crowded. Most have English menus.

Talat Somphet (Somphet Market; Map pp280-1; Th Moon Muang; 6am-6pm) North of the Th Rat-withi intersection, this market sells cheap takeaway curries, *yam*, *lâap* (spicy minced-meat salad), *thâwt man* (fried fish cakes), sweets and seafood.

Chiang Mai Gate Night Market (Map pp280-1; Th Bamrungburi; 6pm-5am) Another good hunting ground is this very large and popular night market near Pratu Chiang Mai. People tend to take their time here, making an evening of eating and drinking – there's no hustle to vacate tables for more customers.

Talat Warorot (Map pp276-7; cnr Th Chang Moi & Th Praisani; 6am-5pm) In the upstairs section are a number of basic stalls for *khâo tôm* (rice soup), *khâo man kài* (chicken rice), *khâo mǔu daeng* ('red' pork with rice), *jóhk* (thick rice soup) and *khâo sawy*, with tables overlooking the market floor. It's not the best cooking in Chiang Mai by a long shot, but it's cheap. A set of vendors on the ground floor specialise in inexpensive noodles – this area is particularly popular.

Food Centres

The food centres at **Kad Suan Kaew Shopping Centre** (Map pp276-7; Th Huay Kaew) and **Central Airport Plaza** (Map pp276-7; Th Mahidon) have vendors selling Thai and Chinese dishes at reasonable prices.

There's a big indoor/outdoor cluster of permanent vendors at **Galare Food Centre** (Map pp280-1; Th Chang Khlan), opposite the main Chiangmai Night Bazaar building. Free Thai classical dancing is featured nightly.

DRINKING

The Glass Onion (Map pp276-7; 0 5321 8479; Th Nim-manhaemin; 8.30pm-late) Tucked at the far end of the 'Room – boutique mall' (an open-air walkway with shops and cafés) is this small, glamorous, James Bondesque lounge bar. Drink decent cocktails at the black lacquer bar, relax in the '60s-style red chairs and listen to the jazz pianist, or the DJ spinning housey jazz. There's an extensive wine list.

Drunken Flower (Map pp276-7; 0 5321 2081; Th Nimmanhaemin, 295/1 Soi 1) This cosy indoor/outdoor bar and restaurant has a mixed Thai and expat crowd, including local NGO staffers. There's plenty to nosh on while drinking (the pumpkin curry is delicious). Live bands perform folk music most nights.

NimMahn Bar (Map pp276-7; Th Nimmanhaemin) A good place to start before heading over to Warm-Up (opposite), this new bar is typical of the places popping up in the area. Catering for trendy Thais and foreigners, it has a cavernous industrial-looking interior, softened with smart leather poufs and sofas. A DJ plays nightly and there's a seating area outside. Food is available.

Writer's Club & Wine Bar (Map pp280-1; 0 5381 4187; 141/3 Th Ratchadamnoen) Run by an ex-foreign correspondent, this simple shopfront bar and restaurant attracts a steady stream of expats and tourists, including a few resident writers. The mainly Australian and Italian house wines change weekly. Also good for watching the Walking Street hubbub on Sunday evenings.

Mix Bar (Map pp280-1; 0 5399 9999; D2 Hotel, 100 Th Chang Klan) You could be in London or Paris here but if you fancy a chic, minimalist bar to sup cocktails in, head to D2 Hotel's slinky Mix Bar. It's right by the night market.

Monkey Club (Map pp276-7; 0 5322 6997; Th Nimmanhaemin, Soi 9) This stylish all-white bar is popular among Thai students. It turns into a club later in the evening (see opposite).

Pinte Blues Pub (Map pp280-1; 33/6 Th Moon Muang) This place deserves some sort of award for staying in business so long (more than 20 years) while serving only espresso and beer, and for sticking to a the blues music format the whole time.

UN Irish Pub (Map pp280-1; 0 5321 4554; 24/1 Th Ratwithi) This is a comfortable place with the food area downstairs and the bar upstairs. There's nothing particularly Irish here other than some kitsch on the walls and a dark-green décor. Heineken, Carlsberg and Thai-brewed beers are on tap, and the Guinness is bottled. There's live music on Tuesday and Friday, plus quiz nights and a TV for watching football.

John's Place (Place on the Corner; Map pp280-1; Th Ratchamankha, cnr Th Moon Muang & Soi 2) This open-air bar is always heaving of an evening due to its proximity to the many backpacker digs nearby.

Kafé (Map pp280-1; Th Moon Muang, btwn Soi 5 & Soi 6) The daily happy hour here is popular among both expats and Thais.

Yoy Pocket (Map pp280-1; Th Ratwithi) This is a funky spot, reminiscent of some of the homier café-pubs along Th Phra Athit in Bangkok.

Darling Wine Pub (Map pp276-7; ☎ 0 5322 7427; 49/21 Th Huay Kaew) Darling serves fine wines by the glass or bottle in a sophisticated but relaxed atmosphere.

The Pub (☎ 0 5321 1550; 189 Th Huay Kaew) In an old Tudor-style cottage set well off the road, this venerable Chiang Mai institution semi-successfully calls up the atmosphere of an English country pub. The Friday evening happy hour is popular.

Behind the building that houses the Yoy Pocket is a cluster of rustic outdoor bars catering to backpackers and expats. **Rasta Café** (Map pp280-1), the first one to open in this area (and still the largest), plays recorded reggae, dub, African and Latin music, and is quite popular in the high season. In the same area, the similarly rustic **Heaven Beach** (Map pp280-1) and **Life House** (Map pp280-1) often feature live local bands.

ENTERTAINMENT
Live Music
Riverside Bar & Restaurant (Map pp280-1; ☎ 0 5324 3239; 9-11 Th Charoenrat; ☺ closes 2am-3am) In a twinkly setting on Mae Nam Ping, this is one of the longest-running live music venues in Chiang Mai. Two cover bands play at either end of the rambling wooden buildings nightly. It's usually packed with both foreigners and Thais on weekends, so arrive early to get a table on the veranda overlooking the river. There are two indoor bars, both full of regulars, and the food is reliably good (see p305).

Le Brasserie (Map pp280-1; ☎ 0 5324 1665; 37 Th Charoenrat; ☺ 11.15pm-1am) A block or so north of the riverside Gallery restaurant, Le Brasserie is a popular late-night spot to listen to live bands play rock and blues. Expect to hear Hendrix, Cream, Dylan, Marley, and other 1960s and '70s classics. Food service is available inside the bar or out the back by the river.

Tha Chang Gallery (Map pp280-1; Th Charoenrat) Next door to the Gallery restaurant, this tiny music venue has great live jazz and blues nights.

Warm-Up (Map pp276-7; ☎ 0 9993 2963; Th Nimmanhaemin) Warm-Up occasionally hosts nationally known Thai bands. On other nights bands

play covers and Thai pop. DJs also play their decks.

Good View (Map pp280-1; ☎ 0 5324 1866; 13 Th Charoenrat) Next door to Riverside, Good View changes bands more frequently than Riverside and is quite popular. It also has a restaurant (see p305).

Clubs
Warm-Up (Map pp276-7; ☎ 0 9993 2963; Th Nimmanhaemin; ☺ 6pm-1am) This relaxed place is filled with Thai trendsters and a smattering of Westerners. Hang out in the pretty decked courtyard area with lots of seating and various bars, or dance manically to the latest tunes in the two glass enclosed dance floors. Regular live music is a feature here too.

Bubbles (Map pp280-1; Pornping Tower Hotel; ☺ 9pm-2am). The newly renovated Bubbles is as popular as ever. The dance floor heaves with a mix of tourists remembering how to do rave moves, locals, some expats and pros. The 100B entry ticket exchanges for a beer or a scarily sweet cocktail.

Monkey Club (Map pp276-7; ☎ 0 5322 6997; Th Nimmanhaemin, Soi 9; ☺ 6pm-12.30am) Although the first thing you see when you walk in is the restaurant, head instead for the glassed-in, trendy looking, all-white bar with sofas and chairs. The furniture is shifted when things get going later. Nightly DJs plus live music attract young Thais and some foreigners.

Spicy (Map pp280-1; Th Chaiyaphum; ☺ 9pm-5am) Near Pratu Tha Phae, people pile into Spicy when everything else has shut. Not the most salubrious place, it is nevertheless fun after 2am – don't go before, it is seediness central.

Fashion House (Map pp276-7; Ground fl, Kad Suan Kaew Shopping Centre; ☺ 9pm-2am) Students fill this two-room club. The hip-hop room is always full, the techno one is quieter. The bands are pretty dodgy but the DJ is good.

Smooth (Map pp280-1; ☎ 0 5330 2340-1; Th Chiang Mai-Lamphun) East of Mae Nam Ping, Smooth is packed full with young Thais dancing to techno.

Cinemas
Major Cineplex (Map pp276-7; ☎ 0 5328 3939; Central Airport Plaza, 2 Th Mahidon; tickets 80-160B) This theatre complex boasts a state-of-the-art sound system and the option of 'honeymoon seats', pairs of seats without a middle armrest for romantic couples. Along with the latest Thai

films, first-run foreign films with English soundtracks are shown.

Chiang Mai University (Map pp276-7) Every Sunday at 3pm there are showings of different foreign films – usually art films of the Bergman and Buñuel variety – at the main auditorium of the Art & Culture Center. Admission is free.

Two other cinemas showing first-run foreign as well as Thai films are the **Vista** (Map pp276-7; Kad Suan Kaew Shopping Centre, Th Huay Kaew) and **Vista 12 Huay Kaew** (Map pp276-7; Th Huay Kaew).

SHOPPING

Chiang Mai is Thailand's handicraft centre, ringed by small cottage factories and workshops. Most of the time the products you see in the outskirts can be bought cheaper in Chiang Mai itself unless you are buying wholesale.

There are numerous shops throughout the city but the main areas to head for are the Night Bazaar and the Walking Streets, which have a huge selection of handicrafts and souvenirs.

There's also Th Thae Pae, with its mix of antiques, jewellery, homewares and clothes, and Warorot Market, which is best for inexpensive fabrics.

If you want to shop where the trendy Thais shop, head to Th Nimmanhaemin, especially the section of the road by the Amari Rincome Hotel, and in Soi 1, which is full of contemporary Thai design.

JJ Market, northeast of town, is the newcomer to the shopping scene. It is not filled with crowds yet, but its mix of fresh new designers and more established Thai names make it worth a visit.

Within 15km of the city, Hang Dong (p336), and San Kampaeng and Bo Sang (p334) are the places to go and see factories and showrooms for antiques, woodcarving, furniture, ceramics, silks and paper umbrellas.

Antiques

Burmese antiques are becoming more common than Thai, as most of the Thai stuff has been bought by collectors, and you can get some great buys on antique Burmese furniture from the British colonial period.

Chiang Mai Night Bazaar (Map pp280-1; Th Chang Khlan). The best place to look for 'copy' antiques is around the bazaar. Inside the Night Bazaar building, towards the back on the 2nd floor, are a few small shops with real antiques.

Lost Heavens (Map pp280-1; ☎ 0 5327 8185; Stall 2, 2nd fl, Chiang Mai Night Bazaar Bldg, Th Chang Khlan; ☎ 0

5325 1557) Among the best of the Night Bazaar's antique shops, Lost Heavens specialises in Mien tribal artefacts. It's in the 'antiques corner' towards the back left of the Night Bazaar building. There's a second store at 234 Th Tha Phae, opposite Wat Bupparam.

Under the Bo (Map pp280-1; ☎ 0 5381 8831; Stall 22-23, Chiang Mai Night Bazaar) Carries many unique pieces, in the form of furniture, antique bronze and wood figures, old doors, woodcarvings and weaving from Africa, South Asia and Southeast Asia. It isn't cheap, but many of the items are one-of-a-kind. There's another shop out on the road to Hang Dong, about 5km southwest of Th Mahidon.

More antique shops can be found along Th Tha Phae. Kesorn (Map pp280-1) has a good reputation. Th Loi Kroh is another good spot for antique shops. **Art Deco** (☎ 0 5320 6878; 51 Th Loi Kroh) has an interesting collection of hill-tribe art – particularly Akha.

Hang Dong, 15km south of Chiang Mai, is even better for antique furniture of all kinds; see p336.

Celadon Ceramics

Celadon ceramics have beautiful deep-crackle glaze finishes in translucent colours of green, blue, white or yellow. Thought to have been developed in China around 907, the celadon you'll find in Chiang Mai are mainly inspired by the Sawankhalok pottery styles that were made hundreds of years ago at Sukhothai and exported all over the region.

Ceramthai (Map pp280-1; ☎ 0 5382 0390; 2nd fl, Chiang Mai Night Bazaar Bldg) Head to the shop in Chiang Mai Night Bazaar building to see some refined examples of celadon, in lovely blue, green or off-white hues. If you want to see more, go to the main workshops in Soi 5, Th Chedi Liam and get some customised pieces.

Mengrai Kilns (Map pp280-1; ☎ 0 5327 2063; www.mengraikilns.com; 79/2 Th Arak) In the southwestern corner of the inner moat area, Mengrai Kilns are particularly focused on keeping the old Thai celadon traditions alive.

Siam Celadon (Map pp280-1; 0 5324 3518; 158 Th Tha Pae) In a lovely teak building, this established celadon company sells its ceramics here plus silk home accessories. There is a pretty garden café out back.

Deco Moda (☎ 0 5321 9576; www.deco-moda.com; Soi 1, Th Nimmanhaemin) Has modern, funky ceramics –

(Continued on page 317)

STU SMUCKER

JOHN ELK III

Reclining Buddha at Wat Pho (p108), Bangkok

Wat Saket's (p113) Golden Mount, Bangkok

A golden *chedi* overlooks Bangkok's Grand Palace (p108)

MICHAEL COYNE

RYAN FOX

Bangkok (p101) by night

MICK ELMORE

Muay thai (Thai boxing; p173) in action, Bangkok

Colourful fabrics of Phahurat Market (p178), Bangkok

RICHARD I'ANSON

Pick your mortar from your pestle at Bangkok's cooking schools (p143)

Lumphini Park (p137), Bangkok

Old Siam Plaza (p162) in Bangkok's Chinatown

DENNIS JOHNSON

Death Railway Bridge (p211) on the River Kwai, Kanchanaburi

The elegant *chedi* of Wat Phra Si Sanphet (p197), Ayuthaya

TOM COCKREM

JULIET COOMBE

Monkeys at home in the ruins of Prang Sam Yot (p205), Lopburi, Lopburi Province

BILL WASSMAN

The tourist hubbub of Pattaya (p232),
Chonburi Province

ANTONY GIBLIN

The seven-tiered Erawan waterfall, Erawan
National Park (p217), Kanchanaburi Province

WOODS WHEATCROFT

Swinging in paradise, Ko Mak (p265), Trat
Province

Beachside dining on Ao Cho, Ko Samet (p243), Rayong Province

FRANK CARTER

Riverside dining in Chiang Mai (p305)

ALAIN EVRARD

JERRY ALEXANDER

Talat Warorot (p306), one of Chiang Mai's buzzing markets

Royal summer palace of Bang Pa-In (p202), Ayuthaya Province

CLAVER CARROLL

DENNIS JOHNSON

Steps leading to Wat Phra That Doi Suthep (p325), Doi Suthep-Pui National Park, Chiang Mai Province

ANTONY GIBLIN

Artist at work in Bo Sang (p334), also known as Umbrella Village, Chiang Mai Province

Flowers, floats and fun at Chiang Mai's Flower Festival (p294)

ALAIN EVRARD

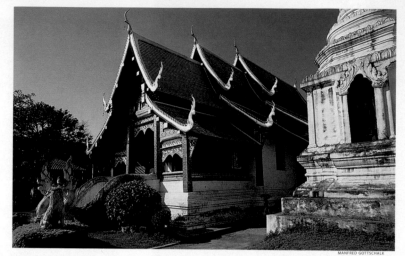

Wat Phra Singh (p284), home of the revered Buddha image, Phra Singh, Chiang Mai

The cave complex of Tham Chiang Dao (p329),
Chiang Mai Province

A still-life painting in the making, Maesa
Elephant Camp (p328), Chiang Mai
Province

(Continued from page 308)

mainly cups and mugs – as well as brightly coloured homeware accessories.

Other homeware shops down Soi 1 are also worth checking out for ceramics.

Clothing & Accessories

All sorts of shirts, blouses and dresses, plain and embroidered, are available at low prices, but make sure that you check on the quality carefully. The Chiang Mai Night Bazaar and shops along Th Tha Phae and Th Loi Kroh have good selections.

Lanes off the north side of Th Tha Phae, near Talat Warorot, boast dozens of shops (signed in Thai only) that offer excellent deals on ready-made Thai cotton and silk clothing, both traditional and modern.

Sri Sanpanmai (Map pp276-7; ☎ 0 5389 4372; G-59 Kad Suan Kaew Shopping Centre, Th Huay Kaew) Sells good ready-made clothing made from northern Thai textiles.

Ginger (Map pp276-7; ☎ 0 5321 5635; 6/21 Th Nimmanhaemin) For something more night-on-the-townish, check out the shimmery dresses, sparkly mules, fabulous jewellery and colourful accessories. Not cheap though. There is another shop attached to House restaurant at 199 Th Moon Muang.

Chabaa (Map pp276-7; www.atchabaa.com; 14/32 Th Nimmanhaemin) Offers a similar style to Ginger, but a bit more hippy. In this funky shop you'll find brightly coloured embroidered tops and skirts plus big-statement jewellery.

Elements (Red Ruby; Map pp280-1; ☎ 0 5387 4277; 400-402 Th Tha Pae) Located next to Roon Ruang Hotel, Elements stocks embroidered bags, a diverse collection of fun jewellery and other trinkets.

TAILORS

There are a number of good tailors off Th Kotchasan near Aroon (Rai) Restaurant, including Florida, Chao Khun, Chaiyo and Progress. Also down Soi 1 off Th Ratchadamnoen, Chok Dee Tailor, next to Herb Garden restaurant, is well-priced.

Another strip for tailors is Th Chang Khlan in the Chiang Mai Night Bazaar area, as well as along Th Tha Phae. However, some of these overcharge. Make sure you shop around first and ask to see some finished work before choosing a shop.

City Silk (Map pp280-1; ☎ 0 5323 4388; 336 Th Tha Phae) More or less opposite Wat Mahawan, City Silk

---

CHIANG MAI NIGHT BAZAAR

Whether you find it tantalising or tourist tat, Chiang Mai's Night Bazaar (Map pp280-1) is one of the city's main attractions and definitely worth experiencing. This buzzing market is the modern legacy of the original Yunnanese trading caravans that stopped here along the ancient trade route between Simao (in China) and Mawlamyaing (on Myanmar's Gulf of Martaban coast). Today the epicentre of the outdoor market is at the Th Chang Khlan and Th Loi Kroh junction. It spreads all the way up to Th Tha Phae, down to Th Si Donchai and east to Th Charoen Prathet. It opens from sunset till midnight every night of the year, rain or dry, holiday or no.

Made up of hundreds of street vendors, several different roofed areas and ordinary glass-fronted shops, the market offers a huge variety of Thai and northern Thai products, as well as designer goods (both fake and licensed, so look carefully) at very low prices – if you bargain well. The fact that there are so many different stalls selling the same merchandise means that competition effectively keeps prices low. Look over the whole bazaar before you begin getting down to haggling.

Popular buys include hill-tribe crafts like hand-woven fabrics and embroidered bags; lacquerware; silver jewellery; woodcarvings; iron and bronze Buddhas; simple cotton clothes; silk cushion covers and scarfs; and other knick-knacks. If the outdoor stalls are looking a bit samey or too busy, head to one of the covered markets. The helpfully named Chiang Mai Night Bazaar building is the best. Inside you will find some shops with more original designs, including fashion, jewellery, textile and ceramic outlets (see p308). On the second floor near the back there are some interesting shops with Thai and Burmese antiques.

If you're not into shopping, the night market still makes an entertaining stroll. Alternatively, head to the outdoor Anusan food market (p305) where you can sit, drink a beer and take in the lively atmosphere of the market surrounding you.

CHIANG MAI PROVINCE

MARKETS

Talat Warorot

Locally called *kàat lǔang* (northern Thai for 'great market'), this is the oldest and most famous **market** (Map pp280-1; off Th Chang Moi; ⏱ 5am-6pm) in Chiang Mai. Although the huge enclosure is quite dilapidated (ignore the scary looking escalators, which haven't functioned for years), it's an especially good market for fabrics and cooking implements, as well as inexpensive cosmetics, clothing, handicrafts and prepared foods (especially northern Thai food).

Across from Talat Warorot is the similar Talat Lamyai, which has the same opening hours.

JJ Market

At the north end of Th Atsadathorn, 200m from the Superhighway, the brand new **JJ Market** (Map pp276-7; Th Atsadathorn) is a street lined with designer shops of various descriptions, from small outlets selling unique jewellery and kitschy homewares, to bigger Thai names selling contemporary furniture and mod-Thai fashion.

Chiang Mai Gate Night Market

Near Pratu Chiang Mai, this **fresh-food market** (Talat Pratu Chiang Mai; Map pp280-1; Th Bamrungburi) is particularly busy with locals shopping for takeaway Thai and northern Thai food. The indoor area is open from 4am until around noon, while outside vendors continue to sell until nightfall. A night food market then sets up next to the moat across the street, and stays open past midnight.

Flower Market

Locally called *tàlàat dàwk mái,* this **market** (Map pp280-1; Th Praisani; ⏱ daily) is a quick stop for flowers only, especially fresh *phuang má-lai* (jasmine garlands).

Talat Kamthieng

East of JJ Market, this picturesque **plant and flower market** (Map pp276-7; Hwy 11/Th Superhighway) is the perfect place to pick up some greenery to feather your Chiang Mai nest if you're settling in long term.

Talat Thanin

North of Pratu Chang Pheuak, this clean and well-run **market** (Map pp280-1; off Th Chotana; ⏱ 5am-early evening) is the best spot for prepared foods.

Talat Ton Phayom

Across from Chiang Mai University, this **market** (Map pp276-7; Th Suthep) features all manner of fresh produce and cooked foods. Because CMU students make up a good portion of the clientele, prices tend to be low. Talat Ton Phayom is slated to be demolished to make room for an expanded road system in the near future.

Talat San Pa Khoi (Map pp276-7; off Th Charoen Muang) and **Talat Thiphanet** (Map pp276-7; Th Thiphanet) are large municipal markets that offer all manner of goods and see few tourists. San Pa Khoi opens around 4am and does a brisk trade until around 10am, then slows until an hour before nightfall.

specialises in silk tailoring for women. English is spoken here, and the service is friendly and professional.

Contemporary Art

Outside of Bangkok, Chiang Mai is Thailand's leading art centre and there are dozens of small galleries offering fine Thai contemporary art in the city. Among the better ones:

Aka Wilai (Map pp276-7; ☎ 0 5330 6521; www .akawalai.com; 35 Th Ratanakosin)

Galerie Panisa (Map pp280-1; ☎ 0 5320 2779; 189 Th Mahidon)

Gongdee Gallery (Map pp276-7; ☎ 0 5322 5032; www .gongdee.com; Th Nimmanhaemin, Soi 1; ⏱ 9am-7pm)

HQ Gallery (Map pp280-1; ☎ 0 5381 4717; www
.hqartgallery.com; 3/31 Th Samlan)
La Luna Gallery (Map pp280-1; ☎ 0 5330 6678; www
.lalunagallery.com; 190 Th Charoenrat)
Semi-apply (Map pp276-7; ☎ 0 5870 6262;
olarn_p@hotmail.com; Th Nimmanhaemin, 24 Soi 1;
🕙 9am-7pm)

Essential Oils & Spa Products

Several shops around town specialise in extracting oils from local herbs such as lemongrass and Thai bergamot to create essential
oils, massage oil, herbal cosmetics and natural
toiletries.

Laan Pai Lin (Map pp276-7; ☎ 0 5322 2036; Nantawan
Arcade, 6/12 Th Nimmanhaemin; 🕙 10am-8pm) This is
one of the better shops, selling products like
Thai herbal compresses, essential oils and
body scrubs. Good sizes for travelling and
also for gifts.

Herb Basics (Map pp280-1; ☎ 0 5341 8289; Th Ratchadamnoen; 🕙 9am-6pm Mon-Sat, 1-9pm Sun) Sells aromatherapy products like lip balm and soaps,
all made in Chiang Mai.

Lacquerware

Decorated plates, containers, utensils and
other items are made by building up layers
of lacquer over a wooden or woven bamboo
base. Burmese lacquerware, smuggled into the
north, can often be seen, especially at Mae Sai,
the northernmost point of Thailand. There
are several lacquerware factories in San Kamphaeng, southeast of Chiang Mai. A lot of
stalls and shops also sell lacquerware in the
Night Market.

For a contemporary angle on lacquerware
Living Space (Map pp280-1; ☎ 0 5387 4156; www.living
spacedesigns.com; 276-278 Th Tha Pae) does some beautiful, brightly coloured boxes, trays and other
accessories.

Local Handicrafts

The Saturday and Sunday **Walking Street** markets on Th Wualai and Th Ratchadamnoen,
respectively, offer a great selection of handicrafts in a fun setting; see p284.

Thai Tribal Crafts (Map pp280-1; ☎ 0 5324 1043; 208
Th Bamrungrat) Near the McCormick Hospital,
this place is run by two church groups on a
nonprofit basis and has a good selection of
quality handicrafts.

Hill-Tribe Products Promotion Centre (Map pp276-7;
☎ 0 5327 7743; 21/17 Th Suthep) This royally sponsored project is near Wat Suan Dok; all the

profits from sales go to hill-tribe welfare
programmes.

The two commercial markets with the wid-
est selections of northern Thai folk crafts are
Talat Warorot (opposite) and the **Chiang Mai Night
Bazaar** (p317).

Rattan

Hangdong Rattan (Map pp280-1; ☎ 0 5320 8167; 54-55
Th Loi Kroh) For better-quality furniture and accessories made from this jungle vine, check
out the many items on display. Custom orders
are also taken.

Two cheaper rattan shops can be found
along the northern side of Th Chang Moi
Kao, two blocks east of the moat. These are
the places to buy chairs, small tables, chaise
longues, planters, floor screens, settees, book-
shelves and other everyday household items.

Shopping Centres & Department Stores

Chiang Mai has more than 15 shopping complexes with department stores. **Central Airport
Plaza** (Map pp276-7; Th Mahidon), centred around a
branch of Bangkok's Central Department Store,
is the best, with **Kad Suan Kaew Shopping Centre**
(Map pp276-7; Th Huay Kaew) a close second. There are
several luxe shops in both complexes.

Computer Plaza (Map pp280-1; Th Mani Nopharat)
and **Pantip Plaza** (Map pp280-1; Th Chang Khlan) are the
places to go for computer supplies. Computer
Plaza is cheaper by far.

Silverwork

Just south of Pratu Chiang Mai, historic Th
Wualai is known for its silversmiths; there
have been **silver workshops** (Map pp280-1) here
for centuries (see Saturday Walking Street
p284).

Sipsong Panna (Map pp276-7; ☎ 0 5321 6096; Nantawan Arcade, 6/19 Th Nimmanhaemin) Opposite the
Amari Rincome Hotel, this upmarket shop is
the place for jewellery collected in Thailand,
Laos, Myanmar and southwestern China. The
chunky hill-tribe jewellery is very nice.

Nova (Map pp280-1; ☎ 0 5327 3058; www.nova-collec
tion.com; 201 Th Tha Phae) For contemporary jewellery. This place does fantastic rings, pendants
and earrings using silver, some gold and precious stones. Pieces can be custom made, or
you can learn to do it yourself at Nova's jewellery workshops (see p293).

Angel (Map pp280-1; ☎ 0 5323 2651; 370 Th Tha Phae)
Also has some original and modern silver
designs.

CHIANG MAI PROVINCE

Textiles

Thai silk, with its lush colours and pleasantly rough texture, is a good bargain and is usually cheaper in Chiang Mai than in Bangkok. Talat Warorot is one of the best and least expensive places to look for fabrics, but take care, as many polyester items are passed off as silk.

If you want to see where and how local cloth is made, go to the nearby town of San Kamphaeng for Thai silk, or to Pasang, south of Lamphun, for cotton.

Studio Naenna (Map pp276-7; ☎ 0 5322 6042; Th Nimmanhaemin, 22 Soi 1) Operated by Patricia Cheeseman, an expert on Thai-Lao textiles who has written extensively on the subject. You can see the production process, using natural dyes, at the **studio** (Map pp276-7 ☎ 0 5322 6042; www.studio-naenna.com; 138/8 Soi Chang Khian, Th Huay Kaew).

Kachama (Map pp276-7; ☎ 0 5321 8495; www.kachama.com; Th Nimmanhaemin, Soi 1) If you're interested in textiles as works of art, visit Kachama. The wall hangings have been created using traditional weaving techniques, mixed with innovative design using natural materials. Even if you can't afford to buy, it's worth coming for a look. Simpler textiles and cushions are also available.

Vila Cini (Map pp280-1; ☎ 0 5324 6246; www.vilacini.com; 30-34 Th Charoenrat) In a couple of beautiful teak houses surrounding a small courtyard garden, Villa Cini sells unique, handmade silks and cotton in an atmospheric setting. You can purchase material by the metre or buy ready-made cushions, wall hangings and other accessories. Antiques are also available.

KukWan Gallery (Map pp280-1; ☎ 0 5320 6747; 37 Th Loi Kroh) Set slightly back from the road, this charming teak building houses natural cotton and silk by the metre. It's a great place to shop for gifts, with scarves, bedspreads and tablecloths available in subtle colours.

Umbrellas

At Bo Sang, the 'umbrella village' 9km east of Chiang Mai, you will find hand-painted paper umbrellas of all kinds, from simple traditional brown ones to giant rainbow-hued parasols. You'll also find textured *sa* paper, made from mulberry tree bark. See p334 for more details about the village.

Woodcarving

Many types of wood carvings are available in Chiang Mai, including countless elephants. Teak salad-bowls are good, and usually cheap. Numerous shops along Th Tha Phae and near the Chiang Mai Night Bazaar stock wood crafts, or you can go to the source – Hang Dong (p336) and Ban Thawai (p336).

GETTING THERE & AWAY

Air

INTERNATIONAL

Regularly scheduled international flights fly into **Chiang Mai International Airport** (Map pp276-7; ☎ 0 5327 0222) from the following cities:

Kuala Lumpur (Air Asia; ☎ 0 2515 9999; www.airasia.com)

Kunming (THAI Airways; ☎ 0 5321 1021; www.thaiair.com)

Singapore (Silk Air; ☎ 0 5327 6459; www.silkair.com)

Taipei (Mandarin Airlines; ☎ 0 5320 1268; www.mandarin-airlines.com)

Vientiane, Luang Prabang (Lao Airlines; ☎ 0 5322 3401; www.laoairlines.com)

Yangon, Mandalay (Air Mandalay; ☎ 0 5381 8049; www.air-mandalay.com)

DOMESTIC

Since 2003 Thailand has been going through a period of air route deregulation which has resulted in several low-fare, no-frills airline start-ups. Fares range from as low as 899B one way from Bangkok to Chiang Mai with Air Asia to as high as 4740B for the same sector on THAI (more in business class). Prices constantly vary depending on factors like season and various promotions. The following have counters at Chiang Mai International Airport; tickets can be booked online.

Air Asia (☎ 0 2515 9999; www.airasia.com) Has four flights between Bangkok and Chiang Mai daily.

Bangkok Airways (☎ 0 5321 0043/4) Has two flights a day to Bangkok, one of which goes via Sukhothai.

Nok Air (☎ 1318; www.nokair.com) A subsidiary of THAI; has the most frequent daily departures to Bangkok. It also flies to Mae Hong Son from Chiang Mai twice a day for 900B.

One-Two-Go (☎ 0 5392 2159; www.fly12go.com) Has five flights a day between Chiang Mai and Bangkok at a fixed price of 1700B.

Siam GA (☎ 0 2664 6099, 0 2641 4190; www.sga.aero) 35-minute flights to and from Chiang Mai and Pai. At the time of writing the fare was one way/return 1450/2900B.

Thai Airways International (☎ 0 5321 1044/7; www.thaiair.com) Operates around eight one-hour flights between Bangkok and Chiang Mai daily, plus four flights a day between Chiang Mai and Mae Hong Son.

Bus

Departing from Bangkok's newer Northern and Northeastern bus terminal (also known

BUS DESTINATIONS FROM CHIANG MAI

Destination	Fare (B)	Duration (hr)	Destination	Fare (B)	Duration (hr)
Chiang Dao*	40	1½	Mae Sai	126	5
Chiang Khong	161	6½	air-con	176	5
air-con	225	6	1st class air-con	227	5
1st class air-con	290	6	VIP	350	5
Chiang Rai	100	4	Mae Sariang	100	4-5
air-con	140	3	1st class air-con	180	4-5
1st class	180	3	Mae Sot	253	6½
VIP	280	3	1st class air-con	326	6
Chiang Saen	126	4	Nan	158	6
1st class air-con	227	3½	air-con	221	6
Chom Thong*	34	2	1st class air-con	284	6
Fang*	80	3	VIP	440	6
van	120	3	Pai	80	4
Hang Dong*	14	½	air-con	142	4
Khon Kaen (via Tak)	335	12	Phayao	87	3
air-con	469	12	air-con	122	2½
1st class air-con	542	12	1st class air-con	157	2½
Khon Kaen (via Utaradit)	267	11	Phrae	115	4
air-con	421	11	air-con	147	3½
1st class air-con	542	11	1st class air-con	189	3½
Khorat	468	12	VIP	290	3½
1st class air-con	601	12	Phitsanulok	227	5-6
VIP	701	12	air-con	292	5
Lampang	51	2	Sukhothai	167	6
air-con	71	2	air-con	234	5
1st class air-con	92	2	1st class air-con	301	5
Lamphun	32	1	Tha Ton*	90	4
Mae Hong Son (via Mae Sariang)	187	8	Udon Thani	313	12
air-con	337	8	air-con	438	12
Mae Hong Son (via Pai)	112	7	1st class air-con	563	12
air-con	199	7	VIP	657	12

*Leaves from Chang Pheuak bus terminal. All other buses leave from the Chiang Mai Arcade bus terminal (also called New Terminal) off Th Kaew Nawarat.

as Moh Chit) there are 12 2nd-class air-con buses a day (434B, 10 to 11 hours), but note that the air-con doesn't always work.

More comfortable 1st-class air-con buses with toilets and 42 seats leave every half hour from 6.45am to 9pm (558B, 10 hours).

The government VIP buses, with seats that recline a bit more than the seats in 1st-class air-con, have about six departures each day, from either Bangkok or Chiang Mai, between 7pm and 9pm plus one in the morning at around 9am (24/32 seat bus 651/863B, 10 hours).

Ten or more private tour companies run air-con buses between Bangkok and Chiang Mai, departing from various points throughout both cities. Return tickets are always cheaper than one-way tickets. The fares cost 400B to 500B, depending on the bus. The government buses from the Northern and Northeastern bus terminal in Bangkok are generally more reliable and on schedule than the private ones booked in Banglamphu and other tourist-oriented places.

Travel agencies in Bangkok are notorious for promising services they can't deliver, such as reclining seats or air-con that works. Several Th Khao San agencies offer bus tickets to Chiang Mai for as little as 300B, including

a night's free stay at a guesthouse in Chiang Mai. Sometimes this works out well, but the buses can be substandard and the 'free' guesthouse may charge 50B to 60B for electricity or hot water, or apply heavy pressure on you to sign up for one of its treks before you can get a room. Besides, riding in a bus or minivan stuffed full of foreigners and their bulky backpacks may not be the best cultural experience.

Several readers have complained of purchasing tickets for large air-con or even VIP buses from Th Khao San and at the last minute being shunted into cramped minivans. We recommend avoiding these buses altogether; use public buses from Bangkok's Northern and Northeastern buses terminal instead.

Government buses between Chiang Mai and other northern towns depart frequently throughout the day (at least hourly), except for the Mae Sai, Khon Kaen, Udon, Ubon and Khorat buses, which have only morning and evening departures.

For buses to destinations within Chiang Mai Province use the **Chang Pheuak bus terminal** (Map pp280-1; ☎ 0 5321 1586; Th Chotana). For buses outside the province use the **Chiang Mai Arcade bus terminal** (Map pp276-7; ☎ 0 5324 2664), also called New Terminal. From the town centre, a túk-túk or chartered såwngthåew to the Chiang Mai Arcade terminal should cost 50B to 60B; to the Chang Pheuak terminal you should be able to get a såwngthåew at the normal 20B per person rate.

Train
Chiang Mai-bound trains leave Bangkok's Hualamphong station daily. To check the most up-to-date timetables and prices call the **State Railway of Thailand** (www.railway.co.th/www.thailandrailway.com; ☎ 0 2220 4334, free hotline 1690; ☉ 24hr) or visit its website.

Rapid trains leave Hualamphong station in Bangkok at 5.50am (2nd/3rd class 391/231B) and 2.30pm (2nd/3rd class 391/231B, 2nd-class sleeper lower/upper 541/491B) arriving at 7.45pm and 5.35am, respectively.

An express train leaves Bangkok at 10pm and arrives in Chiang Mai at 12.25pm (2nd/3rd class 431/271B, 2nd-class air-con 541B, 2nd-class sleeper lower/upper 581/531B, 2nd-class air-con sleeper lower/upper 821/751B).

Sprinter trains leave Bangkok at 8.30am and 7.20pm, arriving in Chiang Mai at 8.20pm and 7.30am respectively (2nd-class air-con 611B).

Special Express trains leave at 6pm and 7.35pm, arriving at 6.30am and 9.20am (1st-class air-con sleeper 1353B, 2nd-class air-con sleeper lower/upper 881/791B).

Berths on sleepers to Chiang Mai are increasingly hard to reserve without booking well in advance; tour groups sometimes book entire cars. The return trip from Chiang Mai to Bangkok doesn't seem to be as difficult, except during the Songkran (mid-April) and Chinese New Year (late February to early March) holiday periods.

Try and book as well in advance as possible and at least a day in advance for seats (rather than sleepers). To book, either go to Bangkok's Hualamphong station, Chiang Mai station or any major train station in person. Alternatively, email the **State Railway of Thailand** (passenger-ser@railway.co.th) at least two weeks before your journey. You will receive an email confirming the booking. Pick up and pay for tickets an hour before leaving at the scheduled departure train station.

Chiang Mai's neat and tidy **train station** (Map pp276-7; ☎ 0 5324 5364; Th Charoen Muang) has an ATM and two advance booking offices: one at the regular ticket windows outdoors (open 24 hours), the other in a more comfortable air-con office (open 6am to 6pm). These booking offices have a computerised reservation system through which you can book train seats for anywhere in Thailand up to 60 days in advance. It's advisable to check out current timetables and prices on www.railway.co.th/www.thailandrailway.com or by calling ☎ 0 2220 4334 or ☎ 1690, but it's not possible to book on the websites or over the phone.

There is a left-luggage facility in the station that is open 4.50am to 8.45pm. The cost is 10B per piece for the first five days and 15B per piece thereafter, with a 20-day maximum.

GETTING AROUND
To/From the Airport
There is only one licensed airport taxi service, charging 120B per car. Pick up a ticket at the taxi kiosk just outside the baggage-claim area, then present your ticket to the taxi drivers outside by the main arrival area exit. The airport is only two to three kilometres from the city centre. Public buses number 4 (red såwngthåew, 15B) and number 10 (white bus, 10B) run from the airport to Th Tha Pae from 6am to 9pm daily.

You can charter a túk-túk or red săwngthăew from the centre of Chiang Mai to the airport for 60B or 70B.

Bicycle

Cycling is a good way to get around Chiang Mai if you don't mind a little traffic and, at the denser intersections, vehicular fumes. The city is small enough so that everywhere is accessible by bicycle, including Chiang Mai University, Wat U Mong, Wat Suan Dok and the Chiang Mai National Museum on the outskirts of town.

If you have your own bicycle with you and need repairs or hard-to-find parts, your best bet is Canadian-owned **Top Gear Bike Shop** (Map pp280-1; ☎ 0 5323 3450; topgearbike@hotmail.com; 173 Th Chang Moi), near Soi 2.

Basic Chinese- or Thai-manufactured bicycles can be rented for around 30B to 50B a day from some guesthouses or from various places along the east moat:

Contact Travel (Map pp280-1; ☎ 0 5381 2444; www.activethailand.com; 73/7 Th Charoen Prathet) Rents rugged 21-speed mountain bikes for 200B a day. Also operates cycling tours around the province.

Velocity (Map pp280-1; ☎ 0 5341 0665; velocity@thaimail.com; 177 Th Chang Pheuak) Rents mountain and racing bikes, offers guided tours and carries all kinds of cycling accessories.

Bus

After much protracted talk and studies concerning a Mass Transit System to alleviate Chiang Mai's traffic congestion (see p324), a bus system has finally emerged. There are four new routes – numbers 2, 4, 6 and 8 – in addition to number 10, an existing bus route.

White air-con buses ply routes 2, 6 and 10. Numbered red săwngthăew follow routes 4 and 8. The air-con buses cost 10B per person and the săwngthăew (on these routes) charge 15B. With no number allotted, yellow săwngthăew (or the purple line on the map) run from Th Praisani (the road running along Mae Ping River near Warorot Market), stop at Chang Pheuak bus station, Rajabhat University and finally, Mae Rim.

Maps of these routes can be found in most free publications around Chiang Mai, or pick one up at TAT. These services run every 15 minutes from 6am to 9pm daily.

BUS ROUTES

No 2 white air-con bus (10B fixed price)
Starts from the Chiang Mai Nong Hoi Area Office; Th Chiang Mai-Lamphun; Th Charoenrat; Th Superhighway 11; Th Chotana; 7th Field Artillery Battalion (Mae Rim).

No 4 red săwngthăew (15B fixed price)
Starts from Carrefour supermarket; Arcade Bus Station, Th Kaew Nawarat; Th Thung Hotel; Th Charoen Muang; Railway Station; Th Chang Moi; Warorot Market; Th Moon Muang; Pratu Tha Pae; Th Bamrungburi; Pratu Chiang Mai; Thanon Wualai; Old Cultural Centre; Central Airport Plaza; Airport.

No 6 white air-con bus (10B fixed price)
Starts from Chiang Mai Nong Hoi Area Office; Th Superhighway 11; Arcade Bus Station; Th Superhighway 11; Th Chotana; Rajabhat University; Th Chang Pheuak, Chang Pheuak Bus Station; Th Superhighway 11; Th Huay Kaew; Chiang Mai University; Th Suthep; Th Arak; Pratu Suan Prung; Th Om Muang; Th Mahidon; Airport; Th Superhighway 11; Th Charoen Prathet; Alliance Française; Th Tha Pae; Th Chang Klan; Chiang Mai Nong Hoi Area Office.

No 8 red săwngthăew (15B fixed price)
Starts from Chiang Mai International Airport; Th Mahidon; Th Bunreuangrit; Th Mani Nopharat; Computer Plaza; Th Cheung Pheuk; Cheung Pheuk bus station; Th Chotana; City Hall.

No 10 white air-con bus (10B fixed price)
Starts from Kwan Wieng Village; Th Wualai; Th Sri Donchai; Th Chang Khlan; Th Tha Phae; Th Chang Moi; Th Moon Muang; Th Ratchawithi; Th Phra Pokklao; Th Mani Nopharat; Th Bunreuangrit; Th Mahidol; Airport; Kwan Wieng Village.

At the time of writing this seemed to be a fledgling service. Most Chiang Mai residents still take the regular såwngthåew and many also own their own bicycles or motorcycles.

Cars & Trucks

Rental cars, 4WDs and minivans are available at several locations throughout the city. Be sure that the vehicle you rent has insurance (liability) coverage – ask to see the documents and carry a photocopy with you while driving. Petrol is always extra.

It's important to choose a car-rental agency carefully, by reputation rather than what's on paper. Whatever happens, you're still responsible for personal injury and medical payments of anyone injured in connection with a traffic accident.

Two of the most well-regarded agencies are **North Wheels** (Map pp280-1; ☎ 0 5387 4478; www .northwheels.com; 70/4-8 Th Chaiyaphum) opposite Talat Somphet, and **Journey** (Map pp280-1; ☎ 0 5320 8787; www.journeycnx.com; 283 Th Tha Phae), near Pratu Tha Phae. Both offer hotel pick-up and delivery as well as 24-hour emergency road service, along with insurance. Sample rentals at North Wheels include a Toyota Soluna for 1000B a day and 4WD pick-up trucks from 1300B a day (plus an extra 500B for driver). Journey rents 4WD Suzuki Caribians for 800B per day.

Both companies offer discounted weekly and monthly rates.

The good-value and highly recommended **Alternative Travel** (☎ 08 1784 4856, 08 9632 6556; noree9000@hotmail.com; 56 Mu, 9 Th Mea Faek Mai) offers customised tours, with English-speaking drivers, in Toyota sedans, 4WD trucks or vans (1500B to 2000B a day). Contact Winai to discuss car or itinerary options.

Other car-rental agencies in town include the following:

Avis Royal Princess Hotel (Map pp280-1; ☎ 0 5328 1033; 122 Th Chang Khlan); Chiang Mai International Airport (Map pp276-7; ☎ 0 5320 1798-9)

Budget (Map pp276-7; ☎ 0 5320 2871; Chiang Mai International Airport)

National Car Rental (Map pp276-7; ☎ 0 5321 0118; Amari Rincome Hotel, 1 Th Nimmanhaemin)

MOTORCYCLES

If you are planning to hire a motorcycle, Honda Dream 100cc step-throughs can be rented for about 150B a day, depending on the season, the condition of the motorcycle and the length of rental. Slightly larger bikes are also available. The 125cc to 150cc Hondas or Yamahas rent for 200B to 250B a day. Motorcycles bigger than 150cc are less ubiquitous but you can usually find 250cc Japanese off-road motorcycles (600B) or 400cc motorcy-

---

MASS TRANSIT FOR CHIANG MAI?

Ever since Chiang Mai's original four-line city bus system was closed down in 1997, both residents and visitors have lamented the lack of regular public transport in the city. In the meantime private vehicle use has grown tremendously, with concomitant traffic jams and noxious auto emissions.

In 2004, the municipal government hired experts at Chiang Mai University to carry out a feasibility study for Chiang Mai mass transit, to be funded in part at the national level. The main objective was to establish a light electric rail system, supplemented by air-conditioned buses and private metered taxis.

The biggest roadblock standing in the way of the plan is the powerful red såwngthåew mafia, who have bribed, cajoled and physically threatened all newcomers who have tried to provide other forms of local transport. As is obvious to everyone who lives in Chiang Mai, the over-abundant såwngthåew tend to exacerbate, rather than relieve, local traffic congestion.

In 2006, a new bus system did finally materialise, with five lines running from 6am to 9pm (see p323). Three of these lines are run by sparkling, white air-con buses. However, the såwngthåew mafia managed to muscle in again, claiming the two other lines for themselves, charging 5B more, and managing to get subsidised by City Hall for doing it! At the time of writing this bus service seemed rather unconvincing and sporadic, and most people were still using their private transport or the usual red såwngthåew to get around.

There is still no sign or real news of the proposed 25 electric trams or 300 metered taxis on the streets of Chiang Mai. But with the pesky reds still with such control over transport in the city it is not a surprise.

cles (700B to 800B) at agencies specialising in larger motorcycles.

Prices are very competitive in Chiang Mai because there's a real glut of motorcycles. For two people, it's cheaper to rent a small motorcycle for the day to visit Doi Suthep than to go up and back in a săwngthăew.

Motorcycle rental places come and go with the seasons. Many of them are lined up along the eastern side of the moat on Th Moon Muang and Th Kotchasan. Among the more established and more reliable are the following:

Dang Bike Hire (Map pp280-1; ☎ 0 5327 1524; 23 Th Kotchasan)

Mr Mechanic (Map pp280-1; ☎ 0 5321 4708; Th Moon Muang, 4 Soi 5)

Pop Rent-A-Car (Map pp280-1; ☎ 0 5327 6014; Th Kotchasan, near Soi 2)

Tony's Big Bikes (Map pp280-1; ☎ 08 6730 1088; cookyboy9@yahoo.com; 17 Th Rachamanka) Rents 125-400cc motorbikes. Also offers motorcycle lessons and tours (see p289).

The motorcycle rental agencies offer motorcycle insurance for around 50B a day, not a bad investment considering you could face a 25,000B to 60,000B liability if your bike is stolen. Most policies have a high deductible (excess), so in cases of theft you're usually responsible for a third to half of the motorcycle's value – even with insurance.

More casual rental places that specialise in quick, easy and cheap rentals of 100cc bikes can be found along Th Moon Muang.

If you're renting a motorcycle for touring the countryside around Chiang Mai, check out the tips and routes at Golden Triangle Rider (www.gt-rider.com).

Metered Taxi

Fares start at 40B for the first 2km, plus 5B for each additional kilometre. However, it is very rare to see a metered taxi to flag down in Chiang Mai. Call for a pick-up instead on **Taxi Meter** (☎ 0 5327 1242/9291).

Săwngthăew, Túk-Túk & Săamláw

Hordes of red săwngthăew ply the streets of Chiang Mai looking for passengers. Flag one down, state your destination and if it is going that way you can ride for 15B to 20B. It's best to board one that already has passengers if you're worried about getting overcharged. If you're going, say, from Pratu Tha Phae to Talat Warorot – a relatively short and well-travelled distance – you shouldn't have to pay more than the normal 15B fare. You can charter (măo) a săwngthăew anywhere in the city for 70B or less.

Túk-túk work only on a charter or taxi basis, at 30B for short trips and 40B to 60B for longer ones. After midnight in entertainment areas such as along Th Charoenrat near the Riverside Bar & Restaurant and Le Brasserie, or down towards Smooth, most túk-túk charge a flat 60B for any trip back across the river.

Chiang Mai still has loads of săamláw (pedicabs), especially in the old city around Talat Warorot. Săamláw cost around 20B to 30B for most trips.

NORTHERN CHIANG MAI PROVINCE

The north of Chiang Mai province is packed with interesting attractions, most of which are within a half day's travel of the city. Among the highlights are the sacred Doi Suthep and its surrounding national park; the beautiful Ma Sa Valley and the many scenic options dotted along its route; and the impressive cave and forest trekking around Chiang Dao.

DOI SUTHEP-PUI NATIONAL PARK

ดอยสุเทพ

Sixteen kilometres northwest of Chiang Mai is Doi Suthep (1676m), a peak named after the hermit Sudeva, who lived on the mountain's slopes for many years. Near its summit is **Wat Phra That Doi Suthep** (entrance fee 30B; tram fee 20B); first established in 1383 under King Keu Naone, it is one of the north's most sacred temples. At the end of the winding road up the mountain, a staircase of 306 steps leads to the wat. You also have the option of riding a tram from the parking lot to the wat grounds.

At the top, weather permitting, there are some fine views of Chiang Mai. Inside the cloister is an exquisite Lanna-style, copper-plated chedi topped by a five-tiered gold umbrella – one of the holiest chedi in Thailand.

Within the monastery compound, the **International Buddhism Center** (IBC; ☎ 0 5329 5012; www .fivethousandyears.org; admission free, donations appreciated) offers informal chats and discussion (1pm to

CHIANG MAI PROVINCE

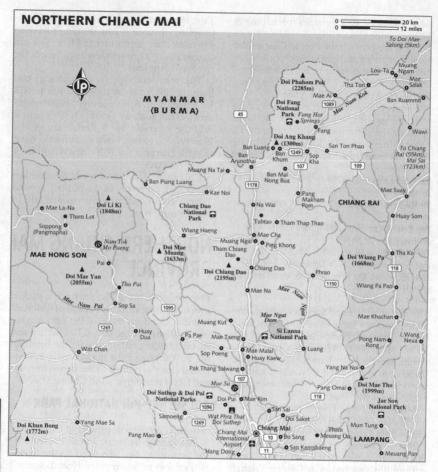

NORTHERN CHIANG MAI

3pm daily) as well as chanting (6pm). It is possible to do a three-day meditation retreat here but it is preferred that meditators start with the 21-day Vipassana foundation course.

About 4km beyond Wat Phra That Doi Suthep is **Phra Tamnak Phu Phing**, a winter palace for the royal family with **palace gardens** (admission 50B; 8.30am-11.30am & 1-3.30pm). It closes if the royal family are visiting.

The road that passes the palace splits off to the left, stopping at the peak of Doi Pui. From there, a road proceeds for a couple of kilometres to **Ban Doi Pui**, a Hmong hill-tribe village. Don't expect much evidence of village life here though – it is basically a paved market selling Hmong crafts and other souvenirs, and there are some Nepalese stalls. There is a tiny **museum** (10B) giving some information about hill tribes and opium production.

Most visitors do a quick tour of the temple, the Hmong village and perhaps the winter palace grounds, altogether missing the surrounding park. This 265-sq-km **reserve** (adult/child under 14 yrs 200/100B; 8am-sunset) is home to more than 300 bird species and nearly 2000 species of ferns and flowering plants. Because of its proximity to urban Chiang Mai, development of the park has become a very sensitive issue. The western side of the park has been severely disturbed by poachers and land encroachers, including around 500 hill-tribe families, and the Night Safari (see p289) has caused controversy by taking over parts of national park land.

There are extensive hiking trails in the park, including one that climbs the 1685m Doi Pui; the summit is a favourite picnic spot. If you're cycling or driving to the summit, you can stop off along the way at **Nam Tok Monthathon** (admission adult/child 400/200B; ☺ 8am-sunset), 2.5km off the paved road to Doi Suthep. The trail is well marked; if you're interested in checking the waterfalls out, have the săwngthăew driver drop you off on the way up the mountain. Pools beneath the falls hold water year-round, although swimming is best during or just after the annual monsoon. The falls can be a little crowded on weekends. The 200B fee allows you to visit other waterfalls on the road to Suthep.

Other trails pass Hmong villages that rarely get foreign visitors. For a less commercialised Hmong village than Doi Pui, instead of going left on the road past the palace head right. Look out for the sign saying 'Kun Chang Kian Mong Village – 7km'. The road is paved until you hit the Doi Pui camp ground, and from there it is dirt track for 3km to the village (difficult to travel along in the rainy season). In between the camp ground and the village is a **coffee plantation** where you can stop and have a cup of coffee or stay the night in basic accommodation (room 150B) with fantastic views.

Accommodation in the national park includes smart **bungalows** (☎ 0 5329 5014; doisuthep_pui@hotmail.com; r from 500B) about 1km north of the wat by the park headquarters. From here a 4km trail leads to the scenic and more isolated Nam Tok Sai Yai (Sai Yai waterfalls), and connects with a trail that leads to Nam Tok Monthathon. There is also the **Doi Pui camp ground** (☎ 0 5329 5014; doisuthep_pui@hotmail .com; 2/4/7 person tent 150/225/300B). Sleeping bags, gas fires, pots and pans are also available to hire. There's a good information centre at the camp ground, with an exhibition of the flora and fauna of the park, and the agricultural calendar of the hill tribes. Mountain bikes (200B) can be hired here for some fat-tyred fun.

Getting There & Away

Săwngthăew to Doi Suthep leave Chiang Mai throughout the day from the western end of Th Huay Kaew in front of Chiang Mai University. Doi Suthep săwngthăew fares are 50B there and 40B back, per person. Săwngthăew also depart from Pratu Chang Pheuak and the Chiang Mai Zoo. To Phra Tamnak Phu Phing

and Doi Pui add 30B in each direction. It is worth hiring a motorbike to get up to the wat and explore the surrounding park.

HUAY TEUNG THAO RESERVOIR

อ่างเก็บน้ำห้วยตึงเฒ่า

Head for this sizeable **reservoir** (admission free; ☺ 8am-sunset), about 12km northwest of the city, if you're in the mood for an all-day swim and picnic, especially during the hotter months. Windsurfing equipment can be rented for around 150B an hour.

If you don't bring your own, food is available from vendors at the lake, who maintain small bamboo-thatch huts over the water's edge for people to sit in. The local speciality is *kûng tên* (dancing shrimp), freshwater shrimp served live in a piquant sauce of lime juice and *phrík lâap* (a northern Thai blend of spicy herbs and chillies). Fishing is permitted if you'd like to try your luck at hooking lunch.

Travelling by car or motorcycle you can reach Huay Teung Thao by driving 10km north on Rte 107 (follow signs towards Mae Rim), then west 2km past an army camp to the reservoir.

Cyclists would do best to pedal to the reservoir via Th Khan Khlong Chonlaprathan. Head west on Th Huay Kaew, then turn right just before the canal. Follow Th Khan Khlong Chonlaprathan north until it ends at a smaller road between the reservoir and the highway; turn left here and you'll reach the lake after another kilometre or so of pedalling. From the northwestern corner of the moat, the 12km bicycle ride takes about an hour.

MAE SA VALLEY & SAMOENG

น้ำตกแม่สา/สะเมิง

This forested loop northwest of Chiang Mai via Mae Rim and/or Hang Dong makes a good day or overnight trip. Although dotted with tourist developments – resorts, orchid farms, butterfly parks, elephant camps, snake farms, botanic gardens, antique and handicraft shops – the Rte 1096/1269 loop through the Mae Sa Valley is very scenic in spots.

The two orchid farms you'll see along this route are the **Mae Rim Orchid Farm** (☎ 0 5329 8801; entrance 40B; ☺ 7am-5pm) and **Sai Namphung Orchid Nursery** (☎ 0 5329 8771; entrance 40B; ☺ 7am-5pm). Both have butterfly enclosures. Mae Rim Orchid Farm is rather run down but sells pretty orchid leaf jewellery at good prices. Sai Namphung is better kept and has more beautiful

orchid displays, but the focus here is more onselling the (overpriced) jewellery rather than giving information on orchids.

Mae Sa Waterfall (Nam Tok Mae Sa; entrance 200B) is only 6km from the Mae Rim turn-off from Rte 107, which in turn is 12km north of Chiang Mai. Further along the loop are several Hmong villages.

There are at least four places along the loop that call themselves elephant 'camp', 'farm' or 'village'. Best of the bunch is the **Maesa Elephant Camp** (☎ 0 5320 6247; www.maesaelephantcamp.com; show adult/child 120/80B), near Mae Sa Waterfall, where the elephants seem to be treated well. One hour shows (8am and 9.40am daily, plus 1.30pm during high season) feature elephants playing musical instruments, painting pictures, kicking footballs and stacking logs. Fun for kids but for adults we found it uncomfortable to watch the elephants perform. Feed the elephants sugar cane and bananas afterwards, and visit the baby elephants in their nursery and training school. Elephant rides in the forest (for two people, 30 minutes/1hour 800/1200B) and mahout courses are also available.

Two kilometres past the elephant camp is the **Queen Sirikit Botanical Gardens** (☎ 0 5384 1000; www.qsbg.org; admission 20B, car 100B (excluding individual admission); ☼ 8.30am-5pm). There are some lovely walks here, such as the Thai Plants and Medicinal Herbs Trail or the Climber Trail. It's a nice place to have a picnic too. The glasshouses and gardens feature an impressive array of plants and flowers. Take the provided bus (30B) or your own car to get around the whole facility. Motorbikes are not allowed in the gardens.

Top-end resorts dot this route (see p300). The drive to Samoeng – at the westernmost extension of the loop (35km from Mae Rim) – is a beautiful one. If you want to stay here before following the loop back down to Chiang Mai, **Samoeng Resort** (☎ 08 9955 6811; r 200-400B; ☒), about 2.5km outside Samoeng village itself, has 15 basic bungalows in a garden setting.

Getting There & Away
You can get a săwngthăew to Samoeng from the Chang Pheuak bus terminal in Chiang Mai for 50B. There are two daily departures, one that leaves around 9am and another at 11am. It takes 2¾ hours to reach Samoeng from Chiang Mai. In Samoeng the vehicles stop near the market, across from Samoeng Hospital.

Since it's paved all the way, the winding loop road makes a good ride by bicycle or motorcycle. From Samoeng you can take a northwest detour along Rte 1265 to Rte 1095 for Pai and Mae Hong Son; the 148km road breaks north at the Karen village of Wat Chan, where fuel is available. The road passes by a few Hmong and Karen villages.

MAE TAENG
แม่แตง

The mountainous area around Mae Taeng – especially southwest of the junction of Rtes 107 and 1095 – has become a major trekking area because of the variety of Lisu, Lahu, Karen and Hmong villages in the region. **White-water rafting** along Mae Taeng is popular. It is often easier to arrange a trip from Chiang Mai through a company like **Chiang Mai Adventure** (☎ 0 5341 8197; www.chiangmaiadventure.co.th; 13/1 Th Sriphoom), who specialise in white-water rafting along this river.

CHIANG DAO
เชียงดาว

Best known for its cave complex, Chiang Dao is also a good base to explore the trekking and bird-watching opportunities of Doi Chiang Dao. The area surrounding Chiang Dao town is scenic and largely unspoiled. From the summit of Doi Chiang Dao (also called Doi Luang; 2195m), allegedly Thailand's highest limestone mountain, there are spectacular views.

There is a market every day at the northern end on the main street through Chiang Dao. It is worth coming into town to see the colourful **Tuesday morning market** (7am-12am), when hill tribes come to sell their wares. Most accommodation is in the vicinity of Tham Chiang Dao, 5km west of town. There is an ATM machine at the 7-Eleven near the bus stop for Fang.

From the main four-way junction at Chiang Dao, those with their own wheels – preferably a mountain bike, motorcycle or truck – can head east to visit Lahu, Lisu and Akha villages, which are all within 15km. Roughly 13.5km east from Rte 107 is the Lisu village of Lisu Huay Ko, where rustic accommodation is available.

Sights
ELEPHANT TRAINING CENTRE CHIANG DAO
The **Elephant Training Centre** (☎ 0 5386 2037; Km 56, Rte 107; show adult/child 60/30B), off Rte 107 be-

tween Mae Taeng and Chiang Dao, is one of several training centres in the area that puts on elephant shows (9am and 10am daily) for tourists. It is in a beautiful spot and feels more intimate than the Maesa Elephant Camp. Elephant rides in the forest (2 people, 30 minutes/1 hour 800/1200B) and bamboo rafting (up to three people, one hour, 400B per person) are also offered. If you haven't seen the elephant training center in Lampang Province (in Thung Kwian), this is a reasonable alternative.

THAM CHIANG DAO
ถ้ำเชียงดาว

The main attraction along the way to Fang and Tha Ton is this **cave complex** (admission 20B), 5km west of Rte 107 and 72km north of Chiang Mai.

The complex is said to extend some 10km to 14km into Doi Chiang Dao; the interconnected caverns that are open to the public include Tham Mah (735m long), Tham Kaew (474m), Tham Phra Non (360m) and Tham Nam (660m).

Tham Phra Non contains religious statuary and is electrically illuminated (and thus easily explored on one's own), while Tham Mah, Tham Kaew and Tham Nam have no light fixtures. A guide with a pressurised gas lantern can be hired for 100B for up to five people. The interior cave formations are quite spectacular in places – more than 100 of them are named.

Local legend says this cave complex was the home of a *reusii* (hermit) for a thousand years. As the legend goes, the sage was on such intimate terms with the deity world that he convinced some *thewádaa* (the Buddhist equivalent of angels) to create seven magic wonders inside the caverns: a stream flowing from the pedestal of a solid-gold Buddha; a storehouse of divine textiles; a mystical lake; a city of *naga* (mythical serpents); a sacred immortal elephant; and the hermit's tomb. No, you won't find any of the seven wonders; the locals say these are much deeper inside the mountain, beyond the last of the illuminated caverns.

The locals also say that anyone who attempts to remove a piece of rock from the cave will forever lose their way in the cave's eerie passages.

There is a wat complex outside the cavern, and a stream with huge carp and catfish you can feed. Vendors by the parking lot sell medicinal roots and herbs.

From the summit of the 2195m **Doi Chiang Dao** (also called Doi Luang), allegedly Thailand's highest limestone mountain, there are spectacular views. Beyond Tham Chiang Dao along the same rural road is a smaller sacred cave retreat complex, **Samnak Song Tham Pha Plong** (Tham Pha Plong Monastic Centre), where Buddhist monks sometimes meditate. A long, steep stairway leads to a large *chedi* beautifully framed by forest and limestone cliffs.

Sleeping

Over the last five years or so, Chiang Dao has enjoyed a surge in popularity among visitors who have discovered there's more to the area than just Tham Chiang Dao.

For arranging activities like hiking and bird-watching, Malee's and Chiang Dao Nest are the most established, although, some of the other guesthouses have better value accommodation.

Pieng Dao Hotel (☎ 0 5345 5165; Ban Chiang Dao, Rte 107; r 150-250B) In town, this old-style wooden hotel has basic but clean rooms with shared hot-water showers and 'ensuites' with cold-water showers. It can get noisy being by the road.

our pick **Chiang Dao Rainbow** (☎ 08 4803 8116; www.chiangdao-rainbow.com; r 300-600B) Down a side road, past the market and the wat (on the way to Fang) is a side road to the sign-posted Chiang Dao Rainbow. The two, great value, recycled teak bungalows, with four-poster bed, smart furniture and terraces, look out onto rice fields, a stream and dramatic views of Doi Chiang Dao. There are also spick-and-span cheaper rooms in the house at the back. Run by an ex-Oxford professor and partner, they do cycle and car tours of the area, with an educational bent. The restaurant here has had great reviews.

Chiang Dao Inn Hotel (☎ 0 5345 5134; 20 Mu 6, Rte 107; r 500-650B, ste 1500B) If you need to stay in the middle of town, this Thai business hotel (an older wooden wing, plus a modern L-shaped wing) is old-fashioned but comfortable, clean and friendly.

our pick **Chiang Dao Nest** (☎ 0 6017 1985; www .chiangdao.com; bungalows 695B; 🖵) About 2km past the entrance to the Tham Chiang Dao, the setting for the ten A-frame bungalows here delivers excellent forest and mountain views. The

friendly owners, an Englishman and his Thai wife, can arrange trekking and bird-watching. Even if you don't stay here, pop over for a meal at the award-winning restaurant.

Chiang Dao Nest 2 (☎ 0 5345 6242; www.chiangdao .com; bungalows 695B; 💻) A slightly newer branch, with the same owners as Chiang Dao Nest, this is a cluster of five bungalows with great views, about 600m past the cave turn-off on the left side of the road. The restaurant at Chiang Dao Nest 2 focuses on Thai cuisine.

Nature Guest House (☎ 08 9955 9074; r 400-700B) The nearest guesthouse to town and 3km from the cave, this quiet place is set in a neat garden with mountain views. The four A-frame wooden bungalows with terraces are simple yet stylish. Breakfast is available.

Malee's Nature Lovers Bungalows (☎ 0 1961 8387; r 250-1100B) The pioneer of eco-friendly tourism in the area, Malee's is about 1.3km past the entrance to Tham Chiang Dao (heading towards the mountains). Friendly and knowledgeable Thai owner Malee has a range of thatch-and-brick bungalows, as well as a restaurant on site. The cheaper rooms could do with a spruce up. Malee can arrange trekking, rafting and bird-watching. Mountain bikes are available for rent.

Eating

You wouldn't have thought it a few years ago – but Chiang Dao is fast becoming a spot for foodies.

Baan Krating Chiang Dao (☎ 0 5345 5577; Km 63, Rte 107; dishes 50-110B) Located 9km before the town of Chiang Dao on Rte 107 (coming from Chiang Mai), this is a good place to stop en route. The restaurant overlooks manicured gardens, pomelo trees and a stream. Dishes like deep-fried chicken in pandanus leaves are served, as well as sandwiches and salads.

Café-café (☎ 08 6179 6300; Ban Chiang Dao; dishes 40-135B), Next to the bus stop for Chiang Mai (and opposite the bus stop for Fang), this café is run by a Thai-French couple. If you crave some Western food, this new modern place has large breakfasts, good coffee, great baguettes and burgers, yummy ice cream, and some Thai food. There is a TV for big sports games, and motorbikes for rent.

Chiang Dao Rainbow (☎ 08 4803 8116; www .chiangdao-rainbow.com; dishes 50-230B) This highly recommended restaurant offers two menus – northern Thai and Greek/Mediterranean. Its Shan pork stew and banana flower salad has

been raved about, and gourmet dishes like stuffed squid and baked prawns with goat cheese work well. There are plenty of vegetarian options too.

Mon and Kurt Restaurant (dishes 40-280B) On the main road near the turn-off for Chiang Dao Rainbow, this place is good for big breakfasts, as well as Thai and Western food.

our pick Chiang Dao Nest (☎ 0 6017 1985; www .chiangdao.com; dishes 95-375B) Included in Thailand Tatler's best restaurant list 2006, Chiang Dao Nest serves sophisticated European food in a relaxed setting. The lunch and dinner menu changes every three to four days, reflecting what's best to be found locally. Dishes like pork tenderloin wrapped in bacon with a roasted shallot sauce are delicious.

Across the main road from Pieng Dao Hotel in Chiang Dao town is **Pon Pen** (dishes 20-25B). Choose from the tasty dishes on display, like chicken and ginger with bamboo shoots, as well as various other curries and salads.

There is a daily **food market** off the main street through Chiang Dao. The Tuesday morning market is the most colourful, with hill tribes bringing wares to sell.

Getting Around

From town you can easily charter sǎwngthǎew (120B) or motorbike taxis (50B) to guesthouses like Malee's or Chiang Dao Nest. To get to the cave from town costs around 100B with a sǎwngthǎew or 30B on a motorbike taxi.

Getting There & Away

Buses to Chiang Dao from Chiang Mai's Chang Pheuak terminal depart every 30 minutes between 6am and 6pm (40B, 1½ hours). From Chiang Dao, departures are the same and leave from next to Café-café. Almost opposite the same café you can catch a bus to Fang (50B).

DOI ANG KHANG

ดอยอ่างขาง

About 20km before Fang is the turn-off for Rte 1249 to Doi Ang Khang, Thailand's 'Little Switzerland'. Twenty-five kilometres from the highway, this 1300m peak has a cool climate year-round and supports the cultivation of flowers, fruits and vegetables that are usually found only in more temperate climates.

A few hill-tribe villages such as Ban Luang, Ban Khum, Ban Pang Ma, Nor Lae and Kob

Dong can be visited on the slopes. Many of these villages are supported by royal agricultural projects. TAT in Chiang Mai has a basic map of Doi Ang Khang outlining cycling routes and treks to villages. A good source of information on Doi Ang Khang is Mr Macku, who runs the eco-friendly Angkhang Nature Resort (see below) and can arrange cycling, mule riding and trekking to hill-tribe villages in the area.

Nineteen kilometres before the turn-off to Doi Ang Khang, you can make a 12km detour west off Rte 107 onto a dirt road to visit Ban Mai Nong Bua, a Kuomintang (KMT) village with an old-fashioned Yunnanese feel.

A more scenic route is the 'back road' to Doi Ang Khang via Rte 1178, which winds along a ridge to the mountain's western slopes. Along this route, Ban Arunothai was until recently visited regularly by United Wa (Myanmar Special Region 2) State Army soldiers who were moving *yaa bâa* (crude amphetamine pills) from across the border in Myanmar to the Thai market. On this road up to Doi Ang Khang, the village of Ban Luang is another interesting stopover for a Yunnanese atmosphere. In the vicinity, you'll see plenty of ponies and mules still used to transport local goods.

Near the summit of Doi Ang Khang and the Yunnanese village of Ban Khum, there are several places to stay.

Part of the Amari Hotel Group, **Angkhang Nature Resort** (☎ 0 5345 0110; www.amari.com/ang khang; 1/1 Mu 5, Ban Khum, Tambon Mae Ngan, Fang; r 3000-3900B; 🖳 🕱) is an unexpectedly plush hotel featuring large, tastefully designed bungalows spread over a slope. The huge, attractive lobby boasts stone fireplaces at either end for use in the cool season. There is a good restaurant on the premises that uses organic produce from the nearby Royal Agricultural Project. Mr Macku, who runs the resort, is a great source of information on the area, and arranges trekking to hill tribe villages, mountain-bike and mule-riding trips, and bird-watching. Call to arrange for transfers to the resort.

Naha Guest House (☎ 0 5345 0008; Ban Khum, Tambon Mae Ngan, Fang; per person 350B) has large eight-person bungalows with shared hot-water shower and toilet.

At the base of the slope are a couple of open-air restaurants serving a variety of dishes with an emphasis on Thai and Yunnanese Muslim cuisine.

Getting There & Away

If not using your own transport to get around Doi Ang Khang, catch a bus heading to Fang from Chiang Mai's Chang Pheuak terminal (every half hour, 8.30am to 4.30pm). About 20km before Fang there is a junction and turn-off for Rte 1249 to Doi Ang Khang. Get off here and take a săwngthăew (50B, or 500B chartered) for the 30 minute/25km trip up to Ban Khum (where the accommodation is) near the summit.

FANG & THA TON
ฝาง/ท่าตอน

North from Chiang Mai along Rte 107, the city of Fang was originally founded by Phaya Mengrai in the 13th century, although as a human settlement and trading centre for *jiin haw* caravans, the locale dates back at least 1000 years. More recently the surrounding district has become a conduit for *yaa bâa* manufactured by the Wa in Myanmar.

Although Fang may not look particularly inviting at first pass, the town's quiet back-streets are lined with some interesting little shops in wooden buildings. The Shan/Burmese-style Wat Jong Paen (near the New Wiang Kaew Hotel) has a very impressive stacked-roof *wíhăan*.

There are Mien and Karen villages nearby that you can visit on your own, but for most people Fang is just a road marker on the way to Tha Ton. Most visitors also prefer Tha Ton's more rural setting to stay overnight. It's only half an hour or so by săwngthăew to the river from Fang or vice versa.

Along the main street in Fang there are two banks offering currency exchange, and four ATMs.

About 10km west of Fang at Ban Meuang Chom, near the agricultural station, is a system of hot springs that are part of Doi Fang National Park. Just ask for the *bàw náam ráwn* (*baw náam háwn* in northern Thai). On weekends there are frequent săwngthăew carrying Thai picnickers from Fang to the hot springs.

Tha Ton is little more than a săwngthăew stand and a collection of river boats, restaurants and tourist accommodation along a pretty bend in Mae Nam Kok. As a tourist destination, the main focus is the river dock, launching point for Mae Nam Kok trips to Chiang Rai, with treks to the many hill-tribe settlements in the region a distant second place.

There is a **tourist police office** (☎ 1155; www
.tourist.police.go.th; ☒ 8.30am-4.30pm) near the bridge
on the river-boat dock side. Opposite the tourist police is an internet shop and there is also a
computer next door in Coffee Cup (opposite).
Both charge 30B an hour.

Sights & Activities
TREKKING & RAFTING
There are some pleasant walks along Mae
Nam Kok. Within 20km of Fang and Tha
Ton you can visit local villages inhabited by
Palaung (a Karennic tribe that arrived from
Myanmar around 16 years ago), Black Lahu,
Akha and Yunnanese on foot, mountain bike
or motorcycle.

Treks and rafting trips can be arranged
through any local guesthouse or hotel in Tha
Ton or go to Taton Tours by the boat dock.
Typical trips aboard bamboo house-rafts with
pilot and cook for three days cost 2500B per
person (minimum four people), including all
meals, lodging and rafting.

On the first day you'll visit several villages
near the river and spend the night in a Lisu
village; on the second day rafters visit hot
springs and more villages, and then spend
the night on the raft; and on the third day you
dock in Chiang Rai.

You could get a small group of travellers
together and arrange your own house-raft
with a guide and cook for a two- or three-day
journey down river, stopping off in villages of
your choice along the way. A house-raft generally costs 700B per person per day, including
simple meals, and takes up to six people – so
figure on 1900B for a three-day trip. Police
regulations require that an experienced boat
navigator accompany each raft – the river
has lots of tricky spots and there have been
some mishaps.

Near the Tha Ton pier, you can rent inflatable kayaks and do your own paddling in
the area. Upstream a few kilometres the river
crosses into Myanmar. See opposite for details
on organised river trips to Chiang Rai.

WAT THA TON
Climb the stairs up the hill to **Wat Tha Ton** (☎ 0
5345 9309; www.wat-thaton.org). There are nine different levels of the wat punctuated by shrines,
Buddha statues, monks and student living-
quarters, and a *chedi*. Each level affords stunning views of the mountainous valley towards
Burma, and the plains of Tha Ton. It is 3km

or a 30-minute walk to the 9th level but it's
sometimes possible to get a lift by car.

The short walk to the first level has a statue
of Kuan Yin, the Chinese goddess of compassion; the international liaison monk has his office here too. Ten-day, silent **Vipassana meditation
retreats** are offered, where you stay in your own
kuti (basic hut) and have one-on-one teaching,
as well as doing your own individual practice.
At the time of writing retreats started from the
1st to the 19th of each month. Visit the website
to check dates and to book. It is also possible
to go to the Wat between 9am and 5pm daily,
where monks can teach meditation.

Sleeping
FANG
Chok Thani (☎ 0 5345 2353; r 290-450B; ☒ ▢) On
the main road by the market, this stark looking hotel has large basic rooms with the option
of air-con.

Baan Sa-Bai Hotel (☎ 0 5345 3453; b-sabai@hotmail
.com; 88 Mu 9 Wieng; r 700B; ☒) Just before coming
into Fang (on the road from Chiang Dao) this
new, three-storey hotel looks a bit hospital
like. Inside though, the large, comfortable
rooms are well furnished with some Thai
touches, and have cable TV.

THA TON
BUDGET TO MIDRANGE
ourpick **Thaton Garden Riverside** (☎ 0 5345 9286; r
300-500B) Next to Thaton Chalet by the bridge,
this spick-and-span place has a choice of air-
con and fan rooms. It's worth paying the extra
baht for the air-con room as you get a river
terrace. There is also a restaurant overlooking the river.

Apple Guest House (r 350-500B) Conveniently
located opposite the boat landing, the rooms
in this two-storey building are spacious, light
and well equipped. There's a restaurant on the
ground floor.

Garden Home (☎ 0 5337 3015; r 300-1500B) A tranquil place along the river, about 150m from
the bridge, with thatch-roofed bungalows
spaced well apart among lots of litchi trees
and bougainvillea. There are also a few stone
bungalows, and three larger, more luxurious
bungalows on the river with small verandas, a
TV and fridge. From the bridge, turn left at the
Thaton River View Hotel sign. Motorbikes and
mountain bikes are available to rent here.

Baan Suan Riverside Resort (☎ 0 5337 3214; fax 0
5337 3215; r incl breakfast 700-800B, bungalow 1200-1500B; ;

🏠) Has small cement air-con bungalows with terraces back from the river; fan rooms in a cement building, also back off the river; and a couple of large air-con wooden bungalows with terraces right on the river. With its cheap furniture the bungalows are overpriced. The grounds are beautifully landscaped and an attached restaurant overlooks the river.

TOP END
our pick **Thaton River View Hotel** (☎ 0 5337 3173; fax 0 5345 9288; r incl breakfast 1530B; 🏠) Further upstream along the river, this quiet resort hotel has 33 rooms facing the river, joined by wooden walkways lined with frangipani trees. The rooms are stylishly decorated but there are no decent chairs on the terraces. The restaurant at the hotel is the best in the area.

Thaton Chalet (☎ 0 5337 3155/7; www.thatonchalet .com; 1400-2200B; 🏠) A four-storey hotel next to the bridge, with stone façade. The comfortable rooms have a good view of the river and standard 4-star facilities but blankets are bobbly and it feels a little old-fashioned. The hotel features a pleasant beer garden right on the river, as well as an indoor restaurant.

Maekok River Village Resort (☎ 0 5345 9355; www .track-of-the-tiger.com; r 2625-4275B; 🖵 🏠) On the boat-dock side, downstream along the river, this sprawling affair offers four-bed family rooms as well as two-bed poolside rooms. On the grounds are a pool and restaurant. A variety of activities including massage, cooking classes, trekking, rafting, mountain biking and caving can be arranged here. It's popular with tour groups.

Eating
FANG
The food stalls on the main street market are good places to eat. There are also a few restaurants serving Yunnanese specialities such as *khâo sawy, man-thoh* (*mantou* in Mandarin; steamed buns) and *khâo mòk kài*, plus *kǔaytǐaw* (rice noodles) and other standards.

THA TON
Most of the top-end hotels have good restaurants, particularly the **Thaton River View Hotel** (mains 60-150B) with its tasty Thai dishes served on a terrace overlooking the river and mountains.

There is a line of basic **Thai/Chinese restaurants** (dishes 20-30B) by the boat dock, and **The Coffee Cup** (dishes 60-90B; ⏲ 7.30am-4.30pm) – a funky looking place that sells good breakfasts and sandwiches as well as iced and hot coffee and tea.

Getting There & Away
BUS & SǍWNGTHǍEW
Buses to Fang (80B, 3½ hours) leave from the Chang Pheuak bus terminal in Chiang Mai every 30 minutes between 6am and 6pm. Aircon minivans make the trip to Fang (120B, 3½ hours) every 30 minutes between 8am and 5pm, leaving from behind the Chang Pheuak bus terminal on the corner of Soi Sanam Kila.

From Fang it's about 23km to Tha Ton. Yellow sǎwngthǎew by the market do the 40-minute trip for 20B; the larger orange buses from Fang leave less frequently and cost 20B. Buses and sǎwngthǎew leave from near the market. Both operate from 5.30am to 5pm only.

The river isn't the only way to get to points north of Tha Ton. Yellow sǎwngthǎew leave from the northern side of the river in Tha Ton to Mae Salong in Chiang Rai Province every 90 minutes between 8am and 12.30pm (60B, 1½ hours). From there you can get another bus to Chiang Rai for 40B.

To get to Mae Sai or Chiang Rai directly take the daily 3pm bus from the bridge. It costs 50B to Mae Sai and 90B to Chiang Rai.

If you're heading west to Mae Hong Son Province, it's not necessary to dip all the way south to Chiang Mai before continuing on. At Ban Mae Malai, the junction of Rte 107 (the Chiang Mai–Fang highway) and Rte 1095, you can pick up a bus to Pai for 55B; if you're coming from Pai, be sure to get off at this junction to catch a bus north to Fang.

MOTORCYCLE
Motorcycle trekkers can travel between Tha Ton and Doi Mae Salong, 48km northeast, over a fully paved but sometimes treacherous mountain road. There are a couple of Lisu and Akha villages on the way. The 27km or so between Doi Mae Salong and the village of Muang Ngam are very steep and winding – take care, especially in the rainy season. When conditions are good, the trip can be done in 1½ hours.

You can take a motorcycle on most boats to Chiang Rai for an extra charge.

RIVER TRIP TO CHIANG RAI
From Tha Ton you can make a half-day long-tail boat trip to Chiang Rai down Mae Nam Kok. The regular passenger boat takes up to

12 passengers, leaves at 12.30pm and costs 350B per person. You can also charter a boat all the way for 2200B, which among six people works out to be about 20B more per person but gives you more room to move. A boat can be chartered any time between 8am and 3pm. The trip is a bit of a tourist trap these days as the passengers are all tourists (what local will pay 350B to take the boat when they can catch a bus to Chiang Rai for less than 90B?), and the villages along the way sell cola and souvenirs – but it's still fun. The best time to go is at the end of the rainy season in November when the river level is high.

The travel time down river depends on river conditions and the skill of the pilot, taking anywhere from three to five hours. You could actually make the boat trip in a day from Chiang Mai, catching a bus back from Chiang Rai as soon as you arrive, but it's better to stay in Fang or Tha Ton, take the boat trip, then stay in Chiang Rai or Chiang Saen before travelling on. You may sometimes have to get off and walk or push the boat if it gets stuck on sand bars.

Some travellers take the boat to Chiang Rai in two or three stages, stopping first in **Mae Salak**, a large Lahu village that is about a third of the distance, or **Ban Ruammit**, a Karen village about two-thirds of the way down. Both villages are well touristed these days (charter boat tours stop for photos and elephant rides), but from here you can trek to other Shan, Thai and hill-tribe villages, or do longer treks south of Mae Salak to **Wawi**, a large multiethnic community of *jiin haw*, Lahu, Lisu, Akha, Shan, Karen, Mien and Thai peoples. The Wawi area has dozens of hill-tribe villages of various ethnicities, including the largest Akha community in Thailand (Saen Charoen) and the oldest Lisu settlement (Doi Chang).

Another alternative is to trek south from Mae Salak all the way to the town of **Mae Suay**, where you can catch a bus on to Chiang Rai or back to Chiang Mai. You might also try getting off the boat at one of the smaller villages. You can also make the trip (much more slowly) upriver from Chiang Rai – this is possible despite the rapids.

Near Ban Ruammit, on the opposite river bank (50B, 1½ hours by boat from Chiang Rai) are some pretty **hot springs**. Don't even think about entering the water – it's scalding.

From here you can hike about an hour to **Akha Hill House** (☎ 0 5374 5140, 08 9997 5505; www

BOAT FARES FROM THA TON	
Destination	Fare (B)
Ban Mai	80
Mae Salak	90
Pha Tai	100
Jakheu	110
Kok Noi	120
Pha Kwang	140
Pha Khiaw	250
Hat Wua Dam	250
Pong Man Ron	300
Ban Ruammit	300
Chiang Rai	350

.akhahill.com; r 120-500B), wholly owned and managed by Akha tribespeople. The rustic guesthouse is in a beautiful setting overlooking a mountain valley; a waterfall and several other villages (Akha, Mien, Lisu, Karen and Lahu) are within walking distance. The guesthouse staff can organise overnight trips into the forest with guides who build banana-palm huts and cook meals using sections of bamboo. All of the profits from the guesthouse and its activities go back into the community and its school. Akha River House (p355) in Chiang Rai is run by the same people and has the same philosophy. Free pick-ups are available from Chiang Rai.

Several of the guesthouses in Tha Ton organise raft trips down the river – see p332.

A boat leaves once daily from **Tha Ton public pier** (☎ 0 5345 9427) at 12.30pm. The table shows boat fares from Tha Ton.

SOUTHERN CHIANG MAI PROVINCE

Get in some extra shopping in the villages east and south of Chiang Mai, learn Vipassana meditation at the famous Wat in Chom Thong, or enjoy the natural environment of Doi Inthanon.

BO SANG & SAN KAMPHAENG
ปอสร้าง/สันกำแพง

Bo Sang (also often spelt 'Baw Sang' or 'Bor Sang'), 9km east of Chiang Mai on Rte 1006, is also known as the Umbrella Village because of its many umbrella manufacturers. Almost

the entire village consists of craft shops selling painted umbrellas, fans, silverware, straw handiwork, bamboo and teak, statuary, china, celadon and lacquerware. You'll also find the textured *sa* paper, made from mulberry tree bark.

The larger shops can arrange overseas shipping at reasonable rates. As at Chiang Mai Night Bazaar, discounts are offered for bulk purchases. Some places will also pack and post parasols, apparently quite reliably.

In late January the **Bo Sang Umbrella Festival** (*thêtsàkaan rôm*) features a colourful umbrella procession during the day and a night-time lantern procession. Although it sounds touristy, this festival is actually a very Thai affair; a highlight is the many northern-Thai music ensembles that perform in shopfronts along Bo Sang's main street.

Four or 5km further down Rte 1006 is San Kamphaeng, which flourishes on **cotton and silk weaving**. Shops offering finished products line the main street, although the actual weaving is done in small factories down side streets. There are some good deals to be had here, especially in silk. For cotton, you'd probably do better in Pasang (p343), a lesser-known village near Lamphun, although you may see shirt styles here not available in Pasang.

Getting There & Away

Săwngthăew to Bo Sang and San Kamphaeng leave Chiang Mai frequently during the day from the stop by the flower market on Th

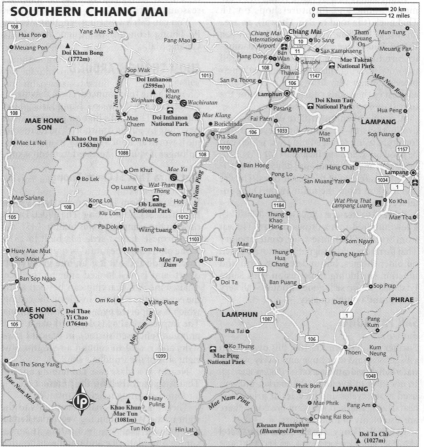

Praisani, near the footbridge. The fare is 10B to Bo Sang and 15B to San Kamphaeng. White săwngthăew leave from Chang Pheuak bus terminal and make the trip to either destination for 10B.

HANG DONG, BAN WAN & BAN THAWAI
หางดง/บ้านวัน/บ้านถวาย

Located 15km south of Chiang Mai on Rte 108, **Hang Dong** is famous for ceramics, wood-carving and antiques. Many of the shops here deal in wholesale as well as retail, so prices are low. Catch a bus from Pratu Chiang Mai to Hang Dong (10B). The shops are actually strung out along Rte 108, starting about 2km before Hang Dong.

Immediately east of Hang Dong there are more antique and furniture shops on Th Thakhilek (the road to Ban Thawai), an area known as **Ban Wan**, and beyond that, in **Ban Thawai**. Ban Wan generally has the best-quality furniture and antiques. Ban Thawai itself is a wood-carving village offering mostly new pieces, though very little is of high quality, as most of the goods churned out are for the tourist or overseas export markets.

A couple of shops in Ban Wan make reproductions of Thai and Burmese antique furniture using salvaged old teak, which can be good buys. **Srithong Thoprasert** (☎ 0 5343 3112; Th Thakhilek) and **Crossroads Asia** (☎ 0 5343 4650; 214/7 Th Thakhilek) are two of the better ones. They're about 500m from the main Hang Dong intersection.

Nakee's Asia Treasures (☎ 0 5344 1357; Th Thakhilek), a few hundred metres towards Ban Thawai from Srithong Thoprasert, has contemporary Thai furniture and designer accessories based on older themes, but updated for form and function (including some fusion with Santa Fe styles). It also sells good antiques – all very tasteful and of high quality.

SAN PA THONG
สันป่าตอง

Further south down Rte 108, this overgrown village is home to a huge and lively weekly **water buffalo and cattle market** (☼ 5.30am-10am Sat). In addition to livestock, the market purveys used motorcycles and bicycles at prices that beat Chiang Mai's. If you want breakfast, there are also plenty of food vendors.

In San Pa Thong, **Kao Mai Lanna Resort Hotel** (☎ 0 5383 4470; www.kaomailanna.com; Km 29, Th Chiang Mai-Hot; r 2600-3000B; ⚅ ⚄) is almost reason enough to travel this far. As southern China supplanted northern Thailand as a major source of tobacco for the world cigarette industry, many tobacco-curing sheds were either abandoned or destroyed. At Kao Mai Lanna, the sheds have been converted into characterful tourist lodging. Built of brick and bamboo, and following designs imported by British tobacco brokers, each building has two floors divided into two units. All rooms are furnished with antiques or reproductions. There is a new pool and spa, and wellness weekends and tours are available. There's also free transport from the airport, train station or bus stations in Chiang Mai. Even if you don't stay here, the outdoor restaurant serves superb Thai food at very reasonable prices.

You can catch a bus or săwngthăew to San Pa Thong from the bus queue near Pratu Chiang Mai.

CHOM THONG & AROUND
จอมทอง

Chom Thong (pronounced 'jawm thawng') is a necessary stop between Chiang Mai and Doi Inthanon (Thailand's highest peak) if you're travelling by public transport. The main temple is worth an hour's stop for its ancient bòt, or longer if you're interested in meditation.

Wat Phra That Si Chom Thong
วัดพระธาตุศรีจอมทอง

Walk down Chom Thong's main street to Wat Phra That Si Chom Thong. The gilded Lanna chedi in the compound was built in 1451 and the Burmese–Lanna-style bòt, built in 1516, is one of the most beautiful in northern Thailand. Inside and out it is an integrated work of art, and is well looked after by the local Thais. Fine woodcarving can be seen along the eaves of the roof and inside on the ceiling, which is supported by massive teak columns. The impressive altar is designed like a small praasàat (enclosed shrine), in typical Lanna style, and is said to contain a relic from the right side of the Buddha's skull.

Nearby is a glass case containing ancient Thai weaponry. Behind the praasàat altar is a room containing religious antiques.

There's a row of small restaurants to the right of the Wat, including **Vegetarian Restaurant** (Watjanee; dishes 25B; ☼ 6am-7pm). It serves simple one-plate rice and noodle dishes that

---

MEDITATION RETREATS

Under the direction of Ajahn Thong, formerly of Wat Ram Poeng in Chiang Mai, Vipassana meditation retreats in the style of the late Mahasi Sayadaw are held regularly in a lay centre at **Wat Phra That Si Chom Thong** (☎ 0 5382 6869, 0 5334 2161; kathrynchindaporn@yahoo.com). The many donations given to the wat are evident in the new meditation centre and numerous *kùtì* (meditation huts). It is preferred that meditation students stay a minimum of two weeks, with the optimum course lasting 21 days. However, it is sometimes possible to come for shorter periods if room is available. Foreign monks and lay people teach these well-regarded retreats. Students, who dress in white, stay in their own *kùtì* at the back of the wat. The schedule is very rigorous.

---

substitute meat with tofu and gluten. Look for the yellow pennants out the front.

Doi Inthanon National Park
อุทยานแห่งชาติดอยอินทนนท์

Thailand's highest peak, the 2565m Doi Inthanon (often abbreviated as Doi In) has three impressive waterfalls cascading down its slopes. Starting from the bottom these are **Nam Tok Mae Klang** (adult/child 400/200B, car/motorbike 30/20B; ⏱ 8am-sunset), **Nam Tok Wachiratan** and **Nam Tok Siriphum**. Admission prices allow entry to all three sights. The first two have picnic areas and food vendors. Nam Tok Mae Klang is the largest and the easiest to get to; you must stop here to get a bus to the top of Doi Inthanon. It can be climbed nearly to the top, as there is a footbridge leading to rock formations over which the water cascades. Nam Tok Wachiratan is also very pleasant, and less crowded.

The views from Doi Inthanon are best in the cool dry season from November to February. You can expect the air to be quite chilly towards the top, so take a jacket or sweater. For most of the year a mist, formed by the condensation of warm humid air below, hangs around the highest peak. Along the 47km road to the top are terraced rice fields, tremendous valleys and a few small hill-tribe villages. The mountain slopes are home to around 4000 Hmong and Karen tribespeople.

The entire mountain is a national park (482 sq km), despite agriculture and human habitation. One of the top destinations in Southeast Asia for naturalists and bird-watchers, the mist-shrouded upper slopes produce abundant orchids, lichens, mosses and epiphytes, while supporting nearly 400 bird varieties, more than any other habitat in Thailand. The mountain is also one of the last habitats of the Asiatic black bear, along with the Assamese macaque, Phayre's leaf-monkey and a selection of other rare and not-so-rare monkeys and gibbons as well as the more common Indian civet, barking deer and giant flying squirrel – around 75 mammal species in all.

Most of the park's bird species are found between 1500m and 2000m; the best bird-watching season is from February to April, and the best spots are the *beung* (bogs) near the top.

Phra Mahathat Naphamethanidon, a *chedi* built by the Royal Thai Air Force to commemorate the king's 60th birthday in 1989, is off the highway between the Km 41 and Km 42 markers, about 4km before reaching the summit of Doi Inthanon. In the base of the octagonal *chedi* is a hall containing a stone Buddha image.

The 400B entry fee collected for Nam Tok Mae Klang near the foot of the mountain is good for all stops on the Doi Inthanon circuit; be sure to keep your receipt.

Park bungalows (☎ 0 5326 8550; bungalow from 1000B), 31km north of Chom Thong, are well-equipped, log-cabin style and can be reserved at the park headquarters or by calling. If you have your own tent camping is 40B a night, or you can hire a tent with sleeping bag for 250B.

Getting There & Away
Buses to Chom Thong leave regularly from just inside Pratu Chiang Mai at the south moat as well as from the Chang Pheuak bus terminal in Chiang Mai. Some buses go directly to Nam Tok Mae Klang and some go only as far as Hot, although the latter will let you off in Chom Thong. The fare to Chom Thong (58km from Chiang Mai) is 34B.

From Chom Thong there are regular sǎwngthǎew to Mae Klang (20B), about 8km north. Sǎwngthǎew from Mae Klang to Doi Inthanon (per person 30B) leave almost

hourly until late afternoon. Most of the passengers are locals who get off at various points along the road, thus allowing a few stationary views of the valleys below.

For another 15B you can go south from Chom Thong to Hot, where you can get buses

west on to Mae Sariang or Mae Hong Son. However, if you've been to Doi Inthanon and the waterfalls, you probably won't have time to make it all the way to Mae Sariang or Mae Hong Son in one day, so you may want to stay overnight in the park.

Northern Thailand

The first true Thai kingdoms arose in northern Thailand, endowing this region with a rich cultural heritage. Whether at the sleepy town of Lamphun or the famed ruins of Sukhothai, the ancient origins of Thai art and culture can still be seen. A distinct Thai culture thrives in northern Thailand. The northerners are very proud of their local customs, considering their ways to be part of Thailand's 'original' tradition. Look for symbols displayed by northern Thais to express cultural solidarity: *kàlae* (carved wooden 'X' motifs) on house gables and the ubiquitous *sêua mâw hâwm* (indigo-dyed rice-farmer's shirt). The north is also the home of Thailand's hill tribes, each with their own unique way of life. The region's diverse mix of ethnic groups range from Karen and Shan to Akha and Yunnanese.

The scenic beauty of the north has been fairly well preserved and has more natural forest cover than any other region in Thailand. It is threaded with majestic rivers, dotted with waterfalls, and breathtaking mountains frame almost every view.

The provinces in this chapter have a plethora of natural, cultural and architectural riches. Enjoy one of the most beautiful Lanna temples in Lampang Province. Explore the impressive trekking opportunities and the quiet Mekong river towns of Chiang Rai Province. The exciting hairpin bends and stunning scenery of Mae Hong Son Province make it a popular choice for trekking, river and motorcycle trips. Home to many Burmese refugees, Mae Sot in Tak Province is a fascinating frontier town. Less visited areas like Um Phang are becoming well known for more remote treks, and provinces like Nan and Phrae are worth the extra hike for the unusual temples and some of the best mountain scenery in the north.

HIGHLIGHTS

- Exploring **caves** (p443) and doing **motorcycle rides** (p443) around Soppong
- Taking in the frontier-town feel of **Mae Sot** (p417) and then heading to Um Phang, where the end of the road leads to **Nam Tok Thilawsu** (p426), Thailand's biggest, most beautiful waterfall
- Learning to be a *mahout* (elephant caretaker) at Lampang's **Elephant Conservation Centre** (p348)
- Getting off the beaten path in Nan to see the beautiful murals at **Wat Phumin** (p388)
- Cycling around the awesome ruins of Thailand's 'golden age' at **Sukhothai** (p403) and **Si Satchanalai-Chaliang Historical Park** (p408)
- Volunteering in an Akha village in **Chiang Rai Province** (p354)

★ Soppong

★ Chiang Rai province

★ Nan

★ Elephant Conservation Centre

★ Si Satchanalai-Chaliang Historical Park

★ Sukhothai Historical Park

★ Mae Sot

★ Um Phang

NORTHERN THAILAND

FAST FACTS

- **Best Time to Visit** November to March
- **Population** 7.8 Million

History

Northern Thailand's history has been characterised by the shifting powers of various independent principalities. One of the most significant early cultural influences in the north was the Mon kingdom of Hariphunchai (modern Lamphun), which held sway from the late 8th century until the 13th century. The Hariphunchai art and Buddha images are particularly distinctive, and many good examples can be found at the Hariphunchai National Museum in Lamphun.

The Thais, who had migrated down from China since around the 7th century, united various principalities in the 13th century – this resulted in the creation of Sukhothai and the taking of Hariphunchai from the Mon. In 1238 Sukhothai declared itself an independent kingdom under King Si Intharathit and quickly expanded its sphere of influence. Sukhothai is considered by Thais to be the first true Thai kingdom. In 1296 King Mengrai established Chiang Mai after conquering the influential Mon kingdom of Hariphunchai.

Later, Chiang Mai, in an alliance with Sukhothai in the 14th and 15th centuries, became a part of the larger kingdom of Lan Na Thai (Million Thai Rice Fields), popularly referred to as Lanna. This extended as far south as Kamphaeng Phet and as far north as Luang Prabang in Laos. The golden age of Lanna was in the 15th century. For a short time the Sukhothai capital was moved to Phitsanulok (1448–86), and Chiang Mai became an important religious and cultural centre. However, many Thai alliances declined in the 16th century. This weakness lead to the Burmese capturing Chiang Mai in 1556 and their control of Lanna for the next two centuries. The Thais regrouped after the Burmese took Ayuthaya in 1767, and under King Kawila, Chiang Mai was recaptured in 1774 and the Burmese were pushed north.

In the late 19th century Rama V of Bangkok made efforts to integrate the northern region with the centre to ward off the colonial threat. The completion of the northern railway to Chiang Mai in 1921 strengthened those links until the northern provinces finally became part of the kingdom of Siam in this early period of the 20th century.

Climate

The mountains in northern Thailand influence the climate. It can get quite cold in the highland town of Mae Hong Son and rain pockets can get stuck in the ranges of Tak Province. The central-plains areas around Sukhothai are less variable.

National Parks

Travellers who make it to one of northern Thailand's national parks usually consider it a highlight of their trip. In a region where the elevation reaches as high as 2000m, the north is home to some of Thailand's rarest geography and wildlife. Chae Son (p349) is known for its waterfalls. Doi Luang (p349) and Thung Salaeng Luang (p401) were designated for wildlife protection. While Phu Hin Rong Kla (p400) is of interest for its ties to Thailand's Communist Party. Other parks in the north include Lum Nam Kong National Park (p433) with its lazy river, and Doi Phu Kha (see p391) with its 2000m peaks. All of the national parks in this section are worth the extra effort if you love nature and want some peace and quiet.

Language

Northern Thais (khon meuang) are known for their relaxed, easy-going manner, which shows up in their speech – the northern dialect (kham meuang) has a slower rhythm than Thailand's three other main dialects.

Getting There & Away

Some travellers make stops in this region en route between Bangkok and Chiang Mai. Others only use Chiang Mai as a point for other destinations. Either way, train access is limited to the northern line out of Chiang Mai. But just about everywhere in the region is accessible by bus, except the outlying communities along the Myanmar border where the sǎwngthǎew (pick-up truck) is the transport of choice.

Getting Around

If you know how to ride a motorcycle, rent one. If you don't know how to ride one it's easy to learn and you'll be glad you did. For around 150B per day, sometimes less,

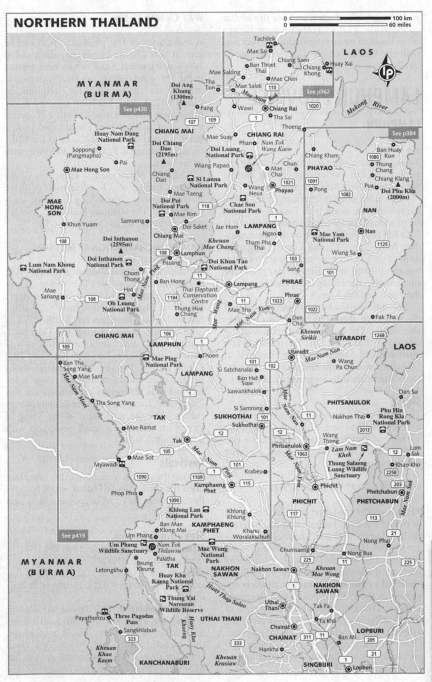

NORTHERN THAILAND

0 — 100 km
0 — 60 miles

MYANMAR (BURMA)

See p430

Huay Nam Dang National Park

Soppong (Pangmapha)

Pai

Mae Hong Son

MAE HONG SON

Khun Yuam

108

Doi Inthanon (2595m) ▲

Lum Nam Khong National Park

Doi Inthanon National Park

108

Mae Sariang

Hot

108

Ob Luang National Park

1184

Ban Hong

Chom Thong

Thai Elephant Conservation Centre

Thung Hua Chang

Tachileik
Mae Sai
Ban Thoet Thai
Mae Salong
Chiang Saen
Huay Xai
Mae Chan
Mae Salak
110
See p362

LAOS

Doi Ang Khang (1300m) ▲

Tha Ton
Fang
107
109
Wawi
Chiang Rai
1020
Thoeng

CHIANG MAI

Mae Suay
CHIANG RAI
Phan
Nam Tok Wang Kaew

Doi Chiang Dao (2195m) ▲

Doi Luang National Park

Wiang Papao
Mae Chai
Chun
Chiang Kham
1080
Ban Huay Kon
Thung Chang

Chiang Dao

Si Lanna National Park

Wang Neua
Phayao
1021
1091
PHAYAO
Pong
Chiang Klang
Pua
1082
Doi Phu Kha (2000m) ▲

Mae Taeng

Doi Pui National Park
Mae Rim
118
Chae Son National Park

NAN

Samoeng
Doi Saket
Jae Hom
LAMPANG
Ngao
Mae Yom National Park
Nan
1125

Chiang Mai
108
Lamphun
Kheuan Mae Chang
Tham Pha Thai
Wiang Sa
101

Pasang
Doi Khun Tan National Park
Song
103
1022
Fak Tha

11
Lampang
PHRAE

Mae Tha
11
Phrae
1023

Den Chai

Kheuan Sirikit
UTARADIT
1268

CHIANG MAI
106
1
Utaradit
Mae Nam Nan
Wang Pa Chun

105
LAMPHUN
Thoen
101
102
Dan Sai

Mae Ping National Park

Si Satchanalai
Ban Hat Siaw
PHITSANULOK
Phu Hin Rong Kla National Park

Ban Tha Song Yang
Mae Sarit
LAMPANG
Sawankhalok
Nakhon Thai
2013

Tha Song Yang
Si Samrong
Wang Thong
12
Lom Sak

TAK
SUKHOTHAI
101
Lam Nam Khek
Khao Kho
2258

Mae Ramat
Sukhothai
12
Thung Salaeng Luang Wildlife Sanctuary
203
Phetchabun

Tak
Phitsanulok
1063
Phichit
PHETCHABUN

Mae Sot
105
PHICHIT
113

Myawadi
Krabeu
101
117
21

1090
1109
Kamphaeng Phet
115
Khlong Khlung
Nong Phai

Phop Phra
1090
Khanu Woralaksaburi
Chumsaeng
225
Nong Bua
225

Khlong Lan National Park
KAMPHAENG PHET

Ban Mae Klong Mai
See p415
Um Phang
Mae Wong National Park
NAKHON SAWAN
Kheuan Mae Wong
11

MYANMAR (BURMA)
Um Phang Wildlife Sanctuary
Nam Tok Thilawsu
Palatha
Nakhon Sawan
NAKHON SAWAN

Beung Kleung
TAK
1
Uthai Thani
Tak Fa

Letongkhu
Huay Kha Kaeng National Park
Huay Thap Salao
Ta Khli

Payathonzu
Three Pagodas Pass
Thung Yai Naresuan Wildlife Reserve
UTHAI THANI
311
11
Ban Mi
LOPBURI
205

Sangkhlaburi
323
Chainat
CHAINAT
1
21

Kheuan Khao Kaem
KANCHANABURI
333
Hankha
Kheuan Krasiaw
SINGBURI
Lopburi

Mekong River

Mae Nam Kok

Mae Nam Wang

Mae Nam Ping

Mae Nam Yom

Mae Nam Nan

Mae Nam Ping

Huay Kha Khaeng

NORTHERN THAILAND

you can get out of town and see the idyllic countryside. This increased independence often leads to more interesting interactions with the locals, outside the normal tourist circuit.

LAMPHUN PROVINCE

LAMPHUN
ลำพูน
pop 15,200
This quiet town, capital of the province of the same name, lies southeast of Chiang Mai on the banks of Nam Mae Kuang.

Best visited as a day trip from Chiang Mai, Lamphun was, along with Pasang, the centre of a small Hariphunchai principality (AD 750–1281) originally ruled by the semilegendary Mon queen, Chama Thewi. Long after its Mon progenitor and predecessor Dvaravati was vanquished by the Khmer, Hariphunchai succeeded in remaining independent of both the Thais and the Khmer.

The enthusiastically run museum is a good place to learn about this quiet town's venerable history. The ancient and vibrant working temple of Wat Phra That Haripunchai is a must see, and August is a lively time to visit Lamphun and sample the fruits of the surrounding fields at its longan festival (right).

Sights
There are many more nearby temples than the two described here. Although none enjoys the fame of Wat Phra That Hariphunchai and Wat Chama Thewi, many of them are quite old and atmospheric.

WAT PHRA THAT HARIPHUNCHAI
วัดพระธาตุหริภุญชัย
Thais consider the tallest *chedi* at this wat to be one of the eight holiest *chedi* in Thailand. Built on the site of Queen Chama Thewi's palace in 1044 (1108 or 1157 according to some datings), this temple lay derelict for many years until Khruba Siwichai, one of northern Thailand's most famous monks, made renovations in the 1930s. It boasts some interesting post-Dvaravati architecture, a couple of fine Buddha images and two old *chedi* of the original Hariphunchai style. The tallest *chedi*, Chedi Suwan, dating from 1418, is 46m high and is surmounted by a nine-tiered gold umbrella weighing 6.5kg.

WAT CHAMA THEWI
วัดจามเทวี
A more unusual Hariphunchai *chedi* can be seen at Wat Chama Thewi (popularly called Wat Kukut), which is said to have been erected in the 8th or 9th century as a Dvaravati monument. It was later rebuilt by the Hariphunchai Mon in 1218. As it has been restored many times since then, it's now a mixture of several schools of architecture. The stepped profile bears a remarkable resemblance to the 12th-century Satmahal Prasada at Polonnaruwa in Sri Lanka.

Each side of the *chedi* – known as Chedi Suwan Chang Kot – has five rows of three Buddha figures, diminishing in size on each higher level. The standing Buddhas, although made recently, are in Dvaravati style.

HARIPHUNCHAI NATIONAL MUSEUM
พิพิธภัณฑสถานแห่งชาติลำพูน
Hariphunchai National Museum (☎ 0 5351 1186; hariphunchao-mu@thaimail.com; Th Inthayongyot; admission 30B; ☼ 9am-4pm Wed-Sun) Across the street from Wat Phra That Hariphunchai, Lamphun's National Museum has a collection of artefacts and Buddhas from the Dvaravati, Hariphunchai and Lanna kingdoms, as well a stone inscription gallery with Mon and Thai Lanna scripts. The curator's passion about her museum and Lamphun's heritage is infectious. The temporary exhibitions are also interesting, focusing on more contemporary subjects like the settlement of the Yong in Lamphun. There is a small bookshop with some English titles.

Festivals
During the second week of August, Lamphun hosts the annual **Lam Yai Festival**, which features floats made of fruit and, of course, a Miss Lam Yai contest.

Sleeping & Eating
Si Lamphun Hotel (no roman-script sign; ☎ 0 5351 1176; Th Inthayongyot, Soi 5; s/d 100/200B) On the main street through town, south of Wat Phra That, this small hotel has very basic rooms with ceiling fans.

Supamit Holiday Inn (☎ 0 5353 4865; fax 0 5353 4355; Th Chama Thewi; s/d 250-400B; ☒) Although it bears no relation to the international hotel chain, this is a solid choice, with 50 spacious, clean and airy rooms. The restaurant on the 5th floor serves good fare, and has floor-to-ceiling

windows giving panoramic views of Lamphun and the surrounding rice fields. It's opposite Wat Chama Thewi.

There is a string of decent **noodle and rice shops** (Th Inthayongyot) south of Wat Phra That on the main street.

Getting There & Away

Blue sǎwngthǎew to Lamphun (15B) from Chiang Mai leave at 30-minute intervals throughout the day from Th Chiang Mai-Lamphun, just south of the Tourist Authority of Thailand (TAT) office on the opposite side of the road. A small bus station on the same road, north of the TAT office, has regular buses going to Lamphun (20B). Buses also go from Chiang Mai Arcade bus terminal (32B).

In the reverse direction, sǎwngthǎew leave Lamphun from the queue near the intersection of Th Inthayongyot and Th Wang Khwa. The 26km ride (15B, one hour) is along a beautiful country road, parts of which are bordered by tall dipterocarp trees. You can also pick up a bus outside the Hariphunchai National Museum (15B) or go to the bus terminal on Th Sanam.

PASANG

ป่าซาง

Not to be confused with Bo Sang, the umbrella village, Pasang is known for its cotton weaving. It's not really a shopping destination, but more of a place to see how the weaving is done. The selection of cotton products is limited mostly to floor coverings, tablecloths and other useful household items.

Wat Chang Khao Noi Neua, off Rte 106 towards the southern end of town, features an impressive gilded Lanna-style *chedi*. Near the wat is a cotton-products store called **Wimon** (no roman-script sign), where you can watch people weaving on looms in the front of the shop. You'll also find a few **shops** near the

main market in town, opposite Wat Pasang Ngam. A few vendors in the **market** also sell blankets, tablecloths, *phâakhamáa* (cotton wraparounds), shirts and other woven-cotton products.

A sǎwngthǎew will take you from Lamphun to Pasang for 10B. If you're heading south to Tak Province using your own vehicle, traffic is generally lighter along Rte 106 to Thoen than on Hwy 11 to Lampang; a winding 10km section of the road north of Thoen is particularly scenic. Both highways intersect Hwy 1 south, which leads directly to Tak's capital.

WAT PHRA PHUTTHABAHT TAHK PHAH

วัดพระพุทธบาทตากผ้า

Regionally famous, this wat belonging to the popular Mahanikai sect is a shrine to one of the north's most renowned monks, Luang Pu Phromma. It's about 9km south of Pasang or 20km south of Lamphun off Rte 106 in the Tambol Ma-Kok (follow Rte 1133 1km east). It contains a lifelike resin figure of the deceased monk sitting in meditation.

One of his disciples, Ajahn Thirawattho, teaches meditation to a large contingent of monks who are housed in a *kùti* (a monk's dwelling or meditation hut) of laterite brick. Behind the spacious grounds are a park and a steep hill mounted by a *chedi*. The wat is named after an unremarkable Buddha footprint *(phrá phútthábàat)* shrine in the middle of the lower temple grounds and another spot where Buddha supposedly dried his *tàak phâa* (robes).

A sǎwngthǎew from Lamphun to the wat costs 20B.

DOI KHUN TAN NATIONAL PARK

อุทยานแห่งชาติดอยขุนตาล

This 225-sq-km **park** (☎ 0 5351 9216-7; www .dnp.go.th; admission 400B) receives around 10,000 visitors a year, making it one of northern Thailand's least visited. It ranges in elevation from 350m at the bamboo forest lowlands to 1363m at the pine-studded summit of Doi Khun Tan. Wildflowers, including orchids, ginger and lilies, are abundant. At the park headquarters there are maps of well-marked trails that range from short walks around the headquarters' vicinity to trails covering the mountain's four peaks; there's also a trail to **Nam Tok Tat Moei** (7km round trip). Thailand's longest train tunnel (1352m), which opened

in 1921 after six years of manual labour by thousands of Lao workers (several of whom are said to have been killed by tigers), intersects the mountain slope.

Bungalows (☎ 0 2562 0760; r 400B, bungalows 4/6/9 people 1500/2200/2700B) are available near the park headquarters. You can pitch your own tent for 30B or rent a two-person tent for 150B. There is a restaurant by the bungalows. The park is very popular on cool season weekends.

This park is unique in that the main access is from the Khun Tan train station (15B, 1½ hours, daily trains from Chiang Mai at 6.45am, 9.20am and 3.40pm). Once at the Khun Tan station, cross the tracks and follow a steep, marked path 1.3km to the park headquarters. By car take the Chiang Mai–Lampang highway to the Mae Tha turn-off, then follow signs along a steep unpaved road for 18km.

LAMPANG PROVINCE

LAMPANG

ลำปาง

pop 50,700

Many Thais visit Lampang for a taste of a more sedate urbane life. The main pull for *faràng* (Western) travellers is the renowned Elephant Conservation Centre (p348), and Wat Phra That Lampang Luang (p348), for many the most beautiful wooden temple in northern Thailand.

History

Although Lampang Province was inhabited as far back as the 7th century in the Dvaravati period, legend says Lampang city was founded by the son of Hariphunchai's Queen Chama Thewi, playing an important part in the history of the Hariphunchai Kingdom (8th to 13th centuries).

Like Chiang Mai, Phrae and other older northern cities, Lampang was built as a walled rectangle alongside a river (in this case Mae Wang). At the end of the 19th and beginning of the 20th centuries Lampang, along with nearby Phrae, became an important centre for the domestic and international teak trade. A large British-owned timber company brought in Burmese supervisors familiar with the teak industry in Burma to train Burmese and Thai loggers in the area. These well-paid supervisors, along with independent Burmese teak

merchants who plied their trade in Lampang, sponsored the construction of more than a dozen impressive temples in the city. Burmese and Shan artisans designed and built the temples out of local materials, especially teak. Their legacy lives on in several of Lampang's best-maintained wats.

Information

There are many banks with ATMs along Th Boonyawat, especially near Wat Suan Dok.

Arabica Coffee Internet (Th Thakhrao Noi; per hr 20B; ⏰ 9am-10pm)

Internet & Games (Th Thip Chang; per hr 20B; ⏰ 10am-10pm)

Post office (Th Thakhrao Noi; ⏰ 8.30am-4.30pm Mon-Fri, 9am-12am Sat)

Tourist information office (☎ 0 5421 9300; Th Thakhrao Noi; ⏰ 8am-12pm, 1-4.30pm Mon-Fri) Locally run, with a decent map of the area and details about local sights.

Sights

WAT PHRA KAEW DON TAO

วัดพระแก้วดอนเต้า

On the northern side of the Mae Wang, this wat housed the Emerald Buddha (now in Bangkok's Wat Phra Kaew, see p108) from 1436 to 1468. The main *chedi* shows Hariphunchai influence, while the adjacent *mondòp* (a square, spire-topped shrine room) was built in 1909. The *mondòp*, decorated with glass mosaic in typical Burmese style, contains a Mandalay-style Buddha image. A display of Lanna artefacts (mostly religious paraphernalia and woodwork) can be viewed in the wat's **Lanna Museum** (admission by donation).

OTHER TEMPLES

Wat Si Rong Meuang and **Wat Si Chum** are two wats built in the late 19th century by Burmese artisans. Both have temple buildings constructed in the Burmese 'layered' style, with tin roofs gabled by intricate woodcarvings. The current abbots of these temples are Burmese.

Apart from the *wíhǎan* (any large hall in a Thai temple) at Wat Phra That Lampang Luang (p348), the *mondòp* at **Wat Pongsanuk Tai** is one of the few remaining local examples of original Lanna-style temple architecture, which emphasised open-sided wooden buildings.

Wat Chedi Sao (☎ 0 5432 0233), about 6km north of town towards Jae Hom, is named for the *sao* (northern Thai for 20) whitewashed

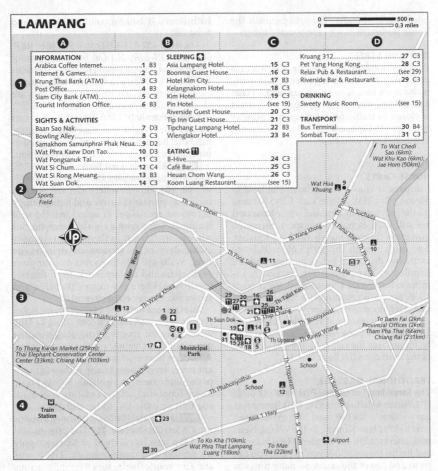

LAMPANG

0 ─────── 500 m
0 ─────── 0.3 miles

INFORMATION		
Arabica Coffee Internet	1	B3
Internet & Games	2	C3
Krung Thai Bank (ATM)	3	C3
Post Office	4	B3
Siam City Bank (ATM)	5	C3
Tourist Information Office	6	B3

SIGHTS & ACTIVITIES		
Baan Sao Nak	7	D3
Bowling Alley	8	C3
Samakhom Samunphrai Phak Neua	9	D2
Wat Phra Kaew Don Tao	10	D3
Wat Pongsanuk Tai	11	C3
Wat Si Chum	12	C4
Wat Si Rong Meuang	13	B3
Wat Suan Dok	14	C3

SLEEPING 🏠		
Asia Lampang Hotel	15	C3
Boonma Guest House	16	C3
Hotel Kim City	17	B3
Kelangnakorn Hotel	18	C3
Kim Hotel	19	C3
Pin Hotel	(see 19)	
Riverside Guest House	20	C3
Tip Inn Guest House	21	C3
Tipchang Lampang Hotel	22	B3
Wienglakor Hotel	23	B4

EATING 🍴		
B-Hive	24	C3
Café Bar	25	C3
Heuan Chom Wang	26	C3
Koom Luang Restaurant	(see 15)	

Kruang 312	27	C3
Pet Yang Hong Kong	28	C3
Relax Pub & Restaurant	(see 29)	
Riverside Bar & Restaurant	29	C3

DRINKING		
Sweety Music Room	(see 15)	

TRANSPORT		
Bus Terminal	30	B4
Sombat Tour	31	C3

Lanna-style *chedi* on its grounds. It's a well-endowed wat, landscaped with bougainvillea and casuarina. At one edge of the wat stands a very colourful statue of Avalokitesvara, while a pavilion in the centre features a gilded Buddha similar in style to the Chinnarat Buddha in Phitsanulok (p395). But the wat's real treasure is a solid-gold, 15th-century seated Buddha on display in a glassed-in **pavilion** (8am-5pm), built over a square pond. The image weighs 150kg, stands 38cm tall and is said to contain a piece of the Buddha's skull in its head and an ancient Pali-inscribed golden palm leaf in its chest; precious stones decorate the image's hairline and robe. A farmer reportedly found the figure next to the ruins of nearby Wat Khu Kao in 1983.

Monks stationed at Wat Chedi Sao make and sell herbal medicines; the popular *yaa màwng* is similar to tiger balm.

BAAN SAO NAK
บ้านเสานัก

In the old Wiang Neua (North City) section of town, **Baan Sao Nak** (Many Pillars House; ☎ 0 5422 7653; admission 30B; 10am-5pm) was built in 1895 in the traditional Lanna style. A huge teak house supported by 116 square teak pillars, it was once owned by a local *khunying* (a title equivalent to 'Lady' in England); it now serves as a local museum. The entire house is furnished with Burmese and Thai antiques; three rooms display antique silverwork, lacquerware, bronzeware, ceramics and other

northern-Thai crafts. The area beneath the house is often used for ceremonial dinners.

WALKING STREET

Perhaps wanting to emulate the success of Chiang Mai's walking streets, Lampang now has its own along the charming **Th Talat Kao**. Dotted with old shophouses, the street is closed to traffic on Saturday and Sunday from 4pm to 10pm and fills up with souvenir, handicraft and food stalls.

Activities
HORSE CARTS

Lampang is known throughout Thailand as Meuang Rot Mah (Horse Cart City) because it's the only town in Thailand where **horse carts** are still used as public transport, although nowadays they are mainly used for tourists. You can't miss the brightly coloured horse carts that drip with nylon flowers, and are handled by Stetson-wearing drivers. A 15-minute horse-cart tour around town costs 150B; for 200B you can get a half-hour tour that goes along beside Mae Wang. For 300B a one-hour tour stops at Wat Phra Kaew Don Tao and Wat Si Rong Meuang. Horse carts can be found near the larger hotels and just east of the market on Th Boonyawat.

TRADITIONAL MASSAGE

The **Samakhom Samunphrai Phak Neua** (☎ 0 6586 0711; Northern Herbal Medicine Society; 149 Th Pratuma; massage per 30min/hr 100/150B, sauna 100B; ☯ 8am-8pm), next to Wat Hua Khuang in the Wiang Neua area, offers traditional northern-Thai massage and herbal saunas. Once you've paid, you can go in and out of the sauna as many times as you want during one visit.

BOWLING

Yep, that's right, Lampang has a **bowling alley** (basement, Th Thipawan shopping centre; 3 games 100B; ☯ 10.30am-11.30pm).

Sleeping
BUDGET

Tip Inn Guest House (☎ 0 5422 1821; 143 Th Talat Kao; r 100-160B; ☒) This place has friendly hosts and very basic rooms. Renovation was starting at the time of writing.

Boonma Guest House (☎ 0 5432 2653; 256 Th Talat Kao; r 250-300B) This family-run place features a couple of rooms in a gorgeous teak home, and cement rooms behind. Some have shared

bathrooms. It lacks a comfortable place to hang out.

Kim Hotel (☎ 0 5421 7721; fax 0 5422 6929; 168 Th Boonyawat; r 250-350B; ☒) On the other side of the road to Kelangnakorn Hotel, the rooms in this three-storey hotel have tiled walls, making the bedrooms feel like bathrooms. Yet they are clean, comfortable and have cable TV.

Kelangnakorn Hotel (☎ 0 5421 6137; Th Boonyawat; r 260-340B; ☒) Popular with travelling salesmen, this hotel has modernish rooms with wooden furniture, cable TV and a friendly reception.

our pick **Riverside Guest House** (☎ 0 5422 7005; www.theriversidelampang.com; 286 Th Talat Kao; r 300-600B, ste 800B; ☒) This traveller-oriented place is tucked away near the river and has tastefully decorated rooms set in upgraded old teak buildings. Some rooms are a bit cramped, but you can stretch out in the pleasant outdoor areas. Many of the terraces are right on the river. Walls are thin so expect to hear your neighbours and nightly music from the riverside bars. There is a midnight curfew and motorbikes are available to rent.

Asia Lampang Hotel (☎ 0 5422 7844; www.asialampang.com; 229 Th Boonyawat; r 390-500B; ☒) All of the wood-accented rooms in this long-running place are great value, especially the large, suite-style rooms on the 5th floor. The pleasant street-level Koom Luang restaurant (opposite) and basement nightclub, Sweety Music Room (opposite), attract a mature crowd. All rooms have cable TV, fridge and desks.

our pick **Pin Hotel** (☎ 0 5422 1509; www.travelideas.net; 8 Th Suan Dok; r from 450; ☒) The pristine and quiet Pin feels like a Hyatt or Marriott, only it's smaller and more intimate. The rooms are very comfortable, super clean, spacious and come with cable TV, minibar and large bathrooms. Staff are professional, there's a decent restaurant and room service, as well as a laundry service. This would easily cost double in Chiang Mai. A travel agent is attached and books domestic and international flights.

MIDRANGE & TOP END

Hotel Kim City (☎ 0 5431 0238-40; 274/1 Th Chatchai; r including breakfast 640-740, ste 1040B) The best thing about this big, modern hotel is the lovely Thai styled spa (treatments 350B to 750B). The rooms have all the amenities but are plain, and some smell a bit musty.

Tipchang Lampang Hotel (☎ 0 5422 6501; www.tipchanghotel.com; 54/22 Th Thakhrao Noi; r incl breakfast 800-1200B, ste 1500-2000B; ☒ 🖳 🐾) This hotel, with

cocktail lounge, conference room and disco, sounds more luxurious than it feels. Rooms are comfortable and have a pool or park view. The cheapest do let in some noise from the disco. Staff are friendly and helpful.

Wienglakor Hotel (☎ 0 5431 6430; 138/35 Th Phahonyothin; r 1500-1800, ste 3500B; ❄ ▣) This massive hotel has replica Thai antiques in the hallways, a tasteful lobby lounge area and a pretty fishpond and garden. But the rooms are overpriced and nothing special.

Eating

Lampang has a good selection of restaurants. It's not ultradiverse like Chiang Mai, but the quality is pretty high. Several of the more expensive hotels have restaurants with a nice atmosphere and above-average food.

Riverside Bar & Restaurant (☎ 0 5422 1861; 328 Th Thip Chang; dishes 45-225B; ❄ 11am-midnight) This rambling old teak structure on the river is definitely the most popular place in town. There's live music, a full bar and an enormous menu of vegetarian, northern-Thai and Western dishes. The homemade gelato and pizza nights (Tue, Thu, Sat-Sun) are favourites but the pasta dishes aren't too good. Prices are reasonable and service is excellent.

Kruang 312 (Th Thip Chang; dishes 30-60B; ❄ 10am-9pm) Set in a charming wooden shophouse and surrounded by black-and-white pictures of Lampang and the king, this tiny, simple restaurant serves delicious curries, noodle and rice dishes.

B-Hive (Th Thip Chang; dishes 30-80B; ❄ 10.30am-10.30pm) You can't miss this funky looking purple café. Sit outside on wooden chairs or inside on brightly coloured pods, and have coffee or tea with ice cream and pancakes.

Koom Luang Restaurant (☎ 0 5422 7844; 229 Th Boonyawat; dishes 50-100B; ❄ 6.30am-midnight; ❄) Choose between air-con or street seating at this northern Lanna–style restaurant. The Thai and Chinese dishes are far more authentic than the European.

Relax Pub & Restaurant (Th Thip Chang; dishes 50-150B; ❄ 6pm-midnight) Just west of the Riverside, Relax is a little more punk-rock, with neon lights, industrial architecture and more amplified music. The food's good and the scene is more energetic than the Riverside.

Pet Yang Hong Kong (Th Boonyawat; dishes 25-60B; ❄ 8am-6pm) This is the best spot for roast duck with rice (or noodles). It's opposite Kim Hotel, near several other rice and noodle joints.

Heuan Chom Wang (☎ 0 5422 2845; 276 Th Talat Kao; dishes 40-120B; ❄ 11am-11pm) This romantic, open-air place fronting the river occupies a beautiful old teak building down an alley off Th Talat Kao. The menu is strictly non-Westernised northern- and central-Thai fare. Service is attentive but English is limited.

Drinking

In addition to the **Riverside Bar** (left) and **Relax Pub** (left), Lampang has a couple of other nightspots.

Café Bar (no sign; Th Talat Kao; ❄ 8am-midnight) This small atmospheric bar next to Tip Inn Guest House is decorated with wooden chairs and old-fashioned glass lamps. If you prefer downtempo to live rock'n'roll, this is a good place to have a drink and a chat.

Sweety Music Room (229 Th Boonyawat; ❄ 7pm-1am) Downstairs from the Koom Luang Restaurant, this retro nightspot plays a good range of Western favourites until 11.30pm, when the mood gets romantic. Dance jams turn on at 12.30am. The room's always dark, the booths are spacious and the house band is lively (but not all that good).

Getting There & Away

AIR

Daily flights between Lampang and Bangkok (2660B, 10.45am & 5pm) are offered by **PB Air** (☎ 0 5422 6238, Bangkok ☎ 0 2261 0220; www.pbair.com; Lampang Airport).

BUS

From Chiang Mai, buses to Lampang (ordinary/2nd class air-con/1st class/VIP 51/71/92/140B, two hours) leave from the Chiang Mai Arcade terminal every half-hour during the day, and also from the small bus station (ordinary 51B) near the TAT office in the direction of Lamphun (19B).

Buses go to Lampang from Phitsanulok's main bus terminal (ordinary/2nd class air-con/1st class/VIP 119/167/214/250B, four hours; ordinary/2nd class air-con/1st class 148/207/214B via Sukhothai, five hours). Buses to Phrae leave hourly from 8am to 6pm (ordinary/2nd class air-con/1st class/VIP 60/84/108/315B). There are regular buses to and from Bangkok (2nd class air-con/1st class/VIP 374/481/748B, 2nd class nine hours, 1st class and above eight hours) running from 7.30am to 9pm. To book a cheaper, 10 hour air-con bus from Lampang to Bangkok head

to **Sombat Tour** (☎ 0 5432 3361; Th Boonyawat; 1st class/
VIP 446/621B).

The bus terminal in Lampang is some way
out of town – 15B by shared săwngthăew.

TRAIN
Trains run between Chiang Mai and Lampang
(2nd/3rd class 50/23B, two hours).

AROUND LAMPANG
Sights
WAT PHRA THAT LAMPANG LUANG
วัดพระธาตุลำปางหลวง

Arguably the most beautiful wooden Lanna
temple found in northern Thailand, Wat Phra
That Lampang is centred on the open-sided
Wihan Luang and is one attraction not to be
missed. Believed to have been built in 1476,
the impressive *wíhǎan* features a triple-tiered
wooden roof supported by teak pillars, and is
considered to be the oldest existing wooden
building in Thailand. A huge, gilded *mondòp* in
the back of the *wíhǎan* contains a Buddha image
cast in 1563. The faithful leave small gold-coloured Buddha figures close to the *mondòp* and
hang Thai Lü weavings behind it.

Early 19th-century *jataka* murals (stories
of the Buddha's previous lives) are painted
on wooden panels around the inside upper
perimeter of the *wíhǎan*. The tall Lanna-style
chedi behind the *wíhǎan*, raised in 1449 and
restored in 1496, measures 24m at its base and
is 45m high. The small and simple **Wihan Ton
Kaew**, to the north of the main *wíhǎan*, was
built in 1476.

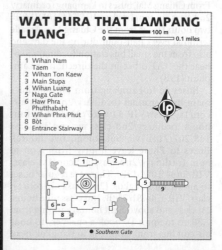

**WAT PHRA THAT LAMPANG
LUANG**

0 —— 100 m
0 —— 0.1 miles

1 Wihan Nam
  Taem
2 Wihan Ton Kaew
3 Main Stupa
4 Wihan Luang
5 Naga Gate
6 Haw Phra
  Phutthabaht
7 Wihan Phra Phut
8 Bòt
9 Entrance Stairway

● *Southern Gate*

Until recently, only men could see a camera
obscura image of the *chedi* in the **Haw Phra
Phutthabaht**, a small white building behind
the *chedi*. Now everyone can see the shadowy
inverted image (which is projected via a small
hole in the wall onto a white sheet) in **Wihan
Phra Phut** (admission 20B), which is south of the
main *chedi*. The 13th-century Wihan Phra
Phut is the oldest structure in the compound
and houses a seated Buddha.

The *wíhǎan* to the north of the *chedi*, **Wihan
Nam Taem**, was built in the early 16th century
and, amazingly, still contains traces of the
original murals.

The lintel over the entrance to the compound features an impressive dragon relief –
once common in northern Thai temples but
rarely seen these days. This gate supposedly
dates to the 15th century.

In the arboretum outside the southern gate
of the wat, there are now three **museums**. One
displays mostly festival paraphernalia, plus
some Buddha figures. Another, called 'House
of the Emerald Buddha', contains a miscellany
of coins, banknotes, Buddha figures, silver betelnut cases, lacquerware and other ethnographic
artefacts, along with three small, heavily gold-
leafed Buddhas placed on an altar behind an
enormous repoussé silver bowl. The third, a
fine, small museum, features shelves of Buddha figures, lacquered boxes, manuscripts and
ceramics, all well labelled in Thai and English.

Wat Phra That Lampang Luang is 18km
southwest of Lampang in Ko Kha. To get there
by public transport from Lampang, flag an
eastbound săwngthăew (20B) on Th Rawp
Wiang. From the Ko Kha săwngthăew station,
it's a 3km chartered motorcycle taxi ride to the
temple (30B). Minibuses outside the temple
go back to the city for 30B.

If you're driving or cycling from Lampang,
head south on the Asia 1 Hwy and take the Ko
Kha exit, then follow the road over a bridge
and bear right. Follow the signs and continue
for 3km over another bridge until you see the
temple on the left. If you're coming from
Chiang Mai via Hwy 11, turn south onto Rte
1034, 18km northwest of Lampang at the Km
13 marker – this route is a 50km shortcut to
Ko Kha that avoids much of Lampang.

THAI ELEPHANT CONSERVATION CENTER
ศูนย์อนุรักษ์ช้างไทย

In Amphoe Hang Chat northwest of Lampang, outside Thung Kwian between Km 28

MAHOUT TRAINING

If you like the idea of elephants being employed again, but not in elephant shows, try one of the highly recommended **Conservation Center programmes** (www.changthai.com; 1-/3-day course 2500/5000B, per day for 10+ days incl training, lodging & food 1500B), where you learn the skills of the *khwaan cháang* (elephant caretaker) or mahout. If you want a quick taste of the mahout's life, you can sign on for a one-day course and learn a few simple commands for leading an elephant, experiment with dung paper, ride an elephant in the jungle and take a tour of the elephant hospital.

A more involved three-day, two-night homestay programme includes all meals, a night's lodging in a well-equipped wood-and-bamboo bungalow and another night at a jungle camp, plus a general introduction to elephant care and training. Those with a higher level of commitment can choose 10- or 30-day programmes.

and 29, this unique **facility** (TECC; ☎ 0 5422 8035, 0 5422 9042; www.changthai.com, www.thaielephant.org; child/adult 30/50B + shuttle bus or own transport 20B; ☺ elephant bathing 9.45am, 1.15pm; public shows 10am, 11am, 1.30pm) promotes the role of the Asian elephant in ecotourism, and provides free medical treatment and care for sick elephants from all over Thailand.

The elephant show at this 122-hectare centre is less touristy and more educational than most, focusing on how elephants work with logs, as well as the usual painting of pictures and playing oversized xylophones. You can feed the elephants afterwards with bananas. There is also an exhibit on the history and culture of elephants as well as elephant rides (8am to 3.30pm, 100/400/800B for 10/30/60 minutes) through the surrounding forest.

All proceeds from the entrance fee and souvenir shops go to the elephant hospital on site, which cares for old, abandoned and sick elephants from all over Thailand, as well as working for the preservation of elephants by various research and breeding programmes (see boxed text p350).

The camp is 33km from town and can be reached by Chiang Mai-bound bus or sǎwngthǎew (25B) from Lampang's main bus terminal. Let the driver know where you are headed and get off at the Km 37 marker. The centre is 1.5km from the highway. Alternatively, you can hire a blue sǎwngthǎew for 350B to 500B at the bus terminal. If you have your own transport, on the way to the elephant camp, 25km from Lampang, is the **Thung Kwian market**. Very popular with Thais, this market has a good selection of food stalls and an interesting range of wares, from bottles of herbs for making whisky to preserved fruit and amulets.

OTHER ATTRACTIONS

North and east of Lampang are the cotton-weaving villages of **Jae Hom** and **Mae Tha**. You can wander around and find looms in action; there are also plenty of shops along the main roads.

Tham Pha Thai (Pha Thai Cave) is 66km north of Lampang, between Lampang and Chiang Rai about 500m off Hwy 1. Besides the usual cave formations (stalagmites and stalactites), Tham Pha Thai has a large Buddha image.

The province is well endowed with waterfalls. Three are found within Amphoe Wang Neua, roughly 120km north of the provincial capital: **Wang Kaew**, **Wang Thong** and **Than Thong** (Jampa Thong). Wang Kaew is the largest, with 110 tiers. Near the summit is a Mien hill-tribe village. This area became part of the 1172-sq-km **Doi Luang National Park** in 1990; animals protected by the park include serow, barking deer, pangolin and the pig-tailed macaque.

In Amphoe Meuang Pan, about halfway between Wang Neua and Lampang, is another waterfall, **Nam Tok Jae Sawn**, part of the 593-sq-km **Chae Son National Park** (☎ 0 5422 9000; Tambon Jae Son, Amphoe Muang Ban, Lampang; admission 400B). Elevations in the park reach above 2000m. Jae Sawn has six drops, each with its own pool; close to the falls are nine hot springs. Small huts house circular baths, recessed into the floor and lined with clay tiles, that are continuously filled with water direct from the spring. For 20B you can take a 20-minute soak, preceded and followed by an invigorating cold-water shower.

Camping is permitted in both Chae Son and Doi Luang National Parks. Chae Son has a visitors centre, 12 bungalows for hire and

NORTHERN THAILAND

THE PLIGHT OF THAILAND'S ELEPHANTS

The elephant is one of the most powerful symbols in Thai culture and until 1917 a white elephant appeared on the Thai national flag. Historically, Thais have worked side-by-side with elephants on farms and in the jungle, and elephants were the superweapons of Southeast Asian armies before the advent of tanks and big guns. Today, elephants are still revered in Thai society and are a strong drawcard for Western tourists.

Currently, experts estimate there are now fewer than 2000 wild elephants in Thailand, more than India but fewer than Myanmar. There are fewer than 3000 domesticated elephants. The numbers of both wild and domestic animals are steadily dwindling. Around 1900 it was estimated that there were at least 100,000 elephants working in Thailand; by 1952 the number had dropped to 13,397. Today, Tak province has the highest number of elephants.

Elephant mothers carry their calves for 22 months. Once they are born, working elephants enjoy a three- to five-year childhood before they begin training. The training, which is under the guidance of their mahouts, takes five years. They learn to push, carry and stack logs, as well as bathing and walking in procession.

Working elephants have a career of about 50 years; so when young they are trained by two mahouts, one older and one younger – sometimes a father-and-son team – who can see the animal through its lifetime. Thai law requires that elephants be retired and released into the wild at age 61. They often live for 80 years or more.

As a mode of jungle transport, the elephant beats any other animal or machine for moving through a forest with minimum damage – its large, soft feet distribute the animal's weight without crushing the ground. Interestingly, an adult elephant can run at speeds of up to 23km/h but puts less weight on the ground per square centimetre than a deer!

In 1989 logging was banned in Thailand, resulting in decreased demand for trained elephants. Some owners, however, continue to work their elephants in the illegal logging industry along the Thai–Myanmar border. Sadly, some animals are pumped full of amphetamines so they can work day and night.

The plight of these unemployed creatures is becoming an issue of national concern. Many domesticated elephants are increasingly neglected, mistreated or abandoned by owners who often cannot afford to care for them. Meanwhile, destruction of forests and ivory-trade poach-

---

a restaurant, but food must be ordered in advance of your visit. Several privately run food/snack stalls provide sustenance as well. For further information, contact the **Royal Forest Department** (☎ 0 2579 7223, 0 2561 4292-3; Th Phahonyothin, Chatuchak, Bangkok) of the Natural Resources Conservation Office.

CHIANG RAI PROVINCE

Chiang Rai, the northernmost province in Thailand, is one of the country's most rural areas. Half of its northern border, separating the province and nation from Laos, is formed by the Mekong River. Mountains form the other half, cleaving Myanmar from Thailand, with the junction of Nam Ruak (Ruak River) and Mekong River at Thailand's peak. The fertile Mekong floodplains to the east support most of the agriculture in the province;

to the west the land is too mountainous for most crops. One crop that thrives on steep mountain slopes is opium and until recently Chiang Rai was the centre for most of the opium in Thailand.

Crop substitution and other development projects sponsored by the late Princess Mother (the king's mother), along with accelerated law enforcement, have pushed much of the opium trade over the border into Myanmar and Laos. While there are undoubtedly still pockets of the trade here and there (even a few poppy patches), Chiang Rai's Golden Triangle fame is now mostly relegated to history books and museums.

CHIANG RAI

เชียงราย

pop 73,300

About 180km from Chiang Mai, the city northern Thais know as 'Siang Hai' has

ing are placing the wild-elephant population in increasing jeopardy. The Asian elephant is now officially classified as an endangered species.

Rising numbers of unemployed elephants also means unemployed mahouts; many mahouts have begun migrating with their elephants to large Thai cities, even Bangkok. They earn money simply by walking the animal through the streets and selling bananas and sugarcane to people to feed the elephants. In these urban environments, the elephants often suffer.

Elephant conservation experts are urging tourists not to feed elephants in the cities. A better way to make contact with these beautiful animals is at the Thai Elephant Conservation Center (TECC) in Lampang Province (p348) or at other bona fide conservation facilities.

One of the problems in the elephant camps around Thailand is inbreeding; due to a lack of males in mainly female camps, baby elephants are being born with disabilities. One of the initiatives of TECC is an artificial insemination programme to avoid this problem, and as a longer-term solution if the population dwindles even more. Apart from its elephant hospital in Lampang, TECC also has mobile health clinics, which travel around Thailand health checking and treating the elephants.

Outside of Thailand the attempt to conserve Asian elephants has caused controversy. In 2004 Australia granted import permits for five Thai elephants to go to Taronga Zoo in Sydney, and three to be sent to Melbourne Zoo. In both zoos breeding programmes have been established aimed at preserving the species. This decision led to two years of legal action and protests, where animal welfare groups alleged that importing the elephants had no conservation benefit, that the zoos were not equipped to meet the needs of the elephants, and their import would potentially be detrimental to the survival and recovery of the species. It was alleged that the import was more about increasing visitor numbers than animal conservation. It was also pointed out that the millions spent on the enclosures should have gone to conservation efforts in the elephant's home country.

However, the tribunal gave the go-ahead to the imports in 2006 after they had been convinced that the zoos were committed and dedicated to the welfare and conservation of the elephants, and that extra conditions put forward by the welfare groups had been met. In June 2006 protests in Bangkok prevented the elephants from leaving but they arrived in their respective Australian zoos in November 2006.

been marketed in tourist literature as 'the gateway to the Golden Triangle'. Thais often tout Chiang Rai as a laid-back alternative to Chiang Mai. Things are on a smaller scale here, from the night market to the amount of sites to see, but the city has a more relaxed atmosphere, less pollution, and its trekking areas are quicker to get to. There are also more volunteering and homestay opportunities outside of Chiang Rai compared to Chiang Mai. Although often compared to the north's capital, Chiang Rai has its own character and attractions, like the unique, sparkling white Wat Rong Khun temple, just outside the city.

Phaya Mengrai founded Chiang Rai in 1262 as part of the Lao-Thai Lanna kingdom and it didn't become a Siamese territory till 1786, then a province in 1910. Lots of wealthy Thais began moving to Chiang Rai in the 1980s, and in the early 1990s the area saw a development

boom as local entrepreneurs speculated on the city's future. Things have calmed down a bit since then but ambitions are still high. Although the airport still doesn't link Chiang Rai with international destinations in the region, there has been talk (but not much action) of the potential of possible roads connecting Chiang Rai and cities in Laos, Myanmar and southern China.

Information
BOOKSHOPS
Gare Garon (869/18 Th Phahonyothin; ✆ 10am-10pm) Mainly new books with a smattering of overpriced used ones; also sells coffee, tea and some handicrafts.

Orn's Bookshop (☎ 08 1022 0318; ✆ 8am-8pm) By far the best used bookshop in Chiang Rai, this place is run by the eccentric and discerning Peter. His superb collection of books are in many languages and at much cheaper prices than Gare Garon. Turn right down the *soi* past Boonbundan Guest House.

NORTHERN THAILAND

EMERGENCY

Tourist Police (☎ 0 5374 0249; ☺ 24hrs) At the new tourist police office next to North Wheels cars; English is spoken and police are on stand-by 24 hours a day

INTERNET ACCESS

Internet access is readily available around town and costs 40B per hour. It's especially abundant around the Wang Come Hotel.
Connect Café (☎ 0 5374 0688; 868/10 Th Phahonyothin; ☺ 10.30am-10.30pm) This colourful, funky internet café serves homemade brownies and good coffee while you're typing away. It has an overseas call service, burns digital photos onto CDs, sells books and maps, and plays chilled-out music.

MEDICAL SERVICES

Overbrook Hospital (☎ 0 5371 1366; www.overbrook hospital.com; Th Singkhlai) English is spoken in this modern hospital that treats foreigners.

MONEY

There is an abundance of banks and ATMs on both Th Phahonyothin and Th Thanalai.

POST

Main post office (Th Utarakit; ☺ 8.30am-4.30pm Mon-Fri, 9am-noon Sat, Sun & holidays) South of Wat Phra Singh.

TELEPHONE

Many internet places offer international call services, including Connect Café (above).
Communications Authority of Thailand office (CAT; cnr Th Ratchadat Damrong & Th Ngam Meuang; ☺ 7am-11pm Mon-Fri) Offers international telephone, internet and fax services.

TOURIST INFORMATION

Tourism Authority of Thailand office (TAT; ☎ 0 5374 4674, 0 5371 1433; tatchrai@tat.or.th; Th Singkhlai; ☺ 8.30am-4.30pm) Staff here are some of the best in north Thailand. Fantastically helpful, they take the time to give detailed advice, and have maps and useful brochures.

Sights

WAT PHRA KAEW

วัดพระแก้ว

Originally called Wat Pa Yia (Bamboo Forest Monastery) in local dialect, this is the city's most revered Buddhist temple. Legend says that in 1434 lightning struck the temple's octagonal *chedi*, which fell apart to reveal the Phra Kaew Morakot or Emerald Buddha (actually made of jade). After a long journey

that included a long stopover in Vientiane, Laos, this national talisman is now ensconced in the temple of the same name in Bangkok (see boxed text p109).

In 1990 Chiang Rai commissioned a Chinese artist to sculpt a new image from Canadian jade. Named the Phra Yok Chiang Rai (Chiang Rai Jade Buddha), it was intentionally a very close but not exact replica of the Phra Kaew Morakot in Bangkok, with dimensions of 48.3cm across the base and 65.9cm in height, just 0.1cm shorter than the original. The image is housed in the impressive Haw Phra Kaew, which sits towards the back of the wat compound.

The main *wíhǎn* is a medium-sized, well-preserved wooden structure with unique carved doors. The *chedi* behind it dates from the late 14th century and is in typical Lanna style.

WAT JET YOT

วัดเจ็ดยอด

The namesake for this wat is a seven-spired *chedi* similar to that in Chiang Mai's Wat Jet Yot, but without stucco ornamentation. Of more aesthetic interest is the wooden ceiling of the front veranda of the main *wíhǎn*, which features a unique Thai astrological fresco.

WAT PHRA SINGH

วัดพระสิงห์

Housing yet another copy of a famous Buddha image, this temple was built in the late 14th century during the reign of Chiang Rai's King Mahaphrom. A sister temple to Chiang Mai's Wat Phra Singh, its original buildings are typical northern Thai-style wood structures with low, sweeping roofs. The impressive dragon-carved gate looks to be of Thai Lü design. The main *wíhǎn* houses a copy of Chiang Mai's Phra Singh Buddha.

WAT PHRA THAT DOI CHOM THONG

วัดพระธาตุดอยจอมทอง

This hilltop wat northwest of Wat Phra Kaew has partial views of the river and gets an occasional river breeze. The Lanna-style *chedi* here was supposedly built in 940, impossible since Lanna hadn't yet been founded. Most likely it dates from the 14th to 16th centuries, and may cover an earlier Mon *chedi* inside. King Mengrai, Chiang Rai's founder, first surveyed the site for the city from this peak.

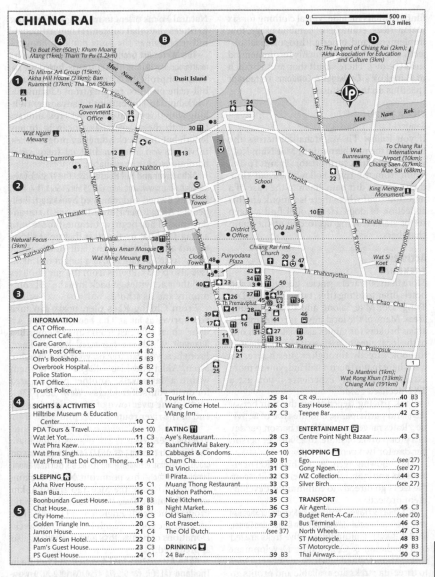

CHIANG RAI

HILLTRIBE MUSEUM & EDUCATION CENTER
พิพิธภัณฑ์และศูนย์การศึกษาชาวเขา

This **museum and handicrafts centre** (☎ 0 5374 0088; www.pda.or.th/chiangrai; 3rd floor, 620/1 Th Thanalai; admission 50B; ☷ 9am-6pm Mon-Fri, 10am-6pm Sat-Sun) is a good place to visit before undertaking any hill-tribe trek. The centre, run by the non-profit Population & Community Development Association (PDA), offers a 20-minute slide show on Thailand's hill tribes with narration in English, French, German, Japanese and Thai. The curator is passionate about his museum, and will talk about the different hill tribes, their histories, recent trends and the community projects that the museum helps

fund. Exhibits include typical clothing for six major tribes, examples of bamboo usage, folk implements and other anthropological objects. The PDA also run highly recommended treks (below). There's a gift shop and a branch of Bangkok's **Cabbages & Condoms restaurant** (p358) is on the premises.

THAM TU PU
ถ้ำตูปู

If you follow Th Winitchaikul across the bridge to the northern side of Mae Nam Kok, you'll come to a turn-off for Tham Tu Pu, 800m from the river. Follow the road 1km, then follow a dirt path 200m to the base of a limestone cliff where there is a monk and his collection of dogs. Here, you'll find a steep set of stairs leading up to one of the main chambers.

Activities
TREKKING

More than 30 travel agencies, guesthouses and hotels offer trekking trips, typically in the Doi Tung, Doi Mae Salong and Chiang Khong areas. Many of the local travel agencies merely act as brokers for guides associated with one of the local guesthouses, so it may be cheaper to book directly through a guesthouse. As elsewhere in northern Thailand, you're more assured of a quality experience if you use a TAT-licensed guide.

Trek pricing depends on the number of days and participants, and the type of activities. Rates range from 950B per person per day in a group of six or more, to 2300B per person per day for two people.

The following agencies in Chiang Rai operate treks and cultural tours where profits from the treks go directly to community-development projects:

PDA Tours & Travel (☎ 0 5374 0088; crpdatour@hotmail .com; 620/1 Th Thanalai, Hilltribe Museum & Education Center; 620/1 Th Thanalai) Culturally sensitive treks are led by Population & Community Development Association-trained hill-tribe members. One-to three-day treks are available and profits go back into community projects that include HIV/AIDS education, mobile health clinics, education scholarships and establishment of village-owned banks.

Natural Focus (☎ 0 5371 5696, 08 1706 7639; www .naturalfocusecotour.com; 129/1 Mu 4, Th Pa-Ngiw, Soi 4, Rop Wiang) Set up by the Hill Area and Community Development Foundation (www.hadf.org),

Natural Focus offers tours ranging from one to fifteen days that concentrate on nature and hill-tribe living.

The Mirror Art Group (☎ 0 5373 7412-3; www.mir rorartgroup.org; 106 Moo 1, Ban Huay Khom, Tambon Mae Yao) This nonprofit NGO does many admirable hill-tribe projects, ranging from educational workshops to Thai citizenship advocacy. Trekking with this group encourages real interaction with the villagers. Trips can be of any length but one-week homestay programmes, in which you learn traditional weaving or bamboo work, are available.

Akha River and Hill House (☎ 08 9997 5505; www .akhahill.com, www.akha.info; 423/25 Mu 21 Soi 1 Th Kohloy) Wholly owned and managed by Akha tribespeople, Akha River House does one- to seven-day treks. They begin at the guesthouse with a long-tail boat up the river, before trekking to and around their Akha Hill House about 23km from Chiang Rai, at a height of 1500m (see also p333). Profits from the guesthouses and their activities go back into the hill community and its school.

From Chiang Rai's pier, boats can take you upriver as far as Tha Ton (see p360). An hour's boat ride east from Chiang Rai is **Ban Ruammit**, which is a fair-sized Karen village. From here you can trek on your own to Lahu, Mien, Akha and Lisu villages – all of them within a day's walk. Another popular area for do-it-yourself trekkers is **Wawi** (see p334), south of the river town of Mae Salak near the end of the river route.

VOLUNTEERING
The Mirror Art Group (☎ 0 5373 7412-3; www.mirrorart group.org/volunteerenglish.html; 106 Moo 1, Ban Huay Khom, Tambon Mae Yao) This nonprofit NGO working with hill tribes in the Mae Yao area is 15km west of Chiang Rai. Its Volunteer Teaching Programme needs English and IT skills. The programme goes for a minimum of one week. Donations of books, toys and clothes are also appreciated.

Akha Association for Education and Culture in Thailand (AFECT; ☎ 0 5371 4250, 08 1952 2179; www .akhaasia.org; 468 Th Rimkok) Volunteer at AFECT's Life Stay and you will be living and working in a village with an Akha family. Depending on the agricultural season, the days can be quite physical – you may be working in the fields, helping build a house, or gathering food in the forest. Stays are from seven days, and places are limited so it is best to

arrange in advance of travel. Proceeds from the Life Stay are put back into the community for programmes that range from health to education.

Hill Area and Community Development Foundation/Natural Focus (☎ 0 5371 5696, 08 1706 7639; www.hadf.org; www.naturalfocusecotour.com; 129/1 Mu 4, Th Pa-Ngiw, Soi 4, Rop Wiang) Contact Natural Focus to find out about possible volunteering opportunities with the Hill Area And Community Development Foundation (HADF). This foundation helps hill tribes deal with problems ranging from environmental management to social development. Currently, volunteering includes teaching English in the Mae Chan/Mae Salong area for six months, but shorter stays may be possible.

Sleeping

The two main areas for accommodation are in the centre, clustered around Th Jet Yot and off Th Phahonyothin, or by the relaxed setting of Mae Nam Kok. Prices are lower in Chiang Rai for comparable comfort in other big towns. Budget accommodation has pulled up its socks in the last couple of years with some good new offerings. The top end is showing signs of leaving the bland four/five-star and going the boutique way.

BUDGET

our pick **Akha River House** (☎ 0 5371 5084; www.akha .info, www.akhahill.com; 423/25 Mu 21 Th Kohloy, Soi 1; s 100-200B, d 150-300B; ▯) Behind the TAT office on the Mae Nam Kok, this wholly Akha-owned guesthouse is a real retreat. Comfortable rooms and bungalows are set in a manicured garden, tastefully designed with warm ochres and Akha textiles. There is a restaurant and seating areas for relaxing by the river, plus a small boat to explore in. Bikes are free of charge to use and free pick-up from the bus station is available. Its treks are raved about (opposite), and part of the profits from the guesthouse goes back into Akha education and community projects.

Chat House (☎ 0 5371 1481; www.chathouse32.com; Th Trairat, 3/2 Soi Saengkaew; s/d without bathroom 80/150B, r from 200-300B; ▨) Out of the way on a residential street, this long-running guesthouse has a relaxed and personable atmosphere. The collection of cheap but run-down rooms are set in a pleasant garden with a small restaurant. Bikes, motorbikes and 4WDs can be rented here.

Tourist Inn (☎ 0 5375 2094; touristinn1@hotmail.com; 1004/4-6 Th Jet Yot; fan s 150-180B, d 200-250B, air-con r 350B; ▨ ▯) Rooms here are a little stark but clean, and set in two buildings – the newer one has the nicer and slightly more expensive rooms. Breakfasts here are fantastic with homemade croissants, wholemeal bread and baguettes. There is a cable TV in the communal area. Car and motorcycle rentals can be arranged and the proprietors speak English, Thai and Japanese.

Pam's Guest House (☎ 08 9433 5134; Th Jet Yot; r 150-250B) This friendly place has a colourful communal area with a small bar and pool table, plus lounging areas with cable TV and DVDs. The cheaper rooms have shared hot water bathrooms; all of them are clean but plain.

Boonbundan Guest House (☎ 0 5375 2413-4; 1005/13 Th Jet Yot; r 170-500B; ▨) Contained in a quiet, walled compound, this old favourite has had many rooms renovated and a new building added. There is something to suit every budget, but the older rooms lack character and could do with a lick of paint. The newer rooms are great value and come with cable TV, fridge and a kitchenette. A laundry service is available. Motorcycles can be rented.

Baan Bua (☎ 0 5371 8880; baanbua@yahoo.com; 879/2 Th Jet Yot; r 250-400B; ▨) This place can be full any time of the year. It's in a quiet location off Th Jet Yot, and offers 17 large, spotless rooms with hot showers, all in a cement row house with a garden out the front. The guide who does its tours has been with them for eight years.

PS Guesthouse (☎ 0 5360 0470, 0 5374 4521; 82/2 Kohloy; r 250-450B; ▨ ▯) Near Akha River House, this new guesthouse has a friendly host and eight fan or air-con, large, good-value rooms. Although not filled with lots of character, the rooms do have cable TV, attractive, well-designed bathrooms, plus a fridge, sink, kettle and free drinks. Bicycles are free to use and motorbikes can be rented.

City Home (☎ 0 5360 0155; 868 Th Phahonyothin; r 400B; ▯) Down a tiny *soi*, smack in the middle of town, this quiet four-storey hotel has 17 large rooms. All have wooden floors, air-con, and cable TV, and are well furnished. There's no garden but a 'relax zone' with brightly coloured chairs surrounded by plants. Fantastic value.

our pick **Janson House** (☎ 0 5371 4552; 897/2 Th Jet Yot; r 450B; ▨) This new three-storey hotel offers

TREKKING IN NORTHERN THAILAND

Thousands of visitors trek into the hills of northern Thailand each year. Most come away with a sense of adventure, but some are disillusioned by the experience. The most important ingredient in having an enjoyable trek is having a good leader-organiser, followed by a good group of trekkers.

Before Trekking

Hill-tribe trekking isn't for everyone. First, you must be physically fit enough to withstand extended uphill and downhill walking, exposure to the elements and unsavoury food. Second, many people feel awkward walking through hill-tribe villages and playing the role of voyeur.

In cities and villages elsewhere in Thailand, Thais and other lowland groups are quite used to foreign faces and foreign ways (from TV if nothing else). But in the hills of northern Thailand the tribes lead largely insular lives. Therefore, hill-tribe tourism has pronounced effects, both positive and negative. On the positive side, travellers have a chance to see how traditional, subsistence-oriented societies function. Also, since the Thai government is sensitive about the image of their minority groups, tourism may actually have forced it to review and sometimes improve its policies towards hill tribes. On the negative side, trekkers introduce many cultural items and ideas from the outside world that may erode tribal customs to varying degrees.

If you have any qualms about interrupting the traditional patterns of life in hill-tribe areas, you probably shouldn't go trekking. If you do go, keep in mind that anyone who promises you an authentic experience is probably exaggerating at the very least, or at the worst contributing to the decline of hill-tribe culture by leading travellers into untouristed areas.

Choosing a Company

Many trekking guides are freelance and float from company to company, so there's no way to predict which companies are going to give the best service. Many guesthouses that advertise their own trekking companies actually act as commission-charging brokers for off-site operations. The Tourism Authority of Thailand (TAT) office in Chiang Mai (p283) maintains a list of licensed agencies and is making efforts to regulate trekking companies.

Make sure that the guides you go trekking with are licensed TAT guides. This means they have had at least regional and survival training, and they are registered, which is useful if there are problems later. The guide should be able to show you their licence and certificate. Green licences are for trekking only, pink are for sightseeing only and silver ones are for guides licensed to do both. Still, with more than 300 companies, it's very difficult to guarantee any kind of control. Ultimately, the best way to shop for a trek is to talk to travellers who have just returned from one.

In short, if you decide to do a trek, choose your operator carefully, try to meet the others in the group (suggest a meeting), and find out exactly what the tour does and does not include; and if there are additional expenses. In the cool season, make sure sleeping bags are provided, as the thin woollen blankets available in most villages are not sufficient for the average visitor. Here's a useful checklist of questions:

- How many people will there be in the group? (Six to 10 is a good maximum range.)
- Can the organiser guarantee that no other tourists will visit the same village on the same day, especially overnight?
- Can the guide speak the language of each village to be visited? (This is not always necessary, as many villagers can speak Thai nowadays.)
- Exactly when does the tour begin and end? (Some three-day treks turn out to be less than 48 hours in length.)
- Does the tour company provide transport before and after the trek or is it by public bus (which may mean long waits)?
- Is the trek (ie number of participants, itinerary and the duration) registered with the tourist police?

In general, the trekking business has become more conscious of the need to tread carefully in hill-tribe villages than in previous decades. Most companies now tend to limit the number of visits to a particular area and are careful not to overlap areas used by other companies. Everyone

benefits from this consciousness: the hill tribes are less impacted, the trekkers have a better experience and the trekking industry is more sustainable.

You might find that places other than Chiang Mai or Chiang Rai offer better and less expensive tours for more remote and less-trekked areas. Also, they are generally smaller, friendlier operations and the trekkers are usually a more determined bunch since they're not looking for an easy and quick in-and-out trek. You can easily arrange treks out of Mae Hong Son, Pai, Mae Sai and Tha Ton. If you have a little time to seek out the right people, you can also join organised treks from Mae Sariang, Khun Yuam, Soppong (near Pai), Mae Sot, Um Phang and various out-of-the-way guesthouses elsewhere in the north.

The downside, of course, is that companies outside Chiang Mai are generally subject to even less regulation than those in Chiang Mai, and there are fewer guarantees with regard to terms and conditions.

Costs

Organised treks out of Chiang Mai average around 2000-2500B for a three-day, two-night trek, including transport, guide, accommodation, three meals per day, sleeping bags, water bottles and rafting and/or elephant riding. Not included are beverages other than drinking water or tea, lunch on the first and last days and personal porters. Rates vary, so it pays to shop around – although these days so many companies are competing for your business that rates have remained pretty stable for the last few years. Elephant rides actually become boring and uncomfortable after an hour or two. Some companies now offer quickie day treks or one-night, two-day programmes – these tend to cost around 900B a day. Don't choose a trek by price alone. It's better to talk to other travellers in town who have been on treks.

Seasons

The best time to trek is November to February, when the weather is refreshing, there's little or no rain and wildflowers are in bloom. Between March and May the hills are dry and the weather is quite hot. The second-best time is early in the rainy season, between June and July, before the dirt roads become too saturated.

Independent Trekking

You might consider striking out on your own in a small group of two to five people. Some guesthouses, like Cave Lodge (p445) near Tham Lot and Shin Sane Guest House in Mae Salong (p363) have good trekking maps and knowledge of their areas.

Gather as much information as you can about the area you'd like to trek in, from the Tribal Museum in Chiang Mai (p287) or the excellent Hilltribe Museum & Education Center in Chiang Rai (p353). Browsing the displays will help you identify different tribes, and the inscriptions offer cultural information. Don't bother staff with questions about trekking as this is not their area of expertise.

Be prepared for language difficulties. Few people will know any English. Usually someone in a village will know some Thai, so a Thai phrasebook can be helpful. Lonely Planet publishes a *Hill Tribes Phrasebook* with phrase sections for each of the six major hill-tribe languages.

Many people now do short treks on their own, staying in villages along the way. It's not necessary to bring a lot of food or gear, just money for food that can be bought en route at small Thai towns and occasionally in the hill-tribe settlements. (Obviously, be sure to take plenty of water and some high-energy snacks.) However, the TAT strongly discourages trekking on your own because of the safety risk. Check with the police when you arrive in a new district so they can tell you if an area is considered safe or not. A lone trekker is an easy target for bandits.

Safety

Thai police mount regular hill-country patrols and we haven't heard of any trekking groups being robbed for several years now. Still, you shouldn't take anything along on a trek that you can't afford to lose. If you leave your valuables with a guesthouse, make sure you obtain a fully itemised receipt before departing on a trek.

NORTHERN THAILAND

some of the best value rooms in town. In a central location, the neat, spacious rooms are set around a small courtyard filled with plants. Each has cable TV, well-designed bathrooms, good furniture and tiled floors. Free coffee in the morning is an extra bonus.

MIDRANGE

Moon & Sun Hotel (☎ 0 5371 9279; 632 Th Singkhlai; r/ste 400-500/700B; 🔅) Bright and sparkling clean, this little hotel offers large modern rooms. Some come with four-poster beds, all come with desks, cable TV and refrigerators (although some don't have bedside tables). Suites have a separate, spacious sitting area.

Golden Triangle Inn (☎ 0 5371 1339/6996; www.gold enchiangrai.com; 590/2 Th Phahonyothin; r includes breakfast 800B; 🔅) This place is more like a home than a hotel. It has 39 rooms with tile or wood floors and stylish furniture. Some rooms have bathtubs, but no rooms have TV. The lush, landscaped grounds include a restaurant, a Budget car-rental office and an efficient travel agency. It's a popular place so book in advance.

TOP END

Wang Come Hotel (☎ 0 5371 1800; www.wangcome .com; 869/90 Th Premawiphat; r 1500-1800B; 🔅 🖳 🏊) In a lively and convenient location, the Wang Come has very comfortable rooms decorated in burgundy and dark wood. Staff members are polite, and there's a funky bar and coffee shop, two restaurants, a banquet room and a disco. The pool is quite small.

Wiang Inn (☎ 0 5371 1533; www.wianginn.com; 893 Th Phahonyothin; s/d/ste from 1800/2200/5000B; ✕ 🔅 🏊) Centrally located, this full-sized hotel offers all the service and comfort you expect from a business-class hotel. The rooms are well maintained and have a few Thai touches. It has a kidney-shaped pool, a pleasant nonsmoking lobby lounge and live music in the restaurant.

Mantrini (☎ 0 5360 1555-9; www.mantrini.com; 292 Moo 13, Robwiang on the superhighway; r 2990-3290B; 🔅 🖳 🏊) Around 1km south of the town centre, this brand new, achingly hip hotel is for design conscious travellers. Lounge music is played in the lobby, where there's a huge plasma screen surrounded by bright curvy Arne Jacobsen-style chairs. The minimalist, chic rooms are gleaming white, contrasted with accents of primary colour, although the superior rooms are slightly cramped. The contemporary bar with floor-to-ceiling windows overlooks the lush

garden and pool. There's also a good restaurant. Discounts are available.

🔖 **Legend of Chiang Rai** (☎ 0 5391 0400; www .thelegend-chiangrai.com; 124/15 Kohloy; studio 3900-5900B, villa 8100B; ✕ 🔅 🖳 🏊) At this elegant and stylish hotel the spacious bungalows exemplify a fine mixture of contemporary rustic Thai architecture. Rooms feel romantic and luxuriously understated with furniture in calming creams and rattan. Each has a pleasant outdoor sitting area, frosted glass for increased privacy and a cool, outdoorlike bathroom with an oversized shower; villas have a small private pool. The riverside infinity pool and spa are the icing on the comfort-filled cake.

Eating

The **night market** has a good collection of food stalls offering snacks and meals, from won ton to fresh fish. Choose a dish and sit at the nearby tables. There are lots of stalls and restaurants on and off Th Phahonyothin by the night market, as well as on the streets around Wang Come Hotel.

THAI

Rot Prasoet (English sign reads 'Muslim food'; Th Itsaraphap; dishes 25-50B; 🕒 7am-8pm) This Thai-Muslim restaurant next to the mosque on Th Itsaraphap dishes up delicious Thai Muslim favourites, including *khâo mòk kài*, a Thai version of chicken briyani. The set lunch is popular.

Cham Cha (Th Singkhlai; dishes 35-100B; 🕒 7am-4pm Mon-Sat) This casual little hole-in-the-wall is good for breakfast or lunch. It has all the usual Thai and Chinese standards, along with a few Isan dishes that are not on the English menu, such as *lâap* (spicy minced-meat salad) and *sôm-tam* (spicy green papaya salad), plus ice cream.

Cabbages & Condoms (C&C; ☎ 0 5395 2314; 620/1 Th Thanalai; dishes 35-200B; 🕒 8am-midnight) Next to the Hilltribe Museum, this restaurant serves hit-and-miss northern-Thai food. With the intention of making condoms as easy to find as cabbages, profits from the restaurant are used by the PDA for family planning and HIV/AIDS education.

Nakhon Pathom (no roman-script sign; Th Phahonyothin; dishes 40-110B; 🕒 8am-3pm) Another local restaurant named after a central-Thailand city, Nakhon Pathom is very popular for inexpensive *khâo man kài* (chicken rice) and *kŭaytĭaw pèt yâang* (roast duck with rice noodles).

Muang Thong Restaurant (☎ 0 5371 1162; Th Phahonyothin; dishes 60-100B; 🕒 24hr) You can't miss

the sidewalk side platters of Thai and Chinese dishes here. It's packed nightly. One of the house specialities is *kaeng pàa phèt*, a delicious duck curry.

our pick Aye's Restaurant (☎ 0 5372 2534; 869/170 Th Phahonyothin; dishes 90-500B; ☺ 7.30am-12pm) Looking for atmosphere and an unbeatable selection of food? This friendly spot draws a big crowd nightly. The ceiling fans, rattan furniture and parasols feel slightly colonial, and everything from the steak schnitzel to the northern Thai curries is tasty and well presented. The extensive wine list is impressive.

our pick Old Siam (☎ 0 5371 4282; 541/2 Th Phahonyothin; dishes 105-250B; ☺ 8am-12pm) Set in a teak house, this gem of a restaurant is tucked in a corner off Th Phahonyothin. It has low lighting and lovely decorating details, like old black-and-white photos, wooden birdcages and ceramics jewelled with colour, which make it a romantic spot. There's a choice of tables and chairs or low tables and mats to sit on for eating the recommended fish and curry dishes.

INTERNATIONAL

BaanChivitMai Bakery (☎ 08 1764 7020; at the bus station, Th Prasopsuk; www.baanchivitmai.com; ☺ 7am-9pm Mon-Sat, 2-9pm Sun) If you want to feel virtuous *and* eat delicious cakes, croissants and bread, then come to this two-storey, superclean Swedish bakery. Profits from the bakery go back into BaanChivitMai, an organisation that runs homes and education projects for vulnerable, orphaned or AIDS-affected children.

The Old Dutch (541 Th Phahonyothin; dishes 50-300B; 8am-12pm) Next to the Old Siam restaurant, The Old Dutch is an atmospheric place with a European café-style décor. A large choice of good Western, Indonesia and Thai dishes are on the menu.

Il Pirata (☎ 08 9758 9173; 868/8 Th Phahonyothin; dishes 50-200B; ☺ 12am-10pm) This simple, Italian-run restaurant serves delicious homemade gnocchi, fettuccine and lasagne, as well as pizza with good, fresh ingredients, and dishes like chicken with cream and mushroom sauce. Located down a *soi* off the night market, this is good spot to drop in after shopping.

Da Vinci (☎ 0 5375 2535; 879/4-5 Th Phahonyothin; mains 125-300B; ☺ 12am-11pm) This slightly pricey, smart Italian restaurant serves fresh pasta, pizza and salads plus some fish and meat dishes. Recommended are the rib fingers with rosemary and the black spaghetti with prawns and chilli.

Nice Kitchen (Th Jet Yot; ☺ 7.30am-8.30pm) Along Th Jet Yot, Nice Kitchen is a good restaurant for breakfast, especially as most places round here don't open till much later. You'll find a large selection of cheap and satisfying breakfasts, as well as sandwiches and Thai dishes.

Drinking & Entertainment

Th Jet Yot is the liveliest area for bars. The dodgy go-go bar centre is at the end of Th Jet Yot on an L-shaped lane between Th Banphaprakan and Th Suksathit.

Teepee Bar (Th Phahonyothin; ☺ 6.30pm-12pm) A hang-out for backpackers and Thai hippies, the Teepee is a good place to exchange information.

CR 49 (Th Jet Yot; ☺ 10.30am-2am) Thais and expats recommended this new, popular, funky-looking bar. Its stays open late and the food is good too.

24 Bar (Th Jet Yot; ☺ 5pm-1am) Next to a couple of girlie bars, this cool bar manages to stand out with its all-black décor, bright squares of light on the floor, glitter balls and DJ. Have a drink at the lacquered bar or flop in the deep sofas surrounded by abstract paintings. There is outdoor seating in the back.

Easy House (☎ 0 5360 0963; Th Premaviphat; ☺ 11am-12pm) On the corner of Th Jet Yot and Th Premawiphat, this laid-back place serves beer and food on chunky wooden tables and chairs.

Centre Point Night Bazaar (off Th Phahonyothin) Free northern-Thai music and dance performances are staged nightly.

Shopping

Adjacent to the bus station off Th Phahonyothin is Chiang Rai's **night market** (☺ 6pm-11pm). On a much smaller scale than Chiang Mai's, it is nevertheless a good place to find an assortment of handicrafts at decent prices. On entering the night market from Th Phahonyothin you'll see **MZ Collection** (☎ 0 5375 0145; www .mzcollection.com; 426/68 Kok Kalair) on the right-hand side. This shop has unusual handmade silver and semiprecious stone jewellery. Each piece is unique so don't expect bargain basement prices.

Antiques and silverwork are sometimes cheaper in Chiang Rai than in Chiang Mai. Several shops worth checking for handicrafts, silver and antiques can be found along Th Phahonyothin, including the following:

Ego (869/81 Th Premawiphat) Carries upmarket items such as antique textiles.

Gong Ngoen (873/5 Th Phahonyothin)
Silver Birch (891 Th Phahonyothin)

Just out of town are two handicraft centres that are worth a look:
Chiangrai Handicrafts Center (☎ 0 5371 3355; ⏲ 9am-6pm) Four kilometres out of town on Rte 101.
Khum Muang Mang (☎ 0 5371 8789; Th Kasalong; ⏲ 9am-6pm) This brand new handicraft centre is 500m past the boat pier.

Getting There & Away

AIR
Chiang Rai Airport (☎ 0 5379 3048-57) is 8km north of the city. Currently, there are just daily connections to Bangkok. The terminal has restaurants, a money exchange, a post office (open 7am to 7pm) and car-rental booths.

In town, **Air Agent** (☎ 0 5374 0445; 863/3 Th Phahonyothin; ⏲ 8.30am-9pm) can book domestic and international flights in advance. Alternatively, book online or go directly to the airport offices listed below:
Air Asia (☎ 0 5379 3545-8275; www.airasia.com) Operates three flights a day between Bangkok and Chiang Rai (from 1400B).
One-Two-Go (☎ 0 5379 3555; www.fly12go.com) has one flight a day to Bangkok at 1950B.
Thai Airways Th Phahonyothin (☎ 0 5371 1179; www .thaiair.com; 870 Th Phahonyothin; ⏲ 8am-5pm Mon-Fri); airport office (☎ 0 5379 8202-3; ⏲ 8am-8pm daily) Does flights to/from Bangkok (3345B, 1¼ hours) four times daily.

Taxis run into town from the airport and cost 200B. Out to the airport you can get a túk-túk for 100B.

BOAT
Another way to reach Chiang Rai is by boat on Mae Nam Kok from Tha Ton (see p333).

(see p333)

LONG BOAT DESTINATIONS FROM CHIANG RAI

Destination	Fare (B)	Duration (hr)
Ban Ruammit	80	1
Hat Yao	150	2¼
Kok Noi	200	3
Mae Salak	210	4
Pha Khwang	180	2½
Pong Nam Rawn	90	1½
Tha Ton	350	5

For boats heading upriver, go to the pier in the northwest corner of town. Boats embark daily at 10.30am. Long boats from Chiang Rai leave at times approximate for ideal river conditions.

You can charter a boat to Ban Ruammit for 700B or all the way to Tha Ton for 2000B at the pier.

BUS
Buses to Chiang Mai leave regularly from 6.30am to 6pm from Chiang Rai's bus terminal, behind the night market. The journey takes around three hours. The fare is 100B ordinary (one departure a day at 7.45am, four hours), 140B 2nd-class air-con, 180B 1st-class air-con or 280B for VIP. Buses from Chiang Mai to Chiang Rai leave from Chiang Mai's Arcade bus terminal. Buses on this route are sometimes stopped for drug searches.

Check the adjacent table for information about fares and duration of journeys to bus destinations from Chiang Rai.

Getting Around
A sǎamláw (three-wheeled pedicab) ride anywhere in central Chiang Rai should cost around 30B. Túk-túk often charge twice that. Shared sǎwngthǎew cost 15B per person.

Bicycles and motorcycles can be hired at **ST Motorcycle** (☎ 0 5371 3652; Th Banphaprakan and Th Wat Jet Yot; per day bicycles 60-100B, motorcycles older Honda Dreams/newer/250cc Yamaha TTR 150/200/700B; ⏲ 8am-6pm), which has two locations and takes good care of its bicycles. Many guesthouses also rent motorcycles.

Several small agencies near Wang Come Hotel rent out cars (around 1200B a day), vans (1300B to 1500B) and Suzuki Caribian 4WDs (800B).

The following companies have good reputations and charge a little more:
Avis Rent-A-Car (☎ 0 5379 3827; www.avisthailand .com; Chiang Rai Airport)
Budget Rent-A-Car (☎ 0 5374 0442-3; www.budget .co.th; 590 Th Phahonyothin) At Golden Triangle Inn.
National Car Rental (☎ 0 5379 3683; Chiang Rai Airport)
North Wheels (☎ 0 5374 0585; www.northwheels .com; 591 Th Phahonyothin; ⏲ 8am-7pm)

AROUND CHIANG RAI
WAT RONG KHUN
Thirteen kilometres south of Chiang Rai is the unusual and popular **Wat Rong Khun** (☎ 0

BUS DESTINATIONS FROM CHIANG RAI

Destination	Bus	Fare (B)	Duration (hr)	Destination	Bus	Fare (B)	Duration (hr)
Bangkok				Mae Sai			
	air-con	511	12		ordinary	33	1½
	1st class	722	11		1st class	58	1½
	VIP	900	11		VIP	85	1½
Ban Huay Khrai				Mae Sot			
(for Doi Tung)					air-con	379	12
	ordinary	20	¾		1st class	488	12
Basang				Mae Suay			
	ordinary	20	¾		ordinary	27	1¼
Chiang Khong				Nan			
	ordinary	57	2½		air-con	176	6
Chiang Saen				Phayao			
	ordinary	32	1½		air-con	66	1½
Fang					1st class	85	1½
	ordinary	64	2½	Phitsanulok			
Khon Kaen					air-con	267	7
	air-con	462	12		VIP	344	7
	1st class	594	12	Phrae			
Khorat					air-con	160	4
	air-con	508	13		1st class	205	4
	1st class	653	12	Tak			
	VIP	767	12		air-con	312	8
Lampang					1st class	401	8
	ordinary	109	5½				
	air-con	153	5				

5367 3579), aka the 'White Wat'. Whereas most temples have centuries of history, this one's construction began in 1997 by noted Thai painter-turned-architect Chalermchai Kosit-pipat. The impressive and quiet temple stands out due to its pure white exterior, sparkling with clear-mirrored chips.

Walk over a bridge and sculpture of reaching arms (symbolising desire) to enter the sanctity of the wat, where inside you can watch Chalermchai Kositpipat's murals still being completed. Instead of the traditional Buddha life scenarios, the artist has added contemporary scenes representing *samsara* (the realm of rebirth and delusion). Check out the plane smashing into the Twin Towers or rockets going into space being held back by demonlike creatures.

Whether you agree with the overheard descriptions calling it, romantically 'a glittering ice castle', or less complimentarily, 'a frosted birthday cake on fire', it is definitely worth seeing this modern spin on the Thai wat.

A gallery sells reproductions of Chalermchai Kositpipat's rather New Age–looking works.

Pick up an entertaining free leaflet where the artist describes his aims and achievements in a simultaneously humble and self-aggrandising way. Londoners may recognise his style from the Wat Buddhapadipa in Wimbledon, where his students did the mural paintings.

To get to the temple, hop on one of the regular buses that run from Chiang Rai to Chiang Mai and ask to get off at Wat Rong Khun (15B).

MAE SALONG (SANTIKHIRI)

แม่สลอง(สันติคีรี)

pop 10,000

Aside from Bangkok's Amphoe Yaowarat, Mae Salong is Thailand's most Chinalike community. The atmosphere here is reminiscent of a small Chinese mountain village. The combination of pack horses, a mainly Yunnanese population, hill tribes (Akha, Lahu, Shan, Mien), red lanterns decorating shops, and southern Chinese-style houses conjure up images of a small town or village in southern China's Yunnan Province.

History

Mae Salong was originally settled by the 93rd Regiment of the Kuomintang (KMT), which fled to Myanmar from China after the 1949 Chinese revolution. After futile intermittent rearguard action against the Chinese communists, the renegades were forced to flee Myanmar in 1961 when the Yangon government decided it wouldn't allow the KMT to remain legally in northern Myanmar. Crossing into northern Thailand with their pony caravans, the ex-soldiers and their families settled into mountain villages and re-created a society like the one they left behind in Yunnan.

After the Thai government granted the KMT refugee status in the 1960s, efforts were made to incorporate the Yunnanese KMT and their families into the Thai nation. Until the late 1980s they didn't have much success. Many ex-KMT persisted in involving themselves in the Golden Triangle opium trade in a three-way partnership with opium warlord Khun Sa and the Shan United Army (SUA). Because of the rough, mountainous terrain and lack of sealed roads, the outside world was rather cut off from the goings-on in Mae Salong, so the Yunnanese were able to ignore attempts by the Thai authorities to suppress opium activity and tame the region.

Infamous Khun Sa made his home in nearby Ban Hin Taek (now Ban Thoet Thai; p365) until the early 1980s when he was finally routed by the Thai military. Khun Sa's retreat to Myanmar seemed to signal a change in local attitudes and the Thai government finally began making progress in its pacification of Mae Salong and the surrounding area.

In a further effort to separate the area from its old image as an opium fiefdom, the Thai government officially changed the name of the village from Mae Salong to Santikhiri (Hill of Peace). Until the 1980s packhorses were used to move goods up the mountain to Mae Salong, but today the 36km road from Basang (near Mae Chan) is paved and well travelled. The Yunnanese immigrants' equestrian history, alien to the Thais, has led the latter to refer to them as *jiin haw* (galloping Chinese).

In spite of the ongoing 'Thai-isation' of Mae Salong, the town is unlike any other in Thailand. It's not unusual for hotels and

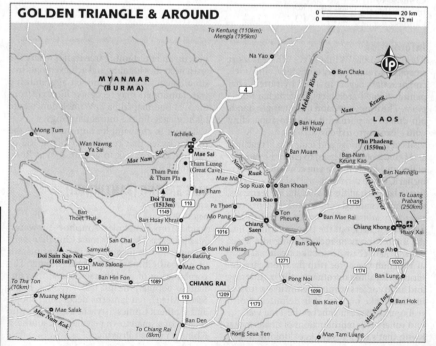

GOLDEN TRIANGLE & AROUND

restaurants in Mae Salong to boast satellite reception of three TV channels from China and three from Hong Kong. Although the Yunnanese dialect of Chinese remains the lingua franca, the new generation of young people look more to Bangkok than Taipei for its social and cultural inspirations. Many have left for greater educational and career opportunities.

In an attempt to quash opium activity, and the more recent threat of *yaa baa* (methamphetamine) trafficking, the government created crop-substitution programmes to encourage hill tribes to cultivate tea, coffee, corn and fruit trees. This seems to be successful as tea and corn are abundant in the surrounding fields, every other shop along the main street is a teashop, and there are tea factories in and around town. In both you can sample the fragrant Mae Salong teas (originally from Taiwan).

The local illicit corn whisky is much in demand – perhaps an all-too-obvious substitution for the poppy. Another local speciality is Chinese herbs, particularly *yaa dawng*, a kind that is mixed with liquor. Thai and Chinese tourists who come to Mae Salong frequently take back a bag or two of assorted Chinese herbs.

Information

There is an ATM at the Thai Military Bank opposite Khumnaiphol Resort.

The weather is always a bit cooler on the peak of Doi Mae Salong than on the plains below. During the cooler and dry months, November to February, nights can actually get cold – be sure to bring sweaters and socks for visits at this time of year.

Minivans full of Thai day-trippers begin arriving in Mae Salong around 10am and leave by 4pm. If you can stay overnight you'll pretty much have the place to yourself in the mornings and evenings.

Sights

An interesting **morning market** convenes from 5am to 7am (5am to 6am is the peak time) at the T-intersection near Shin Sane Guest House. The market attracts town residents and many tribespeople from the surrounding districts.

To get to **Wat Santakhiri** go past the mosque and up a steep hill that affords heady views along the way. The wat is of the Mahayana

tradition and Chinese in style. Go further to the top of the hill to meet the impressive **Princess Mother Pagoda**.

Past the Khumnaiphol Resort and further up the hill is a **viewpoint** with some teashops, and a KMT general's **tomb**. It is guarded by a soldier who will describe (in Thai or Yunnanese) the history of the KMT in the area.

Fifteen kilometres north of Mae Salong is the **Hilltribe Development & Welfare Centre**, which supports the local hill-tribe settlements by selling mainly Akha and Mien handicrafts, such as woven cloth and silverware.

Trekking

Shin Sane Guest House has a wall map showing approximate routes to Akha, Lisu, Mien, Lahu and Shan villages in the area. Nearby Akha and Lisu villages are less than half a day's walk away.

The best hikes are north of Mae Salong between Ban Thoet Thai and the Myanmar border. Ask about political conditions before heading off in this direction (towards Myanmar), however. Shan and Wa armies competing for control over this section of the Thailand–Myanmar border do occasionally clash in the area. A steady trade in methamphetamine and, to a lesser extent, heroin, flows across the border via several conduit villages.

Shin Sane Guest House (below) arranges four-hour **horseback treks** to four nearby villages for around 400B per day. It's possible to hire ponies as pack animals or horses for riding. You could also trek the 4km to an Akha village on your own. A basic guesthouse there offers rooms and two meals a day for 50B per person.

Akha Mae Salong Guest House (p364) also runs treks and can arrange half-day horseriding tours.

Sleeping

Since the road from Mae Salong to Tha Ton opened, fewer visitors are opting to stay overnight in Mae Salong. The resulting surplus of accommodation often makes prices negotiable, except at holidays when they tend to increase.

BUDGET

ourpick **Shin Sane Guest House** (Sin Sae; ☎ 0 5376 5026; 32/3 Th Mae Salong; s/d from 50/100B, bungalow 300B) Mae Salong's original hotel is a wood affair

with a bit of atmosphere. Trekking details are available, including a good trekking map. There is also a little eating area. The rooms are bare but spacious with shared bathrooms. The bungalows are much more comfortable, and have private bathrooms and cable TV. It is noisy in the morning when calls to prayer (from the mosque behind the guesthouse) start up.

Akha Mae Salong Guest House (☎ 0 5376 5103; Th Mae Salong; s/d/tr 50/100/150B) Next door to Shin Sane, this guesthouse occupies a rambling building and is run by a friendly, non-English-speaking Akha family. Shared bathroom rooms are clean and large. Horseback trekking and hiking can be arranged.

ourpick **Saeng A Roon Hotel** (☎ 0 5376 5029; Th Mae Salong; r 200-300B) Next to the teashop of the same name, this brand new hotel has friendly staff, spacious tiled-floor rooms and great views of the hills. The cheaper rooms share spick-and-span hot-water bathrooms.

Golden Dragon Inn (☎ 0 5376 5009; 13/1 Th Mae Salong; dm 50B, r 300-500B) The Golden Dragon has accommodation ranging from dorm beds in basic A-frame bungalows, newer more comfortable bungalows with private bathrooms and balconies, as well as large neat rooms in a concrete building. The more expensive rooms have cable TV. The owner has her own coffee plantation and coffee shop at the hotel. Sample the Arabica coffee in the manicured garden or go visit her plantation 2km away. It's worth a look.

MIDRANGE

ourpick **Mae Salong Villa** (☎ 0 5376 5114/9; maesalongvilla@thaimail.com; 5 Mu 1; r 800-1500B; ☐) Stunning views are the highlight of this collection of well-furnished bungalow-style rooms. Floor-to-ceiling windows and terraces make the most of the garden setting. The on-site Chinese restaurant has high-backed red chairs and lanterns, and the food is good. High-quality tea, grown on the proprietor's tea estate, is for sale.

Khumnaiphol Resort (☎ 0 5376 5001/3; fax 0 5376 5004; 58 Mu 1; r & bungalows 1200B) On the road to Tha Ton, 1km south of town near the afternoon market, this resort has bungalows perched on the hillside. The covered porches give great views of the tea plantations. Further back are some older, hotel-style rooms with mattresses that are distinctly Thai in 'softness' (or the lack thereof).

Eating

Pàa-thâwng-kŏh (Chinese doughnut) and hot soybean milk at the morning market are an inspiring way to start the day. Don't miss the many street noodle vendors who sell *khànŏm jiin náam ngíaw*, a delicious Yunnanese rice-noodle concoction topped with a spicy pork sauce – Mae Salong's most famous local dish and a gourmet bargain at 15B per bowl.

Around town you'll find a variety of places serving simple Chinese snacks such as fluffy *mantou* (plain steamed Chinese buns) and *saalaapao* (pork-stuffed Chinese buns) served with delicious pickled vegetables. Many of the Chinese in Mae Salong are Muslims so you'll find Muslim Chinese restaurants serving *khâo sawy* (egg noodles in a curried broth).

In town, several teahouses sell locally grown teas and offer complimentary tastings in very traditional, elaborate procedures, involving the pouring of tea from a tall, narrow cup into a round cup, said to enhance the tea's fragrance.

Mini Restaurant (Th Mae Salong 25-60B) Further south from Salema, Mini has western breakfasts, as well as Chinese and Thai dishes. There is an English language menu.

Salema Restaurant (Th Mae Salong; dishes 40-120B) Halfway between the Shin Sane Guest House and the day market, Salema serves tasty Yunnanese dishes using locally grown shiitake mushrooms at moderate prices.

Getting There & Away

Mae Salong is accessible via two routes. The original road, Rte 1130, winds west from Ban Basang. Newer Rte 1234 approaches from the south, allowing easier access from Chiang Mai. The older route is definitely more spectacular.

To get to Mae Salong by bus, take Mae Sai bus from Chiang Rai to Ban Basang (20B, 30 minutes, every 15 minutes between 6am and 4pm). From Ban Basang, sǎwngthǎew head up the mountain to Mae Salong (per person 60B, one hour). It's a little cheaper on the way down from Mae Salong – pick up a sǎwngthǎew from outside the 7-Eleven in town. Sǎwngthǎew stop running at around 5pm but you can charter one in either direction for about 400B.

You can also reach Mae Salong by road from Tha Ton (see p333).

BAN THOET THAI
บ้านเทิดไทย

Those with an interest in Khun Sa history (p362) can make a side trip to this Yunnanese-Shan village, 12km off the road between Ban Basang and Mae Salong.

Today, many of Ban Thoet Thai's 3000 residents – a mix of Shan, Yunnanese, Akha, Lisu and Hmong – claim to have fond memories of the man once hunted (but never captured) by heroin-consuming countries. The warlord's former camp headquarters, a simple collection of wood and brick buildings on a hillside overlooking the village, has been turned into a free rustic **museum**. There are no set opening hours, and admission is free so you simply have to turn up and ask one of the caretakers to open the exhibition room for you.

Inside, the walls are hung with maps of the Shan States and Mong Tai (the name the Shan use for the independent nation they hope to establish in the future) homelands, a photograph of the former Kengtung (East Shan State) palace and a few political posters. It's not much considering Khun Sa's six years (1976–82) in the area and, of course, there is no mention of opium.

A busy **morning market**, part of which was once used to store the Shan United Army arsenal, trades in products from Thailand, Myanmar and China. Khun Sa was also responsible for the construction of **Wat Phra That Ka Kham**, a Shan-style monastery near his former camp.

MAE SAI
แม่สาย
pop 25,800

Thailand's northernmost town, Mae Sai can be used as a starting point for exploring the Golden Triangle, Doi Tung and Mae Salong. It's also a good spot to observe border life, as Mae Sai is one of the few official overland crossings between Myanmar and Thailand. Don't come expecting loads of atmosphere; the town is little more than a modern trading post.

Foreigners are permitted to cross the border to Tachileik (the town opposite Mae Sai, spelt Thakhilek by the Thais), then continue to Kengtung, and as far as Mengla on the Thai/China border. It is now possible to travel from Mengla on to Daluo and Jinghong in China, if you have arranged the appropriate visas beforehand (see p371). Chiang Saen to China via boat is another, and relatively easier,

route (see p372). In spite of these opening, Thai tourists are much more commonly seen in Mae Sai than *faràng* (Westerners).

In February 2001 Burmese forces, apparently in pursuit of Shan State Army rebels, shelled and fired on parts of Mae Sai, invoking retaliatory shelling from the Thai army. During the fighting the whole of Mae Sai was evacuated and the border area was subsequently closed for a time. The crossing closed again between May and October 2002 following a political spat between the Thai and Myanmar governments. More recently, the border crossing was closed for a few days immediately after the September 2006 military coup. At the time of writing the border was open again, but it's always a good idea to check the current situation before travelling to Mae Sai.

Information

Immigration (☎ 0 5373 3261; ✹ 8am-5.30pm) At the entrance to the border bridge.

Internet Café (40B per hour) Behind the Wang Thong Hotel by its car park.

Monkey Island Guesthouse (☎ 0 5373 4060; www.mon keyisland.biz; 40/5 Th Sailomjoi) Has internet and free wi-fi if you have your own laptop.

Overbrook Clinic (☎ 0 5373 4422; 20/7 Th Phahonyothin; ✹ 9am-3pm) Connected to the modern hospital in Chiang Rai, this small clinic on the main road has doctors who can speak English.

Tourist police (☎ 115) They have a booth in front of the border crossing before immigration.

Sights & Activities

Take the steps up the hill near the border to **Wat Phra That Doi Wao**, west of the main street, for superb views over Mae Sai and Myanmar. This wat was reportedly constructed in memory of a couple of thousand Burmese soldiers who died fighting the KMT here in 1965 (you'll hear differing stories around town, including a version wherein the KMT are the heroes).

There are also some interesting **trails** in the cliffs and hills overlooking Mae Sai Guest House and the river. Monkey Island Guesthouse (p366) can give out maps detailing motorbike rides and walks to do in the area.

A persistent rumour says there's a gated cave tunnel that crosses to Myanmar beneath Mae Nam Sai; the entrance is supposedly hidden in the grounds of **Wat Tham Phah Jom**. If it's there it must be for locals only, and those staying at Mae Sai Guest House are treated to a constant parade of Burmese guys stripping

MAE SAI

INFORMATION
Immigration	1 B1
Internet Café	(see 14)
Overbrook Clinic	2 C1
Police Station	3 B2
Siam Commercial Bank (ATM)	4 C2
Thai Military Bank (ATM)	5 B1
Tourist Police	6 B1

SLEEPING
Chad House	7 C3
Mae Sai Guest House	8 A1
Mae Sai Riverside Resort	9 A1
Monkey Island Guesthouse	10 B1
Piyaporn Place Hotel	11 C2
S-House Hotel	12 B1
Top North Hotel	13 B1
Wang Thong Hotel	14 B1
Yee Sun Hotel	15 A1
Ying Ping Yunnan Guest House	16 C2

EATING
Food Stalls	17 C2
Khao Tom 25	18 C3
Kik Kok Restaurant	19 C2
Mae Sai Riverside Resort	(see 9)
Night Market	20 C2
Rattana Bakery	21 C2
Ying Ping Yunnan Restaurant	(see 16)

TRANSPORT
Chok-Roong Tawee Tour	22 C3
Pornchai	23 C3
Săwngthăew run to Chiang Saen & Sop Ruak	24 C2

off their *longyi* (sarongs) and wading up to their necks across the river.

If interested in **volunteering**, a company called **I to I International** (www.i-to-i.com) organises community projects around Mae Sai (and in other parts of Thailand), where volunteers teach and look after hill-tribe children. The minimum stay is four weeks and needs to be arranged before leaving your home country. The US$1895 fee includes Teaching English as a Foreign Language (EFL) training, orientation and insurance.

Sleeping
BUDGET
Chad House (☎ 0 5373 2054; Th Phahonyothin, off soi 11; dm/s/d 60/100/150B, bungalows 250B) In an awkward location in a residential neighbourhood, this guesthouse feels like a homestay. The English-speaking Thai-Shan owners are friendly and helpful and the food is good. Simple, clean rooms have shared hot-water shower facilities. There are a couple of bungalows with private cold-water bathrooms. Look for the sign on the left when coming into town.

our pick **Monkey Island Guesthouse** (☎ 0 5373 4060; www.monkeyisland.biz; 40/5 Th Sailomjoi; r with shared bathroom 100-200B, 4-person family room 400B; ▢) This guesthouse has become a gathering point for travellers. Partly because of the English guy who runs it and his in-depth knowledge of the Mae Sai area and Myanmar, but also because of the huge, cheap rooms, the bar/restaurant area with pool table, plus the large terrace

facing Myanmar. Maps are available, trips to Myanmar organised, and motorbikes and mountain bikes rented here.

Mae Sai Guest House (☎ 0 5373 2021; 688 Th Wiengpangkam; bungalows s 100-200B, d 300-500B) This collection of A-frame bungalows ranges from simple rooms with shared cold water showers, to bungalows on the river with terraces and private bathrooms. It is up a narrow, one lane stretch behind Mai Sai Riverside Resort. There is a riverside restaurant on site serving Thai and Western dishes.

Mae Sai Riverside Resort (☎ 0 5373 2630; Th Wiengpangkam; r 350B) Right at the end of Th Sailomjoi, this riverside hotel looks grand from the outside but is disappointing inside. The simple rooms with hot water shower bathrooms could do with a repaint. However, their restaurant overlooking the river serves tasty Thai dishes (see right).

Ying Ping Yunnan Guest House (☎ 0 5364 0507; Th Phahonyothin, Soi 6; r 350B) Above the Ying Ping Yunnan Chinese restaurant (right) are nine sparklingly clean, simple white rooms with pictures of Chinese goddesses on the walls. It's good value.

Top North Hotel (☎ 0 5373 1955; 306 Th Phahonyothin; d 400-600B, tr 900B; 🋑 🖳) A five-minute walk to the bridge to Myanmar, this older hotel has spacious rooms and friendly staff – and a very auspicious red theme going on. Some of the rooms look newer than others and have cable TV; choose the ones at the back of the building to avoid street noise.

S-House Hotel (☎ 0 5364 0670; s_house43234@yahoo .com; Mu 1, 384 Th Sailomjoi; r 500-600B; 🋑) At the end of the covered part of Th Sailomjoi, away from the border crossing, this hotel has spacious rooms with balconies overlooking the hills.

our pick **Yee Sun Hotel** (☎ 0 5373 3455; 816/13 Th Sailomjoi; r 600B; 🋑) This new, 11-room Chinese-run hotel has great value if rather characterless rooms. Find four-star level furnishings with bath, shower and a view of the river.

TOP END

Piyaporn Place Hotel (☎ 0 5373 4511-3; www.piya pornplacehotel; Th Phahonyothin; r/ste 1000/1800B; 🋑) On the main road by Soi 7, this seven-storey hotel is the best place in town and good value. The large, contemporary-styled rooms have wooden floors, a small sofa, and the usual four/five-star amenities like bath, cable TV and minibar. There is a conference room and

a smart, stylish restaurant serving Thai and European food.

Wang Thong Hotel (☎ 0 5373 3389-95; wangthong -hotel@hotmail.com; 299 Th Phahonyothin; r 1200-2500B, ste 4500B; 🋑 🖳) The nine-storey Wang Thong is a comfortable choice and great for its convenient location by the border crossing. The rooms are nothing special but they're spacious and come with amenities you'd expect at this price. In addition to the pool there is a pub, disco and a popular restaurant. Off-street parking is guarded. Discounts are available in low season.

Eating

Many **food stalls** offering everything from *khâo sawy* to custard set up at night on the footpaths along Th Phahonyothin. The **night market** is rather small but the Chinese vendors do good *kŭaytĭaw phàt sii-íu* (rice noodles stir-fried in soy sauce) and other noodle dishes. You can also get fresh *pàa-thâwng-kŏh* and hot soy milk.

Rattana Bakery (☎ 0 5373 1230; 18 Th Phahonyothin; dishes 10-35B; ☯ 8am-5pm) Head here for baked snacks, but don't expect a full meal.

Khao Tom 25 (Th Phahonyothin; dishes 20-45B; ☯ noon-4am) Near Chad House, this is your best bet for late-night eats.

Kik Kok Restaurant (Th Phahonyothin; dishes 25-60B; ☯ 6am-8pm) This simple place serves a good selection of Thai dishes; its rice noodles are particularly good.

Mae Sai Riverside Resort (☎ 0 5373 2630; Th Wiengpangkam; dishes 40-139B) Recommended for its Thai dishes, like the tasty lemongrass fried fish, this restaurant has a great location looking out over the river to Myanmar.

Ying Ping Yunnan Restaurant (☎ 0 5364 0507; Th Phahonyothin, Soi 6; dishes 100-300B) This smart, bustling and authentic Chinese restaurant serves dishes like 'eight hero salad' with prawns, octopus and shiitake mushrooms, as well as Yunnan-style fried duck. Its slow-cooked pork leg in garlic is the house speciality.

Shopping

Burmese lacquerware, gems, jade and other goods from Laos and Myanmar are sold in shops along the main street. Many Burmese come over during the day from Tachileik to work or do business, hurrying back by sunset. Gem dealers from as far away as Chanthaburi frequent the gem market that is opposite the police station.

Getting There & Away

Mae Sai's government **bus station** (☎ 0 5364 437) is 4km south of the frontier immigration office, or an 8B shared săwngthăew ride from the city centre. Buses to Mae Sai leave frequently from Chiang Rai (ordinary/air-con 33B/55B, 1½ hours).

To/from Chiang Mai there are ordinary (126B, at 8.15am and 2pm), 1st class air-con (227B, at 7am, 10.45am and 1.45pm), and VIP (350B, at 9.15am and 3.15pm) buses daily; this trip takes four to five hours.

There is a 2nd-class air-con bus (402B, 6.15am) and a 1st-class air-con bus (516B, 7am) that goes to Mae Sot daily. Six departures go to Nakhon Ratchasima (2nd class air-con 507B, 1st class air-con 652B, VIP 760B, 15 hours) daily.

There is also a direct bus from Mae Sai to Fang (61B, two hours, 7am) and one to Tha Ton (51B, 1½ hours, 7am). Hop on any of the buses to Chiang Rai for Mae Chan (27B, 30 minutes).

For Doi Tung take a bus to Ban Huay Khrai (15B), then a săwngthăew to Doi Tung (60B, one hour).

On the main Th Phahonyothin road, by Soi 8 is a sign saying 'bus stop'. From here blue săwngthăew run to Chiang Saen (40B) and Sop Ruak (40B) every 40 minutes, between 9am and 2pm daily.

BANGKOK

Second-class air-conditioned buses run to Bangkok (483B, 13 hours, depart 5.20pm and 5.45pm). VIP buses (965B, depart 7am, 5pm and 5.45pm) and 1st-class air-con buses (621B, depart 4.30pm, 5pm and 5.45pm) are also available.

Chok-Roong Tawee Tour (☎ 0 5364 0123) With the same prices as the bus station you can buy tickets in advance here. There is no sign in English so look for the large red 'International Telephone' sign.

Getting Around

Săwngthăew around town are 5B shared. Motorcycle taxis cost 20B to 30B. Honda Dreams can be rented between Chok-Roong Tawee Tour and the Shell petrol station at **Pornchai** (☎ 0 5373 1136; 4/7 Th Phahonyothin) for 150B a day. **Monkey Island Guesthouse** (☎ 0 5373 4060; www .monkeyisland.biz; 40/5 Th Sailomjoi) also rents out motorbikes from 200B a day and mountain bikes from 50B a day.

AROUND MAE SAI
Tham Luang
ถ้ำหลวง

About 6km south of Mae Sai off Rte 110, this large cave extends into the hills for at least a couple of kilometres, possibly more. The first cavern is huge, and a narrow passage at the back leads to a series of other chambers and side tunnels of varying sizes. The first kilometre is fairly easy-going, but after that you have to do some climbing over piles of rocks to get further in. At this point the roof formations become more fantastic and tiny crystals make them change colour according to the angle of the light. For 40B you can borrow a gas lantern from the caretakers in front of the cave or you can take someone along as a guide (for which there's no fixed fee; just give them whatever you feel they deserve). Apparently, guides sometimes have better things to do during the week. Charter a săwngthăew or rent a bike in Mae Sai to get to Tham Luang.

Tham Pum & Tham Pla
ถ้ำปุ่ม/ถ้ำปลา

Only 13km south of Mae Sai, just off Rte 110 at Ban Tham, these two caves have freshwater lakes inside. Bring a torch to explore the caves, as there are no lights. Another attraction here is the unique cakelike *chedi* in front of the cave entrance. It's a very large, multi-tiered structure stylistically different from any other in Thailand.

There is a police checkpoint at Ban Tham so bring some ID. To get here either rent a motorbike or charter a săwngthăew to the turn-off on Rte 110 at Ban Tham; from there it is a 1km walk down to the caves.

Doi Tung
ดอยตุง

About halfway between Mae Chan and Mae Sai on Rte 110 is the west turn-off for **Doi Tung**. The name means 'Flag Peak', from the northern Thai word for flag *(tung)*. King Achutarat of Chiang Saen ordered a giant flag to be flown from the peak to mark the spot where two *chedi* were constructed in AD 911; the *chedi* are still there, a pilgrimage site for Thai, Shan and Chinese Buddhists.

But the main attraction at Doi Tung is getting there. The 'easy' way is via Rte 1149, which is mostly paved to the peak of Doi Tung. But it's winding, steep and narrow,

so if you're driving or riding a motorcycle, take it slowly.

Along the way are Shan, Akha and Musoe (Lahu) villages. It is not safe to trek in this area without a Thai or hill-tribe guide, simply because you could be mistaken for a United States Drug Enforcement Agency agent (by the drug traders) or drug dealer (by the Thai army rangers who patrol the area). However, under the royal project development, this area has got safer.

On the theory that local hill tribes would be so honoured by a royal presence that they will stop cultivating opium, the late Princess Mother (the king's mother) built the **Doi Tung Royal Villa** (☎ 0 5376 7011; www.doitung.org; admission 70B; ☯ 6.30am-5pm), a summer palace on the slopes of Doi Tung near Pa Kluay Reservoir, which is now open to the public as a museum. The royal initiative also educated on new agricultural methods to stop slash and burn practices. Opium has now been replaced by crops such as, coffee, teak and various fruits. The rest of the property, including the **Mae Fah Luang Garden** and **Mae Fah Luang Arboretum** (admission 80B; ☯ 7am-5pm), is also open to the public. There is also a top-end hotel (see right), a classy restaurant, coffee kiosk and a Doi Tung craft shop up here. This place is popular with bus tour groups.

Another nearby royal project, **Doi Tung Zoo** (admission free; ☯ 8am-6pm) covers an open space of over 32 hectares. The zoo was first established as a wildlife breeding and animal conservation station, to help reintroduce many species to a reforested Doi Tung. These include Siamese fireback pheasants, peacocks, bears, sambar deer, barking deer and hog deer.

At the peak, 1800m above sea level, **Wat Phra That Doi Tung** is built around the twin Lanna-style *chedi*. The *chedi* were renovated by famous Chiang Mai monk Khruba Siwichai early in the 20th century.

Pilgrims bang on the usual row of temple bells to gain merit. Although the wat isn't that impressive, the high forested setting will make the trip worthwhile. From the walled edge of the temple you can get an aerial view of the snaky road you've just climbed.

A walking path next to the wat leads to a spring and there are other short walking trails in the vicinity.

A bit below the peak is the smaller **Wat Noi Doi Tung**, where food and beverages are available from vendors.

SLEEPING & EATING

If you want to spend the night, **Doi Tung Lodge** (☎ 0 5376 7003; www.doitung.org; Doi Tung Development Project, Mae Fah Luang District; r incl full breakfast per person per 1/2/3 nights 2600/3850/5050B; ☒) is an elegant mountain lodge with 47 deluxe rooms. A semi-outdoor **restaurant** (☯ 7am-9pm; dishes 80-250B) offers excellent meals made with local produce, including lots of fresh mushrooms.

GETTING THERE & AWAY

Buses to the turn-off for Doi Tung are 15B from either Mae Chan or Mae Sai. From Ban Huay Khrai, at the turn-off, săwngthăew run to Ban Pakha (30B, 30 minutes), or all the way to Doi Tung (60B, one hour).

Road conditions to Doi Tung vary from year to year depending on the state of repair; during the bad spells, the section above Baa Pakha can be quite a challenge to negotiate, whether you're in a truck, 4WD or riding a motorcycle.

You can also travel by motorcycle between Doi Tung and Mae Sai along an even more challenging, 16km, unevenly sealed road. It starts in the Akha village of Ban Phame, 8km south of Mae Sai (4km south along Rte 110, then 4km west) and joins the main road about two-thirds of the way up Doi Tung – about 11km from the latter. You can also pick up this road by following the dirt road that starts in front of Mae Sai's Wat Phra That Doi Wao. West of Ban Phame the road has lots of tight curves, mud, rocks, precipitous drops, passing trucks and occasional road-repair equipment – figure on at least an hour by motorcycle or 4WD from Mae Sai.

Although now paved, this is a route for experienced bikers only. The road also runs high in the mountains along the Myanmar border and should not be travelled alone or after 4pm. Ask first in Mae Sai about border conditions. If you want to do a full loop from Mae Sai, ride/drive via Rte 110 south of Mae Sai, then Rte 1149 up to Doi Tung. Once you've had a look around the summit, return to Mae Sai via the Ban Bang Phame aforementioned roads; this means you'll be travelling downhill much of the way.

Cross-Border Trips to Tachileik & Beyond

Foreigners are ordinarily permitted to cross the bridge over Nam Ruak into Tachileik. On occasion the border may close temporarily

for security reasons, so be prepared for possible disappointment if the political situation between Thailand and Myanmar deteriorates again.

Head to the immigration office just before the bridge on the Thai side and state how far you will be going in Myanmar – Tachileik, Kengtung or Mengla. Cross the bridge and enter the Myanmar immigration office, where for a payment of US$10 or 500B you can enter Myanmar at Tachileik, and travel onto Kengtung or Mengla for a period of 14 days. Whether staying for a few hours or 14 days the fee is the same. At this immigration office your picture is taken for your temporary ID card that has your final destination marked on it. If going further afield than Tachileik, this ID card is stamped at every checkpoint along the route. On your return to Thailand, the Thai immigration office at the bridge will give you a new 30-day tourist visa (see p753).

There is little to do in **Tachileik** apart from shop – the prices are about the same as on the Thai side and everyone accepts baht. Around 4000 people cross the bridge to this market town daily; most of these are Thais shopping for dried mushrooms, herbal medicines, swords and daggers, antlers, X-rated DVDs, and other cheap and bootlegged imports from China that could get you loads of attention back home from customs. Shan handicrafts, fake designer bags, gems, CDs and DVDs are some of the other things on offer in this market. Be wary of cheap cartons of Marlboros and other Western-brand cigarettes, as many are filled with Burmese cigarettes instead of the real thing. Also, Thai police have been known to fine travellers in possession of these cigarettes.

If travelling on, money can be changed into Burmese *kyat* for Kengtung and Chinese *yuan* for Mengla at Tachileik. Ask at the **Tourist Office** next to immigration. This same office also gives out free rough maps of Kentung and Mengla.

KENGTUNG

Kengtung (called Chiang Tung by the Thais and usually spelt Kyinetong by the Burmese), 163km north, is a sleepy but historic capital for the Shan State's Khün culture. The Khün speak a northern Thai language related to Shan and Thai Lü, and use a writing script similar to the ancient Lanna script. It's a bit over halfway between the Thai and Chinese

borders. Built around a small lake and dotted with ageing **Buddhist temples** and crumbling British **colonial architecture**, it's a much more scenic town than Tachileik and one of the most interesting towns in Myanmar's entire Shan State. About 70% of all foreign visitors are Thais seeking a glimpse of ancient Lanna. Few Westerners are seen in town save for contract employees working for the UN Drug Control Project (UNDCP).

Five-day, four-night excursions to the town of Kengtung and/or Mengla can be arranged through Monkey Island Guesthouse (p366) on the Thai side. To get to Kengtung independently see opposite.

Harry's Guest House & Trekking (☎ 0 1012 1418; 132 Mai Yang Lan; r per person US$5-10) rents basic rooms in a large house. Harry is an English-speaking Kengtung native who spent many years as a trekking guide in Chiang Mai. The downside is that it is about 2km out of town. **Sam Yawt** (r US$5-10), on the east side of the market and by the lake, is the cheaper, centrally located choice, while **Princess Hotel** (☎ 9 5842 1319; kentung@mail4u.com; 21 Th Zaydankalay; r US$20-30), in a convenient location by the morning market and restaurants, is the relatively up-market option in Kentung.

In order to proceed on to Mengla from Kengtung, you must first register at the Kengtung immigration office. The staff at Harry's Guest House can help you accomplish this or you can stay at the other guesthouses recommended, which are closer to the immigration office.

MENGLA

Eighty-five kilometres north of Kengtung is the Sino-Burmese border district of Mengla (or Mong La as it is sometimes spelt). Although Mengla is mainly a Thai Lü district, in a deal worked out with the Myanmar military it's currently controlled by ethnic Wa, who once fought against Yangon troops but now enjoy peaceful relations with Yangon (it's suspected this is in return for a sizeable share in the Wa's thriving amphetamine and opium trade).

A **Drug Free Museum** contains an exhibit on how to refine heroin from opium. It is worth going up to the hilltop **Wat Jon Kam** for heady views across the border to China.

The district receives lots of Chinese tourists who come to gamble in the district's several casinos. There are also plenty of karaoke bars,

discos and other staples of modern Chinese entertainment life. Mengla's well-known wildlife market, which sells animals such as reptiles and bears, is best avoided.

For a complete description of Kengtung and Mengla, see Lonely Planet's *Myanmar (Burma)* guidebook.

MENGLA TO CHINA?

The obvious question is, can you cross the border from Mengla into Daluo or further afield in China? The answer is now yes, if you have Burmese and Chinese visas arranged in advance, and go through one company. Based in Mengla, **Lyaung Daw Mu Garden** (☎ 186 691 55 69331; shwelinstar@vip.sina.com; Mengla) picks clients up from the border and arranges tours and hotels in China, as far as Jinghong. Email Shwe Lin Star, who speaks English, for more information.

Getting There & Away

Once through immigration at Tachileik, go to the **tourist office** (next to immigration) to organise a seat on a bus or in a taxi for the 163km stretch to Kentung. The 45-seat buses

go at 9am and 1pm, take around four hours and cost 350B per person. The four-seater taxis go between 9am and 6pm, take around three hours and cost 450B per person. Make sure the price includes fuel, and photocopies of your itinerary that the driver shows at checkpoints along the way. The price is the same from Kentung to Mengla. Toll fees from Tachileik to Kengtung are approximately 120B (one way). There is a toll when entering Mengla province – 36 yuan per person and 42 yuan for a small passenger vehicle. The road trip allows glimpses of Shan, Akha, Wa and Lahu villages along the way.

Alternatively, you can organise a tour through Monkey Island Guesthouse in Mae Sai (see p366). According to the tourist office in Tachileik, it is not possible to organise tours from the Myanmar side at this point.

CHIANG SAEN

เชียงแสน

pop 55,000

A sleepy crossroads town on the banks of the Mekong River, Chiang Saen was once the site of an important northern Thai kingdom.

CHIANG SAEN

INFORMATION	
Chiang Saen Hospital	1 A2
Immigration Office	2 C2
Main Immigration Office	3 B2
Police	4 B2
Siam Commercial Bank (ATM)	5 B2
Visitors Centre	6 B2

SIGHTS & ACTIVITIES	
Chiang Saen National Museum	7 B2
Wat Chedi Luang	8 B2
Wat Chom Chang	9 A1
Wat Pa Sak	10 A2
Wat Phakhaopan	11 B2
Wat Phra That Chom Kitti	12 A1

SLEEPING 🛏	
Chiang Saen Guest House	13 C2
Chiang Saen River Hill Hotel	14 B3
Gin's Guest House	15 C1

EATING 🍴	
Evening Food Vendors	16 C2
Food Stalls	17 B3
Food Stalls	18 B2

DRINKING 🍸	
2 be 1	19 B2

TRANSPORT	
Boats to Sop Ruak & Chiang Khong	20 C3
Bus Terminal	21 B2
Săwngthăew to Sop Ruak, Mae Sai & Chiang Khong	22 B2
Xishuangbanna Tianda Tourism and Shipping	23 C3

NORTHERN THAILAND

Scattered throughout the town today are the ruins of the 14th-century Chiang Saen kingdom – surviving architecture includes several *chedi*, Buddha images, *wíhǎan* pillars and earthen city ramparts. A few of the old monuments still standing predate Chiang Saen by a couple of hundred years; legend says this pre-Chiang Saen kingdom was called Yonok. Formerly loosely affiliated with various northern Thai kingdoms, as well as 18th-century Myanmar, Chiang Saen didn't really become a Siamese possession until the 1880s.

Yunnanese trade routes extended from Simao, Yunnan, through Laos to Chiang Saen and then on to Mawlamyine in Burma, via Chiang Rai, Chiang Mai and Mae Sariang. A less-used route proceeded through Utaradit, Phayao and Phrae.

Nowadays huge river barges from China moor at Chiang Saen, carrying fruit, engine parts and all manner of other imports, keeping the old China–Siam trade route open. Despite this trade, and despite commercialisation of the nearby Golden Triangle, the town hasn't changed too much over the last decade.

Chiang Saen is an official border crossing for Thai and Lao citizens travelling by ferry to and from the Lao People's Democratic Republic town of Ton Pheung on the opposite side of the river.

Information

Chiang Saen's immigration office has two branches: the main office on the southwest corner of the town's main intersection, and a smaller one next to the Mekong River pier (for crossings to Ton Pheung).

Chiang Saen Hospital (☎ 0 5377 7017-035) This government hospital is just south of Wat Pa Sak. Staff speak little English. The best hospital nearby is in Chiang Rai (see p352).

Siam Commercial Bank (Th Phahonyothin) On the main street leading from the highway to the Mekong River. Has an ATM and currency exchange.

Visitors Centre (Th Phahonyothin; ⏰ 8.30am-4.30pm Mon-Sat) Has a good relief display showing the major ruin sites as well as photos of various *chedi* before, during and after restoration.

Sights & Activities

Near the town entrance, the small **Chiang Saen National Museum** (☎ 0 5377 7102; 702 Th Phahonyothin; admission 30B; ⏰ 8.30am-4.30pm Wed-Sun) displays artefacts from the Lanna period and prehistoric stone tools from the area, as well as hill-tribe crafts, dress and musical instruments.

Behind the museum to the east are the ruins of **Wat Chedi Luang**, which feature an 18m octagonal *chedi* in the classic Chiang Saen or Lanna style. Archaeologists argue about its exact construction date but agree it dates to some time between the 12th and 14th centuries.

About 200m from the Pratu Chiang Saen (the historic main gateway to the town's western flank) are the remains of **Wat Pa Sak**, where the ruins of seven monuments are visible in a **historical park** (admission 20B). The main mid-14th-century *chedi* combines elements of the Hariphunchai and Sukhothai styles with a possible Bagan influence.

The remains of **Wat Phra That Chom Kitti** and **Wat Chom Chang** can be found about 2.5km north of Wat Pa Sak on a hilltop. The round *chedi* of Wat Phra That Chom Kitti is thought to have been constructed before the founding of the kingdom. The smaller *chedi* below it belonged to Wat Chom Chang. There is nothing much to see at these *chedi*, but there is a good view of Chiang Saen and the river.

Inside the grounds of **Wat Phakhaopan**, a living wat near the river, stands a magnificent Lanna-period *chedi*. The large, square base contains Lanna-style walking Buddhas in niches on all four sides. The Buddha facing east is sculpted in the *mudra* ('calling for rain') pose, with both hands held pointing down at the image's sides – a pose common in Laos but not so common in Thailand.

MEKONG RIVER TRIPS

Boats from China, Laos and Myanmar can be seen unloading their cargoes in the mornings at a boat landing near the customs station stand on the Chiang Saen waterfront.

Six-passenger speedboats jet to Sop Ruak (per boat one way/return 500/600B, 35 minutes), or all the way to Chiang Khong (per boat one-way only 2000B, 1½ hours). Eight-passenger slower boats go to Sop Ruak (per boat one way/return 600/700B, 50 minutes) or Chiang Khong (per boat one way/return 3000/3500B, two hours).

Although it was once possible to travel by cargo ship from Chiang Sean to Jinghong in China, now it's only permitted via passenger boat through **Xishuangbanna Tianda Tourism and Shipping** (☎ 0 5365 1136; 08 9637 1178; one way/return

4000/7000B; ⊙ 8am-5pm daily). The office is located on the main road opposite the Chiang Saen port (1km south of the ferry pier). The 50-seater speedboat goes through Myanmar and Laos but passengers stay on board. To do this trip you must already have your visa for China (quicker to arrange from Chiang Mai or Bangkok). The people at Chiang Saen Guest House (below) can book you a ticket and help you get a visa for China. It takes at least four work days to get the visa.

The trip from Chiang Saen to Jinghong takes 15 hours when conditions are good. During drier months the going is slower, as rocks and shallows can hamper the way. When this is the case a night's stay in Guanlei is included. Boats depart from Chiang Saen on Monday, Wednesday and Saturday at 5am.

Sleeping

Chiang Saen Guest House (☎ 0 5365 0196; s/d 200/250B, bungalows 250B) In a handy location opposite the river and night stalls, this long-running place has basic but good-value rooms and A-frame bungalows. It can get noisy in the evening so choose rooms at the back. Boat tickets to China and visa can be arranged here (see opposite).

Gin's Guest House (☎ 0 5365 0847/1023; 71 Mu 8; r 250-700B) On the northern side of town (about 2km north of the bus terminal), this place has a variety of possibilities (all with attached bathroom) and a variety of prices. Rooms are simple, with those more expensive having more charm. The upstairs veranda is a good place from which to watch the Mekong flow by. Mountain bike and motorcycle rentals are available, as are a variety of tours.

Chiang Saen River Hill Hotel (☎ 0 5365 0826; 714 Mu 3 Tambon Wiang; r incl breakfast 1200B) This clean, four-storey hotel features good service and some nice northern-Thai furnishing touches. All the rooms have a fridge and TV along with a floor sitting area furnished with Thai axe cushions, a Thai umbrella and a small rattan table.

Eating & Drinking

Cheap noodle and rice dishes are available at food stalls in and near the market on the river road and along the main road through town from the highway, near the bus stop. Evening food vendors set up at the latter location and stay open till around midnight.

our pick Evening food vendors (dishes 30-60B; ⊙ 4-11pm) During the dry months these vendors sell sticky rice, green papaya salad, grilled chicken, dried squid and other fun foods for people to eat while sitting on grass mats along the river bank in front of Chiang Saen Guest House – a very pleasant way to spend an evening. Local specialities include fish or chicken barbecued inside thick joints of bamboo, eaten with sticky rice and *sôm-tam* (green papaya salad).

2 be 1 (⊙ 4pm-1am) By the river, this funky bar with inside and outside seating, has colourful lamps and plays house music.

Song Fang Khong (dishes 35-100B; ⊙ 11am-11pm) and **Rim Khong** (dishes 35-100B; ⊙ 11am-11pm) are two *sŭan aahăan* (food garden-style) riverside restaurants in Sop Ruak, off the river road from Chiang Saen. Both offer extensive menus of Thai, Chinese and Isan food. Bring your Thai-language skills.

Getting There & Away

There are frequent buses between Chiang Rai and Chiang Saen (32B, 1½ hours).

Be sure to ask for the *săi mài* (new route) via Chiang Rai from Chiang Mai (ordinary/air-con 126/227B, five hours). The ordinary bus leaves at 7.15am and the air-con bus leaves at 8.30am daily. The *săi kào* (old route) meanders through Lamphun, Lampang, Ngao, Phayao and Phan; a trip that takes between seven and nine hours. Alternatively, you can take a bus first to Chiang Rai then change to a Chiang Saen bus (about 4½ hours).

Opposite the bus terminal are blue săwngthăew that travel to Sop Ruak (20B), Mae Sai (40B) and Chiang Khong (60B).

If you're driving from Mae Sai to Chiang Saen there's a choice of two scenic paved roads (one from the centre of Mae Sai and one near the town entrance), or a wider, busier paved road via Rte 110 to Mae Chan and then Rte 1016 to Chiang Saen.

The roads out of Mae Sai are considerably more direct but there are several forks where you have to make educated guesses on which way to go (signs are occasional). The two roads join not far from the Golden Triangle village of Mae Ma, where you have a choice of going east through Sop Ruak or south through Pa Thon. The eastern route is more scenic.

LAOS

Although boats do travel from here to Laos, the closest crossing open to foreigners is in Chiang Khong (see p379).

Getting Around

Motorbike taxis and sǎamláw do short trips around town for 20B. They gather opposite the bus terminal.

A good way to see the Chiang Saen–Mae Sai area is on two wheels. Mountain bikes (per day 50B) and motorcycles (per day 200B) can be rented at **Gin's Guest House** (☎ 0 5365 0847/1023; 71 Mu 8). If you are heading southwards to Chiang Khong, Rte 1129 along the river is the road to take.

AROUND CHIANG SAEN
Sop Ruak
สบรวก

The borders of Myanmar, Thailand and Laos meet 9km north of Chiang Saen at Sop Ruak, the official 'centre' of the Golden Triangle, at the confluence of Nam Ruak and the Mekong River.

In historical terms, 'Golden Triangle' actually refers to a much larger geographic area, stretching thousands of square kilometres into Myanmar, Laos and Thailand, within which the opium trade is prevalent. Nevertheless hoteliers and tour operators have been quick to cash in on the name by referring to the tiny village of Sop Ruak as 'the Golden Triangle', conjuring up images of illicit adventure even though the adventure quotient here is close to zero. In northern Thai this village is pronounced 'Sop Huak'; many out-of-town Thais don't know either Thai name and simply call it 'Sam Liam Thong Kham' (sǎam lìam thawng kham; Thai for 'Golden Triangle').

Tourists have replaced opium as the local source of wealth. Sop Ruak has in fact become something of a tourist trap, with souvenir stalls, restaurants, a massage place and bus loads of package-tour visitors during the day. In the evenings things are quieter.

There is a Commercial Bank of Siam ATM machine next to the House of Opium.

SIGHTS & ACTIVITIES

The **House of Opium** (☎ 0 5378 4060; www.houseof opium.com; admission 50B; ❤ 7am-8pm), a small museum with historical displays pertaining to opium culture, is worth a peek. Exhibits include all the various implements used in the planting, harvest, use and trade of the *Papaver somniferum* resin, including pipes, weights, scales and so on, plus photos and maps with labels in English. The museum is at Km 30, at the southeastern end of Sop Ruak.

Next to the House of Opium are some steps up to **Wat Phra That Phu Khao**. From here is the best viewpoint to see the Mekong meeting of Laos, Myanmar and Thailand.

On the Burmese side of the river junction stands the **Paradise Resort's Golden Triangle** (☎ 053 652 111; r 2500B), a huge hotel and casino financed by Thai and Japanese business partners who have leased nearly 480 hectares from the Myanmar government. Only two currencies – baht and dollars – are accepted at the hotel and casino.

Ten kilometres north of Chiang Saen on a plot of about 40 hectares opposite the Anantara Resort & Spa, the Mah Fah Luang Foundation has established the 5600-sq-metre **Hall of Opium** (☎ 0 5378 4444; www.goldentrianglepark .com; Mu 1 Baan Sobruak; admission 300B; ❤ 10am-3.30pm). The goal of this impressive facility is to become the world's leading exhibit and research facility for the study of opiate use around the world. This multimedia exhibition includes a fascinating history of opium, and examines the effects of abuse on individuals and society. Well balanced and worth seeing.

For **Mekong River Cruises** (40min cruise max 5 people per boat 400B; Chiang Saen/Chiang Khong per boat 400/1700B, 40min/1½hrs), local long-tail boat trips can be arranged through several local agents. The typical trip involves a circuit around a large island and upriver for a view of the Burmese casino hotel. Longer trips head downriver as far as Chiang Khong. There's a fee of 500B to go onto the casino island for the day (they'll stamp you in and out at the same time).

On longer trips you can stop off at a Lao village on the large river island of **Don Sao**, roughly halfway between Sop Ruak and Chiang Saen. The Lao immigration booth here is happy to allow day visitors onto the island without a Lao visa. A 20B arrival tax is collected from each visitor. There's not a lot to see, but there's an official post office where you can mail letters or postcards with a Laos PDR postmark, a few shops selling T-shirts and Lao handicrafts, and the Sala Beer Lao, where you can quaff Lao beer and munch on Lao snacks.

SLEEPING & EATING

Most budget travellers now stay in Chiang Saen. Virtually all the former budget places in Sop Ruak have given way to souvenir stalls and larger tourist hotels.

NORTHERN THAILAND

CHIANG RAI PROVINCE •• Chiang Khong **375**

Greater Mekong Lodge (☎ 0 5378 4450; www.mae fahluang.org; s/d 1600/1800B; ✗ ✗) This hotel is part of the Doi Tung Hall of Opium project. There are well-equipped rooms with cable TV in the cavernous, stark main building. Its spacious, modern bungalows are the better choice and are perched on the slope of a hill overlooking the museum. Views are 1st class and so is the buffet lunch (130B).

Imperial Golden Triangle Resort (☎ 0 5378 4001/5; www.imperialhotels.com; 222 Ban Sop Ruak; r from 3500B; ✗ 🖳 🍽) Another 1st-class option, this is closer to the cluster of tourist services. Most rooms have impressive river views.

There are several tourist-oriented restaurants overlooking the Mekong River in Sop Ruak.

ourpick Anantara Golden Triangle Resort & Spa (☎ 0 5378 4084; www.anantara.com; r/ste from 9164/12,219B; 🖳 🍽) Anantara sits on a secluded hillside off the road between Sop Ruak and Mae Sai, directly opposite the Hall of Opium (opposite). The 90-room complex combines classic northern-Thai design motifs with recycled teak floors and stylish modern touches such as Jim Thompson fabrics and cathedral ceilings. A Jacuzzi, squash and tennis courts, gym, sauna, library, medical clinic and spa round out the luxury amenities. Special attractions include the King's Cup Elephant Polo Tournament and one- to three-day mahout-training packages. Rates include two tickets to the Hall of Opium.

GETTING THERE & AWAY
From Chiang Saen to Sop Ruak a săwngthăew or share taxi costs 20B; these leave every 20 minutes or so throughout the day. It's an easy bicycle ride from Chiang Saen to Sop Ruak.

CHIANG KHONG
เชียงของ
pop 9000
At one time Chiang Khong was part of a small river-bank *meuang* (city-state) called Juon, founded in AD 701 by King Mahathai. Over the centuries Juon paid tribute to Chiang Rai, then Chiang Saen and finally Nan before being occupied by the Siamese in the 1880s. The territory of Chiang Khong extended all the way to Yunnan Province in China until the French turned much of the Mekong River's northern bank into French Indochina in 1893.

More remote yet more lively than Chiang Saen, Chiang Khong is an important market town for local hill tribes and for trade with northern Laos. Nearby are several villages inhabited by Mien and White Hmong. Among the latter are contingents who fled Laos during the 1975 communist takeover and who are rumoured to be involved in an organised resistance movement against the current Lao government.

Huay Xai, opposite Chiang Khong on the Lao side of the river, is a legal point of entry for Laos. Anyone with a valid visa for Laos may cross by ferry. From Huay Xai it's 250km to Luang Nam Tha, a short distance from Boten, a legal border crossing to and from China – see p379 for more information.

Trade between Thailand and China via Chiang Khong is steady. Thai goods going north include dried and processed food and beverages, cosmetics, machinery, spare parts and agro-industrial supplies.

Information
Si Ayuthaya, Kasikornbank and Siam Commercial Bank have branches in town with ATMs and foreign-exchange services.

Easy Trip (☎ 0 5365 5174, 08 9922 2030; www.disco verylaos.com; Th Sai Klang) On the main street opposite Easy Bar and Restaurant, this very professional travel agency organises boats and buses to Laos (see p379), as well as minibuses to Chiang Mai (220B) and Pai (400B). Flights in Thailand and to Laos can be booked here. Many guesthouses in Chiang Khong offer similar services, including SP Guest House (p376).

Net.com (per hr 40B; ✆ 10am-11pm) Next door to Easy Trip, which also has internet services.

Sights & Activities
The current town of Chiang Khong has several northern Thai-style wats of minor interest. **Wat Luang**, on the main road, was once one of the most important temples in Chiang Rai Province and features a *chedi* dating from the 13th century, which was restored in 1881.

On a hill overlooking the town and the river is a **Nationalist Chinese Soldiers Cemetery**, where more than 200 KMT soldiers are buried. The grave mounds are angled on the hill so that they face China. A shrine containing old photos of KMT soldiers-in-arms stands at the top of the hill.

The village of **Ban Hat Khrai**, about 1km south of Chiang Khong, is famous as being one of the few places where *plaa bèuk* (giant Mekong catfish) are still occasionally caught. During the *plaa bèuk* season, mid-April to

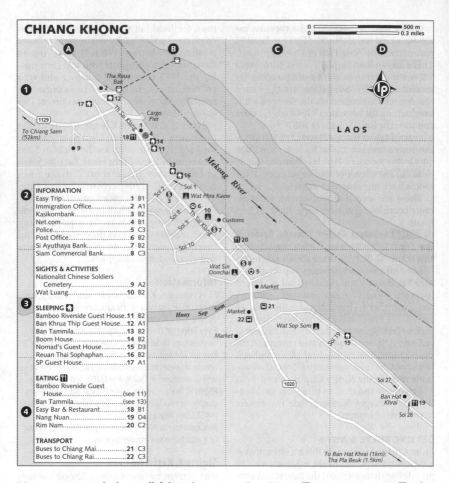

CHIANG KHONG

May, you can watch the small fishing boats coming and going from **Tha Pla Beuk**, about 2km south of Chiang Khong on the Mekong; the turn-off is near Km 137.

Mountain bikes can be rented from Ban Tammila (opposite) and Easy Trip (p375).

Sleeping

SP Guest House (☎ 0 5379 1767; www.spguesthouse.com; dm 80, r100-200B; ☐) The popular SP is a quiet place off the road on a wooded hillside. Rates for rooms vary depending on the number of beds and whether or not there's an en suite bathroom. A laundry service and a restaurant are on site. The owner organises trips through Laos and has a van shuttle that runs twice daily to Chiang Mai (250B; five hours).

Boom House (☎ 0 5379 1310; r 200-400B; ✖) This new place down a side road by Net.com internet café has large, clean, if slightly stark, rooms facing the river. There is a pleasant restaurant right on the riverbank. Rooms are 200B if you just use the fan, air-con costs 400B.

Nomad's Guest House (☎ 0 5365 5537; www.nomadshg.com; 153/4 Mu 3, Baan Sop Som; r 200-500B; ☐) Good rooms, good views, good food and a great philosophy – travel hard, rest easy – are the backbone to this guesthouse. Downside is its inconvenient location.

Reuan Thai Sophaphan (☎ 0 5379 1023; p_durasawang@hotmail.com; 8 Th Sai Klang; r 200-600B; ☐) This guesthouse is a beautiful, multifloor teak building with heaps of character. Rooms are spacious, simply but carefully decorated and all

have their own bathrooms. The cheaper rooms just have cold water though. There are several places to sit and watch the river roll by.

our pick **Ban Tammila** (☎ 0 5379 1234; baantammila@ hotmail.com; 113 Mu 8 Th Sai Klang; garden side/riverside bungalows 250/450B, r 350B) Facing a lush garden and the river, the stylish rooms and well-designed bungalows are decorated in warm colours. This relaxing place has lovely hosts, who also organise bicycle trips. Try their delicious homemade bread at the dining/seating area by the river.

our pick **Bamboo Riverside Guest House** (☎ 0 5379 1621; 71 Mu 1 Hua Wiang; bungalow 300B) This guesthouse has a chilled-out, bohemian atmosphere. Its collections of bungalows are set on a slope that lead down to a restaurant overlooking the river. The simple bamboo, thatched bungalows are surrounded by palms and plants and have hammocks outside.

Ban Khrua Thip Guest House (☎ 0 5379 2010; kruathip2006@hotmail.com; bungalows 300B) This col-lection of basic, sparsely decorated A-frame wooden bungalows near the pier fills up mostly because of location. Each hut has an attached hot-water shower and towels.

Eating

Easy Bar & Restaurant (☎ 08 6913 1144; Th Sai Klang; dishes 20-100B; ⊙ 7am-11pm) On the main street opposite Easy Trip travel agency, this lively place serves fresh, tasty Thai dishes, as well as Western food. It prepares packed lunches for the ferry too. Movies are played here every night at 6pm.

Rim Nam (dishes 30-90B; ⊙ 11am-9pm) On a nar-row road down beside the river, is this simple indoor-outdoor restaurant that overlooks the Mekong. The bilingual menu is much shorter than the Thai menu; yam (spicy salads) are the house specialities, but the kitchen can whip up almost anything.

Ban Tammila (☎ 0 5379 1234; 113 Mu 8 Th Sai Klang; dishes 40-100B; ⊙ 7am-11pm) With a terrace on the

---

MEKONG'S GIANT CATFISH

The Mekong River stretch that passes Chiang Khong is an important fishing ground for the *plaa bèuk* (giant Mekong catfish, *Pangasianodon gigas* to ichthyologists), probably the largest fresh-water fish in the world. A *plaa bèuk* takes at least six and possibly 12 years (no-one's really sure) to reach full size, when it will measure 2m to 3m in length and weigh up to 300kg. Locals say these fish swim all the way from Qinghai Province (where the Mekong originates) in northern China. In Thailand and Laos its meaty but mild-tasting flesh is revered as a delicacy.

These fish are taken only between mid-April and May when the river depth is just 3m to 4m and the fish are swimming upriver to spawn in Erhai Lake, Yunnan Province, China. Before netting them, Thai and Lao fishermen hold a special annual ceremony to propitiate Chao Mae Pla Beuk, a female deity thought to preside over the giant catfish. Among the rituals comprising the ceremony are chicken sacrifices performed aboard the fishing boats. After the ceremony is completed, fish-ing teams draw lots to see who casts the first net, and then take turns casting.

Only a few catfish are captured in a typical season, and the catfish hunters' guild is limited to natives of Ban Hat Khrai. Fishermen sell the meat on the spot for up to 500B or more per kilo (a single fish can bring 100,000B in Bangkok); most of it ends up in Bangkok, since local restaurants in Huay Xai and Chiang Khong can't afford such prices. During harvest season dishes made with giant catfish may be sold in a makeshift restaurant near the fishermen's landing in Ban Hat Khrai.

Although the *plaa bèuk* is on the Convention on International Trade in Endangered Species (CITES) list of endangered species, there is some debate as to just how endangered it is. Because of the danger of extinction, Thailand's Inland Fisheries Department has been taking protective measures since 1983, including a breed-and-release programme. Every time a female is caught, it's kept alive until a male is netted, then the eggs are removed (by massaging the female's ovaries) and put into a pan; the male is then milked for sperm and the eggs are fertilised in the pan. As a result, well over a million *plaa bèuk* have been released into the Mekong since 1983. Of course, not all of the released fish survive to adulthood. Reservoirs elsewhere in Thailand have had moderate success breeding this fish, however.

At the moment the greatest threat to the catfish's survival is the blasting of Mekong River rapids in China, which is robbing the fish of important breeding grounds.

river Ban Tammila does one of the best breakfasts in town with delicious homemade bread, as well as a good selection of Thai dishes with many vegetarian options.

Bamboo Riverside Guest House (☎ 0 5379 1621; 71 Mu 1 Hua Wiang; dishes 40-100B; ☺ 7am-11pm) The restaurant, perched on a riverside deck with views of Laos, serves good Thai and *faràng* food, as well as a few Mexican dishes. It's worth seeking out for a meal or dessert even if you're not staying there.

Nang Nuan (dishes 80-170B; ☺ 9am-midnight) There's no smoking allowed in this pleasant, open-air eating place overlooking the Mekong. Nang Nuan specialises in fresh river fish, including *plaa bèuk*.

Getting There & Away

From Chiang Saen, graded and paved 52km-long Rte 1129 is the quickest way to arrive from the west. A second 65km road curving along the river has also been paved and provides a slower but less trafficked alternative. With mountains in the distance and the Mekong River to one side, this road passes through picturesque villages and tobacco and rice fields before joining Rte 1129 just outside Chiang Khong.

Buses depart hourly from Chiang Khong to Chiang Rai (57B, 2½ hours) from around 4am to 5pm; the same for going to/from Chiang Saen. Buses from Chiang Rai and beyond use roads from the south (primarily Rte 1020) to reach Chiang Khong.

Daily buses going to Bangkok (2nd class air-con/1st class air-con/VIP 493/634/985B, 12 hours) leave at 3pm or 4pm daily. Book tickets with Easy Trip (see p375).

Boats taking up to 10 passengers can be chartered up the Mekong River from Chiang Khong to Chiang Saen for 2700B. Boat crews

---

NORTHERN THAILAND TO YUNNAN, CHINA

If you have already arranged a visa for China in Bangkok, it's possible to travel from Thailand to China's Yunnan Province by road via Laos, a land route that ties together the Golden Triangle and Yunnan's Xishuangbanna district (called Sipsongpanna in Thailand) in southwest China. The Thais, Shan and Lao all consider Xishuangbanna to be a cultural homeland.

One can now cross into Laos from Thailand via five legal border crossings. Once in Laos, head to Luang Nam Tha or Udomxai, then proceed north to the Lao village of Boten on the Chinese border, close to the Xishuangbanna town of Mengla (Mong La). From Mengla an existing road leads to Jinghong.

To reach Luang Nam Tha from northern Thailand you may cross by ferry from Chiang Khong on the Thai side to Huay Xai on the Lao side. Here you can obtain a 30-day Laos visa-on-arrival. From Huay Xai a bus goes to Luang Nam Tha. At the time of writing this road was under construction, and it took eight to 10 hours to do the journey. The road works will be finished around mid-2007, with the trip then taking only four hours. The Boten crossing is legal for all nationalities if you have a pre-arranged visa for China.

Another way to reach Boten is via Pakbeng in Laos' Udomxai Province. Pakbeng is midway along the Mekong River route between Huay Xai and Luang Prabang; from Pakbeng a Chinese-built road system continues all the way to Boten. To facilitate trade and travel between China and Thailand, the Chinese have offered to build a new road directly south to the Thai border (Nan Province) from the riverbank opposite Pakbeng. This has not happened as yet, as for now Thai authorities are not too happy about this proposed road extension, which is seen as a push towards an 'invasion' of Thailand. During the years of Thai communist insurgency, Communist Party of Thailand cadres used the Pakbeng road to reach Kunming, China, for training in revolutionary tactics.

The Mekong River route is also promising. It is now possible to take a speedboat from Chiang Saen in Thailand to Jinghong in China (see p372), which takes around 15 hours when the water is high enough. Chinese barges weighing up to 100 tonnes ply the Mekong eight months a year; from the Chinese border to Chiang Khong and Chiang Saen, Thailand, the trip takes about five days. During the drier months, however, river transport north of Luang Prabang is hampered by rocks and shallows. Blasting and dredging could make way for boats of up to 500 tonnes to travel year-round, but could have devastating effects on the watercourse and the lands downstream.

can be contacted near the customs pier behind Wat Luang, or further north at the pier for ferries to Laos.

BORDER CROSSING (LAOS)

Ferries to Huay Xai, Laos (one way 20B), leave frequently between 8am and 6pm from Tha Reua Bak, a pier at the northern end of Chiang Khong.

Foreigners can now purchase a 30-day visa for Laos upon arrival in Huay Xai for 1500B or US$30. There is an extra US$1 or 50B charge after 4pm and on weekends. Be sure to get an exit stamp from Thai officials before heading to Laos. Travellers who forget to do this find themselves in uncomfortable situations later on. On your return to Thailand, immigration will stamp you passport with a new 30-day tourist visa (see p753 for limits on the amount of times you can do this).

Once on the Lao side you can continue by road to Luang Nam Tha and Udomcai, or by boat down the Mekong River to Luang Prabang and Vientiane. At the time of writing the road trip from Huay Xai to Luang Nam Tha was taking eight to 10 hours due to a new road being constructed. This should be finished around mid-2007, and then the journey should take around four hours.

The more pleasant trip is by slow boat down the Mekong to Luang Prabang. Starting from Huay Xai it takes two days, including staying at a guesthouse in Pak Beng, before continuing on to Luang Prabang. Book with an agent like Easy Trip (p375) or a guesthouse, like SP (900B; p376) or pick up a slow boat (700B) at Huay Xai between 9am and 11am in the morning. Avoid the noisy fast boats (1400B, six to seven hours) that ply the Huay Xai to Luang Prabang route, as there have been reports of bad accidents. From Luang Prabang it's possible to get a boat to Vientiane, which takes another two days. The quicker route is a 13-hour bus ride.

At the time of writing Huay Xai airport was closed for renovation, but it is expected that when it reopens, **Lao Airlines** (☎ 211026, 211494; www.laoairlines.com) will fly from Huay Xai to Vientiane three times a week for US$84.

PHRAE PROVINCE

Phrae Province is probably most famous for the distinctive *sêua mâw hâwm*, the indigo-dyed cotton farmer's shirt seen all over Thai-

land. 'Made in Phrae' has always been a sign of distinction for these staples of rural Thai life, and since the student-worker-farmer political solidarity of the 1970s, even Thai university professors like to wear them. The cloth is made in Ban Thung Hong outside the town of Phrae.

The annual Rocket Festival kicks off the rice-growing season in May. In Phrae, the biggest celebrations take place in Amphoe Long and Amphoe Sung Men. Look for launching towers in the middle of rice fields for the exact location.

Amphoe Sung Men is also known for **Talat Hua Dong**, a market specialising in carved teak wood. Phrae has long been an important teak centre. Along Rte 101 between Phrae and Nan you'll see a steady blur of teak forests (they are the thickest around the Km 25 marker). Since the 1989 national ban on logging, these forests are protected by law. Most of the provincial teak business now involves recycled timber from old houses. Specially licensed cuts taken from fallen teak wood may also be used for decorative carvings or furniture (but not in house construction).

The province of Phrae and its neighbouring province of Nan are often overlooked by tourists and travellers because of their remoteness from Chiang Mai, but from Den Chai – on the train route north – they're easily reached by bus on Rte 101.

PHRAE

แพร่

pop 21,200

Like Chiang Mai and Lampang, Phrae has an old city partially surrounded by a moat beside a river (here it's the Mae Nam Yom). Unlike Chiang Mai, Phrae's old city still has lots of quiet lanes and old teak houses – if you're a fan of traditional Thai teak architecture, you'll find more of it here than in any other city of similar size anywhere in Thailand. The local temple architecture has successfully resisted central-Thai influence over the centuries as well. It's a bit unusual: you'll find a mix of Burmese, northern-Thai (Nan and Lanna) and Lao styles.

Southeast of the old city, the newer, more modern Phrae looks like any other medium-sized town in Thailand.

Information

Bangkok Bank (Th Charoen Meuang; ☼ 8.30am-3.30pm Mon-Fri) Foreign-exchange service and ATM.

PHRAE

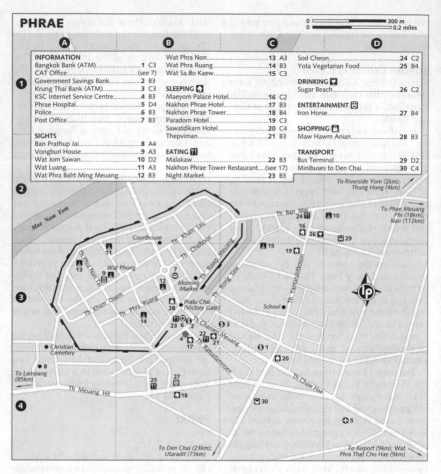

0 ————— 300 m
0 ————— 0.2 miles

INFORMATION
Bangkok Bank (ATM).................................1 C3
CAT Office..(see 7)
Government Savings Bank..................2 B3
Krung Thai Bank (ATM).....................3 C3
KSC Internet Service Centre.............4 B3
Phrae Hospital....................................5 D4
Police...6 B3
Post Office...7 B3

SIGHTS
Ban Prathup Jai..................................8 A4
Vongburi House...................................9 A3
Wat Jom Sawan................................10 D2
Wat Luang..11 A3
Wat Phra Baht Ming Meuang..........12 B3

Wat Phra Non...................................13 A3
Wat Phra Ruang................................14 B3
Wat Sa Bo Kaew...............................15 C3

SLEEPING
Maeyom Palace Hotel......................16 C2
Nakhon Phrae Hotel.........................17 B3
Nakhon Phrae Tower........................18 B4
Paradorn Hotel..................................19 C3
Sawatdikarn Hotel............................20 C4
Thepviman..21 B3

EATING
Malakaw..22 B3
Nakhon Phrae Tower Restaurant....(see 17)
Night Market.....................................23 B3

Sod Cheon...24 C2
Yota Vegetarian Food.......................25 B4

DRINKING
Sugar Beach.......................................26 C2

ENTERTAINMENT
Iron Horse...27 B4

SHOPPING
Maw Hawm Anian.............................28 B3

TRANSPORT
Bus Terminal.....................................29 D2
Minibuses to Den Chai.....................30 C4

Sights

WAT LUANG
วัดหลวง

This is the oldest wat in Phrae, probably dating from the founding of the city in the 12th or 13th century. **Phra That Luang Chang Kham**, the large octagonal Lanna-style *chedi*, sits on a square base with elephants supporting it on all four sides, surrounded by *kùti* and coconut palms. As is sometimes seen in Phrae and Nan, the *chedi* is swathed in Thai Lü fabric.

The veranda of the main *wíhǎan* is in the classic Luang Prabang-Lan Xang style but has unfortunately been bricked in with laterite. Opposite the front of the *wíhǎan* is **Pratu Khong**, part of the city's original entrance

CAT office (Th Charoen Meuang; 8am-8pm) Attached to the main post office. Long-distance calls can be made and you can use a T-card to access the internet.

Government Savings Bank (Th Rong Saw; 8.30am-3.30pm Mon-Fri) The ATM is next to the police station.

Krung Thai Bank (Th Charoen Meuang; 8.30am-3.30pm Mon-Fri) Foreign-exchange service and ATM.

KSC Internet Service Centre (Th Ratchadamnoen; per 30min 10B; 8am-9pm)

Phrae Hospital (0 5452 2444) Just east of Th Chaw Hae, southeast of town.

Post office (Th Charoen Meuang; 8.30am-4.30pm Mon-Fri, 9am-noon Sat) Close to the centre of the old city near the traffic circle.

gate. No longer used as a gate, it now contains a statue of Chao Pu, an early Lanna ruler. The image is sacred to local residents, who leave offerings of fruit, flowers, candles and incense.

Also on the temple grounds is a **museum** displaying temple antiques, ceramics and religious art dating from the Lanna, Nan, Bago and Mon periods. A 16th-century, Phrae-made sitting Buddha on the 2nd floor is particularly exquisite. There are also some 19th-century photos with English labels on display, including some gruesome shots of a beheading. The museum is usually open weekends only, but the monks will sometimes open it on weekdays on request.

WAT PHRA NON
วัดพระนอน

Southwest a few hundred metres from Wat Luang is a 300-year-old wat named after its highly revered reclining *phrá nawn* (Buddha image). The *bòt* (central sanctuary) was built around 200 years ago and has an impressive roof with a separate, two-tiered portico and gilded, carved, wooden façade with Ramayana scenes. The *wíhǎan* behind the *bòt* contains the Buddha image, swathed in Thai Lü cloth with bead and foil decoration.

WAT JOM SAWAN
วัดจอมสวรรค์

Outside the old city on Th Ban Mai, this temple was built by local Shan in the late 19th and early 20th centuries, and shows Shan and Burmese influence throughout. The well-preserved wooden *wíhǎan* and *bòt* have high, tiered, towerlike roofs like those in Mandalay. A large copper-crowned *chedi* has lost most of its stucco to reveal the artful brickwork beneath. A prized possession in the main *wíhǎan* is a Tripitaka section of 16 ivory 'pages' engraved in Burmese.

OTHER TEMPLES

Across from the post office within the old city, **Wat Phra Baht Ming Meuang** houses a Buddhist school, an old *chedi*, an unusual octagonal drum tower made entirely of teak and the highly revered Phra Kosai, which closely resembles the Phra Chinnarat in Phitsanulok. Just outside the northeastern corner of the moat, **Wat Sa Bo Kaew** is a Shan-Burmese–style temple similar to Wat Jom Sawan. **Wat Phra Ruang**, inside the old city, is

typical of Phrae's many old city wats, with a Nan-style, cruciform-plan *bòt*, a Lao-style *wíhǎan* and a Lanna *chedi*. Perhaps this unique mix is actually a coherent design of local (Nan-Phrae) provenance that has yet to be identified.

VONGBURI HOUSE
บ้านวงศ์บุรี

This private **museum** (☎ 0 5462 0153; Th Phra Non Tai; admission 20B; 🕙 8am-5pm) in the two-storey teak house of the last prince of Phrae, is rather worn but still interesting. It was constructed between 1897 and 1907 for Luang Phongphibun and his wife Chao Sunantha, who once held a profitable teak concession in the city. Elaborate carvings on gables, eaves, balconies and above doors and windows are in good condition. Inside, many of the house's 20 rooms display late-19th-century teak antiques, documents (including early-20th-century slave concessions), photos and other artefacts from the bygone teak-dynasty era. Most are labelled in English as well as Thai.

BAN PRATHUP JAI
บ้านประทับใจ

On the outskirts of the town is **Ban Prathup Jai** (Impressive House; ☎ 0 5451 1008; admission 30B; 🕙 8am-5pm), also called Ban Sao Roi Ton (Hundred Pillar-Filled House), a large northern Thai-style teak house that was built using more than 130 teak logs, each over 300 years old. Opened in 1985, the house took four years to build, using timber taken from nine old rural houses. The interior pillars are ornately carved. The house is also filled with souvenir vendors and is rather tackily decorated, so don't take the moniker 'impressive' too seriously.

Sleeping
BUDGET

Thepviman (☎ 0 1595 0153; 226-228 Th Charoen Meuang; r 90-120B) These very basic rooms with cold water showers, some of which come with Western toilets, are a reasonable choice for baht-pinching travellers.

Sawatdikarn Hotel (☎ 0 5451 1032; 76-78 Th Yantarakitkoson; s/d 100/150B) This place has similar basic rooms to the Thepviman, but these come with squat toilets.

Nakhon Phrae Hotel (☎ 0 5451 1122; fax 0 5452 1937; 29 Th Ratsadamnoen; r 290-400B; 🖭) A two-minute

walk from the old city, this hotel's two wings are on opposite sides of the street. Rooms are large with some furniture; the more expensive ones have air-conditioning. Some tourist information and maps are available in the lobbies of both wings.

our pick **Paradorn Hotel** (Pharadon; ☎ 0 5451 1177; www.phrae-paradorn.com; 177 Th Yantarakitkoson; r 290-540B, ste 800B; ❄) By far the best budget option in Phrae, you can't miss this white hotel with the sign 'absolutely clean' outside. All rooms, whether the cheapest fan rooms or the more expensive suites, are decorated in teak furnishings, have cable TVs, hot water and are pristine. There is a wi-fi hot-spot in the lobby, and rates include a simple breakfast.

MIDRANGE & TOP END
Maeyom Palace Hotel (☎ 0 5452 1029-35; wccphrae@ hotmail.com; 181/6 Th Yantarakitkoson; r incl breakfast 1200-1400B, ste incl breakfast 3000-3500B; ❄ ▢ ▣) Opposite the bus terminal, Phrae's top end option has all the modern amenities: carpeted rooms with cable TV, sofa and minibar; although some could do with a few pictures. The pool is a good size and there is a pleasant restaurant on decking outside, as well as an air-conditioned option inside. Discounts of up to 30% are typical in the low season.

Nakhon Phrae Tower (☎ 0 5452 1321; nakornphrae@ yahoo.com; 3 Th Meuang Hit; r incl breakfast 650-750B, ste incl breakfast 1800B; ❄ ▢) Not as luxurious as the Maeyom Palace, it is certainly nicer than other places in town. Rooms are large and tastefully decorated. There is a piano bar and the restaurant has been recommended (right).

Eating
A very good **night market** convenes just outside the Pratu Chai (Victory Gate) intersection every evening. Several food vendors also set up nightly in the lane opposite the Sawatdikarn Hotel. There's another night market a block or two behind the Paradorn Hotel on weekday evenings only. On Th Ratsadamnoen, near the Nakhon Phrae Hotel are several eating options.

Yota Vegetarian Food (Th Saisibut; dishes 15-40B; ⏰ 7am-7pm) This is a reliable Thai vegetarian place.

Sod Cheon (Th Yantarakitkoson; dishes 25-90B; ⏰ 11am-4am) On the crossroads, 50m north of the Maeyom Palace Hotel, is this simple but very popular Chinese/Thai restaurant. Choose from the big pots of Chinese-style soups or duck, or go for your usual Thai dishes. All are superfresh and tasty. Good for late night eats. The menu is in Thai only.

Malakaw (Th Ratsadamnoen; meals 40-80B; ⏰ 6pm-1am) This rustic hole-in-the-wall with its rough-cut tables and chairs is a popular place for socialising with locals. The ceiling is low and so are the lights, but the menu features fresh, seasonal goodies. Locals rave about the *sôm-tam* here.

Nakhon Phrae Tower Restaurant (☎ 0 5452 1321; nakornphrae@yahoo.com; 3 Th Meuang Hit; dishes 40-160B) This recommended restaurant offers tasty Thai dishes, seafood, steaks and sandwiches. Live music is played here from 8pm.

Drinking & Entertainment
Iron Horse (Th Meuang Hit) Opposite the Nakhon Phrae Tower, the Iron Horse has country-and-western décor and plays live music most nights.

Riverside Yom (⏰ 4pm-12am) This cluster of pavilions fashioned from grass thatch and pine fronts the river and features live bluegrass and *phleng phêua chii-wít* (Thai folk music) nightly. It's about 2km northeast of the city centre amid a maze of roads, and thus quite difficult to find; it's best to take a săamláw or săwngthăew.

Sugar Beach, one of the more salubrious local nightspots, is a large, open-air pavilion near the bus terminal. It's basically just a bar-restaurant but on some nights there's live music.

Shopping
A good place to buy *mâw hâwm* in Phrae is **Maw Hawm Anian** (no roman-script sign; 36 Th Chareon Muang; ⏰ 6.30-8.30pm), a shop about 60m from the southeastern gate (Pratu Chai) into the old city.

Getting There & Away
BUS
Most of the buses that depart from Bangkok's Northern and Northeastern bus terminals (2nd class air-con/1st class/VIP 318/409/635B) leave in the evening.

From Chiang Mai's Arcade bus terminal, buses leave at regular intervals (ordinary/2nd class air-con/1st class/VIP 105/147/189/290B, four hours) for Phrae. From Chiang Rai, bus services also take four hours to reach Phrae (ordinary/2nd class air-con/1st class/VIP 105/160/205/239B).

Buses leave from the bus station to Den Chai every hour from 3.30pm to 6.30pm (20B, 30 minutes). Minibuses travel to Den Chai hourly from 6am to 6pm (30B) and depart next to the vocational college. From Den Chai you can catch the northern train line.

There are hourly buses to Nan from the bus station (ordinary/2nd class air-con, 1st class/VIP 62/87/112/170B, two hours), with the last one leaving at 8.30pm.

TRAIN
Tickets to Den Chai station from Bangkok cost 200B for 3rd class. In second class there is the option of a fan seat/fan sleeper lower bunk/fan sleeper upper bunk/air-con sleeper. They cost 317/467/431/767B. There are no 1st-class seats only sleepers, these cost 1191B.

Trains that arrive at a decent hour are the rapid 111 (2nd and 3rd class only, departs Bangkok at 7am and arrives in Den Chai at 5.10pm), the express 9 diesel (2rd class only, leaves at 8.30am and arrives at 3.53pm), and the express 51 (2nd and 3rd class, departs at 10pm and arrives at 7.14am). On the latter service you can get a 2nd-class sleeper. Tickets can be reserved by calling **Den Chai station** (☎ 0 5461 3260), where English is spoken.

Blue sǎwngthǎew and red buses leave the Den Chai station frequently for the 23km jaunt to Phrae (20-30B). You can catch them anywhere along the southern end of Th Yanta-rakitkoson.

Getting Around
A sǎamláw anywhere in the old town costs 30B; further afield to somewhere like Ban Prathup Jai it can cost up to 40B. Motorcy-cle taxis are available at the bus terminal; a trip from here to, say, Pratu Chai should cost around 25B.

Shared sǎwngthǎew ply a few of the roads (mainly Th Yantarakitkoson) and cost 5B to 10B, depending on the distance.

AROUND PHRAE
Wat Phra That Cho Hae
วัดพระธาตุช่อแฮ
On a hill about 9km southeast of town off Rte 1022, this wat is famous for its 33m-high gilded *chedi*. Cho Hae is the name of the cloth that worshippers wrap around the *chedi* – it's a type of satin thought to have originated in Xishuangbanna (Sipsongpanna, literally '12,000 Rice Fields' in northern Thai), China.

Like Chiang Mai's Wat Doi Suthep, this is an important pilgrimage site for Thais living in the north. The **Phra Jao Than Jai** Buddha image here, which is similar in appearance to Phra Chinnarat in Phitsanulok, is reputed to impart fertility to women who make offerings to it.

The *bòt* has a gilded wooden ceiling, ro-coco pillars and walls with lotus-bud mosa-ics. Tiered *naga* (a mythical serpentlike being with magical powers) stairs lead to the temple compound. The hilltop is surrounded by a protected forest of mature teak trees.

Sǎwngthǎew between the city and Phra That Cho Hae (15B) are frequent.

Phae Meuang Phi
แพะเมืองผี
The name Phae Meuang Phi means 'Ghost-Land', a reference to this strange geological phenomenon approximately 18km northeast of Phrae off Rte 101. Erosion has created bi-zarre pillars of soil and rock that look like giant fungi. The area has been made a provin-cial park; a few walking trails and viewpoints are recent additions. There are picnic pavil-ions in the park and food vendors selling *kài yâang* (grilled, spiced chicken), *sôm-tam* and sticky rice near the entrance – you may need a drink after wandering around the baked surfaces between the eroded pillars.

Getting to Phae Meuang Phi by public transport entails a bus ride 9km towards Nan, getting off at the signposted turn-off for Phae Meuang Phi, and then catching a sǎwngthǎew another 6km to a second right-hand turn-off to the park. From this point you must walk or hitch about 2.5km to reach the entrance. Al-ternatively, charter a sǎwngthǎew for around 250B. Sǎwngthǎew drivers seem to hang out at the front of the school.

NAN PROVINCE

Formerly a government-designated 'remote province', Nan before the early 1980s was so choked with bandits and People's Liberation Army of Thailand (PLAT) insurgents that travellers were discouraged from visiting.

With the successes of the Thai army and a more stable political machine in Bangkok during the last two decades, Nan has opened up considerably. The roads that link the pro-vincial capital with the nearby provinces of Chiang Rai, Phrae and Utaradit pass through

NORTHERN THAILAND

NAN PROVINCE

0 ———— 20 km
0 ———— 12 miles

LAOS

Hong Sa

Nam Tok Phu Sang
1021
Thung Kluay
Chiang Kham
Xieng Hon
Muang Ngoen
Ban Huay Kon
Ban Nam Liang
Ngop Nua
Ban Sophit
Tham Luang
Song Khwae
1179
Ban Hae
1148
Ban Sakoen
Hang Thung
Ban Don Kaew
Baeng
Huay Khok
Nam Puk
1091
CHIANG RAI
Pong
Pha Thang
Huay Sing
Ta Fah Tai
Doi Phajik

LAOS

1080
Thung Chang
1081
Na Maen
Wat Nong Daeng
Chiang Klang
Nam Mong
Bo Yuak
Doi Lo (2077m)
Doi Phu Kha National Park
Ban Toei
Doi Phu Kha (2000m)
Pua
1256
Ban Pa Klang
Nam Tok Silaphet
Ban Bo Kleua
Nong Bua
Tha Wang Pha
Pa Tong
1082
Pha Khwang
1257
Lak Lai
Mae Sanan
1080
Ban Nam Yao
Tham Phah Tup Forest Reserve
1169
Santisuk
Mae Nam Yom
Chiang Muan
Pii Neua
Song Khwae
Muang Chang
1125
Ban Luang
Nam Airport
Nan
1168
Phu Fa (1750m)
Sa Iap
Doi Luang (1396m)
Ban Wat Pra That Khao Noi
Pra That Chae Haeng
Ban Kuaeng
Mae Charim
Sop Kaen
Pa Lao Klang
101
Huay Kaew
1168
Nam Phun
Saliam
Nam Phun National Biodiversity & Conservation Area
Wiang Sa
Huay Son
PHRAE
1162
Fang Min
Nam Muap
101
Huay Rong
1026
LAOS
103
Rong Kwang
Hom Chom
Na Noi
Boh Bia
1216
Sao Din
1083
1134
Doi Kusathan (1728m)
Nam Tok Kaeng Luang
1123
Na Moh
Na Meun
Pang Hai
Nam Tok Mae Kam
Ban Muang Jet Dan
Huay Noi Ka
Doi Khun Loen (1247m)
Ban Pak Nai
Ban Khok
Doi Phaya Fo (1465m)
Thaleh Sap Neua
Sak Yai Forest Park
Fak Tha
UTARADIT

Nam Samun
Nam Wa
Nam Haeng
Mae Nam Nan

NORTHERN THAILAND

exquisite scenery of rich river valleys and rice fields. Like Loei in the northeast, this is a province to be explored for its natural beauty and its likeable people.

Nan remains a largely rural province with not a factory or condo in sight. Most of the inhabitants are agriculturally employed, growing sticky rice, beans, corn, tobacco and vegetables in the fertile river plains. Nan is also famous for two fruits: *fai jiin* (a Chinese version of Thailand's indigenous *máfai*) and *sôm sîi thawng* (golden-skinned oranges). The latter are Nan's most famous export, commanding high prices in Bangkok and Malaysia. Apparently, the cooler winter weather in Nan turns the skin orange (lowland Thai oranges are mostly green) and imparts a unique, sweet, tart flavour. Amphoe Thung Chang supposedly grows the best *sôm sîi thawng* in the province. Nan is also famous for its *phrík yài hâeng* (long, hot chillies) similar to those grown in China's Sichuan Province. During the hot season, you'll see heaps of these chillies drying by the roadside.

Geography

Nan shares a 227km border with Laos. Only 25% of the land is arable (and only half of that is actively cultivated), as most of the province is covered by heavily forested mountains; **Doi Phu Kha**, at 2000m, is the highest peak. Half the forests in the province are virgin upland monsoon forest. Most of the province's population of 364,000 live in the Mae Nam Nan Valley, which is a bowl-shaped depression ringed by mountains on all sides.

The major river systems in the province include the Nan, Wa, Samun, Haeng, Lae and Pua. At 627km, Mae Nam Nan is Thailand's third-longest river after the Mekong and Mae Nam Mun.

Population & People

Nan is a sparsely populated province and the ethnic groups found here differ significantly from those in other northern provinces. Outside the Mae Nam Nan valley, the predominant hill tribes are Mien (around 8000), with smaller numbers of Hmong. During the Vietnam War, many Hmong and Mien from Nan (as well as Chiang Rai and Phetchabun) were recruited to fight with the communist Pathet Lao, who promised to create a Hmong-Mien king following a Pathet Lao victory in Laos. Some of these so-called 'Red Meos' even trained in North Vietnam.

Along the southwestern provincial border with Phrae are a few small Mabri settlements. What makes Nan unique, however, is the presence of three lesser-known groups seldom seen outside this province: the Thai Lü, Htin and Khamu.

THAI LÜ

Originally from Xishuangbanna in China's Yunnan Province, the Thai Lü migrated to Nan in 1836 in the wake of a conflict with a local lord. Phra Jao Atityawong, ruler of the Nan kingdom at the time, allowed the Thai Lü to stay and grow vegetables in what is now Amphoe Tha Wang Pha. Their influence on Nan (and to a lesser extent, Phrae) culture has been very important. Like most Siamese Thai, the Thai Lü are Theravada Buddhists, and the temple architecture at Wat Phra That Chae Haeng (p388), Wat Phumin (p388) and Wat Nong Bua – typified by thick walls with small windows, two- or three-tiered roofs, curved pediments and *naga* lintels – is a Thai Lü inheritance. Thai Lü fabrics are among the most prized in northern Thailand and the weaving motifs show up in many Nan handicrafts.

The Thai Lü build traditional wooden or bamboo-thatched houses on thick wooden stilts, beneath which they place their kitchens and weaving looms. Many still make all their own clothes, typically sewn from indigo-dyed cotton fabrics. Many Thai Lü villages support themselves by growing rice and vegetables. In Nan they maintain a strong sense of tradition; most Thai Lü communities still recognise a *jâo meuang* (lord) and *mǎw meuang* (state astrologer), two older men in the community who serve as political and spiritual consultants.

HTIN

Pronounced 'Tin', this Mon-Khmer group of about 3000 live in villages of 50 or so families spread across remote mountain valleys of Amphoe Chiang Klang, Amphoe Pua and Amphoe Thung Chang. A substantial number also live across the border in neighbouring Sayaburi Province, Laos. They typically subsist by hunting for wild game, breeding domestic animals, farming small plots of land and, in Ban Bo Kleua, by extracting salt from salt wells.

Htin houses are usually made of thatched bamboo and raised on bamboo or wooden

stilts. No metal – including nails – is used in the construction of houses because of a Htin taboo.

The Htin are particularly skilled at manipulating bamboo to make everything needed around the house; for floor mats and baskets the Htin interweave pared bamboo with a black-coloured grass to create bold geometric patterns.

They also use bamboo to fashion a musical instrument of stepped pipes (similar to the *angklung* of central Thailand and Indonesia), which is shaken to produce musical tones. The Htin don't weave their own fabrics, often buying clothes from neighbouring Mien.

KHAMU

Like the Thai Lü, the Khamu migrated to Nan around 150 years ago from Xishuangbanna and Laos. There are now more than 5000 in Nan (more than anywhere else in Thailand), mostly in the Wiang Sa, Thung Chang, Chiang Klang and Pua districts. Their villages are established near streams; their houses have dirt floors like those of the Hmong but their roofs sport crossed beams similar to the northern-Thai *kàlae* (locally called *ka-pkri-aak*).

The Khamu are skilled at metalwork and perform regular rituals to placate Salok, the spirit of the forge. Khamu villages are usually very self-sufficient; villagers hold fast to tradition and are known to value thrift and hard work. Ban Huay Sataeng in Amphoe Thung Chang is one of the largest and easiest Khamu villages to visit.

NAN
น่าน

pop 24,300

Just over 668km from Bangkok, little-known Nan is steeped in history. For centuries it was an isolated, independent kingdom with few ties to the outside world. Ample evidence of prehistoric habitation exists, but it wasn't until several small *meuang* consolidated to form Nanthaburi on Mae Nam Nan in the mid-14th century – concurrent with the founding of Luang Prabang and the Lan Xang (Million Elephants) kingdom in Laos – that the city became a power to contend with. Associated with the powerful Sukhothai kingdom, the *meuang* took the title Waranakhon and played a significant role in the development of early Thai nationalism.

Parts of the old city wall and several early wats dating from the Lanna period can be seen in present-day Nan. Meuang Nan's wats are distinctive: some temple structures show Lanna influence, while others belong to the Thai Lü legacy brought from Xishuangbanna, the Thai Lü's historical homeland.

History

Towards the end of the 14th century Nan became one of the nine northern Thai-Lao principalities that comprised Lan Na Thai (now known simply as Lanna). The city-state flourished throughout the 15th century under the name Chiang Klang (Middle City), a reference to its position approximately midway between Chiang Mai (New City) and Chiang Thong (Golden City, which is today's Luang Prabang).

The Burmese took control of the kingdom in 1558 and transferred many of the inhabitants to Burma as slaves; the city was all but abandoned until western Thailand was wrested from the Burmese in 1786. The local dynasty then regained local sovereignty and it remained semi-autonomous until 1931, when Nan finally accepted full Bangkok sponsorship.

Information

Internet services are available around town for 40B per hour.

Bangkok Bank (Th Sumonthewarat) Near the Nan Fah and Dhevaraj hotels. Operates foreign-exchange services and has ATMs.

CAT office (Main post office, Th Mahawong; ⏰ 7am-10pm) Has a Home Country Direct Phone.

Kasikornbank (Th Sumonthewarat) As Bangkok Bank.

Main post office (Th Mahawong; ⏰ 8.30am-4.30pm Mon-Fri, 9am-noon Sat, Sun & holidays) In the centre of town.

Tourist Information Centre (☎ 0 5471 0216; Th Pha Kong; ⏰ 8am-5pm) New centre, complete with coffee shop. Opposite Wat Phumin. Fhu Travel is also a good source of information (p389).

Sights

NAN NATIONAL MUSEUM
พิพิธภัณฑ์สถานแห่งชาติน่าน

Housed in the 1903-vintage palace of Nan's last two feudal lords (Phra Jao Suriyapongpalidet and Jao Mahaphrom Surathada), this **museum** (☎ 0 5477 2777, 0 5471 0561; Th Pha Kong; admission 30B; ⏰ 9am-12pm,1-4pm) first opened its doors in 1973. Relatively recent renovations have

NAN

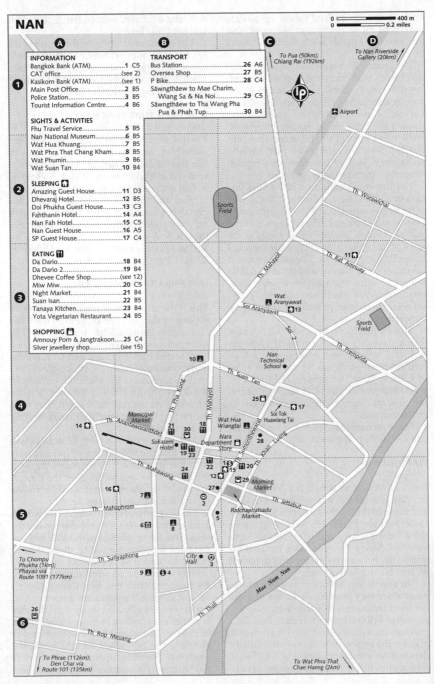

INFORMATION
Bangkok Bank (ATM).................**1** C5
CAT office.................................(see 2)
Kasikorn Bank (ATM)................(see 1)
Main Post Office.......................**2** B5
Police Station...........................**3** B5
Tourist Information Centre.........**4** B6

SIGHTS & ACTIVITIES
Fhu Travel Service.....................**5** B5
Nan National Museum...............**6** B5
Wat Hua Khuang.......................**7** B5
Wat Phra That Chang Kham.......**8** B5
Wat Phumin..............................**9** B6
Wat Suan Tan...........................**10** B4

SLEEPING
Amazing Guest House...............**11** D3
Dhevaraj Hotel.........................**12** B5
Doi Phukha Guest House...........**13** C3
Fahthanin Hotel........................**14** A4
Nan Fah Hotel..........................**15** C5
Nan Guest House......................**16** A5
SP Guest House.........................**17** C4

EATING
Da Dario...................................**18** B4
Da Dario 2................................**19** B4
Dhevee Coffee Shop..............(see 12)
Miw Miw..................................**20** C5
Night Market............................**21** B4
Suan Isan.................................**22** B5
Tanaya Kitchen.........................**23** B4
Yota Vegetarian Restaurant......**24** B5

SHOPPING
Amnouy Porn & Jangtrakoon.....**25** C4
Silver jewellery shop..............(see 15)

TRANSPORT
Bus Station...............................**26** A6
Oversea Shop............................**27** B5
P Bike.......................................**28** C4
Săwngthăew to Mae Charim,
  Wiang Sa & Na Noi..................**29** C5
Săwngthăew to Tha Wang Pha
  Pua & Phah Tup.......................**30** B4

To Pua (50km);
Chiang Rai (192km)

To Nan Riverside
Gallery (20km)

Airport

Sports Field

Th Worawichai

Th Rat Amnuay

Th Mahayot

Wat Aranyawat **13**

Soi Aranyawat

Soi 2

Th Premprida

Sports Field

Nan Technical School

Th Suan Tan

10

25

Soi Tok Huawiang Tai

17

Th Pha Kong

Th Mahayot

Municipal Market

Th Anantaworarittidet

14

21

30

18

Wat Hua Wiangtai

Sukasem Hotel

19 **23**

Nara Department Store

28

Th Sumonthewarat

Th Khao Luang

Th Mahawong

24

22

16

7

6

8

15

20

12

29 Morning Market

27

2

5

Ratchaphatsadu Market

Th Jettabut

Th Mahaphrom

To Chompu
Phukha (1km);
Phayao via
Route 1091 (177km)

Th Suriyaphong

City Hall

9 **4**

3

Mae Nam Nan

26

Th Thai

Th Rop Meuang

To Phrae (112km);
Den Chai via
Route 101 (135km)

To Wat Phra That
Chae Haeng (2km)

made it one of Thailand's most up-to-date provincial museums and, unlike most, this one also has English labels for many items on display.

The ground floor is divided into six exhibition rooms, with ethnological exhibits covering the various ethnic groups found in the province, including the northern Thais, Thai Lü, Htin, Khamu, Mabri, Hmong and Mien. Among the items on display are silverwork, textiles, folk utensils and tribal costumes. On the 2nd floor are exhibits on Nan history, archaeology, local architecture, royal regalia, weapons, ceramics and religious art.

The museum's collection of Buddha images includes some rare Lanna styles as well as the floppy-eared local styles. Usually made from wood, these standing images are in the 'calling for rain' posture (with hands at the sides, pointing down) and they show a marked Luang Prabang influence. The astute museum curators posit a Nan style of art in Buddhist sculpture; some examples on display seem very imitative of other Thai styles, while others are quite distinctive, with the ears curving outwards.

Also on display on the 2nd floor is a rare 'black' (actually reddish-brown) elephant tusk said to have been presented to a Nan lord over 300 years ago by the Khün ruler of Chiang Tung (Kengtung). Held aloft by a wooden *garuda* (mythical bird) sculpture, the tusk measures 97cm long and 47cm in circumference.

The museum sells a few books on Thai art and archaeology at the entrance.

WAT PHUMIN
วัดภูมินทร์

Nan's most famous temple is celebrated for its cruciform *bòt* that was constructed in 1596 and restored during the reign of Chao Anantavorapitthidet (1867–74). Murals depicting the *Khatta Kumara* and *Nimi Jatakas* were executed during the restoration by Thai Lü artists; the *bòt* exterior exemplifies the work of Thai Lü architects as well.

The murals have historic as well as aesthetic value since they incorporate scenes of local life from the era in which they were painted. As well as hell and heavenly realms, Buddha's previous incarnations and Nan's legends and history, the bright, fluid figures refreshingly depict more mundane aspects of life. You'll find scenes like a group of gossips, people

enjoying a smoke, women fixing their hair and amorous lovers.

The ornate altar sitting in the centre of the *bòt* has four sides, with four Sukhothai-style sitting Buddhas in *maan wíchai* ('victory over Mara' – with one hand touching the ground) posture, facing in each direction.

WAT PHRA THAT CHAE HAENG
วัดพระธาตุแช่แห้ง

Two kilometres past the bridge that spans Mae Nam Nan, heading southeast out of town, this temple dating from 1355 is the most sacred wat in Nan Province. It's set in a square, walled enclosure on top of a hill with a view of Nan and the valley. The Thai Lü-influenced *bòt* features a triple-tiered roof with carved wooden eaves and dragon reliefs over the doors. A gilded Lanna-style *chedi* sits on a large square base next to the *bòt* with sides 22.5m long; the entire *chedi* is 55.5m high.

WAT PHRA THAT CHANG KHAM
วัดพระธาตุช้างค้ำ

This is the second-most important **temple (Th Pha Kong)** in the city after Wat Phra That Chae Haeng; the founding date is unknown. The main *wíhǎan*, reconstructed in 1458, has a huge seated Buddha image and faint murals in the process of being painstakingly uncovered. (Sometime in the mid-20th century an abbot reportedly ordered the murals to be whitewashed because he thought they were distracting worshippers from concentrating on his sermons!)

Also in the *wíhǎan* is a set of Lanna-period scrolls inscribed (in Lanna script) not only with the usual Buddhist scriptures but with the history, law and astrology of the time. A *thammâat* (a '*dhamma* seat' used by monks when teaching) sits to one side.

The magnificent *chedi* behind the *wíhǎan* dates to the 14th century, probably around the same time the temple was founded. It features elephant supports similar to those seen in Sukhothai and Si Satchanalai.

Next to the *chedi* is a small, undistinguished *bòt* from the same era. Wat Chang Kham's current abbot tells an interesting story involving the *bòt* and a Buddha image that was once kept inside. According to the venerable abbot, in 1955 art historian AB Griswold offered to purchase the 145cm-tall Buddha inside the small *bòt*. The image appeared to be a crude Sukhothai-style walking Buddha moulded

of plaster. After agreeing to pay the abbot 25,000B for the image, Griswold began removing the image from the *bòt* – but as he did it fell and the plaster around the statue broke away to reveal an original Sukhothai Buddha of pure gold underneath. Needless to say, the abbot made Griswold give it back, much to the latter's chagrin. The image is now kept behind a glass partition, along with other valuable Buddhist images from the area, in the abbot's *kùtì*. Did Griswold suspect what lay beneath the plaster? The abbot refuses to say.

Wat Phra That Chang Kham is also distinguished by having the largest *hǎw trai* (Tripitaka library) in Thailand. It's as big as or bigger than the average *wíhǎan*, but now lies empty.

The wat is located across from the Nan National Museum.

WAT HUA KHUANG
วัดหัวข่วง

Largely ignored by art historians, this small wat diagonally opposite Wat Phra That Chang Kham features a distinctive Lanna/Lan Xang-style *chedi* with four Buddha niches, a wooden *hǎw trai* – now used as a *kùtì* – and a noteworthy *bòt* with a Luang Prabang-style carved wooden veranda.

Inside is a carved wooden ceiling and a huge *naga* altar. The temple's founding date is unknown, but stylistic cues suggest this may be one of the city's oldest wats.

WAT SUAN TAN
วัดสวนตาล

Reportedly established in 1456, **Wat Suan Tan** (Palm Grove Monastery; Th Suan Tan) features an interesting 15th-century *chedi* (40m high) that combines *prang* (Hindu/Khmer-style *chedi*) and lotus-bud motifs of obvious Sukhothai influence. The heavily restored *wíhǎan* contains an early Sukhothai-style bronze sitting Buddha.

Activities

Nan has nothing like the organised trekking industry found in Chiang Rai and Chiang Mai, but there is one company that leads two- or three-day excursions into the mountains. **Fhu Travel Service** (☎ 0 5471 0636, 08 1287 7209; www .fhutravel.com; 453/4 Th Sumonthewarat; per person (2-person min) 'soft' trek 1 day 800-1300B, 2 days & 1 night 1400-2500B, 3 days & 2 nights 1800-3200B) offers treks to Mabri, Hmong, Mien, Thai Lü and Htin villages. The operators have been leading tours for 17 years, and are professional, honest and reliable.

The trekking fees include transport, meals, accommodation, sleeping bag and guide services; and prices vary depending on the number of participants.

Fhu also runs boat trips on Mae Nam Nan in December and January, when the water level is high enough. One-day white-water rubber-rafting trips on the Nam Wa in Mae Charim are offered. The prices run from 1000B per person (for trips of six to eight people) to 2300B per person (for trips of two people). This price includes transport, guide, lunch and safety equipment. Three-day rubber-rafting trips are 4500B to 6000B per person, depending on the number of people. Elephant tours are also available for 1000B per person for half a day. Tours of the city and surrounding area (500B per person), as well as cycling tours are offered (300B per person, three hours). Fhu also runs two-hour kayaking trips on the Mae Nam Nan (1000B).

Festivals & Events

It is worth being in Nan for the **boat races**, held at the end of the rainy season and during the robe-giving ceremonies at Wat Phra That Chang Kham (opposite), between mid-October and mid-November. Even if you arrive too early for the official races, it's possible to see participants practising along the Mae Nam Nan from 5pm to 6pm each evening. It's an impressive sight to watch around 50 oarsmen race in the long, dragon prow boats, decorated with coloured, fluttering flags and paper.

Sleeping
BUDGET

Doi Phukha Guest House (☎ 0 5475 1517; 94/5 Soi 1 Th Aranyawat; s/d 100/150B) This rambling old house in a residential neighbourhood is awkward to get to but offers basic sleep space with clean cold-water bathrooms. It's fairly quiet and the English-speaking owner is very helpful.

Amazing Guest House (☎ 0 5471 0893; 23/7 Th Rat Amnuay; s/d 120/350B; 🛇) In a tidy, two-storey wooden house on a quiet lane off Th Rat Amnuay, this intimate place is a bit like staying with your long-lost Thai grandparents. The hosts are sweet, but may be too personable for some. All rooms have wooden floors, clean beds and hot shared showers. Rooms in concrete rooms out the back have en suite bathrooms. Bicycles and motorbikes can be

rented here, and free pick-up from the bus station is available.

Nan Guest House (☎ 0 5477 1849; www.nan-guest house.com; 57/16 Th Mahaphrom; r 230-350B; 🖳 🖳) This well maintained place has spotless spacious rooms, most with en suite hot water bathrooms. It can be hard to get service and you should not count on eating meals here despite the readily available menus. But for a clean, comfortable place to sleep, it's an excellent choice. It also organises tours, has an international call service and rents out mountain bikes.

ourpick SP Guest House (☎ 0 5477 4897; Soi Tok Huawiang Tai; r 250-350B; 🖳) Excellent value and well situated, this guesthouse is the best deal in town. The six rooms have large, well-equipped bedrooms and bathrooms, with wooden or tiled floors. All come with hot water and cable TV, and a choice of fan or air-con. It's just off Th Sumonthewarat. Eight new rooms were being built at the time of writing.

Nan Fah Hotel (☎ 0 5471 0284; 438-440 Th Sumonthewarat; s/d/tr 350/500/600B; 🖳) This all-wooden hotel feels like a rooming house, with neat, large rooms. They all come with cable TV, fridge and hot-water showers. Being a wooden house you will hear all of your neighbour's movements, so try and get a room away from the road. There's a good restaurant attached, and bicycles, motorbikes and pick-ups can be rented here.

MIDRANGE

Fahthanin Hotel (☎ 0 5475 7322-3; 303 Th Anantaworarittidet; r 600-800B; 🖳) Seven stories tall, modern but tattered, this hotel is a good deal during the low season when rates hover around 500B. Some rooms have excellent views, and all have cable TV, hot shower and mini fridge. Heavy, ugly headboards let them down though. Slightly larger versions have bathtubs.

ourpick Dhevaraj Hotel (☎ 0 5471 0078; 466 Th Sumonthewarat; r incl breakfast 700-1200B; 🖳 🖳 🖳) This four-storey hotel potentially looks good but details have been overlooked. Rooms are built around a tiled courtyard but where seating areas could be, instead there are people dealing with the sorting and folding of laundry. Still, it is the best place in Nan for location and comfort. Rooms are clean with the amenities you'd expect at this price, and there's a restaurant and massage centre on site.

Eating

Yota Vegetarian Restaurant (Th Mahawong; dishes 10-35B; ☺ 7am-3pm) Run by the friendliest lady in town who will not let you leave hungry, this is perhaps the best deal in Nan. It's popular and once the food is gone after lunch, that's it for the day.

Miw Miw (no Roman-script sign; 347/3 Th Sumonthewarat; dishes 20-50B; ☺ 8am-10pm) Opposite Kasikornbank, this place has good *jók* (broken-rice congee), noodles, and real coffee, and it is popular in the afternoon for ice-cold *chaa yen* (Thai iced tea).

Tanaya Kitchen (☎ 0 5471 0930; 75/23-24 Th Anantaworarittidet; dishes 30-80B; ☺ 7am-9.30pm) Neat and tidy, with a creative selection of dishes made without MSG, and a variety of vegetarian (and nonvegetarian) options, Tanaya is a good choice for any diet. It caters to a mostly tourist clientele.

Suan Isan (☎ 0 5477 2913; Th Sumonthewarat; dishes 30-90B; ☺ 11am-11pm) For Isan food, this semi-outdoor spot is 200m up the lane off Th Sumonthewarat past the Bangkok Bank.

Dhevee Coffee Shop (☎ 0 5471 0094; Dhevaraj Hotel, 466 Th Sumonthewarat; dishes 40-140B; ☺ 6am-2am) Modest, clean and reliable, Dhevaraj Hotel's restaurant does good buffets (lunch buffet 59B) and is open when many other places are closed.

Da Dario Th Mahayot (☎ 08 7184 5436; Th Mahayot; dishes 40-160B; ☺ 9am-5pm); Th Anantaworarittidet (Th Anantaworarittidet; ☺ 5pm-10pm) With two locations in town, this Italian restaurant makes great breakfasts, delicious pizza and pasta, as well as other Western treats and some Thai dishes. Prices are reasonable, service is excellent, atmosphere is homey and the food attracts a cadre of regulars. The Th Anantaworarittidet branch sits above the Chinese restaurant Poom Sam.

The **night market**, on Th Anantaworarittidet by the junction with Th Pha Kong, has some tasty food stall offerings.

Shopping

Good buys include local textiles, especially the Thai Lü weaving styles from Xishuangbanna. Typical Thai Lü fabrics feature red and black designs on white cotton in floral, geometric and animal designs; indigo and red on white is also common. A favourite is the *lai náam lǎi* (flowing-water design) that shows stepped patterns representing streams, rivers and waterfalls. Local Hmong appliqué

and Mien embroidery are of excellent quality. Htin grass-and-bamboo baskets and mats are worth a look, too. The best shops for textiles are **Amnouy Porn** and **Jangtrakoon**, next to each other on Th Sumonthewarat.

There's a silver jewellery shop attached to Nan Fah Hotel (☎ 0 5471 0284; 438-440 Th Sumonthewarat). For more choice, and to see the items being made, head to **Chompu Phukha** (☎ 0 5471 0177; www.phukhasilver.com; 254 Mu 4, Th Nan-Phayao), a silver showroom and workshop. It's 1km out of town on the road to Phayao (Rte 1091), opposite a PT petrol station.

Getting There & Away
AIR
PB Air (☎ 0 5477 1729; www.pbair.com; Nan Airport) runs flights from Bangkok to Nan (3160B, once a day). Flights can be booked at the travel agency at **Fahthanin Hotel** (☎ 0 5475 7321-4; 303 Th Anantaworarittidet), online or at its airport office.

BUS
Buses travel from Chiang Mai, Chiang Rai and Phrae to Nan. The fare from Chiang Mai's Arcade terminal is ordinary bus/2nd class aircon/1st class/VIP 158/221/284/440B, six to seven hours. From and to Chiang Rai there's one daily bus at 9am (150B) that takes five to six gruelling hours via treacherous mountain roads – get a window seat as there's usually lots of motion sickness. Buses from Phrae to Nan leave frequently (ordinary/2nd class air-con/1st class/VIP 62/87/112/170B, two to 2½ hours). From Nan all buses, including privately run buses, leave from the main terminal at the southwestern edge of town.

Regular air-con buses to Bangkok cost 388B for 2nd class (7.20am, 8am, 8.30am, 9am, 6.30pm and 7pm), 497B for 1st class (8am, 9am, 7pm) and 770B for VIP (7.30pm). The journey takes 10 to 11 hours. The private Sombat Tour buses are also at the bus terminal. To reserve tickets call **Sombat Tour** (☎ 0 5471 1078) or go to the bus terminal.

SĂWNGTHĂEW
Pick-ups to districts in the northern part of the province (Tha Wang Pha, Pua, Phah Tup) leave from the petrol station opposite the Sukasem Hotel on Th Anantaworarittidet. Southbound sǎwngthǎew (for Mae Charim, Wiang Sa, Na Noi) depart from the car park opposite Ratchaphatsadu Market on Th Jettabut.

TRAIN
The northern railway makes a stop in Den Chai, a 55B, three-hour bus ride from Nan.

A Bangkok-bound Sprinter leaves Den Chai at 12.50pm and arrives in Bangkok at 8.15pm. There are also a couple of evening rapid-train departures each day; to be sure of meeting any of these trains, take an early afternoon (1pm or 2pm) Den Chai-bound bus from the Nan bus terminal.

Trains bound for Chiang Mai depart Den Chai at 3.31pm (2nd and 3rd class, arrives 7.45pm), 3.53pm (2nd class, arrives 8.20pm) and 7.14am (2nd and 3rd class, arrives 12.25pm). The 2nd- and 3rd-class fares to/from Chiang Mai are 208/153B.

Tickets can be reserved by calling the **Den Chai station** (☎ 0 5461 3260), where English is spoken.

See Phrae (p383) for more Den Chai train details.

Getting Around
Oversea Shop (☎ 0 5471 0258; 488 Th Sumonthewarat; bicycles per day 50-80B; motorcycles per day 150B) rents out better bicycles and motorcycles than other places in town. It can also handle repairs.

P Bike (no roman-script sign; ☎ 0 5477 2680; 331-3 Th Sumonthewarat; Honda Dreams incl helmet & 3rd-party insurance per day 150B), opposite Wat Hua Wiangtai, rents out Honda Dreams and bicycles, and also does repair work.

Sǎamláw around town cost 20B to 30B. Green sǎwngthǎew circulating around the city centre charge 5B to 10B per person, depending on distance.

AROUND NAN
Doi Phu Kha National Park
อุทยานแห่งชาติดอยภูคา

This **national park** (☎ 0 5473 1362; www.dnp.go.th; child/adult 200/400B) is centred on 2000m-high Doi Phu Kha in Amphoe Pua and Amphoe Bo Kleua in northeastern Nan (about 75km from Nan). There are several Htin, Mien, Hmong and Thai Lü **villages** in the park and vicinity, as well as a couple of **caves** and **waterfalls**, and endless opportunities for forest **walks**. At the time of writing there were no maps at park headquarters but it's possible to hire a guide (300B a day) there. The park is often cold in the cool season and especially wet in the wet season.

The park offers A-frame **bungalows** (☎ 0 2562 0760; reserve@dnp.go.th; for 2-7 people 300-2500B).

NORTHERN THAILAND

You must bring food and drinking water in from town, as the park office no longer offers food service.

Bamboo Hut (☎ 08 1883 7687; 103 Mu 10, Tambon Phu Kha, Amphoe Pua, Nan 55120; r 200B) in Ban Toei, a Lawa-Thai village near the summit at the edge of the park, is a much better choice than the park bungalows. Bamboo Hut offers five simple and clean, well-spaced bamboo-thatch huts with shared bathroom and stupendous mountain and valley views. It leads guests on one- to three-day treks (600B per day, including all meals). Treks visit local waterfalls, limestone caves (Tham Lawng is the biggest cave – about a one-day walk from the guesthouse) and hill-tribe villages. This area can get quite cool in the winter months – evening temperatures of 5°C to 10°C are not uncommon – so dress accordingly.

To reach the national park by public transport you must first take a bus or săwngthăew north of Nan to Pua (30B), and then pick up one of the infrequent săwngthăew to the park headquarters or Bamboo Hut (35B). The one that goes from Nan to Pua leaves about 6am, the one from Pua to Ban Toei at about 7am.

Ban Bo Kleua is a Htin village southeast of the park where the main occupation is the extraction of salt from local salt wells. It's easy to find the main community salt well, more or less in the centre of the village. Many small shops and vendor stands sell the local salt in 2kg bags for 25B; it's delicious stuff. Rte 1256 meets Rte 1081 near Ban Bo Kleua; Rte 1081 can be followed south back to Nan (107km) via a network of unpaved roads.

Nong Bua
หนองบัว

This neat and tidy Thai Lü village near the town of Tha Wang Pha, approximately 30km north of Nan, is famous for Lü-style **Wat Nong Bua**. Featuring a typical two-tiered roof and carved wooden portico, the *bòt* design is simple yet striking – note the carved *naga* heads at the roof corners. Inside the *bòt* are some noteworthy but faded *jataka* murals thought to have been painted by the same mural artists as Wat Phumin. The building is often locked when religious services aren't in progress, but there's usually someone around to unlock the door. Be sure to leave at the altar a donation for temple upkeep and for its restoration.

You can also see Thai Lü weavers at work in the village. The home of **Khun Janthasom Phrompanya**, a few blocks behind the wat, serves as a local weaving centre – check there for the locations of looms or to look at fabrics for purchase. Large *yâam* (hill-tribe-style shoulder bags) are available for around 60B, while nicely woven neck scarves cost more. There are also several weaving houses just behind the wat.

GETTING THERE & AWAY
Săwngthăew to Tha Wang Pha (20B) leave from opposite Nan's Sukasem Hotel. Or take a bus from the main bus station. Get off at Samyaek Longbom, a three-way intersection before Tha Wang Pha, and walk west to a bridge over Mae Nam Nan, then left at the dead end on the other side of the bridge to Wat Nong Bua. It's 3.1km from the highway to the wat.

If you're coming from Nan via your own transport on Rte 1080, you'll cross a stream called Lam Nam Yang just past the village of Ban Fai Mun but before Tha Wang Pha. Take the first left off Rte 1080 and follow it to a dead end; turn right and then left over a bridge across Mae Nam Nan and walk until you reach another dead end. Turn left and continue for 2km until you can see Wat Nong Bua on the right.

Tham Phah Tup Forest Reserve
ถ้ำผาตูบ

This limestone cave complex is about 10km north of Nan and is part of a relatively new wildlife reserve. Some 17 **caves** have been counted, of which nine are easily located by means of established (but unmarked) trails.

From Nan you can catch a săwngthăew bound for Pua or Thung Chang; it will stop at the turn-off to the caves for 15B. The vehicles leave from the petrol station opposite the Sukasem Hotel.

Sao Din
เสาดิน

Literally 'Earth Pillars', Sao Din is an erosional phenomenon similar to that found at Phae Meuang Phi in Phrae Province – tall columns of earth protruding from a barren depression. The area covers nearly 3.2 hectares off Rte 1026 in Amphoe Na Noi, about 60km south of Nan.

Sao Din is best visited by bike or motorbike since it's time consuming to reach by

NORTHERN THAILAND

public transport. If you don't have your own wheels, take a săwngthăew to Na Noi from the southbound săwngthăew station opposite Ratchaphatsadu Market in Nan. From Na Noi you must get yet another săwngthăew bound for Fak Tha or Ban Khok, getting off at the entrance to Sao Din after 5km or so. From here you'll have to walk or hitch 4km to Sao Din itself. There are also occasional direct săwngthăew from Na Noi.

Northwest of Sao Din, off Rte 1216, is a set of earth pillars called **Hom Chom**.

Other Attractions

Twenty kilometres north of Nan on Route 1080 is the **Nan Riverside Gallery** (☎ 0 5479 8046; www.nanartgallery.com; Km 20 Rte 1080; admission 20B; ☸ 9am-5pm Wed-Sun), where contemporary Nan-influenced art is exhibited in a peaceful setting. Established in 2004 by Nan artist Winai Prabipoo, this two-storey building holds the more interesting temporary exhibitions downstairs – sculpture, ceramics and drawings – as well as a permanent painting collection upstairs – which seems to be mainly inspired by the Wat Phumin murals. The unusual building is a light-filled converted rice barn with an arrow shaped turret. The shop and café have seats right on the Mae Nam Nan and the beautiful manicured gardens are nice to wander around. From Nan, take a bus (20B) or a săwngthăew (30B) to the gallery.

There are a couple of interesting destinations in and around the Thai Lü village of **Pua**, roughly 50km north of Nan. In Pua itself you can check out another famous Thai Lü temple, **Wat Ton Laeng**, which is admired for its classic three-tiered roof. **Nam Tok Silaphet** (Silaphet Waterfall) is southeast of Pua just off the road between Pua and Ban Nam Yao. The water falls in a wide swath over a cliff and is best seen at the end of the monsoon season in November. On the way to the falls and west of the road is the Mien village of **Ban Pa Klang**, worth a visit to see silversmiths at work. This village supplies many silver shops in Chiang Mai and Bangkok. Other silverwork Mien villages can be found on Rte 101 between Nan and Phrae.

In the northwest of the province, off Rte 1148 and north of the village of Ban Sakoen, is a huge, 200m-wide cave called **Tham Luang**. The path to the cave is not signposted, but if you ask at the police checkpoint in Ban Sakoen you should be able to get directions or you might even find a guide.

To the south about 100km, **Thaleh Sap Neua** (Northern Lake) formed by Kheuan Sirikit is an important freshwater fishery for Nan, as well as a recreational attraction for Nan residents. **Ban Pak Nai** on its northwestern shore is the main fishing village. Just before Mae Nam Nan feeds into the lake at its extreme northern end, there is a set of river rapids called **Kaeng Luang**.

Every Saturday morning from around 5am to 11am there's a lively Lao-Thai **market** in Thung Chang.

Border Crossing (Laos)

There have been rumours for years that Ban Huay Kon (140km north of Nan) in Amphoe Thung Chang may some day be open to foreigners. For now, it's for Thais and Lao only.

PHITSANULOK PROVINCE

PHITSANULOK

พิษณุโลก
pop 100,300

Under the reign of Ayuthaya King Borom Trailokanat (1448–88), Phitsanulok served as the capital of Thailand for 25 years. Because the town straddles Mae Nam Nan near a junction with Mae Nam Khwae Noi, it's sometimes referred to as Song Khwae (Two Tributaries). The city was associated with floating houseboats lining the banks, as it's the only city in Thailand where it's legal to reside on a houseboat within municipal boundaries. However, most have now been moved to the outskirts of the city. The central Ekathotsarn Bridge is lit up with blinging red and blue lights, and each night a lively night market lines the banks south of here.

Due to large parts of the town being burned down by a massive fire in 1957, the architecture of the city is pretty nondescript. Yet, this vibrant and extremely friendly city boasts some interesting sites and museums, chief of which is Wat Phra Si Ratana Mahathat, which contains one of Thailand's most revered Buddha images.

Phitsanulok makes an excellent base from which to explore the attractions of historical Sukhothai, Kamphaeng Phet and Si

NORTHERN THAILAND

Satchanalai, as well as the national parks and wildlife sanctuaries of Thung Salaeng Luang and Phu Hin Rong Kla, the former strategic headquarters of the Communist Party of Thailand (CPT). All of these places are within 150km of Phitsanulok.

The name Phitsanulok is often abbreviated as 'Philok'.

Information

Shops offering internet access dot the streets around the railway station, near the Topland Hotel and on the western bank of the river near Saphan Ekathotsarot. Prices range from 15B per hour for slow connections to 60B per hour for the slightly faster connections. Several banks in town offer foreign-exchange

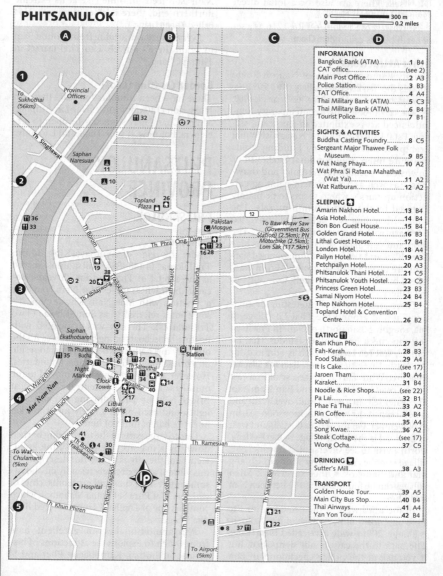

PHITSANULOK

| 0 | 300 m |
| 0 | 0.2 miles |

INFORMATION
Bangkok Bank (ATM).............................**1** B4
CAT office...(see 2)
Main Post Office..................................**2** A3
Police Station.......................................**3** B3
TAT Office..**4** A4
Thai Military Bank (ATM)....................**5** C3
Thai Military Bank (ATM)....................**6** B4
Tourist Police.......................................**7** B1

SIGHTS & ACTIVITIES
Buddha Casting Foundry.....................**8** C5
Sergeant Major Thawee Folk
    Museum...**9** B5
Wat Nang Phaya.................................**10** A2
Wat Phra Si Ratana Mahathat
    (Wat Yai)..**11** A2
Wat Ratburan.....................................**12** A2

SLEEPING
Amarin Nakhon Hotel.......................**13** B4
Asia Hotel..**14** B4
Bon Bon Guest House........................**15** B4
Golden Grand Hotel..........................**16** B3
Lithai Guest House.............................**17** B4
London Hotel......................................**18** A4
Pailyn Hotel.......................................**19** A3
Petchpailyn Hotel..............................**20** A3
Phitsanulok Thani Hotel....................**21** C5
Phitsanulok Youth Hostel..................**22** C5
Princess Green Hotel.........................**23** B3
Samai Niyom Hotel............................**24** B4
Thep Nakhorn Hotel..........................**25** B4
Topland Hotel & Convention
    Centre...**26** B2

EATING
Ban Khun Pho....................................**27** B4
Fah-Kerah..**28** B3
Food Stalls...**29** A4
It Is Cake...(see 17)
Jaroen Tham......................................**30** A4
Karaket...**31** B4
Noodle & Rice Shops.....................(see 22)
Pa Lai...**32** B1
Phae Fa Thai......................................**33** A2
Rin Coffee..**34** B4
Sabai..**35** B4
Song Kwae...**36** A2
Steak Cottage.................................(see 17)
Wong Ocha..**37** C5

DRINKING
Sutter's Mill.......................................**38** A3

TRANSPORT
Golden House Tour............................**39** A5
Main City Bus Stop............................**40** B4
Thai Airways......................................**41** A4
Yan Yon Tour.....................................**42** B4

services and ATMs. There's also an ATM inside the Wat Phra Si Ratana Mahathat compound.

Bangkok Bank (35 Th Naresuan; ☉ to 8pm) An after-hours exchange window.

CAT office (Th Phuttha Bucha; ☉ 7am-11pm) At the post office. Offers phone and internet services.

Left-luggage storage (train station; per day 10B; ☉ 7am-10pm)

Main post office (Th Phuttha Bucha; ☉ 8.30am-4.30pm Mon-Fri, 9am-noon Sat & Sun)

TAT office (☎ 0 5525 2742-3; tatphlok@tat.or.th; 209/7-8 Th Borom Trailokanat; ☉ 8.30am-4.30pm) Off Th Borom Trailokanat, with knowledgeable, helpful staff (some of TAT's best) who hand out free maps of the town and a walking-tour sheet. It also runs a sightseeing tram (see p399). This is the official information office for Sukhothai and Phetchabun Provinces as well. If you plan to do the trip from Phitsanulok to Lom Sak, ask for the 'Green Route' map of Hwy 12, which marks several national parks, waterfalls and resorts along the way.

Tourist Police (☎ 1155; Th Ekathotsarot) 300m north of Topland Hotel.

Sights
WAT PHRA SI RATANA MAHATHAT
วัดพระศรีรัตนมหาธาตุ

The full name of this temple is Wat Phra Si Ratana Mahathat, but the locals call it Wat Phra Si or Wat Yai. The wat stands near the east end of the bridge over Mae Nam Nan (on the right as you're heading out of Phitsanulok towards Sukhothai). The main *wíhǎan* contains the Chinnarat Buddha (Phra Phuttha Chinnarat), one of Thailand's most revered and copied images. This famous bronze image is probably second in importance only to the Emerald Buddha in Bangkok's Wat Phra Kaew. In terms of total annual donations collected (around 12 million baht a year), Wat Yai follows Wat Sothon in Chachoengsao, east of Bangkok.

The image was cast in the late Sukhothai style, but what makes it strikingly unique is the flamelike halo around the head and torso that turns up at the bottom to become dragon-serpent heads on either side of the image. The head of this Buddha is a little wider than standard Sukhothai, giving the statue a very solid feel.

The story goes that construction of this wat was commissioned under the reign of King Li Thai in 1357. When it was completed, King Li Thai wanted it to contain three high-quality bronze images, so he sent for well-known sculptors from Si Satchanalai, Chiang Saen and Hariphunchai (Lamphun), as well as five Brahman priests. The first two castings worked well, but the third required three attempts before it was decreed the best of all. Legend has it that a white-robed sage appeared from nowhere to assist in the final casting, then disappeared. This last image was named the Chinnarat (Victorious King) Buddha and it became the centrepiece in the *wíhǎan*. The other two images, Phra Chinnasi and Phra Si Satsada, were later moved to the royal temple of Wat Bowonniwet in Bangkok. Only the Chinnarat image has the flame-dragon halo.

The walls of the *wíhǎan* are low to accommodate the low-swept roof, typical of northern temple architecture, so the image takes on larger proportions than it might in a central or northeastern wat. The brilliant interior architecture is such that when you sit on the Italian marble floor in front of the Buddha, the lacquered columns draw your vision towards the image and evoke a strong sense of serenity. The doors of the building are inlaid with mother-of-pearl in a design copied from Bangkok's Wat Phra Kaew.

Another sanctuary to one side has been converted into a free **museum** (☉ 9am-5.30pm Wed-Sun), displaying antique Buddha images, ceramics and other historic artefacts. Túk-túk line the entrance street, souvenir stands line the walkways, and there's an ATM and notable tourist police within the walls of the complex. Dress appropriately when visiting this most sacred of temples – no shorts or sleeveless tops.

Near Wat Yai, on the same side of the river, are two other temples of the same period – **Wat Ratburan** and **Wat Nang Phaya**.

WAT CHULAMANI
วัดจุฬามณี

Five kilometres south of the city (bus 5 down Th Borom Trailokanat, 4B), Wat Chulamani harbours some ruins dating to the Sukhothai period. The original buildings must have been impressive, judging from what remains of the ornate Khmer-style tower. King Borom Trailokanat was ordained as a monk here and there is an old Thai inscription to that effect on the ruined *wíhǎan*, dating from the reign of King Narai the Great.

The tower has little left of its original height, but Khmer-style lintels remain,

NORTHERN THAILAND

including one with a Sukhothai walking Buddha and a *dhammacakka* (Buddhist wheel of law) in the background.

As well as the tower and the *wíhǎan*, the only original structures left at Wat Chulamani are the remains of the monastery walls. Still, there is a peaceful, neglected atmosphere about the place.

FOLK MUSEUM, BUDDHA-CASTING FOUNDRY & BIRD GARDEN
พิพิธภัณฑ์พื้นบ้านนายทวี/โรงหล่อพระ

The **Sergeant Major Thawee Folk Museum** (26/43 Th Wisut Kasat; bus 8; admission 50B; 8.30am-4.30pm Tue-Sun) displays a remarkable collection of tools, textiles and photographs from Phitsanulok Province. Sergeant Thawee was a military cartographer turned Buddha caster who recognised that old ways of life were dying so he started collecting items to preserve their place in Thailand. The museum is spread throughout five traditional-style Thai buildings with well-groomed gardens. There's a small, kids' play area behind the two far buildings. Some of the more impressive objects are the bird traps, ceremonial clothing, ancient kitchen utensils and basketry. Perhaps the most unique exhibit is that of a traditional birthing room.

Across the street is a small **Buddha Casting Foundry** (8am-5pm) where bronze Buddha images of all sizes are cast. Most are copies of the famous Phra Chinnarat Buddha at Wat Yai. Visitors are welcome to watch and there are even detailed photo exhibits demonstrating the lost-wax method of metal casting. Some of the larger images take a year or more to complete. The foundry is also owned by Dr Thawee, an artisan and nationally renowned expert on northern-Thai folklore. There is a small gift shop at the foundry where you can purchase bronze images of various sizes.

In addition to the foundry, there is a display of fighting cocks, which are bred and sold all over Thailand. (The official English name for this part of the facility is 'The Centre of Conservative Folk Cock'.)

Attached to the foundry is Dr Thawee's new project, the **Thai Bird Garden** (0 5521 2540; child/adult 20/50B; 8.30am-5pm). This small collection of aviaries contains indigenous Thai birds and some endangered species, like the very pretty pink-chested jamu fruit-dove, and the prehistoric-looking helmeted hornbill. Unfortunately, the cages look too small and most of the birds are caged alone.

Sleeping
BUDGET

Phitsanulok has a good selection of budget lodgings. However, the large hotels in the budget category tend to have a problem with maintenance.

Phitsanulok Youth Hostel (0 5524 2060; www .tyha.org; 38 Th Sanam Bin; dm/tr/q 120/450/600B, s 200-300B, d 300-400;) This is a good choice during the high season when backpackers fill the place. It has a lot of character, with rooms made of salvaged teak, and many intricate details on antique doors and furniture. The outdoor seating area has hammocks and is surrounded by greenery. Rates include breakfast. Starting around January 2007, a one-year renovation is planned – call to check if it is open. To get here take bus 12 or 4 from the train station, and bus 1 from the bus terminal. Buses stop outside the large hotel next door.

London Hotel (0 5522 5145; 21-22 Soi 1, Th Phuttha Bucha; r 150B) This old, wooden, Thai-Chinese hotel is as close to an early-20th-century rooming house as you'll find. These eight clean and colourfully tiled rooms share three cold-water bathrooms.

our pick **Lithai Guest House** (0 5521 9626; 73 Th Phayalithai; s 240-350B, d 460B;) This place is so clean it gleams. The light-filled 60 or so rooms don't have much character but they are the best value in town. Most have large en suite bathrooms with hot water, cable TV, plentiful furniture and a fridge. Rates include breakfast and free bottled water. There is an air ticket agent, coffee shop and restaurant on site.

our pick **Bon Bon Guest House** (0 5521 9058; Th Phayalithai; r 300B;) Don't be discouraged by the building out front, it is worth going inside. The quiet, spotless rooms have some charm and all feature hot-water showers and cable TVs. The communal area is very cutesy with its collection of ceramic pigs and chickens.

Princess Green Hotel (0 5530 4988; Th Phra Ong Dam; r 390-490B;) This brand new 28-room hotel has spacious, spotless rooms that are well furnished, and have cable TVs and mini-bars. Some rooms could do with a few more lights, and the mosque is not far, so early morning wake-up calls may be an issue. There is a restaurant and bar attached.

Petchpailyn Hotel (0 5525 8844; 4/8 Th Athitaywong; s/d 400/450B;) The rooms here are

spacious and clean, but a little dark. A Chinese-style buffet breakfast is included in the rates. Rooms towards the back are considerably quieter.

Both the **Asia** (☎ 0 5525 8378; Th Ekathotsarot; r 250-380B; ❄) and the **Samai Niyom** (☎ 0 5525 8575; 175 Th Ekathotsarot; r 250-380B; ❄) hotels are conveniently located by the train station. Unfortunately, their posh looking lobbies don't reflect the state of the rooms inside. Most are in serious need of a revamp, especially the cheaper rooms. Asia Hotel's rooms have the edge with better furnishings.

MIDRANGE

Golden Grand Hotel (☎ 0 5521 0234; 66 Th Thammabucha; r 690-850B; ⊠ ❄ 💻) A solid midrange hotel, the rooms here are a vision of green, mint and white, and are large, well maintained and feature a private balcony. Staff are friendly and there's a restaurant on site.

Thep Nakhorn Hotel (☎ 0 5524 4070; www.geocities.com/thepnakorn_hotel; 43/1 Th Sithamatraipidok; s/d incl US breakfast 750/840B, ste 3500B; ❄) This six-storey hotel offers great-value, superclean, smart rooms with spacious bathrooms. Professional service but little English is spoken.

TOP END

Discounts at Phitsanulok's top-end hotels are usually available online. Prices below are for walk-in guests.

Pailyn Hotel (☎ 0 5525 2411; 38 Th Borom Trailokanat; s/d/ste incl breakfast 1000/1200/2000B; ⊠ ❄) The conveniently located, thirteen-storey Pailyn has an enormous lobby with an unfortunate looking catfish squashed in a tank. The rooms are spacious, have cable TV, minibars, and are well decorated apart from very loud batik panels above the beds. Some have great river views. There are several restaurants and lounges downstairs, and the staff members are professional and helpful.

Phitsanulok Thani Hotel (☎ 0 5521 1065; www.phitsanulokthani.com; Th Sanam Bin; r/ste incl breakfast 1200/2000-4000B; ⊠ ❄ 💻) At the Folk Museum end of town, this hotel is part of the Dusit chain and offers all the basics, plus a few extras. The rooms are large yet cosy and tastefully decorated. There's a restaurant and cocktail lounge, and the spa is over the road.

Topland Hotel & Convention Centre (☎ 0 5524 7800; www.toplandhotel.com; cnr Th Singhawat & Th Ekathotsarot; r incl breakfast 1400-1600B, ste incl breakfast 2400-4800B; ⊠ ❄ 💻 🏊) The luxurious and well-run Topland has a beauty salon, café, snooker club, fitness centre, several restaurants and other facilities. The upper-floor rooms afford great views of Phitsanulok. Rooms are comfortable, large and have cable TV.

Eating

Phitsanulok takes its cuisine seriously. In addition to one of the most active night markets, there's a solid collection of high-quality restaurants.

DOWNTOWN

As well as the **night market** (see p398) market-style **food stalls** (dishes 20-40B) cluster just west of the London Hotel.

Fah-Kerah (786 Th Phra Ong Dam; dishes 5-20B; 🕑 6am-2pm) There are several Thai-Muslim cafés near the mosque on Th Phra Ong Dam, and this is a popular one. Thick *rotii* is served up with *kaeng mátsàmàn* (Muslim curry), fresh yogurt is made daily and the *rotii kaeng* (set plate) is a steal at 20B.

Jaroen Tham (Vegetarian Food; Th Sithamatraipidok; dishes 15-20B; 🕑 8am-3pm) Around the corner from the TAT office, this simple place serves a choice of vegetarian dishes paired with husky brown rice. Look for a sign saying 'Vegetarian Food'.

Rin Coffee (☎ 0 5525 2848; 20 Th Salreuthai; dishes 15-50B; 🕑 7.30am-9pm, Sat-Sun 9.30am-9pm) This light-filled, glass-fronted café is popular with young Thais. Whole menu pages are dedicated to various green tea, coffee and chocolate drink concoctions. Sit in the brightly coloured seats or perch at the bar and sample the ice cream, hearty breakfasts, waffles, sandwiches or salads.

Karaket (Thai Food; ☎ 0 5525 8193; Th Phayalithai; dishes 20-30B; 🕑 1-8pm) Opposite Bon Bon Guest House, this simple restaurant has a variety of fresh curries and vegetables on display. Choose from the dishes in the metal trays out front. On the walls, there are interesting pictures of Phitsanulok before the 1957 fire.

Steak Cottage (☎ 0 5521 9626; dishes 40-150B; 🕑 7am-2pm & 5-9pm Mon-Sat) In the Lithai Building complex, this air-conditioned eatery serves salmon, beef and chicken steaks. It also serves other high-quality European and Thai dishes.

It is Cake (🕑 9am-9pm) In the same building as the Steak Cottage, this place sells decent cakes, tarts and pies as well as good sandwiches,

salad and pasta. It has an outside seating area, plus a squeaky clean air-con section.

Ban Khun Pho (Th Chao Phraya; dishes 50-90B; ☪ 11am-2pm, 6-11pm) Opposite the Amarin Nakhon Hotel, this clean, cosy place is decorated with antiques. On the menu are Thai, Japanese and Western selections.

Near the Phitsanulok Youth Hostel are some small **noodle and rice shops**. Around the corner, **Wong Ocha** (no roman-script sign; Th Sanam Bin; dishes 15-30B; ☪ 8am-10pm) is a permanent stall dishing delicious *kài yâang, khâo nĭaw* (sticky rice) and *yam phàk kràchèt* (water mimosa salad).

For snacks and self-catering, there's a huge supermarket in the basement of the Topland Shopping Plaza.

ON THE RIVER
Night market (dishes 40-80B; ☪ 5pm-3am) Several street vendors specialise in *phàk bûng lawy fáa* (literally 'floating-in-the-sky morning glory vine'), which usually translates as 'flying vegetable'. Originated in Chonburi, this food fad has somehow taken root in Phitsanulok. The dish isn't especially tasty – basically water spinach stir-fried with garlic in soya-bean sauce – but the preparation is a performance: the cook fires up a batch of *phàk bûng* in the wok and then flings it through the air to a waiting server who catches it on a plate. Some of the places are so performance-oriented that the server climbs to the top of a van to catch the flying vegetable! If you're lucky, you'll be here when a tour group is trying to catch the flying vegetables, but is actually dropping *phàk bûng* all over the place.

Pa Lai (no roman-script sign; Th Phuttha Bucha; dishes 20-60B; ☪ 10am-4pm) Opposite the river, north of Wat Phra Si Ratana Mahathat, this popular open-air restaurant serves *kŭaytĭaw hâwy khàa* (literally, legs-hanging rice noodles). The name comes from the way customers sit on a bench facing the river, with their legs dangling below. There are several copycats nearby.

Floating restaurants light up Mae Nam Nan at night. Good choices include **Phae Fa Thai** (☎ 0 5524 2743; Th Wangchan; dishes 30-120B; ☪ 11am-11pm) and **Sabai** (Th Wangchan; dishes 40-140B; ☪ 11am-11pm), the latter is located by the massive Grand Riverside hotel. Just north of Phae Fa Thai is **Song Kwae** (☎ 0 5524 2167; Th Wangchan; boarding fee 40B; dishes 50-150B; ☪ 11am-11pm) a restaurant boat that cruises Mae Nam Nan

nightly. You pay a fee to board the boat and then order from a menu as you please.

Drinking & Entertainment

Along Th Borom Trailokanat near the Pailyn Hotel is a string of popular, rockin' Thai pubs.

Sutter's Mill (Th Borom Trailokanat) Opposite the entrance to Petchpailyn Hotel, this bar has a cowboy theme going on. It has outdoor and indoor seating areas and features live Thaifolk and pop. Food is available and music starts at 8pm.

Getting There & Away

AIR
Thai Airways (☎ 0 5524 2971-2; 209/26-28 Th Borom Trailokanat; ☪ 8am-5pm Mon-Fri) operates daily connections (55 minutes) to Phitsanulok from Bangkok (2185B). Tickets can also be booked at the travel agent attached to Lithai Guest House (p396).

BUS
Transport options out of Phitsanulok are good, as it's a junction for bus routes both north and northeast. Bangkok is six hours away by bus and Chiang Mai is 5½ hours. Phitsanulok's Baw Khaw Saw bus terminal is 2km east of town on Hwy 12. Second and 1st class air-con buses go to Bangkok every hour from 7.30am to 11.30pm daily (2nd class/1st class air-con 240/297B). VIP buses to Bangkok depart once a day at 11.30pm (347B). Buses to destinations in other northern and northeastern provinces leave regularly from the Baw Khaw Saw bus terminal. See the table (opposite) for fares.

Yan Yon Tour (☎ 0 5525 8647; Th Ekathotsarot) runs 1st class air-con and VIP buses to Bangkok (1st class/VIP 297/407B, 9.15am-12.30pm) from the centre of town.

TRAIN
For most people, reaching Phitsanulok from Bangkok via train rather than bus is more economical and convenient, since you don't have to go out to Bangkok's Northern and Northeastern bus station. Timetables and prices are readily available at Bangkok's Hualamphong station. To check the most up-to-date timetables and prices in advance call the State Railway of Thailand or look at their website (www.railway.co.th; ☎ 0 2220 4334, free 24-hr hotline 1690).

BUS DESTINATIONS FROM PHITSANULOK

Destination	Bus	Fare (B)	Duration (hr)	Destination	Bus	Fare (B)	Duration (hr)
Chiang Mai (via Uttaradit)				Mae Sot			
	ordinary	162	5		air-con minivan	167	5
	2nd class air-con	227	5	Nakhon Ratchasima (Khorat)			
	1st class air-con	292	5				
	VIP	340	5		2nd class air-con	263	6
Chiang Mai (via Tak)					1st class air-con	338	6
					VIP	395	6
	ordinary	191	6	Nan			
	2nd class air-con	267	6		1st class air-con	199	9
	1st class air-con	344	6		VIP	258	8
Chiang Rai (via Sukhothai)				Sukhothai**			
	ordinary	246	6		ordinary	30	1
	2nd class air-con	267	5		air-con	42	1
	1st class air-con	344	5	Tak*			
	VIP	401	5		ordinary	68	3
Kamphaeng Phet*					air-con	95	3
	ordinary	57	3	Udon Thani			
	air-con	80	3		ordinary	167	7
Khon Kaen					1st class air-con	234	7
	ordinary	154	6		VIP	301	7
	2nd class air-con	215	6				
	1st class air-con	277	5				

*Buses to Kamphaeng Phet & Tak leave every hour.
**Buses to Sukhothai leave every half-hour.

Rapid trains (2nd class/3rd class 309/219B) depart from Bangkok five times each day at 5.50am, 7am, 2.30pm, 7.50pm and 8.10pm and take seven hours. There are also three air-con, 2nd-class, express-diesel trains (or 'Sprinter'), at 8.30am, 10.50pm and 7.20pm daily (449B, five hours), which are about two hours quicker than the rapid service. A 1st- and 2nd-class sleeper train (1064/629-699B, six hours) departs at 7.35pm.

If you're continuing straight to Sukhothai from Phitsanulok, take the city bus 10 (fan/air-con 8B/11B) or a túk-túk (50B) from the train station to the bus station 4km away. From there you can catch a bus to Sukhothai.

Getting Around

Săamláw rides within the town centre should cost no more than 50B. Outside the train station there's a sign indicating túk-túk prices for different destinations around town: bus terminal 50B, airport 150B, temples 50B, TAT

office 50B, Folklore Museum 50B, post-office 50B.

Ordinary city buses cost 8B and there are 18 routes, making it easy to get just about anywhere by bus. A couple of the lines also feature air-con coaches for 11B. The main bus stop for city buses is south of the train station, on Th Ekathotsarot.

To get to the bus terminal from town take bus 1 or 8 (ordinary/air-con 8/11B). There is no city bus to the airport but túk-túk go there for 150B. Bus 1 also goes to Wat Phra Si Ratana Mahathat (or Wat Yai) and bus 8 also goes to the Folk Museum and Buddha Foundry.

Run by the TAT, the Phitsanulok Tour Tramway (PTT) is a quick way to see many sights. The ride takes around 45 minutes, with the first departing at 9am and the last at 3pm. The **tram** (child/adult 20/30B) leaves from Wat Yai and stops at 15 sights before returning to the same temple.

The only place in town to rent motorcycles is **PN Motorbike** (☎ 0 5530 3222; Th Mittraphap; 125cc

motorbike per day 200B; ☺ 8.30am-5.30pm Mon-Sat) located next to the bus terminal.

Phitsanulok's **airport** (☎ 0 5530 1002) is 5km south of town. Thai Airways has a door-to-door van service that shuttles incoming flight passengers to accommodation in Phitsanulok (50B per person). **Golden House Tour** (☎ 0 5525 9973; 55/37 Th Borom Trailokanat), has a board at the airport indicating its mini-van service from the airport to hotels (150B per person). Túk-túk go to the airport from town for 150B.

Budget (☎ 0 5525 8556; www.budget.co.th) and **Avis** (☎ 0 5524 2060; www.avisthailand.com) have car-rental offices at the airport. They charge from 1350B per day.

PHU HIN RONG KLA NATIONAL PARK
อุทยานแห่งชาติภูหินร่องกล้า
Between 1967 and 1982, the mountain that is known as Phu Hin Rong Kla served as the strategic headquarters for the Communist Party of Thailand (CPT) and its tactical arm, the People's Liberation Army of Thailand (PLAT). The remote, easily defended summit was perfect for an insurgent army. Another benefit was that the headquarters was only 50km from the Lao border, so lines of retreat were well guarded after 1975 when Laos fell to the Pathet Lao. China's Yunnan Province is only 300km away and it was here that CPT cadres received their training in revolutionary tactics. (This was until the 1979 split between the Chinese and Vietnamese communists, when the CPT sided with Vietnam.)

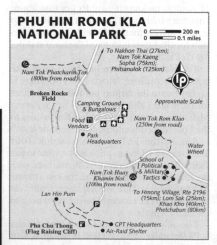

PHU HIN RONG KLA NATIONAL PARK

For nearly 20 years the area around Phu Hin Rong Kla served as a battlefield for Thai troops and the communists. In 1972 the Thai government launched an unsuccessful major offensive against the PLAT. The CPT camp at Phu Hin Rong Kla became especially active after the Thai military killed hundreds of students in Bangkok during the October 1976 student-worker uprising. Many students subsequently fled here to join the CPT, setting up a hospital and a school of political and military tactics. By 1978 the PLAT ranks here had swelled to 4000. In 1980 and 1981 the Thai armed forces tried again and were able to recapture some parts of CPT territory. But the decisive blow to the CPT came in 1982, when the government declared an amnesty for all the students who had joined the communists after 1976. The departure of most of the students broke the spine of the movement, which had become dependent on their membership. A final military push in late 1982 effected the surrender of the PLAT, and Phu Hin Rong Kla was declared a national park in 1984.

Orientation & Information
The **park** (www.dnp.go.th; admission 400B; ☺ 8.30am-5pm) covers about 307 sq km of rugged mountains and forest. The elevation at park headquarters is about 1000m, so the area is refreshingly cool even in the hot season. Attractions on the main road through the park include the remains of the CPT stronghold – a rustic meeting hall, the school of political and military tactics – and the CPT administration building. Across the road from the school is a water wheel designed by exiled engineering students.

Sights & Activities
A trail leads to **Pha Chu Thong** (Flag Raising Cliff, sometimes called Red Flag Cliff), where the communists would raise the red flag to announce a military victory. Also in this area is an **air-raid shelter**, a **lookout** and the remains of the main **CPT headquarters** – the most inaccessible point in the territory before a road was constructed by the Thai government. The buildings in the park are made out of wood and bamboo and have no plumbing or electricity – a testament to how primitive the living conditions were.

There is a small **museum** at the park headquarters that displays relics from CPT days, including weapons and medical instruments. At the end of the road into the park is a small

White Hmong village. When the CPT was here the Hmong were its ally. Now the Hmong are undergoing 'cultural assimilation' at the hands of the Thai government.

If you're not interested in the history of Phu Hin Rong Kla, there are **waterfalls, hiking trails** and **scenic views**, as well as some interesting rock formations – jutting boulders called **Lan Hin Pum**, and an area of deep rocky crevices where PLAT troops would hide during air raids, called **Lan Hin Taek**. Ask at the Visitor Centre (8.30am-4.30pm) for maps.

Phu Hin Rong Kla can become quite crowded on weekends and holidays; schedule a more peaceful visit for midweek.

Sleeping & Eating

Thailand's Royal Forest Department (0 5523 3527; reserve@dnp.go.th; bungalows 800-2400B; tent pitch 30B, 2-8 person tent 150-600B) Bungalows for two to eight people, in three different zones of the park, can be rented from this organisation. You can also pitch a tent or rent one. Sleeping bags (30B) and pillows (10B) are available.

Golden House Tour (0 5525 9973; 55/37 Th Trailokanat; 8am-6.30pm) Near the TAT office in Phitsanulok, it can help book accommodation.

Near the camping ground and bungalows are restaurants and food vendors. The best are **Duang Jai Cafeteria** – try its famous carrot *sôm-tam* – and **Rang Thong**.

Getting There & Away

The park headquarters is about 125km from Phitsanulok. To get here, first take an early bus to Nakhon Thai (35B, two hours, hourly from 6am to 6pm). From there you can catch a *săwngthăew* to the park (30B, three times daily from 7.30am to 4.30pm). If you have your own vehicle, turn at Hwy 12's Km 85 stone to take Rte 2013, then go east on Route 2331 for the Visitor Centre entrance.

A small group can charter a pick-up and driver in Nakhon Thai for around 800B for the day. Golden House Tour (above) charges 1500B for car and driver; petrol is extra. This is a delightful trip if you're on a motorcycle since there's not much traffic along the way, but a strong engine is necessary to conquer the hills to Phu Hin Rong Kla.

PHITSANULOK TO LOM SAK

Hwy 12 between Phitsanulok and Lom Sak is known as the 'Green Route', which parallels the scenic, rapid-studded Lam Nam Khek.

Off this route are waterfalls, resorts, the Phu Hin Rong Kla (opposite) and Thung Salaeng Luang National Parks. The sites tend to be more popular on weekends and holidays.

Any of the resorts along Hwy 12 can organise **white-water rafting** trips on the Lam Nam Khek along the section with the most rapids, which corresponds more or less between Km 45 and 52 of Hwy 12.

The Phitsanulok TAT office (p395) distributes a 'Green Route' map of the attractions along this 130km stretch of road. You may want to bypass the first two waterfalls, **Nam Tok Sakhunothayan** (at the Km 33 marker) and **Kaeng Song** (at the Km 45 marker), which are on the way to Phu Hin Rong Kla and therefore get overwhelmed with visitors. The third, **Kaeng Sopha** at the Km 72 marker, is a larger area of small falls and rapids where you can walk from rock formation to rock formation – there are more or fewer rocks depending on the rains. **Food vendors** provide inexpensive *sôm-tam* and *kài yâang*. In between the Kaeng Song and Kaeng Sopha waterfalls, turning off at Km 49, is the **Dharma Abha Vipassana Meditation Center** (0 5526 8049; www.dhamma.org/en /schedules/schabha.htm), which does regular 10-day meditation retreats.

Further east along the road is the 1262-sq-km **Thung Salaeng Luang National Park** (www.dnp .go.th; admission 400bht; 8am-5pm), one of Thailand's largest and most important wildlife sanctuaries. Thung Salaeng Luang encompasses vast meadows, evergreen and dipterocarp forests, limestone hills and numerous streams. From November through to December the meadows bloom with carpets of wild flowers, and the best place to see wildlife is on these meadows and around the ponds and salt licks. There are over 190 bird species confirmed in the park, most significant of which for bird-watchers is the Siamese fireback pheasant. Thung Salaeng Luang was also once home to the PLAT. The entrance is at the Km 80 marker, where the park headquarters here has information on walks and accommodation.

If you have your own wheels, you can turn south at the Km 100 marker onto Rte 2196 and head for **Khao Kho** (Khao Khaw), another mountain lair used by the CPT during the 1970s. About 1.5km from the summit of Khao Kho, you must turn onto the very steep Rte 2323. At the summit, 30km from the highway, stands a tall **obelisk** erected in memory of the

Thai soldiers killed during the suppression of the communist insurgency. The monument is surrounded by an attractive garden. Gun emplacements and sandbagged lookout posts perched on the summit have been left intact as historical reminders. On a clear day, the 360-degree view from the summit is wonderful.

If you've made the side trip to Khao Kho you can choose either to return to the Phitsanulok–Lom Sak highway, or take Rte 2258, off Rte 2196, until it terminates at Rte 203. On Rte 203 you can continue north to Lom Sak or south to Phetchabun. On Rte 2258, about 4km from Rte 2196, you'll pass **Khao Kho Palace**. One of the smaller royal palaces in Thailand, it's a fairly uninteresting, modern set of structures but has quite a nice rose garden. If you've come all the way to Khao Kho you may as well take a look.

Sleeping & Eating

Thung Salaeng Luang National Park (☎ 0 2562 0760; reserve@dnp.go.th; bungalows 1000-5000B, tent pitch 30B, 2-8 person tent 150-600B) In the park there are 15 well-equipped wooden bungalows that accommodate four to 10 people. Bungalows are available near the headquarters by the Km 80 entrance or in two other park zones. It's also possible to pitch a tent. There's a restaurant and food vendors in the park.

Rainforest Resort (☎ 0 5529 3085-6; www.rainforestthailand.com; Km 42; 2-6 person cottages 1400-4800B; 🔀) There are several resorts just off Hwy 12 and this is the best of the lot. Spacious, tastefully designed cottages spread over a hillside facing Mae Nam Khek accommodate from two to six people. An indoor-outdoor restaurant serves locally grown coffee and good Thai food. Another good choice is **Wang Thara Health Resort & Spa** (☎ 0 5529 3411-4; www.wanathara.com; Hwy 12, Km 46; r 1600-3800B; 🔀), which offers a stylish retreat with the added bonus of a reasonably priced spa. Both resorts have online discounts and arrange activities like white-water rafting and mountain biking.

Getting There & Away

For more freedom it's best to do this route with your own wheels. Buses between Phitsanulok and Lom Sak cost 50B for ordinary and 70B for air-con, each way. So any stop along the way will cost less. During daylight hours it's easy to flag down another bus to continue your journey, but after 4pm it gets a little chancy.

SUKHOTHAI PROVINCE

SUKHOTHAI
สุโขทัย
pop 39,800
As Thailand's first capital, Sukhothai (Rising of Happiness) flourished from the mid-13th century to the late 14th century. The Sukhothai kingdom is viewed as the 'golden age' of Thai civilisation – the religious art and architecture of the era are considered to be the most classic of Thai styles. The *meuang kào* (old city) of Sukhothai features around 45 sq km of ruins, which are one of the most visited ancient sites in Thailand.

Almost 450km from Bangkok, the market town of New Sukhothai with the Mae Nam Yam running through it, is not particularly interesting. Yet its friendly and relaxed atmosphere, good transport links and attractive accommodation make it a good base from which to explore the old city ruins. These can also be visited via a day trip from Phitsanulok.

History

Sukhothai was the first capital of Siam. Established in the 13th century, Sukhothai's dynasty lasted 200 years and had nine kings. The most famous was King Ramkhamhaeng, who reigned from 1275 to 1317 and is credited with developing the first Thai script – his inscriptions are considered the first Thai literature. He also expanded the kingdom to include almost all of present-day Thailand. But a few kings later in 1438, Sukhothai was absorbed by Ayuthaya. See Sukhothai Historical Park for more information (opposite).

Information

There are banks with ATMs scattered all around the central part of New Sukhothai, plus one in Old Sukhothai.

Internet is easy to find in New Sukhothai. Most places connections (40B per hour) are pretty quick. Some guesthouses also offer internet.

Sukhothai's best sources of tourist information are the guesthouses, especially Ban Thai (p406).

CAT office (Th Nikhon Kasem; ☯ 7am-10pm) Offers international phone services; attached to post office.
Police station (Map p403; ☎ 0 5561 1010) In New Sukhothai.

NEW SUKHOTHAI

0 ————— 200 m
0 ————— 0.1 miles

To Airport (27km);
Sawankhalok (36km);
Si Satchanalai (62km)

To Sawankhalok (36km);
Si Satchanalai (56km)

Approximate Scale

Mae Nam Yom

Municipal
Office

To Sukhothai Historical
Park (12km); Tak (78km)

Soi Mae
Ramphan

To Kamphaeng
Phet (77km) Th Jarot Withithong

Soi Paintan
Soi
Wat Chasuwan

Wat
Ratchathani

Municipal
Market

Th Bat Uthit

Th Jarot Withithong

Th Vichian Chamnong

Th Ratchathani

Th Ban Meuang

Th Maharat

Th Tri Chat

Th Singhawat

Th Pawet Nakhon

Mae Nam Yom

Th Nikhon Kasem

Th Si Intharathit

Th Loei Thai

Th Singhawat

To Sangkhalok Museum (1km);
Phitsanulok (56km)

INFORMATION	
Bangkok Bank	1 D3
CAT Office	(see 4)
Kasikorn Bank	2 B3
Police Station	3 D3
Post Office	4 D4
Siam Commercial Bank	5 D3
Sukhothai Hospital	6 A2

SIGHTS & ACTIVITIES	
Aerobics	7 C3
Bicycle Tours	(see 9)
Suan Nam Premsuk	8 A2

SLEEPING	
Ban Thai	9 C3
Cocoon Guest House	10 D3
Garden House	11 B3
J&J Guest House	12 B2
Lotus Village	13 C2
Ninety-Nine Guest House	14 B2
No 4 Guest House	15 B3
River House	16 C3
Ruean Thai	17 D2
Sabaidee Guest House & Homestay	18 A2
Sukhothai Guest House	19 D2
TR Guest House	20 C3

EATING	
Dream Café	(see 10)
Food Stalls	21 C3
Kuaytiaw Thai Sukhothai	22 D2
Night Stalls	23 B3
Night Stalls	24 C3
Poo Restaurant	25 B3
Sukhothai Suki-Koka	26 D3

DRINKING	
Chopper Bar	27 B3

TRANSPORT	
Buses to Sukhothai Historical Park	28 B3
Government Bus Station	29 C2
Sǎwngthǎew to Sukhothai Historical Park	30 C3

Post office (Th Nikhon Kasem; ☻ 8.30am-noon Mon-Fri, 1-4.30pm Sat & Sun, 9am-noon holidays)
Sukhothai hospital (☎ 0 5561 0280; Th Jarot Withithong)
Tourist police (Map p404; Sukhothai Historical Park) Call 1155 for emergencies or go to the tourist police station opposite the Ramkhamhaeng National Museum.

Sights
SUKHOTHAI HISTORICAL PARK
อุทยานประวัติศาสตร์สุโขทัย

The **Sukhothai ruins** (admission 30-150B, plus bicycles/motorcycles/cars 10/20/50B; ☻ 6am-6pm) are one of Thailand's most impressive World Heritage sites. The park includes remains of 21 historical sites and four large ponds within the old walls, with an additional 70 sites within

a 5km radius. The original capital of the first Thai kingdom was surrounded by three concentric ramparts and two moats bridged by four gateways.

The ruins are divided into five zones – central, north, south, east and west – each of which has a 30B admission fee, except for the central section, which costs 40B. For a reasonable 150B you can buy a single ticket (from the kiosk at the south entrance) that allows entry to all the Sukhothai sites, plus Sawanworanayok Museum (p410), Ramkhamhaeng National Museum (p404) and the Si Satchanalai and Chaliang (p408). The ticket is good for repeated visits over 30 days.

The architecture of Sukhothai temples is most typified by the classic lotus-bud *chedi*,

NORTHERN THAILAND

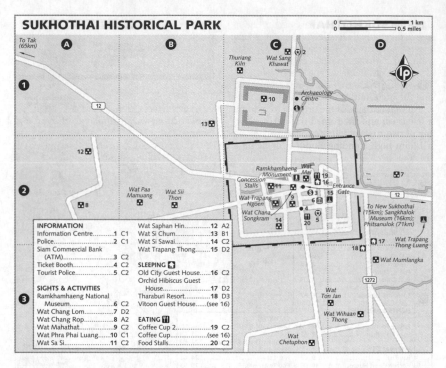

SUKHOTHAI HISTORICAL PARK

featuring a conical spire topping a square-sided structure on a three-tiered base. Some sites exhibit other rich architectural forms introduced and modified during the period, such as bell-shaped Sinhalese and double-tiered Srivijaya *chedi*. Some of the most impressive ruins are outside the city walls, so a bicycle or motorcycle is essential to fully appreciate everything.

See p408 for details on the best way to tour the park.

Ramkhamhaeng National Museum
พิพิธภัณฑสถานแห่งชาติรามคำแหง

A good starting point for exploring the park ruins is **Ramkhamhaeng National Museum** (Map p404; ☎ 0 5561 2167; admission 30B; ☼ 9am-4pm). A replica of the famous Ramkhamhaeng inscription (see Wiang Kum Kam p289) is kept here among an impressive collection of the Sukhothai artefacts.

Wat Mahathat
วัดมหาธาตุ

Finished in the 13th century, Sukhothai's largest wat is surrounded by brick walls (206m long and 200m wide) and a moat that is said to

represent the outer wall of the universe and the cosmic ocean. The *chedi* spires feature the famous lotus-bud motif, and some of the original stately Buddha figures still sit among the ruined columns of the old *wíhǎan*. There are 198 *chedi* within the monastery walls – a lot to explore in what many consider was the spiritual and administrative centre of the old capital.

Wat Si Chum
วัดศรีชุม

This wat is northwest of the old city and contains an impressive *mondòp* with a 15m, brick-and-stucco seated Buddha. This Buddha's elegant, tapered fingers are much-photographed. Archaeologists theorise that this image is the 'Phra Atchana' mentioned in the famous Ramkhamhaeng inscription. A passage in the *mondòp* wall that leads to the top has been blocked so that it's no longer possible to view the *jataka* inscriptions that line the tunnel ceiling.

Wat Saphan Hin
วัดสะพานหิน

Four kilometres to the west of the old city walls in the west zone, Wat Saphan Hin is

on the crest of a hill that rises about 200m above the plain. The name of the wat, which means 'stone bridge', is a reference to the slate path and staircase that leads up to the temple, which are still in place. The site gives a good view of the Sukhothai ruins to the southeast and the mountains to the north and south.

All that remains of the original temple are a few *chedi* and the ruined *wíhăan*, consisting of two rows of laterite columns flanking a 12.5m-high standing Buddha image on a brick terrace.

Wat Si Sawai
วัดศรีสวาย

Just south of Wat Mahathat, this shrine (dating from the 12th and 13th centuries) features three Khmer-style towers and a picturesque moat. It was originally built by the Khmers as a Hindu temple.

Wat Sa Si
วัดสระศรี

Also known as 'Sacred Pond Monastery', Wat Sa Si sits on an island west of the bronze monument of King Ramkhamhaeng (the third Sukhothai king). It's a simple, classic Sukhothai-style wat containing a large Buddha, one *chedi* and the columns of the ruined *wíhăan*.

Wat Trapang Thong
วัดตระพังทอง

Next to the museum, this small, still-inhabited wat with its fine stucco reliefs is reached by a footbridge across the large lotus-filled pond that surrounds it. This reservoir, the original site of Thailand's **Loi Krathong** festival (p406), supplies the Sukhothai community with most of its water.

Wat Phra Phai Luang
วัดพระพายหลวง

Outside the city walls in the northern zone, this somewhat isolated wat features three 12th-century Khmer-style towers, bigger than those at Wat Si Sawai. This may have been the centre of Sukhothai when it was ruled by the Khmers of Angkor prior to the 13th century.

Wat Chang Lom
วัดช้างล้อม

Off Hwy 12 in the east zone, Wat Chang Lom (Elephant Circled Monastery) is about 1km

east of the main park entrance. A large bell-shaped *chedi* is supported by 36 elephants sculpted into its base.

Wat Chang Rop
วัดช้างรอบ

On another hill west of the city, just south of Wat Saphan Hin, this wat features an elephant-base *chedi*, similar to that at Wat Chang Lom.

SANGKHALOK MUSEUM
พิพิธภัณฑ์สังคโลก

If you love ancient, rustically decorated pottery, you might enjoy this **museum** (☎ 0 5561 4333; 203/2 Mu 3 Th Muangkao; child/adult 50/100B; ☼ 8am-5pm). It displays an impressive collection of original 700-year-old Thai pottery found in the area, plus some pieces traded from Vietnam, Burma and China. The 2nd floor features some impressive examples of non-utilitarian pottery made as art.

Activities
BICYCLE TOURS

Belgian cycling enthusiast Ronnie of Ban Thai (p406) offers a variety of fun and educational **bicycle tours** (one hour 100B, half day/full day 400/700B, sunset tour 250B) of the area. Tours range from a 'coffee tour', where you visit plantations and villages, to the 'eccentric hermit tour', where you ride through hills to meet an entertaining hermit. There are tours for those who want to take it slowly (the turtle tour) or those who want a challenging ride (antelope and off-road tours). Rides include stops at lesser seen wats and villages. Personalised itineraries can also be arranged.

AEROBICS

Join the locals in open-air disco aerobics. Over the bridge and opposite Wat Rachthani, a stage is set up among the trees. Here, aerobics instructors put a crowd through their paces from 6.30pm to 7.30pm nightly.

SWIMMING

Suan Nam Premsuk (admission 40B; ☼ 7am-9pm), at Km 4 marker on Rte 101, is a modest sports complex with a clean swimming pool, tennis courts and ping-pong table. The admission includes use of all the facilities. Look for a couple of tall brick pillars supporting a blue-and-white sign. It can get crowded on the weekends.

Festivals

The **Loi Krathong** festival in November is celebrated for five days in historical Sukhothai. In addition to the magical floating lights, there are fireworks, folk-dance performances and a light-and-sound production.

Sleeping

Most accommodation is in New Sukhothai, and is dominated by budget options. A few upmarket choices are coming to town but they are gathered around the historical park. Prices tend to go up during the Loi Krathong festival. Most guesthouses rent motorcycles, bikes and have a laundry service.

BUDGET

The local taxi mafia has its hooks in the guesthouse proprietors. Drivers may say a place is closed if the guesthouse is not paying them commission – check first. Many guesthouses offer free pick-up from the bus terminal. Most also rent bicycles and motorcycles.

New Sukhothai

ourpick Ban Thai (☎ 0 5561 0163; banthai_guesthouse@ yahoo.com; 38 Th Prawet Nakhon; r with shared bathroom 150B, bungalows 250-450B; ⊠) This ultrafriendly place is the closest you'll come to feeling like you are staying with a family. Rooms are in excellent shape and the shared bathrooms sparkle. There's also a choice of simple fan bungalows with private bathroom, or the new air-con ones that come with good furniture and towels. Both sit around an intimate garden. Ban Thai is a great resource for local information, and does a range of interesting bicycle tours. The restaurant is also good.

Sabaidee Guest House & Homestay (☎ 0 5561 6303, 08 9988 3589; www.sabaidee-guesthouse.com; 81/7 Mu 1 Tambol Banklouy; r 150-300B; ⊠) On the way into town from the bus station, this homestay is down a lane off the main road. You can stay upstairs in the family house, where the large separate bathroom is just for guests, or cross a tiny bridge and stay in the spacious bungalows set in a garden. The friendly host speaks French, Thai and English, and offers free use of bicycles. The restaurant here is good too.

River House (☎ 0 5562 0396; riverhouse_7@hotmail .com; 7 Soi Watkuhasuwan; r 150-350B) Operated by a young Thai-French couple, this relaxing place has simple, tidy rooms in an old teak house overlooking the river. Hammocks are dotted about and there is a restaurant attached.

ourpick Garden House (☎ 0 5561 1395; tuigarden house@yahoo.com; 11/1 Th Prawet Nakhon; r 150B, bungalows 250-350B; ⊠ 🖳) This popular and great-value place has bungalows with character, large terraces and private bathrooms. There are also several well-kept rooms in a wooden two-storey house; the shared bathrooms are large and very clean. The restaurant screens movies nightly.

TR Guest House (☎ 0 5561 1663; tr_guesthouse@ thaimail.com; 27/5 Th Prawet Nakhon; r 200-350B; ⊠ 🖳) Set in a concrete building, the large rooms are well furnished and spotlessly clean. Although lacking the character of other options down this street, it is still one of the better choices.

J&J Guest House (☎ 0 5562 0095; jjguest house@hotmail.com; 122 Soi Mae Ramphan; r 300-400B, bungalows 500-700B; ⊠ 🖳) This place is set in a manicured garden, has a large and a small swimming pool plus a pleasant restaurant known for its fresh baguettes and croissants. There are brand new, tastefully decorated wooden bungalows with terraces, cable TV and minibars, as well as spotless, spacious rooms. The friendly staff are multilingual (English, French, Dutch and Thai) and a good source of information.

Sukhothai Guest House (☎ 0 5561 0453; www.su khothaiguesthouse.com; 68 Th Vichien Chamnong; r 450-600B; ⊠ 🖳) This long-running guesthouse has 12 bungalows with terraces packed into a shaded garden. The communal area is filled with an eclectic mix of bric-a-brac and the owners are friendly and very helpful.

Cocoon Guest House (☎ 0 5561 2081; 86/1 Th Sing-hawat; r from 500B; ⊠) The four simple rooms at the back of Dream Café are down a path and set in a junglelike garden.

No 4 Guest House (☎ 0 5561 0165; 140/4 Soi Khlong Mae Ramphan; s/d 200/300B) and **Ninety-Nine Guest House** (☎ 0 5561 1315; 234/6 Soi Panitsan; s/d 120/150B) are managed by the same people. No 4 is by the fields and has bamboo-thatch bungalows. Ninety-nine's rooms are in a two-storey teak house surrounded by gardens. Both places run cookery courses.

Sukhothai Historical Park

The following places are across from the historical park. Both rent out bicycles.

Old City Guest House (☎ 0 5569 7515; 28/7 Mu 3; r 120-600B; ⊠) Set around an old teak house, rooms range from being small and quite dark to large and well-furnished enough to hold a family. A good choice if you want to stay close

to the historic park; unfortunately there isn't a garden area for relaxing.

Vitoon Guest House (☎ 0 5569 7045; 49 Mu 3; r 300-600B; 🔀 🖵) Rooms at Vitoon are comfortable but cluttered and overpriced compared to its neighbour Old City.

MIDRANGE

A number of the following options also offer budget-priced options.

our pick Ruean Thai Hotel (☎ 0 5561 2444; www .rueanthaihotel.com; 181/20 Soi Pracha Ruammit, Th Jarot Withithong; concrete building 250-400B, other rooms 600-2500B; 🔀 🖵 🐾) This antique-filled, two-storey hotel has heaps of character and prices to meet everyone's budget. The romantic-looking rooms that surround the pool have chunky recycled teak floorboards, some antique furniture, cable TV and large well-equipped bathrooms. A teak building has charming, very Thai style rooms, with carved room dividers and a lounging area. There's a concrete building with simple and cheaper air-con rooms out the back. Call for free pick-up from the bus station.

Lotus Village (☎ 0 5562 1484; www.lotus-village.com; 170 Th Ratchathani; r 500-1350B; 🔀 🖵) Set in a lush garden and among lotus ponds is this collection of Thai-style houses. The modern rooms are tastefully decorated and are big enough to host a yoga class. The bungalows on stilts range from simple to super-chic. There's a spa, arty boutique and communal seating area.

Orchid Hibiscus Guest House (Map p404; ☎ 0 5563 3284; orchid_hibiscus_guest_house@hotmail.com; 407/2 Rte 1272; r 800-1200B; 🔀 🐾) Opposite Tharaburi resort, this collection of rooms is set in relaxing, manicured grounds. There are eight cosy rooms with four-poster beds by the pool; behind these are two new, huge multicoloured rooms that would suit families. Across a path away from the pool are teak houses with two floors, living rooms and veranda – another good family choice. The guesthouse is on Rte 1272 about 600m off Hwy 12 – the turn-off is between Km markers 48 and 49.

TOP END

our pick Tharaburi Resort (Map p404; ☎ 0 5569 7132; www.tharaburiresort.com; 113 Th Srisomboon; r 1200-3300B, ste 4600-5800B; 🔀 🖵 🐾) One kilometre from the historical park, this new boutique hotel looks like something out of *Elle Decoration* magazine, with its 12 individually and beautifully styled rooms and villas. Some are themed (Su-

khothai, Japanese, Chinese) and this is done with fine antiques, lush silks and exquisite attention to detail. The cheaper rooms are simpler, the suites feel like a small home, and there are also two-floor family rooms. Definitely the most stylish hotel in Sukhothai.

Eating

Kuaytiaw Thai Sukhothai (Th Jarot Withithong; dishes 20-30B; 🕑 9am-8pm) A good spot to try Sukhothai-style *kŭaytĭaw*, it's located about 20m south of the turn-off for Ruean Thai Guest House. The restaurant is in a nice wooden building with a fountain fashioned from ceramic pots out front.

our pick Poo Restaurant (☎ 0 5561 1735; 24/3 Th Jarot Withithong; dishes 25-80B; 🕑 8am-12pm) Right in the centre of town, this new bar and restaurant is run by a very friendly Thai-Belgian couple. The décor is simple and spotlessly clean, and the menu offers great breakfasts, hearty sandwiches and very tasty Thai dishes. The owners are also really into chocolate – try the delicious *dame blanche* (ice cream covered in Belgian chocolate). A good source of information, this is also the place to rent motorbikes in town.

Sukhothai Suki-Koka (Th Singhawat; dishes 30-90B; 🕑 10am-11pm) Specialising in Thai-style suki-yaki, this bright, homey place is popular for lunch. It serves plenty of Thai dishes but also does sandwiches and pasta.

Coffee Cup (Map p404; Mu 3, Old Sukhothai; dishes 30-150B; 🕑 7am-10pm) If you're staying in the old city or are an early riser, come here for breakfast; the coffee is strong and the bread is fresh. It also serves a variety of snacks and a whopping good hamburger. Internet service is 40B per hour. There's also Coffee Cup 2, just a few doors down, which has a bar inside.

our pick Dream Café (☎ 0 5561 2081; 86/1 Th Singhawat; dishes 60-140B; 🕑 10am-10pm) This romantic, eclectic café is a gem. Decorated with cabinets full of curiosities, and some Thai antiques, it serves a fabulous selection of desserts, pasta and sandwiches, as well as Thai dishes. The food is good and the staff attentive. Alternatively, just pop in for a 'stamina drink' corked in medicine vials. Formula 4 claims to cure insensitivity and increase capability.

Don't miss New Sukhothai's **night stalls**. Most are accustomed to accommodating foreigners and even have bilingual, written menus. On Tuesday nights, there are more lively **night stalls** in the square opposite Poo

Restaurant. Near the ticket kiosk in the historical park, there is a collection of **food stalls** and simple open-air restaurants.

Drinking

Chopper Bar (Th Prawet Nakhon; 🕑 5-12.30pm) Travellers and locals congregate from dusk till hangover for food, drinks, live music and flirtation at this place, within spitting distance from the little guesthouse strip.

Getting There & Away

AIR

The so-called 'Sukhothai' airport is 27km from town off Rte 1195, about 11km from Sawankhalok. It's privately owned by Bangkok Airways and, like its Ko Samui counterpart, is a beautifully designed small airport using tropical architecture to its best advantage. **Bangkok Airways** (☎ 0 5563 3266/7, airport ☎ 0 5564 7224; www.bangkokair.com) operates a daily flight from Bangkok (1700B, 70 minutes). Bangkok Airways charges 120B to transport passengers between the airport and Sukhothai.

Bangkok Airways also flies daily from Chiang Mai to Sukhothai (1440B, 40 minutes). Fares for children are half the adult price.

BUS

Sukhothai is easily reached from Phitsanulok, Tak or Kamphaeng Phet. Buses to/from Phitsanulok (ordinary/2nd class air-con/1st class 30/42/54B, one hour), leave every half hour or so. Buses to Tak (ordinary/2nd class air-con/1st class 40/56/72B, 1½ hours) and Kamphaeng (ordinary/2nd class air-con/1st class 39/55/70B, 1½ hours) leave every 40 minutes.

Departures to Bangkok (2nd class air-con/1st class/VIP 273/349/407B, six to seven hours) leave half-hourly from 7am to 11pm.

Buses to and from Chiang Mai (ordinary/2nd class air-con 167/234B, 5½ hours) via Tak are frequent from 7pm to 2am.

Four air-con buses leave daily for Chiang Rai (ordinary/2nd class air-con 186/260B, nine hours). The 9am one is a good choice for Sawankhalok. Otherwise buses to Sawankhalok (40B, 45 minutes) and Si Satchanalai (38B, one hour) leave every hour from around 6am to 6pm.

Other destinations include Khon Kaen (ordinary/2nd class air-con/1st class 179/251/322B, 6½ hours), Phrae (ordinary/2nd class air-con 83/116B, three hours, four times daily), Lampang (2nd class air-con 162B, four

hours) and Nan (ordinary/2nd class air-con/1st class 132/185/238B, four hours). There are also eight 12-seat minivans to Mae Sot (125B, three hours) between 8.30am and 5.30pm.

Getting Around

A ride by săamláw around New Sukhothai should cost no more than 40B. Săwngthăew run frequently from 6.30am to 6pm between New Sukhothai and Sukhothai Historical Park (15B, 30 minutes), leaving from Th Jarot Withithong near Mae Nam Yom. The sign is on the north side of the street, but săwngthăew actually leave from the south side.

The best way to get around the historical park is by bicycle, which can be rented at shops outside the park entrance for 20B per day, or at any guesthouse in New Sukhothai (30B). Don't rent the first beater bikes you see at the bus stop in the old city as the better bikes tend to be found at shops around the corner, closer to the park entrance. The park operates a tram service through the old city for 20B per person.

Transport from the bus terminal into the centre of New Sukhothai costs 40B in a chartered vehicle, or 10B per person in a shared săwngthăew. Săamláw and motorbike taxis cost 30B. If going directly to the Old Sukhothai, săwngthăew charge 80B.

Motorbikes can be rented at Poo Restaurant (p407) and many guesthouses in New Sukhothai.

AROUND SUKHOTHAI
Si Satchanalai-Chaliang Historical Park

อุทยานประวัติศาสตร์ศรีสัชชนาลัย/ชะเลียง

If you have the time, don't skip this portion of the Sukhothai World Heritage site. Bring your imagination and sense of adventure and you're sure to love this more rustic collection of truly impressive ruins.

Set among the hills, the 13th- to 15th-century ruins in the old cities of Si Satchanalai and Chaliang, about 50km north of Sukhothai, are in the same basic style as those in the Sukhothai Historical Park, but the setting is more peaceful and almost seems untouched. Some people prefer the atmosphere here over that of Sukhothai. The **park** (admission 40B or free if you have the 150B inclusive ticket from Sukhothai, usable for 30 days; plus per bike/motorbike/car 10/30/50B; 🕑 8.30am-5pm) covers roughly 720 hectares and is surrounded by a 12m-wide moat. Chaliang, 1km southeast, is an older city site (dating to the 11th century), though its two temples date to the 14th century.

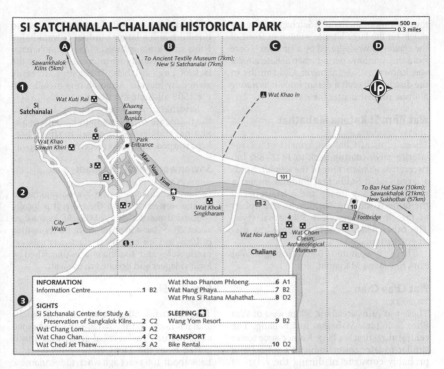

SI SATCHANALAI–CHALIANG HISTORICAL PARK

INFORMATION	Wat Khao Phanom Phloeng..............6 A1
Information Centre.........................1 B2	Wat Nang Phaya..........................7 B2
	Wat Phra Si Ratana Mahathat.........8 D2
SIGHTS	
Si Satchanalai Centre for Study &	SLEEPING
Preservation of Sangkalok Kilns.....2 C2	Wang Yom Resort........................9 B2
Wat Chang Lom............................3 A2	
Wat Chao Chan............................4 C2	TRANSPORT
Wat Chedi Jet Thaew....................5 A2	Bike Rental................................10 D2

Those listed below represent only the more distinctive of the numerous Si Satchanalai ruins.

An **information centre** (8.30am-5pm) at the park distributes free park maps and has a small exhibit outlining the history and major attractions. There are bicycles to rent (20B) near the entrance gate to the park that are slightly better than those rented where the bus stops on the main road. A tram can also be taken around the park (20B).

The nearby town of Sawankhalok (p411) is the main supply centre for the area.

WAT CHANG LOM
วัดช้างล้อม

This fine temple, marking the centre of the old city of Si Satchanalai, has elephants surrounding a bell-shaped *chedi* that is somewhat better preserved than its counterpart in Sukhothai. An inscription says the temple was built by King Ramkhamhaeng between 1285 and 1291.

WAT KHAO PHANOM PHLOENG
วัดเขาพนมเพลิง

On the hill overlooking Wat Chang Lom to the right are the remains of Wat Khao Ph-

anom Phloeng, including a *chedi*, a large seated Buddha and stone columns that once supported the roof of the *wíhǎan*. From this hill you can make out the general design of the once-great city. The slightly higher hill west of Phanom Phloeng is capped by a large Sukhothai-style *chedi* – all that remains of Wat Khao Suwan Khiri.

WAT CHEDI JET THAEW
วัดเจดีย์เจ็ดแถว

Next to Wat Chang Lom, these ruins contain seven rows of *chedi*, the largest of which is a copy of one at Wat Mahathat in Sukhothai. An interesting brick-and-plaster *wíhǎan* features barred windows designed to look like lathed wood (an ancient Indian technique used all over Southeast Asia). A *prasat* (small ornate building with a cruciform ground plan and needlelike spire) and *chedi* are stacked on the roof.

WAT NANG PHAYA
วัดนางพญา

South of Wat Chang Lom and Wat Chedi Jet Thaew, this *chedi* is Sinhalese in style and was built in the 15th or 16th century, a bit later than

the other monuments at Si Satchanalai. Stucco reliefs on the large laterite *wíhǎan* in front of the *chedi* – now sheltered by a tin roof – date from the Ayuthaya period when Si Satchanalai was known as Sawankhalok. Goldsmiths in the district still craft a design known as *naang pháyaa*, modelled after these reliefs.

Wat Phra Si Ratana Mahathat
วัดพระศรีรัตนมหาธาตุ

These ruins at Chaliang consist of a large laterite *chedi* (dating back to 1448–88) between two *wíhǎan*. One of the *wíhǎan* holds a large seated Sukhothai Buddha image, a smaller standing image and a bas-relief of the famous walking Buddha, so exemplary of the flowing, boneless Sukhothai style. The other *wíhǎan* contains some less distinguished images.

There's a separate 10B admission for Wat Phra Si Ratana Mahathat.

Wat Chao Chan
วัดเจ้าจันทร์

These wat ruins are about 500m west of Wat Phra Si Ratana Mahathat in Chaliang. The central attraction is a large Khmer-style tower similar to later towers built in Lopburi and probably constructed during the reign of Khmer King Jayavarman VII (1181–1217). The tower has been restored and is in fairly good shape. The roofless *wíhǎan* on the right contains the laterite outlines of a large standing Buddha that has all but melted away from exposure and weathering.

Sawankhalok Kilns
เตาเผาสังคโลก

The Sukhothai-Si Satchanalai area was once famous for its beautiful pottery, much of which was exported to countries throughout Asia. In China – the biggest importer of Thai pottery during the Sukhothai and Ayuthaya periods – the pieces came to be called 'Sangkalok', a mispronunciation of Sawankhalok. Particularly fine specimens of this pottery can be seen in the national museums of Jakarta and Pontianak in Indonesia.

At one time, more than 200 huge pottery kilns lined the banks of Mae Nam Yom in the area around Si Satchanalai. Several have been carefully excavated and can be viewed at the **Si Satchanalai Centre for Study & Preservation of Sangkalok Kilns** (admission 30B). Two groups of kilns are open to the public: a kiln centre in

Chaliang with excavated pottery samples and one kiln; and a larger outdoor Sawankhalok Kilns site 5km northwest of the Si Satchanalai ruins. The exhibits are interesting despite the lack of English labels. These sites are easily visited by bicycle. Admission is included in the 150B all-inclusive ticket.

Sawankhalok pottery rejects, buried in the fields, are still being found. Shops in Sukhothai and Sawankhalok sell misfired, broken, warped and fused pieces.

Sawanworanayok Museum
พิพิธภัณฑ์สวรรควรนายก

In Sawankhalok town, near Wat Sawankhalam on the western bank of the river, this locally sponsored **museum** (☎ 0 5561 4333; 69 Th Phracharat; admission 30B; ⊙ 8am-4.30pm Wed-Sun) holds thousands of 12th- to 15th-century artefacts, utensils, ceramic wares and Buddha images unearthed by local villagers and donated to the wat.

Ban Hat Siaw
บ้านหาดเสี้ยว

This colourful village southeast of Si Satchanalai is home to the Thai Phuan (also known as Lao Phuan), a Tai tribal group that immigrated from the Xieng Khuang Province in Laos about 100 years ago when the Annamese and Chinese were in northeastern Laos.

The local Thai Phuan are famous for **hand-woven textiles**, particularly the *phâa sîn tiin jòk* (brocade-bordered skirts), which have patterns of horizontal stripes bordered by thickly patterned brocade. The men's *phâa khǎo-mǎa* (short sarong) from Hat Siaw, typically in dark plaids, are also highly regarded.

Practically every stilt house within the village has a loom underneath it; cloth can be purchased at the source or from shops in Sawankhalok. Vintage Hat Siaw textiles, ranging from 80 to 200 years old, can be seen at the **Ancient Textile Museum** (☎ 0 5536 0058; free admission; ⊙ 7am-6pm) opposite the market in New Si Satchanalai, north of the ruins.

Another Thai Phuan custom is the use of **elephant-back** processions in local monastic ordinations; these usually take place in early April.

Sleeping & Eating
SI SATCHANALAI-CHALIANG HISTORICAL PARK
Wang Yom Resort (Sunanthana; ☎ 0 5563 1380; bungalows 600-1000B; ✪) This collection of rustic, worn

bungalows in a mature garden lies just outside the Si Satchanalai-Chaliang Historical Park, 400m before the southeastern corner of the old city. Service lacks enthusiasm but the large restaurant (dishes 50B to 140B) is reportedly very good. Food and drink are also available at a coffee shop in the historical park until 6pm.

SAWANKHALOK
This charming town about 20km south of the historical park has a couple of overnight options.

Saengsin Hotel (☎ 0 5564 1259-1424; 2 Th Thetsaban Damri 3; s/d from 220/360B; ❄) This hotel is about 1km south of the train station on the main street that runs through Sawankhalok. It has clean, comfortable rooms and a coffee shop.

A couple of other options also line the main drag.

This isn't a big town for eating; most food places sell noodles and *khâo man kài* and not much else.

Kung Nam (dishes 40-70B; ❤ 10am-11pm) A Thai and Chinese garden restaurant on the outskirts of Sawankhalok towards Sukhothai, it's probably the best spot to chow down in Sawankhalok.

Sawankhalok's **night market** assembles along its main streets.

Getting There & Away
BUS
Si Satchanalai-Chaliang Historical Park is off Rte 101 between Sawankhalok and new Si Satchanalai. From New Sukhothai, take a Si Satchanalai bus (38B, two hours) and ask to get off at *'meuang kào'* (old city). Alternatively, catch the 9am bus to Chiang Rai, which costs the same but makes fewer stops. The last bus back to New Sukhothai leaves at 4.30pm.

There are two places along the left side of the highway where you can get off the bus and reach the ruins in the park; both involve crossing Mae Nam Yom. The first leads to a footbridge over Mae Nam Yom to Wat Phra Si Ratana Mahathat at Chaliang; the second crossing is about 2km further northwest just past two hills and leads directly into the Si Satchanalai ruins.

TRAIN
Sawankhalok's original train station is one of the main local sights. King Rama VI had a 60km railway spur built from Ban Dara (a small town on the main northern trunk) to Sawankhalok just so that he could visit the ruins.

Amazingly, there's a daily special express (train 3) from Bangkok to Sawankhalok (482B, seven hours), which leaves the capital at 10.50am, stops at Phitsanulok at 4pm and arrives in Sawankhalok at 5.50pm. Train 4 heads back to Bangkok at 7.40pm, arriving in the city at 3.30am. You can also hop this train to Phitsanulok (50B). It's a 'Sprinter', which means 2nd class air-con, no sleepers, and the fare includes dinner and breakfast. It is possible to book in advance via www.railway.co.th.

Getting Around
You can rent **bicycles** (20B per day) from a shop at the gateway to Wat Phra Si Ratana Mahathat.

KAMPHAENG PHET PROVINCE

KAMPHAENG PHET
กำแพงเพชร
pop 27,500
Formerly known as Chakangrao or Nakhon Chum, Kamphaeng Phet (Diamond Wall) was once an important front line of defence for the Sukhothai kingdom but it is now mostly known for producing the tastiest *klûay khài* ('egg banana', a delicious kind of small banana) in Thailand. It's quite a nice place to spend a day or two wandering around the ruins and experiencing a small northern provincial capital that receives few tourists.

Information
Most of the major banks also have branches with ATMs along the main streets near the river and on Th Charoensuk. There are a couple of other internet cafés in town on Th Teresa and Th Ratchadamnoen, otherwise try the main post office.
Tourist Information Centre (❤ 8am-4.30pm) Next to Wat Phra Kaew; has some maps and pamphlets.
Main post office (Th Thesa) Just south of the old city. Has internet.
Police (☎ 0 5571 1199, emergency 1155)

Sights
OLD CITY
เมืองเก่า
A Unesco World Heritage site, the **Kamphaeng Phet Historical Park** (☎ 0 5571 1921; admission 40B, bicycle/motorbike/sǎamláw/car 10/20/30/50B; ❤ 8am-5pm)

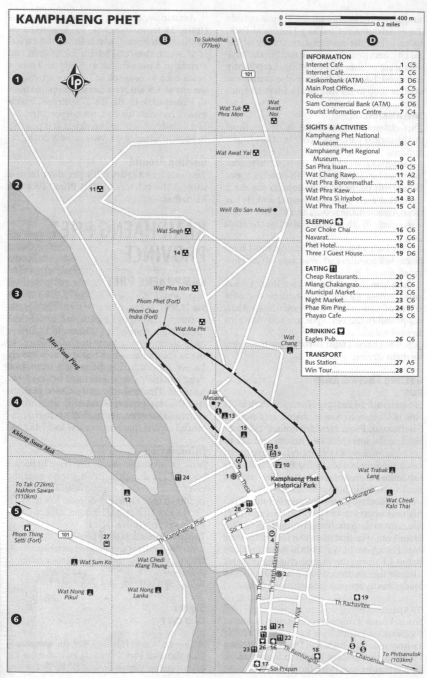

KAMPHAENG PHET

0 ___ 400 m
0 ___ 0.2 miles

INFORMATION
Internet Café.....................................1 C5
Internet Café.....................................2 C6
Kasikornbank (ATM)........................3 D6
Main Post Office..............................4 C5
Police...5 C5
Siam Commercial Bank (ATM)......6 D6
Tourist Information Centre..........7 C4

SIGHTS & ACTIVITIES
Kamphaeng Phet National
 Museum....................................8 C4
Kamphaeng Phet Regional
 Museum....................................9 C4
San Phra Isuan...............................10 C5
Wat Chang Rawp..........................11 A2
Wat Phra Borommathat................12 B5
Wat Phra Kaew..............................13 C4
Wat Phra Si Iriyabot.....................14 B3
Wat Phra That................................15 C4

SLEEPING
Gor Choke Chai..............................16 C6
Navarat...17 C6
Phet Hotel.......................................18 C6
Three J Guest House.....................19 D6

EATING
Cheap Restaurants........................20 C5
Miang Chakangrao........................21 C6
Municipal Market..........................22 C6
Night Market..................................23 C6
Phae Rim Ping................................24 B5
Phayao Cafe....................................25 C6

DRINKING
Eagles Pub.......................................26 C6

TRANSPORT
Bus Station......................................27 A5
Win Tour..28 C5

encloses the old city site where you'll find **Wat Phra Kaew**, which used to be adjacent to the royal palace (now in ruins). It's not nearly as well restored as Sukhothai, but it's smaller, more intimate and less visited. Weather-corroded Buddha statues have assumed slender, porous forms that remind some visitors of the sculptures of Alberto Giacometti (a Swiss artist). About 100m southeast of Wat Phra Kaew is **Wat Phra That**, distinguished by a large round-based *chedi* surrounded by columns. This park is popular with joggers and walkers.

KAMPHAENG PHET NATIONAL MUSEUM
พิพิธภัณฑสถานแห่งชาติกำแพงเพชร

The nearby **national museum** (☎ 0 5571 1570; admission 30B; ⏰ 9am-noon & 1-4pm Wed-Sun) has the usual survey of Thai art periods downstairs. Upstairs there is a collection of artefacts from the Kamphaeng Phet area, including terracotta ornamentation from ruined temples and Buddha images in both the Sukhothai and Ayuthaya styles.

KAMPHAENG PHET REGIONAL MUSEUM
พิพิธภัณฑ์เฉลิมพระเกียรติกำแพงเพชร

The **regional museum** (☎ 0 5572 2341; admission 10B; ⏰ 9am-4pm) is a series of central, Thai-style wooden structures on stilts set among nicely landscaped grounds. There are three main buildings in the museum: one focuses on history and prehistory; one features displays about geography and materials used in local architecture; and the third houses an ethnological museum featuring encased displays of miniature doll-like figures representing various tribes. Push-button recordings in English and Thai explain the displays.

WAT PHRA BOROMMATHAT
วัดพระบรมธาตุ

Across Mae Nam Ping are more neglected ruins in an area that was settled long before Kamphaeng Phet's heyday, although visible remains are postclassical Sukhothai. Wat Phra Borommathat has a few small *chedi* and one large *chedi* of the late Sukhothai period that is now crowned with a Burmese-style umbrella added early in the 20th century.

SAN PHRA ISUAN
ศาลพระอิศวร

Near the Kamphaeng Phet Chaloem Phrakiat Museum, the San Phra Isuan (Shiva Shrine) has

a sandstone base upon which is a Khmer-style bronze sculpture of Shiva (Isvara). The image is a replica: the original is in the Kamphaeng Phet National Museum. In 1886, a tourist stole the idol's hands and head (they were returned).

OTHER TEMPLES

The 40B admission fee to the Kamphaeng Phet Historical Park in the old city also includes access to the forested area just north of it called *Aranyik*. Here, the most notable temples are Wat Phra Si Iriyabot and Wat Chang Rawp.

Northeast of the old city walls, **Wat Phra Si Iriyabot** has the shattered remains of standing, sitting, walking and reclining Buddha images all sculpted in the classic Sukhothai style. Northwest of here, **Wat Chang Rawp** (Elephant-Encircled Temple) is just that – a temple with an elephant-buttressed wall. Several other temple ruins – most of them little more than flat brick foundations, with the occasional weather-worn Buddha image – can be found in the same general vicinity.

Sleeping

Three J Guest House (☎ 0 5571 3129; threejguest@hotmail .com; 79 Th Rachavitee; r 200-500B; ✗ 💻) This pleasant collection of bungalows in a pretty garden has a very hospitable and friendly host. Pathways lead to clean log bungalows with terraces. The cheapest ones share a clean bathroom and the more expensive have aircon. Bicycles and motorcycles are available for rent.

Gor Choke Chai (Kaw Chok Chai; ☎ 0 5571 1247; Th Charoensuk; r from 250B; ✗) The recently renovated Gor Choke Chai is a good budget choice with its large, clean rooms. Popular with Thai businessmen, it's in the centre of the new town not far from the municipal market.

Phet Hotel (☎ 0 5571 2810-5; 189 Th Bamrungrat; r 500-800B; ✗ 💻 ⊕) Near the market, this comfortable hotel features spacious, well-maintained, modern rooms with views over Kamphaeng Phet. There is a small pool, a restaurant and bar. Look for the sign on the top of the building. The street-side sign is only in Thai script.

Navarat (Nawarat; ☎ 0 5571 1211; 2 Soi Prapan; r/ste 600/950B; ✗) Set off the road, this five-storey hotel may lack style, but its carpeted rooms are clean and fairly comfortable. There is a coffee shop downstairs and some rooms have views.

NORTHERN THAILAND

Eating

Miang Chakangrao (☎ 0 5571 1124; 273 Th Ratchadamnoen) Sells local sweets and snacks, particularly the shop's namesake, a fermented tea salad eaten with peanut-rice brittle.

Phayao Cafe (dishes 45-120B; ☺ 10am-midnight) It may look closed with its heavily tinted windows, but inside you'll find a casual, family-friendly atmosphere and great ice cream.

Phae Rim Ping (☎ 0 5571 2767; dishes 40-140B; ☺ 11am-midnight) This place is one of a few floating restaurants on the river.

A **night market** sets up every evening in front of the provincial offices near the old city walls and there are also some **cheap restaurants** near the roundabout. Inexpensive food stalls can be found in a larger **municipal market** (cnr Th Wijit & Th Bamrungrat). Along Th Thesa across from Sirijit Park by the river are several family-friendly, air-con restaurants.

Drinking

There are a number of discos with karaoke around Phet Hotel. Some of them feature live music on the weekends.

Eagles Pub (Th Bamrungrat; dishes 40-120B; ☺ 8pm-1am) A pub with a Western theme, it serves a lot of whisky and a mixture of Thai and Western food. Sometimes the pub hosts live music.

Getting There & Away

The bus terminal is 1km west of town. If coming from Sukhothai or Phitsanulok get off in the old city or at the roundabout on Th Teresa to save getting a sǎwngthǎew back into town. Most visitors arrive from Sukhothai (ordinary/2nd class air-con/1st class air-con 39/55/70B, 1½ hours), Phitsanulok (ordinary/air-con 57/80B, 2½ hours) or Tak (50B, 1½ hours). Regular buses to/from Bangkok (ordinary/air-con/VIP 175/215/274B, five hours) leave throughout the day. You can book tickets in advance at **Win Tour** (☎ 0 5571 1095; Th Kamphaeng Phet).

Getting Around

The least expensive way to get from the bus station into town is to hop on a shared sǎwngthǎew (5B per person) to the roundabout across the river. From there take a sǎamlǎw anywhere in town for 20B to 30B. It is worth renting a bicycle or motorbike to explore areas outside of the old city – Three J Guest House (p413) has both for rent.

TAK PROVINCE

Tak is a wild and mountainous province. Its proximity to Myanmar has resulted in a complex history and unique cultural mix.

In the 1970s the mountains of western Tak were a hotbed of communist guerrilla activity. Since the 1980s the former leader of the local CPT movement has been involved in resort-hotel development and Tak is very much open to outsiders, but the area still has an untamed feeling about it. This province boasts Thailand's largest population of domesticated elephants, which are still commonly used by Karen villagers in western Tak for transport and agricultural tasks.

Western Tak has always presented a distinct contrast with other parts of Thailand because of strong Karen and Burmese cultural influences. The Thailand–Myanmar border districts of Mae Ramat, Tha Song Yang and Mae Sot are dotted with refugee camps, an outcome of the firefights between the Karen National Union (KNU) and the Myanmar government, which is driving Karen civilians across the border. At the time of writing it was estimated that there were 151,000 unregistered migrant workers from Burma in Tak Province alone.

The main source of income for people living on both sides of the border is legal and illegal international trade. The main smuggling gateways on the Thailand side are Tha Song Yang, Mae Sarit, Mae Tan, Wangkha, Mae Sot and Waley. One important contraband product is teak, cut by the Karen or the Karenni (Kayah) and then brought into Thailand from Myanmar on large tractor-trailers at night. As much as 200,000B in bribes per truckload is distributed among local Thai authorities, who conveniently look the other way. None of the trade is legal since the Thai government cut off all timber deals with the Burmese military in 1997.

The majority of Tak province is forested and mountainous and is an excellent destination for those wanting to trek. Organised trekking occurs, some further north out of Chiang Mai, most of it locally organised. There are Hmong, Musoe (Lahu), Lisu and White and Red Karen settlements throughout the west and north.

In Ban Tak, 25km upstream along Mae Nam Tak from Tak, you can visit **Wat Phra**

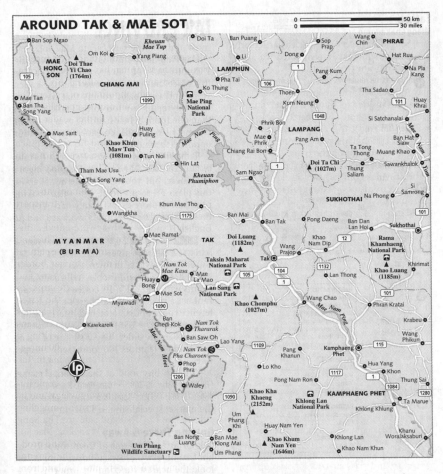

AROUND TAK & MAE SOT

Borommathat, the original site of a Thai *chedi* that, according to legend, was constructed during the reign of King Ramkhamhaeng (1275–1317) to celebrate his elephant-back victory over King Sam Chon, ruler of an independent kingdom once based at or near Mae Sot. The wat's main feature is a large, slender, gilded *chedi* in the Shan style surrounded by numerous smaller but similar *chedi*. Many Thais flock to the temple each week in the belief that the *chedi* can somehow reveal to them the winning lottery numbers for the week.

Approximately 45km north of Tak via Rte 1 and then 17km west (between the Km 463 and Km 464 markers), via the road to Sam Ngao, is **Kheuan Phumiphon** (Bhumibol Dam), which impounds Mae Nam Ping at a height of 154m, making it the tallest dam in Southeast Asia. The shores and islands of the reservoir are a favourite picnic spot for local Thais.

TAK

ตาก

pop 49,200

Tak is not particularly interesting, but it's a good point from which to visit the Lan Sang and Taksin Maharat National Parks to the west or Kheuan Phumiphon to the north. It's also the best place to get up-to-date information about Mae Sot, Um Phang and border activity. Occasionally travellers find themselves stuck here for a night. Luckily there are a couple decent places to stay.

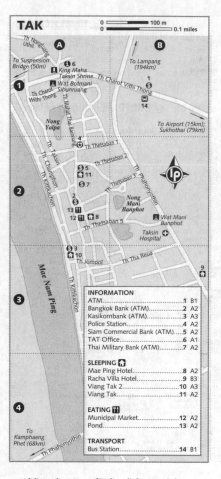

TAK

INFORMATION
ATM......................................1	B1
Bangkok Bank (ATM)..................2	A2
Kasikornbank (ATM)..................3	A3
Police Station.........................4	A2
Siam Commercial Bank (ATM).....5	A2
TAT Office..............................6	A1
Thai Military Bank (ATM)...........7	A2

SLEEPING
Mae Ping Hotel........................8	A2
Racha Villa Hotel.....................9	B3
Viang Tak 2...........................10	A3
Viang Tak.............................11	A2

EATING
Municipal Market....................12	A2
Pond...................................13	A2

TRANSPORT
Bus Station...........................14	B1

Although most of Tak exhibits nondescript, cement-block architecture, the southern section of the city harbours a few old teak homes. Residents are proud of the suspension bridge (for motorcycles, pedicabs, bicycles and pedestrians only) over Mae Nam Ping, which flows quite broadly here even in the dry season.

Information
Several banks have branches along Th Mahat Thai Bamrung and Th Taksin, all of them with ATMs.

You can pick up brochures and some basic maps at the **TAT office** (☎ 0 5551 3584; www.tak.go.th; 193 Th Taksin; ☒ 8.30am-4.30pm), but don't expect much more.

Sleeping & Eating
Few people pause to spend the night in Tak, as most jump on the next bus to Mae Sot.

Mae Ping Hotel (☎ 0 5551 1807; 619 Th Taksin; s 110B, d 140-200B; ☒) Everyone's budget likes this place, but not everyone likes the super-worn and very basic rooms that have gone without repair for too long. Look at more than one room before handing over any baht. It's surprisingly quiet considering its location opposite the market.

Racha Villa Hotel (☎ 0 5551 2361; 307/1 Th Phaho-nyothin; r 220-300B; ☒) You'll get a good night's sleep here, but you won't write home about this plain 58-room hotel. The retro-looking rooms have more extras than you'd expect at these prices. The location is awkward and no English is spoken.

our pick Viang Tak 2 (☎ 0 5551 2507; www.viangtak hotel.com; 236 Th Jompol; r/ste 600-950/2100B; ☒ ☐ ☒) By far the best place in town, this smart eight-storey hotel has comfortable, well-maintained rooms with cable TV. Its coffee shop/restaurant has a river view, and there's a pool, conference room and an attached internet café.

Viang Tak (☎ 0 5551 1950; 25/3 Th Mahat Thai Bamrung; r 490B) is the older, bigger sibling of Viang Tak 2, and it features 100 rooms with cheaper rates.

You can buy food at the **municipal market** (Th Taksin; dishes 10-30B; ☺ 6am-6pm). **Pond** (Th Taksin; dishes 15-30B; ☺ 8am-3pm) is a simple place near the market specialising in Thai curries.

Getting There & Away
Tak airport, 15km out of town towards Sukhothai on Hwy 12, wasn't operating at last look; the nearest functioning airport is Phitsanulok.

Tak's **bus station** (Th Charot Vithi Thong) is just outside town. A túk-túk will take you to the town centre for around 30B, but it's also possible to walk if you packed light. Frequent buses travel between Tak and Sukhothai (ordinary/2nd class air-con/1st class air-con 40/56/72B, 1½ hours).

There is also regular service to Lampang (ordinary/air-con 90/126B, three hours), Chiang Mai (ordinary/air-con 133/186B, four hours), Chiang Rai (ordinary/air-con 176/246B, seven hours).

Ordinary government buses depart for Bangkok (176B, 10 hours) three times daily, while a 2nd-class air-con bus (207B, eight hours) leaves once a day. There are four daily

1st-class air-con departures from Tak to Bangkok and one 10pm departure (275B, six hours) in the reverse direction.

Air-con buses to Mae Sot (74B) leave at 2pm, 4pm and 5pm. Minivans to Mae Sot leave almost hourly (53B, 1½ hours).

AROUND TAK
Taksin Maharat & Lan Sang National Parks
อุทยานแห่งชาติตากสินมหาราช

These small **national parks** (www.dnp.go.th; admission 400B) receive a steady trickle of visitors on weekends and holidays, but they are almost empty during the week. Taksin Maharat (established in 1981) covers 149 sq km; the entrance is 2km from the Km 26 marker on Rte 105/Asia Rte 1 (the so-called Pan-Asian Hwy, which would link Istanbul and Singapore if all the intervening countries allowed land crossings) to Mae Sot.

The park's most outstanding features are the 30m, nine-tiered **Nam Tok Mae Ya Pa** and a record-holding *tàbàak*, a dipterocarp that is 50m tall and 16m in circumference. Birdwatching is said to be particularly good here; known resident and migratory species include the tiger shrike, forest wagtail and Chinese pond heron.

Nineteen kilometres from Tak, Lan Sang National Park preserves a 104-sq-km area of rugged, 1000m-high granite peaks – part of the Tenasserim Range. A network of **trails** leads to several **waterfalls**, including the park's 40m-high namesake.

Lan Sang National Park (☎ 0 5551 9278; bungalows 400-4000B) rents rustic bungalows that can accommodate two to 36 people. Two-person tents (40B) are also available. **Taksin Maharat National Park** (☎ 0 5551 1429; r 1000-2400B) offers utilitarian rooms that sleep between four and 15 people. Taksin Maharat also has a **camping ground** (tent sites 20B). Food service can be arranged in both parks.

The best way to reach the parks is by private car, but the bus to Mae Sot will drop you on the road where you can easily walk to the park entrance. By car take Rte 1103 3km south off Rte 105. Some tour agencies in Mae Sot do trips to the parks.

Kheuan Phumiphon
เขื่อนภูมิพล

This huge reservoir is a favourite canoeing, swimming, fishing and picnicking destination for Tak residents. The **Electrical Generating Authority of Thailand** (EGAT; Bangkok ☎ 0 2436 3179, Ban Phak Rap Rong Kheuan Phumiphon ☎ 0 5554 9509; multibed units 400-1500B) maintains several bungalows and longhouses. On weekends there is bus service from the Tak bus terminal (54B).

Doi Muser Hilltribe Cultural Center
ศูนย์พัฒนาและสงเคราะห์ชาวเขาดอยมูเซอ

At the top of the mountain before you descend into Mae Sot is this small **research and cultural centre** (☎ 0 5551 2131, 0 5551 3614; Km 28 Th Tak-Mae Sot; bungalows 200-700B) where you can visit for the day, or spend the night. Here they grow and sell crops such as tea, coffee, fruits and flowers. Call ahead to find out about seeing a cultural performance. The temperature can go as low as 4°C in the winter. During November and December, *bua tong* (a kind of wild sunflower) blossom around the centre.

MAE SOT
แม่สอด

Mae Sot is a Burmese-Chinese-Karen-Thai trading outpost that has become a small but simmering tourist destination. Although there aren't many formal sites to see in Mae Sot, and most tourists just come for a visa run, many end up staying longer than expected; this laid-back town has a vibrant market, good restaurants and a fascinating cultural mix.

Black-market trade between Myanmar and Thailand is the primary source of local revenue, with most transactions taking place in the districts of Mae Ramat, Tha Song Yang, Phop Phra and Um Phang. Mae Sot has also become the most important jade and gem centre along the border, with most of the trade controlled by Chinese and Indian immigrants from Myanmar.

Walking down the streets of Mae Sot, you'll see an interesting ethnic mixture – Burmese men in their *longyi* (sarongs), Hmong and Karen women in traditional hill-tribe dress, bearded Indo-Burmese men, Thai army rangers, and some foreign NGO workers. Shop signs along the streets are in Thai, Burmese and Chinese. Most of the temple architecture in Mae Sot is Burmese. The town's Burmese population is largely Muslim, while those living outside town are Buddhist and the Karen are mostly Christian.

Border skirmishes between Myanmar's central government and the weakening Karen and Kayah ethnic insurgencies can break out

NORTHERN THAILAND

MAE SOT

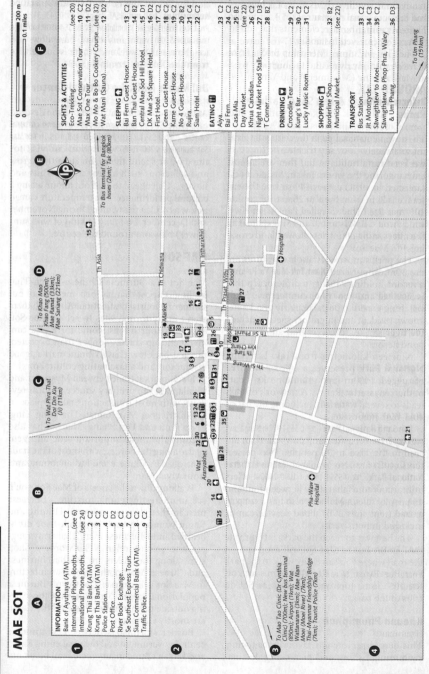

0   200 m
0   0.1 miles

INFORMATION
Bank of Ayutthaya (ATM)........................1 C2
International Phone Booths.................(see 6)
International Phone Booths....................2 C3
Krung Thai Bank (ATM)..........................3 C2
Krung Thai Bank (ATM)..........................4 C2
Police Station...................................5 D2
Post Office......................................6 C2
River Book Exchange............................7 C2
Se Southeast Express Tours....................8 C2
Siam Commercial Bank (ATM)..................9 C2
Traffic Police....................................

SIGHTS & ACTIVITIES
Eco-Trekking.................................(see 20)
Mae Sot Conservation Tour...................10 C2
Max One Tour......................................11 D2
Mo Mo & Bo Bo Cookery Course......(see 32)
Wat Mani (Sauna)................................12 D2

SLEEPING
Bai Fern Guest House...........................13 C2
Ban Thai Guest House...........................14 B2
Central Mae Sod Hill Hotel...................15 D1
DK Mae Sot Square Hotel.....................16 D2
First Hotel..17 C2
Green Guest House..............................18 C2
Kame Guest House...............................19 C2
No 4 Guest House................................20 B2
Rujira...21 C4
Siam Hotel...22 C2

EATING
Aiya...23 C2
Bai Fern..24 C2
Casa Mia..25 B2
Day Market....................................(see 22)
Khrua Canadian.................................26 C2
Night Market Food Stalls....................27 D3
T Corner..28 B2

DRINKING
Crocodile Tear...................................29 C2
Kung's Bar..30 C2
Lucky Music Room..............................31 C2

SHOPPING
Borderline Shop.................................32 B2
Municipal Market...........................(see 22)

TRANSPORT
Bus Station..33 C2
Jit Motorcycle....................................34 C2
Sawngthaew to Moei...........................35 C2
Sawngthaew to Phop Phra, Waley
& Um Phang.......................................36 D3

To Khao Mao
Khao Fang (500m);
Mae Ramat (33km);
Mae Sariang (221km)

To Bus terminal for Bangkok
buses (2km); Tak (80km)

To Wat Phra That
Doi Din Kiu
(Ju) (11km)

To Mao Tao Clinic (Dr Cynthia
Clinic) (700m); New bus terminal
(850m); Airport (1km); Wat
Wattanaram (3km); Mae Nam
Moei (Moei River) (7km);
Thai-Myanmar Friendship Bridge
(7km); Tourist Police (7km)

To Um Phang
(151km)

Th Asia
Th Chidwana
Th Intharakhiri
Th Prasat Withi
Th Tang Kim Chiang
Th Si Wiang
Th Sri Phanit

Market
Hospital
School
Mosque
Wat
Anamvathet
Pha-Waw
Hospital

at any time, sending thousands of refugees – and the occasional mortar rocket – across the Thai–Myanmar border, elements that add to the area's perceived instability.

The Thai-Myanmar Friendship Bridge links Mae Sot with Myawadi and the highway west to Mawlamyine (Moulmein) and Yangon.

Information

Krung Thai Bank, Bank of Ayuthaya and Siam Commercial Bank all have ATMs and are conveniently located in the centre of town. International phone services can be found at Bai Fern restaurant (p421), the River Book Exchange and Se. Southeast Express Tours. There is no official tourist information or TAT office in Mae Sot, but good sources of information are Ban Thai Guest House (p420) and Khrua Canadian (p421).

River Book Exchange (Tourist Information; ☎ 0 5553 4700; Th Intharakhiri; ⏱ 10am-6pm Mon-Fri) Has a fair collection of books to exchange and offers Thai lessons (five days 3000B, personal tutor) and some tourist information.

Se. Southeast Express Tours (Th Intharakhiri; per hr 25B) There are several internet cafés around town, but this is the biggest.

Tourist police (☎ 1155) Has an office at the market by the Friendship Bridge.

Sights & Activities

See p424 for information about visiting Myawadi in Myanmar.

WAT WATTANARAM

วัดวัฒนาราม

At Ban Mae Tao, 3km west of Mae Sot on the road to the Thailand–Myanmar border, lies this Burmese temple, Wat Wattanaram (Phattanaram). Most associate this wat with its huge, modern Burmese-style reclining Buddha. In the main *wíhăn* on the 2nd floor is a collection of Burmese musical instruments, including tuned drums and gongs.

WAT PHRA THAT DOI DIN KIU (JI)

วัดพระธาตุดอยดินกิ่ว(จี)

Wat Phra That Doi Din Kiu (Ji) is a forest temple 11km northwest of Mae Sot on a 300m-high hill overlooking Mae Nam Moei and Myanmar. It's a bit difficult for some to find, and during Myanmar's dry-season offensives against the KNU, this area is sometimes considered unsafe and the road to the temple is occasionally blocked by Thai rangers. Ask

in town about the current situation before heading up the road.

The highlight of this wat is a small *chedi* mounted on what looks like a boulder that has been balanced on the edge of a cliff. It is reminiscent of the Kyaiktiyo Pagoda in Myanmar.

If you're on a motorcycle, or have a car, take Hwy 105 to Wat Thani Wattharam, turn right and drive 3km. The trail that winds up the hill to the *chedi* provides good views of the thick teak forests across the river in Myanmar. There are a couple of small limestone caves in the side of the hill on the way to the peak.

HERBAL SAUNA

Wat Mani has separate herbal **sauna** (admission 20B; ⏱ 3-7pm) facilities for men and women. The sauna volunteers also sell monk-made herbal medicines. The sauna is towards the back of the monastery grounds, past the monks' *kùti*.

COOKERY COURSE

Mo Mo & Bo Bo Cookery Course (Borderline; ☎ 0 5554 6584; borderlineshop@yahoo.com; 674/14 Th Intharakhiri; 400B a day, 3 people min) Held at the Borderline Shop (p422) this course teaches Shan, Burmese and Karen dishes. Running from 8am to 12pm, it includes a trip to the market, food and drink preparation, a cook book, and sharing the results in the adjoining café.

Tours

Several guesthouses arrange tours of the surrounding area. The staff working at the Khrua Canadian restaurant (p421) keep pretty good tabs on the different tours and can book tours with agencies out of Um Phang. Tours from Mae Sot run at about 1800B per person for day tours or 4500B for three-day/two-night trips – not including transport to Um Phang. Be sure to clarify exactly what is included in the price of your tour.

The following are the longest running and most reliable. See p427 for other tour options out of Um Phang.

Eco-Trekking (☎ 0 5554 4976; www.geocities.com /no4guesthouse; No 4 Guest House; 736 Th Intharakhiri) Mr Oom has extensive knowledge of flora and fauna (especially birds) and will design specialised tours based on your interests. One of his specialities is a challenging seven-day trek south to Sangkhlaburi. Check the website for more details.

NORTHERN THAILAND

Mae Sot Conservation Tour (☎ 0 5553 2818; maesotco@cscoms.com; 415/17 Th Tang Kim Chiang) Runs educational tours to Karen and Hmong hill-tribe villages.

Max One Tour (☎ 0 5554 2942; www.maxonetour.com; Mae Sot Sq, Th Intharakhiri) Biggest company with the most elaborate adventure-centric tours.

Se. Southeast Express (☎ 0 5554 7048; 522/3 Th Intharakhiri) Does the usual three- to four-day tours to Um Phang and around, as well as one-day tours around Mae Sot.

Festivals & Events

A big **Thai-Burmese gem fair** is held in April. Around this time Thai and Burmese boxers meet for an annual **Thai-boxing competition**, held somewhere outside town in the traditional style. Matches are fought in a circular ring and go for five rounds; the first four rounds last three minutes, the fifth has no time limit. With their hands bound in hemp, the boxers fight till first blood or knockout. You'll have to ask around to find the changing venue for the annual slugfest.

Sleeping

BUDGET

The lodging market is changing and growing in Mae Sot, especially in the budget category. Most places cater for NGO workers that are staying longer-term and often offer weekly or monthly discounts.

No 4 Guest House (☎ 0 5554 4976; www.geocities .com/no4guesthouse/; 736 Th Intharakhiri; dm/s/d 50/80/100B) This large teak house has very basic rooms with mattresses on the floor. Shared bathrooms are down steep stairs. It's fine if you are short on baht and don't mind the 11pm curfew.

Kame Guest House (☎ 0 5553 5868; kame@picosystems .net; 119/22 Th Chidwana; dm/s/d 60/120/150B; 💻) Tidy but stark, this guesthouse overlooking the bus terminal has clean dorms and 120B rooms with just tatami mats to sleep on. The more expensive rooms have beds and a fan. All share hot-water bathrooms. You can rent a bicycle here for 30B a day.

Green Guest House (☎ 0 5553 3207; 406/8 Th Intara-hakhiri; dm/s/d from 80/150/250B) Run by a teacher and her husband, this peaceful, friendly guest-house offers a variety of good-sized rooms with TV and decent furniture. It's great value, centrally located and has a pretty garden.

Bai Fern Guesthouse (☎ 0 5553 1349; Th Intharakhiri; s/d 150/250) The newly renovated Bai Fern has superclean, large, if rather plain rooms, right

in the middle of town. All have well-equipped shared bathrooms. The service is very friendly and professional with the use of a kitchen, fridge, wireless internet and TV in the communal area.

Siam Hotel (☎ 0 5553 1376; 185 Th Prasat Withi; r 200-500B; ✗) Although it's basically a truckers' and gem traders' haunt, local rumour has it that Myanmar intelligence agents frequent the Siam. It also sees a fair number of families and has clean, if stark, rooms.

DK Mae Sot Square Hotel (Duang Kamol Hotel; ☎ 0 5554 2648/9; 298/2 Th Intharakhiri; r 250-450B; ✗ 💻) The vast rooms in this plain, three-storey hotel range from those with fans, hospital-like beds and cold water, to more comfortable air-con rooms with hot water, a small balcony and some furniture to fill up the space. There is a bookshop next door that occasionally has England-language titles.

First Hotel (☎ 0 5553 1233; fax 0 5553 1340; 44 Th Intharakhiri; r 270-450B; ✗) Just off the main street, this hotel appears to be in shambles from the outside but inside the ceilings and walls of heavy carved teak make it imposingly grand. Large rooms are not at all grand but have cable TV and lots of furniture.

our pick Ban Thai Guest House (☎ 0 5553 1590; banthai_mth@hotmail.com; 740 Th Intharakhiri; r 300-550B; 💻) Popular among volunteers, this neighbourhood of five converted Thai houses down a hibiscus-lined alley has spacious, very stylish wooden rooms with Thai style furniture, axe lounging pillows and Thai textiles. The cheaper rooms have plentiful shared bathrooms; the more expensive have en suite bathrooms, large terraces and some come with a lounge/office. Shared sitting areas have cable TV, DVDs and free wireless internet. There are bicycles and motorbikes to rent and a laundry service.

MIDRANGE & TOP END

our pick Rujira (☎ 0 5554 4969; rujira_tom@hotmail.com; 3/18 Th Buakjoon; r 350-1000B; ✗ 💻) This fantastic value hotel south of the centre, has spacious, light rooms with lots of homely touches. Cable TV, large fridges, good toiletries, bathrobes and slippers are included. More expensive rooms have romantic four-poster beds and sofas. The many communal areas include hammocks around a fountain and a *saalaa* (open-sided covered meeting hall or resting place) with axe cushions. There is a restaurant, cute coffee shop, two conference rooms, wi-

fi access throughout the hotel, and bicycles are free to use. Call for pick up from the bus station (50B).

Central Mae Sod Hill Hotel (☎ 0 5553 2601; www .centralhotelsresorts.com; 100 Th Asia; r/ste incl breakfast 1100/2900B; ❄ ☎) This resort on the highway to Tak is 10 minutes' drive from the town centre. Rooms are spacious and have all the four-star amenities. There's a pool, tennis courts, good restaurant, disco and a bar.

Eating

Mae Sot is a culinary crossroad with plenty of veggie-friendly options.

RESTAURANTS

our pick **Casa Mia** (☎ 08 7204 4701; Th Don Kaew; dishes 30-160B; ❄ 8am-10pm) Tucked down a side street, this simple Italian restaurant is heartily recommended by Italian NGO workers. Homemade pasta, pizzas and focaccia are served here. Try dishes like spinach and ricotta ravioli with sage and butter sauce. They also do a wicked chocolate cake. Lots of vegetarian options plus Thai and Burmese food is on offer. Guesthouse deliveries are also available.

Aiya (☎ 0 5553 0102; 533 Th Intharakhiri; dishes 30-160B; ❄ 10am-10pm) Opposite Bai Fern Guest House, Aiya is a simple place that serves fantastic Burmese food, which is particularly strong on vegetarian options. Try dishes like tealeaf salad with mixed fried peas or the aubergine curry. The sea bass with ginger sauce is good too. Aiya also delivers.

T Corner (☎ 0 5553 4297; 557/2 Th Intharakhiri; dishes 35-60B; ❄ 8am-10pm) This new, fresh looking café has a decked terrace with parasols and a small air-con section. Serving large breakfast, good coffee, sandwiches, salads and Thai food, this is a popular gathering spot.

our pick **Khrua Canadian** (☎ 0 5553 4659; 3 Th Sri Phanit; dishes 40-100B; ❄ 7am-10.30pm) The coffee is strong, the servings are large, the menu is varied, the prices are reasonable and local information is abundant here. It's also the best place to catch up on international news.

Khao Mao Khao Fang (☎ 0 5553 3607; 382 Mu 5, Mae Pa; dishes 50-90B; ❄ 10am-10pm) North of town between the Km 1 and Km 2 markers on the road to Mae Ramat, this is the place for a romantic evening out. A Thai botanist designed this open-air restaurant to make it feel as if you're dining in the forest. The Thai cuisine is equally inventive, with such specialities as *yam hèt khon* (a spicy salad made with for-

est mushrooms only available in September and October) and *mŭu khâo mâo* (a salad of home-cured sausage, peanuts, rice shoots, lettuce, ginger, lime and chilli).

Bai Fern (☎ 0 5553 3343; Th Intharakhiri; dishes 60-240B; ❄ 7.30am-10pm) The cosy, wood-furnished Bai Fern has a pleasant atmosphere and is popular all day long. Many come here for the good coffee and bread. The steaks, salads and Burmese curries have been recommended too. Peruse the *Bangkok Post* or the *Nation* while you wait.

QUICK EATS

For cheap Thai and Burmese takeaway, head to the **day market** behind the Siam Hotel or to the back of the **night market** (furthest away from Th Prasat Withi). Look out for a favourite local snack, *krabawng jaw* (Burmese for 'fried crispy'), a sort of vegetable tempura. Another local food speciality is *kŭaytĭaw meuang*, a rich bowl of rice noodles covered with sliced pork, greens, peanuts, chilli and green beans – very similar to *kŭaytĭaw sùkhŏthai*. Look for rice-noodle vendors along Th Prasat Withi.

Drinking & Entertainment

Mae Sot has a lively nightlife that heats up at the weekends.

Kung's Bar (Th Intharakhiri) Lively on Friday and Saturday nights, this laid-back popular place has a chunky wooden bar, pool table, and a choice of outside or inside seating. Good Thai food is also available.

Crocodile Tear (Th Intharakhiri; ❄ 3pm-1am) Features an extensive selection of mixed drinks, folky live music and many drunken travellers.

Lucky Music Room (Th Prasat Withi) For more local flavour, you can dance yourself silly at Lucky Music Room, which gets going around 10.30pm and sometimes charges a cover (20B).

Shopping

Don't miss the large, lively **municipal market** in Mae Sot. Behind the Siam Hotel, the market sells some interesting stuff, including Burmese clothing, cheap cigarettes, roses, Indian food, sturdy Burmese blankets and velvet thong slippers from Mandalay.

Mae Sot is most famous for its gems trade, and is the most important jade and gem centre along the border. Check out the hustle and bustle among the glittering treasures in the shops and stalls along Th Prasat Withi (beside

the Siam hotel). If looking to buy be prepared to bargain hard.

Borderline Shop (☎ 0 5554 6584; borderlineshop@ yahoo.com; 674/14 Th Intharakhiri; ✆ 8am-6pm Tue-Sun) Selling arts and craft items made by refugee women, the profits of this shop go back into a woman's collective and a child-assistance foundation. All of the products, such as bags, clothes and household items, have labels on them so you know where the money is going. Upstairs a gallery sells paintings. A cookery course (see p419) and outdoor café are also located here.

Getting There & Away

AIR
The Mae Sot airport was not operating at the time of writing.

BUS & SĂWNGTHĂEW
If you're heading anywhere other than Bangkok, go to Tak (minivan/air-con bus 53/74B,

1½ hours) where you can easily connect with buses headed to Lampang, Chiang Mai, Chiang Rai and Mae Sai. Minivans leave for Tak hourly from the station just north of the police station. Buses leave less frequently from the same station. Orange săwngthăew serving the northern destinations of Mae Sarit (70B, 2½ hours), Tha Song Yang (60B, 1½ hours) and Mae Sariang (170B, six hours) also leave this station hourly between 6am and noon.

First-class air-con buses run between Bangkok and Mae Sot six times daily (365B, nine hours); 2nd-class air-con buses (284B, nine hours) have similar departures. VIP buses (24 seats) to/from Bangkok leave four times daily (565B, eight hours). These leave from the bus station that is around 2km out of town by Th Asia. A new bus terminal near the airport was being completed at the time of writing. All buses will stop here when it is finished – reportedly by late 2007. Blue săwngthăew to

---

BURMESE REFUGEES & MIGRANTS

Burmese refugees first crossed into Thailand in 1984, when the Burmese army penetrated the ethnic Karen state and established bases near the Thai–Burma border, from where they launched forced relocation campaigns of the indigenous populations. Large numbers of civilian ethnic minority populations, students and pro-democracy advocates were forced into Thailand following the suppression of pro-democracy demonstrations in 1988 and the overturned 1990 elections. Today, refugees continue to cross the border to escape from ongoing fighting and persecution in eastern Burma.

At present, over 151,000 Burmese refugees live in relative safety in nine refugee camps scattered along the border. In these camps the Thai government allows international organisations to provide humanitarian assistance, including health care and schooling.

Many who flee Burma are not permitted to be registered refugees if not running from active fighting. Those who cross the border because of politically induced economic hardship or human rights violations often become migrant workers, with a precarious political and legal status. Approximately two million Burmese migrant workers and their families live in Thailand – often at way below subsistence levels - performing farm, factory, fishery, construction and domestic work. They are extremely vulnerable to exploitation by employers and deportation by officials, and frequently lack access to basic educational and health services.

It is possible for migrant workers from the region to be legally registered, obtain non-Thai identification cards and be issued work permits once employment is secured. Migrants are allowed to work for one year and the work permits have to be renewed on a yearly basis. However, the majority of the migrants are not registered, as it is an expensive and unclear process and the employer needs to cover some of the costs.

According to Thai government policy, migrant children in Thailand have a right to basic education of up to 12 years, regardless of their nationality, legal status and documentation. Yet many challenges remain to making this law a practical reality for migrant children. These include their lack of legal status making them vulnerable to deportation, language differences and difficulty in accessing transport to the schools. Migrants and registered workers can access a national health insurance scheme, but this is largely unattainable for the majority of migrants, partly because most aren't registered and their legal status makes them avoid Thai institutions. Consequently,

Um Phang (120B, four hours) leave hourly between 7am and 3pm from an office off the southern end of Th Sri Phanit.

Getting Around

Most of Mae Sot can be seen on foot. Regular săwngthăew serve surrounding communities including Moei (10B).

Jit Motorcycle (Th Prasat Withi; motorcycles per day 160B) rents out motorcycles. Make sure you test ride a bike before renting. Ban Thai guesthouse also rents out motorbikes (see p406). Cars and vans can be rented for around 1200B a day; ask at any hotel or Bai Fern restaurant (p421).

Motorcycle taxis and săamláw charge 20B for trips around town.

AROUND MAE SOT
Waley
บ้านวะเลย์

Thirty-six kilometres from Mae Sot, Rte 1206 splits southwest off Rte 1090 at Ban Saw Oh and terminates 25km south at the border town of Waley, an important smuggling point.

The Burmese side was once one of two main gateways to Kawthoolei, the Karen nation, but in 1989 the Yangon government ousted the KNU. Until the Thai government cut off all timber trade with Myanmar's military government, teak was the main border trade. Nowadays there's a brisk trade in teak furniture instead.

One can visit hill-tribe villages near **Ban Chedi Kok**, or the **Highland Farm and Gibbon Refuge** (www.members.tripod.com/highlandfarm; Km 42.8, Rte 1090) near Phop Phra. The latter is a private facility that cares for gibbons and other animals that have been rescued from captivity. It is possible to volunteer and live at the sanctuary, but there is a three-day minimum at a charge of US$25 per person per day, or US$600 per month. The fee includes a very nice room and three meals per day.

---

many grass roots and international nongovernmental organisations are actively working to bridge this gap in health care, often in cooperation with provincial health authorities.

To find out more about the refugees and migrants, as well as the situation in Burma, useful sites are www.burmanet.org and www.irrawaddy.org.

Thanks to the International Rescue Community (www.theirc.org)

HOW TO HELP?

Although many Thai and foreign volunteers have come to the refugees' aid, the camps are very much in need of outside assistance. Tourists, both Thai and foreign, are no longer permitted to visit the camps unless working formally with an aid organisation. However, there are various ways to help:

Mae Tao Clinic (Dr Cynthia's Clinic; ☎ 0 5556 3644; www.maetaoclinic.org, www.burmachildren.org) While many of Burma's refugees that flood over the border end up in refugee camps with access to medical care; those who don't are in a precarious position. The Mae Tao Clinic was established in 1989 by Dr Cynthia Maung, herself a Karen refugee, to meet the health needs of these Burmese migrants. The clinic gives free medical treatment to around 50,000 Burmese migrants a year. One of the best and direct ways of offering help is by donating money to the clinic. Take a săwngthăew to the clinic, which is halfway between Mae Sot and the Friendship Bridge. Here there is a desk with a 'Public Relations Center' sign, where you can give money in return for a receipt. It is also possible to volunteer at the clinic if you apply in advance. Most of the volunteers are health professionals doing internships but there are some English teaching opportunities. In both cases the minimum volunteering period is 3 months. Email win7@loxinso.co.th for more information.

Burma Volunteer Programme (www.geocities.com/maesotbvp) This volunteer programme was set up to provide English teaching to different Burmese social, political and ethnic groups along the Thai–Burmese border, to enable communication of their situation with the international community, and to facilitate access to additional educational opportunities. Teaching placements are for a minimum of three months. As well as English training, volunteers may get involved in editing publications or practical skills training. Placements are mainly in Mae Sot and around, but positions in Mae Hong Son, Mae Sariang and Chiang Mai are possible.

Ban Thai Guest House (p420) Ask at this guesthouse about other volunteering options. Teaching is often in demand, and with 40 schools in and around Mae Sot, an informal teaching post may be arranged. So as not to be disruptive, the minimum commitment is usually one month.

NORTHERN THAILAND

GETTING THERE & AWAY

Săwngthăew to Phop Phra (40B) and Waley (45B) depart from Mae Sot every half-hour, between 6am and 6pm, from the same place as the săwngthăew to Um Phang. If you go by motorcycle or car, follow Rte 1090 southeast towards Um Phang and after 36km take Rte 1206 southwest. From this junction it's 25km to Waley; the last 10km of the road are unpaved. Your passport may be checked at a police outpost before Waley.

Border Market & Myawadi
ตลาดริมเมย/เมียวาดี

Experience a slice of Myanmar, or just go for the sake of an instant 30-day visa, by crossing the Mae Nam Moei to Myawadi. Immigration procedures are taken care of at the **Thai immigration booth** (🕒 8.30am-4.30pm) at the Friendship Bridge, although if you have any problems there's another immigration office in the nearby Mae Moei Shopping Bazaar. It takes around 15 minutes to finish all the paperwork to leave Thailand officially, and then you're free to walk across the arched 420m Friendship Bridge.

At the other end of the bridge is a rustic **Myanmar immigration booth**, where you'll fill out permits for a one-day stay, pay a fee of US$10 or 500B and leave your passports as a deposit. Then you're free to wander around Myawadi as long as you're back at the bridge by 4.30pm to pick up your passport and check out with immigration. On your return to Thailand, the Thai immigration office at the bridge will give you a new 30-day tourist visa (p753).

Before taking the 6km săwngthăew trip to the Friendship Bridge, ask about the border situation in Mae Sot. At the time of writing the crossing was closed for a week due to the September 2006 coup. In addition, sporadic relations between Myanmar and Thailand can sometimes cause the border to close for a few days. If the border is closed and your 30-day visa has run out, it is possible to get a one-day extension for free at the immigration office. For each day's extension after that it costs 500B.

There is a **market** about 100m from the river on the Thai side that legally sells Burmese goods – dried fish and shrimp, dried bamboo shoots, mung beans, peanuts, woven-straw products, teak furniture, thick cotton blankets, lacquerware, tapestries, wooden furniture, jade and gems. However, it's not one of the more exciting markets in Thailand, and the Mae Sot market is much more lively. You can also buy black-market *kyat* (Burmese currency) here at favourable rates.

MYAWADI
เมียวาดี

Myawadi is a fairly typical Burmese town, with a number of monasteries, schools, shops and so on. The most important temple is **Shwe Muay Wan**, a traditional bell-shaped *chedi* gilded with many kilos of gold and topped by more than 1600 precious and semiprecious gems. Surrounding the main *chedi* are 28 smaller *chedi*, and these in turn are encircled by 12 larger ones. Colourful shrines to Mahamuni Buddha, Shin Upagot and other Buddhist deities follow the typical Mon and central-Burmese style, with lots of mirrored mosaics.

Another noted Buddhist temple is **Myikyaungon**, called Wat Don Jarakhe in Thai and named for its crocodile-shaped sanctuary. A hollow *chedi* at Myikyaungon contains four marble Mandalay-style Buddhas around a central pillar, while niches in the surrounding wall are filled with Buddhas in other styles, including several bronze Sukhothai-style Buddhas. Myawadi's 1000-year-old earthen city walls, probably erected by the area's original Mon inhabitants, can be seen along the southern side of town.

It might sound like Myawadi isn't all that different than Thailand – temples, *chedi* and Buddhas – but as soon as you step off the bridge, you'll note the differences. As self-proclaimed guides and energetic săamláw drivers gather around lone travellers in hopes of a few extra baht, you'll feel just how different life is on this side of the river. Few motorised vehicles travel the barely paved main avenue, and just about every woman has something large balanced on her head. Because of long-time commercial, social and religious links between Mae Sot and Myawadi, many local residents can speak some Thai.

GETTING THERE & AWAY

Săwngthăew frequently go to the border (10B), 6km west of Mae Sot: ask for Rim Moei (Edge of the Moei). The last săwngthăew going back to Mae Sot leaves Rim Moei at 5pm.

UM PHANG & AROUND
อุ้มผาง

Route 1090 goes south from Mae Sot to Um Phang, 150km away. This stretch of road used to be called the 'Death Highway' be-

cause of the guerrilla activity in the area that hindered highway development. Those days ended in the 1980s, but lives are still lost because of brake failure or treacherous turns on this steep, winding road through incredible mountain scenery.

Along the way there are short hikes off the highway to two waterfalls, **Nam Tok Thararak**

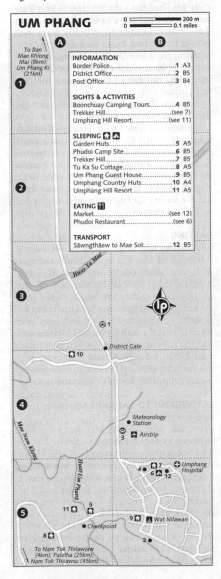

UM PHANG

0 — 200 m
0 — 0.1 miles

To Ban
Mae Khlong
Mai (8km);
Um Phang Ki
(21km)

INFORMATION
Border Police.................................**1** A3
District Office...............................**2** B5
Post Office...................................**3** B4

SIGHTS & ACTIVITIES
Boonchuay Camping Tours...........**4** B5
Trekker Hill...............................(see 7)
Umphang Hill Resort.................(see 11)

SLEEPING
Garden Huts................................**5** A5
Phudoi Camp Site.........................**6** B5
Trekker Hill.................................**7** B5
Tu Ka Su Cottage..........................**8** A5
Um Phang Guest House..................**9** B5
Umphang Country Huts.................**10** A4
Umphang Hill Resort...................**11** A5

EATING
Market.....................................(see 12)
Phudoi Restaurant......................(see 6)

TRANSPORT
Săwngthǎew to Mae Sot..............**12** B5

Huay Ya Mae

District Gate

Meteorology
Station
Airstrip

Umphang
Hospital

Mae Nam Klong

Huay Um Phang

Wat Nilawan

Checkpoint

To Nam Tok Thilawjaw
(4km); Palatha (25km);
Nam Tok Thilawsu (45km)

(26km from Mae Sot) and **Nam Tok Pha Charoen** (41km). Nam Tok Thararak streams over limestone cliffs and calcified rocks with a rough texture that makes climbing the falls easy. It's been made into a park of sorts, with benches right in the stream at the base of the falls for cooling off and a couple of outhouse toilets nearby; on weekends food vendors set up here.

The eucalyptus-lined dirt road leaves the highway between the Km 24 and Km 25 markers. A side road at the Km 48 marker leads to a group of government-sponsored hill-tribe villages (Karen, Lisu, Hmong, Mien, Lahu). Just beyond Ban Rom Klao 4 – roughly midway between Mae Sot and Um Phang – is a very large Karen and Burmese refugee village (called Um Piam) with around 20,000 refugees that were moved here from camps around Rim Moei. There are also several Hmong villages.

Sitting at the junction of Mae Nam Klong and Huay Um Phang, Um Phang is an overgrown village populated mostly by Karen. Many Karen villages in this area are very traditional, and elephants are used as much as oxen for farm work. *Yaeng* (elephant saddles) and other tack used for elephant wrangling are a common sight on the verandas of Karen houses outside of town. You'll also see plenty of **elephants** in other Karen villages throughout the district. The name for the district comes from the Karen word *umpha*, a type of bamboo container in which travelling Karen carried their documents to show to Thai border authorities.

An interesting hike can be done that follows the footpaths northeast of the village through rice fields and along Huay Um Phang to a few smaller Karen villages. At the border where Amphoe Um Phang meets Myanmar, near the Thai-Karen villages of Ban Nong Luang and Ban Huay, is a Karen refugee village inhabited by more than 500 Karen who originally hailed from Htikabler village on the other side of border.

South of Um Phang, towards Sangkhlaburi in Kanchanaburi province, **Um Phang Wildlife Sanctuary** (admission 400B) is a Unesco World Heritage site. One of its most popular attractions is Nam Tok Thilawsu (p426), the largest waterfall in Thailand. Um Phang Wildlife Sanctuary links with the Thung Yai Naresuan National Park and Huay Kha Kaeng Wildlife Sanctuary (another Unesco World Heritage

site), as well as Khlong Lan and Mae Wong National Parks to form Thailand's largest wildlife corridor and one of the largest intact natural forests in Southeast Asia.

Information

There is no bank in Um Phang and businesses are not equipped to deal with credit cards, so bring all the cash you'll need with you. There's a **post office**, which has a couple of long-distance phones. The Umphang Hill Resort (p428) has a slow internet connection for 40B per hour that nonguests can use. Places in town near Wat Nilawan offer the same connection for 20B per hour.

Sights & Activities
NAM TOK THILAWSU
น้ำตกทีลอซู

In Amphoe Um Phang you can arrange trips down Mae Nam Mae Klong to Nam Tok Thilawsu and Karen villages – inquire at any guesthouse. Typical three-day excursions include a raft journey along the river from Um Phang to the falls, then a two-day trek from the falls through the Karen villages of **Khotha** and **Palatha**, where a 4WD picks up trekkers and returns them to Um Phang (25km from Palatha by road).

Some people prefer to spend two days on the river; the first night at a cave or hot springs along the river before Thilawsu and a second night at the falls. On the third day you can cross the river by elephant to one of the aforementioned villages to be met by a truck and returned to Um Phang. Or you can continue 20km further south along the road to Palatha to the Hmong village of **Kangae Khi**. On the way back to Um Phang from Palatha you can stop off at **Nam Tok Thilawjaw**, which tumbles over a fern-covered cliff.

The scenery along the river is stunning, especially after the rainy season (November and December) when the 200m to 400m limestone cliffs are streaming with water and Nam Tok Thilawsu is at its best. This waterfall is Thailand's largest, measuring an estimated 200m high and up to 400m wide during the rainy season. There's a shallow cave behind the falls and several levels of pools suitable for swimming. Part of Um Phang Wildlife Sanctuary, Thais consider Nam Tok Thilawsu to be the most beautiful waterfall in the country

You can **camp** at the Um Phang Wildlife Sanctuary headquarters near the falls any time of year. Between December and May there are also rooms available for 150B per person, but you must bring your own food. The 1.8km trail between the sanctuary headquarters and the falls has been transformed into a self-guided nature tour, with the addition of well-conceived educational plaques. Surrounding the falls on both sides of the river are Thailand's thickest stands of natural forest, and the hiking in the vicinity of Nam Tok Thilawsu can be superb. The forest here is said to contain more than 1300 varieties of palm; giant bamboo and strangler figs are commonplace, and the orchid tree (Bauhinia variegata) can even be seen along the road to Palatha.

Between December and June you can also drive to the falls over a rough 47km road from Um Phang, suitable for 4WD or a skilled dirtbike rider only. Or follow the main paved road south of Um Phang to Km 19; the walk to the falls is a stiff four hours from here via **Mo Phado** village. A săwngthăew goes to the Km 19 marker from Um Phang once daily; ask for kii-loh sìp kâo and expect to pay 20B to 25B per person.

RAFTING

Um Phang Khi is a 'new' area for rafting, northeast of Um Phang. Officially there are 47 (some rafting companies claim 67) sets of rapids rated at class III (moderate) and class IV (difficult) during the height of the rainy season. The rafting season for Um Phang Khi is short – August to October only – as other times of year the water level isn't high enough. Rafting trips arranged in Um Phang typically cost 3500B for a two-night, three-day programme, or 4000B if booked in Mae Sot. See Tours (opposite) for more information.

LETONGKHU TO SANGKHLABURI
เลตองคุ/อำเภอสังขละบุรี

From Ban Mae Khlong Mai, just a few kilometres north of Um Phang via the highway to Mae Sot, a graded dirt road (Rte 1167) heads southwest along the border to **Beung Kleung** (sometimes spelt Peung Kleung) – a Karen, Burmese, Indo-Burmese, Talaku and Thai trading village where buffalo carts are more common than motorcycles. The picturesque setting among spiky peaks and cliffs is worth the trip even if you go no further. Impressive **Nam Tok Ekaratcha** is an hour's walk away. Săwngthăew from Um Phang usually make a

NORTHERN THAILAND

trip to Beung Kleung once a day, and it's possible to stay at the village clinic or in a private
home for a donation of 100B per person. On
the way you can stop off at the small, traditional Karen village of **Ban Thiphochi**.

Four hours' walk from here along a rough
track (passable by 4WD in the dry season),
near the Myanmar border on the banks of
Mae Nam Suriya next to Sam Rom mountain,
is the culturally singular, 109-house village of
Letongkhu (Leh Tawng Khu).

According to what little anthropological information is available, the villagers, although
for the most part Karen in language, belong
to the Lagu or Talaku sect, said to represent
a form of Buddhism mixed with shamanism
and animism. Letongkhu is one of only six
such villages in Thailand; there are reportedly
around 30 more in Myanmar. Each village has
a spiritual and temporal leader called a *pu
chaik* (whom the Thais call *reusii* – 'rishi' or
'sage') who wears his hair long – usually tied
in a topknot – and dresses in white, yellow or
brown robes, depending on the subsect.

The current *pu chaik* at Letongkhu is the
10th in a line of 'white-thread' priests dating back to their residence in Myanmar. The
sage's many male disciples also wear their hair
in topknots (often tied in cloth) and may wear
similar robes. All *reusii* abstain from alcohol
and are celibate. The priests live apart from
the village in a temple and practise traditional
medicine based on herbal healing and ritual
magic. Antique elephant tusks are kept as
talismans.

Evangelistic Christian missionaries have
infiltrated the area and have tried to convert
the Talaku, thus making the Talaku sensitive
to outside visitation. Before heading out here
call **Ban Lae Tongku** (☎ 0 5556 1008) to make sure
this unique community will welcome your
visit. Travellers are said to have been turned
away upon arrival. If you do visit Letongkhu,
take care not to enter any village structures
without permission or invitation. Likewise,
do not take photographs without permission.
If you treat the villagers with respect then you
shouldn't have a problem.

You should also inquire about the border status in Um Phang or at the TAT office
(p416) in Tak. Opposite Letongkhu on the
Myanmar side of the border, the KNU has
set up its latest tactical headquarters. Yangon
government offensives against the KNU can
break out in this area during the dry months

of the year, but when this is happening or is
likely to happen, Thai military checkpoints
will turn all trekkers back.

Sangkhlaburi (p222) is 90km or a four- to
five-day trek from Beung Kleung. On the way
(11km from Beung Kleung), about 250m off
the road, is the extensive cave system of **Tham
Takube**. From Ban Mae Chan, 35km along
the same route, there's a dirt road branching
out across the border to a KNU-controlled
village. The route to Sangkhlaburi has several
branches; the main route crosses over the border into Myanmar for some distance before
crossing back into Thailand. There has been
discussion of cutting a newer, more direct
road between Um Phang and Sangkhlaburi.

Because of the overall sensitive nature of
this border area and the very real potential for
becoming lost, ill or injured, a guide is highly
recommended for any sojourn south of Um
Phang. You may be able to arrange a guide for
this route in Beung Kleung. Otherwise, Eco-
Trekking in Mae Sot (p419) and Umphang
Hill Resort (p428) can arrange seven-day treks
from Umphang to Sangkhlaburi with advance
notice. The best time of year to do the trek is
October to January.

Tours

Several of the guesthouses in Um Phang can
arrange trekking and rafting trips in the area.
The typical three-night, four-day trip costs
from 4500B per person (four or more people).
The price includes rafting, an elephant ride,
food and a guide service.

Longer treks are also possible, as well as
day trips to Nam Tok Thilawsu. If given a
few weeks' notice Umphang Hill Resort does
a seven-day trek down to Sangkhlaburi (minimum four people, per person 9000B); Eco-
Trekking (p419) at No 4 Guest House in Mae
Sot also does a similar and recommended
trip for US$400. It is worth checking to see
what kind of rafts are used; most places have
switched to rubber as bamboo rafts can break
up in the rough rapids. Choose rubber unless
you are really looking for adventure (such as
walking to your camp site rather than rafting there).

Within Um Phang, Umphang Hill Resort
(p428) has the best equipment and trip designs. Most guesthouses arrange treks, as well
as the recommended companies below who
have English-speaking guides. The majority
have rafting and hiking trips to Nam Tok

NORTHERN THAILAND

Thilawsu and beyond, including one itinerary that takes rafters through 11 different sets of rapids on Mae Nam Mae Klong. Longer or shorter trips may also be arranged, and elephant riding instead of walking is always an option.

Boonchuay Camping Tours (☎ 0 5556 1020; boonchuay _umpang@hotmail.com; 360 Mu 1 Th Pravitpaiwan) Its focus is camping and communing with nature.

Trekker Hill (☎ 0 5556 1090; 620 Th Pravitpaiwan) This highly recommended outfit offers a variety of treks running from one day to four.

Umphang Hill Resort (☎ 0 5556 1063; Mae Sot ☎ 0 5553 1409; www.umphanghill.com) Associated with Max One Tour in Mae Sot (p420) this is the longest-running company in Um Phang. Its emphasis is on leading big groups of foreigners who book ahead of time. Can arrange seven-day treks south to Sangkhlaburi.

Sleeping

Accommodation in Um Phang is plentiful, but since the majority of visitors to the area are Thai, room rates tend to be a little higher than normal and all of the beds are rock hard. Most places cater to large groups so their rooms are designed for four or more people. Singles or couples may be able to negotiate lower rates, especially in the wet season.

BUDGET

Umphang Hill Resort (☎ 0 5556 1063, Mae Sot 0 5553 1409; www.umphanghill.com; per person 100-200B, bungalows 500-2000B; 🕸) Set in a pretty garden with views of the mountains, the oversized bungalows are designed to sleep six to 20 people and are in grave need of TLC. There are also tiny basic huts with just a mattress. Plus sides are that it does run the most tours and has the largest number of English-speaking guides in town.

Phudoi Camp Site (☎ 0 5556 1049, Bangkok 0 1886 8783; www.phudoi.com; 637 Th Pravitpaiwan; tent 200B, r 400B) Primarily catering to its prebooked tour clients, Phudoi has bungalows set on a well-landscaped hillside near the village centre. The log cabin-style bungalows are spacious and have verandas. There's also a camping area and a restaurant with the same name (right).

Um Phang Guest House (☎ 0 5556 1073; r 250-450B) Near Wat Nilawan, this place is owned by the local *kamnan* (precinct officer). It has motel-like rooms with squat toilets that sleep up to three, and nicer wood-and-brick cottages with Western toilets and hot water, which sleep up to four. There's a large outdoor restaurant in an open area near the cottages.

Trekker Hill (☎ 0 5556 1090; r 300B) This rustic collection of huts on a steep hillside has views of the valley and Um Phang. The restaurant serves three meals a day and also has satellite TV.

Garden Huts (Boonyaporn Guest House; ☎ 0 5556 1093, in Bangkok ☎ 0 1642 7594; www.boonyaporn.com; 8/1 Mu 6; r 300-500B) Operated by a sweet older couple, this collection of bungalows of varying degrees of comfort and size fronts the river. It features pleasant sitting areas and a well-cared-for garden. The strong, Thai-grown coffee is a perky bonus.

MIDRANGE & TOP END

Midrange options in Um Phang don't have all the bells and whistles of comparably priced places in other areas. They are notably more comfortable and well kept than their cheaper neighbours though, and take good advantage of the natural scenery in Um Phang.

Tu Ka Su Cottage (Kin Ka Tu; ☎ 0 5556 1295; r 600-1500B) West of Huay Um Phang, this is the cleanest and best-run accommodation in Um Phang. The attractive collection of brick-and-stone, multiroom cottages is surrounded by flower and exotic fruit gardens. The largest bungalows sleep 10, but it's possible to rent half of one of the smaller two-room cottages for between 600B and 800B. All of the bathrooms have hot-water showers with an outdoor feel. Tu Ka Su also runs good local trekking-rafting trips, but it only has one English-speaking guide.

Umphang Country Huts (☎ 0 5556 1079; www.um phangcountryhut.com; r 500-1500B) Off the highway 1.5km before Um Phang, these huts enjoy a nice hilly setting. Rooms in a wood-and-thatch, two-storey building facing Huay Mae Klong share a common veranda. There are larger, more atmospheric rooms in another two-storey building with private verandas. The cheapest rooms have cold-water bathrooms.

Eating

Um Phang has three or four simple noodle and rice shops, plus a morning **market** and a small sundries shop. There is a short string of noodle shops along the main road.

At the camp site of the same name (left) you'll find **Phudoi Restaurant** (☎ 0 5556 1049; dishes 20-40B; 🕙 8am-10pm). It has very good food, especially the *phánaeng* (mild curry) dishes. There are also rice dishes, noodles, *tôm yam* (hot-

and-sour Thai soup) and cold beer. There's a bilingual menu and it's often the only place open past 9pm.

Getting There & Away

There are săwngthǎew to Um Phang from Mae Sot (120B, five hours, 165km) departing several times a day between 7am and 3pm. Săwngthǎew usually stop for lunch at windy **Ban Rom Klao 4** on the way.

If you decide to try to ride a motorcycle from Mae Sot, be sure it's one with a strong engine as the road has lots of fairly steep grades. Total drive time is around four hours. The only petrol pump along the way is in Ban Rom Klao 4, 80km from Mae Sot, so you may want to carry 3L or 4L of extra fuel.

MAE SOT TO MAE SARIANG

แม่สอด/แม่สะเรียง

Route 105 runs north along the Myanmar border from Mae Sot all the way to Mae Sariang (226km) in Mae Hong Son Province. The winding, paved road passes through the small communities of **Mae Ramat**, **Mae Sarit**, **Ban Tha Song Yang** and **Ban Sop Ngao** (Mae Ngao). The thick forest in these parts still has a few stands of teak and the Karen villages continue to use the occasional work elephant. Be prepared to show your passport to Thai border patrols often.

If you have your own transport, be sure to stop and check out these friendly, low-key, rarely visited communities. Don't miss **Wat Don Kaew** in Mae Ramat. It's behind the district office and houses a large Mandalay-style marble Buddha. Other attractions on the way to Mae Sariang include **Nam Tok Mae Kasa**, between the Km 13 and Km 14 markers, and extensive limestone caverns at **Tham Mae Usu**, at Km 94 near Ban Tha Song Yang. From the highway it's a 2km walk to Tham Mae Usu; note that it's closed in the rainy season, when the river running through the cave seals off the mouth.

Instead of doing the Myanmar border run in one go, some people opt to spend the night in Mae Sarit (118km from Mae Sot). **Mae Salid Guest House** (Mae Sarit; s/d 50/100B) is related to Umphang Hill Resort and offers six very simple rooms with private toilet and shared cold-water showers. It's east of the main intersection in Mae Sarit.

There is a very basic **guesthouse** (s/d 80/100B) in Ban Tha Song Yang near the săwngthǎew stop on Rte 105. Just follow the signs.

Krua Ban Tai (Th Si Wattana, Ban Tha Sang Yang; dishes 20-50B; ☻ 8am-9pm) is a two-storey wooden restaurant in the centre of Ban Tha Song Yang, around the corner from the main market. The creative menu includes good *yam wún sên* (spicy noodle salad) made with freshwater shrimp, and *khâo phàt phánaeng* (curried fried rice).

Hourly săwngthǎew to Mae Sarit (70B, four hours) leave from Mae Sot between 6am and noon (the same săwngthǎew continue on to Mae Sariang). Frequent săwngthǎew connect Mae Sarit to Ban Tha Song Yang (30B, 30 minutes) where morning and midday săwngthǎew head to Mae Sariang (60B, three hours). If you miss the morning săwngthǎew from Mae Sarit to Mae Sariang, you can usually arrange to charter a truck for 200B to 250B.

If you decide not to stay overnight in Mae Sarit, just stay on the săwngthǎew and eventually you'll land in Mae Sariang (170B, six hours) with an exhausted bum. These orange săwngthǎew leave from Mae Sot's bus station just north of the police station.

MAE HONG SON PROVINCE

Thailand's most northwestern province is a crossroads for ethnic minorities (mostly Karen, with some Hmong, Lisu and Lahu), Shan (known locally as Thai Yai) and Burmese immigrants. Reportedly 75% of the province consists of mountains and forest.

As the province is so far from the influence of sea winds and is thickly forested and mountainous, the temperature seldom rises above 40°C, while in January the temperature can drop to 2°C. The air is often misty with ground fog in the winter and smoke from slash-and-burn agriculture in the hot season.

Mae Hong Son province has undergone a tourist miniboom over the past decade, with many resorts opening in the area around the capital. However, few visitors seem to leave the beaten Mae Hong Son–Soppong–Pai track.

MAE SARIANG

แม่สะเรียง

pop 7800

Many of the hill-tribe settlements in Mae Hong Son province are concentrated in the

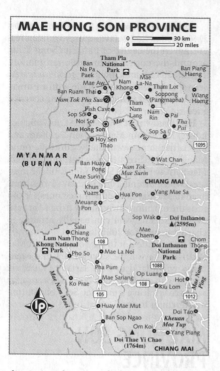

MAE HONG SON PROVINCE

Activities

Little-known Mae Sariang offers amazing **trekking** and **tours**, both scenic and cultural. Because the area around Mae Sariang is far from the popular jumping-off grounds of Mae Hong Son, Chiang Mai or Chiang Rai, you're less likely to see other trekking groups and the communities you visit are going to be less 'prepared' for you. Most tours include or focus on trekking to hill-tribe villages, boat trips to Mae Sam Laep, bamboo rafting, and elephant riding. In November many of the nearby hills bloom with *bua thawng* (literally 'golden lotus'), which look like large yellow daisies. Most guesthouses run tours but these have been particularly recommended:

Salawin Tour (Th Laeng Phanit; one-day trek 1300B, 3-day trek 2200B) With the best reputation in town, the sole trekking guide who runs Salawin Tour is from one of the surrounding hill tribes and knows the mountains like a guide should. He has an 'office' next to Riverside Guest House, and speaks very good English.

Kanchana Tour (☎ 08 1952 2167; kanchanakosai@yahoo .co.uk) This ex-teacher offers half- and full-day cycling tours around Mae Sariang, as well as river trips on the Salawin and 4WD trips to Karen villages. You can find her at Salawin Guest House (below).

Sleeping

BUDGET

Mitaree Guest House (☎ 0 5368 1110; www.mitareehotel .com; Th Mae Sariang; r 120–600B; 🖳) This is Mae Sariang's oldest hostelry. It has rooms in the old wooden wing or rooms with hot-water shower in the new wing. The older wing is popular with Thai truckers.

North West Guest House (☎ 0 5368 1956; Th Laeng Phanit; s/d 150/200B) The rooms in this large wooden house are simple (think mattress on the floor) but get natural light and are a good size. The six rooms come with slippers and towels, and share two spotless hot-water showers.

Salawin Guest House (☎ 0 5368 1490; Th Laeng Phanit; r 300–450B; 🖂 🖳) Although there are no river views here, this simple place is run by a helpful and welcoming couple. Rooms are clean and basic with large bathrooms. The proprietor makes a lovely iced lemon drink, and free coffee and tea is available.

Riverside Guest House (☎ 0 5368 1188; Th Laeng Phanit; r 300–600B; 🖳) This friendly, ramshackle guesthouse keeps growing and improving.

districts and towns of Khun Yuam, Mae La Noi and Mae Sariang, which are good departure points for treks to Hmong, Karen and Shan villages. Of these three small towns, Mae Sariang is the largest and offers the most facilities for use as a base camp.

Although there is not much to see in Mae Sariang, it's a pleasant, laid-back riverside town with a small travel scene. Two Burmese-Shan temples, **Wat Jong Sung** (Uthayarom) and **Wat Si Bunruang**, just off Mae Sariang's main street (not far from the Mae Sariang bus station), are definitely worth a visit if you have time. Built in 1896, Wat Jong Sung is the more interesting of the two temples and has slender, Shan-style *chedi* and wooden monastic buildings.

Information

Mae Sariang has a couple of banks with ATMs and an **immigration office** (☎ 0 5368 1339; Route 108) that will extend your visa by a couple of days if you're in a pinch and on your way to the border. It's opposite the petrol station on the road to Mae Hong Son. Internet is available next to River House Hotel and just south of Renu Restaurant.

Some rooms feel cramped but most share large terraces with fantastic views of a turn in the river and the valley beyond. There is a mediocre restaurant, and the local Salawin Tour trekking guide tends to hang out here if he's not in his place next door.

Kamolsorn Hotel (☎ 0 5368 1524; Th Mae Sariang; r 450-700B; 🟫) A multistorey hotel with clean rooms but zero character. Although spacious, dark wood furniture fills the rooms making them feel cluttered. Limited English is spoken.

MIDRANGE & TOP END

our pick **River House Hotel** (☎ 0 5362 1201; river house@hotmail.com; 77 Th Laeng Phanit; d 550-750B, tr 950B; 🟫) The combo of nostalgia-inducing teak and stylish décor makes this riverside hotel the best spot in town. Air-conditioned 2nd-floor rooms have huge verandas overlooking the river, and floor-to-ceiling windows. Downstairs, fan rooms are also riverside and have hammocks outside. All are well equipped and simply decorated in cream and wood. A very romantic place to stay. There's an excellent restaurant (p432) and recommended tours are run from here.

Garden House Resort (New Mitaree; ☎ 0 5368 1109; www.mitareehotel.com; 24 Th Wiang Mai; s 600-700B, d 700-800B, two-bed cottage 1200B; 🟫) Near the post office, this is run by the same friendly family as Mitaree Guest House. The newer wooden 'resort' cottages at the back have sitting areas in front with great views of the mountains. All have hot water, air-con and cable TV.

River House Resort (☎ 0 5368 3066; www.riverhouse hotels.com; Th Laeng Phanit; r incl breakfast 1700-2800B; 🟫) This large three-storey hotel is run by the same people as the River House Hotel but lacks its charm. New rooms are spacious with contemporary décor, minibar and cable TV. Ask for a river view room as the town-side ones are the same price. Those on the 1st floor open onto the river. There is a lawned garden with deckchairs, a bar with a pool table and a good restaurant.

Eating

Shaw Yang (Th Mae Sariang; snacks 15-49B; 🕙 10am-5pm) This large, modern, airy café serves ice cream by the cone or in a sundae, as well as real coffee. Perch on a bar stool or sit by the window and tuck into scoops of ice cream or a frothy cappuccino.

MAE SARIANG

0 ———— 200 m
0 ———— 0.1 miles

To Ban Mae Waen (36km);
Chiang Mai (185km)

To Mae Sam Laep (44km)

To Mae Sot (221km)

Forestry Department Office

INFORMATION
Immigration Office.................1 D1
Internet Café.......................2 B1
Internet Café.......................3 B2
Krung Thai Bank (ATM)..........4 B2
Police................................5 B2
Post Office..........................6 C2
Siam Commercial Bank
  (ATM)..............................7 B2

SIGHTS & ACTIVITIES
Kanchana Tour..............(see 16)
Salawin Tour.......................8 B1

SLEEPING 🏠
Garden House Resort..........9 D2
Kamolsorn Hotel.................10 B2
Mitaree Guest House............11 B2
North West Guest House........12 B1
River House Hotel................13 B1
River House Resort...............14 B1
Riverside Guest House...........15 B1
Salawin Guest House.............16 B1

EATING 🍴
Inthira Restaurant.................17 B2
Kai Yang Rai Khwan...............18 A2
Renu Restaurant....................19 B2
River House Restaurant.....(see 13)
Sawadee Restaurant &
  Bar...................................20 B1
Shaw Yang...........................21 B1

TRANSPORT
Bus Station...........................22 B1
Sombat Tour.........................23 B1

NORTHERN THAILAND

VISITING VILLAGES

When visiting hill-tribe villages try to find out what the local customs and taboos are, either by asking someone or by taking the time to observe local behaviour. Here are several other guidelines for minimising the impact you can have on local communities:

- Always ask for permission before taking photos of tribespeople and/or their dwellings. You can ask through your guide or by using sign language. Because of traditional belief systems, many individuals and even whole tribes may object strongly to being photographed.
- Show respect for religious symbols and rituals. Don't touch totems at village entrances or any other object of obvious symbolic value without asking permission. Unless you're asked to participate, keep your distance from ceremonies.
- Exercise restraint in giving things to tribespeople or bartering with them. If you want to give something to the people you encounter on a trek, the best thing is to make a donation to the village school or other community fund. Your guide can help arrange this. While it's an easy way to get a smile – giving sweets to children contributes to tooth decay – remember they probably don't have toothbrushes and toothpaste like you do.
- Set a good example to hill-tribe youths by not smoking opium or using other drugs.
- Don't litter while trekking or staying in villages.
- You might also want to check the 'Guidelines for Visitors to Northern Thailand's Mountain Peoples' at www.lanna.com/html/tourists.html.

Kai Yang Rai Khwan (dishes 10-150B; ⏱ 10am-5pm) A great spot for Isan-style grilled chicken (half/whole chicken 72/150B) and sticky rice (10B), this simple place is at the foot of the bridge crossing.

Renu Restaurant (☎ 0 5368 1171; Th Wiang Mai; dishes 25-70B; ⏱ 10am-11pm) Decorated with pics of King Bhumibol playing saxophone, this local spot has a more basic menu than the Inthira. The veggie options are limited to fried rice, but adventurous eaters might enjoy the 'nut-hatch curry'.

Inthira Restaurant (☎ 0 4368 1529; Th Wiang Mai; dishes 40-100B; ⏱ 8am-10pm) This is the town's most popular restaurant for a good reason. Its casual setting with some creative décor is a mere side note to the extensive and tasty menu. Several of the standard Thai and Chinese dishes are available in veggie versions. The mushroom and lemongrass soup is delicious.

Sawadee Restaurant & Bar (Th Laeng Phanit; dishes 40-150B; ⏱ 8am-11pm) At this funky, colourful place sit at the low tables on rattan mats or chill out on the axe cushions. Healthy breakfasts, sandwiches, Thai and fish dishes are served at the river view tables. There are lots of options for vegetarians; it's also a good place just to sip a beer.

ourpick **River House Restaurant** (☎ 0 5362 1201; riverhouse@hotmail.com; 77 Th Laeng Phanit; dishes 45-160B)

For a romantic meal overlooking the wandering river, this is the place to be. It's rustic with antique tables and no white linens, but pleasantly lit and there's plenty of room between the tables. The food is tasty, especially anything including fresh river fish, and the service is great.

Getting There & Around

Ordinary buses to Mae Sariang (100B, four hours) leave Chiang Mai's Arcade terminal at 8am, 1.30pm, 3pm and 8pm. From Mae Sariang to Chiang Mai buses leave at 7am, 9am, 10.30am and 12.30pm. First-class air-con buses (180B, four hours) depart at 6.30am, 11am and 9pm from Chiang Mai and 12pm, 1pm, 3pm and 4.30pm from Mae Sariang.

Buses also regularly connect Mae Sariang to Mae Hong Song (ordinary/air-con 100/180B, four hours), with a stop midway in Khun Yuam (ordinary/air-con 65/110B, two hours).

Săwngthăew leave for Mae Sot (180B, six hours) hourly between 6.30am and 12.30pm, but only leave when full. See the Mae Sot to Mae Sariang section (p429) for more details about the săwngthăew trip.

For a bus to Bangkok head to **Sombat Tour** (☎ 0 5368 1532, 0 5361 8255; Th Mae Sariang). First-class air-con buses leave from here at 4pm, 6pm and 7pm daily (571B, 12 hours).

Destinations anywhere in town are 20B by motorcycle taxi.

AROUND MAE SARIANG

One trekking option out of Mae Sariang is a boat trip on Mae Nam Salawin, with stops in Karen villages and Mae Sam Laep (see p430). In April 2006 it was announced that a new border checkpoint would open at Mae Sam Laep to promote trade and tourism between Thailand and Myanmar. However, at the time of writing the checkpoint had not yet materialised.

From Mae Sam Laep the boat may head upriver to **Lum Nam Kong National Park** (child/adult 200/400B; www.dnp.go.th), a 722-sq-km protected area established in 1994. It takes about half an hour to reach the park headquarters from Mae Sam Laep. There are basic bungalows available (300-800B), and in the dry season you can pitch a tent (30B) on a white-sand beach called Hat Thaen Kaew, along the river in front of the park offices. There are good views of the river and Myanmar from the park headquarters. The park is heavily forested in teak, Asian redwood and cherrywood.

About 36km southeast of Mae Sariang at Ban Mae Waen is **Pan House** (☎ 08 7187 4169; r per person 50B), a wooden house on stilts, where a guide named T Weerapan (Mr Pan) leads local treks. No English is spoken and women and men sleep in separate rooms. Ban Mae Waen itself is a mixed Thai/Karen village in the middle of a Karen district. To get there, take a Chiang Mai-bound bus east on Rte 108 and get out at the Km 65 marker. Ban Mae Waen is a 5km walk south along a mountain ridge and (during the rainy season) across a couple of streams. This is a dirt road so if you're driving a 4WD is necessary, especially if the road is wet.

Khun Yuam

ขุนยวม

About halfway between Mae Sariang and Mae Hong Son, where all northbound buses make their halfway stop, is the quiet mountain town of Khun Yuam. This little-visited town is a nice break from more 'experienced' destinations nearby. There are a couple of places to stay and a few notable sights.

At the northern end of town, a collection of rusted military trucks marks the **World War II Museum** (admission 10B; ☺ 8am-4pm). Here weapons, military equipment, personal possessions

and black-and-white photographs document the period when the Japanese occupied Khun Yuam in the closing weeks of the war with Burma. After they had recovered, some of the Japanese soldiers stayed in Khun Yuam and married. The last Japanese soldier who settled in the area died in 2000.

About 5km to the west of Khun Yuam, the atmospheric **Wat To Phae** sits alongside a country stream and boasts a Mon-style *chedi*, antique wooden monks' residences and an immaculate Burmese-style *wíhàan*. Inside the latter, take a look at the large, 150-year-old Burmese *kalaga* (embroidered and sequined tapestry) that's kept behind curtains to one side of the main altar. The tapestry depicts a scene from the *Vessantara Jataka* and local devotees believe one accrues merit simply by viewing it.

On the slopes of Doi Mae U Khaw is the Hmong village of Ban Mae U Khaw (25km from Khun Yuam via upgraded Rte 1263), and 50km northeast of Khun Yuam is the 100m **Nam Tok Mae Surin** (part of the Mae Surin National Park; child/adult 200/400B), reportedly Thailand's highest cataract. The area blooms with scenic *bua thawng* during November; this is also the best time to view the waterfall.

There is an ATM in town just south of Mit Khoon Youm Hotel, and a few sleeping options.

Ban Farang (☎ 0 5362 2086; banfarang@hotmail .com; 499 Th Ratburana; bungalows 600-1200B) is located off the main road towards the north end of town (look for the signs near the bus stop). The bungalows here are overpriced but set in beautiful, lush grounds. The cheaper fan bungalows are plain and dark but have a terrace. The more expensive ones come with air-con, fridge, cable TV and a terrace looking to the forest. Herbal massage is available and the restaurant on site is reasonable.

On the main road through the town centre, **Mit Khoon Youm Hotel** (☎ 0 5369 1057; 61 Th Chiang Mai-Mae Hong Son; r 300-500B, bungalow 800B; 🖫) has simple, clean rooms. Some have en suite bathrooms and there are a few more expensive bungalows by the garden.

In Khun Yuam you'll find a collection of modest **rice and noodle shops** along the east side, or Rte 108, towards the southern end of town. Most of these close by 5pm or 6pm. Ban Farang has a restaurant and Mit Khoon Youm Hotel can arrange meals.

NORTHERN THAILAND

Buses stop regularly at Khun Yuam (ordinary/air-con 65/110B, two hours) on their runs between Mae Sariang and Mae Hong Song.

MAE HONG SON
แม่ฮ่องสอน

pop 8300

Surrounded by mountains and punctuated by small but picturesque Nong Jong Kham (Jong Kham Lake), this provincial capital is still relatively peaceful despite the intrusion of daily flights from Chiang Mai. Mae Hong Son has become part of northern Thailand's standard tourist circuit, with plenty of guesthouses, hotels and resorts in the area, many of them catering to Thais. However, much of

the capital's prosperity is due to its supply of rice and consumer goods to the drug lords across the border. The town's population is predominantly Shan. Several Karen and Shan villages in the vicinity can be visited as day trips, and further afield are Lisu, Lahu and Musoe villages.

Mae Hong Son is best visited between November and March when the town is at its most beautiful. During the rainy season (June to October) travel in the province can be difficult because there are few paved roads. During the hot season, the Mae Pai valley fills with smoke from slash-and-burn agriculture. The only problem with going in the cool season is that the nights are downright cold – you'll need at least one thick sweater and a good

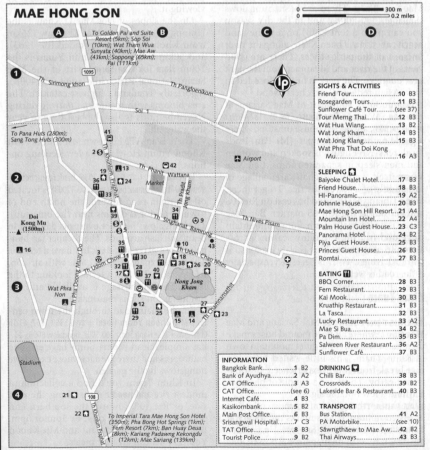

MAE HONG SON

0	300 m
0	0.2 miles

SIGHTS & ACTIVITIES
Friend Tour...............10 B3
Rosegarden Tours..............11 B3
Sunflower Café Tour........(see 37)
Tour Merng Thai..............12 B3
Wat Hua Wiang..............13 B2
Wat Jong Kham..............14 B3
Wat Jong Klang..............15 B3
Wat Phra That Doi Kong
Mu..............16 A3

SLEEPING
Baiyoke Chalet Hotel...........17 B3
Friend House..............18 B3
HI-Panoramic..............19 A2
Johnnie House..............20 B3
Mae Hong Son Hill Resort....21 A4
Mountain Inn Hotel..............22 A4
Palm House Guest House......23 C3
Panorama Hotel..............24 B2
Piya Guest House..............25 B3
Princes Guest House..............26 B3
Romtai..............27 B3

EATING
BBQ Corner..............28 B3
Fern Restaurant..............29 B3
Kai Mook..............30 B3
Kruathip Restaurant..............31 B3
La Tasca..............32 A2
Lucky Restaurant..............33 A2
Mae Si Bua..............34 B2
Pa Dim..............35 B3
Salween River Restaurant......36 A2
Sunflower Café..............37 B3

INFORMATION
Bangkok Bank..............1 B2
Bank of Ayudhya..............2 A2
CAT Office..............3 A3
CAT Office..............(see 6)
Internet Café..............4 B3
Kasikornbank..............5 B3
Main Post Office..............6 B3
Srisangwal Hospital..............7 C3
TAT Office..............8 B3
Tourist Police..............9 B2

DRINKING
Chilli Bar..............38 B3
Crossroads..............39 B2
Lakeside Bar & Restaurant....40 B3

TRANSPORT
Bus Station..............41 A2
PA Motorbike..............(see 10)
Săwngthǎew to Mae Aw......42 B2
Thai Airways..............43 B3

To Golden Pai and Suite Resort (5km); Sop Soi (10km); Wat Tham Wua Sunyata (40km); Mae Aw (43km); Soppong (65km); Pai (111km)

Th Sirimong khon

Th Pangloenikom

Soi 1

To Pana Huts (280m); Sang Tong Huts (300m)

Th Khunlum Praphat

Th Phanit

Wattana

Market

Th Pradit

Th Jong Kham

Th Singhanat Bamrung

Th Nives Pisarn

Doi Kong Mu (1500m)

Th Pha Doong Muay Do

Th Udom Chow

Th Udon Chao Nites

Nong Jong Kham

Th Chamnansathit

Wat Phra Non

Airport

Stadium

To Imperial Tara Mae Hong Son Hotel (350m); Pha Bong Hot Springs (1km); Fern Resort (7km); Ban Huay Deua (8km); Kariang Padawng Kekongdu (12km); Mae Sariang (139km)

Th Khunlum Praphat

pair of socks for mornings and evenings, and a sleeping bag or several blankets.

Information

EMERGENCY
Tourist Police (☎ 0 5361 1812, 1155; Th Singhanat Bamrung; ◷ 8.30am-4.30pm) Report mishaps or file complaints about guesthouses and trek operators here.

INTERNET ACCESS
Where there are travellers, there's internet. But like many places around Thailand, many of Mae Hong Son's places don't last. The **CAT office** (Th Udom Chow) has T-card computers which work out to 15B per hour. Other places charge anywhere from 40B to 60B per hour. Several places around town, including Sunflower Café (p439), and a nameless internet café next to Lakeside Bar & Restaurant (p440), provide internet access by the minute.

MEDICAL SERVICES
Srisangwal Hospital (☎ 0 5361 1378; Th Singhanat Bamrung) A full-service facility that includes an emergency room.

MONEY
Most of the banks on Th Khunlum Praphat have ATMs. Foreign-exchange services are available at Bangkok Bank, Kasikornbank and Bank of Ayudhya.

POST
Main post office (Th Khunlum Praphat; ◷ 8.30am-4.30pm Mon-Fri, closed holidays) Towards the southern end of Th Khunlum Praphat.

TELEPHONE
International telephone service is available at the CAT office, which is attached to the post office – hours are the same. There's a Lenso International Phonecard telephone outside the entrance to the post office.

TOURIST INFORMATION
TAT office (☎ 0 5362 3016; Th Khumlum Praphat; ◷ 8.30am-4.30pm Mon-Fri) In an old two-storey wooden building opposite the post office. With helpful staff, tourist brochures and maps can be picked up here.

Sights

WAT PHRA THAT DOI KONG MU
วัดพระธาตุดอยกองมู
Climb the hill west of town, Doi Kong Mu (1500m), to visit this Shan-built wat, also known as Wat Phai Doi. The view of the sea of fog that collects in the valley each morning is impressive; at other times of the day you get a view of the town. Two Shan *chedi*, erected in 1860 and 1874, enshrine the ashes of monks from Myanmar's Shan state. Around the back of the wat you can see a tall, slender, standing Buddha and catch views west of the ridge.

A good time to visit the wat is at the end of the annual rains retreat, usually late October depending on the lunar calendar, when it fills with townspeople gaining merit by bringing food to feed a large number of monks.

WAT JONG KHAM & WAT JONG KLANG
วัดจองคำ/วัดจองกลาง
Next to Nong Jong Kham in the southern part of town are a couple of mildly interesting Burmese-style wats.

Wat Jong Kham was built nearly 200 years ago by Thai Yai (Shan) people, who make up about half of the population of Mae Hong Son Province. Wat Jong Klang houses 100-year-old glass *jataka* paintings and has small rooms full of wooden reliefs and figures depicting the *Vessantara Jataka* (the popular *jataka* in which the Bodhisattva develops the 'perfection of giving') – all very Burmese in style. The *wíhǎan* containing these is open 8am to 6pm daily. Wat Jong Klang has several areas that women are forbidden to enter – not unusual for Burmese-Shan Buddhist temples.

WAT HUA WIANG
วัดหัวเวียง
Although its wooden *bòt* is in an advanced state of decay, a famous bronze Buddha in the Mandalay style, called Chao Phlalakhaeng, can be seen in this **wat** (Th Phanit Wattana), east of Th Khunlum Praphat.

Activities

TREKKING
The area around Mae Hong Son towards Soppong is also used by tours from Chiang Mai, which means that in the high season it's possible to see other groups of travellers while trekking through the seemingly pristine jungle. Trekking trips can be arranged at several guesthouses and travel agencies. Rates for most treks are about 700B to 800B per person per day (if there are four or more people), with three to five days being the normal duration. Popular routes include the Mae Pai Valley, Amphoe Khun Yuam and north of Soppong.

A straightforward six-day trek from east of Mae Hong Son to near Soppong costs around 700B per person per day. As with trekking elsewhere in the north, be sure to clarify when a trek starts and stops or you may not get your money's worth.

The following tour companies have received good reviews:

Sunflower Café Tour (☎ 0 5362 0549; www.sunflower cafetour.com; Th Udom Chaonithet) The guides here have been highly recommended and are often coming up with new ideas. As well as the usual trek itineraries, they do cycling tours around town and from Maehong Son to Pai, as well as bird-watching.

Tour Merng Thai (☎ 0 5361 1979; Th Khunlum Praphat) Located next to Fern Restaurant and originating from Fern Resort (p438), this company focuses on community-based tourism. It employs guides from the local community and also offers homestays. Treks are very much nature focused.

'LONG-NECKED' PADAUNG VILLAGES

Some come to Mae Hong Son with the intent to visit one of the nearby Padaung refugee villages where 'long-neck' women live. The women wear a continuous coil around their necks, and sometimes their limbs, that can weigh up to 22kg (but 5kg is most common) and stand as tall as 30cm. The neck coils depress the collarbone and rib cage, which makes their necks look unnaturally stretched. A common myth claims if the coils are removed, the women's necks will fall over from atrophy and the women will suffocate. The women attach and remove the coils at will with no such problems. In fact, there is no evidence that this deformation impairs their health at all.

Nobody knows for sure how the coil custom got started. One theory is that it was meant to make the women unattractive to men from other tribes. Another story says it was so tigers wouldn't carry the women off by their throats. The Padaung claim their ancestors were the offspring of a liaison between the wind and a beautiful female dragon, and that the coil-wearing custom pays tribute to their dragon progenitor. This custom was dying out, but money from tourism has reinvigorated it.

The business of the long-neck as a tourist attraction is largely controlled by the Karenni National Progressive Party (KNPP), a Kayah (Karenni) insurgent group whose reported objective is to establish an independent Kayah state in eastern Myanmar. The Padaung are an ethnolinguistic subgroup of the Kayah.

The biggest Padaung village is Nai Soi (also known as Nupa Ah), 35km northwest of Mae Hong Son. It receives an average of 1200 tourists annually and collects an entry fee (250B per person), the bulk of which is believed to go to the KNPP. The 'long-neck' women receive a small portion of the money collected, but make most of their money selling handicrafts (some say as much as 3000B per month). Typically, a visit consists of extended photography sessions of the coil-adorned women posing or standing with visitors. The women tell reporters they aren't bothered by the photography, which they consider to be part of their livelihood. As Nai Soi's Ma Nang was quoted in the *Bangkok Post*, 'We had nothing in Myanmar. I had to work relentlessly in the rice fields. We miss our homes, but we don't want to go back'. These people are usually in Thailand by choice, having fled a potentially worse fate in Myanmar amid ethnic war.

Opinions are sharply divided as to the ethics of 'consuming' the Padaung as a tourist attraction. On the surface, viewing the Padaung seems like crass exploitation, but those who have taken the time to learn more about their lives continue to point out that this gives them an opportunity to make a living under current social conditions in Myanmar and Thailand. Thai authorities view Nai Soi as a self-sustaining refugee camp. For visitors the current set-up beats paying a trek operator for the privilege of photographing tribal people when the latter receive nothing.

If you want to see any of the Padaung settlements, any travel agency in Mae Hong Son can arrange a tour for about 700B. You can choose among Hoy Sen Thao (11km southwest of Mae Hong Son, 20 minutes by boat from the nearby Ban Huay Deua landing), Nai Soi (35km northwest) and Huay Ma Khen Som (about 7km before Mae Aw). A couple of hundred metres beyond Nai Soi is a large Kayah refugee settlement, also controlled by the KNPP.

At the entrance to the village your name, passport number and country of residence will be noted on a payment receipt issued by the 'Karenni Culture Department'.

Friend Tour (☎ 0 5361 1647; 21 Th Pradit Jong Kham) Opposite Friend House, this recommended outfit offers trekking, elephant riding and rafting, as well as day tours.
Rosegarden Tours (☎ 0 5361 1577; www.rosegarden -tours.com; 86/4 Th Khunlum Praphat) English- and French-speaking guides focus on cultural tours.

RAFTING

Raft trips on the nearby Mae Pai are gaining popularity, and the same guesthouses and trekking agencies that organise treks from Mae Hong Son can arrange the river trips. The most common type of trip sets off from Tha Mae Pai (Pai River Pier) in **Ban Huay Deua**, 8km southwest of Mae Hong Son, for a day-long upriver journey of 5km. From the same pier, down-river trips to the 'long-neck' village of **Kariang Padawng Kekongdu** (Hoy Sen Thao) on the Thailand–Myanmar border are also possible.

Another popular rafting route runs between **Sop Soi** (10km northwest of town) and the village of **Soppong** to the west (not to be confused with the larger Shan trading village of the same name to the east). These day trips typically cost 700B to 900B for six people if arranged in Ban Huay Deua, or 900B to 1200B per person if done through a Mae Hong Son agency. Tha Ban Huay Deua (Ban Huay Deua pier) is to the left of the entrance to the large white Mae Hong Son Riverside Hotel in Ban Huay Deua.

The Mae Pai raft trips can be good fun if the raft holds up – it's not uncommon for rafts to fall apart or sink. The Myanmar trip, which attracts travellers who want to see the Padaung or 'long-necked' people (see boxed text opposite), is a bit of a rip-off and, to some, exploitative; it's a four-hour trip through unspectacular scenery to see a few Padaung people who have fled to Mae Hong Son to escape an ethnic war in Myanmar. The admission (250B per person) into the town is not included in the price of the rafting trip. When there is fighting between Shan armies and Yangon troops in the area, this trip may not be possible.

Festivals & Events

Poi Sang Long Festival (March) Wat Jong Klang and Wat Jong Kham are the focal point of this festival, where young Shan boys are ordained as novice monks in the ceremony known as *bùat lûuk kâew*. Like elsewhere in Thailand, the ordinands are carried on the shoulders of friends or relatives and paraded around the wat under festive parasols. But as part of the Shan custom, the boys are dressed in ornate costumes (rather than simple white robes) and wear flower headdresses and facial make-up. Sometimes they ride on ponies.
Jong Para Festival (October) Another important local event, it is held towards the end of the Buddhist Rains Retreat – three days before the full moon of the 11th lunar month, so it varies from year to year. The festival begins with local Shan bringing offerings to monks in the temples in a procession marked by the carrying of models of castles on poles. An important part of the festival is the folk theatre and dance, which is performed on the wat grounds, some of it unique to northwest Thailand.
Loi Krathong (November) During this national holiday – usually celebrated by floating *kràthong* (small lotus floats) on the nearest pond, lake or river – Mae Hong Son residents launch balloons called *kràthong sàwăn* (heaven *kràthong*) from Doi Kong Mu.

Sleeping
BUDGET

New budget options keep springing up in Mae Hong Son. Often the newest places are the best deal, because they're clean and competitively priced. The cheapest rooms share a bathroom, and few places here offer air-con.

Johnnie House (☎ 0 5361 1667; Th Pradit Jong Kham; r 100-250B) The new rooms with private hot-water showers are an excellent deal. They are spacious with tile floors and plenty of natural light, and there are views of the lake. The rooms with shared bathroom are basic and in a dark wooden building.

Princes Guest House (☎ 0 5361 1136; princesguest house@gmail.com; Th Pradit Jong Kham; r 150-400B; ✷ 🖳) It has a collection of spotless, great value rooms with a back door leading to seats on the lake. Two hot-water showers are shared between three large rooms, which have beds with decent mattresses and wooden floors. Upstairs rooms have large bathrooms and river views, plus a shared balcony overlooking the lake to Wat Jong Klang. Motorbikes can be rented here.

Friend House (☎ 0 5362 0119; 20 Th Pradit Jong Kham; r 150-400B) Superclean rooms run from the ultra basic that share hot-water bathrooms to larger en suite rooms. Set in a teak and concrete house, the upstairs rooms have a view of the lake. Breakfast is available and there is a laundry service.

Romtai (☎ 0 5361 2437; Th Chumnanatit; r 250-600; ✷) By the lakeside temples, this place has a choice of spacious, clean rooms or bungalows looking over a lush garden with fishponds.

Mae Hong Son Hill Resort (☎ 0 5361 2475; 106/2 Th Khunlum Praphat; bungalows 250-600B; ❄) Although it doesn't look like much at first, this quiet spot offers 24 well-kept bungalows, each with woven bamboo walls, a bit of furniture, hot showers and a private veranda. It's a friendly, family-run place.

Palm House Guest House (☎ 0 5361 4022; 22/1 Th Chamnansathit; r 300-500B; ❄) Family-run but a bit sterile, Palm House offers spacious modern rooms with hot showers and cable TV. The second-storey common area is a good place to meet travellers. The building is all cement and seems to amplify sound.

HI-Panoramic (☎ 0 5361 1757; www.tyha.org/HI-pano rama.html; 54/1 Th Khunlum Praphat; r 400B) This new, 20-room hostel has spotless, cluttered rooms in an elevated Thai-style house. Instead of a garden it has a parking lot. A laundry service is available.

ourpick Pana Huts (☎ 0 5361 4331, 08 6772 8502; www.panahuts.com; 293/9 Mu 11 Pang Moo; bungalows 400-500B) Although on the edge of town, this new, peaceful place is worth the extra hike. Five cute bamboo huts spaced out on a jungly hill all have attractive hot-water bathrooms and terraces. Rooms look charming with their pots of flowers, Thai textile bed covers and mosquito nets. The communal area feels appropriately rustic, with its thatched teak leaf roof, wooden benches and enclosed campfire for chilly nights. The friendly owner speaks great English, teaches Thai and creates fantastic hearty meals.

Other less convenient places can be found around Mae Hong Son – the touts will find you at the bus station.

MIDRANGE
ourpick Piya Guest House (☎ 0 5361 1260; 1/1 Th Khunlum Praphat; bungalows 600B; ❄) This well-managed place has cement bungalows set around a quiet garden with small lotus ponds. The rooms have wooden floors, air-con and hot showers, and are well furnished and of a decent size. Some are looking a little weathered. There is a pleasant lake view from the restaurant.

Panorama Hotel (☎ 0 5361 1757; www.panorama.8m. com; 51 Th Khunlum Praphat; r 600-800B; ❄) The lobby decorated with Thai details is welcoming, but the dark, wood-panelled rooms have ill-fitted carpet and strange enclosed balconies. The location is quite convenient though.

ourpick Sang Tong Huts (☎ 0 5362 0680; www.sang tonghuts.com; bungalows 700-1600B; ☀) Tucked on a hillside on the edge of town, this eclectic collection of unique huts is a fabulous place to stay. Each and every room is different and decorated using natural materials in variants of contemporary Thai style. Your room may have floor-to-ceiling windows and abstract art, or rattan sofa and chairs with Thai silks. All have terraces and provide a real sense of being in nature. The set, communal five-course dinner is excellent. Call ahead or reserve online – this place is popular.

Baiyoke Chalet Hotel (☎ 0 5361 1536; 90 Th Khunlum Praphat; r incl breakfast 1000-1400B; ❄) Rooms here have a few charming details and are big and modern. It is popular with European tour groups and the restaurant/lounge downstairs can get quite loud, so request a room away from the street or on an upper level. Low-season rates are 30% less and breakfast is included.

TOP END
Southwest of town, a few kilometres towards Ban Huay Deua and Ban Tha Pong Daeng on the river, are several 'resorts', which in the Thai sense of the term means any hotel near a rural or semirural area. Many are quite luxurious, service-oriented hotels with pleasantly groomed grounds. Discounts of up to 40% are common in the low season and online discounts can be found any time of year. Prices listed below are for high-season walk-ins.

ourpick Fern Resort (☎ 0 5368 6110; www.fern resort.info; 64 Mu Bo, Tambon Pha Bong; standard/deluxe/ste 1500/1800/2500B; ✖ ❄ ☀) This ecofriendly resort features Shan-style wooden bungalows with stylishly decorated interiors. Some are set among rice paddies and streams, others are tucked around a lush garden or overlook the pool. Nearby nature trails lead to the adjacent Mae Surin National Park and treks can be arranged. To encourage community-based tourism, most of the employees come from local villages. Free pick-up is available from the airport and bus terminal. Regular shuttles run to/from town stopping at the Fern Restaurant (opposite). To drive here take Rte 108 7km south of town, turn at the sign and follow the winding road 2km.

Golden Pai and Suite Resort (☎ 0 5361 2265; www.goldenpai.com; 285 Moo1 Ban Pang moo; s/d 1400-2300/1500-2500B; ❄ ☀) Five kilometres out of town off the road to Pai, this resort is set on the Pai River and features Shan-style chalets. Set in manicured gardens, rooms are large, tastefully

decorated with textiles and have outside seating areas. The restaurant makes the most of the Pai River location. There is a spa specialising in mud treatments nearby.

Imperial Tara Mae Hong Son Hotel (☎ 0 5368 4444-9; www.imperialhotels.com/taramaehongson; 149 Mu 8; r 2804B, ste 3708-4944B; ✗ 🏵 🗟) Rooms in this upmarket, 104-room hotel all have wood floors and are tastefully decorated. French windows that open onto a terrace make a change from the standard business hotel layout. Facilities include a sauna, swimming pool and fitness centre.

Mountain Inn Hotel (☎ 0 5361 1802; www.mhsmountaininn.com; 112 Th Khunlum Praphat; standard/deluxe/ste incl breakfast 1700/2000/4000B; 🏵) This hotel has clean, cosy rooms with Thai decorative touches. There is a pretty courtyard garden with small ponds, benches and parasols. Standard rooms are a better deal than deluxe as you get a terrace overlooking the garden. All have cable TV.

Eating

Although Mae Hong Son isn't known for culinary delights, there are plenty of places to fill your belly with curry or freshly baked bread.

Mae Si Bua (Thai Yai Food; Th Singhanat Bamrung; dishes 20-45B; 🏵 10am-6pm) Offers delicious Shan and northern-Thai food.

Pa Dim (Th Khunlum Praphat; dishes 25-80B; 🏵 8am-8pm) Everyone loves this place for its extensive variety of well-priced Thai and Chinese options.

Kruathip Restaurant (Th Pradit Jong Kham; dishes 30-150B) Next to Lakeside Bar & Restaurant, this place is a more sedate affair with an equally good view. Tasty Thai dishes and river fish are served. Breakfasts are also available.

ourpick Salween River Restaurant (☎ 0 5361 2050; Th Singhanat Bamrung; dishes 35-150B; 🏵 7am-1am) The local hang-out for NGO workers, this place serves excellent organic hill-tribe coffee, delicate chocolate croissants, local-style Shan specialities and imaginative Western dishes. Try the *kài òp* (baked Shan chicken casserole), fermented green tea salad, or the ginger and honey glazed pork steak. The owners are very friendly and are a good source of information. The menu is also very strong on vegetarian options.

Lucky Restaurant (Th Singhanat Bamrung; dishes 40-100B; 🏵 9am-10pm) Popular with travellers, this place cooks up a lot of savoury meat dishes but has limited offerings for vegetarians. Drinks

seem to be the focus and service is an afterthought. But it's a pleasant place to linger over a meal with friends.

ourpick Sunflower Café (☎ 0 5362 0549; www.sunflowercafetour.com; Th Udom Chaonithet; dishes 40-150B; 🏵 7.30am-9pm) Start your day with an oversized cup of coffee and some fresh-baked bread, or swing by in the afternoon for a light meal of pumpkin soup or stuffed tomatoes. Then again, you could just wait until dinner and munch on a full-sized homemade pizza. This is a cosy place with friendly people. Sunflower also runs recommended tours.

Fern Restaurant (Th Khunlum Praphat; dishes 50-180B; 🏵 10.30am-midnight) The Fern is an upmarket, but casual, option. Service is professional and the food is good. Enjoy a bottle of whisky with friends, French wine with your sweetheart, or just come for the ice cream. There is live lounge music some nights.

Kai Mook (Khai Muk; ☎ 0 5361 2092; 23 Th Udom Chao Nites; dishes 55-160B; 🏵 10am-2pm & 5pm-midnight) This smart, open-air restaurant just off the main street is one of the better Thai-Chinese restaurants in town. It's popular with both Thais and Westerners for house specialities such as *pèt yâang náam phêung* (roast duck with honey gravy), *plaa châwn sâi ùa* (serpent-headed fish with northern-Thai sausage) and *yam bai kùt* (yam with fern leaves). Its set menus are also a good deal.

BBQ Corner (☎ 08 1385 7277; Th Khunlum Praphat; barbecue 69B; 🏵 5pm-12am) This social, open-air place offers table 'BBQ's'. A small hot plate and soup pot is set up on your table where you fling the meat of your choice on the griddle and your noodles and veg in the soup. Good ingredients and a fun way to eat.

La Tasca (☎ 0 5361 1344; Th Khunlum Praphat; dishes 90-145B; 🏵 10am-10pm) This rustic looking place with checked tablecloths and chunky wood serves decent homemade pasta, pizza and calzone.

Drinking

Crossroads (cnr Th Singhanat Bamrung and Th Khunlum Praphat) This two-storey bar, set in a wooden house, is appropriately located at the crossroads of Th Singhanat Bamrun and Khunlum Praphat. Upstairs watch the world go by or shoot some pool; downstairs perch on stools and choose from the huge list of cocktails at the bar. A good selection of mainly Western, as well as Thai dishes (dishes 50B to 200B) are also served at this friendly, laid-back place.

NORTHERN THAILAND

Chilli Bar (Th Pradit Jong Kham; ☼ 7am-1am) This semi-open-air bar is new but already lively. Sit up at the chunky, long, wooden bar and choose from whiskies, beers or shakes. The available food (dishes 30-80B), from bar snacks to sandwiches, is chalked up on boards.

Lakeside Bar & Restaurant (Th Pradit Jong Kham; ☼ 10.30am-midnight) The Lakeside is for those who appreciate live music and a social atmosphere. This is a good choice for groups and for people looking for a little socialising. It's popular with Thai families for dinner, and there's all-you-can-eat dining (buffet 69B). After about 10pm, however, it's a place for drinking.

Shopping

From October to February the walkway around the lake becomes a lively **night market** (☼ 5pm-11pm). Food and a variety of hill-tribe handicraft stalls set up every evening.

Getting There & Away
AIR

For many people the time saved flying from Chiang Mai to Mae Hong Son versus bus travel is worth the extra baht.

Nok Air (☎ 1318; www.nokair.com; airport office) A cheaper subsidiary of Thai Airways, it flies to Chiang Mai twice a day for 900B.

PB Air (☎ 0 5361 4369; www.pbair.com) Flies direct from Bangkok to Mae Hong Son (2370B). Its office is at the entrance to the airport.

Thai Airways (☎ 0 5361 2220/1194; www.thaiairways .com; 71 Th Singhanat Bamrung; ☼ 8am-5pm Mon-Fri) Has flights to Mae Hong Son from Chiang Mai four times daily (1270B, 35 minutes). It also has an office at the airport (open 8.30am to 5.30pm).

BUS

From Chiang Mai there are two bus routes to Mae Hong Son: the 270km northern route through Pai (ordinary/air-con 142/200B, seven to eight hours) and the 368km southern route through Mae Sariang (ordinary/air-con 187/337B, eight to nine hours). The fare to Mae Sariang is (ordinary/air-con 100/180B). Two minivans also run to Chiang Mai via Pai (250B, seven hours) at 8am and 9am.

Although it may be longer, the southern route through Mae Sariang is much more comfortable because the bus stops every two hours for a 10- to 15-minute break, and larger buses – with large seats – are used. Buses to Mae Hong Son via Mae Sariang leave Chiang

Mai's Arcade bus station five times daily between 6.30am and 9pm. In the reverse direction, ordinary buses leave Mae Hong Son for Chiang Mai at 8am, 2pm, 8pm and 9pm; air-con buses depart at 6am, 10.30am and 9pm.

The Pai bus leaves the Chiang Mai Arcade station four times a day at 7am, 9am and 10.30am and 12.30pm. In the opposite direction, buses leave Mae Hong Son at 7am, 8.30am, 10.30am, 12.30pm and 4pm. The 4pm bus only goes as far as Pai. An air-con minivan (Pai 150B, Chiang Mai 250B) departs from Mae Hong Son at 10.30am and 12.30pm.

Buses to Pai (ordinary/air-con/air-con minibus 70/98/150B, three hours) also stop in Soppong (ordinary/air-con/air-con minibus 45/60/150B, 1½ hours), and buses to Mae Sariang stop in Khun Yuam (ordinary/air-con 50/85B, 1½ hours).

The northern route through Pai, originally built by the Japanese in WWII, is very winding and offers spectacular views from time to time. Because the buses used on this road are smaller, they're usually more crowded and the younger passengers tend to get motion sickness.

Getting Around

It's pretty easy to walk around most of Mae Hong Son. Official motorcycle taxi drivers wear a red tunic with a white number and within town they charge 20B; to Doi Kong Mu it's 50B one way or 80B return. Motorcycle drivers will also take passengers further afield but fares out of town are expensive. There are now a few túk-túk in town; most are at the bus stop. They charge 40B per trip and 50B to the airport.

Motorcycles are readily available for rent (150B to 200B per day) around town.

PA Motorbike (☎ 0 5361 1647; 21 Th Pradit Jong Kham) Opposite Friends House, it rents motorbikes (from 150B per day), cars and jeeps (from 1000B per day). Insurance can be bought on top.

Avis Rent-A-Car (☎ 0 5362 0457-8; www.avisthailand .com) Its office is located at the Mae Hong Son airport. Rates start at about 1300B per day.

AROUND MAE HONG SON
Pha Bong Hot Springs
บ่อน้ำร้อนผาบ่อง

Eleven kilometres south of the capital at the Km 256 marker on Rte 108, this public park with **hot springs** (☼ 8am-sunset; private bath/bathing

room 50/400B) covers 12 sq km. You can take a private bath or rent a room. The springs can be reached on any southbound bus.

Mae Aw & Around
แม่ออ

Another day trip from the provincial capital is to Mae Aw, 43km north of Mae Hong Son on a mountain peak at the Myanmar border. The modern Thai name for Mae Aw is Ban Rak Thai (Thai-Loving Village). Mae Aw is a Chinese KMT settlement, one of the last true KMT outposts in Thailand. Filled with old renegade fighters, this is now a quiet place with people going about their business, but the scenery on the way up here, and in the town itself, is stunning.

On the road to Mae Aw, take a left at Ban Na Pa Paek and continue 6km to the Shan village of **Ban Ruam Thai**. Look for the yellow sign indicating the **Guest House and Homestay** (☎ 0 5369 2144, 08 6916 8967; r 200-300B), where simple bamboo huts positioned on a slope are surrounded by coffee plants, fruit trees and stunning scenery. Even if not staying, stop here for a brew. Passionate about coffee, the English-speaking Mr Hilary explains the process of making it, from the picking of beans to the roasting and grinding. There is a roasting room at the homestay where visitors can roast and grind their own beans. Once an opium-growing area, help from the Royal Project, which provided arabica beans and expertise, has transformed this village. Although some miss the 'beautiful flowers' from the opium crops, most see the replacement crop project as a success.

A few kilometres further north is Pang Ung lake where A-frame **wooden huts** (☎ 0 5361 1244; r 200-400B) are perched on its bank. The beautiful scenery here is more reminiscent of Switzerland than Thailand. Bamboo rafts are available here to rent (2 people 100B). Call to book ahead.

Drive back the way you came to Ban Na Pa Paek. From there it is 6km further north to Mae Aw or Ban Tak Thai, past tea and coffee plantations and jaw-dropping scenery. The town sits on the edge of a large reservoir and the faces and signs are very Chinese. At the end of the paved road there are two places to stay. **Tha Law Sue Rak Thai Resort** (☎ 08 9950 0955; r 600-1000B) is quite plush and has large bamboo huts looking over the reservoir to Myanmar, some of which have their own

terraces. There is a restaurant attached serving Yunnan dishes.

Behind the resort restaurant is a shop selling massive bags of tea and pineapple-, lychee- and plum-flavoured palm wine (which you can sample). The friendly family running the store has four, clean simple rooms (300B) with hot-water showers.

There's a dirt road to the border crossing, but it's not advisable to do trekking in this area. Occasionally there's fighting along the border between the KMT and the Mong Tai Army, formerly led by the infamous opium warlord Khun Sa, but now operating as four splinter units under separate leaderships. When this happens, public transport is usually suspended and you shouldn't go without a guide.

Yellow săwngthăew to Mae Aw (60B) and villages on the way (including Ban Na Pa Paek and Ban Ruam Thai), leave from the Mae Hong Son municipal market on Th Phanit Wattana at 9am, 12pm and 3pm. It's necessary to catch one early in the morning coming back from Mae Aw. Because săwngthăew are few and far between it's worth getting a group of people together and chartering a săwngthăew. It will cost you 600B to 1300B (depending on whether the drivers have any paid cargo). Otherwise any tour agency will send you with a driver and room for four for 1300B.

The trip takes two hours and passes Shan, Karen and Hmong villages, the Pang Tong Summer Palace and the Pha Sua waterfall.

THAM PLA NATIONAL PARK
อุทยานแห่งชาติถ้ำปลา

A trip to Mae Aw could be combined with a visit to **Tham Pla Forest Park** (admission free) centred on the animistic Tham Pla or **Fish Cave**, a water-filled cavern where hundreds of soro brook carp thrive. These fish grow up to 1m in length and are found only in the provinces of Mae Hong Son, Ranong, Chiang Mai, Rayong, Chanthaburi and Kanchanaburi. The fish eat vegetables and insects, although the locals believe them to be vegetarian and feed them only fruit and vegetables (which can be purchased at the park entrance).

A path leads from the park entrance to a suspension bridge that crosses a stream and continues to the cave. You can see the fish through a 2-sq-metre rock hole at the base of an outer wall of the cave. A **statue** of a Hindu rishi called Nara, said to protect the holy fish from danger, stands nearby. It's a

bit anticlimactic, but the park grounds are a bucolic, shady place to hang out; picnic tables are available.

The TAT office (p435) in Mae Hong Son has some information about the park. The park is 17km northeast of Mae Hong Son on the northern side of Hwy 1095. October to February is good for star-watching and from November to May is bird-watching season. Buses to Pai pass by, but renting a motorcycle is the best way to get here.

Mae La-Na
แม่ละนา

Between Mae Hong Son and Pai, Rte 1095 winds through an area of forests, mountains, streams, Shan and hill-tribe villages and limestone caves. Some of Mae Hong Son's most beautiful scenery is within a day's walk of the Shan village of Mae La-Na (6km north of Rte 1095 via a half-sealed road), where you can stay overnight. From here you can trek to several nearby Red and Black Lahu villages and to a few caves within a 4km to 8km radius.

It's possible to walk a 20km half-loop all the way from Mae La-Na to Tham Lot and Soppong, staying overnight in Red Lahu villages along the way. Ask for information at MaeLana Garden Home (right). Experienced riders can do this route on a sturdy dirt bike – but not alone or during the rainy season.

Local guides will lead visitors to nearby caves. **Tham Mae La-Na**, 4km from the village, is the largest and most famous – it's threaded by a 12km length of river – and a journey to the cave and through it costs 600B. Tham Paka-

rang (Coral Cave) and Tham Phet (Diamond Cave) all feature good wall formations and cost 200B each for guides. Rates are posted at a small sǎalaa near a noodle stand. At the sǎalaa, and at the social spot of the main village shop, is where you may contact the guides during the day. Some of the caves may not be accessible during the rainy season.

Even if you don't fancy trekking or caving, Mae La-Na can be a peaceful and mildly interesting cul-de-sac for a short stay. Beyond the Shan-style Wat Mae La-Na, a school, some houses and the previously 'downtown' area around the noodle shops and petrol pumps, there's little to see, but the surrounding mountain scenery is quite pleasing.

The Mae La-Na junction is 51.3km from Mae Hong Son, 13.3km from Soppong and 70.5km from Pai. Twelve kilometres west of the three-way junction is a short turn-off for **Wat Tham Wua Sunyata**, a peaceful forest monastery. The village is 6km north of the junction. Infrequent sǎwngthǎew from the highway to the village cost 30B per person – mornings are your best bet.

SLEEPING & EATING

Due to major floods in 2005 most of the accommodation options were wiped out.

MaeLana Garden Home (☎ 0 5361 9028, 0 8706 6021; r 100-200B). The only guesthouse in town, this is a great place to stay. Set among beautifully tended gardens is a two-storey wooden house decorated with colourful Thai paintings and dripping in orchids. Rooms with a shared bathroom are clean, well maintained

---

OPIUM & TREKKING

Some guides are very strict now about forbidding the smoking of opium on treks. This seems to be a good idea, since one problem trekking companies have had in the past is dealing with opium-addicted guides! Volunteers who work in tribal areas also say opium smoking sets a bad example for young people in the villages.

Opium is traditionally a condoned vice of the elderly, yet an increasing number of young people in the villages are now taking opium, heroin and amphetamines. This is possibly due in part to the influence of young trekkers, who may smoke once and a few weeks later be hundreds of kilometres away, while the villagers continue to face the temptation every day.

Addiction has negative effects for the village as well as the individual's health, including a reduced male labour force and corresponding increase in women's workloads (most addicts are men) and reduced overall agricultural production. Also, an increase in the number of villagers injecting heroin (needles are often shared) has led to skyrocketing rates of HIV infection in hill-tribe villages. Given the already high incidence of HIV infection among northern Thai prostitutes, some welfare groups say that entire tribal communities will be wiped out unless the rate of infection can be stopped.

and have mozzie nets and quilts. Out the back are A-frame bamboo bungalows overlooking a huge lotus pond. There is a communal area with a large dining table, where meals can be prepared (50B each). The Thai lady who runs it speaks English and is a good source of information. In the rainy season call ahead to check that someone is there.

Wilderness Lodge (dm/bungalow 50/250B) About 15km before Mae La-Na in Ban Nam Khong is a dirt road leading 1.4km to this lodge. A very basic place overlooking a river valley, it's only really open in the dry season.

Alternatively, Mae La-Na has a **homestay programme** (per person per night 100B), where the money goes back into a community fund. Ask the village head's permission at the *săalaa* and he will place you in a home.

SOPPONG & AROUND
สบปอง

Soppong is a small but relatively prosperous market village a couple of hours northwest of Pai and about 70km from Mae Hong Son. Since the paving of Rte 1095, Soppong and Tham Lot have become popular destinations for minivan tours from Mae Hong Son and Chiang Mai. Soppong in particular is becoming a buzzing travellers' haunt.

Although for many years this town was known only as Soppong, lately the Thai government has been calling it 'Pangmapha', since the Pangmapha District Office is now located here. The two names seem to be used interchangeably.

The area around Soppong is *the* place to come in Northern Thailand for **caving**. There are also several Shan, Lisu, Karen and Lahu **villages** that can easily be visited on foot. The best source of information on caving and trekking in the area is the owner of Cave Lodge (p445) in Tham Lot. The people at Border Bar (p444) in Soppong are also good for reliable information.

The rough back road between Soppong and Mae La-Na is popular with mountain bikers and off-highway motorcyclists.

If you're here on Tuesday, check out the **market**. Next to the Border Bar (p444), a Bangkok Bank was being built at the time of writing.

Sleeping & Eating

All accommodation is on the main road through Soppong or is clearly marked by signs. Every guest house has a restaurant attached.

Lisu Mountain (☎ 08 7175 8581; www.lisumountain.com; dm 90B, r 200-250B) Up in the mountains, four kilometres from Soppong and next to a Lisu village, Mountain Lodge is a peaceful retreat. The thatched huts on stilts have terraces and are simple but comfortable. Run by a friendly English guy and his Thai partner, they offer caving trips and motorbike tours of the area. Call in advance or turn up at Border Bar (p444) to get a pick up from town. Lisu Mountain is closed from mid-July to October.

ourpick Soppong River Inn (☎ 0 5361 7107; www.soppong.com; hut 150B, r 500-1200B; ⬚) With basic huts or stylish rooms in a river-facing two-storey house, this charming place has something for every budget. Set among lush gardens with winding paths, the huts are basic but comfortable. The house has a wonderful shared terrace overlooking a small gorge. Its four rooms have open-air showers, heaps of character and are all different. The 850B one is the best as it has a private balcony dramatically situated right over the river. The restaurant here is very good and massage is available.

Lemon Hill Guest House (☎ 0 5361 7039, 0 5361 7213; lemonhill@thaimail.com; r 200-300B, bungalows 400-1000B; ⬚) Near the bus stop, Lemon Hill has a friendly and funny owner who offers brand new bungalows facing the Nam Lan or rooms near the road. The large concrete and bamboo bungalows are spick-and-span, have hot-water showers, wooden floors and some Thai-style details. The rooms are less attractive but decent. The restaurant overlooking the river serves tasty food using its homegrown organic veggies.

Jungle Guest House (☎ 0 5361 7099; s/d 250/350B) About 500m off the main road, Jungle House has basic bungalows set on a lawned slope. Some need maintenance. The large restaurant here overlooking the river serves great food, including homemade bread.

ourpick Little Eden Guest House (☎ 0 5361 7054; www.littleeden-guesthouse.com; r 420-1500B; ⬚ ⬚ ⬚) The nine A-frame bungalows around a pleasant, grass-decked pool are well kept with hot-water showers. Yet, it's the beautiful two-storey 'houses' that makes this place special. Perfect for families or a group of friends, they are stylishly decorated, have living rooms, interesting nooks and crannies, and terraces with hammocks. One has its own fireplace and

is right on the river. There are also two chic rooms in the owner's house. The owner can speak Thai, English, Danish and German and organises all sorts of activities in the area.

Lisu Homestay (☎ 08 9998 4886; www.lisuhilltribe crafts.blogspot.com; room incl food and 4hrs of classes a day 1000B) This place offers staying in a Lisu village and various holistic programmes, from learning Lisu healing remedies and massage to practising meditation. Check out the website for more details; it needs to be booked in advance.

Border Bar (⏲ 10am-11pm) Next to Lemon Hill, this new, tiny bar is the place to find out about what's going on around Soppong. Perch at the bar or sit by the rustic wood tables and drink beers or wine in a friendly atmosphere. Run by an English and Thai couple, they also run Lisu Mountain (p443).

Tribal Café & Connection (internet per hr 50B; ⏲ 8am-9pm) Opposite Little Eden, this new café has internet and serves good fresh coffee and snacks.

Tham Lot
ถ้ำลอด

About 8km north of Soppong is Tham Lot (pronounced *thâm lâwt* and also known as *thâm náam lâwt*), a large limestone cave with impressive stalagmites and 'coffin caves' (see boxed text below), and a wide stream running through it. Along with Tham Nam Lang further west, it's one of the largest known caves in Thailand. The total length of the cave is 1600m and for 600m the stream runs through it.

At the **Nature Education Centre** (⏲ 8am-5.30pm) and entrance, you must hire a gas lantern and guide for 150B (one guide leads one to four people) to take you through the caverns; visitors are not permitted to tour the caves alone. Apart from the main chamber, there are also three side chambers – Column Cavern, Doll Cave and Coffin Cave – that can be reached by ladders. It takes around two hours to explore the whole thing. Depending on the time of year it is necessary to take a bamboo raft for some or all of the journey through the caves. Access to parts of the cave may be limited between August and October because of water levels.

From the entrance to the exit and taking in the Column Cavern, Doll Cave and Coffin Cave, the rafts (up to four adults) cost 400B return, or 300B one way. If going one way you can walk back from outside of the cave (20 minutes). In the dry season it may be possible to wade to the Doll Cave and then take a raft through to the exit (300B return/200B one way). Try and be at the exit at sunset when hundreds of thousands of cave adapted swifts pour into Tham Lot and cling to their bedtime stalagmites.

Tham Lot is a good example of community-based tourism as all of the guides at the cave are from local Shan villages.

COFFIN CAVES

The 900-sq-km area of Pangmapha district is famous for its high concentration of cave systems, where over 200 have been found. Apart from Tham Lot, one of its most famous is Tham Nam Lang, which is 20km northwest of Soppong near Ban Nam Khong. It's almost 9km long and said to be one of the largest caves in the world in terms of volume.

More than 83 of the district's 200 limestone caverns are known to contain ancient teak coffins carved from solid tree logs. Up to 9m long, the coffins are typically suspended on wooden scaffolds inside the caves. The coffins have been carbon dated between 1200 and 2200 years old. The ends are usually carved and Thai anthropologists have identified at least 50 different design schemes. Pottery remains associated with the sites have also been found, some of which is displayed in the Nature Education Centre (above) at Tham Lot.

The local Thais know these burial caves as *thâm phǐi* (spirit caves), or *thâm phǐi maen* (coffin caves). It is not known who made them or why they were placed where they are, but because most caves have less than ten coffins it indicates that not everyone was accorded such an elaborate burial. Similar coffins have been found in karst areas west of Bangkok and also in Borneo, China and the Philippines, but the highest concentration of coffin caves from this period is in Pangmapha.

The eight coffin caves that scientists are investigating at the moment are off-limits to the public, but John Spies at Cave Lodge (opposite) may know which coffin caves are possible to explore. The most easily accessible one is the coffin cave chamber at Tham Lot.

SLEEPING & EATING

our pick **Cave Lodge** (☎ 0 5361 7203; www.cavelodge
.com; dm 60B, bungalows 300-450B) This popular
place is run by the unofficial expert on the
region's caves, John Spies. Passionate about
caving and fluent in Shan, his book 'Caves,
Coffins and Chaos' details the 25 years of
adventures he has had in the area. The charming bungalows here are all unique and dot a
junglelike hill leading down to the river. The
setting is beautiful and options for adventure
abound. Choose from caving and kayaking
trips, guided or unguided treks (good maps
are available) or just hang out in the beautiful
communal area. The traditional Shan herbal
sauna is an experience and the restaurant is
very good. Tham Lot is a short walk away.

A row of **outdoor restaurants** (dishes 15-40B;
☯ 9am-6pm) outside the Tham Lot park entrance offers simple Thai fare.

Ban Nam Rin
บ้านน้ำริน

At this Lisu village 9km south of Soppong
towards Pai (or 34km coming from Pai to Soppong), you can stay at **Lisu Lodge** (☎ 08 9953 4243;
r 300-600B). This quiet place is set in beautiful
mountain scenery with a garden filled with
fruit trees. Choices range from simple, shared
bathroom A-frames to wood and stone bungalows with lovely recycled teak furniture, tasteful
Thai styling and terraces. A family bungalow is
available too. The owner can give information
on nearby hill-tribe villages to visit, plus he
makes a wicked mulberry liqueur.

Getting There & Around

Pai to Mae Hong Son buses stop in Soppong
and there are six a day in either direction.
From Mae Hong Son to Soppong, buses (or-
dinary/air-con/air-con minibus 45/60/150B)
take 1½ hours. The trip between Pai and Soppong (ordinary/minivan 35/75B) takes one
to 1½ hours.

Motorcycle taxis stationed at the bus stop
in Soppong will take passengers to Tham Lot
or the Cave Lodge for 70B per person; private
pick-up trucks will take you and up to five
other people for 200B.

PAI
ปาย

pop 3000

Pai (pronounced like the English word 'bye',
not 'pie') is something of a travellers' mecca.

It isn't a wat-filled town emanating Thai-ness.
Instead it's a little corner of the world that
happens to be in Thailand that seems to attract artists, musicians and foodies. It's got
a live-music scene you won't find anywhere
else, and some affordable modern art and
a delicious range of international culinary
treats. Oh, and it's in the middle of a gorgeous
green valley with hot springs, rice fields and
a lovely lazy river. However, its popularity
does surpass its capacity and the town can feel
completely overrun by foreigners in the high
season. It remains to be seen what the added
effect of the new Chiang Mai to Pai flight will
do to the laid-back scene of the town.

Most of the town's population are Shan
and Thai, but there's also a small but visible
Muslim Chinese population. Attracted by easy
living, Pai also features a sizeable collection of
long-term visitors – mostly *faràng* and Japanese – who use the town as a place to chill out
between excursions elsewhere in Asia.

Information

There are plenty of places around town, especially on Th Chaisongkhram, that offer
internet services (40B per hour). **Pai Post** (www
.paipost.com) is the free local English language
newspaper. It covers cultural events, travel
destinations, political pieces, and some restaurant and bar openings, and can be picked
up around town.
Krung Thai Bank (Th Rangsiyanon) Has an ATM and
foreign-exchange service.
Siam Books (☎ 0 5369 9075; Th Chaisongkhram) Has a
good selection of new and used books.

Sights
BAN SANTICHON
บ้านสันติชน

Northwest of town, a Shan village, a Lahu vil-
lage, a Lisu village, a KMT village called **Ban
Santichon** (San Ti Chuen in Yunnanese,) and
Nam Tok Mo Paeng can all be visited on foot. The
Shan, Lisu and KMT villages lie within 4km of
Pai, while the Lahu village is near Nam Tok
Mo Paeng, which is another 4km further from
town (8km total).

You can cut the hike in half by taking a Mae
Hong Son-bound bus north about 5km and
getting off at a signpost for the falls; from the
highway it's only 4km. A couple of pools at the
base of the falls are suitable for swimming and
are best just after the rainy season, October to
early December.

NORTHERN THAILAND

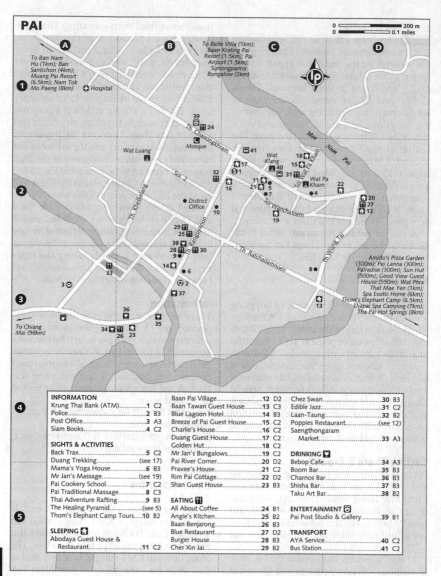

PAI

To Ban Nam
Hu (1km); Ban
Santichon (4km);
Muang Pai Resort
(6.5km); Nam Tok
Mo Paeng (8km)

To Belle Villa (1km);
Baan Krating Resort
(1.5km); Pai
Airport (1.5km);
Sipsongpanna
Bungalow (2km)

Amido's Pizza Garden
(300m); Pai Lanna (300m);
Pairadise (300m); Sun Hut
(500m); Good View Guest
House (550m); Wat Phra
That Mae Yen (1km);
Spa Exotic Home (6km);
Thom's Elephant Camp (6.5km);
Thapai Spa Camping (7km);
Tha Pai Hot Springs (8km)

To Chiang
Mai (98km)

INFORMATION
Krung Thai Bank (ATM)...........1 C2
Police.................................2 B3
Post Office...........................3 A3
Siam Books............................4 C2

SIGHTS & ACTIVITIES
Back Trax.............................5 C2
Duang Trekking..................(see 17)
Mama's Yoga House.................6 B3
Mr Jan's Massage................(see 19)
Pai Cookery School..................7 C2
Pai Traditional Massage............8 C3
Thai Adventure Rafting.............9 B3
The Healing Pyramid..............(see 5)
Thom's Elephant Camp Tours....10 B2

SLEEPING
Abodaya Guest House &
Restaurant..........................11 C2

Baan Pai Village....................12 D2
Baan Tawan Guest House........13 C3
Blue Lagoon Hotel.................14 B3
Breeze of Pai Guest House.......15 C2
Charlie's House....................16 C2
Duang Guest House................17 C2
Golden Hut..........................18 C2
Mr Jan's Bungalows...............19 C2
Pai River Corner...................20 D2
Pravee's House.....................21 C2
Rim Pai Cottage...................22 B3
Shan Guest House.................23 B3

EATING
All About Coffee...................24 B1
Angie's Kitchen....................25 B2
Baan Benjarong....................26 B3
Blue Restaurant...................27 D2
Burger House......................28 B3
Cher Xin Jai.......................29 B2

Chez Swan.........................30 B3
Edible Jazz.........................31 C2
Laan-Taung........................32 B2
Poppies Restaurant............(see 12)
Saengthongaram
Market.............................33 A3

DRINKING
Bebop Cafe........................34 A3
Boom Bar..........................35 B3
Charnos Bar.......................36 B3
Shisha Bar.........................37 B3
Taku Art Bar......................38 B2

ENTERTAINMENT
Pai Post Studio & Gallery.........39 B1

TRANSPORT
AYA Service.......................40 C2
Bus Station........................41 C2

WAT PHRA THAT MAE YEN
วัดพระธาตุแม่เย็น

This temple sits atop a hill and has good views overlooking the valley. Walk 1km east from the main intersection in town, across a stream and through a village, to get to the stairs (353 steps) that lead to the top. Or take the 400m sealed road that follows a different route to the top.

THA PAI HOT SPRINGS
บ่อน้ำร้อนท่าปาย

Across Mae Nam Pai and 8km southeast of town via a paved road is **Tha Pai Hot Springs** (admission free; soaking 50B), a well-kept local park 1km from the road. A scenic stream flows through the park; the stream mixes with the hot springs in places to make pleasant bath-

ing areas. There are also small public bathing houses into which hot spring water is piped. There is a camp site here in the dry season (per pitch 30B; no tents for rent).

Activities

TREKKING & RAFTING

All the guesthouses in town can provide information on local trekking and a few do guided treks for as little as 700B per day if there are no rafts or elephants involved. Among the more established local agencies are **Back Trax** (☎ 0 5369 9739; backtraxinpai@yahoo.com; Th Chaisongkhram) and **Duang Trekking** (at Duang Guest House; p448).

Whatever rafting company you choose in Pai, gauge their attitude about security before you hand over any baht. Make sure they are serious about using safety equipment, that your life jacket fits well and you have a safety helmet. Thai Adventure is considered the most professional outfit in Pai.

Thai Adventure Rafting (TAR; ☎ 0 5369 9111; www .activethailand.com/rafting; Th Rangsiyanon) Run by a French guy who has 18 years' experience on the Mae Pai and other rivers in the region, this is the safest and best place to do white-water rafting in Pai.

It leads excellent two-day white-water Mae Pai rafting trips in sturdy rubber rafts, from Pai to Mae Hong Son for 2400B per person including food, rafting equipment, camping gear, dry bags and insurance. On the way, rafters visit a waterfall, a fossil reef and hot springs; one night is spent at the company's permanent riverside camp. One-day trips are also available for 1500B on slightly easier rapids. The main rafting season runs from mid-June to mid-February; after that the trips aren't usually offered. Thai Adventure Rafting also has offices in Chiang Mai.

ELEPHANT RIDING

Thom's Pai Elephant Camp Tours (☎ 0 5369 9286; www .geocities.com/pai_tours/; Th Rangsiyanon; 1/2hr rides per person 300/450B) offers jungle rides year-round from Thom's camp southeast of Pai near the hot springs. You can choose between riding bareback or in a seat, and some rides include swimming with the elephants – a barrel of laughs on a bouncing elephant in the river. Rides include a soak in the hot-spring-fed tubs afterwards. Thom's can also arrange a variety of trips, including bamboo or rubber rafting, hill-tribe village stays or any combina-

tion of the aforementioned for about 1000B per person per day.

MASSAGE & SPA TREATMENTS

Pai Traditional Massage (☎ 0 5369 9121; pttm 2001@hotmail.com; 1 Th Wiang Tai; 1/1½/2hr massage 150/230/300B, sauna per visit 70B, 3-day massage course around 2500B; ⏰ 4.30pm-8.30pm Mon-Fri, 8.30am-8.30pm Sat & Sun) Being rebuilt after a fire at the time of writing, it should be open again by the time this is published. Pai Traditional Massage has very good northern-Thai massage, as well as a sauna where you can steam yourself in *sàmŭn phrai* (medicinal herbs). The couple that do the massages are graduates of Chiang Mai's Old Medicine Hospital. Massage and sauna services are available on weekends.

Mr Jan's Massage (Soi Wanchaloem 18; per hr 150B) For those into the rougher stuff, this place in town employs a harder Shan-Burmese massage technique.

The Healing Pyramid (☎ 0 9998 2031; Th Chaisongkhram) Using herbal based products, spa packages and one-hour sessions include body scrubs, aromatherapy massage and Reiki, as well as the more dubious sounding psychic surgery and crystal healing. It's located about 6km out of town towards the waterfall. Book at Back Trax (see left) in town.

Thapai Spa Camping (☎ 0 1951 2784; www.thapaispa .com; Ban Mae Hi) Next door to Spa Exotic Home, this hotel has good spa facilities making the most of the nearby hot-spring waters. Come here for the reasonably priced mud wraps, massages and spring-water treatments. The rooms at Thapai, however, are overpriced and plain.

There are plenty of traditional Thai massage places around town charging around 150B an hour.

COOKERY COURSE

Pai Cookery School (☎ 08 1706 3799; Soi Wanchaloem; courses 750-800B per day) offers a choice of three courses (red, green or yellow) with different dishes to learn. The course typically involves a trip to the market for ingredients, learning how to make five meals, getting a free recipe book and, of course, eating your creations at the end. One- to three-day courses are available.

YOGA

Mama's Yoga House (☎ 08 9954 4981; Th Rangsiyanon; one-day course 500B, 100B per hour) Just north of

the police station, Mama offers Hatha Yoga classes and courses in small groups.

VOLUNTEERING

If you want to spend longer in the region and put something back **Travel to Teach** (www .travel-to-teach.org/thai/pai.html) organises affordable programmes where you can teach English in and around Pai. You need to apply at least two months before departure and placements can last from one week to six months.

Sleeping

There's lots of accommodation choice in Pai. If you're coming to enjoy the quiet, idyllic countryside, or plan on staying for a while, head out of town to one of the 'off-map' spots. Budget places are the staple, but more places are moving into the midrange, and the top end has arrived.

There have been massive floods in Pai in the last few years; a particularly bad one was in 2005, in which some riverside bungalows were swept away. If in Pai for the rainy season and you want to stay right on the river, make sure it's a sturdy bungalow.

IN TOWN
Budget

Golden Hut (☎ 0 5369 9949; dm/d 50/100B, r 300-500B) This place is popular for its laid-back atmosphere, garden setting and proximity to town and river. The thatched huts on stilts, dorm beds (not available in rainy season) and double rooms in a large bamboo-thatch building are simple but clean. Some rooms need maintenance because of flood damage. There is a restaurant on site.

Shan Guest House (☎ 0 5369 9162; r 100-300B) If you want to be close to Pai's nightlife, this well-run and well-worn spot on the southern edge of town off Th Rangsiyanon is a decent option. A new, rather grand, dining and lounging pavilion sits in the middle of a big pond. Long-term discounts are available.

Charlie's House (☎ 0 5369 9039; Th Rangsiyanon; r 100-600B; 🐾) The friendly proprietor offers a range of options. Very clean, cheap and in the centre of town but most rooms are quite stark.

Mr Jan's Bungalows (☎ 0 5369 9554; Soi Wanchaloem 18; r from 200B) Although set around a lovely medicinal herb garden, the rooms are very plain and rather dark. Massages and herbal saunas are available in high season.

Pravee's House (☎ 0 5369 9368; Soi Wanchaloem; r with fan 200-300B, r with air con 600B; 🐾) Tucked in the corner, this attractive house offers large, clean rooms with some decent furnishings and small verandas. There is a small garden out front.

Duang Guest House (☎ 0 5369 9101; Th Chaisongkhram; r 200-500B) This rambling complex of two-storey houses, row houses and bungalows is a reasonable choice if you want to be right in town. Being opposite the bus station it can get noisy, so take a room at the back. Shared bathrooms need maintenance.

Abodaya Guest House & Restaurant (☎ 0 5369 9041; Th Chaisongkhram; r 300B) The rooms at this guesthouse are behind the restaurant of the same name. The modern, clean rooms have some cosy touches and are a good deal, with cable TV, hot-water showers and a central location. It lacks a garden though.

Breeze of Pai Guest House (☎ 08 4170 5184, 08 1998 4597; helendavis2@yahoo.co.uk; Soi Wat Pa Kham; r 300-400B) Behind Golden Hut, this brand new place is down a quiet *soi* but right by the action. It has six large A-frame bungalows fitted out in contemporary Thai style, hot-water bathrooms and hammocks. The row of spacious rooms beside them have attractive decking, bamboo plants outside and a simple yet chic décor inside.

Baan Tawan Guest House (☎ 0 5369 8116/7; www .baantawaninpai.com; 114 Mu 4, Wiang Tai; r 300-800B) The older, more charming, more expensive, riverside two-storey bungalows made with salvaged teak are the reason to stay here. The newer, cement rooms hardly compare, but will do in a pinch. It's quite a social place with plenty of balcony hammocks and a pool table. Motorcycles and inner tubes (for floating down the river) are available for rent.

ourpick **Baan Pai Village** (☎ 0 5369 8152; www .baanpaivillage.com; Th Wiang Tai; r 500-650B) Behind Poppies Restaurant, this charming new place has a collection of wooden bungalows set among winding pathways. Beautifully designed, each bungalow has floor-to-ceiling sliding windows, large, quite plush bathrooms, rattan mats and axe cushions for relaxing, plus spacious terraces to enjoy the garden.

Midrange

Blue Lagoon Hotel (☎ 0 5369 9998; Th Rangsiyanon; r 500-750B; 🐾) Clean, characterless motel-like rooms with cable TV and hot-water showers

surround a sizeable pool. There is a restaurant and bar attached with a pool table and big screen to watch movies.

Rim Pai Cottage (☎ 0 5369 9133; www.rimpaicottage .com; Th Chaisongkhram; r & bungalows from 1000B; 🔀) This place feels like a small village from another time period and has a stylish collection of dark wood bungalows and rooms set in a lovely garden. The interiors have a romantic feel with their mosquito nets and Thai decorating details, and the open bathrooms are particularly nice. In the cheaper rooms you may hear your neighbours. There are also some villas on the river. Rim Pai is an excellent deal in low season when the prices drop dramatically.

Top End

our pick **Pai River Corner** (☎ 0 5369 9049; www.pairiver corner.com; Th Chaisongkhram; r 3000-6000B; 🔀) By the river in town, these elegant rooms are exquisitely designed with beautiful Thai furniture, gorgeous colours and lots of deluxe details. Definitely the place for the design conscious, all have river facing balconies and some have lounges and interior spa pool. Discounts are available in low season.

OUT OF TOWN
Southeast of town are a number of places to stay along the road that leads to the hot springs, not very far from Wat Phra That Mae Yen.

Budget
Good View Guest House (Ban Mae Yen; r 100-250B) Near Sun Hut but further up the hill, this sociable place has simple, shared bathroom A-frame bungalows and rooms with views of the mountains and rice fields. There are lots of thatched communal areas with hammocks, and places for campfires.

Sun Hut (☎ 0 5369 9730, 08 1301 3443; pai_the sunhut@yahoo.com; 28/1 Ban Mae Yen; r 350-1100B) Set down a forested pathway, this eclectic collection of zodiac-inspired bungalows is one of the more unique and calming places in the area. Bungalows are nicely spaced apart and more expensive bungalows have porches and lots of charm. There is an attractive communal area with hammocks. The turn-off for Sun Hut comes after a bridge over a stream, about 200m before the entrance to Wat Phra That Mae Yen. Fifty percent discounts are possible in low season.

Midrange
our pick **Pairadise** (☎ 0 9838 7521; www.pairadise .com; 98 Mu 1, Ban Mae Yen; bungalows 650-1000B) Atop the ridge, Pairadise features super-stylish, spacious and cosy bungalows amid a pretty garden. The décor is understated and very chic, with gold leaf lotus murals, beautiful rustic bathrooms, and terraces with hammocks. The more expensive bungalows have a separate living room, desk and day bed. All surround a spring-fed pond that is suitable for swimming.

Spa Exotic Home (☎ 0 1917 9351, 0 5369 8088; 86 Mu 2, Ban Mae Hi; bungalows 850-1000B) All of the charming bungalows here sit around a beautifully landscaped garden. Each has a private tub in partially open-air bathrooms for enjoying the on-site spring water. There are also open-air tubs outside. Service is conscientious and the overall atmosphere is relaxing. Discounts of 35% are available from March to September. The restaurant serves good Thai and Western food.

Pai Lanna (☎ 08 9691 3367; www.pailanna.com; 169 Mu 1, Ban Mae Yen; bungalows ind breakfast 900B) Next to Pairadise, this brand new place has woven bamboo, thatched bungalows with a good view of the mountains. Rooms are simple and neat, and all have hot-water showers, Thai axe cushions for relaxing, mozzie nets and a few stylish touches.

Sipsongpanna Bungalow (☎ 0 5369 8259, 08 1881 7631; sipsongpanna33@hotmail.com; 60 Mu 5, Ban Juang, Wiang Neua; bungalows from 900B) These wooden riverside bungalows are rustic and a bit quirky with a mix of lacy curtains, abstract art and beds on a different level. The front of some bungalows open fully to terraces overlooking the river. Bathrooms have hot water but are basic. There is a vegetarian café and Thai vegetarian-cooking lessons are available.

Muang Pai Resort (☎ 0 5327 0906; www.muangpai -resort.infothai.com; 94 Mu 4, Baan Mor Paeng; bungalows from 1200B; 🔀 🛋) Muang Pai is known for its pleasant, medium-sized swimming pool with loungers. The bungalows and garden are so neat they almost feel plastic. This is a good option for a family with transport.

Top End
Baan Krating Pai Resort (☎ 0 5369 8255, www.baan krating.com/pai; 119 Th Wiang Nua; r 2700-5500B; 🔀 🛋) These bungalows on stilts are all beautifully decorated with white linen, rattan and teak, and have large windows overlooking

NORTHERN THAILAND

manicured gardens or rice paddies. The restaurant serves its home-grown jasmine rice with tasty Thai dishes.

Belle Villa (☎ 0 5369 8226-7; www.bellevillaresort.com; 118 Th Wiang Nua; bungalows 3600B; ✖ ✖ ☎) These tasteful bungalows are very comfortable and have some style but not the 'wow' factor you'd hope for at this price. Attached terraces look over the neatly lawned gardens, and rooms come with cable TV and DVD players. The infinity pool overlooking the river is a nice bonus. There is a restaurant on site and free transfers to town.

Eating

Pai's range of eating options reflects the diversity of international residents and visitors, but there is also a healthy selection of well-priced Thai places. The places that we have selected are located in town.

Cher Xin Jai (Pure Vegetarian Food; Th Ratchadamnoen; dishes 20B; ✆ 8am-5pm) Opposite the District Office, this simple place with low tables on rattan mats serves delicious and cheap vegan and vegetarian Thai food. Choose from the dishes in the metal trays out front, which are filled with much tofu and veg plus brown husky rice. There's good fruit and soya milk shakes too.

Edible Jazz (Soi Wat Pa Kham; dishes 30-90B; ✆ 2-11pm) The cushions-on-the-floor atmosphere make this a good choice for a leisurely late-night pasta, sandwiches or Mexican food. Jazz CDs play in the background and occasionally the Thai owner plays improvisational acoustic guitar. Full cocktail and espresso menu.

Angie's Kitchen (☎ 0 5369 9105; Th Rangsiyanon; dishes 30-100B; ✆ 7.30am-10pm) The 60B set meals are the best deal. The menu includes the typical Thai and Western dishes. It's a nice place to read the paper and catch up on world events over breakfast. Lots of unusual fruit shake mixes too.

Blue Restaurant (Th Chaisongkhram; dishes 30-180B; ✆ 8am-11pm) Next to Pai River Corner resort, this pleasant open restaurant has fantastic lassis, recommended burgers, lots of salads, and vegetarian Thai options.

our pick Baan Benjarong (☎ 0 5369 8010; Th Rangsiyanon; dishes 40-120B; ✆ 11am-10pm) Although this place doesn't look much from outside it serves the best Thai food in Pai. Dishes like stewed, salted crabs in coconut milk, and spicy banana flower salad are delectable. Out the back are tables with views of the rice paddies. There's ice cream too.

our pick All About Coffee (☎ 0 5369 9429; Th Chaisongkhram; dishes 45-75B; ✆ 8.30am-6.30pm) This stylish little bohemian place serves eye-opening coffee drinks and the best French toast in town. Instead of pop music, expect American ragtime, jazz or blues. Yummy open sandwiches are made with homemade bread.

Poppies Restaurant (Th Wiang Tai; dishes 50-70B) This stylish open restaurant serves tasty Thai and Western food on wooden tables surrounded by dark red Chinese parasols and lots of colourful lanterns. The pumpkin soup is really delicious and the salads have been recommended.

Chez Swan (☎ 0 5369 8253, 0 5369 9111; Th Rangsiyanon; dishes 70-190B; ✆ 8am-11pm) Set in an atmospheric wooden house, this cosy, romantic place serves French bistro-style food, like goat cheese salad and chicken in red wine sauce, as well as other European dishes. Try the very English crusty pies or the various Italian pasta dishes. The bar is a friendly place for a drink and there's also a pleasant seating area out back.

Burger House (☎ 0 5369 9093; Th Rangsiyanon; dishes 75-200B; ✆ 9am-9pm) If you are hankering after a big juicy burger this is the place to come. Try the super-high Barbarian Burger with its two quarter pounders, two cheeses and special sauce. Or if you need a fortifying breakfast, go for the Truck Driver Special, which will probably take most of the morning to get through.

Amido's Pizza Garden (dishes 80-160B) The truly great pizza at this open-air restaurant is not to be missed. It also features a variety of pasta dishes and daily specials (including delicious beef Bourguignon). It's about 300m east of the permanent bridge over Mae Nam Pai, near the school on Th Ratchadamnoen.

Laan-Taung (66 Th Rangsiyanon; dishes 129-149B; set menu for two 250B) This elegant restaurant looks very romantically Thai. On two floors, in an attractive wooden building, beautifully presented and tasty Thai dishes are served with the accompaniment of classical music. The downside is it's overpriced and a tad pretentious.

During the day, there's takeaway food at **Saengthongaram Market** (Th Khetkelang).

Drinking & Entertainment

Pai boasts a small but happening live-music scene.

Bebop Cafe (Th Rangsiyanon; ✆ 6pm-1am) This old favourite is popular with travellers and has live

music nightly (from about 9.30pm), playing blues, R&B and rock.

ourpick Charnos Bar (Th Rangsiyanon; ⏰ 8pm-1am) The coolest-looking bar in Pai, this intimate place has a slinky '70s feel with its red easy chairs, bright pink swaying lamps and kitschy toys in display cabinets. Trendy Thais frequent it, and good house and funk are played.

Shisha Bar (Th Rangsiyanon; ⏰ 5pm-1am) By the bridge, this cosy place is filled with people lounging on colourful sofas and smoking hookahs with flavours ranging from mango to cappuccino.

Pai Post Studio & Gallery (Th Chaisongkhram; ⏰ 7.30-9.30pm Sat) Most of the time, the back of this white wooden building is home to Pai's English-language rag, and the front is a white space for photography. But every Saturday night it has another incarnation, when saxophones and bass come out to play some chilled live jazz.

Taku Art Bar (Th Rangsiyanon; ⏰ 10am-11.30pm) Partially owned by a well-known Thai artist, Taku is the main centre for visiting Thai hipsters. It's pop arty décor is really funky and the bartender has a knack for spinning the right CD at the right moment. There's folky/rock live music on Tuesday, Friday and Saturday.

Boom Bar (Th Rangsiyanon; ⏰ 6pm-1am) This big, brand new, partly open-air bar has lots of seating, a pool table and table football. There should be live bands by the time this comes out.

Getting There & Away

AIR

At the time of writing the Pai airstrip renovations had finished and a new terminal had been added. From February 2007 a new Chiang Mai to Pai flight, through a company called Siam General Aviation (Siam GA), is scheduled to commence. It is estimated to cost one way/return 1450/2900B and will take 20 minutes. Contact Siam GA to book (☎ 0 2664 6099, 0 2641 4190; www.sga.aero). The airport is located around 2km north of the city along Rte 1095.

BUS

Buses (ordinary/air-con 80/142B) leave Chiang Mai's Arcade bu station five times a day.

It's only 134km but the trip takes three to four hours due to the steep winding road. From Mae Hong Son there are also five buses a day; this winding 111km stretch takes around three hours (ordinary/air-con/air-con minibus 70/98/150B).

Ordinary buses depart from Pai's bus station for Chiang Mai (80B) at 8.30am, 10.30am, 2pm and 4pm. The air-con minibuses (150B) leave from the same station almost every hour from 9.30am to 6pm. Ordinary buses for Mae Hong Son (70B) leave the bus station at 7am, 8.30am, 11am, 1pm and 4pm. Air-con minibuses to Mae Hong Son (150B) depart almost every hour from 8.30am to 3.30pm. Regular buses from Pai to Soppong cost 35B ordinary and 70B for air-con minivan. The trip takes 1½ hours.

AYA Service (☎ 0 5369 9940; Th Chaisongkhram) Book your ticket in advance at AYA; it runs air-con minivan buses to Chiang Mai (150B, 3hrs), Tham Thom (400B, 5hrs), Mae Sai (500B, 6hrs) and Chiang Khong (600B, 10hrs).

Getting Around

Most of Pai is accessible on foot. For local excursions you can rent bicycles or motorcycles at several locations around town. A place next door to Duang Guest House (p448) rents out bicycles for 80B per day. Motorcycles can be rented at **AYA Service** (☎ 0 5369 9940; Th Chaisongkhram; bikes per 24 hr 100cc/larger 80/100-500B).

Motorcycle taxis wait at the taxi stand at the bus stop. Fares are 30B to Ban Nam Hu and Ban Wiang Neua; 40B to Nam Hu Lisaw and Nam Hu Jin; and 50B to Tha Pai.

AROUND PAI

Pai can be used as a base for excursions to hill-tribe villages, such as Ban Santichon (p445). Further afield, the area northeast of Pai has so far been little explored. A network of unpaved roads – some are little more than footpaths – skirts a mountain ridge and the Mae Taeng valley all the way to the Myanmar border near **Wiang Haeng** and **Ban Piang Haeng**, passing several villages along the way. Near Ban Piang Haeng is a Shan **temple** built by Khun Sa, the opium warlord.

Northeastern Thailand

For most travellers, and many Thais, the northeast is Thailand's forgotten backyard. Isan (or *isăan*), the collective name for the 19 provinces that make up the northeast, offers a glimpse of the Thailand of old: rice fields run to the horizon, water buffaloes wade in muddy ponds, silk weaving remains a cottage industry, peddle-rickshaw drivers pull passengers down city streets, and, even for those people who've had to seek work in the city, hearts and minds are still tied to the village. This colossal corner of the country continues to live life on its own terms: slowly, steadily, and with a profound respect for heritage and history.

If you spend even just a little time here you'll start to find as many differences as similarities to the rest of the country. The language, food and culture are more Lao than Thai, with hearty helpings of Khmer and Vietnamese thrown into the melting pot.

And spend time here you should. Isan saves its finest surprises for those with the patience to come looking for them: Angkor temple ruins pepper the region, superb national parks protect some of the wildest corners of the country, sleepy villages host some of Thailand's wildest celebrations and the scenery along parts of the Mekong is often nothing short of amazing. Thailand's tourist trail is at its bumpiest here (English is rarely spoken), but the fantastic attractions and daily interactions could just end up being highlights of your trip.

HIGHLIGHTS

- Seeking elephants, tigers, monkeys and more in the mountainous forests of **Khao Yai National Park** (p464)

- Soaking up Isan's Angkor-era stone age while wandering through the restored temple complexes of **Phanom Rung** (p468), **Phimai** (p461) and **Prasat Khao Phra Wihan** (p545)

- Watching the Mekong drift by in the soporific riverside village of **Chiang Khan** (p507)

- Succumbing to the surreal in Nong Khai's **Sala Kaew Ku sculpture park** (p493)

- Climbing, and climbing some more, then finally soaking up the beauty from atop **Phu Kradung National Park** (p504)

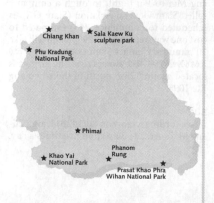

History

The social history of this enigmatic region stretches back at least 5600 years, to the hazy days when the ancient Ban Chiang culture started tilling the region's fields with bronze tools.

Thais employ the term *isǎan* to classify the region (*phâak isǎan*), the people (*khon isǎan*) and the food (*aahǎan isǎan*) of northeast-ern Thailand. The name comes from Isana, the Sanskrit name for the early Mon-Khmer kingdom that flourished in what is now north-eastern Thailand and Cambodia. After the 9th century, however, the Angkor empire held sway over these parts and erected many of the fabulous temple complexes that pepper the region today.

Until the arrival of Europeans, Isan re-mained largely autonomous from the early Thai kingdoms. But as the French staked out the borders of colonial Laos, Thailand was forced to define its own northeastern boundaries. Slowly, but surely, Isan would fall under the mantle of broader Thailand.

Long Thailand's poorest area, the northeast soon became a hotbed of communist activity.

Ho Chi Minh spent 1928 to 1929 proselytising in the area, and in the 1940s a number of Indochinese Communist Party leaders fled to Isan from Laos and helped bolster Thailand's Communist Party. From the 1960s, until an amnesty in 1982, guerrilla activity was rife in Isan, especially in the provinces of Buriram, Loei, Ubon Ratchathani, Nakhon Phanom and Sakon Nakhon. But growing urbanisation drew many peasants to the cities and the various insurgencies evaporated in the glare of Thailand's boom years. Not everyone has benefited though, and the per capita income in Isan is less than one-third of the national average.

Climate

Northeastern Thailand experiences a three-season monsoonal climate, with a relatively cool dry season from November to late February, followed by a hot dry season from March to May (when temperatures can climb to over 40°C) and then a hot rainy season from June to October. The Loei Province experiences the most extreme climatic conditions, with both the hottest temperatures and the coldest – it's one of the few places in Thailand where temperatures dip below zero.

National Parks

Northeastern Thailand has 24 national parks and 21 forest parks. Khao Yai (p464) is its most impressive, covering much of the largest intact monsoon forest in mainland Asia. Other highlights include Phu Kradung (p504) for its wildlife watching and high-altitude hiking; Nam Nao (p481) with its dense forest and unspoilt landscapes; Phu Chong Nayoi (p540), one of Thailand's remotest corners; and Phu Wiang (p481), a must for dinosaur lovers.

Information on all of Thailand's national parks and an online booking service can be found at www.dnp.go.th/parkreserve. You can also book camp sites and bungalows through the **reservations office** (☎ 0 2562 0760; reserve@dnp .go.th). Most lodging can also be reserved by calling the park directly, though you won't always get hold of someone who speaks English.

Language & Culture

Isan language and culture are melting pots of Thai, Lao and Khmer influences. The Khmers left behind Angkor Wat–like monuments across much of the region, but particularly in the Surin, Si Saket, Buriram and Khorat Provinces, while Lao-style temples – most notably Wat Phra That Phanom – are the norm along the Mekong River. Many of the people living in this area speak Lao (which is very similar to the Isan language) as their first language, and, in fact, there are probably more people of Lao heritage in Isan than in all of Laos. Many villages in the far south still speak Khmer as the primary language.

The people of Isan are known by other Thais for their friendliness, work ethic and sense of humour – flip through stations on the radio and you will hear many DJs laughing at their own jokes. Respect and hospitality towards guests is a cornerstone of Isan life and most villagers, plus plenty of city folk, still pride themselves on taking care of other people before themselves. The best food is usually reserved for monks and guests, and if you get invited to a village home your hosts will almost certainly kill one of their chickens to feed you (vegetarians should speak up early). Isan people are less conservative than most Thais, but short shorts and spaghetti-strap tops will earn a lot more stares than most other places in Thailand because of the scarcity of tourists here.

Though this is by far Thailand's poorest region, based on a new government Well-Being Index, the people of the northeast are the nation's happiest. A strong sense of community and close family ties are the main reasons cited, but it also stems from the fact that the people of Isan seek happiness from the inside, not from what they own. In the villages you can almost never tell who is rich and poor because big homes and fancy clothes garner no respect.

The region's music is born out of a distinctive folk tradition and uses instruments such as the *khaen*, a reed instrument with two long rows of bamboo pipes strung together; the *ponglang*, which is like a xylophone and made of short wooden logs; and the *phin*, a type of small three-stringed lute played with a large plectrum. The most popular song form is the *lûuk thûng* (literally, children of the fields), which is far more rhythmic than the classical styles of central Thailand.

The best silk in Thailand is said to come from the northeast, particularly Chaiyaphum, Khon Kaen, Surin and Nakhon Ratchasima. Cotton fabrics from Loei, Nakhon Phanom and Udon Thani are also highly regarded. The defining style uses *mát-mìi* methods (see

EATING ISAN

Isan's culinary creations are a blend of Lao and Thai cooking styles that make use of local ingredients. The holy trinity of northeastern cuisine – *kài yâang* (grilled chicken), *sôm-tam* (papaya salad) and *khâo nǐaw* (sticky rice) – is integral to the culture and reminisced like lost lovers by displaced Isan taxi drivers in Bangkok. Also essential are chillies, and a fistful of potent peppers find their way into most dishes, especially *lâap*, a super-spicy meat salad originating from Laos. *Kaeng om* has more in common with *tôm-yam* than with typical Thai curries as it has *plaa ráa* (a popular fermented fish sauce that looks like rotten mud) instead of coconut and sugar. It is sometimes served with glass noodles, but even then it's still meant to be eaten with rice.

Except at food stalls and the cheapest restaurants, fish dominates Isan-specific menus with *plaa dùk* (catfish), *plaa chawn* (striped snake-head) and *plaa bu* (sand goby) among the most popular dishes. These are mostly caught in the Mekong and a few other large rivers. Fish that families catch themselves are usually small – sometimes so tiny they're eaten bones and all – because they come from streams and rice paddies; as do crabs, frogs and eels. *Plaa bèuk* (giant Mekong catfish) is the most famous fish associated with the northeast, but it is almost never eaten here because it costs too much.

To Westerners and other Thais nothing stands out in Isan cuisine like insects. Even as recently as the 1970s insects composed a large part of the typical family's diet, though it became a fading tradition when the government promoted chicken and pig farming, thus lowering the prices of these now popular meats. Though the younger generations don't bite bugs all that often anymore, they are still very common as snacks and chilli-sauce ingredients. Purple lights shining out in the countryside are for catching giant water bugs, and these, along with crickets, grasshoppers, cicadas, *non maiphai* (bamboo worm) and more, are sold in most municipal and many night markets. In fact, there is still enough of a demand that imports come from Cambodia. Thailand has no shortage of silkworm larvae, which, after they are popped into the boiling water to remove the silk, are popped into the mouth for a literal taste explosion – try one and you'll see what we mean.

box text, p473) in which threads are tie-dyed before weaving. Most large stores stock some fabrics naturally dyed using plant materials, an old process being revived across Isan: some shops in Khon Kaen and Ubon Ratchathani specialise in these. Prices for fabrics can be 20% to 30% cheaper (more than 50% for less-common fabric styles) in the weaving villages than in Bangkok shops, though finished clothes cost about the same. Another handicraft speciality of the northeast is *mǎwn khwǎan* (literally, axe pillow), a stiff triangle-shaped pillow used as an arm support while sitting on the floor. Sticky-rice baskets also make good souvenirs.

Getting There & Away

The main train and bus lines in the northeast are between Bangkok and Nong Khai, and between Bangkok and Ubon Ratchathani. The northeastern region can also be reached from northern Thailand by bus through Phitsanulok, with Khon Kaen as the gateway. Most of the major centres are also connected to Bangkok by air.

Getting Around

If you have time on your side, travelling in the northeast is rarely a problem: all large- and medium-sized towns are linked by bus or train, and sǎwngthǎew (pick-up trucks) services go on to most, but not all, of the smaller villages and temple complexes. If you are short on time, however, remember that distances are large in this part of Thailand and buses are often slow. Consequently, if time is of the essence and you plan to visit the region's more remote sites, a rental car or motorcycle will save a great many headaches and let you see much more of the region with your available time. There are very few flights between cities in the northeast; you generally need to connect through Bangkok.

NAKHON RATCHASIMA PROVINCE

Silk and stone are the cornerstones of the Nakhon Ratchasima tourist industry and it is well worth dipping an inquisitive toe into both

NORTHEASTERN THAILAND

facets of the region's heritage. First up, history aficionados should soak up the stone remains of the region's Angkor-period heyday. Khmer temples dating from this time still pepper the province and while many have been reduced to amorphic piles of rubble, the restored complex of Prasat Phimai provides an evocative glimpse of times past. If you're a fashionista, you should explore the region's silk-weaving industry in Amphoe Pak Thong Chai, Thai silk weaving's spiritual home. Some of the country's best cloth comes out of this area.

Top it all off by getting deep into the jungle at Khao Yai, Thailand's oldest national park and newest World Heritage site. It's one of the best wildlife-watching destinations in Southeast Asia.

NAKHON RATCHASIMA (KHORAT)
นครราชสีมา(โคราช)
pop 215,000
Khorat doesn't wear its heart on its sleeve. Touch down in the brash gateway to the northeast and only those sporting a hefty set of rose-tinted specs will be reaching for their camera as they step off the bus. A bumper dose of urban hubbub reflects the city's growing affluence and Khorat's one-time historic charm has been largely smothered under a duvet of homogenous development.

Khorat is a city you grow to know. Distinctly Isan, with a strong sense of regional identity, this busy centre is at its best in its quieter nooks (inside the east side of the historic moat, for example), where Thai life, largely untouched

NAKHON RATCHASIMA (KHORAT)

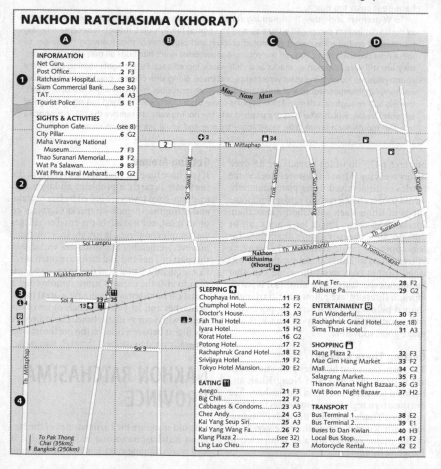

INFORMATION
Net Guru.................................1 F2
Post Office.............................2 F3
Ratchasima Hospital.............3 B2
Siam Commercial Bank......(see 34)
TAT..4 A3
Tourist Police.......................5 E1

SIGHTS & ACTIVITIES
Chumphon Gate.................(see 8)
City Pillar..............................6 G2
Maha Viravong National
    Museum.............................7 F3
Thao Suranari Memorial......8 F2
Wat Pa Salawan....................9 B3
Wat Phra Narai Maharat.....10 G2

SLEEPING
Chophaya Inn......................11 F3
Chumphol Hotel..................12 F2
Doctor's House.....................13 A3
Fah Thai Hotel.....................14 F2
Iyara Hotel...........................15 H2
Korat Hotel...........................16 G2
Potong Hotel........................17 F2
Rachaphruk Grand Hotel....18 E2
Srivijaya Hotel.....................19 F2
Tokyo Hotel Mansion...........20 E2

EATING
Anego....................................21 F3
Big Chili................................22 F2
Cabbages & Condoms..........23 A3
Chez Andy.............................24 G3
Kai Yang Seup Siri................25 A3
Kai Yang Wang Fa................26 F2
Klang Plaza 2...................(see 32)
Ling Lao Cheu.......................27 E3

Ming Ter................................28 F2
Rabiang Pa............................29 G2

ENTERTAINMENT
Fun Wonderful.....................30 F3
Rachaphruk Grand Hotel....(see 18)
Sima Thani Hotel.................31 A3

SHOPPING
Klang Plaza 2........................32 F3
Mae Gim Hang Market.........33 F2
Mall......................................34 C2
Salagrang Market.................35 F3
Thanon Manat Night Bazaar.36 G3
Wat Boon Night Bazaar.......37 H2

TRANSPORT
Bus Terminal 1.....................38 E2
Bus Terminal 2.....................39 E1
Buses to Dan Kwian.............40 H3
Local Bus Stop.....................41 F2
Motorcycle Rental................42 E2

To Pak Thong
Chai (35km);
Bangkok (250km)

Mae Nam Mun

Th Mittaphap

Th Suranari

Th Mukkhamontri

Th Jomsurangyat

Th Kingkan

Soi Sawai Riang

Trok Samoe

Trok Sao Thanonong

Soi Lampru

Nakhon
Ratchasima
(Khorat)

Th Mukkhamontri

Soi 4

Soi 3

Th Mittaphap

by the country's booming tourist industry, goes on in its own uncompromising way.

Information

EMERGENCY & MEDICAL SERVICES

Ratchasima Hospital (☎ 0 4426 2000; Th Mittaphap)
Tourist police (☎ 1155; Th Chang Pheuak) Opposite bus terminal 2.

INTERNET ACCESS

Net Guru (☎ 0 4425 7441; Th Phoklang; per hr 20B; ☻ 24hr)

MONEY

Siam Commercial Bank (Th Mittaphap; ☻ 10.30am-8pm) At the Mall. Many more banks, also with ATM and exchange services, in the city centre open regular hours.

POST

Post office (Th Jomsurangyat; ☻ 8.30am-4.30pm Mon-Fri, 9am-noon Sat & holidays)

TOURIST INFORMATION

TAT (Tourist Authority of Thailand; ☎ 0 4421 3666; www.tourismthailand.org; 2102-2104 Th Mittaphap; ☻ 8.30am-4.30pm) Has information about Khorat, Buriram, Surin and Chaiyaphum Provinces.

Sights

MAHA VIRAVONG NATIONAL MUSEUM

พิพิธภัณฑสถานแห่งชาติมหาวีรวงศ์

Despite an interesting collection of Khmer and Ayuthaya-period artefacts, including stone and bronze Buddhas, woodcarvings from an ancient temple and various domestic

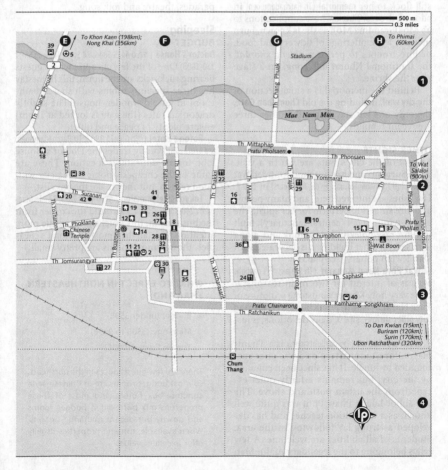

utensils, chances are you will have this interesting little **museum** (☎ 0 4424 2958; Th Ratchadamnoen; admission 10B; ☼ 9am-4.30pm Wed-Sun) to yourself. It is hidden away in the grounds of Wat Sutchinda.

THAO SURANARI MEMORIAL
อนุสาวรีย์ท้าวสุรนารี

Thao Suranari is something of a Wonder Woman in these parts. As the wife of the city's assistant governor, she rose to notoriety in 1826, during the reign of Rama III, when she led a ragtag army of locals to victory against the ravaging Vientiane forces of Chao Anuwong. Some scholars suggest the legend was concocted to instil a sense of Thai-ness in the ethnic-Lao people of the province, but locals still flock to her **memorial** (Th Ratchadamnoen) in adoring droves. Those whose supplications to Ya Mo (Grandma Mo), as she is known, burn incense, leave offerings of flowers and food, or hire troupes to perform *phleng khorâat*, the traditional Khorat folk song, on a stage near the shrine.

Behind the memorial is a small section of the **city wall**, including the old **Chumphon Gate**, the only one left standing – the other three are recent rebuilds.

OTHER SIGHTS

Several of the city's wats are worth a visit. Thao Suranari and her husband founded **Wat Salaloi** (off Th Thanonaosura; ☼ daylight hours) in 1827. Her ashes are interred here, and many people also hire singers to perform for her spirit. The award-winning *bòt* (central sanctuary), built in 1967, resembles a Chinese junk and, along with several other buildings, is decorated with Dan Kwian pottery (see p463).

Wat Phra Narai Maharat (Th Prajak; ☼ daylight hours) is of interest for two main reasons: it has a very holy Khmer sandstone sculpture of Phra Narai (Vishnu) and Khorat's **làk meuang** (city pillar shrine), site of daily devotions, is just outside.

Wat Pa Salawan (☼ daylight hours) is a Thammayut 'forest monastery' and was once surrounded by jungle. It has since been engulfed by the city, but remains a fairly quiet escape from the urban push and shove. The late abbot Luang Phaw Phut was quite well known as a meditation teacher and has developed a strong lay following in the area. Students of all abilities are welcome. A few relics belonging to the legendary Ajahn Man

are on display in the main *wíhǎan* (large hall), a large but simple wooden affair. A cemetery on the grounds has a couple of markers with photos of US veterans who lived out their later years in Khorat – one of seven air bases in Thailand used by the US armed forces to launch air strikes on Laos and Vietnam in the 1960s and 1970s was just outside Khorat.

Festivals & Events

Khorat explodes into life during the **Thao Suranari Festival**, when city dwellers – in addition to legions of villagers from the surrounding area – come together to celebrate Thao Suranari's victory over the Lao (see left). It's held annually from 23 March to 3 April and features parades, theatre and folk song.

Sleeping
BUDGET

Doctor's House (☎ 0 4425 5846; 78 Soi 4, Th Seup Siri; r 150-180B) One of the few cheapies where guests bearing rucksacks are the norm, this homestay has three spacious rooms with shared bathroom in an old wooden house. The slightly draconian rules (the gate is locked at 10pm) ensure plenty of peace and quiet.

Potong Hotel (☎ 0 4425 1962; Th Ratchadamnoen; s/d 170/220B) Potong trades the Doctor's House vibe for an unbeatable location. These are some of the cheapest rooms in the city with good reason, but they make the pass list.

Tokyo Hotel Mansion (☎ 0 4424 2873; 331 Th Suranari; r 240-366B; ☒ ▯) Around the corner from the bus station, this hotel shows a little more attention to detail than most of Khorat's cheapies, though most rooms are pretty small.

WHAT TO EXPECT IN NORTHEASTERN THAILAND

▪ Budget (under 350B)

▪ Midrange (350B to 999B)

▪ Top end (over 1000B)

There are few guesthouses in the northeast, so most budget rooms are in Chinese-style concrete-box hotels, and most of these properties mix both older, budget rooms and dowdy but decent midrange options. When available, top-end properties usually offer excellent value.

Chumphol Hotel (☎ 0 4424 2453; 124 Th Phoklang; r 240-380B; 🅿) Although the dreary corridors are a little reminiscent of an asylum, the rooms are big enough to swing a brace of cats in and the place is generally tidy.

Fah Thai Hotel (☎ 0 4426 7390; 35-39 Th Phoklang; r 250-380B; 🅿) Similar in quality to Chumphol, this Thai-Chinese outfit feels less institutional, but is in bigger need of a paint job.

MIDRANGE

Srivijaya Hotel (☎ 0 4424 2194; 9-11 Th Buarong; r 480-530B; 🅿) The Srivijaya is far too ordinary to justify the 'boutique hotel' label it's given itself; nevertheless the comfy, spic-and-span rooms guarantee a good night's sleep.

Chaophaya Inn (☎ 0 4426 0555; www.chaophayainnkorat.com; 62/1 Th Jomsurangyat; r 490-600B; 🅿 🖳) Rising beyond the jailhouse vibes endemic in many of Khorat's midrange options, the Chaophaya offers cleanliness, comfort and a little atmosphere for a very reasonable price.

Iyara Hotel (☎ 0 4426 8777; theiyara@yahoo.com; 497/1 Th Chumphon; r 500-600B; 🅿) Once a fancy business-class hotel, the Iyara is quite tattered these days, but if you want to soak up the atmosphere of this quiet neighbourhood, it's your only choice. Discounts to 350B are routine.

Korat Hotel (☎ 0 4425 7057; korathotel@hotmail.com; 191 Th Atsadang; r 500-600B; 🅿 🖳) Here's proof that '70s styling made it to Thailand, and stayed way beyond its welcome. Yep, it's not the hippest of hotels, but the rooms are comfy and the welcome cheery. And if you can't sleep you can always pop down to the disco, karaoke or other night-time diversions.

TOP END

Rachaphruk Grand Hotel (☎ 0 4426 1222; www.rachaphruk.com; 311 Th Mittaphap; r 1200B; 🅿 🖳 🛎) 'Grand' is laying it on a little thick, but this slightly dowdy four-star affair, the only hotel in this class in the city centre, is a decent bet if you fancy a few business-style comforts. There is a fitness centre with a sauna, a pair of restaurants and many other attached entertainment options, plus great views from the top floors.

Eating

Kai Yang Seup Siri (no roman-script sign; Th Seup Siri; dishes 30-40B; 🕑 lunch) This spartan spot is famous for its grilled chicken, and reportedly has the best

sôm-tam in town. Just look for the roasting chickens.

Kai Yang Wang Fa (no roman-script sign; Th Ratchadamnoen; whole chicken 75B; 🕑 lunch & dinner) Another famed roast chicken spot, this is takeaway only.

Ling Lao Cheu (no roman-script sign; ☎ 0 4426 0311; dishes 30-100B; 🕑 lunch & dinner; 🅿) This friendly place serves a dizzying array of regional and Chinese seafood dishes. It's down an unnamed street running parallel to Th Jomsurangyat; just look for the bright yellow shopfront.

Cabbages & Condoms (☎ 0 4425 3760; 86/1 Th Seup Siri; dishes 35-180B; 🕑 lunch & dinner; 🅿) This regular favourite offers a leafy terrace, a wine list (something of a rarity in this part of Thailand) and plenty of newspaper clippings celebrating its mostly Thai food. Like the original in Bangkok, this is a nonprofit operation sponsored by the Population & Community Development Association.

ourpick Rabiang Pa (☎ 0 4424 3137; 284 Th Yommarat; dishes 40-220B; 🕑 lunch & dinner; 🅿) The leafiest and loveliest restaurant on this stretch of Th Yommarat is also one of the most low-key. The 2kg picture menu makes ordering the tasty Thai food risk free.

Chez Andy (☎ 0 4428 9556; Th Manat; dishes 50-650B; 🕑 lunch & dinner Mon-Sat; 🅿) Khorat's archetypal expat haunt, this Swiss-managed place – appropriately housed in a red-and-white villa – has a global menu, with fondue, steak and fried rice available.

Other recommendations:

Big Chili (☎ 0 4424 7469; 158/8 Th Chakkri; dishes 70-350B; 🕑 dinner; 🅿 🖳) Pretty good Mexican, for Thailand.

Anego (☎ 0 4426 0530; 62/1 Th Jomsurangyat; dishes 60-600B; 🕑 lunch & dinner; 🅿) For authentic Japanese sushi and noodle dishes, plus some Italian pasta dishes.

Khorat is overflowing with tasty Thai and Chinese restaurants serving cheap meals. Th Ratchadamnoen near the Thao Suranari Memorial and the west end of Th Jomsurangyat are good places to look: two notables are **Ming Ter** (☎ 0 4424 1718; 698 Th Ratchadamnoen; dishes 25-60B; 🕑 breakfast & lunch), a simple vegetarian affair, and the food courts at **Klang Plaza 2** (Th Jomsurangyat; dishes 25-60B; 🕑 lunch & dinner; 🅿). Eating on the hoof is best done at one of the city's many markets (see p460) where Isan specialities can be sampled en masse – keep your eyes open for deep-fried insects and pork sausages.

Entertainment

Sima Thani Hotel (☎ 0 4421 3100; Th Mittaphap; admission free) Hosts touristy cultural shows with Isan folk dances for tour groups; anyone can come along. Call for more details about the current programme.

The **Rachaphruk Grand Hotel** (311 Th Mittaphap) has the dance floor du jour, while **Fun Wonderful** (Th Jomsurangyat) is also popular. Both offer free admission.

The Mall (Th Mittaphap) Has bowling, a mini waterpark and the city's best movie theatre.

Klang Plaza 2 (Th Jomsurangyat) Also has bowling.

Shopping

Khorat has two downtown night markets. Both are at their best from 6pm to 10pm.

Thanon Manat Night Bazaar (Th Manat) Featuring cheap clothes, flowers, sunglasses and food vendors, this is the largest night market.

Wat Boon Night Bazaar (Th Chumphon) The smaller of the two night markets, but better for dining.

Mall (Th Mittaphap; ☺ 10.30am-9.30pm) Isan's largest, glossiest and busiest shopping centre.

Klang Plaza 2 (Th Jomsurangyat; ☺ 10am-9pm) You can find just about anything you need at this place downtown.

Also worth a browse are **Mae Gim Hang Market** (Th Suranari), which has mostly food and clothing, and **Salagrang Market** (Th Mahat Thai), with plenty of handicrafts.

Getting There & Away

BUS

Air-con buses (212B, three hours) leave the Northern bus terminal in Bangkok frequently throughout the day.

There are two bus terminals in Khorat. **Terminal 1** (☎ 0 4424 2899; Th Burin) in the city centre serves Bangkok and towns within the province. Buses to other destinations, plus more Bangkok buses, use **terminal 2** (☎ 0 4425 6006) off Hwy 2.

TRAIN

Eleven trains connect Bangkok to Khorat's two train stations. The express and special express services leave Hualamphong station at 5.45am, 10.05am, 6.30pm, 8.30pm and 9.50pm, arriving in Khorat about 4½ hours later, which is much longer than it takes to travel by bus. The 1st-class fare (express train only) is 230B, 2nd class is 115B and 3rd class is 50B. There are also 10 daily

BUSES TO/FROM KHORAT		
Destination	**Fare (B)**	**Duration (hr)**
Chiang Mai		
air-con	601	13
VIP	701	
Khon Kaen		
ordinary	125	3
air-con	160	
Loei		
ordinary	179	6
air-con	372	
Nong Khai		
ordinary	220	6
air-con	338	
Pattaya		
air-con	255	5
VIP	310	
Sakon Nakhon		
ordinary	220	6
air-con	283	
Ubon Ratchathani		
ordinary	155	7
air-con	279	
Udon Thani		
ordinary	193	4½
air-con	290	
Yasothon		
ordinary	169	4½
air-con	220	

train services, most taking about six hours, to/from Ubon Ratchathani (1st/2nd/3rd class 268/133/58B).

You can get train information at ☎ 0 4424 2044.

Express trains leave for Bangkok from **Khorat Station** (☎ 0 4424 2044) at 10.18am and 6.47pm and take 4½ hours. Normal trains (six hours) leave at 8.22am, 1.10pm, 3.45pm, 8.36pm and 11.28pm. From Bangkok they depart at 5.45am (express), 6.40am, 9.10am, 11.05am (express), 11.45am, 9pm, 9.50pm and 11.40pm. The 1st-class fare (express train only) is 245B, 2nd class is 110B and 3rd class is 50B.

There are also eight ordinary trains (2nd/3rd class 213/138B, five to six hours) and one express (1st class 333B, four hours) daily to/from Ubon Ratchathani.

Getting Around

Săwngthăew (8B) run fixed routes through the city, with most starting at bus terminal 1

and then passing down Th Suranari near the market. Săwngthăew 1 takes you past Th Seup Siri to near the TAT office, while săwngthăew 15 runs to bus terminal 2.

Túk-túk (motorised pedicab) and motorcycle taxis cost between 30B to 70B to most places around town. Several shops on the eastern half of Th Buarong also rent out motorcycles.

AROUND NAKHON RATCHASIMA
Phimai
พิมาย

The innocuous little town of Phimai has one of northeastern Thailand's finest surviving Khmer temple complexes at its heart. Reminiscent of Cambodia's Angkor Wat, which was built a century later, Prasat Phimai once stood on an important trade route linking the Khmer capital of Angkor with the northern reaches of the realm. Peppered with ruins and surrounded by ragged sections of the ancient town wall, modern-day Phimai still offers a little taste of this historic heyday. There is almost nothing to do here once you have wandered through the ruins – which are far less significant than those at Angkor Wat – but if you prefer the quiet life, this sleepy town makes a pleasant base from which to explore the wider region.

INFORMATION
Kasikornbank (Th Chomsudadet; 🕑 8.30am-3.30pm Mon-Fri) Has ATM and exchange facilities.
Tourist police (☎ 1155; Th Anantajinda)

SIGHTS
Phimai Historical Park
อุทยานประวัติศาสตร์พิมาย

Started by Khmer King Jayavarman V during the late 10th century and finished by King Suriyavarman I (AD 1002–49) in the early 11th century, this Hindu-Mahayana Buddhist temple projects a majesty that transcends its size. Although predating Angkor Wat by a century or so, **Prasat Phimai** (☎ 0 4447 1568; Th Anantajinda; admission 40B; 🕑 7.30am-6pm) nevertheless shares a number of design features with its more famous cousin, not least the roof of its 28m-tall main shrine. It may well be wishful thinking, but the tourist brochures claim that it might have been the model for Angkor Wat.

Unlike so many of northeastern Thailand's Khmer temples, Prasat Phimai has been elegantly reconstructed by the Fine Arts Department and is one of the most complete monuments on the circuit. Volunteer guides offer free tours on weekends.

Phimai National Museum
พิพิธภัณฑสถานแห่งชาติพิมาย

Situated on the banks of Sa Kwan, a 12th-century Khmer reservoir, this **museum** (☎ 0 4447 1167; Th Tha Songkhran; admission 30B; 🕑 8.30am-4pm) houses a fine collection of Khmer sculptures from Phimai, Phanom Rung and other ruins, as well as ceramics from nearby Ban Prasat. The museum's most prized possession, a stone sculpture of Angkor King Jayavarman VII, comes from Prasat Phimai and looks very much like a sitting Buddha. A sculpture

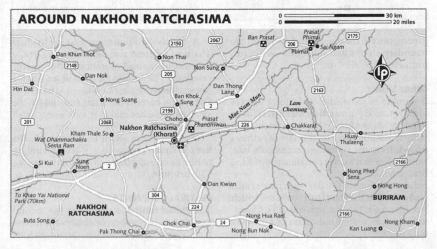

AROUND NAKHON RATCHASIMA

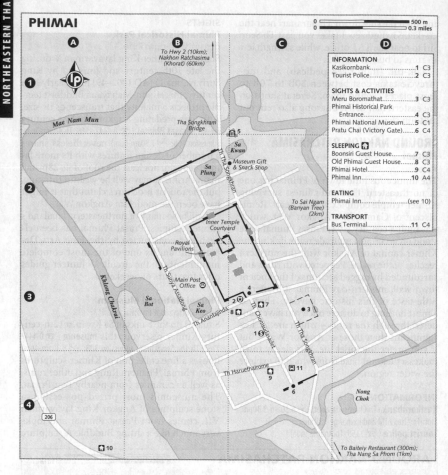

PHIMAI

garden, next to the main hall, displays ornate boundary stones and other Khmer figures from Phimai.

Other Sights

A number of other historic features survive in and around Phimai. **Meru Boromathat** (Th Tha Songkhran; admission free; ⏲ 24hr) is a brick *chedi* (stupa) dating back to the late Ayuthaya period. Its name is derived from a folk tale, which refers to it as the cremation site of King Bramathat.

Large sections of the city walls have crumbled away, but the **Pratu Chai** (Victory Gate), which faces Phimai at the southern end of Th Chomsudasadet, is a good indication of how they once looked.

A couple of kilometres east of town is Thailand's largest and oldest banyan tree, a megaflorum spread over an island in a large reservoir. The locals call it **Sai Ngam** (Beautiful Banyan; admission free; ⏲ 6am-6pm), and the extensive system of roots cascading from all but the smallest branches makes it look like a small forest.

One kilometre south of the town is **Tha Nang Sa Phom** (admission free; ⏲ 24hr), a landing platform constructed out of laterite in the 13th century.

FESTIVALS & EVENTS

The **Phimai Festival**, staged over the second weekend of November, celebrates the town's history and features cultural performances,

light shows and dragon-boat races. A smaller version of the light show is held on the last Saturday of the month from October to April.

SLEEPING

Old Phimai Guest House (☎ 0 4447 1918; off Th Chomsudasadet; dm 80B, r 130-350B; 🔀) This homey place down a *soi* (lane) is a little scruffy, but the backpacker vibe prevails and there's a welcoming atmosphere.

Phimai Inn (☎ 0 4428 7228; r 250-650B 🔀 🖳 🖭) The town's most upmarket option – not that the competition is particularly stiff – sits seemingly in the middle of nowhere on Rte 206, giving you some serious peace and quiet – unless you'd rather rip it up in the karaoke bar. The fan rooms are a bargain.

Boonsiri Guest House (☎ 0 4447 1159; 228 Th Chomsudasadet; dm 150B, r 450-650B; 🔀 🖳) From the front there doesn't seem to be a whole lot to this hotel, but there are plenty of rooms behind the scenes. Pathological spring-cleaning appears to have scrubbed away most of the atmosphere, but standards are high (the dorms have lockers) and the rooms are big and airy.

Phimai Hotel (☎ 0 4447 1306; 305/1-2 Th Haruethairome; r 250-680B; 🔀) Beyond the lobby, this place is letting itself get run-down, but it's the only proper hotel inside the city.

EATING

Sai Ngam (dishes 20-60B; 🕑 breakfast, lunch & dinner) Most of the vendors next to the island serve Thai and Isan basics, including tasty Phimai noodles.

Phimai Inn (dishes 30-180B; 🕑 breakfast, lunch & dinner) This hotel restaurant, serving many Isan dishes, gets good reviews.

Baiteiy Restaurant (☎ 0 4428 7103; Th Phimai-Chumpuang; dishes 40-200B; 🕑 breakfast, lunch & dinner) Appropriately decorated with pseudo-sandstone Khmer carvings, this lovely outdoor eatery, about 500m south of Pratu Chai (Victory Gate), does a decent spread of Thai fare, plus some international staples.

GETTING THERE & AWAY

Buses for Phimai leave from Khorat's bus terminal 2 (37B, 1¼ hours, every half-hour).

GETTING AROUND

Phimai is small enough to stroll but, to see more of the town and environs (eg Sai Ngam) you can rent bicycles from Boonsiri Guest House for 20B per hour or 100B per day.

Ban Prasat
บ้านปราสาท

About 3000 years ago, a primitive agricultural/ceramic culture put down roots at Bat Prasat, near the banks of Mae Nam Than Prasat. It survived for nearly 500 years, planting rice, domesticating animals, fashioning coloured pottery, weaving cloth and, in later years, forging tools out of bronze. The secrets of this early civilisation were finally revealed during extensive archaeological digs, finally completed in 1991. Three of the **excavation pits** (donations appreciated; 🕑 24hr), with skeletons and pottery left *in situ*, are on display throughout the village. A small **museum** (donations appreciated; 🕑 8am-4.30pm) houses some of the better discoveries and explains what life was like in those days.

Many of the houses are part of an award-winning **homestay programme** (per person incl 2 meals 400B), where villagers put up visitors in their homes and show them daily activities, like basketry and farming. Reservations should be made a day or two in advance through Khorat's **TAT office** (☎ 0 4421 3666; www.tourismthailand.org; 2102-2104 Th Mittaphap, Khorat; 🕑 8.30am-4.30pm), or the village headman here, **Khun Thiam** (☎ 0 4436 7075).

GETTING THERE & AWAY

Ban Prasat is 45km northeast of Khorat, off Hwy 2, and ordinary buses (27B, 40 minutes) to Phimai will drop you off. Motorcycle taxis waiting at the highway will zip you around to all the sites, including waiting time of about 15 minutes at each, for 60B.

Prasat Phanomwan
ปราสาทพนมวัน

Even after reconstruction the Khmer ruins of **Prasat Phanomwan** (admission free; 🕑 24hr) are rather tumbledown and the complex lacks the distinctive *prang* (Khmer-style tower) that make so many Khmer temples photogenic. If you're a history buff, however, it's worth a quick trip. Although the structure is thought to have been originally a shrine to the Hindu god Shiva, images of Buddha that have probably been enshrined here since at least the early Ayuthaya period are still in place and remain the objects of veneration. There are direct săwngthăew from Khorat's bus terminal 1 (20B, 30 minutes).

Dan Kwian
ด่านเกวียน

Even if you think you have no interest in **Thai ceramics** you should pay Dan Kwian a visit.

This village 15km southeast of Khorat has been producing pottery for hundreds of years and its creations are famous for the rough texture and rust-like hue – only kaolin sourced from this district produces such results. Myriad shops line the highway and some are as much art gallery as store. It's not all pottery, though. Clay is shaped and fired into all kinds of objects, from jewellery and wind chimes to reproductions of ancient Khmer sandstone sculpture.

Originally the village was a bullock-cart stop for traders on their way to markets in old Khorat (*dàan kwian* means 'bullock-cart checkpoint'). The ramshackle private **Kwian Museum** (☎ 0 4437 5199; donations appreciated; ☽ daylight hours) at the north end of the strip displays a variety of old carts from around the country, plus some farming implements and examples of old-style pottery.

To get here from Khorat, hop on a bus (12B, 30 minutes) from near the south city gate.

Pak Thong Chai
ปักธงชัย

Amphoe Pak Thong Chai became one of Thailand's most famous silk-weaving centres when Jim Thompson started buying silk here (for more on Thompson, see p135). Today there are around 35 silk factories in the district, not to mention the hundreds, if not thousands, of families still weaving on hand-looms under their houses in just about every village in the district; except Ban Pak Thong Chai itself, where families are too busy selling silk to make it. Two outlets worth seeking out are **Chattong** (☎ 0 4428 4465; ☽ 9am-6pm), on the highway across from the Silk Cultural Centre (it's been shuttered for many years but there is talk of reopening it), and **Macchada** (☎ 0 4444 1684; ☽ 8am-5pm), at the southern end of the main road through town. You can watch weavers working at the latter.

Pak Thong Chai is 35km south of Khorat on Rte 304. Buses (30B, 40 minutes) leave terminal 1 every half-hour.

Sandstone Reclining Buddha Image
พระพุทธไสยาสน์หินทราย

Housed inside **Wat Dhammachakra Sema Ram** in Khorat's Amphoe Sung Noen is Thailand's oldest **reclining Buddha** (☽ daylight hours). Thought to date back to the 8th century, the 13.5m-long Dvaravati-style image is unique

in that it hasn't been covered with a layer of stucco and a coat of whitewash. It actually looks as old as it is purported to be. The crude but appealing image is protected from the elements by a huge roof, and an altar has been built before it. Also on display at the wat is a stone rendition of the Buddhist Wheel of Law, also found on the site, which is thought to predate the Buddha image.

Visiting Wat Dhammachakra Sema Ram, 40km southwest of Khorat, is best done as a day trip from there. Sung Noen (6B, 40 minutes) is on the railway line to Bangkok (although only three local trains stop here). It can also be reached by buses from either terminal in Khorat (22B, 30 minutes). From Sung Noen you'll have to hire a săwngthǎew for the final 5km to the wat. Expect to pay nearly 200B for the return trip.

KHAO YAI NATIONAL PARK
อุทยานแห่งชาติเขาใหญ่

Up there on the podium with some of world's greatest parks, **Khao Yai National Park** (☎ 08 1877 3127; admission 400B; ☽ 6am-9pm) is Thailand's oldest and most visited reserve. Covering 2168 sq km, Khao Yai incorporates one of the largest intact monsoon forests remaining in mainland Asia, which is why is was named a Unesco World Heritage site. The mostly English-speaking staff at the **visitor centre** (☽ 8.30am-4.30pm) are very friendly and helpful.

Rising to 1351m with the summit of Khao Rom, the park's terrain covers five vegetation zones: evergreen rainforest (100m to 400m); semi-evergreen rainforest (400m to 900m); mixed deciduous forest (northern slopes at 400m to 600m); hill evergreen forest (over 1000m); and savannah and secondary-growth forest in areas where agriculture and logging occurred before it was protected. Many orchids bloom from the middle of June through the end of July, one of the few benefits of rainy-season visits.

Some 250 wild elephants tramp the park's boundaries; other mammals recorded include sambar deer, barking deer, gaur, Malayan sun bears, Asiatic black bears, tigers, leopards, otters, and various gibbons and macaques. Khao Yai also has one of Thailand's largest populations of hornbills, including the great hornbill (*nók kòk* or *nók kaahang* in Thai), king of the bird kingdom, as well as the wreathed hornbill (*nók graam cháang*; literally, 'elephant-jaw

bird'), Indian pied hornbill *(nók khàek)* and brown hornbill *(nók ngêuak sii nám taan)*. Hornbills breed from January to March, and this is the best time to see them. Over 200 bird species make the park their home and some 315 have been recorded.

There are two primary entrances into the park. The first is the northern entrance through Nakhon Ratchasima Province, with sleeping and transport options originating out of the backpacker town of Pak Chong (see transport information, p466). The second option is the southern entrance in Prachinburi Province (see Southeastern Thailand, p270), which is closer to Bangkok and a popular weekend destination for residents of the capital.

Sights & Activities

The easiest attraction to reach, other than the **roadside overlooks** (Pha Diew Die, on the way to the radar station, is the highest), is **Nam Tok Kong Kaew**, a small waterfall right behind the visitor centre. The biggest waterfall, just a 1km walk from the road in the far south of the park, is **Nam Tok Haew Narok**, whose three levels combine to form a 150m drop, but the beauty award goes to 25m **Nam Tok Haew Suwat**, which scooped a starring role in Danny Boyle's film *The Beach*. You can swim in the pool at the bottom. Though easily reached by car, this forest-encased jewel is best reached via 8km **Trail 1**, a somewhat challenging path (take a compass, you often have to take long detours around fallen trees) that connects it and other waterfalls to the visitor centre. There is a good chance of seeing gibbons and hornbills and it's probably the best footpath (the roads are better) for spotting elephants, though encounters are unlikely.

It's 5.4km from the visitor centre to **Nong Phak Chi observation tower** along **Trail 5**. This tower (there's another close to the visitor centre) overlooks a little lake and a salt lick and is one of the best wildlife-spotting spots in the park. This is the most likely place you'll see a tiger, but you have to be very lucky – like lottery-winner lucky – to do so. Three-kilometre-long **Trail 9** is a seldom-used path to this tower, but it's the better bet for spotting animals on your way. The shortest route to the tower, ideal for getting there at dawn or dusk (the best wildlife-watching times), is a 1km path along a creek bed, starting near Km pillar 35.

Most other hiking trails, some of them formed by the movement of wildlife, are not as well trodden, so guides are recommended. No matter what trail you take, you should wear boots and long trousers – some of the paths get a little rough and during the rainy season leeches are a problem – mosquito repellent also helps keep them away. The staff at the visitor centre gives hiking advice (especially important in the rainy season) and offers **bike rental** (per hr/day 50/200B).

Outside the park, about 10km from the northern gate, is a **bat cave** that begins disgorging millions of rare wrinkle-lipped bats around 5.30pm. Your hotel can direct you to the best viewing point.

Many of the guesthouses around Khao Yai offer **park tours** (Greenleaf Guest House and Khao Yai Garden Lodge have earned widespread praise) and this is really the ideal way to visit. Full-day programmes usually include a 'night safari' (which is your best chance to see elephants); lunch, snacks and water; and, in the rainy season, 'leech socks' (that are actually gaiters). Prices start around 1000B, though do some careful comparison shopping because some companies include the park entrance fee while others do not. Birdwatching, trekking and other speciality tours make good second-day add-ons to the standard tours. Half-day tours are also available, but just too short to be recommended. Reservations are unnecessary, but guides can get booked out by school groups so it's not a bad idea to call ahead. Rangers, if they are free, can sometimes be hired as guides, at the visitor centre. Prices are negotiable, but 500B for a trail walk seems to be the going rate.

Sleeping & Eating

There are also dozens of places to stay in and around the nearby town of Pak Chong. Touts at the train station and bus stops are helpful (if in doubt, call the hotel yourself, most have English-speaking staff), since the best places for visiting the park are south of town along Rte 2090 (Th Thanarat) and they can get you a free ride there.

our pick **Greenleaf Guest House** (☎ 0 4436 5024; www.greenleaftour.com; Th Thanarat, Km 7.5; r 200-300B) Half-home, half-guesthouse, this old favourite has some of the few budget rooms outside town. It's a bit ragged, but the friendly, English-speaking owners keep the rooms spotless.

Khao Yai Garden Lodge (☎ 0 4436 5178; www
.khaoyai-garden-lodge.com; Th Thanarat, Km 7; r 350-2500B;
🅿 🖳 🕲) Previous owners had let standards
slide more than just a little, but the new owners appear to have righted the ship, which is
good news because the lovely garden and individually decorated rooms (available starting at
the mid-price level) make for a lovely stay.

Juldis Khao Yai Resort (☎ 0 4429 7297; juldis@khaoyai
.com; Th Thanarat, Km 17; r 1430-5200B; 🅿 🖳 🕲) This
plush place is one of the Khao Yai area originals, and offers tennis courts, spa treatments,
pleasant gardens and airy rooms.

Kirimaya (☎ 0 4442 6000; www.kirimaya.com; Rte
3052; r 8475-16,575B, tented villa 31,780B; 🅿 🖳 🕲)
The first impression of this luxury resort-spa
is usually either 'Wow!' or stunned silence.
Step 'through' the wooden front doors and
you are greeted by a towering stilted restaurant and other Thai-Bali fusion buildings,
all rising from a lotus- and reed-filled pond.
All rooms have bamboo furniture, balconies
and all the mod cons. We're not too keen on
having an 18-hole golf course on the edge of
the park (even one designed by Jack Nicklaus),
but there is no denying this place is special.
It's 7km east of the park gate.

The best setting for sleeping is, of course,
in the park itself. There are two **camp sites**
(per person 30B, 2-person tent rental 100B), basic two-
sleeper **bungalows** (r 800B) and rather fancier
three-bedroom **villas** (3500B) with air-con and
fridge. Simple **dorms** (50B) are another option,
but only when not in use by groups.

Each of the lodges listed above serve good
food and there are many lovely, garden restaurants near them along Th Thanarat. The
park itself has five restaurants: at the visitor
centre, the Orchid Campsite, the Lam Ta-
khong Campsite, Nam Tok Haew Suwat and
Nam Tok Haew Narok. Even the camp site
ones close early, so plan ahead.

Getting There & Away

From Bangkok take a bus (ordinary/air-con
115/148B, 2½ hours, every 20 minutes) from
the Northern bus terminal to Pak Chong.
From Khorat, just about all Bangkok-bound
buses also stop in Pak Chong (ordinary/air-
con 45/77B, 1½ hours). You can also get to
Pak Chong by train from Bangkok, Ayuthaya
or Khorat, but it is slower than the bus, especially if coming from Bangkok.

Săwngthăew travel the 26km from Pak
Chong to the park's northern gate (25B, 45

minutes) from in front of the 7-Eleven store
that's about 300m west of the ordinary bus
terminal (air-con buses stop at their own
offices at various points on the main road). It's
another 14km to the visitor centre and park
guards are used to talking drivers into hauling
faràng (Westerner) up there.

Some shops on Pak Chong's main road rent
out motorcycles.

BURIRAM PROVINCE

Touch down in the little provincial capital
of Buriram, at the heart of one of Thailand's
larger provinces, and you might wonder what
all the fuss is about. Despite hanging on to half
of its historic moat, the city is a hard sell as a
tourist destination. The best advice is to make
a beeline into the countryside, where you will
find a landscape chock-a-block with tradition and peppered with ruins (143 of them).
Most sit in the southern half of the province,
which is poised to secede from Buriram; some
government offices have already put up Nang
Rong Province signs.

The crowning glory is Phanom Rung, a
beautifully restored Khmer temple complex
straddling the summit of an extinct volcano.
The most spectacular Angkor monument in
Thailand, Phanom Rung is worth the journey
and should impress even those suffering acute
temple overload.

BURIRAM & NANG RONG
บุรีรัมย์
pop 30,000
The forgettable capital of Buriram is a possible base for exploring the region's temples,
but the accommodation scene is poor and
there's very little to keep you occupied so most
people bed down in Nang Rong, 54km to the
south, which has a full range of services and
several good guesthouses, before and after
their ruin runs. Surin is another reasonable
place to base yourself.

Information
Bangkok Bank (Th Thani; 🕙 8.30am-3.30pm) Has ATM
and exchange facilities.
Buriram Comnet (8-10 Th Niwat; per hr 15B; 🕙 8am-
9pm) Check your email here.
Post office (Th E-san; 🕙 8.30am-4.30pm Mon-Fri, 9am-
noon Sat, Sun & holidays)
Tourist police (☎ 1155; Th Niwat)

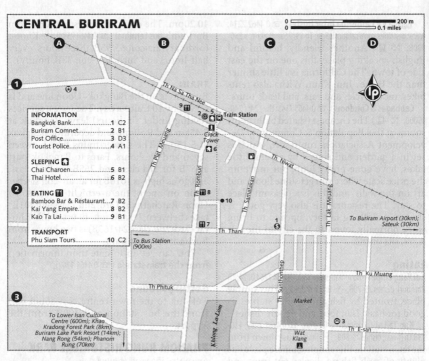

CENTRAL BURIRAM

INFORMATION	
Bangkok Bank.................1	C2
Buriram Comnet.............2	B1
Post Office.....................3	D3
Tourist Police................4	A1

SLEEPING	
Chai Charoen................5	B1
Thai Hotel....................6	B2

EATING	
Bamboo Bar & Restaurant...7	B2
Kai Yang Empire............8	B2
Kao Ta Lai....................9	B1

TRANSPORT	
Phu Siam Tours............10	C2

Sights

Rajabhat University's **Lower Isan Cultural Centre** (☎ 0 4461 1221; Th Jira; admission free; ☒ 8.30am-4.30pm), in the building with the stupa-shaped roof, suffers from neglect, but the elephant-handling display is worth a look.

For panoramic views of the city, join the immense Buddha image atop little **Khao Kradong Forest Park** (Hwy 219; ☒ 6am-6pm). On the drive up you'll see what is assumed to be the crater of an extinct volcano; going down there's a sculpture of an elephant prostrating itself before the Lord Buddha. If you are using public transport, any bus heading south will drop you at the entrance where you can climb the 197-step staircase.

Sleeping

BURIRAM

Chai Charoen (no roman-script sign; ☎ 0 4461 1559; Th Niwat; r 120-180B) This scruffy place next to the train station is fast approaching fleapit, but the rooms aren't as grubby as the rest of the joint.

Thai Hotel (☎ 0 4461 1112; 38/1 Th Romburi; r 180-400B; ☒) The Thai could be quite nice if it just made half an effort. As it is, there are passable rooms, and plenty of them.

Buriram Lake Park Resort (☎ 0 4460 5169; www.birdresort.com; Hwy 219; r 500-1500B; ☒) If you are travelling with kids in tow, they will never be bored at this large resort on Huay Talat Reservoir, 12km south of the city. There is a small zoo, wandering peacocks, a dinosaur slide and thousands of herons and waterfowl living on the lake. The log-cabin bungalows are large and lovely, but a few that we saw needed a bit of repair so look closely before choosing.

NANG RONG

our pick Honey Inn (☎ 0 4462 2825; www.honeyinn.com; 8/1 Soi Si Kun; r 200-350B; ☒ ☐) This welcoming guesthouse, 1km from the bus station, is run by a knowledgeable retired English teacher. The rooms are simple but bright and a lot of travellers tips get shared among guests. Car and motorcycle rental, guided tours and food (with advance notice) are all available at good prices. To find it, walk north from the bus station and cross the main road, then head east until you see the sign; or take a săamláw for 30B.

our pick **P California Inter Hostel** (☎ 0 4462 2214; www.geocities.com/california8gh; Th 59/9 Sangkakrit; r 250-500B; 🔀 🖵) Another friendly, helpful and English-speaking place, this one on the east side of town. The California is a little shinier than the Honey Inn. Khun Wicha also rents bikes, motorcycles and cars, and leads tours.

Cabbages & Condoms (☎ 0 4465 7145; Hwy 24; r 240-1500B; 🔀 🖵) The cheapest (shared bathroom) rooms at this Population & Community Development Association–run resort, which is set in a garden and ringed by several little lakes, have gone pretty limp, but move up the price scale where you get stone floors and art on the walls, and this is a pleasant place to stay. The restaurant is also very good. A shoe and clothing factory, opened to bring work normally found in the city to the villages, sits onsite.

Eating

Kai Yang Empire (no roman-script sign; ☎ 08 1264 0624; Th Romburi; dishes 25-70B; 🕑 lunch & dinner) This simple place, fronted by fish and rooster statues, is good for basic Isan food and noodle dishes.

Kao Ta Lai (no roman-script sign; ☎ 0 4461 2089; 136-138 Th Niwat; dishes 25-80B; 🕑 dinner) Just down from the train station, this simple Chinese place has plenty of fresh fish on display out front and cauldrons of oddities to pick from inside.

Bamboo Bar & Restaurant (☎ 0 4462 5577; 14/13 Th Romburi; dishes 40-290B; 🕑 breakfast, lunch & dinner) With a dartboard, satellite TV and entire walls covered with Heineken and Chang cans, this is the home-away-from-home of Buriram's expat set. It has a lively atmosphere once the drinking starts, and the menu includes Western staples like schnitzel and spaghetti. It rents motorcycles for 200B per day.

There are also some restaurants and simple food stalls at Phanom Rung Historical Park.

Getting There & Away

AIR

PB Air (☎ in Bangkok 0 2261 0222; www.pbair.com) flies to Bangkok (one way 2360B, 50 minutes) five days a week. Buy tickets at **Phu Siam Tours** (☎ 0 4462 5065; Th Romburi; 🕑 8am-5pm) in the back of the Speed Music Complex.

BUS

Air-con buses to Bangkok's Northern bus terminal (227B, six hours) depart all day long; **999 VIP** (☎ 0 4461 5081), with an office at the terminal, has a daily 24-seater (450B) at 10.20pm. The other main destinations from Buriram's **bus terminal** (☎ 0 4461 2534) are Khorat (ordinary/air-con 65/95B, three hours, every half-hour) and Surin (air-con 35B, hourly).

TRAIN

Buriram is on the Bangkok–Ubon line and is served by 10 trains a day. The fastest services (taking under six hours) leave Bangkok at 5.45am and 9.50pm, and depart for Bangkok at 5.15pm. The slower trains take between seven and 8½ hours. Fares to Bangkok start at 67B for 3rd class and 265B for 2nd class, and go as high as 1016B for an air-con sleeper cabin on one of the overnight services. To Ubon Ratchathani (3rd/2nd class 40/201B) takes between 2½ and four hours, while Khorat (3rd/2nd class 24/165B) is two hours from Buriram on most trains.

You can get up-to-date train information from the **train station** (☎ 0 4461 1202).

Getting Around

Túk-túk to the town centre cost about 40B from the bus station and 400B from the airport.

PHANOM RUNG HISTORICAL PARK

อุทยานประวัติศาสตร์เขาพนมรุ้ง

Phanom Rung (Big Hill; ☎ 0 4463 1746; admission 40B; 🕑 6am-6pm) has a knock-me-dead location. Crowning the summit of a spent volcano, this sanctuary sits a good 70 storeys above the flat paddy fields below. To the southeast you can clearly see Cambodia's Dongrek mountains, and it's in this direction that the capital of the Angkor empire once lay. The Phanom Rung temple complex is the largest and best restored Khmer monument in Thailand (it took 17 years to complete the restoration) and, although it's not the easiest place to reach, it more than rewards those who make the effort.

The Phanom Rung temple was erected between the 10th and 13th centuries, the bulk of it during the reign of King Suriyavarman II (r AD 1113–50), which by all accounts was the apex of Angkor architecture. The complex faces east, towards the original Angkor capital. Of the three other great Khmer monuments of Southeast Asia, Cambodia's Angkor Wat faces west, its Prasat Khao Wihan faces north and Thailand's Prasat Phimai faces southeast. Nobody knows for sure whether these orientations have any special significance, especially

as most smaller Khmer monuments in Thailand face east (towards the dawn – typical of Hindu temple orientation).

If you can, plan your visit for one of the four times when the sun shines through all 15 sanctuary doorways. The correct solar alignment happens during sunrise on 3–5 April and 8–10 September and sunset on 5–7 March and 5–7 October. In leap years it begins one day earlier. The park extends its hours during this event. Also, on the first Saturday of April, local people have their own special celebration, the **Climbing Khao Phanom Rung Festival**, which commemorates the restoration of Phanom Rung. During the morning there is a procession up Khao Phanom Rung, and at night-time sound-and-light shows and dance-dramas are performed in the temple complex.

Below the main sanctuary, after the long row of gift shops, an **Information Centre** (admission free; ☽ 9am-4.30pm) houses a scale model of the area, artefacts found at the site, and displays about both the construction and restoration. Guides (fees are negotiable) offer their services at the complex, but when we last visited none spoke English. It's possible that bungalows will be available in the future, but it's unlikely.

Design

One of the most remarkable design aspects of Phanom Rung is the promenade leading to the main gate. This is the best surviving example in Thailand. It begins on a slope 400m east of

the main tower, with three earthen terraces. Next comes a cruciform base for what may have been a wooden pavilion. To the right of this is a stone hall known locally as Rohng Cháng Phèuak (White Elephant Hall) where royalty bathed and changed clothes before entering the temple complex. Flower garlands to be used as offerings in the temple may also have been handed out here. After you step down from the pavilion area, you'll come to a 160m avenue paved with laterite and sandstone blocks, and flanked by sandstone pillars with lotus-bud tops, said to be early Angkor style (AD 1100–80). The avenue ends at the first and largest of three *naga* (mythical serpent-like creature) bridges. The first is flanked by 16 five-headed *naga* in the classic Angkor style – in fact, these figures are identical to those found at Angkor Wat.

After passing this bridge and climbing the stairway you come to the magnificent east gallery leading into the main sanctuary. The central *prasat* (building with a cruciform ground plan and needle-like spire) has a gallery on each of its four sides and the entrance to each gallery is itself a smaller version of the main tower. The galleries have curvilinear roofs and false-balustrade windows. Once inside the temple walls, have a look at each of the galleries and the *gopura* (entrance pavilion), paying particular attention to the lintels over the porticoes. The craftsmanship at Phanom Rung represents the pinnacle of Khmer artistic achievement, on par with the reliefs at Angkor Wat in Cambodia.

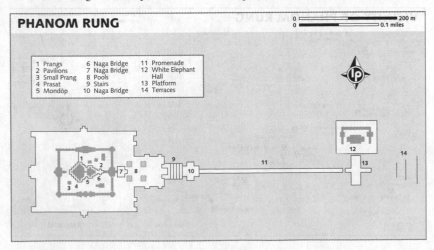

PHANOM RUNG

0 ──── 200 m
0 ──── 0.1 miles

1 Prangs	6 Naga Bridge	11 Promenade
2 Pavilions	7 Naga Bridge	12 White Elephant
3 Small Prang	8 Pools	Hall
4 Prasat	9 Stairs	13 Platform
5 Mondòp	10 Naga Bridge	14 Terraces

Sculpture

The Phanom Rung complex was originally constructed as a Hindu monument and exhibits iconography related to the worship of Vishnu and Shiva. Excellent sculptures of both Vaishnava and Shaiva deities can be seen in the lintels or pediments over the doorways to the central monuments and in various other key points on the sanctuary exterior. On the east portico of the *mondòp* (square, spired building) is found a Nataraja (Dancing Shiva), which is late Baphuan or early Angkor style, while on the south entrance are the remains of Shiva and Uma riding their bull mount, Nandi. The central cell of the *prasat* contains a Shivalingam (phallus image).

Several sculpted images of Vishnu and his incarnations, Rama and Krishna, decorate various other lintels and cornices. Probably the most beautiful is the Phra Narai lintel, a relief depicting a reclining Vishnu (Narayana) in the Hindu creation myth. Growing from his navel is a lotus that branches into several blossoms, on one of which sits the creator god Brahma. On either side of Vishnu are heads of Kala, the god of time and death. He is asleep on the milky sea of eternity, here represented by a *naga*. This lintel sits above the eastern gate (the main entrance) beneath the Shiva Nataraja relief.

Getting There & Away

Phanom Rung can be approached from Khorat, Buriram or Surin. From Buriram take a Chanthaburi-bound bus to Ban Ta Pek

(ordinary/air-con 35/55B, every 40 minutes, 1½ hours), where you'll need to hire a motorcycle taxi (150B) or såwngthåew (three people 300B) to take you the rest of the way. These rates include waiting times while you tour the ruins.

Buses from Nang Rong to Chanthaburi also pass through Ban Ta Pek (20B, 30 minutes, every 40 minutes), or you can take one of the five daily såwngthåew (20B, 45 minutes) from the market on the east end of town that go to the foot of the mountain, while a motorcycle taxi to the top will cost about 30B less.

Those coming by bus from Khorat (air-con 78B, two hours) or Surin (air-con 65B, two hours) should get off at Ban Ta-Ko, a well-marked turn-off about 14km east of Nang Rong. Once in Ban Ta-Ko you can wait for one of the buses or såwngthåew from Nang Rong that will pass through Ban Ta Pek (10B) and then continue as above, or take a motorcycle taxi all the way to Phanom Rung (return 300B).

PRASAT MEUANG TAM

ปราสาทเมืองต่ำ

In the little village of Khok Meuang, the restored Khmer temple of **Prasat Meuang Tam** (Lower City; admission 30B; 🕑 6am-6pm) is an ideal bolt-on to any visit to Phanom Rung, which is only 7km to the northwest. Dating back to the late 10th or early 11th century and sponsored by King Jayavarman V, this is probably Isan's third most interesting temple complex – after Phanom Rung and Phimai; fourth if you

VICINITY OF PHANOM RUNG

0 ——— 20 km
0 ——— 12 miles

count Khao Phra Wihan – in terms of size, atmosphere and the quality of restoration work. The whole complex is surrounded by laterite walls, within which are four lotus-filled reservoirs, each guarded by whimsical five-headed *naga*.

Sandstone galleries and *gopura,* the latter exquisitely carved, surround five *prang.* The principal *prang* could not be rebuilt and the remaining towers, being brick, are not nearly as tall or as imposing as the sandstone *prang* at Phanom Rung. The plan is based on the same design as that of Angkor Wat: the five peaks of Mt Meru, the mythical abode of the Hindu gods. A Shivalingam found in the central tower suggests that the temple was once a shrine to Shiva. Also, a lintel from the principal *prang* depicted Shiva and his consort Uma riding the sacred bull, Nandi. It can be seen, along with other related exhibits labelled in English, in the small **information centre** (admission free; ☺ 8am-5pm), across the road from the temple. Any motorcycle taxi driver will add Meuang Tam onto Phanom Rung for about 100B to 150B.

OTHER RUINS

For those with an insatiable appetite for Khmer ruins, Buriram offers a smorgasbord of lesser-known sites that, taken together, create a picture of the crucial role this region once played in the Khmer empire. Even history buffs will likely find these places of only minor interest, but driving through this rice-growing region offers an unvarnished look at village life and you will surely have an enlightening trip. Note that many roads around here are in terrible shape.

At the time of writing, all of the following sites, restored or stabilised to some degree by the Fine Arts Department, were free of charge and open during daylight hours. **Kuti Reusi Nong Bua Rai** sits right between Phanom Rung and Meuang Tam, so you might as well stop if you are heading to the latter. **Kuti Reusi Khok Meuang** is just south of Prasat Meuang Tam, while you have to hike in to **Prasat Khao Praibat**. Further east, near Ban Kruat, are **Prasat Thong** and **Prasat Baibak**. **Prasat Ban Khok Ngiew** is the only one of these sites that can conveniently be reached by public transport from Nang Rong; any sǎwngthǎew heading south will drop you off.

Archaeologists assume that much of the rock used to build these ancient structures

came from the widely scattered **Ban Kruat Quarry.** Nearby are two restored kilns, **Tao Sawai** and **Tao Nai Chian**, that supplied pottery to much of the Khmer empire.

You can easily tack on **Prasat Ta Meuan** (p542), a secluded Khmer complex on the Thai–Cambodian border that, though it lies in Surin Province, is more conveniently visited from this region. It's 55km from Phanom Rung.

WAT KHAO ANGKHAN
วัดเขาอังคาร

Although the peaceful temple atop this extinct volcano has an ancient past, as evidenced by the 8th or 9th century Dvaravati sandstone boundary markers, it's the modern constructions that make **Wat Khao Angkhan** (☺ daylight hours) worth a visit. The *bòt* and several other flamboyant buildings were erected in 1982 in an unusual nouveau-Khmer style that sort of harkens back to the age of empire. Inside the *bòt,* the *jataka* murals, painted by Burmese artists, have English captions. The wat also hosts a Chinese-style pagoda, a 29m reclining Buddha, and beautiful views of the surrounding mountains and forest.

The temple is about 20km from Nang Rong or Phanom Rung. The route is pretty well signed, but you will have to ask directions at some junctions. There is no public transport. A motorcycle taxi from Ban Ta Pek could cost as little as 150B.

CHAIYAPHUM PROVINCE

Travelling through Chaiyaphum Province, you're almost as likely to run into a tiger as a foreign tourist – and this is not a province with a lot of tigers. Despite its position at the heart of the country, it is a remote region and remains something of a mystery, even to Thais. Famous for its fields of flowers – and not a whole lot else – Chaiyaphum has several sights worth a peep, but its primary appeals are the peace and quiet and sense of straying off the beaten track.

History

In the late 18th century a Lao court official brought 200 Lao from Vientiane to settle this area, which had been abandoned by the

Khmers some 500 years earlier. The community paid tribute to Vientiane but also cultivated relations with Bangkok and Champasak. When Prince Anou (from Vientiane) declared war on Siam in the early 19th century, the Lao ruler of Chaiyaphum, Jao Phraya Lae, wisely switched allegiance to Bangkok, knowing that Anou's armies didn't stand a chance against the more powerful Siamese. Although Jao Phraya Lae lost his life in battle in 1806, the Siamese sacked Vientiane in 1828 and ruled most of western Laos until the coming of the French near the end of the 19th century. Today a statue of Jao Phraya Lae (renamed Phraya Phakdi Chumphon by the Thais) stands at the entrance to the capital city

CHAIYAPHUM & AROUND

ชัยภูมิ

pop 55,500

Chaiyaphum is a bit of a nowhere town and is a base for visiting the surrounding attractions – all just a short hop outside the city – rather than a destination in itself. In brief, silk lovers should head west to the village of Ban Khwao and the outdoorsy should head to the mountains where the relatively unknown Tat Ton National Park is the star of several national parks in the area.

Information

Bangkok Bank (Th Sanambin, Lotus Department Store; 10am-8pm) The city's only late-opening bank does foreign exchange.

Pat Pat (☎ 0 4483 0037; Th Tantawan; per hr 15B; 9.30am-10pm) Friendly internet café and good source of information about Chaiyaphum.

Post office (Th Bannakan; 8.30am-4.30pm Mon-Fri, 9am-noon Sat, Sun & holidays)

Sights
BAN KHWAO
บ้านเขว้า

Most visitors to Chaiyaphum are here for the silk village of **Ban Khwao**, 13km southwest of town on Rte 225, where nearly 50 shops sell fabric and clothing. The **Silk Development Centre** (☎ 0 4489 1101; admission free; 8am-5pm) by the market has displays about silk-making and will soon offer day-long tours: if you've never observed the process – from the cultivation of mulberry trees and propagation of silkworms to the dyeing and weaving of silk thread – you're in for an interesting day. Since over 200 families produce fabric, many using *mát-mìi* methods, you'll also be able to see some of the steps on your own if you wander around. Săwngthăew to Ban Khwao (15B, 20 minutes, every 20 minutes) leave from in front of Pat Pat internet café.

TAMNAK KHEO
ตำหนักเขียว

Tamnak Kheo (Green Hall; ☎ 0 4481 1574; off Th Burapha; admission free; 10am-noon & 2-4pm), built in 1950 as the governor's residence and now restored as a museum, has displays of old *mát-mìi* cloth and photos from King Rama IX's 1955 visit. The classic wooden house itself is more interesting than the displays.

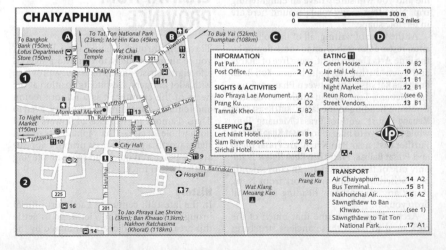

CHAIYAPHUM

0 ——— 300 m
0 ——— 0.2 miles

INFORMATION		
Pat Pat	1	A2
Post Office	2	A2

SIGHTS & ACTIVITIES		
Jao Phraya Lae Monument	3	A2
Prang Ku	4	D2
Tamnak Kheo	5	B2

SLEEPING		
Lert Nimit Hotel	6	B1
Siam River Resort	7	B2
Sirichai Hotel	8	A1

EATING		
Green House	9	B1
Jae Hai Lek	10	A2
Night Market	11	B1
Night Market	12	B1
Reun Rom	(see 6)	
Street Vendors	13	B1

TRANSPORT		
Air Chaiyaphum	14	A2
Bus Terminal	15	B1
Nakhonchai Air	16	A2
Săwngthăew to Ban Khwao	(see 1)	
Săwngthăew to Tat Ton National Park	17	A1

To Bangkok Bank (150m); Lotus Department Store (150m)

To Tat Ton National Park (23km); Mor Hin Kao (45km)

To Bua Yai (52km); Chumphae (108km)

Chinese Temple
Wat Chai Prasit
Th Non Meuang
Th Chaiprasit
Th Niwetrat
Th Yutitham
Municipal Market
Th Ratchathan
Soi Ban Hin Tang
Th Burapha
Th Talord
To Night Market (750m)
Th Tantawan
City Hall
Th Hanthathan
Th Manithan
Th Haruthat
Th Bannakan
Hospital
Wat Klang Meuang Kao
Wat Prang Ku

To Jao Phraya Lae Shrine (3km); Ban Khwao (13km); Nakhon Ratchasima (Khorat) (118km)

MÁT-MÌI

Thanks to growing interest from both Thais and foreigners, the once-fading Isan tradition of *mát-mìi* has undergone a major revival and is now one of Thailand's best-known weaving styles. Similar to Indonesian *ikat*, *mát-mìi* is a tie-dye process (*mát* is 'tie' and *mìi* is 'strands') that results in a geometric pattern repeatedly turning back on itself as it runs up the fabric. The wider the pattern, the more complicated the process. No matter what the design, every *mát-mìi* fabric has an ever-so-slight blur to it, which, more than anything else, makes it so distinct.

To start, the weavers string their thread – either silk or cotton, but usually silk – tightly across a wooden frame sized exactly as wide as the finished fabric will be. Almost always working from memory, the weavers then tie plastic (traditionally the skin of banana plant stalks were used) around bunches of strands in their desired design. The frame is then dipped in the dye (usually a chemical colour, though natural sources such as flowers and tree bark are regaining popularity), which grips the exposed thread but leaves the wrapped sections clean. The wrapping and dipping continues for multiple rounds, which results in intricate, complex patterns that come to life on the loom. The more you see of the process, the more you realise how amazing it is that the finished product turns out so beautifully.

Most of the patterns, usually abstract representations of natural objects such as trees and birds, are handed down from mother to daughter, but increasingly designers are working with weaving groups to create modern patterns, which invariably fetch higher prices. Some silk weavers now fetch outlandish prices for their artistry. On the other hand, a two-colour cotton pattern, which can be turned out in a matter of days, might cost as little as 60B per metre.

PRANG KU
ปรางค์กู่

This hollow Khmer **prang** (⊙ daylight hours), about 800m east of the **Jao Phraya Lae monument**, was constructed during the reign of the final Angkor king, Jayavarman VII (AD 1181–1219), as a place of worship at a 'healing station' on the Angkor temple route between the Angkor capital in Cambodia and Prasat Singh in Kanchanaburi Province. It's not much to look at and has just one poorly preserved lintel, but it's the top ancient site in the province – which is why history buffs don't flock to Chaiyaphum. The Buddha figure inside the *ku* (hollow, cave-like stupa) purportedly hails from the Dvaravati period (6th to 10th centuries).

TAT TON NATIONAL PARK
อุทยานแห่งชาติตาดโตน

It isn't the grandest of reserves, but **Tat Ton National Park** (☎ 0 4485 3293, reservations 0 2562 0760; admission 400B; ⊙ 7am-6pm) gets few weekday visitors and makes a pleasant escape for those who really want to get away from it all. Covering 218 sq km at the edge of the Laen Da mountain range, 23km north of the city, Tat Ton is best known for its photogenic namesake 6m-high waterfall, which stretches 50m wide during the May to October monsoon, but flows year-round. You'll probably be the only sightseer at

the park's other smaller waterfalls, including **Tat Fah**, which is the most beautiful.

The park has **camp sites** (per person 30B, 3-person tent hire 300B) and 13 **bungalows** (4 people from 1200B), plus a restaurant and snack shops.

Some *săwngthăew* pass the park entrance road (25B, 45 minutes) every morning, but you'll have to walk 1.5km to the falls. Or stop in Ban Tat Ton (15B, 30 minutes), and hire a túk-túk for about 200B with an hour or so wait.

MOR HIN KHAO
มอหินขาว

Oddly promoted as the 'Stonehenge of Thailand', **Mor Hin Khao** contains a line of five natural stone pinnacles with tapered bottoms rising to 15m. Two fields of less dramatic, but still oddly sculpted rocks lie further up the mountain, beyond the reforestation office. The route to the rocks, 20km northwest of Tat Ton via rough country roads, will be paved and signed in English sometime in the near future, but until then it's very difficult to find, so inquire at the park visitor centre. Someone from the park might ride with you if you ask. A camp site is also planned, which will be welcome because the site can be spectacular at sunset. Call the **Ministry of Sports & Tourism** (☎ 0 4481 1218) in Chaiyaphum for updates.

Festivals & Events

Chaiyaphum residents celebrate two week-long festivals yearly in honour of **Jao Phraya Lae** (see p471 for more on this ruler). The one starting January 12, the date of his death, takes place at City Hall, near his statue, while activities in mid-May focus on a shrine erected on the spot where he was killed, about 3km southwest of town off the road to Ban Khwao. Both events feature music, dance and an elephant parade.

Sleeping

Lert Nimit Hotel (☎ 0 4481 1522; 447 Th Niwetrat; r 200-800B; ☒) Step past the stylish lobby and this hotel is pretty ordinary, but the rooms are pleasant enough, though the fan-cooled ones are slightly dowdy. Rooms at the back have lovely mountain views.

Sirichai Hotel (☎ 0 4481 1461; 565/1 Th Non Meuang; r 340-1000B; ☒) The Sirichai boasts similar standards as the Lert Nimit, though the cheaper rooms are a little bigger and better. Smiling staff make up for the lack of atmosphere.

Siam River Resort (☎ 0 4481 1999; off Th Bannakan; r 800-1800B, ste 3500B; ☒) Chaiyaphum doesn't cater to droves of tourists, but this shiny new hotel out of earshot of the hubbub of the city (what little there is, anyway) is betting this will change. Free bikes for guest use.

Eating

Jae Hai Lek (no roman-script sign; ☎ 0 4607 7819; Th Tantawan; dishes 20-55B; ☒ breakfast, lunch & dinner) A simple, friendly all-vegetarian affair with a range of Thai and Chinese standards.

Green House (☎ 08 7245 2622; 299/20 Th Nonthankhon; dishes 35-150B; ☒ dinner) The most laid-back of several garden restaurants on this end of Th Nonthankhon, and the only one with an English menu (though it lists just a few of the many dishes available). The food and service are excellent.

Reun Rom (☎ 0 4481 1522; 447 Th Niwetrat; dishes 30-800B; ☒ breakfast, lunch & dinner; ☒) The Lert Nimit Hotel's restaurant serves good Thai and Western food, including pancakes, and the menu lists four pages of seafood. It is open right through to the witching hour.

You might want to try *mahm* (sour beef and liver) sausages in Chaiyaphum's lacklustre **night market** (☒ 5-10pm), a short stroll west of the city centre, since locals claim it makes Isan's best. There are also two food-only night markets by the bus terminal, and the street vendors near the park on Th Ratchathan stay open early to late.

Getting There & Away

Nakhonchai Air (☎ 0 4481 2522), with evening-only services to Ubon Ratchathani (air-con 510B, six hours) and Chiang Mai (VIP 750B, four hours), and **Air Chaiyaphum** (☎ 0 4481 1556), with hourly services to Bangkok, have their own southern offices.

Government buses to/from Khon Kaen (ordinary/air-con 70/85B, 2½ hours, hourly), Khorat (ordinary/air-con 60/108B, two hours, hourly) and Bangkok's Northern bus terminal (air-con 270B, five hours, 14 daily) use Chaiyaphum's bus terminal.

Getting Around

A túk-túk should cost no more than 25B for any destination in town.

KHON KAEN & ROI ET PROVINCES

Khon Kaen and Roi Et, where farming and textiles still dominate life, lie at the heart of Isan and are excellent places to dip a toe into the region's culture without having to rough it. On the flipside, things are booming in Khon Kaen itself and the city makes for a lively stopover if you fancy a quick slug of metropolitan living.

KHON KAEN

ขอนแก่น

pop 145,300

Khon Kaen is the darling of Isan's economic boomtime. The skyline rises high, neon illuminates the night, and a bumper crop of bars and restaurants entertain an expanding middle class. As the site of the northeast's largest university and an important hub for all things commercial and financial, the city is youthful, educated and on the move.

Of course, not everyone will feel the urge to celebrate in Khon Kaen's downtown clubs. With a sterile concrete veneer blanketing most of the centre, this big city has inherited little of Isan's idiosyncratic appeal. Wandering through traffic, with office blocks above, it sometimes takes the elephants, trudging down the busy city-centre streets, to remind you that you are in Thailand at all.

But with fine eateries, swanky hotel rooms and plenty of places to wear holes in your dancing shoes, Khon Kaen is the ideal spot to decompress after humping it through the northeast's quieter corners.

History

The city gets its name from Phra That Kham Kaen, a revered *chedi* at Wat Chetiyaphum in the village of Ban Kham, 32km to the northeast. Legend says that early in the last millennium a *thâat* (four-sided, curvilinear reliquary stupa) was built over a tamarind tree stump that miraculously came to life after a contingent of monks carrying Buddha relics to Phra That Phanom (in today's Nakhon Phanom Province) camped here overnight. There was no room at That Phanom for more relics, so the monks returned to this spot and enshrined the relics in the new That Kham Kaen (Tamarind Heartwood Reliquary). A town developed nearby, but was abandoned several times until 1789 when a Suwannaphum ruler founded a city at the current site, which he named Kham Kaen after the *chedi*. Over the years the name has changed to Khon Kaen (Heartwood Log).

Orientation & Information

Khon Kaen has two nearly adjacent tourist centres. Most budget and midrange hotels lie between the bus stations, on or near Th Klang Meuang. The upmarket choices are all a quick hop to the southeast in the city's nightlife district. There are good eats in both places.

CONSULATES

Laos (☎ 0 4324 2858; 171 Th Prachasamoson; ⊙ 8am-noon & 1-4pm Mon-Fri) Normal turnaround for visas is three days, but for an extra 200B you can get immediate service. It only accepts baht, and at a poor exchange rate.

Vietnam (☎ 0 4324 1586; Th Chatapadung; ⊙ 8.30-11.30am & 2-4pm Mon-Fri) Visas ready next day.

EMERGENCY & MEDICAL SERVICES

Khon Kaen Ram Hospital (☎ 0 4333 3800; Th Si Chan) For specialist and 24-hour emergency care.
Tourist police (☎ 1155; Th Mittaphap) Next to HomePro.

INTERNET ACCESS

There are dozens of internet cafés in town.
Meeting Net (no roman-script sign; 54/6 Th Klang Meuang; per hr 15B; ⊙ 24hr)

MONEY

There are banks with exchange and ATM facilities across Khon Kaen.
Siam Commercial Bank (Th Si Chan, Oasis Plaza; ⊙ 10.30am-8pm) One of several banks in this area.

POST

Main post office (Th Klang Meuang; ⊙ 8.30am-4.30pm Mon-Fri, 9.30am-noon Sat, Sun & holidays)

TOURIST INFORMATION

TAT (☎ 0 4324 4498; www.tourismthailand.org; 15/5 Th Prachasamoson; ⊙ 8.30am-4.30pm) Distributes maps of the city and can answer queries on Khon Kaen and the surrounding provinces. It has information about an informal temple-stay programme at Wat Tee Pak Sonk Sa Wang Porn in Amphoe Khao Suan Kwang.

TRAVEL AGENCIES

Air Booking & Travel Centre (☎ 0 4324 4482; 403 Th Si Chan; ⊙ 8.30am-6pm Mon-Sat) Books flights and makes other travel arrangements.

Sights

Although it doesn't seem like it at first look, there is more to do in Khon Kaen than revel in

---

TIES THAT BIND THAIS

To occupy yourself on long bus rides through Isan, do a survey of passengers wearing thin white strings around their wrists. In rural villages in Isan, elders and family members assemble to tie *fâi phùuk khâen* (sacred thread) as a bon voyage measure. The strings act as leashes for important guardian spirits and ensure safety during a trip or success in a new venture. The ceremony is also used on newlyweds.

Strings are also strung on wrists in a similar ceremony, known as *phùuk siaw* (friend bonding), most famously celebrated in Khon Kaen (see p477) to cement friendships with one's closest confidants. More than just a symbolic ritual, the friends gain a standing on par with siblings in each other's families.

Some people believe that these strings must fall off naturally rather than be cut, but this can take weeks, turning sacred thread into stinky thread.

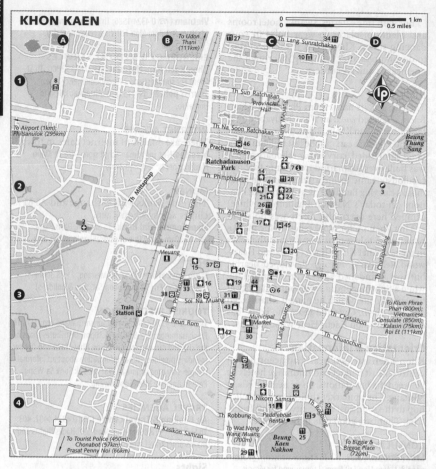

KHON KAEN

the nightlife and shop for souvenirs. First stop should be the **Khon Kaen National Museum** (☎ 0 4324 6170; Th Lang Sunratchakan; admission 30B; ☼ 9am-4pm), which has an interesting collection of artefacts from prehistoric times to the present, including a Dvaravati *sěmaa* (temple boundary marker) from Kalasin depicting Princess Pimpa washing Lord Buddha's feet with her hair, and Ban Chiang painted pottery.

The National Museum's household and agricultural displays shed light on what you'll see out in the countryside, but for a more indepth introduction to Isan, visit the excellent and engaging **Khon Kaen City Museum** (Hong Munmung; ☎ 0 4327 1173; Th Rop Buengkaen Nakhon; admission 90B; ☼ 9am-5pm Mon-Sat), with dioramas and displays going back to the Jurassic period.

The **Art & Culture Museum** (☎ 0 4333 2035; admission free; ☼ 10am-7pm) at Khon Kaen University is also informative about Isan history and culture, but only if you read Thai. The ground-floor gallery sometimes has art exhibits.

Beung Kaen Nakhon (Kaen Nakhon Pond), a 100-hectare lake lined with eateries and walkways, attracts early-evening strollers and smoochers to its banks. At the northern end of the lake is **Wat That** (Th Robbung; ☼ daylight hours), with elongated spires typical of this area, and at the south end is **Wat Nong Wang Muang** (Th Robbung; ☼ daylight hours), with its gorgeous nine-tier *chedi*. Inside you'll find enlightening murals depicting Khon Kaen history, historical displays and a staircase to the top.

Festivals & Events

The **Silk Fair** and the **Phuk Siaw Festival** are held simultaneously over 12 days starting in late November. Centred on the Provincial Hall (*săalaa klaang*), the festival celebrates, and seeks to preserve, the tradition of *phùuk sìaw* (friend bonding), a ritual renewal of the bonds of friendship during which *fai phuk kan* (sacred thread) are tied around one's wrists (see p475). Other activities include parades, Isan music, folk dancing, and the preparation and sharing of Isan food.

Khon Kaen kick-starts **Songkran**, the Thai New Year, on 8 April, with parades of floats bedecked with flowers.

Sleeping

BUDGET

Saen Sumran Hotel (☎ 0 4323 9611; 55-59 Th Klang Meuang; s 150-200B, d 250B) The city's oldest hotel is also it's most charismatic with the wooden front holding onto its once-upon-a-time glory. The rooms are a little shaky, but scrubbed spotless, and an eclectic mix of decoration provides colour downstairs.

First Choice (☎ 0 4333 2374; 18/8 Th Phimphaseut; r 150-200B) This friendly little café is the city's proto backpacker hostel, with no-frills rooms upstairs and a traveller-friendly eatery below. Plane tickets, massage and travel advice are available. Bathrooms are shared.

Sri Mongkol Hotel (no roman-script sign; ☎ 0 4323 7939; 61-67 Th Klang Meuang; r 150-300B; 🅿️) The wooden front of this place also has a certain tumbledown charm, but you'll have to be a

sound sleeper – the walls are thin. There are concrete-block air-con rooms at the back.

Grand Leo Mansion (☎ 0 4332 7745; 62-62/1 Th Si Chan; r 350-450B; 🅿️) This homogenous place, around the corner from Disco Street, is functional and a little frumpy, but the spotless rooms promise a good night's sleep no matter at what hour you stumble back.

Roma Hotel (☎ 0 4333 4444; 50/2 Th Klang Meuang; r 230-550B; 🅿️) The Roma's air-con rooms are good value, spotless and comfy, and the fan rooms are…well, good value and comfy. Unfortunately, the hotel has some noisy neighbours, so you might get an early wake-up call.

MIDRANGE

Europe Guesthouse (☎ 0 4327 1083; www.europe -khonkaen.com; 23/5 Th Nikorn Samran; r 440-490B; 🅿️ 🖥️) This Dutch-owned place is no fancier than the big places in this class, but its six rooms are far cosier. A tiny fan room goes for just 150B, but, like the others, still has TV and fridge.

Phu Inn (☎ 0 4324 3174; off Th Lang Meuang; r 350-500B; 🅿️) The views of the car park at the centre of this Chinese-oriented place don't look so good but, at these prices, the rooms do.

Chaipat Hotel (☎ 0 4333 3055; 106/3 Soi Na Meuang; r 370-600B; 🅿️) Housed in a plain white tower just off Th Na Meuang, this reasonable place features smiley staff, marble floors and, if the brochure is to be believed, a uniformed lady clutching a cocktail in every room.

Biggie & Biggoe Place (☎ 0 4332 2999; Th Robbung; r 550-650B; 🅿️ 🖥️) If you're in Khon Kaen to

relax rather than live it up, this midsize hotel at the foot of the lake is a good bet. Rooms are rather simple and bland, but as it went up in 2005 there are none of the irritating quirks so common in older hotels.

Rossukond Hotel (☎ 0 4323 7797; 1/11 Th Klang Meuang; r 600-700B; 🞩) With wood-panelled walls and womb-red décor, the lobby of this good-value midranger has more character than most of the other options combined. The balconied rooms are also relatively fresh on the décor front, and if you're a stickler for detail, there's a 'hygienic' paper cover on every toilet seat.

Khon Kaen Hotel (☎ 0 4333 3222; 43/2 Th Phimphaseut; r 650-1200B; 🞩) This seven-storey place also bags a few points for atmosphere, with a pleasant maroon paint job downstairs and the odd nod to traditional décor throughout. The hotel remains functional rather than fabulous, but the lower-priced rooms, each with a private balcony, are definitely above average for this class.

Kaen Inn (☎ 0 4324 5420; kaeninnhotel@yahoo.com; 56 Th Klang Meuang; r 660-1400B; 🞩 ▯) Long since toppled as the town's top spot, the Kaen Inn is looking rather sorry for itself on the outside, but get through the door and you'll find an excellent midranger.

TOP END

Kosa Hotel (☎ 0 4332 0320; www.kosahotel.com; 250-252 Th Si Chan; s 1140-1380B, d 1260-1500B; 🞩 ▯ 🞩) Only a little less glitzy than its neighbour the Sofitel, this fantastic-value place (unless it's full and jacks up the rates) is a good top-end choice and offers excellent facilities and slick service.

Hotel Sofitel (☎ 0 4332 2155; www.sofitel.com; 9/9 Th Prachasumran; r 2600B; 🞩 ▯ 🞩) A stunning lobby sets the tone for one of Isan's best hotels. This international-standard Accor-run place in the heart of the city's nightlife district has plenty of razzle-dazzle, big well-equipped rooms, a gym and even its own microbrews.

Eating & Drinking

Khon Kaen has a fabulous array of restaurants and is the place to satisfy your cravings before heading back out into the countryside.

our pick Tawantong (☎ 0 4333 0389; 227/129 Th Lang Sunratchakan; per plate 40B; � breakfast & lunch) This large all-veggie, health-food restaurant sits across from the National Museum. The food is so good it gets many carnivorous diners.

Kai Yang Rabeab (no roman-script sign; ☎ 0 4324 3413; Th Lang Sunratchakan; chicken 90B; ☑ lunch) Many locals believe Khon Kaen has Thailand's best *kài yâang* (grilled chicken) and this simple joint, serving an all-Isan menu, gets the most nods as best of the best.

First Choice (☎ 0 4333 2374; 18/8 Th Phimphaseut; dishes 30-180B; ☑ breakfast, lunch & dinner) This traveller-style eatery-hostel has some tasty breakfasts, smoothies, and a good range of Western and Thai dishes, including vegetarian options. Eat inside or on a little terrace surrounded by potted plants.

Kao Tom Pae Tee (no roman-script sign; ☎ 0 4324 1932; Th Klang Meuang; dishes 50-150B; ☑ dinner) This no-frills local haunt lacks a little in décor, but serves up a mean *tôm yam* (spicy and sour soup made with seafood or chicken) until 3am, and has an English menu.

Plaa Pha Noi (no roman-script sign; ☎ 0 4322 4694; Th Robbung; dishes 40-200B; ☑ lunch & dinner) This large, alfresco spot near Beung Kaen Nakhon specialising in seafood is where locals bring out-of-town guests to sample Isan food. Elephants sometimes perform in the park out the front.

Restaurant Didine (☎ 08 7189 3864; Th Prachasumran; dishes 40-200B; ☑ lunch & dinner) As much a bar as a restaurant, as the two-page drinks list attests, the French chef whips up superb food, like tuna steak with saffron, that belies the simple surrounds. It's also got pub grub and Thai standards.

Bualuang Restaurant (☎ 0 4322 2504; Th Rop Buengkaen Nakhon; dishes 60-350B; ☑ lunch & dinner; 🞩) Ask a local out for dinner and they will probably want to go here. Perched on a pier over Beung Kaen Nakhon, it serves up a great spread of Thai, Isan and Chinese dishes in a largely alfresco setting.

Also recommended:

Kiwi Café (☎ 0 4322 8858; 311/13 Th Robbung; 50-115B; ☑ dinner Mon-Fri, lunch & dinner Sat & Sun) Coffee, wine, cottage pie and, we swear, the best cakes and pies in Isan.

Pizza Uno (☎ 0 4322 0604; 340/3 Soi Na Muang; large pizza 189B; ☑ lunch & dinner) Might be the best 'za in the city, and the rooftop patio is a nice touch.

Kosa Coffee Shop (☎ 0 4332 0320; 250-252 Th Si Chan; dishes 100-600B; ☑ breakfast, lunch & dinner; 🞩) Serves an excellent lunch buffet (179B) and the beer garden out the front is pleasant.

Two **night markets** (☑ 5pm-midnight), a covered one near the air-con bus terminal and an open-air affair on Th Reun Rom on the south side

of the Municipal Market, are the life and soul of the budget eating scene. Many **food stalls** (Th Klang Meuang) also open up between Th Ammat and the Roma Hotel in the late afternoon. For cheap eats around the high-priced hotels, hit the 5th-floor food court at **Oasis Plaza** (Th Si Chan; dishes 20-40B; ☺ lunch & dinner) shopping centre.

Entertainment

Khon Kaen's exuberant nightlife is centred on Th Prachasumran, also known as Disco Street, where clubs and bars run wild to mild. Most get going around 10pm and few charge a cover.

Rad Pub (☎ 0 4322 5987; Th Prachasumran) One anchor is this multifaceted place, with two rooms of live music, one loud and one soft, 'coyote' dancers, and an alfresco restaurant and coffee shop.

U-Bar (☎ 0 4332 0434; off Th Prachasumran) Has a student-filled dance floor, behind the Sofitel.

our pick **Iyara** (☎ 0 4332 2855; 43 Th Robbung; dishes 55-250B; ☺ dinner) This place has a *ponglang* (percussion instrument made of short logs) music, dance and comedy show every night at 7.30pm, but if the show is cancelled, don't worry – with a Khmer-style art theme, this is the loveliest restaurant in the city so it's worth the trip anyway.

The cineplexes at **Fairy Plaza** (Th Na Meuang) and **Oasis Plaza** (Th Si Chan) shopping centres often screen films in English. **Kosa Bowl** (per game 59B; ☺ 11am-2am) has 30 lanes atop Oasis Plaza.

Shopping

Khon Kaen is the best places to buy Isan handicrafts; the selection of shops is excellent.

Klum Phrae Phan (☎ 0 4333 7216; 131/193 Th Chatapadung; ☺ 9am-6pm Mon-Sat) Run by the Handicraft Centre for Northeastern Women's Development, this out-of-the-way store has a superb collection of natural-dyed, hand-woven silk and cotton produced in nearby villages.

Sueb San (no roman-script sign; ☎ 0 4334 4072; Th Klang Meuang; ☺ 8am-6.30pm) More accessible than Phrae Phan, this store also stocks natural-dyed fabrics, plus some atypical Isan souvenirs.

Lao Khao (☎ 0 4333 2035; ☺ 10am-7pm) The gift shop at the Art & Culture museum (p476) carries both traditional crafts and modern art, and some interesting combinations of the two.

Rin Thai Silk (☎ 0 4322 0705; 412 Th Na Meuang; ☺ 8am-7pm) Locals, especially brides-to-be, looking for top-quality silk shop here.

Prathamakhan Local Goods Center (☎ 0 4322 4080; 79/2-3 Th Reun Rom; ☺ 9am-8.30pm Thu-Tue) This outlet has both textiles and handicrafts (including plenty of silver) and is a good one-stop shop if you don't have the time or inclination to spend the day trawling through the smaller stores. Don't miss the knick-knack and handicraft display at the back.

Khon Kaen OTOP Center (☎ 0 4332 0320; Th Si Chan; ☺ 9am-8pm) This large handicrafts store is most convenient to the top-end hotels, but is predictably touristy and pricey as well.

Naem Laplae (no roman-script sign; ☎ 0 4323 6537; 32 Th Klang Meuang; ☺ 6am-9.30pm Mon-Thu, 6am-10pm Fri-Sun) You can follow the fabulous aromas to this old-school Isan food store (if you've got a cold, look out for the bright yellow-and-red shopfront), the largest of several in this area, which sells everything from dried fish to fat, flavoursome sausages, most notably *năem*, made of raw pickled pork.

The most enjoyable souvenir-shopping experience is looking for the handful of people selling traditional baskets and wooden items hidden away within the food, clothes and household-goods stalls in **Talat Bobae** (Th Klang Meuang).

Getting There & Away

AIR

THAI (Thai Airways International; ☎ 0 4322 7701; www .thaiairways.com; 9/9 Th Prachasumran, Hotel Sofitel; ☺ 8am-5pm Mon-Fri) operates three services daily between Bangkok and Khon Kaen (one way 2305B, 55 minutes). The **airport** (☎ 0 4324 6345) is just west of the city off Hwy 12.

BUS

Both the **ordinary bus terminal** (☎ 0 4323 7472; Th Prachasamoson) and the **air-con bus terminal** (☎ 0 4323 9910; Th Klang Meuang) are central and convenient.

Air-con buses leave to/from Bangkok's Northern bus terminal (329B, 6½ hours, every half-hour) from 6am to midnight. VIP service starts at 440B. Other air-con destinations from Khon Kaen include Chiang Mai (542B, 12 hours, 8pm and 9pm only), Nakhon Phanom (238B, five hours, four daily), Nong Khai (148B, 3½ hours, four daily), Pattaya (416B, nine hours, 10 daily), Roi Et (99B, two hours, four daily) and Udon Thani (104B, two hours, every 20 minutes).

There are ordinary buses from Khon Kaen to Chaiyaphum (70B, 2½ hours, hourly), Khorat

(125B, three hours, every 30 minutes) and Roi Et (50B, two hours, every 40 minutes).

TRAIN

Khon Kaen is on the Bangkok–Nong Khai line. Express trains leave from Bangkok's Hualamphong station for the Khon Kaen **train station** (☎ 0 4322 1112) at 8.20am, 6.30pm and 8.45pm, arriving about eight hours later. Bangkok-bound express trains leave Khon Kaen at 8.37am, 8.11pm and 9.05pm. The fares to Bangkok are 227/399/1068B for a 3rd-class seat/2nd-class seat/1st-class sleeper.

Getting Around

A regular, colour-coded sǎwngthǎew system plies the city for 8B per ride. The TAT office has a city map showing all the routes, but ask if it's the old, outdated one or an updated version before relying on it too heavily. Motorcycle taxis charge about 25B for a medium-length trip though town, while túk-túk drivers will want 40B to 60B. A shuttle runs from the airport to most hotels for 60B.

There's a plethora of car-rental outlets around the Kosa Hotel and Sofitel, and First

Choice Guesthouse has a bike for rent for 50B per day.

AROUND KHON KAEN
Chonabot
ชนบท

This small town located 55km southwest of Khon Kaen is one of Thailand's most successful silk villages. The easiest place to see the fabrics is at **Sala Mai Thai** (Thai Silk Pavilion; no roman-script sign; ☎ 0 4328 6160; donations appreciated; ⏰ 8am-5pm), a resource centre for the local silk industry on the campus of Khon Kaen Industrial & Community Education College. There are a couple of traditional northeastern wooden houses with looms and other artefacts (ask the staff to unlock them), plus an exhibition hall cataloguing traditional *mát-mìi* patterns. The campus is 1km west of Chonabot on Rte 229.

The pavilion sells silk, too, but most people buy from the shops on **Th Sribunreung** (aka Silk Road), though textiles can be purchased directly from silk-weaving houses in Chonabot – look for the tell-tale looms beneath the wooden homes. Even if you're not interested

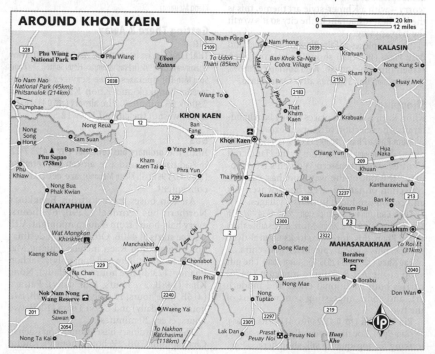

in buying, it's worth wandering around to look at the amazing variety of simple wooden contraptions devised to spin, tie, weave and dry silk.

Some well-known **weaving households** include those belonging to Khun Suwan, Khun Songkhram, Khun Chin and Khun Thongsuk. Very little English is spoken in Chonabot, so it helps considerably if you bring someone along who knows Thai.

GETTING THERE & AWAY

Buses bound for Nakhon Sawan, departing hourly from Khon Kaen's ordinary bus terminal, will drop you in Chonabot (50B, one hour).

Prasat Peuay Noi
ปราสาทเปือยน้อย

Also known as Ku Peuay Noi, and locally as That Ku Thong, the 12th-century Khmer temple **Prasat Peuay Noi** (admission free; ☼ daylight hours) is the largest and most interesting Khmer ruin in northern Isan, though it can't compete with the famous sites further south. About the size of Buriram's Prasat Meuang Tam, the east-facing monument, rich in sculpted lintels, comprises a large central sandstone sanctuary surmounted by a partially collapsed *prang* and surrounded by laterite walls with two major gates.

GETTING THERE & AWAY

If you have your own wheels, head 44km south from Khon Kaen on Hwy 2 to Ban Phai, then east on Hwy 23 (signposted to Borabu) for 11km to the turn-off to Rte 2301. Follow it and Rte 2297 for 24km southeast through a scenic tableau of rice fields to Ban Peuay Noi. The ruins are at the western end of town.

By public transport from Khon Kaen, catch a bus (35B, one hour) or the 7.55am local train (9B, 30 minutes) to Ban Phai, then a săwngthăew to Peuay Noi (25B, 30 minutes). The last săwngthăew back to Ban Phai leaves Peuay Noi around 2pm.

Phu Wiang National Park
อุทยานแห่งชาติภูเวียง

When uranium miners discovered a dinosaur's patella bone in this region in 1976, palaeontologists were soon to follow, excavating the top of Phu Pratutima and unearthing a fossilised 15m-long herbivore later named *Phuwianggosaurus sirindhornae* (after Her

Royal Majesty, Princess Sirindhorn). Dinosaur fever followed (explaining the epidemic of model dinosaurs in Khon Kaen), more remains were uncovered and **Phu Wiang National Park** (☎ 0 4324 9052, reservations 0 2562 0760; admission 400B; ☼ 8.30am-4.30pm), northwest of Khon Khaen, was born.

Four enclosed excavation sites, including one with a partial skeleton of *Siamotyrannus isanensis*, an early ancestor of Tyrannosaurus Rex, can be easily reached by trail from the visitor centre or nearby parking areas. Park guides (some speak a little English) offer free tours of the bone sites if you call in advance. Those who want to explore further (best done by car or mountain bike) will find dinosaur footprints, waterfalls and prehistoric cave paintings.

The **Phu Wiang Museum** (☎ 0 4343 8204; admission free; ☼ 9am-5pm), 5km before the park, has geology and palaeontology displays, including full-size models of the dinosaur species that have been found in the area.

The park has **camp sites** (per person 30B, 3-sleeper tent hire 225B) and a **bungalow** (up to 12 people 1800B).

GETTING THERE & AWAY

The park entrance is 90km west of the provincial capital. Nong Bualamphu–bound buses from Khon Kaen's ordinary bus terminal stop in Phu Wiang town (ordinary/air-con 38/50B, 1½ hours, hourly). It's best to get off downtown, not at the bus terminal, where you can hire a túk-túk (one way/return 200/400B) or motorbike taxi (50B less each way) for the remaining 19km to the park entrance. If you only pay for a one-way trip you'll risk not being able to get a ride back, and hitching is tough.

Nam Nao National Park
อุทยานแห่งชาติน้ำหนาว

One of Thailand's most beautiful and valuable parks, **Nam Nao National Park** (☎ 0 5672 9002, reservations 0 2562 0760; admission 400B; ☼ 6am-10pm) covers nearly 1000 sq km at an average elevation of 800m across the border of Chaiyaphum and Phetchabun Provinces, just beyond Khon Kaen Province. Although it covers remote territory – this remained a People's Liberation Army of Thailand (PLAT) stronghold until the early 1980s – Hwy 12 makes access easy. Temperatures are fairly cool year-round, especially nights and mornings, and

frost occasionally occurs between November and February.

Marked by the sandstone hills of the Phetchabun mountains, the park features dense, mixed evergreen-deciduous forest on mountains and hills; open dipterocarp pine-oak forest on plateaus and hills and dense bamboo mountain forest with wild banana stands in river valleys, plus scattered savannah on the plains. Three rivers are sourced here: the Chi, Saphung and Phrom. A fair system of trails branches out from the visitor centre to several scenic viewpoints. The park also features waterfalls and caves, some of which are easily reached by car along the highway. Nam Nao's highest peak, **Phu Pha Jit**, reaches a height of 1271m and, with a park service guide leading the way, you can camp on the top.

The 1560-sq-km **Phu Khiaw Wildlife Sanctuary** lies adjacent to the park so wildlife is abundant, but the animals here are more timid than at nearby Phu Kradung National Park, and so are sighted less often. Elephants and *banteng* (wild cattle) are occasionally seen, as well as Malayan sun bears, leopards, tigers, Asian jackals, barking deer, gibbons, pangolins and flying squirrels. Over 200 species of bird, including parrots and hornbills, fly through the park.

Accommodation includes a **camp site** (per person with own tent 30B, 2-person tent hire 50B), **huts** (2 people 300B) and 17 **bungalows** (4-person 1000B). There are restaurants next to the visitor centre.

GETTING THERE & AWAY
Buses between Khon Kaen (102B, 2½ hours) and Phitsanulok travel through the park frequently. The visitor centre is a 1.5km walk from the highway.

Ban Khok Sa-Nga Cobra Village
โครงการอนุรักษ์งูจงอาง
The self-styled 'King Cobra Village' of **Ban Khok Sa-Nga** has a thing about snakes. Locals rear hundreds of the reptiles, and most houses have some in boxes under their houses. The strange custom began when a herb farmer Phu Yai Ken Yongla began putting on snake shows to attract customers to the village, and the art of breeding and training snakes has been nurtured ever since. Today the **King Cobra Club** (donations expected; ☼ 8am-6pm) hosts short shows where handlers taunt snakes and tempt fate: they often lose, as the many missing fingers show. Medicinal herbs are still sold and other animals are on display in pitiful little cages.

GETTING THERE & AWAY
The village is northeast of Khon Kaen via Hwy 2 and Rte 2039. By bus, leave from Khon Kaen's ordinary bus terminal to the turn-off to Ban Khok Sa-Nga (40B, one hour) and then walk or take a túk-túk (50B) for the remaining 2km to the stage. If you're driving from Khon Kaen, you can't miss it as there are many signs.

ROI ET
ร้อยเอ็ด
pop 36,000
Three centuries ago, Roi Et served as a buffer between the clashing Thai and Lao armies. Back at that time, it had 11 city gates, one for each of its 11 vassal colonies; its name, which means 'one hundred one', is probably a typically macho exaggeration of this number.

Roi Et's long history hasn't followed it into the 21st century; orderly and modern, you can almost smell the drying paint on some of the city's grander buildings. But while most of its historic monuments have vanished into foggy memory, Roi Et retains a charm and sense of identity all of its own. You can't call Roi Et sleepy, but, perhaps taking its cue from the walking Buddha on an island in the middle of Beung Phlan Chai, it does seem to move to its own urban beat.

Roi Et Province is known for the crafting of the quintessential Isan musical instrument, the *khaen*, a kind of panpipe made of the *mái kuu* reed and wood. The best *khaen* are reputedly made in the village of Si Kaew, 15km northwest of Roi Et. It takes about three days to make one *khaen*, depending on its size.

Information
Bangkok Bank (Th Suriyadet Bamrung; ☼ 8.30am-3.30pm Mon-Fri) Has an ATM and exchange facilities.
Main post office (Th Suriyadet Bamrung; ☼ 8.30am-4.30pm Mon-Fri, 9am-noon Sat & holidays)
Planet (Th Santisuk; per hr 15B; ☼ 9am-9pm) Check your email here.
Police station (☎ 1155; Th Suriyadet Bamrung)

Sights
The large **Roi Et National Museum** (☎ 0 4351 4456; Th Ploenchit; admission 30B; ☼ 9am-4pm Wed-Sun) gives equal billing to ancient artefacts unearthed in the district and Isan cultural displays. The 3rd floor shows materials used to produce a rainbow of colours in natural-dyed silks.

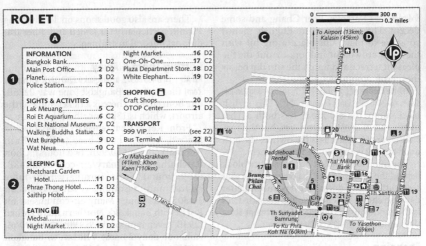

The tall, standing Buddha towering above Roi Et's minimal skyline is the **Phra Phuttha Ratana Mongkon Mahamuni** (Phra Sung Yai for short) at **Wat Burapha** (Th Phadung Phanit; ☾ daylight hours). Despite being of little artistic significance, it's hard to ignore. From the ground to the tip of the *ùtsànít* (flame-shaped head ornament) it's 67.8m high, while head to toe he stands 59.2m.

Wat Neua (Th Phadung Phanit; ☾ daylight hours), in the northern quarter of town, is worth seeing for its 1200-year-old *chedi* from the Dvaravati period, Phra Satup Jedi. This *chedi* has an unusual four-cornered bell-shaped form that is rare in Thailand. Around the *bòt* are a few old Dvaravati *sĕmaa* (temple boundary marker stones) and to one side of the wat is an inscribed pillar, erected by the Khmers when they controlled this area during the 11th and 12th centuries.

Walking paths criss-cross islands in the lake of **Beung Phlan Chai** and attract the usual crowd of doting couples, joggers and picnickers. The **walking Buddha statue** is on the north side and the **lak meuang** (city pillar) is to the south; many more monuments and interesting statuary stand between.

There are a few odd-looking fish in the little **Roi Et Aquarium** (☎ 0 4351 1286; Th Sunthornthep; admission free; ☾ 8.30am-4.30pm Wed-Sun) and the walk-through tunnel is a nice touch.

Sleeping

Saithip Hotel (☎ 0 4351 1742; 133 Th Suriyadet Bamrung; r 210-310B; ⌗) The architect tried, and failed, to splash a smidgen of glamour onto this simple place, but take a room here and your baht will be well spent. Enter from the car park.

Phrae Thong Hotel (☎ 0 4351 1127; 45-47 Th Ploenchit; r 180-350B; ⌗) Insomniacs will bemoan the noise drifting up from the road (and perhaps the adjoining quarters since its has a three-hour rate), but this tidy no-frills spot has some good-value, little rooms with plenty of natural light and, less appealingly, squat toilets and very hard mattresses.

Phetcharat Garden Hotel (☎ 0 4351 9000; Th Chotchaplayuk; r 540-700B; ⌗ ⌗) Some genuinely chic styling earns this attractive place several gold stars. The lobby showcases serene East-meets-West décor, with wooden shutters and tall ceilings, and the immaculate staff (the men sport cool trousers) are tirelessly attentive. The standard rooms don't really capture the atmosphere, but are still fantastic value. If you can, shell out for the deluxe rooms.

Eating

A lot of large, lively outdoor restaurants sit on Th Chotchaplayuk south of the Phetcharat Garden Hotel.

One-Oh-One (☎ 0 4351 4070; Th Sunthornthep; dishes 40-140B; ☾ lunch & dinner) You'll almost always find an expat or two lounging over a beer at Joey's, as this little lakeside place is also known. It's got a full Western menu, but pizza predominates.

Medsai (no roman-script sign; ☎ 0 4352 0338; 160/9 Th Ploenchit; dishes 30-180B, lunch buffet 49B; ☾ lunch

& dinner; [☺]) Karaoke, Beer Chang and some decent Thai cooking (no English menu) conspire to make this place a big hit with the local crowd. Sit indoors or out on the pleasant terrace and watch the sun dip below the…erm…rooftops.

White Elephant (☎ 0 4351 4778; Th Robmung Dannok; dishes 40-240B; [☺] lunch & dinner; [☺]) This stylish place, along the old moat, has both a Thai menu and many Western faves, but the specialities are German, as is the owner. The outdoor terrace is surrounded by greenery.

The main **night market** (5pm-midnight), a block behind the Saithip Hotel, is a covered spot that sees a little action during the day, too. A better daytime choice for cheap soups and stir-fries is the food court at the **Plaza Department Store** (Th Ploenchit; dishes 20-40B [☺] lunch & dinner).

Shopping

OTOP Center (Th Pranpratcharat) Construction had not quite finished on this handicrafts mall when we last checked, but surely this will be the place to shop for silks and souvenirs.

There are also good shops on Th Phadung Phanit, particularly for *khaen* and other traditional musical instruments.

Getting There & Away

PB Air (☎ 0 4351 8572, in Bangkok 0 2261 0222; www.pbair .com) flies to/from Bangkok (one way 2225B, one hour) daily. There is a ticket office at the airport, which is 13km north of the centre.

From Roi Et's **bus terminal** (☎ 0 4351 1466; Th Jangsanit), frequent buses head to Khon Kaen (ordinary/air-con 50/99B, two hours), Ubon Ratchathani (ordinary/air-con 80B/148B, three hours), Surin (ordinary 50B, three hours) and Yasothon (ordinary/air-con 30/50B, one hour). Many air-con buses link Roi Et with Bangkok's Northern bus terminal (293B, seven hours) and **999 VIP** (☎ 0 4351 1466) runs one daily 24-seat VIP bus to Bangkok (585B, seven hours) at 9.30pm.

Getting Around

Sǎamláw usually cost 20B. For a túk-túk, you'll pay 10B to 20B more.

MǍW LAM & THE KHAEN

Among villages in Isan, the up-tempo Lao-Thai musical tradition of *mǎw lam* – roughly 'master of verse' – rules. Performances always feature a witty, topical combination of singing and improvised or recited speech that ranges across themes as diverse as politics and sex. Very colloquial, even bawdy language is employed; this is one art form that has always bypassed government censors and provides an important outlet for grassroots expression. *Mǎw lam* is most commonly performed at temple fairs and local festivals.

There are four basic types of *mǎw lam*. The first, *mǎw lam lǔang* (great *mǎw lam*), involves an ensemble of performers onstage in costume, and these days the dancing sometimes eclipses the music. *Mǎw lam khûu* (couple *mǎw lam*) features a man and woman who engage in flirtation and verbal repartee. *Mǎw lam jòt* (duelling *mǎw lam*) has two performers of the same gender who 'duel' by answering questions or finishing an incomplete story issued as a challenge. Finally, *mǎw lam dìaw* (solo *mǎw lam*) involves only one performer.

The backbone of *mǎw lam* is the *khaen*, a wind instrument consisting of a double row of bamboo-like reeds fitted into a hardwood soundbox. The rows can be as few as four or as many as eight (for a total of 16 pipes), and the instruments vary in length from around 80cm to 2m. Around the turn of the 20th century there were also nine-course *khaen*, but these have all but disappeared. Melodies are almost always pentatonic; ie they feature five-note scales. The *khaen* player blows (as with a harmonica, sound is produced whether the breath is moving in or out) into the soundbox while covering or uncovering small holes in the reeds that determine the pitch for each. An adept player can produce a churning, calliope-like music that inspires dancing. The most popular folk dance is the *lam wong*, the 'circle dance', in which couples dance circles around one another until there are three circles in all: a circle danced by the individual, the circle danced by the couple and one danced by the whole crowd.

Traditionally the *khaen* was accompanied by the *saw* (a bowed string instrument), although the plucked *phin* is much more common today. In modern *mǎw lam*, the *khaen* and *phin* are electrically amplified, and electric bass and drums are added to the ensemble to produce a sound enjoyed by both young and old.

AROUND ROI ET
Ku Phra Koh Na
กู่พระโกนา

Around 60km southeast of Roi Et town are the minor ruins of **Ku Phra Koh Na** (admission free; daylight hours), an 11th-century Khmer shrine. The monument comprises three brick *prang* facing east from a sandstone pediment surrounded by a sandstone-slab wall that once had four gates. The middle *prang* was replastered in 1928 and Buddha niches were added. A Buddha footprint shrine, added to the front of this *prang*, is adorned with the Khmer monument's original Baphuon-style *naga* sculptures. The two other *prang* have been restored (though they still look like they might tumble over any time) but retain their original forms. The northern *prang* has a reclining Narai (Vishnu) lintel over one door and a *Ramayana* relief on the inside gable. The ruins themselves are neither impressive nor well restored, but it's interesting to see how they've been incorporated into the modern temple. And if that doesn't thrill you, spend your time watching the hundreds of monkeys that live here; they are part of the everyday fabric of the grounds.

GETTING THERE & AWAY
Any Surin-bound bus from Roi Et can drop you off at Wat Ku (ordinary/air-con 40/52B, 1½ hours), as the compound is known locally, which is 6km south of Suwannaphum on Rte 215.

UDON THANI PROVINCE

UDON THANI
อุดรธานี
pop 227,200

Udon Thani has one foot on the highway and the other off the beaten track. The city boomed on the back of the Vietnam War, exploding into life as US air bases opened nearby. Today it's become the region's primary transport hub and commercial centre, and you have to dig deep behind its prosperous concrete veneer to find any flashes of its past. Because it lacks the urban chutzpah of Khon Kaen and the touristy appeal of Nong Khai, which is equally convenient for visiting wonderful surrounding attractions, Udon sees few travellers other than a growing number of sex tourists.

Information
EMERGENCY & MEDICAL SERVICES
Aek Udon International Hospital (☎ 0 4234 2555; 555/5 Th Pho Si) One of the best medical facilities in the upper Northeast.
Tourist police (☎ 1155; Th Naresuan)

INTERNET ACCESS
Awo Internet (Th Teekathanont; per hr 20B; 10am-midnight) One of several internet cafés on this block.

MONEY
Kasikornbank (Th Teekathanont, Charoensri Complex; 11am-8pm) One of several banks in the mall. Many more banks, open regular business hours, are lined along Th Pho Si.

POST
Main post office (Th Wattananuwong; 8.30am-4.30pm Mon-Fri, 9am-noon Sat, Sun & holidays)

TOURIST INFORMATION
TAT (☎ 0 4232 5406; www.tourismthailand.org; Th Thesa; 8.30am-4.30pm) Has information on Udon, Loei, Nong Khai and Nong Bualamphu Provinces.

TRAVEL AGENCIES
Ultinet Travel (☎ 0 4224 8606; 277/44 Th Teekathanont 8am-6.30pm) For plane tickets and car rental.

Sights
UDORN SUNSHINE NURSERY
อุดรชันชายน์เนอร์สรี
Ever seen a plant dance? If not, this is the place to do it. Originally earning notoriety for producing the first ever orchid made into a perfume, the **Udorn Sunshine Nursery** (☎ 0 4224 2475; 127 Th Udorn-Nong Samrong; 8am-6.30pm), just west of town, has since developed a hybrid of *Codariocalyx motorius ohashi leguminosae*, which curiously 'dances' to music. The mature gyrant has long oval leaves, plus smaller ones of similar shape. If you sing or talk to the plant in a high-pitched voice (saxophone or violin works even better), a few of the smaller leaves will shift back-and-forth. This is no hype; we've seen it for ourselves, although it's much more of a waltz than a jig. The plants are most active from November to February, the cool season, and between 7am to 10am and 4.30pm to 6.30pm.

The plants are not for sale, and all flowers from plants on public display are removed so nobody can pilfer them and grow their own. You can, however, buy Udon Dancing Tea,

CENTRAL UDON THANI

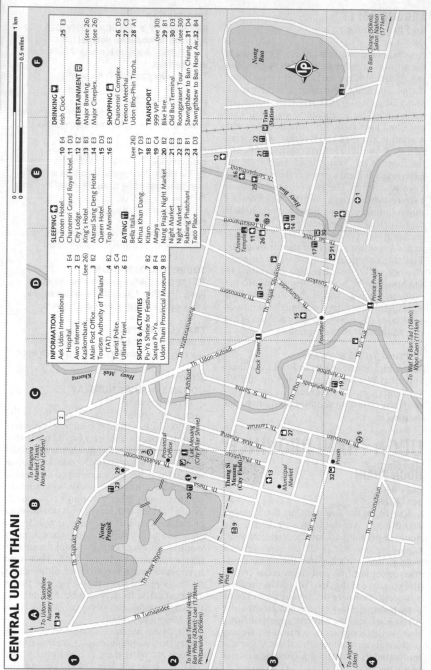

INFORMATION	
Aek Udon International Hospital	**1** E4
Awo Internet	**2** E3
Kasikornbank	(see 26)
Main Post Office	**3** B2
Tourism Authority of Thailand (TAT)	**4** B2
Tourist Police	**5** C4
Ulinet Travel	**6** E3

SIGHTS & ACTIVITIES	
Pu-Ya Shrine for Festival	**7** B2
Sanjao Pu-Ya	**8** F4
Udon Thani Provincial Museum	**9** B3

SLEEPING	
Charoen Hotel	**10** E4
Charoensri Grand Royal Hotel	**11** D3
City Lodge	**12** E2
King's Hotel	**13** B3
Marasi Sang Deng Hotel	**14** E3
Queen Hotel	**15** D3
Top Mansion	**16** E3

EATING	
Bella Italia	(see 26)
Khrua Khan Dang	**17** D3
Kitaro	**18** E3
Maeya	**19** C4
Nang Prajak Night Market	**20** B2
Night Market	**21** E3
Night Market	**22** B1
Rabiang Phatchani	**23** B1
Taco Place	**24** D3

DRINKING	
Irish Clock	**25** E3

ENTERTAINMENT	
Major Bowling	(see 26)
Major Cineplex	(see 26)

SHOPPING	
Charoensri Complex	**26** D3
Teenon Meechai	**27** C3
Udon Bho-Phin Tracha	**28** A1

TRANSPORT	
999 VIP	(see 30)
Bike Hire	**29** B1
Old Bus Terminal	**30** D3
Roongpraisert Tour	(see 30)
Sǎwngthǎew to Ban Chiang	**31** D4
Sǎwngthǎew to Ban Nong Aw	**32** B4

made from the plant, along with the more famous Miss Udorn Sunshine orchids and perfumes. The nursery's newest product is Toob Moob, a perfume derived (using a secret recipe and process they won't discuss) from an insect.

To get here, go under the Ban Nong Sam-rong sign on Rte 2024, then after 150m follow the Udon Sunshine Fragrant Orchid sign. The Yellow Bus and several sǎwngthǎew pass here. A túk-túk from Udon's city centre should cost about 60B.

SANJAO PU-YA CHINESE TEMPLE
ศาลเจ้าปู่ย่า

The garish **Sanjao Pu-Ya** (Th Pho Si; ☼ daylight hours) on the southern shore of Nong Bua is a particularly colourful Chinese temple that attests to the wealth of the local Thai-Chinese merchant class. At its heart, the **Pu-Ya Shrine** houses small images of the God and Goddess of Mercy.

During December's **Thung Si Meuang Festival**, which features Isan music and dance performances and a fair to promote local products, Pu (Grandpa) and Ya (Grandma) are moved to a temporary home in the northwest corner of City Field. There is dragon and lion dancing on several days during the festival.

UDON THANI PROVINCIAL MUSEUM
พิพิธภัณฑ์เมืองอุดรธานี

Filling a 1920s colonial-style building that used to be a girls' school, **Udon Thani Provincial Museum** (☎ 0 4224 5976; Th Pho Si; donations appreciated; ☼ 8am-4pm) has a catch-all collection spanning geology to handicrafts.

Sleeping
BUDGET

King's Hotel (☎ 0 4224 1444; 57 Th Pho Si; r 190-220B; ⊠) A construction crew could probably convert this Vietnam War–era veteran into a prison in a couple of hours; nevertheless, cheery staff and cheap prices make it a good budget choice.

Queen Hotel (☎ 0 4222 1451; 6-8 Th Udon-dutsadi; r 120-240B; ⊠) Located in a busy market area, this place is basic with a double-decker 'B', though the owner is friendly.

Top Mansion (☎ 0 4234 5015; topmansion@yahoo.com; 35/3 Th Sampanthamit; r 310B; ⊠ 💻) Mix the quality, location and well-appointed rooms and this newly erected tower is the best bargain for your baht in town. The only thing missing is some style, but at these prices, who cares?

Marasi Sang Deng Hotel (☎ 0 4234 4131; Th Prajak Silpakorn; r 250-350B; ⊠) Location, location, location. This noisy, slightly scruffy place would surely be cheaper if it didn't sit smack between the bus terminal and the Charoensri Complex. On the other hand, the wood floors and good mattresses are worth a little extra and it's much better than the other cheapies right around this corner.

MIDRANGE & TOP END

Charoen Hotel (☎ 0 4224 8155; charoenhotel@hotmail .com; 549 Th Pho Si; r 800-900B; ⊠ 💻 🖵) A few rungs down the glamour ladder from the top, this large business-class hotel is a little dated, but still offers plenty of trimmings and evening entertainment options.

City Lodge (☎ 0 4222 4439; 83/14-15 Th Wattananu-wong; r 600-1000B; ⊠ 💻) This British-owned property is a good example of the new breed of small hotel springing up in this area that deliver more charm and value than the big boys. The already bright and colourful rooms are cheered up even more with wicker furniture.

Charoensri Grand Royal Hotel (☎ 0 4234 3555; www .charoensrigrand.com; Th Teekathanont; s/d 1300/1400B; ste 2000-2500B; ⊠ 💻 🖵) At the hub of Udon's main shopping and nightlife district, this is the town's glossiest top-ender. The rooms are spacious and immaculate, the facilities are top-notch and the service is swift.

Eating

Khrua Khan Dang (no roman-script sign; ☎ 0 4224 0596; 296/43 Th Sai Uthit; dishes 25-30B; ☼ breakfast, lunch & dinner) No sign, no menu, no atmosphere, but the noodle dishes are simply superb.

Taco Place (☎ 08 1369 8936; 19/3 Th Jamnusorn; dishes 40-155B; ☼ lunch & dinner) A south-of-the-border experience? Of course not, this is Thailand; it can't be done. But Tu, who studied Mexican food while running a Thai restaurant in Mexico, makes a pretty good stab at it. She also makes sub sandwiches, from her time in New Jersey.

Rabiang Phatchanee (☎ 0 4224 1515; 53/1 Th Su-phakit Janya; dishes 45-250B; ☼ lunch & dinner; ⊠) On the lake's east shore, this classy Thai place whips up a fabulous array of local dishes on the deck or in air-conditioned dining rooms.

our pick Maeya (no roman-script sign; ☎ 0 4222 3889; 79/81 Th Ratchaphatsadu; dishes 38-310B; ☼ lunch & dinner) One part Thai restaurant and three parts English tearoom, this labyrinth has waiters

dressed in black tie and a menu stretching from burgers to ice creams to Oriental mains. The curries are divine, though the translations are a little cryptic (the 'rice with spit in sauce' is really 'rice with liver in sauce').

Also recommended:

Bella Italia (☎ 0 4234 3134; Th Teekathanont, Charoensri Complex; dishes 80-500B; ✆ lunch & dinner; ✖) As close to Italy as you'll get in Isan, and as fancy as you'll get in Udon.

Kitaro (☎ 0 4224 3094; Th Prajak Silpakorn; dishes 40-880B; ✆ lunch & dinner) A long-term Japanese favourite.

Vendors in the city's side-by-side **night markets** (Th Prajak Silpakorn; ✆ 4-11pm) in front of the train station serve a good groove of Thai food; and you can watch football on the big screen. A bevy of massage and paint-your-own pottery stands joins the small food shops (which go all day long) on the sunset-watching side of Nang Prajak Park, a favourite jogging and socialising spot, to form the **Nang Prajak Night Market** (Th Thesa; ✆ 4-10pm).

Drinking & Entertainment

Udon's growing expat population makes its presence felt on the city's eating and drinking scene. If you are anywhere near the Charoensri Complex, you can't avoid passing a *faràng*-owned or -aimed bar. Most of those in the block right across the street from the mall are aimed at people looking to meet new friends, if you catch our drift.

Irish Clock (☎ 0 4224 7450; Th 19/5-6 Th Sampanthamit; ✆ 8am-midnight) A wood-trimmed, Guinness-infused pub on the backside of this block is lower key and higher class.

Major Bowling and **Major Cineplex** (☎ 0 2515 5555) sit atop the Charoensri Complex on Th Teekathanont.

Shopping

Teenon Meechai (☎ 0 4222 2838; 206-208 Th Pho Si; ✆ 2-5pm Mon-Sat) This souvenir shop has so much quirky style you'll forget you're a tourist.

Udon Bho-Phin Tracha (no roman-script sign; ☎ 0 4224 5618; Th Phaw Niyom; ✆ 9am-6pm Mon-Sat) There is a very good selection of silk and cotton, including some natural-dyed fabrics, at this spot northwest of Nong Prajak Lake. Look for the sign with the wooden roof.

Charoensri Complex (Th Teekathanont) One of Isan's largest shopping centres and the hub of the city. It has the standard department store,

supermarket, designer-clothing boutiques and dining options.

Getting There & Away

AIR

THAI (www.thaiairways.com), **Nok Air** (www.nokair.com) and **Air Asia** (www.airasia.com) together make 10 daily flights to Bangkok (one hour). One-way fares average 2200B. Nok Air also flies three times a week to Chiang Mai (1½ hours) for the same price as to Bangkok.

BUS

For most destinations, including Bangkok's Northern bus terminal (air-con 443B, eight hours, every 15 minutes), buses use Udon's **old bus terminal** (☎ 0 4222 1489; Th Sai Uthit) or the street in front of it. Other air-con buses include those to Khorat (193B, 4½ hours, every 20 minutes), Sakon Nakhon (109B, 3½ hours, every 15 minutes), Khon Kaen (104B, 2½ hours, every 20 minutes), Pattaya (504B, 10 hours, 10 daily) and Vientiane (80B, two hours, six daily; you must already have a Lao visa). Many companies, including **999 VIP** (☎ 0 4222 1489) and **Roongprasert Tour** (☎ 0 4234 3616), operate 24-seat VIP buses (640B) to Bangkok in the evening.

The **new bus terminal** (☎ 0 4224 7788) is on the Ring Rd on the western outskirts of the city (take the Yellow Bus or såwngthåew 6) and has buses to western destinations, including Loei (ordinary/air-con 60/110B, three hours, every 30 minutes) and Chiang Mai (air-con/32-seat VIP 563/657B, 12 hours, eight daily).

For Nong Khai (ordinary 40B, one hour) you can use either terminal, but the most frequent departures are from Rungsina Market.

TRAIN

Udon Thani is on the Bangkok–Nong Khai line. Express trains leave Hualamphong station in Bangkok at 8.20am, 6.30pm and 8.45pm arriving at Udon's **train station** (☎ 0 4222 2061) about 10 hours later. Express departures in the reverse direction leave at 6.47am, 6.40pm and 7.20pm. The fares to Bangkok are 245/369/1177B for a 3rd-class seat/2nd-class seat/1st-class sleeper.

Getting Around

Såwngthåew (8B) run regular routes across town; TAT hands out free city maps that show the routes. There are also two city buses (8B),

the Yellow and the White. The former runs up and down Th Pho Si and the later tracks Hwy 2. Túk-túk short trips start at 40B (såamláw rates are a little less) and it's 100B to the airport or the new bus terminal.

There are almost as many car-rental outlets around Charoensri Complex as there are bars. Rates start at 1000B, but this is for an older car: for an extra couple hundred you'll get a better quality car and for 1500B you can get a car with a driver.

A couple of **bike rental outlets** (Th Thesa) by Nong Prajak Park have one-, two- and three-seaters starting at 100B per day.

AROUND UDON THANI PROVINCE
Ban Chiang
บ้านเชียง

This town, 50km east of Udon, was once the hub of the ancient Ban Chiang civilisation and archaeological digs here have uncovered a treasure-trove of artefacts dating as far back as 5600 years.

What is now one of the most important archaeological sites in Southeast Asia was discovered quite accidentally in 1966. Stephen Young, an anthropology student from Harvard, tripped while walking through the area and found the rim of a buried pot right under his nose. Looking around he noticed many more and speculated that this might be a burial site – he was right. The first serious excavations took place in 1974–75 and they uncovered over a million pottery pieces as well as 126 human skeletons. Researchers later uncovered the earliest evidence of both farming and the manufacture of metal tools in the region.

The Ban Chiang culture, an agricultural society that once thrived in northeastern Thailand, is now famous for its early bronze metallurgy and clay pottery, especially pots and vases with distinctive burnt-ochre swirl designs, most of which were associated with burial sites. Seven layers of civilisation have been excavated; the famous swirl-design pottery comes from the third and fourth layers. The area was declared a Unesco World Heritage site in 1992.

The excellent **Ban Chiang National Museum** (☎ 0 4220 8340; admission 30B; ☯ 8am-5pm) exhibits pottery from all Ban Chiang periods, plus myriad bronze objects recovered from various

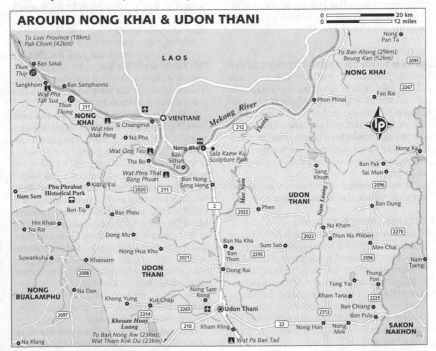

AROUND NONG KHAI & UDON THANI

0   20 km
0   12 miles

excavation pits, including spearheads, sickles, axe heads, fish hooks, chisels, ladles, neck rings and bangles. The displays (with English labels) offer excellent insight into the region's distant past and how its mysteries were unravelled. An original **burial ground excavation pit** (same hours as the museum, and admission included in the museum ticket) displaying 52 skeletons, in whole or part, and lots of pots is at nearby Wat Pho Si. The museum is currently closed for renovation, but will be open soon after publication.

Rice cultivation remains the town's primary livelihood, but the site has made souvenir selling a close second. On the way into town you'll pass many villages specialising in handicrafts, such as pottery, silk weaving, rice baskets and clothes sewn with a distinctive thick, handwoven cotton fabric; all of these and more can be bought from shops facing the museum. Locals also attempt to sell Ban Chiang artefacts, real and fake, but neither is allowed out of the country, so don't buy them.

The **University of Pennsylvania Museum of Archaeology & Anthropology** (www.museum .upenn.edu) has a good page on the archaeological discoveries at Ban Chiang on its website. From the home page type Ban Chiang Project into the search engine.

SLEEPING & EATING

Lakeside Sunrise Guest House (☎ 0 4220 8167; www .banchianglakeside.com; r 200B) On the west side of the lake, within easy striking distance of the museum, this homey, nicely landscaped place is the village's best bet for a budget sleep. Clean, shared facilities are downstairs, while the wooden upper floor boasts a spacious veranda. The joyful owner, an encyclopaedia of Ban Chiang knowledge, speaks English and rents bikes.

There are several simple restaurants across from the national museum entrance.

GETTING THERE & AWAY

A few săwngthăew run between Ban Chiang and Udon (35B, one hour) each morning before 10am. In Udon, catch them on Th Pho Si southwest of the old bus terminal. In Ban Chiang, they stop in front of the museum. Alternatively, take a bus bound for Sakon Nakhon or Nakhon Phanom and get off at the Ban Pulu (45B, one hour) turn-off, a 15-minute săamláw ride (per person 50B) from Ban Chiang.

Phu Phrabat Historical Park

อุทยานประวัติศาสตร์ภูพระบาท

Steeped in local legend and peppered with bizarre rock formations daubed with ancient cave paintings, **Phu Phrabat Historical Park** (☎ 0 4225 1350; admission 30B; ☉ 8.30am-4.30pm) is one of the region's highlights, offering great views from the crags of the Phu Phrabat escarpment and plenty of mythical intrigue. For Isan residents, this is an important place of pilgrimage. For visitors, the side-by-side progression from rock art to Buddhist stupa represents a localised evolution of thought and aesthetics.

The formations are a collection of balanced rocks, spires, whale-sized boulders and caves (more like grottoes or rocky overhangs) with several shrines and wats built in and around them. Prehistoric paintings in several grottoes feature wild animals, humans and cryptic symbols. There are also some small but sophisticated rock carvings of Buddha images dating back to when the Mon and, later, Khmer ruled this area. A climb beyond the rock formations to **Pha Sa Dej** at the edge of the escarpment ends with dramatic views of the valley below and the mountains of Laos beyond. A well-marked web of trails trail meanders past these sites and you can see all of them in about an hour.

Near the entrance to the area is the largest temple in the historical park **Wat Phra That Phra Phutthabaht Bua Bok**, with its namesake Lao-style *chedi* covering a Buddha footprint. It also has some odd temple buildings in the general mood of those in the park.

Most of the bizarre rock formations to be found here are featured in an enchanting local legend about a king (Phaya Kong Phan), his stunningly beautiful daughter (Nang Usua), a hermit (the Rishi Chantra) and a love-struck prince from another kingdom (Tao Baros). The most striking rock formation, **Hoh Nang-Usa**, an overturned boot-shaped outcrop with a shrine built into it, is said to be the tower where the beautiful princess was forced to live by her overprotective father. Many of these rock formations are signposted with names in Thai and English alluding to the legend, but, unless you're familiar with it, they'll make little sense. There's a short version in the museum, but if you're staying at the Mut Mee Garden Guest House in Nong Khai (p496), you can read the whole tale.

The park has three simple **dormitories** (per person 150B) if you want to spend some time

here, but they're geared more towards groups of Thai students. Ask at the office if you want to pitch a tent.

GETTING THERE & AWAY
The park is 70km northwest of Udon Thani and Nong Khai, near the small town of Ban Pheu, and can be visited as a long day trip from either city. From Udon's Rungsina Market it's a 40B, 1½-hour bus ride; it's 35B and two hours from Nong Khai. From Ban Pheu take a săwngthăew (8B) to Ban Tiu, the village at the base of the hill, and then a motorcycle taxi or túk-túk the final 4km to the park itself. If you're using public transport, you should plan on leaving the park by 3.30pm.

Weaving Villages
Ban Na Kha, 16km north of Udon right on Hwy 2, is renowned for *khít*-pattern fabrics. *Khít* is a geometric, diamond-grid minimal weft brocade traditionally used in pillows and other decorative items, but now commonly used in clothing. Dozens of shops line the highway and the main road through town: **Wongduan** (☎ 0 4220 6089; Hwy 2) and **Chanruan Nakha** (☎ 0 4220 6276; cnr Hwy 2 & Mu 1) are used to dealing with foreigners.

Before leaving, take a peek at **Wat Na Ka Taewee** (Hwy 2; ◔ daylight hours), which was founded before the village after a wandering monk found a hole from which bellowed the sound and smoke of a *naga*. He plugged the hole with a rock and built the small *bòt* over it. The hall by the entrance displays pottery, gold Buddhas and human skeletons unearthed during various construction projects at the temple. Udon's Yellow bus runs to the village; catch it anywhere on Hwy 2.

Ban Thon, just 2km east of Ban Na Kha, is a much more peaceful weaving village, though you'll only find looms spinning in the winter since the full-time weavers moved to the highway where most of the customers are found.

The best (and most expensive) *khít* comes from **Ban Nong Aw**, about 40km southwest of Udon via Rte 210 in Nong Bualamphu Province, but there is less available for sale to the public. Săwngthăew (27B, one hour) depart from next to Udon's prison.

Wat Pa Ban Tad
วัดป่าบ้านตาด
Luang Ta Maha Bua, now in his 90s and a former disciple of Ajahn Man, is one of Thailand's most revered monks. Though he earned his reverence as a meditation master, he gained universal celebrity after the 1997 economic crisis by collecting over 10,000kg of gold (people turned in jewellery to be melted down) and US$10 million in baht to help pay the country's international debts. He has been heavily involved in other charity work and in 2005 made unprecedented criticisms of Thaksin, the now-deposed prime minister.

Over 250 monks and *mâe chii* (Thai Buddhist nuns) – all taking ascetic vows in addition to the regular 227 precepts – live and meditate at **Wat Pa Ban Tad** (◔ daylight hours), a vast, humble forest wat 16km south of Udon (take Hwy 2 south and, after a U-turn, follow the signs), including about a dozen Westerners. Hundreds come every morning to hear his simple, direct talks on Buddhism, and thousands more listen via a nationally broadcast radio programme (103.25FM in Udon) or at www.luangta.com.

NONG KHAI PROVINCE

Nong Khai Province, occupying a narrow, 320km-long sweep along the banks of the Mekong, is a beautiful, intriguing region. The capital, Nong Khai, is where the Friendship Bridge crosses into Laos – only the second bridge to be erected anywhere along the Mekong's entire length; the first was in the People's Republic of China. The town is one of northeastern Thailand's most popular tourist destinations and features the surreal Sala Kaew Ku sculpture park, a must-see on any jaunt through the region.

NONG KHAI
หนองคาย
pop 61,500
Spread out along the leafy banks of the Mekong River, Lady Luck certainly smiles on the location. As a major staging post on the tourist trail north, Nong Khai benefits from a steady stream of travellers, and a clutch of excellent places to stay and eat have sprung up to accommodate them, making this the only Isan town with a full-fledged backpacker scene; albeit a modest one. But Nong Khai's popularity is about more than just its proximity to Laos and bounty of banana pancakes. Seduced by its dreamy river views, sluggish pace of life and surrounding attractions, many who mean to stay a day end up bedding down for many more.

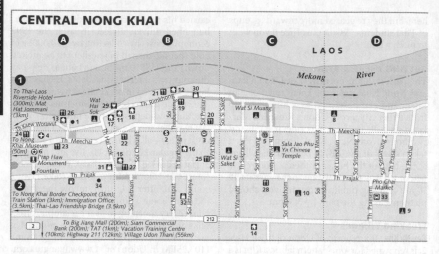

CENTRAL NONG KHAI

Developers have stuck their concrete boots into some of the city's prettier historic districts, but compared to Udon Thani and Khon Kaen further south, Nong Khai has managed to keep at least one of its feet firmly rooted in the past. Cut through with a sprinkling of French colonial villas and a starburst of wats, time, like the Mekong, appears to flow a little more slowly here.

History

Crammed between nations, Nong Khai is both a historic and physical bridgehead between Thailand and Laos. Nong Khai once fell within the boundaries of the Vientiane (Wiang Chan) kingdom, which itself vacillated between independence and tribute to either Lan Xang (1353–1694) or to Siam (late 18th century until 1893). In 1827 Rama III gave a Thai lord Thao Suwothamma the rights to establish Meuang Nong Khai at the present city site, which he chose because the surrounding swamps ('Nong' in Thai) would aid in the city's defence. In 1891, under Rama V, Nong Khai became the capital of *monthon* Lao Phuan, an early Isan satellite state that included what are now Udon, Loei, Khon Kaen, Sakon Nakhon, Nakhon Phanom and Nong Khai Provinces, as well as Vientiane.

The area came under several attacks by *jiin haw* (Yunnanese) marauders in the late 19th century. The 1886-vintage Prap Haw Monument (*pràap haw* means 'defeat of the Haw') in front of the former Provincial Office (now used as a community college) commemorates Thai-Lao victories over Haw invasions in 1874, 1885 and 1886. When western Laos was partitioned off from Thailand by the French in 1893, the *monthon* capital was moved to Udon, leaving Nong Khai to fade into a provincial backwater.

The opening of the US$30 million, 1174m-long Saphan Mittaphap Thai-Lao (Thai-Lao Friendship Bridge) on 8 April 1994 marked the beginning of a new era of development for Nong Khai as a regional trade and transport centre and the skyline has been creeping slowly upwards ever since.

Orientation & Information

Nong Khai follows the curve of the Mekong River, and most of the hotels and restaurants are along, or just off, the three parallel streets of Th Rimkhong, Th Meechai and Th Prajak on the western side of the centre of town. The Friendship Bridge is about 3km west of the centre.

BOOKSHOPS

Hornbill Bookshop (☎ 0 4246 0272; Th Kaew Worawut; ☻ 10am-7pm) Buys, sells and trades English-language books.

EMERGENCY & MEDICAL SERVICES

Nong Khai Hospital (☎ 1669; Th Meechai)
Tourist police (☎ 1155; Hwy 2) In the OTOP Center, 1km south of town.

IMMIGRATION OFFICES

Immigration Office (☎ 0 4242 0242; ☻ 8.30am-4.30pm Mon-Fri) On the highway bypass that leads to the Friendship Bridge; offers Thai visa extensions.

INTERNET ACCESS

Mekong Internet Services (519 Th Rimkhong; per hr 30B; 10am-10pm) At the Maekhong Guest House.
Oxy.Net (569/2 Th Meechai; per hr 25B; 10am-midnight)

MONEY

There are banks with ATM and exchange facilities across town.
Krung Thai (Th Meechai; 8.30am-4.30pm Mon-Fri) A Travelex money-transfer agent.
Siam Commercial Bank (Hwy 2, Big Jiang Mall; 10.30am-8pm) An agent for Moneygram.

POST

Main post office (Th Meechai; 8.30am-4.30pm Mon-Fri, 9am-noon Sat, Sun & holidays) An agent for Western Union.

TOURIST INFORMATION

TAT (0 4242 1326; www.tourismthailand.org; Hwy 2; 8.30am-4.30pm Mon-Fri) In the OTOP Center, 1km south of town.

TRAVEL AGENCIES

Family Corp 2 (0 4241 1526; Th Prajak; 9am-7pm Mon-Sat)
Go Thasadej (0 4242 3921; www.gothasadej.com; 387/3 Soi Thepbunterng; 10am-10pm) Books air tickets and visa-run tours (from Bangkok). At the Café Thasadej.

Sights & Activities

SALA KAEW KU SCULPTURE PARK

ศาลาแก้วกู่

Nong Khai's most enigmatic attraction, **Sala Kaew Ku Sculpture Park** (Pavilion of Kaew Ku; 08 1369

5744; admission 10B; 7.30am-5.30pm) is a surreal, sculptural journey into the mind of a mystic shaman. Built over a period of 20 years by Luang Pu Boun Leua Sourirat, who died in 1996, the park features a weird and wonderful array of gigantic sculptures ablaze with Hindu-Buddhist imagery.

As his own story goes, Luang Pu, a Lao national, tumbled into a hole as a child, where he met an ascetic named Kaewkoo. Kaewkoo introduced him to the manifold mysteries of the underworld and set him on course to become a Brahmanic yogi-priest-shaman. Shaking up his own unique blend of Hindu and Buddhist philosophy, mythology and iconography, Luang Pu developed a large following in northeastern Thailand, where he had moved following the 1975 communist takeover in Laos, and had been working on a similar project.

The park is a real smorgasbord of bizarre cement statues of Shiva, Vishnu, Buddha, and every other Hindu and Buddhist deity imaginable, as well as numerous secular figures, all supposedly cast by unskilled artists under Luang Pu's direction. Some of the sculptures are quite amusing: if you're travelling with kids they'll enjoy the serene and stately elephant wading though a pack of anthropomorphic dogs. The tallest sculpture, a Buddha seated on a coiled *naga* with a spectacular multi-headed hood, is 25m high. Also of interest is the Wheel of Life, entered through a giant mouth, which boils Luang Pu's philosophies down to a single, slightly baffling, image – an

explanation is available on the **Mut Mee Garden Guest House website** (www.mutmee.com).

The main shrine building, almost as bizarre as the sculpture park, is full of framed pictures of Hindu and Buddhist deities, temple donors and Luang Pu at various ages, plus smaller bronze and wooden figures of every description and provenance guaranteed to throw an art historian into a state of disorientation. Luang Pu's corpse lies under a glass dome ringed by flashing lights in the upper room.

To get to Sala Kaew Ku, board a bus heading to Phon Phisai or any other eastern destination and ask to get off at Wat Khaek (10B), as the park is also known; it's about a five-minute walk from the highway. Chartered túk-túk cost 120B return with a one-hour wait, or you can reach it by bike in about 30 minutes: Mut Mee Garden Guest House distributes handy maps if you want to take the scenic route.

WAT PHO CHAI
วัดโพธิ์ชัย

Luang Pu Phra Sai, a large Lan Xang–era Buddha, awash with gold, bronze and precious stones, sits at the hub of **Wat Pho Chai** (Th Phochai; 7am-7pm). The head of the image is pure gold, the body is bronze and the ùtsànìt is set with rubies. The altar on which the image sits features gilded wooden carvings and mosaics, while the ceiling bears wooden rosettes in the late Ayuthaya style.

This was one of three similar statues and the murals in the bòt depict their travels from the interior of Laos to the banks of the Mekong where they were put on rafts. A storm sent one to the bottom of the river where it remains today: it was never recovered because, according to one monk at the temple, the naga like having it. The third statue, Phra Soem, is at Wat Patum Wanaram in Bangkok.

WAT NOEN PHRA NAO
วัดเนินพระเนาว์

A forest wat on the south side of town, **Wat Noen Phra Nao** (daylight hours) boasts a Vipassana (insight meditation) centre on pleasant, tree-shaded grounds. It serves as a spiritual retreat for those (Westerners included, if they are serious about meditation) facing personal crises. Some extremely ornate temple architecture, including perhaps the most rococo bell tower we've ever seen, stands in contrast with the usual ascetic tone of forest monasteries. There's

a Chinese cemetery and some of the statuary wouldn't be out of place at Sala Kaew Ku.

WAT LAM DUAN
วัดลำดวน

You can easily pick **Wat Lam Duan** (Th Rimkhong; daylight hours) out of the skyline since an immense Buddha image sits on top of the bòt. You are welcome to climb up (shoes off) and gaze over the Mekong with it.

WAT TUNG SAWANG
วัดทุ่งสว่าง

The bòt at **Wat Tung Sawang** (Soi Silpakhom; daylight hours) is one of the city's smallest, but the exceptional artistic flair put into the decoration makes it one of the most attractive. Nine Buddhist and Hindu sculptures sit on fanciful pedestals alongside the chapel.

PHRA THAT NONG KHAI
พระธาตุหนองคาย

Also known as **Phra That Klang Nam** (Holy Reliquary in the Middle of the River; admission free), this Lao chedi is submerged in the Mekong River and can only be seen in the dry season when the Mekong lowers about 13m. The chedi slipped into the river in 1847 and continues to slide – it's near the middle now. Once the top of the chedi has cleared the water during the dry season, coloured flags are fastened to the top. **Phra That La Nong**, a replica erected on the original site, glows brightly at night.

NONG KHAI MUSEUM
พิพิธภัณฑ์หนองคาย

The little **Nong Khai Museum** (0 4241 3658; Th Meechai; admission free; 9am-4pm Mon-Fri) once had little to hold your interest, but a renovation ongoing during our last visit could change that, or maybe not.

HAT JOMMANI
หาดจอมมณี

It only makes a seasonal appearance during the dry season, but the sandy beach of **Hat Jommani** under the Thai-Lao Friendship Bridge is a favourite with picnickers, sunsoakers and those who just like to feel the Mekong running between their toes; perhaps from a rented inner tube. During the dry season a rustic thatched shelter with straw mats becomes a restaurant serving delicious kài yâang, plaa pîng (grilled fish), sôm-tam (papaya salad) and cold beer.

MUAY THAI

Several *faràng* have trained in *muay thai* (Thai boxing) with **Seksorn Kupradit** (☎ 042460184), who knows enough English to get his ideas across. It's not a typical hard-nosed camp; instead students get two hours a day of one-to-one lessons. A three-month course costs 12,000B and you'll get into the ring at the end.

VOLUNTEERING

While volunteer opportunities usually require a fairly long commitment, you can do a whole lot of good in just a couple of hours by stopping at one of the orphanages near town, including **Sarnelli House** (http://sarnelli.siam .de) for HIV-positive children, run by Father Mike Shea, to play with the children on weekend mornings. Inquire at Mut Mee Garden Guest House if you're interested. Mut Mee also has information on English-teaching opportunities.

Festivals & Events

During the annual **Songkran Festival** (in April), the priceless image of Luang Pu Phra Sai, a Lan Xang–era Buddha, is paraded around town.

Like many other cities in the northeast, Nong Khai has a **Rocket Festival** (Bun Bâng Fai),

---

GREAT BALLS OF FIRE

Mass hysteria? Methane gas? Drunken Lao soldiers? Or perhaps the fiery breath of the sacred *naga*, a serpent-like being that populates folkloric waterways throughout Theravada Buddhist Southeast Asia. For the Lao and Thai who live along a certain stretch of the Mekong River in Thailand's Nong Khai Province, it's not a matter of whether or not to believe. Since 1983 (or for ages, depending on who you ask), the sighting of the *bâng fai pháyaa nâak* (loosely translated 'naga fireballs') has been an annual event. Sometime in the early evening, at the end of the Buddhist Rains Retreat (October), which coincides with the 15th waxing moon of the 11th lunar month, small reddish balls of fire shoot silently from the Mekong River just after dusk and float fly a hundred or so metres into the air before vanishing without a trace. Most claim the *naga* fireballs are soundless, but others say a hissing can be heard if one is close enough to where they emerge from the surface of the river. People on both sides of the Mekong see the event as a sign that the resident *naga* is celebrating the end of the holiday.

Naga fireballs have only recently come to the attention of the rest of Thailand. TV news has been reporting the annual sightings for years, but it wasn't until the 2002 release of a film based on the phenomena that Thais really began to take notice. Entitled *Sìp Hâa Khâm Deuan Sìp-èt*, or *Fifteenth Waxing Moon of the Eleventh Lunar Month* (the film was released with English subtitles under the curious title *Mekhong Full Moon Party*), the debut of the film not long before the scheduled event had an expected effect. Thousands of Thais from Bangkok and the rest of the country converged on the banks of the Mekong in Nong Khai Province and waited for the show to begin. Sadly, it rained that year. But that didn't dampen enthusiasm and *naga* fireballs were witnessed right on schedule.

So what, you might ask, is the real cause behind *naga* fireballs? Thais have various theories. One, which was aired on a Thai TV exposé-style programme, claimed that Lao soldiers taking part in festivities on the other side of the Mekong were firing their rifles into the air. Interestingly, the reaction to the TV programme was anger and a storm of protest from both sides of the river. Others suggest that a mixture of methane gas and phosphane, trapped below the mud on the river bottom, reaches a certain temperature at that time of year and is released. Whatever the real cause, few Thais will even entertain the suggestion of a hoax.

Naga fireballs have become big business in Nong Khai Province. Every year some 40,000 people invade little Phon Phisai, the locus of fireball watching, and thousands more converge on about two dozen other riverside spots between Sangkhom and Nakhom Phanom in hopes of sightings. Traffic is so bad that public transport isn't a viable option, but Mut Mee Garden Guest House in Nong Khai runs trucks (200B) to the festivities.

The fireball experience is much, much more than just watching a few small lights rise from the river; it's mostly about watching Thais watching a few small lights rise from the river. And even if the *naga* doesn't send his annual greeting on the day you come (it is sometimes delayed by a day), it will be an interesting experience.

which begins on Visakha Puja day (Buddha's birth and enlightenment day) in late May/ early June.

At the end of Buddhist Lent (Okk Paan Saa) in late October/early November, there is a large **Rowing Festival** featuring long-boat races on the Mekong. It corresponds with the October full moon, which is when **naga fireballs** can be seen (see the boxed text, p495).

The **Anou Savari Festival** on March 5 marks the end of the 'Hau' rebellions and boasts the city's biggest street fair.

Sleeping
BUDGET

Catering to the steady flow of backpackers heading across the border, Nong Khai's budget offerings are some of the best in the region and, in fact, these guesthouses also have the best midrange rooms available.

Rimkhong Guest House (☎ 0 4246 0625; 815/1-3 Th Rimkhong; s/d 120/180B) Sparse rooms, some in a shaky wooden house, with shared bathrooms and plenty of hush are standard at this unassuming outfit. A friendly old dog pads around the leafy courtyard and sets the sluggish pace, while the owners provide the warm welcome.

Ruan Thai Guest House (☎ 0 4241 2519; 1126/2 Th Rimkhong; r 120-400B; ✖) Once little more than a small private home, this pleasant spot has grown with the boomtime, boasting a good variety of good-quality rooms with some simple shared bathroom basics out the back to a family room in a little wooden cottage. Factor in the tangle of flower-filled garden greenery and it's a winner.

Pong Vichitr Hotel (☎ 0 4241 1583; 1244/1-2 Th Banthoengjit; r 200-400B; ✖) With a lobby stacked floor to ceiling with boxes of ramen noodles, you sure don't expect much out of this old-school concrete block, but open the door to your room and you'll find…OK, they're just as drab as you expected. But the price is right: air-con starts at 270B and all rooms have private bathroom with hot water.

Khiang Khong Guest House (☎ 0 4242 2870; 541 Th Rimkhong; r 300-400B; ✖) Rooms in this newly built concrete block sparkle and shine, and you can lament the lack (not the loss; it was an empty lot before construction) of history with river views from the 3rd-floor terrace or your private balcony.

Sawasdee Guest House (☎ 0 4241 2502; 402 Th Meechai; r 140-420B; ✖) If you could judge a hotel by its cover, this charismatic place in an old, Franco-Chinese shophouse would come up trumps. The tidy rooms (the fan options share bathrooms) lack the exterior's old-school veneer, but at least you'll sleep well in the knowledge that you're bedded down in a little piece of living history.

Maekhong Guest House (☎ 0 4246 0689; www.me kongguesthouse.com; 519 Th Rimkhong; dm 150B, r 300-500B; ✖ 💻) This revamped riverside outfit serves up little bonuses like decorative headboards and plush towels, rarely found at these prices. Its position, right on the river, also scoops a few credits.

OUR PICK Mut Mee Garden Guest House (☎ 0 4246 0717; www.mutmee.com; 1111/4 Th Kaew Worawut; dm 90B, r 130-600B; ✖) Occupying a sleepy stretch of the Mekong riverbank, Nong Khai's budget old-timer has a garden so relaxing you may not want to leave. A huge variety of rooms (some on a raft on the river are planned) are clustered around a thatched-roof restaurant where the owner, Julian, holds court with his grip of local legend and his passion for all things Isan. A little floating bar, named Gaia, sits on the river. Perhaps unsurprisingly, the alleyway leading to Mut Mee has developed into a self-contained travellers village with yoga instruction, internet cafés and a bookshop at hand.

MIDRANGE & TOP END

Thai-Laos Riverside Hotel (☎ 0 4246 0263; 51 Th Kaew Worawut; r 500-800B; ✖) Built a year before the Friendship Bridge opened, this is a good example of unmet expectations. If you don't mind peeling paint and torn carpets, you'll get good views. And, if you're into tacky hotel clubs, you'll find three of them here.

Pantawee Hotel (☎ 0 4241 1568; www.nongkhaiho tel.com; 1049 Th Hai Sok; r 800-1800B; ✖ 💻 ⚇) The Pantawee brand is something of a cartel along Th Hai Sok, with a string of accommodation options plus a spa, travel agency and 24-hour restaurant. The main hotel is somewhat homogenous but spotless, with a big choice of air-con rooms, almost all with DVD players and internet-connected PCs.

Nong Khai Grand (☎ 0 4242 0033; www.nongkhai grandhotel.com; Hwy 212; r 1290B, ste 3700B; ✖ 💻 ⚇) This slick, modern place has plenty of sparkle. A big hit with passing suits, 'executive' standards are maintained throughout and swanky suites (usually available at 40% discount) are on offer for those after the Midas touch.

Eating

Khrua Sukapap Kwan Im (☎ 0 4246 0184; Soi Wat Nak; dishes 20-30B; ☺ breakfast & lunch) The owners of this simple little vegetarian place make a mumsy fuss over *faràng* diners, and serve Thai and Chinese standards (from a buffet counter and an English-language menu) that are good enough for carnivores. The juices are excellent, too.

Darika (no roman-script sign; ☎ 0 4242 0079; 668-669 Th Meechai; dishes 25-60B; ☺ breakfast & lunch) If you're an early riser this spartan, English-speaking outfit will be waiting for you from 5am with cheap egg-and-toast breakfasts, banana pancakes, real Thai coffee, Lao-style baguette sandwiches and all the usual Thai choices.

Mut Mee Garden Guest House (☎ 0 4246 0717; 1111/4 Th Kaew Worawut; dishes 35-135B; ☺ breakfast, lunch & dinner) Mut Mee's food is very popular, especially the breakfasts, but keep in mind that the Thai dishes are toned down to European tastes. But whether you like it hot or not, you simply cannot beat this riverside location, and there are sometimes cultural performances.

Nagarina (☎ 0 4246 0717; dishes 35-75B; ☺ lunch & dinner) There is no paucity of peppers in the kitchen of Mut Mee's riverboat, which docks below the guesthouse. It offers sunset and night cruises for 100B (check at the guesthouse for times), but serves its superb Thai cuisine throughout the day.

Rom Luang (no roman-script sign; ☎ 08 7853 7136; 45/10 Th Prajak; dishes 40-120B; ☺ dinner) Though the menu is mainly Thai, most of the Yellow Umbrella's best known dishes, like sausages and pork neck, are Isan specialities. The handmade tables and chairs add flair, and the grills stay smoking until 4am.

José Ramon's (1128/11 Th Takai; dishes 80-140B; ☺ lunch & dinner Mon-Sat) A trace of Latin Americana prevails at this hole-in-the-wall diner. And the south-of-the-border menu, cooked up by the gregarious and hilarious José himself, isn't just a Nong Khai novelty – the food's not half bad.

Daeng Namnuang (☎ 0 4241 1961; 526 Th Rimkhong; dishes 30-180B; ☺ breakfast, lunch & dinner) This Vietnamese place has grown into an Isan institution and hordes of out-of-towners head home with car boots and carry-on bags (it's got an outlet at the Udon Thani airport) stuffed with Vietnamese *namnuang* (pork spring rolls).

Café Thasadej (☎ 0 4242 3921; 387/3 Soi Thepbunterng; dishes 50-310B; ☺ breakfast, lunch & dinner) Sophistication is in short supply in Nong Khai, but it oozes out of this little restaurant. Both the menu and liquor list, the latter among the best in town, go global. Gyros, weinerschnitzel, fish and chips, lasagne, tuna salad and smoked salmon are some of the most popular options.

Also recommended:

Pizza Mister Bentz (☎ 08 7806 8930; 1121 Th Hai Sok; pizza 99B; ☺ dinner) A pretty good pizza at a very good price.

Bird's Eye View Terrace (☎ 0 4242 0033; Hwy 212; dishes 55-200B; ☺ dinner) You can sample Isan food and see nearly the whole city from the Nong Khai Grand hotel's rooftop restaurant.

For quick, colourful eats swing by the **Hospital Food Court** (no roman-script sign; Th Meechai; ☺ breakfast, lunch & dinner) where about a dozen cooks whip up the standards, or visit the **night vendors** (Th Prajak) who set up their stalls each evening between Soi Cheunjit and Th Hai Sok. During the day, grilled fish reigns supreme at the lunch-only **riverside restaurants** (Th Rimkhong) tucked behind Tha Sadet Market.

Drinking

our pick **Surreal** (☎ 08 1391 3828; 476/4 Th Rimkhong; ☺ noon-1am Nov-April, 7pm-1am May-Oct) This little place rises above, both figuratively and literally, the other bars on this end of Th Rimkhong. It looks out over the river, has a free pool table and book exchange, and the owner Mark nearly never stops smiling.

Coco-Na Coffee (☎ 0 4241 1362; Th Meechai; ☺ 5pm-midnight; 🖳) This coffeehouse-nightclub hybrid attracts a youthful crowd. Gabber away with the other caffeinated punters inside, or take in a live band (November to May) with a glass of whiskey in the terrace out back.

Shopping

Tha Sadet Market (Th Rimkhong) This huge market runs for most of the day and offers the usual mix of dried food, electronic items, souvenirs and assorted bric-a-brac; most of it imported from Laos and China.

Village Weaver Handicrafts (☎ 0 4242 2651; www .villageweaver.net; 1020 Th Prajak; ☺ 8am-7pm) Selling high-quality, moderately priced hand-woven fabrics and ready-made clothing, this shop was established by the Good Shepherd Sisters as part of a project to encourage local girls to stay in the villages and earn money by weaving. The *mát-mìi* cotton is particularly good here. Its **workshop** (☎ 0 4241 1236; 1151 Soi Jittapanya;

🕑 9am-4pm Mon-Sat), where some of the products are produced, is located off Th Prajak, and visitors are welcome. The Thai name for the project is Hatthakam Sing Thaw.

Village Vocational Training Centre (☎ 0 4241 1860; 🕑 8am-5pm Mon-Sat) Though separate from Village Weaver, this school 7km south of town (take Hwy 2 and follow the sign east) has similar goals. It's a great place to see the *mát-mii* process from start to finish, and it also has a pottery workshop and mushroom farm.

Getting There & Away
AIR
The nearest airport is 55km south in Udon Thani. Regular flights operate from there to Bangkok. See p488 for more details. Several travel agencies run shuttles to the airport (150B, one hour); **Family Corp 2** (☎ 0 4241 1526; Th Prajak; 🕑 9am-7pm Mon-Sat), one of these agencies, runs five a day.

BUS
Nong Khai's main **bus terminal** (☎ 0 4241 1612) is located just off Th Prajak, over 1km from the riverside guesthouses.

Buses to Udon Thani (ordinary 40B, one hour) leave Nong Khai about every half-hour throughout the day. There are also regular air-con buses to Khon Kaen (148B, 3½ hours), Bangkok (482B, 11 hours) and Rayong (600B, 12 hours). For Chiang Mai, you have to change at Udon's New Bus Terminal. **Roongprasert Tour** (☎ 0 4241 1447) and **999 VIP** (☎ 0 4241 2679), with offices on opposite sides of the bus terminal, also offer daily 24-seat VIP services (700B, 10 hours) services to Bangkok at 7.45pm and 8pm respectively.

The ordinary bus 507 travels to Loei (105B, six hours), via Sangkhom (47B, 2¾ hours) throughout the morning; the last bus departs at 3pm.

Laos
Take a túk-túk to the border crossing where you get stamped out of Thailand. From there regular minibuses ferry passengers across the bridge (15B) between 6am and 9.30pm to the Lao immigration checkpoint. From there it's 22km to Vientiane – there will be plenty of buses, túk-túk and taxis waiting for you. If you already have a visa for Laos, there are also six direct buses a day to Vientiane from Nong Khai's bus terminal (55B, one hour).

VISAS FOR LAOS

Despite what travel agents in Bangkok might tell you, the Lao government issues 30-day tourist visas on arrival at Nong Khai's Friendship Bridge and the other border crossings open to those who are not Thai or Lao citizens. Most *faràng* pay either US$30 or US$35, though Canadians get socked with a US$42 fee. You are also allowed to pay in baht, but the price works out much higher. Beside the fee, you'll need a passport photo and the name of a hotel you will be staying at in Laos. Lonely Planet's *Laos* guidebook contains extensive travel information.

TRAIN
From Bangkok, express trains leave Hualamphong station daily at 6.30pm and 8.45pm, arriving in Nong Khai at 5.05am and 9.10am respectively. Going the other way, the express train services depart from Nong Khai at 6am and 6.20pm, arriving at 5.10pm and 6.25am respectively. The fares range from 1217B for a 1st-class sleeper cabin to 498/253B for a 2nd-/3rd-class seat. There is also one rapid train (348/213B 2nd/3rd class) leaving Bangkok at 6.40pm (arriving at 7.35am) and leaving for Bangkok at 6.20pm (arriving at 6.25am).

For information you can call Nong Khai **train station** (☎ 0 4241 1592), which is 2km west of town.

Getting Around
If your guesthouse doesn't rent bikes (30B to 100B) or motorcycles (150B to 200B), someone nearby will. And it pays to shop around a bit, since brakes aren't necessarily standard equipment. Village Weaver Handicrafts has a Jeep available for 1000B per day, which is about the going rate for car rental in Nong Khai.

A short túk-túk trip around the town centre will probably cost about 25B.

AROUND NONG KHAI PROVINCE
The Mekong region west of Nong Khai is madly obsessed with **topiary** and along the entire length of Rte 211 you'll pass hedges and bushes sculpted by ambitious gardeners into everything from elephants to *naga* to boxing matches.

Wat Phra That Bang Phuan

วัดพระธาตุบังเผือน

Boasting a beautiful and ancient Indian-style stupa, **Wat Phra That Bang Phuan** (daylight hours) is one of the region's most sacred sites, not least because some of the Buddha's bones are supposedly buried here. It is similar to the original *chedi* beneath the Phra Pathom Chedi in Nakhon Pathom, but while it is presumed that this stupa dates back to the early centuries AD, no one really knows when either was built.

In 1559 King Jayachettha of Chanthaburi (not the present Chanthaburi in Thailand, but Wiang Chan – now known as Vientiane – in Laos) extended his capital across the Mekong and built a newer, taller Lao-style *chedi* over the original as a demonstration of faith (just as King Mongkut did in Nakhon Pathom). Rain caused the *chedi* to lean precariously and in 1970 it finally fell over. The Fine Arts Department restored it in 1976 and 1977. The current *chedi* stands 34.25m high on a 17.2-sq-metre base and has several unsurfaced *chedi* around it, which give the temple an ancient atmosphere.

GETTING THERE & AWAY

From Nong Khai, catch the 507 Loei-bound bus and ask for Ban Bang Phuan (20B, 40 minutes).

Tha Bo

ท่าบ่อ

pop 16,000

Surrounded by banana plantations and tobacco fields that flourish in the fertile Mekong floodplains, prosperous Tha Bo is the most important market centre between Nong Khai and Loei. The covered market, which spills out to the surrounding streets, is full of tobacco, tomatoes and other locally grown products.

The area's largest Vietnamese population lives here, and they've cornered the market on noodle production. You don't have to travel far before you'll see sheets of *kŭaytĭaw* (wide, flat noodles) drying in the sun. It used to be mostly spring-roll wrappers laid out on the bamboo racks, but noodles are a better export product and most businesses are making the switch. Si Chiangmai, just upriver and directly across the Mekong from Vientiane, has picked up the slack and is now the area's spring-roll wrapper capital.

Hotels are still something of an oddity in Tha Bo, but you'll be well cared for at the **Gasalong Resort & Guest House** (☎ 0 4243 1227; Rte 2020; 250-500B;), 1km out of town, where bright and cheery bungalows (plus two 250B fan rooms) rest in a quiet little compound filled with trees and flowers and surrounded by rice paddies. There is a handful of food stalls and basic restaurants on the main street through the town.

GETTING THERE & AWAY

The 'yellow bus' runs regularly between Nong Khai and Tha Bo (25B, one hour), taking the scenic riverside route – look for fish cranes along the way. Pick it up in Nong Khai at the bus station or near the Hospital Food Court on Th Meechai. Alternatively, take bus 507 (25B, 40 minutes).

Wat Hin Mak Peng

วัดหินหมากเป้ง

Wat Hin Mak Peng (daylight hours) is worth a trip if only for the scenery along Rte 211 as the riverside mountains begin to rise here. The vast forest temple is nationally known for its *thúdong* (*dhutanga* in Pali) monks who have taken ascetic vows in addition to the standard 227 precepts, eating only once a day and wearing robes sewn by hand from torn pieces of cloth. There are also several *mâe chii* living here. This place is very quiet and peaceful, set in a cool forest with lots of bamboo groves overlooking the Mekong. It was built above three giant boulders that form a cliff rising out of the river. From this point, a Lao forest temple can be seen directly across the river and fisherfolk occasionally drift by on house rafts. Several monuments honour Luang Pu Thet, the wat's deeply revered founding abbot, including a glistening *chedi* housing all his earthly possessions.

The current abbot requests that visitors dress politely – no shorts or sleeveless tops. Those who don't observe the code may be turned away.

GETTING THERE & AWAY

The temple is midway between Si Chiangmai and Sangkhom, on the river side of Rte 211. Bus 507 passes the wat en route between Nong Khai (45B, two hours) and Loei.

Sangkhom

สังคม

Seductively sleepy, the little town of Sangkhom, facing the Lao island of Don Klang

Khong, is a convenient staging post for those taking the high (river) road (Rte 211) between Nong Khai and Loei. The Mekong dominates life here, but there are also some lovely waterfalls in the area.

The largest local waterfall is three-tiered **Nam Tok Than Thip** (admission free; ☉ daylight hours), 13km west of Sangkhom (2km off Rte 211). The lower level drops 30m and the second, easily reached via stairs, falls 100m. The 70m-top drop is only barely visible through the lush forest. **Nam Tok Than Thong** (admission free; ☉ daylight hours), 11.5km east of Sangkhom off the northern (river) side of Rte 211, is a wider but shorter drop with a swimmable pool at the bottom. The short nature trail takes you down by the Mekong. Than Thong is more accessible than Than Thip, but can be rather crowded on weekends and holidays.

The forest wat peering down on the town from the eastern hills, **Wat Pa Tak Sua** (☉ daylight hours), lies about 4km as the crow flies (ask someone to point you to the footpath to the top), but it's 18km to drive (take the turn-off across from Nam Tok Than Thong). It has a very good sunset-over-the-Mekong view.

Bouy's Guest House (☎ 0 4244 1065; Rte 211; r 160-190B; 💻) is an Isan word association game; Sangkhom and the town's veteran guesthouse are rarely more than a breath apart. Rusticity is the buzzword here and the riverside thatched bungalows, the cheaper ones sharing bathrooms, are pretty basic, but in better shape than much of the competition. The owner is a great big bag of smiles and the location just west of town is wonderfully relaxing.

Vanda House (☎ 0 4244 1088; Rte 211; r 500-600B; 🍽) offers some swankier digs 1km east of town. The resort doesn't make good use of the river views and isn't really great value, but its beds will satisfy those who demand a certain level of comfort. The resort's adjoining **Pu-Pae Restaurant** (dishes 30-140B; ☉ breakfast, lunch & dinner; 🍽) recently relocated out here from a great spot across from the police station in the centre of town; which is a shame because its atmospheric old post had a wooden terrace dining room over the Mekong, with two cosy timber rooms above. It's worth seeing what has moved in.

A couple of surrounding villages, Ban Pha Tang and Ban Pak Som, participate in a home-stay (☎ 0 4242 3783) programme. For 300B you get three meals and one night's sleep. Extras, like walks in the forest and cultural performances, are available. The TAT office in Nong Khai can help with arrangements.

GETTING THERE & AWAY
Bus 507 passes through Sangkhom on its way between Nong Khai (47B, 2¾ hours) and Loei (58B, 3½ hours).

BEUNG KAN
บึงกาฬ
Beung Kan is a small dusty town on the Mekong River, 136km east of Nong Khai by Rte 212. You may want to break your journey here if you are working your way around the northeastern border from Nong Khai to Nakhon Phanom (as opposed to the easier but less interesting route via Udon Thani and Sakon Nakhon).

Amphoe Beung Kan itself isn't much, but it has banks, an internet café and most other services you might need, plus a nice promenade along the waterfront. During the dry season the Mekong River recedes from Beung Kan and reaches its narrowest point along the Thai-Lao border. People picnic on the sand-bar that comes exposed at this time. The surrounding countryside has several waterfalls.

If you're saving your baht for sundowners, consider the **Mekong Guest House** (☎ 0 4249 1341; 202/1 Th Chansin; r 200-300B; 🍽), but look carefully because it treads a fine line between dirty and filthy. Three doors down, the **Maenam Hotel** (☎ 0 4249 1052; 107/1 Th Chansin; r 350-450B; 🍽) is a big step up in quality and service, offering spotless rooms with lots of little extras. Just about all the restaurants on Th Chansin serve inside or riverside (which can be buggy), including **Chowdin** (no roman-script sign; ☎ 08 7863 4170; Th Chansin; dishes 30-100B; ☉ dinner), a *jim jam* restaurant (cook your own soup over a wood-burning fire at your table) where you sit on cushions at short tables. For a menu in English, try **Joy's Restaurant** (Th Chansin, Mekong Guest House; ☉ breakfast, lunch & dinner).

Getting There & Away
Ordinary buses (70B, three hours, three daily) to Nong Khai park in front of the 'Thai Beauty' shop near the clocktower. Air-con buses (110B, two hours, four daily) use the petrol station about 100m south.

AROUND BEUNG KAN
Wat Phu Tok
วัดภูทอก
Accessed via a network of rickety staircases built in, on and around a giant sandstone out-

crop, **Wat Phu Tok** (☾ 6.30am-5pm, closed 10-16 April) is one of the region's true wonders, with fabulous vistas over the surrounding countryside and a truly soporific atmosphere. Six levels of steps, plus a seventh-level scramble up roots and rocks to the thick forest at the summit, represent the seven factors of enlightenment in Buddhist psychology. Monastic *kùtì* (meditation huts) are scattered around the mountain, in caves and on cliffs. It is the cool and quiet isolation of this wat that entices monks and *mâe chii* from all over the northeast to come and meditate here – many of them do so on the summit, so be quiet and respectful up there.

This wat used to be the domain of the famous meditation master Ajahn Juan, a disciple of the fierce Ajahn Man (see p515) who died in 1949. Ajahn Juan died in a plane crash in 1980 along with several other highly revered forest monks who were flying to Bangkok for Queen Sirikit's birthday celebration. A marble *chedi* containing his belongings and some bone relics sits below the mountain.

Visitors who impress the monks by acting and dressing respectfully are permitted to stay the night here. Dorms are single sex and you should not forget that this is a holy place. Another, perhaps better, option is the **homestay programme** (☎ 08 6086 1221; per person 200B) in **Ban Kom Kan Phat Tana**, the village just outside the wat. Just ask around and you'll get pointed in the right direction.

GETTING THERE & AWAY

Túk-túk can be hired to get to Wat Phu Tok from the clocktower in Beung Kan – fares cost around 600B for the return journey, plus a two-hour wait at the wat itself. Better still, take bus 225 from the clocktower south to Si Wilai (20B, 45 minutes) where túk-túk drivers charge around 250B to the wat. If you catch an early bus to Beung Kan, Wat Phu Tok can be visited as a day trip from Nong Khai. If you're driving or pedalling, a more direct route to the monastery is to continue southeast along Rte 212 from Beung Kan for 27km until you reach Chaiyaporn, then turn right (south) at Rte 3024, the road signed for Jet Si, Tham Phra and Chut Na waterfalls. After 17.5km make a right (southwest) and continue 4km more.

Ban Ahong

บ้านอาฮง

A nice alternative to staying in Beung Khan, Ban Ahong is a pretty little riverside village

at the Km 115 marker on Rte 212. **Wat Ahong Silawat** (☾ daylight hours), on the village's west side, is built around ruddy boulders at a river bend known as 'The Navel of the Mekong' because of the large whirlpool that spins here. A 7m-tall copy of Phitsanulok's Chinnarat Buddha gazes over the Mekong from next to the simple little *bòt*. This is considered a highly auspicious spot to spend the evening of *wan àwk phansǎa,* the end of the Buddhist Rains Retreat (Buddhist Lent), because the *bâng fai pháyaa nâak* (*naga* fireballs) were first reported here (see the boxed text, p495).

The **Ahong Mekong View Hotel** (☎ 0 4290 1112; r 350-650B; ❄) sits along the river on the temple grounds and does most of its business with tour groups – so you'll likely either find it booked out or you'll be the only guests. The prices are a bit high, but each of the 14 large rooms is well appointed and has a balcony.

A better overnight option is the village's new **homestay programme** (☎ 08 7223 1544; per person 150B, per meal 50B). About two dozen families have guestrooms in their houses and you can join in village life as much as you like, perhaps joining your hosts out in the surrounding rubber plantations. Either call ahead or stop by to see Khun Win at house number 74, a little west of the school on the river road.

The bus between Beung Kan and Ban Ahong costs 25B (30 minutes).

LOEI PROVINCE

Stretching south from the sleepy arc of the Mekong River near Chiang Khan to the undulating hilltops of Phu Kradung National Park, Loei is a diverse, beautiful province untouched by mass tourism, despite all it has to offer. This isn't the wildest place in Thailand, but potholes definitely pepper a still relatively untrammelled trail that will lead you from the hush of the region's tranquil national parks to the hubbub of Dan Sai's annual Phi Ta Khon Festival.

The terrain here is mountainous and temperatures fluctuate from one extreme to the other – hotter than elsewhere in Thailand during the hot season and colder than anywhere else during the cold season. This is the only province in Thailand where temperatures can drop below 0°C, a fact the tourist brochures love to trumpet. For hiking, the best time to visit Loei is during the cool months of mid-October through February.

LOEI PROVINCE

LOEI

เลย

pop 33,000

Arrive here after a sojourn in the region's dreamy countryside and Loei, the capital of the province, is little more than a reminder that concrete and congestion still exist. Efforts to upgrade the town, including a large city-centre lake and a plush new hotel, have done little to haul Loei out of the doldrums, and, as the Tourism Authority of Thailand itself says: 'The city of Loei has little to hold the traveller's interest.'

Information

Bangkok Bank (Th Charoenrat; ☑ 8.30am-3.30pm Mon-Fri) Has an ATM and exchange service.

Faster Zone (22/38 Soi Pia Th Chumsai; per hr 15B; ☑ 8am-10pm) Surf the web here.

Loei Ram Hospital (☎ 0 4283 3400; Th Maliwan) South of the city centre.

Loei Tourism Coordination Centre (☎ 0 4281 2812; Th Charoenat; ☑ 8.30am-4.30pm)

Loei Travel (☎ 0 4283 0741; 167/4 Th Charoenrat) In the Loei Palace Hotel.

Main post office (Th Charoenat; ☑ 8.30am-4.30pm Mon-Fri, 8am-noon Sat, Sun & holidays)

Tourist police (☎ 1155; Rte 203) West of town.

Sights

If you've been to any other Isan museum, the little **Cultural Centre of Loei** (☎ 0 4283 5224; Rte 201; admission free; ☑ 8.30am-4.30pm), 4km north of town at Rajabhat University, is hardly worth

the trip, though if you won't be stopping in Dan Sai, there are Phi Ta Khon festival masks and photos to see.

Wang Saphung, 24km south of Loei, is the strange and unlikely location of the **Sirindhorn Arts Centre** (☎ 0 4284 1410; Rte 210; admission free; 🕑 8.30am-4.30pm). It was built to honour Sangkom Thongmee, a famous local teacher (since retired) at the adjoining school whose students, mostly farmers' children, have won thousands of awards for their work. There's a sculpture garden and gallery and sometimes student work on display, which is invariably more interesting that the professionals' exhibits.

Festivals & Events
Though Loei's farmers are fast switching to other crops, the end of January/start of February still sees a **Cotton Blossom Festival** that culminates in a parade of cotton-decorated floats.

Sleeping
Sugar Guest House (☎ 0 4281 2982; 4/1 Th Wisut Titep Soi 2; r 150-350B; 🗙) The cheapest place in town is also the friendliest. The fan rooms share a hot-water bath. The English-speaking owner arranges trips around the province at reasonable prices and rents motorcycles (200B) if you'd rather get there yourself.

King Hotel (☎ 0 4281 1701; 11/9-12 Th Chumsai; r 240-600B; 🗙) Fit for a king? No, but business travellers love it. The pleasant rooms surround a small courtyard and shining surfaces, even in the fan rooms, bear testament to a clutch of hard-working, behind-the-scenes cleaners.

AP Court Hotel (☎ 0 4286 1627; www.apcourthotel .com; 31/29 Th Ruamphattana; r 350-600B; 🗙) The rooms at this newly built property, hidden away in the centre of the block, are a bit of a letdown compared to the plant- and art-filled lobby (where you can use wi-fi), but the value is undeniable.

Loei Palace Hotel (☎ 0 4281 5668; loeipalace@amari .com; 167/4 Th Charoenrat; s/d/t 3060/3296/4002B; 🗙 🖥 🖳) Loei's flagship hotel sports some wedding-cake architecture, helpful staff, plenty of mod cons and 40% discounts when business is slow, which is almost always. Check out the flood marker and photos next to the reception desk to see what the city suffered in September 2002.

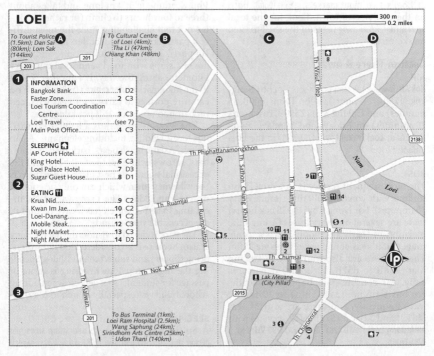

LOEI

0 —————— 300 m
0 —————— 0.2 miles

To Tourist Police (1.5km); Dan Sai (80km); Lom Sak (144km)

To Cultural Centre of Loei (4km); Tha Li (47km); Chiang Khan (48km)

INFORMATION
Bangkok Bank.........................1 D2
Faster Zone............................2 C3
Loei Tourism Coordination
  Centre................................3 C3
Loei Travel ....(see 7)
Main Post Office....................4 C3

SLEEPING 🏠
AP Court Hotel.......................5 C2
King Hotel.............................6 C3
Loei Palace Hotel....................7 D3
Sugar Guest House...................8 D1

EATING 🍴
Krua Nid...............................9 C2
Kwan Im Jae.........................10 C2
Loei-Danang.........................11 C2
Mobile Steak.........................12 C3
Night Market.........................13 C3
Night Market.........................14 D2

Th Wisut Titep
Th Phiphattanamongkhon
Th Sathon Chang Khan
Th Ruamjai
Th Ruamphattana
Th Ruamjit
Th Charoenrat
Nam
Loei
Th Ua Ari
Th Chumsai
Th Nok Kaew
Lak Meuang (City Pillar)
Th Maliwan
Th Charoenrat

To Bus Terminal (1km); Loei Ram Hospital (2.5km); Wang Saphung (24km); Sirindhorn Arts Centre (25km); Udon Thani (140km)

Eating

Kwan Im Jae (☎ 0 4281 4863; Soi Pia Th Chumsai; dishes 15-30B; ☺ breakfast & lunch) A small, friendly vegetarian restaurant.

Krua Nid (no roman-script sign; ☎ 0 4281 3013; Th Charoenrat; dishes 20-45B; ☺ breakfast, lunch & dinner) Basic and striplit, this no-frills eatery serves *hàw mòk* (soufflé-like curry steamed in banana leaves) and other central-Thai dishes. Look for the banana-leaf balls or the 'Welcome' sign.

Loei-Danang (☎ 0 4283 0413; 22/58-60 Soi Pia Th Chumsai; dishes 25-120B; ☺ lunch & dinner; ☒) This friendly restaurant, on what's commonly called Soi Night Plaza, adds Thai dishes and ice cream to its wonderful Vietnamese menu. There are a few pictures in the menu to help you order.

Mobile Steak (no roman-script sign; ☎ 08 5008 8288; Th Chumsai; dishes 30-159B; ☺ lunch & dinner) One of Snow White's dwarves welcomes you to this alfresco eatery that serves tasty Thai, as well as slabs of beef, at wooden tables surrounded by pot plants and the sounds of golden oldies.

Most of the city's culinary razzmatazz – and a whole host of cheap eats – can be found at Loei's two **night markets** (☺ 4-10pm), both on the east side of town. Look for the local speciality, *khài pîng* (eggs in the shell toasted on skewers).

Getting There & Away

AIR

Nok Air (www.nokair.com) connects Loei to Bangkok (1750B, 1½ hours), Udon Thani (600B, 35 minutes) and Chiang Mai (2550B, two hours 20 minutes) on Fridays and Sundays. Book tickets at **Loei Travel** (☎ 0 4283 0741) in the Loei Palace Hotel.

BUS

The most frequent service is to Udon Thani (ordinary/air-con 60/110B, three hours, every 30 minutes). For Nong Khai (105B, six hours) there are several ordinary buses through the morning and early afternoon; this is a scenic route, but it's easier and faster to go via Udon Thani. There are also four air-con Chiang Mai (438B to 657B, 10 hours) departures daily. Air-con buses to Bangkok's Northern bus terminal (344B, nine to 10 hours) leave frequently, and there are also 24-seat (685B) and 32-seat (521B) VIP services with **Air Muang Loei** (☎ 0 4283 2042) and **999 VIP** (☎ 0 4281 1706).

Getting Around

Săwngthăew (7B) run from the bus station into town about every five minutes, or you can take a túk-túk for 20B.

AROUND LOEI PROVINCE
Phu Kradung National Park

อุทยานแห่งชาติภูกระดึง

Capped off by its eponymous peak, **Phu Kradung National Park** (☎ 0 4287 1333; admission 400B; ☺ trail to summit 7am-2pm Oct-May) covers a high-altitude plateau, cut through with trails and peppered with cliffs, waterfalls and montane forests. Rising to 1316m, Thailand's second national park is always cool at its highest reaches (average year-round temperature 20°C; dropping as low as 1°C to 2°C at night in December and January), where its flora is more typical of a temperate zone. The maple trees paint some corners red in December and January. Lower down are mixed deciduous and evergreen monsoon forests as well as sections of cloud forest.

A small visitor centre at the base of the mountain distributes detailed maps and collects your admission fee, but almost everything else is on the top. The **main trail** scaling Phu Kradung is 5.5km long and takes about three to four hours to climb (or rather walk – it's not that challenging since the most difficult parts have bamboo ladders and stairs for support). The hike is quite scenic and there are rest stops with food vendors about every kilometre along the way. It's another 3.5km to the main park **visitor centre** (☺ 8am-5pm). You can hire porters to carry your gear balanced on bamboo poles for 15B per kilogram.

The 359-sq-km park is a habitat for various forest wildlife, including elephants, Asian jackals, Asiatic black bears, barking deer, sambars, serows, white-handed gibbons and the occasional tiger. The best place to see them is the **wilderness area**, which can only be entered in April and May. The many waterfalls, including **Tham Yai**, which has a cave behind it, are accessible year-round.

The park is closed to visitors during the rainy season because it is considered too hazardous, being slippery and subject to mudslides. Spending the night atop Phu Kradung is a rite of passage for students, so it gets crowded during school holidays (especially March to May).

SLEEPING & EATING

Atop the mountain there are **camp sites** (per person 30B, 2-person tent hire 150B) and 13 swanky

bungalows (4 people 1600B). There are also several small open-air eateries serving the usual stir-fry dishes for 40B. If you are arriving late in the afternoon, there is one bungalow at the bottom and a few resorts outside the entrance.

GETTING THERE & AWAY

Buses on the Loei–Khon Kaen line go to the district town of Phu Kradung (55B, 1½ hours, every half-hour). From Phu Kradung, hop on a săwngthăew (20B) to the park visitor centre at the base of the mountain, 10km away. The last bus back to Loei from Phu Kradung leaves around 8pm.

Tham Erawan

ถ้ำเอราวัณ

High up the side of a beautiful limestone mountain, **Tham Erawan** (donations appreciated; ☽ daylight hours) is a large cave shrine, featuring a vast seated Buddha. Gazing out over the plains below, the Buddha is visible from several kilometres away and can be reached by a winding staircase of some 600 steps. There's not much to admire in the cave itself, but the views are photogenic and it's a good place to stretch your legs if you happen to be travelling along Rte 210.

The cave is at the back of **Wat Tham Erawan** (☽ daylight hours), which is 2km north of a turn-off on Rte 210 just across the Nong Bualamphu Province line. A túk-túk will shuttle you there for about 20B.

Phu Reua National Park

อุทยานแห่งชาติภูเรือ

Phu Rua means 'boat mountain', a moniker that owes its origins to a cliff that juts out of the peak sort of in the shape of a Chinese junk. At only 121 sq km, **Phu Reua National Park** (☎ 0 4288 1716, reservations 0 2562 0760; admission 400B; ☽ 8am-8pm) isn't one of Thailand's most impressive reserves, but it does offer some dreamy vistas from the summit of the mountain it surrounds. Few visitors do more than make the easy 30-minute hike from the upper visitor centre through pine forest to the summit (1365m), where in December and January temperatures can drop below freezing at night. There are some fine views of a mountain range in Sainyabuli Province, Laos, up here. **Hin San** waterfall is just a 300m walk from the parking area.

If you want solitude, head out from the lower visitor centre. **Huai Phai** waterfall is an easy 2.5km hike or take a roundabout route to the summit starting down here.

SLEEPING & EATING

The park offers a number of accommodation options, and if they are all full, don't worry, the town seemingly has more hotel rooms than houses. As well as a **camp site** (per person 30B, 2-person tent hire 250B), there are also some comfortable **bungalows** (4 people 1500B) with fan, hot water and fridge, as well as simpler **rooms** (3 people 500B). There are restaurants at both visitor centres.

GETTING THERE & AWAY

The park is about 50km west of the provincial capital on Rte 203. Although buses heading west from Loei can drop you in the town of Phu Reua (ordinary/air-con 40/55B, 1½ hours), you'll have to charter a săwngthăew for around 600B (including a few hours wait) to the park.

Dan Sai & Around

ด่านซ้าย

For 362 days a year, Dan Sai is an innocuous little town, a borderline backwater community where life revolves around a small market and a dusty main street. For the remaining three days, however, it is the site of one of the country's liveliest and loudest festivals.

Falling during the fourth lunar month (usually June), Dan Sai's **Phi Ta Khon Festival** (also called Bun Phra Wet) combines the Phra Wet Festival – during which recitations of the *Mahavessantara Jataka* (past-life stories of the Buddha) are supposed to enhance the listener's chance of being reborn in the lifetime of the next Buddha – with Bun Bâng Fai (Rocket Festival). For those wishing to plunge headlong into Isan life, this curious cross between the drunken revelry of Carnival and the spooky imagery of Halloween is a must-see.

The origins of the Phi Ta Khon Festival are shrouded in ambiguity, but some aspects of the festival appear to be related to tribal Thai – possibly Tai Dam – spirit cults. In fact, the dates for the festival are divined by Jao Phaw Kuan, a local spirit medium who channels the information from Jao Saen Meuang, the town's guardian deity.

INFORMATION

Information centre (☎ 0 4289 1094; Th Kaew Asa; ☽ 8.30am-4.30pm Mon-Fri) In the library by the market.

THE ARRIVAL OF THE SPIRITS

Dan Sai's three-day **Phi Ta Khon** (*phǐi taa khǒhn*) **Festival** – known as Bun Phra Wet in other towns – is one of the most colourful and unique annual events in Thailand. On the first day the village shaman, Jao Phaw Kuan, assisted by his shaman wife Jao Mae Nang Tiam, plus a group of male and female lesser mediums, leads the propitiation of the all-important *tiam*. The *tiam* are a class of spirits similar to the Lao-Thai *khwǎn* (guardian spirits) but perceived to be at a higher level.

Ceremonies begin around 3.30am in a procession from Dan Sai's Wat Phon Chai to Mae Nam Man. Rites are performed at the riverside to coax Phra Upakhut – a water spirit supposedly embodied in an invisible piece of white marble – to join the proceedings. Phra Upakhut is believed to have once been a monk with supernatural powers, who transformed himself into white marble 'to live a solitary and peaceful existence below the water'. The procession – accompanied by the spirit – then returns to the wat, where resident monks receive ceremonial food at around 7am.

Shortly thereafter the summoning of additional spirits takes place at Jao Phaw Kuan's home, which doubles as the most important spirit shrine in Dan Sai. After some incantations and lighting of candles, villagers crawl up to Jao Phaw and Jao Mae, now in states of semitrance, and tie lots of sacred thread on their arms. The attendants also tie sacred thread around one wrist of everyone present. While all this is taking place, free food is served and everyone downs shots of *lào khǎo* (white spirit) to get in the mood for what comes next.

As the thread tying finishes up, the attendants don special costuming and gather in front of the house. Most of the outfits look like something from Shakespearean theatre meant for beggar or jester roles – ragged and tattered but very colourful. To complete the transformation into *phǐi taa khǒhn* (an untranslatable term basically meaning 'Phra Wet spirits'), each attendant dons a huge mask made from a *hûat* (crescent-shaped basket used for steaming sticky rice), cut and reshaped to fit atop the head, and a thick sheath from the base of a coconut palm frond. On the typical mask small eye-openings are cut into the palm sheath and a large curving wooden nose added; the whole affair is custom painted, to suit the wearer, with all manner of designs.

Two of the attendants, however, wear tall bamboo frames assembled in vaguely human shapes, covered with white cloth and topped with giant heads standing perhaps 2m above their own heads. One figure is male, the other female, as is obvious from the huge, exaggerated sexual organs attached to the outfits. These are the *phǐi taa khǒhn yài* (big Phra Wet spirits), and exactly what they represent is anyone's guess nowadays. The costumed figures, as well as 'civilians', then begin a boisterous, dance-filled procession – fuelled by more *lào khǎo* – back to the monastery.

Once the cavalcade reaches the wat grounds, the participants begin circumambulating the main *wíhǎan* (large hall) and continue for a couple hours, becoming increasingly rowdy with each turn. There's abundant sexual innuendo and older village women take turns grabbing the lengthy penis of the male *phǐi taa khǒhn y'ài* and giving it a few good shakes, laughing all the while. The whole thing ends around noon and people stagger back home to sleep it off.

On day two all the locals get into costume and accompany Jao Phaw and Jao Mae in a procession from Chum Chon Dan Sai School to the temple. In earlier years the shaman court rode on wood or bamboo palanquins, but these days they sit on colourful dais in the back of pick-up trucks. Bamboo rockets ride along with them. As on the first day, there's plenty of music and dancing, but this time there are hundreds more participants, and spectators marvel at the many different costume designs cooked up for this year's event. Many of the costumed *phǐi taa khǒhn*, both men and women, carry carved wooden phalli (or a knife or sword with a phallic handle) in one or both hands, waving them about as talismans or using them to tease the crowd while they dance and strut down the street. Tin cans and wooden cowbells hang from some costumes to increase the racket.

Once again, when they reach the wat, the participants dance round the *wíhǎan* for hours, becoming more raucous and spontaneous as the day wears on. At the same time in front of the wat there's live *mǎw lam* (an Isan musical tradition). If it has rained recently, participants will revel in the mud. As one Western observer remarked: 'It's like Woodstock and Halloween rolled into one'. Come late afternoon the bamboo rockets are fired off to the sky.

The celebration ends with a more solemn third day as the villagers assemble at the temple to listen to *Mahavessantara Jataka* recitations (past-life stories of the Buddha) and Dhamma sermons by local and visiting monks. By custom, 13 sermons are delivered in a row.

Has festival photos and free internet. The staff speaks a little English, but if it's not enough, stop by City Hall just up the road.

Krung Thai Bank (Rte 203; ☼ 8.30am-4.30pm Mon-Fri) Changes dollars and euros only.

Post office (Th Kaew Asa; ☼ 8.30am-4.30pm Mon-Fri, to noon Sat & holidays)

SIGHTS & ACTIVITIES

On the main road through town, **Wat Phon Chai** (Th Kaew Asa; ☼ daylight hours) plays a major role in the Phi Ta Khon festivities. The small **Dan Sai Folk Museum** (donations appreciated; ☼ 9am-5pm) here features a collection of costumes worn during the celebrations.

Phra That Si Songrak (Rte 2113; ☼ daylight hours) is the most highly revered stupa in Loei Province. The whitewashed Lao-style *chedi* stands 30m high and was built in 1560 as a gesture of unity between the Lao kingdom of Wiang Chan (Vientiane) and the Thai kingdom of Ayuthaya in their resistance against the Burmese. A pavilion in front of it contains a very old chest that supposedly contains an even older carved stone Buddha about 76cm long. You can't wear shoes or the colour red, or carry food or umbrellas anywhere on temple grounds.

Wat Neramit Wiphatsana (☼ daylight hours), on a wooded hill overlooking Phra That Si Songrak, is a gorgeous (it almost looks like a Buddhist-themed resort) meditation wat where most of the buildings are made of unplastered laterite blocks. Famous Thai temple muralist Pramote Sriphrom spent years painting images of jataka tales on the interior walls of the *bòt*. The wat is dedicated to the memory of the late Ajahn Mahaphan (also known as Khruba Phawana), a much-revered local monk.

Out of town on Rte 203 near the Km 60 marker is **Chateau de Loei Winery** (☎ 0 4280 9521; www.chateaudeloei.com; ☼ 8am-5pm), Thailand's most respected vineyard. The winery released the first commercially produced Thai wine in 1995 and scooped a silver medal for its Chenin Blanc dessert wine in the 2004 International Wine & Spirits Competition. Visitors are welcome and you can taste its wines, grape juices and brandies back in the main winery building. There is a restaurant and gift-gourmet shop on the main road.

SLEEPING & EATING

As very few people stay in Dan Sai outside the festival season, accommodation is extremely limited within the town itself, though out on Rte 203 towards Loei there's a good selection if you can spend a little more and have your own transport.

Homestay (☎ information centre 0 4289 1094; per person 150B) The information centre places visitors in homes in nearby villages. The families dote on *faràng* guests and will take you out to give food to the monks in the morning and share other typical daily activities. The information centre can also set you up to stay at Wat Neramit Wiphatsana for a small donation.

Yen Suk Guest House (☎ 0 4289 2281; Rte 203; r 250-600B; ☼) The only guesthouse in town (though another is supposedly coming soon) is a bright orange affair built in 2006. The rooms, including the cheap fan rooms, are fine, but the neighbours give you a very early wake-up call.

Rangyen Resort (☎ 0 4280 9511; www.rungyenresort.com; Rte 203; r 1090-9200B; ☼ ☐ ☼) When you crest the hill, this resort, owned by Chateau de Loei, makes a great first impression. Spread out over several hectares, this pleasant spot boasts a sizable pond, a swimming pool, tennis courts and manicured gardens. The large rooms have nice decorations and the bungalows (sleeping up to 10) have fireplaces. Off-season (April to September) discounts are nearly 50%. There's a big restaurant and a karaoke bar on the premises as the place is geared towards convention business. It's a 10km drive off the highway, so you can forget about using public transport to get here.

Aim Aun (no roman-script sign; ☎ 0 4289 1586; Rte 203; dishes 25-200B; ☼ lunch & dinner) Sizzling Thai favourites, like *kaeng páa* (forest curry), are served under a thatched roof in a garden setting, on the edge of town.

There are a few noodle and rice shops near Wat Phon Chai and a market filled with food stalls opposite the information centre.

GETTING THERE & AWAY

Thirteen buses from Loei (ordinary/air-con 50/60B, 1½ hours) to Phitsanulok (ordinary/air-con 71/99B, three hours) stop in Dan Sai daily. Buses leaving Dan Sai depart from the entrance of Yen Suk Guest House.

CHIANG KHAN

เชียงคาน

Traditional timber houses line the streets, old ladies sit nattering in their shadow and the Mekong drifts slowly by: if you had an image of a northern riverside town where nothing much

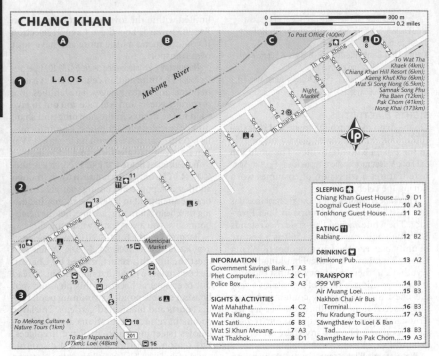

CHIANG KHAN

SLEEPING
Chiang Khan Guest House.......9 D1
Loogmai Guest House...........10 A3
Tonkhong Guest House.........11 B2

EATING
Rabiang................................12 B2

DRINKING
Rimkong Pub.......................13 A2

INFORMATION
Government Savings Bank...1 A3
Phet Computer...................2 C1
Police Box.........................3 A3

TRANSPORT
999 VIP..............................14 B3
Air Muang Loei..................15 B3
Nakhon Chai Air Bus
    Terminal........................16 B3
Phu Kradung Tours............17 A3
Săwngthǎew to Loei & Ban
    Tad................................18 B3
Săwngthǎew to Pak Chom.....19 A3

SIGHTS & ACTIVITIES
Wat Mahathat....................4 C2
Wat Pa Klang.....................5 B2
Wat Santi..........................6 B3
Wat Si Khun Meuang.........7 A3
Wat Thakhok.....................8 D1

happens and no one seems to care, Chiang Khan may just be it. Pretty and peaceful, with photogenic views of the river and the mountains of Laos beyond, this little town has a good spread of cheap accommodation and makes a restful stopover if you fancy a couple of days of doing…well…nothing.

Information

Government Savings Bank (Rte 201; 8.30am-3.30pm Mon-Fri) Has an ATM, but there are no foreign-exchange facilities in town.

Phet Computer (Th Chiang Khan; per hr 40B; 10am-11pm) Check your email here.

Police box (1155; cnr Rte 201 & Th Chiang Khan) On the main road through town.

Post office (Soi 26; 8.30am-4.30pm Mon-Fri, to noon Sat, Sun & holidays)

Tourist Information Centre (Kaeng Khut Khu; 9am-5pm) Your guesthouse would be a better source of information on the area.

Sights
TEMPLES

Chiang Khan's wats are modest, but feature a particularly idiosyncratic style of wat ar-

chitecture rarely seen in Thailand. Featuring colonnaded fronts and painted shutters, the *wíhǎan* temples echo the French architectural influences of Laos. A good example in the centre of town is **Wat Pa Klang** (Th Chiang Khan; daylight hours), which is about 100 years old and features a new glittery superstructure. On the grounds of this wat is a small Chinese garden with a pond, waterfall, and Chinese-style sculptures of Buddha and Kuan Yin. Temple structures at **Wat Santi** (Soi 9; daylight hours) and **Wat Thakhok** (Th Chai Khong; daylight hours) are similar to those at Wat Pa Klang (minus the Chinese garden, etc).

Wat Mahathat (Th Chiang Khan; daylight hours), in the centre of town, is Chiang Khan's oldest temple; the *bòt*, constructed in 1654, has a new roof over old walls, with faded original murals on the front.

Wat Si Khun Meuang (Th Chai Khong; daylight hours) contains a Lao-style *chedi* and *bòt*, fronted by an unusual mural style, plus a topiary garden.

Wat Tha Khaek (daylight hours) is a lovely and peaceful 600- to 700-year-old temple housing three very old stone Buddha images.

They sit on a ledge over a larger, modern Buddha in the wat's modern *bòt*. The temple is 2km outside town on the way to Kaeng Khut Khu.

Another well-known monastic centre in the area is **Samnak Song Phu Pha Baen** (☉ daylight hours), 12km east of Chiang Khan (no English signage), where monks meditate in caves and on tree platforms.

Activities
KAENG KHUT KHU
แก่งคุดคู้

Next to nobody in Bangkok has ever heard of Chiang Khan, but most know the rapids at **Kaeng Khut Khu** (admission free; ☉ 24hr), a popular spot (at its most beautiful in the dry, hot season) for paddling, picnicking and sunsoaking, about 6km downstream from Chiang Khan. The surrounding park has thatched-roof shelters with reed mats on raised wooden platforms where **food vendors** sell delicious Isan food and drinks into the late afternoon. The local speciality is coconut candy *(má-prów ków)*, and this is also a good place to try *kûng ten* ('dancing shrimp'), little bowls of live shrimp meant for slurping down just as they come. Săwngthăew rarely come out here, so rent a bike in town.

BOAT TRIPS & TOURS

Most guesthouses listed here arrange boat trips to Kaeng Khut Khu (per person 200B to 300B) or further afield, and the mountain scenery makes these highly recommended. Most guesthouses also rent bikes (200B to 280B for a mountain bike, 50B for a clunker)

and motorcycles (around 200B). Mekong Culture & Nature Tours, which plans to open an office in town, has kayaks for rent (two hours 400B, full-day trip with shuttle 1500B) and, if *faràng* are ever allowed to cross the border here, will offer boat services to Vientiane.

Both Chiang Khan Guest House and Mekong Culture & Nature Tours arranges a host of customised regional tours. Huub at Chiang Khan Guest House can also set you up with a map if you're a do-it-yourselfer.

Festivals & Events

Chiang Khan comes alive during *wan àwk phansăa*, the end of the **Buddhist Rains Retreat** (Buddhist Lent) in late October and early November. There's a week-long festival that features a parade of large carved wax *prasat* from each of the temples in town, as well as boat races on the river and a carnival with *măw lam* (an Isan musical tradition) performances at night.

Sleeping

our pick **Chiang Khan Guest House** (☎ 08 4282 1691; www.thailandunplugged.com; 282 Th Chai Khong; s/d/t 200/250/300B) Run by a Dutch tour guide (you'll never be short of local info) and his affable Thai wife (you'll never stop laughing), this traditional-style place with shared bathrooms is all creaking timber and tin roofing. Scores of pot plants and bucolic views from the terrace round out the scene.

Tonkhong Guest House (☎ 08 1670 2729; 299/3 Th Chai Khong; s 150, d 200-380B; ✍) Modern modifications have robbed this old wooden place of most of its charm, but the owner scores high marks for bonhomie and it's the homiest

---

TAI DAM

The village of Ban Napanard, near Chiang Khan, is home to many Tai Dam people who migrated here from Laos sometime around 1885, though their ancient cultural home is in Vietnam.

Locals run a little-known **homestay** (☎ 0 4281 4664; per person 200B) where you get to learn about Tai Dam culture and history and join in village life. The price includes three meals of Tai Dam food, which is similar to Isan food, but with different sauces. Also available, whether you do the homestay or not, is a partial performance of their *Sair Pang* cultural dance show, which colourfully tells the story of a witch doctor healing the sick. The money (1200B) from these shows, which require a few days notice to arrange, goes to maintain a small **Tai Dam Cultural Centre** (admission free; ☉ daylight hours), with an old-style bamboo and thatch house that needed several shows worth of repairs when we last saw it. In their free time, women come down here to weave.

Two săwngthăew make the trip from Chiang Khan (25B, 30 minutes) daily and some guesthouses in Chiang Khan run tours (which may be the more educational option if you don't speak Thai). If you are coming on your own, head down Rte 201 for 5km and then follow Rte 3011 for 11.5km to the village.

choice facing the river. Doors close at 11pm. Cooking classes and massage are available.

our pick Loogmai Guest House (☎ 0 4282 2334; 112 Th Chai Khong; r 300-400B) Combining some minimalist modern artistic styling with oodles of French colonial class, this old school villa offers a handful of sparse but atmospheric rooms, an airy terrace with river views and a real sense of history. The owner leaves the villa at 9pm (you get the key) and chances are you'll have the place to yourself. It also has one 'large room', where there's enough space to swing cats by the dozen. Bathrooms are shared.

Mekong Culture & Nature Tours (☎ 0 4282 1457; mcn_thailand@hotmail.com; 407 Th Chiang Khan; camp sites per person 100B, r 800-900B; 🖳) If you want some Siamese serenity, head 1km upstream to this riverside home with six shared-bath guestrooms and a bungalow in the forest out the back. Rooms are quite pricey for what you get, but you're paying for the setting, and off-season discounts are available. If you are travelling by bus, staff will pick you up in town.

Eating & Drinking

The guesthouses and hotels offer the best dining options.

Rabiang (no roman-script sign; ☎ 0 4282 1532; 299 Th Chai Khong; dishes 30-150B; 😋 breakfast, lunch & dinner) It's not the cheeriest of venues, but the views of the river are pleasant and all the usual Thai favourites are represented on the English-language menu.

Chiang Khan Hill Resort (☎ 0 4282 1285; dishes 25-230B; 😋 breakfast, lunch & dinner) The best views of Kaeng Khut Khu are from the area's only swank resort. Dine riverside, inside, or on a dry-docked boat.

Rimkong Pub (☎ 0 4282 1125; 294 Th Chai Khong; 😋 breakfast, lunch & dinner) French expat Pascal will tell you all you want to know about the area (or the bungalows he rents) over beer or breakfast.

Entertainment

Chiang Khan Guest House (☎ 0 4282 1691; www.thai landunplugged.com; 282 Th Chai Khong; 😋 lunch & dinner with advance notice) On weekends and school holidays this place can organise a *ponglang* show (2000B) with local students, who keep all the cash to put towards their studies.

Getting There & Away

Săwngthăew to Loei (30B, 1¼ hours) depart about every 15 minutes from a stop on Rte 201, while nine buses (36B, 45 minutes) leave

from Nakhon Chai Air's bus terminal about 100m further south.

No transport runs direct to Nong Khai, so you'll have to get out of town to catch the bus headed there from Loei. It may be possible to take a săwngthăew to Pak Chom (25B, one hour), but these only run if they're full, and they rarely fill up these days since the road is in terrible shape (though you could always just buy up the remaining seats). The surer option is to take the Loei săwngthăew south to Ban Tad (20B, 30 minutes) and get the bus there. Ask at your guesthouse if things have changed.

Three companies make the run to Bangkok (about 10 hours) daily from their own offices. **Air Muang Loei** (☎ 0 4282 1002; Soi 9), with an office at a pharmacy, has two buses (1st/2nd class 479/372B) each morning at 8am and again at 6.30pm. **999 VIP** (☎ 0 4281 1706; Soi 9) includes ordinary services (193B) at 6pm and 6.50pm, and a 24-seat VIP (540B) at 6.30pm. **Phu Kradung Tours** (☎ 0 9696 2845; Rte 201) charges 372B for its 6.30pm trip.

If you're heading west and you've got your own wheels, consider following the seldom-seen back roads along Mae Nam Heuang; they will eventually deposit you in Dan Sai.

NAKHON PHANOM PROVINCE

Lao, Vietnamese and, in the capital, Chinese influences dominate Nakhon Phanom, a province bordered by the Mekong and dotted with Lao-style *thâat*. Though just about every person you see working in the rice fields or herding buffalo along the road is ethnically Thai, most wear the conical Vietnamese-style straw hats. It's not a region bristling with attractions, but there are plenty of fine river views, and the colossal Wat Phra That Phanom, in That Phanom, is an enchanting talisman of Isan culture.

NAKHON PHANOM

นครพนม

pop 31,700

In Sanskrit-Khmer, Nakhon Phanom means 'city of hills'. Unfortunately, they're all across the river in Laos. But that doesn't stop you from admiring them. With fabulous views across the Mekong to the undulating, sugarloaf peaks on

the other side of the border, this slightly scruffy little provincial capital can sure sell its postcards. The bad news is that there's not a whole lot to do once you've written them.

Information

Bangkok Bank (Lotus Department Store; Th Nittaya; ☾ 10am-8pm) Changes cash only. There are many more banks, open normal banking hours, in the town centre that also do travellers cheques.

Crab Internet (Th Si Thep; per hr 10B; ☾ 8.30am-10pm)

Immigration office (☎ 0 4251 1235; Th Sunthon Wijit; ☾ 8.30am-4.30pm Mon-Fri) For visa extensions.

Main post office (Th Sunthon Wijit; ☾ 8.30am-4.30pm Mon-Fri, 9am-noon Sat, Sun & holidays)

North By North-East Tours (☎ 0 4251 3572; www .north-by-north-east.com; 746/1 Th Sunthon Wijit; ☾ 9am-5pm Mon-Sat) Specialises in bird-watching and other ecotours, especially across the river in Laos' mountains. It can also help arrange volunteer placements in the area.

TAT (☎ 0 4251 3490; www.tourismthailand.org; Th Sunthon Wijit; ☾ 8.30am-4.30pm) The handiest thing it has is a rough City Tour map that leads you past a few grand old buildings.

Tourist police (☎ 1155; Th Sunthon Wijit) In the park next to the Nakhon Phanom River View Hotel.

Sights

Most of Nakhon Phanom's wats feature bas-relief carvings on the exterior walls, a distinctive temple style that spilled over from the Lan Xang kingdom in southern Laos around the 17th century. Later a vivid French influence crossed the Mekong. One good example is **Wat Maha That** (Th Sunthon Wijit; ☾ daylight hours), founded along with the city in the 6th century. Its 24m-tall, gold and white Phra That Nakhon *chedi* resembles the second *chedi* built at That Phanom.

Wat Okat Si Bua Ban (Th Sunthon Wijit; ☾ daylight hours) predates the town and also has a touch of Chinese influence. The *wíhǎan* houses Phra Taew and Phra Tiam, two sacred wooden Buddha images, and the murals show the story of them floating across the Mekong from Laos.

The interior murals of the *bòt* at **Wat Si Thep** (Th Si Thep; ☾ daylight hours) show the *jataka* along the upper portion, and kings of the Chakri dynasty along the lower part. On the back of

NAKHON PHANOM

| 0 | 200 m |
| 0 | 0.1 miles |

INFORMATION
Bangkok Bank...................................1 A3
Crab Internet.....................................2 B3
Immigration Office............................3 C3
Main Post Office................................4 C1
Tourism Authority of Thailand (TAT)..5 C1

SIGHTS & ACTIVITIES
Wat Okat Si Bua Ban.........................6 C2
Wat Si Thep.......................................7 B3

SLEEPING 🏠
First Hotel..8 C2
Grand Hotel..9 B3
Sritep Hotel......................................10 B3
Windsor Hotel..................................11 B2

EATING 🍴
Indochina Market.............................12 C2
Luk Tan...13 B2
O-Hi-O..14 B2
Tex-Italia Restaurant........................15 B2
Vietnamese Food Shop.....................16 B2

TRANSPORT
999 VIP...(see 17)
Bus Terminal....................................17 A2
Ferry Terminal..................................18 C2
Koo Yong Long................................19 C2
Sangpatip.....................................(see 17)
Thai Airways International Agent.....20 B3

the *bòt* is a colourful triptych done in modern style.

The *bòt* at **Wat Noi Pho Kham** (Th Si Thep; ☼ daylight hours), just off the highway bypass south of town (turn at the lumberyard), has bas-relief carvings inside and out and a 12m-tall Buddha in the subduing mara posture sitting on top.

The Vietnamese community in Ban Na Chok, about 4km west of town, has restored the simple wooden house where Ho Chi Minh lived (1928–29) and planned his resistance movement. There are a few more Ho Chi Minh displays, some labelled in English, around the block from **Uncle Ho's House** (donations appreciated; ☼ daylight hours) at the **Friendship Village** (donations appreciated; ☼ 8am-5pm) community centre.

From February to April **Hat Sai Thong** (Golden Sand Beach) rises just south of the Mae Nam Khong Grand View Hotel.

If you are coming from or heading to the north along Hwy 212, take a short break at **Nam Song Si**, 45km north, where the greenish water of Huay Songkhram meets the muddy brown Mekong. The highway road sign calls this the 'Two Bi-Coloured River'.

Sleeping

First Hotel (☎ 0 4251 1253; 16 Th Si Thep; r 160-300B; ❄) Set back slightly from the road, this bare-bones place has little decoration, but at least offers some peace and quiet.

Grand Hotel (☎ 0 4251 1526; 210 Th Si Thep; r 190-390B; ❄) 'Grand' is a popular euphemism for 'modest' among Thailand's budget hotels. This is no duff option though, and while the interior is rather spartan, potted plants and animal sculptures bring a lick of colour and the rooms are perfectly comfortable.

Windsor Hotel (☎ 0 4251 1946; 272 Th Bamrung Meuang; r 250-400B; ❄ ▢) Housed in a rather intimidating concrete block, this is nevertheless one of the friendlier options in town. The rooms are functional – and the fan rooms are a bit noisy – but remain quite good value.

Sritep Hotel (☎ 0 4251 2395; 197 Th Si Thep; r 320-500B; ❄) This twin-towered hotel is one of the few in town that sits squarely in the midrange. Rooms are ever so ordinary, but it's not bad for the night. The city's only cinema shares the parking lot.

Mae Nam Khong Grand View Hotel (☎ 0 4251 3564; www.mgvhotel.com; 527 Th Sunthon Wijit; r 700-2600B; ❄ ▢) The town's former chart-topping hotel has a little less pizzazz than the Nakhon Phanom River View, but since it's also priced a little bit less you can't really go wrong. There's a pleasant terrace overlooking the river, plus the staff are helpful and polite.

Nakhon Phanom River View Hotel (☎ 0 4252 2333; Th Sunthon Wijit; r 900-2700B; ❄ ▢ ▤) This place is a bit of a hike south of the centre, but it's the town's glossiest hotel, with fresh, well-appointed rooms and the usual business-class amenities. All rooms deliver on the name's promise.

Eating

There are plenty of restaurants along the river, but most of the better eateries are back in the centre of town.

Indochina Market (Th Sunthon Wijit; ☼ breakfast, lunch & dinner) The food court's 2nd-floor terrace has choice seats that frame the mountain views.

Luk Tan (no roman-script sign; ☎ 0 4251 1456; 83 Th Bamrung Meuang; buffet 69-89B; ☼ dinner) This quaint little spot oozes quirky charm, with tables made from old sewing machines and a carefully constructed model train built into the wall. Quirkiest of all is the food; an American home-style buffet featuring mashed potatoes and a salad bar.

Vietnamese Food Shop (no roman-script sign; ☎ 0 4251 2087; 165 Th Thamrong Prasit; dishes 25-100B; ☼ lunch & dinner) With coloured lights and Ronaldinho posters, this little corner shop takes a half-hearted attempt at being fashionable, but the food stays classic, serving the same family recipes, including *namnuang* (assemble-it-yourself pork spring rolls) and spicy Thai salads, for over 50 years now.

O-Hi-O (☎ 0 4252 1300; 24 Th Fuang Nakhon; dishes 30-220B; ☼ dinner; ❄ ▢) This airy bar/eatery has plenty of wood, food (the usual Thai, Isan and Chinese), rivers of whisky and movies on the big screen.

Tex-Italia Restaurant (☎ 0 4251 5516; Th Thamrong Prasit; dishes 55-289B; ☼ lunch & dinner; ❄) What does a Thai woman who fell in love with Italian food while cooking in Bangkok and then moved to Texas do when she returns home? Open this little restaurant-bar. There are no culinary fireworks, but some of the East-meets-West mergers are fun; and the pool table is free.

our pick Pak Nam Chaiburi (no roman-script sign; ☎ 0 4257 3037; dishes 25-200B; ☼ lunch & dinner) This bucolic restaurant right at the confluence of Nam Song Si serves fish on a shaky wooden

deck. The food is fine and the scenery is superb.

Getting There & Away

AIR

Thai Airways doesn't fly to Nakhon Phanom, but the **THAI agent** (☎ 0 4251 2494; 85 Th Nittaya; ⏰ 8am-5pm Mon-Fri, to 1pm Sat & Sun) sells tickets for **PB Air** (☎ in Bangkok 0 2261 0222; www.pbair.com), which flies daily to/from Bangkok (one way 2905B).

BOAT

Between 8am and 6pm, you can catch a boat (one way 60B) from the **ferry terminal** (Th Sunthon Wijit) across the Mekong to Tha Khaek in Laos. Thirty-day visas are *usually* available at the border.

BUS

Nakhon Phanom's **bus terminal** (☎ 0 4251 3444) is east of the town centre, down Th Fuang Nakhon. From here buses head to Nong Khai (ordinary/air-con 160/205B, five hours, nine daily until 11.30am); Udon Thani (ordinary/air-con 90/164B, five hours, 17 daily) via Sakon Nakhon (ordinary/air-con 47/85B, 1½ hours); and Mukdahan (ordinary/air-con 52/94B, two hours, hourly) via That Phanom (ordinary/air-con 27/49B, one hour).

   999 VIP (☎ 0 4251 1403) and **Sangpatip** (☎ 0 4252 0411), both with terminals at the airport, together send three VIP buses to Bangkok (32/24 seat 664/820B, 13 hours) daily.

Getting Around

Túk-túk drivers want 100B per hour, which is about how long it takes to visit Ban Na Chok and Wat Noi Pho Kham. A better bet is renting a bike from **Koo Yong Long** (☎ 0 4251 1118; 363 Th Sunthon Wijit; per hr/day 10/50B; ⏰ 6.30am-7pm).

RENU NAKHON

เรณูนคร

The village of Renu Nakhon is known for cotton weaving and there are many places around the village where you can watch the process. The local Phu Thai, a Thai tribe separate from mainstream Siamese and Lao, make and market their designs here. The finished products are sold in the big **handicrafts market** on the grounds of **Wat Phra That Renu Nakhon** (⏰ daylight hours), as well as at a string of nearby shops. The temple's 36m tall *thâat* is a replica of the second *chedi* built in That Phanom and is considered very holy.

During local festivals, the Phu Thai sometimes hold folk-dance performances called *fáwn lám phu thai,* which celebrate their unique heritage.

GETTING THERE & AWAY

The turn-off to Renu Nakhon is only 8km north of That Phanom, so you could visit Renu on the way there from Nakhon Phanom or even make it a day trip from That Phanom. From Rte 212, it's 7km west on Rte 2031 (20B by túk-túk from the junction). To charter a túk-túk from That Phanom costs around 150B, though the price will rise if you want them to show you around and bring you back.

THAT PHANOM

ธาตุพนม

Towering over the small town, the spire of the colossal Lao-style *chedi* of Wat Phra That Phanom is one of the region's most emblematic symbols and one of the great flagpoles of Isan identity. In comparison, the little town of That Phanom itself is rather forgettable. Divided neatly in two, with the older half to the east, next to the river, it does, however, make a relatively peaceful base for exploring the wider region.

Information

Jane Internet (45 Th Phanom Phanarak; per hr 20B; ⏰ 8am-9pm)

Siam Commercial Bank (Th Chayangkun; ⏰ 8.30am-3.30pm Mon-Fri) Offers an ATM, foreign exchange and Moneygram wire-transfer services.

Sights

WAT PHRA THAT PHANOM

วัดพระธาตุพนม

Wat Phra That Phanom (Th Chayangkun; ⏰ 5am-8pm) is a potent and beautiful symbol of Isan identity and has at its hub a *thâat,* or Lao-style *chedi,* more impressive than any in present-day Laos and highly revered by Buddhists all over Thailand. The *thâat* is 53m high and a five-tiered, 16kg gold umbrella laden with precious gems adds 4m more to the top. Surrounding it is a cloister filled with Buddha images and behind the wat is a shady park.

   Many Thais truly believe the legend that the Lord Buddha came to Thailand and directed that one of his breast bone relics be enshrined in a *chedi* to be built on this very site – and so it was, eight years after his death

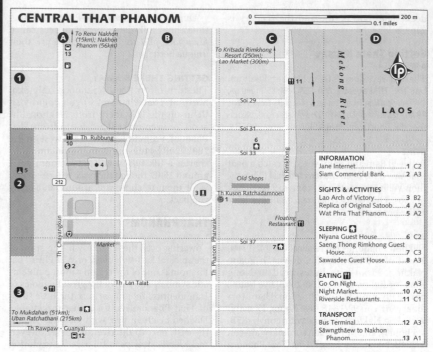

CENTRAL THAT PHANOM

in the 5th century BC. Some historians date the first construction, a short **satoob** (there's a replica of it in a pond in front of the temple) to the 6th century BC. Modifications have been routine since then, but there have been four major constructions. The first *thâat* was 24m tall and went up in the 1st century BC, and it was raised to 47m in 1690 – you'll find copies of this design all over Isan. The current design was built in 1941, but it toppled during heavy rains in 1975 and was rebuilt in 1978. A large **museum** (8.30am-4pm) tells both the legend and history of the *thâat,* and also displays a hodge-podge collection of pottery, gongs, statues, US presidential commemorative coins and many other old items.

OTHER SIGHTS
Hundreds of Lao merchants cross the river for a **market** (8.30am-noon Mon & Thu) north of the pier. Exotic offerings include Lao herbal medicines, forest roots and animal skins. The maddest haggling occurs just before the market closes, when Thai buyers try to take advantage of the Lao's reluctance to carry unsold merchandise back home.

The short road between Wat Phra That Phanom and the old town on the Mekong River passes a large **Lao arch of victory**, which is a miniature version of the arch on Th Lan Xang in Vientiane (which leads to Vientiane's Wat That Luang). The short stretch of Th Kuson Ratchadamnoen between the arch and the river is interesting, with a smattering of French-Chinese architecture that is reminiscent of old Vientiane or Saigon and many shops selling Vietnamese foodstuffs. A couple of the old shop interiors are nearly museum-quality timeless.

Festivals & Events
During the **That Phanom Festival** in February visitors descend from all over Isan and Laos to pay respect to the *thâat.* The streets fill with market stalls, many top *mǎw lam* troupes perform and the town hardly sleeps for 10 days.

Sleeping & Eating
Few tourists stick around town very long, so there are only a handful of sleeping options. During the February That Phanom Festival accommodation rates soar and rooms are booked out a month in advance.

Niyana Guest House (☎ 0 4254 0880; 65/14 Soi 33; r 140B) The town's backpacker original has moved into new digs, but it's just as chaotic as ever. Undoubtedly the friendliest and most helpful place in town, it's little more than someone's house with an English school on the ground floor – with all the good and bad that goes with that. Rooms are spartan, but kind of cosy; bathrooms are shared. Bike rental costs 40B per day.

Saeng Thong Rimkhong Guest House (no roman-script sign; ☎ 0 4254 1396; 507 Th Rimkhong; r 250B) This so-so place steals the centre ground, with less sparkle than Kritsada and less atmosphere than Niyana. It's fine for a night's sleep though.

Sawasdee Guest House (no roman-script sign; ☎ 0 4254 0148; off Th Lan Talat; r 400B; 😵) This brand-new place just a stone's throw from the bus stop has a motel-style strip of well-appointed rooms.

Kritsada Rimkhong Resort (☎ 0 4254 0088; www .kritsadaresort.com; 90-93 Th Rimkhong; r 400-600B; 😵) The shiny rooms at this resort are a mix of sterile modern rooms and traditional wood-style buildings, which are more atmospheric outside than in. Many of the rooms are colossal and have separate sitting rooms. Call and someone will pick you up at the bus stop.

Go On Night (no roman-script sign; ☎ 0 4254 1014; 419 Th Chayangkun; dishes 50-200B; 😯 lunch & dinner) There is no English menu, but most ingredients are on display so just point and let them serve it, Thai or Chinese style. They don't stop stir-frying until 3am or 4am.

Every evening a small **night market** (😯 3-9pm) takes over Th Robbung. Also come nightfall, lots of small **riverside eateries** (Th Rimkhong), perched on stilts and ablaze in fairy lights, open their doors between the pier and Kritsada Rimkhong Resort. They are all much of a muchness foodwise – although some turn the karaoke machine up louder than others – so have a wander and pick your place.

Getting There & Away

From the bus terminal on the south side of town there are regular services to Ubon Ratchathani (ordinary/air-con 102/178B, 4½ hours, hourly) via Mukdahan (ordinary/air-con 28/50B, one hour), Sakon Nakhon (ordinary/air-con 38/68B, 1¼ hours, hourly) and Nakhon Phanom (ordinary/air-con 27/49B, one hour, five daily). Nakhon Phanom also has regular săwngthăew services (36B, 90 minutes, every 10 minutes). Up to six air-con buses go to Bangkok (588B, 10 hours) daily, including a 24-seat VIP service (800B, 5.50pm).

Only Thai and Lao citizens are permitted to cross the river to/from Laos here.

SAKON NAKHON PROVINCE

Many famous forest temples sit deep in the Phu Pan Mountain range that runs across Sakon Nakhon Province, and among Sakon Nakhon's famous sons are two of the most highly revered monks in Thai history. Both Ajahn Man Bhuridatto and his student, Ajahn Fan Ajaro, were ascetic *thúdong* monks who were thought to have attained high levels of proficiency in Vipassana meditation and are widely recognised among Thais as having been *arahants* (fully enlightened beings). Although born in Ubon Ratchathani, Ajahn Man spent most of his later years at Wat Pa Sutthawat in Sakon Nakhon.

SAKON NAKHON

สกลนคร

pop 68,000

Workaday Sakon Nakhon is primarily an agricultural market and Th Ratpattana is chock-a-block with shops selling farming equipment. And though the city centre is the usual concrete mess, neighbourhoods on the fringes are full of old wooden houses, and this is where you will find the two historic temples of Wat Phra That Choeng Chum and Wat Pa Sutthawat, the town's main attractions.

Information

Bangkok Bank (Th Makkhalai, Lotus Department Store; 😯 10am-8pm) Has an ATM and exchange services (cash only). Plenty of banks in the town centre keep regular banking hours.

CT Com (no roman-script sign; 1871/12-13 Th Prem Prida; per hr 15B; 😯 8.30am-10pm) Surf the web here.

Police station (☎ 1155; Th Makkhalai)

Post office (Th Charoen Meuang; 😯 8.30am-4.30pm Mon-Fri, to 9am-noon Sat, Sun & holidays)

Sights

WAT PA SUTTHAWAT

วัดป่าสุทธาวาส

The grounds of Wat Pa Sutthawat, on the southwestern outskirts of town, are essentially a shrine to two of Thailand's best-known monks. Most famous of all is Ajahn Man Bhuridatto who died here in 1949. The final resting place of Ajahn Man's personal effects, the

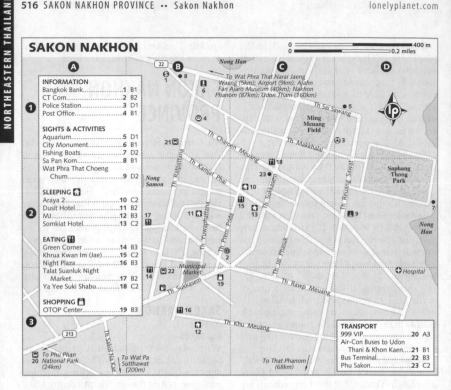

SAKON NAKHON

INFORMATION
Bangkok Bank.................1 B1
CT Com..........................2 B2
Police Station..................3 D1
Post Office......................4 B1

SIGHTS & ACTIVITIES
Aquarium........................5 D1
City Monument................6 B1
Fishing Boats...................7 D2
Sa Pan Kom.....................8 B1
Wat Phra That Choeng
  Chum..........................9 D2

SLEEPING
Araya 2..........................10 C2
Dusit Hotel.....................11 B2
MJ.................................12 B3
Somkiat Hotel.................13 C2

EATING
Green Corner 14 B3
Khrua Kwan Im (Jae).......15 C2
Night Plaza....................16 B3
Talat Suanluk Night
  Market........................17 B2
Ya Yee Suki Shabu...........18 C2

SHOPPING
OTOP Center..................19 B3

TRANSPORT
999 VIP..........................20 A3
Air-Con Buses to Udon
  Thani & Khon Kaen.....21 B1
Bus Terminal..................22 B3
Phu Sakon......................23 C2

Ajahn Man Museum (donations appreciated; ☻ 8am-6pm), bizarrely looks a bit like a modern Christian church, with arches and etched-glass windows. A bronze image of Ajahn Man, surrounded by flowers, sits on a pedestal at the back

Ajahn Lui Chanthasaro, who died in 1989, was one of Ajahn Man's most famous students and King Rama IX designed the *chedi* that holds the **Ajahn Lui Museum** (donations appreciated; ☻ 8am-6pm). Ajahn Lui's likeness, also surrounded by flowers, is in wax.

Both museums showcase all the monks' worldly possessions, as well as photographs and descriptions of their lives; Ajahn Man's displays, signed in English, give a good description of a typical monk's life.

WAT PHRA THAT CHOENG CHUM
วัดพระธาตุเชิงชุม

The most visible highlight at **Wat Phra That Choeng Chum** (Stupa of the Gathering of the Footprints; Th Reuang Sawat; ☻ daylight hours) is the 24m-high Lao-style *chedi*, which was erected during the Ayuthaya period over a smaller 11th-century Khmer *prang*. It was built over four Buddha footprints where, legend has it, four different incarnations of Lord

Buddha had a meeting. To view the *prang* you must enter through the adjacent *wíhăan*. If the door to the *chedi* is locked, ask one of the monks to open it; they're used to having visitors.

Also on the grounds are a Lan Xang–era *bòt* and a *wíhăan* built in the cruciform shape reminiscent of Lanna styles found in northern Thailand. *Lûuk nímít* (spherical ordination-precinct markers that look like cannonballs and are buried under the regular boundary markers that surround most *bòts*) are lined up near the *wíhăan*. The wax castles carved during the Buddhist Rains Retreat (Buddhist Lent) resemble the top of the west gate, and next to the east gate is the base for an original Khmer Shivalingam (phallic object).

WAT PHRA THAT NARAI JAENG WAENG
วัดพระธาตุนารายณ์แจงแวง

About 5km west of town at Ban That, this wat (known as Phra That Nawaeng, a contraction of the words Narai Jaeng Waeng) has a 10th- to 11th-century Khmer *prang* in the early Bapuan style. Originally part of a Khmer-Hindu

(Continued on page 525)

The 11th-century Hindu–Mahayana
Buddhist temple complex, Prasat Phimai
(p461), Nakhon Ratchasima Province

A masked participant of the Phi Ta Khon festival
(p506) in Dan Sai, Loei Province

Wat Phu Tok (p500), near Beung Kan, Nong Khai Province

TOM COCKREM

Wat Si Chum, Sukhothai Historical Park (p403), Sukhothai

Gilded *mondòp* of Wat Phra That Lampang Luang (p348), Lampang Province

TOM COCKREM

FRANK CARTER

A Padaung girl from Nai Soi wears a traditional neck coil (p436), Mae Hong Son Province

MARGIE POLITZER

Akha villagers, Chiang Rai
Province (p350)

FRANK CARTER

Thailand's largest waterfall, Nam Tok Thilawsu (p426), near
Um Phang, Tak Province

Some of Tak Province's (p414) large population of domesticated elephants

FRANK CARTER

Hat Sai Ri, Ko Tao (p616)

Ao Thong Ta Khian, a secluded cove between Ko Samui's Hat Chaweng Noi and Hat Lamai (p586)

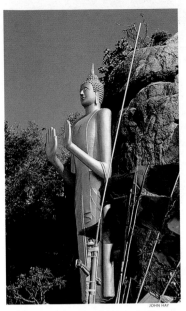

JOHN HAY

Golden statue at a seaside temple, Hua
Hin (p556), Prachuap Khiri Khan Province

RICHARD NEBESKY

Entrance to a wat in Songkhla (p631), Songkhla Province

Local fishermen, Hua Hin (p556), Prachuap Khiri Khan Province

JOHN HAY

A săamláw passes an elephant in Surin (p541), Surin Province

Phuket Town's vegetarian festival (p668) in action, Phuket Province

A fisherman casts his net off Hat Patong (p676), Phuket Province

ANDERS BLOMQVIST

Cliffs loom over Hat Phra Nang (p700), Railay, Krabi Province

Wat Tham Seua (p694), set in limestone caves and cliffs near Krabi, Krabi Province

RICHARD I'ANSON

DOMINIC BONUCCELLI

Visitors partying in Patong (p676), Phuket Province

Rock-climbing off Hat Phra Nang (p700), Railay, Krabi Province

SCOTT DARSNEY

(Continued from page 516)

complex, the five-level sandstone *prang* is missing most of its top, but still features a reclining Vishnu lintel over its northern portico and a dancing Shiva over its eastern one. This is not a particularly evocative temple, but it's the most complete Khmer ruin in the province.

To get here by public transport catch săwngthăew 3 (8B) heading north on Th Ratpattana from the bus terminal, get off at Talat Ban That Nawaeng and walk 500m north.

OTHER SIGHTS

The **city monument** (Th Ratpattana) at the northwestern corner of town was obviously inspired by Vientiane's Patuxai or That Phanom's gate. The arch-like structure consists of four thick cement pillars standing over a bowl filled with *naga*.

Across the park from the monument, little **Sa Pan Kom** (Khmer Bridge; Th Sai Sawang) was once part of a Khmer road leading to Wat Phra That Narai Jaeng Waeng.

Along the eastern and northern edges of town is **Nong Han**, Thailand's largest natural lake. Fishermen, who tie up their boats behind Saphang Thong Park, will take you out sightseeing, including a stop to visit the monks on **Ko Don Sawan** (Paradise Island), the lake's largest island. The going rate is 500B for as long as a tank of gas lasts; the Dusit Hotel can help make arrangements. *Don't* swim in the lake: it's infested with liver flukes, which can cause a nasty liver infection known as opisthorchiasis.

The freshwater **aquarium** (☎ 0 4271 1447; Th Sai Sawang; admission free; ☼ 8.30am-4.30pm) at the Sakon Nakhon Fishery Station displays fish from Nong Han, as well as the Mekong and Songkhram rivers. There is a pitiful little crocodile pond nearby.

Festivals & Events

The end of the **Buddhist Rains Retreat** (Buddhist Lent) in late October/November is fervently celebrated in Sakon, with the carving and display of wax castles in Ming Meuang Field the highlight. The festival also features demonstrations of *muay-boron*, the old, bare-knuckle style of Thai boxing.

Sleeping

Araya 2 (☎ 0 4271 1054; 354 Th Prem Prida; r 150-250B) This basic concrete bolthole is inching towards decrepit, but it won't break your budget.

Somkiat Hotel (☎ 0 4271 1740; 1348 Th Kamjat Phai; r 200-400B; ⊠) The Somkiat is no beauty queen, but for just a few baht more it takes the tiara from Araya. The fan rooms in the main building have the hot water turned on only during the winter. The air-con rooms at the back are motel style and fronted by carports.

Dusit Hotel (☎ 0 4271 1198; www.dusitsakhon.com; 1784 Th Yuwaphattana; r 400-700B; ⊠ ⬚) This oldtimer has the loveliest lobby and cheeriest staff in town. The most expensive rooms have some character built in while the rest are more ordinary, but each price category offers good value. The restaurant is pretty good and there's free wi-fi in the lobby.

MJ (☎ 0 4273 3771; 399/2 Th Khu Meuang; r 630-3360B; ⊠ ⬚) Prices have dropped over the years making this place pretty good value, and the facilities (restaurant, cocktail lounge, pub, café, massage, snooker club and karaoke) earn a few extra brownie points as well. If you are in the mood to part with a few extra baht, the superior rooms are well worth the extra.

Eating

Khrua Kwan Im (Jae) (no roman-script sign; ☎ 0 4271 1599; Th Prem Prida; dishes 25-50B; ☼ breakfast & lunch) This simple place distinguishes itself by offering veggie versions of many Isan favourites, like *láap* (a super-spicy salad).

Ya Yee Suki Shabu (no roman-script sign; ☎ 0 4273 2011; 349 Th Charon Meuang; buffet 89B; ☼ lunch Sat & Sun, dinner daily) Walk the buffet line at this colourful Chinese place and cook up your creations at your table, or order some scrumptious Thai and Chinese food off the menu.

Green Corner (☎ 0 4271 1073; 1773 Th Ratpattana; dishes 35-250B; ☼ breakfast, lunch & dinner; ⬚) The first choice for a fix of *faràng* food really distinguishes itself with its Thai and Isan choices – mao berry juice, Chiang Mai pork sausage, spicy catfish salad – and we've never seen ants' egg omelettes on an English-language menu before.

Sakon Nakhon's biggest night market, the **Night Plaza** (Th Khu Meuang), has an excellent selection of food, but it's all bagged up for takeaway and the action starts to fade around 8pm. If you want to sit down and stay out late, hit the **Talat Suanluk Night Market** (Th Tor Pattana) in the thick of the city's nightlife district.

Shopping

OTOP Center (☎ 0 4271 1533; Th Sukkasem; ☼ 8.30am-5pm) Has a good selection of natural-dyed,

hand-woven fabrics and clothes dyed with indigo and other natural colourants. You can also pick up mao-berry and black-ginger wines here and in many other shops, hotels and restaurants.

Getting There & Away

Phu Sakon (☎ 0 4271 2259; 332/3 Th Sukkasem; ◷ 8.30am-5pm) is the agent for **PB Air** (☎ in Bangkok 0 2261 0222; www.pbair.com), which flies once or twice daily to/from Bangkok (one way 2745B, one hour).

Buses serve Ubon Ratchathani (ordinary/air-con 125/225B, five hours, eight daily), That Phanom (ordinary/air-con 38/68B, 1¼ hours, 14 daily), Nakhon Phanom (ordinary/air-con 47/85B, 1½ hours, hourly), Udon Thani (ordinary/air-con 78/109B, 3½ hours, every half-hour), Khon Kaen (ordinary/air-con 92/166B, four hours, five daily) and Bangkok's northern bus terminal (air-con/32-seat VIP 360/540B, 11 hours, every half-hour).

There are also departures for Udon Thani (every half-hour) and Khon Kaen (six daily) from the Esso petrol station north of the bus terminal, while **999 VIP** (☎ 0 4271 2860) has 24-seat buses to Bangkok (715B, 8.30am, 7.30pm, 7.45pm) from its office on the road out of town.

AROUND SAKON NAKHON
Ajahn Fan Ajaro Museum
พิพิธภัณฑ์พระอาจารย์ฝั้นอาจาโร

Ajahn Fan Ajaro, a famous student of Ajahn Man, lived at Wat Pa Udom Somphon in his home district of Phanna Nikhom from 1963 until his death in 1987. His **museum** (donations appreciated; ◷ 8am-5pm), inside a *chedi* with a triple-layer lotus design, commemorates his life with the usual display of relics, photos and worldly possessions. Unlike Wat Pa Sutthawat, which has become a *wát thîaw* (tourist wat), this is still a strict forest meditation monastery, so only those with a serious interest in Buddhism should walk back to the adjacent monastery. The museum is 40km from Sakon Nakhon toward Udon Thani on Hwy 22, then 1.5km north of Ban Phanna on Th Srisawadwilai.

Phu Phan National Park
อุทยานแห่งชาติภูพาน

Swathed in forest and tumbling over the pretty Phu Phan mountains, **Phu Phan National Park** (☎ 08 1263 5029; reservations 0 2562 0760; free admission; ◷ 24hr) remains relatively undeveloped and

isolated – it's no surprise that the area once provided cover for Thai resistance fighters in WWII and People's Liberation Army of Thailand (PLAT) guerrillas in the 1970s. **Tham Seri Thai** (Seri Thai Cave) was used by the Thai Seri (Thai underground resistance; see p35) during WWII as an arsenal and mess hall. As well as being a stomping ground for barking deer, monitor lizards and monkeys, the 645-sq-km park also hosts a few elephants.

There are two main places to visit. **Pha Nang Moem** is a vista point just 700m from the visitor centre and you can climb down to **Lan Sao E** plateau just below it. **Nam Tok Kam Hom**, one of four petite falls along a 600m stretch of stream (the water is only from August to October), is 9km north (near Thailand's largest kilometre pillar). Seldom-visited **Tang Pee Parn** natural rockbridge can be reached by 4WD. A park guide is recommended for trekking deep into the gorgeous mountains in the south end of the park; if you want to do it yourself, discuss your plans at the headquarters before setting out. For spending the night, there is a **camp site** (per person 30B, 3-person tent hire 150B) and eight **bungalows** (4 people 500B) available.

Both of the principal attractions sit right off Rte 213 and any Kalasin-bound bus (ordinary/air-con 20/25B, 45 minutes, every 40 minutes) from Sakon Nakhon will drop you off or shuttle you between them.

Talat Klang Dong Sang Kaw
ตลาดกลางดงสร้างค้อ

Twenty-five kilometres past Phu Phan National Park on Rte 213, **Talat Klang Dong Sang Kaw** (Sang Kaw Jungle Market) stocks custard apples and other foods grown on small village farms, but it's best known for the products gathered sustainably in the surrounding forest, like fruits, roots, honey, insects, bird nests (for good luck – well, not for the birds) and mushrooms. There are also locally produced whiskies and mao-berry wines.

YASOTHON & MUKDAHAN PROVINCES

YASOTHON
ยโสธร
pop 23,000

Yasothon Province has little of interest to the average traveller, though people look-ing

to nose a little deeper into Isan culture will want to peek at Phra That Kong Khao Noi and purchase some pillows in Ban Si Tham. The provincial town of Yasothon saves all of its fireworks for the annual Rocket Festival, which completes a trifecta of Isan icons. The city has nothing to offer outside the official whizz-bang period of late May and neither looks nor acts like a capital city. In fact, it barely feels like a city at all.

Sights

PHRA THAT KONG KHAO NOI

พระธาตุก่องข้าวน้อย

A rather sinister myth surrounds **Phra That Kong Khao Noi** (Small Rice Basket Stupa; ☼ daylight hours), a brick-and-stucco *chedi* dating from the late Ayuthaya period found along Hwy 23 about 9km out of town towards Ubon. According to one legend (which is taught to school children around the country as an example of why it's important to keep your emotions in check) a young, and no doubt ravenously hungry, farmer who had toiled all morning in the hot sun murdered his mother here when she brought his lunch to the fields late – and in the smallest of sticky-rice baskets. The farmer, eating his lunch over his mother's dead body, realised that the small basket actually contained more sticky rice than he could manage to eat. To atone for his misdeed, he built a *chedi*.

Or perhaps not. Others say it was built by people who were travelling to Phra That Phanom to enshrine gold and gems, but got to Ban Tat Thong and learned they were too late, so they built this *chedi* instead.

Further complicating matters, many claim that the real Small Rice Basket Stupa is a little further north in the back of Wat Ban Sadow, located 7km east of Yasothon on Rte 202. All that remains is the base; when the original tumbled over shortly after the redeemed son's death, locals built another petite *chedi* next to it.

BAN SI THAN

บ้านศรีฐาน

Residents of **Ban Si Than** can't leave their work behind when they go to sleep – this is a pillow-making village. Almost everywhere you look as you walk through the village (and most of those surrounding it, too) you'll see people sewing, stuffing or selling *măwn khít* (pillows decorated with diamond-grid *khít* patterns),

most famously the triangular *măwn khwăan* (literally 'axe pillow'). They couldn't possible meet demand without using machine-made fabric, but most of the shops in town also stock some of the old-style hand-woven pillows. Prices here are almost half what you'll pay elsewhere in Thailand, and this is also one of the few places you can buy them unstuffed (*yang măi sài nûn*; literally 'no kapok inserted'), which makes the big ones viable as souvenirs.

If you want to see monkeys, have someone point you to **Don Ling**, 4km out of town at Ban Tao Hi.

Ban Si Than was set to launch a **homestay programme** (☎ 08 7243 2278) when we last stopped by; call for details. The village is 20km from Yasothon, then 2.5km south of Rte 202 from Ban Nikom. Any Amnat Charoen bus can drop you at the junction (30B, 45 minutes) where a motorcycle taxi will zip you in for about 20B.

OTHER SIGHTS

In town, **Phra That Phra Anon** (Th Wariratchadet; ☼ daylight hours), also known as Phra That Yasothon, at Wat Mahathat is a highly venerated Lao-style *chedi*. It's said to be more than 1200 years old and to enshrine holy relics of Phra Anon (Ananda), the Buddha's personal attendant monk and one of his chief disciples. The scripture hall, dating to the 1840s, sits on stilts in a pond.

Wat Singh Ta (Th Uthai Rammarith; ☼ daylight hours) is rather ordinary, but the block fronting its south side is a treasure-trove of classic Chinese shophouses.

Festivals & Events

The **Rocket Festival** (Bun Bâng Fai) rain and fertility rite is celebrated on the second weekend of May. Rocket Festivals are held to herald the rainy season across Isan, but nowhere as fervently as in Yasothon where it involves local dances, parades and rocket-launching contests. The largest rockets, called *bâng fai saen,* are packed with 120kg of nitrate. Those whose homemade rockets fail to launch get tossed in the mud.

Sleeping & Eating

In Town Hotel (no roman-script sign; ☎ 0 4571 3007; 614 Th Jangsanit; r 220-380B; ⊠) This place, on the main road through town, is far enough south that it almost loses the rights to its name, but

for Yasothon, it's far better than the budget average.

Yasothon Orchid Garden (no roman-script sign; ☎ 0 4572 1000; 219 Th Prachasamphan; r 400-450B; ⚡ 🖵) The eye-catching exterior hides some fairly drab rooms at this newly built place by the old bus terminal, but it makes a reasonable midranger.

JP Emerald Hotel (☎ 0 4572 4848; 36 Th Prapa; r 800-1600B; ⚡ 🖵) The lobby is lovely (even with the tacky plastic greenery) and the rooms comfy, but they are a bit behind on the upkeep of everything in between. Still, you could do a lot worse at these prices and the staff is at the top of their game. It's at the Roi Et end of town.

our pick **Rim Chi** (no roman-script sign; ☎ 0 4571 4597; dishes 50-200B; ☽ breakfast, lunch & dinner) Enjoy superb Isan and Thai food and bucolic Chi River views from either the shady terrace or your own thatched-roof raft. It's 700m west of Krung Thai Bank.

For some more colourful eats, head to the dually misnamed **Night Barza** (Th Jangsanit; ☽ breakfast, lunch & dinner), on the north end of downtown, or the proper **night market** (Th Wariratchadet), one block north.

Getting There & Away

Until a new bus terminal is built most buses stop at random points around town. Only Khorat (ordinary/air-con 169/220B, five hours, 14 daily) buses and **999 VIP** (☎ 0 4571 2965) to Bangkok (32/24 seat 449/595B, 8pm/8.30pm) use the current terminal on Th Rattanakhet. Most regular air-con rides to Bangkok (350B, nine hours, 26 daily) leave from two spots near the Night Barza: one on Hwy 23 and one just north of it on Th Wariratchadet. Khon Kaen (ordinary/air-con 70/155B, 3½ hours, nine daily) buses stop 500m south of the old terminal, while Ubon Ratchathani (ordinary/air-con 50/90B, 1½ hours, 20 daily) buses are nearby, in front of Mitsubishi on Hwy 23.

MUKDAHAN

มุกดาหาร

pop 34,300

On the banks of the Mekong, directly opposite the Lao city of Savannakhet, Mukdahan is one of the region's prettier towns. Known for its riverfront Talat Indojin (Indochina Market), which stretches under as well as along the riverfront park, Mukdahan is mainly a trade

centre and on weekends, when the market really kicks off, you'll wonder how the locals manage to find time to do anything but trawl the Chinese, Vietnamese, Thai and Lao stalls.

The December 2006 opening of the Thai-Lao Friendship Bridge 2 formalised Mukdahan's status as a trade hub, but the city has not gone bridge crazy like Nong Khai did when that Mekong span was planned, and Savannakhet has reaped most of the economic reward.

Information

Bangkok Bank (Hwy 212, Lotus Department Store; ☽ 10am-8pm) Changes cash only, but many banks in the centre of town open regular banking hours and exchange travellers cheques.

Huanam Hotel (☎ 0 4261 1137; 36 Th Samut Sakdarak; per hr 30B; ☽ 6am-10pm) Check your email here. It sometimes stays open later than 10pm.

Immigration office (☎ 0 4261 1074; 2 Th Song Nang Sathit; ☽ 8.30am-4.30pm Mon-Fri, to noon Sat) Visa extensions are available here.

Main post office (Th Phitak Santirat; ☽ 8.30am-4.30pm Mon-Fri, 9am-noon Sat, Sun & holidays)

Police station (☎ 1155; Th Phitak Santirat)

Sights

One of the most oddly out-of-place landmarks in all of Thailand, **Ho Kaeo Mukdahan** (☎ 0 4263 3211; Th Samut Sakdarak; admission 20B; ☽ 8am-6pm) is a 65m-tall tower built for the 50th anniversary of King Rama IX's ascension to the throne. The nine-sided base has a good museum with displays (labelled in English) on typical Isan village life and the eight ethnic groups living in the province. There are great views and a few more historical displays in 'The 360° of Pleasure in Mukdahan by the Mekong' room up at the 50m level. The ball on the top holds a locally revered Buddha image supposedly made of solid silver.

The 2m tall Phra Chao Ong Luang Buddha image at **Wat Si Mongkhon Tai** (Th Samron Chaikhongthi; ☽ daylight hours) is older than the city itself and, according to one of the legends associated with it, was unearthed during Mukdahan's construction. The striking ceramic-encrusted northern gate was built as a gesture of friendship by the city's Vietnamese community in 1954.

Wat Yod Kaeo Sivichai (Th Samron Chaikhongthi; ☽ daylight hours) just down the street stands out for having its enormous Buddha inside

a glass-walled *wíhǎan,* and not one, but two small-sized copies of Phra That Phanom.

Festivals

The **Mukdahan Red Cross Fair,** held from 9 to 15 January in the field fronting the Provincial Hall, is a chance to see the dances and clothing of Mukdahan's eight ethnic groups, though this aspect has been de-emphasised in recent years in favour of a more ordinary carnival and trade fair.

Sleeping

Bantomkasen Hotel (no roman-script sign; ☎ 0 4261 1235; 25/2 Th Samut Sakdarak; r 140-250B; ✖) From the outside this place looks just like your usual concrete block, but louvred doors and wooden floors give it some back-in-the-day charm. And, if you don't want to squat on the pot, have a look at several rooms before taking a key.

Huanam Hotel (☎ 0 4261 1137; 36 Th Samut Sakdarak; r 150-320B; ✖ 💻) At first glance you might think the posted prices are a bait-and-switch ploy. It turns out the rooms just aren't quite as slick as the lobby. They are, nonetheless, good

value in a good location. Mountain bikes are available for rent per day for 100B.

Kimjeckin Hotel (☎ 0 4263 1041; 40/5 Th Pitak Phanomkhet; r 250-350B; ✖) This travelling-salesperson's favourite is completely ordinary, except for the low prices. Rooms at the back have a limited view of the lake.

Submukda Grand Hotel (☎ 0 4263 3444; 72 Th Samut Sakdarak; r 500B; ✖) This shiny new tower was erected in 2006 to cash in on the expected rise in tour-bus business that the bridge might bring. Rooms are boxy, but they're good.

Mukdahan Grand Hotel (☎ 0 4261 2020; 78 Th Song Nang Sathit; r 900-2500B; ✖) A little less 'Grand' than the Palace, this upmarket outfit nevertheless offers high standards (a swimming pool is planned) and some of the most cheerful staff on the circuit. The restaurant sometimes serves Phu Thai cuisine, though it differs very little from regular Isan food.

Ploy Palace Hotel (☎ 0 4263 1111; www.ploypalace .com; 40 Th Pitak Phanomkhet; r 1050-3000B; ✖ 💻 🛜) With business coming through at a trickle, rooms at this executive sleepeasy are good value. There's plenty of marble and wood for that 'swanky' feel, a decent spread of creature

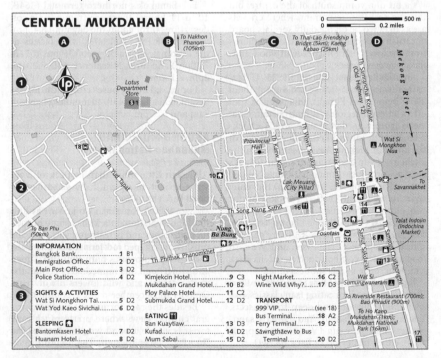

CENTRAL MUKDAHAN

0   500 m
0   0.2 miles

comforts (including a sauna, swimming pool and rooftop restaurant) and some friendly staff. For something out of the ordinary, ask for the 9th-floor rooms with beehives on the balcony.

Eating

Ban Kuaytiaw (no roman-script sign; ☎ 08 1523 3595; 5/1 Soi Jaeng Waeng; dishes 20-35B; ☒ breakfast & lunch) Nothing fancy, but the cooks whip up tasty *khâo phàt* (fried rice) and noodle soups under a thatch roof.

ourpick Wine Wild Why? (☎ 0 4263 3122; 11 Th Samron Chaikhongthi; dishes 40-130B; ☒ lunch & dinner) Housed in an atmospheric wooden building right on the river, this romantic little spot serves delicious Thai food and has bags of character, though the wine list is history. The sociable owners, transplants from Bangkok, just add to the charm.

Kufad (no roman-script sign; ☎ 0 4261 2252; 36 Th Samut Sakdarak; dishes 20-150B; ☒ breakfast, lunch & dinner) This spic-and-span Vietnamese café is rightly quite popular; and the picture menu takes the guesswork out of ordering.

Bao Phradit (no roman-script sign; ☎ 0 4263 2335; 123/4 Th Samron Chaikhongthi; dishes 20-160B; ☒ dinner) It's a bit of a yomp south of the centre, but this is a real Isan restaurant, where crickets are as likely to be on the daily specials board as catfish and many ingredients are gathered from the forest. It's got a peaceful wood-and-thatch riverside deck.

Riverside Restaurant (☎ 0 4261 1705; 103/4 Th Samron Chaikhongthi; dishes 65-180B; ☒ lunch & dinner) About 200m before Bao Phradit, this popular spot offers an eager legion of attentive staff, great views from a garden terrace and is chock-a-block with tanks filled with examples of the kinds of Mekong River fish it has in the kitchen – if you don't want to eat the fish, it's almost worth just coming here for a biology lesson. The menu lists (in English) the many styles in which the chefs can cook it up for you, plus some non-fish dishes.

Mum Sabai (☎ 0 4263 3616; 1 Th Song Nang Sathit; dishes 35-250B; ☒ lunch & dinner; ☒) There's a good spread of Japanese, Thai, Isan and Western food and a few combos, such as sirloin steak with Isan sauce in this spotless diner.

Night market (Th Song Nang Sathit; ☒ 5pm-10pm) Particularly good for eating Isan classics, like *kài yâang*, *sôm-tam* and deep-fried insects. You'll also find *khâo jìi* (Lao baguette sandwiches) and *pàw-pía* (Vietnamese spring rolls), either fresh *(sòt)* or fried *(thâwt)*.

Getting There & Away
BOAT

Even with the bridge, boats continue to connect Mukdahan's **ferry terminal** (☎ 0 4261 4926) with Savannakhet, Laos, though the frequency of the service may soon be reduced. There are nine ferries daily during the week (9am to 4.30pm), eight on Saturday (9.30am to 4.30pm) and six on Sunday (9.30am to 3pm). Tickets cost 50B each way. Thirty-day Lao visas are available on arrival.

BUS

Mukdahan's **bus terminal** (☎ 0 4261 1421) is on Rte 212, west of town; to get there from the centre, take a yellow sǎwngthǎew (8B) from Th Phitak Phanomkhet near the fountain. There are regular buses to Nakhon Phanom (ordinary/air-con 52/93B, two hours, every 40 minutes) going via That Phanom (ordinary/air-con 28/50B, one hour), and also service to Khon Kaen (air-con 155B, 4½ hours, every half-hour), Ubon Ratchathani (ordinary/air-con 80/144B, 3½ hours, every 45 minutes) and Yasothon (air-con 104B, two hours, 13 daily).

For Bangkok's northern terminal (364B, 10 to 11 hours) there are frequent air-con departures throughout the day until 8.45pm, and **999 VIP** (☎ 0 4261 1478), with offices at the terminal, runs a 32-seat VIP bus (571B, 7.20pm) and three 24 seaters (760B, 8.30am, 8pm, 8.15pm).

For Laos, 12 daily buses cross the bridge to Savannakhet, Laos (45B, 40 minutes), between 7am and 5.30pm.

AROUND MUKDAHAN
Mukdahan National Park
อุทยานแห่งชาติมุกดาหาร

Although little more than a speck of a reserve at just 48 sq km, hilly **Mukdahan National Park** (☎ 0 4260 1753; reservations 0 2562 0760; admission 400B; ☒ 5am-6pm), also known as Phu Pha Thoep National Park, has some beautiful landscapes and is scattered with unusual mushroom-shaped **rock formations**. The main rock group, known as both Phu Pha Thoep and Hin Thoep, sits immediately behind the visitor centre, and wildflowers bloom from October to December.

Besides the rock formations there are several clifftop views where pretty much only forest is visible around you and **Nam Tok Phu Tham Phra**, a scenic waterfall with a grotto atop

it holding hundreds of small **Buddha images**. It only takes a couple of hours on the well-marked trails to see all of these. **Than Fa Mue Daeng**, a cave with 5000-year-old hand paintings, is an 8km walk through the forest and must be visited with a park guide; you might see flying squirrels, barking deer, wild boar, monkeys or civets along the way.

For accommodation, you have a choice of **camping** (camp sites per person 30B, 3-person tent hire 80B) or simple rooms in **bungalows** (500B) that can sleep seven.

The park is 15km south of Mukdahan off Rte 2034. Săwngthăew (15B, 20 minutes) to Amphoe Don Tan (which leave from the bus terminal in Mukdahan every half-hour) pass the turn-off to the park entrance, and for an extra 20B the driver will take you the remaining 1.5km to the visitor centre. The less frequent Kham Marat buses also pass the park entrance and the 4pm service is your last guaranteed ride back to town, though hitching shouldn't be tough.

Old Highway 212
หนองแอก–บ้านนาโพธิ

Old Highway 212 (Nong Ak Na Po Yai), which never strays far from the Mekong, offers a lovely look at traditional Thai life and makes a fantastic bike trip. Leaving Mukdahan you'll follow a long line of fish farms on the river before passing the 1.6km long **Thai-Lao Friendship Bridge 2**. This is the widest reach of the Mekong along the Thai border, so this bridge stretches over 400m more than the Friendship Bridge 1.

At the Km 12 mark, where the greenish Chanode River meets the muddy Mekong (if you're lucky, you'll see men unloading their fish traps here), is **Wat Manophirom** (☼ daylight hours), one of Mukdahan Province's oldest temples. The original *bòt*, now a *wíhǎan*, was built in 1756 in Lan Xang style with a bas-relief front and painted wooden eave brackets. It holds many ancient Buddha images, including eight carved into an elephant tusk.

Wat Srimahapo (☼ daylight hours), sometimes called Wat Pho Si, is another 5km north. You'd never expect its tiny *bòt* to be worth a look, but inside, elaborately carved beams hold up the tin roof and interesting naive murals cover the walls. The Buddhas that greet you have holes cut over their hearts to receive blessings, and a couple of long boats are stored here between races.

After a further 7km you'll pass the modern, glass-walled **Church of Our Lady of the Martyrs of Thailand** (☼ daylight hours Mon-Sat, 7am mass on Sun), locally called Wat Song Khan, built in 1995 to commemorate seven Thai Catholics killed by the police in 1940 for refusing to renounce their faith. Wax sculptures of the martyrs lie under glass in back.

Just beyond the church is **Kaeng Kabao**, a stretch of rocky shore and islets, turning to rapids when submerged during the rainy season. A variety of restaurants have set up on and along the river here making this a good place to refuel before riding back to Mukdahan. During April its waters are clean enough for swimming and inner-tubing.

Ban Phu
บ้านภู

Ban Phu is a quaint village in the shadow of Phu Jaw Kor Puttakiri where wooden houses and the Phu Thai dialect still dominate – no matter how boned up you are on your Isan, Thai or Lao, expect a few verbal trip ups here. Of all Isan's minority groups, the Phu Thai, who trace their heritage to southern China, near the Laos and Vietnam border, are known for having clung closest to their culture. Most villagers still don traditional duds for festivals and funerals, and all children wear the old-style clothes to school every Thursday. This is a well-known silk- and cotton-weaving village and you'll find a loom under most of the 300 houses. Most women supply *mát-mìi* designs to meet demand, but the little shop in front of the temple stocks some traditional designs.

The village **homestay programme** (☎ 08 9570 8161; per person per day 250B) is designed for large groups, but all are welcome and Khun Anan, who speaks some English, can help set you up. The typical programme is three days and two nights, including meals, and lets you get involved in daily life: cooking, weaving and farming, for example. If you want some adventure with your culture, someone can take you up the mountain and into a cave.

Ban Phu is 50km west of Mukdahan via Rtes 2042 and 2370. The only direct public transport is a lone săwngthăew that heads to/from Mukdahan (40B, 90 minutes) early every morning, but buses go throughout the day to Nong Sung (air-con 60B, 90 minutes), where you can get a motorcycle taxi (50B) or hire a săwngthăew (about 100B) for the last 6km.

UBON RATCHATHANI PROVINCE

This varied province, famous across Thailand for its forest wats, pushes down into the tri-border region where Laos, Thailand and Cambodia come together. To bolster the region's tourist profile TAT has labelled this the 'Emerald Triangle' in recognition of its magnificent green landscapes and drawing obvious – but rather hopeful – parallels with northern Thailand's 'Golden Triangle'. However successful this may be, Ubon remains one of the region's more attractive cities, while the surrounding countryside has plenty to entertain the rustic rover. Phu Chong Nayoi and Pha Taem National Parks are two of Isan's remotest corners.

History

Ubon's Mae Nam Mun and Mae Nam Chi river basins were centres for Dvaravati and Khmer cultures many centuries ago. Following the decline of the Khmer empires, the area was settled by groups of Lao in the late 18th century and they founded the capital city. By the early Ratanakosin era it had become part of *monthon* Ubon, a southeastern Isan satellite state extending across what are now Surin, Si Saket and Ubon Provinces – as well as parts of southern Laos – with Champasak, Laos, as *monthon* capital. Today the Lao influence in the province dominates the Khmer.

UBON RATCHATHANI

อุบลราชธานี

pop 115,000

Survive the usual knot of choked access roads and Ubon will reveal an altogether more attractive face. Racked up against Mae Nam Mun, Thailand's second-longest waterway, the southern portions of the city have a pedestrian, sluggish character rarely found in the region's big conurbations. Temples pepper the surrounding area, the urban push-and-shove is easily escaped and despite the quick-time march of modernisation, a deep sense of Isan identity continues to live on. Few cities in Thailand reward aimless wandering as richly as Ubon.

A US air base during the Vietnam era, 21st-century Ubon is primarily a financial, educational and agricultural market centre for eastern Isan. With the nearby Thai–Lao border crossing at Chong Mek drawing a steady stream of foreigners, Ubon is an increasingly popular travel destination. The hotel scene is glum, but there are plenty of good restaurants and well-stocked stores that offer a chance to enjoy the good life before heading off into rural Laos.

Orientation & Information

Most of the activity in Ubon takes place to the north of Mae Nam Mun and east of the main north–south thoroughfare, Th Chayangkun/Th Uparat. The train station, more places to stay and a good few restaurants are south of the Mae Nam Mun in Warin Chamrap.

EMERGENCY & MEDICAL SERVICES

Saphasit Prasong Hospital (☎ 0 4524 0074; Th Saphasit) Has a 24-hour casualty department.
Tourist police (☎ 1155; Th Suriyat) Directly behind the police station.

INTERNET ACCESS

Internet Pirch (382 Th Phrom Rat; per hr 10B; ☺ 9am-11pm)

MONEY

Bangkok Bank (Th Chayangkun, Lotus Department Store; ☺ 10am-8pm) Only changes cash. There are many more banks that are open normal business hours in the town centre and take travellers cheques.

POST

Main post office (Th Si Narong; ☺ 8.30am-4.30pm Mon-Fri, 9am-noon Sat, Sun & holidays)

TOURIST INFORMATION

TAT (☎ 0 4524 3770; www.tourismthailand.org; 264/1 Th Kheuan Thani; ☺ 8.30am-4.30pm) Has information about Ubon, as well as Si Saket and Yasothon Provinces.

TRAVEL AGENCIES

Sakda Travel World (☎ 0 4524 3560; Th Phalorangrit; ☺ 8am-6pm) Books plane tickets, rents cars and leads tours.

Sights & Activities

UBON NATIONAL MUSEUM

พิพิธภัณฑสถานแห่งชาติอุบลราชธานี

Once you've dropped your bags in the hotel and slipped on a clean shirt, your first stop in town should be the informative **Ubon National Museum** (☎ 0 4525 5071; Th Kheuan Thani; admission 30B; ☺ 9am-4pm Wed-Sun). Occupying a pretty former palace from the Rama VI era, this is the spot to

come to swot up on background information before venturing out into the wider province. And there's plenty on show, from Buddhist ordination-precinct stones from the Dvaravati period and a 2500-year-old Dong Son bronze drum to Ubon textiles and betel-nut sets. The museum's most prized possession is a 9th-century Ardhanarisvara, a composite statue combining Shiva and his consort Uma into one being; one of just two ever found in Thailand.

Just north of the museum is **Thung Si Meuang Park**, the centrepiece of which is a huge concrete replica of an elaborate **votive candle**. The park is the venue of Ubon's annual Candle Parade (see p535).

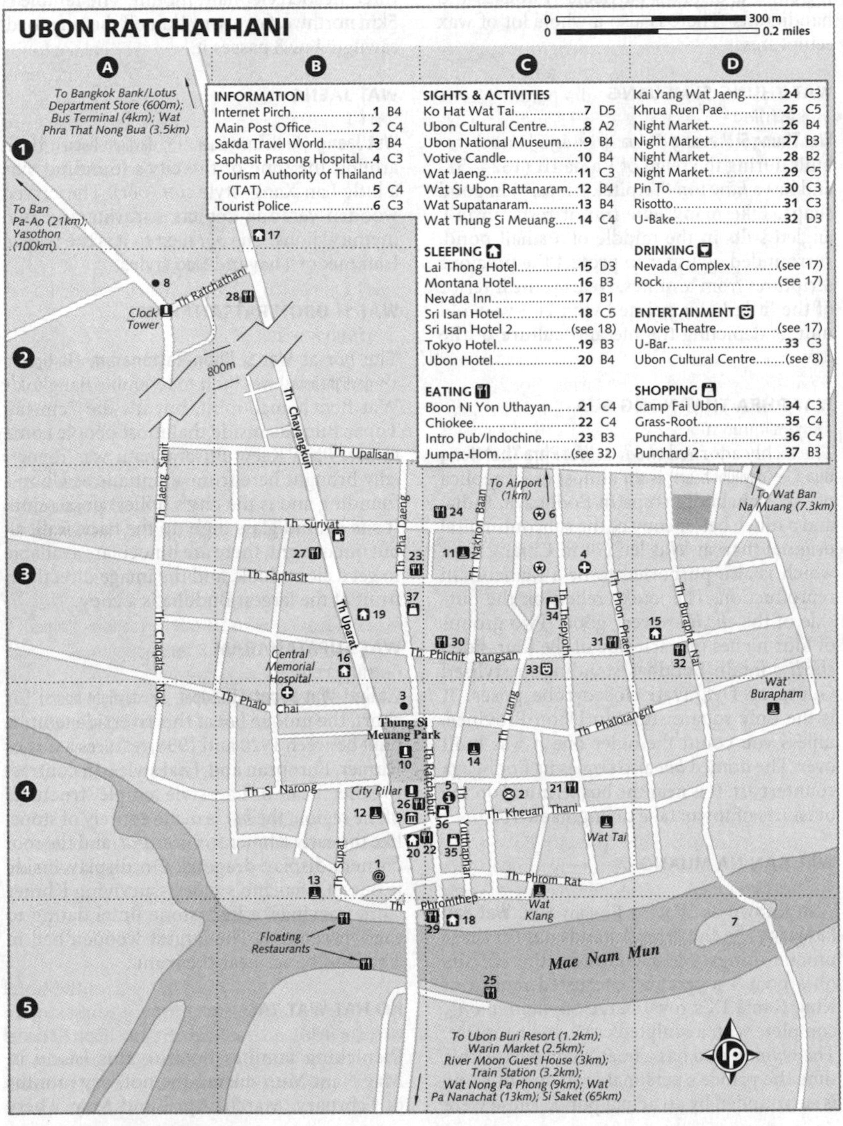
UBON RATCHATHANI
0 300 m
0 0.2 miles
INFORMATION
Internet Pirch 1 B4
Main Post Office 2 C4
Sakda Travel World 3 B4
Saphasit Prasong Hospital 4 C3
Tourism Authority of Thailand (TAT) 5 C4
Tourist Police 6 C3
SIGHTS & ACTIVITIES
Ko Hat Wat Tai 7 D5
Ubon Cultural Centre 8 A2
Ubon National Museum 9 B4
Votive Candle 10 B4
Wat Jaeng 11 C3
Wat Si Ubon Rattanaram 12 B4
Wat Supatanaram 13 B4
Wat Thung Si Meuang 14 C4
SLEEPING
Lai Thong Hotel 15 D3
Montana Hotel 16 B3
Nevada Inn 17 B1
Sri Isan Hotel 18 C5
Sri Isan Hotel 2 (see 18)
Tokyo Hotel 19 B3
Ubon Hotel 20 B4
EATING
Boon Ni Yon Uthayan 21 C4
Chiokee 22 C4
Intro Pub/Indochine 23 B3
Jumpa-Hom (see 32)
Kai Yang Wat Jaeng 24 C3
Khrua Ruen Pae 25 C5
Night Market 26 B4
Night Market 27 B3
Night Market 28 B2
Night Market 29 C5
Pin To 30 C3
Risotto 31 C3
U-Bake 32 D3
DRINKING
Nevada Complex (see 17)
Rock (see 17)
ENTERTAINMENT
Movie Theatre (see 17)
U-Bar 33 C3
Ubon Cultural Centre (see 8)
SHOPPING
Camp Fai Ubon 34 C3
Grass-Root 35 C4
Punchard 36 C4
Punchard 2 37 B3
To Bangkok Bank/Lotus Department Store (600m); Bus Terminal (4km); Wat Phra That Nong Bua (3.5km)
To Ban Pa-Ao (21km); Yasothon (100km)
Clock Tower
Th Ratchathani
800m
Th Chayangkun
Th Upalisan
Th Jaeng Sanit
To Airport (1km)
To Wat Ban Na Muang (7.3km)
Th Suriyat
Th Pha Daeng
Th Nakhon Baan
Th Saphasit
Th Uparat
Th Thepyothi
Th Phon Phaen
Th Burapha Nai
Th Chagala Nok
Central Memorial Hospital
Th Phichit Rangsan
Th Phalo Chai
Thung Si Meuang Park
Th Luang
Th Phalorangrit
Wat Burapham
Th Si Narong
City Pillar
Th Ratchabut
Th Kheuan Thani
Wat Tai
Th Supat
Th Yutthaphan
Th Phrom Rat
Th Phromthep
Wat Klang
Floating Restaurants
Mae Nam Mun
To Ubon Buri Resort (1.2km); Warin Market (2.5km); River Moon Guest House (3km); Train Station (3.2km); Wat Nong Pa Phong (9km); Wat Pa Nanachat (13km); Si Saket (65km)

UBON CULTURAL CENTER
ศูนย์วัฒนธรรมอุบลฯ

The **museum** (☎ 0 4535 2000; Th Jaeng Sanit; admission free; ☿ 8.30am-4pm) in the lower level of the striking Ubon Cultural Centre, a seven-story contemporary Isan-design tower at Rajabhat University, is more scattershot than the National Museum, but there are some interesting cultural displays, particularly houses and handicrafts. There is also a whole lot of wax sculptures.

WAT THUNG SI MEUANG
วัดทุ่งศรีเมือง

Wat Thung Si Meuang (Th Luang; ☿ daylight hours) was built during the reign of Rama III (1824–51) and has a *hǎw trai* (Tripitaka library) in good shape. Like many *hǎw trai*, it rests on tall, angled stilts in the middle of a small pond, surrounded by water to protect the precious scriptures from termites. Nearby, the interior of the little *bòt* is painted with 200-year-old murals depicting the life and culture of the day.

WAT PHRA THAT NONG BUA
วัดพระธาตุหนองบัว

The richly adorned *chedi* at **Wat Phra That Nong Bua** (☿ daylight hours) is an almost exact replica of the Mahabodhi stupa in Bodhgaya, India; and a much better copy of the subcontinental original than at Wat Jet Yot in Chiang Mai, which is also purported to be a Mahabodhi reproduction. The *jataka* reliefs on the outside of the *chedi* are very good. Two groups of four niches on each side of the four-sided *chedi* contain Buddhas standing in stylised Gupta or Dvaravati closed-robe poses. It is the only square stupa in Ubon Province, unless you count the older one it was built over. The domed *bòt* also copies its Bodhgaya counterpart. It is near the bus terminal on the outskirts of town; take sǎwngthǎew 10.

WAT BAN NA MUANG
วัดบ้านนาเมือง

Also known as Wat Sa Prasan Suk, **Wat Ban Na Muang** (☿ daylight hours) stands out for three unique things. Most famously, the *bòt* sits on a boat – a ceramic encrusted replica of King Rama IX's royal barge *Suphannahong*, complete with a sculpted crew, to be precise. The *wíhǎan* also has a boat-shaped base, this time the prince's personal craft and this one is surrounded by an actual pond. These were

not just artistic endeavours, rather the water represents our desires and the boats represent staying above them. The commissioner of these creations, Luang Pu Boon Mi, died in 2001 and his body is on display behind glass in the big hall next to the boat *bòt*. Finally, to reach all of these, you must pass under an immense statue of Airavata, Hindu God Indra's three-headed elephant mount. The temple is 5km northwest of town, 1km off the ring road; sǎwngthǎew 8 passes it.

WAT JAENG
วัดแจ้ง

Wat Jaeng (Th Nakhon Baan; ☿ daylight hours), built around the time of the city's founding, has a little Lan Xang–style *sìm* (*bòt*). The carved wooden veranda depicts Airavata and two mythical lions. The *bòt* next to it is the typical Isan mix of Thai and Lao styles.

WAT SI UBON RATTANARAM
วัดศรีอุบลรัตนาราม

The *bòt* at **Wat Si Ubon Rattanaram** (Th Uparat; ☿ daylight hours) was built to resemble Bangkok's Wat Benchamabophit, but it's the 7cm-tall Topaz Buddha inside that most people come to see. Phra Kaew Busarakham was reportedly brought here from Vientiane at Ubon's founding and is the city's holiest possession. It sits behind glass high up the back wall, all but out of sight; there are binoculars available to get a closer look, and the image directly in front of the largest Buddha is a copy.

WAT SUPATANARAM
วัดสุปัฏนาราม

Called **Wat Supat** (Th Supat; ☿ daylight hours) for short, the unique *bòt* at this riverside temple, built between 1920 and 1936, features a mix of Khmer, European and Thai styles. In contrast to other Thai- or Lao-style temple structures of the region, the *bòt* is made entirely of stone, like the early Khmer stone *prasat*, and the roof corners display dragons. On display inside is one of Thailand's oldest-surviving Khmer stone carvings, a lush stone lintel dating to the 7th century. The largest wooden bell in Thailand hangs near the front.

KO HAT WAT TAI
เกาะหาดวัดใต้

Picnicking families flock to this island in Mae Nam Mun during the hot, dry months of February, March, April and May. There

are beaches for swimming and sunbathing. A makeshift bamboo bridge connects it to the northern shore.

WARIN CHAMRAP DISTRICT TEMPLES
The famous monk and meditation master Ajahn Cha was quite a name in these parts. He founded the two well-known forest monasteries detailed below, and students of his have opened a long list of temples across Thailand, and even about a dozen in Europe, North America, Australia and New Zealand.

Known for his simple and direct teaching method, the venerable *ajahn* (teacher), a former disciple of the most famous northeastern teacher of them all, Ajahn Man, died in January 1992, aged 75. His funeral, held at Wat Nong Pa Phong, drew thousands of followers from around the world.

Wat Nong Pa Phong
วัดหนองป่าพง
Peaceful **Wat Nong Pa Phong** (☺ daylight hours) is known for its quiet discipline and daily routine of work and meditation. Dozens of Westerners have lived here over recent decades, and several still do, but if you have an interest in Buddhism you'll be steered to Wat Pa Nanachat unless you are fluent in Thai. The wat features the *chedi* where Ajahn Cha's ashes are interred and a large **museum** (admission free; ☺ 8am-4.30pm) displaying an odd assortment of items, from Ajahn Cha's worldly possessions to world currencies to a foetus in a jar. The temple is about 10km past the river – take săwngthăew 14 from the Warin Market.

Wat Pa Nanachat
วัดป่านานาชาติบุ่งหวาย
Wat Pa Nanachat (www.watpahnanachat.org; Ban Bung Wai, Amphoe Warin, Ubon Ratchathani 34310; ☺ daylight hours) is a Western-oriented wat, opened in 1975 specifically for non-Thais, and English is the primary language. Those with a *serious* interest in Buddhism and previous meditation experience are welcome to apply (write using the above address or the website) to stay here. Guests must follow all temple rules (including eating just one meal a day, rising at 3am, and shaving heads and eyebrows after the third day). During the March-to-May hot season, monks go into retreat and overnight guests aren't usually accepted.

There is nothing really to see here, but visitors are welcome to drop by. A senior monk

is available most days after the 8am meal to answer questions. A săwngthăew from Warin Market or any Si Saket bus can drop you on Hwy 226, about 500m from the entrance. The wat is in the forest behind the rice fields.

Festivals & Events
Ubon's **Candle Parade** (Hae Tian) features gigantic, elaborately carved wax sculptures and is a part of Khao Phansa, a Buddhist holiday marking the commencement of *wan àwk phansăa*, the Rains Retreat (Buddhist Lent) in July. You can see the floats the rest of the year on most temple grounds, where they are kept until it's time to melt them down for the next parade. The festival is very popular with Thai tourists and the city's hotel rooms are often all booked for the event.

Sleeping
BUDGET
River Moon Guest House (☎ 0 4528 6093; 43 Th Sisaket 2; r 120-150B) Parts of this rustic, wooden spot are falling apart, the chairs in the lounge are from an old train and old musical instruments lean against the walls – yet somehow it all adds up to pretty cool. It's about 200m from the train station in Warin Chamrap. Facilities are shared.

Sri Isan Hotel 2 (☎ 0 4525 4544; 60 Th Ratchabut; r 160-350B; ✖) This older, dishevelled place, hidden behind its flashier sister sleeper, is, for the price, one of the city's better budget hotels.

Tokyo Hotel (☎ 0 4524 1739; 360 Th Uparat; r 220-600B; ✖) Besides being a popular though dour midranger, the Tokyo is a good budget bet in the centre of Ubon, with the highest-priced rooms in a new tower and some relatively humble air-con and fan affairs in the old.

Ubon Hotel (☎ 0 4524 1045; 333 Th Kheuan Thani; r 280-700B; ✖ ▢) The plain Jane of Ubon's hotels is too old and tired to recommend as the midranger it wants to be, but the budget fan rooms offer reasonable value, and the balcony views from upper floors are a nice bonus.

MIDRANGE
Montana Hotel (☎ 0 4526 1748; 179/1-4 Th Uparat; r 400B; ✖) The focal point of this central hotel is the 'VIP' Piano Karaoke Bar, and the porter is an enthusiastic 'boom-boom' salesman. But if you can escape the potential shenanigans down below, you'll find the rooms are spotless and well appointed, with little balconies, TV and fridge.

Nevada Inn (☎ 0 4531 3351; 436 Th Chayangkun; r 550-800B, ste 1500B; 🖭) North of the centre, ensconced in the city's busiest entertainment complex, the lower-level rooms have wooden floors and frilly bedspreads giving it a fair amount of va-va-voom for the price – but only by Ubon's low standards. If you are looking to move up the price range, you'd probably be better off moving across the parking lot to its big brother, the Nevada Grand.

our pick **Sri Isan Hotel** (☎ 0 4526 1011; www .sriisanhotel.com; 62 Th Ratchabut; r 550-1300B; 🖭 🖵) The exception to the rule of Ubon's typical uninspired midrangers, this bright, cheerful place is full of natural light, which streams down through the atrium and gives the lobby an open, airy feel. The rooms, which come with fridge and TV, are small and the décor is a little twee – a knitted toilet roll cover wouldn't be out of place – but standards are high and an orchid comes gratis on every pillow.

TOP END

Ubon Buri Resort (☎ 0 4526 6777; www.ubonburiresort .com; Th Srimongkol; r 1140-1330B, bungalow 1500B, ste 2500B; 🖭 🖵 🖭) This bona fide, self-contained resort is the place to come if you're planning on staying in Ubon without really *being* in Ubon. With rooms and bungalows set in acres of lush, tropical greenery, Isan folk-art styling and tip-top staff, this is Ubon's best-value top-ender. It's just off the main road between Ubon and Warin Chamrap.

Lai Thong Hotel (☎ 0 4526 4271; www.laithongho tel.net; 50 Th Phichit Rangsan; s/d 1200/1300B; ste 3000B; 🖭 🖵 🖭) A tourist office favourite, this swanky spot offers attentive staff, all the usual 'executive' facilities and the odd token nod to traditional Isan design. There is a 3rd-floor outdoor swimming pool.

Eating

Boon Ni Yon Uthayan (☎ 0 4524 0950; Th Si Narong; per plate 15B; 🕙 breakfast & lunch) One of Ubon's most famous restaurants has an impressive vegetarian buffet under a giant roof. Most of the food is grown organically just outside the city.

U-Bake (☎ 0 4526 5671; 49/3 Th Phichit Rangsan; chocolate cake 40B; 🕙 lunch & dinner; 🖭 🖵) The French-Lao influence means Ubon is more accustomed to pastries than many parts of Thailand and U-Bake is as good as it gets. It shares a water-and-plant filled wooden deck with its sister restaurant, Jumpa-Hom.

Kai Yang Wat Jaeng (☎ 08 1709 9393; 228 Th Suriyat; dishes 20-100B; 🕙 lunch) It looks like a tornado whipped through this no-frills spot, but the chefs cook up a storm of their own. This is considered by many to be Ubon's premier purveyor of *kài yâang, sôm-tam*, sausages and other Isan food.

Intro Pub/Indochine (☎ 0 4524 5584; 168-170 Th Saphasit; dishes 40-100B; 🕙 lunch & dinner; 🖭) It's difficult to see the wood for the trees at this popular two-in-one place – the exterior of the timber building is cloaked in leaves. The deliciously fresh Vietnamese food is served downstairs in Indochine until 6pm, when the action and the chefs move to the slightly swankier Intro Pub venue above. The menu – featuring favourites such as *ban hoi thit nuong* (grilled pork with vermicelli) – remains the same, but you get live music upstairs after dark.

Chiokee (☎ 0 4525 4017; 307-317 Th Kheuan Thani; dishes 25-160B; 🕙 breakfast, lunch & dinner) Offering a slightly incongruous blend of East (darkwood styling and a decorative Chinese shrine) and West (Heinz ketchup and white tablecloths), this popular spot whips up a wide range of dishes, from eel soup to English breakfasts.

Pin To (no roman-script sign; ☎ 0 4524 4473; 298-300 Th Phichit Rangsan; dishes 40-180B; 🕙 lunch & dinner; 🖭) This snug, wooden diner has oodles of cosy character, live music in the evening, a scattering of tables on the street out the front and a reasonable selection of Thai food. The cooking is not the ace card, but it remains a pleasant spot for an after-dinner beer and snack.

Khrua Ruen Pae (no roman-script sign; ☎ 0 4532 4342; dishes 60-250B; 🕙 lunch & dinner) One of four floating restaurants on Mae Nam Mun, Krun Ruen Pae serves up tasty food and a relaxed atmosphere. You can drive here (exit to the west and then go under the bridge) but it's easier to find if you walk.

Risotto (☎ 08 1879 1869; Th Phichit Rangsan; dishes 70-300B; 🕙 lunch & dinner; 🖭) The dining room can't pull off an Italian vibe, but the kitchen offers a dash of *la dolce vita*. Risotto makes one of the best pizzas in Isan.

Jumpa-Hom (☎ 0 4526 0398; 49/3 Th Phichit Rangsan; dishes 65-1500B; 🕙 dinner; 🖭) Sharing premises with U-Bake, this restaurant serves pricey Thai, Chinese and Western cuisine.

Ubon has many small **night markets** (🕙 4.30pm-midnight) rather than one large one. The *tàlàat yài* (big market) down by the river is much smaller than the market up Th Ratch-

abut next to Thung Si Meuang or the market on Th Uparat north of the Tokyo Hotel.

Entertainment

U-Bar (☎ 0 4526 5141; 97/8-10 Th Phichit Rangsan; ☺ 6pm-1am) This has long been Ubon's ubertrendy (well, for Isan anyway) nightspot. It offers hip styling, plenty of shiny, happy people and a drink called Blue Kamikaze, which is served out of a sinister-looking slush machine behind the bar. The bands (and they get some pretty good ones) usually kick off around 9pm and the club is packed soon after.

Ubon Cultural Centre (☎ 0 4535 2000; Th Jaeng Sanit) There are sometimes Isan song and dance performances here.

Ubon's nightlife nexus is the **Nevada Complex** (Th Chayangkun), a multibar and restaurant area anchored by a seven-screen **movie theatre** (☎ 0 4531 3351) and the **Rock** (☎ 0 4528 0999; ☺ 10pm-2am), a rough and ready dance club that doesn't get going until midnight.

Shopping

Grass-Root (☎ 0 4524 1272; 87 Th Yutthaphan; ☺ 9am-6pm) The speciality of Ubon Province is natural-dyed, hand-woven cotton and you'll find a fantastic assortment here.

Camp Fai Ubon (☎ 0 4524 1821; 189 Th Thepyothi; ☺ 8am-8pm Mon-Sat) Signed as Peaceland, this is another good place for hand-woven cotton.

Punchard (☎ 0 4524 3433; 158 Th Ratchabut; ☺ 8am-8pm Mon-Sat) and **Punchard 2** (☎ 0 4526 5751; 156 Th Pha Daeng; ☺ 9.30am-8.30pm) stock a wider array of handicrafts. Shop carefully though, prices are high.

Getting There & Away

AIR

THAI (www.thaiairways.com) has three daily flights to/from Bangkok (one way 2700B), while **Air Asia** (www.airasia.com) has one flight (1650B).

BUS

Ubon's **bus terminal** (☎ 0 4531 6085) is north of the town centre, just off Th Chayangkun – take săwngthăew 2, 3 or 10. Buses link Ubon with Bangkok's northern terminal (air-con 411B, eight hours) frequently. **Nakhonchai Air** (☎ 0 4526 9777), with an office at the terminal, has VIP buses to Bangkok (594B, 10 daily), Rayong (687B, 14 hours, five daily) and Chiang Mai (960B, 17 hours, four daily). Other fares to/from Ubon are in the table on right.

BUSES TO/FROM UBON

Destination	Fare (B)	Duration (hr)
Kantharalak (for Khao Phra Wihan)		
ordinary	37	1½
Khon Kaen		
ordinary	147	4½
air-con	230	
Khorat		
ordinary	155	7
air-con	279	
Mukdahan		
ordinary	80	3
air-con	144	
Pakse, Laos		
air-con	200	3
Roi Et		
ordinary	82	3
air-con	148	
Sakon Nakhon		
ordinary	125	5
air-con	225	
Si Saket		
ordinary	40	1¼
air-con	59	
Surin		
ordinary	80	3
air-con	144	
Yasothon		
ordinary	50	1½
air-con	90	

Phibun (25B, 1½ hours, hourly) and Khong Jiam (60B, three hours, five daily) buses stop briefly at the Warin Market after leaving the terminal, but they're sometimes already full when they get there.

TRAIN

The **train station** (☎ 0 4532 1004) is in Warin Chamrap; săwngthăew 2 connects it to Ubon.

The Ubon express leaves Bangkok nightly at 8.30pm, arriving in Ubon at 6.35am the next day while the Bangkok-bound train leaves Ubon at 6.30pm arriving at Hualamphong station at 5.25am. Nine other trains also make the run throughout the day taking just as long, except the 2.50pm express service that makes the trip in 8½ hours.

Fares for 1st-class air-con sleeper/2nd-class fan sleeper/2nd-class seat/3rd-class seat are 1180/471/221/95B.

NORTHEASTERN THAILAND

These train services also stop in Khorat (1st/2nd/3rd class 268/133/58B, six hours).

Getting Around

Numbered and colour-coded săwngthăew (8B) run throughout town. The free city map TAT hands out has the routes marked. A normal túk-túk trip will cost about 40B and a săamláw will be about 20B.

The Lai Thong Hotel rents mountain bikes for 200B per day.

AROUND UBON RATCHATHANI PROVINCE
Ban Pa-Ao
บ้านผาอ่าว

Ban Pa-Ao, northwest of Ubon on Hwy 23, is a silk-weaving village, but it is best known for producing brass and bronze items using the lost-wax casting method. Between December and July you can see workers making bowls and bells at a cooperative workshop in the centre of the village – most people work in the rice fields the rest of the year. There's a village-run **homestay programme** (☎ 08 1967 0225; per person per night incl 2 meals 500B), which offers the chance to try silk weaving.

Ban Pa-Ao is 3km off the highway, near the Km 19 pillar. Buses to Yasothon pass this way and a motorcycle taxi from the highway will cost about 15B.

Phibun Mangsahan to Khong Jiam
พิบูลมังสาหาร/โขงเจียม

Visitors often stop in the dusty town of Phibun Mangsahan to see a set of rapids called **Kaeng Sapheu**, just downstream of the Mae Nam Mun river crossing. The rocky islets make 'Python Rapids' rise only from end of January until June, but the shady park here makes it a pleasant stop year-round. It's got a Chinese temple, several simple restaurants (most serving frog skins and fish) and countless souvenir shops. Many fishermen work here and they'll take you on **boat trips** (per hour 400B, all day 1500-1800B) where you can see water birds and visit island wats. Phibun Mangsahan is also the location of the Ubon **immigration office** (☎ 0 4544 1108; ☼ 8.30am-4.30pm Mon-Fri), where visa extensions are available. The office is 700m south of the bridge on the way to Chong Mek.

The villages just over the bridge, as you drive east to Khong Jiam along Rte 2222, are famed for forging iron and bronze **gongs**, both

for temples and classical Thai-music ensembles. You can watch the gong-makers hammering the flat metal discs and tempering them in rustic fires at many houses and simple roadside shelters. Small gongs start at around 500B and the huge 2m gongs fetch as much as 200,000B. People make many drums and cymbals around here too.

Five kilometres before Khong Jiam you can cross the Pak Mun Dam to little **Kaeng Tana National Park** (☎ 0 4540 6886, reservations 0 2562 0760; admission 200B; ☼ 6am-6pm). After circling thickly forested Don Tana, linked to the mainland by footbridge, Mae Nam Mun roils through the beautiful namesake rapids, which lie underwater during the rainy season. The island has a beach at the north end and the 2km clifftop trail to **Lan Pha Phueng** viewpoint is serene. Bikes cost 50B per hour and, if you call a day in advance, park staff can arrange canoe rental (per hour 100B) and horseback riding. Five kilometres south of the **visitor centre** (☼ 8am-6pm) is **Nam Tok Tad Ton**, a wide waterfall just a 300m walk from the road. There is a **camp site** (per person 30B, 2-person tent hire 150B) and restaurant by the rapids. The park is 14km from Khong Jiam; there is no public transport.

Khong Jiam sits on a picturesque peninsula at the confluence of the Mekong and Mun Rivers, which Thais call **Mae Nam Song Si** (Two Colour River) after the contrasting coloured currents formed at the junction. Huge conical fish traps are made here for local use; they look very much like the fish traps that appear in the 3000-year-old murals at Pha Taem National Park (p539). You can charter long-tail boats to take you out to Mae Nam Song Si (300B, up to 10 people), Kaeng Tana (600B) or Pha Taem (1200B).

Thais can cross the Mekong to Laos and though this is not an official crossing for foreigners, it is possible to persuade the Lao immigration police (all it takes is 50B) to let you visit the market in the Lao village across the river. First you should get a border pass from Thai immigration, which officials will give you if you are polite and dressed nice.

SLEEPING & EATING

There are a few passable places to stay in Phibun Mangsahan, but Khong Jiam offers better options.

Phiboonkit Hotel (☎ 0 4544 1201; 65/1-3 Th Phiboon, Phibun Mangsahan; r 200-300B; ☒) In the centre of town, midway between the bus stop and the

bridge, this is your usual, slightly chaotic, budget hotel.

Apple Guest House (☎ 0 4535 1160; 267 Th Kaewpradit, Khong Jiam; r 150-300B; 🗱) Down a tiny little alley, the Apple has old wooden buildings with bathrooms shared between two rooms, and concrete rooms below with private bathroom for the same price. Both are pretty basic.

Mongkon Guest House (☎ 0 4535 1352; 595 Th Kaewpradit, Khong Jiam; r 200-800B; 🗱) From the simple fan rooms to the four cute wooden cottages, this place near the highway is a good choice for any budget. It rents bikes (per day 100B) and motorcycles (per day 200B).

Tohsang Khong Jiam Resort (☎ 0 4535 1174; www .tohsang.com; Khong Jiam; r 2000-2500B; villas 3000-6000B; 🗱 🖳 🖳) The glitz and gloss at this large resort-spa are a little incongruous for this stretch of rural Thailand, but this looming place holds all the aces in the posh-accommodation stakes. It's 3km out of town, in a lush garden on the south bank of Mae Nam Mun.

Tom Reung Ruang (no roman-script sign; 🕑 breakfast & lunch) This ramshackle shop right at the bridge in Phibun is famous for *saalaapao* (large Chinese buns), *năng jip* (small porkfilled wraps) and *năng kòp* (frog skin, usually fried). Thais visiting Pha Taem National Park like to stop here to stock up on these items (5B each)

There are plenty of simple restaurants in Khong Jiam, some floating down on the Mekong. The row of **food vendors** (🕑 6am-midnight) in front of market, at the junction of the highway and the main road, is the closest thing Khong Jiam has to a night market.

GETTING THERE & AWAY
Five Khong Jiam buses leave Ubon (50B, three hours) daily; you can also take a Phibun bus (25B, 1½ hours) and continue by săwngthăew (30B, one hour, every half-hour) from the bridge, which is about 1km (10B by túk-túk) from the Khong Jiam bus stop.

Pha Taem National Park
อุทยานแห่งชาติผาแต้ม
Up the Mekong from Khong Jiam is a long stone cliff named Pha Taem – the centrepiece of **Pha Taem National Park** (☎ 0 4526 6333, reservations 0 2562 0760; admission 400B; 🕑 24hr). From the top you get an amazing bird's-eye view of Laos, and you can see the first sunset in Thailand. Down below, reached via a trail, the cliff

features prehistoric rock paintings that are at least 3000 years old. Mural subjects include fish traps, *plaa bèuk* (giant Mekong catfish), elephants, human hands and geometric designs. The second viewing platform fronts the most impressive pictographs. A clifftop **visitor centre** (🕑 8am-5pm) contains exhibits pertaining to the paintings and local geology.

Nam Tok Soi Sawan, a 25m-tall waterfall flowing from June to November, is another popular spot. It's a 19km drive from the visitor centre, but it's best reached by the 9km hiking trail tracing the cliff. What the park calls **Thailand's largest flower field** (blooming late October to end of December) lies just beyond the falls. The far north of the park, where roads are so bad they are best travelled on two wheels, holds many more waterfalls and wonderful views. **Pa Cha Na Dai** cliff serves Thailand's first sunrise. Scattered across the 340-sq-km park are several areas called **Sao Chaliang**, mushroom-shaped stone formations similar to Phu Pha Thoep in Mukdahan National Park.

Pha Taem has **camp sites** (per tent 30B, 2-person tent hire 150B) and six **bungalows** (6-bed with fan 1200B, 4-bed with air-con 2000B). Vendors sell snacks and beverages near the visitor centre.

GETTING THERE & AWAY
Pha Taem is 18km beyond Khong Jiam via Rte 2112, but there's no public transport there. The best way to get there on your own is to rent a motorcycle in Khong Jiam, which will set you back 150B to 200B.

Chong Mek & the Emerald Triangle
ช่องเม็ก/สามเหลี่ยมมรกต
South of Khong Jiam, at the end of Rte 217, is the small trading town of **Chong Mek** on the Thai–Lao border, the only place in Thailand where *faràng* can cross into Laos by land (that is, you don't have to cross the Mekong). The southern Lao capital of Pakse is about 45 minutes by road from Vangtao, the village on the Lao side of the border, where you can now buy a 30-day visa on the spot. Buses crossing here wait for passengers to complete the paperwork. The border is open from 6am until 6pm, but Lao border officials charge a 40B 'overtime' levy/bribe (it doesn't appear to be an official charge) if you arrive before 8am or after 4pm or anytime on a weekend. They also try to extract a 50B 'stamping fee' no matter what the hour.

Thai travellers come to Chong Mek to browse through cheap goods from China, Vietnam and Laos. Foreign visitors won't find much of interest to purchase here, unless they're in the market for toiletries (from China), camouflage clothing (from Vietnam) or CDs (from Laos), though skirts and fabrics are priced very low. If you get here after hours, the **Nonthaveth & Ounchith Guest House** (☎ 0 4548 5237; r 200-500B; 🅿 💻) is clean and friendly, though the fan rooms are a little overpriced.

About 5km west of Chong Mek is the northeastern shore of the huge **Kheuan Sirinthon** reservoir, an impoundment of a Mae Nam Mun tributary. Local aquaphiles and picnickers frequent a recreation area on forested hills near the dam at its northern end.

GETTING THERE & AWAY
Sǎwngthǎew run between Phibun and Chong Mek (35B, one hour) every 20 minutes. There is no public transport between Chong Mek and Khong Jiam; you must go through Phibun or hire a túk-túk for about 400B. If you are continuing on to Pakse, catch a bus (50B) on the Lao side.

Phu Chong Nayoi National Park
อุทยานแห่งชาติภูจองนายอย
Stretching across the 'Emerald Triangle', the jungle-clad intersection of the Lao, Thai and Cambodian borders, is the little-known **Phu Chong Nayoi National Park** (☎ 0 4541 1515, reservations 0 2562 0760; admission 400B; ⏱ 24hr), one of Thailand's wildest parks and healthiest forests. Fauna includes barking deer, monkeys, gibbons, Malayan sun bears, Asiatic black bears, black hornbills, red jungle fowl and the endangered white-winged ducks. Elephants and tigers often cross over the border into the park.

The park's primary attraction is **Nam Tok Huay Luang**, which plunges 40m over a cliff in two separate but parallel streams. A short trail leads to the top, and you can walk down 272 steps to the bottom. Another 170m downstream is little **Nam Tok Pa On La-Oe**, also a pretty picture. You can swim below both, though they dry up around March. Rangers love taking visitors on short **bamboo raft trips** (price negotiable) above the falls where they insist you might see a python; but water levels are often too high or too low to make the trip,

AROUND SI SAKET & UBON RATCHATHANI

especially from February to April. At the far end of the 687-sq-km park, there are superb vistas of the surrounding countryside (it looks a lot like the view from Pha Taem cliff, but with jungle instead of the Mekong at the bottom of the valley) from atop **Pha Hin Dang**. It's a 50km drive from the main park entrance and then a 2km hike.

Stargazing is superb here, so consider spending the night. There are four three-bed **bungalows** (600B) with hot water and electricity, plus a **camp site** (per person 30B). During our visit there was no tent hire, but this may change. A couple of restaurants operate on weekends and holidays only, but park staff will cook for overnight guests with advance notice. Snacks and drinks are available daily.

GETTING THERE & AWAY

From Ubon catch one of the three morning buses to the town of Najaluay (60B, three hours). From Najaluay, túk-túk can be hired for about 300B for the return journey to Nam Tok Huai Luang with a short wait. If you have your own wheels, the turn-off to the park is 9km beyond Najaluay, and Huai Luang is another 11km after the turn-off.

SURIN & SI SAKET PROVINCES

The adjacent provinces of Surin and Si Saket are dotted with Angkor-era Khmer ruins. Most are now looking rather tatty, but Khao Phra Wihan ranks among the northeast's best attractions.

The region's towns are rather less interesting, but Surin in particular makes a comfortable base for exploring the temples and provides the backdrop for the raucous Annual Elephant Roundup, held each November.

SURIN & AROUND

สุรินทร์

pop 41,200

Quiet Surin doesn't have much to say for itself until November, when the provincial capital explodes into life for the **Annual Elephant Roundup** when giant scrums of pachyderm come to town – you'll never see so many well-dressed tuskers. The city celebrates for 10 days, but the massive crowds come on just the last weekend for the main event, which

features 300 elephants showing their skills and taking part in a battle re-enactment. Tickets start at 40B, but VIP seats, which get you closest to the action, English commentary and guaranteed shade cost 500B. Arguably the festival's best event is the free buffet for the elephants and parade on the Friday before the big show.

Just outside the capital city you'll find more elephantine entertainment and some interesting handicraft villages. Further afield are some ruins worth the effort to reach for those with a history habit.

Information

Microsys (Th Sirirat, Surin; per hr 15B; ✆ 24hr) You can access email here.

Post office (Th Tanasan, Surin; ✆ 8.30am-4.30 Mon-Fri, 9am-noon Sat, Sun & holidays)

Ruamphet Hospital (☎ 0 4451 3192; Th Thesaban 1, Surin)

Siam Commercial Bank (Th Sratara, Surin; ✆ 10.30am-8pm) Has ATM and exchange facilities inside Surin Plaza shopping centre.

Sights & Activities

BAN THA KLANG

บ้านตากลาง

To see Surin's elephants during the low season, visit the **Elephant Study Centre** (☎ 08 1879 2773; donations appreciated; ✆ 9am-5pm) in Ban Tha Klang, about 50km north of Surin. Displays inside and out discuss elephants and elephant training, and dozens of the performers at the annual festival live here – some in traditional Suai homes sheltering both elephants and humans. There are one-hour **shows** (donations expected) daily (except during the festival, but there are plans to change that) at 10am and 2pm.

The village hosts an **Elephant Parade**, with all the pachyderms brightly painted, around May's full moon, for the new monks' ordination ceremony.

Buses from Surin (30B, two hours) run hourly. If you are driving, take Rte 214 north for 40km and follow the 'Elephant Village' signs down Rte 3027.

CRAFT VILLAGES

There are many silk-weaving villages in easy striking distance of Surin town. By far the most famous is **Ban Tha Sawang**, where **Chansoma** (☎ 08 1726 0397) makes exquisite brocade fabrics incorporating threads coated in silver

or gold. You can't buy them here – they are only made to order; prices start at 30,000B per metre – but the weaving process, which takes two to three months, is mighty impressive. Four women, including one sitting on a floor below the others, work the loom simultaneously. Dozens of other shops selling more typical silks serve the masses disgorged by a steady stream of tour buses. The village is 8km west of the city via Rte 4026, and săwngthăew (12B, 20 minutes) run regularly from the market in Surin.

Ban Khwao Sinarin and **Ban Chok**, next door neighbours 18km north of Surin via Rtes 214 and 3036, are known for silk and silver respectively, though you can buy some of both in each village. One of the silk specialities is *pha hole*, a distinctive tightly woven *mát-mìi*. Also popular is *yok daw*, a much simpler brocade style that requires up to 35 footpedals on the looms. Neither fabric style is readily available in other parts of Thailand, and prices here (as well as in other Surin villages) can be over 50% cheaper. The silver standout is *prakueam*, a Cambodian style of bead brought to Thailand by Ban Chok's ancestors many centuries ago. You can see both products being made at shops and homes in the villages, and Khun Manee, who runs **Phra Dab Suk** (☎ 08 9865 8720) on the main drag, often takes customers (or non-customers for a small fee) out to see the entire silk-weaving process, from cocoon to loom. Săwngthăew go from Surin (20B, 1½ hours) hourly.

The residents of **Ban Buthom**, 14km out of Surin on Rte 226, on the way to Sikhoraphum, weave sturdy, unlacquered rattan baskets, including some rather flat ones that pack well.

PRASAT TA MEUAN
ปราสาทตาเมือน
The most atmospheric – and most difficult to reach – of Surin's temple ruins is a series of three sites known collectively as **Prasat Ta Meuan** (admission free; ☉ 6am-5pm) in Amphoe Ban Ta Miang on the Cambodian border. It lines the ancient route linking Angkor Wat to Phimai.

The first site, **Prasat Ta Meuan** proper, was built in the Jayavarman VII period (AD 1181–1210) as a rest stop for pilgrims. It's a fairly small monument with a two-door, 10-window sanctuary constructed of laterite blocks; only one sculpted sandstone lintel over the rear door remains.

Just 300m south, **Prasat Ta Meuan Toht**, which is said to have been the chapel for a 'healing station' or 'hospital' like Prang Ku outside Chaiyaphum, is a bit larger. Also built by Jayavarman VII, the ruins consist of a *gopura, mondòp* and main *prang*, which are surrounded by a laterite wall.

Nearly a kilometre further south, next to the army base at the end of the road, is the largest site, **Prasat Ta Meuan Thom**, which predates the other two sites by as much as two centuries. Despite a somewhat haphazard reconstruction, this one nearly justifies the effort it takes to get here. Three *prangs* and a large hall are built of sandstone blocks on a laterite base and several smaller buildings still stand inside the wall. Many carvings encase the principal *prang*, but the best were pried or blasted away and sold to unscrupulous Thai dealers by the Khmer Rouge who occupied the site in the 1980s. A stairway on the southern end drops into Cambodian territory. Land mines and undetonated hand grenades still litter the thick jungle surrounding the complex, which is why the red signs (in Thai only) warn you of 'danger'.

The sites begin 10.5km south of Ban Ta Miang (on Rte 224, 23km east of Ban Kruat) via a winding road used by far more cows than cars. You need your own transport to get here, and a visit is more convenient from Phanom Rung Historical Park (p468) than from Surin town.

OTHER KHMER-TEMPLE RUINS
The southern reach of Surin Province along the Cambodian border harbours several minor Angkor-period ruins, including **Prasat Hin Ban Phluang** (admission 30B; ☉ 7.30am-6pm), 33km south of Surin. It's just a solitary sandstone *prang* with most of its top gone sitting on a laterite base that once held three; but some wonderful carvings, including a lintel above the entrance with the Hindu god Indra riding his elephant, Airavata, make it worth a trip. It was probably built in the 11th century and a U-shaped moat rings it. The site sits 600m off Rte 214; the turn-off is 1.5km south of Hwy 24. Any vehicle bound for the border can drop you nearby, but it's easier to get to the town of Prasat and hire a motorcycle taxi there.

A larger Khmer site is seen 30km northeast of town at **Prasat Sikhoraphum** (admission 30B; ☉ 7.30am-6pm), in the town of the same name. Built in the 12th century, Sikhoraphum

features five brick *prang*, the tallest of which reaches 32m. Two of the *prang* still hold their tops, including the central one whose doorways are decorated with stone carvings of Hindu deities following the Angkor Wat style. Locals are keenly proud of this site and sell DVDs of student music and dance shows and T-shirts to raise money for a small museum that would house two Sikhoraphum lintels currently consigned to museums in Surin and Phimai. Sikhoraphum can be reached by bus (20B, one hour) or train (7B, 40 minutes) from Surin town. If driving out here, you may as well take a 300m detour off Rte 226 for a peep at **Prasat Muang Thi** (admission free; ☾ daylight hours), 15km from Surin. The three remaining brick *prang* are in sad shape (one looks like it's ready to topple), but they're so small they're actually kind of cute.

The ruined **Prasat Phumpon** (admission free; ☾ daylight hours) in Amphoe Sangkha (9km south of Hwy 24 on Rte 2124; veer right through the village at the fork in the road), dating from the 7th or 8th century, is the oldest Khmer *prasat* in Thailand; though that is its only claim to fame and you will likely be disappointed in this simple brick *prang*.

Surin can also be used as a base to visit the Khmer ruins at Phanom Rung about 75km southwest of Surin in Buriram Province (see p468).

SURIN NATIONAL MUSEUM
พิพิธภัณฑสถานแห่งชาติสุรินทร์

As has been the case ever since this museum, about 5km south of town on Rte 214, was constructed in 2000, the best guess anyone can give for when it will open is 'next year'. Displays will focus on Surin's ethnic groups, including the Suai, the region's renown elephant herders, and the province's Khmer ruins.

VOLUNTEERING
Starfish Ventures (☎ 0 4453 0601; www.starfishvent ures.co.uk; Th Thrayrong, Mu 6) runs four projects in Surin that require as little as a two-week commitment. The most popular is a nursing programme where nurses or nursing students visit village health clinics. Also available year-round is a school development programme to renovate and construct buildings; those who can paint fun pictures for young children on the walls are especially welcome. English teachers for grades 1 to 6 can work during the school year (June to September and November to February) and a conservation programme, mostly involving tree planting, runs in July and August.

All work is done in surrounding villages, but volunteers get private rooms in the provincial capital. Starfish also has volunteering opportunities in other Thai cities; see Responsible Travel (p45) for more information.

Tours
Pirom, at Pirom-Aree's House (see below), offers a wide range of tours, from a half-day in Ban Tha Klang and the craft villages (per person 1200B with four people) to a four-day Isan immersion (per person per day with four people 2100B) from the back of his Land Rover. All the well-known Khmer temples (and many others) are also available. Prices are high, but the tours are good.

Saren Travel (☎ 0 4452 0174; sarentour@yahoo.com; 202/1-4 Th Thesaban 2; ☾ 8am-5pm Mon-Sat) offers customised day tours in and around Surin Province from 1500B. It is planning to create audio-tour CDs for those who want to drive themselves.

Sleeping
The hotels fill up fast during the Elephant Roundup (and prices skyrocket), so book as far in advance as you can.

our pick Pirom-Aree's House (☎ 0 4451 5140; Soi Arunee, Th Thungpo, Surin; r 120-200B) The location, 1km west of the city, is a little inconvenient, but the new setting for this long-time budget favourite can't be beat. Simple wooden rooms (all with shared bathroom) in two new houses and a shady garden overlook an old flower-filled rice paddy. Aree cooks some pretty good food and Pirom is one of the best sources of information on the region.

Ban Tha Klang Homestay (☎ 08 1879 2773; per person 250B) The price of this village homestay programme includes three meals and a little elephant time. For 1000B more you can spend a whole day working with them.

Sangthong Hotel (☎ 0 4451 2009; 279-281 Th Tanasan, Surin; r 80-500B; 🌀) This labyrinthine older property is run with jet-engine precision by smiling staff. The 125 rooms range from some rachitic shared-bathroom cheapies on the roof to large and comfy midrangers. Air-con starts at 240B.

Phetkasem Hotel (☎ 0 4451 1274; 104 Th Jit Bamrung, Surin; r 690-850B; 🌀 🖳 🕸) It's a bit frumpier than

the Majestic, but this reasonable midranger scratches good-value terrain and features Bond-villain-meets-Benidorm architecture and plenty to keep you occupied, including an adjacent movie theatre.

Surin Majestic Hotel (☎ 0 4471 3980; www.surin majestic.net; 99 Th Jit Bamrung, Surin; r 800-1800B, ste 3000B; ❄ ☐ ☎) This shiny new top-ender, which sits right behind the bus terminal, has plenty of extras, like a fitness centre. The rooms are nothing special, but aren't bad for the price.

Eating

Surin Chai Kit (no roman-script sign; Th Tanasan; dishes 20-60B; ❤ breakfast & lunch) This no-frills spot whips up a tasty breakfast – try a plate of pan eggs and Isan sausages. The owner wears a welcoming permagrin and speaks enough English to guide you through the Thai menu. It's three doors south of the Sangthong Hotel.

Petmanee 2 (☎ 0 4451 6024; Th Munrasat; dishes 20-80B; ❤ lunch) This simple spot between Ruamphet Hospital and Wat Salaloi is Surin's most famous purveyor of *sôm-tam* and *kài yâang*. The smaller original is around the corner.

Larn Chang (☎ 0 4451 2869; 199 Th Siphathai Saman; dishes 30-180B; ❤ dinner) Tasty and low-priced Thai and Isan dishes are served in an old wooden house overlooking a surviving stretch of the city moat, now known as Sŭan Rak (Love Park), where couples come to hold hands at night. The garden is great, but the rooftop patio is the place to be. It's a shortish walk south of the centre.

Farang Connection (☎ 0 4451 1509; off Th Chit Bamrung; dishes 30-600B; ❤ breakfast, lunch & dinner; ❄ ☐) Tucked away behind the bus station, and not far from Surin's surprisingly wild nightlife district, this aptly named British-owned place has a thick list of foreign favourites, like Cornish pasties, weiner schnitzel and BLTs. The liquor list is even more global, and the Thai food is pretty good too.

Surin's principal **night market** (Th Krung Si Nai; ❤ 5-10pm) is just south of the Sangthong Hotel. Two blocks west, vendors fronting the municipal market serve until 2am. Both markets whip up an excellent selection of Thai and Isan dishes, including, as always, barbecued insects.

Getting There & Away

BUS

From Surin's **bus terminal** (☎ 0 4451 1756; Th Chit Bamrung) buses head to/from Roi Et (ordinary

50B, three hours, hourly), Khorat (ordinary/air-con 93/130B, four hours, every half-hour), Si Saket (ordinary 50B, 2½ hours, hourly), Chiang Mai (air-con/VIP 690/960B, 14 hours, seven daily) and Pattaya (air-con/VIP 321/626B, eight hours, nine daily). Most of the frequent buses to Bangkok's northern bus terminal (ordinary/air-con 248/342B, eight hours) also use Surin's bus terminal, including **999 VIP** (☎ 0 4451 5344), which has a 24-seat VIP service (495B, 9.30pm), but one company has an office three blocks west by Surin Plaza shopping mall.

If you are heading to the Cambodian border at Chong Jom, where visas are available on the spot, you have a choice of eight săwngthăew (40B, 3½ hours) or eight minibuses (60B, two hours).

TRAIN

Surin is on the Bangkok–Ubon train line and there are nearly a dozen daily services to either destination. A 1st-/3rd-class seat to Ubon (three hours) starts at 140/31B; to Bangkok (eight hours) 1st-/3rd-class prices begin at 346/73B.

Surin can also be reached by train from any other station along the Ubon line, including Buriram and Si Saket.

Getting Around

Surin is a very convenient city for travellers: virtually everything you would want or need is within a few blocks of the bus and train stations. If you don't want to walk, săamláw charge 20B to 30B for a trip around the centre.

Pirom-Aree's House, Saren Travel and Farang Connection all rent cars, plus the latter has motorcycles.

SI SAKET & AROUND

ศรีสะเกษ

pop 42,800

There's not a whole lot to do in the perennially humdrum town of Si Saket, but a visit to the Angkor-period temple complex of Khao Phra Wihan (Preah Vihear in Khmer), just over the border in Cambodia, is more than enough to warrant a visit.

Information

Kasikornbank (Th Khukhan, Si Saket; ❤ 8.30am-3.30pm Mon-Fri) Located south of the train station. Has ATM and change facilities.

Si Saket Tourism Coordination Centre (☎ 0 4561 1283; www.pao-sisaket.go.th; cnr Th Lak Muang & Th

Tepa, Si Saket; ⊗ 8.30am-4.30pm) The staff are really enthusiastic about Si Saket; pity the province doesn't have more to promote. There are English-speaking staff on weekdays only.

TP Internet (Th Ratchakanrodfai 3; per hr 15B; ⊗ 9am-10pm) Just west of the train station, on the south side of the tracks.

Sights

PRASAT KHAO PHRA WIHAN NATIONAL PARK

อุทยานแห่งชาติเขาพระวิหาร

Just inside Cambodia, and all but inaccessible from that side of the border, Khao Phra Wihan (Preah Vihear in Khmer) is one of the region's great Angkor-period monuments. Straddling a 600m-high cliff on the brow of the Dangrek (Dong Rek) escarpment and accessed via a series of steep stepped *naga* approaches, the large temple complex towers over the plains of Cambodia, offering dreamy views and some beautiful and evocative ruins. Access, however, is a relatively confusing and expensive business.

Claimed by both countries, the temple was finally awarded to Cambodia in a 1962 World Court ruling. But the only access is through Thailand's **Prasat Khao Phra Wihan National Park** (☎ 0 4581 6000; admission 400B; ⊗ 8am-5pm, last entry 4pm), where a **visitor centre** (⊗ 8am-4pm) marks the path into Cambodia and up to the temple, about 1km away. On the Thai side you have to pay 5B for a border pass (passports are not necessary, but it would be wise to bring it anyway in case things change) and just after the border the Cambodian authorities collect their 200B fee (total cost 605B).

On the Thai side of the border, the 130-sq-km Prasat Khao Phra Wihan National Park contains a number of sights that are worth a peep before tramping over the border to Khao Phra Wihan itself. Near the visitor centre, which includes a model of the temple and some interesting exhibits on its history, the **Pha Mo I Daeng** cliff face features some fabulous views and the oldest bas-relief in Thailand. The relief depicts three figures, sitting below a roughly carved pig (which might represent Vishnu), whose identities are an enigma to archaeologists and art historians. Although they give the general impression of representing deities, angels or kings, the iconography corresponds to no known figures in Thai, Mon or Khmer mythology. Stylistically the relief appears to date back to the Koh Ker (AD

921–45) period of Khmer art, when King Jayavarman IV ruled from his capital at Koh Ker. The carving is on an overhanging section of the cliff and is accessed via a walkway. Across the parking lot is **Nam Tok Khun Si**, a waterfall flowing over a cave large enough to hold an orchestra. There is usually only water in the stream from late June through October, and you should visit with a park ranger because it is assumed land mines are still buried in the area.

Khao Phra Wihan itself was constructed over three centuries under a succession of Khmer kings, beginning with Rajendravarman II in the mid-10th century and ending with Suryavarman II in the early 12th century – it was the latter who also commanded the construction of Angkor Wat. The hill itself was sacred to Khmer Hindus for at least 500 years before the completion of the temple complex, however, and there were smaller brick monuments on the site prior to its construction.

The temple complex is only semirestored and the Cambodians appear to have little interest in completing the job any time soon – which makes one wish the World Court had found in favour of the Thais. During Khmer Rouge occupation, which lasted until Pol Pot's death in 1998, the site suffered from the pilfering of artefacts – lintels and other carvings in particular – although some of this smuggled art has been intercepted and may eventually be returned to the site.

One *naga* balustrade of around 30m is still intact; the first two *gopura* have all but fallen down and many of the buildings are roofless, but abundant examples of stone carving are intact and visible. The doorways to the third *gopura* have been nicely preserved and one (the inner door facing south) is surmounted by a well-executed carved stone lintel depicting Shiva and his consort Uma sitting on Nandi (Shiva's bull) under the shade of a symmetrised tree. A Vishnu creation lintel is also visible on the second *gopura;* in contrast to the famous Phanom Rung lintel depicting the same subject, this one shows Vishnu climbing the churning stick rather than reclining on the ocean below.

The main *prasat* tower in the final court at the summit is in need of major restoration before the viewer can get a true idea of its former magnificence. Many of the stone carvings from the *prasat* are missing while others lie buried in nearby rubble. The galleries surrounding the

prasat have fared better and have even kept their arched roofs.

The area around the temple witnessed heavy fighting between Khmer Rouge guerrillas and the Phnom Penh government, and land mines and artillery pieces still litter the surrounding forest – heed the skull and crossbones signs around the temple and stick to well-trodden paths everywhere else.

Getting There & Away

Route 221 leads 95km south from Si Saket to Phum Saron – 10km before the temple – via Kantharalak. Take a bus first to Kantharalak (40B, 1½ hours) and then pick up a såwngthåew to Phum Saron (30B, 40 minutes); both depart every half-hour. From Phum Saron you'll have to hire a motorcycle taxi to the park; figure on 200B return with a couple of hours waiting there. A truck will cost 400B for four people. Drivers in Phum Saron are well aware that visitors who have already come this far are unlikely to skip visiting the ruins and so hold all the cards in bargaining. Hitching to the park is possible, but could take a long time, especially on weekdays.

You can also catch a bus from Ubon Ratchathani to Kantharalak (37B, 1½, every half-hour) and continue from there as above.

OTHER KHMER RUINS

Thirty kilometres west of Si Saket via Rte 226 in Amphoe Uthumphon Phisai, **Prasat Hin Wat Sa Kamphaeng Yai** (admission free; ☾ daylight hours) features four 11th-century *prang* and two *wíhåan*. The *prang* (including the main one, which was built of sandstone but restored with brick) have lost their tops, but many lintels and other carvings, some in excellent condition, remain. The ruined sanctuary can be found on the grounds of Wat Sa Kamphaeng Yai's modern successor.

About 8km west of Si Saket on the way to Kamphaeng Noi, on the north side of the highway in a temple with no sign in Thai or English, is **Prasat Sa Kamphaeng Noi** (admission free; ☾ daylight hours). Like many other Khmer ruins in the area, it was built as a healing station by Angkor King Jayavarman VII. These days it is barely more than a pile of laterite blocks.

OTHER SIGHTS

Officially it's Wat Pa Maha Chedi Kaeo, but these days nearly everyone calls it **Wat Lan Khuad** (☾ daylight hours), the 'Million Bottle Temple'. In the 1990s the abbot dreamt of a *prasat*

in heaven made entirely of glass and he longed to copy it. Since that wasn't possible he did the next best thing: he covered nearly every surface of nearly every building, from the *bòt* to the bell tower, of his current temple with glass bottles. The more you look around, the less the name seems like an exaggeration. It's on the west side of Amphoe Khun Han, 12km south of Hwy 24 via Rte 2111.

Wat Phra That Rueang Rong (☾ daylight hours) is another unusual temple. A previous abbot, lamenting the loss of the old ways, built the *bòt* like an oxcart being pulled by two giant cows and created a **museum** (donations appreciated; ☾ 7.30am-5pm) with old tools, musical instruments and the like from the province's four cultures: Lao, Khmer, Suai and Yer. Concrete statues of people on the grounds wear traditional clothes, while oversized animals offer life lessons (lead a bad life and you might come back as a gorilla the next time around). The wat is 7km north of town; take a såwngthåew (10B, 15 minutes) from in front of the train station. The last ride returns to the city at 3pm.

Sleeping & Eating
SI SAKET

Si Saket Hotel (☎ 0 4561 2582; 384 Th Si Saket; r 100-350B; 🐱) Just a stone's throw north of the train station, this place isn't bad for the price. Even the cheapest rooms have satellite TV – great if you want to have a TV party, though that money would have been better spent on quality mattresses.

Phrompiman Hotel (☎ 0 4561 2677; 849/1 Th Lak Meuang; r 230-490B; 🐱 🖳) You won't get the four-star facilities you'd expect at first sight and the fan rooms are a tad rough, but this hotel just west of the train station still offers fantastic value, which is why it is sometimes full.

There are several restaurants just north of the train station and a big **night market** (☾ 5pm-midnight) convenes immediately to the south. There is a more varied roster of restaurants a little further south, principally along Th Ubon.

KANTHARALAK

A såamláw from the bus station to these hotels costs 20B to 30B.

Rose Inn Resort (no roman-script sign; ☎ 0 4566 3310; Th Sinpadit Soi 1; r 250-350B; 🐱) The closest lodging to the bus terminal (it's about 1km away down a *soi* next to the Government Savings Bank) doesn't deliver on the sign's promise of

VIP services, but it does have shades to draw around your car so your wife doesn't know you are here with your girlfriend. Rooms are clean and colourful.

SB Hotel (☎ 0 4566 3103; 136 Th Anan Ta Pak Dee; r 250-550B; ✷ ❑) The rooms are rather dull, but this family-run place with a coffee shop and bakery out the front is very friendly. It's just south of the main street.

Kantharalak Palace Hotel (☎ 0 4566 1085; 131/35-36 Th Sinpadit; r 300-550B; ✷) This place on the main street through town greets you with an attractive wood-lined lobby, and then serves very ordinary rooms, but the higher-priced offerings are the best the city has to offer.

PRASAT KHAO PHRA WIHAN NATIONAL PARK

The park has a few new air-conditioned **bungalows** (prices unconfirmed at time of writing) and a **camp site** (per person 30B; 2-person tent hire 150B).

There are many restaurants across from the visitor centre, and vendors in the ruins themselves sell drinks and snacks.

Getting There & Away

From Bangkok's Northern bus terminal there are frequent departures to Si Saket (ordinary/air-con 314/423B, eight hours) stopping at either the bus terminal or on Th Si Saket just north of the train station. There are also regular buses to/from Ubon Ratchathani (ordinary/air-con 40/59B, 1¼ hours) and Surin (ordinary/air-con 50/80B, 2½ hours). **999 VIP** (☎ 0 4561 2523), departing from the bus terminal, has 24-seat VIP service (610B) to Bangkok at 7.40pm.

A 2nd-/3rd-class train from Ubon to Si Saket costs 29/13B (1½ hours, six daily); from Bangkok a 2nd-/3rd-class train costs 281/147B (10½ hours, six daily).

There are about a dozen daily trains to Bangkok (2nd-/3rd-class 311/197B, eight to 10 hours) including overnight express service (1st-class air-con sleeper 651B, 10 hours) departing Hualamphong station at 8.30pm and departing Si Saket at 7.30pm. A 2nd-/3rd-class train to Ubon Ratchathani (one hour, 11 daily) costs as little as 139/13B.

Upper Southern Gulf

Here's an interesting question. What percentage of foreign tourists that traverse this coastline en route to Thailand's southern islands actually stop here? The answer? Definitely not enough.

Long popular with local tourists, Thailand's upper southern gulf region showcases beach resorts that run from relaxed to raucous, two stunning national parks, and plenty of historical intrigue just waiting to be explored. And if your Thai experience sometimes resembles a roll-call of other travellers, you'll find it easy to detour off the *faràng* (Westerner) trail for a few days.

On weekends, sleepy Cha-am is jolted into action by bus loads of Bangkok types, keen to shake off the big city's cobwebs at nicely noisy beach parties. On the secluded beaches of Ban Krut and Bang Saphan Yai, the ambience is more subdued, but no less Thai. And the seafood is just as fresh and just as affordable. Hua Hin's sandy, boulder-strewn beaches come with a royal seal of approval (the Thai king lives here for part of the year), and a buzzy cosmopolitan vibe.

Wilderness and wildlife junkies can escape to the Khao Sam Roi Yot and Kaeng Krachan National Parks, but if you like your fauna slightly more domesticated, the curious monkeys of Phetchaburi's caves and Prachuap Khiri Khan's hilltop temple will gladly trade a banana for a photo.

Getting between the major cities is a breeze, but travel around the rest of the area requires an infusion of travellers' ingenuity, curiosity and initiative. Trust us, it'll be well worth it.

HIGHLIGHTS

- Experiencing a moment of quiet contemplation in Phetchaburi's **cave temples** (p550) amid sun-dappled Buddhas

- Appreciating the culinary choices in **Hua Hin** (p562) – the bustling night market one night followed by excellent European food the next

- Feeling elated and loving the views after completing the climb to Khao Krachom in **Khao Sam Roi Yot National Park** (p564)

- Returning the curious stares of troops of monkeys as you negotiate the 418 steps to **Wat Thammikaram** (p567) in Prachuap Khiri Khan

- Relaxing in your deckchair on **Cha-am beach** (p555) while you put together an alfresco Thai dinner party with the help of friendly seafood vendors

★ Phetchaburi

★ Cha-am

★ Hua Hin

★ Khao Sam Roi Yot
  National Park

★ Prachuap Khiri Khan

FAST FACTS

■ **Best Time to Visit** February to June

■ **Population** 1.4 million

Climate

The best time to visit is during the hot and dry season (February to June). From July to October (southwest monsoon) and from October to January (northeast monsoon) there is occasional rain and strong winds. However, because this region is between the three-monsoon season that rules northern, northeastern and central Thailand, and the two-monsoon season in the country's south, it remains drier than elsewhere in the country, even during the rainy months. During the monsoon season, beach resorts such as Hua Hin and Cha-am may be cloudy, but are not as wet as destinations further south like Ko Samui or Phuket.

National Parks

Kaeng Krachan (p553), the largest national park in Thailand, covers nearly half of Phetchaburi Province and is known for its waterfalls and bird-watching. From the tall peaks of Khao Sam Roi Yot (p564) there are views of the gulf, the coast and limestone cliffs.

Getting There & Away

Frequent air-con buses from Bangkok's southern bus station travel to all major cities in the region including Phetchaburi, Hua Hin and Chumphon. Air-con services also connect to smaller destinations such as Prachuap Khiri Khan, Hat Ban Krut and Bang Saphan Yai on at least a daily basis. Thai Railways' southern line from Bangkok conveniently stops at most points of interest for the independent traveller. Chumphon is the major departure point for boats to Ko Tao, and there are three flights per day to/from Bangkok's Suvarnabhumi airport and Hua Hin.

Getting Around

Public transport is not as prolific or well organised as further south, but it's still relatively easy to get to most places. Buses and trains connect the region's major cities, and motorcycle taxis and săwngthăew (small pick-up trucks) cater for shorter trips. The exception is reaching the two national parks where you'll

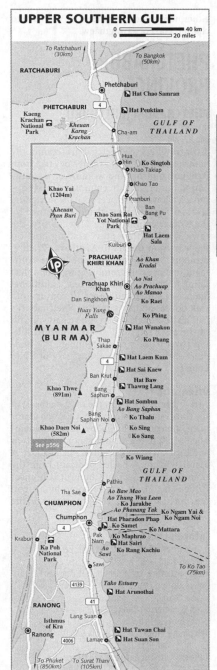

UPPER SOUTHERN GULF

either need your own wheels, or will have to charter a taxi or săwngthăew.

PHETCHABURI PROVINCE

PHETCHABURI (PHETBURI)

เพชรบุรี

pop 47,000

Most travellers see Phetchaburi (commonly known as Phetburi) as a rushed day trip from Bangkok or from the window of a southbound bus or train, but a more leisurely approach allows you to peel back the intriguing layers of Thai history. Originally settled by the Khmer empire in the 11th century, the town was a 17th-century trading post on the way from Burma to Ayuthaya. Trading brought wealth, still evident in the commanding array of crumbling wat (temples) lining Phetchaburi's waterfront. Traditional Siam can still be glimpsed in century-old teak houses and by sampling Phetchaburi's culinary heritage. When you've had your fill of the town's tasty desserts, climb to hilltop royal palaces or contemplate the Buddhist shrine in the cave sanctuary of Khao Luang.

Orientation

Arriving by train, follow the road southeast of the tracks until you come to Th Ratchadamnoen, then turn right. Follow Th Ratchadamnoen south to the second major intersection and turn left towards central Phetchaburi. A săamláw (three-wheeled pedicab) from the train station to Saphan Chomrut (Chomrut Bridge) is 20B. If you've come by air-con bus, you'll stop near the night market on the northern edge of the centre.

Information

3 Girls Internet (Th Damnoen Kasem; per hr 20B; ☺ 7am-9pm)

Main post office (cnr Th Ratwithi & Th Damnoen Kasem)

Police station (☎ 0 3242 5500; Th Ratwithi) Near the intersection of Th Ratchadamnoen.

Siam Commercial Bank (2 Th Damnoen Kasem) Other nearby banks also offer foreign exchange and ATMs.

Telephone office (cnr Th Ratwithi & Th Damnoen Kasem; ☺ 7am-10pm) Upstairs at the post office.

Tourism Authority of Thailand Office (TAT; ☎ 0 3242 5987; Th Ratwithi; ☺ 8.30am-4.30pm) Directly opposite Khao Wang. Ask staff for the informative 'Variety in One – Phetchaburi' booklet.

Sights & Activities

There are scores of wats in town, so take a wander if this interests you. In the 'Variety in One' brochure from the TAT office there is detailed coverage and walking instructions for exploring the town's many wats.

KHAO LUANG & KHAO BANDAI-IT CAVES

ถ้ำเขาหลวง

The main cavern in the cave sanctuary of **Khao Luang** (donation appreciated; ☺ 8am-6pm) is lined with impressive stalactites and old Buddha statues (including a large reclining Buddha), many of which were put in place by Rama IV. Sunlight from a hole in the chamber ceiling illuminates the images and makes for great photos. To the rear of the main cavern is an entrance to a third, smaller chamber. On the right of the entrance is Wat Bunthawi, with a săalaa (meeting hall) designed by the abbot of the wat himself and a bòt (central sanctuary) with impressively carved wooden door panels. Around the cave you'll meet brazen monkeys looking for handouts. The cave is 5km north of town.

An even more magical cave sanctuary is **Khao Bandai-It** (donation appreciated; ☺ 9am-4pm), 2km west of town. English-speaking guides lead tours through the caves. From Phetchaburi catch a săamláw (60B) or motorcycle taxi (40B) to the sanctuaries.

KHAO WANG & PHRA NAKHON KHIRI HISTORICAL PARK

เขาวัง/อุทยานประวัติศาสตร์พระนครคีรี

Cobblestone paths lead up and around Khao Wang, which is studded with wat and crowned with King Mongkut's palace. **Phra Nakhon Khiri** (Holy City Hill; ☎ 0 3240 1006; admission 40B; ☺ 9am-4pm), the palace area on the top, is a national historical park and a good spot to take in views of the town while curious monkeys look at you. The walk up looks easy, but is fairly strenuous. A tram (adult/child 30/10B one way) is the easier way.

PHRA RATCHAWANG BAN PEUN

พระราชวังบ้านปืน

Just over 1km south of the city centre, and inside a Thai military base, is **Phra Ratchawang Ban Peun** (Ban Peun Palace; ☎ 0 3242 8083; admission 50B; ☺ 8am-4pm Mon-Fri). Construction began in 1910 at the behest of Rama V (who died just after

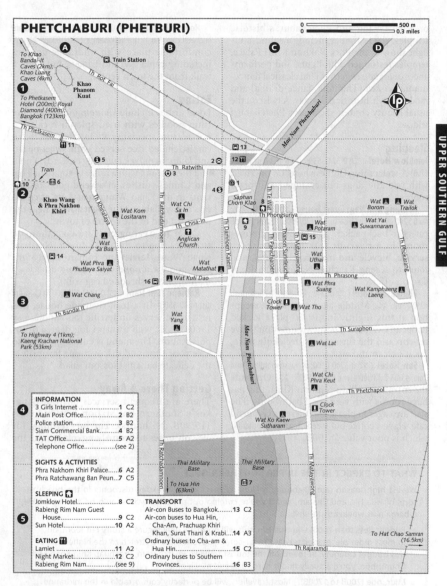

PHETCHABURI (PHETBURI)

0 — 500 m
0 — 0.3 miles

INFORMATION
3 Girls Internet 1 C2
Main Post Office.................2 B2
Police station.....................3 B2
Siam Commercial Bank........4 B2
TAT Office..........................5 A2
Telephone Office................(see 2)

SIGHTS & ACTIVITIES
Phra Nakhom Khiri Palace...6 A2
Phra Ratchawang Ban Peun...7 C5

SLEEPING
Jomklow Hotel.....................8 C2
Rabieng Rim Nam Guest
 House.............................9 C2
Sun Hotel..........................10 A2

EATING
Lamiet 11 A2
Night Market.....................12 C2
Rabieng Rim Nam............(see 9)

TRANSPORT
Air-con Buses to Bangkok.......13 C2
Air-con buses to Hua Hin,
 Cha-Am, Prachuap Khiri
 Khan, Surat Thani & Krabi...14 A3
Ordinary buses to Cha-am &
 Hua Hin.............................15 C2
Ordinary buses to Southern
 Provinces............................16 B3

the project was started) and was completed in 1916. The German architects used the opportunity to showcase contemporary German innovations in construction and interior design. The structure is typical of the early-20th century, a period that saw a Thai passion for erecting European-style buildings in an effort to keep up with the 'modern' architecture of its colonised neighbours. The outside of the two-storey palace is not that exciting, but it's worth visiting to see the exquisite glazed tiles in the interior.

Festivals & Events

The **Phra Nakhon Khiri Fair** takes place in early February and lasts about eight days. Centred

UPPER SOUTHERN GULF

on Khao Wang and Phetchaburi's historic temples, the festivities include a sound-and-light show at the Phra Nakhon Khiri Palace, temples festooned with lights, and performances of *lákhon chaatrii* (Thai classical dance-drama), *lí-keh* (Thai folk dance-drama) and modern-style historical dramas. A twist on the usual beauty contest showcases Phetchaburi widows.

Sleeping

Jomklow Hotel (☎ 0 3242 5398; 1 Th Te Wiat; r 130-170B) A welcoming Chinese hotel on the river, with friendly dogs but cramped and basic rooms.

Rabieng Rim Nam Guest House (☎ 08 9919 7446; fax 0 3240 1983; 1 Th Chisa-In; s/d 120/240B) This place caters to backpackers and offers bare-bones rooms in a riverside teak house. Laundry service, bicycle and motorcycle rental, and tours to Kaeng Krachan National Park are also on offer.

Phetkasem Hotel (☎ 0 3242 5581; 86/1 Th Phetkasem; r 250-350B; 🔀) Middle-aged dogs loll in reception at this slightly industrial place tucked under an overpass. Cheaper rooms don't have air-con and the furniture is decidedly retro, but it's clean and airy.

Sun Hotel (☎ 0 3240 0100; www.sunhotelthailand .com; 43/33 Soi Phetkasem; r 800-1500B; 🔀) Opposite the entrance to Phra Nakhon Khiri, this has huge rooms with very good bathrooms. The staff are eager to please and there's a colourful café. Have a coffee but steer clear of breakfast which is poor value at 100B.

Royal Diamond (☎ 0 3241 1061; www.royaldiam ondhotel.com; Mu 1, Th Phetkasem; r 1200-1800B; 🔀) A comfortable place with midrange goodies including cable TV and fridges, but quite a walk from the town centre.

Eating

Local dishes include *khànom jiin thâwt man* (thin noodles with fried spicy fish cake), a hot-season speciality *khâo châe phétbùrii* (moist chilled rice served with sweetmeats) and *khànom màw kaeng* (egg custard). You'll find these, along with a range of standard Thai and Chinese dishes, at several good restaurants in the Khao Wang area. Lots of cheap eats are available at the **night market**, near the northern end of the centre of town.

Other good eating spots are along the main street leading to the clock tower. North of Khao Wang, **Lamiet** (no roman-script sign) sells good *khànom màw kaeng* and *fawy thawng* (sweet shredded egg yolk).

Rabieng Rim Nam (☎ 0 3242 5707; 1 Th Chisa-In; dishes 40-180B) In a teak riverside house, this restaurant serves up terrific food and cruisy 1960s music with a surprising degree of sophistication. The menu is enticingly long, so take your time and discover our favourite – the delicate banana blossom salad.

Getting There & Away

There are frequent services to/from Bangkok's Southern bus station (1st/2nd class 115/90B, 2½ hours). The bus terminal for air-con buses to/from Bangkok is near the

---

WHAT TO EXPECT IN THE UPPER SOUTHERN GULF

We list high-season rates (February to June). Expect good weekday discounts in the beach resorts of Hua Hin and Cha-am, and if you're coming out of season you should be able to secure a bargain at weekends as well.

- Budget (less than 700B) – In Hua Hin, this will normally only secure a stuffy fan room, but in most other places look forward to air-con if you're willing to stretch to the higher end of this budget category. In towns off the tourist trail like Phetchaburi, Prachuap Khiri Khan and Chumphon, you'll actually find it hard to spend much more.

- Midrange (700B to 1700B) – Most travellers will be perfectly comfortable in the midrange category. In good-value Cha-am, and even more expensive Hua Hin, newly opened hotels with spacious rooms, air-con, swimming pools and cable TV are readily available at the upper end of this category.

- Top End (over 1700B) – How much do you want to spend? Luxury resorts like the Anantara and the Chiva-Som near Hua Hin quote their rates in US dollars, but if you're willing to spend just a little over the 1700B mark there are some very comfortable places to stay which would be considerably more expensive in other countries.

night market. Other air-conditioned bus destinations to/from Phetchaburi include: Cha-am (35B, 40 minutes), Hua Hin (50B, 1½ hours), Prachuap Khiri Khan (105B, three hours), Surat Thani (300B, eight hours) and Krabi (385B, 10 hours). These destinations are served from the bus station just east of Khao Wang.

Ordinary buses to the southern provinces leave from the corner of Th Banda-It and Th Ratchadamnoen. Local buses to Hua Hin and Cha-am depart in the town centre, on Th Matayawong.

Frequent services run to/from Bangkok's Hualamphong train station. Fares vary depending on the train and class (3rd class 74B to 115B, 2nd class 143B to 210B, three hours).

Getting Around

Săamláw and motorcycle taxis go anywhere in the town centre for 40B, or charter them for the whole day from 300B. Săwngthăew cost 10B around town. It's a 20-minute walk (1km) from the train station to the town centre.

Rabieng Rim Nam Guest House rents out bicycles (120B per day) and motorbikes (250B per day). It also offers a one-day tour visiting Phetchaburi's wats and palaces (400B to 600B per person).

KAENG KRACHAN NATIONAL PARK

อุทยานแห่งชาติแก่งกระจาน

At 3000 sq km, Thailand's largest park (☎ 0 3245 9291; www.dnp.go.th; admission 400B; visitors centre ⊙ 8.30am-4.30pm) is home to the stunning Pa La-U waterfalls, and includes long-distance hiking trails that snake through forests and savannah-like grasslands, and past cliffs, caves and mountains. Two rivers, Mae Nam Phetchaburi and Mae Nam Pranburi, a large lake, and abundant rainfall keep the place green year round. Animal life includes wild elephants, deer, tigers, bears, gibbons, boars, hornbills, dusky langurs, gaurs and wild cattle. To explore Kaeng Krachan you really need your own transport, but it's worth the effort as this majestic place sees few tourists. The best months to visit are between November and April.

Sights

Hiking is the best way to explore the park. Try the 4km (three hours) walk from the Km 36 marker on the park road to the 18-tiered **Nam Tok Tho Thip** waterfall. A longer 6km hike ascends the summit of **Phanoen Thung**, the park's highest point. From the top, there are lush forest views in all directions. It can be particularly spectacular in late autumn, when surrounding valleys are shrouded in early morning mist. The hiking trail starts at the 'Km 27' marker on the park road. Note that some trails, including the one to Phanoen Thung, are closed during the rainy season (August to October).

To the south, near La-U Reservoir, are the spectacular twin waterfalls of **Pa La-U Yai** and **Pa La-U Noi**. Water flows over their 15 tiers year round. The waterfalls can be reached by 4WD from the south (closer to Hua Hin) along Hwy 3219.

Near the visitors centre is a reservoir where boats can be hired for 400B per hour.

Sleeping & Eating

There are various **bungalows** (☎ 0 3245 9291; reserve@dnp.go.th; from 1200B) within the park, mainly near the reservoir. These sleep from four to six people and are simple affairs with fans and fridges. There are also **camp sites** (per person 50B), including a pleasant one near the reservoir at the visitors centre (where there's also a modest restaurant). Tents (150B to 300B) can be rented at the visitors centre.

On the road leading to the park entrance are several simple resorts and bungalows. About 3.5km before reaching the visitors centre, **A&B Bungalows** (☎ 08 9891 2328; r 650B, bungalow 1300B) is scenic, and popular with bird-watching groups. There is a good restaurant here that can provide you with a packed lunch.

Getting There & Away

Kaeng Krachan is 53km southwest of Phetchaburi, with the southern edge of the park 35km from Hua Hin. From Phetchaburi, drive 20km south on Hwy 4 to the city of Tha Yang. Turn right (west) and after 40km you'll reach the visitors centre (follow the 'Special Forces Training Camp' signs). You'll need a 4WD vehicle if you want to explore the dirt roads within the park.

There is no direct public transport all the way to the park, but you can get a săwngthăew (50B, 1½ hours) from Phetchaburi (near the clock tower) to the village of Ban Kaeng Krachan, 4km before the park. Go early as the last săwngthăew leaves at 2pm. Motorcycle

taxis (40B) run from Ban Kaeng Krachan to the visitors centre. An alternative is to join a trip from Phetchaburi, Hua Hin or Cha-Am. In Phetchaburi, the Rabieng Rim Nam Guesthouse (p552) runs one- and two-day trips (2600B to 3950B) that include bird- and animal-watching, and trekking. Most travel agencies in Hua Hin and Cha-am offer daytrips (1200B to 1850B).

CHA-AM
อำเภอชะอำ

pop 65,000

If you've come to Thailand to experience modern Thai culture then look no further. At weekends and on public holidays, Cha-am is a getaway spot for provincial families and Bangkok students. Buses deliver holidaymakers firmly in party mode, fuelled by cheesy pop music and ready to kick back for a couple of days. Mix in beach parties under shady casuarina trees, fresh seafood and cold beers delivered to your deck chair, and rip-snorting banana boats up and down the beach and you begin to see the attraction. Subtle it's not, but hey, there's nothing wrong with a bit of raucous Thai fun.

If you're looking for something quieter, then come during the week when Cha-am returns to being a relaxed resort town and you'll get an even better deal at the good-value guesthouses and midrange hotels. Chances are it will be just you and the ladies selling deep fried shrimps and grilled squid. Bliss…

Orientation
Phetkasem Hwy runs through Cha-am's busy centre, and includes the main stop, banks, the main post office, an outdoor market and the train station. About 1km east, via the main connecting road, Th Narathip, is the long beach strip where you'll be headed. The road along the beach (and where beach accommodation and services are located) is Th Ruamjit. Air-con buses from Bangkok stop one block from the beach on Th Chao Lai.

Festivals & Events
The **Cha-am Feast-Fish-Flock Seafood Festival** is a riot of Thai food stalls and kitschy pop music. It's all set in a beachfront beer garden at the eastern end of Th Narathipand not to be missed if you're around while it's on in late September/early October.

Information
For internet access, see **C.V.Net** (Th Ruamjit; per hr 30B; ☻ 8am-8pm) on the beach road just before Soi North 7. The **post office** (Th Ruamjit) is also on the main beach strip. For international phone calls go to the CAT office on Th Narathip.

The **Tourism Authority of Thailand** (TAT; ☎ 0 3247 1005; tatphet@tat.or.th; 500/51 Th Phetkasem; ☻ 8.30am-4.30pm) is located on Phetkasem Hwy, 500m south of town. The staff speak good English. Along Th Ruamjit, you'll find banks with ATMs and exchange services.

Sleeping
Cha-am has two basic types of accommodation: low-grade apartment-style hotels along the beach road (Th Ruamjit) and more expensive 'condotel' developments (condominiums with a kitchen and operating under a rental programme). True bungalow operations are quite rare. Expect a 20% to 40% discount on posted rates for weekday stays. Compared to flashier Hua Hin, your money will go further in Cha-am.

BUDGET
Charlie House (☎ 0 3243 3799; Soi 1 North, 241/60-61 Th Ruamjit; r 650B; ☒) Downstairs, the reception is funky; upstairs the rooms are crisp and modern with sleek wooden floors. Calling it budget is almost a misnomer, but the rates don't lie.

Memory Guest House (☎ 0 3247 2100; 241/29 Th Ruamjit; r 450-650B; ☒) The décor here is nicely beachy if you wake up and forget where you are. With air-con rooms this friendly guesthouse is excellent value.

Nirundorn Resort (☎ 0 3247 1038; www.nirundorn .com; 26/171 Th Ruamjit; r 500-700B; ☒) This beachside spot's been around for a while, but it's got a brand new lease of life with coolly minimalist white interiors and bathrooms transplanted from somewhere much flashier. A two-room bungalow is also available for 2200B.

Baan Thai (☎ 0 3247 0596; www.ban-thai.net; 222/14-16 Th Ruamjit; r 600-800B; ☒ 🖵) There's a family atmosphere at this Thai-Norwegian owned guesthouse with five older rooms and a couple of new ones being completed at the time we visited.

MIDRANGE
Cha-Am Villa Beach (☎ 0 3247 1079; www.chaamvil lahotel.com; 241/2 Th Ruamjit; r 800-1000B; ☒ 🖵 🖲) With a pool, air-con and wi-fi, the Villa Beach

knows exactly what travellers want. At the time of writing, some snazzy two-storey bungalows were being built.

Dee Lek (☎ 0 3247 0145; www.deelek.com; 225/30-33 Th Ruamjit; r 800-1200B; ✷) Spotless rooms with crisp bed linen, spacious bathrooms, and terracotta tiles sit above a good restaurant (below). Mind your head on the arty lampshade when you're coming downstairs.

Sweet Home (☎ 0 3241 1039; 279/1 Ruamjit; bungalows 1500B; ✷) Sweet Home's traditional wooden bungalows sit in a tropical garden. Inside things are a little cramped, but there is no denying their rustic charm at the right price.

Rungaran de Challet (☎ 0 3247 1226; www.rungaran-chaam.com; 279/1 Th Ruamjit, 263/26 Soi Cha Am 4; r 1200-1500B; ✷) Cha-am's best value midranger is at the beach's southern end. An Asian vibe highlights chic bathrooms and secluded gardens, with hidden alcoves purpose built for relaxation.

Kaenchan Beach Hotel (☎ 0 3247 0777; www.kaenchanbeach.com; 241/4 Ruamjit; r 2150-3300B, bungalows 1350-3260B; ✷ ✷) Cherry-coloured wooden buildings glow under soft lighting at this well-designed place that's recommended for serial romantics. Ferns and shrubs bubble from a collage of terracotta and timber, and whisper 'take…it…easy'.

TOP END

Casa Papaya (☎ 0 3247 0678; www.casapapayathailand.com; 810/4 Phetkasem; r 2500-4500B; ✷ ✷) Designer Mexican chic runs riot at this terrific spot right on the beach 6km towards Hua Hin. The beachfront and seaview bungalows have rooftop decks to enjoy the sunlight (or the moonlight), but with king-size beds and bathrooms in wonderfully brave colours, some days you may not make it that far.

Dusit Resort & Polo Club (☎ 0 3252 0009; www.dusit.com; 193 Th Phetkasem; r from 6500B; ✷ ✷ ✷) The leader in Thailand's luxury chains, the Dusit has 300 rooms, all with private balcony, overlooking either the sea or lush gardens. Included is a fitness centre, minigolf course, horse riding, tennis and squash courts, as well as, of course, polo. After all that we recommend a drink in the Polo Bar.

Eating

Beach vendors sell barbecued and fried seafood, and at the far northern end of the beach reasonably priced **seafood restaurants** can be found at the fishing pier. Along the beach road are simple Thai restaurants, all similar in ambience and price. The following are a bit different.

Rang Yen Garden (☎ 0 3247 1267; 259/40 Th Ruamjit; dishes 50-180B; ✸ lunch & dinner Nov-Apr) This lovely patio-style restaurant serves up Thai favourites under the stars. It's only open in the high season.

Da Vinci's (☎ 0 3247 1871; 274/5 Th Ruamjit; pizza 120-210B, pasta 180-210B; ✸ lunch & dinner) Trimmed with a Euro-Asian mix of old-style lamps and shady palms, Da Vinci's chic patio is easily the classiest spot to dine in Cha-am.

Poom Restaurant (☎ 0 3247 1036; 274/1 Th Ruamjit; dishes 90-220B; ✸ lunch & dinner) Slightly more expensive than other nearby beach restaurants, but worth it for the fresh seafood served under tall sugar palms – the restaurant of choice for weekending Thais.

Crawfords (☎ 0 3247 1774; 252/6 Th Chao Lai; dishes 80-400B; ✸ breakfast, lunch & dinner; ✷ 💻) Irish owner John (formerly a chef) and his friendly cat (always a cat) are great hosts at this garden restaurant/bar with Guinness and Kilkenny on tap. Saturdays feature American barbecues and on Sundays cross the Atlantic for traditional roast dinners. There's live music every night and special parties for everything from St Patrick's Day to Halloween. It's one block from the beach near the stop for air-con buses to Bangkok. Bookings are recommended on Friday and Saturday nights. Say gidday to the cat for us.

Dee-Lek (☎ 0 3247 0145; 225/33 Th Ruamjit; dishes 80-400B; ✸ breakfast, lunch & dinner) Run by a Thai-English couple, Dee-Lek serves up good Thai and Euro dishes in modern surroundings. The servings are generous.

Getting There & Away

Most hotels have shuttles to Hua Hin for 150/300B one-way/return.

Ordinary and air-con buses stop in the town centre, on Phetkasem Hwy. Some air-con buses to/from Bangkok go to the beach, stopping on Th Chao Lai a few hundred metres south of the Th Narathip intersection.

Frequent bus services operating to/from Cha-am include Bangkok (air-con/ordinary 140/105B, three hours), Phetchaburi (35B, 40 minutes) and Hua Hin (25B, 30 minutes).

The train station is inland on Th Narathip, west of Phetkasem Hwy, and a 30B motorcycle ride to/from the beach. From Bangkok three

train stations have daily services to Cha-am; Hualamphong (3.50pm), Sam Sen (9.27am) and Thonburi (7.15am, 1.30pm and 7.05pm). Tickets cost from 60B to 150B and the journey is around four hours. Cha-am isn't listed on the English-language train schedule.

Getting Around

From the city centre to the beach it's a quick motorcycle (30B) or sǎwngthǎew (10B) ride. Motorcycle taxis around town cost 30B. Some drivers will try and take you to another hotel that offers them a commission. Be firm.

You can rent motorcycles for 300B per day all along Th Ruamjit. Bicycle rentals are available everywhere for 20B per hour, or 100B per day, and are a good way to get around. Travel agencies hire cars or jeeps for 1500B to 2000B per day.

AROUND CHA-AM

Midway between Cha-am and Hua Hin is **Phra Ratchaniwet Marukhathayawan** (☎ 0 3247 2482; admission 90B; ⏲ 8.30am-4.30pm), a summer palace built during the reign of Rama VI. The one- and two-storey buildings are constructed of teak and interlinked by covered boardwalks, all high above the ground on stilts. Incorporating high tiled roofs and tall shuttered windows, the design maximises air circulation.

Unlike the current summer palace situated further south at Hua Hin, this palace is open to the public. Camp Rama VI, a military post, surrounds the palace grounds, and you need to check in at the gate. If you catch a Cha-am–Hua Hin bus to get here, ask to be dropped at the road to this place. There are often motorcycle taxis waiting, or you can walk 2km the rest of the way.

PRACHUAP KHIRI KHAN PROVINCE

HUA HIN

อำเภอหัวหิน

pop 48,700

Hua Hin's inevitable rise to become Thailand's first glamorous getaway began in 1922 when King Rama VII instructed his Italian architect to construct Phra Ratchawang Klai Kangwon ('Far from Worries' Palace) in what was then just a humble fishing village. Today's royal family still commutes regularly to the palace to unwind from the pressures of keeping the army and politicians in line in Bangkok. Rama VII's endorsement made the town the place for be for Thai society, and Hua Hin, (like Cha-am), settled into a low-key role as a favourite spot for holidaying Thais.

In the 1980s the renovation of the Hua Hin Railway Hotel by the luxury hotel group Sofitel sparked overseas interest and ignited development geared towards foreigners. Today all the big hotel chains have properties in Hua Hin, and in recent years a growing number of expats have chosen to live in the seaside town that's fast-forwarding to become one of Thailand's most cosmopolitan cities. High-rise

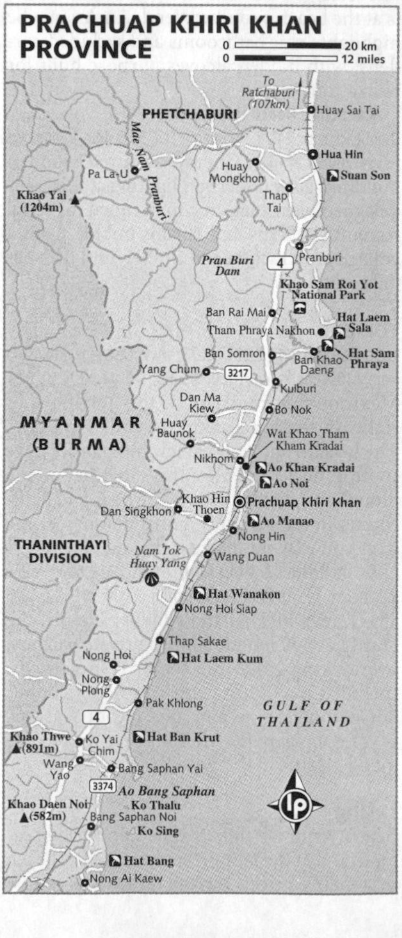

PRACHUAP KHIRI KHAN PROVINCE

condominiums and planned housing subdivisions are creeping across the surrounding hinterland, and French, Italian, German and Scandinavian restaurants create a little slice of home for sun-kissed escapees from the European winter.

With rapid development comes challenges, and Hua Hin has witnessed the growth of a small sex industry, and the fishing-village ambience of the old piers is largely masked by hotels, restaurants and tailor shops. Development has encroached onto government land, and trying to spot the sea is a frustrating exercise along many parts of the beach road.

Despite the development Hua Hin is bravely clinging to the beachside atmosphere that kicked things off back in 1922. Compared to Pattaya, the other main beach destination near Bangkok, Hua Hin is (relatively) serene, and is a favourite with families and older travellers. Don't come looking for a party-at-all-costs backpacker scene. Instead you can fill your time with 18 holes at the Royal Hua Hin Golf Course or go horseback riding on the beach. After dark there's a cosmopolitan restaurant scene to explore, rustic seafood restaurants on the pier to visit, or the simple culinary charms of one of Thailand's best night markets to sample. The city's 5km of beaches are the cleanest they've been for many years, swimming is safe, and Hua Hin continues to enjoy some of the peninsula's driest weather.

And the following day when you're relaxing on a deckchair drinking cold beer and steamed crab, you might think not much has changed in Hua Hin after all.

Orientation

Thanon Naresdamri is the tourist backbone and home to restaurants, souvenir stalls, and persistent tailors trying to tempt passers-by into an 'original' Armani suit. Guesthouses and outdoor restaurants line the waterfront area, and small *soi* (lanes) veer off concealing more guesthouses, lively bars and travel agencies. Hua Hin is gradually moving upmarket, and every year more midrange hotels, Western restaurants and designer eyewear shops open. It's a lively place and if you want some quiet time it may be best to stay elsewhere.

The best beach is in front and south of the Sofitel resort. This pleasant stretch of sandy beach is broken up by round, smooth boulders (Hua Hin means 'stone head') and is ideal for year-round swimming. The train station lies at the western end of town and features a beautifully restored royal waiting room. The airport (www.huahinairport.com) is 6km north of town.

Information

BOOKSHOPS
Bookazine (☎ 0 3253 2071; 166 Th Naresdamri; ☽ 9am-10pm) Has maps, books and magazines in English, and travel books – including Lonely Planet guides.

EMERGENCY
Tourist police (☎ 0 3251 5995, emergency 1155; Th Damnoen Kasem) At the eastern end of the street.

INTERNET ACCESS
Internet access is available all over Hua Hin.
Buffalo Bill's Steak & Grill (8 Th Naresdamri; ☽ 8am-midnight) Has a wi-fi network.
Sunshine Internet (Th Amnuaysion; per 150 min 40B, per 350 min 100B; ☽ 8.30am-midnight) Its wi-fi hotspot, your laptop.
World News Coffee (Th Naresdamri; per hr 40B; ☽ 8am-11pm) Has fast internet connection in air-con comfort.

INTERNET RESOURCES
www.huahinafterdark.com A good resource for night-time shenanigans.

MEDIA
Free maps, pamphlets and brochures can be found in restaurants and hotels.
Hua Hin Observer (www.observergroup.net) A free, home-grown, expat-published magazine with features in English & German. Available at most hotels around town, it contains info on dining, culture and entertainment.

MEDICAL SERVICES
Hospital San Paolo (☎ 0 3253 2576; 222 Th Phetkasem) Just south of town with emergency facilities.

MONEY
There are exchange booths and ATMs up and down Th Naresdamri. Near the bus stations, there are banks on Th Phetkasem.
Bank of Ayudhya (Th Naresdamri) Most convenient to the beach; near the corner of Th Damnoen Kasem.

POST & TELEPHONE
Main post office (Th Damnoen Kasem) Includes the CAT for international phone calls. Most internet cafés have Skype.

HUA HIN

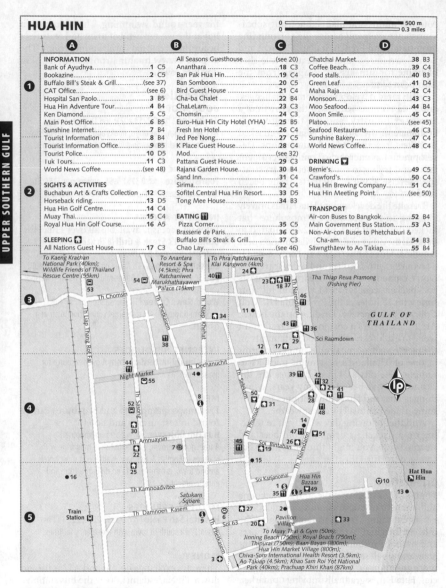

INFORMATION	
Bank of Ayudhya	1 C5
Bookazine	2 C5
Buffalo Bill's Steak & Grill	(see 37)
CAT Office	(see 6)
Hospital San Paolo	3 B5
Hua Hin Adventure Tour	4 B4
Ken Diamond	5 C5
Main Post Office	6 B5
Sunshine Internet	7 B4
Tourist Information	8 B4
Tourist Information Office	9 B5
Tourist Police	10 D5
Tuk Tours	11 C3
World News Coffee	(see 48)

SIGHTS & ACTIVITIES	
Buchabun Art & Crafts Collection	12 C3
Horseback riding	13 D5
Hua Hin Golf Centre	14 C4
Muay Thai	15 C4
Royal Hua Hin Golf Course	16 A5

SLEEPING	
All Nations Guest House	17 C4

All Seasons Guesthouse	(see 20)
Ananthara	18 C4
Ban Pak Hua Hin	19 C4
Ban Somboon	20 C5
Bird Guest House	21 C4
Cha-ba Chalet	22 B4
ChaLeLarn	23 C3
Chomsin	24 C3
Euro-Hua Hin City Hotel (YHA)	25 B5
Fresh Inn Hotel	26 C4
Jed Pee Nong	27 C5
K Place Guest House	28 C4
Mod	(see 32)
Pattana Guest House	29 C3
Rajana Garden House	30 B4
Sand Inn	31 C4
Sirima	32 C4
Sofitel Central Hua Hin Resort	33 D5
Tong Mee House	34 B3

EATING	
Pizza Corner	35 C5
Brasserie de Paris	36 C3
Buffalo Bill's Steak & Grill	37 C3
Chao Lay	(see 46)

Chatchai Market	38 B3
Coffee Beach	39 C4
Food stalls	40 B3
Green Leaf	41 D4
Maha Raja	42 C4
Monsoon	43 C3
Moo Seafood	44 B4
Moon Smile	45 C4
Platoo	(see 45)
Seafood Restaurants	46 C4
Sunshine Bakery	47 C4
World News Coffee	48 C4

DRINKING	
Bernie's	49 C5
Crawford's	50 C4
Hua Hin Brewing Company	51 C4
Hua Hin Meeting Point	(see 50)

TRANSPORT	
Air-con Buses to Bangkok	52 B4
Main Government Bus Station	53 A3
Non-Air-con Buses to Phetchaburi & Cha-am	54 B3
Săwngthăew to Ao Takiap	55 B4

TOURIST INFORMATION

Tourist Information Office (☎ 0 3251 1047; cnr Th Phetkasem & Th Damnoen Kasem; ☻ 8.30am-4.30pm) Provides advice about Hua Hin and its surrounding area, and sells bus tickets. There's another branch under the clock tower on the cnr of Th Phetkasem & Th Naep Khehat (☻ 8.30am-4.30pm).

TRAVEL AGENCIES

There are many travel agencies, most offering day trips to nearby places such as Khao Sam Roi Yot (p564) and Kaeng Krachan National Park (p553). Unless you're in a group, you may have to wait a day or two until enough people sign up for the trip of your choice so keep that in mind when you make a booking.

Alternatively, try forming a group with fellow tourists you've meet on the trip to ensure a prompt trip.

Hua Hin Adventure Tour (☎ 0 3253 0314; www
.huahinadventuretour.com; Th Naep Khehat; ☺ 8.30am-
7pm) Runs kayaking trips in the Khao Sam Roi Yot National
Park (1900B). Offers more active excursions than other
travel agencies.
Ken Diamond (☎ 0 3251 3863; 162/6 Th
Naresdamri; ☺ 8.30am-7pm) Offers dozens of trips to
nearby destinations, including waterfalls and national
parks, and organises diving and snorkelling packages.
Also rents cars.
Tuk Tours (☎ 0 3251 4281; www.tuktours.com; 33/5
Th Phunsuk; ☺ 8.30am-7pm) Can book activities and
transport all around Thailand.

Activities

A long-time favourite golf-holiday destination for Thais, Hua Hin has recently begun
receiving attention from international golf-
ers. **Hua Hin Golf Centre** (☎ 0 3253 1096; www
.huahingolf.com; Th Naresdamri; ☺ noon-10pm) rents

golfing equipment and organises golfing
tours.

The **Royal Hua Hin Golf Course** (☎ 0 3251 2475;
green fee weekend/weekday 1500/1200B), near the train
station, offers ocean and temple views on an
elegant course.

Head to Bernie's (p563) and ask the British
owner for the lowdown on the local golfing
scene.

Horseback riding (per hr 450B) is on offer on
the beach at the end of Th Damnoen Kasem.
Prices are reasonable and the lessons are conducted in a safe fashion.

Muay Thai matches (☎ 0 3251 5269; 8/1 Th Phunsuk; Tue & Sat 350B, Wed & Fri 400B) take place every
Tuesday and Saturday at 9pm. On Wednes-
day and Friday at 9pm the action moves to
the Grand Plaza on Th Phetkasem. The **gym**
(☎ 08 9754 7801; www.grandsporthuahin.com; admission
180B; muay thai lessons 300B; ☺ 9am-9pm) is a good
place to burn off last night's Singha beers in
authentic Thai style. See the gym's website
for information on sporting activities in and
around Hua Hin.

GAME OF ELEPHANT POLO, ANYONE?

In early September for the past few years, the ancient Indian sport of elephant polo has been a highlight of the Hua Hin social scene. The game was revived in 1982 by Englishman Jim Edwards and Scotsman James Mann-Clark, who popularised it in Sri Lanka and Nepal. Christopher Staf-ford, general manager of Anantara Resort and a keen polo fan and player, brought the game to Thailand in 2001. From 2001 to 2005, the Anantara Resort & Spa was the setting for the King's Cup Elephant Polo Tournament. In September 2006 the tournament was moved to the Antantara Resort & Spa in Chiang Rai in Northern Thailand to widen the appeal of this unique sport, and at the time of writing it was envisaged that future tournaments would be held in Hua Hin or Chiang Rai on alternate years.

Elephant polo is much like horse polo in the sense of the rules, but the differences are striking. The game is obviously slower paced, but if you tire of watching the lumbering jumbos, you can focus on the spirited pooper-scoopers who flit around the field, harvesting the animals' grassy dumps. In a royal game rife with etiquette, the audience members usually aren't too keen to be regaled with flying elephant shit.

Each elephant bears a player, who hits the ball, and a mahout, who directs the animal using voice and body. The equipment of course is much different, too: the polo sticks are 2m to 2.5m in length, depending on the size of the elephant. The umpire takes it all in from the back of the largest pachyderm.

Because the sport is still so new, the players are usually trained horse-polo players, who still have much to learn and old habits to break. For example, flapping your legs on an elephant doesn't make it go any faster.

Elephants for the tournament are treated well, seem to enjoy the game, and are provided by the Thai Elephant Conservation Centre, in whose aid the event is held.

If you're in Hua Hin or Chiang Rai in early September, it's certainly worth checking out a unique spectacle. For more information visit www.anantara.com.

Aspiring chefs should visit **Buchabun Art & Crafts Collection** (☎ 08 1572 3805; www.siambeing. com/restaurant/cookingcourse; 22 Th Dechanuchit) where you can sign up for a half-day Thai cooking class. Classes cost 1000B and include a market visit and recipe book. They only run if several people are interested.

Volunteering

If you love animals and aren't afraid of a bit of hard work, then a stint at the **Wildlife Friends of Thailand Rescue Centre** (☎ 0 3245 8135; rescue cen tre www.wfft.org, volunteering www.wildlifevolunteer.org) could be a good, fun and unique way to break up your travels. Based 35km northwest of Cha-am, the centre cares for an entire menagerie of animals that have been rescued from animal shows and exploitative owners. An average day could involve feeding sun bears, building enclosures for macaques and establishing island refuges for gibbons. Volunteering costs US$140 per week, including all accommodation and meals. Volunteers are expected to stay for two to three months, although one-month stays are also considered. Travel agencies in Cha-am and Hua Hin can organise daytrips (1200B) to the centre or you can phone the centre directly, and staff can arrange return transport from Hua Hin (600B) or Cha-am (900B).

Sleeping

All budgets are catered for in Hua Hin. Expect discounts of 20% to 40% off these rates in the low season. Prices may be hiked up on weekends and at holidays.

BUDGET

Euro-Hua Hin City Hotel YHA (☎ 0 3251 3130; www .tyha.org; 15/15 Th Sasong; r incl breakfast 200-1000B; ✵) Is a barbecue and beer garden mandatory for a good youth hostel? If so, this friendly spot delivers. All rooms have air-con, even the eight-person dormitories (200B). If you're a snorer we recommend a single room (1000B). You'll need to be a YHA member to get these room rates.

All Nations Guest House (☎ 0 3251 2747; www.ge ocities.com/allnationsguesthouse/; 10-10/1 Th Dechanuchit; r 175-500B; ✵) Feed the backpacker within at this friendly spot with loads of information, cheap 50B beers and homemade pies. The cheaper rooms have shared bathrooms, and there is a bar with televisions tuned to an all-day diet of sport.

Pattana Guest House (☎ 0 3251 3393; huahin pattana@hotmail.com; 52 Th Naresdamri; r 250-450B) The rooms are small and there's no air-con, but the real highlight is the lusciously verdant bar and courtyard area in this restored fisherman's house. Book ahead as it's very popular.

Ban Pak Hua Hin (☎ 0 3251 1653; fax 0 3253 3649; Th Phunsuk, 5/1 Soi Bintaban; r 350-550B; ✵) 'Ezy-kleen' tiles and modern styling make this an acceptable budget choice in a street that's a tad noisy after dark. The cheapest rooms only have fans.

Pier Guesthouses

There are several pier guesthouses lining Th Naresdamri with simple rooms overlooking the sea. You're paying more for the location, and the shared areas can be noisy, but the first three places listed all have an echo of old Siam.

Mod (☎ 0 3251 2296; cnr Th Naresdamri & Th Naresdamri; r 200-450B; ✵) Next to Sirima, this two-storey place has fading wooden charm. The upstairs rooms cost more, but are airy and have better views. The cheapest rooms just have fans.

Bird Guest House (☎ 0 3251 1630; birdguesthouse huahin@hotmail.com; 31/2 Th Naresdamri; r 400-600B; ✵) Bird is smaller, quieter and nicer than the other pier guesthouses, with a homely family atmosphere and a more-relaxed clientele. There's a secluded pier-end deck.

Sirima (☎ 0 3251 1060; Th Naresdamri; r 250-650B; ✵) Sirima is decked out in pastel tones, with a long hallway leading to its only highlight: a common deck overlooking the water. The rooms are small and gloomy so hang out on the deck instead.

Tong Mee House (☎ 0 3253 0725; tongmeehuahin@ hotmail.com; 1 Soi Raumpown; r 450-550B; ✵ 🖳) Hidden away in a quiet residential *soi*, this boutique hotel could be the best value in town. The rooms are small but very well-kept, and most have balconies to gaze down on the everyday goings-on of families on the lane below.

Cha-ba Chalet (☎ 0 3252 1181; www.chabachalet .com; 1/18 Th Sasong; r 700B; ✵) The exterior's designer promise is not quite fulfilled with the functional rooms. Still, at only 700B and very close to the bustling night market, it's a good choice.

Ban Somboon (☎ 0 3251 1538; 13/4 Soi Damnoen Kasem; r 600-900B; ✵) With family photos, a com-

pact garden and a tiny Buddhist shrine, this place is like staying at your favourite Thai auntie's house.

In the same *soi* there are a couple of other good value guesthouses.

MIDRANGE

Hua Hin's midrange places are small, sedate, modern hotels with air-con, fridges and cable TV. A handful of new openings are making everyone lift their game.

Rajana Garden House (☎ 0 3251 1729; www.rajana -house.com; 3/9 Th Sasong; r 900B; 🔀) The rooms may lack the designer touches of other midrangers in town, but it's a little cheaper and the air-con bus from Bangkok stops nearby. Ask for a room at the back to counter road noise from busy Th Sasong.

K Place Guest House (☎ 0 3251 1396; kplaceus@yahoo .com; 116 Th Naresdamri; r 800-1000B; 🔀) Right in the heart of things on Th Naresdamri, but tucked away behind a minimart. The spacious rooms are good value, but not all have natural light.

All Seasons Guesthouse (☎ 0 3251 5151; www .hotelthailand.co.uk; 77/18-19 Th Phetkasem, Soi 63; r 1000-1300B; 🔀) The rooms are big and bright (and the bathrooms even brighter) in this popular spot run by Richard the friendly Brit. He'll even rent you a DVD player so you can watch your pirated purchases from the nearby night market. There are only seven rooms so book ahead.

Sand Inn (☎ 0 3253 2060; www.ourweb.info/sand inn_hotel; 38/1-4 Th Phunsuk; r 1000-1600B; 🔀) The contemporary lobby is adorned with Thai artefacts, and upstairs the classy rooms come with balconies and trendy minimalist design. Good bars await you outside on Th Phun-suk.

Jed Pee Nong (☎ 0 3251 2381; www.jedpeenong hotel-huahin.com; 17 Th Damnoen Kasem; r 1500-1800B; 🔀 🏊) This place is great for families. It has a small kid-friendly pool (they'll love the waterslides) and larger three-bed family rooms to squeeze the whole clan into. It's centrally located and is walking distance to the beach.

Fresh Inn Hotel (☎ 0 3251 1389; freshinnhuahin@ yahoo.com; 132 Th Naresdamri; r 1500-1800B; 🔀 🏊) New rooms with sea-views and a pool have boosted this long-standing place in the comfort stakes. Downstairs is Lo Stivale Italian restaurant, and if you're travelling with the whole mob, book one of the family rooms (2600B).

On Th Chomsin, three excellent new guesthouses have opened, all a short stroll from some of Hua Hin's best restaurants.

Ananthara (☎ 0 3251 6650; ananthara@hotmail.com; 1/8 Th Chomsin; r 1200B; 🔀 🖥) It's a fine line but this sparkling place delivers the perfect mix of old style Thai charm (courtesy of the antiques in reception) and subtle 21st-century style, (courtesy of the chic bathrooms and wi-fi internet access in the lobby).

Chomsin (☎ 0 3251 5348; www.chomsinhuahin.com; 130/4 Th Chomsin; r 1200B; 🔀 🖥) Another new opening, the Chomsin has super comfortable rooms with chic wooden floors, sparkling bathrooms, and cable TV channels to burn. It's close to the beach and night market.

ChaLeLarn (☎ 0 3253 2889; www.chalelarn.com; 11 Th Chomsin; r 1000-1200B; 🔀) Just up the road from Ananthara, ChaLeLarn has a beautiful lobby with wooden floors and 'lazy-days-in-the-tropics' cane furniture. Upstairs is a plant-filled rooftop, and the spacious rooms are classily decorated in a subtle collage of Asian and Western styles.

About 1km south of Hua Hin is a small traveller's enclave of midrange guesthouses. Prices (rooms from 600B to 900B July to September, from 1000B to 1350B October to June) and facilities (clean, comfortable, modern) are the same at almost every one. We recommend the following, all with pools, but the beach is just a short walk away.

Jinning Beach (☎ 0 3251 3950; www.jinningbeach guesthouse.com; r 1000B; 🔀 🏊)

Royal Beach (☎ 0 3253 2210; royalbeach@hotmail .com; r 1000B; 🔀 🏊)

Thipurai (☎ 0 3251 2210; www.thirupai.com; r 1350B; 🔀 🏊)

TOP END

Hua Hin has an impressive selection of luxury hotels. You'll also find other top-end places just north or south of the town centre.

Sofitel Central Hua Hin Resort (Hua Hin Railway Hotel; ☎ 0 3251 2021, Bangkok office 0 2541 1125; www .accorhotels-asia.com; 1 Th Damnoen Kasem; r from 7000B; 🔀 🖥 🏊) A magnificent, two-storey colonial-style place with three pools, expansive grounds along the beach, a spa and sporting facilities. Rooms, either in the original colonial wing or in the new modern wing, are luxurious with old-world touches. Discounts of up to 40% may be possible during the week and in the low season, or if you book through the office in Bangkok. Also worth visiting is

the lobby café, which doubles as a museum of the hotel's fascinating history.

Anantara Resort & Spa (☎ 0 3252 0800; www .anantara.com; r from 7350B; 🔀 🖭) Located about 4km from town, and featuring exquisite Thai-style villas and suites on 14 landscaped acres, this place is romantic with a capital 'R', and pulls off the effortless trick of being low key and luxury at the same time. Gorgeous teak bungalows conceal pampering spa facilities, and the more active traveller can choose between tennis, golf and a whole raft of water sports.

Baan Bayan (☎ 0 3253 3544; www.baanbayan.com; 119 Th Phetkasem; r 6000-11,000B; 🔀 🖭) Housed in a colonial beach house built in the early 20th century, Baan Bayan is perfect for travellers seeking a luxury experience without the over-kill of a big resort. The airy, high-ceilinged rooms feature a delicious mix of Asian antiques and modern facilities, and the location is absolute beachfront, just a few minutes from central Hua Hin.

Chiva-Som International Health Resort (☎ 0 3253 6536; www.chivasom.com; 74/4 Th Phetkasem; 3 nights from US$1530; 🔀 🖭) Set on a private lake 3.5km south of town, Chiva-Som is the ultimate hideaway for over-worked, over-stressed (and just maybe over-paid) high-flying business folk and celebrities. The name means Haven of Life in Thai-Sanskrit, and the staff of 200 fuse Eastern and Western approaches to health with planned nutrition, step and aqua aerobics, and Thai, Swedish or underwater massage. Rates include three meals per day along with health and fitness consultations, massage and all other activities. One-week, 10-day and two-week packages are also available, including specialist detox and fitness programmes.

Eating

One of Hua Hin's major attractions is the inexpensive Chatchai Market in the centre of town, where vendors gather nightly to cook fresh seafood for hordes of hungry Thais. It's also excellent for Thai breakfasts – there's very good *jóhk* and *khâo tôm* (both rice soups). Fresh-fried *paa-thâwng-koh* (Chinese dough-nuts in the Hua Hin-style – small and crispy, not oily) cost 3B for three. A few vendors also serve hot soy milk in bowls (5B) – break a few *paa-thâwng-koh* into the soy milk for an authentic local breakfast. Starting at 5pm there is a bustling night market along Th

Dechanuchit. Gradually the food stalls are being outnumbered by DVD stalls and T-shirt vendors, but it's still a buzzy scene. Moo Seafood on the corner of Th Dechanuchit and Th Sasong has busy alfresco tables. If you're after 100% authentic eats, check out the food stalls that set up around 5pm in the soi on the northern side of Th Chomsin.

The best seafood in Hua Hin is *plaa sam-lii* (cotton fish or kingfish), *plaa kràphong* (perch), *plaa mèuk* (squid), *hawy málaeng phûu* (mussels) and *puu* (crab). Fresh seafood is all over town, but the concentration of wharfside outdoor seafood restaurants is on Th Naresdamri, at the intersection with Th Dechanuchit. On the beach you can order a cold Singha and cracked crab without leaving your deckchair.

Coffee Beach (98 Th Naresdamri; snacks 40-80B; ☺ breakfast & lunch) Fruit shakes, fair-trade coffee and tasty sandwiches make this a great spot for an energising breakfast or a relaxing lunch.

Hua Hin Market Village (Th Phetkasem; dishes 70-120B; ☺ 10.30am-10pm) It's OK. Once in a while you're allowed to visit a big shopping centre with a good value and diverse foodcourt. But only once OK?

World News Coffee (☎ 0 3253 2475; 130/2 Th Naresdamri; dishes 70-130B; ☺ breakfast, lunch & dinner) This Starbucks-esque café serves Western breakfasts, including bagels, croissants and lots of different coffees. You can surf the web for 40B per hour and there are magazines and newspapers to complement your first cup of the day. Just like being at home really.

Sunshine Bakery (130/5 Th Naresdamri; breakfast 100-130B; ☺ breakfast, lunch & dinner) This German-Thai bakery whips up good value breakfasts in a variety of accents – German, English, American – you choose.

Green Leaf (Th Naresdamri; meals 100-190B; ☺ breakfast, lunch & dinner) Excellent coffee, fruit lassis (50B to 60B) and a good selection of veggie delights are the go at this New-Agey café looking out onto a small cove. There's an attached shop selling ethnic prints and world music CDs.

Maha Raja (☎ 0 3253 0347; 25 Th Naresdamri; dishes 90-200B; ☺ lunch & dinner) Indian cuisine usually travels well and this reasonably priced shrine to Bollywood bling is no exception. When you arrive you'll be offered a welcome drink, and when you leave you might be offered a great deal at the tailors next door.

Moon Smile (Th Phunsuk; meals 80-200B; 😋 lunch & dinner) On Th Phunsuk opposite Soi Bintaban there is an enclave of well-priced Thai restaurants that will respect your request for 'Thai spicy, please'. Moon Smile is the best of them – try the grilled beef and eggplant salad. A few doors up, Platoo is another good choice.

Pizza Corner (☎ 0 3235 2084; cnr Th Naresdamri & Th Damnoen Kasem; pizza 120-200B; 😋 breakfast, lunch & dinner) People-watching, pizza eating or pasta twirling – this bustling corner spot is good for all three.

Monsoon (☎ 0 3253 1062; 62 Th Naresdamri; dishes 120-300B, afternoon tea 100B; 😋 2pm to midnight) An excellent wine list and mood lighting makes this Vietnamese restaurant, located in a lovingly restored two-storey teak house, Hua Hin's most romantic spot. There's also Thai and European food, and your can surprise your loved one with a purchase from the attached homeware shop, or treat them to afternoon tea from 3pm.

Buffalo Bill's Steak & Grill (☎ 0 3253 0082; 8 Th Naresdamri; dishes 100-380B; 😋 breakfast, lunch & dinner) Heaven for carnivores is this expat-friendly spot with Aussie and Kiwi steaks, and huge Brit-style fry-ups for brekkie. The burgers are only so-so – you're better off to go the whole hog (or cow) and have a steak. Most nights Bill himself will provide you with a recommendation for wine. Laptop toters can feast on its wi-fi network.

Chao Lay (☎ 0 3251 3436; 15 Th Naresdamri; dishes 60-400B; 😋 breakfast, lunch & dinner) Downstairs there's enough different marine species in tanks to keep *The Undersea World of Jacques Cousteau* in syndication for decades. Upstairs this very popular teak-wood restaurant has two levels which are often packed full of fans of excellent seafood.

Brasserie de Paris (☎ 0 3253 0637; 3 Th Naresdamri; dishes 350-500B) France comes to town with a real French chef cooking up authentic French flavours in a light and airy space with good views of *la mer* upstairs. Local crab is the standout dish. Reassuringly expensive.

Drinking

There are several *faràng* bars under European management in the Hua Hin Bazaar. Some offer the familiar Thai-hostess atmosphere, but a few bill themselves as 'sports bars' and have wide-screen TVs. Soi Bintaban is lined with girlie bars doing their best to attract clientele. It's not a dangerous place per se, just a glimpse into the seedier side of tourism. Nearby Th Phunsuk is a bit more salubrious with a couple of classier drinking holes.

Hua Hin Brewing Company (☎ 0 3251 2888; 33 Th Naresdamri; beer 180B; 😋 open 5pm) Operated by the Hilton, the HHBC serves three microbrews in a faux fishing village atmosphere. Try the Sabai Sabai Wheat Beer with a slice of lime or the hoppy Dancing Monkey Lager. Most nights there's a live band, followed by a relatively clued-up DJ. Inside is as dark as the belly of Jonah's whale, so park yourself outside on the spacious decks and watch the passing parade on Th Naresdamri.

Crawford's (☎ 0 3251 1517; 5 Th Phunsuk; 😋 8.30am-midnight) Pretty authentic for so far from the Blarney Stone, Crawford's offers good *craic* amid two levels of moody wood, with lots of hideaway nooks and crannies. Live sport is on offer on several tellies, and there's a robust menu including fish and chips. Draught beers are cheaper Monday to Thursday. *Slainte!*

Hua Hin Meeting Point (☎ 0 3253 1132; 3 Th Phunsuk; 😋 8.30am-midnight) This versatile place is good for a quick bite to eat any time of the day, and is a popular…er…meeting point for a few drinks. Inside the décor is slick and modern, and outside is a rustic garden bar. Somehow it all hangs together nicely.

Bernie's (Hua Hin Bazaar, Th Damnoen Kasem) The owner is a big golf nut with loads of info on swinging a club in the area. Wall-to-wall TVs show wall-to-wall sport – especially golf.

Getting There & Away

There are air-con buses to/from Bangkok's Southern bus station (171B, 3½ hours, every half hour). These leave Hua Hin 70m north of Rajana Garden House on Th Sasong (outside the Siripetchkasem Hotel).

The main government bus station, on Th Liap Thang Rot Fai, has air-con buses to many destinations throughout the country. Be sure to ignore the touts here and go to the window for assistance and ticket purchase. There is at least one air-con bus per day to each destination: Phetchaburi (80B, 1½ hours), Cha-am (40B, 30 minutes), Prachuap Khiri Khan (80B, 1½ hours), Chumphon (160B, four hours), Phuket (378B, eight hours), Krabi (389B, eight hours), Koh Samui (320B, nine hours) and Songkhla (457B, 11 hours). Frequent non-air-con buses to Phetchaburi (50B, 1½ hours)

and Cha-am (25B, 30 minutes) leave from near the intersection of Th Chomsin and Th Phetkasem.

There are frequent trains running to/from Bangkok's Hualamphong train station (2nd class 292B to 382B, 3rd class 234B to 294B, four hours) and other stations on the southern railway line.

SGA (Hua Hin office ☎ 0 3252 2300, Bangkok Office 0 2134 3233; www.sga.aero) flies a 12-seat shuttle three times a day (one way 3100B, 40 minutes, 11.45am, 3pm and 6.30pm) from Bangkok's Suvarnabhumi airport to Hua Hin.

Getting Around

Local buses (10B) and sǎwngthǎew (12B) to Ao Takiap leave from the corner of Th Sasong and Th Dechanuchit.

Even though sǎamláw fares in Hua Hin have been set by the municipal authorities, haggling is usually required. Some sample fares: from the train station to the beach 30B; from the air-con bus terminal to Th Naresdamri 40B to 50B (depending on size of your bags). Most drivers will push for at least twice this much.

Motorcycles (250B to 500B per day) and bicycles (100B per day) can be rented from a couple of places on Th Damnoen Kasem near the Jed Pee Nong Hotel. Car and 4WD drive rental can be arranged at most travel agencies including Ken Diamond (p558). Expect to pay around 1500B per day for a Suzuki 4WD and around 2000B per day for a small sedan.

KHAO SAM ROI YOT NATIONAL PARK

อุทยานแห่งชาติเขาสามร้อยยอด

Towering limestone cliffs, caves and beaches produce a dramatic landscape at this 98-sq-km **park** (☎ 0 3261 9078; adult/child 400/200B), which means Three Hundred Mountain Peaks in English. The park's lagoons and coastal marshlands are excellent for birdwatching, and with a little exercise you'll be rewarded with magnificent views of the gulf coastline.

Bring your mosquito repellent, especially during the rainy season (June to November). Rama IV and a large entourage of Thai and European guests came here on 18 August 1868 to see a total solar eclipse (apparently predicted by the monarch himself) and to enjoy a feast prepared by a French chef. Two months later the king died from malaria, contracted from mosquito bites inflicted here. Today the risk of malaria in the park is low, but the mosquitoes can be pesky.

Orientation & Information

There are three park headquarter locations: Hat Laem Sala, Ban Rong Jai and Ban Khao Daeng; and three visitors centres at Hat Laem Sala, Hat Sam Phraya and Ban Khao Daeng. A nature studies centre lies at the end of a 1km road leading north from Ban Rong Jai. There are a couple of checkpoints – on the road south from Pranburi and on the road east of Hwy 4. You'll need to pay admission or show proof that you already have.

Sights & Activities

BEACHES

Both of the park's beaches have plenty of facilities – from food stalls to picnic areas and bathrooms.

Hat Laem Sala is a sandy beach flanked on three sides by dry limestone hills and casuarinas. It has a small visitors centre, restaurant, bungalows and camp sites. Boats, taking up to 10 people, can be hired from Bang Pu to the beach (250B return, 15 minutes). The beach is about a 20-minute hike from Bang Pu, via a steep trail.

Hat Sam Phraya, 5km south of Hat Laem Sala, is a 1km-long beach with a restaurant and bathrooms.

CAVES

Khao Sam Roi Yot has three caves, all well worth visiting. **Tham Phraya Nakhon** is the most popular and can be reached by boat (250B return) or on foot. By foot, hike along a steep and rocky trail from Hat Laem Sala for 430m. Once there you'll find two large caverns with sinkholes allowing light in. In one cave is a royal sǎalaa (meeting hall) built for Rama V, who would stop here when travelling between Bangkok and Nakhon Si Thammarat.

Tham Kaew, 2km from the Bang Pu turn-off, features a series of chambers connected by narrow passageways; you enter the first cavern by means of a ladder. Stalactites and limestone formations glittering with calcite crystals (hence the cave's name, 'Jewel Cave') are plentiful. Lamps can be rented, but Tham Kaew is best visited with a park guide because of the dangerous footing.

Tham Sai is in a hill near Ban Khung Tanot, 2.5km from the main road between Laem Sala

and Sam Phraya beaches. Villagers rent out lamps (40B) at a shelter near the cave mouth. A 280m trail leads up the hillside to the cave, which features a large single cavern. Be careful of steep drop-offs in the cave.

HIKING

For spectacular views of limestone cliffs against a jagged coastline, take the 30-minute step trail from the park headquarters at Ban Khao Daeng to the top of **Khao Daeng**. At sunset you might see a serow (Asian goat-antelope). If you have more time and energy, climb the 605m to the top of **Khao Krachom** for even better views.

KAYAKING

In the fishing village of Ban Khao Daeng, **Horizon Adventure** (☎ 08 1820 9091) rents out kayaks for 400B per day, allowing you to explore the wildlife-filled mangroves of the area at your leisure.

WILDLIFE-WATCHING

Wildlife includes barking deer, crab-eating macaques, slow lorises, Malayan pangolins, fishing cats, palm civets, otters, serows, Javan mongooses, monitor lizards and dusky langurs. Possibly due to the rise in tourism, it can be difficult to actually spot any wild animals.

Because the park is at the intersection of the East Asian and Australian flyways, as many as 300 migratory and resident bird species have been recorded here, including yellow bitterns, cinnamon bitterns, purple swamphens, water rails, ruddy-breasted crakes, bronze-winged jacanas, grey herons, painted storks, whistling ducks, spotted eagles and black-headed ibises. The park contains Thailand's largest freshwater marsh (along with mangroves and mudflats), and is one of only three places in the country where the purple heron breeds.

Waterfowl are most commonly seen in the cool season. Encroachment by shrimp farmers in the vicinity has sadly destroyed substantial portions of mangroves and other wetlands, thus depriving the birds of an important habitat. November to March are the best waterfowl-watching months. The birds come from as far as Siberia, China and northern Europe to winter here. You can hire a boat in the village of Khao Daeng for a cruise (400B, 45 minutes) along the canal

in the morning or afternoon to spot them. Before heading out, chat with your prospective guide to see how well they speak English. Better guides will know the English names of common waterfowl and point them out to you.

Sleeping & Eating

Forestry Department (☎ Bangkok 0 2562 0760; campsite per person 30B, bungalow 5-6 people 1200-1400B, 6-9 people 1600-2200B) The forestry department hires out bungalows at Hat Laem Sala and at the visitors centre near the Khao Daeng viewpoint. Two-person tents are available for rent at these spots for 150B per night. You can pitch your own tent at camp sites near the Khao Daeng Viewpoint, Hat Laem Sala or Hat Sam Phraya. There are basic restaurants at all these locations.

There are also a few private resort-style accommodation options.

Dolphin Bay Resort (☎ 0 3255 9333; www.dolphin bayresort.com; 227 Mu 4, Phu Noi; r & bungalows from 1290B; ✖ ⊗) Choose between hotel-style rooms or well-appointed bungalows at this family-friendly place, with an excellent restaurant that understands the true meaning of spicy. A wide range of trips is on offer to nearby islands and the national park. From February to May pink dolphins are sometimes seen off the beach.

Long Beach Inn (☎ 0 3255 9068; www.longbeach-thai land.com; 223/4 Mu 4; Phu Noi; r 1800B; ✖ ⊗) A short walk from the eponymous Long Beach, but comfortable with air-con rooms in new villas around a pretty pool.

Brassiere Beach (☎ 08 1734 4343; www.brassier ebeach.com; 210 Mu 5, Cosy Beach; villas 4200-8200B; ✖) Nine stunning Mexican-style villas have (white)washed ashore at a private cove, and the funky owners have equipped them with retro furniture, CD players and playful names like La Perla, Victoria's and Secret. Brassiere Beach's uniqueness deserves your support.

Getting There & Away

The park is about 40km south of Hua Hin, and best visited by car. From Hua Hin, take Hwy 4 (Th Phetkasem) to Pranburi. In Pranburi, turn left at the main intersection, drive 2km, stay right at the fork in the road, and go another 2km. At the police substation, turn right. From there, it's 19km to the park's entrance and then another 4km to the headquarters

at Hat Laem Sala. If you're trying to reach the park from the south, there's an entrance off Hwy 4 – turn right at highway marker 286.5, where there's a sign for the park, then drive another 13km to the headquarters at Ban Khao Daeng.

If you don't have your own wheels, catch a bus or train to Pranburi and then a såwngthåew (50B, every half hour between 8am and 4pm) to Bang Pu, the small village inside the park. From Bang Pu you can walk to Hat Laem Sala.

You can also hire a såwngthåew (400B) or a motorcycle taxi (250B) from Pranburi all the way to the park. Be sure to mention you want to go to the ùtháyaan hàeng châat (national park) rather than Ban Khao Sam Roi Yot. Transport can also be arranged at travel agencies in Hua Hin (p558), most of which also run tours. Hua Hin Adventure Tour has the best selection of more intrepid activities.

PRACHUAP KHIRI KHAN
ประจวบคีรีขันธ์
pop 27,700

Framed by limestone cliffs and islands, and studded with colourful fishing boats, the sleepy seaside town of Prachuap Khiri Khan is a charming place to get off the faràng trail for a while. The town is actually the provincial capital, but the ambience is nicely small-town relaxed. Attractions, with a small 'a', include climbing to a hill-top wat while being shadowed by a troop of monkeys, taking a leisurely motorbike ride to the excellent beaches north and south of town, or just enjoying some of Thailand's freshest (and cheapest) seafood.

Development is coming slowly to Prachuap, and a few recent guesthouse openings have improved the level of accommodation. The local council has even splashed out on a ritzy new corniche (beachfront walkway). Blur your eyes just a bit (well, maybe a bit more), and you could almost be in the south of France.

Prachuap, specifically Ao Manao, was one of seven points on the gulf coast where Japanese troops landed on 8 December 1941 during their invasion of Thailand. Several street names around town commemorate the ensuing skirmish: Phithak Chat (Defend Country), Salachip (Sacrifice Life) and Suseuk (Fight Battle).

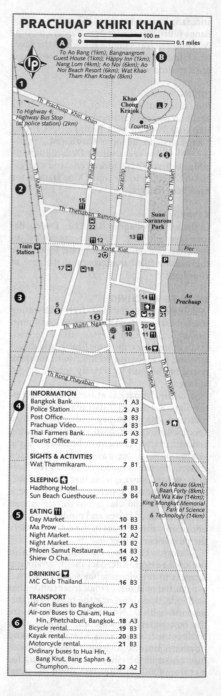

PRACHUAP KHIRI KHAN

To Ao Bang (1km); Bangnangrom Guest House (1km); Happy Inn (1km); Nang Lom (4km); Ao Noi (6km); Ao Noi Beach Resort (6km); Wat Khao Tham Khan Kradai (8km)

To Highway 4; Highway Bus Stop (at police station) (2km)

Khao Chong Krajok

Fountain

Suan Saranrom Park

Train Station

Pier

Ao Prachuap

Th Maharat
Th Phithak Chat
Th Salachip
Th Suseuk
Th Chai Thaleh
Th Thetsaban Bamrung
Th Kong Kiat
Th Maitri Ngam
Th Rong Phayaban
Th Suseuk
Th Chai Thaleh

To Ao Manao (6km); Baan Forty (8km); Hat Wa Kaw (14km); King Mongkut Memorial Park of Science & Technology (14km)

INFORMATION		
Bangkok Bank	1	A3
Police Station	2	A3
Post Office	3	B3
Prachuap Video	4	B3
Thai Farmers Bank	5	A3
Tourist Office	6	B2

SIGHTS & ACTIVITIES		
Wat Thammikaram	7	B1

SLEEPING		
Hadthong Hotel	8	B3
Sun Beach Guesthouse	9	B4

EATING		
Day Market	10	B3
Ma Prow	11	B3
Night Market	12	A2
Night Market	13	B2
Phloen Samut Restaurant	14	B3
Shiew O Cha	15	A2

DRINKING		
MC Club Thailand	16	B3

TRANSPORT		
Air-con Buses to Bangkok	17	A3
Air-con Buses to Cha-am, Hua Hin, Phetchaburi, Bangkok	18	A3
Bicycle rental	19	B3
Kayak rental	20	B3
Motorcycle rental	21	B3
Ordinary buses to Hua Hin, Bang Krut, Bang Saphan & Chumphon	22	A2

Information

Bangkok Bank (cnr Th Maitri Ngam & Th Sarachip)
Police station (Th Kong Kiat) Just west of Th Sarachip.
Post office (cnr Th Maitri Ngam & Suseuk) By the telephone office.
Prachuap Video (Th Sarachip; per hr 30B; 🕙 9am-9pm) For internet access; near Th Maitri Ngam.
Thai Farmers Bank (Th Phitak Chat) Just north of Th Maitri Ngam.
Tourist office (☎ 0 3261 1491; Th Chai Thaleh; 🕙 8.30am-4.30pm) At the northern end of town. The staff speak English.

Sights & Activities

Visible from almost anywhere in Prachuap Khiri Khan is **Khao Chong Krajok** (Mirror Tunnel Mountain – named after the hole in the mountain that appears to reflect the sky). At the top of a long flight of stairs up the small mountain is **Wat Thammikaram**, established by Rama VI. From here, there are perfect views of the town and the bay – even the border with Myanmar, just 11km away. Along the way you'll be entertained by hordes of monkeys. At the base of the mountain, the more fastidious monkeys bathe in a small pool.

Continue 4km north along the beach road and you'll come to a small village on **Ao Bang Nang Lom**, where wooden fishing vessels are still made using traditional Thai methods. The industrious folk here also catch a fish called *plaa ching chang*, which they dry and store for Sri Lankan traders. A couple of kilometres north of Ao Bang Nang Lom is another bay, **Ao Noi**, with a small fishing village and the comfortable Ao Noi Beach Resort (right).

Six kilometres south of the city is island-dotted **Ao Manao**, a scenic bay ringed by a clean white-sand beach. A Thai air-force base guards access to the bay and every week the beach is given a military-grade clean up. There are several *săalaa* (rest stops) here, along with a hotel and restaurant. You can rent chairs, umbrellas and inner tubes, and buy food and drink, while Thailand's Top Guns relax on a golf course and driving range. The beach itself is 2km to 3km past the base entrance, where you may need to show your passport. The beach closes at 8pm.

Nine kilometres south of Ao Manao, **Hat Wa Kaw** is a pleasant, casuarina-lined beach that's even quieter and cleaner than Ao Manao. Here you'll find the **King Mongkut Memorial Park of**

Science & Technology (☎ 0 3266 1098; admission free; 🕙 8.30am-4.30pm) which commemorates the 1868 solar eclipse that the king and his 15-year-old son Prince Chulalongkorn came south to witness. Unfortunately not much is translated into English, but there is a good aquarium.

Sleeping

Accommodation hasn't been Prachuap's biggest asset, but a few new places are lifting standards. Head north and south for a few interesting places to stay on quieter beaches.

Sun Beach Guesthouse (☎ 0 3260 4770; www.sun beach-guesthouse.com; 160 Th Chai Thaleh; r 1000B; 🖭 🖳) The neo-classical styling is a bit OTT, but the rooms at this new place are discreet and trimmed in blue to match the pool and Jacuzzi out front. There's a real family atmosphere brought to life by the energetic kids of the Thai-German owners.

Hadthong Hotel (☎ 0 3260 1050; www.hadthong .com; 21 Th Suseuk; r 675-1060B; 🖭 🖳) The beach-front five-storey Hadthong is PKK's only 'real' hotel. The rooms are looking a bit tired, but friendly staff and good value 100B buffet breakfasts easily compensate. It's worth shelling out a bit more for a room facing the sea.

One kilometre north of town (just across the bridge) is a quiet beach which gets lots of Thai visitors at the weekend.

Happy Inn (☎ 0 3260 2082; 149-151 Th Suanson; bungalows 500B) There's no English spoken at this spot, and the slightly charmless bungalows are down a driveway, but the beach is just over the road, and shy smiles come as standard.

Bangnangrom Guest House (☎ 0 3260 4841; 137 Th Suanson; r 700-1000B; 🖭) The owner was cleaning his car when we dropped by, and it looked like he'd given the spotless rooms a makeover as well. All rooms have air-con and cable TV, and there's a good-value triple room.

AO NOI BEACH

Heading 5km north from town, you reach Ao Noi Beach.

Ao Noi Beach Resort (☎ 0 3260 1350; 206 Tambon Ao Noi; r 650-800B; 🖭) Set in pleasant, leafy grounds next to a secluded beach, this laid-back place is miles away from anything or anywhere touristy. Fan rooms face the sea, but unfortunately air-con rooms face a wall.

UPPER SOUTHERN GULF

AO KHLONG WAN

To the south of town is Ao Khlong Wan.

Baan Forty (☎ 0 3266 1437; 555 Th Prachuap-Khlong Wan; bungalows 1000-1200B; ▨) It's a simple recipe. Spend your nights in simple concrete bungalows on a private beach, and spend your days relaxing on the sand or in the shady garden waiting for another huge meal. With not much else to do, bring loads of books. Weekends are busy with holidaying Thais.

Eating & Drinking

Because of its reputation for fine seafood, Prachuap Khiri Khan has many restaurants. A local speciality is *plaa samlii dàet diaw* – whole cottonfish that's sliced lengthways and left to dry in the sun for half a day. It's then fried quickly and served with mango salad. It may sound awful, but the taste is sublime. An all-day market lines the street on Th Maitri Ngam, starting early in the morning. There are two excellent night markets; the more atmospheric is opposite the pier, but both are good with lots of different stalls.

Shiew O Cha (☎ 0 3260 1732; cnr Ths Phitak Chat & Thetsaban Bamrung; meals 50-90B; ☾ breakfast, lunch & dinner) A friendly Saint Bernard holds fort at this cavernous Chinese-Thai restaurant that occasionally has live music and always has good seafood. Look for the big cream-and-green building on the corner.

Phloen Samut Restaurant (☎ 0 3261 1115; 44 Th Chai Thaleh; dishes 50-120B; ☾ breakfast, lunch & dinner) With sea views and loads of seafood, this is another good option. The service would be better if the staff stopped watching Thai soap operas on the telly.

Ma Prow (☎ 08 5293 7278; 48 Th Chai Thaleh; dishes 80-160B; ☾ lunch & dinner) The Thai flavours are spicily authentic at this airy wooden pavilion across from the beach. The music is an intriguing mix of Western and Thai – kind of like the clientele you'll see here on a busy weekend.

MC Club Thailand (Th Chai Thaleh; ☾ noon-late) Decorated with motorcycle memorabilia, this bar is a good place to kick start a big night in PKK. During the high season, the club sets up across the road beside the beach.

Getting There & Away

There are frequent air-con buses to/from Bangkok (230B, five hours), Hua Hin (80B, 1½ hours), Cha-am (90B, 2½ hours) and Phetchaburi (105B, three hours) leaving from Th

Phitak Chat near the centre. For southern destinations such as Phuket or Krabi, hike 2km northwest out to the police station on the highway to catch passing buses (motorcycle taxis will take you for 40B). Ordinary buses to Hua Hin (65B), Bang Krut (55B), Bang Saphan (65B) and Chumphon (160B, 3½ hours) leave from the southeast corner of Ths Thetsaban Bamrung and Phitak Chat.

There are frequent train services to/from Bangkok (2nd class 220B to 357B, 3rd class 128B, six hours). Trains also run to Ban Krut (one hour) and Bang Saphan Yai (1½ hours).

Getting Around

Prachuap is small enough to get around on foot, but you can hop on a motorcycle taxi around town for 30B. Other destinations include Ao Noi (50B) and Ao Manao (40B). At Ao Manao motorcycles aren't permitted past the gate unless both driver and passenger are wearing helmets.

You can rent motorbikes in front of the Hadthong Hotel for 200B per day. The roads in the area are very good and it's a great way to see the surrounding beaches.

Kayaks are available to rent at a pet supplies store beside the Hadthong Hotel. A two-person kayak is 100B per hour, and a trip to the nearby islands should take around three hours. Opposite the post office, bicycles can be rented for 100B per day.

AROUND PRACHUAP KHIRI KHAN

Wat Khao Tham Khan Kradai

วัดเขาถ้ำคานกระได

About 8km north of town, following the road beyond Ao Noi, is this small cave wat at one end of **Ao Khan Kradai** (also known as Ao Khan Bandai) – a long, beautiful bay. A trail at the base of the limestone hill leads up and around the side to a small cavern and then to a larger one that contains a reclining Buddha. If you have a torch you can proceed to a larger second chamber also containing Buddha images. From this trail you get a good view of Ao Khan Kradai. The beach here is suitable for swimming and is usually deserted. A motorcycle ride here costs 50B.

Dan Singkhon

ด่านสิงขร

Just south of Prachuap Khiri Khan is a road leading west to Dan Singkhon, on the My-

anmar border. This is the narrowest point in Thailand between the Gulf of Thailand and Myanmar – only 12km across. The border is open to Thai-Burmese citizens only.

HAT BAN KRUT & BANG SAPHAN YAI
หาดบ้านกรูด/บางสะพานใหญ่

These two low-key destinations lie about 80km and 100km south of Prachuap Khiri Khan, respectively, and are a popular weekend and holiday destination for Thai tourists. During the week you'll have the beaches largely to yourself and a few long-tail boats.

The main beach of **Hat Ban Krut** is right beside a road, making the 10km beach handy to cars and services, but detracting from a 100% peaceful beach experience. North of the headland topped by the Disneyland-like spires of **Wat Tan Sai**, you'll find **Hat Sai Kaew**, which is quieter but slightly out of the way, making it a better beach experience.

Bang Saphan Yai, 20km south of the town, is nothing special, but its coastline is now experiencing development. Islands off the coast to the south, including **Ko Thalu** and **Ko Sing**, offer good **snorkelling** and **diving** from the end of January to mid-May. Coral Hotel and Suan Luang Resort in Bang Saphan Yai can arrange half-day diving excursions to these islands.

When booking transport, don't confuse Bang Saphan Yai with Bang Saphan Noi, which is 15km further south.

Sleeping
HAT BAN KRUT
You'll struggle to find true budget options here, but if you visit on a weekday you should secure a discount of 20% to 30%. Bicycles (100B per day) and motorcycles (300B per day) can be rented to see the surrounding area, and most accommodation places arrange snorkelling trips (350B to 450B) to nearby islands.

The following are on the beach road south of the wat-topped headland.

Ban Rim Haad Resort (☎ 0 3269 5205; www.ban rimhaad.com; bungalows 600-1500B; ✷) Near a few bars and restaurants, this friendly family-run accommodation has a veritable village of different sized bungalows. Most travellers will be happy with the standard bungalows, but there are 10-person bungalows (2500B to 3000B) if you're a member of a volleyball team or have a large family.

Ban Klang Aow Beach Resort (☎ 0 3269 5086; www.baanklangaowresort.com; bungalows incl breakfast 2000-3500B; ✷ ☖) Further south on the same beach, the one- and two-bedroom bungalows have large verandas, and are hidden in leafy glades. Bicycles, kayaks and two swimming pools will get you hungry for your next meal at the resort's restaurant.

The following places are on **Hat Sai Kaew**, north of the headland. Count on running up a substantial tab on motorcycle taxis if you want to frequent the wider range of restaurants on the main beach. An alternative is to rent your own two wheels.

Ban Kruit Youth Hostel (☎ 0 3269 5525; www .thailandbeach.com; dm 300-400B; bungalows 600-2600B; ✷ ☖) More like a resort than a hostel, this place has bungalows in a wide range of sizes. The cheapest are wooden huts with shared bathroom, and the ritzy beachfront ones have TV, air-con and hot water. Cheaper dorm rooms are available in the main building. There's lots of greenery beside the long empty beach, and a postage stamp-sized tiny pool. Breakfast is included and YHA cardholders get a discount.

Bayview Beach Resort (☎ 0 3269 5566; www.bay viewbeachresort.com; bungalows 1300-4000B; ✷ ☖) Sharing the same beach as the youth hostel, Bayview has fine bungalows amid shady grounds with a beachside pool. The spick-and-span bungalows range from small wooden numbers to large, concrete ones with huge bay windows.

BANG SAPHAN YAI
There is accommodation on the beaches north and south of town. To the north are mainly midrange places, while to the south there is one flash resort, and a few budget-priced bungalows. A good source of local information is www.bangsaphanguide.com; it's worth checking out before your trip.

The following are north of the town.

Van Veena Hotel (☎ 0 3269 1251; www.vanveena.com; r 400-800B; ✷) The rooms are unexciting, but undeniably spacious, and downstairs there is a well-stocked minimart with all the essentials for beach life. Across the road is a beachfront restaurant.

Sailom Resort (☎ 0 3269 1003; www.sailomresortbang spahan.com; r 1900B; ✷ ☖) Manicured grounds, a huge swimming pool, Asian chic décor – this new spot has certainly shaken things up in sleepy Bang Saphan.

The following are about 5km south of town. There is more budget accommodation here than on the northern beach, or at Hat Ban Krut.

Lola Bungalows (☎ 0 3269 1963; bungalows 300B) Beachfront location – check. Lazydays hammocks – check. Corrugated iron roof…mmm. OK, they don't get things 100% right at this chilled spot near Coral Hotel, but after a few days' beachside, you won't care what the roof is made of.

Suan Luang Resort (☎ 0 3269 1663; www.suanluang .com; bungalows 400-600B; 🕸) You're 700m from the beach here, but the friendly welcome from the young Thai-French owners more than makes up for that. Located in a coconut grove, simple wooden bungalows with fans blend with air-con concrete ones with TV and hot water. The restaurant's menu speaks Thai and French, and there are daytrips to waterfalls and islands to give you something to talk about over dinner.

Coral Hotel (☎ 0 3269 1667; www.coral-hotel.com; 171 Mu 9; r 1525B, bungalows 2730-3525B; 🕸 🖭) Set amid a coconut grove, this upmarket French-managed hotel is right on the beach. There's a huge pool, a very good restaurant and all rooms have TV, fridge and hot water. Fill your days with water-sports, or exploring the area on an organised tour. Four-person bungalows are also available for families.

Getting There & Around

Buses depart at least once daily from Bangkok's Southern bus terminal to Ban Krut (255B, five hours) and Bang Saphan Yai (290B, six hours). Get a direct bus, otherwise you may be left on Hwy 4 (Th Phetkasem) and will need to get a motorbike taxi to the beaches (60B). Frequent buses run from Prachuap Khiri Khan to Ban Krut (55B) and Bang Saphan Yai (65B), and a local bus (15B) trundles from Ban Krut to Bang Saphan Yai.

Ban Krut and Bang Saphan Yai are both on Thailand's southern railway line and there are at least daily departures to/from Chumphon, Prachuap Khiri Khan, Hua Hin and Bangkok. Ban Krut's train station is 4km from the beach and in Bang Saphan Yai you'll be dropped off in town. In both places you'll need to hire a motorcycle taxi (around 60B) to get to the beach.

Getting around can be a problem, as there's not much public transport between the beaches. Once you get to the beaches, most resorts rent out motorcycles for around 300B per day.

CHUMPHON PROVINCE

CHUMPHON

ชุมพร

pop 81,000

Chumphon features on many travellers' itinerary as they flit in and out of the busy transport hub en route to Ko Tao, or head west for Ranong and Phuket. Around 500km south of Bangkok, Chumphon is where Southern Thailand begins and you'll begin to see mosques and start to hear different dialects.

While there's not a lot in town to keep you amused, the surrounding beaches are good places to step off the treadmill of travel for a few days. **Hat Tha Wua Laen** (12km north of town) is renowned for windsurfing and kiteboarding, and has a developing travellers' scene with some good bungalows and beachside bars. Pretty **Hat Sairi** (22km east of town) is a more traditional Thai beach resort, and the best spot to arrange day trips to offshore islands.

When you're ready to move on again, Chumphon's array of enterprising travel agencies can help you book transport to Ko Tao, as well as bus and train connections further south to Krabi and Surat Thani.

Information

There are banks along Th Sala Daeng with exchange facilities and ATMs.

Communications Authority of Thailand office (CAT; Th Poramin Mankha) About 1km east of the post office; has international call facilities.

CS Leisure Travel (☎ 7750 3001; www.geocities.com /cs_leisure; 68/10 Th Tha Taphao; 🕑 8am-10pm) Food and drink, travel information and internet. Its website is an excellent resource for information on Chumphon and the surrounding area.

DK Book Store (☎ 0 7750 3876; Soi Sala Daeng; 🕑 8am-9pm) Opposite the Janson Chumphon Hotel. Carries a few titles in English.

iNet (Th Tha Taphao; 30B per hr; 🕑 9am-9pm) Internet access near most guesthouses.

Main post office (Th Poramin Mankha) In the south-eastern part of town.

New Infinity Travel (☎ 0 7750 1937; new_infinity@hotmail.com; 68/2 Th Tha Taphao;

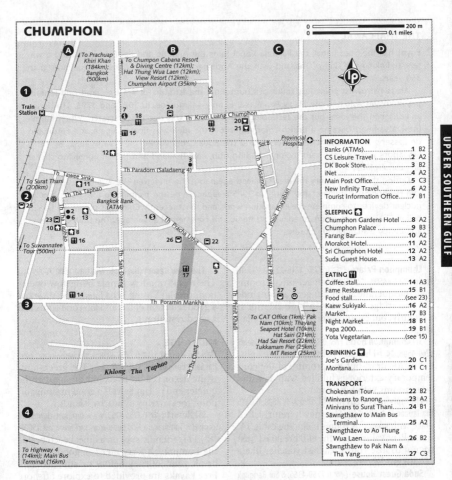

⏰ 8am-10pm) Has a good selection of secondhand
paperbacks.

Tourist Information Office (cnr Th Sala Daeng & Th
Krom Luang Chumphon; ⏰ 8.30am-5pm) Speaks English
and supplies good information, especially about transport
to/from Chumphon.

Festivals & Events
From mid-March to the end of April the
Chumphon Marine Festival features folk-art
exhibits, a windsurfing competition at Hat
Thung Wua Laen and a marathon. In Octo-
ber, the five-day **Lang Suan Buddha Image Parade
& Boat Race Festival** includes a procession of
temple boats and a boat race on Mae Nam
Lang Suan (Lang Suan River), about 60km
south of Chumphon.

Sleeping
Most people overnighting in Chumphon are
backpackers on the way to Ko Tao, so accommodation is budget priced. Instead of jumping
on the next boat to Ko Tao or the overnight
train back to Bangkok, consider breaking your
journey on the beaches at Hat Thung Wua
Laen or Hat Sairi.

BUDGET
Farang Bar (☎ 0 7750 1003; farngbar@yahoo.com; 69/36
Th Tha Taphao; r 150-300B) Everything for the independent traveller is under one funky roof,
including car and motorbike rental, a pool
table and cheap beer. Rooms are a bit ramshackle but cheap and clean. Have a shower
before catching the boat for 20B.

THE THAI CANAL

Egypt has the Suez Canal, the Panama Canal joins the Atlantic and Pacific oceans, and a waterway linking the Gulf of Thailand with the Andaman Sea has been discussed for more than 350 years.

At its narrowest point just south of Chumphon, the Isthmus of Kra (the land bridge joining mainland Asia and the Malay Peninsula) is only 44km wide. In 1677 and 1793, Thai kings championed the idea, but the technology of the times was not up to scratch. When Burma (now Myanmar) became a British colony in 1863, the idea was floated again and Ferdinand de Lesseps, the successful engineer behind the Suez Canal visited the area in 1882. By 1897, Singapore was an important regional trading hub, and Thailand and Britain agreed to shelve any canal plans.

During the 20th century the idea surfaced again, but the preferred site was moved south to join Nakhon Si Thammarat and Trang. In 1985 a Japanese design planned to use more than 20 nuclear devices to complete the excavation work, and most recently China has planned a US$25 billion Thai canal to secure a regional strategic and commercial advantage. The United States is apparently watching very closely.

Chumphon Palace (☎ 0 7757 1715-22; 328/15 Th Pracha Uthit; r 450B; 🕸) The budget-priced rooms here masquerade as midrangers, and include TV and fridge. Its pretty-in-pink exterior is a bit girly, but business travellers seem to lap it up.

Sri Chumphon Hotel (☎ 0 7751 1280; Th Sala Daeng; r 260-450B; 🕸) The dark hallways feel like lights out at Alcatraz, but the promise of the contemporary exterior is fulfilled with airy and clean rooms with big windows.

Chumphon Gardens Hotel (☎ 0 7750 6888; 66/1Th Tha Taphao; r 490B; 🕸) This newly refurbished place with spacious rooms including cable TV is excellent value – as is the 60B breakfast. Just try not to lose your breakfast voucher like a certain guidebook author.

Suda Guest House (☎ 0 7750 4366; 8 Soi Bangkok Bank; r 200-500B; 🕸) Suda, the friendly English-speaking owner, proudly advertises 'Probably the best guesthouse in town' from an earlier edition of Lonely Planet. We're happy to report she's maintaining her impeccable standards at this cosy spot with wooden floors, and a few elegant touches you wouldn't expect for the price. It's very popular so phone ahead.

Morakot Hotel (☎ 0 7750 3629; fax 0 7757 0196; 102-112 Th Tawee Sinka; r 310-590B; 🕸) Despite a strange location behind a motorcycle dealership, the young, friendly staff make this a welcoming place. The rooms were undergoing a facelift when we visited, and the budget priced bathrooms should really come with a midrange price tag.

The View Resort (Hat Thung Wua Laen, r 500-700B; 🕸) The nicest of a few simple bungalow operations on Hat Thung Wua Laen, The View has a good selection of fan and air-con rooms and a good restaurant.

MIDRANGE

Had Sai Resort (☎ 0 7755 8028; www.hadsairesort.com; Hat Sairi; bungalows 800-1500B; 🕸) The green-and-white décor is a bit twee, but this spot at the quieter end of Hat Sairi is a good jumping off point for daytrips to nearby islands.

MT Resort (☎ 0 7755 8153; www.mtresort-chumphon .com; Hat Tummakam Noi; bungalows incl breakfast 1500B; 🕸) This friendly spot on a quiet beach beside the Lomprayah ferry pier is a good place to break your journey before or after Ko Tao. Free kayaks are provided to explore offshore islands and the mangroves of the nearby Mu Ko Chumphon National Park. There's no public transport and a taxi from Chumphon will cost around 300B. Call to organise transport.

Chumphon Cabana Resort & Diving Center (☎ 0 7756 0245; www.cabana.co.th; 1; Hat Thung Wua Laen; r 1350-1540B, bungalows 1650B; 🕸 🛈) This is Hat Thung Wua Laen's flashiest spot. It's big with 110 rooms and 18 bungalows, and also showing its age a little, but it's great for PADI dive tuition. Instructors are experienced. The beach is blissfully unsullied by deckchairs and motorised watersports, so there's no rampaging jet skis or banana boats. Breakfast is included. A regular shuttle bus (120B) runs to/from Chumphon.

Eating & Drinking

Chumphon's **night market** (Th Krom Luang Chumphon) is excellent, with a huge variety and good street light. Come for the delicious food and linger for good photographs. A day market runs between Th Pracha Uthit and Th Poramin Mankha.

Beside Farang Bar on Th Tha Taphao, there is an unnamed **food stall** which sets up nightly at 4pm. Look for the white plastic furniture. A couple of curries with rice costs 30B. On the corner of Th Tha Taphao and Th Poramin Mankha, a **coffee stall** selling Chinese doughnuts (10B) opens at dawn.

Fame Restaurant (☎ 0 7757 1077; 188/20 Th Sala Daeng; ⏰ breakfast, lunch & dinner) Also known as the Khao San Restaurant, (gee, I wonder who they're targeting), Fame has tasty sandwiches using freshly baked bread, and real-deal cheeses like mozzarella and gorgonzola. Mmmm. A travel agency is attached, so you might get the hard sell mid-sandwich. Get takeaway or say no if you're not interested.

Yota Vegetarian (Th Sala Daeng; ⏰ 7am-5pm) Located beside Fame, this hole-in-the-wall eatery has delicious self-serve vegetarian dishes. Add your own touch with overflowing plates of Vietnamese mint, holy basil and sliced cucumber.

Kaew Sukiyaki (☎ 0 7750 6366; Th Tha Taphao; dishes 40-110B; ⏰ breakfast, lunch & dinner) Sukiyaki noodles of all kinds (cooked at your table) are the speciality here, but the huge menu also has everything from sashimi to macaroni. There's a good bar that's popular with locals and travellers.

Papa 2000 (☎ 0 7751 1972; 188/181 Th Krom Luang Chumphon; dishes 70-150B; ⏰ lunch & dinner) The food (mainly seafood) is good, without being exceptional, but it's a great local hangout. Retro tunes are delivered nightly and after a few drinks you'll be singing along to songs you're ashamed to know the words to. Don't worry as everyone else will be doing the same.

Montana (☎ 7750 2864; 116 Th Suksamoe; ⏰ 6pm-1am) This bar has relatively authentic Western décor including stuffed animal heads (don't worry, they're fake), Budweiser neon and nightly gigs with the Big Boss Blues Band from 9.30pm. In the kitchen there are no concessions to the West with a zingy Thai menu.

Around the corner **Joe's Garden** (Th Krom Luang Chumphon; ⏰ 4pm-late) is good for a few quiet ones after the night market.

Getting There & Away

BOAT

The small island of Ko Tao (p616) can be reached by boat from one of three piers south of town.

The Lomprayah express catamaran (www.lomprayah.com; 550B, 1½ hours) leaves Tummakam pier (25km from town) at 7am and 1pm. Transfers between Chumphon and Tummakam pier are included in the ticket price. The Songsrem Express (450B, 2½ hours) leaves Tha Yang pier (7km from town) at 7am. Most travel agencies provide free transfers to this pier as well.

There is a midnight boat that leaves from Pak Nam pier (10km from town) arriving at Ko Tao at 6am (200B). If you fancy sleeping on the deck of a slow boat, this could be a memorable trip. However, if it's raining or the seas are rough, it could be a long and uncomfortable night. A shared taxi to Pak Nam pier costs 50B. Săwngthăew to Pak Nam pier or Tha Yang pier are 20B.

If you get stuck at Tha Yang pier and don't want to return to Chumphon, try the **Thayang Seaport Hotel** (☎ 0 7755 3052; r 200-300B; ☒).

BUS

The main bus terminal is on the main highway, 16km from Chumphon. To get there you can catch a local bus or săwngthăew (25B) from Th Nawaminruamjai.

Much more convenient is **Chokeanan Tour** (☎ 0 7751 1757; Th Pracha Uthit), in the centre of town, with six buses a day to Bangkok (air-con 373B, VIP 435B) or **Suwannatee Tour** (☎ 0 7750 4901), 700m southeast of the train station, with 12 departures per day (2nd class 290B, air-con 373B, VIP 435B). Most Bangkok buses stop in town so get off there and save yourself the săwngthăew fare from the bus station. Ask the driver or local passengers to tell you where to disembark.

Other destinations from Chumphon include Hua Hin (230B, five hours), Bang Saphan (100B, two hours), Prachuap Khiri Khan (160B, 3½ hours), Ranong (130B, three hours), Surat Thani (170B, 3½ hours), Krabi (270B, eight hours), Phuket (320B, eight hours) and Hat Yai (310B, 10 hours). Tickets can be bought at travel agencies.

TRAIN

There are frequent services to/from Bangkok (2nd class 292B to 382B, 3rd class 234B, 7½

hours). Overnight sleepers range from 440B to 770B.

Other destinations from Chumphon (all in 3rd-class berths) include Prachuap Khiri Khan (56B, three hours), Surat Thani (58B, three hours) and Hat Yai (110B, six to seven hours). Southbound rapid and express trains – the only trains with 1st and 2nd class – are less frequent and can be difficult to book out of Chumphon from November to February.

Getting Around

Săwngthăew and motorcycle taxis around town cost a flat 20B per trip. Săwngthăew to Hat Sairi and Hat Thung Wua Laen cost 30B.

Motorcycles can be rented at travel agencies and guesthouses for 200B to 250B per day. Car rental costs around 1500B per day from travel agencies or from Suda Guesthouse (p571).

Lower Southern Gulf

If you're shopping for penny-pinching paradises, Ko Samui, Ko Pha-Ngan and Ko Tao proffer fabulous bang for your baht. Bobbing like plump, green apples in the Gulf of Thailand, the Samui archipelago epitomises an exotic Eden fantasy for a fraction of the price. Calm, gin-clear seas, warm as a bath and sparkling a million shades of green, stretch on forever. Swaying palms and long stretches of porcelain sand give you the choice of basking until bronze, reading trashy romances or sipping juice from a coconut. When it comes to turning beach dreams into reality, these islands are master magicians.

Ko Samui is best for pampering, attracting a crowd of jetsetters, honeymooners, families and, unfortunately, men searching for love with Thai prostitutes. The villas here can come with private pools, restaurants are Michelin-star worthy and water sports are plentiful.

Citizens of the world wanting to twirl firesticks and dance till dawn will find their answer in Ko Pha-Ngan. Not only is the backpacker Mecca legendary for throwing the planet's best Full Moon parties, its ramshackle bungalows can go for less than three Singha's at the bar.

Divers enjoy mellow Ko Tao where open-water certification is cheap and the snorkelling is the best in the gulf.

For an entirely different angle, head south along the mainland's coast. Off the madly trodden 'banana pancake trail', the Deep South is the crucible of Buddhist and Muslim cultures. Unfortunately, at the time of research, continued violence made travel to this region dicey. See the travel warning on p636 for more.

HIGHLIGHTS

- Lazing the day away on Ko Samui's sun-kissed **Chaweng Beach** (p586), then indulging in an oceanside massage
- Experiencing the legendary Ko Pha-Ngan **Full Moon party** (p615)
- Sleeping in a boutique hotel on tranquil and gorgeous **Hat Bo Phut** (p586), Ko Samui's rising seashore star
- Tramping around lost waterfalls and million-year-old rainforests in impressive **Khao Sok National Park** (p582)
- Relishing the solitude on a picturesque beach along the coast of **Nakhon Si Thammarat Province** (p626)

★ Ko Pha-Ngan
★ Ko Samui

Khao Sok
★ National Park

Nakhon Si ★
Thammarat
Province

FAST FACTS

- **Best Time to Visit** November to April
- **Population** 5.2 million

History

Indian traders first visited the Gulf of Thailand around 600 BC and introduced Hinduism, which rapidly became the principal faith in the area. By 230 BC, when Chinese traders showed up on southern shores, large parts of Thailand had been incorporated into the kingdom of Funan, the first state in Southeast Asia. At its peak the state included large parts of Thailand, Laos, Cambodia and Vietnam and had active trade with agrarian communities along the Malay Peninsula, as far south as modern-day Pattani and Yala. Funan peaked as a nation under Jayavarman I, who ruled from AD 478 to 514, and then went into rapid decline.

Following this decline a series of city-states developed in the upper southern gulf. Tambralinga, which had its capital at Ligor on the site of present-day Nakhon Si Thammarat, was one of the most notable. It became part of the Srivijaya kingdom, a confederation of maritime states that ruled southern Thailand and Malaysia from the 7th to 13th centuries. The Srivijaya became hugely wealthy from tolls extracted from traffic through the Strait of Melaka. Tambralinga and nearby states adopted Buddhism in the 13th century, while those further south fell under the influence of Islam, creating a religious boundary that persists to this day in southern Thailand.

Islam came to southern Thailand from Malaysia during the reign of Sultan Iskandar, reaching Pattani by 1387 and spreading as far north as Songkhla. The Malay dialect of Yawi became the main language of the Deep South and Islam replaced Buddhism through the region.

Songkhla, Pattani, Narathiwat, Yala and the Andaman coast province of Satun were not officially a part of Thailand until 1902, when Rama V annexed them in an attempt to prevent Thai territory from being ceded to the British, who were then in control of Malaysia. Culturally quite different from the rest of the country, these provinces were comprehensively neglected by the central government over the next 50 years. Islamic traditions and the Yawi language were discouraged by the region's non-Malay administrators and systematic abuses of power contributed to growing separatist sentiments.

In 1957 Muslim resentment against the ruling Buddhist government reached boiling point and separatists initiated a guerrilla war with the aim of creating a separate Muslim state in southern Thailand. The main armed faction was the Pattani United Liberation Organisation (PULO), which launched a campaign of bombings and armed attacks throughout the 1970s and '80s. The movement began to decline in the 1990s, when Bangkok presented a peace deal consisting of greater cultural freedom and autonomy for the south and an amnesty for PULO members.

For a while the situation in the south subsided and it seemed the separatist movement had diffused, but after Thaksin Shinawatra became prime minister in 2001 PULO resumed its activities.

Violence in this region increased markedly in the month leading up to the 19 September coup, when Thaksin and his government were peacefully ousted (see p40). It was hoped with the end of Thaksin's regime and his hard-line approach with Muslim separatists, bloodshed would decrease. But at the end of 2006 the situation remained dire and the death toll had climbed above 1800. Most of the victims were innocent Thai bystanders, although a few foreigners were also killed. The increase in terrorist brutality in November 2006 led the government to close all schools in Yala, Pattani and Narathiwat Provinces indefinitely.

On 22 November Wan Kadir Che Wan, leader of an umbrella organisation for southern separatist groups, told Arab TV network Al Jazeera that an Al-Qaeda-linked terrorist network was helping local insurgents stage the attacks. It is believed that much of the violence is linked to younger separatists, but as yet no specific group has been identified.

For more on politics and safety in this region, see the travel warning on p636.

Climate

The best time to visit the Samui group of islands is during the hot and dry season, from February to late June. From July to October (southwest monsoon) it can rain on and off, and from October to January (northeast

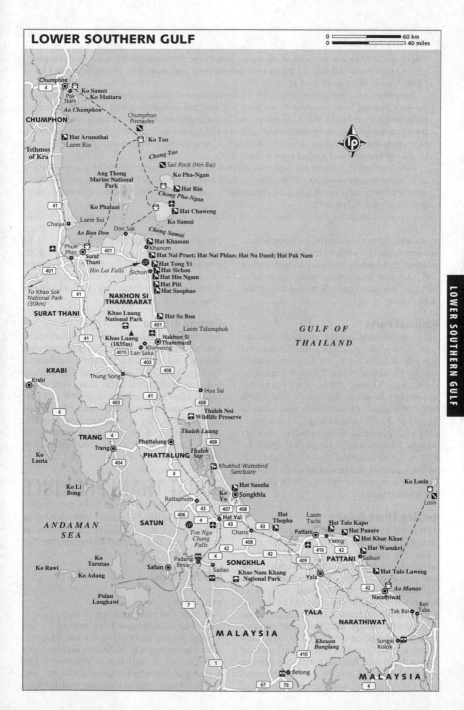

LOWER SOUTHERN GULF

0 ————————————— 60 km
0 ————————————— 40 miles

Chumphon
Pak Nam
Ko Samet
Ko Mattara
Ao Chumphon
CHUMPHON
Hat Arunothai
Laem Riu
Isthmus of Kra
Chumphon Pinnacles
Ko Tao
Chong Tao
Sail Rock (Hin Bai)
Ang Thong Marine National Park
Ko Pha-Ngan
Hat Rin
Chong Pha-Ngan
Ko Phaluai
Hat Chaweng
Chaiya
Laem Sui
Don Sak
Ko Samui
Chong Samui
Ao Ban Don
Hat Khanom
Khanom
Phun Phin
Surat Thani
Hat Nai Praet; Hat Nai Phlao; Hat Na Dand; Hat Pak Nam
Hin Lat Falls
Sichon
Hat Tong Yi
Hat Sichon
Hat Hin Ngam
Hat Piti
Hat Saophao
To Khao Sok National Park (30km)
SURAT THANI
NAKHON SI THAMMARAT
Khao Luang National Park
Hat Sa Bua
Laem Talumphuk
GULF OF THAILAND
Khao Luang (1835m)
Nakhon Si Thammarat
Lan Saka
Khiruong
KRABI
Krabi
Thung Song
Hua Sai
Thaleh Noi Wildlife Preserve
Thaleh Luang
TRANG
Trang
Phattalung
Thaleh Sap
PHATTALUNG
Ko Lanta
Khukhut Waterbird Sanctuary
Ko Li Bong
Rattaphum
Hat Samila
Ko Yo
Songkhla
Ko Losin
Losin
ANDAMAN SEA
SATUN
Ton Nga Chang Falls
Hat Yai
Chana
Hat Thepha
Laem Tachi
Hat Talo Kapo
Hat Panare
Pattani
Yaring
Hat Khae Khae
Ko Rawi
Ko Tarutao
Ko Adang
Satun
Padang Besar
Sadao
SONGKHLA
Khao Nam Khang National Park
Yala
PATTANI
Hat Wasukri
Saiburi
Hat Talo Laweng
Pulau Langkawi
Ao Manao
Narathiwat
Ban Taba
Tak Bai
YALA
NARATHIWAT
MALAYSIA
Kheuan Banglang
Sungai Kolok
Betong
MALAYSIA

ISLANDS FOR CHEAP

You're on Th Khao San in Bangkok, shopping around for combination tickets to Ko Pha-Ngan (or Ko Tao or Ko Samui) and the prices seem unbelievable: Bangkok to Ko Pha-Ngan straight for 350B? Sounds like a good deal, right?

Sometimes it is…and sometimes it's not. Some unscrupulous bus companies make their profits by, well, stealing from travellers. Ruses have included bus personnel going below and rifling through bags (while the bus is en route) and picking pockets while everyone is asleep (and the lights are off). Some travellers show up and don't get the bus they were expecting. Others have extra transport charges added to their fare. A very few have even reported being gassed to unconsciousness and robbed right in their seats.

We're not saying that this happens with cheap bus/boat tickets, but remember that no-one's in business to lose money. It's always best to have a chat with other travellers who've recently returned from where you're going before choosing a dirt-cheap company. Otherwise cough up the extra few hundred baht.

---

monsoon) there are sometimes strong winds. However, many travellers have reported fine weather (and fewer crowds) in September and October. November tends to receive some of the rain that affects the east coast of Malaysia.

National Parks

There are several notable parks in this region. Khao Sok (p582) is a thick rainforest glory land with plenty of accommodation and lazy rivers flowing through limestone cliffs. Ang Thong (p589), the setting for the perfect beach in the movie *The Beach* (although much of the movie was actually filmed on Ko Phi-Phi Leh; p713), is a stunning archipelago of 40 small picture-perfect islands. Khao Luang National Park (p630) is known for its beautiful mountain and forest walks, waterfalls and fruit orchards. It is also home to a variety of species, from clouded leopards to tigers.

Getting There & Away

Travelling to the lower southern gulf is fairly straightforward. It's extremely easy to hop on a bus or train and then catch a ferry to the islands from Bangkok, the Andaman coast and numerous other Thai destinations, as well as neighbouring Malaysia. Aeroplanes also ply the skies between Bangkok and Ko Samui. Bus and train travel from Bangkok is generally cheap, relatively efficient and mostly takes place overnight. Almost any travel agency can sell you a combination bus or train and boat ticket to the islands, which should get you to your destination with little effort on your part. Beware of the

cheapest tickets as they often prove to be scams. Pay a few more baht and you'll arrive with few hassles. For more information on travelling into and out of the region, see the individual destinations or check out the Transport chapter (p761).

Getting Around

An intricate public-transport network takes you almost everywhere. Numerous boats shuttle back and forth between Ko Samui, Ko Pha-Ngan, Ko Tao and Surat Thani, while buses and trains link Surat Thani with destinations further south. Săwngthăew and motorcycle taxis will take you around the islands for little cost. If you want to drive yourself, motorcycles can be rented for about 200B a day. Car rental, at about 1500B per day, is also an option.

SURAT THANI PROVINCE

Southern Thailand's largest province is home to Ko Samui, Ko Pha-Ngan and Ko Tao, as well as the stunning Ang Thong Marine National Park.

SURAT THANI

สุราษฎร์ธานี

pop 132,324

Not many travellers include a stop in Surat Thani on holiday itineraries, instead it's just a point you zip through on the way to somewhere better, namely Ko Samui, Ko Pha-Ngan and Ko Tao. If your bus or minivan is late arriving in Surat (a common problem), and you don't have time to make the shuttle trip to

the main pier – some 84km away – before the last ferry for Ko Samui heads out, you'll end up sleeping in Surat for the night. (Usually, an effective way of avoiding this dilemma is by grabbing the earliest bus from your original destination, lessening the possibility of not boarding the boat.)

There's a string of banks – one on every block for five blocks – along Th Na Meuang southwest of Th Chonkasem; all have ATMs and most offer foreign exchange. Check your email at **Miss Tuka Cappucino** (☎ 0 7721 2723; 442/307 Th Talat Mai; per hr 30B; ⏱ 9am-midnight; ✉), which also serves real coffee, sandwiches and smiles.

Be wary of Surat Thani travel agencies, many of which have a shady track record for innovative scams involving substandard buses, nonexistent bookings and surprise 'extra' fees. **Phantip Travel** (☎ 0 7727 2230; 442/24-5 Th Talat Mai) is one of the more reliable full-service travel agencies in town.

Sleeping

At some of Surat Thani's cheaper hotels, business consists largely of 'by the hour' trade. This doesn't make them any less suitable as regular hotels – it's just that there's likely to be more noise as guests arrive and depart with some frequency.

Ban Don Hotel (☎ 0 7727 2167; 268/2 Th Na Meuang; r 200-350B; ✉) Surat's best bet for budget beds is a relatively quiet place with squeaky-clean rooms. Those with air-con are a great deal. The

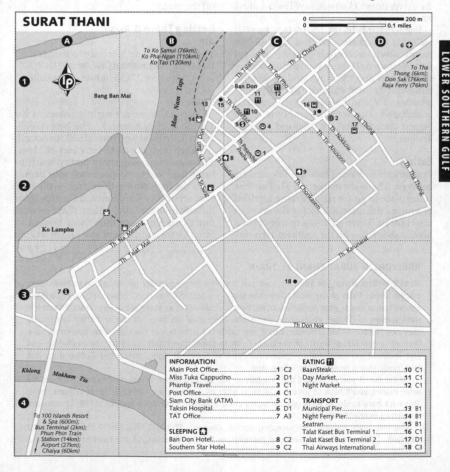

SURAT THANI

INFORMATION	
Main Post Office	1 C2
Miss Tuka Cappucino	2 D1
Phantip Travel	3 C1
Post Office	4 C1
Siam City Bank (ATM)	5 C1
Taksin Hospital	6 D1
TAT Office	7 A3

SLEEPING 🏠	
Ban Don Hotel	8 C2
Southern Star Hotel	9 C2

EATING 🍴	
BaanSteak	10 C1
Day Market	11 C1
Night Market	12 C1

TRANSPORT	
Municipal Pier	13 B1
Night Ferry Pier	14 B1
Seatran	15 B1
Talat Kaset Bus Terminal 1	16 C1
Talat Kaset Bus Terminal 2	17 D1
Thai Airways International	18 C3

LOWER SOUTHERN GULF

entrance is through a Chinese restaurant – quite a good one for inexpensive rice and noodle dishes, so you don't have to wander far after dark.

our pick **100 Islands Resort & Spa** (☎ 0 7720 1150; www.roikoh.com; 19/6 Muu 3, Bypass Rd; r 800B; 🕸 🖳) Set in a gorgeous teakwood palace of sorts, the public areas are fabulous – think lofty ceilings, leafy plants and even a trickling waterfall. The garden out back is lush with shady outdoor seating and even a lagoon pool. Rooms are large and very sleepable, even if they smell a bit musty and lack decorative charm. The on-site restaurant stays open late. The menu is for the most part Thai, which is quite good, although it lists a few Western dishes. Take a sǎwngthǎew there; if the driver doesn't know it, say 'Tesco-Lotus', which is opposite.

Southern Star Hotel (☎ 0 7721 6414-24; fax 0 7721 6427/8; 253 Th Chonkasem; r 800-2700B; 🕸) All 150 rooms, which are relatively elegant in a sort of Best Western or Holiday Inn fashion, feature sitting areas and the same kind of familiar home-on-the-road comfort (like carpeting, minibar, TV and hot showers). Breakfast is included. The hotel is also home to the biggest disco in southern Thailand, the Star Theque.

Eating

Restaurants in Surat Thani are few and far between. The night market on Th Ton Pho is the place to go for fried, steamed, grilled or sautéed delicacies – look for the crunchy insect titbits. There are also a couple of good noodle shops: one on the southwestern corner of Th Chonkasem and Th Na Meuang; and one on the southern side of Th Talat Mai.

During the day you can eat very well at the day market in and around the bus terminal. Although stalls serve most local staples, they specialise in tasty *khâo kài òp* (marinated baked chicken on rice).

BaanSteak (☎ 0 7728 5744; Th Witeetad; dishes 50-130B; ☯ breakfast, lunch & dinner) Ever craved a pork-flavoured steak? No, well how about chicken? This small restaurant serves reasonably priced steaks in marinades you never knew (and perhaps never wanted to know) existed. The food is tasty, but portions are on the small side. If you don't favour meat-flavoured meat, order pasta or sandwiches off the menu.

Getting There & Away

AIR
There is a twice daily service to Bangkok on **Thai Airways International** (THAI; ☎ 0 7727 2610; 3/27-28 Th Karunarat) for 2745B; it takes 70 minutes.

BOAT
From Surat there are nightly ferries to Ko Tao (500B, eight hours), Ko Pha-Ngan (200B, seven hours) and Ko Samui (150B, six hours). All leave from the night ferry pier at 11pm. These are cargo ships, not luxury boats, so bring food and water and watch your bags.

In the high season there are usually bus/boat services to Ko Samui and Ko Pha-Ngan directly from the train station. These services don't cost any more than those booked in Surat Thani and can save you a lot of waiting

---

ARRIVING IN SURAT THANI BY TRAIN

Most travellers arriving in Surat by train don't realise they'll actually be debarking in Phun Phin, a town about 14km to the west where the station is located. You don't necessarily have to leave Phun Phin to reach your Andaman coast beach destination as there are buses directly from the train station to Phuket, Phang-Nga and Krabi. They may not have air-con and their departures may not fit your arrival schedule, but if you catch the right bus at the right time you could save yourself a few hours' worth of back-and-forth-to-Surat travel time. Look for the big white wall just south of the train station – there's a Pepsi symbol and sign proclaiming 'Coffee shop and fast food'. This is where those buses stop.

Of course, if you've missed the last bus (or Ko Samui is your actual destination – it's on the *other* coast), you'll have to hike it into Surat after all, as there are more transport options there. This isn't hard to do, as local orange buses chug between Phun Phin and Surat (9B, 25 minutes, departing every 10 minutes).

The tiny town has just one sleeping option, **Queen** (☎ 0 7731 1003; 916/10-13 Th Mahasawat; r 200-400B; 🕸). Look for it around the corner from the train station, on the road to Surat Thani.

around. **Seatran** (☎ 0 7727 5060-2; www.seatranferry
.com; 45/1 Th Talat Luang), whose office is near the
night ferry pier, operates a bus/boat combination to Ko Samui (180B, three hours, departing hourly from 5.30am to 5.30pm) and a
combo to Ko Pha-Ngan (280B, four hours,
3.30pm). **Raja Ferry** (☎ 0 7747 1151; Don Sak) also
operates bus/boat combinations to Ko Tao
(500B, four hours, at least two daily), Ko Pha-
Ngan (280B, 3½ hours, hourly) and Ko Samui
(180B, 2½ hours, hourly). You can buy any of
these boat/bus tickets at **Phantip Travel** (☎ 0 7727
2230; 442/24-5 Th Talat Mai).

BUS & MINIVAN
Most long-distance public buses run from
the Talat Kaset bus terminals 1 and 2. Air-con
minivans leave from Talat Kaset 2; they tend

BUS & MINIVAN SERVICES FROM
SURAT THANI

Services to/from Surat include the following, although unless you specify which
class of minivan or bus you'd like, you will
likely be on the first one to leave. The prices
below are a guide only; prices are sometimes given arbitrarily.

Destination	Bus type	Fare	Duration
Bangkok	VIP	660B	10hr
	1st class	450B	10hr
	2nd class	370B	11hr
	ordinary	270B	11hr
Hat Yai	1st class	310B	4hr
	2nd class	210B	5hr
	minivan	190B	3½hr
Krabi	1st class	340B	3hr
	2nd class	170B	4hr
	minivan	160B	2hr
Nakhon Si	1st class	130B	2hr
Thammarat	2nd class	90B	2hr
	minivan	95B	2hr
Phang-Nga	1st class	200B	3hr
	2nd class	170B	4hr
	minivan	210B	3hr
Phuket	1st class	240B	5hr
	2nd class	200B	6hr
	minivan	220B	4hr
Ranong	1st class	150B	4hr
	2nd class	120B	5hr
	minivan	130B	3½hr
Trang	2nd class	120B	3hr
	minivan	130B	2½hr

to have more frequent departures than buses,
though they're not always cheaper.

There's a bus terminal 2km west of town
(on the way to Phun Phin train station), but
it's used less frequently than the two terminals
in town. To get into town from there, take an
orange local bus (15B), which comes by every
10 minutes. Just make sure it's going back into
town rather than out to Phun Phin (it does a
loop). Săwngthăew are another option into
town; they also cost 15B.

Air-conditioned buses and minibuses to
Khao Sok (two hours) can be booked through
travel agencies and should cost no more than
80B to 100B. You can also catch certain Phuket-
bound buses from the two bus terminals in
town and ask to be let off at Khao Sok – a
better option since some pushy minivan drivers
double as touts for Khao Sok hotels.

TRAIN
There are several trains from Bangkok
to Phun Phin. Fares for fan/air-con are:
227/297B in 3rd class, 368/478B in a 2nd-class
seat, 498/658B in an upper 2nd-class sleeper,
568/748B in a lower 2nd-class sleeper, and
1179B in 1st-class. The trip takes around 11 to
12 hours, so if you take an early evening train
from Bangkok you'll arrive in the morning.

The train station has a 24-hour left-luggage
room that charges 20B a day. The advance
ticket office is open from 6am to 6pm (with
an 11am to noon lunch break) daily.

At certain busy times it's difficult to book
long-distance trains out of Phun Phin; taking
the bus can be easier, especially if heading
south. Trains are often full, and it's a pain
to take a bus to the train station just to be
turned away – though you could buy a 'standing room only' 3rd-class ticket and see if a
seat becomes available. Many travel agencies
in town make advance train reservations, so
if you have a fixed return schedule you can
make an onward reservation before getting
on a boat to the islands.

Getting Around
Vans with air-con to/from the Surat Thani
airport cost around 70B per person. They'll
drop you off at your hotel. Purchase tickets
at travel agencies.

Orange buses run from Phun Phin train
station to Surat Thani every 10 minutes from
6am to 8pm (15B, 25 minutes). For this ride
taxis charge 200B. Other taxi rates are posted

just north of the train station (at the metal pedestrian bridge).

Taxis from Surat Thani to Don Sak pier cost around 500B; **Phantip Travel** (☎ 0 7727 2230; 442/24-5 Th Talat Mai) runs frequent vans for 60B per person, but this is included when you buy a ferry ticket.

Around town, sǎwngthǎew cost 20B, while sǎamláw (three-wheeled vehicles) charge about 150B to 200B per trip.

AROUND SURAT THANI

Chaiya

ไชยา

pop 12,500

Most folks visit tiny Chaiya, 60km north of Surat Thani, to partake in an excellent monthly meditation retreat. One of the oldest cities in Thailand, dating back to the Srivijaya Empire, it is a calm and friendly spot offering a glimpse into small-town life not often found in this region. Browse the vibrant day market and small stores or stop into one of the plentiful Chinese teashops.

Wat Suan Mokkhaphalaram (Wat Suanmok; ☎ 0 7743 1522) is a famous Buddhist meditation centre renowned for its monthly retreats. A very calm and nonshowy modern forest wat, it was founded by Ajahn Buddhadasa Bhikkhu, arguably Thailand's most famous monk.

Buddhadasa's philosophy was ecumenical in nature, comprising Zen, Taoist and Christian elements, as well as the traditional Theravada schemata. Today the hermitage is spread over 120 hectares of wooded hillside and features huts for up to 70 monks, a 'spiritual theatre' and a museum-library.

A MOST FAMOUS MONK

Born in Chaiya in 1906, Buddhadasa was ordained as a monk when he was 21 years old. He spent many years studying Pali scriptures before retiring to a forest for six years of solitary meditation. Returning to ecclesiastical society, he was made abbot of Wat Phra Boromathat, a high distinction, but conceived of Suanmok as an alternative to orthodox Thai temples. During Thailand's turbulent 1970s he was branded a communist because of his critiques of capitalism, which he saw as a catalyst for greed. Buddhadasa died in July 1993 after a long illness.

This latter building has bas-reliefs on the outer walls that are facsimiles of sculptures at Sanchi, Bharhut and Amaravati in India. The interior walls feature modern Buddhist painting – eclectic to say the least – executed by the resident monks.

The retreats cost 1500B for 10 days of teaching, food and accommodation. Just show up on the evening of the last day of any given month to sign up (retreats are always during the first 10 days of each month).

To get to Chaiya you can catch one of the frequent 3rd-class local trains from Phun Phin (10B, one hour) or a sǎwngthǎew (50B, 45 minutes) from Surat's Talat Kaset bus terminal 2. Alternatively, if you're heading to Surat Thani by train from Bangkok, you can get off at the small Chaiya train station. From Chaiya, Wat Suan Mokkhaphalaram is about 7km. Until late afternoon there are sǎwngthǎew from Chaiya's train station to Wat Suan Mokkhaphalaram for 15B per passenger. If those aren't running, you can hire a motorcycle taxi for 50B anywhere along Chaiya's main street

KHAO SOK NATIONAL PARK

อุทยานแห่งชาติเขาสก

You'll feel as if you've stepped into a *George of the Jungle* movie when you take the time to visit extraordinary **Khao Sok National Park** (☎ 0 7739 5025; www.khaosok.com; admission 200B). It offers a good break from dozing in the sand and encompasses 646 sq km of thick native rainforest and rugged mountains. Here, waterfalls tumble over soaring limestone cliffs and hiking trails follow rivers to an island-studded lake. Enjoy the solitude as your feet squish through deep brown dirt and the sun filters through gnarled and ancient trees. Keep an eye out for the plethora of wildlife the park shelters – wild elephants, leopards, serow, banteng, gaur, dusky langurs and, if you're really lucky, tigers and Malayan sun bears, not to mention more than 180 species of bird.

Established in 1980, Khao Sok lies in the western part of Surat Thani Province, off Rte 401 about a third of the way from Takua Pa to Surat Thani. According to Thom Henley, author of the highly informative *Waterfalls and Gibbon Calls*, the Khao Sok rainforest is in fact a remnant of a 160-million-year-old forest ecosystem that is much older and richer than the forests of the Amazon and central African regions.

Khao Sok is connected to two other national parks, Kaeng Krung and Phang-Nga, as well as the Khlong Saen and Khlong Nakha wildlife sanctuaries. Together, these reserves form the largest contiguous nature preserve – around 4000 sq km – on the Thai peninsula. A major watershed for the south, the park is filled with lianas, bamboo, ferns and rattan, including the *wăi tào phráw* (giant rattan) with a stem more than 10cm in diameter. A floral rarity in the park is the *Rafflesia kerrii* Meijer, known to the Thais as *bua phút* (wild lotus), one of the largest flowers in the world. Found only in Khao Sok and an adjacent wildlife sanctuary (different varieties of the same species are present in Malaysia and Indonesia), mature specimens can reach 80cm in diameter. The flower has no roots or leaves of its own; instead it lives parasitically inside the roots of the liana, a jungle vine. From October to December buds burst forth from the liana root and swell to football size. When the bud blooms in January and February it emits a potent stench resembling rotten meat, which attracts pollinating insects.

Orientation & Information

The park headquarters and visitors centre are 1.8km off Rte 401, close to the Km 109 marker.

The best time of year to visit Khao Sok is December to May, when trails are less slippery, river crossings easier and river-bank camping safer due to the lower risk of flash flooding. On the other hand, during the June to November wet season you're more likely to see Malayan and Asiatic black bears, civets, slow loris, wild boar, gaur, deer and wild elephants, and perhaps even tigers, along the trail network. During dry months the larger mammals tend to stay near the reservoir in areas without trails.

Leeches are quite common in certain areas of the park, so make sure to take the usual precautions – wear closed shoes when hiking and apply plenty of repellent (see also p778).

Sights & Activities

Various trails from the visitors centre lead to the waterfalls of **Sip-Et Chan** (4km), **Than Sawan** (9km) and **Than Kloy** (9km), among other destinations. A rough map showing trails and sights can be obtained at the visitors centre, or any guesthouse in the area will happily arrange guided tours and hikes.

An hour's drive east of the visitors centre is the vast **Chiaw Lan Lake**, 165km at its longest point. It was created in 1982 by the 95m-high, 700m-long, shale-clay dam of Ratchaprapha (Kheuan Ratchaprapha or Kheuan Chiaw Lan). Limestone outcrops protruding from the lake reach a height of 960m, over three times higher than the formations in the Phang-Nga area. A cave known as **Tham Nam Thalu** contains striking limestone and subterranean streams, while **Tham Si Ru** features four converging passageways used as a hideout by communist insurgents between 1975 and 1982. The caves can be reached on foot from the southwestern shore of the lake. You can rent boats from local fishermen to explore the coves, canals, caves and cul-de-sacs along the lakeshore.

The recommended, environmentally conscious Khao Sok Rainforest Resort runs a variety of tours in and around the park starting at 350B – visit its website for an entire list. This would be a good spot to try **elephant trekking**, as the company has a holistic reputation. There is only one elephant, 40-year-old Linda, but she takes guests on short, but invigorating, trail rides in rainforest near the park (800B). Afterwards help the mahout wash her down.

Spending a night on a **floating lodge** (per person 2500B) in the river is another popular option. The price includes three meals and optional activities like hiking. The best bit is stepping out of your bedroom and into the warm water.

Sleeping & Eating

Along the road from Hwy 401 to the visitors centre and down a dirt side road are several private, simple guesthouses and their restaurants. All have rooms with fans; there are no rooms with air-con in these parts. Prices rise in the high season from about November to February. The following accommodation options are on the highway.

Khao Sok Rainforest Resort (☎ 0 7739 5006; www.krabidir.com/khaosokrainforest; bungalows 400-600B) Blending easily into the jungle where they reside, these bungalows have some rather appalling coloured polyester bedspreads, but many resemble ultracool crosses between huts high on stilts and tree houses. The resort is right on the river, which is perfect for cooling down on hot afternoons. It's big on conservation and offers slide lecture

programmes and tips on low-impact hiking. It also runs rehabilitation and forest-restoration projects.

Bamboo House II (☎ 0 7739 5013; r 300-500B) On the other side of the river from the Rainforest Resort, Bamboo House II has bright, well-built concrete and brick bungalows with tiled floors and verandas.

The following are on the dirt side road leading off the highway.

Our Jungle House (☎ 0 9909 6814; www.losthorizons asia.com; bungalows 400-600B) In a brilliant location across from a limestone cliff, this Australian-run place is another ecotourism venture. It offers a variety of riverside bungalows and tree houses with simple décor and oil lights set on junglelike paths along a river. The restaurant serves Western and Thai food, including a nightly Thai buffet with lots of fresh fruit.

Art's Riverview Jungle Lodge (☎ 0 7739 5009; bungalows 350-550B) Art's has a pleasant range of simple, solid and airy rooms with mosquito nets. The more expensive ones have verandas and hammocks, and all are in a beautiful, tranquil and lush setting. You can watch wild macaques from the riverside restaurant.

Getting There & Around

Khao Sok is about 100km from Surat Thani. Transport to the park by minivan from Surat Thani (80B, one hour, at least twice daily) can be arranged through most travel agents in Surat, but be aware that some minivan companies work with specific bungalow outfitters and will try to convince you to stay at that place. Otherwise, from the Surat Thani area you can catch a bus going towards Takua Pa – you'll be getting off well before hitting this destination (tell the bus driver 'Khao Sok'). You can also come from the west coast by bus, but you'll have to go to Takua Pa first. Buses from Takua Pa to the park (25B, one hour, nine daily) drop you off on the highway, 1.8km from the visitors centre. If guesthouse touts don't meet you, you'll have to walk to your chosen guesthouse (from 50m to 2km).

To arrive at Chiaw Lan Lake, go east on Rte 401 from the visitors centre and take the turn-off between the Km 52 and Km 53 markers, at Ban Takum. It's another 14km to the lake. If you don't have your own wheels, you'll have to bus it to Ban Takum, then hope to hitch a ride to the lake. The best option without private transport would be to join a tour, which any guesthouse can arrange for 1000B (2000B to 2500B with an overnight stay).

KO SAMUI

เกาะสมุย
pop 39,000

In 1971 two tourists arrived on Thailand's third-largest island via a coconut boat from Bangkok and stumbled upon paradise – white-sand beaches with palms blowing in the wind and clear green seas sparkling in the sunlight. It was a picture-perfect background of lush green hills and brown roads interspersed with rough wooden structures.

More than 30 years after the first rough-hewn hut went up on Ko Samui, the island and the archipelago that includes 80 smaller islands, has become the Asian travel markets' most enigmatic chameleon – as attractive to fire-twirling backpackers as to flashpackers toting Louis Vuitton. On the map alongside places like Goa and Bali, Samui has polished its reputation as a hippy island paradise that remembers to provide the best of the creature comforts from home.

In the last five years, Samui has become as popular as Phuket, and at times as trendy – Bo Phut has become the romantic boutique darling of Samui, if not any beach destination in Thailand. But it's also managed to retain the legendary status among Asian backpackers that it has held for the past quarter century.

The Ko Samui of today is changing however, and the cheap fan bungalows are hard to come by this decade. Most accommodation is midrange and top-end options, beachfront properties boasting beautifully decorated rooms, crisp white sheets, lush gardens and lavish pools.

Despite its upmarket trend, Ko Samui still offers something for everyone. There are crowded beaches where young boys peddle coconuts and mangoes to oil-slicked, bikini-clad tourists, and jet skis churn up whitewash on clear seas. There are isolated spots where serenity and seclusion are the name of the game and you can escape the sun in simple air-con cottages and check out the latest MTV video. There are cheap food stalls and top-class restaurants, crowded modern shopping strips with Starbucks, McDonald's and store after store featuring knock-off Von Dutch T-shirts and Gucci sunglasses, and stretches of rough dirt roads and ramshackle huts. Western bars dish up burgers and chips and pump

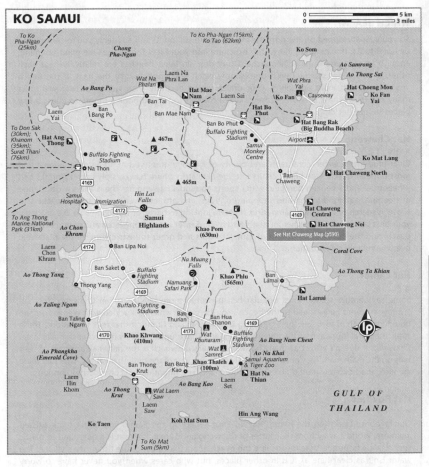

See Hat Chaweng Map (p590)

LOWER SOUTHERN GULF

classic tunes from giant speakers late into the night. Lady-boys and beautiful girls in strappy sandals and tight skirts seek out customers in side alleys, while drunken Westerners pound the keyboards at late-night internet cafés.

Some travellers plan to stay a week and three months later are still entranced. Others look around, say 'it's done', and move on. Popularity doesn't come without a price – more people means more traffic, more noise and more rubbish. Whatever your opinion, however, no one can deny Ko Samui is a beautiful place. You'll have to visit for yourself to decide whether it's worth staying.

The best time to visit is during the hot and dry season, from February to late June. From July to October it can be raining on and off, and from October to January there are sometimes heavy winds. On the other hand, many travellers have reported fine weather (and fewer crowds) in September and October. November tends to get some of the rain that also affects the east coast of Malaysia at this time. Prices soar from December to July, whatever the weather.

Orientation

Samui has plenty of beaches to choose from, with bungalows popping up around more small bays all the time. The most crowded beaches are Chaweng and Lamai, both on the eastern side of the island. Bo Phut is quickly developing into an upmarket boutique destination, with some of the coolest lodging

---

WHICH BEACH?

So you've just stepped off the ferry (or maybe you're still on it) and suddenly you're surrounded by hotel touts, thrusting brochure after brochure into your face. The choices are mind-boggling, enough to give you a major headache. Don't despair. Most beaches are relatively near each other; if you're not satisfied with one, simply catch a săwngthăew to the next. If the beach you've arrived at looks appealing, your driver should be more than willing to take you to as many resorts as you'd like to see (they make a commission if you book a room), so check a few places before deciding.

Hat Chaweng

หาดเฉวง

Clear blue-green water, coral reefs and plenty of nightlife greet you at Ko Samui's longest and most popular beach. Free beach chairs line the 6km strip where hawkers ply anklets, drinks and pineapples, and adrenalin-pumping water sports abound. Chaweng has the island's widest range of sleeping, eating, drinking and shopping options, and attracts everyone from backpackers to those in search of top-notch pampering. If you're looking to party, or travelling solo, it's probably your best bet for meeting other folks. It's also by far Samui's most congested and commercialised beach, and the constant onslaught of touts, vendors and other tourists can make the place feel overwhelmingly claustrophobic.

Hat Lamai

หาดละไม

Some say Samui's second most popular beach is even more beautiful than Chaweng. You can swim year-round here – head to the beach's southern end, which is studded with elegant granite boulders. South of town are the interesting Grandfather and Grandmother rock formations. These explicit natural formations attract plenty of giggling Thai tourists. Slightly quieter and smaller than Chaweng, it doesn't attract as many hawkers. Lamai's drawback is the rather sleazy strip of beer bars on the main road. They're not necessarily offensive, just of the girlie-bar variety. That said there are also good expat watering holes and high-quality restaurant and accommodation options.

Hat Bo Phut

หาดบ่อผุด

Our favourite beach on the island, Hat Bo Phut serves up the Samui you didn't think existed anymore. World's away from the clutter of Chaweng and Lamai, Bo Phut is a quiet and romantic spot. Mainly boutique-style resorts line the beach about 2km west of the fishermen's village. The water isn't as clear here as it is in other places, but who cares when you never have to worry about throbbing discos, crowds and in-your-face hawkers.

---

on the island. Other less crowded beaches include Mae Nam (popular with backpackers) and Hat Bang Rak (Big Buddha Beach) on the island's northern end near the pier. Ao Thong Yang, on the island's western side, is even more secluded. The southern part of the island now has many bungalows that are set in little out-of-the-way coves – it's worth seeking them out if you are looking for total isolation. On the northwestern side of Ko Samui you'll find Na Thon, which is the arrival point for express and night passenger ferries from the piers in Surat Thani. If you're not travelling on a combination ticket, you'll probably end up spending some time in Na Thon on your way in and/or out, waiting for the next ferry.

Car ferries from Don Sak and Khanom land at Thong Yang, about 10km south of Na Thon.

For descriptions of what these places have to offer, see the boxed text, above.

Information
BOOKSHOPS
Book Corner & Coffee World (Map p590; ☎ 0 7741 3908) Stock up on English novels and espresso at this bookstore, which has branches around Samui.

Bo Phut has been popular with the French for the last decade, but it's now attracting a growing number of tourists from all nationalities. The village is a charming strip of old Chinese shophouses, many of which have been converted into upmarket bars, restaurants, guesthouses and galleries. The place has a distinctly Mediterranean feel, but doesn't offer much for solo travellers or those seeking to party. From October to April the water may become too shallow for swimming.

Hat Mae Nam
หาดแม่น้ำ
Still a good choice for budget accommodation, with a long strip of cheap bungalows, it's also home to several five-star resorts. The beach is rather quiet and secluded, but the water isn't as stunning as at Chaweng and can become too shallow for swimming from October to April. The beach in front of Wat Na Phalan is undeveloped; please avoid going topless here.

Hat Bang Rak
หาดพระใหญ่
Very close to the airport and the main pier Hat Bang Rak (Big Buddha Beach) isn't even close to being a runner-up for Samui's most pretty beach. However, it is convenient if you've got an early plane to catch or are seeking out two of the islands better budget bets - both located on this beach.

Ao Bang Po
อ่าวบางปอ
This secluded, quiet bay has fair snorkelling and swimming, and two new-age resorts featuring everything from meditation to tarot card reading (see p593).

Ao Thong Sai & Hat Choeng Mon
อ่าวท้องทราย/หาดเชิงมน
Clean and quiet, this large cove and beach is recommended for families or those who don't need nightlife and a plethora of restaurants (easily found at nearby Hat Chaweng) to survive.

Na Thon
หน้าทอน
The beach is smelly and otherwise pierlike, and there's really no reason to stay here. The town is mostly just a ferry departure point. If you want to look around it sports a few old teak Chinese shophouses, cafés and a colourful day market.

Saai Bookshop (Map p590; ☎ 0 7741 3847) Friendly small bookstore selling new and used books, and magazines in several languages.

EMERGENCY
Tourist police (Map p588; ☎ emergency 1155, non-emergency 0 7742 1281) Located at the southern end of Na Thon.

IMMIGRATION OFFICES
Ko Samui Immigration office (Map p588; ☎ 0 7742 1069; 🕑 8.30am-noon & 1-4.30pm Mon-Fri, closed public holidays) Extends tourist visas by 30 days (500B). It's about 2km south of Na Thon.

INTERNET ACCESS
There are places all over the island offering internet access, even at the less popular beaches. The going rate is between 1B and 2B per minute.

INTERNET RESOURCES
The following websites cover dive centres, accommodation and tours, as well as having timetables for Bangkok Airways, ferries, trains and VIP buses.
Ko Samui Thailand (www.sawadee.com)
Tourism Association of Ko Samui (www.samuitourism.com)

MEDIA

A locally produced, tourist-oriented newspaper with articles in German, English and Thai, *Samui Welcome* is published monthly (free). *What's on Samui*, *Samui Guide* and the pocket-sized *Accommodation Samui* are also free and have listings of hotels, restaurants and suggestions of things to do – buried beneath a heap of ads.

MEDICAL SERVICES

There are several hospitals on the island and nursing-care units for stubbed toes, scraped knees, pregnancy tests and earaches.

Hyperbaric chamber (Map p585; ☎ 0 7742 7427) The only hyperbaric chamber on the island is in Hat Bang Rak (Big Buddha Beach).

Samui International Hospital (Map p585; ☎ 0 7723 0781, 0 7742 2272; www.sih.co.th) For any medical or dental problem. Emergency ambulance service is available 24 hours and credit cards are accepted. Opposite the Muang Kulaypan Hotel.

MONEY

Changing money isn't a problem in Na Thon, Chaweng or Lamai, where several banks (with ATMs) or exchange booths offer daily exchange services. See the maps for some locations.

POST

There are privately run post-office branches on the island. Many bungalow operations also sell stamps and can mail letters, but they often charge a commission. If you're heading to the mainland, it's probably a good idea to wait until you get there to post something – island mail doesn't have an outstanding reputation.

Main post office (Map p588; ☺ 8.30am-4.30pm Mon-Fri, 9am-noon Sat) In Na Thon.

TELEPHONE

Many private telephone offices on the island will make a connection for a surcharge above the Telephone Organisation of Thailand (TOT) or Communications Authority of Thailand (CAT) rates.

CAT (Map p588; ☺ 7am-10pm) Provides international telephone service at the main post office.

TOURIST INFORMATION

TAT (Map p588; ☎ 0 7742 0504; ☺ 8.30am-4.30pm) Friendly and helpful, it has scores of brochures and maps.

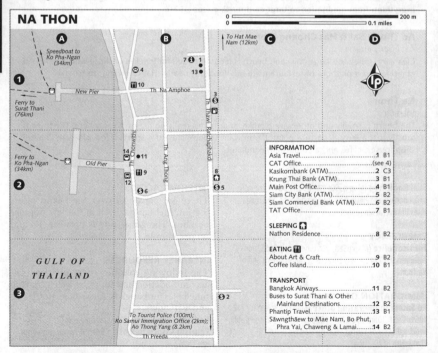

NA THON

0 ————————————————— 200 m
0 ————————————————— 0.1 miles

To Hat Mae Nam (12km)

Speedboat to Ko Pha-Ngan (34km)

New Pier

Ferry to Surat Thani (76km)

Th Na Amphoe

Ferry to Ko Pha-Ngan (34km)

Old Pier

Th Chonwithi

Th Ang Thong

Th Thawi Ratchaphakdi

GULF OF THAILAND

To Tourist Police (100m); Ko Samui Immigration Office (2km); Ao Thong Yang (8.2km)

Th Preeda

INFORMATION	
Asia Travel...1	B1
CAT Office...............................(see 4)	
Kasikornbank (ATM)..........................2	C3
Krung Thai Bank (ATM)....................3	B1
Main Post Office...............................4	B1
Siam City Bank (ATM)........................5	B2
Siam Commercial Bank (ATM)..........6	B2
TAT Office...7	B1

SLEEPING	
Nathon Residence...............................8	B2

EATING	
About Art & Craft................................9	B2
Coffee Island.....................................10	B1

TRANSPORT	
Bangkok Airways.............................11	B2
Buses to Surat Thani & Other Mainland Destinations.................12	B2
Phantip Travel..................................13	B1
Sǎwngthǎew to Mae Nam, Bo Phut, Phra Yai, Chaweng & Lamai........14	B2

TRAVEL AGENCIES

Asia Travel (Map p588; ☎ 0 7723 6120) Deals especially with airline tickets.

Travel Solutions (Map p590; ☎ 0 7723 0203; ttsolutions@ hotmail.com) Efficient and reliable, it's on Chaweng beach. It can help with international travel plans, transport bookings, accommodation and visa arrangements. Languages spoken include English, Spanish, French and Thai.

Dangers & Annoyances

Several travellers have written to warn others to take care when making train, bus and air bookings. These sometimes aren't made at all, the bus turns out to be far inferior to the one expected or other hassles develop. We too have had trouble with buses/boat combos, and our last research trip included a harrowing minibus ride from Phuket to Surat Thani that left us biting our nails and screaming for our money back. Unfortunately there is little you can do to avoid this, except make sure to ask as many questions as possible when booking tickets. Air scams include travel agents telling customers that economy class on planes is fully booked and only business class is available; the agent then sells the customer an air ticket – at business-class prices – that turns out to be economy class.

As on Phuket, the rate of fatalities on Samui from road accidents is quite high. This is due mainly to the large number of tourists who rent motorcycles only to find out that Samui's winding roads, stray dogs and coconut trucks can be lethal to those who have never dealt with them. If you feel you must rent a motorcycle, protect yourself by wearing a helmet, shoes and appropriate clothing when driving.

Theft isn't unknown on the island. If you're staying in a beach bungalow, consider depositing your valuables with the management while off on excursions around the island or swimming at the beach.

Sights

Most people come to Samui to laze on the beaches, snorkel in its azure water or churn life up with a whirl on the jet ski. There are a few options if you tire of bronzing and massages on the beach (sounds terrible…).

ANG THONG MARINE NATIONAL PARK

อุทยานแห่งชาติหมู่เกาะอ่างทอง

Easily the most popular activity in Samui is a boat trip around this picture-perfect archi-

pelago made up of around 40 small islands. Sheer limestone cliffs, white-sand beaches, hidden lagoons and dense vegetation all add to the cosmetic beauty. The park lies 31km northwest of Ko Samui and encompasses 18 sq km of islands, plus 84 sq km of marine environments.

Any travel agency can book a day trip to Ang Thong, and tours usually include pick-up from your hotel. Travel agencies simply act as booking agents for the tour companies, which all offer nearly identical trips in terms of quality and itineraries. Lunch and snorkelling are included, along with a climb to the top of a 240m hill to view the whole island group; some tours visit **Tham Bua Bok**, a cavern containing lotus-shaped cave formations, and other tours offer sea kayaking. There's officially a 200B admission fee for foreigners, though it should be included in your tour. Bring shoes with good traction, a hat, plenty of sunscreen and drinking water. Tours cost about 1700B. Overnight tours are also available. At the **park headquarters** (☎ 0 7728 6025), on Ko Wat Ta Lap, there are bungalows, but you may not be able to reserve them unless you go with a tour.

MUMMIFIED MONK

Samui's strangest attraction by far is the ghostly mummified monk at Wat Khunaram, south of Rte 4169 between Ban Thurian and Ban Hua Thanon. The monk, Luang Phaw Daeng, has been dead over two decades but his corpse is preserved sitting in a meditative pose and sporting a pair of sunglasses.

Activities

Water sports are big on Hat Chaweng; you can hire sailboards, go diving, sail a catamaran, charter a junk and so on. Parasailing costs around 450B. Jet skis cost 700B or 800B per 20 minutes, depending if you want a one- or two-person boat.

DIVING & SNORKELLING

The best diving is in the Ko Tao area and plenty of dive trips from Samui end up there. Better-known shops are often good, but smaller shops may try harder – and some go out with smaller groups as well. The hyperbaric chamber on the island is at Hat Bang Rak.

Beach dives cost as little as 800B per dive, but then again there's very little to see. Dives from boats range from 3500B to 5000B, and

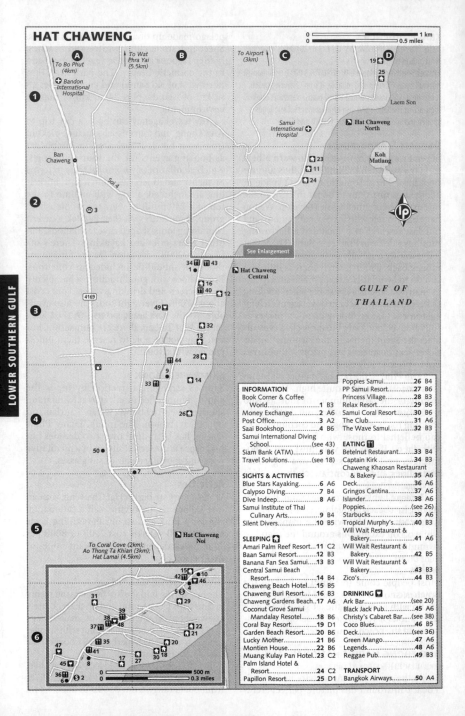

HAT CHAWENG

0 _____ 1 km
0 _____ 0.5 miles

INFORMATION
Book Corner & Coffee
  World..........................1 B3
Money Exchange.............2 A6
Post Office....................3 A2
Saai Bookshop................4 B6
Samui International Diving
  School.....................(see 43)
Siam Bank (ATM)............5 B6
Travel Solutions..........(see 18)

SIGHTS & ACTIVITIES
Blue Stars Kayaking..........6 A6
Calypso Diving................7 B4
Dive Indeep...................8 A6
Samui Institute of Thai
  Culinary Arts..............9 B4
Silent Divers.................10 B5

SLEEPING
Amari Palm Reef Resort...11 C2
Baan Samui Resort..........12 B3
Banana Fan Sea Samui......13 B3
Central Samui Beach
  Resort.....................14 B4
Chaweng Beach Hotel.....15 B5
Chaweng Buri Resort.......16 B3
Chaweng Gardens Beach..17 A6
Coconut Grove Samui
  Mandalay Resotel........18 B6
Coral Bay Resort.............19 D1
Garden Beach Resort........20 B6
Lucky Mother.................21 B6
Montien House...............22 B6
Muang Kulay Pan Hotel...23 C2
Palm Island Hotel &
  Resort.....................24 C2
Papillon Resort..............25 D1

Poppies Samui...............26 B4
PP Samui Resort..............27 B6
Princess Village..............28 B3
Relax Resort..................29 B6
Samui Coral Resort..........30 B6
The Club.....................31 A6
The Wave Samui.............32 B3

EATING
Betelnut Restaurant..........33 B4
Captain Kirk 34 B3
Chaweng Khaosan Restaurant
  & Bakery 35 A6
Deck...........................36 A6
Gringos Cantina..............37 A6
Islander.......................38 A6
Poppies.....................(see 26)
Starbucks.....................39 A6
Tropical Murphy's...........40 B3
Will Wait Restaurant &
  Bakery.....................41 A6
Will Wait Restaurant &
  Bakery.....................42 B5
Will Wait Restaurant &
  Bakery.....................43 B3
Zico's.........................44 B3

DRINKING
Ark Bar.....................(see 20)
Black Jack Pub...............45 A6
Christy's Cabaret Bar....(see 38)
Coco Blues....................46 B5
Deck........................(see 36)
Green Mango.................47 A6
Legends.......................48 A6
Reggae Pub...................49 B3

TRANSPORT
Bangkok Airways............50 A4

To Bo Phut (4km)
To Wat Phra Yai (5.5km)
To Airport (3km)
Bandon International Hospital
Laem Son
Hat Chaweng North
Koh Matlang
Samui International Hospital
Ban Chaweng
Soi 4
GULF OF THAILAND
Hat Chaweng Central
4169
Hat Chaweng Noi
To Coral Cove (2km);
Ao Thong Ta Khian (3km);
Hat Lamai (4.5km)
See Enlargement
500 m
0.3 miles

LOWER SOUTHERN GULF

CARING FOR FIDO

If you've been on the islands for a while, you can't help but notice the roving packs of dogs. They wander from restaurant to restaurant looking for scraps, chill next to you on the beach or start nightly street brawls with other mutts. As is the case throughout Thailand (especially on the islands), an influx of animal-loving tourists and the resulting excess of food scraps have led to an abundance of stray dogs on Ko Samui and Ko Pha-Ngan. The stress of living in an overpopulated environment, however, leads to disease and injuries, which fester easily in the tropical climate and can end up threatening humans. Thais have been trying to keep the dog population under control through annual poisoning, which is administered by blowing poison-tipped darts through bamboo poles – not a very nice way for the poor animals to die.

The dog rescue centre, appropriately called **Dog Rescue Centre Samui** (☎ 0 1893 9443; www .samuidog.org), is the original organisation and has played an integral role in keeping the island's dog population down through an aggressive spaying and neutering programme. The centre has also vaccinated thousands of dogs against rabies, and Samui is now proud to claim its canine friends are 100% rabies free! The rescue centre is always in need of donations. If you want to adopt one of the island strays, this can also be arranged – one European woman had arranged to adopt and transport more than one older dog across a few oceans when we were in town. The Wave Samui (p596) in Chaweng is super supportive of the dog rescue; ask owners Dave or Pete for the low-down.

Thanks to the sponsorship of the Dog Rescue Centre Samui and the Animals Asia Foundation, **Pha-Ngan Animal Care** (PAC; ☎ 0 9875 7513; www.pacthailand.org) was opened by veterinary surgeon Shevaun Gallwey in September 2001. Since then almost 20% of the island's female dogs have been sterilised. Perhaps most importantly, the organisation has managed to convince the island government to refrain from the annual stray-dog executions as long as it continues to perform sterilisation procedures. Nurses who can stay and work here for at least three months are offered free accommodation and a basic wage.

two- to four-day certification courses cost from 8600B to 14,000B. An overnight dive trip to Ko Tao, including food and accommodation, can be done for about 4000B to 5000B.

The highest concentration of dive shops is at Hat Chaweng. We recommend the following centres:

Calypso Diving (Map p590; ☎ 0 7742 2437; www.calypso -diving.com; Hat Chaweng)

Dive Indeep (Map p590; ☎ 0 7723 0155; www.divein deep.com; Hat Chaweng)

Samui International Diving School Hat Chaweng (SIDS; Map p590; ☎ 0 7724 2386; www.planet-tec.net); Hat Lamai (☎ 0 7723 2069; www.planet-tec.net)

Silent Divers (Map p590; ☎ 0 7742 2729/30; www .silentdivers.com; Hat Chaweng)

KAYAKING

Any travel agency worth its salt should be able to book a sea-kayak tour.

Blue Stars Kayaking (Map p590; ☎ 0 7741 3231; www .gallerylafayette.com/bluestars; Hat Chaweng) offers guided sea-kayak trips in Ang Thong National Marine Park (1990B) as well as two-day overnight tours to a spectacular bay (4750B). There are free pick-ups and drop-offs from your hotel.

MASSAGES, SPAS & YOGA

When it comes to pampering Samui is in a spa renaissance. With around 25 classy spas, offering everything from private treatment suites with lotus-filled Jacuzzis built for two to salt-water floatation tanks, relaxation is unavoidable. Nearly all the posh hotels have spas attached, and most accept clients even if they are not staying at the hotel. Treatments and massages start at around 800B.

The **Spa Samui Village** (☎ 0 7723 0976; www .spasamui.com) was the island's original health destination, and is still known for its original 'clean me out' fasting programme.

For a unique and truly special experience, try **Tamarind Springs** (p598). This gorgeous place features a dip pool tucked against limestone boulders, in a natural setting filled with waterfalls, canals and wooden walkways. Tamarind offers plenty of packages designed especially for couples.

The **Health Oasis Resort** (p593) on the island's quiet north shore, offers one- to eight-day courses and certification in Thai and Swedish massage, aromatherapy, reiki, meditation, yoga and 'life training' for 6000B to 30,000B.

LOWER SOUTHERN GULF

The length and tuition of all courses can be adjusted to suit the individual. The place also features day rejuvenation packages, including deep colon cleansing, and Thai massage for mental and physical wellbeing.

For up-to-date info on the latest hot spas check out the free *Samui Health & Spa Guide* (released four times a year) or visit www.siam spaguide.com.

At the other end of the spectrum, you can get a more informal massage on a mattress on a raised platform overlooking the action on Hat Chaweng (among other spots). These only cost around 250B to 300B for one hour, and if you get the right therapist a Thai massage can be just as beneficial as the fancy spas. There are also plenty of beauty shops offering massage for 250B per hour, along with manicures and pedicures (100B for both).

Many spas incorporate yoga into regimens – the ancient art of stretching and toning is an integral part of Thai massage. For straight up yoga, head to the Bo Phut Fisherman's Village and check out **Absolute Yoga** (☎ 0 7743 0290; www .absoluteyogasamui.com), which offers hot, flow and yin yoga classes. There's no need to reserve in advance, just show up. Check the website for prices.

COOKING

It seems as if everyone wants to learn how to cook Thai cuisine these days, and Samui offers a fine place to try your hand at cooking local specialities.

Samui Institute of Thai Culinary Arts (SITCA; Map p590; ☎ 0 7741 3434; www.sitca.net; 46/6 Soi Colibri, Hat Chaweng) offers daily Thai-cooking classes, as well as courses in the aristocratic Thai art of carving fruits and vegetables into intricate floral designs. Quick lunchtime classes cost 1600B (three courses), while dinner classes are 2000B (four courses). Of course, you get to eat your work, and even invite a friend along for the meal. DVDs with Thai-cooking instruction are also available so you can practise at home.

Sleeping

There is a mind-boggling array of sleeping options on Ko Samui, and the following list is by no means exhaustive. Budget places offering simple bungalows with thatched roofs and walls of local materials are nearly nonexistent now on Hat Chaweng, which is pretty much the domain of midrange and top-end joints. Hat Lamai is also changing. Most midrange places do, however, offer the option of renting smaller fan rooms for under 700B.

Prices on the island fluctuate depending on the time of year and demand. At peak times operators have been known to triple their prices, but then you can find some good deals when the going is slow.

In this section, we start with Na Thon, the point of entry for most travellers (although far from the nicest place on the island) and then work our way clockwise around Ko Samui.

WHAT TO EXPECT IN KO SAMUI

We list high-season rack rates for midrange and top-end hotels. Search online booking agencies or individual hotel websites for lower promotional rates.

The difference between budget and midrange places on Samui is whether the place has a fan or air-con. Most operations in these price brackets offer both.

- Budget (under 800B) – Don't expect much in the low end of this price range. From 100B to 300B, you'll get a bed and four walls. You'll share a bathroom (no hot water) and a rickety fan will chase the hot air around the room. Once you step up to the 400B range, you should start to expect air-con, private bathroom with hot-water shower and walls thick enough to block out noise.

- Midrange (800B to 1200B) – Sleeping options in this bracket are larger than the budget huts and usually come with real beds, nicer furnishings and less claustrophobic bathrooms. Nearly all have air-con and many have on-site swimming pools, spas and restaurants.

- Top end (over 1200B) – Places in this price range come with all the mod cons and will generally have an upmarket restaurant, bar, and some sort of luxury-oriented spa and Thai-massage facility on site. You can expect room service, big swimming pools, tasteful furnishings and international standards.

To get an idea about which beach offers what, see p586.

NA THON

The island's main settlement is dominated by the ferry pier and is not much to look at. There's really no reason to stay here, but if for some reason you feel compelled, try the following.

Nathon Residence (Map p588; ☎ 0 7723 6058; Th Thawi Ratchaphakdi; r 500B; 🗙) Most places in this town are on the drab side, but this is your best bet. There are big, sparkling tiled rooms here as well as a downstairs café and great staff. The rooms all come with satellite TV.

AO BANG PO

This bay, with its main town of Ban Tai, has fair snorkelling and swimming. There's a small enclave of charming and isolated budget places resisting the urge to upgrade – though their prices have been creeping up.

Health Oasis Resort (☎ 0 7742 0124; www.health oasisresort.com; bungalows 675-4000B; 🗙) If the term 'Vortex Astrology' scares you, you should probably give this place a miss. New Age is all the rage here and this resort is geared towards cleansing (both of the physical and mental variety). There are bright, modern bungalows as well as plenty of greenery and sunshine. There's also a vegetarian restaurant on site (of course).

Also recommended:

Moon (☎ 0 7744 7129; bungalows 250-800B)
Ban Tai (☎ 0 9874 7357; bungalows 350-450B)
Sunbeam (☎ 0 7742 0600; bungalows 500-800B)

HAT MAE NAM

When it comes to Samui standards, Hat Mae Nam's accommodation is still refreshingly cheap and backpacker-esque, although it doesn't occupy the best beach in town and spreads inland along sand tracks. There are a couple of bars and restaurants here that should keep you from having to stray too far.

Harry's (☎ 0 7742 5447; www.harrys-samui.com; bungalows 800-1200B; 🗙 🖳) If you ever wanted to hang out in a miniature teak-wooden palace, then this is your chance. In the traditional Thai lobby polished teak abounds, pointed roofs reach for the sky and the dining area is punctuated by massive twisting trees providing shade. The basic concrete bungalows lie scattered around a verdant garden.

Sea Fan (☎ 0 7742 5204; www.seafanresort.com; r 2400-3300B; 🗙 🖳) Offering huge luxury thatch and wood bungalows connected by wooden walkways, with colourful flora abounding, this is a fine place to stay. The beautiful beachside pool has a small kid's area.

Paradise Beach Resort (☎ 0 7724 7727-32; www .samuiparadisebeach.com; r 5500-12,000B; 🗙 🖳) A classy, child-friendly place, Paradise Beach Resort features Thai-style bungalows and rooms with private balconies in a tropical garden setting. There are two swimming pools, a Jacuzzi, a children's playground, an on-site dive centre, all sorts of water sports and a seaside restaurant.

HAT BO PHUT

Now is the time to visit Bo Phut, a lovely beach with fabulous boutique hotels that, unlike most bungalows in Thailand, actually differ from each other. More relaxed and isolated than Samui's east coast beaches, look for accommodation off the main road and west of the central village area, and on the inland side of the road/village, just a few steps from the beach. Most resorts have snazzy restaurants attached, or you can wander down to the charming fisherman's village, home to a range of wonderful old Chinese shophouses perfect for a cocktail or a romantic dinner. You can rent kayaks and kite-boards on the beach, or grab a massage on a platform overlooking the sea.

Chalet Villa (☎ 08 9591 7340; bungalows 400-600B) The yard here is swampy looking and littered with hulks of old motorboats, but the bungalows are cheap and popular. One traveller described the place as 'primitive but plenty comfortable'. The most expensive huts have TV but no air-con. Many have porches facing the ocean.

Free House (☎ 0 7742 7516; bungalows 400-1200B; 🗙) Yes, the fan rooms are the size of a shoebox, but they have windows on two sides, which make them far from claustrophobic and some of the best in their class on Samui. The floors are made from simple wood planks and the bed is just a mattress on a raised platform covered by a mozzie net. Considering the price the baths are positively spacious, with no rot and a shower separated from the toilet. The air-con rooms are biggish and beds have real comforters, but otherwise are nothing special. We liked the loungy pillows and book-recycle area at the restaurant serving

LOWER SOUTHERN GULF

lots of curries. Look for it to the east of the Samui Palm Beach.

Eden (☎ 0 7742 7645; www.sawadee.com/samui/eden; bungalows 800-1600B; ❌ 🗨) Eden is an exceptional find. Another boutique-style place, it has 12 spacious and creative rooms, and a gorgeous garden with a pool. Reconfirm reservations before you arrive.

Sandy Resort (☎ 0 7742 3534; fax 0 7742 5325; bungalows 800-2600B; ❌ 🗨 🖳) The old adage, you get what you pay for is true at Sandy's. The fan bungalows have the saggiest mattresses, while the most expensive places are quite roomy with nicer baths, beds and sheets. Even the smallest bungalows are far from crummy, however, and come with nice touches like art on the walls. The public areas are well maintained and the place is popular even in low season.

World Resort (☎ 0 7742 5355; www.samuiworldresort .com; bungalows incl breakfast 1500-3500B; ❌ 🗨 🖳) World Resort is a step down in luxury, but we found it quite peaceful. The bungalows are old-style Samui, with rattan-woven walls, thick mattresses and nonscratchy sheets. They are very spacious and clean, although bathrooms could use an upgrade and the walls tend to be a tad thin. The swimming pool is lovely and you can partake in a massage overlooking the sea. A Philippine band plays twice a week at the on-site restaurant. The selection of bungalows is huge – the ones closest to the beach are best.

Zazen (☎ 0 7742 5085; www.samuizazen.com; r from 3500B; ❌ 🗨) Off the main road and west of the village area, Zazen is an absolute stunner, possibly our favourite boutique hotel in Thailand and still very affordable. The 28 artistically decorated, multilevel abodes are trimmed in wood and beautiful painted. Public spaces feature fabulous attention to detail. We loved the open-air spa in the middle of a lagoon, where massages are given on beds of silk. Other highlights include a billiard-table pavilion, swimming pool and a restaurant known for excellently presented world cuisine. The only downer was suspicious, and at times surly, staff.

Samui Palm Beach Resort (☎ 0 7742 5494; r from 6500-24,000B; ❌ 🖳 🗨) This swanky, Mediterranean-style place has white villas on manicured grounds, multiple swimming pools, a restaurant, a bar with cabaret shows, and an icy-cold lounge where you can check your email or watch a movie on the flatscreen TV. Abodes are luxurious and have a maritime theme. It's popular with Europeans.

HAT BANG RAK

Otherwise known as Big Buddha Beach, this area around one of Samui's main ferry piers is rather ugly and the only reason to sleep here is for two particularly good budget resorts. The moniker comes from the huge golden Buddha that acts as overlord from the small nearby island of Ko Fan, which is connected to Samui by a causeway.

Shambala (☎ 0 7742 5330; www.samui-shambala .com; bungalows 500-1000B) A laid-back, English-run place, Shambala has plenty of communal cushion seating and a hip beachside wooden sundeck. The grounds are spacious, the bungalows are bright and roomy, and the spiritual ambience has a slightly hippy feel to it.

Secret Garden Bungalows (☎ 0 7724 5255; www .secretgarden.co.th; bungalows 500-1800B; ❌) Another English-run establishment, Secret Garden has a great big restaurant and bar as well as lovely A-frame bungalows. The cheaper fan bungalows are as nicely finished in wood trimmings as the much pricier air-con rooms and offer the best value. There's live music and a party scene on weekends, but it's fairly subdued the rest of the time.

AO THONG SAI & HAT CHOENG MON

The largest cove following Ao Thong Sai has several names, but the beach is generally known as Hat Choeng Mon. This area also boasts a few luxury resorts – see the boxed text, p 595.

White House (☎ 0 7724 5315; info@samuidreamholiday .com; r 4500-7000B; ❌ 🗨) Perfect for a cosy getaway, beautifully appointed rooms at the White House are artistically decorated with creative wooden details and peaked roofs. Duvets top every bed, and on arrival there are fresh fruit and flowers. Water-filled urns dot the lush garden paths and there's an elegant pool, restaurant and private spa areas – it's simply a gorgeous place.

HAT CHAWENG

Packed end-to-end with hotels and bungalows, Hat Chaweng is the eye of the tourist storm in Samui. Snazzy resorts rule. While most real budget places have long since been squeezed out, a few remain hidden in the masses.

Central Hat Chaweng is an urban strip that is home to plenty of video-playing restaurants, bars (including the girlie kind), discos, minimarts, film-processing labs, tailors, souvenir shops and foreign-exchange booths. Despite

the havoc and chaos on the main road, the beautiful stretch of beach (about 400m away) and many places to stay are well protected from street sounds.

North Chaweng is far enough from the noise, but still close enough to the action, and houses mostly midrange to top-end resorts along the still leafy beachfront. Meanwhile, around a headland south of central Hat Chaweng, there is a fetching little area known as Hat Chaweng Noi, which offers respite of the luxurious kind.

North

Amari Palm Reef Resort (Map p590; ☎ 0 7742 2015; www.amari.com; r & bungalows from 5500B; 🔀 🖳 🖳) A luxurious, ultra tastefully decorated resort, this place has a gorgeous pool area, spacious, comfortable rooms and public lounge areas feature silk-pillow day beds. It's the most environmentally conscious luxury resort on the island, using filtered sea water for most first uses and recycled grey water for landscaping. The place fills quickly, probably because it's such a good deal considering its amenities and *haute couture* style.

Chaweng Beach Hotel (Map p590; ☎ 0 7742 2747; chawengbeachhotel@yahoo.com; r 800-1200B; 🔀 🖳) On the opposite side of the road from the beach is this very good-value hotel – much better than many of the cheap bungalow operations right on the beach and less noisy. You have to climb a few stairs to reach it, but once you do you'll find rooms larger than expected. Beds

---

SAMUI'S TOP FIVE TOP-END RESORTS

There's no shortage of places on Samui willing to help you live the rock-star lifestyle. If hearing prices quoted in US dollar triple figures doesn't give your accountant a heart attack, then the following list of unique top-end resorts might be for you.

Imperial Boat House Hotel (☎ 0 7742 5041-52; www.imperialhotels.com; Hat Choeng Mon; r US$160-220, boat ste US$270; 🔀 🖳) This place is something else. It has a three-storey hotel as well as free-standing, two-storey bungalows made from teak rice barges complete with separate lounge areas and a patio on each bow. There's also a boat-shaped swimming pool. It's a sophisticated and unique place.

Le Royal Meridien Baan Taling Ngam (☎ 0 7634 0480; www.lemeridien.com; Ao Taling Ngam; r & villas US$180-800; 🔀 🖳 🖳) The finest resort on Samui and arguably one of the best in Thailand, Le Meridien dominates the northern end of this shallow curving bay from its perch atop a steep hill. It boasts tennis courts, two swimming pools, a fitness centre and a full complement of equipment and instructors for kayaking, windsurfing and diving. Luxuriously appointed guest accommodation contains custom-made Thai-style furnishings and the service here is impeccable. As it's not right on the beach, a shuttle service transports guests back and forth; airport and ferry transfers are also provided.

Central Samui Beach Resort (Map p590; ☎ 0 7723 0500; www.centralhotelsresorts.com; Hat Chaweng; r US$188-1000; 🔀 🖳 🖳) One of Samui's best, this place has what you would expect at an internationally rated four-plus star resort. The green palm-studded garden rolls into the sea, your bath comes filled with aromatherapy bits and bobs, and there are childcare facilities, a spa, library, fitness room, outstanding service and four restaurants. All the hotel-style rooms have sea views and balconies.

Tongsai Bay (☎ 0 7724 5480-5500; www.tongsaibay.co.th; Hat Choeng Mon; ste 11,000-30,000B; 🔀 🖳) For serious pampering, head to this secluded, luxurious place. Expansive, impeccably maintained with hilly grounds make buildings here look like a small village, and golf carts are employed to zoom guests around. All the swanky suites have day-bed rest areas, gorgeous romantic décor, stunning views, large terraces and creatively placed tubs (you'll see). Facilities include salt- and fresh-water pools, a tennis court, spa and three restaurants.

Muang Kulay Pan Hotel (Map p590; ☎ 0 7723 0849-51; www.kulaypan.com; Hat Chaweng; r 12,000B; 🔀 🖳 🖳) This resort has a distinctive style; it's designed with minimalist Japanese, Thai and Indonesian influences that are fused in an unassuming but very elegant look. Sleek villas are gracefully appointed and include original works of art. The pool is fabulous with a waterfall and an artificial beach that allows you to walk down an inclined entrance to the water – allowing you to get wet at your own speed. Fish-filled canals run around the foliage-heavy property.

have firm mattresses and bathrooms feature separate shower stalls.

Coral Bay Resort (Map p590; ☎ 0 7742 2223; www .coralbay.net; r & bungalows 4000-7000B; ✺ ⚉) Accommodation here is fabulous, sporting natural materials and unique wooden details in spacious surroundings. Gardens are lush, hilly and meandering, and there's an enticingly designed pool area with an overlooking restaurant. Other facilities include a spa and an overhead projector showing news and movies.

Papillon Resort (Map p590; ☎ 0 7723 1169; www.pap illonsamui.com; r & bungalows 1600-5500B; ✺ ⚉) This place offers imaginative, two-level rooms with elegant décor and lofts, along with a lush garden, beautiful restaurant and a tiny pool.

Central

The Wave Samui (Map p590; ☎ 0 7723 0803; www .thewavesamui.com; r from 350-850B; ✺) The only true backpackers on Samui, the Wave is a relatively new place run by two friendly Brits. The fan rooms are some of the best on the island; they are all decent sized and freshly painted (although baths are shared), and come with cable TV and fridge. Air-con rooms are also fairly priced. There is a single two-storey suite (1650B) that is a real steal; it sleeps four, has a private rooftop deck and a TV with a DVD player. The bar and restaurant offers cheap beers, solid food and lively ambiance. The owners are huge supporters of the Samui Dog Rescue, so you'll see plenty of four-legged friends hanging around.

The Club (Map p590; ☎ 0 1894 2327; bungalows 450-1200B, villas 3500B; ⚉) The drive up the roughshod dirt road to this isolated mountain getaway is totally worthwhile once you get a load of the awesome views. The bungalows in this French-Thai–run place have unpretentious back-to-nature design and a share of the magnificent vistas. There's a great horizon pool and French restaurant, and you can call ahead for a pick-up. This is easily the best value on this beach.

Lucky Mother (Map p590; ☎ 0 7723 0931; bungalows 400-600B; ✺) Lucky Mother offers some of the cheapest, and smallest, rickety old Samui bungalows left on this beach – an alternative if the Wave is full. These are pretty bad as far as bungalows go –the cheapest ones have rotting walls, broken fans and grimy bathrooms, and the air-con ones are similar only larger – but considering Samui's serious lack of budget

accommodation they remain popular with the backpacking crowd and can fully book out.

Relax Resort (Map p590; ☎ 0 7742 2280; fax 0 7742 2113; r 600-1200B; ✺) The resort has nice rooms with fans in an appalling location off a driveway. On the other hand, the rooms with air-con are gorgeous and charming, with attractive architecture (some have wonderful lofts) and creative details. They're in the back, along nice garden paths.

Coconut Grove Samui Mandalay Resotel (Map p590; ☎ 0 7723 1157; bungalows 800-1000B; ✺ ⚉) Good value for its central location, this place has cosy wooden bungalows with satellite TV and mattresses on the floor. They don't let in a lot of light but they're large enough. The on-site bar and restaurant is very popular and the place can be really loud at night – ask for a bungalow away from the bar and down the beach, as these are quieter and nicer.

Samui Coral Resort (Map p590; ☎ 0 7742 2364; www .samuicoralresort.com; bungalows incl breakfast 800-1500B; ✺ ⚉) The bungalows closest to the beach are dark wooden stilt boxes with slats missing from the floors and weathered woven rattan walls, but they're as tidy as can be and the mattress doesn't sink too bad. Further back, two-storey whitewashed modern bungalows have big glass windows and more space. The cement exterior fronting the beach is far from attractive, but the bar in the sand attracts plenty of people; plus the pool is clean and bigger than most.

Palm Island Hotel & Resort (Map p590; ☎ 0 7741 3140; www.palmislandsamui.com; bungalows from 1100B; ✺) It's far from special, but a good deal for this part of Chaweng. Rooms are not just big enough to move in, they even have space for a night table and a TV with a wide range of channels in English. The décor may not be to everyone's taste, and lends a sort of black-leather studded dog-collar accent to the chipped furnishings. The two-tiered pool right off the beach is a plus.

Garden Beach Resort (Map p590; ☎ 0 7741 3798; www.ark-bar.com; bungalows r from 1200B; ✺ ⚉) Although we're not sure why, the Garden Beach Resort is a huge hit with the 20-something crowd. The cement bungalows are small, overpriced and far from special, featuring cheap brown furniture. The location, right in the middle of the beach, is pretty killer though. The bar and restaurant on the sand is also wildly popular with backpackers, and it makes sense to sleep where you party. It's often fully booked.

Princess Village (Map p590; ☎ 0 7742 2216; www
.samuiprincess.com; bungalows 4100-6000B; ⊠) Stunning
Ayuthaya-period Thai stilt homes lie among
ponds and a sea of green in this romantic
getaway. The bungalows are beautifully constructed and decorated, and the whole place
is hushed with silence. It's a very special place,
perfect for honeymooners.

Baan Samui Resort (Map p590; ☎ 0 7742 2415; www
.see2sea.com; r from 4500B; ⊠ ⊠) Whether you
consider Baan Samui eccentrically charming
or a major eyesore, one thing is for sure – you
can't miss this pink adobe joint with blue trim.
The décor is southwest USA meets Miami Art
Deco. The rooms continue the theme with
bright colours, Navajo rugs and clean white
duvets. The Moon Dance restaurant lets you
dine under the stars and does a seafood barbecue for about 350B.

Poppies Samui (Map p590; ☎ 0 7742 2419; www.pop
piessamui.com; r 7200B; ⊠ ⊠) The gorgeous garden
at Poppies comes with a bubbling stream,
while the cottages are luxuriously comfortable. Boulders edge the small swimming pool
and the restaurant is top-notch. It has been a
long-time Samui favourite for jet-setters.

Also recommended:

Chaweng Gardens Beach (Map p590; ☎ 0 7742 2265;
bungalows 600-2200B; ⊠) A long-time establishment.

PP Samui Resort (Map p590; ☎ 0 7742 2540; fax 0
7742 2324; r 1050-2500B; ⊠)

Montien House (Map p590; ☎ 0 7742 2169;
montien@samart.co.th; r & bungalows 1700B) A special
place with a beautiful pool by the beach.

Banana Fan Sea Samui (Map p590; ☎ 0 7741 3483-6;
www.bananafansea.com; r & bungalows 4000-14,000B;
⊠ ⊠) Appealing upmarket option; wonderful Thai-
style rooms.

Chaweng Buri Resort (Map p590; ☎ 0 7742 2466;
www.chawengburi.com; bungalows 4500B; ⊠ ⊠)
Romantic atmosphere and great grounds.

HAT LAMAI

After Chaweng became too crowded, travellers started to turn up to this much mellower
location, which boasts super calm waters
thanks to an offshore reef. However, its
popularity today – just look around – means
those looking for solitude have moved on to
more secluded spots. The Lamai nightlife is
Samui's most tawdry, attracting tourists by
the boatload to down buckets of booze while
go-go dancers 'polish poles' in the open-air
hostess bars. Generally, attractive accommodation at the northeastern end of the beach

is quieter and moderately priced in the low
season, though the beach is a bit rougher and
the water deeper. The action centres on Ban
Lamai. The vibe here is more laid-back than
Chaweng, and sleeping options tend to be
less claustrophobic and better value. All the
usual traveller services and provisions exist
here. Hinta Hinyai, at the southern end of
Lamai, is famous for its suggestive, giggle-
inspiring formations called the Grandmother
and Grandfather rocks.

Budget

Heaps of cheap fan bungalows scattered about
on Hat Lamai mean there's no shortage of
options for any length of stay, but if you need
air-con expect to pay at least 600B.

Amity (☎ 0 7742 4084; amitytravel@yahoo.com; bungalows 350-1200B; ⊠) Another welcome cheapie in
a constantly upward-moving market, the most
expensive bungalows at Amity are large, updated and on the beach. B-level rooms include
air-con, while the dirt-cheap ones seem rather
neglected and share bathrooms. Basic, comfortable and economical are the tenets, so go
ahead, have those extra Singha's and relax.

Beers House (☎ 0 7723 0467; bungalows 350-6000B)
Popular and friendly, with an old-school feel,
Beers House has closely situated shady bungalows (the best ones right on the beachfront),
a welcoming restaurant and helpful staff. The
cheapest accommodation shares bathrooms.

Magic Resort (☎ 0 7742 4229; bungalows 400-1200B;
⊠) The teal bungalows are newly painted while
the older structures resemble tiny wooden
thatched-roof houses perched on stilts. All have
a front porch and are within walking distance to
the sea. Put simply, it's a good deal on no-frills
accommodation. Don't expect a TV or minifridge; however, the renovated units have additional living space with newer bathrooms.

Utopia (☎ 0 7723 3113; www.utopia-samui.com; bungalows from 500B; ⊠) Sleep in fan-only Thai-style
cottages or fancier air-con teak-appointed
rooms with terraces overlooking exotic tropical gardens. Dine on fresh seafood, Thai or
international cuisine while sitting under the
stars at the in-house restaurant. The beach
here is Samui's best as far as sand, sea and
scenery go.

Midrange

Midrange options are plentiful on Hat Lamai,
but check out a few places because quality
changes very quickly here.

LOWER SOUTHERN GULF

Spa Resort (☎ 0 7723 0976; www.spasamui.com; bungalows 500-3000B; ✷ ☎) Though this place has gone more upscale of late, it still maintains bargain-priced rustic beach bungalows. New Age and holistic treatments like herbal sauna packages, body wraps, clay facials, and colon cleansing are available for guests and nonguests alike. Thai herbal massage, cleansing fasts and more intensive programmes (minimum three-night stay) are also available. Activities include *taijiquan* (tai chi), meditation, yoga and cooking classes. Reserving a place ahead of time (email is best) is advised as it's often fully booked.

Long Island Resort (☎ 0 7742 4202; www.longisland resort.com; bungalows 750-3000B; ✷ ☎) A well-liked establishment, the Long Island features nicely situated thatched-roof bungalows alongside brick pathways spanning over three acres of tropical landscape. Affordable luxury, a peaceful vicinity and friendly, attentive staff are all reasons why we like it.

Bill Resort (☎ 0 7742 4403; www.thebillresort.com; r & bungalows from 1000B; ✷ ☎) Colourful materials and textures mix freely, complementing the blossoming overgrown garden, Jacuzzi and pool areas. Accommodation ranges from wicker beds and furniture to platform beds, with handcrafted features like funky spiralling bedposts made from local timber.

Sand Sea Resort (☎ 0 7723 1127; www.samuisandsea .com; bungalows 1000-4700B; ✷ ☎) Contemporary upmarket Thai furnishings, unpretentious comfort and convenience is what to expect at the newly renovated Sand Sea. Laze contentedly under coconut palm canopies then pamper yourself with a spa treatment, or indulge at the weekly beach barbecue.

Golden Sand (☎ 0 7742 4031/2; www.goldensand -resort.com; r & bungalows 1470-4800B; ✷) On the main road and easy to find, two types of accommodation are offered here set amid beautiful expansive grounds. Take your pick of modern hotel rooms inside a low-rise building, or bungalows surrounded by coconut trees, some with glass fronts that get heaps of light. The restaurant overlooks the central garden, while the bar sits on the beach.

Galaxy Resort (☎ 0 7742 4441; www.samui-hotels .com/galaxy; r & bungalows incl breakfast 1500-3800B; ✷ ☎) Thai-style architecture, huge bathtubs and beautifully presented interior décor are featured in the most lavish rooms at this resort. The cheaper ones are clean, adequate and comfortable, although they can be a little rough around the edges.

Jungle Park Hotel (☎ 0 7741 8034-7; www.jungle -park.com; r incl breakfast 1500-4800B; ✷ ☎) Luxury for less, need we say more? Rooms are tidy, well maintained and attractively decorated. Leafy foliage abounds creating an inviting atmosphere coupled with an intimate sense of exclusivity. A brilliant amoeba-shaped pool near the beach, with a restaurant and bar situated alongside, make this an excellent choice.

Aloha (☎ 0 7742 4418; www.alohasamui.com; r & bungalows from 2000B; ✷ ☎) Soft waxen sand, cerulean water, coconut trees and serene forested hills swathe you in idyllic tranquillity at Aloha. Sadly, the rooms are very plain with modest furnishings and do not live up to the amazing natural beauty just outside your door. The greatest asset is the wonderfully tropical, blue-tiled pool that overlooks the beach.

Top End

There are several top-end places to stay on Hat Lamai, many of the spa-resort variety.

Star Bay Beach & Garden (☎ 0 7742 4546; www .starbay-beach.com; 1- & 2-bedroom houses from US$50 per day; ✷ ☎) Travellers with children or in small groups looking for extended stays on the island will likely enjoy these lodgings. It caters to longer-term guests (two weeks or so) with fully furnished, roomy and striking residences near the beach, combining the best of Thai character and Western comfort. There is a beachside restaurant and the gardens are tropical paradises. If business is slow, shorter stays may be possible.

our pick Tamarind Retreat Resort (☎ 0 7742 4221; www.tamarindretreat.com; r & villas from 3200B; ✷ ☎) Resting against a forested hillside oasis, Tamarind offers gorgeously designed and crafted holiday homes – each with a distinctive theme. Some integrate boulders into walls and floors, private ponds or inventive open-air bathrooms in the vein of the appropriately named 'Rock 'n Wood' suite. There is a five-night minimum stay, seven nights during peak season, including free airport round-trip transfer and breakfast. Tamarind Springs is the attached day spa that has all the usual services and packages. It's regularly fully booked, so reserve well in advance.

Pavilion Resort (☎ 0 7742 4420; www.pavilionsamui .com; r & bungalows incl breakfast from 9500B; ✷ ☎) Chalet-chic Pavilion caters exclusively to travellers' privacy and pampering whims. Even though the boutique cottages seem commu-

nally heaped, they still endow an exceptionally cosy, handsome and airy interior feel. The spacious pool mirrors, the sky overhead and the turtle statuette fountains trickling azure rivulets of water create an atmosphere of tranquillity.

In the following places, just south of Hat Lamai, you pay for the atmosphere and ecological sensitivity more than for amenities.

Laem Set Inn (☎ 0 7723 3299; www.laemset.com; bungalows 1200-15,950B; 🛱 🌊) A secluded place connected by stairways and waterways, and surrounded by a tropical garden, it has a minor art gallery on the premises and a good Thai restaurant, as well as a full-service spa.

Central Samui Village (☎ 0 7742 4020; www.central hotelsresorts.com; bungalows 4500-5500B; 🛱 🌊) These chic, modern wooden cottages are linked by wooden walkways over a rocky landscape. The village has well-designed grounds, a pool and a mixed Thai and foreign clientele. Cottages have either a garden or sea view.

WEST COAST

Several bays along Samui's western side have places to stay, including Thong Yang, where the Don Sak and Khanom ferries dock. The beaches here turn to mudflats during low tide, however, so they're not very popular with beach fans. With the exception of Samui's most exclusive resort, Le Royal Meridien Baan Taling Ngam (see box text, p595), there is little reason to stay here.

Simple Life Bungalow (☎ 0 7733 4191; bungalows 300-800B; 🛱) Around Laem Hin Khon, on the southern end of Samui's west, is a little bay called Emerald Cover. Here you'll find Simple Life Bungalows, which delivers on its promise. The reasonable, bare-bones rooms set around a flora-filled path are far from pretty much anywhere. The owner can arrange day trips to Ko Taen for 1000B per boat.

Coconut Villa (☎ 0 7733 4069; coconutvilla@sawadee .com; bungalows 400-1200B; 🛱 🌊) Not far from Simple Life, these perky-coloured little huts are a slightly fancier affair. The beach here is slim but enticing, and the isolation can be bliss after spending time in the rush-hour of the east coast. There's a restaurant on the premises.

Wiesenthal (☎ 0 7723 5165; wisnthal@samart.co.th; bungalows 500-1500B; 🛱) Located on Ao Taling Ngam, this place sits amid a pleasant garden with coconut palms. The well-spaced bungalows have either partial or full sea views.

Eating

The number of eating establishments on Samui is overwhelming. Fans of Italian food will not be disappointed, especially on Chaweng, where it seems Italian-owned restaurants outnumber everything else combined. Nearly all bungalow operations have their own restaurant, but because the ownership and management of various lodgings around the island change so frequently it's difficult to name favourites.

NA THON

There are several good restaurants and watering holes in Na Thon, many of which fill quickly with travellers waiting for the night ferry. A giant supermarket and a day market are on Th Thawi Ratchaphakdi, the third street back from the harbour.

About Art & Craft (Map p588; ☎ 0 1499 9353; Th Chonwithi; dishes 20-120B; ☒ breakfast, lunch & dinner) This is a jewellery and art gallery that also serves delicious organic and sugar-free vegetarian food and juices. There is a peaceful, spiritual atmosphere here – surprising for Na Thon.

Coffee Island (Map p588; ☎ 0 7742 0153; Th Chonwithi; dishes 30-190B; ☒ breakfast, lunch & dinner) Great if you arrive at the pier early morning and need a real espresso to wake up. Coffee Island also has cures to settle queasy tummies, the huge menu offers baked goods, full breakfasts, and Thai and Western staples such as sandwiches and curry. It's run by the Ruang Thong restaurant chain in Na Thon.

HAT BO PHUT

Hat Bo Phut is as wonderful for eating as it is for sleeping. The romantic Fisherman's Village is host to a number of trendy restaurants serving food that tastes as good as the surroundings look. Resorts further to the west along the beach also boast a few great restaurants.

Billabong Surf Club (☎ 0 7743 0144; Fisherman's Village; dishes from 100B; ☒ breakfast, lunch & dinner) An Aussie restaurant that serves giant portions of steaks, barbecue ribs and lamb chops, along with burgers, bar snacks, Aussie-rules football and, for some reason, Indian curries. The beer flows late into the night.

The Shack Bar & Grill (☎ 0 7724 5041; Fisherman's Village; dishes from 200B; ☒ breakfast, lunch & dinner) Well-presented flame-grilled dishes are served in intimate settings at this restaurant featuring Californian cuisine and a lengthy wine list.

LOWER SOUTHERN GULF

SAMUI'S TOP FIVE EATS

When dining options are plentiful and varied, one has to consider the overall experience: the food, the service and the ambience, before deciding what and where to eat. Ko Samui has some of the best chefs in the world plying their trade and delighting gastronomes with their inspired creations. Below are our favourite five.

Betelnut Restaurant (Map p590; ☎ 0 7741 3370; Hat Chaweng; dishes 200-650B; ☾ dinner) With one of Samui's top reputations for seriously fine dining, Betelnut owner-chef Jeffrey Lord honed his chops at Poppies before going it alone, and the island's foodies remain loyal throughout. Imagine a highly innovative menu fusing Californian, European and Chinese styles with distinctive Thai twists. Reservations recommended.

Poppies (Map p590; ☎ 0 7742 2419; Hat Chaweng; 250-700B; ☾ lunch & dinner) A long-time Samui institution, Poppies creates the ultimate balance: delectable, inspired cuisine presented in a relaxed but cordial beachside atmosphere in Chaweng. The romantic ambience with its candlelit tables, elegantly attired conscientious staff and unobtrusive live music provides the perfect setting for a memorable night.

Zico's (Map p590; ☎ 0 7723 1560-3; Hat Chaweng; 250-700B; ☾ lunch & dinner) A contemporary and sleekly modern restaurant, Zico's gleams in the Brazilian national colours of green and yellow, and has concealed romantic alcoves, loveseats, waterfalls, under-lit glass terrazzo, and loads of plants. Its signature dish is the carnivorous churrasqueria gaucho-style barbecue, with passadors bearing laden skewers of every variety of meat conceivable doing a steady round of the tables. A genuine Brazilian samba band and dancers entertain guests nightly. The cocktail bar is well worth visiting in itself and for the chance of joining one of the scantily clad samba girls on the dance floor. It's on the beach road at the southern end of Chaweng.

Laem Set Inn (☎ 0 7742 4393; Ban Hua Thanon; 250-700B; ☾ lunch & dinner) This place offers upscale dining featuring classical Thai cuisine, as well as creative Pacific Rim fare at one of the most well-established boutique resorts on Samui. The short menu changes daily and meals are always served in a traditional Thai wooden thatched *sǎalaa* where the sea views are fantastic.

The Lai Thai Restaurant (☎ 0 7742 9201; Hat Mae Nam; dishes 480-800B; ☾ dinner) Located on the northern end of idyllic Mae Nam in the Napasi Resort, Lai Thai overlooks a romantic sheltered beach and combines elegant natural surroundings with 1st-class Thai service. Dining here is a memorable culinary treat. French chef Michel Chlaustre produces a brilliant selection of delicious European seafood and meat dishes entwining flavours and ingredients with enviable talent, while his sous chefs prepare a fine medley of classic Thai dishes, many of which were originally conceived in the kitchens of the Royal Palace. Reserving ahead in high season is highly recommended.

Jazz and blues music complement the dining experience.

Baia (☎ 0 7724 5566; Fisherman's Village; dishes 120-300B; ☾ lunch & dinner) Baia smells delicious from the moment you step into its airy, environs. Grab a wooden table overlooking the water and scope out the Italian and Mediterranean menu. We liked the pizza here so much we ordered a second slice – it has a thin crust and is served with a delicious hot pepper dipping sauce.

Zazem Restaurant (☎ 0 7742 5085; Fisherman's Village; dishes 150-500B; ☾ breakfast, lunch & dinner) The restaurant at this cool boutique hotel offers a fabulous fusion of Mediterranean and Thai food served in a stunning, romantic location right on the beach or under a private Thai *sǎalaa* (an open-sided, covered meeting space)

by the lagoon. The salads are mouthwatering and ultra fresh and there don't seem to be any bad choices on the menu. The cocktail menu is long and sweet.

Villa Bianca (☎ 0 7724 5041; Fisherman's Village; dishes 150-400B; ☾ lunch & dinner) Serving classic Italian cuisine with a seafood slant, Villa Bianca is nestled among the old converted Chinese shophouses overlooking the water in Bo Phut Fisherman's Village. Its stark white walls, classy *objets d'art* and well-spaced candlelit tables covered in crisp white linen give the restaurant an unmistakably Mediterranean feel.

HAT BANG RAK

The Mangrove (☎ 0 7742 7584; dishes from 200B) For an exceptional meal, check out the Mangrove on Ko Fan (the island connected to the mainland

by a causeway). An ex-Poppies chef runs the kitchen and cooks up an ever-changing menu of French cuisine. Reservations are highly recommended as seating is limited.

HAT CHAWENG

Back on the 'strip' are dozens of restaurants and cafés serving Western cuisine. Italian places outnumber the rest, but many types of food are accounted for from stalls serving cheap Thai to Starbucks and McDonald's. For the best ambience get off the strip and head to the beach where many bungalow operators set up tables on the sand and have glittery fairy lights at night. With the waves providing the background soundtrack, you can't get much more relaxed.

The following places are only a start – there are literally hundreds more. Also make sure to check out the boxed text on Samui's Top Five Eats (opposite).

Will Wait Restaurant & Bakery (Map p590; ☎ 0 7742 2613; dishes 50-200B; ☯ breakfast, lunch & dinner) It's been around forever it seems, and never loses popularity, which says a lot in Samui's fickle eating market. The eatery has a few locations on Chaweng's main strip. In addition to cakes and pastries, it serves pizza, Thai food and decent Western breakfasts at three locations in south and central Chaweng.

Chaweng Khaosan Restaurant & Bakery (Map p590; dishes from 60B; ☯ breakfast, lunch & dinner) Big and airy with a congenial atmosphere, it seems as popular with *faràng* (Westerners) as with Thais. The menu has everything you could be craving and then some – from savoury pancakes to pizza, pasta, baguettes and seafood. It shows movies at night, does big breakfasts in the morning and always seems to be filled.

Starbucks (Map p590; ☎ 0 7742 1234; coffee & snacks 60-185B; ☯ breakfast, lunch & dinner) When you're feeling homesick and can't stomach another fried breakfast tasting vaguely of last night's *phàt thai*, come home to Starbucks. Sure, it's a global corporate conglomerate, but sometimes you just need to regroup over a vanilla latte and blueberry scone that tastes the same in Ko Samui as it docs in Los Angeles or London.

Captain Kirk (Map p590; ☎ 08 1270 5376; dishes 140-400B; ☯ dinner) A tropical rooftop garden restaurant in the heart of Chaweng, Captain Kirk's is as popular for its ambiance as it is for its food. A mixture of high quality, well-presented, fresh food from Thailand and the world is on the diverse menu – which has

more than 80 different choices. After dinner linger over cocktails on bamboo cushioned chairs.

Deck (Map p590; ☎ 0 7723 0897; dishes 80-200B; ☯ breakfast, lunch & dinner) Eat upstairs in Thai-style, with loads of cushions, or downstairs off the sidewalk, so you can check out the street traffic. The three-course 170B breakfast is served all day and is a good deal – choose from healthy (fruit, salad and yoghurt with toast and juice) to unhealthy (we're not kidding this is the name, and it includes Coke, fried eggs, fried toast, bacon and French fries). At lunch and dinner it cooks up Thai food, burgers, souvlaki, pasta and salad, among other dishes. The bar is popular at night.

Gringos Cantina (Map p590; ☎ 0 7741 3267; dishes 145-230B; ☯ dinner) This is a popular Mexican *cocina* serving quesadillas, tacos, tostadas and burritos that are best washed down with margaritas, piña coladas and tequila shooters. Of course, it has the requisite pizzas and burgers as well.

Islander (Map p590; ☎ 0 7723 0836; dishes 90-210B; ☯ breakfast, lunch & dinner) *Faràng* pack this partially al fresco joint off the busy beach road day or night. The brekkies are served all day long and include coffee and lots of meats. Starting at 135B, these are a good sop-up-the-booze morning fuel. Other choices take you around the world and include quesadillas, pizza, Thai and lots of Brit staples, and veggie options. Service is slow.

Tropical Murphy's (Map p590; ☎ 0 7741 3614; dishes 150-350B; ☯ breakfast, lunch & dinner) This place is fairly similar to the Islander and just as popular with *faràng*. On the menu are steak-and-kidney pie, fish and chips, lamb chops, Irish stew and desserts. The décor is dark old-world pub; fans keep the inside cool even when it's steaming outside. There is a great brew selection and live music four times per week.

HAT LAMAI

Lamai has less variety than Chaweng when it comes to eating. Dining in your hotel's restaurant is agreeable for some, but endeavouring to go out for a meal is well worth the short walk. Fresh seafood, Italian and pub grub is nearly ubiquitous. However, several local Thai food stalls in the central beach are a superb means for sampling local flavours while saving baht.

Rising Sun (☎ 0 7741 8015; dishes 60-300B; ☯ breakfast, lunch & dinner) Popular with *faràng* for its

LOWER SOUTHERN GULF

open-air, informal tables and chairs, this place does respectable burgers, steaks, veggie stuff, coffees and drinks.

Bauhaus Bistro (☎ 0 7741 8797; dishes 80–350B; ☯ breakfast, lunch & dinner) Inside this intricate woody behemoth, the regular carte du jour includes burgers, salads, sandwiches, munchies, and European and Thai food.

Eldorado (www.eldoradolamai.com; dishes 120–210B; ☯ breakfast, lunch & dinner) West of the central crossroads, this popular, inexpensive Swedish restaurant blends international cuisine with Thai specialities and an all-you-can-eat barbecue every Wednesday at 7pm.

Samui Shamrock (☎ 0 1597 8572; dishes 120–500B; ☯ breakfast, lunch & dinner) Thai-erd of *phàt thai*? Then head to the Samui Shamrock and fill up on generous, hearty portions of Irish fare while quaffing it down with a Guinness. Featuring live music five nights a week, a new stage and lighting system, the ever-hip Samui Shamrock is your ticket for entertainment in Lamai. It does a wonderful breakfast special/ hangover cure called the 'Irish Fry-up' that's perfect for the morning after a big night out.

Il Tempio (☎ 0 7723 2307; dishes 130–230B; ☯ lunch & dinner) Il Tempio's area of expertise is Italian cooking, but it also does savoury Thai dishes and has a gelataria. It has appealing open courtyard seating that is straightforward and relaxing. If interested, you can watch *muay thai* (Thai boxing) action across the street.

Drinking & Entertainment

Hat Chaweng and Hat Lamai have the most nightlife, but many bungalows and hotels all over the island have small- to medium-sized bars.

HAT BO PHUT

Quiet and completely lacking in girly bars, Bo Phut's nightlife scene is mellow. That said, the place is hardly lacking in entertainment, with a few great pubs along its waterfront and in the Fisherman's Village. Most double as restaurants.

The Frog & Gecko Pub (☎ 0 7742 5248) This tropical British watering hole has become a bit of a Samui institution, famous for its 'Wednesday Night Pub Quiz' competitions and its wide selection of music. Live sporting events are shown on the big screen. There is a slate-bed pool table and the pub claims to serve the coldest beer on the island. It also does great pub grub (100B to 200B).

Billabong Surf Club (☎ 0 7743 0144) Great views across to Ko Pha-Ngan, as well as plenty of Aussie sports memorabilia make this restaurant (p599) and bar a popular drinking spot. Of course, the telly is always tuned to the sport.

HAT CHAWENG

Soi Green Mango is the heart of Chaweng's pumping nightlife scene, with loads of bars concentrated on one long alleyway. All the watering holes, some sleazier than others, seem to constantly change names – in Thailand if a business doesn't work in the first month the owners often just cut their losses and pack up shop. At the time of research you could drink your way around the world on this strip, from the London Inn to the Kangaroo Bar to Henry's Africa; take a wander to see what's around.

Reggae Pub (Map p590; ☎ 0 7742 2331) Looming like a gorgeous monster at the end of a girlie-bar line-up, this two-storey, tastefully done, open building has been a hit for seemingly forever. A virtual Bob Marley shrine, it packs in nightly crowds to watch sports at the long bars or shoot a game of pool. There are plenty of places to sit, great lake views and live music played on the stage.

Green Mango (Map p590; ☎ 0 7742 2148) This place is so popular it has a whole soi named after it! Another Samui power drinking house, it is cavernous, very loud and very *faràng*. Green Mango has blazing lights, soccer on TV, expensive drinks and masses of sweaty bodies swaying to dance music.

Coco Blues (Map p590; ☎ 0 7742 2248; ☯ 10am-2am) Some of Samui's best live talent and international players can be found here (every night) if they're touring. This place is actually a promotional vehicle for the nearby Coco Real Estate company – after a few drinks we were pretty keen on some beachfront property.

Deck (Map p590; ☎ 0 7723 0897) An open-air, multiterraced bar with comfortable lounging platforms, the deck has good views of the street scene below. This place has recently been refurbished to have even more terraces and more lounging platforms. There is also a smaller related pub directly opposite called the Quarterdeck.

Ark Bar (Map p590; ☎ 0 7741 3798) One of the most popular of the beach bars, the Ark is lit up with paper lanterns at night. There are cushions on the sand, whiskey buckets, and

Wednesday night dance parties with live DJs and a free barbecue starting at 4pm.

Legends (Map p590) Right on the main strip, this bar is run by a friendly expat and draws in fistfuls of *faràng* for strong cocktails (try the Long Island Iced Tea to knock your socks off) and sport on the TV. It has a casual outdoor seating area.

Black Jack Pub (Map p590; ☎ 0 1748 3740) Small and cosy with sports TV and two pool tables, the Black Jack is run by an expat. Internet access is free from 5pm to 11pm.

Christy's Cabaret Bar (Map p590; admission free; show time 11pm) This bar offers transvestite cabaret nightly and attracts a mixed clientele of both sexes. Inside, the music's outdated and the show's not great, but it's something different.

HAT LAMAI

Touristy seaside towns are infamous for their seedy Pattaya-style hostess bars, but there *are* other avenues for meeting, eating and partying in more tasteful settings. Lamai is beginning to lean away from that scene in areas. The Samui Shamrock (opposite) on the main strip has a great bar, a large dance floor, live music five nights a week and heaps of chilled-out ambience. Next door, the long-time favourite Bauhaus Bistro (opposite) looks like some sort of bacchanal resort in its own right and throws hugely popular foam dance parties on Fridays.

Getting There & Away

AIR

Bangkok Airways (Map p590; ☎ 0 7742 2512) flies about 16 times daily between Ko Samui and Bangkok. The flight takes about one hour and 20 minutes. Other destinations from Samui include Phuket, Pattaya and Chiang Mai. During high season flights may be booked out six weeks in advance, so plan accordingly. If Samui flights are full, you might try flying to Surat Thani first, then taking a boat. Delays are also common, so plan accordingly for connecting flights.

The Samui airport departure tax is 500B for domestic and international flights. The attractive open-air airport has a nice bar, restaurant, money-exchange outlet and hotel-reservations counter.

There are almost 10 daily departures between Samui and Ko Pha-Ngan. These leave either from the Na Thong, Mae Nam or Bang Rak piers and take from 20 minutes to one hour (130B to 250B). On Ko Pha-Ngan there are two piers (Hat Rin and Thong Sala), with the boats departing from Hat Bang Rak servicing Hat Rin, and the other boats Thong Sala. From the same piers, there are also around six daily departures between Samui and Ko Tao. These take 1¼ to 2½ hours and cost 345B to 550B.

Car ferries from Don Sak and Khanom land at Thong Yang, about 10km south of Na Thon.

BUS

It can be cheaper and less stressful to get bus/ferry combination tickets that take you all the way to (and from) Ko Samui.

The government-bus fares from Bangkok's Southern bus terminal include the cost of the ferry. These are 900/700/500B for VIP/1st class/2nd class. Most private buses from Bangkok charge around 450B for the same journey and include the ferry fare. From Th Khao San in Bangkok it's possible to get bus/ferry combination tickets for as little as 280B, but service is substandard and theft occurs more frequently than on the more expensive buses. If an agency on Th Khao San claims to be able to get you to Samui for less, it is almost certainly a scam as no profit can be made at such low prices. The Surat Thani travel agency **Phantip Travel** (☎ 0 7742 1221) has offices in Na Thon.

From Na Thon, air-con buses fan out over Thailand and there are at least three daily departures for any given destination, the first one being at 7.30am.

BUSES FROM NA THON	
Destination	**Price**
Bangkok	400-875B
Hat Yai	400B
Khao Sok	360B
Krabi	270-380B
Penang	650-800B
Phuket	350-380B
Ranong	350-380B
Surat Thani	180B
Trang	400-450B

TRAIN

You can buy train/bus/ferry tickets straight through to Samui from Bangkok. Buying these combination tickets saves you some hassle, though you really don't save much money –

especially if you include getting to the train station. For details on train travel, see p581.

Getting Around
TO/FROM THE AIRPORT
Private taxi fares from the airport are as follows: Chaweng (300B to 400B), Lamai (400B) and Na Thon (400B to 500B). Minivans also do the run. Destinations and rough prices: Bang Rak (80B), Bo Phut (100B), Chaweng (200B), Mae Nam (200B), Na Thon (200B to 250B) and Lamai (200B to 250B). Cheapest are the săwngthăew: Chaweng (100B), Lamai (100B), Mae Nam (100B) and Na Thon (150B).

CAR & MOTORCYCLE
You can rent motorcycles (and bicycles) from several places in Na Thon, Chaweng and Lamai, as well as from various bungalows around the island. The going rate is 150B per day for a small motorcycle, but for longer periods try to negotiate a better rate. Take it easy on the bikes; every year several *faràng* die or are seriously injured in motorcycle accidents on Samui. A helmet law is enforced with occasional vigour.

Suzuki Caribbean jeeps can be hired for around 1500B per day from various travel agencies.

SĂWNGTHĂEW
Fares from Na Thon include Mae Nam (30B), Bo Phut (50B), Hat Bang Rak (50B), Lamai (70B), Chaweng (70B) and Choeng Mon (70B). Săwngthăew drivers love to try to overcharge you, so it's always best to ask a third party for current rates, in case these have changed. Săwngthăew run regularly during daylight hours only.

A rough rate for motorcycle taxis is around 25B for a five-minute ride.

KO PHA-NGAN
เกาะพะงัน
pop 10,500
Ko Pha-Ngan is famous for its ability to party, attracting a crowd of nature lovers and shoestring wanderers – the kind of folks happy to sleep in a simple reed woven bungalow or in a hammock strung between two palms. Ko Samui's rebellious little sister attracts backpackers like no other place in Thailand for its no-worries attitude and famous Full Moon parties. This is the kind of place where young revellers can slurp their booze buckets

without interruption until dawn, then nurse terrible hangovers while snoozing on white hot sand.

A half-hour boat ride north, 193-sq-km Ko Pha-Ngan boasts the same stupendous scenery found on Ko Samui, minus the glitz. The lack of an airport and relative absence of good roads have spared it from package-tour development, although the island is changing and one top-end resort has already set up shop. The view from the island's most popular beach, Hat Rin, yields rows of rather ramshackle bungalows and colourfully painted beach bars. Long-tail boats float alongside lazy swimmers in the clear green water. And while there are comfortable air-conditioned places, you'll have to look long and hard to find an in-room satellite TV or ornate furnishings.

Despite the throngs that flock here on a daily basis, Ko Pha-Ngan is a casual island with a sort of hippy fun-loving vibe, where backpackers still dominate the tourist trade. Those searching for a remote paradise can find it on many of the island's secluded beaches, where simple huts are the only accommodation and nights are passed in a make-your-own-fun fashion. If you're looking to party, as many coming to Ko Pha-Ngan are, head to Hat Rin, home of the legendary Full Moon parties (see p615), the biggest beach party in the world. Although nowadays it seems any phase of the moon is an excuse to get out the fire sticks, set up the mats on the sand and pump up the trance music – nightlife is huge here, and scantily clad revellers party on buckets of cheap Thai whisky on a regular basis.

Orientation
Ko Pha-Ngan is approximately 20km from Ko Samui and 100km from Surat Thai.

About half of Ko Pha-Ngan's population lives in and around the small port of Thong Sala. This is where the ferries to and from Ko Tao, Surat Thai and Ko Samui dock. It's a taking-care-of-business town, with restaurants, travel agencies, banks, clothing shops and general stores.

The long cape of Laem Hat Rin is at the southeastern tip of the island and has beaches along both its western and eastern sides – this is officially the most popular place on Ko Pha-Ngan. Travel agencies, minimarts, tattoo shops and discos crowd the small streets off the pretty beaches. The eastern side has

the best beach, Hat Rin Nok (Sunrise Beach), a long, sandy strip lined with coconut palms, but there's more boat traffic than at the western beach. The snorkelling here is good, but between October and March the surf can be a little risky. Hat Rin Nok is famous for its monthly Full Moon parties. The western side of the cape, Hat Rin Nai (Sunset Beach), is more isolated and serves as an accommodation overflow if Hat Rin Nok is full. A pier on Hat Rin Nai serves boats from the northeastern coast of Ko Samui.

There are plenty of other places to stay on the island, although you will find many spots to be very remote (perfect if this is what you're looking for, but not if you're expecting to party). The northern destinations of

Hat Khuat (Bottle Beach) and Ao Thong Nai Pan/Yai are good if you're looking for beach options between 'too busy' and 'too isolated', while the beaches on the island's east coast are the most remote.

There are few paved roads on Pha-Ngan, so transport between places can be a bit of a hassle, although the situation is constantly improving as enterprising Thais set up taxi and boat services between beaches.

Information

Thong Sala and Hat Rin are centres for internet activity, but every beach with development should have access. Rates are generally 1B to 2B per minute, with a 20B minimum. There are also numerous ATMs to withdraw baht.

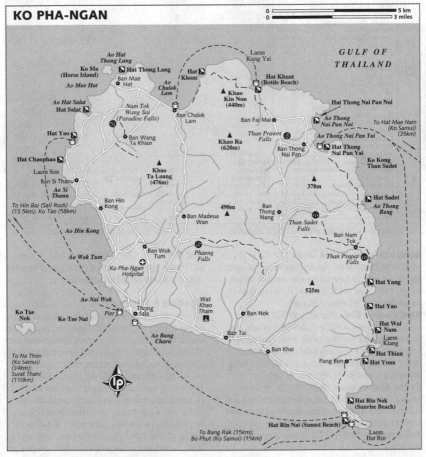

KO PHA-NGAN

GULF OF THAILAND

LOWER SOUTHERN GULF

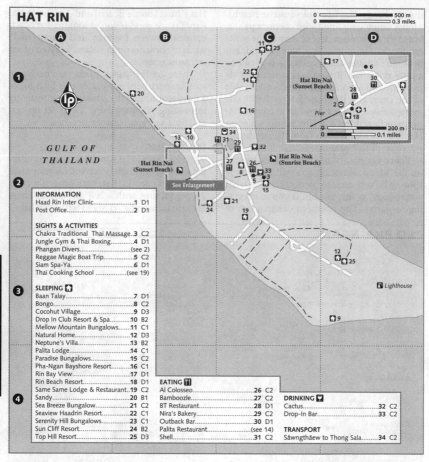

HAT RIN

0   500 m
0   0.3 miles

Hat Rin Nai
(Sunset Beach)

Pier

0   200 m
0   0.1 miles

GULF OF
THAILAND

Hat Rin Nai
(Sunset Beach)

Hat Rin Nok
(Sunrise Beach)

See Enlargement

Lighthouse

INFORMATION	
Haad Rin Inter Clinic...............1	D1
Post Office................................2	D1

SIGHTS & ACTIVITIES	
Chakra Traditional Thai Massage..3	C2
Jungle Gym & Thai Boxing..........4	D1
Phangan Divers.......................(see 2)	
Reggae Magic Boat Trip............5	C2
Siam Spa-Ya...........................6	D1
Thai Cooking School ....(see 19)	

SLEEPING	
Baan Talay..............................7	D1
Bongo...................................8	C2
Cocohut Village.......................9	D3
Drop In Club Resort & Spa........10	B2
Mellow Mountain Bungalows....11	C1
Natural Home........................12	D3
Neptune's Villa.......................13	B2
Palita Lodge..........................14	C1
Paradise Bungalows.................15	C2
Pha-Ngan Bayshore Resort........16	C1
Rin Bay View.........................17	D1
Rin Beach Resort....................18	D1
Same Same Lodge & Restaurant..19	C2
Sandy..................................20	B1
Sea Breeze Bungalow..............21	C2
Seaview Haadrin Resort............22	C1
Serenity Hill Bungalows...........23	C1
Sun Cliff Resort......................24	B2
Top Hill Resort......................25	D3

EATING	
Al Colosseo...........................26	C2
Bamboozle............................27	C2
BT Restaurant........................28	D1
Nira's Bakery.........................29	C2
Outback Bar..........................30	D1
Palita Restaurant...................(see 14)	
Shell...................................31	C2

DRINKING	
Cactus.................................32	C2
Drop-In Bar...........................33	C2

TRANSPORT	
Sǎwngthǎew to Thong Sala........34	C2

Backpacker's Information Centre (☎ 0 7737 5535; www.backpackersthailand.com; Hat Rin) Stands out for its friendly, UK-born, ex-backpacker owner who will not only sell you a ticket, but also fill you in on all there is to do on Ko Pha-Ngan and in the rest of Thailand.

Haad Rin Inter Clinic (Map p606; ☎ 0 7737 5342; 24hr) Formerly 'Sang's Clinic', this has long been the spot to fix your 'Ko Pha-Ngan tattoo' (motorcycle accident scrape) in Hat Rin. It's expanded and now has 24-hour service (although head to the hospital for life-threatening emergencies). Look for the clinic near the pier.

Ko Pha-Ngan Hospital (☎ 0 7737 5103; 24hr) About 2.5km north of Thong Sala off the road to Chalok Lam, it offers 24-hour emergency services. Anything that can wait until Bangkok should, where medical facilities are better.

Police station (☎ 0 7737 7114) About 2km north of Thong Sala.

Post offices (8.30am-4.30pm Mon-Fri, 9am-noon Sat) There is a post office south of Thong Sala, and another at Hat Rin Nai on the road to Hat Rin Nok.

Dangers & Annoyances

Doing drugs in Thailand is risky. Among other things it could land you in the mental ward. Over the past five years Suan Saranrom (Garden of Joys) psychiatric hospital in Surat Thai has to take on extra staff during full-moon periods to handle the number of travellers who freak out on magic mushrooms, acid or other abundantly available hallucinogens.

Those who come specifically seeking an organic buzz should take note: a hallucinogenic plant, newly exploited on the island, has caused a number of travellers to pay an

LOWER SOUTHERN GULF

unscheduled visit to the local psychiatric hospital. Called *ton lamphong* in Thai, the plant is possibly related to datura, a member of the highly toxic nightshade family. Eating any part of the plant causes some people to be completely out of it for a couple of days.

Sampling the local herb could turn equally scary. There are constant reports of travellers being offered and sold marijuana and other drugs by restaurant or bungalow owners, and then being promptly busted by police officers who somehow know exactly, who, when and where to check.

The Thai government's war on drugs is no joke, and the police take it *extremely* seriously. There is a good chance that you could go to jail for more than just a few days for even possessing half a joint. Once in jail, you won't necessarily be able to count on your embassy, your daddy or even bribery to get you out. You'll probably have to wait in the cell until your paperwork creeps its way to the top before anything even starts to happen.

Police road blocks between Thong Sala and Hat Rin are becoming more common, especially in the week leading up to the Full Moon party on Hat Rin. These aren't cursory checks either; if you're on a motorcycle, the police look in the fuel tank, check the tyres and search all your gear.

As elsewhere in Thailand, riding motorcycles in Ko Pha-Ngan can be dangerous. Roads are hilly, narrow and unpaved in portions.

Sights
WATERFALLS
In the interior of this island are four year-round waterfalls and a number of seasonal ones. Boulders carved with the royal insignia of Rama V, Rama VII and Rama IX, all of whom have visited the falls, can be found at **Than Sadet Falls**, which cascades along Khlong Than Sadet in the eastern part of the island. Rama V liked this island so much that he made 18 trips here between 1888 and 1909.

Phaeng Falls is off the main road between Thong Sala and Ban Chalok Lam, almost in the centre of the island. A third waterfall, **Than Prapat Falls**, is situated near the eastern shore in an area that can be reached by road or boat, while **Than Prawet Falls** is in the northeast near Ao Thong Nai Pan.

A fun way to get to experience the falls (and get to know some other travellers in the process) is by joining one of the 'Reggae Magic

Boat Trips' offered by **Cactus** (☎ 0 7737 5308; cruise 500B; ☺ departs noon), a bar in Hat Rin. The cruise includes an opportunity to see the falls and stops for snorkelling. Food, refreshments and snorkel gear are provided. Contact Cactus if you want to book, as the trips only depart when people are interested.

WAT KHAO THAM
วัดเขาถ้ำ
This cave temple is beautifully situated on top of a hill near the little village of Ban Tai. An American monk lived in this temple for over a decade and his ashes are interred on a cliff overlooking a palm field below. It's not a true wat, since there are only a couple of monks and a nun in residence (among other requirements, a quorum of five monks is necessary for a temple to reach wat status).

Ten-day meditation retreats taught by an American-Australian couple are run during the latter half of most months – there are no retreats during the rainy season between September and November. The cost is 2900B. Check out the website of **Wat Khao Tham** (www .watkowtahm.org) for more information. Anyone under 25 years of age must talk with the teachers before being accepted for the retreat. A bulletin board at the temple also has information.

Activities
DIVING & SNORKELLING
As at Ko Samui, coral reefs can be found intermittently at various points around the island. The better bay-reef spots are at the island's northwestern tip and are suitable for snorkelling. There are also some rock reefs of interest on the eastern side of the island.

An outstanding site for scuba divers, a pinnacle called **Hin Bai** (Sail Rock) lies about 13.5km north of the island. An abundance of corals and tropical fish can be seen at depths of 10m to 30m and there's an interesting vertical swim-through called 'The Chimney'. Conditions are best from April to October, when divers sometimes enjoy visibility of up to 20m or more. Hin Bai can also be reached from Ko Tao, although the boating distance from the latter adds 4km to 5km to the trip.

Phangan Divers (☎ 0 7737 5117; www.phangandivers .com; 2 dives incl lunch 2000-3000B) has its main office near the pier at Hat Rin Nai. Its price depends on the distance of the dives. Full certification runs at 11,500B to 13,500B.

Snorkelling day trips (which often include trips to the waterfalls mentioned above) are popular. These circumnavigate the island, stopping at the best snorkelling spots, and include lunch and equipment. The following company departs daily at noon and returns around 6pm, unless the weather is bad. If you've booked ahead only to find it's windy and wet, you'll get a full refund.

Reggae Magic Boat Trip (Map p606; ☎ 08 1085 9137; Cactus Club; trips 500B) is the original around-the-island tour company, and offers the same long-tail trips it always has. Part of the popular bar Cactus, on the beach at Hat Rin, it is very popular with backpackers.

TREKKING
Jungle trekking is taking off on Ko Pha-Ngan in a big way – the trails up to the 620m Khao Ra, the island's biggest mountain, are reasonably well marked. Those with eagle-eyes will spot wild crocodiles, monkeys, deer and boar along the way, and the views from the top are spectacular – on a clear day you can see Ko Tao. This long, sometimes steep trail begins at the village of Ban Madeua Wan; be sure to bring plenty of high-energy food and drinking water. Guides for this trek and to the Phaeng Falls can be arranged at the village for 500B per trip or you can contact **Phaeng Waterfall National Park** (☎ 0 7723 8275).

YOGA & MASSAGE
The yoga retreat on Hat Chaophao, **Agama Yoga** (☎ 0 9233 0217; www.agamayoga.com; Bovy Resort), gets rave reviews from Lonely Planet readers for its holistic approach to the study of tantric yoga. Full day programmes start at 250B per day and longer workshops are also available. The centre is often closed from September to December while its instructors travel to India to work on their craft.

Chakra Traditional Thai Massage (Map p606; ☎ 0 7737 5401; 1/2hr 200/300B), located on a side street near the pier at Hat Rin Nai, offers expert massage. Yan, the proprietor, studied massage as a monk and is adept at traditional Thai massage as well as deep tissue techniques. Staff also practice reflexology, acupressure and reiki, and are adept at realigning chakras.

OTHER ACTIVITIES
There are loads of opportunities to try your hand at water sports, including jet-skiing, kite-boarding, water-skiing, sea-kayaking,

wind-surfing and sailing. Back on land, alternative modes of transport include all-terrain vehicles (ATVs) or quad-bikes, and elephants. The friendly staff at the **Backpacker's Information Centre** (☎ 0 7737 5535; www.backpackersthailand.com; Hat Rin) can help you arrange any of these.

The island's newest high-calibre activity is paintball. **Paintball Warfare** (☎ 08 1804 6059; Thong Sala) offers six varieties of games, including the always popular capture the flag – where you try to capture the other teams flag. It costs 500B to play all day, and up to 12 folks can play at once. Afterwards chill out at the on-site bar that plays a range of tunes over the speakers and has both Thai and Western staff.

If you want to try your foot at kick boxing or work up a sweat on the Stairmaster, head to **Jungle Gym & Thai Boxing** (Map p606; ☎ 0 7737 5155), which has facilities in Hat Rin and Thong Sala. The gym offers day visitors a range of weights and cardio equipment, along with yoga (one- to three-day workshops) and personal fitness training. The gym's instructors have been teaching and training fighters for more than eight years now and offer all levels of training – from novice to prefight. Stop by or give them a ring for rates.

Courses
Same Same Lodge runs a **Thai Cooking School** (Map p606; ☎ 0 7737 5200; www.same-same.com) and has one-/three-/five-day courses for 900/2500/4200B respectively. **Siam Spa-Ya** (☎ 0 7737 5563) runs 30-hour Thai massage certification courses over five or 10 days. These cost 4500B. You can also learn how to cook a multicourse Thai meal (800B; half-day classes beginning at 1pm).

Sleeping
Beach-bungalow operations are concentrated to the north and southeast of Thong Sala and especially on the southern end of the island at Hat Rin, but there are many other places to stay. Pha-Ngan has just one top-end resort of the calibre found on Ko Samui, but that's likely to change soon. Although the budget bracket still predominates on this backpacker Mecca, quite a few more than decent mid-range options with air-con, hot showers and real décor are also present.

The following sleeping options are listed in a clockwise direction starting with Thong Sala. Remember, when you jump off the boat you may be surrounded by hotel touts push-

ing small (and sometimes larger) operations all over the island. However, many of these bungalows will be on very remote beaches, some may lack electricity or running water, and you could feel quite isolated. If you're looking for lots of other travellers, multiple eating options or the chance to party hard, head to Hat Rin.

THONG SALA

There really is no reason to stay here unless you don't feel like having to worry about making an ultra early boat. If this is the case, we've listed our fave option below, although this pier town has many more places to rest your head.

Bua Kao Inn (☎ 0 7737 7226; buakao@samart.co.th; r 550-700B; ✳) Fastidiously maintained by an expat, this is a guesthouse with awesome showers. The five rooms are clean and nicely decorated and there's a popular restaurant downstairs. The inn is on the right-hand side of the first main intersection in town, about 100m straight ahead of the pier.

AO HIN KONG & AO WOK TUM

This long bay – sometimes divided in two by a stream that feeds into the sea (hence the two names) – is just a few kilometres north of Thong Sala and has relatively subdued tourist development. Bungalows are cheap; most don't have air-con. Săwngthăew here cost 30B, but you'll see them only at ferry departure and arrival times. A sign warns not to take seashells and corals from the bay, please respect this as it is not only illegal but bad for the ecosystem.

Woktum Cabana (☎ 0 7737 7430; bungalows 150-250B) The bit of sand at the front of this diverse collection of shacks and bungalows is one of the big draws. The friendly owner offers smaller, older concrete bungalows and newer, larger wooden ones.

Sea Scene (☎ 0 7737 7516; www.seascene.com; bungalows 400-1000B; ✳) This place is beautiful with upscale, modern bungalows in a well-tended garden. The top rooms here are air-con family bungalows sleeping up to four people.

HAT CHAOPHAO & AO SI THANU

One of the more tranquil beaches on this coast, Hat Chaophao is a rounded beach two headlands south of Hat Yao; Ao Si Thanu sits south of this beach. There's a charming lagoon at the southern end of Hat Chaophao as well as a few bars and minimarts scattered along

the road, so you're never far from essentials like water or beer.

Laem Son I & II (☎ 0 7734 9032; laemson1200@yahoo.com; Ao Si Thanu; bungalows 200-400B) On the rounded, pine-studded cape of Laem Son, at the northern end of Ao Si Thanu proper, these two places have small but passable bungalows, some with hammocks. Most are on the beach and there's a definite backpacker feel. The seaside restaurant has decent music and lots of pillows.

Pha-Ngan Cabana (☎ 0 1958 0182; Hat Chaophao; bungalows 300-1200B; ✳ 🖳 🖵) These sturdy, tidy villa-style bungalows are lined up inland from the beach. Outdoor bathrooms are cute. The restaurant is just OK, but it shows two movies a day and attracts people from around the beach – it's a real treat for rainy days.

HAT YAO

The coral-fringed beaches here are getting more developed as the road from Thong Sala gets paved. Hat Yao is a very long, pretty beach with a reasonable drop-off that makes it one of the islands best swimming beaches. There are a few diving outfits and several ATMs along the beaches but, as yet, no 7-Eleven.

Tantawan Bungalows (☎ 0 1956 0700; yup_pat@hotmail.com; bungalows 450-500B; 🖵) On a hillside, this place is fantastic but it's a bit of a trek down to the beach. It has a good French-Thai restaurant and beautiful views over the bay, as well as plenty of tree shade and soothing music.

Long Bay Resort (☎ 0 7734 9057; bungalows 700-2660B; ✳ 🖳 🖵) This is the fanciest place on the beach, with adequate fan bungalows and larger, beautiful air-con bungalows. It's good for families and the pool has a wading area. There's a five-person house that can be rented for 3500B. Laundry and massages are possible, and a minimart is within reach.

Ibiza (☎ 0 1968 4727; ibiza_thailand@hotmail.com; bungalows 150-1200B; ✳) Bungalows are cramped and basic, but its popular with backpackers, mostly because of the appealing garden and the chilled restaurant that plays movies nightly. The cheapie fan rooms are all the rage, but there are also pricier brick bungalows available with hot water and air-con.

AO MAE HAT, KO MA & AO HAT THONG LANG

Ban Mae Hat is a small fishing village with a few bungalow resorts. The beach at Ao Mae Hat isn't fantastic, but there is a bit of

LOWER SOUTHERN GULF

coral offshore and good snorkelling. Nam Tok Wang Sai, also known as Paradise Falls, is nearby. Ao Thong Lang is exceptionally quiet and devoid of development except for one midrange operation. Săwngthăew to/from Ban Chalok Lam cost 30B.

Pha-Ngan Divers Ko Ma Resort (☎ 0 1892 4835; bungalows 200-300B) This is the only place to stay on the small island of Ko Ma, opposite the beach. There are some bungalows of the standard Pha-Ngan variety here and not much else – it's perfect if you're into rustic isolation. During low tide you can walk to this little isle; at other times a small boat can ferry you across. There's excellent snorkelling here as well as a satellite dive-shop operation.

Wang Sai Resort (☎ 0 7737 4238; Ban Mae Hat; bungalows 200-1000B; ⊠) Decent bamboo huts along with more solid bungalows, some with air-con, are the trademarks here. There are boulders and a garden, and the beach is over the footbridge. All have views of the beach and bay. Rates depend on position on the slope. An open-air restaurant is situated well away from the huts, down on the beach, and a dive operation here offers instruction and guided trips.

Pha-Ngan Utopia Resort (☎ 0 7737 4093; www .phanganutopia.com; Hat Thong Lang; bungalows 1000-1500B; ⊠ ⊠) Recently upgraded, this place has neat bungalows high atop a cliff overlooking Hat Thong Lang – the views from the rooms are excellent and some even have bathtubs next to windows with grand sea panoramas. All rooms come with DVD players, and there's good snorkelling below.

AO CHALOK LAM

Ko Pha-Ngan's second-largest settlement is a laid-back little fishing village on the north coast. There are a couple of piers here and eager boatmen happy to take tourists to surrounding beaches, such as Hat Khuat. The beach is fairly shallow and not one of the island's best, but there's a couple of decent sleeping options, good restaurants and plenty of amenities, like grocery stores, laundry, internet cafés and motorbike-rental places. Săwngthăew ply the route from here to Thong Sala for 50B per person.

Fanta (☎ 0 7737 4132; fantaphangan@yahoo.com; bungalows 200-500B) The several rows of huts here take up a fair chunk of beach frontage, and there's a good travellers vibe.

North Beach Bungalows (☎ 0 7737 4258; bungalows 300-400B) These cute beachside cabanas have

two hammocks on each porch with perfect sea views, so you no longer have to take turns.

HAT KHUAT & HAT KHOM

Hat Khuat (also known as Bottle Beach) is the more stunning of the two bays, although Hat Khom is still quite the beauty queen. Both are becoming more popular by the hour, attracting tourists for their gorgeous beaches, calm waters and low-key atmosphere. These bays are backed by lush, thick jungle and the relative isolation is exactly what many people look for in an island getaway. During the high season both fill fast. In fact, after Hat Rin they're probably the second most popular sleeping destination. The clientele is still mostly backpackers – the type that thinks Hat Rin is too built up, but still craves a little action. Both beaches offer decent snorkelling around the points, and some places only have electricity at night.

In Chalok Lam there are regular long-tail boats to Hat Khom and Hat Khuat (50B to 150B). You can also walk to Hat Khom in about 20 minutes or take a taxi. Motorcycles should be able to negotiate the hard, sandy road – though it can get a little tricky after heavy rains. You can also hike the 2.5km from Hat Khom to Hat Khuat (approximately one hour).

Ocean Bay (☎ 0 7737 7231; Hat Khom; bungalows 200-450B) Up on the headland, this friendly place offers 30 comely abodes with great views. They range from basic huts with shared bathroom to large, ritzy and creatively decorated bungalows with balconies. The on-site restaurant has a splendid deck and serves vegetarian food. Call for free pick-up.

Ocean View Resort (☎ 0 7737 7231; Hat Khom; bungalows 200-450B) The best rooms are still basic but have enough room to swing two cats and then some. The beach garden setting looks like its manicured daily and the staff are exceptionally amiable.

Bottle Beach I (☎ 0 7744 7572; Hat Khuat; bungalows 350-700B; ⊠) Midrange rooms here are the best value: although they don't have air-con, the floors are made from polished wood and they are roomier than the low-priced huts. The air-con bungalows are cheap if keeping cool is your main objective, but they are far from good-looking concrete affairs.

Bottle Beach III (☎ 0 7744 5127; Hat Khuat; bungalows 350-850B) Also known as BB3, the cheapie huts these guys offer aren't the best deal in town,

but their deluxe two-level wooden bungalows are lovely and come with windows galore. **Bottle Beach II** (☎ 0 7744 5156; Hat Khuat; bungalows 150-350B) is the most rustic of the three; its plain huts come in colour combinations of aqua/dark brown or natural nipa/dark brown. They're all lined up in neat rows either along the beach or along the small river that feeds into the bay.

AO THONG NAI PAN YAI & NOI

This bay is really made up of two smaller bays, Ao Thong Nai Pan Yai (*yai* means 'big') and Ao Thong Nai Pan Noi (*noi* means 'little'). The latter is the best all-round swimming beach. Thong Nai Pan Yai has a relaxed vibe and a good set of rocks for advanced climbers. Many places have recently upgraded and offer some luxurious air-con choices – two of the swankiest places on the island are here. Otherwise, there's always the old, ramshackle fan-room variety for budgetarians.

Săwngthăew from Thong Sala to Thong Nai Pan cost 100B. Getting here by motorbike is easier than it once was since the dirt road has been resurfaced.

AD View (☎ 0 7744 5047; Ao Thong Nai Pan Yai; bungalows 150-400B) This place has a very relaxed restaurant on the beach and 12 bungalows ranging from small and rustic to larger and cute. All sit on lovely grounds.

Star Hut (☎ 0 7744 5085; Ao Thong Nai Pan Noi; bungalows 200-1800B; 🍴) Options here go from simple thatched huts with shared bathroom to more expensive, better versions with air-con. There's a reasonably priced, popular restaurant that offers some traveller services.

Panviman Resort (☎ 0 7744 5101-9; www.panviman.com; Ao Thong Nai Pan Noi; r & bungalows 2500-15,000B; 🍴 🛒 🛍) Sitting on top of the headland separating the two bays, this is Ko Pha-Ngan's other ultra fancy sleeping option with fine accommodation on hilly, lush grounds interlaced with brick paths and a spa on site. Rooms have balconies and elegant furniture, and there's a taxi service from Thong Sala.

Santhiya Resort & Spa (☎ 0 7723 8333; www.santhiya.com; Ao Thong Nai Pan Noi; bungalows r from 10,000B; 🍴 🛒 🛍) This sparkling new luxury resort is the most decadent place on Ko Pha-Ngan – even though the villas and bungalows blend into the lush environs and sit around a scenic cove – it's still kind of shocking to see something this posh on this shabby-chic island. All the plush and comfy small homes come

with sea views and direct access to the resort's private beach. Arrange for a speedboat to transfer you directly from the ferry pier to the resort.

EAST COAST BEACHES

There are areas of the east coast of Ko Pha-Ngan that are still undeveloped, which is great if you're trying to avoid the big party scene. For the most part, you'll have to hire a boat to get to these places, but that's not difficult. The road from Thong Sala to Ban Nam Tok is partially paved and only partially traversable by motorcycle; it's best to take a boat. Another dirt track (traversable on foot but only partially by motorcycle) runs along the coast from Hat Rin before heading inland to Ban Nam Tok and Than Sadet Falls. Think about how much isolation you really want before heading out here; some people can't get enough of the remoteness, others go crazy when they realise there's nothing to do but sit in the hammock and read all day (and night) long.

Hat Sadet

Hat Sadet sits past a rocky headland and is a large but relaxed beach cove that has some reasonable snorkelling. Here lies a string of modestly simple places – the remoteness of these places makes them perfect for a romantic getaway. All the bottom-rung options here share bathrooms.

Grookoo (bungalows 150-500B) Has hillside bungalows sporting excellent views.

Mai Pen Rai (☎ 0 7744 5090; www.thansadet.com; bungalows 300-700B)

Ao Thong Reng

The pretty coast of Ao Thong Reng has a striking, intimate beach that is touted as having been visited by many of Thailand's kings. Most travellers only come here to see the waterfalls, but basic accommodation can be found during the high season. Both of the places below offer basic bungalows with paper-thin walls, slightly off smells and mattresses on the floor. Dingy but cheap.

Thong Reng Resort (bungalows 100-300B)
Than Sadet Resort (bungalows 150-250B)

Hat Thian

Around a headland, Hat Thian is a small, quiet beach with a couple of very good places to stay. Boats from Hat Rin cost 80B; by rough trail it's a 1½-hour hike.

The Sanctuary & Wellness Centre (☎ 0 1271 3614; www.thesanctuary-kpg.com; dm 70B, bungalows 350-3000B) There's a great community feeling here. The main office incorporates impressive massive boulders into its structure and has a small library nestled above one of them. There's also a creatively built restaurant that serves wonderful vegetarian dishes and seafood. On offer are daily yoga and full spa treatments, including fasting and colonic irrigation, as well as body cleansing programmes.

Also recommended:

Haad Tien Resort (☎ 0 7737 7231; bungalows 100-350B) Beautiful peaked wood and bamboo bungalows.

Beam Restaurant & Bungalows (☎ 0 7927 2854; bungalows 300-500B) Charming wooden huts with hammocks and big bay windows looking out over the ocean.

Hat Yuan

This beach is rapidly becoming cool, which means crowds are increasing.

Bamboo Hut (☎ 0 7737 5139; bungalows 350-400B) High above the rocks at the beach's northern end, it has a scenic atmosphere surrounding its garden bungalows. Ideal for endless lounging is the huge, recently renovated restaurant and chill-space – it has awesome views of the bay.

HAT RIN (NOK & NAI)

This is the place to see and be seen on Ko Pha-Ngan. The island's most popular area is made up of two beaches, separated by a small shopping and eating district jam-packed with travel agencies, internet cafés, funky bars, retro clothing shops and unique jewellery stores. It's an exciting little scene that's especially crowded on cloudy days.

Hat Rin Nok (Sunrise Beach), on the east side, is along a sandy bay lined with bungalows and coconut palms, and is busy with boat traffic. It's the better of the two beaches, and the snorkelling here is good, but between October and March the surf can be a little hairy. This is the Full Moon party beach, so forget about sleeping on party nights.

Hat Rin Nai (Sunset Beach), on the western side, has a less-enticing beach, and is where the pier is located. It's a straighter beach than Hat Rin Nok and pleasantly relaxed, with much less activity and a more isolated feeling, but the beach tends to collect rubbish when the wind blows. It also has a number of bungalow operations. It's only a five-minute walk between the two beaches, so it doesn't really matter which side you stay on.

We've divided the following places into price categories; often the only difference between budget and midrange is air-con, and many places offer both cheaper and more expensive accommodation. Almost all operations have bars and restaurants, which show movies throughout the afternoon and evening.

Budget

Natural Home (☎ 0 1326 1552; dm 100B, bungalows 250-350B) This place is unique in that it offers dorm rooms – perfect for solo travellers on a serious budget. It too is high on the same sparse and shady hill as Top Hill, and is a bit of a hike towards the lighthouse from the main beach. There are great views of the sunrise and main beach from the restaurant. It may be deserted in low season. Insect repellent is a must.

Serenity Hill Bungalows (Map p606; ☎ 0 9937 1066; bungalows 200-350B) The best part about this place on the rocks at the far northern end of Hat Rin is the restaurant-bar perched precariously on stilts. It offers awesome sea views and a chilled-out atmosphere. The bungalows themselves are rather ratty. It throws Full Moon parties.

Mellow Mountain Bungalows (Map p606; ☎ 0 7737 5347; bungalows 300-600B) Right next to Serenity Hill, Mellow Mountain has similar views, a hip vibe and also hosts Full Moon parties. The bungalows are decently maintained and sit on a grassy hill. The bar is pretty cool – loads of cushions, hammocks, delicious milkshakes and soothing tunes. Check it out at sunset.

Rin Bay View (☎ 0 7737 5188; bungalows 300-700B; ❄) A great location means it's often full. The bungalows are simple but well maintained. They border a fertile garden strip and come in many price ranges.

Same Same Lodge & Restaurant (☎ 0 7737 5200; www.same-same.com; r 350-700B; ❄) This relative newcomer is often fully booked. It is a busy, friendly backpacker hang-out with a lounge full of comfy pillows, a book exchange and a TV on which to watch videos. A Thai-Danish couple run the peach-coloured, modern accommodation, and the restaurant serves everything from *phàt thai* to Frikadeller (Swedish meatballs). A Thai cooking school (p608) is also run from here.

Top Hill Resort (☎ 0 7737 5327; bungalows 500B) The moniker fits here; this place is way off the beach on the top of a very long dirt road

(basically walk uphill from Hat Rin Nok until you feel you've gone too far, keep going for another 10 minutes and you'll find Top Hill). Those who make it are rewarded with the most wonderful views and peace and quiet. The large and rickety log-pole bungalows with unique stone baths sit high on stilts at the edge of a cliff and have hammocks on their sea-facing porches. Those afraid of heights should steer clear – at times it feels as if you are going to fall through the floor. Bring insect repellent; the mozzies are vicious.

Midrange

Sun Cliff Resort (Map p606; ☎ 0 7737 5134; bungalows 250-1500B; 🛋) Perched on a hillside, Sun Cliff overlooks the sea and catches sunset rays amid huge boulders and lots of vegetation. It offers a variety of nicely appointed bungalows, each of a different design and décor. To get here walk five minutes south of the pier.

Paradise Bungalows (Map p606; ☎ 0 7737 5244; bungalows 400-800B; 🛋) This is where the Full Moon parties started, and the place remains popular (it's right on the beach at the centre of all the action). Maybe it's the nostalgia appeal, because past the fancy entrance sign are unattractive grounds and some seriously ramshackle bungalows (although the more expensive ones are nicer).

Sea Breeze Bungalow (Map p606; ☎ 0 7737 5162; bungalows 500-1000B; 🛋 🛋) This place gets a good report card from other travellers, and is our choice in this price bracket. There's a romantic feel created by well-spaced, secluded bungalows, some built high on stilts. Strategically strewn about the thick jungle on the hill overlooking Hat Rin Nai, many of these huts have dramatic views of the sunset from their patios. The new swimming pool, complete with whirlpool, is another reason to stay.

Bongo (Map p606; ☎ 0 7737 5268; bongomoo@yahoo .com; bungalows 500-1200B; 🛋) Rooms here are very simple and the cheaper ones have lumpy mattresses, but it's set in a peaceful, shady garden a few blocks from the beach. Check out a few rooms as some are much nicer than others.

Pha-Ngan Bayshore Resort (Map p606; ☎ 0 7737 5227; bungalows 500-3000B; 🛋) Set on spacious grassy grounds, just seconds from the beach, the more expensive bungalows here are quite lovely and large – with hardwood floors and duvets on the beds (a rarity around these parts). Try for the bungalow closest to Sun-

rise Resort – it has two sides of floor-to-ceiling windows and a giant porch.

Baan Talay (Map p606; ☎ 0 7737 5083; www.phangan .info/baantalay; bungalows 800-1000B; 🛋) A solid option if you just want an air-con place to crash, not too far from the pier but close to the action in town (it is not on the beach). Rooms in a motel block sport soft, but not lumpy, mattresses, clean sheets and blue-tiled floors, and are big enough to not feel in the least bit claustrophobic. Walls could use a new paint job and a few decorations. The air-con gets the room ice cold, and the place was relatively quiet. The lack of minifridge is a bummer.

Palita Lodge (Map p606; ☎ 0 7737 5172; www.palita lodge.com; bungalows with breakfast 800-3000B; 🛋) A friendly place with a good range of well-maintained bungalows, some of which are newly renovated and very posh – these come with suave furnishings like giant TVs, skylights, floor-to-ceiling windows, modern art and trickling fountains to sooth you to sleep. The regular air-con and cheap fan bungalows are kind of dark, but clean with nice porches. The garden is sparse rather than lush, and the restaurant serves up tasty food and screens movies.

Cocohut Village (Map p606; ☎ 0 7737 5368; www .cocohut.com; r 600B, bungalows 1200-3500B; 🛋 🛋) Located on a dazzling stretch of beach, this well-designed garden resort offers a range of accommodation diverse enough to accommodate everyone, from grandma and the family to the young couple on honeymoon. There are rooms in a hotel-style building as well as beachside bungalows with cheery interiors. The pool is a nice touch and employees are eager to please.

The following places are also recommended and all have similar facilities.

Seaview Haadrin Resort (Map p606; ☎ 0 7737 5160; bungalows 250-1500B; 🛋)

Sandy (Map p606; ☎ 0 7737 5138; bungalows 300-1500B; 🛋)

Rin Beach Resort (Map p606; ☎ 0 7737 5112; bungalows 500-2500B; 🛋)

Neptune's Villa (Map p606; ☎ 0 7737 5251; bungalows 850-1500B; 🛋)

Top End

Drop In Club Resort & Spa (Map p606; ☎ 0 7737 5444; dropinclub@kohsamui.com; bungalows from 2500B; 🛋 🛋) This newish place started the island's slow trend towards swankier accommodation. The resort is tastefully laid-out and features 46 luxury bungalows with teak furnishings and Thai décor throughout, as well as all the usual

upmarket amenities – satellite TV, safe, mini-bar. There's a restaurant, a lovely pool and spa facilities. The only drawback is it's not right on the beach.

BAN TAI & BAN KHAI

Between the villages of Ban Tai and Ban Khai is a series of sandy beaches with quite a few well-spaced bungalow operations. From the main road, the signs to these places can be small and hard to see. A săwngthăew from Thong Sala costs 30B per person to this area. These are not the best beaches on the island, and quite remote, so if you choose to stay here pick a place with amenities to keep you entertained.

Milky Bay Resort (☎ 0 7723 8566; www.milkybay .com; bungalows from 1500B; 🌂 🖳 🗩) This newer South African–Thai venture can be a great deal, some of the bungalows are really beautiful with welcome touches, bamboo bed frames and mosquito nets, but others seem cramped and overpriced. Just check out a few before deciding to stay. It was popular when we visited, despites its remote location on a not so great beach. We liked the pool, jungle fitness centre, sauna and pool tables. It's very family friendly, and the on-site restaurant and bar keep you from having to stray.

Eating

Many bungalows operators have restaurants attached, but there is a burgeoning eating scene scattered around the island. Make a beeline for Hat Rin for the biggest selection of eateries.

THONG SALA

A's Coffee Shop and Restaurant (☎ 0 7737 7336; dishes 40-170B; 🌂 breakfast & lunch Mon-Sat) The perfect place to spend a few hours if you're stuck in town waiting for the ferry, it offers everything from homemade breads to big breakfasts, and throws in sandwiches, pasta and salads for good measure. Strong coffee and a long cocktail menu are an added bonus.

HAT CHAOPHAO

The Village Green (☎ 0 7734 9217; dishes 60-200B; 🌂 breakfast, lunch & dinner) Run by the ludicrously informative Ben Green, this place serves excellent Thai and Western fare in a two-storey teak structure. Its 'build your own breakfast' menu is enough to satisfy anyone's morning munchies.

HAT RIN (NOK & NAI)

There's no shortage of Thai, Western or seafood restaurants in the Hat Rin area.

Nira's Bakery (Map p606; ☎ 0 7737 5109; dishes 25-200B; 🌂 24hr) This bakery and restaurant combo is a very popular breakfast spot, brewing up fancy coffees such as iced mocha (70B) and double espresso (60B). The food is also good and includes sandwiches, quiches, donuts, pizza, Israeli dishes, salads and Thai dishes. The service could use some improvement, though.

Palita Restaurant (Map p606; ☎ 0 7737 5172; www .palitalodge.com; dishes 60-200B; 🌂 breakfast, lunch & dinner) On a prime spot on the beach, the restaurant at the resort by the same name has a giant TV playing all the latest pirated blockbusters. It is set back from the beach and catches a breeze. The grounds are a bit messy, but it has billiard and ping-pong tables. Its breakfasts range from American to Israeli dishes (100B to 200B), and it also serves loads of salads, soups and spaghetti.

BT Restaurant (Map p606; ☎ 0 1797 8815; Hat Rin; dishes 60-200B) The usual Thai and Western specialities as well as barbecues and set-price meals are served here. It was packed when we stopped by.

Bamboozle (Map p606; dishes 70-180B; 🌂 lunch & dinner) Take your pick of Mexican food such as chilli *rellenos*, burritos and nachos served on a lofty platform.

Shell (Map p606; ☎ 0 7737 5149; dishes 90-130B, pizzas 140-220B; 🌂 lunch & dinner) Serves good Italian food such as gnocchi, ravioli and pizza, along with gelato, tiramisu and Italian coffees. It's in an open, peaceful area beyond the lily ponds.

Outback Bar (Map p606; ☎ 0 7737 5126; dishes 120-220B; 🌂 breakfast, lunch & dinner) This is an expat-run eatery, which in this case means the Western food is reasonably authentic – order Caesar salad, lamb chops, Swedish meatballs and shepherd's pie, followed by a good selection of beer. It plays movies and Full Moon party footage throughout the day and night. It's an ambient place, with modern art on the walls and fat cushions on the floor. Escape the sun for a few hours, and spend the afternoon watching a movie or footy on the big TVs. At night, however, it can get hot and cramped.

Al Colosseo (Map p606; ☎ 0 7883 8569; dishes 200-400B; 🌂 lunch & dinner) Sit in the air-con, indoor environs or out on the porch, while Al Colosseo prepares authentic Italian food. Order

FULL MOONING

According to legend, Ko Pha-Ngan's first Full Moon party took place in either 1987 or 1988 – no-one can quite remember – although it was meant to be a celebration of someone's birthday. It took place at the Paradise Bungalows. The party turned out so well the gang decided to meet up again for the next full moon, and thus began a tradition that has since turned into the world's largest monthly rave. Some 3000 to 8000 ravers – sometimes over 30,000 during the December-to-February peak season – turn up to dance, drink and smoke the night away. Although the moon parties used to be casual affairs, these days they are quite impressively planned extravaganzas, with more than 10 major sound systems on the beach playing everything from psy-trance to drum'n'bass – each represents a different genre. Popular venues include Paradise Bungalows, The Rock, Drop-In Bar (below), Vinyl, Zoom Bar and Cactus (below) – all are within stumbling distance of each other on the beach. Fire dancing and fireworks light up the night and the number of party goers peaks at around 2am to 3am (the last DJs don't shut down till around 11am). As you can guess, it's a pretty wild and hazy time for everyone.

And what would the world's biggest beach party be without drugs? Yes, they're still available these days, though the more hardcore partakers have moved on to other beaches due to a pumped-up police presence (both uniformed and undercover). More than a few deaths have been attributed to drug use at this party.

The whole event is well organised by Thai residents who run the bungalows and bars along Hat Rin. And these same proprietors, along with some of the more conscientious foreign travellers, come together to clean the beach of substantial morning-after litter when the party is finally over.

Theft has been a problem at Full Moon parties in recent years (the bungalows in Ko Pha-Ngan are simply too rickety in most cases to be fully secure), so much so that many folks are visiting the party via one of the all-night shuttles departing from various points in Ko Samui. Tickets cost 400B one way or 550B return. If you choose to stay on the island for the party, arrive a few days earlier – accommodation books out fully, especially during the peak months.

Check your lunar calendar for upcoming Full Moon party dates. The website, www.fullmoon.phangan.info/, is also a good resource.

Ko Pha-Ngan has done a good job of cashing in on its Full Moon fame and there are now moon parties for every phase. Ban Tai has **Half Moon Festival** (www.halfmoonfestival.com) twice a month, with lots of psychedelic tunes and quality trance.

---

pizza, pasta or fresh seafood – they are all equally delicious. There are daily specials.

Drinking

For the most part, where there's bungalows, there's booze, although Hat Rin is the only place where there's really a bar scene.

Drop-In Bar (Map p606; Hat Rin) Claiming to be the island's original beach bar, Drop-In is the kind of place that uses any excuse for a party. The walls are colourful, the staff strangely eclectic and the drinks list includes piña coladas, kamikazes and Long Island iced teas. Tunes run from rock to hip hop, pop, house and trance – 'every night is different', says the Rasta dude. There are plenty of mats in the sand with cheap buckets of whisky to imbibe, someone is always throwing around a fire stick, and there are frequent parties with bonfires to celebrate any phase of the moon.

Cactus (Map p606; ☎ 0 7737 5308) Very similar to the Drop-In, this popular place serves a range of cocktails and beer, has nightly pounding DJ music for dancing and more mats in the sand for lounging.

Lazy House (Map p606; ☎ 0 7737 5432) This is a cool place to veg out and watch a movie on a giant projector screen. Run by a friendly English man, it serves food from around the globe and has loads of cushions for just chilling.

There are also a bunch of bars at Ao Thong Nai Pan Noi, including the Jungle Bar, Rasta Bar and Outlaw Bar.

The Pirates Bar (☎ 0 4728 6064) A popular and wacky drinkery at Hat Chaophao, it is a replica of a pirate ship built into the cliffs. When you're sitting on the deck and the tide is high you can almost believe you're out at sea – watch out for men overboard. These guys have an immense sound system and host moon-set parties.

Getting There & Away

The exact number of boat departures is determined by the weather and season. Slower boats tend to be no frills and cheaper, while faster ones are more expensive and more comfortable.

There are almost 10 daily departures between Ko Pha-Ngan and Ko Samui (180B to 250B). These boats leave throughout the day from 7am to 4pm and take from 30 minutes to an hour. All leave from either Thong Sala or Hat Rin on Ko Pha-Ngan and arrive either in Na Thon, Mae Nam or the Bang Rak pier on Ko Samui. If the final location matters, state your preferences while buying your ticket.

There are over six daily departures between Ko Pha-Ngan and Surat Thani (250B to 380B, 2½ hours). These boats leave from Thong Sala throughout the day from 7am to 10pm.

You can also take a slow night ferry direct to Pha-Ngan from Th Ban Don in Surat at 11pm (200B, seven hours). The night ferry can be a rough ride – November is the worst month. As with the night ferry to Samui, don't leave your bags unattended on the boat and remember that you'll arrive *very* early in the morning, but this can be pleasant and you'll save the cost of a night's accommodation.

There are several daily departures between Ko Pha-Ngan's Thong Sala and Ko Tao (180B to 350B, one to 1½ hours). These boats leave throughout the day from 8.30am to 1pm.

Getting Around

Roads on the island are being paved at a rapid rate, which will no doubt mean fewer low-speed accidents and more high-speed ones. The worst place for motorcycle riding is between Ban Khai and Hat Rin, which is a paved but very hilly road; don't attempt this unless you're very good on a motorcycle. Also, the unpaved midsection to Ao Thong Nai Pan can get pretty rough.

You can rent motorcycles all over the island for about 250B per day. Wear a helmet, especially if you're going to be taking on dirt or steep roads. Bicycles are sometimes available for rent for 100B a day. Car rentals are around 1300B a day.

Some places can be reached only by boat, such as Hat Khuat and some sections of the eastern coast. If you do find trails, bear in mind that they can be overgrown and are not recommended for walking if you're wearing a heavy pack.

To and from Thong Sala, săwngthăew cost 50B per person to anywhere on the island except for Ao Thong Nai Pan (100B). Rates jump at sunset or if petrol happens to be particularly expensive that week. The best time to move around the island, whether by boat or săwngthăew, is around midday. This is when the majority of the boats from Surat Thani and other islands arrive and săwngthăew and boats swarm in to move people to their final destinations. At other times you may have to charter the whole săwngthăew or boat if there are not enough people.

Long-tail boats from Ao Chalok Lam to Hat Khuat cost around 50B per person with at least six people; otherwise it's 350B to charter the whole thing. Boats between Thong Sala and Hat Yao or Hat Rin cost about 150B per person from January to September (in calm weather only), though there are rarely enough people to warrant these boats running. From Hat Rin to Ao Thong Nai Pan Yai by long-tail boat expect to pay around 250B. You can charter a boat ride from beach to beach for about 200B per 15 minutes of travel.

KO TAO

เกาะเต่า

pop 5500

Scuba virgins from all over flock to Ko Tao to learn how to dive. Not only is this lush, pistachio-coloured island blessed with crystal clear water and trippy coral reefs shallow enough for beginners to explore; it's also is one of the world's cheapest and most popular places to get your open-water dive certification – only Cairns in Australia issues more PADI diving certificates each year. Diving is definitely the island's mainstay, and on its busiest areas you can't walk 100m without tripping over a shop. Once you choose an outfitter, there are dozens of spectacular reefs with plentiful marine life to swim through. Experienced divers should note, however, that while Ko Tao may be advertised as Thailand's diving Mecca, when it comes to truly awesome dive sites, the island can't compete with the world-famous Similan Islands (p655) or even the fishy waters off of Ko Phi Phi (p705).

Once considered exclusively a dive destination, these days Ko Tao is nearly as popular with nondivers as it is with scuba enthusiasts. Small (it measures just 21 sq km) and laidback, it's become a haven for those seeking the beauty found on big sisters Ko Samui and

---

KEEPING IT CLEAN

Like in many closed ecosystems, Ko Tao's popularity is starting to strain resources; litter is a common problem and there is an ongoing water shortage. Here are a few ways that you can help:

▪ Follow the 'when its yellow let it mellow, when it's brown flush it down' rule of toilet flushing. Turn the water off while shampooing and conditioning and keep your showers just short enough to wash the salt off – you know you're just going back in the ocean anyway.

▪ Although bins are often hard to come by, make the effort to find one rather than depositing your cigarette butts and empty bottles on the beach – cigarette butts take years to break down and spoil the sand. And if you purchase a small item at the store, think about whether you need the plastic bag it's automatically placed in.

Ko Pha-Ngan without the chaos. Fast and frequent ferries make travel to Ko Tao easy, and once you arrive there's plenty of entertainment – from lounging on pristine beaches to mountain biking through the lush and rugged interior. All in all Ko Tao is a romantic place, where nights are casual affairs, usually involving a quiet drink by candlelight on a cushion near the edge of the sea.

Even though Ko Tao has become more hip with each season, it hasn't let this celebrity status go to its head. Although there are pockets of frenetic activity in the main tourist ghettos of Ban Hat Sai Ri and Ban Mae Hat, much of the island retains an easy-going pace. Infrastructure on Ko Tao is still pretty basic, with much of the east coast only accessible by 4WD or boat, and 24-hour electricity blanketing only about 75% of the island.

Orientation & Information

Ko Tao is about 60km of the coast of Surat Thani and part of the Samui archipelago. As it is only 21 sq km, it's possible to walk to most parts, providing you get an early start.

Ban Mae Hat, a one-street town with a busy pier, is where the boats dock. It is on the island's western side and is the main commercial centre. Here you'll find travel agencies, dive shops, restaurants, internet cafés, shops, boutiques and motorcycle rentals. Boat tickets can be purchased at a booking office by the harbour as well as from travel agencies. Two second-hand bookshops are here as well.

Both Krung Thai Bank and Siam Commercial Bank have a money exchange window near the pier, and several ATMs and moneychangers can also be found around town.

The **police station** (☎ 07745 6631) is just north of Mae Hat. There's a post and telephone office in Ban Mae Hat. Watch out for private phone offices, which charge exorbitant rates. **Badalveda** (☎ 0 7745 6664; www.badalveda.com), on the main road in Mae Hat, has a hyperbaric chamber. There are also clinics throughout the island to treat minor ailments.

Ban Hat Sai Ri, about midway up the western coast, is where most travellers choose to crash. It has the same selection of tourist services as Ban Mae Hat, plus countless bungalow operations and a lovely beach.

Ban Chalok Ban Kao to the south is the only other village on the island, but not

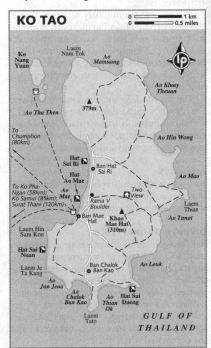

KO TAO

> ## KO TAO – THE BACK STORY IN FIVE LINES
>
> Ko Tao's name means 'Turtle Island' and it is called this because of the swarms of turtles that used to nest here. Drifting further from land than either Ko Samui or Ko Pha-Ngan, Ko Tao lays claim to a chequered past and has been a favourite hideout for pirates, a lay-over point for weary fishermen and even a detention centre for political prisoners. The descendants of the original inmates still make up a large part of the local community.

nearly as appealing as Ban Hat Sai Ri. Ko Nang Yuan, just 1km off the northwestern side of Ko Tao, is really three islands joined by a sand bar. It has just one place to stay. The east and north coasts are fairly undeveloped, with only a few bungalow enterprises on each little bay offering a truly rugged retreat. The steep, rutted roads that connect these bays are best navigated by sǎwngthǎew or an off-road motorbike handled by an experienced rider.

The granite promontory of Laem Tato at the southern tip of Ko Tao makes an enjoyable hike from Ban Chalok Ban Kao. About the only thing of historic interest on the island is a large boulder that King Rama V had his initials carved into to commemorate a royal visit in 1900.

The *Ko Tao Info* booklet, available all over the island, is updated four times a year and is a great resource. It lists virtually every business here, and includes details about Ko Tao's history, culture and social issues.

Activities

Ko Tao has little to offer in the area of cultural attractions. But if you're into being active, you won't get bored anytime soon.

DIVING & SNORKELLING

Ko Tao is one of Thailand's main underwater playgrounds, which is no surprise considering its high visibility and clean waters. Some of the best sites here are offshore islands or pinnacles (see Top Five Dive Sites, opposite). Underwater wildlife includes grouper, moray eels, batfish, titan triggerfish, angelfish, bluespotted stingrays, sea snakes, reef sharks and the occasional whale shark.

Courses are taught in many different languages other than English and the quality of your dive experience will ultimately depend on the experience and abilities of your dive shop's staff. It's a good idea to ask around for a recommendation. Some of the dive shops are small and just offer dive services, while others are 'dive resorts' that also have accommodation (sometimes only available to clients).

These days rates are standardised around the island – there's little need to spend your time hunting around for the best deal. Typical rates charged are from 900B to 1000B per dive or 7000B for a 10-dive package (including gear, boat, guide, food and beverages). If you bring all your own gear, it's 700B per dive. An all-inclusive introductory dive lesson will set you back 2000B, while a four-day, PADI Open Water certificate course costs 9000B – these rates include gear, boat, instructor, food and beverages, and sometimes a discount on accommodation.

Ask at your accommodation or one of the travel agencies (often doubling as internet cafés) in the villages about snorkelling trips; they usually run at about 450B to 700B per day including lunch and snorkelling gear. A snorkel, mask and fins are typically hired as a set for 100B per day and can be rented almost anywhere.

OTHER WATER SPORTS

If hanging out underwater doesn't appeal to you, there are a few things you can do on the surface. Both **Black Tip Divers** (☎ 0 7745 6204; www.black-tip.com) and the friendly folks at **MV Sports** (☎ 0 7745 6065; www.mvsports.net) in Mae Hat can pull you behind a speedboat on all manner of things, including water skis, wakeboards or even an inflatable sumo suit. Two exhausting 10-minute sessions will cost you 1000B. Fishing enthusiasts can swing their tackle at sea by contacting the **Adventure Centre** (☎ 0 9019 1761; Mae Hat), which arranges all-day fishing *sea*faris for 1500B (minimum two people). A number of bungalow operations also rent out kayaks for around 350B per day.

SPAS

There are half-a-dozen places on Ko Tao to get wonderful massages or spa treatments. Many bungalows offer more rustic, but sometimes equally good, Thai massages. A one-hour massage costs about 300B.

Jamahkiri Resort & Spa (☎ 0 7745 6400/1; www
.jamahkiri.com), near Ao Tanot, does aloe-vera
wraps (great for sunburn), massage and
facials atop a huge island peak. The resort is
large, peaceful and gorgeously designed. It's
a truly luxurious experience that's very good
value (450B for an aloe wrap). Call for free
transport.

Here & Now (☎ 0 7745 6730; www.hereandnow.be),
at CFT (p620), offers classes in two Chinese
martial arts, *taijiquan* and *qi gong*, taught by a
German expat. Nine-session early morning or
evening courses cost 3100B. The owner's wife
and his daughter also offer traditional Thai
yoga massage for 680B for 2½ hours.

OTHER ACTIVITIES

Ko Tao Bowling (☎ 0 5150 3485; per hr 240B; ☼ noon-
midnight) is on the main road between Mae Hat
and Chalok Ban. It offers island-style bowling on homemade lanes or you might like
to test your putting skills on the miniature
golf course.

Sleeping

Now that Ko Tao has established itself as
a full-scale diving resort destination, the
island has gone construction crazy. The
days of the thatched hut are over, especially
along Hat Ao Mae and Hat Sai Ri, but so far
there are still only a couple of true luxury
options. Many operations are fronted by a
dive shop.

There are several dazzling, lonely bays scattered around Ko Tao that still offer escapists
a true getaway experience. Getting to these
places takes patience, however, due to the
dismal road network that connects them. If
you want to sleep in Ko Tao's more remote
beaches, it is probably better to decide on a
resort – at least for the first night – in advance.
That way you can call ahead of time and usually arrange to be picked up from the pier –
this may save you having to charter a whole
taxi for 350B to 450B.

Unless stated, rates here are approximates
for April to November; expect them to skyrocket from December to March and vacan-
cies to disappear regardless. Many simple
places have electricity only at night and not
even all the fancy places have electricity 24
hours a day (at least not yet). Midrange operations here don't tend to offer air-con unless
you fork out at least 1500B.

Practically all bungalows on the island have
their own restaurant; some places can even get
miffed if you don't take the majority of your
meals at their restaurant.

HAT AO MAE

As the home of Ko Tao's ferry pier, this is
not the most appealing beach on Ko Tao (the
pier generates a lot of rubbish). Home to numerous shops, restaurants, bars and internet
cafés, Hat Ao Mae is noisy, but a fun place to
party. It also has plenty of coral in its shallow
bay, just stay away from the southern edge
where most of the rubbish clusters. The village spreads to the north and south of the
pier.

TOP FIVE DIVE SITES

With so many excellent dive sites within easy reach, it's no wonder diving is *de rigueur* here. If
you're lucky, you may spot some of the increasingly elusive whale sharks that have been known
to frequent this region. The following are a sample of some of the better dives here (with their
maximum depths in brackets).

- Sail Rock (45m) – The most famous site here is closer to Pha-Ngan than Ko Tao, and has a
  massive rock chimney with vertical swim-through, as well as barracuda, kingfish and the occasional manta ray.

- Chumphon Pinnacle (40m) – The base of these four pinnacles is covered in anemones and
  you will see bat fish, big groupers, barracuda and possibly whale sharks (in season).

- Shark Island (28m) – Made of massive boulders and rock formations, you can spot leopard
  and reef sharks at the lower depths and the occasional hawksbill turtle.

- White Rock (22m) – Lots of hard and soft corals are home to butterfly fish, clown fish, angel
  fish, morays and the territorial trigger fish.

- Southwest Pinnacles (33m) – A good advanced dive, the rocky pinnacles here are home to
  colourful tropical fish, leopard sharks, blue-spotted rays and occasional whale sharks.

LOWER SOUTHERN GULF

South of the Pier

To get to the following places, take a right as soon as you get off the main pier

Save Bungalow (☎ 0 7745 6180; bungalows 250-650B) As far as cheapies go, this is one of the better values close to the pier. Wooden and concrete bungalows line a green pathway leading away from the beach, and the better rooms have kitchenettes (although none are exceptional).

Ko Tao Royal Resort (☎ 0 7745 6156; fax 0 7745 6157; bungalows 950-3500B; 🔀) A great choice, this is a chic place with beautiful, contemporary bungalows (everything's teak) and 24-hour electricity. Each bungalow sits in a garden and has a hammock.

Sensi Paradise Resort (☎ 0 7745 6244; www.sensi paradise.com; bungalows 1050-8820B; 🔀) The Thai-style bungalows at this artsy upmarket spot can be gorgeous, done up in masculine dark wood. The indoor/outdoor paths are a romantic plus, while covered decks (excellent for lounging) overlook the sea. The bigger villas are perfect for families. There are a few basic bungalows.

North of the Pier

Take a left at Café del Sol to reach these establishments.

Crystal Dive Resort (☎ 0 7745 6107; www.crystal dive.com; bungalows 250B-900B; 🔀 🖵) You must dive here to sleep at Crystal (hence the ultra cheap rates). Prices vary not on amenities, but on what sort of diving you do – a beginner's course garners the cheapest rate. The bungalows are lean, modern and lined in neat rows. The pool is a plus. During the off season nondivers may be accommodated, but expect rates to rise quite a bit.

Tommy's Dive Resort (☎ 0 7745 6039; bungalows 400-2500B) The deck restaurant has a fun vibe, but sadly the bungalows feel sterile. They are bright and quite modern, however, and terraced down to the water. Most have hammocks and balconies. The priciest options are probably not worth the baht, as none have air-con.

HAT SAI RI

Look for our favourite stretch of sand on Ko Tao around the headland to the north of the pier. It is the longest and most developed beach on the island, with a string of dive operations, bungalows, travel agencies, minimarkets and internet cafés. The narrow, shady pathway here is now paved with bricks the whole way; just watch out for motorcycles.

Budget

Here and Now (CFT) Resort (☎ 0 7745 6730; www .hereandnow.be; bungalows 100-600B) This German-run place offers traditional Thai yoga massage (700B for 2½ hours) and *qi gong*/tai chi courses. CFT doesn't focus on creature comforts, but instead on spiritual enlightenment, and is best for those who don't mind roughing it a bit. All bungalows are basic and the cheapest share baths. The junglelike grounds are strewn with magnificent boulders. Look for CFT on the far northern end of the road a few hundred metres past Sun Lord.

Big Blue Resort (☎ 0 7745 6050; www.bigbluediving .com; r 200-500B; 🔀) A good variety of accommodation is offered at Big Blue, but it only takes nondivers during the low season and charges them higher rates. Even if you aren't staying, the deck bar is a good spot for happy hour (5pm to 8pm).

North of the beach, in a hilly area called Ao Ta Then, are several operations with very inexpensive and very basic bungalows – most high above the water. All charge about 200B to 400B and the majority have outstanding views. These places are very isolated, but could be your deal if you love the ultra rustic and aren't afraid of dust or a few bugs on your bed. Don't expect many amenities up here (like restaurants).

Blue Wind (☎ 0 7745 6116; bungalows 250-800B; 🔀) Offering basic fan bungalows, Blue Wind also has slightly nicer, air-con bungalows that stand out from the competition. They're still small, but are built out of higher quality wood that blends in with the environs. There's a great feeling of seclusion here, and yoga classes (300B) are held twice a day if you need even more peace of mind. Most of the huts aren't beachfront, however.

Sai Ree Cottages (☎ 0 7745 6126; bungalows 300-500B) These thatched-roof bungalows are excellent value and go pretty quickly – book ahead or get here early to score one of the huts facing out onto a grassy lot with palm trees. There's also a popular, tranquil restaurant.

Also recommended:

Sun Lord (☎ 0 7745 6139; bungalows 300B) Our pick of the bunch, look for Sun Lord below Sun Sea. Bungalows seem to be a bit sturdier than the other places.

Silver Cliff (☎ 0 9290 7546; bungalows 300B) Up a rough driveway.

Sun Sea (☎ 0 9037 4195; bungalows 300B) High on top of the rocks.

Midrange

AC Resort I (☎ 0 7745 6197; bungalows 350-1500B; 🍴 🍸) This place can't be missed – look for the massive sign with a waterfall spilling over it. It features small fan bungalows and air-con ones with huge beds, all located on pleasantly grassy, hilly and palm-tree laden grounds. If you dive with the resort's dive shop, you can get 30% to 40% off.

Ban's Diving Resort (☎ 0 7745 6061; www.amazing kohtao.com; r & bungalows 400-1200B; 🍴 🍸) The best deal in its price range, Ban's has fabulously manicured grounds filled with pools, fountains and lush vegetation. The more expensive rooms are in sets of white colonial-style hotel buildings with balconies, while the cheaper options are decent no-frills bungalows. The most expensive rooms have TVs. If you want to stay in a fan room, you need to book a dive trip.

Seashell Resort (☎ 0 7745 6299; www.kohtaoseashell .com; bungalows 450-1550B) The pricier bungalows here come with lovely tiled floors and floor-to-ceiling windows looking out onto the ocean. On the downside they are a bit small and the sheets don't match. The porches are great, however, and the grounds beautiful.

Also recommended:

Lotus Resort (☎ 0 7745 6271; r 400-850B, bungalows 1200-1600B; 🍴)

Silver Sand Beach Resort (☎ 0 7745 6303-6; silver-sand_kohtao@hotmail.com; bungalows 400-1500B; 🍴)

Sunset Buri Resort (☎ 0 7745 6266; bungalows 700-1800B; 🍴 🍸)

Top End

Thipwimarn (☎ 0 7745 6409; thipwimarn@excite.com; bungalows 1750-3500B; 🍴) Probably the best deal on this beach, Thipwimarn lies 200m beyond the cheapies and is at the other end of the comfort spectrum. A circular restaurant with an outstanding view offers intimate, floor-level tables. Attractive bungalows spill down the hillside among boulders and greenery, with a myriad of stairs to keep you fit!

Koh Tao Coral Grand Resort (☎ 0 7745 6431-4; www .kohtaocoral.com; bungalows 2000-7200B; 🍴 🍸) A posh and newish resort, a bit beyond Hat Sai Ri proper, it has pastel-coloured, double-peaked bungalows in geometric shapes. The air-con abodes are really comfortable and boast wooden floors, huge sliding glass doors and porches facing right out over the water. Linens are bright and there are wooden tubs.

Koh Tao Cabana (☎ 0 7745 6250; www.kohtaocabana .com; bungalows 2700-3500B; 🍸) This place can be a luxury winner as long as you score a room with air-con – make sure to ask before shelling out nearly 3000B for a fan. There's a lovely grassy bit leading up to the water with wooden sun beds to laze on. The bungalows are large and Flintstone-like with tropical décor and creative indoor/outdoor bathrooms. All are smooth and circular and overlook the sea from under shady palms.

AO MAMUANG

An isolated rocky bay, Ao Mamuang offers great snorkelling and a dramatic setting of jungle and rocky hills.

our pick **Mango Bay Grand Resort** (☎ 0 7745 6097; www.mangobaygrandresortkohtaothailand.com; bungalows 800-2500B; 🍸) Blending sublimely into its wild surroundings, this is a well-liked Italian-run little gem. The very neat, burnt-red bungalows are finished with smart wooden fixtures, have excellent views and are well spread out along the hill. They're reached by gently curving walks and mosaic-lined paths. There's a massive restaurant/deck here to laze away the time between snorkelling sessions.

AO HIN WONG

On the eastern side of Ko Tao is serene Ao Hin Wong. There isn't much of a beach, but the water is crystal clear and the snorkelling is quite good. The road here is paved but still risky on a motorcycle. Several places rent out kayaks for around 150/350B for a half-/full-day; these provide a great way to explore the area.

View Rock (☎ 0 7745 6548/9; viewrock@hotmail .com; bungalows 300-500B) Located 600m up the dirt road from Green Tree, you climb the hill to get to the entrance, but climb back down (it's around a headland) to reach the seaside bungalows and restaurant. The place is a little rickety, with a mishmash of wooden bungalows on stilts snaking up a steep hill. It's not without its charm, though, and there's a feeling of complete seclusion.

Hin Wong Bungalows (☎ 0 7745 6006; bungalows 300-700B) There are some beautiful new wooden bungalows here with great big modern bathrooms; older bungalows are OK too, but obviously not as fancy. There's also an agreeable seaside restaurant.

LAEM THIAN

South of Ao Hin Wong, past Ao Mao, is the scenic cape of Laem Thian.

Laem Thian (☎ 0 7745 6477; r 350-1000B, bungalows 150-1500B; ✗) The best part about this place is its grounds, which are strewn with huge boulders. Check out the ones on the edge of the hillside above the sea – they are perfect for ocean jumps if you're brave enough. Laem Thian is in an isolated location, so it's not the best choice if you want to go out at night. Rooms here tend to be better than the bungalows, as long as you don't judge them from the outside (which is rather depressing looking). Inside they feature contemporary furnishings and balconies. The best have sea views. The road here is very rough; you can call for a pick-up.

AO TANOT

Heading south from Laem Thian is Ao Tanot – one of the island's best spots for snorkelling. Two dive operators compete in this small, boulder-strewn cove, while several bungalow ventures line the beachfront. There are a few simple shops in the area.

Bamboo Hut (☎ 0 7745 6531; bungalows 150-500B) Surrounded by trees, but the older they are, the smaller they are. The restaurant is very laid-back and the kitchen specialises in spicy southern Thai-style food.

Diamond Beach (☎ 0 7745 6591/2; bungalows 400-500B) These bungalows are relatively new, modern and comfortable. They have interesting designs with windows placed on the hut's corners. It's a good spot, with upbeat music playing and an appealing restaurant near the beach.

Tanote Bay Resort (☎ 0 7745 6757; tanotebay@hotmail .com; bungalows 400-3000B; ✗) The most upmarket joint on this stretch of beach, bungalows here range from wood to concrete construction and sit at the northern end of the beach. It's a good choice, and the hillside rooms are modern and hygienic. Its rates stay the same year-round.

Black Tip Dive Resort (☎ 0 7745 6488; www.blacktip -kohtao.com; bungalows 800-1700B; ✗) Part of a dive shop and water-sports centre, Black Tip has a handful of lovely bungalows. If you fun dive with them, you get 25% off the room rates; if you do a course, it's 50% off. The dive centre has a wacky, white adobe design with strange geometrical configurations.

KHAO MAE HAT

On the southern road to Ao Tanot from Ban Mae Hat, a path forks off the main track and leads up the slopes of 310m Khao Mae Hat, in the centre of the island. Even 4WD vehicles in the dry season hesitate to climb this road, but strong (unburdened) hikers can reach the top in about 30 minutes.

Two View (twoview@hotmail.com; bungalows 150B) It's a trek to get here – you'll have to hike for one hour uphill along the path from Ao Tanot – but if you're looking for a room with a view away from it all, Two View is worth the climb. It's a back to nature place affording sunrise and sunset views of both sides of the island. There are only six bungalows and no electricity or generator: kerosene lamps and candles provide light at night. Organically grown vegetarian food and herbal teas are available in the restaurant. Two View has three-day meditation retreats, as well as courses in massage, yoga, chakra-balancing, rebirthing, natural colon-cleansing and sessions to help you recall past lives. Consider reserving a spot during the high season.

AO LEUK TO AO THIAN OK

The dirt road to Ao Leuk gets steep, rough and rutty, especially towards the end; don't attempt it on a motorcycle unless you're an expert. This little bay has good snorkelling with amazing visibility on calm days. These beaches are isolated, so don't expect much nightlife outside your resort.

Coral View Resort (☎ 0 7745 6058; bungalows 500-700B) Run by a friendly Aussie-Thai couple, Coral View features well-built bungalows. It's best to get here by long-tail boat from Ban Mae Hat, as the road is rough and you may be required to hike a little.

Jamahkiri Resort & Spa (☎ 0 7745 6400-01; www .jamahkiri.com; bungalows 7900-10,900B) Halfway between Hat Sai Daeng and Ao Thian Ok, this spa has some of the most impressive bungalows on the island. Mushrooming out of the cliffs, these whitewashed, rounded abodes have curvy roofs and large balconies, and all come with their own Jacuzzis. There are some two-level options, and all are decorated with Thai art and lovely furniture and have sweeping views of the ocean. The spa here is highly recommended.

AO CHALOK BAN KAO

Ao Chalok, about 1.7km south of Ban Mae Hat by road, has the second largest concentra-

tion of accommodation on Ko Tao and can get quite crowded.

Freedom Beach (☎ 0 7745 6539; bungalows 100-250B) On its own secluded beach at the eastern end of Ao Chalok, these little huts are as basic as they come – wooden boxes with mattresses on the floor. However, if you crave solitude with great view for pennies, then Freedom might be for you. The bungalows are a 10-minute walk from the action on the main beach.

Viewpoint Bungalows (☎ 0 7756 6445; bungalows 200-1000B) A friendly, family-run place just past Taraporn Restaurant, it feels like it's almost at the end of civilisation on this beach. The cheap bungalows were supposedly designed by a hot-shot Bangkok architect and are spartan but airy and well maintained. Some have partial sea views; others are in a gorgeous hillside garden that thrums with cicadas at night. The restaurant has excellent views and a wonderful, mellow ambience, as well as attentive staff.

Buddha View Dive Resort (☎ 0 7745 6074; www.buddhaview-diving.com; r 300-1000B; ☒) The positive vibe is the reason to stay at Buddha View, a very popular resort both for diving and for hanging out. The bungalows are just OK, but there's a fantastic barbecue here every night, weather permitting, and celebrations often spring up for people passing their PADI tests (virtually every night). Rooms are even cheaper if you do a dive course here.

AO JUN JEUA TO HAT SAI NUAN

A trail follows past Viewpoint Bungalows, going both along the beach and inland, eventually turning into a full-on, steep hiking trail. This remote part of the island is a small backpacker haven for those wishing to escape the dive-focused hubbub of the more accessible beaches. Long-tail boats are a good form of transport to this coastal area; with a decent number of people they cost 100B per person to these destinations. Or you can take a taxi to the Hat Sai Nuan area and find your way on the trail from there. The following are located on Jun Juea Beach.

Orchid Cliff Bungalows (☎ 0 1956 9332; bungalows 250B) The bungalows are well constructed and perched atop a steep cliff overlooking Hat Jun Juea. Check out the balconies, which have marvellous views and a sheer drop to the sea below.

Sunset (☎ 0 9202 4937; www.earth2marsh.com/sunset; bungalows 400B) With a perfect seaside location and large, polished-wood bungalows sitting a little way up a grassy hill, Sunset probably has some of the choicest huts on this beach. There's a vegetarian restaurant, good swimming and snorkelling offshore, and yoga classes.

Closer to Ban Mae Hat, the following places are along the rocks and small beach of Sai Nuan:

Tao Thong Villa (☎ 0 7745 6078; bungalows 100-500B) Very popular with long-termers seeking peace and quiet, this place has funky, no-frills bungalows with views. Laem Je Ta Kang, the headland on which this place is located, straddles two tiny swimming beaches; it's a great spot if you can make it here. There's also an agreeable, lofty restaurant.

Sai Thong Resort (☎ 0 7745 6476; www.sai-thong.com; bungalows 150-1400B; ☒) Ranging from basic hillside huts to creatively designed beachside abodes, Sai Thong is big on variety. It also features a relaxing restaurant complete with hammocks and sun deck, and sits on a small, private beach. The pool here is salt water and there is also a spa. The cheapest bungalows are a fabulous deal considering the deluxe amenities.

KO NANG YUAN

This private little tripartite island has one resort. Daily boats from Ban Mae Hat leave at 10.30am, 3pm and 5.30pm (100B return). Note that it's a private island that levies a 100B users' fee for anyone landing ashore.

Ko Nangyuan Dive Resort (☎ 0 7745 6088-93; www.nangyuan.com; bungalows 1200-3200B; ☒) This dive resort monopolises the trio of islands, about 1km offshore to the northwest, connected by an idyllic sand bar. Bungalows are quite comfortable and well spaced. The emphasis here is on diving, with a four-day dive course for around 9000B (rates depend on the season). It's probably a little overpriced for what you get and the restaurant here isn't the best – but then again, it's the only one on the island.

Eating

Just five years ago eating in Ko Tao was still in its infancy, but today the restaurant scene is up and rocking with dining places offering choices from around the globe. If you're lazy, practically all bungalow operations have their own restaurants. Most of the following restaurants are in Ban Mae Hat or Hat Sai Ri.

BAN MAE HAT

Mae Hat has Ko Tao's largest selection of restaurants.

Baan Yaay (☎ 0 7745 6262; dishes 40–200B; ⏰ lunch & dinner) We liked the casual, airy deck overlooking the water at Baan Yaay – kick back with a cocktail from the long menu. The restaurant serves yummy salads, soups, and fried rice and noodle dishes.

Café del Sol (☎ 0 7745 6578; dishes 60–300B; ⏰ breakfast, lunch & dinner) This café serves delicious 'world' cuisines, with a focus on Italian. Every day there is a special set meal of a different cuisine. It gets consistently good reviews.

Zest Coffee Lounge (☎ 0 7745 6178; dishes 70–190B; ⏰ breakfast & lunch) This place corners Ko Tao's sandwich and breakfast market, which it follows up with the best lemon meringue pie in town. It's a great place to live the street-café lifestyle, while nibbling on fresh-baked wholemeal breads and sipping quality coffee. It's open until 6pm.

Noori Indian (☎ 0 7892 9970; dishes 80–250B; ⏰ lunch & dinner) This nearly new eatery is Ko Tao's first and only Indian restaurant. It serves up authentic curries, and there are plenty of options for those who spurn meat.

La Matta (☎ 0 7745 6517; dishes 90–235B; ⏰ lunch & dinner) On the uphill road, this Italian-run place serves freshly made pasta, sandwiches, salads and omelettes – all apparently prepared to ancient family recipes. Some locals prefer it to Faràngo Pizzeria next door. There's a second La Matta on Hat Sai Ri.

HAT SAI RI

This is just a sampling of the restaurants unattached to bungalows now open in Hat Sai Ri. If you don't like the choices listed below, don't fear, it seems something new is opening nearly every day.

Simple Life (☎ 0 7745 6742; dishes 50–200B; ⏰ breakfast, lunch & dinner) Oozing good vibes, Simple Life has people hanging around for a drink long after the last *phàt thai* has been tucked away. The most popular dish by far is the Barbecue Kebab (180B), and there are also killer pool competitions.

Chopper's Bar & Grill (☎ 0 7745 6641; Soi Sopaa; dishes 60–230B; ⏰ breakfast, lunch & dinner) Plenty of local and imported draught beers and big-screen sports drag the punters into this multi-level pub. Hearty pub food, including big, greasy, English breakfasts, is what keeps them coming back.

El Gringo Funky Mexican House (☎ 0 7745 6323; dishes 80–250B; ⏰ breakfast, lunch & dinner) A big menu of Mexican dishes is served along with steak and pizza. The quality of the Mexican is questionable – some love it, others think its crap. El Gringo is popular for live sports on the telly and daily happy hours (5.30pm to 8.30pm), and screens nightly movies on a giant screen. It stays open until midnight. There's a second location.

Mango Pub & Steakhouse (☎ 0 9727 2278; dishes 80–430B; ⏰ breakfast, lunch & dinner) It claims to have the best burger on the island – taste for yourself. Ostrich, crocodile and kangaroo meat are also on the menu here. If you're in the mood, New Zealand lamb is another popular item.

Drinking

Ko Tao has a surprisingly large number of hip bars. If you're looking to shake your money-maker, check out the ubiquitous party fliers posted on trees and walls; venues are always changing but there is usually some sort of dance party or rave happening every night – expect the usual whisky buckets and fire shows on the beach, although interesting sand sculptures and flame jugglers add an extra twist. The following bars are strung out between Ban Hat Sai Ri and Ban Mae Hat, mostly along the beachfront.

Pure Beach Lounge (☎ 0 6972 0494) Next to Orchid Spa, this place brings a touch of the smooth, New York bar scene to Thailand. Here you can lounge on the comfy red bean-bags and cushions strewn about three levels of deck, while taking in some seriously smooth beats. Framed by boulders and right on the beach, it's great for watching gorgeous sunsets. Parties held several nights a week.

Whitening (☎ 0 7745 6199) A groovy bar-restaurant right on the beach, the 'floors' are sandy, the music is moody and the lighting glitters romantically at night (think tiki torches). A variety of mixed drinks is served and house music usually wafts in the background. It has a definite upscale feel, but it's comfortable; there's a great deck over the water.

Dry Bar (☎ 0 6972 0494; btwn Lotus Resort & Big Blue Resort) Also on the beach, the Dry Bar has a friendly atmosphere and is a good place to hang out with both *faràng* and locals. There are sand-side cushions and lanterns, as well as a huge cocktail menu to help you unwind after a hard day's scuba action.

Tattoo (☎ 0 9728 4656) Just 30m south of Whitening (at the edge of town), Tattoo is a more casual and intimate bar, with some tables and a TV-watching lounge area. Breezes blow through the friendly, laid-back spaces and there are plans to build a barbecue patio alongside. If you're hungry, try massive burgers (120B) or homemade meat pies and sausages.

Dragon Bar (☎ 0 7745 6423) This bar caters to those seeking snazzy, cutting-edge surroundings in which to be seen. It's an exception to other places in Ban Mae Hat and may start an upmarket trend. There's retro styling throughout, a large, modernistic communal area, and everything's dimly lit, moody and relaxing (not a party atmosphere). There's a large variety of cocktails and plans to add tapas to the food menu.

Getting There & Away

As always, the cost and departure times are in flux.

BANGKOK

Bus/boat combination tickets from Bangkok cost 800B to 1000B and are available from travel agencies on Th Khao San. Promotional bus/boat combination tickets in the opposite direction are sometimes offered for as little as 650B.

Beware of travel agencies on Ko Tao selling boat/train combinations, like a 'voucher' that you are supposed to be able to exchange for a train ticket in Surat Thani or Chumphon – more than a few travellers have found the vouchers worthless. If you book a train a few days (or more) in advance, legitimate agencies on Ko Tao should be able to deliver the train tickets themselves.

CHUMPHON

There are three departures a day from Chumphon to Ko Tao (see also p573). From Ko Tao, a high-speed catamaran departs for Chumphon at 10am and 3pm (550B, 1½ hours) and a Songserm fast boat makes the same journey at 2.30pm (400B, three hours). There may be fewer departures if the swells are high.

There's also a midnight boat from Chumphon (200B) arriving early in the morning. It returns from Ko Tao at 11pm. Don't take this boat if there's a good chance of rain; some boats leak and you'll be wet, cold and miserable. Otherwise, sleeping on a slow boat (on mats on the floor) is excellent.

SURAT THANI

A Songserm Express Boat departs from Surat Thani (500B, 6½ hours) at 8am daily and returns from Ko Tao at 10am. Every night, depending on the weather, a boat runs between Surat Thani (Tha Thong) and Ko Tao (500B one way, nine hours). From Surat, these night boats depart at 11pm. From Ban Mae Hat the departure time is 8.30pm.

KO PHA-NGAN

There are several express boats to Ko Pha-Ngan (180B to 300B, two hours), departing Ko Tao at around 10am and 2pm. There's also a high-speed catamaran (250B to 350B, one hour), which departs at 9.30am and at 3pm.

KO SAMUI

Two express boats (345B) leave Ko Tao at 10.30am and 2pm and arrive in Samui 2½ hours later. Speedboats (580B) leave at 9.30am and 3pm, include hotel pick-ups, and arrive in Ko Samui 1½ hours later.

Getting Around

Assuming you have at least three to four people, the following are approximate prices (per person) for săwngthăew from Mae Hat: Sai Ri (50B), Chalok Ban Kao (50B), Tanot (100B), Hin Wong (100B), Ao Leuk (100B) and Thian Ok (100B). You will be asked to pay for the whole taxi if there is only one or two of you (350B to 450B to most destinations). Many guesthouses will send representatives to the pier, or alternatively you can call for a pick-up if you know where you intend to stay. Săwngthăew from Sai Ri cost approximately 80B to Chalok Ban Kao and 120B to Ao Leuk.

There are boat taxis from Mae Hat to Chalok Ban Kao (200B per person), Nang Yuan (150B) and Tanot (400B). Long-tail boats can be chartered for around 1500B a day, depending on the number of passengers carried.

Walking is an easy way to get around the island, but some remote trails aren't clearly marked and can be difficult to follow. You can walk around the whole island in a day, although the hilly paths make it a challenge. Consider renting a mountain bike if you're in good shape.

Many tourists rent motorcycles on Ko Tao (150B per day). If you're confident on two wheels then this is a good way to get around,

LOWER SOUTHERN GULF

though there aren't a lot of roads on the island. The main ones are paved, but the more remote ones are rutty, sometimes steep, dirt paths. These shouldn't be attempted by novices.

NAKHON SI THAMMARAT PROVINCE

If you're searching for less-trodden paths and fewer *faràng*, then this relatively non-touristy province might be the gem you're looking for. Much of it is covered with rugged mountains and forests, its verdant jungles teem with lush vegetation and it was once the last refuge of Thailand's communist insurgents. Its eastern border is formed by the Gulf of Thailand, and much of the provincial economy is dependent on fishing and prawn farming. Along the north coast there are picturesque beaches and pristine waterfalls where solitude and serenity rule the day and Western tourists are few and far between. The province also boasts Khao Luang National Park; known for its beautiful mountain and forest walks, cool streams, waterfalls and orchards. Besides fishing, Nakhon residents earn a living by growing coffee, rice, rubber and fruit (especially *mangkhút*, or mangosteen).

AO KHANOM
อ่าวขนอม

Four almost deserted white-sand beaches – Hat Nai Praet, Hat Nai Phlao, Hat Na Dand and Hat Pak Nam – are along the bay of Ao Khanom, about 70km from Surat Thani and close to the town of Khanom. Tourism along this beautiful coastline is minimal, with just a few places to stay. In some areas prawn farms are starting to develop and, while these threaten to damage the environment and local tourism, so far the farms haven't multiplied too dramatically.

If you're searching for Ko Samui's beauty without its crowds, head to Nai Phlao, the best beach, about 8km south of Khanom. Here, the mountains meet the aquamarine waters of the Gulf of Thailand and the sand is pristine white. Coconut palms blow gently in the wind, and you'll be left with the impression that a chunk of Ko Samui somehow cut loose and drifted ashore. Two kilometres south of Nai Phlao is scenic Nam Tok Hin Lat – another Samui echo.

There's a stunning, 8km stretch of beach along the southern half of Hat Nai Phlao, where most of the sleeping options are located.

Supar Villa (☎ 0 7552 8552; fax 0 7552 8553; bungalows 850-1500B; 🛏 🖭) is on prime beachfront real estate and offers great brick bungalows and very friendly staff. On weekends Thai conferences are often held here, as well as shows and entertainment that are usually free to watch if you sleep at the hotel.

Another good option is **Khanom Hill Resort** (☎ 0 7552 9403; bungalows 1500B). The red-roofed bungalows on stilts overlook the sea, with large areas of decking for sitting outside and enjoying the view.

You can catch a share taxi from Nakhon Si Thammarat's share-taxi terminal to Khanom for 100B. If you're driving, pedalling or riding, get off Rte 401 at the junction marked for Rte 4014 and follow the latter to Rte 4232, which runs parallel to the coast all along Ao Khanom (as far south as Sichon).

HAT SICHON & HAT HIN NGAM
หาดสิชล/หาดหินงาม

Few foreigners turn up at these mellow side-by-side beaches along a small curving bay about 65km north of Nakhon Si Thammarat in Amphoe Sichon. Anyone looking for a low-key local scene, eye-catching rocks strewn along the sand or the chance to peruse the market in a picturesque fishing village won't be disappointed.

Hat Sichon ends at a pier in the small hamlet of Sichon. Coconut is a major local product, so there are plenty of palms to set the tone. The beach is quiet and you can easily walk into town. Head to the harbour and check out the large, colourful fishing boats lined up along spindly wooden piers, and the old one-storey weathered shophouses made from the same rough wood.

Hin Ngam is found south of Hat Sichon. Marked by a cluster of unique-looking boulders at its northern end, perfect for those who enjoy isolation – there are few services here. If you journey further south, you'll come to the lesser-known beaches of Hat Piti and Hat Saophao. Hat Piti is a pretty stretch of white sand with one midrange resort. Hat Saophao stretches for 5km and could be the most beautiful beach in the area if it weren't for the prawn farms just inland, which use the most environmentally unfriendly techniques for raising the pink crustaceans.

Sleeping & Eating

Prasarnsuk Villa (☎ 0 7553 6299; bungalows 350-1200B; ⊠) Swaying palms and lovely green lawns grace this solid find. The 30 bungalows are well constructed, and the simple open-air seafood restaurant out front is pleasant for a beer and meal. Look for it at the end of the sandy part of Hat Sichon, with easy access to the rocky headland (with fair snorkelling) that starts at Hat Hin Ngam.

Hat Piti Beach Resort (☎ 0 7533 5301-4; bungalows 1500-3000B; ⊠ ⊠) An upmarket resort set on sprawling grounds, it not only looks pretty (think whitewashed walls, and large fully equipped bungalows), but it's all well run. It sits on the lengthy, unspoiled Hat Piti and has a good open-air restaurant. Discounts of up to 50% can be found when the place is empty.

There are a number of small restaurants scattered about these beaches, although quality often changes with the year. Ask your host to recommend this year's best eats.

Getting There & Away

Get a bus for Sichon from the Nakhon Si Thammarat bus terminal for 20B to 50B or take a share taxi for 50B to 80B. From Sichon, you can take a motorcycle taxi to Hat Sichon, Hat Hin Ngam or Hat Piti for around 30B to 60B per person.

NAKHON SI THAMMARAT

นครศรีธรรมราช

pop 121,059

The area around Nakhon Si Thammarat is a breathtaking collage of mountainous scenery and thriving rainforest, yet the city itself is a dreary mix of modern Thai buildings and Muslim, Buddhist and Hindu temples. It is steeped in history, however, and was the centre of Buddhist study during the Sivichaya period nearly 1700 years ago. If you're in need of cultural immersion after fun and frivolity on the islands, this is a good place to soak up fascinating wat architecture or glimpse the rare handmade shadow puppets the region is famed for.

Hundreds of years ago, an overland route between the western port of Trang and eastern port of Nakhon Si Thammarat functioned as a major trade link between Thailand and the rest of the world. At that time, Nakhon Si Thammarat became an important centre of religion and culture: the Thai *năng tàlung* (shadow play) and *lákhon* (pronounced

'lagor'; classical dance-drama) art forms were developed here.

Today the city is a mix of dreary modern Thai buildings and Buddhist, Muslim and Hindu temples, remnants of the international influences that created this city.

Orientation & Information

Nakhon Si Thammarat can be divided into two sections: the historic section south of the clock tower, and the new city centre north of the clock tower and Khlong Na Meuang. The newer part of the city has all the hotels and most of the restaurants, as well as more movie theatres per square kilometre than any other city in Thailand. There are several interesting handicraft stores near the City Park.

There are several banks at the northern end of town. Check the **Bovorn Bazaar** (Th Ratchadamnoen) for internet cafés.

Main post office (Th Ratchadamnoen; ⊠ 8.30am-4.30pm Mon-Fri)

TAT (☎ 0 7534 6515; tatnakon@nrt.cscoms.com; ⊠ 8.30am-4.30pm) Housed in a 1960s building near the police station. The friendly staff can help with transport information.

Sights & Activities

Most foreign travellers, and even Thai visitors, come to Nakhon Si for the shadow puppets (see the boxed text, p629), but the national museum here is surprisingly well done, and there is also a trip-worthy wat in town. Those interested in mosques, temples, churches or wats should take a look at the map for more places of worship, the most important being Phra Phutta Sihing Chapel and Shiva Shrine.

NAKHON SI THAMMARAT NATIONAL MUSEUM

พิพิธภัณฑสถานแห่งชาตินครศรีธรรมราช

When the Tampaling (or Tambralinga) kingdom traded with Indian, Arabic, Dvaravati and Champa states, much art from these places found its way to the Nakhon Si Thammarat area, and some is now on display in the **national museum** (Th Ratchadamnoen; admission 30B; ⊠ 9am-4pm Wed-Sun). Notable are Dong-Son bronze drums, Dvaravati Buddha images and Pallava (south Indian) Hindu sculptures. Locally produced art is also on display.

The museum is well south of the principal wat on Th Ratchadamnoen, and is located across from Wat Thao Khot and Wat Phet Jarik (it's 5B by *săwngthăew*).

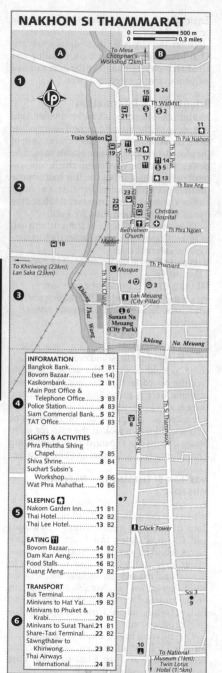

NAKHON SI THAMMARAT

WAT PHRA MAHATHAT
วัดพระมหาธาตุ

In a land of endless wats, Wat Phra Mahathat stands out with the distinction of being the largest wat in southern Thailand – it's comparable to Wat Pho and other grand Bangkok wats. If visiting wats is a pastime for you, this one should be on your temple itinerary. As the city's most historic site, it was supposedly founded by Queen Hem Chala more than 1000 years ago. Bronze statues representing the queen and her brother stand in front of the east wall facing Th Ratchadamnoen, and her spirit is said to be associated with the large standing Buddha in the southeastern cloister. Locals make daily offerings of flower garlands to this Buddha image and the statue of the queen, believing her spirit watches over the city and its residents. It's both majestic and beautiful at the same time.

Reconstructed in the mid-13th century, the huge complex features a 78m *chedi*, crowned by a solid-gold spire weighing several hundred kilograms. Numerous smaller grey-black *chedi* surround the main one. A *mondòp*, the fortress-looking structure towards the northern end of the temple grounds, holds a Buddha footprint – one of the better designs in Thailand.

It's approximately 2km south of the new town centre – hop on any bus or sǎwngthǎew going down Th Ratchadamnoen (10B).

Festivals & Events

Every year during mid-October there is a southern-Thai festival called **Chak Phra Pak Tai** held in Nakhon Si Thammarat (as well as Songkhla and Surat Thani). In Nakhon Si the festival is focused around Wat Phra Mahathat and includes performances of *nǎng tàlung* and *lákhon*, as well as the parading of Buddha images around the city to collect donations for local temples.

In the third lunar month (February to March) the city holds the colourful **Hae Phaa Khun That**, in which a lengthy cloth *jataka* painting is wrapped around the main *chedi* at Wat Phra Mahathat.

Sleeping

Most of Nakhon Si Thammarat's hotels are within walking distance of the train station and easy to locate.

Thai Lee Hotel (☎ 0 7535 6948; 1130 Th Ratchadamnoen; r 120-200B) This hotel has friendly staff and

residents, but its rooms are a bit of a trade-off – you either get bright but noisy, or really dark but quiet (good for folks wanting to sleep day and night we suppose). The location is secure, however, and you can't beat the price, especially if cleanliness is part of your criteria.

Nakorn Garden Inn (☎ 0 7531 3333; fax 0 7534 2926; 1/4 Th Pak Nakhon; r 445B; 🅿) Rooms have brick walls, TV, fridge, and furniture that's less scratched than usual. It's tidy, homey and quite fair in value. Accommodation is set around a gentle, sparse garden, and there's plenty of parking.

Twin Lotus Hotel (☎ 0 7532 3777; fax 0 7532 3821; 97/8 Th Phattanakan Khukhwang; r from 1000B; 🖳) A 16-storey, 413-room hotel offers all the top amenities in its class and gets good reviews from previous guests. The décor pays a little too much homage to the glittering '80s, but it's a very comfortable option. Twin Lotus is a few kilometres southeast of town.

Thai Hotel (☎ 0 7534 1509; fax 0 7534 4858; 1375 Th Ratchadamnoen; r 220-450B; 🖳) Rooms here come with TVs and just a few scratches. The more expensive ones with air-con are larger, better furnished and have a fridge. There's a small lobby café and the place is central.

Eating

At night the entire block running south from Th Neramit is lined with cheap food stalls – Muslim stands sell delicious *khâo mòk* (chicken briyani), *mátàbà* (pancakes stuffed with chicken or vegetables) and Nakhon's famous *rotii* in the evening, and by day there are plenty of rice and noodle shops.

Dam Kan Aeng (☎ 0 7534 4343; 1979 Th Ratchadamnoen; dishes 30-90B; 🕑 lunch & dinner) The Thai and Chinese food here is authentic and simple. This explains the packed crowds of hungry diners on a nightly basis. Look for it on the northwestern corner of Th Ratchadamnoen and Th Watkhit.

Kuang Meng (no roman-script sign; 343/12 Th Ratchadamnoen; dishes 20-70B; 🕑 breakfast, lunch & dinner) Opposite the Siam Commercial Bank, this is a very small Hokkien coffee shop with marble tabletops and tasty pastries.

Bovorn Bazaar on Th Ratchadamnoen is a *faràng* hang-out that hosts several other culinary delights:

Hao Coffee (☎ 0 7534 6563; Bovorn Bazaar; dishes 30-60B; 🕑 breakfast & lunch) Excellent Nakhon coffee and breakfasts served in an antique Hokkien-style coffee shop.

Khrua Nakhon (☎ 0 7531 7197; Bovorn Bazaar; 🕑 breakfast & lunch) Large cafeteria-style place serving

---

SHADOW-PUPPET WORKSHOPS

Performances of Thai shadow theatre are rare nowadays and usually seen only during festivals, but there are two places in Nakhon Si Thammarat where you can see the puppets being made.

Traditionally, there are two styles of the shadow puppets: *nǎng tàlung* and *nǎng yài*. The former are similar in size to the Malay- and Indonesian-style puppets and feature movable appendages and parts (including genitalia), while the latter are unique to Thailand, nearly life size and lacking moving parts. Both are intricately carved from buffalo hide. The puppet masters use light against the puppets to create silhouettes (hence the name 'shadow puppets'), and also employ their own voices in dialogue and song to tell the story, while musicians play instruments, including gongs, drums and cymbals.

The acknowledged master of shadow-puppet manufacture and performance is Suchart Subsin, a Nakhon resident with a **workshop** (☎ 0 7534 6394; Soi 3, 110/18 Th Si Thammasok; 🕑 9am-4pm) not far from Wat Phra Mahathat. He has received several awards for his mastery and preservation of the craft, and has performed for the king. His workshop is open to the public; if enough people are assembled he may even be talked into providing a performance at his small outdoor studio. Puppets can also be purchased at reasonable prices – and here only, as he refuses to sell them through distributors. On some puppets the fur is left on the hide for additional effect – these cost a bit more as special care must be taken when tanning them. Bring your camera; you may be able to see a puppet being carved by hand.

Another craftsperson, Mesa Chotiphan, has a **workshop** (☎ 0 7534 3979; 558/4 Soi Rong Jeh, Th Ratchadamnoen; 🕑 9am-4pm) in the northern part of town; visitors are also welcome. Call if you would like to be picked up from anywhere in Nakhon Si. To get there on your own, go north from the city centre on Th Ratchadamnoen and, 500m north of the sports field, take the *soi* opposite the Chinese cemetery (before reaching the golf course and military base).

Nakhon cuisine; order *khâo yam* (southern-style rice salad) or *kaeng tai plaa* (spicy fish curry).

Getting There & Away

AIR
Thai Airways International (☎ 0 7534 2491; 1612 Th Ratchadamnoen) has flights between Nakhon Si and Bangkok (3520B, one hour, twice daily).

BUS & MINIVAN
There are buses to/from Bangkok (from 325B, 13 hours, twice daily). One VIP departure leaves nightly (705B). Ordinary buses to Bangkok leave from the bus terminal, but a couple of private bus companies on Th Jamroenwithi sell air-con bus tickets to Bangkok and these buses leave from here. Look for Saphan Tour or Moung Tai Tours, which are both easy to find.

Other destinations from the bus terminal include Hat Yai (102B, three hours, daily), Phuket (125B to 200B, seven hours, daily), Krabi (67B to 94B, three hours, daily), Songkhla (70B to 98B, three hours, daily), Surat Thani (45B to 90B, one hour, daily) and Trang (72B, 1½ hours, daily).

There are frequent minivans to Krabi (120B, 2½ hours) and Phuket (200B, five hours) that leave from Th Jamroenwithi. Minivans to Surat Thani (95B, one hour) depart from Th Watkhit. Minivans to Hat Yai (90B, three hours) leave from Th Yommarat. Look for small desks set near the footpath (minivans and waiting passengers may or may not be present nearby).

TRAIN
Most southbound trains from Bangkok stop at Thung Song, about 40km west of Nakhon, from where you must take a bus or taxi to the coast. However, two trains (2nd class 468B to 688B) go all the way to Nakhon Si Thammarat: the rapid 173, which leaves Bangkok's Hualamphong train station at 5.35pm, arriving in Nakhon Si at 8.50am; and the express 85, which leaves Bangkok at 7.15pm and arrives in Nakhon at 10.50am. There are two daily trains (air-con 2nd-class sleepers 643B) to Bangkok, departing at 1pm and 2pm.

There are two trains each day to/from Hat Yai and one each to Yala and Sungai Kolok.

Getting Around
Săwngthăew run north–south along Th Ratchadamnoen and Th Si Thammasok for 6B (a bit more at night). Motorcycle-taxi rides cost between 20B and 50B.

AROUND NAKHON SI THAMMARAT
Khao Luang National Park
อุทยานแห่งชาติเขาหลวง

Known for its beautiful mountain and forest walks, cool streams, waterfalls and fruit orchards, this 570-sq-km park (☎ 0 1228 2051; admission 200B) surrounds **Khao Luang** (1835m), the highest peak in peninsular Thailand. Along with other forested igneous peaks to the west, Khao Luang provides a watershed that feeds Mae Nam Rapi. Local Thais practise a unique form of agriculture called *sŭan rôm* (shade garden, or shade farm). Instead of clear-cutting the forest, they leave many indigenous trees intact, randomly interspersing them with betel, mangosteen, rambutan, langsat, papaya, durian and banana trees. Cleverly placed bamboo and PVC pipes irrigate the mixed orchards without the use of pumps.

Wildlife includes clouded leopard, tiger, elephant, banteng, gaur, tapir, serow, musk deer, macaque, civet, binturong and Javan mongoose, plus more than 200 bird species. An excess of 300 orchid varieties (including several indigenous species) find roots in the humid environments here, along with begonias and a wide variety of ferns.

The best time to visit Khao Luang is January to April, when it's cooler and drier. If you're coming from Nakhon Si Thammarat, visit the **TAT office** (p627) and pick up a small informative English booklet to the park.

ACTIVITIES
Hiking is the park's biggest attraction. You can hike 2.5km through dense tropical forest to the top of **Nam Tok Karom** from the national park headquarters near Lan Saka (25km from Nakhon Si Thammarat), off Rte 4015. Every 500m or so there are shelters and seats. To reach seven-tiered **Nam Tok Krung Ching**, a half-day walk, you'll have to take the Krung Ching nature trail from Nopphitam at the northeastern border of the park, off Rte 4140.

Along the way you'll pass the world's largest tree ferns, an old communist insurgent camp, **Tham Pratuchai** (a cave also used by the communists) and a mangosteen forest. This trail, too, is lined with seats and shelters. The falls are most impressive after the rainy season has ended in November and December.

A more challenging trail leads from a car park near Khiriwong to the summit of **Khao Luang**, a 14-hour walk best divided into two or more days. Night temperatures at the sum-

mit can drop to 5°C, so come prepared with plenty of warm clothing. At 600m, Kratom Suan Sainai offers a simple-roofed shelter and also marks the upper limit of the fruit plantations. In the dry season you can camp next to a riverbed at Lan Sai, about a six-hour walk from the car park. Five hours further on, along a section of very steep trail, you'll enter a cloud forest full of rattan, orchids, rhododendrons, ferns and stunted oaks. From here it's another three hours to the summit, where, if the weather is clear, you'll be rewarded with stunning views of layer after layer of mountains rolling into the distance.

The best and safest way to appreciate the Khao Luang trek is to go with a guide from the **Khiriwong Village Ecotourism Club** (☎ 0 7530 9010, 0 9501 2706; trek 1500B) in Khiriwong. For this price the villagers will arrange a three-day, two-night trek that includes all meals and guide services. The guides can point out local flora and fauna that you might otherwise miss. The only time you can complete this hike is between January and June, when the trails are dry and the leeches are not too bad. During heavy rains the trail can be impassable for days.

SLEEPING

There are **park bungalows** (☎ reservations 0 7530 9664; 6-12 people 600-1200B) available, and camping is permitted on the trail to the summit of Khao Luang. There are a few private bungalows and restaurants on the road to the park offices that offer accommodation and food.

GETTING THERE & AWAY

To reach the park take a sǎwngthǎew (20B) from Nakhon Si Thammarat (on Th Jamroenwithi) to the village of Khiriwong at the base of Khao Luang. The entrance to the park and the offices of the Royal Forest Department are 33km from the centre of Nakhon on Rte 4015, an asphalt road that climbs almost 400m.

SONGKHLA PROVINCE

SONGKHLA & AROUND

ส งขลา

pop 87,822

Despite a delightful location buttressed by Thale Sap Songkhla (Lake Songkhla) on one side and the Gulf of Thailand on the other, Songkhla isn't seeing much tourist traffic these days. Although 'the great city on two seas' hasn't experienced any of the Muslim separatist violence plaguing nearby Hat Yai, it's still catching the same bad press. Which is a bit of a shame, as Songkhla is the last safe (at least for the moment – always check the situation before travelling around here) city where you can experience the unique flavour of Thailand's predominately Muslim Deep South.

Even though Songkhla is the capital of the region, it feels like a backwards country town. The city is surrounded by beaches on all sides, has several green parks dotted around and has a pretty historical centre – it's a pleasant place to pass a few days and partake in the beachside city life. The seafood served along Hat Samila is exceptional. Though the white beach is not that great for swimming, the sand and casuarina trees along Hat Samila can be visually striking. The population is a mix of Thais, Chinese and Malays, and the local architecture and cuisine reflect this fusion at every turn.

Big-name international petroleum companies and their exploration interests offshore bring an influx of multinational (particularly British and American) oil-company employees. The result is a strong Western presence in Songkhla that has helped create a relatively wealthy and prosperous town.

Orientation

The city has a split personality, with the charming older section west of Th Ramwithi towards the waterfront, and a modern mix of business and suburbia to the east. Towards the north is a scenic promontory, Laem Songkhla; the eastern side of the jutting piece of land is Hat Son Awn, along which there is a lovely path for strolling. Further north is Hat Samila, which is attractive and peaceful, too. If you enter town from the north or leave town heading north, you'll go through Ko Yo (see the boxed text, p633) and cross the Tinsulanonda Bridges –the longest concrete bridges in Thailand.

There's a large golf course in town, along the coast next to the BP Samila Hotel.

Information

Banks can be found all over town.
Corner Bookshop (☎ 0 7431 2577; cnr Th Saiburi & Th Phetchakhiri; ◷ 7am-7.30pm) English-language novels, maps, newspapers, magazines and Lonely Planet guides.
Dotcom Internet (☎ 0 7432 5049; 28/20 Th Ramwithi; per hr 40B; ◷ 8am-10pm)

Immigration office (☎ 0 7431 3480; Th Laneg Phra Ram; ☾ 8.30am-4.30pm Mon-Fri) Visa extensions can be filed here.

Indonesian Consulate (☎ 0 7431 1544; Th Sadao)

Malaysian Consulate (☎ 0 7431 1062; 4 Th Sukhum)

Police Station (☎ 0 7431 2133) Corner of Hat Samila.

Post office (Th Wichianchom) Opposite the market; international calls can be made upstairs.

Sights & Activities

Songkhla's top site is the excellent **national museum** (☎ 0 7431 1728; Th Wichianchom; admission 30B; ☾ 9am-4pm Wed-Sun, closed public holidays), which was constructed in 1878 using a Thai-Chinese architectural style that's as delightful as the art inside. Design highlights include curved rooflines and thick walls. The grounds are quiet and shady with a tranquil garden at the front – sit under a tree and write in your journal. Inside there are exhibits from all national art-style periods. The most intriguing is on Srivijaya, a 7th- to 9th-century Shivalingam found in Pattani.

If museums aren't your style, head to the beach. The residents have begun taking better care of the strip of white sand along **Hat Samila**, and it is now quite pleasant for strolling or early morning reads on one of the benches sitting in the shade of casuarina trees. A **bronze mermaid**, depicted squeezing water from her long hair in tribute to Mae Thorani (the Hindu-Buddhist earth goddess), sits atop some rocks at the northern end of the beach. Locals treat the figure like a shrine, tying the waist with coloured cloth and rubbing the breasts for good luck. Next to that are the **cat and rat sculptures**, named for the Cat and Rat Islands (Ko Yo and Ko Losin). The rustic seafood restaurants at the back of the beach supply food and cold beverages.

Th Nang Ngam is another attraction. It has a large Chinese community and is lined with quaint, rickety old Thai houses and several multicoloured Chinese temples.

Sleeping

The following listings are only a start, there are many more. Songkhla's hotels tend to be lower priced than other areas in the gulf, which makes going up a budget level a relatively cheap splurge.

Amsterdam Guest House (☎ 0 7431 4890; 15/3 Th Rong Meuang; r 150-200B) This homey, quirky Dutch-run place is popular and clean, with plenty of cushions, wandering pet dogs and cats, and a caged macaque that is said to bite the unwary. All rooms share bathrooms.

Guest House Romantic (☎ 0 7430 7170; 10/1-3 Th Platha; r 250-390B; ❄) Substantial, airy abodes smell fresh and all come with TVs. Even the air-con rooms are cheap, and the bamboo wood beds are impressive for this price range. Overall a good budget choice if you're willing to pay more than 200B.

Green World Palace Hotel (☎ 0 7443 7900-8; 99 Th Samakisukson; r 750-900B; ❄ ☕) Green World Palace is not only the best value in town, it's also classy, boasting chandeliers, a spiralling staircase in the lobby and a 5th-floor swimming pool with views. Rooms are immaculate and filled with enough amenities to keep you comfortable and entertained. The hotel is immensely popular, so book ahead. Look for it a few hundred metres south of town.

Rajamangala Pavilion Beach Resort (☎ 0 7448 7222; www.pavilionhotels.com; 1 Th Rajdamnoen Nok; r 1400B; ❄ ☕) This miniresort is actually owned by the local university and looks over the road to Songkhla's eastern beach. The enormous lobby is filled with water features and Thai artefacts, and the rooms are elementary but stylish. This place is often fully booked, so you may want to call ahead.

BP Samila Hotel (☎ 0 7444 0222; www.bphotelsgroup .com; 8 Th Ratchadamnoen; r 2500B; ❄ ☐) Songkhla's most posh hotel is actually a really good deal – you'd pay nearly double for the same amenities on the islands. The beachfront establishment offers large rooms with IDD phone, fridge, satellite TV, and a choice of sea or mountain views. Internet access costs 60B per hour. BP can arrange a caddie for the neighbouring golf course.

Eating

The seafood in Ko Yo (see opposite) has a reputation for being some of the best in the area. The seafood restaurants on Hat Samila are pretty good and well priced – try the curried crab claws or spicy fried squid. There's a string of cheap, excellent seafood restaurants around the beach close to where Th Ratchadamnoen and Th Son Awm intersect. And at the southern end of Th Sisuda is a night market called Rot Fai Night Plaza – on Sunday, a morning market pops up here.

Nai Wan Restaurant (☎ 0 7431 1295; Th Ratchadamnoen; dishes 40-220B; ☾ lunch & dinner) Popular for its crab dishes (bring moist wipes!), the menu also offers Thai salads, soups and other

seafood offerings, as well as a few veggie entries. The large, casual space is near the little mermaid sculpture.

Sea Sport Restaurant (☎ 0 7432 7244; Th Ratchadamnoen; dishes 50-200B; ☯ breakfast, lunch & dinner) The ambience here is great, at least when it's not raining: outside wooden benches (some shaped like boats) are set on a grassy, bricked terrace while a cloth tarp blows overhead. At night everything's lit up romantically. Highly recommended by locals for its seafood.

Dokkeaw (☎ 0 7431 6226; Th Rajadamnoen; dishes 60-220B; ☯ breakfast, lunch & dinner) This busy Thai eatery is over the road from the mermaid statue and has plenty of outdoor terrace seating where you can enjoy the sea breeze. The seafood here is splendid and you can enjoy your meal while being serenaded by nightly live singers.

Drinking

A string of bars just east of the Indonesian consulate is jokingly referred to among local expats as 'The Dark Side'. Not as ominous as it sounds, this strip caters mainly to oil company employees and other Westerners living in Songkhla. The Office, the bar nearest Soi 5, is run by an Englishman and not too seedy.

A few other casual bars, interspersed with restaurants, are worth checking out on nearby happening Th Sisuda: Corner Bier is where Songkhla's Canadian community hangs out; and the Parlang Restaurant and Bar is another popular expat place. To see how the locals party, head to Dr Cool Radio, which has great sea views and is filled most nights by Thai students listening to local DJs spinning pop hits.

Getting There & Around

From Songkhla you'll have to go to Hat Yai to reach most long-distance destinations in the south. There are a few destinations with transport originating in Songkhla, though.

The government bus station is a few hundred metres south of the Viva Hotel. Four 2nd-class buses go daily to Bangkok (550B), stopping in Chumphon (320B), Nakhon Si Thammarat (150B) and Surat Thani (210B), among other places. One VIP bus to Bangkok leaves at 4.45pm (1050B), while three 1st-class buses (572B) leave late afternoon and evening.

DETOUR: KO YO

เกาะยอ

An island on the inland sea, Ko Yo (kaw yaw) is worth visiting just to see the cotton-weaving cottage industry there. The good-quality, distinctive *phâa kàw yaw* is hand woven on rustic looms and is available on the spot at 'wholesale' prices – meaning you still have to bargain but have a chance of undercutting the usual city price.

Cotton weaving is a major household activity around this forested, sultry island, and there is a central market off the highway so you don't have to go from place to place comparing prices and fabric quality. At the market, prices for cloth and ready-made clothes are excellent if you bargain and especially if you speak Thai. If you're more interested in observing the weaving process, take a walk down the road behind the market where virtually every other house has a hand-operated loom or two – listen for the clacking sound.

At the northern end of the island, about 2km past Ban Ao Sai, the must-see **Folklore Museum** (☎ 0 7433 1185; admission 60B; ☯ 8.30am-5.30pm) aims to promote and preserve the culture of the region. Be ready to hike – the museum ripples down a hillside, each display room connected by stairs, stairs and more stairs. Displays include pottery, beads, shadow puppets, basketry, textiles, musical instruments, jewellery, boats, religious art, weapons, and various agricultural and fishing implements.

If you'd rather just meander around the island, you can hire a motorcycle in Songkhla (make sure you know how to operate one first) and tour the quiet back roads of Ko Yo: tiny villages, scenic coastline, forested hills, spiritual wats – it's a very local treat and way off the beaten track. If you've made it to the island, don't leave without trying Ko Yo's famous seafood; look for shorefront restaurants along the island's main road.

Frequent săwngthăew to Ko Yo depart from Th Platha in Songkhla (15B, 30 minutes). To stop at the market ask for *nâa tàlàat*, 'in front of the market'. To get off at the museum, about 2km past the market, ask for *phíphítháphan*. Buses to Ranot pass through Ko Yo for the same fare.

To Hat Yai, buses (18B), minivans (25B) and share taxis (30B) take around 40 minutes and leave from Th Ramwithi. Minivans to Pattani (90B) and Yala (90B) leave from the southern part of Th Ramwithi, while ordinary buses to Nakhon Si Thammarat (86B) leave from a different bus terminal in the southern part of town.

Share taxis to the Hat Yai airport cost 250B to 300B per taxi. Private taxis charge up to 500B.

Săwngthǎew circulate around town and to Ko Yo for 12B. Motorcycle taxis cost around 20B; rates double at night. There are numerous places along the streets to rent bicycles or motorcycles. Bikes go for about 100B per day, while motorcycles cost 200B to 250B.

HAT YAI
หาดใหญ่
pop 193,732

Songkhla's liveliest town is a fun, if slightly dodgy, place with a bit of a buzz to it. The main pastime here seems to be eating critters from the sea. There are literally hundreds of restaurants serving sweet seafood, prepared either in Chinese, Muslim or Thai style, and every street seems to be packed with shops and street stalls. Markets are also plentiful and several large, air-con shopping malls offer a chilly respite from the heat. The nightlife scene buzzes nightly and you can hang out in some cosy pubs or dance the night away before heading off to the surrounding region.

Most travellers only visit Hat Yai while in transit to Malaysia, but since terrorists started targeting it for bombings within the last few years its seeing fewer and fewer folks passing through; many people are choosing to fly straight on to Kuala Lumpur or Singapore rather than do the traditional overland route through Thailand's Deep South. Violence comes in spurts, however, so it might very well be quiet again before this book is retired. If you do visit, just be vigilant about your surroundings and stay away from large demonstrations or crowded spaces, which are more likely to be targets, but don't worry too much.

Information
Bangkok Hatyai Hospital (☎ 0 7436 5780-9; bhhimc@bgh.co.th; 75 Soi, 15 Th Pechkasam) One of the best health-care providers in southern Thailand, it offers full medical care and has English-speaking staff.

Cathay Tour (☎ 0 7423 5044; 93/1 Th Niphat Uthit 2) One of many travel agencies in town, it stands out for its friendly staff and full range of services, from tickets to tours to visa runs.
Immigration office (☎ 0 7425 7079; Th Phetkasem) Near the railway bridge; handles visa extensions.
TAT (☎ 0 7424 3747; tatsgkhla@tat.or.th; 1/1 Soi 2, Th Niphat Uthit 3) Very helpful staff here speak excellent English and have loads of info on the area.
Tourist Police (☎ 0 7424 6733; Th Niphat Uthit 3; ☯ 24hr)

Sights

Hat Yai is rather short in the attraction department. During festivals and special events **Muay Thai boxing matches** (admission 200B) are held in the boxing stadium just north of Hat Yai's sports stadium. Times vary, so check with the TAT office to confirm the schedule. If you're interested in boxing, you'll be thrilled with the low admission price – seats at matches in other cities can go for as much as 1500B.

If you're bored, you could hop on a săwngthǎew and head about 1.5km out of town to **Wat Hat Yai Nai** (ณะงหดฟพดพนทข้าทนหะรทยพ่าหหรอ้า); it features a 35m reclining Buddha (Phra Phut Mahatamongkon). Inside the image's gigantic base is a curious little museum and mausoleum with a souvenir shop. To get here, grab the săwngthǎew that passes near the intersection of Th Niphat Uthit 1 and Th Phetkasem and get off after crossing Saphan U Taphao – it costs about 12B.

Sleeping

For some reason hotels in Hat Yai take a disproportionate leap upward in quality once you pay another 100B to 200B a night. There are endless Chinese-run midrange hotels offering pretty much exactly the same thing – it's often easiest to go with the first one you come across. If you're at the tail end of a long trail ride and just want to crash cheap, there are dozens of budget hotels within walking distance of the train station.

Cathay Guest House (☎ 0 7424 3815; 93/1 Th Niphat Uthit 2; dm/r 100/250B) Even though it has seen better days, this has become the travellers headquarters in Hat Yai because of its good location, helpful staff and plentiful information about onward travel. It's a great place to meet other travellers, leaf through mountains of brochures and catch up on overdue laundry. Inexpensive breakfasts and lunches are served in an on-site café and there's a reliable travel agency downstairs.

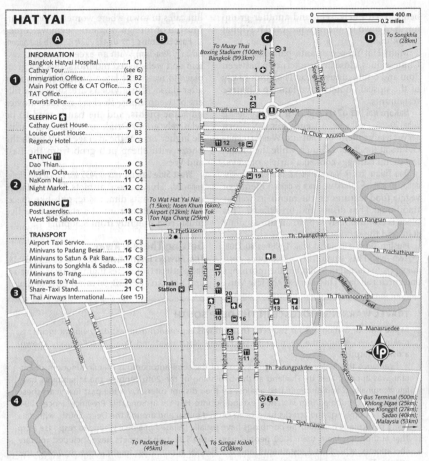

HAT YAI

0 — 400 m
0 — 0.2 miles

INFORMATION
Bangkok Hatyai Hospital...............1 C1
Cathay Tour.............................(see 6)
Immigration Office....................2 B2
Main Post Office & CAT Office.....3 C1
TAT Office...............................4 C4
Tourist Police..........................5 C4

SLEEPING
Cathay Guest House...................6 C3
Louise Guest House....................7 B3
Regency Hotel..........................8 C3

EATING
Dao Thian................................9 C3
Muslim Ocha...........................10 C3
NaKorn Nai.............................11 C4
Night Market...........................12 C2

DRINKING
Post Laserdisc.........................13 C3
West Side Saloon......................14 C3

TRANSPORT
Airport Taxi Service....................15 C3
Minivans to Padang Besar...........16 C3
Minivans to Satun & Pak Bara......17 C3
Minivans to Songkhla & Sadao....18 C2
Minivans to Trang.....................19 C3
Minivans to Yala......................20 C3
Share-Taxi Stand.......................21 C1
Thai Airways International........(see 15)

To Muay Thai Boxing Stadium (100m); Bangkok (993km)

To Songkhla (28km)

Th Niphat Songkhran 1
Th Niphat Songkhran 2

Th Pratham Uthit

Fountain

Th Chuti Anuson

Khlong Toei

Th Montri 1

Th Sang See

Th Rattakan

Th Phetkasem

To Wat Hat Yai Nai (1.5km); Noen Khum (6km); Airport (12km); Nam Tok; Ton Nga Chang (25km)

Th Suphasan Rangsan

Th Duangchan

Th Prachathipat

Th Phetkasem

Train Station

Th Roitai

Th Rattakan

Th Saeng Chan

Th Supharasm

Th Thamnoonvithi

Khlong Toei

Th Manasruedee

Th Tephsongkroh

Th Niphat Uthit 1
Th Niphat Uthit 2
Th Niphat Uthit 3

Th Padungpakdee

Th Soonthjawithi

Th Rat Uthit

To Bus Terminal (500m); Khlong Ngae (25km); Amphoe Klonggit (27km); Sadao (40km); Malaysia (53km)

Th Siphunawat

To Padang Besar (45km)

To Sungai Kolok (208km)

Louise Guest House (☎ 0 7422 0966; 21-23 Th Thamnoonvithi; r 300-400B; ✕) This place is conveniently located and has more appealing rooms than the Cathay Guest House – but lacks its buzz. With more of an apartment-style layout, the rooms here aren't very big but are well maintained and you have the option of air-con.

Regency Hotel (☎ 0 7435 3333-47; www.regency -hatyai.com; 23 Th Prachathipat; r from 900B; ✕ ▣ ✕) This beautiful hotel has that grand old-world charm that's so rare nowadays. There's a softly lit lounge dotted with artefacts and all that's missing are the retired colonels from the queen's navy, talking about their days in Batavia over gin and tonics. The rooms are stuffed with modern amenities, and there's a coffee shop, dim sum restaurant, huge swim-

ming pool with bar, and a gym on site. It's extremely well priced.

Eating & Drinking

Hat Yai is southern Thailand's gourmet Mecca, offering Muslim *rotii* and curries, Chinese noodles and dim sum, and fresh seafood from both the Gulf of Thailand and the Andaman Sea. Lots of good, cheap restaurants can be found along the three Niphat Uthit roads, in the markets off side streets, between them and near the train station.

The extensive **night market** (Th Montri 1) specialises in fresh seafood, where you can dine on two seafood dishes and one vegetable dish for around 200B. There's an excellent gathering of veggie focused food stalls at the

bend in Th Phetkasem, and another group north of town by the mosque, off Th Niphat Songkhrao.

Many Hat Yai restaurants, particularly the Chinese ones, close in the afternoon between 2pm and 6pm – unusual for Thailand. Many of the upscale hotels have fancier Chinese restaurants.

NaKorn Nai (☎ 0 7423 2550; 16-17 Th Niphat Uthit 2; dishes 30-60B; ☺ Thu-Tue) A trendy joint, NaKorn serves a large menu of Thai and Western specialties at lunch and dinner, while the breakfast menu has eggs cooked a variety of ways.

Dao Thian (cnr Th Niphat Uthit 3 & Th Thamnoonvithi; dishes 40-80B; ☺ breakfast, lunch & dinner) Plenty of veggie food features on the menu, as well as traditional Thai dishes and breakfasts. This place is continuously kept in an immaculate state and the service is great.

Muslim Ocha (Th Niphat Uthit 1; dishes 40-210B; ☺ 6am-7pm) This small, tidy place does *rotii kaeng* (*rotii chanai* in Malay) in the mornings and curries all day. This is one of the few Mus-

lim cafés in town where women – even non-Muslim or foreign women – seem welcome.

Post Laserdisc (☎ 0 7423 2027; 82/83 Th Thamnoonvithi; ☺ 9am-1am) With an excellent sound system and well-placed monitors, this is a great place to watch the latest pirated blockbuster after dark. Music videos are shown as fillers between films. Rockers replace movies on some nights, and the bands tend to be relatively good. Drink prices are only a little higher than at the average bar. Quash the booze with cheap pub grub from the East and West.

West Side Saloon (☎ 0 7435 4833; 135/5 Th Thamnoonvithi) This 'saloon' attracts Thais, Malays and *faràng* to its dim, rustic, pub-like space. Tables are set in front of a stage, where live music rocks nightly from 8.30pm.

Getting There & Away

Thai Airways International (THAI; ☎ 0 7423 3433; 182 Th Niphat Uthit 1) operates flights between Hat Yai and Bangkok (3395B, 90 minutes, four daily).

TRAVEL WARNING: VIOLENCE IN THE DEEP SOUTH

At the time of writing, the far south of Thailand was experiencing almost daily violent incidents, making travel around the Deep South (as Pattani, Narathiwat and Yara are collectively known) a risky enterprise.

Ever since this Malay region, originally part of the semi-autonomous Islamic Kingdom of Pattani, was appropriated by Thailand at the beginning of the 20th century, the inhabitants have felt marginalised and discriminated against by their distant rulers. Over the past few years these feelings have bubbled into violence, extending into Hat Yai in Songkhla Province. Since 2004, dozens of bombings and attacks have been carried out in and around the Deep South, with Yala being particularly hard hit. The bombings have usually resulted in a heavy-handed response from Thai authorities. More than 1000 people have been killed and targets have included military checkpoints, schools and restaurants, and the Hat Yai airport (two tourists were injured in this attack). The violence increased markedly in the month leading up to the 19 September coup (see p40). On 31 August 2006, 22 bombs exploded inside commercial banks in Yala Province, injuring 28 people. A second series of bombs were detonated in a commercial district of Hat Yai on 17 September 2006. The region has been under martial law since 2005, and more than 1815 people have been killed and another 2729 wounded between January 2004 and October 2006 – most have been innocent bystanders, Buddhists and, ironically, Muslims. The increased violence forced the government to shut all schools in Yala, Pattani and Narathiwat Provinces indefinitely from 27 November 2006.

On 22 November Wan Kadir Che Wan, leader of the umbrella organisation for southern separatist groups, told the Arab TV network Al Jazeera that the Al-Qaeda-linked Jemaah Islamiyah terrorist network was helping local insurgents stage the attacks. However, as yet no group has been identified by the Thai government.

To date tourists have not been directly targeted (although at least one American and one Canadian have been killed in the violence), and it is difficult to predict which way the situation will turn; by the time you read this, things could be back to normal. If you are planning to travel in this region, be sure to check the latest security situation with your embassy and local authorities before you head out.

MAKING A (VISA) RUN FOR THE BORDER FROM HAT YAI

The Malaysian border is about 50km south of Hat Yai, and many travellers come through town just to extend their Thai visas.

To get an in-and-out stamp, head to Padang Besar, the nearest Malaysian border town. Private taxis cost 600B return (one hour), share taxis are 150B (one hour, leave when full), minivans 80B (1½ hours, hourly) and buses 40B (1½ hours, every 25 minutes). It's also possible to take the train, but this option is not very fast or frequent.

If you need a longer Thai visa, you'll have to see the Thai consulate in Georgetown, on Penang Island (accessible through the mainland town of Butterworth). Buses from Hat Yai to Butterworth cost 250B (four hours). Again, trains from Hat Yai to Butterworth are slower and less frequent.

There is also a daily THAI flight to/from Phuket (6400B) and Singapore (15,100B).

The bus terminal is 2km southeast of the town centre, though many buses make stops in town. Destinations from Hat Yai include Bangkok (550B, 14 hours), Krabi (200B, five hours), Ko Samui (combined bus/boat 300B, seven hours), Kuala Lumpur (350B to 450B, nine hours), Phuket (250B to 450B, eight hours) and Singapore (450B to 600B, 16 hours). The above quotes are for air-con buses. There are multiple buses each day to all the destinations.

Cathay Tour (☎ 0 7423 5044; 93/1 Th Niphat Uthit) runs express minivans to Krabi (180B), Ko Samui (400B), Phuket (350B), Surat Thani (230B), Sungai Kolok (190B) and Trang (140B). There's also a direct night bus to Bangkok (680B).

There are five daily overnight trains to/from Bangkok. Sample fares include: 3rd-class seat with fan/air-con 269/339B, 2nd-class seat 465/575B, 2nd-class sleeper (lower berth) 665/845B, and a 1st-class sleeper 1394B. There are also daily trains to Sungai Kolok (42B to 184B, seven daily), Butterworth (322B, two daily) and Padang Besar (57B, two daily).

There is an advance-booking office and left-luggage office at the train station; both are open 6am to 6pm daily.

Getting Around

An **Airport Taxi Service** (☎ 0 7423 8452) makes the run to/from the airport (60B, seven daily). The service leaves for the airport from the THAI office on Th Niphat Uthit 1; coming into Hat Yai, the service offers hotel drop-off. A private taxi for this run costs about 200B.

Săwngthăew run along Th Phetkasem and charge 5B per person. A túk-túk around town should cost 10B per person, though they like to charge foreigners 20B instead.

YALA PROVINCE

Yala is the most prosperous of the four predominantly Muslim provinces in southern Thailand, mainly due to income from rubber production. It is also the prime business and education centre for the region. See the travel warning on opposite before visiting.

YALA

ยะลา

pop 99,954

Unless you are a wat fanatic there is absolutely no reason to visit this province's capital city. It may be known for its cleanliness, but otherwise it is not an exciting place, not to mention the fact that it is slightly dangerous these days.

That said if you are a wat fanatic, then you'll probably love **Wat Khuhaphimuk** (also called Wat Na Tham or Cave-Front Temple), 8km west of town on the Yala–Hat Yai road. This Srivijaya-period cave temple dates to AD 750. Inside the cave you'll find a long, reclining Buddha image known as Phra Phutthasaiyat. For Thais, this is one of the three most venerated Buddhist pilgrimage points in southern Thailand (the other two are Wat Boromathat in Nakhon Si Thammarat and Wat Phra Boromathat Chaiya in Surat Thani). To get to the temple, take a săwngthăew (7B) going west towards Yala via Rte 4065 and ask to get off at the road to Wat Na Tham. It's about a 1km walk to the wat from the highway.

If you happen to be in the area in March, then it might also be worth popping into Yala for the **Asean Barred Ground Dove Competition**. This is the World Cup for songbirds, and attracts dove lovers from across Southeast Asia. Over 1000 feathered competitors are literally 'pitched' against each other, judged on stamina, melody, volume and pitch.

ISLAM IN SOUTHERN THAILAND

Whether it is the beautiful, haunting echo of the muezzin's call to prayer curling into your room at dawn, or the smile of a woman in a softly coloured headscarf as she deftly kneads and winds a traditional *rotii* – during a trip to Thailand's southern islands and beaches you are very likely to encounter the presence and influence of Islam.

At approximately 4% of the population, Muslims make up Thailand's largest religious minority, living side by side with the majority who are Theravadin Buddhists. There are some 3000 mosques in Thailand – over 200 in Bangkok alone. Of these mosques 99% are associated with the Sunni branch of Islam (in which Islamic leadership is vested in the consensus of the Ummah, or Muslim community), and 1% with the Shi'ite branch (in which religious and political authority is given to certain descendants of the Prophet Mohammed).

Islam was introduced to the area that comprises modern Thailand between AD 1200 and AD 1500 in the south, through the influence of Indian and Arab traders and scholars. To this day, most of Thailand's Muslims reside in the south, concentrated in the regions of Pattani, Narathiwat, Satun and Yala, where the population is up to 85% Muslim. These southerners trace their heritage to the former Kingdom of Pattani, an Islamic kingdom whose territory straddled the present-day border between Thailand and Malaysia. Accordingly, the south shares both a border and a cultural heritage with its predominantly Muslim neighbour. Most of Thailand's southern Muslims are ethnically Malay and speak Malay or Yawi (a dialect of Malay written in the Arabic script) in addition to Thai.

These cultural differences, inflamed by a history of perceived religious and linguistic discrimination, have led to a feeling of disconnection with the Buddhist mainland among a radical few of the southern Muslims. Some have called for secession, and fewer still have, in the past, taken up armed insurgency.

The most notable of these insurgent groups was known as the Pattani United Liberation Organisation (PULO), active in the 1970s and 1980s, whose goal was the formation of an independent Muslim state. In 1998 joint efforts by the Thai and Malaysian governments effectively crippled PULO and the separatist movement as a whole, but economic and cultural factors continue to feed the sort of residual feelings of dissatisfaction that have led to more-recent spurts of violence (see boxed text, p636).

Proper etiquette in Thai Muslim communities is simple and predictable. Islam forbids the consumption of pork and alcohol – obvious public intoxication is frowned upon (and thus asking for a beer and *muu* – pork – in an obviously Muslim restaurant will not be productive or polite). In very conservative communities, multigender groups will be split off into separate rooms upon arrival. Men and women will be reunited as they depart.

Just as is the case when visiting wat, mosques will not permit entry to those in shorts or shoes. Women should not wear short skirts, sleeveless tops or any particularly revealing clothing; simply remain conservative. Unless invited to do so, avoid entering the mosque's main prayer hall as this is a sacred space intended for Muslims. Do not bring cameras and remember to turn off mobile phones.

Friday is the day of the Sabbath, with religious activities culminating between 11am and 2pm. Locals may be too busy on Friday for visitors and most restaurants close down during this time.

You'll find Yala's best beds at rock-bottom prices at the **Chang Lee Hotel** (☎ 0 7324 4597; fax 0 7324 4599; 318 Th Siriros; r from 300B; ❆ ❂). The rooms here are plush and come with carpets and TV, while facilities include a business centre, karaoke nightclub and coffee shop. The downer is it's not central (a 15-minute walk from the train station). If it's empty, ask about promotions and bargain. Rooms can go for as low as 300B, which is a damn good deal.

Yala is hardly a culinary destination, though there are a couple of decent eateries in town. Chinese restaurants proliferate along Th Ratakit and Th Ranong. The Muslim day market, in the northern part of town, sells fresh fruit and vegetables; try to wear modest clothing around here to avoid

offending and to help blend in. Look for delicious seafood restaurants, where your meal is cooked right on the sidewalk in front of your table, around Th Pitipakdee and Th Sribumrung. Ratchapat night market, south of town about 1km (turn left at the clock tower), is the place to head to for cheap eats (a túk-túk there costs 25B).

Daily buses between Bangkok and Yala (500B to 900B, 15 hours) leave from Th Phumachip in Yala, a side road off Th Siriros, about 250m south of Th Kotchaseni 1. Buses to Hat Yai (100B, 2½ hours) stop several time a day on Th Siriros, outside the Prudential TS Life office. Across the street is the stop for other short- to medium-distance buses north.

Daily train destinations from Yala include Bangkok (1st class 1500B, 2nd class 500B to 800B) and Sungai Kolok (3rd class 50B).

PATTANI PROVINCE

PATTANI
ปัตตานี

pop 44,800

Pattani is a sprawling, casual town and, while it conceals an interesting past, there's little of interest here for the traveller except its access to nearby beaches.

With a history of independence, Pattani has never quite adjusted to being a part of the Kingdom of Thailand. Pattani was the centre of an independent principality that included Yala and Narathiwat. Today Pattani is a predominantly Muslim town that has traditionally had more in common with its Malaysian neighbours in the south than the central government in Bangkok. The Portuguese established a trading post here in 1516, the Japanese in 1605, the Dutch in 1609 and the British in 1612. During these times Pattani's allegiances shifted several times and rebellions were not uncommon. This fierce independence continues and is a driving force behind some of the problems that are currently plaguing Thailand's southern region (see the travel warning on p636).

Several banks are found along the southeastern end of Th Pipit, near the intersection of Th Naklua Yarang. For medical services try the **Pattani Hospital** (☎ 0 7332 3411-14; Th Nong Jik). The **police station** (☎ 0 7334 9018; Th Pattani Phirom) is central.

Sights
Pattani has some of the prettiest beaches in southern Thailand – space constraints have allowed us to list only our favourites here, but there are plenty more. Ask around in town or buy a local map at any convenience store. Out of respect for the local Muslim culture, women should wear T-shirts over their swimsuits when at the beach or swimming.

The only beach near town is at **Laem Tachi**. Although it has 11km of white sand, it is far from the best beach in the area (if you want to visit anyway, take a boat taxi from the Pattani pier or Yaring Amphoe). Instead we'd suggest heading out along Rte 4136 for 53km. **Hat Wasukri** (Chaihat Ban Patatimaw) is a beautiful white-sandy spot with plenty of shade. You'll find more of the same along stretches of deserted beach further down Rte 4136, just a few kilometres before you reach the Narathiwat provincial border.

Sleeping & Eating
A night market with plenty of food vendors convenes on Th Charoenpradit nightly; another one lies along Soi Thepiwat 2.

Sakom Bay Resort (☎ 0 1277 1202; Hat Thepha; r 300-700B; ❄) This resort, which often has English speakers on the staff, might be the best choice in Pattani for budget travellers. Rooms in a hotel-style building are cheapest and there are comfortable air-con bungalows. An open-air restaurant that does seafood completes the offerings here.

CS Pattani Hotel (☎ 0 7333 5093/4; cspatani@cscoms .com; 299 Muu 4 Th Nong Jik; r from 1100B; ❄ ▯ ▣) If you are spending the night in Pattani, you might as well enjoy it. The CS Pattani features a gorgeous colonial lobby, two pools, an excellent restaurant, a sauna and steam room…the list goes on. Breakfast is included. Ask about discounts.

Getting There & Around
Săwngthǎew go anywhere in town for 15B per person. Daily buses to Bangkok depart from the small lot beside a petrol station near the CS Pattani Hotel – call ☎ 0 7334 8816 for ticket purchase and reservations. The trip is 15 to 16 hours and costs between 600B and 1500B, depending on the fanciness of the bus – if amenities like bathrooms and reclining seats matter, ask what kind of bus you're paying for, otherwise you'll likely be thrown on the first to depart.

NARATHIWAT PROVINCE

NARATHIWAT

นราธิวาส

pop 44,200

Sitting on the banks of the Bang Nara River, the provincial capital is a friendly town that exudes the sort of charisma that many modern Thai cities are leaving behind in the name of modernisation.

Some of the Sino-Portuguese buildings lining the riverfront are over a century old and you are as likely to hear Yawi, a local dialect, as Malay and Thai spoken around town. If you are making a visa run for the Malaysian border 1½ hours south, this town is a more favourable place to stay overnight than the rough and tumble border town of Sungai Kolok.

The security situation in this part of the country (see the travel warning on p636) has suffocated the little tourism that this region used to see. Be sure to check the latest situation before travelling here and take necessary precautions.

Narathiwat is right on the sea, and some of the prettiest beaches on southern Thailand's eastern coast stretch between it and Pattani – see p639 for more information. Just north of town is a small Thai-Muslim fishing village at the mouth of the Bang Nara river, lined with the large, painted fishing boats called *reua kaw-lae*, which are peculiar to Narathiwat and Pattani. Near the fishing village is **Hat Narathat**, a 5km-long sandy beach, which serves as a kind of public park for locals, with outdoor seafood restaurants, tables and umbrellas.

It's not very fancy, but **Ao Manao Resort** (☎ 0 7351 3640; bungalows 250-400B), located 7km south of town, features large, super-clean cement cottages in a small compound. It's only about 400m from the beach. Consider calling ahead, as it might be hard to find staff, especially in the low season. Nearby is a large batik shop selling painted fabric wall hangings that are this region's speciality.

At the other end of the scale, the **Imperial Narathiwat** (☎ 0 7351 5041; www.imperialhotels.com /narathiwat; 228 Th Pichitbamrung; r 1200-3000B; 🅿 🏊) is the town's new posh option and includes all the goodies you'd expect from a top-end hotel, including overly attentive staff and very comfy finishings.

Chow down at the night market off Th Chamroonnara behind the Bang Nara Hotel. There's also a cluster of food stalls on Th Sophaphisai at Th Puphapugdee serving inexpensive noodle dishes.

At **Ang Mo** (cnr Th Puphapugdee & Th Chamroonnara; dishes 30-80B; 🕑 lunch & dinner), you know the food must be good, because it's packed every night. The Thai food is cheap but tasty, and you can point to the displayed dishes.

Kopiitiam (dishes 30-100B; 🕑 breakfast, lunch & dinner) serves breakfast, snacks and light meals – try the refreshing fruit frappes or the good selection of coffee and teas. It's a tiny place, with just four small tables.

Air-con buses to Bangkok and Phuket leave from two separate small shop terminals on Th Suriyapradit, south of town a few hundred metres past the police station. The buses to Phuket (475B, 12 hours) originate in Sungai Kolok, pass Narathiwat three times daily (7am, 9am and 6.30pm) and continue via Pattani, Hat Yai, Songkhla, Trang, Krabi and Pha-Ngan. Buses to Bangkok (from 650B) run four times a day. You can buy tickets at the terminal or on the bus.

Narathiwat is easy to navigate on foot. If you don't feel like walking, motorcycle taxis will take you around for 15B to 30B, depending on the distance.

SUNGAI KOLOK

สุไหงโกลก

pop 40,500

Thailand's Wild West border town is a dusty spot that's more than a little rough around the edges. As the main southern coastal gateway between Malaysia and Thailand, Sungai Kolok oozes seediness and the main industries here revolve around catering to a weekend crowd of Malaysian men looking for sex.

Most of the hotels here cater to the 'by the hour' market. If you must stay the night in town, it's well worth shelling out a few extra baht to get away from the short-time trade scene. Some places in Sungai Kolok will take Malaysian ringgit as well as Thai baht for food or accommodation.

The best middle-of-the-road option in Sungai Kolak is probably the **Grand Garden Hotel** (☎ 0 7361 3600; gghotel@cscoms.com; 66 Soi, 3 Th Pratchatiwat; r from 585-1020B; 🅿 🏊). It features fine, clean, modern rooms that are well maintained and quite comfortable. There's a small pool outside and karaoke inside.

Three daily air-con buses make the 18-hour run to Bangkok (from 750B). The first bus leaves around 11.30am.

To Phuket (520B), buses head off at 6am, 8am and 5.30pm, and stop in Krabi (410B). These buses leave from Th Wongwiwat, west of the town centre. Buses to Krabi or Surat Thani go through Hat Yai first.

The border is about 1km from the centre of Sungai Kolok or the train station. Transport around town is by motorcycle taxi – it's 20B for a ride to the border. Coming from Malaysia, just follow the old train tracks to your right or, if looking for the town, turn left at the first junction and head for the high-rises.

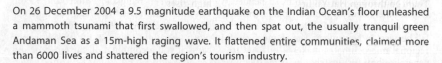

Andaman Coast

On 26 December 2004 a 9.5 magnitude earthquake on the Indian Ocean's floor unleashed a mammoth tsunami that first swallowed, and then spat out, the usually tranquil green Andaman Sea as a 15m-high raging wave. It flattened entire communities, claimed more than 6000 lives and shattered the region's tourism industry.

But even the world's second most powerful earthquake couldn't shake the Andaman Coast's super-sized natural beauty. With a face of soaring jagged limestone peaks, jade water for eyes and long sun-kissed golden beaches for legs, this bit of Thailand is positively dreamy.

The Andaman Coast encourages you to design your own adventure, with choices as endless as the sparkling sea. Surf Thailand's best breaks in Kata, Phuket, which dazzles with fine resorts, fine cuisine and fine beaches. Check out the otherworldly, underwater marine life on a live-aboard dive trip around the Similan Islands. Or really get off the beaten path and go to Ko Tarutao National Marine Park, where you can camp on wild, pristine beaches. For lazy beach days there's dramatic Ko Phi Phi or laid-back backpacker sweetheart Ko Lanta. And if you want to test your limits on some of the best rocks in the world, head to our favourite beach in Thailand, beautiful Railay. (Think water sparkling like an emerald brooch, specked with bits of sapphire and swirls of turquoise.)

Reminders of the tsunami linger. On Patong's streets one passes as many evacuation route signs as vendors toting fake Chanel. But while the clatter of construction is a constant, sadly, tourists are not. Which is a shame, because there is no reason not to visit. Residents are thinking forward, not back, and so should you.

HIGHLIGHTS

- Scaling limestone cliffs rising from emerald seas in pin-up-worthy **Railay** (p700)
- Riding morning waves at **Kata** (p683) then sipping Singha at a beachside bar, watching others wipe out worse than you
- Snorkelling crystal clear waters and lazing on honey-hued beaches at lovely **Ko Phi Phi** (p705)
- Doing the trash-with-cash thing in **Phuket** (p660), indulging your sinful side in Patong's seedy bars before bedding down at one of the island's luxury resorts
- Discovering the underwater world of the beautiful **Similan Islands Marine National Park** (p655), one of the planet's top dive sites

★ Similan Islands Marine National Park

Phuket ★   ★★ Krabi Province / Railay
Kata ★
★ Ko Phi Phi

Climate

A main concern when visiting Thailand's southern provinces is the weather. The Andaman coast receives more rain than the southern gulf provinces – with May to October being the months of heaviest rainfall. During this time passenger boats to some islands, such as the Surin, Similan and Ko Tarutao, are suspended. On the other hand, the southern gulf provinces are comparatively dry until October, with rainfall heaviest in November. The abundance of regional microclimates makes it difficult to generalise but, fortunately, the peninsula on which southern Thailand sits is somewhat narrow. If you find the weather on the Andaman coast unpleasant, you can easily travel to the other side and hope to find the sun shining.

National Parks

This region has more than its share of national parks. Ao Phang-Nga (p659) offers limestone cliffs, islands and caves to explore by sea-kayaking, scuba-diving or snorkelling. Khao Lak/Lamru (p653) has lots of hiking past cliffs and beaches, while multiple islands and kilometre after kilometre of mangroves and jungle make Laem Son (p649) perfect for birding. The Similan Islands Marine National Park (p655) is a world-class diving and snorkelling destination. In the Surin Islands Marine National Park (p651) you'll find granite islands and coral reefs, and whale sharks and manta rays to dive or snorkel with. Hat Jao Mai (p721) has sand beaches, mangroves and coral islands, while Khao Phanom Bencha (p704) is a hiker's paradise with mountain jungle, tumbling waterfalls and monkeys. Wild islands, pristine beaches and azure seas provide plenty of opportunities for snorkelling and diving in remote Ko Tarutao Marine National Park (p730). Sa Nang Manora Forest Park (p658) has a fairyland setting of moss-encrusted roots and rocks, plus multilevel waterfalls. Than Bokkharani (p704) offers a similar setting – emerald waters, caves and cliffs. On the border between Thailand and Malaysia, Thaleh Ban has the region's best-preserved section of white meranti rainforest.

Getting There & Away

Getting to the Andaman coast is straightforward. From Bangkok, the islands on the lower southern gulf and numerous other Thai destinations (as well as neighbouring Malaysia), it's easy to hop on a bus or train and then catch a ferry to the islands. Aeroplanes also ply the

skies between Bangkok, Phuket and Krabi. Bus and train travel from Bangkok is generally cheap, relatively efficient and mostly takes place overnight. Almost any travel agency can sell you a combination bus or train and boat ticket to Ko Phi Phi or Ko Lanta, which should get you to your destination with little effort. Beware of the cheapest tickets as they often prove to be scams. Pay a few more baht, however, and you'll likely arrive with few hassles. For more information on getting into and out of the region, see the destination sections or check out the Transport chapter (p761).

Getting Around

An intricate public transportation network takes you almost everywhere. Numerous boats shuttle back and forth between Ko Phi Phi and Ko Lanta and other more far-flung islands. Boats to more remote destinations – like the Surin Islands, Similan Islands and Ko Tarutao Marine National Parks – only run during the dry season (that would be November through May). Minivans and buses to just about anywhere make frequent trips throughout the day (and sometimes night). Basically, if you need to get from one tourist hot spot to another, it will take very little planning. Cheap săwngthăew (small pick-up truck) and motorcycle taxis are also abundant and are used for short trips around the islands and mainland. If you want to drive yourself, motorcycles can be rented for about 250B to 300B per day. Car rental, at about 1500B per day, is another option.

RANONG PROVINCE

Rising out of the murky, otherworldly waters of Myanmar's hinterland, Thailand's least populated province is also its most rainy, logging in with up to eight months of it per year. As a result the heavily forested and mountainous province is lush and green (although it's swampy near the coastline and mainland beaches are almost nonexistent).

There are really only two reasons to visit Ranong: visa runs to Myanmar or a trip to

ANDAMAN COAST

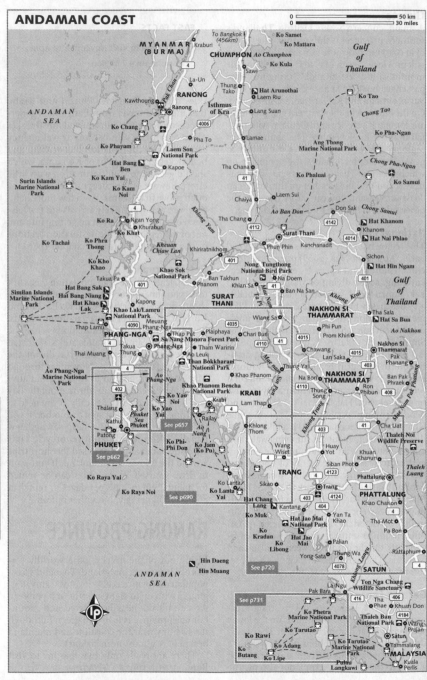

ANDAMAN COAST

ANDAMAN COAST

EARLY WARNING SYSTEM

In 2005, Thailand officially inaugurated a national disaster warning system, which was created in response to the country's lack of preparedness during the 2004 Asian tsunami. The Bangkok-based centre is staffed by a team of scientists and crisis-management staff who will evaluate the intensity of natural disasters and issue warnings to the general public. It is anticipated that a tsunami warning can be issued within 30 minutes of the event being detected by existing international systems that monitor seismic activity in the Pacific Ocean. The public will be warned via the nationwide radio network, Channel 5 army TV network, the state-operated TV pool, and SMS messages. For non-Thai speakers, the centre has installed warning towers along the high-risk beachfront areas that will broadcast pre-recorded announcements in various languages accompanied by flashing lights. The **call centre** (☎ 1860) also handles questions and tips from the public regarding potential or unfolding disasters.

---

the laid-back island of Ko Phayam, part of the Laem Son National Park, which includes the longest protected shoreline in the country.

RANONG

ระนอง

pop 24,500

On the east bank of the Chan River's tea brown estuary, the frontier town of Ranong is no more than a short boat ride – or a filthy swim – from Myanmar. In many ways, the capital of Ranong Province is a stereotypical border town: shabby, frenetic and ever so slightly seedy. But while most visitors roll into town for visa services, the town has a thriving Burmese population – keep an eye out for men wearing traditional *longyi* (Burmese sarong) – a clutch of natural hot springs and a handful of tumbledown historic buildings. In fact, even if you're not here to renew your visa, it's well worth taking the opportunity to have a cup of afternoon tea in Myanmar.

An increasing number of travellers are showing up specifically to dive the spectacular Burma Banks, 60km north of the Surin Islands. A number of dive operators have established themselves in Ranong (which does lend the city a bit of an expat feel), using it as a jumping-off point for live-aboard trips to the aforementioned Burma Banks.

Orientation & Information

Most of Ranong lies just west of Hwy 4, about 600km south of Bangkok and 300km north of Phuket.

BOOKSHOPS

Chuan Aksam bookshop (☎ 0 7781 1154; Th Ruangrat; ⏰ 8am-9.30pm) Near the corner of Th Tha Meuang, it has some reading material in English.

IMMIGRATION OFFICES

The main Thai immigration office is on the road to Saphan Plaa, about halfway between town and the main piers, across from a branch of the Thai Farmer's Bank. If entering Thailand from Myanmar via Kawthoung, you'll have to visit this office to get your passport stamped with a visa on arrival.

There is also a smaller immigration post in the vicinity of the Saphan Plaa pier. If you're just going in and out of Myanmar's Kawthoung for the day, a visit to the small post will suffice.

For details on renewing a visa or making a trip to Victoria Point (Myanmar), see p647.

INTERNET ACCESS

J Net (☎ 0 7882 2877; Th Ruangrat; per hr 40B; ⏰ 9am-9pm)

MONEY

Most of Ranong's banks are on Th Tha Meuang (the road to the fishing pier), near the intersection with Th Ruangrat, Ranong's main north–south street. Many have ATMs.

POST

Main post office (Th Chonrau; ⏰ 9am-4pm Mon-Fri, 9am-noon Sat)

TRAVEL AGENCIES

Plenty of agencies along Th Ruangrat offer visa services, bus and boat tickets, make accommodation arrangements for the nearby islands of Ko Chang and Ko Phayam, and run day trips to Kawthoung (in Myanmar).

Pon's Place (☎ 0 7782 3344; Th Ruangrat; ⏰ 7.30am-midnight) Also rents out motorcycles and cars.

Tanatwan Tours (☎ 0 7782 2807; tanatwan@hotmail.com; 16/8 Th Chonrau; ⏰ 9am-8pm) Visa trips cost 350B (plus visa costs) per person and depart daily at 9am.

Sights & Activities

HOT SPRINGS
บ่อน้ำร้อน

Ranong may lack the sophisticated pizzazz of your typical spa town, but it is well known for its hot springs. You can sample the waters at Wat Tapotaram, where **Ranong Mineral Hot Springs** (Th Kamlangsap; admission 10B; ⏰ 8am-5pm) offers pools hot enough to boil eggs in (65°C). Almost, but not quite, like the three bears of *Goldilocks* fame, the names of the three springs translate as Father Spring, Mother Spring and Baby Spring and each has its own distinct flavour (all horrid). The spring water is thought to be sacred, as well as having miraculous healing powers.

You can bathe in rustic rooms where you scoop water from separate hot and cool water tanks and sluice the mixed water over your body Thai-style. Don't get inside the tanks and spoil the water. Several local hotels pipe water directly from the springs into rooms.

WATERFALLS

Of the several well-known waterfalls in Ranong Province, **Ngao Falls** and **Punyaban Falls** are within walking distance of Hwy 4. Ngao is 13km south of Ranong, while Punyaban is 15km north. Just take a săwngthăew in either direction and ask to be let off at the *náam tòk* (waterfall).

DIVING

Live-aboard diving trips run from Ranong to world-class bubble-blowing destinations

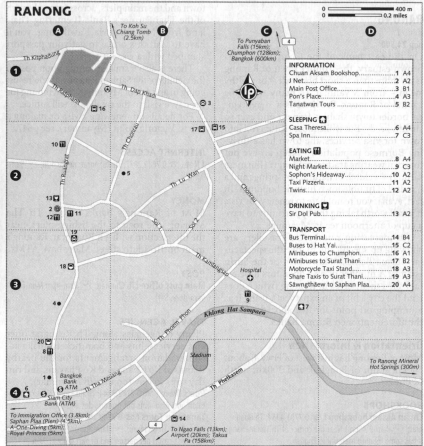

RANONG

| 0 | 400 m |
| 0 | 0.2 miles |

INFORMATION
Chuan Aksam Bookshop	1	A4
J Net	2	A2
Main Post Office	3	B1
Pon's Place	4	A3
Tanatwan Tours	5	B2

SLEEPING
| Casa Theresa | 6 | A4 |
| Spa Inn | 7 | C3 |

EATING
Market	8	A4
Night Market	9	C3
Sophon's Hideaway	10	A2
Taxi Pizzeria	11	A2
Twins	12	A2

DRINKING
| Sir Dol Pub | 13 | A2 |

TRANSPORT
Bus Terminal	14	B4
Buses to Hat Yai	15	C2
Minibuses to Chumphon	16	A1
Minibuses to Surat Thani	17	B2
Motorcycle Taxi Stand	18	A3
Share Taxis to Surat Thani	19	A3
Săwngthăew to Saphan Plaa	20	A4

RENEWING YOUR VISA AT VICTORIA POINT

The dusty, tumbledown port at the southernmost tip of mainland Myanmar was named Victoria Point by the British, but is known as Ko Song (Second Island) by the Thais. The Burmese appellation, Kawthoung, is most likely a corruption of the Thai name. Most travellers come here to renew their visas, but the place also makes an interesting day trip.

Fishing and trade with Thailand keep things ticking over, but Kawthoung also churns out some of Myanmar's best kick boxers. Nearby islands are inhabited by bands of nomadic *chao leh* (sea gypsies).

The easiest way to renew your visa is to opt for one of the 'visa trips' (from 350B per person plus visa fees) offered by travel agencies in Ranong, or you can do the legwork yourself.

When the Thai–Myanmar border is open, boats to Kawthoung leave from the pier at Saphan Plaa (Pla Bridge) about 5km from the centre of Ranong. Take săwngthăew 2 from Ranong (10B) and get off at the **immigration office** (☎ 0 7782 2016; Th Ruangrat; ⊗ 8.30am-6pm), 700m north of the pier, to get your passport stamped. From there, groups of people will be waiting to take you on a boat trip (one-way/return 50/100B) to Myanmar immigration. When negotiating the price, confirm whether it is per person or per ride, and one-way or return. At the checkpoint, you must inform the authorities that you're a day visitor – in which case you will pay a fee of US$5 or 300B for a day permit. If you have a valid Myanmar visa in your passport, you'll be permitted to stay for up to 28 days.

If you're just coming to renew your Thai visa, the whole process will take a minimum of two hours. Bear in mind when you are returning to Thailand that Myanmar time is 30 minutes behind Thailand's. This has caused problems in the past for returning visitors who got through Burmese immigration before its 6pm closing time only to find the Thai office closed. Though the Thai immigration department seems to have changed its hours in order to avoid this unpleasantness, it's a good idea to double-check closing hours when leaving the country.

including the Burma Banks and the Surin and Similan Islands. Prices start at around US$200 for a two-day, two-night package. Try **A-One-Diving** (☎ 0 7783 2984; www.a-one-diving .com; 77 Saphan Plaa).

Sleeping

Ranong's hotels don't exactly get your blood racing; they are more likely to make it boil. Most offer little more than bare bones amenities.

The places on or near Th Phetkasem (Hwy 4) can be reached from town by săwngthăew 2.

Kiwi Orchid (☎ 0 7783 2812; www.kiwiorchid.com; Th Phetkasem; r 250B) Right by the bus station – expect late night rumblings – this ramshackle backpacker place boasts plenty of greenery, guitars on the walls of the downstairs café and heavily tattooed staff. The atmosphere is good, but business is slow and the rooms are looking a little downtrodden.

Spa Inn (☎ 0 7781 1715; fax 0 7782 3384; 25/11 Th Phetkasem; r 300-500B; ☒) Walls here could do with a rubdown with the local mineral water, but this so-so hotel takes a step up the price (and quality) escalator, with large rooms and water pumped in from the springs. The back rooms look out on the lush green mountainside.

Casa Theresa (☎ 0 7781 1135; 119/18 Th Tha Meuang; r 200-700B; ☒) There's no question the beds here might be too firm for some people's tastes. However this clean off-the-street guesthouse redeems itself with quite authentic Thai massages and friendly, knowledgeable staff.

Royal Princess (☎ 0 7783 5240; www.royalprincess .com; r 800-1200B; ☒ ☒) Our choice for sleeping, although the amenities are better than the rooms (which are looking a bit tatty these days). The place has a pool and gym, and mineral water in the bathrooms. Rates vary with the wet and dry(er) seasons.

Eating & Drinking

On Th Kamlangsap, not far from Hwy 4 and the Spa Inn, is a night market with several food stalls selling great Thai dishes at low prices; across the street is a modest noodle stand. The day market, on Th Ruangrat towards the southern end of town, offers inexpensive Thai and Burmese meals, as well as fresh produce, fish and meats. A cluster of decent eateries can also be found at the northern end of Th Ruangrat.

Twins (Th Ruangrat; mains 40-80B; ⊗ dinner) Thai and Western dishes are served amid wind

ANDAMAN COAST

WHAT TO EXPECT ON THE ANDAMAN COAST

■ Budget (under 600B)

■ Midrange (600 to 2000B)

■ Top End (more than 2000B)

High-season rates have been quoted. Ranong tends to be cheaper than other provinces of the Andaman Coast. Expect to pay between 150B and 600B for a budget bungalow or room. Midrange options go for around 600B to 800B while top-end places start at around 1000B.

In 2006, prices in tsunami-affected regions of Phang-Nga were still severely discounted (lots of places were still under construction). Budget places cost under 600B, midrange options go for 600B to 2000B and top-end places start at 2000B. Prices drop by 50% in the rainy season (when, frankly, the province can be pretty darn depressing. Save your visit here for the sunny season).

If you are coming from parts of the gulf during the high season, Phuket may seem a bit pricey. Budget digs on the beaches go between 400B and 600B on average. Midrange hotels go between 800B and 3500B, with top-end places costing more than 3500B per night. Phuket has some of the most luxurious resorts in Thailand. Prices can drop by as much as 50% during the low season. Accommodation on Phi Phi is ridiculously expensive compared with much of Thailand – a fan room in the low season costs 900B, double what it costs in Phuket!

---

chimes and the odd foreign football game on the TV at this timber alfresco joint. If you take a table at the back, you can just about sneak a view of green fields.

Taxi Pizzeria (☎ 0 7782 5730; Th Ruangrat; dishes 60-180B; ☾ lunch & dinner) Completed framed jigsaws provide the decoration at this spartan pizzeria. The food won't have mama amending her recipe book, but the chef does make an attempt at rustling up a reasonable margarita.

Sophon's Hideaway (☎ 0 7783 2730; Th Ruangrat; mains 60-200B; ☾ lunch & dinner) This little spot has everything, including internet access, a free pool table, a pizza oven, water features and rattan furnishings aplenty. The menu spans the East–West divide and cocktails are served come sundown.

Sir Dol Pub (☎ 0 9471 0884; Th Ruangrat; ☾ 8pm-2am) Proudly boasting a heritage stretching all the way back to the sepia-tint days of 1994, this parochial drinking den offers blacked-out windows, Thai tunes and live bands from 9pm.

Getting There & Away

AIR

Ranong airport is 20km south of town, off Hwy 4. **Phuket Airlines** (☎ 0 7782 4591; www.phuket airlines.com) has two flights to Bangkok (one-way around 2700B) in the morning.

BUS

The bus terminal is on Th Phetkasem towards the southern end of town, though some buses stop in town before proceeding to the terminal. Săwngthăew 2 (blue) passes the terminal.

Tanatwan Tours (☎ 0 7782 2807; tanatwan@hotmail .com; 16/8 Th Chonrau; ☾ 9am-8pm) offers privately operated 2nd-class (360B, 11 hours, 10 daily), 1st-class (510B, 10 hours, 8am and 8pm) and 24-seat VIP (720B, 10 hours, 8pm) buses to Bangkok.

The bus terminal also has services to the following destinations:

BUSES FROM RANONG

Destination	Bus type	Price (B)	Duration (Hr)
Bangkok	VIP	389-515	10
	1st class	333	10
	2nd class	259	10
	ordinary	185	10
Chumphon	2nd class	70	3
	ordinary	50	3
Hat Yai	2nd class	300	5
Khuraburi	air-con	60	1½
	ordinary	40	1½
Krabi	air-con	106	6
Phang-Nga	ordinary	90	5
Phuket	air-con	185	5-6
	ordinary	103	5-6
Surat Thani	1st class	180	4-5
	2nd class	80	4-5

ANDAMAN COAST

Getting Around

From Ranong take a săwngthăew (15B) to Saphan Plaa pier. Motorcycle taxis will take you almost anywhere in town for 15B, to the hotels along Th Petchkasim for 20B and to the Saphan pier for boats to Ko Chang, Ko Phayam and Myanmar for 50B. **Pon's Place** (☎ 0 7782 3344; Th Ruangrat; ☾ 7.30am-midnight) can assist with motorcycle and car rentals.

AROUND RANONG
Ko Chang
เกาะช้าง

Ko Chang feels a world apart from most of Thailand's islands. There are no megaphone announcements for Thai boxing (even though some of the country's best fighters hail from Ranong Province), no streets designed entirely for faràng. No, Ko Chang isn't selling knock-off Ray-Bans and Playstation games. Its marketing scheme focuses squarely on seducing buyers with an older, slower version of Thailand. Electricity is sporadic, and tourists few and far between.

Pass the time exploring the island's tiny village capital (where boats dock during the dry season) or wind your way around the island on one of the dirt trails. Sea eagles, Andaman kites and hornbills all nest here and, if you're lucky, you'll catch sight of them floating above the mangroves. Keen sunbathers can lie out on one of the island's reasonable west coast beaches.

Bungalow operators can arrange boat trips to Ko Phayam and other nearby islands for around 250B per person (including lunch) in a group of six or more. Dive trips are also possible. **Aladdin Dive Cruise** (☎ 0 7782 0472; www .aladdindivecruise.de), on Ko Chang, runs PADI courses and offers a range of live-aboard dive safaris. A three-day live-aboard trip to the Surin Islands costs 11,250B; four-day trips to the Similan Islands cost 15,000B.

SLEEPING & EATING

Basic bungalows are the norm on rustic Ko Chang and, for the most part, they're only open from November to April. There is limited electricity and the cheaper rooms inevitably come with shared bathroom.

Ko Chang Contex (☎ 0 7782 0118; bungalows 100-250B) North of the village, this spartan outfit is run by a welcoming Thai family and features basic bungalows on a rocky headland. It's homey and the beach is a stone's throw away.

Hornbill Bungalow (☎ 0 7783 3820; bungalows 150-250B) On an isolated beach in the island's north, this is a good spot for solitude seekers. It's a bit of a hike to get here, but the owner has a boat for ferrying guests around.

Cashew Resort (☎ 0 7782 4741; bungalows 200-600B) Cashew is Ko Chang's most venerable resort. Choose from cheap A-frame huts or larger, more robust bungalows.

Eden Bistro Cafe (☎ 0 7782 0172; bungalows 250-300B) Feast on a fab phàt thai (thin noodles with vegetables, tofu and egg) in the café before falling into bed in one of the basic bungalows. Most of the digs come with shared bathroom, but there is one 'VIP' suite with attached shower. Eden is southwest of Ko Chang Contex.

GETTING THERE & AWAY

From Ranong take a săwngthăew (15B) to Saphan Plaa pier, getting off at the PTT petrol station and toll booth. Look for the lane on the left just before the toll booth (there may be a sign referring to Ko Chang) and follow it down a few hundred metres, zigzagging along the way; turn left at the T-junction and walk about five minutes to reach the pier.

Two or three boats leave every morning from November to April; turn up around 9am to see when they're going, as they don't usually leave before this hour. During the high season (December to March) there's a regular noon departure daily. Boats return to Ranong at 8am the next day. The boat fare is 150B per person, but can be included in the cost of your accommodation if you book ahead.

LAEM SON NATIONAL PARK
อุทยานแห่งชาติแหลมสน

The **Laem Son National Park** (☎ 0 7782 4224; www .dnp.go.th; adult/child 200/100B) covers 315 sq km of the Kapoe district of Ranong and Khuraburi district in Phang-Nga. This area includes about 100km of Andaman Sea coastline – the longest protected shore in the country – as well as over 20 islands. Much of the coast here is covered with mangrove swamps, home to various species of birds, fish, deer and monkeys (including crab-eating macaques) often seen while driving along the road to the park headquarters.

The most accessible beach is **Hat Bang Ben**, where the park headquarters are. This long, sandy beach, backed by shady casuarinas, is said to be safe for swimming year-round.

From Hat Bang Ben you can see several islands, including the nearby Ko Kam Yai, Ko Kam Noi, Mu Ko Yipun, Ko Khang Khao and, to the north, Ko Phayam. The park staff can arrange boat trips out to any of these islands for 800B per boat per day. During low tide you can walk to an island just a couple of hundred metres from Hat Bang Ben.

Ko Phayam is a friendly, demure little island which supports about 500 inhabitants, mostly Thais and Burmese, with a smattering of expats and a few dozen ethnic *chao leh* (sea gypsies) thrown into the mix. While spotlighted by two main bays and their pretty beaches, Ko Phayam also has a couple of sizeable forested hills and plenty of scenic agricultural land to boot. Interesting fauna in the area include wild pigs, hornbills, monkeys and snakes. Locals support themselves prawn-fishing, farming cashews and working the rubber plantations.

The island has one 'village', where you will find the main pier, a couple of simple eateries, some small grocery stalls and a bar. From the pier area, motorcycle taxis scoot you to the 15 or so basic bungalow operations around the island, almost all of which are on the picturesque bay of Ao Khao Fai. A new motorcycle 'highway', running down the middle of Ko Phayam, augments smaller concrete roadways and dirt driveways.

Ko Khang Khao is known for a beach on its northern end, which is covered with colourful pebbles. Although underwater visibility isn't great here, it's a little better than on Ko Chang as it's further from the mouth of the Chan River. The beach on **Ko Kam Noi** has relatively clear water for swimming and snorkelling (April is the best month), plus the added bonus of fresh water year-round and plenty of grassy areas for camping. One island on the other side of Ko Kam Yai, which can't be seen from the beach, is **Ko Kam Tok** (also called Ko Ao Khao Khwai). It's only about 200m from Ko Kam Yai, and, like Ko Kam Noi, has a good beach, coral, fresh water and a camping ground. **Ko Kam Yai** is 14km southwest of Hat Bang Ben. It's a large island with some accommodation (camping and bungalows), a pretty beach and great snorkelling.

About 3km north of Hat Bang Ben, across the canal, is another beach, **Hat Laem Son**, which is almost always deserted. The only way to get here is to hike from Hat Bang Ben. In the opposite direction, about 50km south of Hat Bang Ben, is **Hat Praphat**, very similar to Bang Ben, with casuarinas backing the long beach. Sea turtles lay eggs on Hat Praphat. There is a second park office here, which can be reached by road via Hwy 4 (Phetkasem Hwy).

In the canals you ford coming into the park, you may notice the large wooden racks that are used for raising oysters.

Sleeping & Eating

It's best to stay in Ko Phayam if you're going to spend the night – the options are more appealing than the dingy national park bungalows at Hat Bang Ben. Fan cooled, rustic bungalows are the staple on Ko Phayam; electricity is usually available from sunset to 10pm or 11pm. Most of the bungalow operations stay open throughout the year – although the shutters will come down if business becomes too slow – and many have attached eateries serving standard backpacker fare.

The following places are on Ao Yai, a pleasant 3km-long sweep of sandy beach, and Ao Khao Fai. The water tends to be choppier at Ao Yai than at Ao Khao Fai, which is a little further north. Though the beach is more sheltered at Ao Khao Fai, the bay is not quite as good for swimming and tides tend to be stronger. That said it's still a scenic spot for soaking up the sunshine and admiring the view.

Vijit (☎ 0 7783 4082; www.geocities.com/vijitbungalows; Ao Khao Fai; bungalows 100-200B) This place, towards the southern end of the bay, has about a dozen basic bungalows around a sandy lot planted with young trees. Each bungalow has been built in a slightly different style. At high tide, the beach here thins out. Contact the staff for free transport from Ranong.

JPR (Ao Khao Fai; bungalows 150-200B) Further north, JPR has nine simple bungalows spread out between trees, on a dusty hillside above the beach. It's friendly, pretty isolated and down a long driveway.

Mountain Resort (☎ 0 7782 0098; Ao Khao Fai; bungalows 350B) Located in a shady palm grove, this has some of the glossiest bungalows on the island – they are also some of the most pleasant. With only a handful of bungalows on offer, you can count on plenty of privacy and lashings of peace and quiet. Mountain Resort is at the northern end of the bay.

Bamboo Bungalows (☎ 0 7782 0012; Ao Yai; bungalows 100-500B) Opt for more expensive, but sturdier (read: monsoon-proof) concrete-

and-tile bungalows. It is run by an Israeli/ Thai couple, offers oodles of atmosphere and attracts plenty of backpackers – when they are in town. There's a solid eatery, a pleasant, leafy garden and you can hire bodyboards if you fancy a boogie in the surf.

Drinking

Oscar's (☎ 0 7782 4236; Ao Khao Fai; ☯ 10am-11pm) Located in the main village, this modern bar looks a little incongruous in its backwater setting. If you're after late-night (for a remote island) shenanigans, however, it is *the* place to go – the beer might even be cold.

Getting There & Away

The turn-off for Laem Son National Park is about 58km from Ranong down Hwy 4 (Phet-kasem Hwy), between the 657km and 658km markers. Buses heading south from Ranong can drop you off here (ask for Hat Bang Ben). Once you're off the highway, however, you'll have to flag down a pick-up truck going towards the park. If you can't get a ride all the way, it's a 10km walk from Hwy 4 to the park entrance. At the police box at the junction you may be able to hire a motorcycle taxi for 30B; the road is paved, so if you're driving it's a breeze.

See p649 for details on getting to Ranong's Saphan Plaa, from where boats head to Ko Phayam.

There are daily boats from Saphan Plaa to Ko Phayam's pier at around 8am and 3pm (100B, 1½ to two hours). From Ko Phayam back to Ranong the boats run at 9am and 2pm. During the high season there may be three runs daily. Long-tail boat charters to the island cost 1500B to 2000B.

There has been sporadic talk of a boat service running directly from Ranong to the two main bays on Ko Phayam (per person one way 100B), saving you a hefty motorcycle fare. This service would run from November to May only; ask around Ranong for the latest on this venture.

Boats out to the various islands can be chartered from the park's visitors centre; the general cost is 800B per day. You can arrange to go as far as the Similan or Surin Islands for 900B and 1200B per person, respectively.

Getting Around

Motorcycle taxis provide the transport around Ko Phayam, there are no cars or trucks (yet), and roads are pleasantly motorcycle-sized. A

ride to your bungalow will cost 50B to 100B. Walking is possible but distances are long – it's about 45 minutes from the pier to Ao Khao Fai, the nearest bay.

Motorcycle rentals are available at **Oscar's** (☎ 0 7782 4236; per day approx 250B), the only bar in Ko Phayam's village – you can't miss it. Some of the bigger guesthouses might be able to arrange rentals, too.

PHANG-NGA PROVINCE

More than anywhere else in Thailand, the Phang-Nga coastline is still reeling from the devastation of the 2004 tsunami. In fact about 6,000 of the deaths – well over half the national count – occurred along this section of the An-daman coast, particularly in the Thai Muang, Khao Lak, Bang Niang and Bang Sak regions.

From November to April the water is very clear, the sun shines, soda-white beaches beckon. In the rainy season, however, many places shut down and the area can feel a bit haunted and depressing.

Offshore, the Surin Islands and Similan Islands Marine National Parks harbour some of the world's top diving destinations.

For an overview on accommodation costs see the boxed text on p648.

SURIN ISLANDS MARINE NATIONAL PARK (MU KO SURIN NATIONAL PARK)

อุทยานแห่งชาติหมู่เกาะสุรินทร์

The five gorgeous islands that make up **Surin Islands Marine National Park** (www.dnp.go.th; admission 400B; ☯ mid-Nov–mid-May) sit 60km offshore, just 5km from the Thai–Burma marine border. Healthy rainforest, pockets of white-sand beach in sheltered bays and rocky headlands that jut into the ocean characterise these granite-outcrop islands. The clearest of water makes for great marine life, with underwa-ter visibility often up to 20m. The islands' sheltered waters also attract *chao náam* – sea gypsies – who live in a village onshore during the May–November monsoon season. Here they are known as Moken, from the local word *oken* meaning 'salt water'.

Ko Surin Nuea (north) and Ko Surin Tai (south) are the two largest islands. Park head-quarters and all visitor facilities are at Ao Chong Khad on Ko Surin Nuea, near the jetty.

Khuraburi is the jump-off point for the park. The pier is about 9km north of town,

as is the mainland **national park office** (☎ 0 7649 1378; ⊙ 8am-5pm) with good information, maps and helpful staff.

Sights & Activities

DIVING & SNORKELLING
Dive sites in the park include **Ko Surin Tai**, and **HQ Channel** between the two main islands. In the vicinity is **Richelieu Rock** (a seamount 14km southeast) where whale sharks are often spotted during March and April. Sixty kilometres northwest of the Surins – but often combined with dive trips to the park – are the famed **Burma Banks**, a system of submerged seamounts. The three major banks, **Silvertip**, **Roe** and **Rainbow**, provide five-star diving experiences, with coral gardens laid over flat plateaus and large oceanic and, smaller, reef marine species. There's presently no dive facility in the park itself, so dive trips (four-day live-aboards around 20,000B) must be booked from the mainland; see Getting There & Away, right, for more information.

Snorkelling is excellent due to relatively shallow reef depths of 5m to 6m, and most coral survived the tsunami intact. Two two-hour snorkelling trips by boat (per person 70B; gear per day 150B) leave island headquarters daily.

WILDLIFE & WALKS
Around park headquarters you can explore the forest fringes, looking out for the crab-eating macaques (cheeky monkeys!) and some of the 57 resident bird species which include the fabulous Nicobar pigeon, endemic to the islands of the Andaman Sea. Along the coast you're likely to see the chestnut Brahminy kite soaring, and reef herons on the rocks. Twelve species of bat live here, most noticeably the tree-dwelling fruit bats, also known as flying foxes.

A rough-and-ready **walking trail** – not for the unsteady – winds 2km along the coast and through forest to the beach at **Ao Mai Ngam**, where there's good snorkelling. At low tide it's easy to walk between the bays near headquarters.

OTHER ACTIVITIES
On Ko Surin Tai, the **Moken village** at Ao Bon welcomes visitors; take a long-tail boat from headquarters (80B). Post-tsunami, Moken have settled in this one sheltered bay where a major ancestral worship ceremony (Loi Reua) takes place in April. Painted *law bong* – protective totem poles – stand at the park entrance.

Sleeping & Eating
Accommodation is simple and fine, but because of the island's short, narrow beaches it's *very* close together and can feel seriously crowded when full (around 300 people). For park accommodation, book online at www .dnp.go.th or with the **mainland park office** (☎ 0 7649 1378) in Khuraburi.

Bungalows (incl fan, bathroom & balcony 2000B) and **on-site tents** (1-person/2-person tents 300/450B) are available at Ao Chong Khad; tents should be available at Ao Mai Ngam from 2006. You can pitch your own **tent** (per night 80B). There's generator power until about 10pm.

A park **restaurant** (dishes from 60B) serves Thai food.

If you need to stay overnight in Khuraburi, try the new **Country Hut Riverside** (☎ 08 6272 0588; r from 300-500B; ☒) or long-standing **Tararin Resort** (☎ 0 7649 1789; r from 300-500B; ☒). On either side of the bridge at the north end of town, each has clean, basic, tiny fan/air-con rooms. A more luxurious option, **Kuraburi Greenview Resort** (☎ 0 7640 1400; www.kuraburigreenview.co.th; d from 1900B; ☒ ▢ ☒) is 15km south of town, set among forest and river, with curious but comfortable wood, slate-and-cobblestone bungalows.

Getting There & Away
A 'big boat' (return 1200B, 2½ hours one-way) leaves the Khuraburi pier at 9am daily, returning at 1pm. Tour operators use speedboats (return 1600B, one hour one way) and will transfer independent travellers on their daily runs.

Several tour operators, all located near the pier, run day/overnight tours (around 2600/3500B) to the park; agencies in Khao Lak and Phuket can make bookings for these and for dive trips. In Khuraburi town, try the affable **Tom & Am Tour** (☎ 08 6272 0588; www .surinislandtour.com) for on-spec bookings. Tour operators include transfers from Khao Lak in their prices.

Buses run three times daily between Phuket and Khuraburi (160B, 3½ hours) and between Khuraburi and Ranong (60B, 1½ hours).

HAT BANG SAK
หาดบางสัก

Pre-tsunami the long, sleepy stretch of sand at Bang Sak had been attracting an ever-growing number of tourists striking north from the more heavily developed resorts of Phuket

and nearby Khao Lak. While most areas had recovered from the tsunami by the end of 2006, Bang Sak was still trying to rebuild its tourist infrastructure. Rehabilitation efforts will likely continue well into 2008. That said, the beach is open for business and the best way to help out the locals is to stop over for the night to get the economy rolling again. For the latest on the region's reconstruction, including details of the hotels that are open, visit www.khaolak-info.net.

There are just a few hotels along this pretty stretch of beach, making it an ideal romantic hideaway.

Similana Resort (☎ 0 7648 7166; www.similanare sort.com; r from 1300B; 🅿) is a unique resort getting rave reviews from guests. Each bungalow is a small work of art, with handcrafted furnishings, waxed dark-wood floors, cotton quilted bedcovers, bay windows and private decks with panoramic views. Try the traveller-recommended tree houses nestled in the forest, which descends into the sand. Similana is a romantic place that is rather secluded – if you don't have private transport it's a pricey (300B) taxi ride into Khao Lak. The beach here is lovely, however, and there's an on-site restaurant so there's little reason to leave.

The **Le Meridien Khao Lak Beach & Spa Resort** (☎ 0 7642 7500; www.khaolak.lemeridien.com; Hwy 4; r 3000-8000B; 🅿 🖥 🅿) just may be the swankiest resort on the mainland Andaman Coast. Rooms are spacious and stylish, there's a fabulous spa for days of pampering and there's every amenity you could hope for.

Buses running between Takua Pa and Phuket will get you here; just ask to be let off at Hat Bang Sak.

KHAO LAK

เขาหลัก/บางเนียง/นางทอง

Post-tsunami construction and rebuilding are underway, but two years after the event, locals worry they've been forgotten. Hotels remain unfinished, restaurants empty and the lack of tourists is all too obvious.

It's a pity, because the beautiful diver's haven of Khao Lak was experiencing a tourist gold rush before the fateful events of December 2004 which washed away years of progress.

Backpacker accommodation predominates in the centre of town, where tourists congregate to rehash diving yarns in a string

of bars and restaurants. Grand resorts have set up shop on the outskirts of town, and offer some of the swankiest beds this side of Phuket.

Ready access to the Surin and Similan Islands Marine National Parks is one reason to visit Khao Lak, as these islands offer some of Thailand's most exhilarating diving. For shorter trips, a coral reef suitable for snorkelling lies 45 minutes offshore by long-tail boat, and many dive shops offer excursions.

Orientation & Information

This area, which actually encompasses three main beaches (Khao Lak, Nang Thong, Bang Niang), is generally referred to as Khao Lak. Most businesses are concentrated on the beachfront, and along Highway 4 (Th Phetkasem, which runs parallel to the beach) in Nang Thong. Resorts and hotels are also found on Bang Niang beach to the north and Khao Lak beach proper, to the south. Khao Lak/Lamru National Park is just north of Khao Lak Beach.

There are numerous 'travel agencies' scattered about – many just a desk on the side of the road – and most of these do laundry and rent motorbikes for around 250B per day.

Khao Lak Inn (☎ 0 7642 3056; Th Phetkasem; per min 2B; 🕙 9am-9pm) Offers internet access.

O.A.Sis Tour (☎ 08 7644 3292, 0 7271 4326) Run by long-time Khao Lak resident Su, who speaks great English. She can arrange all sorts of lodging, transport and activities. Ring for her current location.

Siam Commercial Bank (Th Phetkasem; 🕙 9am-3.30pm Mon-Fri) On the main road; has ATM and change facilities.

Tsunami Volunteer Center (☎ 08 9882 8840; www .tsunamivolunteer.net; Th Phetkasem) For information about the reconstruction effort in the surrounding area.

Sights & Activities

The area immediately south of Hat Khao Lak has been incorporated into the 125-sq-km **Khao Lak/Lamru National Park** (☎ 0 7642 0243; www.dnp.go.th; adult/child 200/100B; 🕙 8am-4.30pm), a beautiful collection of sea cliffs, 1000m hills, beaches, estuaries, forested valleys and mangroves. Wildlife seen in the park includes hornbills, drongos, tapirs, gibbons, monkeys and Asiatic black bears. The visitors centre, just off Hwy 4 between the 56km and 57km markers, has little in the way of maps or printed information, but there's a very nice

open-air restaurant perched on a shady slope overlooking the sea.

Guided treks along the coast or inland can be arranged through Poseidon Bungalows, as can long-tail boat trips up the scenic **Khlong Thap Liang** estuary. The latter afford opportunities to view mangrove communities of crab-eating macaques. Between Khao Lak and Bang Sak is a network of sandy beach trails – some of which lead to deserted beaches – which are fun to explore on foot or by rented motorcycle. Most of the hotels in town rent out motorbikes for 250B per day.

Since both the Surin and Similan islands are relatively far from the mainland – around 60km away – most dive shops offer live-aboard trips. These trips cost around 3700/9000/12,000B for one-/two-/three-day packages. Trips to local coral reefs start at around 1300B.

Sea Dragon Dive Center (☎ 0 7642 0420; www.sea dragondivecenter.com; Th Phetkasem), on the main road through Khao Lak, is extremely helpful, with Western staff and a range of packages on offer. Poseidon Bungalows also organises live-aboard **snorkelling tours** (2 nights 6500B) to the Similan Islands, departing on Tuesday and Friday from November to May. If you are not a certified diver, this is a great opportunity to sample many of the best underwater sights from the surface.

About 2.5km north of Hat Khao Lak, **Hat Bang Niang** was also flattened by the tsunami, but is well worth a trip if you are looking for a little more peace and quiet.

Sleeping

Khao Lak was hard hit by the tsunami and most of the beachfront hotels were destroyed. By late 2006, the reconstruction effort was well underway, but some of the seaside outfits had yet to open for business – they were scheduled to open over the course of 2007.

BUDGET

Jai Restaurant & Bungalow (☎ 0 7642 0390; Th Phetkasem; r 350-500B) Shack up at Jai's if you don't need air-con or other frills to survive, and are just looking for a cheap place to lay your head. A thatched, leafy eatery serves tasty local fare in front; the bungalows are out back.

Happy Lagoon (☎ 0 7642 3408; bungalows 600B; 🞩) The best part about Happy Lagoon is the fabulous old-fashioned bar. The garden area

is also great; full of tucked-away benches and gnarled old trees. Just a short hop from the beach, the bungalows are spartan, but large and perfectly comfortable, at a very reasonable price. When it's busy, Happy Lagoon has great personality.

Khao Lak Inn (☎ 0 7642 3056; juju311@hotmail.com; Th Phetkasem; s/d 600/700B; 🞩 🖳) Above a row of shops on the main road at the southern edge of town, Khao Lak Inn is hardly glamour incarnate, but offers comfy, backpacker-friendly digs in tidy surrounds.

MIDRANGE & TOP END

Poseidon Bungalows (☎ 0 7644 3258; www.similan tour.com; bungalows 900B) On the other side of the headland of Khao Lak/Lam Ru National Park, about 5km south of Hat Khao Lak, this quiet spot has huts discreetly dispersed among huge boulders and coastal forest, affording quiet and privacy. The proprietors dispense information on the area and organise boat excursions and dive trips to the local reef and to the Similan Islands.

Suwan Palm Resort (☎ 0 7648 5830; www.suwan palm.com; Hat Nang Thong; r from 1500B; 🞩 🖳 🞩) Rechristened after the tsunami (it used to be the Khaolak Orchid Resortal), this hotel has rooms with floor-to-ceiling glass doors opening onto a patio overlooking the water. Beautiful! The rooms are tastefully decorated with light teak furniture. The sheets are not too scratchy, but beds seem ultrafirm and the air-con can be a tad noisy. The on-site restaurant and Irish pub add lively ambience come dark. There is free internet (only one computer though).

Khao Lak Countryside Resort & Spa (☎ 0 7648 5474; www.khalak-countryside.com; Hat Nang Thong; bungalows 1600B; 🞩 🖳 🞩) A medium-sized resort on grassy grounds; rates drop by half in the low season. Done in a country Thai style, rooms come in various shapes and sizes and feature lovely blue-tiled baths. Check out the large pool with the water spouts shaped as dolphins.

Khao Lak/Lam Ru National Park Bungalows (☎ 0 2562 0760; reserve@dnp.go.th; bungalows 1200-2000B) There are a handful of four- and six-bed bungalows in the national park. Standards are basic, but the setting will suit those after the nature experience. Perfect for ramblers.

Khao Lak Seaview Resort (☎ 0 7642 9800; www .khaolak-seaviewresort.com; Hat Nang Thong; r from 3500B; 🞩 🞩) Completely rebuilt after the tsu-

nami, this upmarket resort features beautiful grounds draped with sculptures of elephants and laced with decorative canals. Check out the sunken tubs in the bathroom, and elegant dark-wood floors, teak furniture and firm beds in the spacious, fresh abodes. We liked the raised pool. There is an on-site restaurant, bar and spa.

Khao Lak Baan Krating Resort (☎ 0 7642 3088; www.baankrating.com; Hwy 4; r 1600-4000B; 🄫 🄫) Spacious, gracious and stylish, this boutique-style outfit is perched on the cliffs to the south of Khao Lak, just 50m from the ocean. It gets rave reviews from visitors, many of whom use 'beautiful' when describing the place, and we concur. There's a restaurant with views and a lovely pool. Very good low-season rates are often offered to those who haggle.

Khao Lak Merlin (☎ 0 7642 8300; www.merlin phuket.com; Hwy 4; r 2500-5000B; 🄫 🄫 🄫) Brand new and sparkling, this is one of the Merlin chain's flagship properties. It features a maze of swimming pools, well-maintained, stylish rooms and creature comforts aplenty. It was very quiet at the time of research, but as the tourists flood back, this is bound to become something of a favourite. Look for it 7km south of town.

Eating

Eating options are limited in the area, but more restaurants are opening each season. Independent restaurants are concentrated on Th Phetkasem and nearly all hotels and guesthouses have some kind of eating establishment attached.

Discovery Café (Th Phetkasem; mains 50-200B; breakfast, lunch & dinner) Chill here on a rainy day. The chairs are covered with pillows, so bring a book and get comfortable. Pizza, pasta and breakfast options, along with the usual Thai staples (cooked for foreign palates) fill the long menu. There are loads of cocktails to start with.

Viking Steakhouse (☎ 0 7642 0815; Th Phetkasem; mains 50-300B; 🕑 breakfast, lunch & dinner) A long-standing favourite, it offers a fine line in pizza, pasta and Nordic meat feasts. The cosy, open-fronted interior features all sorts of welcome trimmings, including…wait for it…table-cloths and candles. There's also a little bar for a pre- or post-dinner tipple.

Two good choices (even if you're not staying) are the Le Meridien Khao Lak Beach & Spa Resort (p653) in Bang Sak and Khao Lak Baan Krating Resort (left). Both places offer gourmet dining – a mixture of Thai and international cuisine – in congenial environs. Prices for dishes range from 200B to 600B.

Getting There & Away

Any bus running along Hwy 4 between Takua Pa (30B, 45 minutes) and Phuket (60B, two hours) will stop at Hat Khao Lak if you ask the driver (for the latter, look for Sea Dragon Dive Center on the eastern side of the highway). Buses will also stop near the Merlin resort and the Khao Lak/Lam Ru National Park headquarters.

If you're heading to Poseidon Bungalows, your best bet is to get off the bus at Thap Lamu and then take a motorcycle taxi from there (40B).

SIMILAN ISLANDS MARINE NATIONAL PARK (MU KO SIMILAN NATIONAL PARK)

อุทยานแห่งชาติหมู่เกาะสิมิลัน

Renowned by divers the world over, beautiful **Similan Islands Marine National Park** (www.dnp .go.th; admission 400B; 🕑 Nov-May) is 70km offshore. Its smooth granite islands are as impressive above water as below, topped with rainforest, edged with white-sand beaches, and fringed with coral reef.

Two of the nine islands, Ko Miang (Island 4) and Ko Similan (Island 8), have ranger stations and accommodation; park headquarters and most visitor activity centres on Ko Miang. 'Similan' comes from the Malay word *sembilan*, meaning nine, and while each island is named they're just as commonly known by their numbers.

Khao Lak is the jump-off point for the park. The pier is at Thap Lamu, about 10km south of town, where you'll find a cluster of tour operators. The **mainland park office** (☎ 0 7659 5045; 🕑 8am-4pm) is about 500m before the pier, but there's no information in English available.

Sights & Activities
DIVING & SNORKELLING
The Similans offer exceptional diving for all levels of experience, at depths from 2m to 30m. There are seamounts (at **Fantasy Rocks**), rock reefs (at **Ko Payu**) and dive-throughs (at **Hin Pousar** or 'Elephant-head'), with marine life ranging from tiny plume worms and soft

ANDAMAN COAST

corals to schooling fish and whale sharks. There are dive sites at each of the six islands north of Ko Miang; the southern part of the park is off-limits to divers. No facilities for divers exist in the national park itself, so you'll need to take a dive tour. Agencies in Khao Lak and Phuket book dive trips (three-day live-aboards from around 11,000B).

Snorkelling is good at several points around **Ko Miang**, especially in the main channel; you can hire snorkel gear from the park (per day 100B). Day-tour operators usually visit three or four different snorkelling sites. **Poseidon Bungalows** (☎ 076 443258; www.similantour.com) at Khao Lak offers snorkelling-only trips (three-day live-aboard trips around 6500B).

WILDLIFE & WALKS

The forest around park headquarters on Ko Miang has a couple of walking trails and some great wildlife. The fabulous Nicobar pigeon, with its wild mane of grey-green feathers, is common here. Endemic to the islands of the Andaman Sea, it's one of some 39 bird species in the park. Hairy-legged land crabs and flying foxes (or fruit bats) are relatively easily seen in the forest, as are flying squirrels.

Small Beach Track, with information panels, leads about 400m to a tiny, pretty snorkelling bay. Detouring from it, the **Viewpoint Trail** – 500m or so of steep scrambling – has panoramic vistas from the top. A 500m walk to **Sunset Point** takes you through forest to a smooth granite platform facing – obviously – west.

On Ko Similan there's a 2.5km forest hike to a **viewpoint**, and a shorter, steep scramble off the main beach to the top of **Sail Rock**.

Sleeping & Eating

Accommodation in the park is available for all budgets. Book online at www.dnp.go.th or with the **mainland park office** (☎ 076 595045) at Khao Lak.

On Ko Miang there are sea view **bungalows** (r 2000B; ✷) with balconies; two dark five-room wood-and-bamboo **longhouses** (r 1000B) with fans, and crowded on-site **tents** (2-person 570B). There's electricity from 6pm to 6am.

On-site tents are also available on Ko Similan. You can pitch your own **tent** (per night 80B) on either island.

A **restaurant** (dishes 100B) near park headquarters serves simple Thai food.

Getting There & Away

There's no public transport to the park, but independent travellers can book a speedboat transfer (return 1700B, one-way 1½ hours) with a day-tour operator. They will collect you from Phuket or Khao Lak but if you book through national parks (who use the same tour-operators' boats anyway) be aware that you'll have to find your own way to their office, and then wait for a transfer to the pier.

Agencies in Khao Lak and Phuket book day/ overnight tours (from around 2500/3500B) and dive trips (three-day live-aboards from around 11,000B).

Public buses run regularly between Phuket and Khao Lak (60B, 1½ hours), and Khao Lak and Ranong (100B, three hours).

AO PHANG-NGA & PHANG-NGA

อ่าวพังงา/พังงา

pop 9700

If Eden had an ocean, it would look a little like this. A turquoise bay, peppered with craggy limestone rock towers, soda-white beaches and tumbledown fishing villages, Ao Phang Nga is one of the region's most spectacular great escapes and full of picture-postcard flavour. It's pretty easy to see why James Bond choose this locale, among towering cliffs and swifts' nests, to build his lair in *The Man with the Golden Gun*. Much of the bay, along with portions of the coastline, have now been incorporated into the Ao Phang-Nga Marine National Park and can be explored by boat or kayak. The area is desperately lacking in quality accommodation, so it may be best to visit on a day trip – there are heaps of tours out of Phuket; ask at any travel agency on the island. Most trips are advertised on chalkboards and posters as 'trips to James Bond Island.' Tours start at 450B depending on season and demand.

Information

Phang-Nga town doesn't have a tourist office, but the **TAT office** (Tourist Authority of Thailand; ☎ 0 7621 2213; www.tat.or.th; 73-65 Th Phuket; ✷ 8.30am-4.30pm) in Phuket Town provides maps and good information on the region. Head to the town centre if you need to catch a bus or pull cash out of the ATM. The post and telephone offices are about 2km south of the centre. There are numerous places to log on for your emails.

Immigration office (☎ 0 7641 2011; ⊙ 8.30am-4.30pm Mon-Fri) A few kilometres south of town; you'll probably never find it on your own, so take a motorcycle taxi.
Siam Commercial Bank (Hwy 4; ⊙ 9am-4pm Mon-Fri) On the main road through town; has an ATM and change facilities.

Sights & Activities
The old 'city of contrasts' cliché really does apply to the town of Phang-Nga: it is a scruffy, luckless town in a sublime location. The main street is a downtrodden, rather sad-looking strip, but it backs up against breathtaking limestone cliffs.

About 8.5km south of the town centre is **Tha Dan**. From here, you can charter boats to see half-submerged caves, oddly shaped islands and Ko Panyi, a Muslim village on stilts (see p661). There are tours to **Ko Phing Kan** ('James Bond Island'; the island rock depicted in Roger Moore's Bond escapade, *The Man with the Golden Gun*). These tours also visit Ao Phang-Nga National Park (per person for a two- to three-hour tour 400B to 500B). **Takua Thung**, another pier area about 10km further west of Tha Dan, also has private boats for hire, for similar prices; ask at the restaurants. The park office inside Ao Phang-Nga Marine National Park offers boat tours as well.

Unless you enjoy haggling with boatmen, it's much easier (and not that expensive) to go with an organised tour through an agency in town. **Sayan Tours** (☎ 0 7643 0348) has been doing tours of Ao Phang-Nga for many years

now, and continues to receive good reviews from travellers. Half-day/day tours cost from 400/700B per person and include **Tham Lawt** (a large water cave), **Ko Phing Kan** and **Ko Panyi**, among other destinations. Meals and very rustic accommodation on Ko Panyi are part of the longer packages.

The overnight trip is recommended over either half-day or full-day trips, which feel rushed but are more affordable at 200B and 500B respectively. Sayan Tours also offers canoe trips and tours to other nearby destinations, including Sa Nang Manora Forest Park and the various caves near town.

MR Kean Tours (☎ 0 7643 0619) is another option. Check for its offices at the bus terminal in the centre of town.

Sleeping
Phang-Nga doesn't have much in the way of quality sleeping, and many folks choose to visit on a day trip. If you do decide to shack up, there are only a handful of places to which we'd allocate precious review space.

Old Lukmuang Hotel (☎ 0 7641 2125; fax 0 7641 1512; 1/2 Muu 1 Th Phetkasem; r 450B) This choice is rather dingy, but Bond fanatics will be interested to know that it housed some of the crew from *The Man with the Golden Gun* when they based themselves here during filming.

Phang-Nga Guest House (☎ 0 7641 1358; Th Phetkasem; r 250-1000B; ✷) It's a little less charismatic, but this is a great budget back-up. On the whole, it's a gloom-free zone and there's a room to suit most budgets – this is not a town for those after luxury digs.

Phang-Nga Inn (☎ 0 7641 1963; 2/2 Soi Lohakit; r 350-1000B; ✷) This converted residential villa comes up trumps in the town's hotel stakes. Expect pleasant surrounds, comfy beds and homey welcomes. It's well furnished and there's a little eatery out front. Rooms range from basic fan options to swish air-con suites.

Eating
Cha-Leang (☎ 0 7641 3831; Th Phetkasem; dishes 40-90B; ⊙ lunch & dinner) The best – and often busiest – eatery in town cooks up a smorgasbord of well-priced seafood dishes – try the 'clams with basil leaf and chilli' or 'edible inflorescence of banana plant salad'. There's a pleasant veranda out back.

Bismilla (☎ 08 1125 6440; Th Phetkasem; dishes 60-120B; ⊙ lunch & dinner) With dishes like 'yum fish's spawn' on the menu, how can you resist

AO PHANG-NGA

a night at this basic, Thai-Muslim outfit? The food is good, the prices are excellent and the crowds are boisterous.

Phang-Nga Satay (184 Th Phetkasem; satay 40B; ☻ lunch & dinner) Two doors down from Chai Thai (past the wedding dress store), this tiny shack specialises in Malay-style satay; the shrimp satay is particularly good.

Several food stalls on the main street of Phang-Nga sell delicious *khànom jiin* (thin wheat noodles) with chicken curry, *náam yaa* (spicy ground-fish curry) or *náam phrík* (spicy sauce). *Rotii kaeng* (fried flatbread dipped in mild curry sauce, served with jam or fruit fillings) is available from the morning market, which is open daily from 5am to 10am. There's also a small night market on Tuesday, Wednesday and Thursday evenings just south of Soi Lohakit.

Getting There & Around

If you're arriving in the Ao Phang-Nga area from Krabi on Hwy 4, you can go two ways. After Thap Put, you can either continue straight on Hwy 4 or go left onto Hwy 415. Turning onto 415 will keep you on the shorter, straighter path, while staying on Hwy 4 will take you onto a narrow, very curvy and pretty stretch of highway that is 5km longer than the direct route. It's your choice between boring but straight or pretty but longer.

Phang-Nga's bus terminal is located just off the main street on Soi Bamrung Rat. Buses between Bangkok and Phang-Nga include VIP (685B, 12 hours, once daily), 1st class (441B to 459B, 12 to 13 hours, twice daily) and 2nd class (357B, 12 hours, three to four daily). There are several other services available:

BUSES FROM AO PHANG-NGA

Destination	Price (B)	Frequency (hr)	Duration
Hat Yai	200	2 daily	6
Ko Pha-Ngan	400	2 daily	6
Ko Samui	240	2 daily	5
Krabi	65	frequent	1½
Phuket	50	frequent	1½
Ranong	100	4 daily	5
Satun	225	2 daily	6
Surat Thani	110	9 daily	3
Trang	145	frequent	3½

AROUND PHANG-NGA
Sa Nang Manora Forest Park
สวนป่าสระนางมโนราห์

The fairyland setting at this beautiful and little-visited **park** (admission free) is nothing short of fantastic. Moss-encrusted roots and rocks, dense rainforest and rattan vines provide a delicious backdrop for swimming in pools beneath multilevel waterfalls. Primitive trails meander along (and at times through) the falls, climbing level after level, and seem to go on forever – you could easily get a full day's hiking in without walking along the same path twice. Bring plenty of drinking water – although the shade and the falls moderate the temperature, the humidity in the park is quite high.

The park's name comes from a local folk belief that the mythical Princess Manora bathes in the pools when no one else is around. Facilities include some picnic tables, plus a small restaurant. To get here, catch a motorcycle taxi from Phang-Nga (50B). If you have your own wheels head north out of town on Hwy 4, go 3.2km past the Shell petrol station, then turn left and go down a curvy road another 4km.

Wat Tham Suwankhuha
วัดถ้ำสุวรรณคูหา

About 10km south of Phang-Nga is **Wat Tham Suwankhuha** (Heaven Grotto Temple; admission 10B), a cave wat full of Buddha images. The shrine consists of two main caverns: a larger one containing a 15m reclining Buddha and tiled with *laikhraam* and *benjarong* (two-coloured patterns more common in pottery) and a smaller cavern displaying spirit flags and a *rishi* (*reusii*; Hindu sage) statue. Royal seals of several kings, including Rama V, Rama VII and Rama IX – as well as those of lesser royalty – have been inscribed on one wall of the latter cave. Monkeys hang around the area, so lock your car doors or they'll break in to get at your snacks.

To get here without your own transport, hop on any *săwngthǎew* running between Phang-Nga and Takua Thung (20B). The wat is down a side road.

On this same side road, about 6km beyond the cave wat, is **Raman Forest Park** (admission free), a pretty little park with a beautiful waterfall running through a small valley. Follow the gorgeous trail running alongside this cascade for about 3km, and refresh yourself with a dip in a couple of the pools along the way.

The park is relatively isolated, so it's difficult to get here without your own transport. Try hitching from the cave wat or you could rent a motorcycle in Phang-Nga; however, because you'd be riding along the busy highway, ensure you have decent riding skills.

Ao Phang-Nga Marine National Park

อุทยานแห่งชาติอ่าวพังงา

Established in 1981 and covering an area of 400 sq km, **Ao Phang-Nga Marine National Park** (admission 200B) is noted for its classic karst scenery, created by mainland fault movements that pushed massive limestone blocks into geometric patterns. As these blocks extend southward into Ao Phang-Nga, they form more than 40 islands with huge vertical cliffs. The bay itself is composed of large and small tidal channels that originally connected with the mainland fluvial system. The main tidal channels – Khlong Ko Phanyi, Khlong Phang-Nga, Khlong Bang Toi and Khlong Bo Saen – run through vast mangroves in a north–south direction and today are used by fisher folk and island inhabitants as aquatic highways. These mangroves are the largest remaining primary mangrove forest in Thailand. The Andaman Sea covers more than 80% of the area within the park boundaries.

The biggest tourist spot in the park is so-called James Bond Island, known to Thais as **Ko Phing Kan** (Leaning on Itself Island). Once used as a location setting for *The Man with the Golden Gun*, the island is now full of vendors hawking coral and shells that should have stayed in the sea, along with butterflies, scorpions and spiders encased in plastic.

The Thai name for the island refers to a flat limestone cliff that appears to have tumbled sideways to lean on a similar rock face, which is in the centre of the island. Off one side of the island, in a shallow bay, stands a tall slender limestone formation that looks like a big rock spike that has fallen from the sky. There are a couple of caves you can walk through and a couple of small sand beaches, often littered with rubbish from the tourist boats.

Please remember to take only pictures and leave only footprints, ie make sure to dispose of your used water bottles and other rubbish in bins – if you can't find a bin, wait until you return to your bungalow to get rid of it. Improve your trash karma and pick up someone else's junk on the beach.

About the only positive development has been the addition of a concrete pier so that tourist boats don't have to moor directly on the island's beaches, but this still happens when the water level is high and the pier is crowded with other boats.

For information on Ko Yao, which is part of Ao Phang-Nga Marine National Park, see p689.

Two types of forest predominate in the park: limestone scrub forest and true evergreen forest. The marine limestone environment favours a long list of reptiles, including the Bengal monitor, flying lizard, banded sea snake, dogface water snake, shore pit viper and Malayan pit viper. Keep an eye out for the two-banded (or water) monitor *(Varanus salvator)*, which looks like a crocodile when seen swimming in the mangrove swamp and can measure up to 2.2m in length (only slightly smaller than the Komodo dragon, the largest lizard in the Varanidae family). Like its Komodo cousin, the water monitor (called *hĩa* by the Thais, who generally fear or hate the lizard) is a carnivore that prefers to feed on carrion but occasionally preys on live animals.

Amphibians in the Ao Phang-Nga area include the marsh frog, common bush frog and crab-eating frog. Avian residents of note are the helmeted hornbill (the largest of Thailand's 12 hornbill species, with a body length of up to 127cm), the edible-nest swiftlet *(Aerodramus fuciphagus)*, osprey, white-bellied sea eagle and Pacific reef egret.

Over 200 species of mammal reside in the mangrove forests and on some of the larger islands, including the white-handed gibbon, serow, dusky langur and crab-eating macaque.

SLEEPING & EATING

National Park Bungalows (☎ 0 2562 0760; reserve@dnp .go.th; bungalows 700-900B; 🔀) The cheaper bungalows sleep four and are fan-cooled; the pricier air-con bungalows sleep two. Camping is permitted in certain areas within park boundaries but you should ask permission at the bungalow office first.

There's a small, clean restaurant in front of the bungalow office with views over the mangroves.

GETTING THERE & AROUND

From the centre of Phang-Nga drive south on Hwy 4 about 6km, then turn left onto Rte

ANDAMAN COAST

ROCK ART

Many of the limestone islands in Ao Phang-Nga feature prehistoric rock art painted or carved onto the walls and ceilings of caves, rock shelters, cliffs and rock massifs. In particular you can see rock art on Khao Khian, Ko Panyi, Ko Raya, Tham Nak and Ko Phra At Thao. Khao Khian (Inscription Mountain) is probably the most visited of the sites. The images are of human figures, fish, crabs, shrimp, bats, birds and elephants, as well as boats and fishing equipment – it's obvious this was some sort of communal effort tied to the all-important harvesting of sustenance from the sea. Some drawings also contain rows of lines thought to be some sort of cabbalistic writing. The rock paintings don't fall on any one plane of reference; they may be placed right side up, upside-down or sideways. Most of the paintings are monochrome, while some have been repeatedly traced several times over in orange-yellow, blue, grey and black.

4144 and go 2.6km to the park headquarters; 400m beyond here is the visitors centre. Without your own transport you'll need to take a săwngthăew to Tha Dan (20B).

Plenty of private boats, ready to zoom off on Ao Phang-Nga tours, await your bargaining skills (1000B, four-person maximum for a two- to three-hour tour).

PHUKET PROVINCE

pop 82,800

Hedonistic Phuket seduces honeymooners, heiresses, surfer babes and middle-aged men trying to score with a smooth blend of ostentation and seediness. Thailand's largest and most popular island, Phuket is as colourful as it is cosmopolitan and one of the world's most famous dream destinations. Phuket (poo-get) boasts some lush inland vistas, including a few remote swathes of rainforest, but the island really comes into its own along its western shoreline, where hunter-green foliage meets the turquoise waters of the Andaman Sea. The mile upon sandy mile of coastline boasts tons of water sports, delectable restaurants and decadent resorts. In fact, travellers named four of Phuket's hotels among the world's best in a recent magazine poll.

Heavily developed, Phuket can, at times, feel a little like Bangkok-on-Sea, a Costa del Farang, with all the hubbub and brouhaha of a Club 18-to-30 sundowner sing-along. High-rise developments bear testament to the hegemony of the holiday buck, package tourists dramatically outnumber independent travellers and if you stick to the well-worn highways, quiet corners are few and far between.

But if you can do without the beer halls and girlie bars of Patong, Phuket's uber-resort, there's a whole other island to discover. Whether it's swanky resorts of the Laguna complex, the relaxed surfer vibe at friendly Kata, or the night markets of old Phuket Town, Phuket has something to satisfy every appetite. Just don't forget your Speedos.

Information
INTERNET RESOURCES
Phuket.com (www.phuket.com) All sorts of information, including accommodation on the island.
Phuket-Info.com (www.phuket-info.com) You'll find more info on Phuket Province here.
Phuket.Net (www.phuket.net) An internet service that provides forums for tourism and business-oriented exchange, and has limited listings.

MEDIA
The weekly English-language *Phuket Gazette* (20B) publishes lots of information on activities, events, dining and entertainment in Phuket Town, as well as around the island. It can be accessed online at www.phuketgazette .net. The same publisher issues *Gazette Guide* (140B), a sizeable tome listing businesses and services on the island.

MEDICAL SERVICES
Both hospitals listed are equipped with modern facilities, emergency rooms and outpatient-care clinics. For dive-related medicine, see opposite.
Bangkok Phuket Hospital (Map p662; ☎ 0 7625 4425; Th Yongyok Uthit) Reputedly the favourite with locals.
Phuket International Hospital (Map p662; ☎ 0 7624 9400, emergency 7621 0935; Airport Bypass Rd) International doctors rate this hospital as the best on the island.

Dangers & Annoyances

Drownings are common on Phuket's beaches, especially on the western coast (Surin, Laem Singh and Kamala). Red flags are posted on beaches to warn bathers of riptides and other dangerous conditions. If a red flag is flying at a beach, don't go into the water. Especially during the May to October monsoon, the waves on the western coast of Phuket sometimes make it too dangerous to swim. Hat Rawai, on the southern edge of the island, is usually a safe bet at any time of year.

Keep an eye out for jet-skis when you're in the water. Although the Phuket governor declared jet skis illegal in 1997, the ban didn't seem to be enforced in 2006.

Renting a motorcycle can be a high-risk proposition. Thousands of people are injured or killed every year on Phuket highways. Some have been travellers who weren't familiar with riding motorcycles and navigating the island's roads, highways and traffic patterns. If you must rent a motorcycle, make sure you at least know the basics and wear a helmet.

Activities

DIVING & SNORKELLING

Although there are scores of dive sites around Thailand, Phuket is at the heart of the Thai scuba-diving industry and is one of the world's top 10 dive destinations. Good-to-excellent dive sites ring the island, including several small islands to the south – Ko Hae, Ko Raya (Noi and Yai), Hin Daeng and Hin Muang – and to the east – Ko Yao (Noi and Yai). Live-aboard excursions to the fantastic Surin and Similan islands, or to the Burma Banks/Mergui Archipelago off the southern coast of Myanmar, are also possible from Phuket.

Phuket has heaps of 'dive' shops – at last count there were over 100, though most of them are the equivalent of a booking agency. The more serious ones often operate their own boat(s) while others send you off with another operator, so ask if you're concerned. And it doesn't hurt if an operator is a five-star PADI dive centre, though this isn't always the best criterion for dive shops. Many of these operations are centred at Hat Patong or Ao Chalong, though the smaller beach towns certainly have their share. Some of the bigger (but not necessarily better) places have multiple branch offices all over Phuket.

Typical one-day dive trips to nearby sites cost 1600B to 2500B. This includes two dives and equipment. Nondivers (and snorkellers) are permitted to join such dive trips for a significant

---

DETOUR: KO PANYI

Home to one of Thailand's most extraordinary Muslim fishing villages, Ko Panyi makes an interesting detour if you've had your fill of Phuket's glitzy beach life. Built on stilts in a nook in the limestone cliffs, it's something of a tourist trap during the day. Stay overnight, however, and you will sample the best of its unique charms.

The 200 households here – home to perhaps a total of 2000 people – are said to descend from two seafaring Muslim families who arrived from Java around 200 years ago. Besides alcohol, dogs and pigs are also forbidden on the island. Houses mixed in with the shops vary from grubby little shacks to homes with fancy tile fronts and curtained windows. The people are generally quite friendly, especially if you can speak a little Thai. Village men often gather to gossip and watch the sunset over the western side of the village near the turquoise mosque.

There are a few places to stay on the island. **Thawisuk Hotel** (r 100-150B), near the island's northern pier, is a slightly tatty budget hideaway.

Along with the more expensive seafood restaurants built out over the sea in front of the village (which are generally open for lunch only), there are some smaller cafés and restaurants along the interior alleys where locals eat. *Khâo yam* (southern-Thai rice salad) and *rotii* (fried flatbread) are available in the morning. The villagers raise grouper in floating cages, selling them to the island and mainland restaurants. A local culinary speciality is *khànom bâo lâng*, a savoury dish made with black sticky rice, shrimp, coconut, black pepper and chilli steamed in a banana leaf – a breakfast favourite.

You can organise a tour from Phuket or Krabi, or from the bus terminal in Phang-Nga. To go solo, take a *săwngthăew* from the bus terminal to Tha Dan pier (10B) and then catch a long-tail boat (30B, 25 minutes) to Ko Panyi.

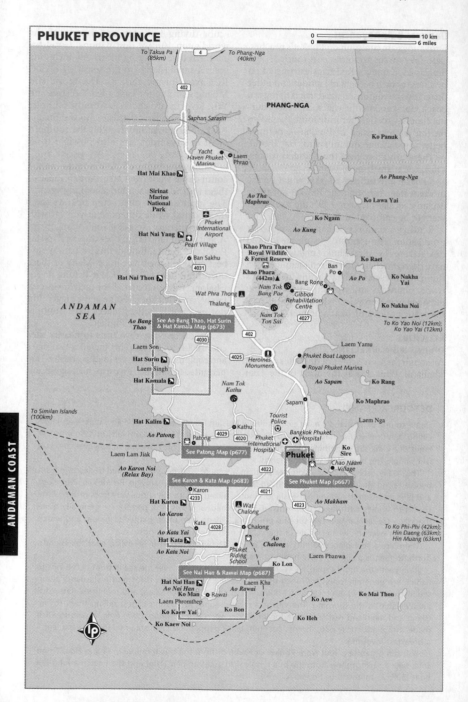

PHUKET PROVINCE

discount. A four-day PADI Open Water certification course costs around 9000B to 12,500B.

It's very wise to obtain your own private diving insurance before travelling. PADI or DAN is best – regular insurance doesn't often cover diving accidents or decompression costs, but you could check with your insurance representative. Your dive shop will also have some insurance, but some shops have better insurance than others; ask.

There are three hyperbaric chambers on Phuket. **Wachira Hospital** (Map p667; ☎ 0 7621 1114) and **Phuket International Hospital** (Map p662; ☎ 0 7624 9400, emergency ☎ 0 7621 0935) are both just outside Phuket Town; a private **hyperbaric chamber** (Map p677; ☎ 0 7634 2518; 231-233 Th Rat Uthit) is in Patong. The chamber at Phuket International Hospital is considered the best of the three. Dive shop affiliation with the private hyperbaric chamber in Patong mostly means that clients who need to use that chamber will be charged US$200 rather than US$800 per hour of treatment (five-hour minimum), though if a dive shop has the right kind of insurance it will cover much of this cost. Again, ask for specifics if you're concerned.

Snorkelling is best along Phuket's western coast, particularly at the rocky headlands between beaches. Mask, snorkel and fins can be rented for around 250B a day. As with scuba diving, you'll find better snorkelling, with greater visibility and variety of marine life, along the shores of small outlying islands such as Ko Raya Yai and Ko Raya Noi.

The best diving months are December to May, when the weather is good and the sea is at its clearest (and boat trips are much safer).

There are numerous dive shops with equipment supplies.

All 4 Diving (☎ 0 7634 4611; 5/4 Th Sawatdirak, Patong) This is Phuket's largest dive store.

Andaman Sea Sport (☎ 0 7621 1752; 69 Th Phuket, Phuket Town) Stocks diving and snorkelling supplies.

Dive Supply (Map p677; ☎ 0 7634 2513; www.divesupply .com; 189 Th Rat Utith, Patong) Has a great variety of diving equipment and offers a good service in several languages.

HORSE RIDING

Phuket Riding School (☎ 0 7628 8213; horsy_maliwan@ yahoo.com.hk), near Chalong, offers one-hour (per person 650B) and two-hour (1250B) rides in the jungle and along nearby beaches.

KAYAKING

Several companies based in Phuket offer canoe tours of scenic Ao Phang-Nga.

In Phuket Town, **Sea Canoe Thailand** (Map p667; ☎ 0 7621 2172; www.seacanoe.net; 367/4 Th Yaowarat) was

---

WHICH DIVE SHOP TO PICK?

Choosing the right dive shop can be an intimidating business. After all, there are so many flashy storefronts advertising the wonders of the diving world – over 100 in Phuket alone. How on earth can you be sure you're making the right choice?

When choosing a dive company on Phuket (or anywhere in Thailand, for that matter) there are a few key questions you should ask. For example, how long has the dive shop existed? How many divers will be on the boat? Does the shop have access to a hyperbaric chamber should an accident occur (you'd be surprised to know some smaller shops are not linked up with a hospital)? What is the dive instructor-to-client ratio? What kind of insurance do they have and what does it cover? Is it a licensed Tourism Authority of Thailand (TAT) operator? If it's a live-aboard trip, is there oxygen on board?

Talk to the staff: how experienced are they and how much of this experience is local? Do they make you feel comfortable and confident? If you're taking a class, what kind of certification do the instructors have? And do they speak your language well enough that you understand each other? One last thing: look at the equipment – is it in good shape and well maintained?

Perhaps the best way to choose an excellent dive operation, however, is to get a glowing recommendation from other divers who've already done the underwater deed. Word-of-mouth is often the best indicator of the quality of a company – and in the competitive diving world, a good reputation can really make or break a business.

Also of note, check out how eco-friendly a dive shop is. Questions to ask include, do you encourage wreck dives (these are super-friendly to the environment as you are not interacting with coral)? Do you allow divers to wear gloves (another no-no, as gloves allow divers to touch coral they otherwise wouldn't lay a hand on, something which is really bad for already-suffering reefs)?

ANDAMAN COAST

the first and is still the most famous. The kayaks are able to enter semi-submerged caves (which Thai fishermen have called *hâwng* or 'room' for centuries) inaccessible by long-tail boats. A day paddle costs 3200B per person and includes meals, equipment and transfer; also available are all-inclusive, three-day (from 9500B) camping trips.

Another canoe company with an excellent reputation is **Paddle Asia** (☎ 0 7624 0952; www .paddleasia.com; 19/3 Th Rasdanusorn), also based in Phuket Town. It caters to beginners and those who don't enjoy being surrounded by noisy tour groups. Groups are small (two to six people) and multiday tours are offered. Prices are similar to Sea Canoe Thailand.

YACHTING
Phuket is one of Southeast Asia's main yacht destinations, and you'll find all manner of craft anchored along its shores – from 80-year-old wooden sloops that look like they can barely stay afloat to the latest in hi-tech motor cruisers. Marina-style facilities with year-round anchorage are presently available at a few locations.

The US$25 million **Royal Phuket Marina** (Map p662; ☎ 0 7623 9762; www.royalphuketmarina.com) is located just south of Phuket Boat Lagoon. Luxury villas, townhouses and a hotel join 190 berths and a spa here.

Phuket Boat Lagoon (Map p662; ☎ 0 7623 9055; fax 0 7623 9056) is located at Ao Sapam, about 10km north of Phuket Town on the eastern shore. It offers an enclosed marina with tidal channel access, serviced pontoon berths, 60- and 120-tonne travel lifts, hard stand area, plus a resort hotel, laundry, coffee shop, fuel, water, repairs and maintenance services.

Yacht Haven Phuket Marina (Map p662; ☎ 0 7620 6705; www.yacht-haven-phuket.com) is at Laem Phrao on the northeastern tip. The Yacht Haven boasts 130 berths and a scenic restaurant, and also does yacht maintenance.

If you need sails, **Rolly Tasker Sailmakers** (☎ 0 7628 0347; www.rollytasker.com; 26/2 Th Chaofa, Ao Chalong) can outfit you with these; riggings, spars and hardware are also available.

Port clearance is rather complicated; the marinas will take care of the paperwork (for a fee of course) if notified of your arrival in advance. For information on yacht charters (both bareboat and crewed), yacht sales and yacht deliveries, contact the following:

Faraway Sail & Dive Expeditions (☎ 0 7628 0701; www.far-away.net; 112/8 Muu 4, Th Taina, Hat Karon)

SEAL (☎ 0 7634 0406; www.seal-asia.com; 225 Th Rat Uthit, Hat Patong)
Sunsail Yacht Charters (☎ 0 7623 9057; www.sun sailthailand.com; Phuket Boat Lagoon)
Thai Marine Leisure (☎ 0 7623 9111; www.thaimarine .com; Phuket Boat Lagoon)
Yachtpro International (☎ 0 7623 2960; www.sailing -thailand.com; Yacht Haven Phuket Marina)

Expect to pay from US$300 per day for a high season, bareboat charter.

The **TAT office** (Map p667; ☎ 0 7621 2213; www.tat .or.th; 73-65 Th Phuket; 🕑 8.30am-4.30pm) in Phuket Town also has an extensive list of yacht charters and brokers. For insurance purposes, it's a good idea to see if the boat you want to charter is registered in Thailand.

Tours
Siam Safari (☎ 0 7628 0116) and **Adventure Safaris** (☎ 0 7634 1988) combine 4WD tours of the island's interior with short elephant rides and hikes for around 2200B per day. Half-day trips are also available, although the difference in price is not that great.

For a bird's-eye view of the island, **Blue Water Air** (☎ 0 7635 1438; www.bluewaterair.com; Phuket International Airport) offers scenic flights (per person from 2000B), as well as charters to Ko Phi Phi (3000B per person one-way) and Ko Yao Noi (per person one way 3000B).

Courses
Pat's Home (☎ 0 1538 8276, 0 7626 3366; thaicooking class@hotmail.com) Pat, who worked as a chef at a Thai restaurant in California for six years, offers Thai cooking courses at her home just outside Phuket Town. Half-day courses for either lunch or dinner cost 1200B.

Pum Thai Cooking School (Map p662; ☎ 0 7634 6269, 0 1521 8904; info@pumthaifoodchain.com; 204/32 Tha Rat Uthit, Hat Patong) Runs Thai restaurants in both Phuket and France; at the Phuket branch you can learn *haute cuisine* the Thai way, starting at 900B for a 1½-hour, three-dish class, and up to 3750B for a six-hour, five-dish class.

Accommodation
Phuket's beaches used to be some of Thailand's most expensive, but post-tsunami it seems like many places are still slashing their prices and deals abound at even the ritziest resorts.

Overbuilding has made it easier to find bargains at midrange and top-end places, especially from May to October – try booking via websites like www.sawasdee.com or www

THE LOW DOWN ON THE BEST RUB DOWN

The Thais are known for splendid massages and Phuket is known for posh pampering, so it's no surprise the country's number one island is home to some number one spas. There seems to be a spa of sorts on every corner in Phuket. Most are low-key family affairs where traditional Thai massage goes for about 250B per hour, and a basic pedi-mani costs around 100B – a real steal. The quality of service at these places varies, and changes rapidly as staff turnover is high. Try asking exiting customers about the quality of the massage. Most of the places in this price range offer similar services and massages can be tailored to *faràng* tastes (less strong).

If you're looking for a more Westernised spa experience, head to one of Phuket's plentiful spa resorts. These places are often affiliated with a ritzy hotel (but nearly all are open to nonguests). They are haute couture affairs with gorgeous Zen designs – Thai massage is after all a spiritual affair. Proper spas offer a range of massages, including Thai, along with a host of treatments. Aromatherapy, steam baths, facials, relaxation therapies and rejuvenation packages are just a few. Prices vary depending on location, but treatments generally start at around 1000B and go up from there.

We've listed our top five Phuket spas below.

■ At the new JW Marriott resort (p672), the **Mandara Spa** is perfect for couples. There are 10 couples' treatment suites that include indoor and outdoor space. The Healing Hot Stones massage (US$175) is one of the signature treatments. Resident Thai massage therapist Upadee Tansom is also excellent.

■ The **Six Senses Spa** at the Evason Resort & Spa (p688) is the kind of back-to-nature place you go to do yoga on a platform in a pond with water lilies. It also has great treatments. Try the Sensory Spa Journey (90 minutes, 8000B), which includes a four-hand massage (two therapists), luxurious footbath and goody bag of product samples used in your treatment.

■ Try the signature three-hour Royal Banyan treatment (US$195) at the **Banyan Tree Spa** at the Banyan Tree Phuket (p673). It includes a mint footbath, a cucumber and lemongrass rub, Thai herbal massage and a soak in a flower-filled tub.

■ One of Phuket's first spas, **Hideaway Day Spa** (p672) still enjoys an excellent reputation. More reasonably priced then many hotel counterparts, the Hideaway offers traditional Thai massage, sauna and mud body wraps in a tranquil wooded setting at the edge of a lagoon. Treatments start at 1500B. It also has its own line of spa products, which make perfect birthday gifts for the girls back home.

■ As posh as it gets: at the **Trisara Spa** at Trisara (p672) six over-the-top private treatment suites face the ocean and open onto breezy pavilions surrounded by ponds. Try one of the holistic oil massages (from 2000B). The oils used were made without chemicals or preservatives.

.planetholiday.com to score swank properties for as little as 2000B! Also check the hotel websites themselves or try Lonely Planet's Haystack booking service at www.lonely planet.com. During the holidays, prices can zoom skywards, although when we checked in late December 2006 the same property was still at just 2200B. It seems, for now at least, post-tsunami low prices are sticking.

Haggling over walk-in rates during low season is not unheard of – ask for a discount if the place is empty. If the price is still too high, ask if you can take the room without breakfast, it usually saves around 300B.

For accommodation costs see the boxed text on p648.

PHUKET TOWN

ภูเก็ต

Centuries before Phuket began attracting sand-and-sea hedonists, it was an important centre for Arab, Indian, Malay, Chinese and Portuguese traders who came to exchange goods for tin and rubber with the rest of the world. Francis Light, the British colonialist who made Penang the first of the British Straits Settlements, married a native of Phuket and tried unsuccessfully to pull this island into the colonial fold. Although this polyglot, multicultural heritage has all but disappeared from most of the island, a few vestiges can be seen and experienced in the province's *amphoe meuang* (provincial capital), Phuket.

As in many growing Thai towns, homogeneity is now the buzzword and you'd have to drink long and hard from the nostalgia potion to get a sense of the city's multicultural heyday. That doesn't mean Phuket Town isn't worth a visit. Evocative traces of Sino-Portuguese architecture remain and the city streets, which move to the rhythm of everyday Thai life, feel a long way from the prefabricated hubbub of Patong. If you fancy a glimpse of the Phuket behind the tourist traps, go-go bars and beaches, this isn't a bad place to start.

Information

BOOKSHOPS
Books (☎ 0 7621 1115; www.thebooksphuket.com; 53-55 Th Phuket; ☯ 8.30am-9.30pm) Offers English-language magazines, guidebooks and novels.

EMERGENCY
Police (☎ 191, 0 7622 3555; cnr Th Phang-Nga & Th Phuket)

INTERNET ACCESS
i-Business (☎ 0 9119 4779; Th Takua Pa; per hr 20B; ☯ 8am-10pm)
Phuket CAT office (Th Phang-Nga; per hr 30B; ☯ 8am-midnight)

MAPS
There's really no need to buy Phuket maps; nearly all hotels and restaurants offer free tourists maps. These are of surprisingly high quality and generally include most businesses. If you'd rather purchase one, *Phuket Island* (1:100,000) by Periplus is a good bet for navigating your way around the island and costs 125B.

MEDIA
Phuket Gazette (www.phuketgazette.net) Posts articles and updated information along with its searchable Gazette Guide on its website.

MEDICAL SERVICES
Bangkok Phuket Hospital (☎ 0 7625 4425; www .phukethospital.com; Th Yongyok Uthit) This private hospital is the best bet within easy reach of Phuket Town.
Boots (☎ 0 7623 0083; Th Tilok Uthit; ☯ 10am-10pm) An outlet of the British pharmacy.

MONEY
Several banks along Th Phuket and Th Ranong offer exchange services and ATMs.
Bangkok Bank (Th Ranong; ☯ 8.30am-4.30pm Mon-Fri)
Bank of Asia (Th Phuket; ☯ 9.30am-3.30pm Mon-Fri)

POST
DHL World Wide Express (☎ 0 7625 8500; 61/4 Th Thepkasatri) Swift and reliable courier service (everything goes by two-day delivery), but rates are about 25 percent higher than at the post office.
Main post office (Th Montri; ☯ 8.30am-4pm Mon-Fri, 9am-noon Sat)

TELEPHONE
Phuket CAT office (Th Phang-Nga; ☯ 8am-midnight) Home Country Direct dialling service.

TOURIST INFORMATION
TAT office (☎ 0 7621 2213; www.tat.or.th; 73-65 Th Phuket; ☯ 8.30am-4.30pm) Maps, information brochures, a list of standard săwngthăew fares out to the various beaches, and also the recommended charter costs for a vehicle.

TRAVEL AGENCIES
Phuket Centre Tour (☎ 0 7621 2892; centre@e-mail .in.th; Th Rasada; ☯ 8am-5pm Mon-Fri, 8am-4pm Sat) Car-hire, airline ticketing and tour packages.

Sights
Phuket's historic **Sino-Portuguese architecture** is the town's most evocative sight: stroll along Ths Thalang, Dibuk, Yaowarat, Ranong, Phang-Nga, Rasada and Krabi for a glimpse of some of the best on offer. The most magnificent examples in town are the **Standard Chartered Bank** (Th Phang-Nga), Thailand's oldest foreign bank; the **THAI office** (Th Ranong); and the **old post office building**, which now houses the **Phuket Philatelic Museum** (Th Montri; admission free; ☯ 9.30am-5.30pm), a first-stop for stamp boffins. The best-restored residential properties are found along Th Dibuk and Th Thalang.

For a bird's-eye view of the city, climb up pretty **Khao Rang** (Phuket Hill), northwest of the town centre. It's at its best during the week, when the summit is relatively peaceful, but keep an eye out for the mobs of snarling dogs. If, as many people say, Phuket is a corruption of the Malay word *bukit* (hill), then this is probably its namesake.

Phuket's main **day market** (Th Ranong) is worth a wander and is the spot to invest in the requisite Thai and Malay sarongs, as well as baggy Shan fishermen's pants.

A handful of Chinese temples inject some added colour into the area. Most are standard issue, but the **Shrine of the Serene Light** (Saan Jao Sang Tham; ☯ 8.30am-noon & 1.30-5.30pm), tucked away at the end of a 50m alley near the Bangkok Bank of Commerce on Th Phang-Nga, is

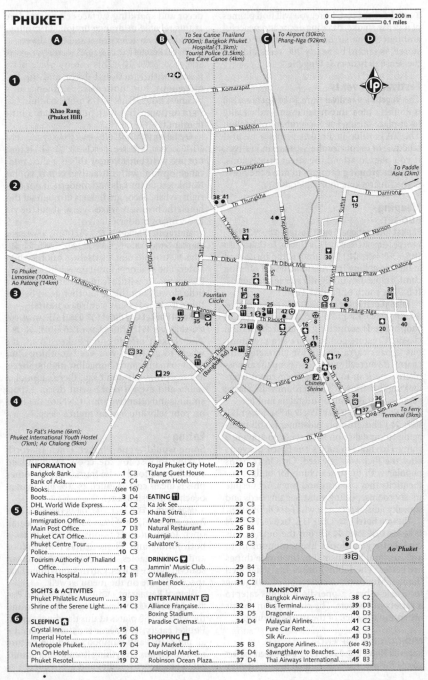

PHUKET

INFORMATION
Bangkok Bank	1 C3
Bank of Asia	2 C4
Books	(see 16)
Boots	3 D4
DHL World Wide Express	4 C2
i-Business	5 C3
Immigration Office	6 D5
Main Post Office	7 D3
Phuket CAT Office	8 C3
Phuket Centre Tour	9 C3
Police	10 C3
Tourism Authority of Thailand Office	11 C3
Wachira Hospital	12 B1

SIGHTS & ACTIVITIES
Phuket Philatelic Museum	13 D3
Shrine of the Serene Light	14 C3

SLEEPING 🏠
Crystal Inn	15 D4
Imperial Hotel	16 C3
Metropole Phuket	17 D4
On On Hotel	18 C3
Phuket Resotel	19 D2

Royal Phuket City Hotel	20 D3
Talang Guest House	21 C3
Thavorn Hotel	22 C3

EATING 🍴
Ka Jok See	23 C3
Khana Sutra	24 C4
Mae Porn	25 C3
Natural Restaurant	26 B4
Ruamjai	27 B3
Salvatore's	28 C3

DRINKING 🍷
Jammin' Music Club	29 B4
O'Malleys	30 D3
Timber Rock	31 C2

ENTERTAINMENT 🎭
Alliance Française	32 B4
Boxing Stadium	33 D5
Paradise Cinemas	34 D4

SHOPPING 🛍
Day Market	35 B3
Municipal Market	36 D4
Robinson Ocean Plaza	37 D4

TRANSPORT
Bangkok Airways	38 C2
Bus Terminal	39 D3
Dragonair	40 D3
Malaysia Airlines	41 C2
Pure Car Rent	42 C3
Silk Air	43 D3
Singapore Airlines	(see 43)
Săwngthăew to Beaches	44 B3
Thai Airways International	45 B3

ANDAMAN COAST

a cut above the rest. Here, you will find plumes of incense smoke, dazzling décor and peaceful ambience. The shrine, which has been restored, is said to be nearly 200 years old and the sense of history is tangible.

Festivals & Events

The **Vegetarian Festival** (www.phuketvegetarian.com) is Phuket's most important event and usually takes place during late September or October. The TAT office in Phuket prints a helpful schedule of events for the Vegetarian Festival. If you plan to attend the street processions, consider bringing earplugs to make the noise of the firecrackers more tolerable.

Sleeping

BUDGET

Phuket International Youth Hostel (☎ 0 7628 1325; www.phukethostel.com; 73/11 Th Chao Fa, Ao Chalong; dm 180B, r 360-440B; 🐱) 'Reliable' is the buzzword at this Hostelling International hostel offering comfortable digs in slightly sterile surrounds. It is 7km south of Phuket Town.

Talang Guest House (☎ 0 7621 4225; talanggh@phuket .ksc.co.th; 37 Th Thalang; r 250-420B; 🐱) This decrepit shophouse is something of an architectural classic. Creature comforts are at a premium, but it bags extra points for character and charm. If you really want to soak up the atmosphere, check in to the 3rd-floor room overlooking the street. It's a fan room with a large veranda and is ideal for nostalgia junkies.

On On Hotel (☎ 0 7621 1154; 19 Th Phang-Nga; r 150-400B; 🐱) This crumbly old-timer is still managing to capitalise on its success portraying a shitty Thai hotel in 2000's *The Beach*. Six years after the flick was released, On On remains popular with those searching for budget authenticity they can taste and smell. Yet despite musty rooms, peeling paint, sagging beds and squeaky fans, it retains a whiff of Old Phuket.

Thavorn Hotel (☎ 0 7621 1333; fax 0 7621 5559; 74 Th Rasada; r 230-550B; 🐱) From the outside this city-centre giant looks like a monument to architectural Stalinism. On the inside things are better. The lobby houses the self-styled 'Phuket Museum' – a collection of intriguing local bric-a-brac. Upper-floor rooms cater to a variety of budgets. The cheapest fan rooms are round the back of the main building.

MIDRANGE & TOP END

Imperial Hotel (☎ 0 7621 2311; www.imperialphuket .com; 51 Th Phuket; r 800B; 🐱) Piped music, chintzy décor and sparkling surfaces come standard at this reliable midrange option. Trimmings include colour televisions and hair dryers.

Phuket Resotel (☎ 0 7622 0965; phuketresotel@yahoo .com; r 650-1000B; 🐱) This roomy place plays it safe, with functional décor and the homogenous, but inoffensive, ambience of a business hotel. Fans of US motels should feel right at home, but may find the staff a little inanimate.

Crystal Inn (☎ 0 7625 6789; www.phuketcrystalinn.com; 2/1-10 Soi Surin, Th Phuket; r from 1400B; 🐱 💻) It may not age well, but for now this is a slick midrange option, with attractive, comfy rooms Rothkoesque murals and modern, if not outright stylish, décor are themes throughout this hotel (the brochure waxes lyrical about the yin and yang of modern design).

Metropole Phuket (☎ 0 7621 5050; www.metro polephuket.com; 1 Soi Surin, Th Montri; r 2000-3200B; 🐱 💻) The Metropole fancies itself as another bighitter. The seahorse fountain is a little kitsch, the rooms are a little frumpier and the staff a little slower, but this is another good bet for those looking for city-centre comforts.

Royal Phuket City Hotel (☎ 0 7623 3333; www.royal phuketcity.com; 154 Th Phang-Nga; r 3500-8500B; 🐱 💻) The slickest offering in Phuket Town, it's where to go when you need soothing after one too many sandy bungalow nights. Sheets are smooth, beds don't sag, there's a pool, a sauna and even a zebra-print disco. Expect smiling and attentive staff, CNN or the BBC on your telly and a great night's sleep.

Eating

Some would argue Phuket Town is worth staying in just for the chow. And indeed there's good food to be found here. Another plus is meals cost as much as 50% less than at beachfront restaurants.

Mae Porn (☎ 0 7621 1389; cnr Th Phang-Nga & Soi Pradit; dishes 10-150B; 🕙 9am-9.30pm) In a casual, open location, this popular eatery attracts both *faràng* and Thais. It has both indoor and outdoor tables, and cooks up some mean seafood at nice prices. Curries and other Thai specialities are on the menu as well.

Natural Restaurant (☎ 0 7622 4287; 62/5 Soi Phuthon; dishes 50-200B; 🕙 lunch & dinner) Travel round the world in 80 plates at this dazzlingly green Phuket eatery. The décor is nature oriented – all pot plants and bamboo – and the picture menu promises everything from wiener schnitzel to Singapore noodles and green curry.

Ruamjai (☎ 0 7622 2821; Th Ranong; dishes 50-200B; ☯ lunch & dinner) Delicious veggie eats are offered at this spartan, open-fronted Chinese restaurant. It's a bit noisy with the background traffic noise, and very popular. The service is quite swift, some say too swift.

Khana Sutra (☎ 0 7625 6192; 18-20 Th Takua Pa; dishes 80-250B; ☯ lunch & dinner; ☒) Rumour has it the curries here have aphrodisiac properties. Either way, they are authentically Indian and are served among the decorative jiggery-pokery of an authentic Delhi diner.

Ka Jok See (☎ 0 7621 7903; kajoksee@hotmail.com; 26 Th Takua Pa; dishes 180-480B; ☯ dinner Tue-Sun) Dripping old Phuket charm and creaking under the weight of the owner's fabulous trinket collection, this atmospheric little eatery offers great food, top-notch music and – if you're lucky – some sensationally camp cabaret. Enjoy your dinner, sip down some wine and then dance the night away. Book ahead.

Salavatore's (☎ 08 9871 1184; 15 Th Rasada; dishes 140-620B; ☯ lunch & dinner Tue-Sun; ☒) This authentic (read: check tablecloths, giant peppergrinders, opera and a portly owner) Italian restaurant cooks up all of mama's favourites, from a mean pizza to a sizzling fillet steak.

Southeast of the centre, on Th Ong Sim Phai, is the town's municipal market where you can buy fresh fruit and vegetables. Around three sides of this market you'll find a night market that features Thai and Chinese food.

Drinking

Phuket Town is no Mecca for nightlife junkies. The major hotels, however, have discos and/or karaoke clubs.

Zanzibar (www.royalphuketcity.com; 154 Th Phang-Nga) For a full-blown boogie, try this spot in the Royal Phuket City hotel (opposite).

O'Malleys (☎ 0 7622 0170; 2/20-21 Th Montri; ☯ 4pm-1am) Travelling thousands of miles to sink a Guinness in an Irish pub always feels a little daft, but Phuket's homesick flock to this cosy Celtic watering hole for pool and assorted shenanigans. It has a generally welcoming atmosphere and the interior is almost authentic, if a little too clean.

Jammin' Music Club (☎ 0 7622 0189; 78/28-29 Th Krung Thep; ☯ 8pm-2am) Gun owners and under-20s are prohibited entry, but this live-music venue is a good bet for a late night knees-up. Expect bands playing everything from rock and pop to jazz, but call ahead to see what's

on. The action usually kicks off around 10pm and Thai youngsters are at the heart of it.

Timber Hut (☎ 0 7621 1839; 118/1 Th Yaowarat; ☯ 6pm-2am) This red-brick spot features Wild West décor and live music from 10pm. The tunes can be deafeningly loud but it's popular with Thai 20-somethings and there's usually plenty of entertainment on offer.

Collector's Pub (☎ 0 7621 1333; 74 Th Rasada; ☯ 6pm-midnight) Drink amid relics at this little bar in the Thavorn Hotel. It's full of museum pieces and is a good bet for a quieter tipple.

Entertainment

Paradise Cinemas (☎ 0 7622 0174; Th Tilok Uthit; tickets 80B) For those addicted to celluloid, Paradise plays English-language blockbusters.

Alliance Française (☎ 0 7622 2988; 3 Soi 1, Th Phattana; ☯ 2.30-6pm Mon, 9.30am-12.30pm & 2.30-6pm Tue-Fri, 9am-noon Sat) Weekly screenings of French films (subtitled in English); it also has a library and a TV with up-to-date news broadcasts.

Boxing Stadium (tickets 500/700/1000B) Thai boxing can be seen Tuesday and Friday nights at 8pm. Ticket prices vary depending on where you sit and include one-way transport. The stadium is at the southern edge of town near the pier; a túk-túk (motorised pedicab) costs 70B. Get your tickets at the On On Hotel (opposite).

Shopping

There's some reasonable shopping in the provincial capital.

Day Market (Th Ranong) Near the town centre, this market can trace its history back to the days when pirates, Indians, Chinese, Malays and Europeans traded in Phuket. You might still find some Southeast Asian fabrics, though for the most part it sells food now.

Municipal Market (Th Ong Sim Phai) Southeast of the centre, the focus of this market is on fresh produce and other things to eat.

Robinson Ocean Plaza (36 Th Tilok Uthit; ☯ 9am-10pm) Look for this air-con shopping mall near the municipal market.

Getting There & Around
TO/FROM THE AIRPORT

There are direct international flights to Phuket from Hong Kong, Singapore, Kuala Lumpur and Osaka. All other international flights arrive via Bangkok. Many of these (if you are coming from North America or are routed through Tokyo in particular) arrive in Bangkok too late to connect with an outgoing domestic flight

ANDAMAN COAST

to Phuket. This means even if you buy tickets directly to Phuket you will likely have to spend one night in Bangkok first – it will likely appear as a layover on your ticket. The good news is there are a number of hotels near the airport in Bangkok where you can shack up for the night (p148).

Phuket Airport is about 45 minutes from Patong, Kata and Karon beaches. There is a minibus service at the airport that will take you into Phuket Town for 80B per person; trips to Patong, Kata and Karon beaches cost 120B. If you would rather not wait for the minibus, grab a metered taxi from the rank outside – skip the set-price taxi booth inside as it is much more expensive. It costs about 500B to go from the airport to Kata, Karon or Patong.

Thailand's budget airline, **Air Asia** (www.airasia .com) had some of the cheapest flights out of Phuket at the time of research. Daily flights include Bangkok (one-way from 1600B) and Kuala Lumpur (one-way from 2200B). The later is great if you want to visit the Andaman Coast and lower southern gulf before heading to Malaysia but no longer want to go by train due to the violence in the deep south (see boxed text, p636).

BUS

You'll find the **bus terminal** (☎ 0 7621 1977) just to the east of the centre, within walking distance of the many hotels. Services from here include the following:

BUSES FROM PHUKET

Destination	Bus type	Fare (B)	Duration (hr)
Bangkok	air-con	400-500	13-14
	VIP	900	13
Chumphon	air-con	250	6½
Hat Yai	ordinary	150	8
	air-con	210-270	6-7
Ko Samui	air-con	260	8 (bus & boat)
Krabi	air-con	120	3½
Nakhon Si Thammarat	air-con	175-200	7
Phang-Nga	air-con	100	2½
Ranong	air-con	185	5
Surat Thani	air-con	160-170	5
Takua Pa	air-con	110	3
Trang	air-con	150-200B	5

CAR

There are cheap car rental agencies on Th Rasada near Pure Car Rent. Suzuki jeeps go for about 1600B per day (including insurance), though in the low season the rates can go down to 1100B. If you rent for a week or more, you should get a discount.

The rates are always better at local places than at the better-known international agencies, though you may be able to get deals with the familiar companies if you reserve in advance.

Avis Rent-A-Car (☎ airport 0 7635 1243; www.avis thailand.com) Charges a premium (around 1500B per day) but has outlets at some bigger resort hotels.

Pure Car Rent (☎ 0 7621 1002; www.purecarrent.com; 75 Th Rasada) A good choice in the centre of town.

MOTORCYCLE

You can rent motorcycles on Th Rasada near Pure Car Rent, or from various places at the beaches. Costs are between 250B and 350B per day, and can vary depending on the season. Bigger bikes (over 125cc) can be rented at a couple of shops in Patong and Karon.

Take care when riding a bike and use common sense. People who ride around in shorts, T-shirt, a pair of thongs and no helmet are asking for trouble – a minor spill while wearing reasonable clothes would leave you bruised and shaken, but for somebody clad in shorts it could result in enough skin loss to end your travels right there. If you do have an accident, you're unlikely to find that medical attention is up to international standards.

Phuket now has a helmet law that police claim will be enforced without exception: those caught not wearing one will be fined 300B. When we last visited there still seemed to be plenty of 'exceptions', but then again, it's just stupid to ride without a helmet so don't take the risk (on your wallet and life).

SĂWNGTHĂEW & TÚK-TÚK

Large bus-sized sǎwngthǎew run regularly from Th Ranong near the market to the various Phuket beaches for 50B per person – see the respective destination for details. These run from around 7am to 5pm; outside these times you have to charter a túk-túk to the beaches, which will set you back 250B to Patong, 300B to Karon and Kata, and 350B for Nai Han and Kamala. You'll probably have to bargain. Many drivers will ask you to make

a stop at a gem shop for a discount (they get a gas voucher from the shop for this). If you do, be clear about how many stops (one is enough) and for how long you'll be stopping. Beware of tales about the tourist office being 5km away, or that the only way to reach the beaches is by taxi, or even that you'll need a taxi to get from the bus terminal to the town centre (it is more or less in the town centre). For a ride around town, túk-túk drivers should charge 25B, although with rising petrol prices many won't go for less than 50B.

Motorcycle taxis around town should cost about 25B, but like túk-túks fares are sometimes inflated based on petrol prices (or so we were told).

KHAO PHRA THAEW ROYAL WILDLIFE & FOREST RESERVE

อุทยานสัตว์ป่าเขาพระแทว

This mountain range, in the northern interior of the island, protects 23 sq km of rainforest (evergreen monsoon forest). There are nice jungle hikes in this reserve and a couple of waterfalls, **Ton Sai** and **Bang Pae**. The falls are best seen in the rainy season between June and November; in the dry months they slow to a trickle. Because of its royal status, the reserve is better protected than the average Thai national park.

A German botanist, Dr Darr, discovered a rare and unique species of palm in Khao Phra Thaew about 50 years ago. Called the white-backed palm or langkow palm, the fan-shaped plant stands 3m to 5m tall and is found only here and in Khao Sok National Park. The highest point in Khao Phra Thaew Royal Wildlife & Forest Reserve is 442m **Khao Phara**.

Tigers, Malayan sun bears, rhinos and elephants once roamed the forest here, but nowadays resident mammals are limited to humans, gibbons, monkeys, slow loris, langurs, civets, flying foxes, squirrels, mousedeer and other smaller animals. Watch out for cobras and wild pigs.

Near Nam Tok Bang Pae (Bang Pae Falls) is the **Phuket Gibbon Rehabilitation Centre** (☎ 0 7626 0492; www.warthai.org/projects; admission by donation; ☼ 9am-4pm). Financed by donations and run by volunteers, the centre cares for gibbons that have been kept in captivity and reintroduces them to the wild. Visitors who wish to help may 'adopt' a gibbon for 1500B, which

will pay for one animal's care for a year. The programme includes keeping you updated on your adopted gibbon's progress throughout the year of adoption. Check the website for more information.

HAT NAI THON, HAT NAI YANG & HAT MAI KHAO

หาดในทอน/หาดในยาง/หาดไม้ขาว

If you're looking for isolation, then the remote beaches of Phuket's northwestern coast might be your tonic.

Near the northwestern tip of Phuket, Hat Mai Khao is Phuket's longest beach. Sea turtles lay their eggs here between November and February each year. Please respect the turtles and do not touch them or their eggs. A visitors centre with toilets, showers and picnic tables is found at Mai Khao. Here you'll also find some short trails through the casuarinas to a steep beach. Take care when swimming here, as there's a strong year-round undertow. Except for weekends and holidays you'll have this place almost entirely to yourself; even during peak periods, peace and solitude are usually only a few steps away, as there's so much space here.

About 5km to the south, improved roads to Hat Nai Thon have brought only a small amount of development to this broad expanse of pristine sand backed by casuarinas and pandanus trees. Down on the beach, umbrellas and sling chairs are available from vendors. Swimming is quite good here except at the height of the monsoon, and there is some coral near the headlands at either end of the bay. The submerged remains of a wrecked 50m-long tin dredger lie further off the coast near tiny Ko Waew at a depth of 16m. Naithon Beach Resort at Hat Naithon can arrange dive trips in the vicinity.

Hat Nai Yang is renowned for snorkelling and it is very popular with Thai tourists. About 1km off Nai Yang is a large reef at a depth of 10m to 20m. Snorkelling and scuba equipment can be hired at many resorts so check for best prices and quality.

Sleeping & Eating
HAT NAI THON
Tien Seng Guest House (Th Surin; r 400-800B; ☒) This so-so place has rooms in a modern shophouse building, just south of the Naithon Beach Resort, and is the best bet in its price bracket. There is also a restaurant that serves Thai and

672 PHUKET PROVINCE •• Ao Bang Thao

Chinese dishes. The more expensive rooms come with air-con.

Naithon Beach Resort (☎ 0 7620 5379; fax 0 7620 5381; 22/2 Th Surin; cottages 1000-1500B; ☒ Nov-May; ☒) This resort has large, tastefully designed wooden cottages. A small restaurant serves sandwiches and Thai food. The resort closes in the rainy season. It is on the opposite side of the access road from the beach.

Trisara (☎ 0 7361 0100; www.trisara.com; villas from US$565; ☒ ☐ ☒) If you can afford to stay here, do so. A tranquil oasis far removed from Patong's chaos, ultra-exclusive Trisara became a hit the minute it opened. Must have been something about the villas coming with private pools and steam rooms (for the spa review see p665). Honeymoon, anyone? We loved the true infinity pool, which blends effortlessly into the sea.

HAT NAI YANG & HAT MAI KHAO

Camping is allowed on both Nai Yang and Mai Khao beaches without any permit.

Phuket Camp Ground (tents per person 100B) Privately operated, this camp site rents out tents with rice mats, pillows, blankets and a torch. A light mangrove thicket separates the camp site from the beach, but the proprietors don't mind if you move the tents onto the beach crest. A small outdoor restaurant-bar provides sustenance. Other amenities include a shower and toilet, hammocks, sling chairs, beach umbrellas and a campfire ring.

Golddigger's Resort (☎ 0 7632 8424; crown@phuket.com; 72/12 Th Surin; r 1100-1600B; ☒ ☒) Despite its unsavoury name, Golddigger's is one of the best midrange options on this beach. The Swiss-run hotel has just 16 rooms, and their décor, spaciousness and choice furniture take them a step above most beachside joints in this price bracket. A poolside bar and a restaurant serving great Thai and international fare are other bonuses. Don't bother spending more on air-con; the fan rooms are often just as cool, thanks to ocean breezes. Prices don't vary between seasons.

Nai Yang Beach Resort (☎ 0 7632 8300; nai _yang@ phuket.ksc.co.th; 65/23-24 Th Hat Nai Yang; bungalows 650-1800B; ☒) This resort is clean, quiet and near the beach. It sets itself apart from the hundreds of other bungalows looking exactly like it by pulling together a great nightly barbecue.

JW Marriott Phuket Resort & Spa (☎ 0 7633 8000; www.marriott.com; 231 Moo 3; r from US$400; ☒ ☐ ☒)

This hot new Marriott was named one of the best hotels in the world in 2006 by readers of *Condé Nast Traveler*. Among the most appreciated assets are mammoth rooms boasting superior sea views, raised *sǎalaa* (open-sided resting place) areas, triangular back cushions, massage mats and polished wood floors. A cooking school and pub with live music round out the deal. Don't miss the spa (see boxed text, p665).

Along the dirt road at the very southern end of Hat Nai Yang is a seemingly endless strip of seafood restaurants and, as always, tailor shops. There is a small minimart near the entrance to the Indigo Pearl Resort.

Getting There & Away

Sǎwngthǎew from Phuket cost 50B per person and run between 7am and 5pm only. If you're coming from the airport a taxi costs about 250B. There is no regular sǎwngthǎew stop for Mai Khao but a túk-túk charter from Phuket Town costs about 300B.

AO BANG THAO

อ่าวบางเทา

Home to some of the islands mega-resorts (serious pampering at serious prices), Ao Bang Thao laps against a lovely 8km-long crescent of white-sand beach on Phuket's western coast. A steady breeze makes the bay ideal for windsurfing; since 1992 the annual **Siam World Cup windsurfing championships** have been held here in January. A system of lagoons inland from the beach has been incorporated into Laguna Phuket, a complex of five upmarket resorts dominating the central portion of the beach. Even if you can't afford to stay, the beach makes a nice day trip.

Activities

Hideaway Day Spa (☎ 0 7627 1549; ☒ 11am-9pm) offers traditional Thai massage, sauna, mud body wraps and other treatments beginning at 1500B for a 90-minute massage. The facility is nicely laid out in a tranquil wooded setting next to one of Bang Thai's lagoons. Reservations for any treatments are recommended. Look for Hideaway about 800m west of Hwy 4030.

Sleeping

With one exception (although this may change in the near future), Bang Thao is strictly for the rich. The resorts in Laguna Phuket have more

AO BANG THAO, HAT SURIN & HAT KAMALA

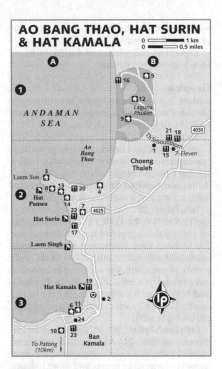

than 1100 rooms and 30 restaurants between them (the gargantuan Sheraton Grande alone has 335 rooms and eight restaurants). The complex also boasts an 18-hole golf course. Guests at any one of the resorts can use the dining and recreation facilities at all of them. Frequent shuttle buses make the rounds of all the hotels, as do pontoon boats (via the linked lagoons).

Bangtao Lagoon Bungalows (☎ 0 7632 4260; www.phuket-bangtaolagoon.com; Ao Bang Thao; bungalows 400-1800B; ✄ 🖳 🖭) It's still looking a bit ramshackle from the tsunami, but Bangtao Lagoon is toughing it out and remains the only cheapie in the region. Fabulously friendly staff, and a location on an almost deserted stretch of beach make up for the slightly worn, but passable, rooms.

Dusit Laguna Resort (☎ 0 7632 4324; r US$150-280, ste US$250-400; ✄ 🖳 🖭) There are 226 guest rooms and suites offered at this well-appointed luxury resort (although it's nowhere near as swanky as the Banyan Tree), as well as a spa, fitness centre and tennis courts, and free use of sailboards and sailboats.

Sheraton Grande Laguna Phuket (☎ 0 7632 4101; www.starwoodhotels.com; r US$200-1000; ✄ 🖳 🖭) At the other end of the atmosphere scale, the Sheraton will appeal to a livelier, more active crowd. With plans for further expansion, it already features a gigantic 323m pool, water sport facilities galore and 335 rooms.

Banyan Tree Phuket (☎ 0 7632 4374; www.banyantree .com; villas US$550-2500; ✄ 🖳 🖭) One of Asia's finest hotels, the Banyan Tree Phuket is an oasis of sedate, understated luxury. Accommodation is in private villas – many with private pools and massage areas – and the on-site spa is one of the continent's best (see boxed text, p665). In 2006 the Banyan Tree Phuket was once again voted one of the world's best places to stay by readers of *Condé Nast Traveler*.

Eating & Drinking

Despite what some local hoteliers would have you believe, there is good food to be had outside the confines of Bang Thao's luxury hotels. You will find much of it just outside Laguna's main gate.

Lotus Restaurant (dishes 50-100B; 🕑 lunch & dinner) A clean, breezy and friendly open-walled eatery serving an amazing assortment of live crab, shrimp, lobster, fish and other visual and culinary delights in quite well-tended tanks. Look for Lotus 500m west of the entrance to

ANDAMAN COAST

Banyan Tree Phuket. It is the first in a row of beachside Thai and seafood restaurants that stretches to the south.

Tatonka (☎ 0 7632 4349; Th Srisoonthorn; dishes 250-300B; ☺ dinner Thu-Tue) This is the home of 'globetrotter cuisine', which owner-chef Harold Schwarz developed by taking fresh local products and combining them with cooking and presentation techniques learned in Europe, Colorado and Hawaii. The eclectic, tapas-style selection includes creative vegetarian and seafood dishes. There's also a tasting menu (per person 750B, minimum two people) which lets you try a little of everything. Call ahead in the high season. Tatonka arranges free transportation for guests of the resort complex.

English Pub (☎ 08 9872 1398; Th Srisoonthorn; dishes 100-300B; ☺ lunch & dinner) This timber and thatch watering hole is the most authentic English pub on the island – even the toilets smell. It has a sunny beer garden, a snug interior, a good range of beers and some decent pub grub. Shoot darts or kick back with Premiership footy.

Peppers (☎ 0 7632 5112; Th Srisoonthorn; dishes 150-400B; ☺ lunch & dinner) A spicier take on the Hard Rock Café theme, Peppers features bare, red-brick walls, a pool table, music memorabilia and a splash of neon. Food is Tex-Mex meets Thai and there's cold beer on tap.

Getting There & Away

A sǎwngthǎew between Bang Thao and Phuket Town's Th Ranong costs 50B per person. Túk-túk charters are 250B.

HAT SURIN
หาดสุรินทร์

Little more than a gear change and a slow right-hander north from Laem Singh, Hat Surin is on the up and up. Showcasing a trio of top-end resorts, as well as a starburst of cheap imitators, this busy beach is big on variety. Trees line the shore and dozens of cheap food shacks (offering some of the best-value seafood on Phuket) take shelter beneath them. Money is pouring in, new places are opening all the time and the murmur among expats is that this is the beach to watch.

The downside of all this, of course, is ever-growing crowds. Hat Surin is extremely pretty, but stretches have already become a car crash of snack stalls and souvenir salesmen. For the celebrities, at least, the only way to do Surin today is from behind the guarded gates of the exclusive Amanpuri.

Expect big, dangerous seas during the monsoon – swimmers beware.

Sleeping

Budget digs are at a real premium, but there are some excellent midrange operations and several fabulous luxury choices.

Surin Bay Inn (☎ 0 7627 1601; r 1000-1500B; ☒ ☐) Right next to Capri Beach, this is another welcoming midrange option. There's an eatery serving fabulous breakfasts below; clean, spacious rooms above (although a sea view costs 400B extra); and a useful book exchange.

Twin Palms (☎ 0 7631 6500; www.twinpalms-phuket .com; r US$160-1200; ☒ ☐ ☒) There is a youthful vibe about this seductive spa hotel; there are lots of clean lines to its contemporary, stylish façade and minimalist décor in its posh rooms. If you want A-grade pampering without paying the earth, this is one of Phuket's best bets (hint: it's a great alternative to the nearby Laguna Beach complex, on an equally appealing beach).

Capri Beach Resort (☎ 0 7627 0597; www.phuket.com /thecapri; r 600-2200B; ☒) A little yellow temple to Italian kitsch, this welcoming spot offers great home cooking, snug rooms and more Italiana than you can likely stomach. Expect opera, giant pepper grinders and high standards. It's a short hop from the beach.

Chedi (☎ 0 7632 4017; www.ghmhotels.com; r 7200-15,200B; ☒ ☒) Boasting one of the best private beaches on Phuket, the Chedi offers a range of chi-chi bungalows scattered across a forested hillside. Facilities are a little limited, but there is a restaurant, the requisite infinity pool and a small bar.

Amanpuri Resort (☎ 0 7632 4333; www.amanresorts .com; villas US$700-8200; ☒ ☐ ☒) Phuket's number one celebrity magnet, the Amanpuri offers lashings of glamour and palatial luxury (what else would you expect from the former Shah of Iran's winter palace architect?) With a staggering three-and-a-half members of staff assigned to every guest, this is exclusive service with bells. Accommodation is in private villas and you can even book your own maid and cook.

Eating

There are plenty of excellent restaurants in and around Surin. For cheap seafood, your first stop should be the seafront snack stalls on the main beach.

Twin Brothers (☎ 0 9591 1274; mains 40-200B; ☽ lunch & dinner) Another of Hat Surin's more substantial food shacks, this airy eatery specialises in Australian steaks, pizzas and antipasto. The tables come clothed and there's a sign telling you how far it is to home – apparently, it's 9887km to London.

Mr Crab (☎ 0 7632 5000, ext 1710; mains 50-200B; ☽ breakfast, lunch & dinner) Crab cooked every way imaginable is offered at this no-frills beach-front joint. You pay by the weight and gobble it down in front of fabulous seaside vistas.

Silk (☎ 0 7627 1705; Rte 4025; mains 200-450B; ☽ lunch & dinner) Expats from across Phuket flock to Silk for a hip cocktail amid burgundy walls and exotic flowers. The menu focuses on beautifully executed Thai specialities. The expansive, stylish restaurant is one of several upmarket dining options in Surin Plaza, just east of the beach, on Rte 4025.

Getting There & Away

A regular såwngthåew from Phuket Town's Th Ranong to Hat Surin costs 50B per person, and túk-túk or såwngthåew charters cost 250B to 350B.

Rent cars from **Andaman Car Rental** (☎ 0 7632 4422; ☽ 9am-9pm), opposite the entrance to the Chedi. A jeep costs from 1200B per day.

HAT KAMALA
หาดกมลา

This photogenic bay is one of Phuket's prettiest, but recovery has been a little slower here than elsewhere on the island. And while it is now business as usual, Kamala has lost ground – in terms of tourist arrivals – to nearby Patong and Hat Surin. As a result, Kamala is a pretty good deal. Resorts are newer and the beaches are quieter than almost anywhere else on Phuket – make the most of it now, before it gets rediscovered.

Sights & Activities

Local beach bums will tell you that **Laem Singh**, just north of Kamala, is one of the best capes on the island. Walled in by cliffs, there is no road access so you have to park on the headland and clamber down a narrow path. You could camp here and eat at the rustic roadside seafood places at the northern end of Singh or in **Ban Kamala**, a village further south. If you're renting a motorbike, this is a nice little trip down Rte 4025 and then over dirt roads from Surin to Kamala.

Phuket Fantasea (☎ 0 7638 5000; www.phuket -fantasea.com; admission with/without dinner 1600/1100B; ☽ 5.30-11.30pm Wed-Mon) is a US$60 million 'cultural theme park' found just north of Hat Kamala. Despite the billing, there aren't any rides, but there is a truly magical show that manages to capture the colour and pageantry of traditional Thai dance and costumes and combine them with state-of-the-art light-and-sound techniques rivalling anything found in Las Vegas (think 30 elephants). All of this takes place on a stage dominated by a full-scale replica of a Khmer temple reminiscent of Angkor Wat. Kids especially will be captivated by the spectacle. There is a good collection of souvenir shops in the park offering Thai handicrafts. The Thai buffet dinner is surprisingly good. Tickets can be booked through most hotels and tour agencies.

Don't bother bringing your camera to catch the splendour and spectacle on film – they are not allowed and if you do bring it, you'll have to deposit it for safekeeping before you enter.

Back in Kamala, you can organise diving through expat-run **Scuba Quest** (☎ 0 7627 9016; www.scuba-quest-phuket.de).

Sleeping

Kamala is seeing a fair bit of development as small places expand and go upscale.

Benjamin Resort (☎ 0 7638 5145; www.phuketdir .com/benjaminresort; r 350-600B; ☒) This aging hotel with a laid-back air has the best budget digs in town. Air-con rooms are particularly good value (some of the cheapest on the island). Aside from appalling pink bedspreads in some rooms, there's little to complain about.

Kamala Dreams (☎ 0 7629 1131; www.kamala-beach .net; r 1200-1800B; ☒) This old-timer, only a few seconds from the beach, is looking slick again thanks to a massive renovation project. Rooms are spotless, floors are made from cool tiles, walls have bright new paint and everything sparkles.

Kamala Beach Hotel (☎ 0 7627 9580; www.kamala beach.com; r 1800-3900B; ☒ ▢ ☒) The best bet in its price range, Kamala Beach offers spacious well-kitted rooms, a couple of glassy pools and more than one restaurant. Service is commendable.

Eating

Aew Seafood (☎ 0 7627 9843; dishes 70-200B; ☽ lunch & dinner) Settle in at this breezy eatery where fresh fish steals the limelight. Whether you

are in the mood for a plate of cuttlefish or grilled king prawns, simple home cooking has a fabulous fresh taste.

Voyage One World (☎ 0 5787 6515; dishes 200-400B; ❧ lunch & dinner) A moderately priced French restaurant that gets good reviews. Voyage One World offers an early-bird special between 5.30pm and 7pm featuring a three-course set menu (price varies). The à la carte menu is small but varied, split nearly evenly between seafood and meat. There's chocolate fondue for dessert.

Getting There & Away
A regular săwngthăew from Kamala to Patong costs 50B per person, while a săwngthăew charter (necessary after dark) costs 250B. You can rent vehicles in Hat Kamala at **Via Rent-A-Car** (☎ 0 7638 5718; www.via-phuket.com; various locations).

PATONG
ป่าตอง

Chaotic Patong's beautiful curved beach sparks with frenetic electricity. The steamy streets seethe with souvenir shops, girlie bars, pricey seafood restaurants, dive shops, travel agencies, hotels and everything in between. Scantily clad golden-brown travellers pay homage to the neon gods, dancing the night away to booming sound systems in sweaty, pulsating clubs, or sipping Singha under the stars at sandy beachside bars. Demurely dressed diners dine on giant prawns and Italian wines at decadent, romantic restaurants where the views are as worthwhile as the food.

Hat Patong is the island's most popular beach, and it seems to be trying to become the next Pattaya – the streets are filled with flashy fluorescent signs lighting the night sky with a lurid red glow – but it's not nearly as creepy and by day it's quite fine for kids. The sort of people drawn to this teeming, neon-lit atmosphere will adore Patong, while the more peace-loving souls (you know who you are) might want to stay far, far away.

Although most of Patong has been spruced up, some reconstruction continues.

Information
Money-exchange booths and internet cafés are commonplace. There are two post offices in Patong; one is towards the northern end of Th Rat Uthit, the other is near the centre of Th Thawiwong.

Bookazine (☎ 0 7634 5833; 18 Th Bangla; ❧ 9.30am-11.30pm) Head here to buy English-language maps, guidebooks, magazines and newspapers.
Immigration office (☎ 0 7634 0477; Th Kalim Beach; ❧ 10am-noon & 1-3pm Mon-Fri) Does visa extensions.
Tourist police (☎ 0 7634 0244) At the beach road's intersection with Th Bangla.

Activities
Patong is a diving centre on the island. For a list of established dive shops, see p661. Yachts, sailboats and catamarans sometimes can be chartered here, with or without crew. To find out more on this, see p664.

Sleeping
While Patong was once Phuket's most expensive beach, prices are stabilising as the local accommodation market becomes saturated with new places to stay.

BUDGET
On the beach there is nothing in the budget range, but on and off Th Rat Uthit, especially in the Paradise Complex and along Soi Saen Sabai, there are several nondescript guesthouses with rooms for 300B to 500B.

Touch Villa (☎ 0 7634 4011; touchvilla@hotmail.com; 151/4 Th Rat Uthit; r 350-600B; 🏠) A slightly crumbly spot with a twee garden setting and holiday-camp ambience. It's cheap, cheerful and refreshingly un-seedy. The pricier rooms have air-con.

M's Guesthouse (14/13 Soi Ratchaphatanuson; r 400-800B; 🖳) There is nothing subtle about M's gaudiness: it sports verandas with pink porcelain balusters and there is glazed tile covering nearly all flat surfaces. Rooms have all the mod cons, but share baths and porches. Check out the outlandishly furnished common area. It's a 10-minute walk from the beach.

Tatum Mansion (☎ 0 7634 4332; tatummansion@hotmail.com; 66/7-8 Soi Kepsap; r from 600-1200B; 🏠) On a street packed with budget offerings, this expat-owned outfit comes up trumps. You get cable TV and a bed that won't groan when you clamber into it. You can also get the low-down on town from the management.

C&N Hotel (☎ 0 7634 5949; www.cnhotelpatong.com; r 800-1200B; 🏠 🖳) The original features (it looks like it might once have posed as a spa hotel) are now looking a bit hung over, but this remains solid value for the price. The rooms feel almost cosy with wood panels on some

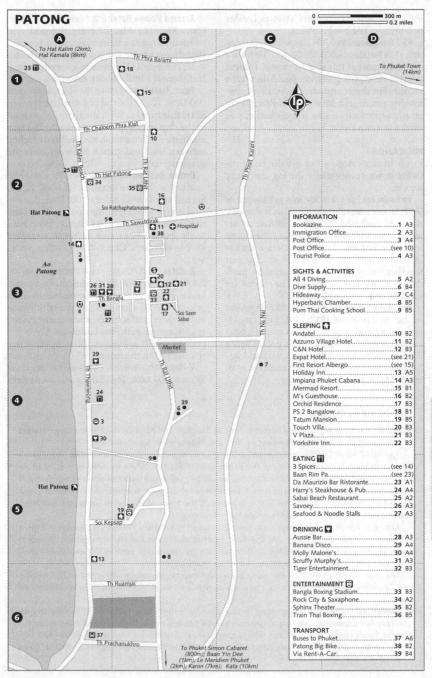

PATONG

0 — 300 m
0 — 0.2 miles

To Hat Kalim (2km);
Hat Kamala (8km)

Th Phra Barami

To Phuket Town
(14km)

Th Chaloem Phra Kiat

Th Hat Patong

Th Kalim Beach

Th Rat Uthit

Th Phisit Karani

Soi Ratchaphatanuson

Hat Patong

Th Sawatdirak

Hospital

Ao
Patong

Th Bangla

Soi Saen
Sabai

Market

Th Na Nai

Th Thawiwong

Th Rat Uthit

Hat Patong

Soi Kepsap

Th Ruamjai

Th Prachanukhro

To Phuket Simon Cabaret
(800m); Baan Yin Dee
(1km); Le Meridien Phuket
(2km); Karon (7km); Kata (10km)

INFORMATION
Bookazine	1 A3
Immigration Office	2 A3
Post Office	3 A4
Post Office	(see 10)
Tourist Police	4 A3

SIGHTS & ACTIVITIES
All 4 Diving	5 A2
Dive Supply	6 B4
Hideaway	7 C4
Hyperbaric Chamber	8 B5
Pum Thai Cooking School	9 B5

SLEEPING
Andatel	10 B2
Azzurro Village Hotel	11 B2
C&N Hotel	12 B3
Expat Hotel	(see 21)
First Resort Albergo	(see 15)
Holiday Inn	13 A5
Impiana Phuket Cabana	14 A3
Mermaid Resort	15 B1
M's Guesthouse	16 B2
Orchid Residence	17 B3
PS 2 Bungalow	18 B1
Tatum Mansion	19 B5
Touch Villa	20 B3
V Plaza	21 B3
Yorkshire Inn	22 B3

EATING
3 Spices	(see 14)
Baan Rim Pa	(see 23)
Da Maurizio Bar Ristorante	23 A1
Harry's Steakhouse & Pub	24 A4
Sabai Beach Restaurant	25 A2
Savoey	26 A3
Seafood & Noodle Stalls	27 A3

DRINKING
Aussie Bar	28 A3
Banana Disco	29 A4
Molly Malone's	30 A4
Scruffy Murphy's	31 A3
Tiger Entertainment	32 B3

ENTERTAINMENT
Bangla Boxing Stadium	33 B3
Rock City & Saxaphone	34 A2
Sphinx Theater	35 B2
Train Thai Boxing	36 B5

TRANSPORT
Buses to Phuket	37 A6
Patong Big Bike	38 B2
Via Rent-A-Car	39 B4

walls and American-motel style polyester bedspreads. The pool is a plus.

PS 2 Bungalow (☎ 0 7634 2207; www.ps2bungalow.com; 21 Th Rat Uthit; r 400-1500B; ⚋ ⚌) There's a dearth of gloss at this slightly dowdy budget offering. The pink paint job could do with a facelift, but the rooms are modern and reasonably priced, if a little scruffy. Prices vary greatly depending on season and whether you want a fan or air-con.

MIDRANGE
Prices in this category can usually be negotiated down substantially during the rainy season.

Yorkshire Inn (☎ 0 7634 0904; www.yorkshireinn.com; 169/16 Soi Saen Sabai; r 800B; ⚋ ⚌) This is one of a string of unabashedly British outfits, courting visitors that insist on putting the home in their comforts. This one offers a flicker of homey B&B charm and can at least put together a mean fry-up…the Yorkshire pudding is a little less successful. The rooms are spotless and come with cable TV.

First Resort Albergo (☎ 0 7634 0980; firsthotel@hotmail.com; 19/12 Th Rat Uthit; r 800B; ⚋ ⚌) This pleasant, Italian-run spot is solid as mama's bust and offers stylish rooms around a pool. There's TV, a terrace restaurant (expect pizza and bolognese made with Thai basil) and plenty of warm Mediterranean hospitality.

Azzurro Village Hotel (☎ 0 7634 1811; 107 Th Rat Uthit; r 900B; ⚋) Also offering the odd nod to Mediterranean design, Azzurro features slightly over-priced, comfortable rooms in a quiet courtyard. The owners are multilingual and there is a little on-site eatery.

Expat Hotel (☎ 0 7634 0300; expat@loxinfo.co.th; r 490-1200B; ⚋) At the end of a small bar-packed alley, this hotel is surprisingly quiet, at least in the daytime. Popular with young foreigners, there's a communal, buddy-buddy feeling between staff and guests. Monthly rates are available, too.

Orchid Residence (☎ 0 7634 5176; www.orchid-residence.com; 171/22 Soi Saen Sabai; r 580-1700B; ⚋ ⚌) Spread across both sides of the lane, this orchid is now looking a little droopy. That said, there's certainly plenty of choice, from relatively spartan fan rooms to much swankier air-con offerings. Check it out if other places are full.

Andatel (☎ 0 7629 0489; www.andatelhotel.com; 419 Th Rat Uthit; r 1000-1800B; ⚋ ⚌) Andatel is a good-looking place and one of the best deals in its price range. It offers great rooms with patios or balconies, and some creative touches in the traditional peaked Thai buildings. There is a pool to splash around in, plus an attractive restaurant out the front.

V-Plaza (☎ 0 7629 2556; www.valhalla-th.com; 163/24 Soi Sunset; r 800-2000B; ⚋) This place is pretty darn

---

GAY PRIDE IN PHUKET

Although there are big gay pride celebrations in Bangkok and Pattaya, the **Phuket Gay Festival** is considered by many to be the best in Thailand, maybe even Southeast Asia.

The first Phuket Gay Festival started as a small community project in November 1999, in response to plans for similar events in the capital and in Pattaya. When the festival proved to be very successful, the planners realised Phuket would be competing with the other similar festivals across the country so it was moved from November to February – a drier month in Phuket anyway. Since then, in early February the whole island, but the town of Patong in particular, has been packed with (mostly male) revellers from the world over.

Although Bangkok and Pattaya both have prominent gay scenes, Phuket's is possibly the most pleasing, for both the scenery and the light-hearted, open and friendly atmosphere. In recent years, the festival has also included social responsibility campaigns, such as HIV awareness, staying clean and sober, and the fight against child prostitution.

The main events of the four-day party are a huge beach volleyball tournament and, of course, the Grand Parade, featuring floats, cheering crowds and beautiful costumes in the streets of Patong.

Pre-festival parties start happening in late January, and include things such as **Gay Diving** and **Gay Sea Canoeing**. Great package tours can be booked through many companies, including **Utopia Tours** (www.utopia-tours.com), which specialises in gay/lesbian trips in Southeast Asia.

For updates on future festivals, or to sign up for the spectacular volleyball tournament, go to www.phuketgaypridefestival.com.

unique; think of it as a mini Viking-theme park. In a large indoor space, there are 13 comfortable rooms facing the restaurant/bar area (could be noisy at night), highlighted by a giant Viking helmet. All have TV and fridge; two come with private whirlpool (700B extra). Expect to see some hookers hanging out with Western men here: the place advertises that 'there are no additional costs for overnight visitors' – hey at least they're honest, most hotels allow prostitutes inside, you just have to pay a 1000B extra...

Mermaid Resort (☎ 0 7634 5670; www.mermaid -resort.com; Th Rat Uthit; r 1200-2200B; 🐾 🖭) The piped music echoing through the marble lobby is a little cheesy, but the rooms offer the kind of reliability you can expect from a chain three-star hotel. Count on a minibar, mini shampoo bottles, cable TV and a rather garish, shiny bedspread.

TOP END

Holiday Inn (☎ 0 7634 0608; Th Rat Uthit; r 3200-5200B; 🐾 🖳 🖭) This brand new resort is a little glitzier than your run-of-the-mill Holiday Inn, offering all the usual amenities, plus one or two extra. There's a glossy spa featuring a smorgasbord of restorative treatments and the open-air bar faces out on the street for fashionable people watching.

Impiana Phuket Cabana (☎ 0 7634 0138; www .impiana.com; Th Thawiwong; r 3000-7500B; 🐾 🖳 🖭) A small village of opulent bungalows set on the sand, the Impiana Phuket Cabana has one of the best locations in Patong. The gorgeous cabanas fuse Thai and Balinese styles and privacy is of utmost importance. It's very easy to wander from your cabana, through a tropical garden to the beach without seeing a soul. Don't miss the 3 Spices restaurant (right).

Baan Yin Dee (☎ 0 7629 4104; www.baanyindee.com; 7/5 Th Muean Ngen; r US$180-490; 🐾 🖭) On a hill overlooking town, this is Patong's premier boutique getaway. It's small but perfectly put together. Spacious rooms come with balconies, magazine-worthy styling and a trickle of beautiful young things hanging out around the pool. If you're partying all night, come here to repair your soul (plus there's a fabulous restaurant providing hangover-curing culinary delights).

Le Meridien Phuket (☎ 0 7634 0480; www.lemeridien .com; r US$230-250; 🐾 🖳 🖭) Just outside town, this swanky resort has everything the international globetrotter could ask for – from

tennis courts and swimming pools (both very much in the plural), to fabulous rooms and palatial rooms. There's even volleyball, minigolf and a climbing wall. It remains one of Phuket's most popular great escapes.

Eating

Patong has stacks of restaurants, some of them quite good. Patong's most glamorous restaurants are in a little huddle above the cliffs on the northern edge of town. Back in town, expect the usual spread of expat diners.

Sabai Beach Restaurant (dishes 70-120B; ⏲ break-fast, lunch & dinner) The tables are set right on the sand at this beachfront place run by a friendly Thai staff. The fried rice and calamari dishes are good, but so are the Western choices. If you are craving a good, simple meal, the food is better than average. We liked the spaghetti with garlic and chilli.

Savoey (☎ 0 7634 1171; 136 Th Thawiwong; dishes 120-350B; ⏲ lunch & dinner) A perennially popular seafood haunt, it subscribes to the 'slay 'em and weigh 'em' fish restaurant philosophy. Cast an eye over the mountain of seafood piled up on ice outside, or the fish gulping away in tanks inside, point out your prey and then take a seat to enjoy your quarry. If you want something more upscale, try the swank, white-tableclothed new addition next door featuring a smaller menu of mostly seafood.

Baan Rim Pa (☎ 0 7634 4079; dishes 215-475B; ⏲ lunch & dinner) Soft piano music sets the mood for a romantic evening at this restaurant built high above a thicket of mangrove trees. It offers stunning ocean-view tables (make reservations) and specialises in Thai cuisine that's only slightly toned down for foreign palates. Dress accordingly to dine at this high-class restaurant.

Harry's Steakhouse & Pub (☎ 0 1787 3167; 110/2 Soi Big One; dishes 100-495B; ⏲ breakfast, lunch & dinner) There are no surprises at Harry's; it's the usual air-conditioned tourist boozer. If you fancy a slab of steak in fresh, clean surrounds, however, you could do a lot worse than a table here.

3 Spices (☎ 0 7634 2100; Impiana Phuket Cabana; dishes 175-600B; ⏲ lunch & dinner) Part of the newly opened Impiana Phuket Cabana resort, 3 Spices serves sumptuous food in a fun location right on Patong's busy main beach road. Chow down on gourmet fusion like New Zealand green shell mussels in a sweet chilli and cilantro sauce served on dill-mashed potatoes,

ANDAMAN COAST

while checking out the hustle and bustle on the street. Meals are complemented by live music played at conversation level.

Da Maurizio Bar Ristorante (☎ 0 7634 4079; dishes 450-950B; ⊙ lunch & dinner) Another very classy and romantic restaurant, this one serves delicious Italian cuisine. Call for reservations and a complimentary ride to the restaurant. It's set down on the rocks.

Bargain seafood and noodle stalls pop up across town at night – try the lanes on and around Th Bangla.

Drinking

Some visitors may find that Patong's bar scene is enough to put them off their *phàt thai*, but if you're in the mood for plenty of beer, winking neon and short skirts, it is sure worth sampling.

Th Bangla is Patong's beer-and-bar girl Mecca, featuring a number of spectacular, go-go extravaganzas, where you can expect the usual mix of gyrating Thai girls and red-faced Western men. The music is loud – expect techno – the clothes are all but non-existent and the décor is typically slapstick – expect plenty of phallic imagery. That said, the atmosphere is more carnival than carnage and you'll find plenty of Western girls pushing their way through the throng to the bar.

Molly Malone's (☎ 0 7629 2771; Th Thawiwong; ⊙ noon-2am) Wildly popular with tourists and *faràng*, this pub rocks with Irish gigs every night at 9.45pm. There's a good atmosphere, lots of pub food and some great tables out the front from which to admire the ocean and legions of tourist passers-by. Guinness is available for a mere 349B per pint.

Tiger Entertainment (☎ 0 7634 5112; Th Bangla; ⊙ noon-2am) The strangest building in Phuket features a concrete cave styling and a menagerie of unsettling – and extremely well endowed – anthropomorphic tigers. More a congregation of go-go bars – topped with a nightclub – than a single entity, this is the first, and often last, stop on any odyssey through Patong's bar scene.

Scruffy Murphy's (☎ 0 7629 2590; 5 Th Bangla; ⊙ noon-2am) This place competes with Molly Malone's by offering its own live Irish music and cover bands at 9.45pm. It's also clean and air-conditioned. It cooks up pub grub and Thai food and offers big screens for watching sports. Although it's located amid the strips of cheap girlie bars, the older male *faràng*

clientele that frequent the place seem more interested in flirting with young *faràng* women than Thai prostitutes. Still, it can be harmless fun and you may find yourself here more than once in a span of days.

Aussie Bar (Th Bangla; ⊙ noon-2am) This Australian-style bar is bedecked with kangaroos and is a good spot for a pre-wiggle tipple.

Banana Disco (☎ 0 1271 2469; 96 Th Thawiwong; admission 200B) Phuket's most sophisticated nightclub was closed for renovations when we stopped by, but it's bound to look great when it reopens (we dug the spiral metal staircase and brightly painted murals we viewed while peeking through the floor-to-ceiling glass windows.)

Entertainment

Once you've done the go-go, there's plenty more to see. Cabaret and Thai boxing, in particular, are something of a speciality here.

Phuket Simon Cabaret (☎ 0 7634 2011; www.phuket-simoncabaret.com; admission 550B) About 300m south of town on Th Sirirach, this cabaret offers entertaining transvestite shows. The 600-seat theatre is grand, the costumes are gorgeous and the ladyboys are convincing. It's often a full house. Performances are at 7.30pm and 9.30pm nightly – book ahead.

Sphinx Theatre (☎ 0 7634 1500; 120 Th Rat Uthit; admission 350B) There's more cabaret on offer at the Sphinx, where shows kick off at 9pm and 10.30pm daily.

Rock City & Saxaphone (Th Kalim Beach Rd) These two new venues, next door to each other, have nightly live music. Rock City, well rocks, with local and Western hard-rock bands. Saxaphone focuses on jazz, funk and soul, and books acts from Bangkok on a regular basis.

Bangla Boxing Stadium (☎ 0 7275 6364; Th Bangla; admission 1000B) You can't miss this stadium's match advertising – announcements are blasted every few minutes from giant speakers in passing pick-up trucks. The announcements are so annoying they may turn you off, but if you're into *muay thai* (Thai boxing), boxing bouts are held a few times per week (usually Wednesday and Sunday) at 8.45pm.

Train Thai Boxing (☎ 0 7629 2890; Soi Kepsap; ⊙ 8am-9pm) *Muay thai*/mixed martial arts fighting is taking off in a big way on television screens across the world. Learn a few moves of your own at Train Thai Boxing. Cost for a 90-minute lesson? A lot of bruises plus 300B. Cool quotient with your friends back home? Priceless.

Getting There & Around

Túk-túk around Patong should cost 25B per ride – the driver may try to charge you more as a *faràng*, so it's best to have the money already out before he or she can say anything. There are numerous places to rent 125cc motorcycles and jeeps – you'll find them at nearly every street corner. **Patong Big Bike** (☎ 0 7634 0380; Th Rat Uthit) rents proper motorcycles (per day 500B to 1000B), not scooter/motorbikes, as well as off-road motorbikes (per day 350B). Keep in mind that the helmet law is strictly enforced in Patong. For car rental, **Via Rent-A-Car** (Map p677; ☎ 0 7638 5718; www.via-phuket.com; 189/6 Th Rat Uthit, Patong) is a good choice and can deliver cars to anywhere on the island.

Såwngthåew to Patong from Phuket Town leave from Th Ranong, near the day market and fountain circle; the fare is 50B. The after-hours charter fare is 250B. Buses from Patong to Phuket Town leave from the southern end of Th Thawiwong and cost 50B.

KARON
กะรน

Karon's gorgeous beachfront is developing rapidly, but the area still has an isolated feel. The beach road, once nearly void of development, now features a string of mainly top-end resorts. Luckily, most are tasteful and set far enough back from the sand to blend into the background hills. Karon is just a few minutes' taxi ride from Kata, but has none of Kata's noisy buzz. If you want to slumber in quiet, without being too far from the party, Karon is the beach for you.

During the monsoon season the surf is too rough for swimming here, so you'll have to head to Kata for that as well. As a result Karon's hotels are absurdly cheap during the rainy season: we're talking luxury resorts for 2000B.

You'll find most of the restaurants in the village of Karon, just north of the beachfront where many hotels are clustered. Karon is still a fairly peaceful place and relatively devoid of the overwhelming commercialisation, neon lights and loud music found on nearby Patong, although you're still likely to be propositioned by the ladyboys hanging outside the restaurants come dark.

Sights

If you're looking for fun away from the sand, or are travelling with the kids, try **Dino Park** (Map p683; ☎ 0 7633 0625; adult/child 120/90B, incl use of golf course 240/180B; ⊙ 10am-midnight), next to Marina Phuket. It features an 18-hole minigolf course and a fake waterfall, among other things. The theme is Flintstones – the staff dress in caveman outfits, the restaurant serves Bronto Burgers and you can drink at the Dino Bar.

Sleeping

Hat Karon is lined with inns and deluxe bungalows, along with some cheaper places. Karon sees a disproportionately large number of guests from Scandinavia and as a result the beach is home to quite a few Scandinavian run simple hotels. These places tend to be clean and cheap, and most have attached restaurants specialising in fare from these northern finger countries.

BUDGET & MIDRANGE

Less expensive places will naturally be found well off the beach, often on small hillocks to the east of the main road.

Karon Guest House (Map p683; ☎ 0 7639 6860; r 400-500B; ✗ ✦) Furniture is of the scratched mismatched variety and bathrooms are tiny, but this family-run hotel is very cheap, the staff is friendly and beds are firm. It offers free left-luggage service and safe deposit, plus satellite TV in the lobby. Guests have pool privileges at the nearby Golden Sands Hotel.

Bazoom Hostel (Map p683; ☎ 0 7639 6914; www.bazoomhostel.com; 64/76-77 Th Patak East; dm 240B, r 500B; ✗ 🖳) One of Phuket's bona fide backpacker haunts, Bazoom offers plenty of banter and staff who are savvy with the intricacies of doing Phuket on the cheap. The dorm is basic (with 14 beds), or you can opt for one of the no-frills, but still comfy rooms. Air-con is available in the pricier doubles. Såwngthåew drivers may pretend they've never heard of this place, as Bazoom doesn't pay them commissions – be adamant. From Phuket Town, you can catch the Kata/Karon bus (25B). Alternatively, call for a pick-up (150B).

Fantasy Hill Bungalow (Map p683; ☎ 0 7633 0106; bungalows 200-1000B; ✗) Sitting in a lush garden on a hill, the bungalows here are good value and of the type that's pretty much disappeared from this beach. Fantasy Hill isn't a fancy spot, but it's somewhat better than average for the price.

Best Western Phuket Orchid Resort (Map p683; ☎ 0 7639 6599; www.bestwestern.com; 562 Th Patak; r from 1000B; ✗ 🖳 ✦) This Best Western, with sleek architecture effortlessly blending into the hill upon which it sits, gives you more than your

money's worth. The amenities, along with the spacious, posh rooms feel as if they belong at a much pricier place. The hotel is family oriented, with babysitting services. The pool is the most popular hangout for sunbathers.

TOP END

Many of the remaining places to stay in Karon are newer resort-type hotels with all the posh amenities.

our pick Woraburi Resort & Spa (Map p683; ☎ 0 7639 6638; www.woraburiphuket.com; 198-200 Th Patak West; r from 2200B; 🕸 🖵 🕭) We loved this gorgeous southern Thai styled resort for offering five-star amenities at three-star prices. Everything about the Woraburi was impeccable, from the smiling, ultra-attentive staff to the large, beautifully appointed rooms featuring richly coloured silk pillows and bed runners and polished dark-wood furnishings. The gorgeously tiled bathrooms have big tubs and separate showers with great water pressure. The 207 rooms are in low-rise buildings that melt into the lush environment surrounding the beachfront property. The swimming pool is a work of art, resembling a cross between a lazy river and a Venetian canal complete with a swim-up bar. The morning buffet breakfast (included in the room rate) is immense, tasty and served in a giant open-air pavilion. The Woraburi consistently gets rave reviews from guests.

Movenpick (Map p683; ☎ 0 7639 6 139; www.moven pick-hotels.com; 509 Th Patak West; r from 3500B; 🕸 🕭) Grab a secluded villa and choose from a private plunge pool or outdoor rainforest shower; alternatively chill in the cubelike rooms with huge floor-to-ceiling glass windows (in some cases covering two entire walls) in the swank ultramod white hotel. Besides a prime location across the street from a pretty stretch of the beach, the Movenpick offers artistic décor, top-end linens, a big pool with swim-up paposo bar, spa and an alfresco restaurant and bar with a giant selection of wood-fired pizzas.

Eating & Drinking

As usual, almost every place to stay has a restaurant. There are a few cheap Thai and seafood places off the Th Patake roundabout (including beachside seafood stalls 100m north), but overall you'll find a better selection further south at Hat Kata Yai and Hat Kata Noi.

Red Onion (Map p683; ☎ 0 7639 6827; dishes 80-160B; 🕙 4-11pm) This shotgun eatery in half of a garage with a tin roof is a bona fide *faràng* magnet. There is Thai food on the menu, along with Western tidbits like schnitzel and spaghetti. Cocktails and wine selections complement the meals, so try to forget the bad music. Dine at cheery red-clothed tables, on chairs padded with silk pillows. It's about 300m east of the roundabout – look for the coloured lights.

Karon Seafood (Map p683; ☎ 0 7639 6797; cnr Th Patak East & Th Vitak; dishes 80-250B; 🕙 lunch & dinner) Bright coloured lights woo you towards this popular seafood joint that also does pizza, steak and vegetarian dishes. You'll find both Thais and Westerners dining here. Choose your dinner from the pictures on the huge seafood menu. There are daily drink specials to wash down the shrimp and crab.

Little Mermaid (Map p683; ☎ 0 7639 6580; 643 Th Patak East; dishes 80-300B; 🕙 breakfast, lunch & dinner) Scandinavia rules the roost at this eatery. The menu features pretty much everything from schnitzel and baked beans to *phàt thai* and *tom yum* (hot and sour soup), but beer (and plenty of it) tends to be the drink of choice. A bar atmosphere prevails as the night wears on, but you are guaranteed a lively ambience and a steady stream of slightly bored-looking local gals.

Harry's Pub (Map p683; ☎ 0 7635 7656; Th Patak East; dishes 100-300B; 🕙 lunch & dinner) Harry's is at its best in high season, when it is one of the area's most popular watering holes. Whenever the doors are open though, you can count on big portions of anything that comes with fries. The beer's good, if a little expensive.

Buffalo Steak House (Map p683; ☎ 0 7633 3013; Th Patak West; dishes 80-450B; 🕙 lunch & dinner) At the southern end of the town, this old-timer swears it serves the best steak in Phuket. It's not wildly off the mark and if you fancy large slabs of red meat, this is your place. The open front keeps the air fresh, and wood décor brings a taste of the Wild West to the place.

Bang Bar II (Th Patak East; Map p683; 🕙 noon-midnight) Built from flotsam and jetsam collected on the beach, this chilled-out bar is perfect for sundowners. It features your standard brand of Rastafarian décor and a collection of surfboards. A sun-bleached tarpaulin provides shelter during monsoon downpours.

Getting There & Away

For details on transport to Karon, see p686.

KATA
กะตะ

With a sunny disposition and an all around good-time vibe, unpretentious Kata is our pick for Phuket's best beach. Don't confuse unpretentious with not being prestigious: Kata boasts some of the isle's most swank hotels and gourmet restaurants. Plus with the only sets of waves in Thailand, Kata has a burgeoning surf culture (the surfing is best from April to November). Fly-by-night board shops have set-up on the beach, and the ocean is littered with surf virgins and pros trying to hang ten.

The beach here is actually divided into two distinct parts, separated by a rocky headland: Hat Kata Yai to the north and Hat Kata Noi to the south. Both offer plenty of soft, golden sand and attract a more bohemian crowd than neighbouring Karon.

Orientation & Information

The main commercial street of Th Thai Na is perpendicular to the shore and has most of the restaurants and shops, along with some cheaper places to stay. Expats have moved into the area in large numbers, but Scandinavians appear to be holding most of the best cards and you won't get five paces without passing a 'Viking' this or a 'Horned Helmet' that.

The second main part of town is concentrated behind Hat Kata Yai, around the Kata Beach Resort. Here you'll find more upmarket hotels and resorts, numerous restaurants and tailor shops, and hundreds of stalls and vendors

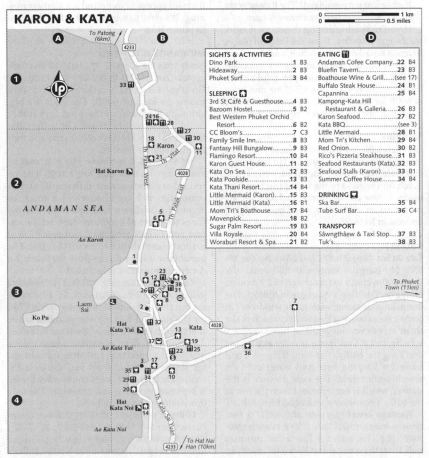

KARON & KATA

0 ———————— 1 km
0 ———————— 0.5 miles

To Patong (6km)

To Phuket Town (11km)

To Hat Nai Han (10km)

ANDAMAN SEA

Ao Karon

Hat Karon

Laem Sai

Ko Pu

Hat Kata Yai

Ao Kata Yai

Hat Kata Noi

Ao Kata Noi

Karon

Kata

SIGHTS & ACTIVITIES
Dino Park..........................1 B3
Hideaway..........................2 B3
Phuket Surf.......................3 B4

SLEEPING
3rd St Café & Guesthouse.....4 B3
Bazoom Hostel....................5 B2
Best Western Phuket Orchid
    Resort...........................6 B2
CC Bloom's.........................7 C3
Family Smile Inn.................8 B3
Fantasy Hill Bungalow.........9 B3
Flamingo Resort................10 B4
Karon Guest House............11 B2
Kata On Sea.....................12 B3
Kata Poolside...................13 B3
Kata Thani Resort..............14 B4
Little Mermaid (Karon).......15 B3
Little Mermaid (Kata).........16 B1
Mom Tri's Boathouse..........17 B4
Movenpick........................18 B2
Sugar Palm Resort.............19 B3
Villa Royale......................20 B4
Woraburi Resort & Spa.......21 B2

EATING
Andaman Cofee Company...22 B4
Bluefin Tavern...................23 B3
Boathouse Wine & Grill......(see 17)
Buffalo Steak House............24 B1
Capannina........................25 B4
Kampong-Kata Hill
    Restaurant & Galleria.......26 B3
Karon Seafood..................27 B3
Kata BBQ.........................(see 3)
Little Mermaid..................28 B1
Mom Tri's Kitchen..............29 B4
Red Onion........................30 B2
Rico's Pizzeria Steakhouse...31 B3
Seafood Restaurants (Kata).32 B3
Seafood Stalls (Karon).......33 B1
Summer Coffee House.........34 B4

DRINKING
Ska Bar..........................35 B4
Tube Surf Bar...................36 C4

TRANSPORT
Sǎwngthǎew & Taxi Stop....37 B3
Tuk's..............................38 B3

ANDAMAN COAST

selling fake Chanel sunglasses, Louis Vuitton wallets and pirated DVDs. This is our favourite part of Kata and it's very easy to spend an entire afternoon browsing the side streets.

Both places have numerous ATMs to grab cash.

Activities

If you feel like firing up the stove, **Mom Tri's Boathouse** (☎ 0 7633 0015; www.boathousephuket.com; Th Patak West) offers a popular two-day Thai cooking class each weekend for 3200B per person; one-day courses are 2000B. The first day focuses on appetisers and salads, the second on mains and desserts. A total of 10 recipes are taught during the half-day sessions, and you get to eat your creation.

Rather just get pampered? The **Hideaway spa** (Map p683; ☎ 0 7633 0914) has a branch here.

If you're visiting during the rainy season, we'd suggest **surfing**. There are loads of places to rent a board on Kata's beach, and the waves are often gentle enough for beginners (avoid red flag days when there are powerful undertows). Board rental costs 150B for one hour or 600B for the whole day. Lessons can also be arranged. For more on surfing, see opposite.

Sleeping

In general, the less expensive places tend to be off the beach between Kata Yai (to the north) and Kata Noi (to the south) or well off the beach on the road to the island interior. The places below are recommended, but are by no means an exhaustive list of good lodging options in Kata.

BUDGET

Kata On Sea (Map p683; ☎ 0 7633 0594; bungalows 300-800B; 🛏) Bargain hunters should make the steep 100m climb to this clutch of 29 modest bungalows dotting a quiet green hilltop. The bungalows are large with giant windows (in some cases covering two walls), which make them seem even bigger. The furniture isn't splashy, but it's adequate and the mattresses don't sag too badly. The mini fridge is a real score for keeping beer and water cold on scorching hot days. The only downer is the shower, which is not separated from the rest of the bath. The owner speaks good English.

Flamingo Resort (Map p683; ☎ 0 7633 0776; www .flamingo-resort.com; 5/19 Th Patak West; bungalows 600-1000B; 🛏) This resort is just a few minutes walk from the scene at Hat Kata Yai (a rarity in this price bracket). It offers a handful of large, pleasantly decorated bungalows on a hillside. Most have fridges, sizeable verandas and good views. There is a restaurant downstairs.

Little Mermaid (Map p683; ☎ 0 7633 0730; www .littlemermaidphuket.net; 94/23-25 Th Thai Na; r 465-665, bungalows 700-1500B; 🛏 🖵 🛏) Not to be confused with the other Little Mermaid in Karon, this guesthouse is an eclectic, brightly painted spot. Accommodation is of the mismatched furniture, slightly saggy mattress variety, although the bungalows facing the pool are slightly more upscale. Bathrooms in the main house can feel claustrophobic. Popular with male German tourists (and in many cases their female Thai escorts), it has a big pool and a raucous (though not sleazy) party vibe that will appeal to some and send others running. It's next to a gym, if you feel the need to pump iron.

MIDRANGE & TOP END

Family Smile Inn (Map p683; ☎ 0 7633 9268; www.family innphuket.com; 147-151 Th Thai Na; r 1000-1500B; 🛏) Great value, especially in the low season when rooms go for just 600B. The beds are big, although the mattresses aren't as firm as they could be and the sheets are a little thin. But the multistorey hotel is void of sand and feels comfortable and secure.

3rd St Café & Guesthouse (Map p683; www.3rd streetcafe.com; 100 3/4 Th Patak West; r 2000B) The six rooms are each styled differently at this personality-rich guesthouse with a knack for decorating. Walls are done up in muted earthy tones with lots of bright modern art. Furniture and fixings are classy, and make use of natural materials like rich red Thai silk. The guesthouse is just minutes from the beach. An American breakfast is included.

Kata Poolside (Map p683; ☎ 0 7633 3175; www.kata poolside.com; 36/38 Th Kata; r 2000-3800B; 🛏 🛏) Rooms are big and with lots of lounging space. Chill on the day bed to keep the starched white sheets from getting sandy. Beds are on raised dark-wood modern platforms whose colour matches the wood trim and other furnishings; tile floors are made from real stone. Bathrooms are large and when you shower the lip is high enough not to soak the room! The only downside was too-firm beds.

CC Bloom's (Map p683; ☎ 0 7633 3322; www.beaches thairesort.com; 84/21 Th Patak; r 3900-5000B; 🛏 🖵 🛏) This American-run gay-friendly boutique hotel (strangely named after Bette Midler's

ANDAMAN COAST

SURF'S UP, THAILAND

During the monsoon season (May to October), the rocky headland at the northern end of Hat Kata Noi makes a clean right point break and attracts numerous surfers. Although a long-time favourite beach destination, Thailand hasn't really been associated with surfing in the same way as other countries, such as South Africa, Australia, Hawaii and Indonesia. But the surf is definitely looking up for wave runners in Hat Kata in early September. That's when the annual surfing competition comes to town. The four-day event offers three types of contest for amateur surfers – shortboard, longboard and longboard paddling race. The entry fee is around 500B and if you think you've got the skills, you can register at www.phuketsurf.com, which also has info about the local surfing community. **Phuket Surf** (Map p683; ☎ 08 1002 2496; www.phuketsurf.com), on Hat Kata Yai's southern cove, offers surf lessons starting at 1500B, as well as board rentals. Look for it on the beach next to Kata BBQ.

Speaking of Hat Kata Yai, the main beach is a great place to catch beginner breaks on a long foam board (experienced surfers will have fun riding here as well, especially on big wave days). Phuket Surf has plenty of rentals for all levels, but if you don't see a board to your liking there are plenty of other vendors offering similar goods all along the beach. The southern cove is the best place to catch waves, but watch out for the gnarly rocks on the extreme southern edge.

---

character in the movie *Beaches*) has a fab location overlooking Kata. Stylish rooms are done up in creamy Indochina yellow with crimson silk panels draped from the ceiling. They are festooned with orchids and face out onto a small pool decorated with a waterfall. The layout is conducive to lounging poolside by day then curling up in bed with a Singha and a movie picked from the huge in-house library – DVD players are available free on request. If you tire of the isolation (it is a bit of a hike from the beach) a free shuttle makes multiple runs to the waves. Rooms go for as little as 2400B during the rainy season.

our pick **Sugar Palm Resort** (Map p683; ☎ 0 7628 4404; www.sugarpalmphuket.com; 20/10 Th Kata; r 1800-6100B; 🏊 🖳 🍴) One of Kata's newest boutique ventures, Sugar Palm is as sugary as its name and bound to become popular with trendsetters. The ultramod design is reminiscent of Miami Art Deco with glittery purple panels and clean white lines centred about a U-shaped swimming pool with Jacuzzi and swim-up bar. All rooms come with private balconies overlooking the pool and the sweetest ones have direct access. Digs are spacious with hip designs and feature very sleepable mattresses.

Kata Thani Resort (Map p683; ☎ 0 7633 0124; www.katathani.com; 14 Th Kata Noi; r US$140-220; 🏊 🍴) An enormous, three-storey, 530-room resort that commands most of the beach at Kata Noi, this place sits on one of the choicest bits of beach anywhere along Karon or Kata. Rooms are upmarket and stylish, and the grounds are beautifully landscaped with tennis courts,

four swimming pools, a fitness centre and six restaurants.

Mom Tri's Boathouse (☎ 0 7633 0015; www.theboathousephuket.com; 2/2 Th Patak West; r 4000-7500B; 🏊 🍴) For Thai politicos, pop stars, artists and celebrity authors, the intimate boutique Boathouse is still the only place to stay on Phuket. Rooms were remodelled after the tsunami and are spacious, gorgeous affairs, some sporting large breezy verandas. Critics complain the Boathouse is a bit stiff-lipped old-fashioned for this century, but no one can deny that the main reason to sleep at the Boathouse is for the food. The three on-site restaurants are the best on the island.

Villa Royale (Map p683; ☎ 0 7633 3568; www.villaroyalephuket.com; ste incl breakfast from 11,500B; 🏊 🖳 🍴) Tucked away in a secluded Kata Noi location with the grandest of views, Villa Royale (the newest venture by the folks from the Boathouse) opened in 2006 to nearly instant acclaim. The romantic place with fabulous food offers beautiful rooms straight out of the pages of *Architectural Digest*. Guiltless pleasures include an attached spa and a saltwater pool, if you deign to a tamer version of the real thing – which is just steps away.

Eating

If none of the places listed here sound appealing, there are plenty more eateries on Th Thai Na, which has more than its share of Italian and Scandinavian restaurants. A cluster of affordable, casual seafood restaurants can be found on Th Patak West near the shore,

though unfortunately they're not within view of the sea.

Summer Coffee House (Map p683; ☎ 0 7628 4584; Th Patak West; cakes 50B; ☺ breakfast, lunch & dinner) Lounge music, cappuccinos, wi-fi – this is where passing media types come to download new tracks for their iPod and get their daily vanilla frappucino lift. The menu is pretty much limited to cakes and coffee, but it does serve the biggest croissants on the planet.

Andaman Coffee Company (Map p683; ☎ 0 7628 5180; dishes 40 80B; ☺ breakfast, lunch & dinner; ▣) The frozen coffee concoctions are delish at this Western-style coffeeshop with muted colours and lots of computers. Buy a cup of Java and get 15 minutes of free internet access – not a bad deal. It has a big selection of espresso drinks and tea as well as light snacks. The sidewalk seating is good for people watching.

Kata BBQ (Map p683; ☎ 0 7633 0989; dishes 60-150B; ☺ lunch & dinner) The terrace is a prime spot to watch the surfers play or just chill out with a cocktail from the loooooonnnnggg list – the place even has pastis! The seafood is what to order. It's prepared in every manner you can imagine – from crab with pineapple and ginger to barbecue shrimp. We loved the fried squid. Spaghetti, pizza, egg breakfasts and baguette sandwiches round out the menu.

Bluefin Tavern (Map p683; ☎ 0 7633 0856; dishes 40-165B; ☺ 3-11pm) A popular restaurant and bar, it grills up surprisingly palatable Tex-Mex like quesadillas and tacos along with pizza, burgers, steak and, of course, Thai food. Come for dinner, or just for a margarita – either way the small front deck is nice and laid-back.

Kampong-Kata Hill Restaurant & Galleria (Map p683; ☎ 0 7633 0103; Th Patak West; dishes 80-260B; ☺ lunch & dinner) Choc-a-block with Thai antiques and serving some fabulous local dishes, this excellent little eatery is up a long stairway. Finding good, well-priced Thai food in these parts can be a bit of a headache – this is a great place to start.

Rico's Pizzeria Steakhouse (Map p683; www.ricos.se; Th Thai Na; mains 90-300B; ☺ lunch & dinner) The smartest kid on the Th Thai Na block features fine New Zealand steaks, pizzas and a huge collection of black-and-white film star snaps (very 1980s). Everything, from the door handles to the sparkling condiment trays, is spotless and – guess what? – the chefs are Scandinavian.

Capannina (Map p683; dishes 150-350B; ☺ lunch & dinner) We just couldn't get enough of this Italian eatery tucked away amid the venues. With warm red accents, an open kitchen and a wood-fired oven, Capannina has intimate ambience and delicious food. Garlic- and chilli-infused pasta dishes, tender grilled calamari in a rich marinara and homemade stuffed ravioli are just a few of the treats. Wash it all down with a glass of rough country grappa.

Mom Tri's Kitchen (Map p683; ☎ 0 7633 0015; Th Kata Noi; dishes 180-500B; ☺ lunch & dinner) Another link in the Boathouse chain, this delightful restaurant offers more of the same. Fine wines and *haute cuisine* are served in gorgeous grounds and the atmosphere is a little less formal than its slightly stuffier cousin.

our pick **Boathouse Wine & Grill** (Map p683; ☎ 0 7633 0015; www.boathousephuket.com; Th Patak West; mains 450-850B; ☺ lunch & dinner) The perfect place to wow a fussy date, the Boathouse is the pick of the bunch for most local foodies. The atmosphere can be a little stuffy – this is the closest Phuket gets to old-school dining – but the food is fabulous, the wine list is expansive and the sea views are sublime.

Drinking

Kata's nightlife tends to be pretty mellow.

The super-mellow Ska Bar, tucked into the rocks at Kata's southernmost cove, is our choice for oceanside sundowners. It's also one of the coolest bars we've ever seen, literally built around, and seemingly intertwined with, the trunk of a sturdy old tree. It's a very simple spot with ramshackle stools and delicious piña coladas. Pot-leaf flags, Reggae music and dreadlocked Thai bartenders all add to Ska's funky Rasta vibe. It stays open late.

Tube Surf Bar (Map p687; ☎ 0 7285 4718; dishes from 30B) This surf bar gets going on Tuesday and Friday nights (in particular), when surf videos are screened and all-you-can-eat barbecues (150B) or chilli nights (100B for a bottomless bowl of chilli, plus a beer) take place. If you're looking to find out more about local surfing culture, this is where to head. It's sometimes closed on seemingly random nights. It's a bit difficult to find – if you get lost ask for directions (during the day) from Phuket Surf (which runs the Tube), next to the Ska Bar.

Getting There & Around

Săwngthăew and buses to both Kata and Karon (per person 50B) leave frequently from the Th Ranong market in Phuket from 7am to 5pm. The main săwngthăew stop is in front of Kata Beach Resort.

Taxis from Kata go to Phuket Town (300B), Patong (250B) and Karon (150B).

Motorcycle rentals are available at **Tuk's** (☎ 0 7628 4049) for 300B.

NAI HAN
ในหาน

Rimming a picturesque bay only a few kilometres south of Kata, this beach at the near southern tip of the island is less developed than neighbouring strips of sand. This is partly due to topography, but also to the presence of **Samnak Song Nai Han**, a monastic centre in the middle of the beach that claims most of the beachfront land. The Meridien resort occupies other prime seaview property not owned by the monks, so to make up for the lack of saleable beachfront, developers started cutting away the forest on the hillsides overlooking the beach. Recently, however, the development seems to have come to a halt. This means that Nai Han is usually one of the least crowded beaches on the southern part of the island.

Hat Nai Han can be a dangerous place to swim in the monsoon season (May to October), but it really varies according to daily or weekly weather changes – look for the red flag, which means dangerous swimming conditions. Beach chairs and umbrellas can be rented for 60B.

Sleeping & Eating

Except for the Le Royal Meridien, there's not much accommodation with views of the beach.

Nai Harn Garden Resort (Map p687; ☎ 0 7628 8319; www.naiharngardenresort.com; 15/12 Muu 1 Th Viset; r 800-2000B; 🅿 🖳 🛋) Back from the beach, on the far side of the reservoir, this resort offers a range of bungalows and villas in a spacious garden setting. The atmosphere is a little suburban cul-de-sac, but standards are high, there are plenty of masseuses at hand – massage is something of a hotel speciality – and prices are reasonable.

Sabana (Map p687; ☎ 0 7628 9327; www.sabana-resort.com; 14/53 Muu 1 Th Viset; r 2000-6500B; 🅿 🖳 🛋) If Le Meridien's full, Sabana is a great back up option. The décor is all primary colours and Thai motifs, and, while the cheaper rooms are a little ordinary, the pricier 'Thai Sala' options are beautifully designed. There's also an on-site spa.

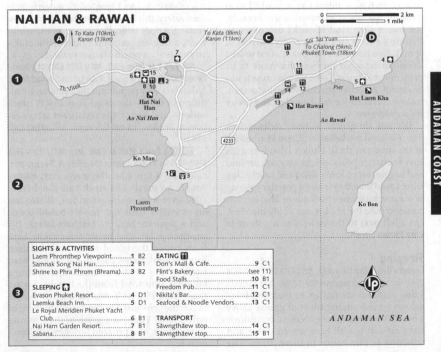

NAI HAN & RAWAI

ANDAMAN SEA

ANDAMAN COAST

Le Royal Meridien Phuket Yacht Club (Map p687; ☎ 0 7638 0200; www.lemeridien.com; 23/3 Muu 1 Th Viset; r US$190-500; ❄ ☐ ☎) There's not a yacht in sight, but Le Meridien's signature Phuket property is grand indeed. Rooms feature fabulously large terraces and stunning bay views, and there's every creature comfort you can imagine somewhere on site. If you can cadge one of the low-season discounts, it really is excellent value.

Le Meridien's restaurants cater for expensive appetites, while a handful of beachside food stalls will fill you up for a pittance.

Getting There & Away

Nai Han is 18km from Phuket Town and a săwngthǎew (leaving from the intersection of Phuket Town's Th Krung Thep and the fountain circle) costs 50B per person. Túk-túk charters are about 250B one way. From Nai Han to Rawai, expect to pay about 25B in a túk-túk.

RAWAI

ราไวย์

Okay, we won't lie, there's really no reason to stay on Rawai unless you're booked in at Evason, spa resort extraordinaire. Frankly, the beach here kind of sucks compared to Patong or Kata (it can be really narrow at spots). Rawai was one of Phuket's first tourist developments, but this was due more to its proximity to Phuket Town than because it was beautiful. As better beaches were discovered, tourist travel to Rawai dwindled and today it's a quiet spot.

It's not altogether without redemption. There is good **snorkelling** off Laem Phromthep at the southern tip of Phuket Island, and it's easy to charter boats (prices vary, ask around and haggle) for offshore **diving** and snorkelling trips. **Laem Phromthep** is also a popular viewing point at sunset, when busloads of Thai tourists come to pose for photos and enjoy the view. On a hill next to the viewpoint is a **shrine to Phra Phrom** (Brahma).

Sleeping

Laemka Beach Inn (Map p687; ☎ 0 7638 1305; fax 0 7628 8547; Hat Laem Ka; bungalows 500-1200B; ❄) Good-value accommodation in 30 thatched bungalows spread among coconut groves above a beach. Only the more expensive bungalows have air-con but all have screen doors and windows (a rare bonus in these parts). The

shoreline along the rounded cape is an interesting mix of clean sand and large boulders, with good swimming. Many speedboats depart from here for nearby islands, and it's a favourite local picnic spot.

Evason Phuket Resort (Map p687; ☎ 0 7638 1010; www.sixsenses.com; 100 Th Vised; r 4500-38,000B; ❄ ☐ ☎) Hip, smartly designed and offering copious amounts of luxury, Evason appeals to rock stars and moneyed media types. Expect beautiful people tapping away at their wireless gadgetry beside the infinity pool and immaculately turned-out staff. For a review of its spa see p665.

Eating & Drinking

Besides the restaurants attached to the resorts in Rawai, there are oodles of seafood and noodle vendors along the roadside near Hat Rawai. The following listings are sit-down restaurants.

Flint's Bakery (Map p687; ☎ 0 7628 9210; Hat Rawai; ☽ breakfast, lunch & dinner) Cakes, coffees and pizzas are on offer at this little bakery. It's right next door to Freedom Pub.

Freedom Pub (Map p687; ☎ 0 7628 7402; Hat Rawai; dishes 80-200B; ☽ lunch & dinner) More watering hole than eatery, this Rawai boozer features outdoor seating, a pool table, live music on the weekends, a free barbecue on Friday night and – strangely – an on-site tattoo parlour.

Nikita's Bar (Map p687; ☎ 0 7628 8703; Hat Rawai; dishes 80-225B) With quirky décor and good food, Nikita's is very popular in the evening. In addition to food – the usual Thai and Western melee – and booze, the restaurant serves espresso drinks. It's on the main road through town.

ourpick Don's Mall & Cafe (Map p687; ☎ 0 7638 3100; 48-5 Soi Sai Yuan; dishes 100-650B) A Texan-run café with a fun vibe, the menu stars hearty American meals like steak and ribs barbecued over a mesquite-wood fire. It also has an extensive wine list, freshly baked goods and a separate bar, the **Longhorn Saloon**. It's super popular, and many folks come here from round the island to eat and socialise. From Rawai, drive past the Wall and turn right at the next two main intersections (about 3.4km total from the beach). To get there from Phuket Town (and many people make the trip just for the food), turn right onto Th Sai Yuan, just south of the Chalong roundabout, and proceed for 3km; you can't miss it.

Getting There & Away

Rawai is about 18km from Phuket Town and getting there costs 50B by săwngthăew from Phuket's fountain circle at Th Ranong. Túk-túk charters cost at least 250B from Phuket Town. The túk-túk trip from Rawai to Nai Han should be around 25B.

Long-tail boats are available for charter right along Hat Rawai – a charter to Ko Phi Phi costs 3500B (maximum six passengers).

KO YAO

เกาะยาว

Ko Yao Yai (Big Long Island) and Ko Yao Noi (Little Long Island) are actually part of the Ao Phang-Nga Marine National Park, but are more easily accessible from Phuket. Together they encompass 137 sq km of forest, beach and rocky headland with views of the surrounding karst formations characteristic of Ao Phang-Nga.

In spite of being smaller, **Ko Yao Noi** is the main population centre of the two. Fishing as well as coconut, rice and rubber cultivation sustain the locals. **Hat Pa Sai** and **Hat Tha Khao**, both on Yao Noi, are the best beaches. **Ta Khai**, the largest settlement on the island, is a subdistrict seat and a source of minimal supplies.

Ko Yao Yai is more isolated and rustic than its smaller sister island. Please remember to respect the Muslim culture on both islands by wearing modest clothing outside beach areas.

Boat trips to neighbouring islands, bird-nest caves and *chao náam* funeral caves are possible. **Ko Bele**, a small island east of the twin Ko Yao, features a large tidal lagoon, three white-sand beaches, and easily accessible caves and coral reefs.

Sleeping

Ko Yao Noi has only a handful of places to stay.

Sabai Corner Bungalow (☎ 0 1892 7827; bungalows 350-550B) Sturdy thatch-and-wood bungalows with small verandas are offered here. The restaurant is pretty good and comes with fabulous views.

Tha Khao Bungalow (☎ 0 1676 7726; bungalows 500-1200B) On Hat Tha Khao, this small place features five solid thatch-and-wood bungalows, including two family-size ones (with three bedrooms). The small restaurant does tasty food and also rents out bicycles and kayaks – a recommended way to explore the area.

DETOUR: ISLANDS AROUND PHUKET

There are several islands off the coast of Phuket that make for quieter, more romantic getaways. **Ko Heh** (also known as Coral Island and sometimes spelled Ko Hae) is a few kilometres south of Ao Chalong. It's a good spot for diving and snorkelling (the coral is beautiful) if you don't plan on going further out to sea, although jet skis and other pleasure craft can be an annoyance. The island gets lots of day-trippers from Phuket, but at night it's pretty quiet. **Coral Island Resort** (☎ 0 7628 1060; fax 0 7638 1957; coral.island.resort@phuket.com; bungalows 1500-3000B; 🛠 🐷) is about the only place to stay on the island. Most of the 64 concrete bungalows are arranged around the swimming pool, but you can pay extra for a seaside cabin. There's a pool and karaoke lounge, and cable TV in the lobby (in case you can't live without your daily dose of CNN International).

Southeast of Laem Phanwa you'll stumble across the similar, but smaller, **Ko Mai Thon**. Again, there is only one place to stay, and it's a whopper. **Maiton Resort** (☎ 0 7621 4954; fax 0 7621 4959; maiton@phuket.com; bungalows 2800-4000B; 🛠 🖳 🐷) offers semi-luxurious hillside or beachside bungalows, two pools (indoor and outdoor), a sauna, fitness centre, tennis court and five restaurants. This is the kind of self-contained place that could be anywhere, and lacks charisma.

Ko Raya Yai and **Ko Raya Noi**, about 1½ hours south of Phuket by boat, are also known as Ko Racha Yai/Noi. They are highly favoured by divers and snorkellers for their hard coral reefs, which are found in both shallow and deep waters, making it a good area for both novices and pros. Accommodation is available on both islands.

Most people use travel agencies in Phuket Town to get to these islands. If you want to go it alone, boats leave Ao Chalong and Hat Rawai for Ko Heh; the trip takes 30 minutes and costs 80B. You can also charter a long-tail boat or speedboat from Rawai or Ao Chalong for 600B to 1500B.

Songserm Travel (☎ 0 7622 2570) runs passenger boats to Ko Raya Yai from Phuket Town port every morning. The trip takes 30 minutes and costs 350B one way or 750B return. **Pal Travel Service** (☎ 0 7634 4920) runs a similar service. Both companies suspend service from May to October.

ANDAMAN COAST

Long Beach Village (☎ 0 7659 7472; bungalows 500-1500B; ⊠) The 40 fan and air-con bungalows are typical of Thai beach bungalows (think wooden walls, creaky beds, wooden nightstands and slightly grungy baths), but the grounds are lush and tropical. Plus it feels very friendly.

Koyao Island Resort (☎ 0 1606 1517; www.koyao.com; villas from 4000B; ⊠) With some of the most glamorous beds on the island, this outfit features slick service, luxurious villas and a fine line of sundowners at the bar. If you're fed up with the stunning views (unlikely), you can always go and watch satellite TV and crank up the air-con.

On Ko Yao Yai there are three places to stay that have very similar, basic wood-and-thatch fan bungalows:

Halawee Bungalows (☎ 0 1607 3648; bungalows 400B)
Thiw Son (☎ 0 1956 7582; bungalows 350-500B)
Long Island Family Bungalows (☎ 0 1979 2273; bungalows 500B)

HOMESTAY
Koh Yao Noi Eco-Tourism Club (☎ 0 7659 7409, 0 1089 5413; www.koh-yao-noi-eco-tourism-club.com), in partnership with Responsible Ecological Social Tours Project (REST), a Bangkok-based NGO, has developed a model ecotourism project on the Muslim fishing island of Ko Yao Noi. Participants stay with a host family and learn about small-scale fishing methods and local ecology. With postcard views of Ao Phang Nga's limestone mountains, the island is poised between a traditional way of life and a mushrooming tourist industry. Through the homestay programme visitors can contribute to the island's economic development without undermining the village atmosphere. A night of accommodation costs 400B per person and includes meals. A 100B mandatory donation, towards a fund for helping preserve the island's environment, is also required.

Getting There & Around
Although both islands fall within the Phang-Nga Province boundaries, the easiest places to find boat transport are Phuket Town and Ao Leuk and Ao Nang (both in Krabi Province). In Phuket, catch a săwngthăew from in front of the day market to Bang Rong (on Ao Po) for 50B. From the public pier there are up to four boats (50B, one hour) at 11am, noon, 2.30pm and 5pm. Between departures or after

hours you can charter a long-tail boat for about 1000B one way.

To go from Ko Yao Noi to Ko Yao Yai, catch a shuttle boat from Tha Manaw (20B, 15 minutes). On the islands, túk-túk provide transport for about 50B.

KRABI PROVINCE

Krabi is the most beautiful province in Thailand. It's the kind of place that comes to mind when you're daydreaming about paradise. A fairytale creation of dramatic giant karst formations juxtaposed, and sometimes enveloped, by a warm emerald silk sea.

Krabi is always up for a good adventure, and it attracts a mixed bag of travellers. Not-to-be-missed destinations in Krabi include Ko Phi Phi and Railay. The latter boasts some of the world's best rock climbing and our favourite beach in all of Thailand.

December to March are the best times to visit and hotels and bungalows tend to fill up during these months. During the rainy season (June to November), accommodation prices

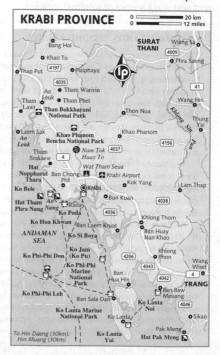

can drop by 50 percent, places are a lot less crowded and you may luck out with windows of decent weather – it usually rains for four or five days and then you get two or three absolutely gorgeous days.

Along with coastal beaches, Krabi has over 150 attractive islands. Once the favourite hide-outs of Asian pirates, today these islands offer excellent recreational opportunities. Many of the islands belong to Hat Noppharat Thara/ Ko Phi Phi Marine National Park, including Ko Phi Phi Don (probably the most popular island in this region).

The interior of the province, noted for its tropical forests and the Phanom Bencha mountain range, has barely been explored.

KRABI

กระบี่

pop 29,300

Most travellers just breeze through Krabi (gra-bee), using the provincial capital as a jumping-off point for wonderful surrounding destinations – Ko Lanta to the south, Ko Phi Phi to the southwest and Ao Nang, Railay and Tham Phra Nang to the west. Although Krabi isn't high on many travellers' priority lists, some folks are charmed enough by the friendly people, delicious food and lack of tourists to want to stay the night.

The town sits on the western bank of the Mae Nam Krabi, about 1000km from Bangkok and 180km from Phuket. The eastern bank of the river is covered in dense mangroves and north of town are the twin limestone massifs of Khao Khanap Nam, which emerge from the water like breaching whales. The population is mainly Taoist-Confucianism and Muslim, and Krabi is an important transport hub for ferries to the islands along the coast.

Orientation & Information

Th Utarakit is the main road into and out of Krabi and most places of interest are on the *soi* (lanes) that branch off it. Ferries to Ko Phi Phi and Ko Lanta leave from a passenger jetty at Khlong Chilat, about 5km north of town. Krabi's bus terminal is 4km north of the centre at Talat Kao, near the junction of Th Utarakit and the main Trang to Phang-Nga road.

Many Krabi budget travel agencies and restaurants offer internet access for 40B to 60B per hour. There are numerous banks and ATMs.

Pakaran (☎ 0 7561 1164; 151 Th Utarakit; ☺ 9am–8pm) Good place to stock up on second-hand books before

you head for the islands. Has a large selection in English and many European languages, as well as some quality handicrafts and antiques.

Immigration office (☎ 0 7561 1350; Th Chamai Anuson; ☺ 8.30am–4pm Mon–Fri) Handles visa extensions.

Krabi Hospital (☎ 0 7561 1210; Th Utarakit) It is 1km north of town.

Krabi You & I Travel (☎ 0 7883 6399; www.krabiinform ation.com; 181 Th Utarakit) Travel agency offering air, boat and bus tickets, tours and island-accommodation booking.

Sights & Activities

Krabi does activities better than sights. If you want to paddle, check out **Sea Kayak Krabi** (☎ 0 7563 0270; www.seakayak-krabi.com; 40 Th Ruen Rudee), which offers a wide variety of sea-kayaking tours, including to Ao Thalane (half-/full-day 700/1200B), which has looming sea cliffs; Ko Hong (full day 1500B), famed for its emerald lagoon; and Ban Bho Tho (full day 1500B), which has sea caves with 2000- to 3000-year-old cave paintings. All rates include guides, lunch, fruit and drinking water.

Reefwatch Worldwide (☎ 0 1979 0535; www.reef watchworldwide.com; Th Utarakit) is one of the few in-town dive shops and has two-dive packages to local islands (2600B) and to Phi Phi (3200B). It also runs Open Water courses (11,900B).

Krabi town also has two wonderful spas, worth visiting if you're looking for a luxurious treatment with a slightly less than luxurious price tag. The **Adora Spa** (☎ 0 7562 0028) at the posh Krabi Maritime Park & Spa Resort offers its signature Aromatic Adora Massage (a Thai massage blend that costs 1500B for 60 minutes) in outdoor garden pavilions around a peaceful lake with mountain vistas.

The **Kantanwan Spa** (☎ 0 7562 3362; Th Maharat) is also good. Try its Coco scrub; the one-hour (1500B) treatment includes a herbal application to open pores followed by a stimulating aromatic body scrub.

Tours

Chen Phen Tour (☎ 0 7561 2004; Th Utarakit) and others offer bird-watching tours in the mangroves around Krabi for about 500B per boat per hour (early morning is best); alternatively, you can hire a boat at the main pier for around 300B per hour. Keep an eye out for fiddler crabs and mudskippers on the exposed mud.

Various companies offer day trips to Khlong Thom, about 45km southeast of Krabi on Hwy 4, taking in some nearby hot springs and freshwater pools. Expect to pay around 950B,

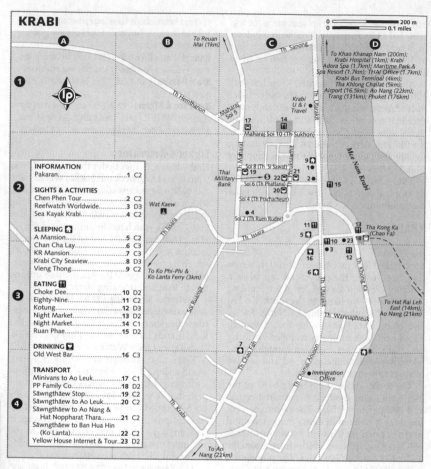

KRABI

including transport, lunch and beverages; bring a swimsuit and good walking shoes. Various other 'jungle tour' itineraries are available.

Sleeping

New guesthouses are appearing all over Krabi and most offer large, clean, tiled rooms with windows and shared bathrooms.

A Mansion (☎ 0 7563 0511; fax 0 7563 0513; 12/6 Th Chao Fah; r from 300B; ☒) Another friendly spot, this relative newcomer offers modern, clean and beautiful (if very pink) rooms, with TV. There's a café, bar and laundry nearby.

KR Mansion (☎ 0 7561 2761; krmansion@yahoo.com; 52/1 Th Chao Fah; r 280-450B; ☒ 🖳) There's a great funky rooftop beer garden with panoramic views over Krabi, just perfect for a sundowner.

The rooms in this bright-pink building are quite comfortable.

Chan Cha Lay (☎ 0 7562 0952; www.geocities.com /chan_cha_lay; 55 Th Utarakit; r 200-500B; ☒ 🖳) This place has very helpful staff, and its relaxing white and baby blue décor has an appealing Mediterranean feel. The tiled rooms are immaculate and the café has dainty trimmings, artistic photos and other bits of art on the walls. It's a great place to stay.

Vieng Thong (☎ 0 7562 0020; fax 0 7561 2525; 155 Th Utarakit; r 550-1000B; ☒ 🖳) Attracting a mixture of tourists and Thai businessmen, the Vieng Thong is an acceptable (but unremarkable) choice in this range. It has quite good facilities, however, including a tour desk and large restaurant. Rooms are simple but spacious

with private bathrooms, TVs and phones. Prices vary throughout the year.

Krabi City Seaview (☎ 0 7562 2885; krabicityseaview@ hotmail.com; 77/1 Th Khong Ka; r 600-1200B; ❄) The best midrange hotel in town, it offers beautifully modern rooms that are tastefully decorated; the better rooms are larger and sport views of the water. It's an excellent place in a quiet part of town, but still within walking distance of the centre. There is a very chilled lounge downstairs that faces out on the river.

Krabi Maritime Park & Spa Resort (☎ 0 7562 0028, ☎ Bangkok 0 2719 0034; www.maritimeparkandspa .com; r from 4500B; ❄ ▢ ▣) On lovely riverside grounds, this swanky hotel about 2km from Krabi town proper is the area's best bet. It sports a nightclub, stylish pool, fitness centre, spa and even a lake on which you can pedal swan-shaped boats. Rooms are classy and the balconies sport impressive views. Promotional rates of 1500B are usually available. There are free shuttle buses to Krabi town and Ao Nang, and shuttle boats to Railay. It may actually be smart to stay here, instead of Railay or Ao Nang, in the high season as it's better value for money and you can easily make day trips to the aforementioned beaches.

Eating & Drinking

Some might say the town's less than appetising, but they don't say the same about the food. Krabi offers a number of quality venues.

Night market (Th Khong Kha; meals 20-50B; ❄ dinner) Found near the Khong Kha pier, this is one of the best places to eat. The menus are in English but the food is authentic and excellent. Stalls here sell papaya salad, fried noodles, *tôm yam kûng* (prawn and lemon-grass soup with mushrooms), fresh seafood and all manner of things on satay sticks, plus sweet milky Thai desserts. There's a similar night market just north on Th Sukhon, near the intersection with Th Phruksauthit.

Choke Dee (cnr Th Chao Fah & Utarakit; dishes 45-70B; ❄ breakfast, lunch & dinner) There's a good backpacker vibe at Choke Dee, where you can dine on Thai and Western dishes at outdoor tables amid lots of potted plants.

Kotung (☎ 0 7561 1522; 36 Th Khong Kha; dishes 40-80B; ❄ dinner) Locals mob this excellent and reasonably priced Thai-Hainanese restaurant every evening for *tôm yam kûng*, *khâo man kài* (Hainan-style chicken with rice), *khâo múu daeng* (red pork with rice), *kǔaytǐaw* (wide rice noodles) and *bà-mìi* (wheat noo-

dles). It has a selection of fresh seafood laid out on ice so you can select your own dish.

Eighty Nine (Th Chao Fah; dishes 40-80B; ❄ breakfast, lunch & dinner; ▢) Most travellers end up in this pleasant eatery at the end of the evening to watch free video movies. The food is unusually good for this kind of place and there's a popular internet café.

Ruan Pae (☎ 0 7561 1956; Th Utarakit; dishes 60-150B; ❄ lunch & dinner) This old-fashioned floating restaurant is a fine place to watch the evening mist gather around the mangroves, though the atmosphere is sometimes better than the food. Mosquitoes can be a problem in the evening.

Old West Bar (Th Chao Fah; ❄ 1pm-2am) Bamboo and wood inside and out, this Wild West–themed bar booms music nightly and is one popular place for a tipple. There's a lively scene most nights and the cocktail list is long enough to keep you sampling for a while.

Getting There & Away

AIR

Thai Airways International (THAI; ☎ 0 7562 2439; Th Utarakit) has four daily flights between Bangkok and Krabi (one-way around 3500B, 1¼ hours). The THAI office is at the entrance to the Krabi Maritime Park & Spa.

BOAT

Boats to Ko Lanta and Ko Phi Phi leave from the new passenger pier at Khlong Chilat, about 3km southwest of Krabi. Travel agencies will arrange free transfers when you buy a boat ticket with them.

The largest boat operator is **PP Family Co** (☎ 0 7561 2463; Th Khong Kha), which has a ticket office right beside the pier in town. In the high season, there are boats to Ko Phi Phi (300B, 1½ hours) at 9am, 10.30am and 2.30pm. In the low season, boats run at 9am and 2.30pm only.

From September to May, there are boats to Ko Lanta (300B, 1½ hours) leaving Krabi at 10.30am and 1.30pm. These can also stop at Ko Jam (one hour), where long-tails will shuttle you to shore (though you'll pay the full 300B fare). During the off season, boats to Ko Lanta are replaced by air-con vans (250B, 2½ hours), which leave at 9am, 11am, 1pm and 4pm.

If you want to get to Railay, long-tail boats leave from Krabi's Khong Kha pier to Hat Rai Leh East from 7.45am to 6pm (150B, 45 minutes) – from Hat Rai Leh East it is only a five-minute walk along a paved path to the more appealing Hat Rai Leh West. The boatmen will

wait until they can fill a boat with 10 people before they leave; if you want go before then you can charter the whole boat for 1000B.

BUS
Government Buses
With fewer eager touts and guaranteed departure times, taking a government bus from the **Krabi bus terminal** (☎ 0 7561 1804; cnr Th Utarakit & Hwy 4) in nearby Talat Kao, about 4km from Krabi, is an altogether more relaxing option than taking a private bus. Air-con government buses leave for Bangkok (451B to 567B, 12 hours) at 7am, 4pm and 5.30pm. There's a very plush 24-seat VIP bus to Bangkok (850B) departing at 5.30pm daily. From Bangkok's Southern bus terminal, buses leave at 7.30am and between 7pm and 8pm.

Other services for regular, air-con government buses:

BUSES FROM KRABI

Destination	Price (B)	Duration (hr)	Frequency
Hat Yai	173-203	5	frequent
Nakhon Si Thammarat	89	3	frequent
Phang-Nga	60-78	2	hourly
Phuket	105-135	3½	hourly
Ranong	150-180	6	2 hourly
Surat Thani	103-130	2½	frequent
Trang	85-106	2	frequent

Minivan
Dozens of travel agencies in Krabi run air-con minivans and VIP buses to popular tourist centres throughout southern Thailand, but staff can be very pushy and you may end up crammed cheek to jowl with other backpackers. Destinations from Krabi:

MINIVANS FROM KRABI

Destination	Price (B)	Duration (hr)
Ao Leuk	40	1
Hat Yai	250	3
Ko Lanta	200-250	1½
Phuket	250	2-3
Satun	420	5
Trang	250	2

SĂWNGTHĂEW
Useful săwngthăew run from the bus station to central Krabi and on to Hat Noppharat Thara (40B), Ao Nang (40B) and the Shell Cemetery at Ao Nam Mao (50B). There are services from 6am to 6.30pm. In the high season there are less frequent services until 10pm for 70B. For Ao Leuk (50B, one hour) there are frequent săwngthăew from the corner of Th Phattana and Th Phruksauthit; the last service leaves at around 3pm. Occasional săwngthăew to Wat Tham Seua leave from opposite the 7-Eleven (on Th Maharat) and cost 25B.

Getting Around
Downtown Krabi is easy to explore on foot, but the bus terminal and airport are both a long way from the centre. A taxi from the airport to town will cost 500B. In the reverse direction, taxis or túk-túk cost 400B. Agencies in town can also arrange minivans to the airport for 150B. Săwngthăew between the bus terminal and downtown Krabi cost 20B.

CAR & MOTORCYCLE
Most of the travel agencies and guesthouses in town can rent you a Honda Dream motorcycle for around 150B per day. **Yellow House Internet & Tour** (☎ 0 7562 2809; 5 Th Chao Fa) hires out reliable bikes and provides helmets. A few of the travel agencies along Th Utarakit rent out small 4WDs for 1200B to 2000B per day.

MINIVAN
Minivans are booked through travel agencies in town. Prices can vary widely; shop around to get an idea. Some sample fares are Ao Leuk (40B, one hour), Hat Yai (200B, three hours), Ko Lanta (180B, 1½ hours), Trang (220B, two hours) and Satun (350B, five hours). Minivans leave when full.

SĂWNGTHĂEW
Services to Ban Hua Hin (the ferry pier for Ko Lanta) leave from the intersection of Th Phattana and Th Phruksauthit. They run fairly frequently, cost 40B and take 40 minutes.

AROUND KRABI
Wat Tham Seua
วัดถ้ำเสือ

Thailand has a lot of wats, but **Wat Tham Seua** (Tiger Cave Temple), in the forest 8km northeast of Krabi, is pretty unique. The main *wíhǎan* (hall) is built into a long, shallow lime-

stone cave. On either side of the cave, dozens of *kùtì* (monastic cells) are built into various cliffs and caves. You may see a troop of monkeys roaming the grounds.

The most shocking thing about Wat Tham Seua is found in the large main cave. Alongside large portraits of Ajahn Jamnien Silasettho, the wat's abbot who has allowed a rather obvious personality cult to develop around him, are close-up pictures of human entrails and internal organs, which are meant to remind guests of the impermanence of the body. Skulls and skeletons scattered around the grounds are meant to serve the same educational purpose.

Ajahn Jamnien, who is well known as a teacher of Vipassana (insight meditation) and Metta (loving kindness), is said to have been apprenticed at an early age to a blind lay priest and astrologer who practised folk medicine, and has been celibate his entire life. On the inside of his outer robe, and on an inner vest, hang scores of talismans presented to him by his followers – altogether they must weigh several kilograms, a weight Ajahn Jamnien bears to take on his followers' karma. Many young women come to Wat Tham Seua to practise as eight-precept nuns.

The best part of the temple grounds can be found in a little valley behind the ridge where the *bòt* (central sanctuary) is located. Walk beyond the main temple building keeping the cliff on your left and you'll come to a pair of steep stairways. The first leads to a truly arduous climb of over 1200 steps – some of them extremely steep – to the top of a 600m karst peak. The fit and fearless will be rewarded with a Buddha statue, a gilded stupa and great views of the surrounding area; on a clear day you can see well out to sea.

The second stairway, next to a large statue of Kuan Yin (the Mahayana Buddhist Goddess of Mercy), leads over a gap in the ridge and into a valley of tall trees and limestone caves. Enter the caves on your left and look for light switches on the walls – the network of caves is wired so that you can light your way, chamber by chamber, through the labyrinth until you rejoin the path on the other side.

If you go to the temple, please dress modestly: pants down to the ankles, shirts covering the shoulders and nothing too tight. Travellers in beachwear at Thai temples don't realise how offensive they are and how embarrassed they should be.

GETTING THERE & AWAY
Take a săwngthăew from Krabi's Th Utarakit to the Talat Kao junction for 20B, then change to any bus or săwngthăew heading east on Hwy 4 towards Trang – these can be rather infrequent, so if you can drive a motorcycle it may be best to rent one in Krabi for the 8km drive. Get off at the road on the left just past the small police station – if you're on the săwngthăew tell the driver 'Wat Tham Seua'. Motorcycle taxis hang out here and charge 25B to the wat, or you can walk 2km straight up the road. Private taxis to the wat from Krabi cost 250B each way; túk-túk charge about 200B.

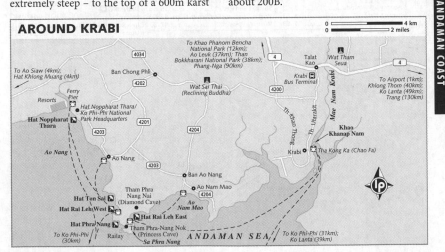

AO NANG

อ่าวนาง

pop 12,400

Ao Nang attracts the two-week jet-set pack to its showy resorts, which outshine the beaches. Sadly, the beach is nothing spectacular and the wide 'European'–style esplanade that tourism-boosters boast about is really just one large mall with souvenir shops, tailors and restaurants. Still, there are some spiffy midrange and top-end resorts with lovely garden pools, appealing enough to make the location irrelevant.

Ao Nang serves as the main jumping-off point for Railay, only a 20-minute long-tail ride away. For your money, Railay is a heaps nicer place to stay. Ao Nang is appealing, however, if you want to partake in popular island-hopping tours or sea-kayaking adventures, as most companies are based here. Plus, if having booze with meals is paramount, Ao Nang will do a better job quenching your thirst: many of Railay's resorts are Muslim owned and don't serve alcohol in their restaurants (although you can buy beer at the local store and bring it into restaurants that don't serve).

Orientation & Information

Ao Nang is not a very large place, and most services and hotels are crammed along either the main beach road or on short side streets. Basically, Hwy 4203 heads west into town, then runs north along the beach about 500m and then heads back inland for a bit before curving towards the coast again at Hat Noppharat Thara.

All the information offices on the strip are private tour agencies and most offer international calls and internet access for around 1B per minute. Several banks have ATMs and foreign-exchange windows on the main drag, open from 10am to 8pm daily. For more extensive services, including medical emergencies, you will need to head into Krabi.

Activities

Loads of activities are possible at Ao Nang, and children under 12 typically get a 50% discount. **Elephant trekking** is a popular activity in Ao Nang, and most tour operators arrange jungle excursions. Before you participate, however, make sure the elephants don't look abused.

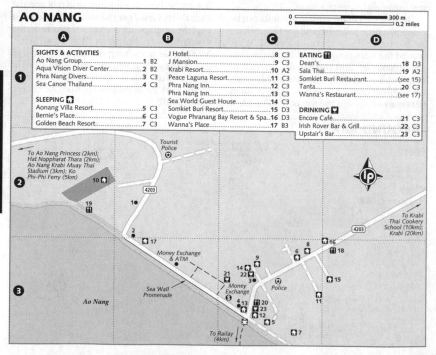

AO NANG

SIGHTS & ACTIVITIES		
Ao Nang Group	1	B2
Aqua Vision Diver Center	2	B2
Phra Nang Divers	3	C3
Sea Canoe Thailand	4	C3

SLEEPING		
Aonang Villa Resort	5	C3
Bernie's Place	6	C3
Golden Beach Resort	7	C3

J Hotel	8	C3
J Mansion	9	C3
Krabi Resort	10	A2
Peace Laguna Resort	11	C3
Phra Nang Inn	12	C3
Phra Nang Inn	13	C3
Sea World Guest House	14	C3
Somkiet Buri Resort	15	D3
Vogue Phranang Bay Resort & Spa	16	D3
Wanna's Place	17	B3

EATING		
Dean's	18	D3
Sala Thai	19	A2
Somkiet Buri Restaurant	(see 15)	
Tanta	20	C3
Wanna's Restaurant	(see 17)	

DRINKING		
Encore Café	21	C3
Irish Rover Bar & Grill	22	C3
Upstair's Bar	23	C3

KAYAKING

At least seven companies offer sea-kayaking tours to mangroves and islands around Ao Nang. Popular destinations include the lofty sea cliffs and wildlife-filled mangroves at Ao Thalane (half-/full-day 700/1000B), and to the sea caves and 2000- to 3000-year-old paintings at Ban Bho Tho (1000B) – the caves are also filled with layers of archaeological shell formations. All rates include lunch, fruit, drinking water, sea kayaks and guides. **Sea Canoe Thailand** (☎ 0 7569 5387) and **Ao Nang Group** (☎ 0 7563 7660/1) are two recommended companies.

DIVING & SNORKELLING

Ao Nang has numerous dive schools offering trips to dive sites at nearby Railay's Laem Phra Nang. It costs about 2200B for two dives. Ko Mae Urai is one of the more unique local dives, with two submarine tunnels lined with soft and hard corals. Other trips run further afield to sites around Ko Phi Phi or Hin Daeng and Hin Muang, southwest of Ko Lanta (2900B for two dives). A PADI Open Water course will set you back 13,000B to 15,000B. Reliable dive schools include **Phra Nang Divers** (☎ 0 7563 7064; www.pndivers.com) and **Aqua Vision Dive Center** (☎ 0 7563 7415; www.aqua-vision.net). Dive companies can also arrange snorkelling trips in the area.

Courses

About 10km from Ao Nang between Wat Sai Thai and Ao Nam Mao, **Krabi Thai Cookery School** (☎ 0 7569 5133; www.thaicookeryschool.net; 269 Muu 2, Ao Nang, Rte 4204) offers one-day Thai-cooking courses for 1000B; transfers are included in the price.

Tours

Any agency worth its salt can book you on one of the popular four-/five-island tours, which cost between 400B and 500B for a day trip. Several tour agencies offer tours to **Khlong Thom**, including visits to freshwater pools, hot springs and the **Wat Khlong Thom Museum**; the price per adult/child is 750/400B. So-called 'mystery tours' visit local snake farms, rural villages, crystal pools and rubber, pineapple, banana and papaya plantations and cost around 900/450B. Tour agencies also offer trips to attractions around Ao Phang-Nga and to a number of dubious animal shows around Ao Nang.

You can also arrange day tours to Ko Phi Phi on the **Ao Nang Princess** (per adult/child 1100/850B). The boat leaves from the Hat Noppharat Thara National Park headquarters at 9am and visits Bamboo Island, Phi Phi Don and Phi Phi Leh.

Sleeping

Ao Nang has become rather overdeveloped in recent years and the strip is creeping upmarket, though a few budget options are hanging on further back from the seafront. Prices at all these places drop by 50% during the low season.

BUDGET

There are several guesthouses that are tightly crammed together in a small alley. You'll find them just up from the beach at the eastern end of the strip.

Bernie's Place (☎ 0 7563 7093; r 200-600B) Bernie's will excite the penniless in high season – rooms max out at just 600B. You'll have to share a bathroom, but the rooms themselves are actually quite decent considering the price. They are big and bright with ceiling fans. The mattresses were ultrasoft, but we'll take saggy over claustrophobic any day. Bernie's was advertising heavily when we stopped by, and truthfully, pretty empty. But the big bar and backpacker priced buffets (all you can eat for 190B) mean it will likely have a travellers' vibe once word gets out.

our pick **J Mansion** (☎ 0 7563 7876, 7569 5128; j_mansion10@hotmail.com; r 350-1500B; ✷ 🖵) You know a place is doing something right when it's fully booked in low season. Rooms at J Mansion are big and spotless and let in lots of light; top-floor digs have sea views. The rooftop is the best asset. Head up here with a few beers at sunset and check out fabulous views across to Railay (constant breezes make it almost as cool as swimming in a pool). J Mansion also runs an honest, fairly priced travel agency and does day trips to Ko Phi Phi on its speedboat for 1400B (low season 1000B). These include a buffet lunch, guide, snorkelling and hotel pick-up.

J Hotel (☎ 0 7563 7878; j_hotelo@hotmail.com; r 350-1800B; ✷ 🖵) J Mansion's sister property (owned by the same friendly family), J Hotel is nearly as good as the original and just up the street. Rooms in an old shophouse are huge, atmospheric and endearingly shabby chic. Our mattresses were a bit too soft for our liking, but everything else is top-notch for the price.

MIDRANGE & TOP END

Most accommodation at Ao Nang falls into this bracket. The following places are recommended, but they are by no means your only options; there are dozens more.

Peace Laguna Resort (☎ 0 7563 7345; www.peace lagunaresort.com; r 1300-2200B, bungalows 2500-6000B; ✗ ☒) Looks a little like Eden. Sweet, modern cottages, some boasting polished ceramic floors, sit around a large lagoon on gorgeous, well-maintained grounds while a limestone cliff basks in the background. The priciest rooms (deluxe and superior cottages) have open-air Balinese style showers, in-room Jacuzzis and huge windows. You can score great deals in the off-season.

Somkiet Buri Resort (☎ 0 7563 7320; www.somkiet buri.com; r 2000-3000B; ✗ ☒) This place just might inspire you to slip into a yoga pose. The lush jungle grounds are filled with ferns and orchids, while lagoons, streams and meandering wooden walkways guide you to the 26 large and creatively designed rooms. A great swimming pool is set amid it all – balconies either face this pool or a peaceful pond. The service everywhere is first rate.

Phra Nang Inn (☎ 0 7563 7130; phranang@sun.phuket .ksc.co.th; r incl breakfast 2300-5500B; ✗ ☒) The beautiful interior décor – a unique bamboo theme with eclectic designs in shell and tilework – is Phra Nang's forte. There are two pools, and a second, similarly designed branch is across the road from the original.

Vogue Phranang Bay Resort & Spa (☎ 0 7563 7635; www.vogueresort.com; r 2100-6800B; ✗ ☒) Rooms have big windows – ask for one facing the sea – and mix tiles and wooden floors in a Zen architectural collage. Baths have separate showers (complete with doors – rare here). The only fault was the softness of the mattress. We really liked the grounds, however. They were peaceful with lots of jungle foliage. There is a big round swimming pool, with sea and sunset views.

Krabi Resort (☎ 0 7563 7030; in Bangkok 0 2208 9165; www.krabiresort.com; r & bungalows 4200-8900B; ✗ ☒) The original Ao Nang luxury resort is ageing gracefully, maintaining quality rooms and luxury bungalows on peaceful, landscaped grounds, some right near the beach. There is an on-site dive school, a restaurant and a bar.

Golden Beach Resort (☎ 0 7563 7870-74; www.krabi goldenbeach.com; r 4500-6000B, bungalows 6000-10,000B; ✗ ☒) This swanky modern resort is made up of large hotel blocks and stylish bunga-

lows arranged in a tidy garden around a big pool. The outdoor restaurant is lit up like a Christmas tree at night and hosts slightly cheesy live music (think electric keyboards and '80s covers).

Also recommended:

Sea World Guest House (☎ 0 7563 7388; seaworld999@ hotmail.com; r 500-1000B; ✗ ☐) A clean budget choice.

Wanna's Place (☎ 0 7563 7322; www.wannasplace.com; r 1875-1975B, bungalows 2290-2390B; ✗) It's quite popular.

Aonang Villa Resort (☎ 0 7563 7270; www.aonang villaresort.com; r 3400-7500B; ✗ ☒) A swank seaside joint.

Eating

At the western end of the beach is Soi Sunset, a narrow alley housing a number of identical seafood restaurants. They all have bamboo seating abutting the ocean, and model boats at the entrance showing off the day's catch. For other options, check out the restaurants listed below.

Wanna's Restaurant (dishes 45-110B; ☒ breakfast, lunch & dinner) Casual and inexpensive, it's worth stopping by for the variety of food on offer – everything from burgers to cheese selections to Swiss specialities, along with Thai cuisine and breakfast.

Somkiet Buri Restaurant (☎ 0 7563 7574; dishes 60-220B; ☒ breakfast, lunch & dinner) Located at the resort of the same name, it cooks up great Thai food and has very attentive service. The lush open-air dining pavilion is an added bonus.

Tanta (☎ 0 7563 7118; dishes 60-250B; ☒ lunch & dinner) The thin-crust pizza is delicious and not too doughy, the service is discreet (you get your meal but aren't pushed to order every 10 minutes). Tanta offers a great selection of Thai and international dishes. It's a popular modern place with a raised covered terrace and wood accents.

Sala Thai (dishes 60-300B; ☒ lunch & dinner) The best (and most popular) of a series of seafood restaurants on decks overlooking the beach. Crab, lobster, prawns and fish are on display for your selection. This restaurant – along with its neighbours – has a wonderfully romantic atmosphere with open wooden deck, sea breezes and great views.

Dean's Restaurant (dishes 80-300B; ☒ lunch & dinner) Locals recommend this restaurant for its mishmash menu of authentic northeastern Thai specialities along with Scandinavian and

European favourites. A low-key place with pleasant outdoor seating, Dean's makes its own bread and imports fresh meat.

Drinking

Have a drink; there's no shortage of bars in Ao Nang.

Upstair's Bar, a 2nd-floor bar next to Tanta, is woven around an old tree and feels like the kind of place hobbits would gather for a round of mojitos (which, coincidentally, are delicious here). It's a mellow place with pebble floors, wooden tables and for some reason a song list of American top 40 hits dubbed into Spanish. Peanuts are served with cocktails (picked off a long menu), and these go for just 100B during nightly happy hour.

Irish Rover Bar & Grill (☎ 0 7563 7607) Readers like this typical Irish pub specialising in draught Guinness and Kilkenny, along with brews like Singapore's Tiger and Thailand's high-alcohol content (but headache inducing) Chang. Sports fans will appreciate the telly broadcasting English footy matches and South African cricket. The place also features live music, tropical cocktails and pool tables.

Encore Café (☺ 4pm–2am in high season) Very popular with holidaying Thais, this live-music club is a fun and modern spot. It has pool tables and special themed evenings – from ladies' night to speed pool. Readers like the Tex-Mex pub food.

Aonang Krabi Muay Thai Stadium (☎ 0 7562 1042; admission 500B, ringside incl 1 beer 1000B) If you get tired of the beach-bars and video movies on the strip, this place has boisterous *muay thai* (Thai boxing) bouts on during multiple nights each week from 8.45pm. A free săwngthăew runs along the strip at Ao Nang, collecting punters before the bouts. You won't be able to miss knowing about upcoming events, as a truck outfitted with massive speakers roars up and down the streets announcing matches.

Getting There & Around

A ferry service to Ko Phi Phi runs year-round (350B, two hours, 9am) and includes a ride to/from the pier in nearby Hat Noppharat Thara.

Long-tail boats to the Hat Rai Leh area run daily in good weather and cost 50B. In bad weather take a săwngthăew to Ao Nam Mao (10B) and then a long-tail boat (30B), which runs even in choppy weather. Long-tail boats from Ao Nang to Krabi (50B) run only in high season.

A good way to get around is by săwngthăew. Destinations include Krabi (25B), Hat Noppharat Thara (15B) and Ao Nam Mao (15B). Look for them on the main road. Taxis from Ao Nang *to* Krabi airport cost 500B, but *from* the airport can cost up to 800B.

HAT NOPPHARAT THARA

หาดนพรัตน์ธารา

About 4km from Ao Nang, at the end of Rte 4203, this appealing casuarina-backed beach is the headquarters for Ko Phi Phi Marine National Park – a popular picnic spot on weekends. There is little development along this northern part of the coastline and exploring leisurely can be a welcome antidote to Ao Nang's mass tourism. There's a small visitors centre with displays on coral reefs and mangrove ecology, labelled in Thai and English.

Laughing Gecko (☎ 0 7569 5115; bungalows 100–500B) is one of several basic bungalow operators down a lane just before the national park office. It features uber-rustic rooms and an artistically decorated restaurant filled with chattering backpackers.

At the other end of the scale, **Sabai Resort** (☎ 0 7563 7791; www.sabairesort.com; r 1100-2600B; ✖ ⚟) is an upmarket Italian-run place with a very neat garden and solid little bungalows. There's a restaurant serving hearty, authentic Italian dishes cooked up by the mama of the family.

The **Government bungalows** (☎ 0 7563 7200; 2-6–person tents 300B, 2-person bungalows 600B, 6–8–person bungalows 1200B or per person 200B) at park headquarters are another option. Well maintained, they come with fans, bathrooms and mosquito nets on the windows. Tents are also available if you want the full primitive experience. A small canteen serves meals in the evenings.

Around the national park headquarters there are several restaurants serving snacks such as fried chicken and papaya salad.

Săwngthăew between Krabi and Ao Nang stop in Hat Noppharat Thara; the fare is 30B from either Krabi or Ao Nang. From October to May the *Ao Nang Princess* runs between Ko Phi Phi Marine National Park headquarters and Ko Phi Phi (300B, two hours). The boat leaves from the national park jetty at 9am, returning from Ko Phi Phi at 3.30pm. It also stops at Railay's Hat Rai Leh West. This boat can also be used for day trips to Ko Phi Phi. During the high season

there's also a direct boat to Phuket, leaving from the same pier at 3.30pm (450B).

RAILAY
ไร่เล

Hiding behind a layer of impenetrable cliffs, the gorgeous isthmus of Railay (also spelled Rai Leh) could easily serve as a fantasy cover for a Harlequin romance. It is possibly the most stunning beach location in all of Thailand, home to emerald silk water punctured by surreal limestone formations, honey-hued beaches and psychedelic sunsets. Railay may be just around the corner from Ao Nang and Krabi but it feels oceans away. Accessible only by boat, for now it remains a mellow place where serenity trumps chaos, there is no motorised transport and the beach is free of stalls selling knock-offs. Life is changing quickly. Construction was in full swing when we visited, and we doubt it will be long before Railay becomes Thailand's new superstar.

For adventure seekers Railay is best known for the hundreds of excellent rock-climbing routes up the surrounding cliffs. Loads of climbing shops cater to visitors wishing to scramble up the karsts, providing equipment rental and instruction for beginners and advanced climbers alike.

Information
The website www.railay.com has lots of information about Railay. There are now a couple of ATMs in Railay – an easy one is on the path between Hat Rai Leh West and Hat Rai Leh East. Several of the bigger resorts can also change cash and travellers cheques. Internet access is available at Sand Sea Resort, on Hat Rai Leh East, for a whopping 180B per hour, but the connections are unreliable; you may be better off checking your email in Ao Nang or Krabi town. For minor climbing injuries there's a small clinic at Railay Bay Resort on Hat Rai Leh West.

Sights
BEACHES
The more alluring beach is **Hat Rai Leh West**. It's also the best place to watch the sun go down (bring a camera, sunsets can be orgasmic). Tastefully designed midrange resorts line a long stretch of golden sand beach and dozens of long-tail boats make pick-ups and drop-offs from here to nearby Ao Nang. The water is perfect for swimming (even at low tide it's deep

enough), and we'd suggest floating on your back, staring up at the cliffs and contemplating life for a while – it's very Zen. At the southern end of the beach is the mighty Thaiwand Wall, a sheer limestone cliff offering some of the most challenging routes at Railay.

Boats from Krabi arrive at **Hat Rai Leh East**. The shallow, muddy beach is lined with mangroves and is not really suitable for swimming, but there are plenty of bungalows, bars and facilities onshore. It's only a short walk (less than five minutes) across the deer neck of Laem Phra Nang to Hat Rai Leh West, so don't feel you're trapped on this beach if you're arriving from Krabi.

Hat Ton Sai is the backpacker retreat and is reached by long-tail (either directly from Ao Nang or from Hat Rai Leh West) or by a sweaty 20-minute scramble over limestone rocks. While the beach here is mediocre, the dozens of cheap bungalow outfits and excellent access to some of the best climbs around keeps it lively with climbers and backpackers. There are occasional full-moon parties here during the high season.

Near the tip of the peninsula is **Hat Phra Nang**, a splendid strip of whispering white sand, framed by looming cliffs. If you just want to sunbathe, Hat Phra Nang is the spot to go – it's the most beautiful beach around and just a few minutes' walk from Hat Rai Leh East. The plush Rayavadee resort dominates the eastern end of the beach but the rest of Hat Phra Nang is untouched. A huge cavern punches straight through the cliffs at the western end of the beach, emerging halfway up Thaiwand Wall. Immediately offshore are Happy Island and Ko Rung Nok (Bird Nest Island), which offer some good snorkelling.

OTHER SIGHTS
At the eastern end of Hat Phra Nang is **Tham Phra Nang** (Princess Cave), an important shrine for local fishermen. Legend has it that a royal barge carrying an Indian princess foundered in a storm here during the 3rd century BC. The spirit of the drowned princess came to inhabit the cave, granting favours to all who came to pay respect. Local fishermen – Muslim and Buddhist – place carved wooden phalluses in the cave as offerings in the hope that the spirit will provide plenty of fish.

About halfway along the path from Hat Rai Leh East to Hat Phra Nang, a crude path leads up the jungle-cloaked cliff wall to a hidden

lagoon known as **Sa Phra Nang** (Holy Princess Pool). There's a dramatic viewpoint over the peninsula from the nearby cliff top, but be warned that this is a strenuous hike with some serious vertigo-inducing parts.

Above Hat Rai Leh East is another large cave called **Tham Phra Nang Nai** (Inner Princess Cave; adult/child 20/10B; ☻ 5am-8pm), also known as Diamond Cave. A wooden boardwalk leads through a series of illuminated caverns full of beautiful limestone formations, including a splendid 'stone waterfall' of sparkling gold-coloured quartz.

Activities
ROCK CLIMBING
With nearly 700 bolted routes and unparalleled cliff-top vistas, it's no surprise these dramatic rock faces are among the top climbing spots in the world. There are routes here ascending to the roofs of massive caverns and following cascades of stalactites up 300m-high cliffs. Climbing options are so plentiful, ranging from beginner routes to challenging advanced climbs, that you could spend months climbing and exploring – and many people do.

Most climbers start off at **Muay Thai Wall** and **One, Two, Three Wall**, at the southern end of Hat Rai Leh East, which have at least 40 routes graded from 4b to 8b on the French system. The mighty **Thaiwand Wall**, a sheer limestone cliff, sits at the southern end of Hat Rai Leh West and has some of the most challenging climbing routes. For a list of some of the best climbs here see the boxed text, below.

The going rate for climbing courses is 800B to 1000B for a half-day and 1500B to 2000B for a full day. Three-day courses (5000B to 6000B) involve some lead-climbing (where you clip into bolts on the rock face as you ascend) as well as multipitch routes. Experienced climbers can hire lead kits from any of the climbing schools for 600/1000B for a half-/full day – the standard kit consists of a 60m rope, two climbing harnesses, two pairs of rock boots, a belaying device and 12 quickdraws. You could consider bringing your own climbing boots and a collection of loose slings, nuts and cams to provide extra protection on thinly bolted routes. If you leave anything at home, all the climbing schools sell imported climbing gear.

Several locally published books detail climbs in the area, but the *Thailand Rock Climbing Guidebook* (800B), published by a local climbing school called **Rock Shop** (☎ 0 1978 3023; Hat Ton Sai), is one of the more popular guides. The book focuses on Railay and has great sketches of each climbing route. There are at least six other climbing shops at Railay – when choosing which to go with, the best thing to do is take a walk around and find one that appeals to you.

Hot Rock (☎ 0 7562 1771; www.railayadventure.com; Hat Rai Leh West) is one school with a good reputation and is run by friendly Luang, one of the granddaddies of Railay climbing, and his Swedish wife Saralisa. Luang arrived in the area in the 1980s, before there was much of a scene. He lived for a while in a cave he reached by climbing, before descending back onto the

---

TOP FIVE CLIMBS

With 700 climbs to choose from, picking a few of the best ones is no easy task – here's a list we've whittled down. Grades are based on the French grading system.

Climb	Grade	Height	Description
Groove Tube	6a	25m	A great climb for beginner to intermediate levels; lots of big gaps and pockets to grab.
Humanality	6a-6b	120m	This multipitch scramble is one of the most popular here; you may have to queue to climb it.
Lion King	6b+	18m	A good, challenging climb, with a slight overhang and zigzags up a crack; requires lots of strength and agility.
Narsillion	6c+	30m	Accessible only at low tide, this climb has a steep wall with small pockets. The beach below this rock is lovely.
Ao Nang Tower	6b-6c	68m	You have to start this climb from a long-tail boat! The last 6c stretch here is a long one so save your strength.

sand where he began guiding the few tourists trickling in for the climbing. The sport took off in the 1990s, and Luang founded Hot Rock in 1994. If you run out of steam halfway up a cliff, you can contact Luang and his staff for free-of-charge emergency rescue.

WATER SPORTS

Several **dive** operations in Railay run trips to Ko Poda and other neighbouring sites. **Krabi Divers** (☎ 0 7562 1686/7; www.viewpointresort66.com; Hat Rai Leh East), at Railay Viewpoint Resort, charges 1500B for two local dives and 2500B for dives at outlying islands. A three- or four-day PADI Open Water dive course is 9900B.

Snorkelling trips to Ko Poda and Ko Hua Khwan (Chicken Island) can be arranged through any of the resorts for about 600B by long-tail or 900B by speedboat. Longer multi-island trips cost 800/1500B per half-/full-day. If you just want to snorkel off Railay, most resorts can rent you a mask set and fins for 50B each.

The Flame Tree Restaurant/Bobo's Bar at Hat Rai Leh West, rents out **sea kayaks** for 150B per hour, or 400B for four hours. Overnight trips to deserted islands can be arranged with local boat owners but you'll need to bring your own camping gear and food.

Sleeping & Eating

Many resorts in Railay are owned or managed by Muslims and do not serve alcohol. Most places will, however, let you bring your own booze in. You can buy takeaway drinks at one of the beach bars (although unless you have alcohol with you, you'll be limited mostly to takeaways like beer or bottles of Thai rice whiskey – unless of course you want to haggle, and then shell out big baht, for an entire bottle of imported gin).

HAT RAI LEH WEST

Railay's first developed beach faces west, so the sunsets are fabulous. It's all pretty much midrange and top-end options on this beach, but rates can drop by 30% in the low season. All the resorts have decent restaurants.

Sand Sea Resort (☎ 0 7562 2170; www.krabisandsea .com; bungalows 1300-4000B; 🛏 🖳 🕾) Solid, well-appointed concrete bungalows with verandas line a snaking, foliage-laced pathway. A full buffet breakfast at the hotel restaurant is included; non-guests should stop by at lunch or dinner, as the food is quite good. We

especially liked the garlic and pepper squid (100B). You'll need to pick up beer at the Flame Thrower Bar two doors down; Sand Sea is alcohol free.

our pick **Railay Bay Resort & Spa** (☎ 0 7562 2571; www.railaybayresort.com; bungalows 2000-4000B; 🛏 🕾) It's worth staying here for the pool alone. The amoeba shaped sparkling blue creation faces onto the best bit of the beach so you can easily switch between its salt and fresh water. In the middle of major renovations when we stopped by, it has expanded and now stretches between Hat Rai Leh East and West. Digs are in swank bungalows with big glass windows and white walls. The restaurant was closed for redecorating when we visited, but we remember its yummy pizzas from the last trip. The spa, which also overlooks the sea, offers a host of treatments at very reasonable prices.

Railay Princess Resort & Spa (☎ 0 7562 2571; www.railaybayresort.com; bungalows 2500-4000B; 🛏 🕾) Railay Bay Resort's sister property has refreshing rooms with teak framed beds, Thai silk runners and crisp white linens. Muted lighting, big windows and a creamy colour scheme lend a serene touch. And bungalows look out onto a peaceful Lotus pond. Private ferry service to Krabi or Ao Nang, a minimart, restaurant, spa and travel agency round out this new luxury resort's amenities. You'll want for nothing.

Railei Beach Club (☎ 0 7562 2582; www.raileibeach club.com; houses 3700-9000B) Hidden away in forested grounds at the northern end of the beach, this is a collection of beautiful Thai-styled homes, each unique in size, style and design. The Beach Club is a conglomerate of foreign-owned houses: the owners rent out their vacation property when they are back home. Each place comes with patio and kitchen. Some houses sleep up to eight people. You'll need to book well in advance for the high season.

Flame Tree Restaurant/Bobo's Bar (dishes 70-150B) Some people call this place Bobo's; others refer to it by the new sign out front – Flame Tree. Whatever you call it, it's the only real bar in Hat Rai Leh West and serves dripping ice-cold beers alongside a long list of cocktails. After dark, sit on a mat on the sand and drink by candlelight. Flame Tree/Bobo's does a short menu of Thai and Western pub grub including good brekkies and real espresso drinks.

ANDAMAN COAST

HAT RAI LEH EAST

Often referred to as Sunrise Beach, the beach along here tends towards mud flats during low tide. It's not too big of a deal though, as Hat Rai Leh West is just a five-minute walk away. The resorts on the hillside above the beach get sea breezes, but down by the water it can feel like a sauna in the evenings. The following rates drop by half in the low season.

Rapala Bungalows (☎ 0 7562 2586; bungalows 400B) The delightful bamboo bungalows sit atop a hill, far removed from the whir of long-tail boats below, and many have winning sea views. This is budget accommodation at its best, but don't expect anything too flash. The intricately woven bungalows feature mattresses on the floor and hammocks on the porch, but that's about it. There's a cushion-lined restaurant that's perfect for chilling – it serves Thai and Indian food that guests have raved about.

Railay Highland Resort (☎ 0 7562 1732; bungalows 750B) This respectable resort sits in the middle of a natural basin above Hat Rai Leh East (it's about a 10-minute walk to the water), surrounded by immense cliffs. There's a very stylish bar and restaurant raised high on stilts in the centre, surrounded by thoughtfully designed wood-and-bamboo bungalows. In low season bungalows go for just 300B.

Diamond Private Resort (☎ 0 7562 1729; www .diamondprivate-railay.com; r 2000-4000B; 🕸 🖭) This resort has a pool high on the hilltop with a deck that sports great views of the bay below. The rooms and bungalows come with TVs, hot showers and minibars, and are set in well-landscaped gardens.

Sunrise Tropical Resort (☎ 0 7562 2599; www.sunrise tropical.com; bungalows 4000-5500B; 🕸 🖭) Likely the first place you'll come across after disembarking from the Krabi boat (look for it just beyond the mooring area). Sunrise has stylish Thai villas with neat décor and very swanky bathrooms. Breakfast is included. The restaurant does not serve alcohol.

HAT PHRA NANG

There's only one place to stay on this beautiful beach.

Rayavadee (☎ 0 7562 0740; www.rayavadee.com; r 42,000-55,000B; 🕸 🖭) Yes, you read those prices right. But if you have serious baht to burn, this exclusive colonial-style five-star resort monopolises 26 acres of stunning beachfront property. Seven types of luxury bungalow dot

the perfectly landscaped grounds; all are two-storey and fabulously decked out in a traditional Thai style. Champagne breakfast, afternoon tea and dinner are included, as are water sports and airport transfers. There's a luxurious pool and great security – guards won't let you enter the area to 'just have a look around'.

HAT TON SAI

The beach here isn't much to look at but with so many good climbs all around, most people don't mind. With the cheapest digs on the isthmus, Ton Sai has become Railay's backpacker ghetto, and there's a fun vibe in high season. Despite the number of places to sleep, Hat Ton Sai has managed to retain a peaceful unspoiled atmosphere, and its resorts lie hidden away among the trees behind the beach. In the low season, rates for bungalows plummet as low as 150B.

There are also a couple of very basic bungalow operations along the beach, though none have huts with sea views. The other resorts at Ton Sai, Dream Valley and Andaman Nature Resorts, are tucked behind the beach on the path next to Ton Sai Bungalows. There are a few other similar resorts along this path offering bamboo bungalows with bathrooms for around 500B.

Mambo (☎ 0 9652 1862; bungalows 500B) The most organised of the basic beach bungalows, Mambo's huts are bare bones – fan, mattress and toilet – with little in the way of decoration, but they are clean. The seaside restaurant is really popular (although the food isn't so great), and the place has a lively energy. In low season prices plummet to 200B, but electricity is often available only at night.

Andaman Nature Resort (☎ 0 7562 1667; fax 0 7561 1842; bungalows 200-500B) Offering the usual bungalow deal, the big attraction here is the popular multilevel restaurant – it's huge, shady and made of funky knotted wood.

Ton Sai Bungalows (☎ 0 7562 2584; bungalows 700-1200B; 🕸) The pricier bungalows are wood and concrete affairs painted a bright mustard colour, and are some of the nicest digs on Ton Sai. There's also a diving centre, climbing school and minimart here.

Dream Valley Resort (☎ 0 7562 2583; iad16@hotmail .com; r 400-1200B; 🕸) This old-style wooden place has a variety of trim and proper wooden bungalows, as well as a restaurant serving decent seafood. There's a minimart and a motorcycle taxi to transfer you to the beach with your bags.

Drinking

Although many of the resorts don't serve alcohol, there are a few places on the beaches where you can get nicely inebriated.

Rock Bar (Hat Rai Leh East) Up the hill towards the Railay Highland Resort, the Rock has an awesome setting under a massive climbing wall, is enveloped by jungle and has a drinking gazebo perched atop a boulder. This place also has yoga most mornings or afternoons and one of the better nightly fire-shows around.

Bamboo Bar (Hat Rai Leh East) One of several bars scattered around this beach, Bamboo Bar has comfy cushions and a driftwood design ethos that makes for interesting décor. It hosts the occasional glass-blowing demonstration, and the staff is fun and helpful.

Flame Thrower/Bobo's (Hat Rai Leh West) The place for a sunset cocktail at Hat Rai Leh West. Flame Thrower (or Bobo's, as it's also called) has cushions and candles on the sand and a long cocktail menu. You can buy takeaway beer here.

Chillout Bar (Hat Ton Sai) Climbers like to chill here after a long day on the rocks. The place flies Rasta colours and serves cold beers as fast as you can drink them.

Getting There & Around

The only way to get to Railay is by long-tail boat, either from Tha Kong Ka (Chao Fa) in Krabi or from the seafront at Ao Nang. Boats between Krabi and Hat Rai Leh East leave every 1½ hours from 7.45am to 6pm (100B, 45 minutes).

Boats to Hat Rai Leh West or Ton Sai (60B, 15 minutes) leave from the eastern end of the promenade at Ao Nang during daylight hours. After dark you'll pay 100B. If seas are rough, boats leave from a sheltered cove just west of Krabi Resort in Ao Nang. You can be dropped at Hat Phra Nang or Hat Ton Sai for the same fare.

During exceptionally high seas, the boats from both Ao Nang and Krabi stop running, but you may still be able to get from Hat Rai Leh East to Ao Nam Mao (30B, 15 minutes), where you can pick up a săwngthăew to Krabi or Ao Nang. Even if boats are running all the way to Ao Nang, you can expect a drenching on any boat ride during the monsoon.

From October to May, the *Ao Nang Princess* runs between Hat Noppharat Thara National Park headquarters and Ko Phi Phi with a stop in Hat Rai Leh West. Long-tails run out to meet the boat at around 9.15am from in front of the Sand Sea Resort; the fare from Railay is 250B.

KHAO PHANOM BENCHA NATIONAL PARK

อุทยานแห่งชาติเขาพนมเบญจา

This 50-sq-km **park** (admission 200B) protects a dramatic area of virgin rainforest along the spine of 1350m-high Khao Phanom Bencha, just 20km north of Krabi. The name means Five-Point Prostration Mountain, a reference to the mountain's profile, which resembles a person prostrate in prayer, with hands, knees and head touching the ground.

The park is full of scenic waterfalls, including the 11-tiered **Nam Tok Huay To**, just 500m from the park headquarters. Close by and almost as dramatic are **Nam Tok Huay Sadeh** and **Nam Tok Khlong Haeng**. On the way into the park, you can visit **Tham Khao Pheung**, a fantastic cave with shimmering mineral stalactites and stalagmites. Numerous trails snake through the park providing excellent opportunities for hiking. You can discover lesser-known streams and waterfalls, too.

Clouded leopards, black panthers, tigers, Asiatic black bears, barking deer, serow, Malayan tapirs, leaf monkeys, gibbons and various tropical birds – including the helmeted hornbill, argus pheasant and extremely rare Gurney's pitta – make their home here.

There is no public transport to the park, and it doesn't offer any lodging or eating options. But the park is an easy day trip from Krabi by hired motorcycle; just follow the signposted turn-off from Hwy 4. Alternatively, you can hire a túk-túk for around 300B return.

THAN BOKKHARANI NATIONAL PARK

อุทยานแห่งชาติธารโบกขรณี

If you visit this national park just after the monsoons, you'll be treated to a lush and surreal experience – almost like you've stepped onto the set of a Disney movie. At the park headquarters, close to the small town of Ao Leuk and 46km northwest of Krabi, emerald-green waters flow out of a narrow cave in a tall cliff and into a large lotus pool, which spills into a wide stream and then divides into many smaller rivulets. At each rivulet there's a pool and a little waterfall; the effect is magical. The park was established in 1991 and protects a large area of islands, mangroves and limestone caves throughout the Ao Leuk area.

Thais from Ao Leuk come to bathe at these pools on weekends, when it becomes full of people playing in the streams – and shampooing their hair, which seems to be a favourite activity here. During the week there are only a few people about – mostly kids fishing. Vendors sell noodles, excellent roast chicken, delicious battered squid and *sôm-tam* (green papaya salad) under a roofed area to one side.

Activities

Caving is the name of the game in this park. Among the protected caves scattered around the Amphoe Ao Leuk, one of the most interesting is **Tham Hua Kalok** (also called Tham Pee Hua Toe or Big-Headed Ghost Cave), reached by long-tail boat or sea kayak from the pier at Ban Bho Tho, 7km south of Ao Leuk. Set in a limestone hill, legend has it that a huge human skull was found in the cave, but the ghost story probably has more to do with the 2000- to 3000-year-old paintings of human and animal figures that adorn the cave walls.

Nearby **Tham Lawt** (Tube Cave) is distinguished by the navigable stream flowing through it and can also be reached by boat. Both caves are popular destinations for sea-kayaking tours from Krabi or Ao Nang, but you can also hire sea kayaks and guides at Tha Bho Tho for 800B. Long-tails are available for 300B.

There are no less than seven other similar limestone caves in the park, including **Tham Sa Yuan Thong**, a few kilometres southeast of Ao Leuk, which has a natural spring bubbling into a pool at its mouth. The park also includes the uninhabited island of **Ko Hong**, with fine beaches, jungle-cloaked cliffs and a scenic hidden lagoon. Sea kayak and long-tail boats come here from Ao Nang.

Sleeping

Ao Leuk has a few places to bed down, or you can camp with permission from the park headquarters.

Ao Leuk Resort (☎ 0 7568 1133; r 300-500B; ✕) Right beside the park headquarters, this place has old rooms with bathrooms and TVs in a motel-like block.

PN Mountain Resort (☎ 0 7568 1554; r 400-1200B; ✕ ✍) This is a newer place with modern rooms and a dramatic backdrop: a lush limestone cliff wall with a hole in the middle. It's on Hwy 4, 1km north of the park turnoff.

Getting There & Away

Than Bok, as the locals call it, is near the town of Ao Leuk. The park headquarters is about 1.5km south of Ao Leuk town along Rte 4039. Buses and sǎwngthǎew from Krabi cost 25B and stop on Hwy 4. From here you can walk about 1.3km to the park headquarters or take a motorcycle taxi for 15B. The easiest way to visit the caves is to join a sea-kayaking tour from Krabi or Ao Nang (that way you don't have to worry about transportation).

To get to Ban Bho Tho from Ao Leuk on your own steam (to organise your own sea-kayak tour), take a motorcycle taxi (50B) to the 'Tham Phee Huato' turn-off on Rte 4039. From the junction it's about 2km to Ban Bho Tho along the first signposted road on the left.

KO PHI PHI DON
เกาะพีพีดอน

Ko Phi Phi is quickly returning to its pre-tsunami status as Thailand's Shangri-la: a hedonistic paradise where tanned couples frolic in glassy green seas and snap pictures of colourful long-tails puttering between craggy slate cliffs.

Unlike other tsunami-affected regions, this island seems to have had less trouble getting the word out. Following a massive rebuilding effort, bungalows are once again fully booked between December and March, and tourists are returning to the curving bays, white sand beaches and dense tropical jungle that made Ko Phi Phi the darling of the Andaman Coast in the first place.

Prior to the tsunami, the island was growing too rapidly for its existing infrastructure and fragile ecosystem to sustain. Immediately following the tsunami the Thai government put on hold any rebuilding on the island's sand bar, and it was hoped, with the slate wiped clean, that lessons could be learned from past mistakes. Several local agencies attempted to educate developers and residents about sustainable growth, and rumours circulated that the area would be turned into a public park.

But none of these things came to pass and Ao Ton Sai now looks almost exactly as it did before 24 December 2004. In the Tourist Village, street vendors and souvenir shops are back in full swing, as are dozens of booking agencies, restaurants and dive operators. On most of the other bays, it's business as usual.

ANDAMAN COAST

Expat James Hood, owner of the new 007 Bar, explained it this way:

'It isn't like anyone actually has permission from the government to build, but it is happening anyway, and no one is doing anything to stop it. One family has a lot of influence on the island and in the provincial government in Krabi,' he said.

There seems to be light at the end of the tunnel, however. A new water-treatment plant, opened in 2006, should eliminate water-supply issues for now. Trash is starting to head into rubbish bins – a local bar owner has taken it upon himself to place bins on the main tourist beaches. Do you part in recycling – look for the new rubbish bins and deposit as much garbage as you can find.

And while Phi Phi may look the same as it did pre-tsunami, it certainly doesn't cost the same.

'Ko Phi Phi is changing, there has been a drop in the backpacker population and an increase in the suitcase brigade,' Hood said. 'Backpackers can't afford to stay here anymore.'

It's true. Although Ko Phi Phi retains a mellow backpacker vibe, cheap bungalows are few and far between, and those that exist seem overpriced for the cramped, dark and dank environs you get. The outlook is only slightly less dismal in the midrange and top-end bracket – expect to pay nearly double what you would on the mainland, for half the amenities and swankness. Why is Phi Phi so expensive these days?

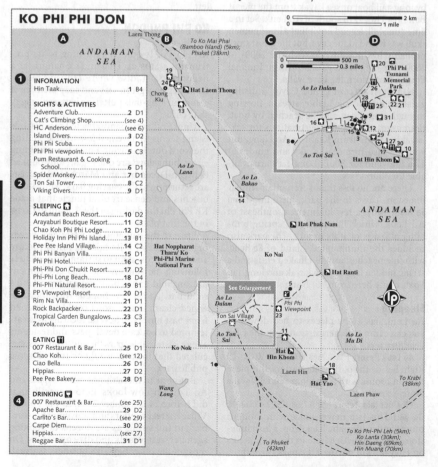

For two reasons, Hood says. First, electricity is hugely expensive on Phi Phi because the island is not supplied with electricity from the mainland and has to rely on generators. Ferry and long-tail boat prices are also increasing – rates are tied to the price of petrol, so if petrol prices drop drastically in the next two years, expect prices to go down (we wish!).

On the plus side, Phi Phi is building sounder structures these days (probably another reason prices are going up). Instead of fly-by-night bungalows, Western style buildings, constructed to withstand a tsunami, are going up. Designs include open-air staircases people can use to climb onto the roof in a hurry.

And even though Ko Phi Phi will seem expensive compared to the rest of Thailand, if you compare it to other gorgeous islands around the planet, we think you'll discover this paradise actually comes pretty damn cheap.

Orientation & Information

Ko Phi Phi Don (usually just referred to as Ko Phi Phi) is part of the Ko Phi Phi Marine National Park, which also includes uninhabited Ko Phi Phi Leh. Development is forbidden on Phi Phi Don's little sister, but it can be visited on immensely popular day trips.

Ko Phi Phi Don is actually two islands joined by a narrow isthmus with the prized beaches **Ao Ton Sai** and **Ao Lo Dalam** on either side. It's here that the tsunami wreaked the most havoc. Boats dock at the large concrete pier at Ao Ton Sai and a sandy path, crammed full of tour operators, bungalows, restaurants, bars and souvenir shops, stretches along the beach towards **Hat Hin Khom**. The maze of small streets in the middle of this sand bar is equally packed and is called 'Tourist Village'. **Hat Yao** (Long Beach) faces south and has some of Phi Phi Don's best coral reefs and one of its most impressive swimming beaches. The beautifully languid and long eastern bays of **Hat Laem Thong** and **Ao Lo Bakao** are reserved for several top-end resorts while the smaller bays of **Hat Phak Nam** and **Hat Ranti** play host to a few simple, low-key bungalow affairs.

Prices vary wildly by season on Ko Phi Phi Don. As soon as you arrive at the pier you'll be assaulted by touts trying to book you into one of the bungalow operations (they all give the same spiel about it being the last available bungalow on the island in your price range; it's usually not). The touts will direct you to an official-looking info desk at the pier (in reality it's just a private tourist booking office) and try to force you into booking a room. Unless you're travelling alone with tons of luggage and desperately need someone to carry your luggage – Ko Phi Phi is vehicle free, so luggage is transported by porters pushing wheeled carts; travellers hike alongside or if you're staying further from the pier you may both go by long-tail boat – don't book here. It's not that the prices are worse, but you'll be forced to pay in advance, thus will be unable to see your room first. As prices in Ko Phi Phi are ridiculously high and quality isn't always great, it's best to see what you're booking first (unless you book in advance over the internet, when you'll likely get a lower rate; or it's the holiday season and it really might be the last room. If the boat's half empty in October though, hoof it).

Scattered throughout Ao Ton Sai are numerous ATMs and internet cafes, and travel agencies that can book day trips and onward tickets.

Activities

The strenuous climb to the **Phi Phi viewpoint** is a rewarding short hike. The trail is off the path to the dam – look for Phi Phi Dream (heading towards the dam, the resort will be on your right) and take the path on the opposite side of the road. Follow the signs from here. The viewpoint is reached via a 1000ft vertical climb that includes hundreds of steep steps and narrow twisting paths. The hike will get your blood pumping and sweat pouring, but it's worth the effort. The views from the top are amazing – the marine park vistas stretch on forever, resembling a shimmering tapestry of aqua and emerald, turquoise and jade.

DIVING & SNORKELLING

With crystal-clear water, abundant coral and tons of fish, Ko Phi Phi is a kick-ass place to dive. In fact, when it comes to Thailand's best scuba sites, many say only the Similans rate above Ko Phi Phi.

Phi Phi's dive shops all charge the same price – an Open Water certification course costs 12,500B, while the standard two-dive trips cost 2200B, or 3200B if you want to visit the *King Cruiser* wreck. A Discover Scuba dive (for those not certified) costs 3100B.

Phi Phi Scuba (☎ 0 7561 2665; www.ppscuba.com) and **Island Divers** (☎ 075 601 082; www.islanddiverspp.com) are the biggest operators. Both churn out dive certifications by the boatload, and some

folks complain about the less-than-personalised service. On the plus side, Island Divers, in particular, pushes ecofriendly scuba – the company encourages wreck dives and doesn't allow clients to touch the coral. Both shops have access to a hyperbaric chamber. **Viking Divers** (☎ 0 1719 3375; www.vikingdiversthailand.com) is a much smaller outfit that helped with the post-tsunami clean-up of the reefs and comes with good recommendations. A friendly Brit, who is married to a local woman, owns the place.

Snorkelling around Ko Phi Phi is equally amazing, especially off Ko Phi Phi Leh. It is worth shelling out the 600B to 2000B (depending on whether you want a long-tail or speedboat, and the duration of the trip) to join a day trip. Most trips include lunch and take you to a number of spots around the marine park. Popular destinations include Ko Mai Phai (Bamboo Island), north of Phi Phi Don. There's a shallow area here where you may see small leopard sharks (very common in this area). All travel agencies can arrange snorkelling day trips. Many snorkelling tours on bigger boats include short kayaking side trips, but some of these tours use mini cruise ships that carry up to 100 people at a time – peace and quiet on these behemoths may not be an option.

If you're going on your own, most bungalows and resorts rent out a snorkel, mask and fins for 100B to 150B per day. There is good snorkelling along the eastern coast of **Ko Nok**, near Ao Ton Sai, and along the eastern coast of **Ko Nai**.

ROCK CLIMBING
Yes, there are good limestone cliffs to climb on Ko Phi Phi, and the view from the top is spectacular. The main climbing areas are **Ton Sai Tower**, at the western edge of Ao Ton Sai, and **Hin Taak**, a short long-tail boat ride around the bay. There are at least six good climbing shops on the island and most places charge around 800B to 1000B for a half-day of climbing or 1500B for a full day, including instruction and gear. **Spider Monkey** (☎ 0 9728 1608) is a tiny new climbing shop run by Soley, one of the most impressive climbers on Phi Phi. One of the bigger outfits around is **Cat's Climbing Shop** (☎ 0 1787 5101; www.catsclimbingshop .com) in the Tourist Village. Cat's gets good reports for safety and service.

Courses
Thai-food fans can take cooking courses at the newly renovated **Pum Restaurant & Cooking School** (☎ 0 1521 8904; www.pumthaifoodchain.com; full

---

WORKING & DIVING IN KO PHI PHI

The dive sites around Ko Phi Phi are filled with marine life. Leopard sharks and hawksbill turtles are very common; whale sharks sometimes make cameo appearances around Hin Bida (Phi Phi Sub Shark Point) and Ko Bida Nok in February and March.

The top five dives at Ko Phi Phi:

Dive Site	Depth	Features
Hin Bida (Phi Phi Sub Shark Point)	15-30m	Submerged pinnacle with hard coral, turtles, leopard sharks and occasional whale sharks.
Ko Bida Nok	18-22m	Karst massif with gorgonians, leopard sharks, barracuda and occasional whale sharks.
Anemone Reef	17-26m	Hard coral reef with plentiful anemones and clownfish.
Hin Musang (Phuket Shark Point)	19-24m	Submerged pinnacle with a few leopard sharks, grouper, barracuda and moray eels.
Phi Phi Leh	5-18m	The whole island rim is covered in coral and oysters where you can see moray eels and seahorses, and do lots of swim-throughs.

Nearly all the dive shops are Western run. By law, unless you are American – don't ask, it's the result of an obscure treaty – foreigners cannot be full owners of businesses in Thailand, so many companies operate under Western-Thai partnerships. Most hire *faràng* to work as touts and dive instructors. If you're interested in work, stop by one of the shops. Both Island and Viking Divers told us they are usually hiring, and interested travellers should stop in and chat with the manager – there didn't seem to be much worry about having work permits. Dive Instructors make around 30% of the price of the course they teach.

HELPING HANDS ON PHI PHI

Nigel and Christine Clifford chose to honeymoon in Ko Phi Phi instead of Bali because they wanted to support the local economy. Holding hands at a beachside bar on a warm October night in 2006, they talked with a group of travellers about their decision.

'We thought about going to Bali, but then we decided on Ko Phi Phi because we just wanted to do something to help. (A local) rugby team had visited Ko Phi Phi because one of their players was killed in the tsunami, so we had heard about a school here that they were helping...so we came here and tomorrow we're going to go to the school and give them this money. It's not much but it's what we have,' Nigel Clifford says.

The Clifford's story of compassion is only one of thousands. Weeks after the tsunami washed through the heart of Ko Phi Phi Don, the island remained nearly deserted and covered in shoulder-high rubble. Survivors were in shock at the devastation and loss of lives. In those early stages, international aid agency help and government funding were still thin on the ground and much of the island was shut down. Those who stayed – locals, expat residents and tourists alike – decided to take matters into their own hands and began the monumental task of cleaning up Ko Phi Phi Don. Word was sent to locals, volunteers and Thai workers from the mainland, and over the following months more than 2000 international volunteers came to lend Phi Phi residents a hand. People stayed from one day to several months. Regular visitors to the island and first-time tourists decided that it was time to give something back.

Help International Phi Phi (www.hiphiphi.com) was set up as an umbrella group that coordinated the volunteer and early aid efforts across the island. By July much of the debris had been removed, shops were renovated and opening again for business, and volunteers kept arriving to help out. The **Phi Phi Dive Camp** (www.phiphidivecamp.com) was set up to direct clean-up operations underwater – it organised volunteer divers in a huge effort to remove the debris that had swept into the sea.

Phi Phi is looking good these days, but there is still work to be done. If you're interested in volunteering, contact either of the above organisations or simply show up and ask around.

For updates on reconstruction efforts and how you can help, see www.lonelyplanet.com/tsunami /thailand.

day 2500B) in the Tourist Village. You'll learn to make some of the excellent dishes that are served in its restaurant.

Tours

As well as the popular long-tail tours to Phi Phi Leh and Ko Mai Phai (Bamboo Island), tour agencies can arrange sunset tours to Monkey Bay and the beach at Wang Long (500B to 650B).

Adventure Club (☎ 0 1895 1334; www.phi-phi-adventures.com) is a green organisation that was instrumental in helping clean up Phi Phi's underwater habitat after the tsunami. It runs educational, eco-focused tours and dive trips, including shark-watching snorkelling trips, reef restoration dive trips, cliff jumping and hiking.

Sleeping

Finding accommodation on this ever-popular island has never been easy, and now with a reduced number of facilities you can expect serious room shortages during peak holiday times. It's best to book ahead if possible; otherwise be prepared for some legwork once you get here. If you choose to go with the touts meeting incoming boats, be sure to find out where the accommodation is, or you may end up on a remote part of the island – which may be just what you're after.

For accommodation costs see the boxed text on p648. The prices quoted here are for high season they drop between 25% and 50% in the low season.

AO TON SAI & AO LO DALAM

Business in Ao Ton Sai and the Tourist Village is pretty much normal again. Redevelopment of Ao Lo Dalam has been slower. There are still lovely, long stretches of sand devoid of bungalow operations, although this could change at any moment.

Rock Backpacker (☎ 0 7561 2402; therockbackpacker@ hotmail.com; dm 350B, r 800B) Backpackers looking for company will like this place. The funky

ANDAMAN COAST

restaurant, on a boat dry-docked on the hillside, is conducive to mingling. The 16-bed dorm room is a real rarity on Ko Phi Phi, and digs are clean, if rather cramped. Rock Backpacker is inland, but close to Ao Lo Dalam.

Tropical Garden Bungalows (☎ 0 9729 1436; r 800B; ⊠) If you don't mind walking 10 minutes to eat, drink or sunbathe, then you'll find Tropical Garden fabulous value. At the far end of the main path from Ao Ton Sai, it feels pretty isolated in its fragment of flourishing hillside jungle. The great cabins are frontier-style log affairs and there's even a lofty pool, surrounded by flora, halfway up the hill.

Rim Na Villa (☎ 0 1894 2668; bungalows 600-1500B; ⊠) Local expats consistently recommend this long-time backpacker favourite to those looking for cheap digs. Be aware though, the bungalows, while clean, are rickety old affairs that are not particularly comfortable – it's best to use them just for sleeping. Insect repellent is a must as the mosquitoes can be vicious.

Chao Koh Phi Phi Lodge (☎ 0 7562 0800; www .chaokohphiphi.com; bungalows 1000-2800B; ⊠ ⊠) There's no way you can miss these concrete duplex bungalows with powder-green paint jobs, gaudy Corinthian columns and oversized A-frame roofs. Interiors are clean and come with TV and personal safes, but are a bit deficient in the charm stakes – the artwork is downright garish. Baths are good though. The tub is separate from the shower. Plus the fan bungalows are a steal for this beach, considering the swimming pool.

Phi Phi Hotel (☎ 0 7561 1233; www.phiphi-hotel .com; r 1800-3000B; ⊠ ⊠) Guests love this hotel that has all the amenities of a posh place and amazing views from your balcony – choose mountain or sea. The place can't be missed – it's a three-storey monolith – but it's tastefully decorated and the rate includes a big breakfast.

SHELL OUT

Numerous souvenir shops on Ko Phi Phi Don sell seashells, but these are poached from the surrounding marine national parks. Shell species are becoming extinct here faster than you can say 'she sells seashells', so please don't buy souvenirs made from tropical shells.

TIP: GOING ECOFRIENDLY UNDERWATER

Ko Phi Phi's reef isn't as healthy as it used to be, and divers often contribute to the problem (they bump against, or blatantly touch the coral, which can be fatal for this fragile living organism). If you want to be positive you're not contributing to the reef's demise, opt for a wreck dive. You'll be away from the coral, but still get to explore some pretty cool stuff. There's something adventurous and slightly chilling (but in a good way) about snooping around the hulking body of a wrecked ship.

Phi Phi Banyan Villa (☎ 0 7561 1233; www.phiphi -hotel.com; r 2500-3300B; ⊠ ⊠) There are lots of rooms snaking inland from the beach here, but even so, the place doesn't feel too squishy. The comfy quarters have all the mod cons and some have a balcony overlooking a garden-lined path. There's a seaside restaurant and the hotel's namesake, a large gnarled banyan tree, sits out front.

PP Viewpoint Resort (☎ 0 7562 2351; www.phi phiviewpoint.com; bungalows 1500-8000B; ⊠ ⊠) At the far end of Ao Lo Dalam, this place rests on a rise with marvellous views of the bay. Wooden bungalows sit high on stilts and share the views. There is a small swimming pool that practically drops into the ocean below and a glass-walled tower with 360-degree views where you can pamper yourself with a Thai massage.

HAT HIN KHOM

Although the beach here was never Phi Phi's best, the abodes in this area are generally far enough removed (although still easily accessible) from Ao Ton Sai's bustle to get a quiet night's sleep. Stunning Hat Yao is also nearby.

Andaman Beach Resort (☎ 0 7562 1427; www.anda manbeachresort.com; bungalows 1450-2550B; ⊠ ⊠) A U-shape of neat, tiled huts sits around a large spartan lawn. The best asset is the small amoeba-shaped pool with great Phi Phi Leh views. The fan bungalows are a good deal – large, airy and modern with oscillating fans that keep the room relatively cool (even if they are rather loud). The air-con digs come with TV, fridge and a teal colour scheme. The baths are a bit grimy, but the bungalows themselves

are roomy. Mattresses are just soft enough and breakfast is included. Staff can be surly.

Arayaburi Boutique Resort (☎ 0 7628 1360; www .phiphibayview.com; bungalows 2700-4300B; ❄) This, formerly Bay View Resort, recently swallowed a neighbouring resort and now offers a cornucopia of huts straddling the lush hill and rocky headland of the coast. Most of the bungalows are modern in design, come stacked with amenities and have excellent ocean views from their front decks. Breakfast is included.

Phi Phi Don Chukit Resort (☎ 0 7561 8126; ppdon chukit@yahoo.com; bungalows 2000-5000B; ❄) One Australian couple described Don Chukit's most expensive bungalows as 'the equivalent of staying in a five-star motel room.' The huts are roomy, face the water and have marble floors. The cheapest bungalows (even those with ocean views) are less memorable. Although these have nice porches, it's cramped and right on a noisy street. The huts themselves are tiny with too-soft mattresses. Breakfast is included.

HAT YAO

Hat Yao (also known as Long Beach) takes effort to reach. You'll either have to take a boat (80B) or hike 45 minutes from Ao Ton Sai village. Do so and you'll be rewarded with a stunning stretch of white sand seashore and perfect swimming water. Budget travellers will appreciate some of Phi Phi's best cheap accommodation (although you will be limited when it comes to nightlife, as it's a long way to the nearest bar).

Phi Phi Long Beach (☎ 0 1510 6541; bungalows 300-600B; 🖵) The wooden bungalows at Phi Phi Long Beach are looking a little rundown, but it's certainly cheap and has a bit of a vibe, with an internet café, restaurant and dive school (free accommodation if you take its dive course). If you'd rather go for a hike, ask staff for walking directions to beautiful and secluded Ao Lo Mu Di.

AO LO BAKAO

Ao Lo Bakao is a beautiful and secluded beach on Phi Phi's remote northeastern shore. The palm-backed sand is ringed by dramatic hills and home to just one resort. Ao Lo Bakao can only be reached by boat. Pee Pee Island Village arranges transfers for guests. If you want to visit for the day, charter a long-tail taxi in Ao Ton Sai. Expect to pay around 500B (one way). Try to negotiate a return rate.

Pee Pee Island Village (☎ Phuket 0 7621 5014, Bangkok 0 2276 6056; www.ppisland.com; bungalows from 5300B; ❄ ✺) This place really is a village unto itself: its whopping 104 bungalows take up much of the beachfront with only a few lonely palms swaying between them. This is the full-service deal with all the trimmings – it's particularly popular with the Japanese jet set.

HAT LAEM THONG

At the northern end of Ko Nai, the beach here is long and pretty with several showy resorts. There's also a small *chao leh* (sea gypsy) settlement of corrugated metal shacks at the end of the beach. A long-tail charter from Ao Ton Sai costs 600B. The following resorts can arrange transfers.

Phi Phi Natural Resort (☎ 0 7561 3010, in Bangkok 0 2982 7575; www.phiphinatural.com; bungalows 1900-5850B; ❄ ✺) At the northern end of the beach, this is a laid-back resort with spacious grounds, a pool and shipshape wooden bungalows with either sea or mountain views. Be sure to look up at the peaked wooden roof of the huge restaurant above; it provides a habitat for a range of wild birds. The resort runs daily boats to Phuket and Krabi in the high season.

Holiday Inn Phi Phi Island (☎ 0 7521 1334; www .phiphi-pambeach.com; bungalows 5500-8000B; ❄ ✺) At the southernmost point of the beach, this tastefully decorated resort has large Thai/Malay-style bungalows on 2m-high stilts spread over spacious, landscaped grounds with lots of coconut palms. Bungalows come with neat little details, such as pots of fresh water in which to clean your feet before entering. On the grounds are tennis courts, a spa, dive centre, restaurant and hilltop bar.

Zeavola (☎ 0 7562 7024; www.zeavola.com; bungalows 16,000-37,000B; ❄ 🖵 ✺) If you have money to burn, let this be your pyre. Gorgeous teak bungalow mansions incorporate traditional Thai style with simple, sleek modern design. Each comes with glass walls on three sides (with remote-controlled bamboo shutters for privacy), beautiful 1940s fixtures and antique furniture, a patio and impeccable service. Some villas have a private pool. There's a 25% discount if you book online. This place was formerly known as Phi Phi Coral Resort.

Eating

Most of the resorts, hotels and bungalows around Phi Phi have attached restaurants. One of the cheapest eating options is at the

Thai pancake stalls scattered about Ao Ton Sai. The thin crepe-style pancakes (20B) are served savoury or sweet, and stuffed with everything from ham and cheese to banana and honey.

Pee Pee Bakery (dishes 40-150; ☺ breakfast, lunch & dinner) It's best at breakfast, when you'll be lucky to find an open table at which to sip your espresso. Also on tap are pizza, steak and Thai food. The atmosphere is modern and movies are shown on the tube. The bakery has two branches; one is on the main walkway east of the piers, while the other is further inland near PP Pavilion Resort.

007 Restaurant & Bar (dishes 100-200B; ☺ breakfast, lunch & dinner) Owned by a talkative Scot named James, 007 is the unique choice on the island. It features ultramodern chrome tables, red cushion booths and, of course, all the Bond paraphernalia you could want. There's a big selection of beer (including British favourites) on tap, and solid food cooked in a very clean kitchen. Pies, salads, fish-and-chips and baked potatoes are on the menu. Sport is shown on the TV by day; the latest blockbusters are played at night. James has plans to open an Indian restaurant, called the Hot Spot, on the ground floor.

Hippies (☎ 0 1970 5483; dishes 80-250B; ☺ breakfast, lunch & dinner) Rebuilt after the tsunami, Hippies is once again a laid-back beachfront hang-out spot serving food from around the globe. It offers tables on the beach or in its thatched restaurant. Hippies serves spicy and non-spicy Thai dishes, along with lots of brekkies, Israeli food, pizza and pasta. The Thai choices are better than the Western offerings. Skip the pizza.

Chao Koh (☎ 075 601 083; dishes 80-300B; ☺ lunch & dinner) Right on the beach, this is an open-air seafood place that displays its freshly caught critters on ice. It's popular and offers well-priced and tasty food. A self-service salad bar is included with most entrées.

Ciao Bella (dishes 150-300B; ☺ breakfast, lunch & dinner) Italian-run Ciao Bella is our favourite place to eat on Ko Phi Phi. It's a long-time expat and traveller fave that recently reopened after extensive post-tsunami renovations. The pizza, pasta and seafood dishes are authentic and as mouth-watering as the super romantic location by the sea. At night, twinkling candles and stars provide the atmosphere for alfresco dining, while lapping waves provides the soundtrack. Ciao Bella is in Ao Lo Dalam.

HC Anderson (☎ 0 1894 5287; dishes 90-200B, steaks 320-280B; ☺ lunch & dinner) A very reliable Scandinavian restaurant serving delicious imported New Zealand steaks, among other creative dishes. It's on the most easterly path from Ao Ton Sai to Ao Lo Dalam.

Drinking & Entertainment

Most of Phi Phi's old-school watering holes have reopened and nightlife on the island is raging.

If you need distraction with your drink 007 Restaurant & Bar shows nightly movies; see Eating, left.

Carpe Diem (☎ 048 401 219; Hat Hin Khom) Sit on pillows in the upstairs lounge and watch the sun go down (locals say this is the best spot on the island for sundowners). Carpe Diem rocks well into the night with fire shows, dance parties and live music on the beach. It's very popular, and an easy spot for mingling if you're travelling alone.

Reggae Bar (Tourist Village; ☺ 10pm-late) The most popular nightspot on the island recently expanded. It has three floors of Rasta colours, drinking competitions, a *muay thai* boxing ring with regular show bouts (where you can fight for free booze) and the occasional *kàthoey* (ladyboy) cabaret – you either love it or hate it.

Apache Bar (Ao Ton Sai) With a strange Native American theme (think Indian from the *Village People*) lit by fluorescent lights, this pre-and-post tsunami favourite is definitely campy. Happy hour is from 4pm to 10pm. It fills up quickly and blasts loud music to all hours (to the annoyance of people sleeping nearby).

Carlitos (☎ 0 9927 3772; Ao Ton Sai) This fairy-lit beachside bar, which puts on impressive fire shows, attracts *faràng* seeking beers and a chair in the sand. It gets rowdy and packs in major crowds on dance-party nights. We like how Carlitos does its bit for the environment by recycling.

Hippies (☎ 0 1970 5483; Hat Hin Khom) Hippies is a good place to end the evening. There are candle-lit tables on the beach and chill-out tunes on the sound system. Moon parties are thrown throughout the month.

Getting There & Away

Ko Phi Phi can be reached from Krabi, Phuket, Ao Nang and Ko Lanta. Most boats moor at Ao Ton Sai, though a few from Phuket use the

isolated northern pier at Laem Thong. The Phuket and Krabi boats operate year-round while the Ko Lanta and Ao Nang boats only run in the October to April high season.

Boats depart from Krabi for Ko Phi Phi at 9.30am, 10.30am and 2.30pm (500B, 1½ hours). From Phuket, boats leave at 8.30am, 1.30pm and 2.30pm, and return from Ko Phi Phi at 9am, 2.30pm and 3pm (550B to 650B, 1¾ to two hours). To Ko Lanta, boats leave Phi Phi at 11.30am and 2pm, and return from Ko Lanta at 8am and 1pm (300B, 1½ hours). A boat departs from the Ko Phi Phi Marine National Park headquarters jetty at 9am, returning from Ko Phi Phi (via Railay) at 3.30pm (550B, two hours). Prices may drop by 50B in the low season.

Getting Around
There are no roads on Phi Phi Don so transport is mostly by foot. If you want to visit a remote beach, long-tails can be chartered at Ao Ton Sai (for prices see the relevant beach in the Sleeping section). Speedboats can be chartered at a cost of 4000B to 6500B for six hours. Chartering a long-tail boat costs 900B for three hours or 1800B for the whole day.

KO PHI PHI LEH
เกาะพีพีเล
Rugged Ko Phi Phi Leh is the smaller of the two islands and protected on all sides by soaring cliffs. The island's translucent water and gorgeous coral reefs teeming with marine life make snorkelling here phenomenal. Two gorgeous lagoons lie in wait in the island's interior – **Pilah** on the eastern coast and **Ao Maya** on the western coast. Ao Maya became famous in 1999 after producers used it as the setting for *The Beach*, based on the popular novel by Alex Garland. It remains wildly popular to this day.

At the northeastern tip of the island, **Viking Cave** (Tham Phaya Naak; admission 20B) is a major collection point for swiftlet nests. Bamboo scaffolding reaches its way to the roof of the cave as nimble collectors scamper up to gather the nests built high up the cliffs. Before ascending the scaffolds, the collectors pray and make offerings of tobacco, incense and liquor to the cavern spirits. This cave gets its misleading moniker from the 400-year-old graffiti made by crews of passing Chinese fishing junks.

There are no places to stay at on Phi Phi Leh and most people come here on one of the ludicrously popular day trips out of Phi Phi Don. Tours last about half a day and include snorkelling stops at various points around the island, with detours to Viking Cave and Ao Maya. Long-tail trips cost 400 to 650B depending on season and demand; by motorboat you'll pay around 2000B.

KO JAM (KO PU) & KO SI BOYA
เกาะจ๋า(ปู) /เกาะศรีบอยา
If you're yearning to escape the crowds, Ko Jam (also called Ko Pu) and its neighbour Ko Si Boya might just be your tonic. Both offer kicked-back, small-island ambience and plenty of solitude. There's not much to do other than swim and sunbathe, and the focus here is on relaxation. If you get tired of reading, wander around the small fishing villages. Most locals are Muslim, so please respect their customs – don't go topless here.

Public transport to Ko Jam and Ko Si Boya is very limited in the low season so most resorts close down between May and November.

Sleeping & Eating
Accommodation on Ko Jam is spread out along the beaches at the southern end of the island. Some places rent out sea kayaks and most have a restaurant on the grounds. Ko Si Boya has one place to stay, Siboya Bungalows, on the western coast just south of the main village, Ban Lang Ko.

Siboya Bungalows (☎ 0 7561 8026; www.siboyabungalows.com; bungalows 150-300B, occasional private houses 400-1200B) The well-designed huts sit on a lush lawn and are covered in heaps of shade by expansive palm and rubber trees. Verandas and hammocks come as standard, and there are also a couple of self-contained houses that are ideal for long-term rentals.

Woodland Lodge (☎ 0 1893 5330; www.woodland-koh-jum.tk; bungalows 300-800B) The bamboo huts sit on shaded grounds and come with shiny, polished wood verandas and mosquito netting. The friendly owners organise boat-tours and fishing trips and run a cooking course in the high season. The lodge has larger family bungalows priced from 400B to 1300B and it stays open year round. At night oil lamps light the property.

Joy Bungalow (☎ 0 1464 6153; www.andaman-island-hopping.com/hotels/joybungalow.htm; bungalows 1000-2000B) On the southwestern coast of Ko Jam, Joy has great thatch-and-wood stilt bungalows on grassy, palm-shaded grounds. The beach

ANDAMAN COAST

restaurant here has a good vibe but the popularity of this place has become a turnoff for some (prices have also skyrocketed in the last few years).

Getting There & Away

From October to May, boats between Krabi and Ko Lanta can drop you at Ko Jam, but you'll pay full fare (350B, one hour). There are also small boats to Ko Jam and Ko Si Boya a few times a day from Ban Laem Kruat, a village about 30km from Krabi, at the end of Rte 4036, off Hwy 4. The cost is 60B to Ko Si Boya and 70B to Ban Ko Jam.

KO LANTA

เกาะลันตา

pop 20,000

A long-time sweetheart with the intrepid backpacking crowd, Ko Lanta is steadily changing, with upmarket resorts replacing the cheap bungalows. The carefree, hippiesque backpacker vibe still prevails, for now, although the laid-back atmosphere has been kicked up a notch, and you'll find plenty of bars blaring the latest hits late into the night, along with a string of *faràng* restaurants showing the newest blockbusters. Travellers pour in daily, ferried from Krabi by a convoy of air-con minivans, or boats in the high season.

Beaches on Lanta's western shores are pleasantly soft, flat and sunny, and in isolated spots there's still some of that 'get away from it all' atmosphere that started attracting travellers in the first place. In recent years the island has been playing catch-up in the development stakes and now has loads of accommodation for pockets of all depths. However, Ko Lanta remains a friendly, relaxing place to stay. The 20,000 residents are mixed descendants of Muslim Malay and seafaring *chao leh*.

Ko Lanta is an *amphoe* (district) within Krabi Province that consists of 52 islands, of which 12 are inhabited. The geography here is typified by stretches of mangrove interrupted by coral-rimmed beaches, rugged hills and huge umbrella trees. Other than tourism, the main livelihood for the local folk includes the cultivation of rubber, cashews and bananas, along with a little fishing. When travellers refer to Ko Lanta, they are referring to Ko Lanta Yai. There's also a Ko Lanta Noi – just off Yai's northeastern tip – but it holds little interest for travellers, as it's ringed with mangroves rather than beaches.

During the wet season rain drenches Ko Lanta and the tide washes right up to the front of the resorts, bringing plenty of driftwood and rubbish with it. Only a few resorts remain open during this time and transport connections get thin on the ground.

Orientation & Information

Ban Sala Dan, a dusty two-street town at the northern tip of the island, is Ko Lanta's largest settlement with restaurants, minimarts, internet cafés, souvenir stores, travel agencies, dive shops, motorcycle rentals and even a 7-Eleven. There's a petrol station just outside town. There is one ATM at the bank and another at the 7-Eleven. However, it's still a good idea to bring money with you to the island. There are more restaurants and internet cafés along the island's main road.

Sights

Although Ko Lanta is primarily a beach destination, there are some interesting sights to explore inland if you tire of the sea and sand.

KO LANTA MARINE NATIONAL PARK

อุทยานแห่งชาติเกาะลันตา

Established in 1990, this **marine national park** (adult/child 200/100B) protects 15 islands in the Ko Lanta group, including the southern tip of Ko Lanta Yai. However, the park is increasingly threatened by the runaway development on the western coast of Ko Lanta Yai. The other islands in the group have fared slightly better – **Ko Rok Nai** is still very beautiful, with a crescent-shaped bay backed by cliffs, fine coral reefs and a sparkling white-sand beach. Camping is permitted on Ko Rok Nok and nearby **Ko Ha**, with permission from the national park headquarters. On the eastern side of Ko Lanta Yai, **Ko Talabeng** has some dramatic limestone caves that you can visit on sea-kayaking tours. The national park fee applies if you visit any of these islands.

The **national park headquarters** is at Laem Tanod, on the southern tip of Ko Lanta Yai, reached by a steep and corrugated 7km dirt track from Ao Nui. There are some basic hiking trails and a **scenic lighthouse**, and you can hire long-tails here for island tours during the low season.

BAN KO LANTA

Halfway down the eastern coast, **Ban Ko Lanta** (Lanta Old Town) was the island's original port and commercial centre, and provided

ANDAMAN COAST

a safe harbour for Arabic and Chinese trading vessels sailing between the larger ports of Phuket, Penang and Singapore. Some of the gracious and well-kept wooden stilt houses and shopfronts here are over 100 years old and are a pleasure to stroll through. A few pier restaurants offer up fresh catches of the day and have prime views over the sea.

A few kilometres past the hospital lies the **Gypsy House**, a Bohemian driftwood creation replete with ponds and traditional music, where artisans sell handicrafts and jewellery. There are a few pamphlets here on the *chao leh* of Ko Lanta, but it's mainly just a pleasant waterside chill-out space.

THAM KHAO MAIKAEO
ถ้ำเขาไม้แก้ว
Monsoon rains pounding away at limestone cracks and crevices for millions of years created this complex of forest caverns and tunnels. There are chambers as large as cathedrals, dripping with stalactites and stalagmites, and tiny passages that you have to squeeze through on hands and knees. There's even a subterranean pool you can take a chilly swim in. Sensible shoes are a must and total coverage in mud is almost guaranteed.

Tham Khao Maikaeo is reached via a guided trek through the jungle. A local family offers guided treks to the caves (with torches) for around 200B. The best way to get here is by rented motorcycle, or most resorts can arrange transport.

Close by, but reached by a separate track from the dirt road leading to the marine national park headquarters, **Tham Seua** (Tiger Cave) also has interesting tunnels to explore; elephant treks run up here from Hat Nui.

Activities
Horse riding, sea kayaking and deep-sea fishing can be arranged through resort tour desks or travel agencies in Ban Sala Dan.

DIVING & SNORKELLING
Several dive shops run two-dive trips to local sights for 2800B, while PADI Open Water courses cost 12,500B. The best diving is around Ko Phi Phi and the undersea pinnacles at **Hin Muang** and **Hin Daeng**, about 45 minutes from Ban Sala Dan by speedboat. These world-class dive sites have lone coral outcrops in the middle of the sea and act as important feeding stations for large pelagic fish such as

sharks, tuna and occasionally whale sharks and manta rays. Dive trips out here cost 3300B for two dives. The sites around **Ko Ha** have consistently good diving conditions, depths of 18m to 34m, plenty of marine life and a cave known as 'the Cathedral'. Reliable dive companies include **Laguna Fun Divers** (☎ 0 9291 4311; www.lagunafundivers.com) and the Scandinavian-run **Lanta Diver** (☎ 0 7568 4208; www.lantadiver .com; Ban Sala Dan). November to April is the best season for diving at Ko Lanta; the rest of the year most dive shops close down.

Numerous tour agencies along the strip can organise snorkelling trips out to Ko Rok Nok, Ko Phi Phi and other nearby islands. **Petpailin Co** (☎ 0 7568 4428), near the passenger jetty at Ban Sala Dan, offers day trips to Ko Phi Phi for 700B and four-island tours to Ko Muk, Ko Kradan, Ko Ngai and Ko Cheuk in Hat Chao Mai National Park for 800B.

Courses
Time for Lime (☎ 0 7568 4590; www.timeforlime.net), on Hat Khlong Dao, has a huge, professional kitchen with plenty of room to run amok. It offers cooking courses with a slightly more exciting selection of dishes than most cookery schools in Thailand; half-day courses cost from 1400B to 1800B.

Sleeping
Ko Lanta has many long stretches of good-looking beach packed with accommodation. However, because of the island's size, you don't get the feeling of 'peak hour' on the sand – even at busy times. Only the west coast is developed for tourism and, while Hat Khlong Dao can feel like package-tour mania, the further south you go the less crowded things get. Many resorts close during the May to October low season; those which stay open discount rooms by as much as 50%. Most places have restaurants and tour-booking facilities.

HAT KHLONG DAO
With perfect white sand stretching for over 2km, it's no wonder this was one of the first beaches to attract tourists and developers. There are numerous small lanes snaking from the main road towards the beach, all chock-a-block with bungalows offering similar facilities and charging midrange prices. The beach here is great for swimming.

Southern Lanta Resort (☎ 0 7568 4174-7; www.south ernlanta.com; bungalows incl breakfast 1600-2200B; 🖳 🖳)

KO LANTA & AROUND

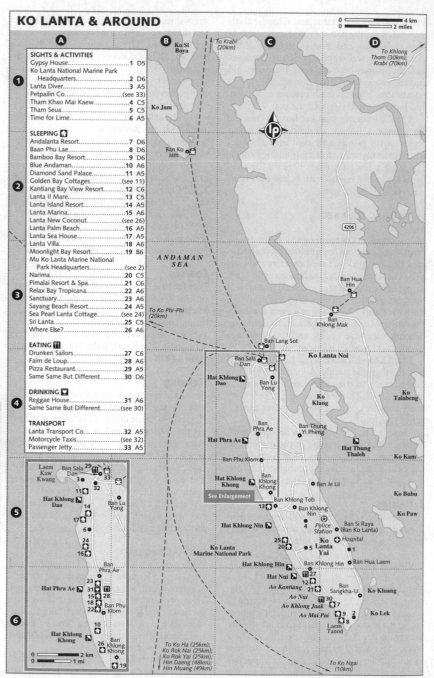

SIGHTS & ACTIVITIES
Gypsy House.................................1 D5
Ko Lanta National Marine Park
  Headquarters............................2 D6
Lanta Diver..................................3 A5
Petpailin Co.........................(see 33)
Tham Khao Mai Kaew..................4 C5
Tham Seua..................................5 C5
Time for Lime..............................6 A5

SLEEPING
Andalanta Resort........................7 D6
Baan Phu Lae..............................8 D6
Bamboo Bay Resort.....................9 D6
Blue Andaman............................10 A6
Diamond Sand Palace.................11 A5
Golden Bay Cottages............(see 11)
Kantiang Bay View Resort..........12 C6
Lanta Il Mare.............................13 C5
Lanta Island Resort....................14 A5
Lanta Marina..............................15 A6
Lanta New Coconut................(see 26)
Lanta Palm Beach.......................16 A5
Lanta Sea House.........................17 A5
Lanta Villa..................................18 A6
Moonlight Bay Resort................19 B6
Mu Ko Lanta Marine National
  Park Headquarters...............(see 2)
Narima......................................20 C5
Pimalai Resort & Spa..................21 C6
Relax Bay Tropicana...................22 A5
Sanctuary..................................23 A5
Sayang Beach Resort.................24 A5
Sea Pearl Lanta Cottage.......(see 24)
Sri Lanta....................................25 C5
Where Else?...............................26 A6

EATING
Drunken Sailors.........................27 C6
Faim de Loup............................28 A6
Pizza Restaurant........................29 A5
Same Same But Different...........30 D6

DRINKING
Reggae House............................31 A5
Same Same But Different......(see 30)

TRANSPORT
Lanta Transport Co....................32 A5
Motorcycle Taxis..................(see 32)
Passenger Jetty.........................33 A5

ANDAMAN COAST

Loads of shade in the tropical garden and a good-sized beachfront. The pool has a waterslide and the bungalows come with TVs, hot showers and minibars. The resort is family friendly and you can organise horse riding from here for 600B per hour.

Golden Bay Cottages (☎ 0 7568 4161; www.krabidir .com/goldenbaycottage; bungalows 1200-2700B; ⬛ ⬛) One of the better options on this beach. The trim little cottages surround a leafy courtyard and come in various sizes. The air-con bungalows on the beach are nicest and offer the best bang for your baht. Skip the overpriced fan bungalows. Breakfast is included.

The following places are recommended.

Diamond Sand Palace (☎ 0 7568 4135; bungalows 700-1000B; ⬚ Oct-Apr; ⬛)

Lanta Villa (☎ 0 7568 4129; www.lantavillaresort.com; bungalows 1500-1800B; ⬛ ⬛)

Lanta Sea House (☎ 0 7568 4073/4; www.lanta.de /seahouse; bungalows 2000-3800B; ⬛ ⬛)

Lanta Island Resort (☎ 0 7568 4124-7; www.lanta islandresort.com; bungalows 400-2000B; ⬛ ⬛)

HAT PHRA AE

The beach at Hat Phra Ae is only mediocre, but the ambience is lively. A large travellers' village has set up camp and there are loads of *faràng*-oriented restaurants, beach-bars, internet cafés and tour offices.

Sanctuary (☎ 0 1891 3055; bungalows 400-800B) A delightful place to stay. There are artistically designed wood-and-thatch bungalows with lots of grass and a hippyish atmosphere that's low-key and friendly. The restaurant offers Indian and vegetarian eats among the Thai usuals. The resort holds yoga classes and has a small art gallery displaying local talent.

Sea Pearl Lanta Cottage (☎ 0 1737 0159; seapearl lanta@hotmail.com; bungalows 250-900B) Despite facing a sandy car park, Sea Pearl manages to remain atmospheric with decent thatch-and-bamboo bungalows under shady palms. A cool restaurant sits by the beach.

Lanta Marina (☎ 0 1677 4522; lantamarina@hotmail .com; bungalows 600-1000B; ⬚ Oct-Apr) For something different check out these giant bungalows, which almost look like towering hay bales. It has a tribal feel: breezy sleeping options have bamboo crossbars for windows and are linked by an elevated boardwalk.

Relax Bay Tropicana (☎ 0 7568 4194; www.relax bay.com; bungalows 900-1600B; ⬚ Oct-Apr; ⬛) This French-run place is spread out over a tree-covered headland, by a small beach. It's pretty

funky and has great wooden bungalows on stilts with large decks overlooking the bay, and a huge bar and restaurant.

Also recommended:

Sayang Beach Resort (☎ 0 7568 4156; bungalows 500-1000B; ⬚ Oct-Apr; ⬛)

Lanta Palm Beach (☎ 0 1606 5433; bungalows 700-1500B; ⬚ Oct-Apr; ⬛ ⬛)

HAT KHLONG KHONG

Only the resorts at the northern end of this rather rocky beach are worth looking at.

Lanta New Coconut (☎ 0 1537 7590; bungalows 250B) The coconut has a small farm of simple huts surrounded by swaying palms. It's not much, but it's darn cheap.

Blue Andaman (☎ 0 1719 4951; bungalows 500-1000B; ⬚ Oct-Apr; ⬛ ⬛) Blue Andaman's friendly staff put lots of effort into making your stay memorable. The brick bungalows are chintzy but comfortable. They all feature balconies and are set around a well-tended garden.

Where Else? (☎ 0 1536 4870; www.whereelse-lanta .com; bungalows 500-1500B) Make your way here for Ko Lanta's little slice of Bohemia. The bungalows may be a bit shaky but there is great mojo here and the place swarms with backpackers. The restaurant is a growing piece of art in itself, but the bamboo and coconut knick-knacks are threatening to take over. The pricier bungalows are all unique, multilevel abodes sleeping up to four people.

Moonlight Bay Resort (☎ 0 7568 4401; www.mlb-resort .com; bungalows 3000-6900B; ⬛ ⬛ ⬛) A Scandinavian resort that plays up the eco-resort angle with natural materials, simple Nordic design and gorgeous bungalows either along a lush river, facing verdant greenery, or right on the beach. It's on a private rocky cove where most of the flora is labelled for your edification.

HAT KHLONG NIN

Halfway down the island the tarmac road turns inland towards Ban Khlong Nin and is replaced by a corrugated dirt track that continues south along the coast to the marine national park headquarters at Laem Tanod. The first beach here is lovely Hat Khlong Nin, which gets progressively nicer the further south you travel.

Lanta II Mare (☎ 0 1540 7257; www.lantariversand .com; bungalows 1200-1900B, f 4500B; ⬛ ⬛) The bungalows are fairly deluxe deals with pretty verandas surrounded by garden greenery. The resort has an intimate feel that's often missing

from larger places. Lanta II sits on one of Hat Khlong Nin's best swimming beaches.

Sri Lanta (☎ 0 7569 7288; www.srilanta.com; villas 3200-5500B; ✖ ▣) On the southern (and best) bit of the beach, this sophisticated, upmarket resort consists of roomy wooden villas in a hillside garden, set back from the shore. There's a very stylish beachside area with a restaurant and pool. Head to the shaded private pavilions for a traditional Thai massage or to stretch them bones at the daily yoga class. Breakfast is included.

HAT NUI

There are several small beaches around here with upmarket places to stay.

Narima (☎ 0 7560 7700; www.narima-lanta.com; bungalows 1800-2900B; ✖ ▣ ▣) This is an excellent, eco-sensitive resort run by an exceptionally friendly woman. The large huts are made from natural materials and feature funky bamboo furniture. The wooden restaurant is lit by lanterns and has some massive gnarled wood furniture. There's also a kiddie pool and a Jacuzzi.

AO KANTIANG

This bay's tip-top beach has a good sprinkling of sand, and several nearby tour offices provide internet access and rent out motorcycles.

Kantiang Bay View Resort (☎ 0 1787 5192; bungalows 400-1500B; ✖) Sharing the bay's fantastic beach, this resort has tidy, modern, concrete air-con bungalows with tiled roofs and a stand of old-fashioned wooden bungalows with bathrooms and fans. There's a beachside restaurant and bar, and lots of tours can be arranged. It's popular even in the low season.

Pimalai Resort & Spa (☎ 0 7560 7999; www.pimalai.com; r 11,500-15,500B; ste 22,000-31,000B; ✖ ▣) The sprawling, manicured gardens are interspersed with splendid water features and fountains. The Thai villas all have slick, modern Thai furnishings and excellent views of the beautiful bay below. There are several pools and restaurants on the grounds, a spa and small library.

AO KHLONG JAAK

There's a splendid beach here at Ao Khlong Jaak and the namesake waterfall is inland along Khlong Jaak.

Andalanta Resort (☎ 0 1836 4877; www.andalanta.com; bungalows 2200-4500B; ✖) You'll find comfortable and modern air-con bungalows

(some with loft) and some simple fan-cooled ones made of bamboo and wood, which face the sea. The garden is a delight, there's an alluring restaurant and the waterfall is a 30- to 40-minute walk away; this resort was formerly Waterfall Bay Resort. Call ahead and the staff will pick you up at Ban Sala Dan.

AO MAI PAI

There are only three resorts on this lovely isolated beach.

Bamboo Bay Resort (☎ 0 7561 8240; www.bamboobay.net; bungalows 700-1000B) Clinging to the hillside above Ao Mai Pai beach, this place has a variety of brick and concrete bungalows on stilts and a fine restaurant down by the beach. The best bungalows come with balconies and grand sea views – it's worth paying the extra baht to stay in one.

Baan Phu Lae (☎ 0 1201 1704; www.baanphulae.co.th; bungalows 400-1500B; ✖) The restaurant and many of the bungalows sit right on a private beach and have perfect sunset views. The thatch bungalows come with bamboo-framed beds and rustic porches made for slinging up a hammock. You can rent mountain bikes here.

LAEM TANOD

The road leading to the marine national park headquarters fords the *khlong* (canal), which can get quite deep in the wet season. Be careful if you're driving.

Mu Ko Lanta Marine National Park Headquarters (☎ Bangkok 0 2561 4292; camping with own tent per person 40B, camping with tent hire 200-300B) The secluded grounds of the national park headquarters are a serene place to set up camp –the sound of the ocean lapping up the rocks will lull you to sleep. The flat camping areas are shaded and sit in the wilds of the tropical jungle. There are toilets and running water, but you should bring your own food. You can also get permission for camping on Ko Rok Nok or Ko Ha here. National park entry fees apply.

Eating

The best places to eat are the seafood restaurants along the little lane at the northern end of Ban Sala Dan. With tables on verandas over the water, they offer fresh seafood sold by weight (which includes cooking costs). Expect to pay 600B per kilo for prawns and 300B per kilo for squid, fish and crabs. The best option is Rimnum Seafood, but come early if you want to get a table.

Most restaurants close in the low season.

Drunken Sailors (☎ 0 7011 0683; mains 40-90B; ☺ breakfast, lunch & dinner) Run by two friendly sisters, this hip, ultra-relaxed, octagonal pad is decked out with beanbags. It serves basic Thai and Western dishes and yummy, refreshing drinks like the banana-choc frappé (40B) – Starbucks, eat your heart out.

Faim de Loup (Hat Phra Ae; mains 50-100B; ☺ lunch & dinner) This little French bistro serves real filtered coffee and baguette sandwiches, as well as Thai food.

Same Same But Different (☎ 0 1787 8670; Ao Khlong Jaak; mains 50-120B; ☺ breakfast, lunch & dinner) In a perfect seaside setting, with tables right on the sand, you can sample some of the tastiest Thai cuisine on the island. Driftwood furniture and pieces of art pop up all over the place and the ambience is hard to beat.

Pizza Restaurant (Ban Sala Dan; pizzas from 140B; ☺ lunch & dinner) At the western end of the alley, this friendly place serves convincing pizzas and has quirky knick-knacks on the walls. There's also a bar and pool table.

Drinking & Entertainment

During the high season Ko Lanta has a positively buzzing nightlife, but this fizzles out almost completely during low season when everything shuts down.

Reggae House (Hat Phra Ae) A perennial favourite, Reggae House is one of dozens of beach-bars along the strip, particularly around Hat Phra Ae, pumping out boisterous reggae and dance anthems at peak times.

Same Same But Different (☎ 0 1787 8670) The lantern-lit open-air pavilions and chilled music make this a star choice if you are looking for a quiet evening of drinks and conversation.

Getting There & Away

Most people come to Ko Lanta by boat or air-con minivan. If you're coming under your own steam, you'll need to use the vehicle ferries between Ban Hua Hin and Ban Khlong Mak (Ko Lanta Noi) and on to Ko Lanta Yai. These run frequently between 7am and 8pm daily (motorcycle and driver 10B; car/4WD and driver 50/100B).

BOAT

There are two piers at Ban Sala Dan. The passenger jetty is about 300m from the main strip of shops; vehicle ferries leave from a second jetty that's several kilometres further east.

Passenger boats between Krabi's Khlong Chilat passenger pier and Ko Lanta run from September through May and take 1½ hours. Boats depart from Ko Lanta at 8am and 1pm (350B). In the reverse direction boats leave at 10.30am and 1.30pm. These boats will also stop at Ko Jam (for the full 350B fare).

Boats between Ko Lanta and Ko Phi Phi run as long as there are enough passengers, which means that services peter out in the low season. Boats usually leave Ko Lanta at 8am and 1pm (400B, 1½ hours); in the opposite direction boats leave Ko Phi Phi at 11.30am and 2pm.

There's also a high-season boat to Ko Ngai (400B, two hours), in Trang Province, that leaves Ban Sala Dan at 8.30am and returns from Ko Ngai at 3pm.

MINIVAN

This is the main way of getting to/from Ko Lanta: vans run year-round. **Lanta Transport Co** (☎ 0 7568 4121) and others have daily minivans to Krabi between 7am and 8am (250B, 1½ hours). Check for afternoon services at 1pm and 3.30pm. From Krabi vans depart at 9am, 11am, 1pm and 4pm. **KK Tour & Travel** (☎ Trang 0 7521 1198) has several daily air-con vans between Trang and Ko Lanta (220B, two hours).

Getting Around

Most resorts send vehicles to meet the ferries and you'll get a free ride *to* your resort. In the opposite direction expect to pay 50B to 100B. Alternatively you can take a motorcycle taxi from opposite the 7-Eleven in Ban Sala Dan; fares vary from 50B to 150B depending on distance.

Motorcycles can be rented at most resorts, restaurants, shops, farms, private houses… you name it. Unfortunately very few of these places provide helmets and none provide insurance, so take extra care on the bumpy roads. The going rate is 250B per day.

Lanta Transport Co is one of several places renting out small 4WDs for around 2000B per day, including insurance.

TRANG PROVINCE

Trang has mellow islands that offer good-value accommodation and the chance to escape the peak-season crowds. You're more likely to see tall rubber plantations here than rows of vendors selling the same T-shirts.

ANDAMAN COAST

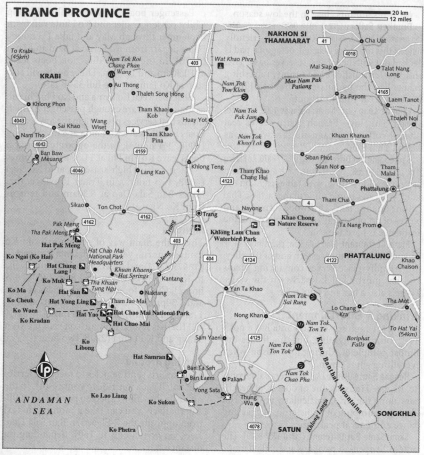

TRANG PROVINCE

0 ————— 20 km
0 ————— 12 miles

ANDAMAN COAST

TRANG
ตรัง
pop 77,200

Chances are you'll have to come through Trang at least once if venturing to or from the islands. The sprawling metropolis doesn't have much in the way of must-see attractions, it's more of a transport hub and important trading centre for fish (locally caught), palm oils and rubber. There are, however, lots of travel agencies in town dedicated to helping you hop to your island of choice as fast as possible. Many of the Trang island resorts maintain satellite offices here that can assist with bookings and transfers to their island. Trang often wins awards for being the 'Cleanest City in Thailand' and is also popular for Thais to tie

the knot before heading off to honeymoon in nearby Hat Chao Mai National Park.

Information
BOOKSHOPS
Ani's (☎ 0 1397 4574; 285 Th Ratchadamnoen; ♥ 9am-10pm) Stock up on English and European language titles here.

INTERNET ACCESS
There are internet cafés on Th Praram IV.
Tosit (285 Th Visetkul; per hr 20B) Fast computers, knowledgeable staff and a café serving real coffee.

POST
Post office (cnr Th Praram VI & Th Kantang) Also sells CAT cards for international phone calls.

TOURIST INFORMATION

TAT office (☎ 0 7521 5867; tattrang@tat.or.th; Th Ruen-rom) New tourist office located near the night market.

TRAVEL AGENCIES

As well as resort offices, Trang has some good travel agencies that can arrange tours.

Chaomai Tour (☎ 0 7521 6380; 15 Th Praram IV)
Libong Travel (☎ 0 7521 4676; 59/1 Th Tha Klang)
Trang Travel Co (☎ 0 7521 9598/9; 9 Th Praram IV)

Sights

Trang is more of a business centre than a tourist town. If you need to kill time, stroll over to **Wat Tantayaphirom** (Th Tha Klang). The huge white chedi enshrining a Buddha footprint is mildly interesting. The Chinese **Meunram Tem-**ple, between Soi 1 and Soi 3, sometimes sponsors performances of southern Thai shadow theatre, which are worth seeing. You'll have to stop in to check the schedule. It's also worth strolling around the large **wet & dry markets** on Th Ratchadamnoen and Th Sathani.

Activities

Boat trips to **Hat Chao Mai National Park** start at 700B per person and take in Ko Muk, Ko Cheuk and Ko Kradan, with lunch and drinks thrown in. National park fees are extra. There are also **sea-kayaking** tours to Tham Chao Mai (850B), where you can explore mangrove forests and canoe under commanding stalactites. **Snorkelling** trips to Ko Rok (1200B to 1500B) and minivan trips to local **caves** and **waterfalls** (850B) can also

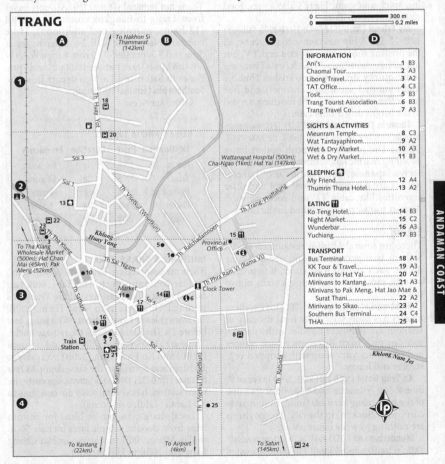

TRANG

| 0 | 300 m |
| 0 | 0.2 miles |

INFORMATION
Ani's...1 B3
Chaomai Tour..............................2 A3
Libong Travel...............................3 A2
TAT Office...................................4 C3
Tosit...5 B3
Trang Tourist Association...........6 B3
Trang Travel Co...........................7 A3

SIGHTS & ACTIVITIES
Meunram Temple........................8 C3
Wat Tantayaphirom.....................9 A2
Wet & Dry Market......................10 A3
Wet & Dry Market......................11 B3

SLEEPING 🏠
My Friend...................................12 A4
Thumrin Thana Hotel................13 A2

EATING 🍴
Ko Teng Hotel............................14 B3
Night Market..............................15 C2
Wunderbar.................................16 A3
Yuchiang....................................17 B3

TRANSPORT
Bus Terminal.............................18 A1
KK Tour & Travel.......................19 A3
Minivans to Hat Yai..................20 A2
Minivans to Kantang.................21 A3
Minivans to Pak Meng, Hat Jao Mae &
  Surat Thani.............................22 A2
Minivans to Sikao.....................23 A2
Southern Bus Terminal.............24 C4
THAI..25 B4

ANDAMAN COAST

be arranged by most agencies. For a cultural fix you can spend a day trekking in the **Khao Banthat Mountains** to visit villages of the mountain Sa Kai people (1500B). This includes a visit to waterfalls, lunch and a knowledgeable local guide. Most of these trips need at least two to three people; otherwise you may have to pay extra.

Sleeping

A number of hotels grace the city's two main thoroughfares, Th Praram VI and Th Visetkul, which intersect at the clock tower.

Ko Teng Hotel (☎ 0 7521 8148; 77-79 Th Praram VI; s/d 180/300B, with TV 280/380B; 😰) The undisputed king of backpacker lodgings in Trang. The corridors may look a little dank, but the rooms here have the magic combination of being big, spick *and* span. There's also a very good restaurant downstairs.

My Friend (☎ 0 7522 5447; 25/17-20 Th Sathani; r 430B; 😰 🖳) A hip newcomer to the scene, all the pristine rooms have air-con and TV, but not all have windows – check first. There are some quirky decorative flourishes (bubble wall-mounted aquarium, anyone?) and free tea, coffee and biscuits in the morning, served in the bright downstairs café.

Thumrin Thana Hotel (☎ 0 7521 1211; www.thumrin.co.th; 69/8 Th Huay Yot; r 1200-1600B; ste 3000-5000B; 😰 🖳) The town's most posh option has a gleaming marble lobby, three restaurants (one serves Japanese) and even its own bakery! Rooms are comfortable, well kept and offer amenities like cable TV and room service. Airport transfers are included in the rate.

Eating

There are several Muslim restaurants on Th Sathani that serve tasty and cheap Malay dishes, such as *rotii* with curry, if you need a quick meal before catching a train out of town.

Night market (noodles per bowl 10B) This excellent market has stalls selling the local delicacy of *khànŏm jiin* (Chinese noodles with curry) – you can pick from three spicy curry sauces and spruce up your soup with chopped vegetables and leaves.

Ko Teng Hotel (☎ 0 7521 8622; 77-79 Th Praram VI; dishes 40-70B; 😾 breakfast, lunch & dinner) Serves some of the best *kaeng kàrìi kài* (mild, Indian-style curry with chicken) in the city. The environs are nothing to write home about.

Wunderbar (☎ 0 7521 4563; 24 Th Sathani; mains 40-100B; 😾 breakfast, lunch & dinner) This *faràng*-owned

place by the train station serves good Thai dishes and convincing European food, plus cold beer in the evening.

Getting There & Away
AIR

THAI operates daily flights from Bangkok to Trang (around 3500B), but there have been some problems with landing at this airport in rain. The **THAI office** (☎ 0 7521 9923; 199/2 Th Visetkul) is open weekdays only. The airport is 4km south of Trang; air-con minivans meet flights and charge 80B to town. In the reverse direction a taxi or túk-túk will cost 100B to 150B.

BUS

Public buses leave from the well-organised Trang **bus terminal** (Th Huay Yot). Air-con buses from Trang to Bangkok cost 449B to 578B (12 hours, morning and afternoon). More comfortable are the VIP 24-seater buses at 5pm and 5.30pm (895B). From Bangkok, VIP/air-con buses leave between 6.30pm and 7pm. Buses to Satun and La-Ngu depart from the **Southern bus terminal** (Th Ratsada).

Other services:

BUSES FROM TRANG

Destination	Price	Duration	Frequency
Hat Yai	100B	3hr	frequent
Krabi	120B	2hr	frequent
Phang-Nga	210B	3½hr	hourly
Phuket	250B	4hr	hourly
Satun	100B	3hr	frequent

MINIVAN & SHARE TAXI

There are share taxis to Krabi (180B, two hours) and air-con minivans to Hat Yai (160B, two hours) from offices just west of the Trang bus terminal. Hourly vans to Surat Thani (200B, 2½ hours) leave from a **depot** (Th Tha Klang), just before Th Tha Klang crosses the railway tracks. There are also departures directly to Ko Samui (220B) and Ko Pha-Ngan (320B) every day at 12.30pm and 3pm from the same depot. **KK Tour & Travel** (☎ 0 7521 1198; 40 Th Sathani), opposite the train station, has several daily air-con vans to Ko Lanta (220B, two hours).

Local share taxis can be hired for custom trips from depots; sample fares include 500B to Pak Meng, 700B to Hat Yao or Hat Chang Lang and 800B to Hat Samran.

Local transport is mainly by air-con mini-van rather than săwngthăew. For Ko Sukorn there are air-con vans from Th Ratsada to the jetty at Palian (45B). Alternatively, take a van to Yanta Khao (30B) and change to a Ban Ta Seh săwngthăew (50B); boats can be chartered on the shore at Ta Seh.

TRAIN
Only two trains go all the way from Bangkok to Trang: the express 83, which leaves from Bangkok's Hualamphong station at 5.05pm and arrives in Trang at 7.35am the next day; and the rapid 167, which leaves from Hualam-phong station at 6.20pm, arriving in Trang at 10.11am. From Trang, trains leave at 1.45pm and 5.30pm. Fares are 1280B/731B for a 1st-/2nd-class air-con sleeper and 521B for a 2nd-class (fan) sleeper.

Getting Around
Túk-túk can be found near the intersection of Th Praram VI and Th Kantang and charge 30B for local trips. Motorcycles can be rented at travel agencies or at **Ani's** (285 Th Ratchadamnoen) for about 200B per day. Most agencies can also help you arrange car rental for around 1500B per day.

TRANG BEACHES & ISLANDS
Trang Province has a string of delightful sandy beaches along the coast. The coast here gets some of Thailand's biggest surf (probably the source of Trang's original unshortened name, 'City of Waves'), but it's really only worth investigating in March or after big storms during the rainy season – you'll also need to bring your own board.

There are dozens of tropical islands off-shore and transport connections are improving yearly. Some islands here are protected by the Hat Chao Mai National Park, including Ko Muk, Ko Kradan and Ko Cheuk. The beaches of Hat Pak Meng to Hat Chao Mai also fall under its jurisdiction.

Hat Pak Meng
หาดปากเมง
Thirty-nine kilometres from Trang in Sikao District, Hat Pak Meng serves as the main jumping-off point for the nearby island of Ko Ngai. There's a wild-looking stretch of coastline here, with a couple of so-so pockets of sand, but much of the seashore is rather marred by a big concrete sea wall. The main

pier is at the northern end of the beach, where Rte 4162 meets the coast. There are good fresh seafood restaurants in the vicinity.

Tour agencies at the jetty and the Lay Trang Resort organise one-day boat tours to Ko Muk, Tham Morakot (Emerald Cave, on Ko Muk), Ko Cheuk, Ko Ma and Ko Kradan for 750B per person (minimum three people), including lunch and beverages. There are also snorkel-ling day tours to Ko Ngai (650B) and Ko Rok (1000B to 1200B, plus national park fees).

Run by a staunch supporter of the Thai royal family, **Lay Trang Resort** (☎ 0 7527 4027/8; www.laytrang.com; bungalows 1000-1500B; ✿) boasts smart bungalows in a tidy garden and a very good patio restaurant.

There are several daily boats from Pak Meng to Ko Ngai at 10am, returning from Ko Ngai between 8am and 9am. You have a choice of a 30-minute ride by speedboat (350B) or a slower ride by 'big boat' (150B, one hour).

There are very regular air-con minivans from Th Kha Klang in Trang to Hat Pak Meng (80B, 45 minutes). You may have to take a motorcycle taxi from the Rte 4162 junction to the pier. Heading south from Pak Meng, the coast road passes Hat Chang Lang, Hat Yao and Hat Chao Mai National Park.

Ko Ngai
เกาะไหง(ไห)
To live out the Robinson Crusoe deserted-island fantasy, head to Ko Ngai (Ko Hai). It's a fetching island with a dramatic interior and squeaky-clean sandy beach along its eastern coast. There is no indigenous population on the island, but there are a few spiffy resorts. A ring of bright coral, excellent for snorkel-ling, circles Ko Ngai and the visibility in the turquoise water is excellent. Mask and snorkel sets and fins can be rented from resorts for 50B each, or you can take half-day snorkelling tours to nearby islands (per person 650B). Trips to Ko Rok Nok, 29km southwest of Ko Ngai, cost 1200B by speedboat (plus the ma-rine national park fee).

Even though it's technically a part of Krabi Province, the island is most easily accessible from Pak Meng.

SLEEPING
There's little here for budgetarians, most places are decidedly midrange and come with restaurants and 24-hour electricity. The boat pier is at Koh Ngai Resort, but if you book

ahead, resorts on the other beaches will arrange transfers.

Koh Hai Villa (☎ 0 7520 3263; bungalows 500-800B) Pretty much the only budget place on offer, the bungalows here are starting to show their age and the staff seem ambivalent about the whole endeavour. The wooden rooms have a little more character than the featureless concrete ones and all come with fans, bathrooms and mosquito nets.

Thapwarin Resort (☎ 0 1894 3585; www.thapwarin .com; bungalows 1550-3500B; 🔀) This place has a small village of very gracious huts made from natural materials – it's rustic done with style. Only the top options offer air-con, but all rooms have chic bathrooms filled with rock and plant features. The 1940s-style fans are a nice touch. It also rents sea kayaks for 150B per hour.

Koh Ngai Resort (☎ 0 7520 6924; bungalows 1500-3600B; 🔀 🖳) In a separate cove at the southern end of the island, this resort has its own private jetty and elegant wooden bungalows with huge verandas. The garden is immense and the resort has a small beach all to itself.

GETTING THERE & AWAY
The resorts provide daily boats from Hat Pak Meng to Ko Ngai at 10am, returning from Ko Ngai between 8am and 9am. Speedboat transfers cost 350B (30 minutes), while the slower 'big boats' cost 150B (one hour). Unless you're staying at Koh Ngai Resort you'll have to take a long-tail for the ship-to-shore ride (80B) or arrange for one of the other resorts to provide transfers. You can also privately charter a long-tail from Pak Meng for 1200B (up to three people). In the high season, Koh Ngai Resort has boats to Ban Sala Dan on Ko Lanta at 3pm (350B), returning from Ko Lanta at 8.30am.

Ko Muk
เกาะมุก

Ko Muk has several appealing beaches along with good-value accommodation. The interior is filled with soaring rubber plantations.

The main development action is based around the west coast beach of **Hat Faràng** (Hat Sai Yao), where one continually growing resort dominates much of the beachfront. Good **snorkelling** opportunities lie offshore and one of the island's star attractions, **Tham Morakot** (Emerald Cave), hides at the northern end of the island. This cave is a beautiful limestone tunnel that leads 80m to a sea lagoon. You have to swim through here at high tide, part of the way in pitch blackness, to a small concealed white-sand beach surrounded by lofty limestone, with a chimney that lets in a piercing shaft of light around midday. Boats can enter at low tide and the cave features on most tour itineraries, so it can get pretty crowded.

GETTING BUZZED IN TRANG

Trang is famous for its coffee shops (ráan kaa-fae or ráan ko-píi), which are usually run by Hokkien Chinese. These shops serve real filtered coffee (called kaafae thŭng in the rest of the country) along with a variety of snacks, typically paa-thâwng-kŏh, saalaapao (Chinese buns), khànŏm jìip (dumplings), Trang-style sweets, mǔu yâang (barbecued pork) and sometimes noodles and jók (thick rice soup).

When you order coffee in these places, be sure to use the Hokkien word ko-píi rather than the Thai kaafae, otherwise you may end up with Nescafé or instant Khao Chong coffee – the proprietors often think this is what faràng want. Coffee is usually served with milk and sugar – ask for ko-píi dam for sweetened black coffee, ko-píi dam, mâi sài náam-taan for black coffee without sugar or ko-píi mâi sài náam-taan for coffee with milk but no sugar. A few of our favourite shops are listed below.

▪ Atmospheric **Yuchiang** (no roman-script sign; Th Praram VI; dishes 20-30B) is a beautiful, hard-core and classic Hokkien coffeeshop with marble-topped round tables in an old wooden building. Food counters sit in front. Yuchiang roasts its own pork, so the pork saalaapao are particularly tasty here.

▪ Next to the train station, **Sin Ocha Bakery** (Th Sathani; dishes 25-50B) is the most convenient ráan ko-píi around and is very popular with travellers. Simple Thai dishes and breakfast are served, along with huge coffee drinks (10B to 40B) and teas. Décor is pleasantly unpretentious, though the service could use a shot in the arm.

Between Ko Muk and Ko Ngai are the small karst islets of **Ko Cheuk** and **Ko Waen**, which have good snorkelling and small sandy beaches. Boats to Ko Muk leave from the new Kuantungku pier just south of the Hat Chao Mai National Park headquarters, docking at Hua Laem on the eastern coast. Hat Faràng is a 60B motorcycle taxi ride across the island.

SLEEPING

The following places are a short walk north from the pier on a shallow beach. Note that much of Ko Muk shuts down in the low season.

Ko Mook Resort (☎ in Trang 0 7520 3303; www.ko mookresort.com; 45 Th Praram VI; bungalows 400–800B) These comfortable huts are excellent value and lie concealed in a thick garden covered with wild-looking ferns. The design here is unadorned and the tropical isolation is perfect for those searching for a romantic getaway. There's a free daily boat to Hat Faràng and snorkelling can be arranged for 300B.

Ko Mook Charlie Beach Resort (☎ 0 7520 3281-3; www.kohmook.com; bungalows 700–2400B; ✷ ▣) This place has become so big of late that it's trying to change the name of the beach from Hat Faràng to Hat Charlie. There's a bunch of different bungalow options, ranging from basic shacks to swish air-con deals with little decorations and big porches. It's starting to get a little crowded, but the beach here is lovely. Staff can organise snorkelling tours to Tham Morakot and other islands for 850B to 1050B. It's open year-round.

GETTING THERE & AWAY

Boats to Ko Muk now leave from the pier at Kuantungku, a few kilometres south of the national park headquarters. There are several ferries to Ko Muk leaving around noon and returning at 8am (80B, 30 minutes). A chartered long-tail from Kuantungku to Ko Muk costs from 700B (800B to Hat Faràng). Air-con vans run frequently from Trang to Kuantungku for 150B (one hour).

It's also possible to charter a long-tail to Ko Muk from either Pak Meng or Hat Yao for around 1000B to 1500B; resorts can arrange cheaper transfers for guests.

Hat Yao
หาดยาว

A laid-back fishing hamlet just south of Hat Yong Ling, Hat Yao is sandwiched between the sea and imposing limestone cliffs. A rocky headland at the southern end of Hat Yao is pockmarked with caves and there's good snorkelling around the island immediately offshore. The best beach in the area is the tiny **Hat Apo**, hidden away among the cliffs; you can get here by long-tail or wade around from the sandy spit in front of Sinchai's Chaomai Resort.

Apparently pirates used to hoard their treasure south of Hat Yao at **Tham Chao Mai**, a vast cave, full of crystal cascades and impressive stalactites and stalagmites, which can be explored by boat. To visit Tham Chao Mai, you can charter a long-tail for 300B per hour from Yao pier. Haad Yao Nature Resort offers sea-kayaking trips to the cave, including lunch, for around 700B to 900B per person, including guide. You can also rent a kayak and self-explore the cave for 500B (map included).

Just south of the headland in Ban Chao Mai is the new concrete Yao pier, the main departure point for Ko Kradan and Ko Libong. Currently there are a few boats offering day trips to Ko Kradan and other islands in the bay for 700/450B per adult/child, or you can make arrangements with local long-tail boatmen.

The **Haad Yao Nature Resort** (☎ 0 1894 6936; www .trangsea.com; r 300–500B, bungalows 800B; ✷) is run by enthusiastic naturalists and offers a variety of environmental tours in the region. Very orderly and homey bungalows come with shared baths, while the better self-contained bungalows have verandas and frilly extras. There's also a great pier restaurant here where you can watch the fishermen ply their trade over tasty Thai victuals.

Sinchai's Chaomai Resort (☎ 0 7520 3034; bungalows 300–1500B; ✷) is an activity oriented place that offers a handful of bungalows nestled under the rocky cliffs at the northern end of Hat Yao. The family that owns it arranges kayaking tours (600B), rents mountain bikes (per day 100B) and runs multiday-tour packages around Trang and the Andaman coast – prices vary.

GETTING THERE & AROUND

From Hat Yao you can charter a long-tail to Ko Kradan (1200B, one hour) or catch one of the regular long-tail boats to Ko Libong (80B to 70B, 20 minutes). A charter to Ko Libong is 300B.

Motorcycles can be rented for 250B per day – ask at your hotel. Sinchai's Chaomai Resort rents mountain bikes for 100B per day.

Ko Kradan
เกาะกระดาน

The remote Ko Kradan may well be the jewel in the crown of Trang Province. The beach here is spectacular and has sweeping views over aqua waters to the other islands scattered about the Andaman. There are great, untouched coral reefs just offshore, and rubber plantations fill large tracts of the island's core. Ko Kradan is part of Hat Chao Mai National Park and has so far been spared major developments. At the moment there is only one place to stay on the island, though plans are in the wind for a huge-scale top-end Amari resort – visit while you can. Camping is possible with permission from the national park staff.

Unfortunately Ko Kradan's sole resort, **Koh Kradan Paradise Beach** (☎ 0 7521 1391; www .kradanisland.com; bungalows with bathroom 600-1200B; 🐾), is overpriced. The wooden bungalows lined up behind the main beach are far from charming.

It's probably best to visit Ko Kradon, as most people do, on a snorkelling tour from Hat Yao or Ko Muk. The Koh Kradan Paradise Beach resort provides a daily transfer bus and boat from its **office** (☎ 0 7521 1391) opposite the train station in Trang (300B). A chartered long-tail from Hat Yao costs around 1000B one way.

Ko Libong
เกาะลิบง

Trang's largest island is just 15 minutes by long-tail from Hat Yao. Less visited than neighbouring isles, Ko Libong is known for its flora and fauna as much as for its beaches. The island is home to a small Muslim fishing community and has a few resorts on the western coast. The sensitive development here is a real breath of fresh air compared with other islands in the bay.

On the eastern coast of Ko Libong at **Laem Ju Hoi** is a large area of mangroves protected by the Botanical Department as the **Libong Archipelago Wildlife Reserve** (☎ 0 7525 1932). The sea channels here are one of the last habitats of the rare dugong, and around 40 of them graze on the sea grass that flourishes in the bay. The nature resorts in Hat Yao and Ko Libong offer dugong-spotting tours by sea kayak, led by trained naturalists, for 900B. Sea kayaks can also be rented at most resorts for 100B per hour.

If you want to spend the night, try **Libong Nature Beach Bungalow** (☎ 0 1894 6936; www.trangsea .com; bungalows 600-1000B; 🐾). Set on a lovely grassy garden and surrounded by rubber plantations, this place is owned by the same friendly and environmentally conscious people running the nature resort in Hat Yao. There's a simple restaurant with tasty food and the owners run excellent sea-kayaking tours of the mangroves. The resort is closed in the low season.

GETTING THERE & AWAY
Long-tail boats to Ban Ma Phrao on the eastern coast of Ko Libong leave regularly from Hat Yao (per person 60B to 70B) during daylight hours; the long-tail jetty at Hat Yao is just before the new Yao pier. On Ko Libong, motorcycle taxis run across to the resorts on the western coast for 70B. A chartered long-tail directly to either resort will cost 500B each way.

SATUN PROVINCE

If you're dying to explore uncharted territory, get off the beaten path and head to Satun. Bumped up against Malaysia, the Andaman coast's southernmost region is too far off the tourist trail to see much action. The largely undeveloped Ko Tarutao Marine National Park encompasses some of the most pristine untamed islands in the Andaman, all drenched in luxuriant greenery and edged by stereotypically splendid tropical beaches. Plucky explorers willing to put forth the effort it takes to get there will not be disappointed.

Until 1813 Satun was a district of the Malay state of Kedah, but the region was ceded to Britain in 1909 under the Anglo-Siamese Treaty and became a province of Siam in 1925. Largely Muslim in make-up, Satun has seen little of the political turmoil that plagues the neighbouring regions of Yala, Pattani and Narathiwat. Around 60% of people here speak Yawi or Malay as a first language, and the few wat in the region are small, impoverished and vastly outnumbered by mosques.

SATUN
สตูล
pop 33,400

Lying in a valley surrounded by limestone cliffs, the isolated town of Satun is a relaxing, if slightly ordinary, coastal settlement that makes a good base for visiting surrounding sights. The nearby Tammalang pier has boats to Kuala Perlis and Pulau Langkawi in Malaysia.

ANDAMAN COAST

Housed in a lovely old Sino-Portuguese mansion just off Th Satun Thanee, the excellent **Ku Den Museum** (Satun National Museum; Soi 5, Th Satun Thanee; ⏰ 8.30am-4.30pm Wed-Sun) is the only real attraction in Satun. The building was constructed to house King Rama V during a royal visit and the museum has exhibits and dioramas with soundtracks in Thai and English, covering every aspect of southern Muslim life.

Sleeping & Eating

There are various Chinese and Muslim restaurants on Th Burivanich and Th Samanta Prasit that will do for a basic, cheap meal. The Chinese food stalls specialise in *khâo mǔu daeng* (red pork with rice), while the Muslim restaurants offer *rotii* with southern-style chicken curry (around 50B each).

Sinkiat Thani Hotel (☎ 0 7472 1055-8; fax 0 7472 1059; 50 Th Buriwanit; r 450-665B; ❄️) It is housed in a tall building with amiable rooms right in the middle of town. Rooms come with TVs and hot showers, and are decent value. There's a good restaurant downstairs serving Thai food from an extensive English menu.

Pinnacle Wangmai Hotel (☎ 0 7471 1607/8; 43 Th Satun Thanee; r 500-1200B; ❄️) Satun's best sleeping bet, it runs the gamut of rooms – from simple fan to a big block of spiffier abodes with air-con. Try for a room in the back; they're a little quieter.

Phrik-Thai Steak & Food (☎ 0 7472 3777; Th Satun Thanee; meals 50-180B; ⏰ breakfast, lunch & dinner) If

SATUN

0 --------- 300 m
0 --------- 0.2 miles

To Khao Phaya Wang (500m)

Th Khuhaprawat

To Thale Ban National Park (30km); Pak Bara (60km); Hat Yai (97km); Trang (145km)

Khao Phaya Wang ▲

Khlong Bambang

Th Reuangit Jaton

Th Satun Thani

Soi 5

Th Yatrasawat

Th Hatthatham Seuksa

Hospital

Immigration Office

Th Phuminat

Th Sinwithi

Th Buriwanit

Kasikornbank

Th Samanta Prasit

To Jepilang (16km)

Wat Chanathipchaloem

4051

Th Wiset Mayura

Th Sulakanukorn

To Amm Guest House (2km); Tha Tammalang (Pier) (7km)

ANDAMAN COAST

steak with garlic-butter sauce and fries is what you're craving, look no further. It also serves plenty of Thai dishes either in its smart air-con restaurant or at outside tables.

Time (☎ 0 7478 1176; 43 Th Satun Thanee; dishes 80-220B; ☺ breakfast, lunch & dinner) This highly recommended air-con restaurant has a TGI Friday thing going on, with chirpy staff and a fun atmosphere. It serves the best Thai food in town.

Night market (Th Satun Thanee) This excellent market, just north of Satun Tanee Hotel, comes to life around 5pm and serves great Thai fast food, including southern-style curries – spicy!

Getting There & Away
BOAT
Boats to Malaysia and Tarutao leave from Tammalang pier, about 7km south of Satun along Th Sulakanukoon. Large long-tail boats run regularly to Kuala Perlis in Malaysia (200B, one hour) between 8am and 2pm. From Malaysia the fare is RM$20. A chartered boat to Kuala Perlis costs around 2000B for up to 15 people.

For Pulau Langkawi in Malaysia, boats leave from Tammalang pier daily at 8am, 9am, 1.30pm and 4pm (250B, 1½ hours). In the reverse direction, boats leave from Pulau Langkawi at 9am, 10am, 2pm and 4pm and cost RM$25. Remember that there is a one-hour time difference between Thailand and Malaysia. You can buy tickets in Satun town at the **Thai Ferry Center** (☎ 0 7473 0511; Th Sulakanukoon), near Wat Chanathipchaloem.

Due to lack of tourist demand, the boats that usually depart to Ko Tarutao and Ko Lipe from Tammalang pier now only run from Pak Bara (see opposite), though you may want to confirm this with the Thai Ferry Centre before you arrive.

BUS
Buses to Bangkok leave from a small depot on Th Hatthakham Seuksa, just east of the centre. Air-con services (522B to 671B, 14 hours) leave at 7am and half-hourly from 2.30pm to 4pm. A single VIP bus leaves at 4.30pm (1030B). From Bangkok's Southern bus terminal, buses leave at 6pm and 6.30pm. Ordinary and air-con buses to Hat Yai (60B, two hours) and Trang (80B, 1½ hours) leave regularly from in front of the 7-Eleven on Th Satun Thanee.

MINIVAN & SHARE TAXI
There are regular vans to the train station in Hat Yai (80B, one hour) from a depot just south of Wat Chanathipchaloem on Th Sulakanukoon. Occasional minivans run to Trang, but buses are much more frequent. If you're arriving by boat at Tammalang pier, there are direct air-con vans to Hat Yai (100B), Hat Yai airport (180B) and Trang (180B).

Share taxis can be hired from next to the Masjid Mambang Satul to Pak Bara (350B, 45 minutes), La-Ngu (240B, 30 minutes) or Hat Yai (350B, one hour).

Getting Around
Small orange sǎwngthǎew to Tammalang pier (for boats to Malaysia) cost 40B and leave every 20 minutes or so between 8am and 5pm from a depot opposite the Thai Ferry Centre. A motorcycle taxi from the same area costs 50B.

AROUND SATUN
Pak Bara
ปากบารา
The coast northeast of Satun has a few small towns that serve as jumping-off points for the islands in the Mu Ko Phetra and Ko Tarutao Marine National Parks, but the small fishing community of Pak Bara is the main transit point. Tourist facilities are slowly improving as Pak Bara becomes increasingly busy with travellers discovering these dazzling isles in the south Andaman. The peaceful town has some decent sleeping options and great seafood and is even turning into a popular place to hang out for a while.

The main road from La-Ngu terminates at the pier where there are several travel agencies, internet cafés, cheap restaurants and shops selling beach gear. There's a **visitors centre** (☎ 0 7478 3485) for Ko Tarutao National Park just back from the pier, where you can book accommodation and obtain permission for camping. Travel agencies here can arrange tours to the islands in the national park.

TOURS
There are several travel agencies near the pier that will vie for your transport custom. **Adang Sea Tours** (☎ 0 1276 1930; www.adangseatour.com) is one of the more reliable agencies in town; it also runs one of the boat services to Ko Tarutao. The friendly owner, Decha, is very helpful and also has day trips kayaking through the impressive caves at Tham Chet Khok (per

person including lunch 1500B); and two-day snorkelling and island-hopping tours around the region (per person from 2300B). You can arrange car hire here for 1000B per day.

In the high season, the **Satun Pakbara Speedboat Club** (☎ 0 7478 3643-5; www.tarutaolipeisland.com) runs speedboat tours to Ko Tarutao, Ko Bulon Leh and Ko Lipe – visit the website for the latest details.

SLEEPING & EATING

Both of these guesthouses have restaurants attached.

Bara Guest House (☎ 0 9654 2801; r 200B) On the beach and just up from the pier, the rooms here are colourful, if a little bare, and sit off a green path leading to the ocean. It's the groovy touches and hippy feel to the rooms, and beachside restaurant, that earn this place its biggest thumbs up.

Best House Resort (☎ 0 7578 3058; bungalows 450-590B; 🔀) This place has tidy new concrete bungalows around a pond. They almost look like moored boathouses.

There are several basic restaurants near the Pak Bara pier that serve good Malay Muslim food for 30B to 50B; the best of these is next to Andrew Tour, just back from the pier.

GETTING THERE & AWAY

There are hourly buses from Hat Yai to the pier at Pak Bara (80B, 2½ hours) between 7am and 4pm. Coming from Satun, you can take an ordinary bus towards Trang and get off at La-Ngu (40B, 30 minutes), continuing by sǎwngthǎew to Pak Bara (25B, 15 minutes). You can also charter a taxi to Pak Bara from Satun for 350B.

Air-con minivans leave hourly for Hat Yai (120B, two hours) from travel agencies near Pak Bara pier. There are also vans to Trang (250B, 1½ hours) and Krabi (400B, four hours).

There are boats directly to Ao Pante Malacca on Ko Tarutao at 10.30am and 3pm (250B, 1½ hours); in the reverse direction, boats leave at 9am and 11.30am. The 10.30am boat also continues on to Ko Lipe. For Ko Bulon Leh and Ko Lipe, boats depart at 1.30pm, arriving in Ko Bulon Leh one hour later (350B) and at Ko Lipe at 3.30pm (450B to 550B). These boats return from Ko Lipe at around 9am. A different, big-boat service runs to Ko Bulon Leh at around 2pm if there are enough takers (250B). None of these services

---

> **IT'S A NICE DAY FOR A WET WEDDING**
>
> Each Valentine's Day, Ko Kradan is the setting for a rather unusual wedding ceremony. Around 35 brides and grooms don scuba gear and descend to an underwater altar amid the coral reefs, exchanging their vows in front of the Trang District Officer. How the couples manage to say 'I do' underwater has never been fully explained, but the ceremony has made it into the Guinness Book of Records for the world's largest underwater wedding. Before and after the scuba ceremony, the couples are paraded along the coast in a flotilla of motorboats. If you think this might be right for your special day, visit the website www.underwaterwedding.com.

run in the low season when the national park is officially closed.

Ko Bulon Leh
เกาะบุโหลนเล

Now is the time to visit Ko Bulon Leh. This gorgeous island, 23km west of Pak Bara, is surrounded by the Andaman's signature clear waters and has its share of faultless white-sand beaches with swaying casuarinas. Gracious **Ko Bulon Leh** is in that perfect phase of being developed enough to offer comfortable facilities, yet not so popular that you have to book umbrella beach-time days in advance.

The southern part of the island is where you'll find the alluring beaches of **Mango Bay**, while in the north there is a rocky bay that's home to small settlements of *chao leh*. The island is perfect for hiking – the interior is interlaced with tracks and trails. The tracks are lined with rubber plantations that are thick with birds, and you can reach most places on the island within half an hour. There are some bizarre rock formations along the coastline reminiscent of a Salvador Dali dream. A fine golden-sand beach runs along the eastern coast of the island with good coral reefs immediately offshore.

Resorts can arrange **snorkelling** trips to other islands in the Ko Bulon group for around 900B, and **fishing** trips for 300B per hour. You can also rent masks and snorkels (100B), fins (70B) and **sea kayaks** (150B per hour).

ANDAMAN COAST

SLEEPING & EATING

Most places here shut down in the low season, though during the swing season between rainy and dry the caretakers at some resorts might rent you a room at a discount rate – although it can be slightly creepy having a whole place to yourself, especially after it's been closed up for months.

Bulone Resort (☎ 0 1897 9084; www.bulone-resort.com; bungalows 500-900B) The pick of the bunch when it comes to budget options, Bulone has airy cottages in various sizes, all with plenty of shade under the tall casuarinas that line the northern part of the beach. It's a simple affair – not all rooms have attached bathroom – but the restaurant here is highly recommended.

Marina Resort (☎ 0 9811 3072; www.marina-kobulon .com; bungalows 500-1000B) Inland from Pansand Resort, this unique place is built from natural materials, and has lovely thatched huts on stilts and a funky castaway-style restaurant with tables on a large bamboo veranda.

Pansand Resort (www.pansand-resort.com; 82-84 Th Visetkul; cottages 1200-1700B) Hands down the best place to stay on Bulon Leh, Pansand sits on the island's prime bit of beach. There are amiable colonial-style bungalows, cottages lined up along green grounds and a well-kept garden, and breakfast is included. The restaurant here is great and staff can arrange snorkelling trips to White Rock Island (1500B for up to eight people). It's popular – call ahead. Book through First Andaman Travel (☎ 0 7521 8035) on Th Visetkul in Trang.

There are a few local restaurants and a small shop in the Muslim village next to Bulon Viewpoint.

GETTING THERE & AWAY

Big boats to Ko Bulon Leh leave from Pak Bara between 2pm and 3pm daily in the high season if there are enough takers; the fare is 250B. In the reverse direction, the boat moors in the bay in front of Bulone Resort at around 9am; you may have to wave your arms around to get the pilot's attention. In the low season these boats often stop altogether. If you must get to the island, you can charter a long-tail from Pak Bara for 2000B.

From November to May there are also boats to Ko Bulon from Ko Lipe in Ko Tarutao Marine National Park; these leave from Ko Lipe at 9am, reaching Ko Bulon at 10am (350B, one hour) and then continuing on to Pak Bara (350B, one hour). In the opposite direction, boats leave from Pak Bara at 1.30pm, stopping at Ko Bulon Leh one hour later.

KO TARUTAO MARINE NATIONAL PARK

อุทยานแห่งชาติหมู่เกาะตะรุเตา

Protected partly by its national park status, and mostly by its relative inaccessibility, **Ko Tarutao Marine National Park** (☎ 0 7478 1285; adult/child under 14 200/100B; ☺ mid-November–Apr) is one of the most exquisite and unspoiled regions in Thailand. This massive park encompasses 51 islands covered with well-preserved virgin rainforest teeming with fauna, as well as sparkling coral reefs and radiant beaches.

One of the first marine national parks in Thailand, Ko Tarutao is the epitome of environmentally sound tourist management. The only accommodation in the park involves small, ecofriendly government-run cabins and longhouses, and great emphasis is placed on preserving the natural resources of the area. Pressure from big developers to build resorts on the islands has so far been mercifully ignored, though concessions were made for the filming of the American reality-TV series *Survivor* in 2001. Within the islands of the park you can spot dusky langurs, crab-eating macaques, mouse deer, wild pigs, sea otters, fishing cats, water monitors, tree pythons, Brahminy kites, sea eagles, hornbills and kingfishers.

Ko Tarutao is the biggest and most visited island in the group and home to the park headquarters and government accommodations. Many travellers choose to stay on Ko Lipe, which has managed to evade the park's protection and is fast becoming a popular resort with tourist facilities and bungalows aplenty. Long-tail tours to other outlying islands can be arranged through travel agencies in Satun or Pak Bara, through the national park headquarters on Ko Tarutao or through resorts and long-tail boat operators on Ko Lipe. Note that there are no foreign exchange facilities at Ko Tarutao – you can change cash and cheques at travel agencies in Pak Bara and there's an ATM at La-Ngu. The park officially closes in the low season (May through early November), when all boats stop running.

Ko Tarutao

เกาะตะรุเตา

Most of Ko Tarutao's whopping 152 sq km is covered in dense, old growth jungle that rises sharply up to the park's 713m peak. Mangrove swamps and typically impressive

KO TARUTAO MARINE NATIONAL PARK & AROUND

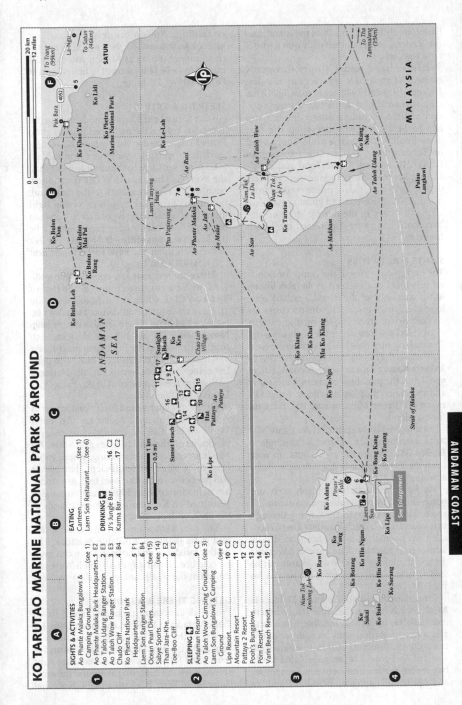

SIGHTS & ACTIVITIES

Ao Phante Malaka Bungalows & Camping Ground	(see 1)
Ao Phante Malaka Park Headquarters.1	E2
Ao Taloh Udang Ranger Station.2	E3
Ao Taloh Wow Ranger Station.3	E3
Chado Cliff.4	B4
Ko Phetra National Park Headquarters.5	F1
Laem Son Ranger Station.6	B4
Ocean Pearl Divers	(see 15)
Sabye Sports	(see 14)
Tham Jara-Khe.7	E2
Toe-Boo Cliff.8	E2

SLEEPING

Andaman Resort.9	C2
Ao Taloh Wow Camping Ground	(see 3)
Laem Son Bungalows & Camping Ground	(see 6)
Lipe Resort.10	C2
Mountain Resort.11	C2
Pattaya 2 Resort.12	C2
Pooh's Bungalows.13	C2
Porn Resort.14	C2
Varin Beach Resort.15	C2

EATING

Canteen	(see 1)
Laem Son Restaurant	(see 6)

DRINKING

JJ's Jungle Bar.16	C2
Karma Bar.17	C2

limestone cliffs circle much of the island, and the western coast is lined with quiet white-sand beaches.

Tarutao has a sordid history that partly explains its great state of preservation today. Between 1938 and 1948, more than 3000 Thai criminals and political prisoners were incarcerated here, including interesting inmates like So Setabutra, who compiled the first Thai–English dictionary while imprisoned on Tarutao, and Sittiporn Gridagon, son of Rama VII. During WWII, food and medical supplies from the mainland were severely depleted and hundreds of prisoners died from malaria. The prisoners and guards mutinied, taking to piracy in the nearby Strait of Malacca until they were suppressed by British troops in 1944.

SIGHTS & ACTIVITIES

The overgrown ruins of the camp for political prisoners can be seen at **Ao Taloh Udang**, in the southeast of the island, reached via a long overgrown track. The prison camp for civilian prisoners was over on the eastern coast at **Ao Taloh Waw** where the big boats from Tammalang pier now dock. A concrete road runs across the island from Ao Taloh Waw to **Ao Pante Malacca** on the western coast, where you'll find the park headquarters, bungalows and the main camping site. Boats travel between Ao Pante Malacca and Pak Bara on the mainland.

Next to the visitors centre at Ao Pante Malacca, a steep trail leads through the jungle to **Toe-Boo Cliff**, a dramatic rocky outcrop with fabulous views towards Ko Adang and the surrounding islands.

Ao Pante Malacca has a lovely alabaster beach shaded by pandanus and casuarinas. If you follow the large stream flowing through here inland, you'll reach **Tham Jara-Khe** (Crocodile Cave), which was once home to deadly saltwater crocodiles. The cave is navigable for about a kilometre at low tide and can be visited on long-tail tours from the jetty at Ao Pante Malacca.

Immediately south of Ao Pante Malacca is **Ao Jak**, which has another fine sandy beach; and **Ao Molae**, which also has fine white sand and a ranger station with bungalows and a camp site. A 30-minute boat ride or 8km walk south of Ao Pante is **Ao Son**, an isolated sandy bay where turtles nest between September and April. You can camp here but there are

no facilities. Ao Son has decent snorkelling, as does **Ao Makham**, further south. From the small ranger station at Ao Son you can walk inland to **Lu Du Falls** (about 1½ hours) and **Lo Po Falls** (about 2½ hours).

SLEEPING & EATING

All the formal park accommodation on Ko Tarutao is around the park headquarters at Ao Pante Malacca and at Ao Molae. The accommodation (open mid-November to mid-May) is far more sensitive to the environment than the average Thai resort. Water is rationed, rubbish is transported back to the mainland, lighting is provided by power-saving light bulbs and electricity is available between 6pm and 7am only. Accommodation can be booked at the **park office** (☎ 0 7478 3485) in Pak Bara, or through the **Royal Forest Department** (☎ 0 2561 4292/3) in Bangkok.

There are spacious fan-cooled **cabins** (r 600-1200B) with two or three rooms at the foot of Toe-Boo Cliff, while at Ao Molae there are 10 recently constructed deluxe **bungalows** (up to 4 people 1000-2000B). There are also simple **longhouse rooms** (r 500B) at Ao Pante Malacca, with four mattresses on the floor (you must take a whole room). All rooms have mosquito nets, but bring some repellent as backup. National park entry fees can be paid at Ao Pante Malacca or Ao Taloh Waw.

Camping is permitted under casuarinas at Ao Pante Malacca, Ao Molae and Ao Taloh Waw, where there are toilet and shower blocks, or on the wild beaches at Ao Son, Ao Makham and Ao Taloh Udang, where you'll need to be totally self-sufficient. The cost is 50B per person with your own tent, or you can hire tents for 100B to 300B. Camping is also permitted on Ko Adang and other islands in the park, with permission.

The park authorities run an excellent **canteen** (dishes 40-120B) at Ao Pante Malacca. The food is satisfying and tasty and you can even get cold beer. If you stay at Ao Taloh Waw you can eat at the small canteen by the jetty.

GETTING THERE & AROUND

From Pak Bara there are boats directly to Ao Pante Malacca at 10.30am and 3pm (200B, 1½ hours); in the reverse direction, boats leave at 9am and 11.30am. Satun Ferry and **Adang Sea Tours** (☎ 0 1276 1930; www.adangseatour.com) runs several boats, all departing at around the same time; Satun Ferry is a little pricier. Note that

most boat transport stops from mid-May to mid-November, when the park is officially closed.

During the high season you can also come here on speedboat day-tours from Pak Bara for 2000B, including national park fees, lunch, drinks and snorkelling. It's possible to charter a long-tail boat for the same price from Pak Bara, or from little Jepilang pier, 13km west of Satun (30km from Tarutao).

Long-tails can be hired from the jetty at Ao Pante Malacca for trips to Tham Jara Khae or Ao Son for around 600B. To Ao Taloh Udang you'll pay about 1500B for a round-trip.

Ko Khai & Ko Klang
เกาะไข่/เกาะกลาง

Between Ko Tarutao and Ko Adang is a small cluster of three islands collectively known as **Muu Ko Klang** (Middle Island Group). Most interesting is **Ko Khai**, which has a very neat white-sand beach and a scenic rock arch. The coral here has suffered a bit due to boat anchors, but both Ko Khai and **Ko Klang** have crystal-clear water for swimming. You can get here by chartered long-tail from either Ao Pante Malacca on Ko Tarutao, or Ko Lipe; a round-trip will cost around 1500B from either end.

Ko Lipe
เกาะหลีเป๊ะ

Encircled by sandy beaches and filled with mountainous woodland, Ko Lipe is home to a 700-strong community of *chao leh* villagers and a growing legion of private developers. Falling outside the protection of the national park (but grouped here for simplicity), partly because of the entrenched local population, this little isle is rapidly emerging as the tourist centre for the far-southern Andaman. However, things are still a lot more low-key than at islands like Ko Lanta or Ko Phi Phi.

SIGHTS & ACTIVITIES
Most of the developments are either at **Hat Pattaya** on the southern coast or near the *chao leh* village on the eastern coast. Luckily, the rest of Ko Lipe is still very mellow, with peaceful jungle trails and some delightful secluded beaches that have a romantic *Gilligan's Island* feel. Probably the most beautiful is **Sunset Beach**, which has fabulous views to Ko Adang. A footpath leads here from behind the village school. Another nifty spot is the northern end

of **Sunlight Beach**, where a lovely curved sand bar carves out a tranquil, translucent cove of emerald water.

There are no banks or ATMs on the island, though several of the bigger resorts can change travellers cheques, cash or do advances on credit cards – all for a hefty fee. It's also a good idea to stock up on necessities such as insect repellent before you arrive, as things can be quite pricey on the island.

There's good coral all along the southern coast and around **Ko Kra**, the little island opposite the *chao leh* village. Most resorts rent out mask and snorkel sets and fins for 50B each and can arrange long-tail trips to Ko Adang and other coral-fringed islands for around 1500B. On Sunset Beach **Sabye Sports** (☎ 0 7412 8026; www.sabye-sports.com) offers PADI Open Water dive courses for about 1200B, and day trips with two dives for 2500B. **Ocean Pearl Divers** (☎ 0 9733 8068) is based out of the Varin Beach Resort and does similar trips.

SLEEPING & EATING
All resorts on Ko Lipe close from May through October, when the boats stop running. Most restaurants have their own restaurants but the village also has several rustic local restaurants. Hat Pattaya is a great spot, despite being crammed with resorts.

Porn Resort (☎ 0 7472 8032; bungalows 350-450B) This lovely old-fashioned bamboo place is the only resort on the comely Sunset Beach – the restaurant is highly recommended. Its bungalow verandas are ideal for admiring the sun's nightly dip into the ocean.

Andaman Resort (☎ 0 7472 8017; camping per site 50B, tent hire 150B, bungalows 350-700B) Just north of the village, this place has plain wooden bungalows under the shade of casuarinas, as well as rather incongruous blue-roofed concrete bungalows closer to the village. The beach here is pretty average.

Pooh's Bungalows (☎ 0 7472 8019; www.poohlipe .com; r 450-900B; 🖳) The rooms here – two per bungalow – have no beach view, and are in a rather breeze-less spot inland from Hat Pattaya. However, they're popular because of easy access to Pooh's accommodating restaurant, dive shop, travel agent and internet café.

Mountain Resort (☎ 0 7472 8131; bungalows 450-1200B; 🌀) This big resort has outstanding views from its hillside location. Winding wooden walkways lead down to the beach, where you'll find a terraced restaurant with

equally spectacular vistas. The huts are intricately designed from thatch and wood and come with verandas, some right on the beachfront. It's best avoided during Thai holidays, when it can be overcrowded.

Varin Beach Resort (☎ 0 1543 0505; www.varin beachresort.com; bungalows 500-1200B; 🐾) This new enterprise has, you guessed it, thatch and wooden bungalows, near the beach, with varying levels of comfort. Look for the big blue marlin monument.

Pattaya Song (☎ 0 7472 8034; www.pattayasongresort .com; bungalows 1000-1500B) Above the rocks at the western end of the beach, this Italian-run pad has decent wood and concrete huts strung out either along the ocean or a little way up the hill. The Pattaya Seafood restaurant here serves excellent food and the resort can organise fishing and island-hopping trips around the area.

Lipe Resort (☎ 0 7472 4336; bungalows 600-2000B) The biggest player at Hat Pattaya, Lipe has a slightly haphazard selection of wood-and-concrete bungalows and a large bamboo restaurant on the beach. The top rooms here have massive windows looking out to sea, but the restaurant doesn't get great reviews.

DRINKING

Karma Bar (☎ 0 5199 3101) This bar lies nestled against the base of a limestone cliff below Mountain Resort and serves fresh cocktails, cold beer and toasties (jaffles) while spinning a great selection of MP3s.

A little bit inland, JJ's Jungle Bar is another good place for a tipple.

GETTING THERE & AWAY

The boats from Pak Bara (see p729) are currently the only way to reach Ko Lipe. The 10.30am boat from Pak Bara to Ko Tarutao continues on to Ko Lipe (450B, two hours). Other boats leave Pak Bara for Ko Lipe at 1.30pm (from 450B to 550B), stopping on the

way at Ko Bulon Leh. These boats return from Ko Lipe at around 9am. The fare between Ko Lipe and Ko Bulon Leh is 300B (one hour). None of these services run in the low season, but you can charter a boat to Ko Lipe from Pak Bara for a hefty 4000B each way.

Ko Adang & Ko Rawi

เกาะอาดัง/เกาะราวี

The island immediately north of Ko Lipe, **Ko Adang**, has brooding, densely forested hills, white-sand beaches and healthy coral reefs. Lots of snorkelling tours make a stop here but there are mooring buoys to prevent damage from anchors. Inland are jungle trails and tumbling waterfalls, including **Pirate's Falls**. Legend has it pirates used the waterfalls as a freshwater source, hence the name. There are great views from **Chado Cliff**, above the main beach, and green turtles lay their eggs here between September and December. The only accommodation is provided by the national park service, near its ranger station at **Laem Son** in the southeast of the island. There are **bungalows** (3-9 people 300-1500B), **longhouses** (4-bed r 400B) and facilities for **camping** (camping with own tent per person 20B, camping with tent hire 100-300B). A small restaurant provides basic meals.

Ko Rawi is 11km west of Ko Adang and has similar limestone hills and dense jungle, with first-rate beaches and large coral reefs offshore. Wild camping is allowed, with permission from the national park authorities. Other excellent snorkelling spots include the northern side of **Ko Yang** and tiny **Ko Hin Ngam**, which is known for its unique stripy pebbles. Legend has it that the stones are cursed and anyone who takes one away will experience bad luck until the stones are returned to their source.

You can get to Ko Adang on any of the boats that run to Ko Lipe (see left) and for the same fare; just tell the boat driver that you want to go to Ko Adang.

Directory

CONTENTS

ACCOMMODATION

Thailand offers the widest and best-priced variety of accommodation of any country in Southeast Asia.

Most hotels and resorts, and all guesthouses, quote their rates in Thai baht (B). A few top-

---

PRACTICALITIES

- *Bangkok Post* and the *Nation* publish national and international news daily.

- More than 400AM and FM radio stations; and short-wave radios can pick up BBC, VOA, Radio Australia, Deutsche Welle and Radio France International.

- Five VHF TV networks with Thai programming, plus UBC cable with international programming.

- The main video format is PAL.

- Thailand uses 220V AC electricity; power outlets most commonly feature two-prong round or flat sockets.

- Thailand follows the international metric system. Gold and silver are weighed in *bàat* (15g).

---

end places quote only in US dollars and where that is the case we have followed suit.

Accommodation prices listed in this book are high-season prices for either single or double rooms. Icons are included to indicate where air-con, swimming pools or internet access are available; otherwise, assume that there's a fan. Rooms under 200B or 250B a night will typically have a shared bathroom.

In this guide we place accommodation costing less than 600B a night in the Budget category, 600B to 1500B in the Midrange category and over 1500B in Top End. Exceptions occur in the Bangkok, Chiang Mai, Andaman and Lower Southern Gulf areas, where midrange is around 800B to 2500B or 3000B.

Beach Bungalows

Beach bungalows occupy much of the Thai coastline, especially in old-fashioned backpacker destinations such as Ko Pha-Ngan and Ko Tao. They range from simple palm thatch and bamboo huts to wooden or concrete bungalows. As travellers' budgets have become more generous in recent years many of the cheap bungalow shacks have been upgraded to more sturdy and comfortable concrete huts. Regardless of quality, many bungalows are

---

BOOK ACCOMMODATION ONLINE

For more accommodation reviews and recommendations by Lonely Planet authors, check out the online booking service at www.lonelyplanet.com. You'll find the true, insider lowdown on the best places to stay. Reviews are thorough and independent. Best of all, you can book online.

DIRECTORY

smack dab on the beach or built on a hillside overlooking the ocean.

Guesthouses

Guesthouses are generally the cheapest accommodation in Thailand and can be found wherever travellers go throughout central, northern and southern Thailand, and to a much lesser extent in the southeast and northeast. Rates vary according to facilities, from a rock-bottom 100B to 150B per room with shared toilet and shower to over 500B with private facilities and air-con. Most guesthouses cultivate a travellers' ambience with minor amenities like tourist information and book exchanges. Many guesthouses make their bread-and-butter from their onsite restaurants that serve some of the classic backpacker meals (banana pancakes and fruit shakes). Don't measure Thai food based on dishes you've eaten in guesthouses; all standard dishes have been adjusted to accommodate the foreigner palate.

Most guesthouses are not equipped to handle advance reservations and there are usually plenty of options grouped together so accommodation can be found upon arrival.

Hotels & Resorts

In provincial capitals and small towns, the only options are often older Chinese-Thai hotels, once the standard in all of Thailand. These are multistorey buildings usually with private bathrooms and air-con, although a few have shared bath facilities and fan rooms. Most cater to Thai guests and English is usually limited. Rates tend to be higher here than at guesthouses as these hotels don't typically have onsite restaurants to subsidise room rates.

For a room sans air-con, you should ask for *hâwng thammádaa* (ordinary room) or *hâwng phát lom* (room with fan); these usually start at 200B. *Hâwng ae* (air-con room) can range from 300B to 750B, depending on the location of the hotel and size of the room. In some of the older hotels, the toilets are squats and the 'shower' is a *khlong* jar (large water jar).

The midrange hotels offer many amenities, such as cable TV, air-con and hot showers, but unless the establishment has been recently refurbished, we've found that they are too old and worn to represent good value. Most midrange hotels start at 1000B or more.

International chain hotels can be found in Bangkok, Chiang Mai, Phuket and other high-end beach resorts. In recent years, there

has been a push for stylish and plush accommodation rather than the utilitarian options of the past. Many of these upscale resorts incorporate traditional Thai architecture with modern minimalism.

Most top-end hotels and some midrange hotels add a 7% government tax (VAT) and an additional 10% service charge. The additional charges are often referred to as 'plus plus'. A buffet breakfast will often be included in the room rate. If the hotel offers Western breakfast, it is usually referred to as 'ABF', a strange shorthand meaning American breakfast.

Midrange and chain hotels, especially in major tourist destinations, can be booked in advance and some offer internet discounts through their websites or online agents.

In most countries, 'resort' refers to hotels that offer substantial recreational facilities (eg tennis, golf, swimming, sailing) in addition to accommodation and dining. In Thai hotel lingo, however, the term simply refers to any hotel that isn't in an urban area. Hence a few thatched beach huts or a cluster of bungalows in a forest may be called a 'resort'. Several places in Thailand fully deserve the resort title under any definition – but it will pay for you to look into the facilities before making a reservation.

National Parks Accommodation

Most national parks have bungalows or campsites available for overnight stays. Bungalows typically sleep as many as 10 people and rates range from 600B to 2000B, depending on the park and the size of the bungalow. These are popular with extended Thai families who bring enough provisions to survive the apocalypse. A

NATIONAL PARKS FEE HIKE

As of late 2006, entrance fees to all national parks have been raised from 200B to 400B for foreigners. A pricing scheme for national parks was introduced some 20 years ago as a way to offset diminishing maintenance funds from the government. Since the late 1990s, entrance fees have split into a double-tiered scheme: one price for Thais and another price for foreigners. The most recent fee hike represents a 100% increase over the last. Although officials cited increased maintenance costs as justification for the recent hikes, issues involving funds are never that transparent.

few parks also have *reuan thăew* (longhouses), where rooms are around 250B for two people.

Camping is available at many parks for 30B per person per night. Some parks hire tents (100B a night), but always check the condition of the tents before agreeing to rent. It's a good idea to take your own sleeping bag or mat, and other basic camping gear.

Advance bookings for accommodation is necessary at the more popular parks, especially on holidays and weekends. To make reservations, contact the **National Park Office** (☎ 0 2562 0760; www.dnp.go.th/parkreserve; 61 Th Phahonyothin, Chatuchak, Bangkok 10900).

ACTIVITIES

Thailand has developed a fairly thriving activities sector to its tourism industry but the majority of options are often classified as 'soft' adventure.

Cycling

Many cyclists have traversed the roads of Thailand on a Southeast Asia tour. **Biking Southeast Asia with Mr Pumpy** (www.mrpumpy.net) contains route suggestions, tips and other details from real-life cyclists. Cycling around certain cities in Thailand is a great alternative to public transport; for details on bicycle hire see p761. There are also countrywide cycling tour programmes available through **SpiceRoads** (spiceroads .com) as well as bike tours of Bangkok (p147).

Diving & Snorkelling

Thailand's two coastlines and countless islands are popular among divers for their warm and calm waters and colourful marine life. Lonely Planet's richly illustrated *Diving & Snorkelling Thailand* is full of vital information for serious divers.

On the Andaman coast, the most spectacular diving is in the Similan (p655) and Surin Islands (p651). Most dive operators running tours to this area are based in Phuket (p660), and to a lesser extent Khao Lak (p653) and Ko Chang (p257). Most dive trips to the Surin and Similan islands are multiday live aboards. One-day trips are also offered at almost every Andaman beach resort.

Reef dives in the Andaman are particularly rewarding – some 210 hard corals and 108 reef fish have so far been catalogued in this understudied marine zone, where thousands more species of reef organisms probably live. Some parts of Thailand's Andaman coast were heavily affected by the December 2004 tsunami, but actual damage to reef systems in Thailand has been very minimal.

Diving on the Gulf coast is available just about anywhere foreigners rest their luggage. Ko Tao (p616) has the reputation of providing the cheapest dive training but because of the numbers of tourists these instructions can feel like you're in a factory line. Although the water conditions are not the best, Pattaya (p232) is the closest dive spot to Bangkok, with several reefs just a short boat ride offshore.

Most islands have easily accessible snorkelling amid offshore reefs that are covered by water no deeper than 2m. Local fisherman will also take out groups for day-long snorkelling tours to various sites around the islands.

SAFETY GUIDELINES FOR DIVING

Before embarking on a scuba diving, skin diving or snorkelling trip, carefully consider the following points to ensure a safe and enjoyable experience:

- Possess a current diving-certification card from a recognised scuba diving instructional agency.
- Obtain reliable information about physical and environmental conditions at the dive site (eg from a reputable local dive operation).
- Be aware of local laws, regulations and etiquette about marine life and the environment.
- Dive only at sites within your realm of experience; if available, engage the services of a competent, professionally trained dive instructor or dive master.
- Be aware that underwater conditions vary significantly from one region, or even site, to another. Seasonal changes can significantly alter any site and dive conditions. These differences influence the way divers dress for a dive and what diving techniques they use.
- Ask about the environmental characteristics that can affect your diving and how local-trained divers deal with these considerations.

Masks, fins and snorkels are readily available for rent at dive centres and guesthouses in beach areas. If you're particular about the quality and condition of the equipment you use, however, you might be better off bringing your own mask and snorkel – some of the stuff for rent is second rate.

Kayaking

The most dramatic scenery for kayaking is along the Andaman coast. It's littered with bearded limestone mountains and semisubmerged caves. Many sea-kayaking tours are based in Phuket (p660) and take visitors to scenic Ao Phang-Nga (p659). For the sporty types, Krabi (p690) is the one-stop beach destination with sea-kayaking tours to emerald lagoons and sea caves.

Most tour operators use open-deck kayaks since water and air temperatures in Thailand are warm. When signing up for a tour, find out if you or the guide is the primary paddler; some tours are more sightseeing than exercise.

Rock Climbing

Way back before the Stone Age, Thailand sat at the bottom of a vast ocean that lapped against the Tibetan Plateau. When the ocean eventually receded and mainland Southeast Asia popped up, the skeletons of deceased marine life left behind a swath of chalk-white caves and cliffs the whole length of Thailand. While the Tibetans lost backyard surfing rights, the Thais got the milky-white, pock-marked, medium-hard limestone perfect for chalky fingers and Scarpa-clad toes. *Faràng* backpackers were the first to slam bolt to stone in the mid-1980s, but the Thais have quickly followed suit. Rock climbing has become so popular that the Thais have begun sending climbers to amateur contests in the USA and Australia.

Krabi's Hat Railay (p700) and Hat Ton Sai are Thailand's limestone mecca. The huge headland and tiny islands nearby offer high-quality limestone with steep, pocketed walls, overhangs and the occasional hanging stalactite. But what makes climbing here so popular are the views. Your reward for a vertical assault on a cliff isn't just the challenge to gravity but also a bird's eye view of a sparkling blue bay and humpbacked mountains.

If the crowds in Krabi are too much, check out Ko Phi-Phi or head north to Chiang Mai (p290), which has access to jungle-choked Crazy Horse Buttress.

Trekking

Wilderness walking or trekking is one of northern Thailand's biggest draws. Many routes feature daily walks through forested mountain areas coupled with overnight stays in hill-tribe villages and elephant rides to satisfy both ethno- and ecotourism urges. Chiang Mai and Chiang Rai are the primary base points for these tours, but Mae Hong Son, Nan and Um Phang also offer trekking tours and are less inundated with tourists. Kanchanaburi is also an outdoor trekking destination and is closer to Bangkok than the other trekking centres. These adventures rank high on most travellers' to-do list, but the final verdict is often mixed. Hill-tribe trekking has many detractors because of concerns over exploitation and tourism overload. For a discussion about the responsibility issues of entering these sensitive communities, see the Thailand & You chapter (p41).

Other trekking opportunities are available in Thailand's larger national parks, including Khao Yai and Khao Sok.

Windsurfing

The best combination of rental facilities and wind conditions are found on Pattaya (p232) and nearby Jomtien, on Phuket's Ao Bang Thao (p672) and on Ko Samui (p584).

In general the windy months on the Gulf of Thailand are from mid-February to April. On the Andaman Sea side of the Thai-Malay peninsula winds are strongest from September to December.

BUSINESS HOURS

Most government offices are open from 8.30am to 4.30pm weekdays. Some government offices close from noon to 1pm for

---

TYPICAL OPENING HOURS

■ Bars – 6pm-midnight or 1am (times vary depending on local enforcement of national curfew laws)

■ Department stores – 10am-8pm Mon-Sun

■ Discos – 8pm-2am

■ Live music venues – 6pm-1am

■ Restaurants – 10am-10pm

■ Local shops – 10am-5pm Mon-Sat, some open Sun

lunch, while others have Saturday hours (9am-3pm). Banking hours are typically 9.30am to 3.30pm Monday to Friday.

Privately owned stores usually operate between 10am and 5pm daily. Most local restaurants are open 10am until 10pm, with an hour's variation on either side. Some restaurants, specialising in morning meals, close by 3pm.

Please note that all government offices and banks are closed on public holidays (see p747).

CHILDREN

Travelling with children in Thailand, in some ways, is easier than a trip to the grocery store. Thais love children and in many instances will shower attention and sweets on your offspring. Children can easily find ready playmates among their Thai counterparts and a 'temporary' nanny service at practically every stop. Thais are so family focused that you'll find otherwise disinterested parties wanting to help you across the street or pinching at your children's cheeks.

To smooth out the usual road bumps of dragging children from place to place, check out Lonely Planet's *Travel with Children*, which contains useful advice on how to cope with kids on the road, with a focus on travel in developing countries.

Health & Safety

For the most part parents needn't worry too much about health concerns, although it pays to lay down a few ground rules (such as regular hand washing) to head off potential medical problems. Children should be warned not to play with animals as rabies is relatively common in Thailand and many dogs are better at being barkers and garbage eaters than pets. All the usual health precautions apply (see p771).

Practicalities

Amenities specially geared towards young children – such as child-safety seats for cars, high chairs in restaurants or nappy-changing facilities in public restrooms – are virtually nonexistent in Thailand. Therefore parents will have to be extra resourceful in seeking out substitutes or just follow the example of Thai families (which means holding smaller children on their laps much of the time).

Baby formula and nappies (diapers) are available at minimarkets in the larger towns and cities, but for rural areas you'll need to bring along a sufficient supply.

Sights & Activities

Of the many destinations in Thailand, kids will especially enjoy the beaches, as most are gentle bays good for beginner swimmers. Animal amusements abound in Thailand, but the conditions and treatments are often below par compared with the standards in the West. Elephant rides, bamboo rafting and other outdoor activities around Chiang Mai and Kanchanaburi are more animal and kid friendly. Older children might enjoy the northeastern town of Khon Kaen, which is decorated with dinosaur statues and boasts a national park and museum with dinosaur bones in situ. For other itinerary ideas, p27.

CLIMATE CHARTS

See p19 for further information on choosing the best time of year for your visit to Thailand.

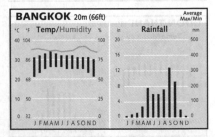

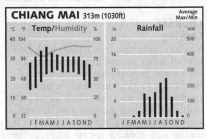

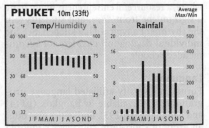

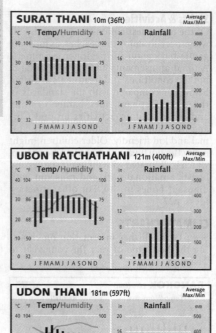

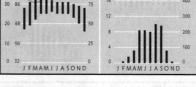

COURSES
Cooking
You too can amaze your friends back home after attending a course in Thai cuisine. Cooking courses pop up wherever there are tourists willing to dice some shallots. Bangkok's courses (p143) tend to be more formal, with dedicated kitchen facilities and individual work stations; but Chiang Mai (p293) is the undisputed cooking-course capital. Elsewhere, a resourceful entrepreneur might hang a sign on the front door, and students join the rhythm of a typical Thai kitchen. See the individual destination chapters for recommended schools.

Language
Formal, university-affiliated language programmes are available in Bangkok (p144) and Chiang Mai (p293). Both cities also offer an array of short-term coursework tailored to suit different communication needs from business Thai to reading and writing.

Muay Thai (Thai Boxing)
One of the fastest growing sectors of Thailand's educational tourism, *muay thai* (Thai boxing) training takes place at dozens of camps around the country. Before the global surge in interest, most *muay thai* camps were unable to accommodate short-term foreign fighters. Traditional *muay thai* camps, especially in the rural areas, are in the business of training winning fighters, who elevate the prestige and earnings of the teacher and the school. The training sessions are gruelling, the diet is rudimentary and the facilities are little more than a dusty ring for sparring and a few shared cabins. Some foreign fighters with the potential for competitive success have trained in these schools but they did so through personal introductions and a dedication to the sport.

Better suited for the athlete interested in the sport rather than becoming a potential prize fighter are the camps that specialise in training Westerners. Many of these facilities have English-speaking trainers and better equipment, and subsidise the training through increased tuition fees. Training periods can range from a one-day course to multiweek sessions. Do be aware that the potential for some camps to be interested only in tuition fees is a concern and it pays to do a lot of advance research. Bangkok and Chiang Mai have long-established foreigner-friendly training camps. Phuket and other resort towns have less serious schools intended for less serious students.

The website www.muaythai.com contains useful information including the addresses of training camps.

Meditation
Thailand has long been a popular place for Buddhist meditation study. Unique to Buddhism, particularly Theravada and to a lesser extent Tibetan Buddhism, is a system of meditation known as *vipassana* (*wípàtsànaa* in Thai), a Pali word that roughly translates as 'insight'. Foreigners who come to Thailand to study *vipassana* can choose from dozens of temples and meditation centres specialising in these teachings. Teaching methods vary but the general emphasis is on observing mind-body processes from moment to moment. Thai language is

usually the medium of instruction but several places also provide instruction in English.

Contact details for some of the more popular meditation-oriented temples and centres are given in the destination sections of this guide. Instruction and accommodation are free of charge at temples, although donations are expected.

Some places require that you wear white clothes when staying overnight. For even a brief visit, wear clean and neat clothing (ie long trousers or skirt and sleeves that cover the shoulders).

For a detailed look at *vipassana* study in Thailand, read *A Guide to Buddhist Monasteries & Meditation Centres in Thailand*, which is available from the World Fellowship of Buddhists in Bangkok (p143).

Thai Massage

Thai massage is more like a yoga workout than a deep-tissue massage. The theory behind the tradition is to promote health by manipulating certain *sên* (pressure points) along the body meridians so that energy is distributed evenly throughout the nervous system. The dynamic aspects of Thai massage also address the muscular-skeletal system in a way that is often compared to modern physiotherapy and chiropractice.

Since a Thai massage usually involves pulling, twisting, thwacking and elbowing, most masseuses are small but powerfully strong women who use different angles and positions as leverage. Training in Thai massage is available in Bangkok and in Chiang Mai. The centre of Thai massage pedagogy is at Wat Pho (p139) in Bangkok.

CUSTOMS

Thailand prohibits the import of firearms and ammunition (unless registered in advance with the police department), illegal drugs and pornographic media. A reasonable amount of clothing for personal use, toiletries and professional instruments are allowed in duty free. Up to 200 cigarettes and 1L of wine or spirits can be brought into the country duty free. The **customs department** (www.customs.go.th) maintains a helpful website with more specific information.

When leaving Thailand, you must obtain an export licence for any antiques or objects of art, including newly cast Buddha images (exported for religious or cultural purposes).

Export licence applications can be made by submitting two front-view photos of the object(s), with no more than five objects to a photo, and a photocopy of your passport, along with the object(s) in question, to the **Department of Fine Arts** (DFA; ☎ 0 2628 5032). Allow three to five days for the application and inspection process to be completed.

DANGERS & ANNOYANCES

Although Thailand is in no way a dangerous country to visit, it is smart to exercise caution, especially when it comes to dealing with strangers (both Thai and foreigners) and travelling alone. In reality, you are more likely to be ripped off or have a personal possession surreptitiously stolen than you are to be physically harmed.

Assault

Assault of travellers is very rare in Thailand, but it does happen. More and more, we've received letters from travellers detailing fights between themselves and Thai guesthouse workers. While both parties are probably to blame (alcohol is often involved), do be aware that causing a Thai to 'lose face' (feel public embarrassment or humiliation) might elicit an inexplicably strong and violent reaction. While a good cuss-out might be an acceptable way to vent anger in the West, it is an invitation for fisticuffs, a sneak attack or worse by a Thai.

There have been incidents of assault on lone female travellers on Ko Samui and Ko Pha-Ngan. Some of these crimes are purely opportunistic, but others often involve confusion over acceptable courtship behaviour that is not consistent between the two cultures. Women should be guarded about flirtations with strangers, especially at night and at bars.

Border Issues

Currently Thailand's southernmost provinces (Yala, Pattani and Narathiwat) are in the midst of a separatist movement. Since 2002, violence has escalated from government and military targets to schools and temples. To a lesser extent periodic bombings have occurred in the southern commercial hub of Hat Yai. It was hoped that the ouster of Thaksin, an unpopular figure in the south, would ease tensions, but this has not been the case. The current government is keen to

negotiate with separatist leaders but none have come forward to begin talks.

As of writing, no tourists have been directly targeted but civilian attacks have increased and it is uncertain what direction future violence will take. As for crossing the Thai–Malaysian border at Sungai Kolok border by train, we advise careful monitoring of the situation. Trains are still running and foreign travellers are still making the crossing but this train station has been bombed in the past and is still considered a target.

The Myanmar border has been quiet for about five years now, but in the past conflicts between Karen or Mon rebels and the Burmese national army would spill over into Thailand. Fighting can break out at any time and border crossings into sensitive areas are often closed as a result. Mae Hong Son Province in northern Thailand borders the Myanmar territories of the Shan and Wa armies, minority groups that control the amphetamine and opium trade in the area. The involvement of these groups in legitimate businesses and with legitimate governments has significantly blurred their otherwise outlaw status. The average tourist will not interact or be affected by the inner workings of this clandestine economy, but one should still be aware that armed conflict can occur in more remote regions.

Druggings & Drug Possession

Less common now than in the past, male travellers, especially, should be suspicious of flirtatious Thai women offering them cigarettes, drinks or food. Several travellers have reported waking up sometime later with a headache, only to find that their valuables have disappeared. Inviting a prostitute to your hotel room can result in the same effect.

It is illegal to buy, sell or possess opium, heroin, amphetamines, hallucinogenic mushrooms and marijuana in Thailand. A new era of vigilance against drug use and possession was ushered in by former prime minister Thaksin's 2003 war on drugs; during the height of the campaign police searched partygoers in Bangkok nightclubs and effectively scared many of the recreational drug users into abstinence.

Belying Thailand's anything-goes atmosphere are severely strict punishments for possession and trafficking that are not relaxed for foreigners. Possession of drugs can result

in at least one year or more of prison time. Drug smuggling – defined as attempting to cross a border with drugs in your possession – carries considerably higher penalties, including execution.

Ko Pha-Ngan is one of Thailand's leading centres for recreational drug use, and the Thai police have taken notice. Particularly on days leading up to Hat Rin's famous monthly full-moon rave, police often set up inspection points on the road between Thong Sala and Hat Rin. Every vehicle, including bicycles and motorcycles, is stopped and the passengers and vehicles thoroughly searched.

Scams

Thais can be so friendly and laid-back that some visitors are lulled into a false sense of security that makes them vulnerable to scams of all kinds. Scammers tend to haunt the areas where first-time tourists go, such as Bangkok's Grand Palace and Wat Pho area. Though you could come across them anywhere in Thailand, the overwhelming majority of scams take place in Bangkok with Chiang Mai a very distant second.

Most scams begin in the same way: a friendly and well-dressed Thai, or sometimes even a foreigner, approaches you and strikes up a conversation. Invariably your destination is closed or being cleaned, but your new friend offers several alternative activities, such as sightseeing at smaller temples or shopping at authentic markets.

The most common scam involves gems. The victims find themselves invited to a gem and jewellery shop – your new-found friend is picking up some merchandise for himself and you're just along for the ride. Somewhere along the way he usually claims to have a connection, often a relative, in your home country (what a coincidence!) with whom he has a regular gem export-import business. One way or another, victims are convinced (usually they convince themselves) that they can turn a profit by arranging a gem purchase and reselling the merchandise at home. After all, the jewellery shop just happens to be offering a generous discount today – it's a government or religious holiday, or perhaps it's the shop's 10th anniversary, or maybe they've just taken a liking to you!

There is a seemingly infinite number of variations on the gem scam, almost all of which end up with the victim making a purchase

of small, low-quality sapphires and posting them to their home countries. Once you return home, of course, the cheap sapphires turn out to be worth much less than you paid for them (perhaps one-tenth to one-half).

Many have invested and lost virtually all their savings; some admit they had been scammed even after reading warnings in this guidebook or those posted by the Tourism Authority of Thailand (TAT) around Bangkok. The Thai police are usually no help whatsoever, believing that merchants are entitled to whatever price they can get. The main victimisers are a handful of shops who get protection from certain high-ranking government officials. These officials put pressure on police not to prosecute or to take as little action as possible.

Card games are another way to separate suckers from their money. A friendly stranger approaches the lone traveller on the street, strikes up a conversation and then invites them to their house or apartment for a drink or meal. After a bit of socialising a friend or relative of the con arrives on the scene; it just so happens a little high-stakes card game is planned for later that day. Like the gem scam, the card-game scam has many variations, but eventually the victim is shown some cheating tactics to use with help from the 'dealer', some practice sessions take place and finally the game gets under way with several high rollers at the table. The mark is allowed to win a few hands first, then somehow loses a few, gets bankrolled by one of the friendly Thais, and then loses the Thai's money. Suddenly your new-found buddies aren't so friendly any more – they want the money you lost. Sooner or later you end up cashing in most or all of your travellers cheques or making a costly visit to an ATM. Again the police won't take any action because gambling is illegal in Thailand – you've actually broken the law.

Other minor scams involve túk-túk drivers, hotel employees and bar girls who take new arrivals on city tours; these almost always end up in high-pressure sales situations at silk, jewellery or handicraft shops. In this case the victim's greed isn't the ruling motivation – it's simply a matter of weak sales resistance.

Follow TAT's number-one suggestion to tourists: *Disregard all offers of free shopping or sightseeing help from strangers* – they invariably take a commission from your purchases. We would add: beware of deals that seem too good to be true. You might also try lying whenever a stranger asks how long you've been in Thailand – if it's only been three days, say three weeks! Or save your Bangkok sightseeing until after you've been up north. The con artists rarely prey on anyone except new arrivals.

Contact the **tourist police** (☎ 1155) if you have any problems with consumer fraud.

Touts

Touting is a long-time tradition in Asia, and while Thailand doesn't have as many touts as, say, India, it has its share.

ACCOMMODATION TOUTS

In the popular tourist spots it seems like everyone – young boys waving fliers, túk-túk drivers, sǎamláw (three-wheeled pedicab) drivers, schoolgirls – is touting something, usually hotel or guesthouse accommodation. For the most part they're completely harmless and sometimes they can be very informative. But take anything a tout says with two large grains of salt. Since touts work on commission and get paid just for delivering you to a guesthouse or hotel (whether you check in or not), they'll say anything to get you to the door.

The better hotels and guesthouses refuse to pay tout commissions – so the average tout will try to steer you away from such places. Hence don't believe them if they tell you the hotel or guesthouse you're looking for is closed, full, dirty or 'bad'. Sometimes (rarely) they're right but most times it's just a ruse to get you to a place that pays more commission.

Always have a look yourself before checking into a place recommended by a tout. Túk-túk & sǎamláw drivers often offer free or low-cost rides to the place they're touting. If you have another place you're interested in, you might agree to go with a driver only if he or she promises to deliver you to your first choice after you've had a look at the place being touted. If drivers refuse, chances are it's because they know your first choice is a better one.

This type of commission work is not limited to low-budget guesthouses. Travel agencies at the airport and Hualamphong train station are notorious for talking newly arrived tourists into staying at badly located, overpriced hotels.

BUS TOUTS

Watch out for touts wearing fake TAT or tourist information badges at Hualamphong train station. They have been known to coerce travellers into buying tickets for private bus rides, saying the train is 'full' or 'takes too long'. Often the promised bus service turns out to be substandard and may take longer than the equivalent train ride due to the frequent changing of vehicles. You may be offered a 24-seat VIP 'sleeper' bus to Chiang Mai, for example, and end up stuffed into a minivan all the way. Such touts are bounty hunters who receive a set fee for every tourist they deliver to the bus companies. Avoid the travel agencies (many of which bear 'TAT' or even 'Lonely Planet' signs) just outside the train station for the same reason.

Theft & Fraud

Exercise diligence when it comes to your personal belongings. Ensure that your room is securely locked and carry your most important effects (passport, money, credit cards) on your person. Take care when leaving valuables in hotel safes.

Follow the same practice when you're travelling. A locked bag will not prevent theft on a long-haul bus when you're snoozing and the practiced thief has hours alone with your luggage. This is a common occurrence on the tourist buses from Khao San to the south or north to Chiang Mai.

When using a credit card, don't let vendors take your credit card out of your sight to run it through the machine. Unscrupulous merchants have been known to rub off three or four or more receipts with one purchase. Sometimes they wait several weeks – even months – between submitting each charge receipt to the bank, so that you can't remember whether you'd been billed by the same vendor more than once.

To avoid losing all of your travel money in an instant, always use a credit card that is not directly linked to your bank account back home so that the operator doesn't have access to immediate funds.

DISABLED TRAVELLERS

Thailand presents one large, ongoing obstacle course for the mobility impaired. With its high curbs, uneven pavements and nonstop traffic, Bangkok can be particularly difficult. Many streets must be crossed via pedestrian bridges flanked with steep stairways, while buses and boats don't stop long enough for even the fully abled. Rarely are there any ramps or other access points for wheelchairs.

A number of more expensive, top-end hotels make consistent design efforts to provide disabled access to their properties. Other deluxe hotels with high employee-to-guest ratios are usually good about accommodating the mobility impaired by providing staff help where building design fails. For the rest, you're pretty much left to your own resources. Counter to the prevailing trends, **Worldwide Dive & Sail** (www.worldwidediveandsail.com) offers liveaboard diving programmes for the deaf and hard of hearing, and can work with wheelchair users.

Some organisations and publications:
Accessible Journeys (☎ 610 521 0339; www.disabilitytravel.com; 35 West Sellers Ave, Ridley Park, Pennsylvania, PA 19078, USA)
Mobility International USA (☎ 541 343 1284; www.miusa.org; 132 E Broadway, Suite 343, Eugene, OR 97401, USA)
Society for Accessible Travel & Hospitality (☎ 212 447 7284; www.sath.org; Ste 610, 347 Fifth Ave, New York, NY 10016, USA)

EMBASSIES & CONSULATES
Thai Embassies & Consulates

The website www.thaiembassy.org links to Thai diplomatic missions abroad. Here is a sample of Thai embassies worldwide.
Australia (☎ 02 6273 1149; www.thaiembassy.org.au; 111 Empire Circuit, Yarralumla, Canberra, ACT 2600); Consulates in Adelaide, Brisbane, Melbourne, Sydney and Perth
Cambodia (☎ 023 726 306; 196 MV Preah Nordom Blvd, Sangkat Tonle Bassa, Khan Chamkar Mon, Phnom Penh)
Canada (☎ 613 722 4444; www.magma.ca/~thaiott/mainpage.htm; 180 Island Park Dr, Ottawa, ON K1Y 0A2); Consulate in Vancouver.
France (☎ 01 56 26 50 50; thaipar@micronet.fr; 8 rue Greuze, 75116 Paris)
Germany (☎ 030 794 810; www.thaiembassy.de; Lepsiusstrasse 64-66, 12163 Berlin); Consulate in Frankfurt.
Israel (☎ 972 3 695 8980; www.thaiembassy.org/telaviv; 21 Shaul Hamelech Blvd, Tel Aviv)
Laos (☎ 21 214581 3; www.thaiembassy.org/Vientiane; Kaysone Phomvihane Ave, Xaysettha, Vientiane); Consulate in Savannakhet.
Malaysia (☎ 603 248 8222; 206 Jalan Ampang, Kuala Lumpur); Consulates in Penang and Kota Bahru.

Myanmar (Burma; ☎ 01 512017, 512018; 437 Pyay Rd, 8 Ward, Kamayut township, Yangon)
UK (☎ 020 7589 2944; www.thaiembassyuk.org.uk; 29-30 Queen's Gate, London SW7 5JB); Consulates in Birmingham, Cardiff & Liverpool.
USA (☎ 202 944 3608; www.thaiembdc.org/index.htm; 1024 Wisconsin Ave NW, Washington, DC 20007); Consulates in Chicago, New York and Los Angeles.
Vietnam (☎ 04 823 5092-94; fax 04 823 5088; 63-65 Hoang Dieu St, Hanoi); Consulate in Ho Chi Minh City.

Embassies & Consulates in Thailand

Foreign embassies are located in Bangkok; some nations also have consulates in Chiang Mai and Khon Kaen.
Australia Embassy (Map p127; ☎ 0 2344 6300; www .austembassy.or.th; 37 Th Sathon Tai)
Cambodia Embassy (Map p127; ☎ 0 2254 6630; 185 Th Ratchadamri, Lumphini)
Canada Embassy (Map p127; ☎ 0 2636 0540; www .dfait-maeci.gc.ca/bangkok; 15th fl, Abdulrahim Bldg, 990 Th Phra Ram IV)
China Embassy (Map pp114-15; ☎ 0 2245 7044; www .chinaembassy.or.th/chn; 57 Th Ratchadaphisek)
Denmark Embassy (Map pp114-15; ☎ 0 2343 1100; www.ambbangkok.um.dk; 10 Soi 1, Th Sathon Tai)
EU Delegation (Map p127; ☎ 0 2305 2645; Kian Gwan Bldg, 19th fl, 140/1 Th Withayu)
France Embassy (Map pp124-5; ☎ 0 2657 5100; www .ambafrance-th.org; 35 Soi 36, Th Charoen Krung); Consular Section (Map p127; ☎ 0 2627 2150; 29 Th Sathon Tai)
Germany Embassy (Map p127; ☎ 0 2287 9000; www .german-embassy.or.th; 9 Th Sathon Tai)
India Embassy (Map pp122-3; ☎ 0 2258 0300-6; www .visatoindia.com/indian-embassy-in-thailand.html; 46 Soi Prasanmit/Soi 23, Th Sukhumvit); Consulate (Map pp276-7; ☎ 0 5324 3066; 344 Th Charoenrat, Chiang Mai)
Indonesia Embassy (Map pp128-9; ☎ 0 2252 3135; www.kbri-bangkok.com; 600-602 Th Phetburi Tat Mai)
Ireland Embassy (Map p127; ☎ 0 2677 7500; www .irelandinthailand.com: 28th fl, Q House, Th Sathon Tai)
Israel Embassy (Map pp122-3; ☎ 0 2204 9200; Ocean Tower 2, 25th fl, 25 Soi 19, Th Sukhumvit)
Japan Embassy (Map p127; ☎ 0 2207 8500; www.th .emb-japan.go.jp; 177 Th Withayu)
Laos Embassy (Map pp114-15; ☎ 0 2539 6679; www .bkklaoembassy.com; 502/1-3 Soi Sahakarnpramoon, Th Pracha Uthit/Soi 39, Th Ramakamhaeng)
Malaysia Embassy (Map pp124-5; ☎ 0 2679 2190-9; 33-35 Th Sathon Tai)
Myanmar Embassy (Burma; Map pp124-5; ☎ 0 2233 2237, 0 2234 4698; www.mofa.gov.mm; 132 Th Sathon Neua)
Nepal Embassy (Map pp114-15; ☎ 0 2391 7240; www .immi.gov.np; 189 Soi 71, Th Sukhumvit)

Netherlands Embassy (Map pp128-9; ☎ 0 2309 5200; www.netherlandsembassy.in.th; 15 Soi Tonson, Th Ploenchit)
New Zealand Embassy (Map pp128-9; ☎ 0 2254 2530; www.nzembassy.com; 14th fl, M Thai Tower, All Seasons Pl, 87 Th Withayu)
Philippines Embassy (Map pp122-3; ☎ 0 2259 0139; www.philembassy-bangkok.net; 760 Th Sukhumvit)
Singapore Embassy (Map pp124-5; ☎ 0 2286 2111; www.mfa.gov.sg/bangkok; 129 Th Sathon Tai)
South Africa Embassy (Map p127; ☎ 0 2253 8473; www.dfa.gov.za; 6th fl, Park Pl, 231 Th Sarasin)
Spain Embassy (Map pp122-3; ☎ 0 2661 8284; www .embesp.or.th; 193 Th Ratchadaphisek)
Switzerland Embassy (Map pp128-9; ☎ 0 2253 0156; 35 Th Withayu)
UK Embassy (Map pp128-9; ☎ 0 2305 8333; www .britishembassy.gov.uk; 14 Th Withayu)
USA Embassy (Map pp128-9; ☎ 0 2205 4000; http://bang kok.usembassy.gov; 120-22 Th Withayu); Consulate (Map pp280-1; ☎ 0 5325 2629; 387 Th Wichayanon, Chiang Mai)
Vietnam Embassy (Map pp128-9; ☎ 0 2251 5836-8; www.vietnamembassy.or.th; 83/1 Th Withayu)

FESTIVALS & EVENTS

Thai festivals tend to be linked to the agricultural seasons or to Buddhist holidays and are most frequent from February to March, after the main rice harvest is in.

The general word for festival in Thai is *ngaan thêtsàkaan*. The exact dates for festivals may vary from year to year, either because of the lunar calendar or because local authorities have decided to change festival dates. For specific dates, contact TAT.

January/February

That Phanom Festival A 10-day-long homage to the northeast's most sacred Buddhist stupa (Phra That Phanom) in Nakhon Phanom Province. Pilgrims from all over the country, as well as from Laos, attend.
Bangkok International Film Festival (www.bangkok film.org) Films from around the world, with an emphasis on Asian cinema, are screened in the capital city. Events end with the awarding of the festival's Golden Kinnaree in a range of categories.
Chiang Mai Flower Festival During this festival, colourful floats and parades exhibit Chiang Mai's cultivated flora.
Magha Puja (*maakhá buuchaa*) Held on the full moon of the third lunar month to commemorate Buddha preaching to 1250 enlightened monks who came to hear him 'without prior summons'. A public holiday throughout the country, it culminates with a candle-lit walk around the *wian thian* (main chapel) at every wat.

DIRECTORY

Phra Nakhon Khiri Diamond Festival This is a week-long celebration of Phetchaburi's history and architecture focused on Phra Nakhon Khiri Historical Park (also known as Khao Wang), a hill topped by a former royal palace overlooking the city. It features a sound-and-light show on Khao Wang; the temples are festooned with lights and presentations of Thai classical dance-drama.

Chinese New Year Called *trùt jiin* in Thai, Chinese all over Thailand celebrate their lunar New Year with a week of house-cleaning, lion dances and fireworks.

April

Prasat Hin Khao Phanom Rung Festival A festival to commemorate Prasat Hin Khao Phanom Rung Historical Park, an impressive Angkor-style temple complex in Buriram Province. It involves a daytime procession up Phanom Rung and spectacular sound-and-light shows at night. The actual date depends on the lunar cycles – be prepared for very hot weather.

Songkran Held from 13 to 15 April, this is the celebration of the lunar New Year. Buddha images are 'bathed', monks and elders receive the respect of younger Thais by the sprinkling of water over their hands, and a lot of water is tossed about. Bangkok and Chiang Mai became watery battlegrounds. Songkran generally gives everyone a chance to release their frustrations and literally cool off during the peak of the hot season.

May

Visakha Puja (*Wísǎakhà buuchaa*) Falling on the 15th day of the waxing moon in the sixth lunar month, this day commemorates the date of the Buddha's birth, enlightenment and *parinibbana* (passing away). Activities are centred around the wat, with candle-lit processions, much chanting and sermonising.

June

Bun Phra Wet (Phi Ta Khon) Festival An animist-Buddhist celebration, held in Loei's Amphoe Dan Sai, in which revellers dress in garish 'spirit' costumes, wear painted masks and brandish carved wooden phalleses. The festival commemorates a Buddhist legend in which a host of spirits (*phǐi*) appeared to greet the Buddha-to-be upon his return to his home town, during his penultimate birth.

Rocket Festival (*bun bang fai*) In the northeast, villagers craft large skyrockets of bamboo, which they then fire into the sky to bring rain for rice fields. This festival is best celebrated in Yasothon, Ubon Ratchathani and Nong Khai.

Royal Ploughing Ceremony To kick off the official rice-planting season, the king participates in this ancient Brahman ritual at Sanam Luang in Bangkok.

July

Asalha Puja (*àsǎanhà buuchaa*) This festival commemorates the Buddha's first sermon.

Khao Phansa (*khâo phansǎa*) A public holiday and the beginning of Buddhist 'lent', this is the traditional time of year for young men to enter the monkhood for the rainy season and for all monks to station themselves in a monastery for three months. It's a good time to observe a Buddhist ordination. Khao Phansa is celebrated in the northeast of Ubon Ratchathani by parading huge carved candles on floats in the streets.

August

Queen's Birthday In Bangkok, Th Ratchadamnoen Klang and the Grand Palace are festooned with coloured lights. Held on 12 August.

September/October

Narathiwat Fair An annual week-long festival celebrating local culture in Narathiwat Province, with boat races, dove-singing contests, handicraft displays and traditional southern Thai music and dance.

Thailand International Swan-Boat Races These take place on Mae Nam Chao Phraya outside of Ayuthaya near the Bang Sai Folk Arts Centre.

Vegetarian Festival A nine-day celebration most notably in Bangkok, Trang and Phuket during which devout Chinese Buddhists eat only vegetarian food. There are various ceremonies at Chinese temples and merit-making processions that bring to mind Hindu Thaipusam in its exhibition of self-mortification. Smaller towns throughout the country also celebrate the veggie fest in the Chinese business sections of town.

November

Kathin (*thâwt kàthǐn*) A month at the end of the Buddhist lent during which new monastic robes and requisites are offered to the *Sangha* (monastic community). In Nan Province longboat races are held on Mae Nan.

Loi Krathong On the proper full-moon night, small lotus-shaped baskets or boats made of banana leaves containing flowers, incense, candles and a coin are floated on Thai rivers, lakes and canals. This is a peculiarly Thai festival that probably originated in Sukhothai and is best celebrated in the north. In Chiang Mai, where the festival is called Yi Peng, residents also launch paper hot-air balloons into the sky.

Surin Annual Elephant Roundup Held on the third weekend of November, Thailand's biggest elephant show is popular with tourists. If you have ever had the desire to see a lot of elephants in one place, then here's your chance.

River Khwae Bridge Week Sound-and-light shows at the Death Railway Bridge in Kanchanaburi. Events include historical exhibitions and vintage-train rides on the infamous railway.

December
King's Birthday This public holiday is celebrated with some fervour in Bangkok. As with the Queen's Birthday, it features lots of lights and other decorations along Th Ratchadamnoen Klang. Other Thai cities hold colourful parades. Some people erect temporary shrines to the king outside their homes or businesses. Held on 5 December.

FOOD
Most restaurants in Thailand are inexpensive by international standards, hence we haven't divided them into Budget, Midrange and Top End categories. A typical meal for one at a street stall should cost 25B to 40B; a restaurant meal for one should be about 100B to 150B. Guesthouses and restaurants catering to foreigners tend to charge more than local restaurants. See p75 for thorough descriptions of the cuisine and the kinds of restaurant you'll find in Thailand.

GAY & LESBIAN TRAVELLERS
Thai culture is relatively tolerant of both male and female homosexuality. There is a fairly prominent gay and lesbian scene in Bangkok (see p170) and in Phuket. With regard to dress or mannerism, lesbians and gays are generally accepted without comment. However, public displays of affection – whether heterosexual or homosexual – are frowned upon. The **Utopia** (www.utopia-asia.com) website posts lots of Thailand information for gay and lesbian visitors.

HOLIDAYS
Government offices and banks close on the following days:
Jan 1 New Year's Day
Apr 6 Chakri Day, commemorating the founder of the Chakri dynasty, Rama I
May 5 Coronation Day, commemorating the 1946 coronation of HM the King and HM the Queen
Jul (date varies) Khao Phansa, the beginning of Buddhist 'lent'
Aug 12 Queen's Birthday
Oct 23 Chulalongkorn Day
Oct/Nov (date varies) Ok Phansa, the end of Buddhist 'lent'
Dec 5 King's Birthday
Dec 10 Constitution Day

INSURANCE
A travel-insurance policy to cover theft, loss and medical problems is a good idea. Policies offer differing medical-expense options. There

is a wide variety of policies available, so check the small print. Be sure that the policy covers ambulances or an emergency flight home.

Some policies specifically exclude 'dangerous activities', which can include scuba diving, motorcycling or even trekking. A locally acquired motorcycle licence is not valid under some policies.

You may prefer a policy that pays doctors or hospitals directly rather than you having to pay on the spot and claim later. If you have to claim later make sure you keep all documentation.

See p771 for recommendations on health insurance and p766 for details on vehicle insurance.

INTERNET ACCESS
You'll find plenty of internet cafés in most larger towns and cities, and in many guesthouses and hotels as well. The going rate is anywhere from 30B to 80B an hour. Bangkok typically has fast connections and new machines, while the provinces are a little bit behind. Wi-fi is available in some upscale hotels but the daily charge is usually around 500B to 600B.

Most hotels use RJ11 phone jacks, though in older hotels and guesthouses the phones may still be hard-wired. In the latter case you may be able to use a fax line in the hotel or guesthouse office, since all fax machines in Thailand are connected via RJ11 jacks.

Temporary internet accounts are available from several Thai ISPs. One of the better ones is WebNet, offered by **CSLoxinfo** (www.csloxinfo .com).

LEGAL MATTERS
In general Thai police don't hassle foreigners, especially tourists. If anything they generally go out of their way not to arrest a foreigner breaking minor traffic laws, instead taking the approach that a friendly warning will suffice.

One major exception is drugs, which most Thai police view as either a social scourge against which it's their duty to enforce the letter of the law, or an opportunity to make untaxed income via bribes.

If you are arrested for any offence, the police will allow you the opportunity to make a phone call to your embassy or consulate in Thailand, if you have one, or to a friend or relative if not. There's a whole set of legal codes governing the

length of time and manner in which you can be detained before being charged or put on trial, but a lot of discretion is left to the police. In the case of foreigners the police are more likely to bend these codes in your favour. However, as with police worldwide, if you don't show respect you will make matters worse.

Thai law does not presume an indicted detainee to be either 'guilty' or 'innocent' but rather as a 'suspect', whose guilt or innocence will be decided in court. Trials are usually speedy.

The **tourist police** (☎ 1155) can be very helpful in cases of arrest. Although they typically have no jurisdiction over the kinds of cases handled by regular cops, they may be able to help with translation or with contacting your embassy. The tourist police can also help with most serious hassles regarding rip-offs or thefts. You can call a hotline number 24 hours a day to lodge complaints or to request assistance with regards to personal safety.

MAPS
The Roads Association of Thailand publishes a good large-format, 48-page, bilingual road atlas called *Thailand Highway Map*. The atlas, which is updated every year, includes dozens of city maps, distance charts and an index. It also gives driving distances and a lot of travel and sightseeing information. Beware of inferior copies. A big advantage of the *Thailand Highway Map* is that the town and city names are printed in Thai as well as Roman script.

ThinkNet (www.thinknet.co.th) produces high-quality city and country series, including bilingual maps and interactive CDs to Bangkok and Thailand.

Do-it-yourself trekkers, or anyone with a keen interest in geography, may find sheet maps issued by the Thai military to be helpful. These maps are available at a number of scales, complete with elevations, contour lines, place names (in both Thai and Roman script) and roads. These maps can be purchased at the **Royal Thai Survey Department** (Krom Phaen Thi Thahan; Map p130; ☎ 0 2222 8844; Th Kanlayana Maitri, Bangkok), opposite the Interior Ministry on the western side of Th Ratchini in Ko Ratanakosin.

MONEY
The basic unit of Thai currency is the *baht*. There are 100 *satang* in one baht; coins include 25-satang and 50-satang pieces and baht

in 1B, 5B and 10B coins. Older coins have Thai numerals only, while newer coins have Thai and Arabic numerals.

Paper currency is issued in the following denominations: 10B (brown), 20B (green), 50B (blue), 100B (red), 500B (purple) and 1000B (beige). 10B bills are being phased out in favour of the 10B coin.

ATMs & Credit/Debit Cards
Debit and ATM cards issued by a bank in your own country can be used at ATM machines around Thailand to withdraw cash (in Thai baht only) directly from your account back home. ATMs are widespread throughout the country and can be relied on for the bulk of your spending cash. You can also use ATMs to buy baht at foreign exchange booths at some banks.

Credit cards as well as debit cards can be used for purchases at many shops, hotels and restaurants. The most commonly accepted cards are Visa and MasterCard, followed by Amex and Japan Card Bureau (JCB).

To report a lost or stolen credit/debit card, call the following telephone hotlines in Bangkok:
American Express (☎ 0 2273 5544)
Diners Club (☎ 0 2238 3660)
MasterCard (☎ 001 800 11887 0663)
Visa (☎ 001 800 11535 0660)

Changing Money
Banks or the more rare private moneychangers offer the best foreign-exchange rates. When buying baht, US dollars are the most accepted currency, followed by British pounds and Euros. Most banks charge a commission and duty for each travellers cheque cashed.

Current exchange rates are printed in the *Bangkok Post* and the *Nation* every day, or you can walk into any Thai bank and ask to see a daily rate sheet.

See p19 for information on the cost of travel in Thailand.

Exchange Control
There is no limit to the amount of Thai or foreign currency you may bring into the country.

There are certain monetary requirements for foreigners entering Thailand; demonstrations of adequate funds varies per visa type but typically does not exceed a traveller's estimated trip budget. Rarely will you be

asked to produce such financial evidence, but do be aware that such laws do exist. For specific amounts for each visa type, visit the website of the **Ministry of Foreign Affairs** (www .mfa.go.th).

Upon leaving Thailand, you're permitted to take out no more than 50,000B per person without special authorisation; export of foreign currencies is unrestricted. An exception is made if you're going to Cambodia, Laos, Malaysia, Myanmar or Vietnam, where the limit is 500,000B.

It's legal to open a foreign currency account at any commercial bank in Thailand. As long as the funds originate from out of the country, there are not any restrictions on maintenance or withdrawal.

Tipping

Tipping is not generally expected in Thailand. The exception is loose change from a large restaurant bill; if a meal costs 488B and you pay with a 500B note, some Thais will leave the 12B change. It's not so much a tip as a way of saying 'I'm not so money grubbing as to grab every last baht'. On the other hand, change from a 50B note for a 44B bill will usually not be left behind.

At many hotel restaurants or other upmarket eateries, a 10% service charge will be added to your bill. When this is the case, tipping is not expected. Bangkok has adopted some standards of tipping, especially in restaurants frequented by foreigners.

PHOTOGRAPHY & VIDEO
Film & Equipment

Print film is fairly inexpensive and widely available throughout Thailand. Slide film can be hard to find outside Bangkok and Chiang Mai, so be sure to stock up before heading out to rural areas.

Memory cards for digital cameras are generally widely available in the more popular formats.

Photographing People

In some of the regularly visited areas hill-tribe people expect money if you photograph them, while certain hill tribes will not allow you to point a camera at them. Use discretion when photographing villagers anywhere in Thailand as a camera can be a very intimidating instrument. You may feel better leaving your camera behind when visiting certain areas.

Processing

Film processing is generally quite good in the larger cities in Thailand and also quite inexpensive. Dependable E6 processing is available at several labs in Bangkok but is untrustworthy elsewhere. Kodachrome must be sent out of the country for processing, so it can take up to two weeks to get it back.

Professionals will find a number of labs in Bangkok that offer same-day pick-up and delivery at no extra cost within the city. **Image Quality Lab** (IQ Lab; Map pp124-5; ☎ 0 2266 4080; 160/5 ITF Bldg, Th Silom, Bangkok) offers the widest range of services, with all types of processing (except for Kodachrome), slide duplication, scanning and custom printing.

POST

Thailand has a very efficient postal service and local postage is inexpensive. Typical provincial post offices keep the following hours: 8.30am to 4.30pm weekdays and 9am to noon on Saturday. Larger main post offices in provincial capitals may also be open for a half-day on Sunday.

Most provincial post offices sell do-it-yourself packing boxes, and some will pack your parcels for you for a small fee. Don't send cash or other valuables through the mail.

Thailand's poste restante service is generally very reliable, though these days few tourists use it. When you receive mail, you must show your passport and fill out some paperwork.

SHOPPING

Many bargains await you in Thailand if you have the luggage space to carry them back. Don't go shopping in the company of touts, tour guides or friendly strangers as they will inevitably take a commission on anything you buy, thus driving prices up.

Antiques

Real antiques cannot be taken out of Thailand without a permit. No Buddha image, new or old, may be exported without the permission of the Fine Arts Department. See p741 for information.

Merchandise in the tourist antique shops are, predictably, fantastically overpriced. Northern Thailand has become the best source of Thai antiques as many items are brought into Thailand from Myanmar and offer good value.

DIRECTORY

BARGAINING

Items sold by street vendors in markets or in many shops are flexibly priced – that is, the price is negotiable. Prices in department stores, minimarts, 7-Elevens and so forth are fixed. If the same kind of merchandise is offered in a department store and a small shop or market, check the department-store price for a point of reference.

Thais respect a good haggler. Always let the vendor make the first offer then ask 'Is that your best price?' or 'Can you lower the price?'. This usually results is an immediate discount from the first price. Now it's your turn to make a counteroffer; always start low but don't bargain at all unless you're serious about buying. Negotiations continue until a price is agreed – there's no set discount from the asking price as some vendors start ridiculously high, others closer to the 'real' price.

Do your homework by shopping around, and the whole process becomes easier with practice. It helps immeasurably to keep the negotiations relaxed and friendly, and to speak slowly, clearly and calmly. Vendors will almost always give a better price to someone they like. Try smiling and being jovial as it often helps relax the seller.

Ceramics

Many kinds of hand-thrown pottery, old and new, are available throughout the kingdom. The best-known ceramics are the greenish Thai celadon products from the Sukhothai–Si Satchanalai area, red-earth clay of Don Kwian, and central Thailand's *benjarong* or 'five-colour' style. Benjarong is based on Chinese patterns while celadon is a Thai original that has been imitated throughout China and Southeast Asia. Rough, unglazed pottery from the north and northeast can also be very appealing. For international styles, the many ceramic factories of Lampang are the best places to look for bargains.

Clothing

Tailor-made and ready-to-wear clothes tend to be inexpensive. If you're not particular about style you could pick up an entire wardrobe of travelling clothes at Bangkok's Siam Square or Pratunam street markets for what you'd pay for one designer shirt in New York, Paris or Milan.

You're more likely to get a good fit if you visit a tailor, but be wary of the quickie 24-hour tailor shops; they often use inferior fabric and have poor workmanship. It's best to ask Thai or long-time foreign residents for a recommendation and then go for two or three fittings.

Fakes

In Bangkok, Chiang Mai and other tourist centres there is black-market street trade in fake designer goods branded with names such as Benetton, DKNY, Lacoste, Von Dutch, Ralph Lauren, Levi's, Reebok, Rolex, Cartier and more. No-one pretends they're the real thing, at least not the vendors.

In some cases foreign-name brands are produced under licence in Thailand and represent good value. A pair of legally produced Levi's jeans, for example, costs a lot less from a Thai street vendor, than in the company's home town of San Francisco.

Furniture

Rattan and hardwood furniture items are often good buys and can be made to order. Bangkok and Chiang Mai have the best selection. With the ongoing success of teak farming and recycling, teak furniture has again become a bargain in Thailand if you find the right places. Asian rosewood is also a good buy.

Gems & Jewellery

Thailand is the world's largest exporter of gems and ornaments, rivalled only by India and Sri Lanka. Although rough-stone sources in Thailand have decreased dramatically, stones are now imported from Australia, Sri Lanka and other countries to be cut, polished and traded.

Be wary of special 'deals' that are offered for one day only or that set you up as a 'courier' in which you're promised big money. Shop around and *don't be hasty*. Remember, there's no such thing as a 'government sale' or 'factory price' at a gem or jewellery shop; the Thai government does not own or manage any gem or jewellery shops. See p742 for a detailed warning on gem fraud.

If you know what you are doing you can make some really good buys in both unset gems and finished jewellery. Buy from reputable dealers only, preferably members of the Jewel Fest Club, a guarantee programme established by TAT and the Thai Gem & Jewellery Traders Association (TGJTA). When you purchase an item of jewellery from a shop that is identified as a member of the Jewel Fest Club, a certificate detailing your purchase will be issued. This guarantees a refund, less 10%, if you return the merchandise to the point of sale within 30 days. You can obtain a list of members direct from **Jewel Fest Club** (☎ 0 2630 1390; www.jewelfest.com) or from TAT.

Lacquerware

Lacquer comes from the *Melanorrhea usitata* tree and in its most basic form is mixed with paddy-husk ash to form a light, flexible, waterproof coating over bamboo frames. To make a lacquerware object, a bamboo frame is first woven. If the item is top quality, only the frame is bamboo and horse or donkey hairs will be wound round it. With lower-quality lacquerware, the whole object is made from bamboo. The lacquer is then coated over the framework and allowed to dry. After several days it is sanded down with ash from rice husks, and another coating of lacquer is applied. A high-quality item may have seven layers of lacquer.

The lacquerware is engraved and painted, then it is polished to remove the paint from everywhere except in the engravings. Multicoloured lacquerware is produced by repeated applications. From start to finish it can take five or six months to produce a high-quality piece of lacquerware, which may have as many as five colours. Flexibility is one characteristic of good lacquerware: a well-made bowl can have its rim squeezed together until the sides meet without suffering damage. The quality and precision of the engraving is another thing to look for.

Good lacquerware, much of which is made in Myanmar (although it originated in Chiang Mai) and sold along the northern Myanmar border, can be found in Thailand. Try Mae Sot, Mae Sariang and Mae Sai for the best buys. Common lacquerware includes bowls, trays, plates, boxes, cups, vases and many other everyday items, as well as pure objects of art.

Textiles

Thai silk is considered the best in the world – the coarse weave and soft texture of the silk means it is more easily dyed than harder, smoother silks, resulting in brighter colours and a unique lustre. Silk can be purchased cheaply in the north and northeast, especially Surin, where it is made, typically by handicraft villages. Every region of Thailand has developed a distinctive silk pattern that can often be divided even further into village characteristics.

Traditional Thai cotton shirts, known as *máw hâwm* (Thai work shirt), are part of the weaving culture and village fashion; this type of cotton is popular in the northeast. The northeast is also famous for *mát-mìi* cloth – thick cotton or silk fabric woven from tie-dyed threads – similar to Indonesia's *ikat* fabrics.

Each hill tribe has a tradition of embroidery that has been translated into the modern market place as bags and jewellery. Much of what you'll find in the marketplaces have been machine made but there are many NGO cooperatives that help villagers get their goods to the consumers. Chiang Mai and Chiang Rai are good places to start.

In the north you can also find Lanna-style textiles based on intricate Thai Daeng, Thai Dam and Thai Lü patterns from Nan, Laos and China's Xishuangbanna.

Fairly nice *paa-té* batik is available in the south in patterns that are more similar to the batik found in Malaysia than in Indonesia.

The colourful *mǎwn khwǎan* – a hard, triangle-shaped pillow made in the northeast – makes a good souvenir and comes in many sizes.

TELEPHONE

The telephone system in Thailand is operated by the government-subsidised, privately owned Telephone Organisation of Thailand (TOT) under the Communications Authority of Thailand (CAT). It is efficient if costly, and from Bangkok you can direct dial most major centres with little difficulty.

The telephone country code for Thailand is ☎ 66. Thailand no longer uses separate area codes for Bangkok and the provinces, so all phone numbers in the country use eight digits (preceded by ☎ 0 if you're dialling domestically). When dialling Thailand from outside the country, you must first dial whatever international access code is necessary (eg from

the USA dial ☎ 011 first for all international calls), followed by ☎ 66 and then the phone number in Thailand.

International Calls

If you want to direct-dial an international number from a private telephone, just dial ☎ 001 before the number. Dial ☎ 100 for operator-assisted international calls.

In addition to the standard direct-dial access number, telephone providers also have various connection prefixes with variable but cheaper calling rates. These include ☎ 007, 008 and 009.

A service called Home Country Direct is available at Bangkok's main post office (Map pp124–5). Home Country Direct phones offer easy one-button connection to international operators in 40-odd countries around the world.

Hotels usually add surcharges (sometimes as much as 50% over and above the CAT rate) for international long-distance calls. Private long-distance phone offices with international service always charge more than the government offices, although they are usually lower than hotel rates. Some guesthouses will have a mobile phone or landline that customers can use for a per-minute fee.

The Communications Authority of Thailand (CAT) does not offer long-distance services to Malaysia or Laos. To call these countries you must go through TOT. For Laos, you can direct-dial ☎ 007 and country code 856, followed by the area code and number you want to reach. Malaysia can be dialled direct by prefixing the Malaysian number (including area code) with the code ☎ 09.

Mobile (Cellular) Phones

Thailand is on a GSM network. Cellular operators in Thailand include AIS, Orange and DTAC – all of which will allow you to use their SIM cards in an imported phone, as long as your phone isn't SIM-locked. For short-term visitors, one route is to buy a phone in Thailand along with a SIM card, telephone number and refill used minutes with prepaid phone cards. Bangkok is the best place to get started: MBK (p174) has a whole section dedicated to new and used phones and phonecards can be bought from 7-Elevens. Rates are typically around 3B per minute anywhere in Thailand and between 5B to 7B for international calls.

To accommodate the growth in cell phone usage, Thailand has introduced an '8' prefix to all mobile numbers; ie ☎ 01 234 5678 is now ☎ 081 234 5678.

Pay Phones & Phonecards

Basically there are two kinds of coin-operated public pay phones in Thailand: 'red' (local city calls) and 'blue' (both local and long-distance calls within Thailand). Then there are the phonecard phone booths that accept only certain kinds of card: 'green' takes domestic TOT phonecards, 'yellow' takes Lenso international phonecards and most major credit cards.

Local calls from pay phones cost 1B for 164 seconds (add more coins for more time). Long-distance rates within the country vary from 3B to 12B per minute, depending on the distance.

Rates for international calls using phonecards are usually around 7B per minute and can be bought from 7-Elevens in varying denominations (300B to 500B). A CAT-issued, prepaid international phonecard, called ThaiCard, comes in 300B and 500B denominations and allows calls to many countries at standard CAT rates. You can use the Thai-Card codes from either end, for example calling the UK from Thailand or calling Thailand from the UK.

TIME

Thailand's time zone is seven hours ahead of GMT/UTC (London). At government offices and local cinemas, times are often expressed according to the 24-hour clock, eg 11pm is written 2300. See also the World Time Zone map (pp818-19).

The official year in Thailand is reckoned from 543 BC, the beginning of the Buddhist Era, so that AD 2005 is BE 2548, AD 2006 is BE 2549 etc.

TOILETS

As in many other Asian countries, the 'squat toilet' is the norm except in hotels and guesthouses geared towards tourists and international business travellers. These sit more-or-less flush with the surface of the floor, with two footpads on either side. For travellers who have never used a squat toilet, it takes a bit of getting used to.

If there's no mechanical flush, toilet users scoop water from an adjacent bucket or tank with a plastic bowl and use it to clean their nether regions while still squatting over the

toilet. A few extra scoops of water must be poured into the toilet basin to flush waste into the septic system.

More rustic yet are toilets in rural areas, which may simply consist of a few planks over a hole in the ground.

Even in places where sit-down toilets are installed, the plumbing may not be designed to take toilet paper. In such cases the usual washing bucket will be standing nearby or there will be a waste basket where you're supposed to place used toilet paper.

TOURIST INFORMATION

The government-operated tourist information and promotion service, **Tourism Authority of Thailand (TAT)**, was founded in 1960 and produces excellent pamphlets on sightseeing, accommodation and transport. There are information offices overseas and in major tourist destinations in Thailand.

TAT Offices Abroad

Check TAT's website for contact information in Hong Kong, Taipei, Seoul, Tokyo, Osaka, Fukuoka, Stockholm and Rome.

Australia (☎ 02 9247 7549; info@thailand.net.au; Level 2, 75 Pitt St, Sydney, NSW 2000)

France (☎ 01 53 53 47 00; tatpar@wanadoo.fr; 90 ave des Champs Elysées, 75008 Paris)

Germany (☎ 069 138 1390; tatfra@tat.or.th; Beth-mannstrasse 58, D-60311 Frankfurt/Main)

Malaysia (☎ 603 216 23480; sawatdi@po.jaring.my; Ste 22.01, Level 22, Menara Citibank, 165 Jalan Ampang, 50450 Kuala Lumpur)

Singapore (☎ 65 6235 7901; tatsin@singnet.com.sg; c/o Royal Thai embassy, 370 Orchard Rd, 238870)

UK (☎ 020 7925 2511; tatuk@tat.or.th; 3rd fl, Brook House, 98-99 Jermyn St, London SW1Y 6EE)

USA New York (☎ 212 432 0433; tatny@tat.or.th; 61 Broadway, Ste 2810, New York, NY 10006); Los Angeles (☎ 323 461 9814; tatla@ix.netcom.com; 1st fl, 611 North Larchmont Blvd, LA, CA 90004)

Tourist Offices in Thailand

TAT's head office is in Bangkok and there are 22 regional offices spread throughout the country. Check the destination chapters for the TAT office in the towns you're planning to visit.

VISAS

The **Ministry of Foreign Affairs** (www.mfa.go.th) oversees immigration and visas issues. Check the website or the nearest Thai embassy or consulate for application procedures and costs.

The Thai government allows 41 different nationalities, including those from most of Europe, Australia, New Zealand and the USA, to enter the country without a prearranged visa for 30 days at no charge. This status is called a 'visa exemption' and in your passport you'll receive an entry and exit stamp that indicates the period you are allowed to remain in country.

Without proof of an onward ticket and sufficient funds for one's projected stay any visitor can be denied entry, but in practice your ticket and funds are rarely checked if you're dressed neatly for the immigration check.

Non-Immigrant Visas

The Non-Immigrant Visa is good for 90 days and is intended for foreigners entering the country for business, study, retirement and extended family visits. If you plan to apply for a Thai work permit, you'll need to possess a Non-Immigrant Visa first.

Tourist Visas

If you plan to stay in Thailand more than a month, you should apply for the 60-day Tourist Visa before arrival.

Visa Extensions & Renewals

You can apply at any immigration office for visa extensions. Most foreigners use the **Bangkok immigration office** (☎ 0 2287 3101; Soi Suan Phlu, Th Sathon Tai; ☯ 9am-noon & 1-4.30pm Mon-Fri, 9am-noon Sat) or the **Chiang Mai immigration office** (Map pp276-7; ☎ 0 5320 1755-6; Th Mahidon; ☯ 8.30am-4.30pm Mon-Fri) for extensions of most types of visa. The usual fee for a visa extension is 1900B.

The 30-day, visa exemption can be extended for seven to 10 days (depending on the immigration office). Prior to October 2006, there was no limit on the number of times within a year that a national from a visa-exempt country could leave Thailand and reenter in order to receive another 30-day entry stamp. Under new regulations, entry stamps will be renewable two consecutive times for a maximum stay of 90 days, after which the visitor must remain outside of the country for at least 90 days before being able to reenter. As of early 2007, travellers were reporting that some border officials were inconsistent in the enforcement of these new regulations and allowing for a third consecutive stamp. But it is unclear how long this practice will continue.

The 60-day Tourist Visa can be extended up to 30 days at the discretion of Thai immigration

authorities. The fee for extension of a Tourist Visa is 1900B.

For all types of visa extensions, bring along two passport-sized photos and one copy each of the photo and visa pages of your passport. Remember to dress neatly and do all visa extensions yourself, rather than hiring a third party.

If you overstay your visa, the usual penalty is a fine of 500B per day, with a 20,000B limit. Fines can be paid at the airport or in advance at an immigration office. If you've overstayed only one day, you don't have to pay. Children under 14 travelling with a parent do not have to pay the penalty.

WOMEN TRAVELLERS

Women make up nearly half of all foreign visitors to Thailand, a much higher ratio than the worldwide average, and female travellers generally face few problems. With the great amount of respect afforded to women, an equal measure should be returned.

In the provincial towns, it is advisable to dress conservatively, covering shoulders and belly buttons. Outside of Bangkok, most Thai women cover up in the sun to avoid unneces-

sary exposure since white skin is considered more beautiful. That Westerners believe the opposite is an endless source of amusement and confusion.

Attacks and rapes are less common in Thailand than in many Western countries, but incidents do occur especially when an attacker observes a vulnerable target; a drunk or solo woman. If you return home from a bar alone, be sure to have your wits about you. The full-moon parties at Ko Pha-Ngan are common trouble spots. Avoid taking dodgy gypsy cabs or accepting rides from strangers late at night – common sense stuff that might escape your notice in a new environment filled with hospitable people.

While Bangkok might be a men's paradise, foreign women are finding their own Romeos on the Thai beaches. As more couples emerge, more Thai men will make themselves available. Women who aren't interested in such romantic encounters should not presume that Thai men have platonic motives. Oftentimes, Thai men ignore their own culture's strictures regarding mingling of the sexes when it comes to dealing with a foreign women. There's no threat of danger, just misconceptions.

Transport

GETTING THERE & AWAY

ENTERING THE COUNTRY

Entry procedures for Thailand, by air or by land, are straightforward. You'll have to show your passport, with any visa you may have obtained beforehand (see p753). You'll also need to present completed arrival and departure cards. These are usually distributed on the incoming flight or, if arriving by land, can be picked up at the immigration counter.

You do not have to fill in a customs form on arrival unless you have imported goods to declare. In that case you can get the proper form from Thai customs officials at the point of entry.

See p748 for Thai customs information about minimum currency requirements.

AIR
Airports

The new **Suvarnabhumi Airport** (Bangkok International Airport; www.bangkokairportonline.com) – pronounced *sùwannáphuum* – opened in September 2006 and has replaced the former airport at Don Muang for all Bangkok-arriving and -departing domestic and international flights. It is located in the Nong Ngu Hao area of Samut Prakan – 30km east of Bangkok and 60km from Pattaya.

The Bangkok International Airport at **Don Muang** was retired from commercial service in September 2006 only to be partially reopened five months later to handle overflow from Suvarnabhumi. As of March 2007, Don Muang began servicing some domestic carriers, but it was unclear at the time of writing what the operating duration or capacity of the old airport would be once construction problems at Suvarnabhumi.were resolved.

While most international flights arrive at and depart out of Bangkok, there are a few routes servicing Thailand's other 'international' airports. Moderately up-to-date information about these airports is available online at www.airportthai.co.th. Besides

THINGS CHANGE

The information supplied in this chapter is particularly vulnerable to change: Prices for international travel are volatile, routes are introduced and cancelled, schedules change, special deals come and go, and rules and visa requirements are amended. Airlines and governments seem to take a perverse pleasure in making price structures and regulations as complicated as possible. You should check directly with the airline or a travel agent to make sure you understand how a fare (and ticket you may buy) works. In addition, the travel industry is highly competitive and there are many lurks and perks.

The upshot of this is that you should get opinions, quotes and advice from as many airlines and travel agents as possible before you part with your hard-earned cash. The details given in this chapter should be regarded as pointers and are not a substitute for your own careful, up-to-date research.

DEPARTURE TAX

At the time of writing, all passengers leaving Thailand on international flights are charged a departure tax (officially called an 'airport service charge') of 500B, which is not included in the price of air tickets, but paid at a booth near the passport control area. Only baht are accepted. However, the departure tax is slated to rise to 700B, the cost of which will be included in ticket prices.

Bangkok, the **Chiang Mai International Airport** (p320) has scheduled flights to many regional capitals. **Phuket** (p669) has a few flights to certain European destinations without a layover in Bangkok. Additional international airports include **Chiang Rai** (p360), which is designated as international but is not currently receiving flights from abroad, Hat Yai, Samui and **Sukhothai** (p408). Samui and Sukhothai airports are privately owned by Bangkok Airways. There are plans to add international flights to **Udon Thani** (p488; the closest provincial airport to the Friendship Bridge between Thailand and Laos), and **Khon Kaen** (p479).

Airlines Travelling to/from Thailand

Bangkok is one of the cheapest cities in the world to fly out of, due to the Thai government's loose restrictions on air fares and close competition between airlines and travel agencies. Thailand's national carrier is Thai Airways International (THAI), which also operates many domestic air routes.

Air Asia (☎ 0 2515 9999; www.airasia.com; Suvarnabhumi Airport)

Air China (Map pp124-5; ☎ 0 2634 8991; www.fly-airchina.com; Bangkok Union Insurance Bldg, 175-177 Th Surawong)

Air France (Map pp124-5; ☎ 0 2635 1191; www.airfrance.fr; 20th fl, Vorawat Bldg, 849 Th Silom)

Air New Zealand (Map pp124-5; ☎ 0 2254 8440; www.airnewzealand.com; 11th fl, 140/17 ITF Tower, Th Silom)

American Airlines (Map pp128-9; ☎ 0 2263 0225; www.aa.com; 11th fl Ploenchit Tower, 898 Th Ploenchit)

Bangkok Airways (☎ 0 2265 5555; www.bangkokair.com)

British Airways (Map pp124-5; ☎ 0 2627 1701; www.britishairways.com; 21st fl, Charn Issara Tower, 942/160-163 Th Phra Rama IV)

Cathay Pacific Airways (Map pp128-9; ☎ 0 2263 0606; www.cathaypacific.com; Ploenchit Tower, 898 Th Ploenchit)

China Airlines (Map pp128-9; ☎ 0 2253 4242; www.china-airlines.com; 4th fl, Peninsula Plaza, 153 Th Ratchadamri)

Garuda Indonesia (Map p127; ☎ 0 2679 7371; www.garuda-indonesia.com; 27th fl, Lumphini Tower, 1168/77 Th Phra Ram IV)

Gulf Air (Map pp128-9; ☎ 0 2254 7931-4; www.gulfairco.com; Maneeya Center, 518/5 Th Ploenchit)

Japan Airlines (Map pp128-9; ☎ 0 2649 9555; www.jal.co.jp; Nantawan Bldg, 161 Th Ratchadamri)

KLM-Royal Dutch Airlines (Map pp124-5; ☎ 0 2635 2300; www.klm.com; 20th fl, Vorawat Bldg, 849 Th Silom)

Korean Air (Map pp124-5; ☎ 0 2635 0465; www.koreanair.com; 1st fl, Kongboonma Bldg, 699 Th Silom)

Lao Airlines (Map pp124-5; ☎ 0 2236 9822; www.laoairlines.com; Silom Plaza, Th Silom)

Lufthansa Airlines (Map pp122-3; ☎ 0 2264 2484, reservations 0 2264 2400; www.lufthansa.com; 18th fl, Q House, Soi 21/Asoke, Th Sukhumvit)

Malaysia Airlines (Map pp128-9; ☎ 0 2263 0565; www.mas.com.my; 20th fl, Ploenchit Tower, 898 Th Ploenchit)

Myanmar Airways International (Map pp122-3; ☎ 0 2630 0334-8; www.maiair.com; 8th fl, BB Bldg, 54 Soi 21/Asoke, Th Sukhumvit)

Northwest Airlines (Map pp128-9; ☎ 0 2254 0789; www.nwa.com; 4th fl, Peninsula Plaza, 153 Th Ratchadamri)

Orient Thai (Map p127; ☎ 0 2229 4260; www.orient-thai.com; 18 Th Ratchadaphisek)

Qantas Airways (☎ 0 2236 2800, reservations 0 2636 1747; www.qantas.com.au; Tour East, 21st fl, Charn Issara Tower; 942/160-163 Th Phra Ram IV)

Royal Brunei Airlines (Map p127; ☎ 0 2637 5151; www.bruneiair.com; 17th fl, U Chu Liang Bldg, 968, Th Phra Ram IV)

Royal Nepal Airlines (☎ 0 2216 5691-5; www.royalnepal.com; 9th Floor Phayathai Plaza Bldg, 128 Th Phayathai)

Scandinavian Airlines (Map pp122-3; ☎ 0 2645 8200; www.scandinavian.net; 8th fl, Glas Haus B Bldg, Th Sukhumvit)

Singapore Airlines (Map pp124-5; ☎ 0 2353 6000, reservations ☎ 2236 5301; www.singaporeair.com; 12th fl, Silom Center Bldg; 2 Th Silom)

South African Airways (Map pp124-5; ☎ 0 2635 1414; www.flysaa.com; 20th fl, Vorawat Bldg, 849 Th Silom)

Thai Airways International Silom (Map pp124-5; ☎ 0 2232 8000; www.thaiair.com; 485 Th Silom); Banglamphu (Map pp120-1; ☎ 0 2356 1111, 6 Th Lan Luang)

United Airlines (Map pp128-9; ☎ 0 2296 7752; www.ual.com; 14th fl, Sindhorn Bldg, Tower 3, 130 Th Withayu)

TRANSPORT

Vietnam Airlines (Map pp122-3; ☎ 0 2656 9056-8; www.vietnamair.com.vn; Th Sukhumvit)

Tickets

Tickets can be purchased cheaply on the internet through booking and airline websites. Online ticket sales work well if you are doing a simple one-way or return trip on specified dates. However, online fare generators are no substitute for a travel agent who knows all about special deals; has strategies for avoiding layovers; and can offer advice on everything from picking the airline with the great vegetarian food to the best travel insurance to bundle with your ticket.

In Thailand, most travel arrangements are done through an agent. Most firms are honest and solvent, but there are some rogue fly-by-night outfits around. Paying by credit card generally offers protection, as most card issuers provide refunds if you can prove you didn't get what you paid for. Agents who accept only cash should hand over the tickets straight away and not tell you to 'come back tomorrow'. After you've made a booking or paid your deposit, call the airline and confirm that the booking was made.

Booking flights in and out of Bangkok during the high season (December to March) can be difficult and expensive. For air travel during these months you should make your bookings as far in advance as possible.

Also, be sure to reconfirm return or ongoing tickets when you arrive in Thailand. Failure to reconfirm can mean losing your reservation.

ROUND-THE-WORLD (RTW) TICKETS

If you're travelling to multiple countries, then an round-the-world (RTW) ticket – where you pay a single discounted price for several connections – may be the most economical way to go.

Here are a few online companies that can arrange RTW tickets:

Airstop & Go (www.airstop.be)
Airtreks (www.airtreks.com)
Air Brokers International (www.airbrokers.com)
Around the Worlds (www.aroundtheworlds.com)

Asia

There are regular flights to Suvarnabhumi Airport from almost every major city in Asia. With the emergence of budget airlines, quick hops from, say, Bangkok to Kuala Lumpur, Singapore or Hong Kong are part of the Asian yuppies' weekend budget. Air Asia and Dragon are two discount carriers that run frequent promotions. A very good internet source for discounted fares leaving from Bangkok is www.bangkoktickets.com.

CLIMATE CHANGE & TRAVEL

Climate change is a serious threat to the ecosystems that humans rely upon, and air travel is the fastest-growing contributor to the problem. Lonely Planet regards travel, overall, as a global benefit, but believes we all have a responsibility to limit our personal impact on global warming.

Flying & Climate Change

Pretty much every form of motor transport generates CO_2 (the main cause of human-induced climate change) but planes are far and away the worst offenders, not just because of the sheer distances they allow us to travel, but because they release greenhouse gases high into the atmosphere. The statistics are frightening: two people taking a return flight between Europe and the US will contribute as much to climate change as an average household's gas and electricity consumption over a whole year.

Carbon Offset Schemes

Climatecare.org and other websites use 'carbon calculators' that allow travellers to offset the greenhouse gases they are responsible for with contributions to energy-saving projects and other climate-friendly initiatives in the developing world – including projects in India, Honduras, Kazakhstan and Uganda.

Lonely Planet, together with Rough Guides and other concerned partners in the travel industry, supports the carbon offset scheme run by climatecare.org. Lonely Planet offsets all of its staff and author travel.

For more information check out our website: www.lonelyplanet.com.

Recommended booking agencies for reserving flights from Asia include **STA Travel** (www.statravel.com), which has offices in Bangkok, Hong Kong, Japan and Singapore. Another resource in Japan is **No1 Travel** (www.no1-travel.com); in Hong Kong try **Four Seas Tours** (www.fourseastravel.com). For India, try **STIC Travels** (www.stictravel.com), which has offices in dozens of Indian cities.

Australia

THAI and Qantas both have direct flights to Bangkok; in 2006, Jetstar announced that it would add more flights during peak travel times between Sydney and Melbourne to Thailand. Garuda Indonesia, Singapore Airlines, Philippine Airlines, Malaysia Airlines and Royal Brunei Airlines also have frequent flights with stopovers to Bangkok.

Shop for cheap tickets from **STA Travel** (☎ 134 782; www.statravel.com.au) and **Flight Centre** (☎ 133 133; www.flightcentre.com.au), both of which have offices throughout Australia.

Canada

Air Canada, THAI, Cathay Pacific and several US-based airlines fly from different Canadian cities to Bangkok. **Travel Cuts** (☎ 800-667-2887; www.travelcuts.com) is Canada's national student travel agency. For online bookings try www.expedia.ca and www.travelocity.ca.

Continental Europe

Following are some recommended agencies across Europe.

France
Anyway (☎ 0 892 302 301; www.anyway.fr)
Lastminute (☎ 0 899 785 000; www.lastminute.fr)
Nouvelles Frontières (☎ 0 825 000 747; www.nouvelles-frontieres.fr)
OTU Voyages (www.otu.fr) This agency specialises in student and youth travellers.
Voyageurs du Monde (www.vdm.com)

Germany
Expedia (www.expedia.de)
Just Travel (☎ 089 747 3330; www.justtravel.de)
Lastminute (☎ 0 180 528 4366; www.lastminute.de)
STA Travel (☎ 0 697 430 3292; www.statravel.de) Good choice for travellers under the age of 26.

Italy
CTS Viaggi (☎ 06 462 0431; www.cts.it) Specialises in student and youth travel.

Netherlands
Airfair (☎ 0 900 7717 717; www.airfair.nl)

Spain
Barcelo Viajes (☎ 902 116 226; www.barceloviajes.com)

Middle East
Some recommended agencies include the following:
Egypt Panorama Tours (☎ 2-359 0200; www.eptours.com) In Cairo.
Orion-Tour (www.oriontour.com) In Istanbul.

New Zealand
Air New Zealand, British Airways, THAI and Australian-based airlines have direct flights to Bangkok. Malaysian Airlines, Qantas and Garuda International also have flights to Bangkok, with stopovers.

Both **Flight Centre** (☎ 0800 243 544; www.flightcentre.co.nz) and **STA Travel** (☎ 0800 474 400; www.statravel.co.nz) have branches throughout the country. The site www.goholidays.co.nz is recommended for online bookings.

South America
Some recommended agencies include the following:
ASATEJ (www.asatej.com) In Argentina, Mexico and Uruguay.
Student Travel Bureau (☎ 3038 1555; www.stb.com.br) In Brazil.

UK
At least two dozen airlines fly between London and Bangkok, although only three of them – British Airways, Qantas and THAI – fly nonstop. Discount air-travel ads appear in *Time Out*, the *Evening Standard* and in the free magazine *TNT*.

Recommended travel agencies include the following:
Bridge the World (☎ 0800 082 5000; www.b-t-w.co.uk)
Flight Centre (☎ 0870 499 0040; flightcentre.co.uk)
Flightbookers (☎ 0800 082 3000; www.ebookers.com)
North South Travel (www.northsouthtravel.com) Part of this company's profit is donated to projects in the developing world.
Quest Travel (☎ 0871 423 0135; www.questtravel.com)
STA Travel (☎ 0871 230 0040; www.statravel.co.uk) Popular with travellers under 26, sells tickets to all. Branches throughout the UK.

Trailfinders (☎ 0845 058 5858; www.trailfinders.co.uk)
Travel Bag (☎ 0800 082 5000; www.travelbag.co.uk)

USA

It's cheaper to fly to Bangkok from West Coast cities than from the East Coast. You can get some great deals through the many bucket shops (which discount tickets by taking a cut in commissions) and consolidators (agencies that buy airline seats in bulk) in Los Angeles and San Francisco.

The airlines that generally offer the lowest fares from the USA include China Airlines, EVA Airways, Korean Air and Northwest. EVA Airways (Taiwan) offers the 'Evergreen Deluxe' class between the USA and Bangkok, via Taipei, which has business-class-sized seats and personal movie screens for about the same cost as regular economy fares on most other airlines.

One of the most reliable discounters is **Avia Travel** (☎ 800 950 2842, 510 558 2150; www.aviatravel.com), which specialises in custom-designed RTW fares.

The following agencies are recommended for online bookings:

www.cheaptickets.com
www.expedia.com
www.itn.net
www.lowestfare.com
www.orbitz.com
www.sta.com (For travellers under the age of 26.)
www.travelocity.com

LAND

Thailand shares land borders with Laos, Malaysia, Cambodia and Myanmar. Travel between all of these countries can be done by land via sanctioned border crossings. With improved highways, it is also becoming easier to travel from Thailand to China. See Border Crossings (right) for specific immigration points and transport summaries.

Bicycle

Many visitors bring their own touring bicycles to Thailand. No special permits are needed for bringing a bicycle into the country, although it may be registered by customs – which means if you don't leave the country with your bicycle, you'll have to pay a huge customs duty. See p761 for more information about travelling by bike.

It's essential to bring a well-stocked repair kit and be sure to have your bike serviced before departure.

Bus

You can enter Thailand by bus through Laos and Malaysia at the moment – your bus will stop at a Thai immigration post at your point of entry so that each foreign passenger can receive an entry stamp in their passport. Thai visas are not normally included in bus fares. For overland routes through Cambodia, you'll need to hire a shared taxi. You can exit Thailand into portions of Myanmar by bus or shared taxi.

Car & Motorcycle

Road passage into Thailand is possible through Malaysia, Cambodia and Laos.

Passenger vehicles (eg car, van, truck or motorcycle) can be brought into Thailand for tourist purposes for up to six months. Documents needed for the crossing are a valid International Driving Permit, passport, vehicle registration papers (in the case of a borrowed or hired vehicle, authorisation from the owner) and a cash or bank guarantee equal to the value of the vehicle plus 20%. For entry through Khlong Toey Port or Suvarnabhumi Airport, this means a letter of bank credit; for overland crossings via Malaysia, Cambodia or Laos a 'self-guarantee' filled in at the border is sufficient.

Train

The only rail option into and out of Thailand is via Malaysia. The **State Railway of Thailand** (www.railway.co.th) and **Malaysian Railway** (www.ktmb.com.my) meet at Butterworth, 93km south of the Thai–Malaysian border, a transfer point to Penang or Kuala Lumpur.

BORDER CROSSINGS
Cambodia

Thai–Cambodian border crossings are typically straightforward. Most visitors cross at

---

CHECKPOINTS

Military checkpoints are common along highways throughout northern, southern and northeastern Thailand, especially in border areas. Always slow down for a checkpoint – often the sentries will wave you through without an inspection, but occasionally you will be stopped and briefly questioned. Use common sense and don't act belligerently or you're likely to be detained longer than you'd like.

Poipet (Cambodia) to Aranya Prathet (Thailand; p270). This is the most direct land route between Bangkok and Angkor Wat.

You can also cross by boat from Ko Kong in southern Cambodia to the coastal town of Hat Lek in Trat Province (p256).

Several more remote crossings have opened between southeastern Thailand and southwestern Cambodia including: Kap Choeng-Chom Som, Chong Sa Ngam-Anlong Veng; Ban Laem-Daun Lem, Ban Phakkat-Pailin. Private or hired transport is required to access most of these crossings.

China

Plans for land and rail links between China and member countries of ASEAN, including Thailand, Laos, Myanmar and Vietnam, have been increasing since the turn of the new millennium.

The China–Thailand highway will link Kunming, in China's Yunnan Province, with Bangkok. As of 2006, 60% of the route (from Kunming to the Laos border town of Boten) has been completed. The routes from Boten, Laos across to Chiang Khong, Thailand, can be done relatively easily now, although roads between Boten and Huay Xai are rough.

Other roads emanating from China's Yunnan Province will link to Myanmar and to Vietnam and then on to Thailand. The China–Myanmar highway stretches between Tachileik, which is on the border with Mae Sai, Thailand, to the Chinese town of Daluo (see p369).

It is possible to float along the Mekong River from the northern Thai town of Chian Saen to Jinghong in China's Yunnan Province. See p372 for more information.

Laos

The Thai-Lao Friendship Bridge (1174m) spans a section of the Mekong River between Nong Khai, Thailand, and Tha Na Leng (near Vientiane, Laos) and is the main transport gateway between the two countries. You can easily reach the Thai border crossing from Vientiane by bus, taxi or săamláw (three-wheeled motorcycle taxi).

The construction of a second Mekong bridge between Mukdahan and Savannakhet opened in 2006 and creates a link between Thailand and Vietnam through Laos.

It's legal for non-Thais to cross the Mekong River by ferry between Thailand and Laos at the following points: Beung Kan (opposite Paksan), Nakhon Phanom (opposite Tha Khaek), Chiang Khong (opposite Huay Xai).

Malaysia

Due to the unrest in the southern provinces of Thailand, many border crossers are opting for flights from Bangkok to Kuala Lumpur, Penang or Singapore instead of crossing by land.

There are very regular public buses and private minivans between Hat Yai in Thailand and various destinations in Malaysia, which include immigration stops at the border.

The train heading into Malaysia from Bangkok splits at Hat Yai with one spur heading east toward the border town of Sungai Kolok (p640) and on to Kota Bahru. The western spur trundles travellers to Butterworth, the transfer point to Penang or other destinations along the west coast of Malaysia.

There are several ways of travelling between Thailand's southern peninsula and Malaysia by sea. The simplest is to take a boat from Satun to Kuala Perlis or the island of Langkawi. For more details, see p728).

PRIVATE BOAT

All foreign-registered vessels, skippers and crew must check in with the relevant Thai authorities as soon as possible after entering Thai waters. Although major ports throughout Thailand offer port check-ins, most leisure boating visitors check in at Phuket, Krabi, Samui, Pranburi or Pattaya. Because Phuket's Tha Ao Chalong brings customs, immigration and harbourmaster services together in one building, Phuket is the most popular check-in point nationwide.

Before departing from Thailand by boat, you must also check out with immigration, customs and harbourmaster. Vessels caught without harbour clearance may be fined up to 5000B. **Lee Marine** (www.leemarine.com) is a brokerage and dealership in Phuket.

Myanmar

The land crossings into Myanmar have peculiar restrictions that often don't allow full land access to the country. Of the four border crossing open to foreigners, only two allow more than a day's access into the country. These borders are also the most sensitive to periodic closures due to fighting on the

Myanmar side between ethnic armies and the Burmese government, or other unstable factors.

The crossing at Mae Sai–Tachileik is the only land point through which foreigners can really travel into Myanmar. From the border you can continue to Kengtung, as far as Mengla on the Thai–China border and into China as long as you have arranged the appropriate visas beforehand (see p365). Interestingly, the bridge that spans the two border towns is Lo Hsing-han's former 'Golden Triangle' passageway for opium and heroin. Many travellers use this border as a way to renew their Thai visas.

In the past, Mae Sai immigration officials have been known to ask travellers to produce evidence of sufficient funds (10,000B cash, the legal requirement for a tourist visa) before issuing an entry stamp.

The Mae Sot–Myawadi border crossing is open to foreigners only as a day trip into a border market, even though the road continues to Mawlamyaing (Moulmein) via Kawkareik. Unlike Three Pagodas Pass, this crossing can be used for visa renewal. For more information, see p424.

Once a gateway for various invading armies and an important smuggling route, Three Pagodas Pass is accessible to foreigners only as a day trip to a Burmese border market. You must surrender your passport on the Thai side and are unable to use this point for renewing your Thai visa. For more information, see p224.

In the southern part of Thailand, you can legally enter Myanmar by boat from Ranong to Kawthoung via the Gulf of Martaban and Pakchan estuary. You'll need to arrange the appropriate visas before arrival in Myanmar. Many people use this crossing only as a day trip in order to renew their Thai visas; for day passes, no Myanmar visa is required. See the boxed text on p647 for more information.

GETTING AROUND

AIR
Hopping around the country by air is becoming more and more affordable these days thanks to airline deregulation. Most routes originate from Bangkok, but Chiang Mai, Ko Samui and Phuket both have routes to other Thai towns. See the Thai Airfares and Rail Lines map (p762) for routes and estimated costs; for airline contact information, see the respective city sections.

Thailand's national carrier is Thai Airways International (THAI), which operates many domestic air routes from Bangkok to provincial capitals. Bangkok Air provides some alternatives between Chiang Mai and the south that bypass Bangkok. One-Two-Go, Nok Air and Air Asia all tend to be cheaper than the older, more established carriers.

BICYCLE
For travelling just about anywhere outside Bangkok, bicycles are an ideal form of local transport – cheap, nonpolluting and slow moving enough to allow travellers to see everything.

Bicycle touring is also a popular way to see the country as most roads are sealed with roomy shoulders. Grades in most parts of the country are moderate; exceptions include the far north, especially Mae Hong Son and Nan Provinces. There is plenty of opportunity for dirt-road and off-road pedalling, especially in the north, so a sturdy mountain bike would make a good alternative to a touring rig. Favoured touring routes include the two-lane roads along the Mekong River in the north and northeast – the terrain is largely flat and the river scenery is inspiring.

You can take bicycles on the train for a little less than the equivalent of one 3rd-class fare. On ordinary buses they'll place your bike on the roof, and on air-con buses it will be put in the cargo hold.

The 2500-member **Thailand Cycling Club** (☎ 08 1555 2901; www.thaicycling.com), established in 1959, serves as an information clearing house on biking tours and cycle clubs.

See p759 for more information on bringing a bike into Thailand.

Hire
Bicycles can be hired in many locations; guesthouses often have a few for rent at only 30B to 50B per day. In northern Thailand, particularly in Chiang Mai and Pai, sturdier mountain bikes can be rented for 80B to 100B a day. A security deposit isn't usually required.

Purchase
Because duties are high on imported bikes, in most cases you'll do better to bring your own bike to Thailand rather than purchase one here.

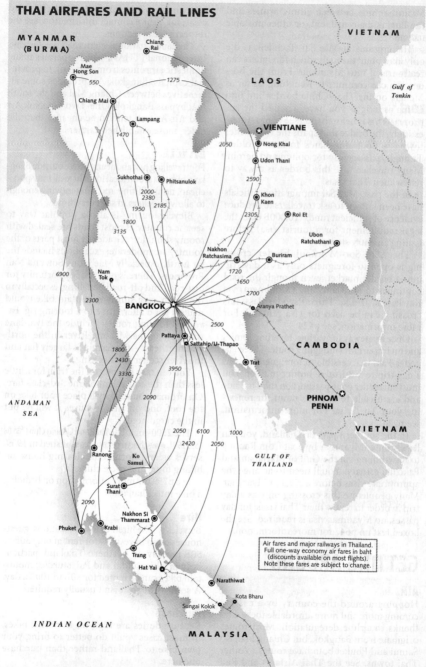

THAI AIRFARES AND RAIL LINES

TRANSPORT

MYANMAR
(BURMA)

Chiang Rai

Mae Hong Son
550

LAOS

Gulf of Tonkin

VIETNAM

Chiang Mai

Lampang

1275

2050

VIENTIANE

Nong Khai

Udon Thani

1470

Sukhothai

Phitsanulok

2590

Khon Kaen

2000-2380

1950

2185

2305

Roi Et

1800

3135

Ubon Ratchathani

Nam Tok

Nakhon Ratchasima

Buriram

6900

2300

1720

1650

2700

BANGKOK

Aranya Prathet

2500

Pattaya

Sattahip/U-Thapao

CAMBODIA

ANDAMAN SEA

1800
2430
3330

3950

Trat

2090

PHNOM PENH

VIETNAM

Ranong

Ko Samui

2050   6100   1000

2420   2050

GULF OF THAILAND

Surat Thani

2090

Nakhon Si Thammarat

Phuket

Krabi

Trang

Air fares and major railways in Thailand.
Full one-way economy air fares in baht
(discounts available on most flights).
Note these fares are subject to change.

Hat Yai

Narathiwat

Kota Bharu

Sungai Kolok

INDIAN OCEAN

MALAYSIA

One of the best shops for cycling gear in Thailand is the centrally located **Probike** (Map p127; ☎ 0 2253 3384; www.probike.co.th; 237/1 Soi Sarasin, Bangkok) opposite Lumphini Park. Probike carries bikes and parts for Gary Fisher, Klein, Challenger, + LeMond and Trek. See p323 for details on bike shops in Chiang Mai.

BOAT
The true Thai river transport is the *reua hǎang yao* (long-tail boat), so-called because the propeller is mounted at the end of a long drive shaft extending from the engine. Long-tail boats can travel at a phenomenal speed.

The long-tail boats are a staple of transport on rivers and canals in Bangkok and neighbouring provinces. See p182 for details on canal travel around the city.

Between the mainland and islands in the Gulf of Thailand or Andaman Sea, the standard craft is an all-purpose wooden boat, 8m to 10m long, with a large inboard engine, a wheelhouse and a simple roof to shelter passengers and cargo. Faster, more expensive hovercraft or jetfoils are sometimes available in tourist areas.

BUS
Bus Companies
The bus network in Thailand is prolific and reliable and is a great way to see the countryside and sit among the locals. The Thai government subsidises the **Transport Company** (bàw-rí-sàt khǒn sòng; ☎ 0 2936 2841; www.transport.co.th), usually abbreviated to Baw Khaw Saw (BKS). Every city and town in Thailand linked by bus has a BKS station, even if it's just a patch of dirt by the side of the road.

The service on the government air-con buses is usually quite good and sometimes includes beverage service and video courtesy of an 'air hostess', a young woman dressed in polyester uniform. Some privately run buses have concessions to operate out of the government-run BKS bus stations and are more reliable than the private companies operating out of the tourist centres like Th Khao San in Bangkok.

On overnight journeys the buses usually stop somewhere en route and passengers are awakened to get off the bus for a free meal of fried rice or rice soup. A few companies even treat you to a meal before a long overnight trip.

Out of Bangkok, the safest, most reliable private bus services are the ones that operate from the three official BKS terminals rather than from hotels or guesthouses. See p180 for information on the main bus terminals in Bangkok.

CLASSES
The cheapest and slowest are the fan-only *rót thammádaa* (ordinary buses) that stop in every little town and for every waving hand along the highway. Many of these ordinary buses are being replaced by air-con buses. But a few lines, especially in fairly rural locations, are still in operation.

The bus companies also run faster, more comfortable but less frequent air-con buses called *rót ae* (air bus), *rót pràp aakàat* (air-con bus) or *rót thua* (tour bus). Longer routes offer at least two classes of air-con buses: 2nd class and 1st class; the latter have toilets. 'VIP' and 'Super VIP' buses have fewer seats so that each seat reclines more. Sometimes these are called *rót nawn* or sleepers. For small- to medium-sized people they are more comfortable. Most private companies offer similar air-con classes.

ON THE BUSES – WARNING

The service on many private lines can be very unreliable, especially on the Bangkok–Chiang Mai, Bangkok–Ko Samui, Surat–Phuket and Surat–Krabi routes.

Sometimes the cheaper lines – especially those booked on Th Khao San in Bangkok – will switch vehicles so that instead of the roomy air-con bus advertised, you're stuck with a cramped van with broken air-con. We've had reports of buses stopping for lunch halfway to Chiang Mai and then abandoning passengers – leaving them to finish the journey on their own. To avoid situations such as this, *always* book bus tickets directly at a bus office – or at the government Baw Khaw Saw (BKS) public bus terminal.

Private buses that leave from nonstandard locations (ie not a government bus terminal) generally spend time cruising the city for passengers, so they rarely leave at the advertised departure time. It's actually illegal for buses to do this, which is why the bus attendants often pull the curtains while driving around the city (so that police can't see that they're carrying passengers).

SAMPLE BUS FARES			
Destination from Bankok	**VIP**	**1st class**	**2nd class**
Chiang Mai (686km)	625–860B	558B	434B
Loei (560km)	685–521B	344B	(n/a)
Krabi (817km)	850B	459B	(n/a)
Hat Yai (993km)	1050B	768B	550B
Trat (313km)	(n/a)	223–257B	188B

It is handy to bring along a light jacket, especially for long-distance trips, as the air-con can turn the cabin into a deep freeze.

SAFETY

The most reputable bus companies depart from Baw Khaw Saw (BKS) public bus terminals. Private buses and minivans that pick up customers from tourist centres such as Th Khao San experience a higher incidence of reported theft, lateness and unreliability. Sometimes these tourist-oriented services pick up passengers from their guesthouse only to drop them off at the public bus terminal. Other complaints include the alleged VIP bus turning out to be a cramped minibus that arrives four hours late.

Readers have also consistently reported having their stowed bags rifled through. Theft is a serious problem on long-haul tourist buses originating out of Bangkok. Keep all valuables on your person, not stored in your luggage as even locked bags can be tampered with and you won't realize anything is missing until days later.

Reservations

You can book air-con BKS buses at any BKS terminal. Ordinary (nonair-con) buses cannot be booked in advance. Privately run buses can be booked through most hotels or any travel agency, but it's best to book directly through a bus office to be sure that you get what you pay for.

CAR & MOTORCYCLE
Bring Your Own Vehicle

See p759 for information on how to bring a private vehicle into Thailand for tourist purposes.

Driving Licence

Short-term visitors who wish to drive vehicles (including motorcycles) in Thailand need an International Driving Permit. Long-term visitors can apply for a Thai driver's licence through the provincial office of the Department of Land Transport. In Bangkok, there are five district offices. Contact the main office (☎ 0 2272 5322) to determine the location of your assigned office based on residence.

Fuel & Spare Parts

Modern petrol (gasoline) stations are in plentiful supply all over Thailand wherever there are paved roads. In more-remote, off-road areas *bensin/náam-man rót yon* (petrol) is usually available at small roadside or village stands. All fuel in Thailand is unleaded, and diesel is used by both trucks and some passenger cars. Due to the global increase in petrol prices, Thailand has introduced several alternative fuels, including gasohol (a blend of petrol and ethanol) as well as compressed natural gas, used by taxis with bifuel capabilities. For news updates about fuel options and other car talk, see **BKK Auto** (www.bkkautos.com).

If you're driving a motorcycle for distances of over 100km, take an extra supply of motor oil, and if riding a two-stroke machine carry two-stroke engine oil.

If you're bringing your own vehicle, you'd be wise to bring a box of crucial spare parts that might not be available in Thailand. The same goes for motorcycles – especially so for bikes larger than 125cc.

Hire & Purchase

Cars, jeeps and vans can be rented in most major cities and airports. The international chains have offices in most of the major cities and can be booked prior to arrival via their websites. Local companies are located in major tourist destinations and tend to have cheaper rates than the international chains, but their fleets of cars tend to be older and not as well maintained. Check the tyre treads and general upkeep of the vehicle before committing.

Motorcycles can be rented in major towns and many smaller tourist centres from guesthouses and small mum-and-pop businesses. Renting a motorcycle in Thailand is relatively easy and a great way to independently tour the countryside, especially in northern Thailand and on the southern beaches. For daily rentals, most businesses will ask that you leave your passport as a deposit. Before renting a motorcycle, check the vehicle for condition

TRANSPORT

ROAD DISTANCES (KM)

	Aranya Prathet	Ayuthaya	Bangkok	Chiang Mai	Chiang Rai	Chumphon	Hat Yai	Hua Hin	Khon Kaen	Mae Hong Son	Mae Sai	Mukdahan	Nakhon Ratchasima	Nakhon Sawan	Nong Khai	Phitsanulok	Phuket	Sungai Kolok	Surat Thani	Tak	Trat	Ubon Ratchathani
Aranya Prathet	⋮	246	275	844	1014	727	1268	458	432	1013	1082	601	239	409	598	535	1125	1555	927	581	285	444
Ayuthaya		⋮	79	607	777	531	1072	262	397	767	845	524	204	163	563	377	929	1359	731	335	392	367
Bangkok			⋮	686	856	452	993	183	450	846	924	577	257	242	616	377		1280	652	414	313	420
Chiang Mai				⋮	191	1138	1679	869	604	225	259	917	744	444	720	309	1536	1966	1338	280	999	881
Chiang Rai					⋮	1308	1849	1039	774	406	68	1087	914	614	890	479	1706	2136	1508	460	1169	1051
Chumphon						⋮	555	269	902	1298	1376	1029	709	694	1068	829	412	866	214	765	872	
Hat Yai							⋮	810	1443	1839	1917	1570	1250	1235	1609	1370	474	287		1407	1306	1413
Hua Hin								⋮	633	1029	1107	760	440	425	799	560	667	1097	597	496	603	
Khon Kaen									⋮	829	842	313	193	408	166	295	1300	1730	1102	441	717	277
Mae Hong Son										⋮	474	1142	969	604	945	578	1696	2126	1498	432	1397	1106
Mae Sai											⋮	1155	982	682	958	547	1774	2204	1576	528	1237	1119
Mukdahan												⋮	320	692	347	608	1427	1857	1229	754	886	157
Nakhon Ratchasima													⋮	372	359	435	1107	1522	909	544	524	163
Nakhon Sawan														⋮	546	135	1092	1896	894	172	555	535
Nong Khai															⋮	411	1466	1896	1263	557	883	443
Phitsanulok																⋮	1227		1029	146	690	572
Phuket																	⋮	761	286	1264	1163	1270
Sungai Kolok																		⋮	688	1694	1593	1700
Surat Thani																			⋮	1066	965	1072
Tak																				⋮	727	707
Trat																					⋮	729
Ubon Ratchathani																						⋮

and ask for a helmet (which is required by law in some provinces).

Many tourists are injured riding motorcycles in Thailand because they don't know how to handle the vehicle and are unfamiliar with road rules and conditions. Be sure to have adequate health insurance and drive sensibly to avoid damage to yourself and to the vehicle. If you've never driven a motorcycle before, stick to the smaller 100cc step-through bikes with automatic clutches. Remember to distribute weight as evenly as possible across the frame of the bike to improve handling.

It is also possible to buy a new or used motorcycle and sell it before you leave the country. A used 125cc bike can be purchased for as low as 25,000B; you'll pay up to 60,000B for a reconditioned Honda MTX or AX-1, and more for the newer and more reliable Honda Degree or Yamaha TTR 250. If you're looking for a more narrowly defined dirt bike, check out the Yamaha Serow.

Insurance

Thailand requires a minimum of liability insurance for all registered vehicles on the road. The better hire companies include comprehensive coverage for their vehicles. Always verify that a vehicle is insured for liability before signing a rental contract; you should also ask to see the dated insurance documents. If you have an accident while driving an uninsured vehicle, you're in for some major hassles.

If you need auto insurance, a policy can be purchased through local companies inexpensively. Two of the more reliable ones are **Bangkok Insurance** (☎ 0 2285 8888; www.bki.co.th) and **AIA Thailand** (www.aiathailand.com).

Road Rules & Hazards

Thais drive on the left-hand side of the road (most of the time!). Other than that seemingly just about anything goes, in spite of road signs and speed limits.

The main rule to be aware of is that right of way belongs to the bigger vehicle; this is not what it says in the Thai traffic law, but it's the reality. Maximum speed limits are 50km/h on urban roads, 80km/h to 100km/h on most highways – but on any given stretch of highway you'll see vehicles travelling as slowly as 30km/h or as fast as 150km/h. Speed traps are common along Hwy 4 in the south and Hwy 2 in the northeast.

Indicators are often used to warn passing drivers about oncoming traffic. A flashing left indicator means it's OK to pass, while a right indicator means that someone's approaching from the other direction.

You'll need to have nerves of steel to drive around Bangkok and we really don't recommend it. Traffic is chaotic, roads are poorly signposted, and motorcycles and random contra flows mean you can suddenly find yourself facing a wall of cars coming the other way.

Outside of the capital city, the principal hazard when driving in Thailand, besides the general disregard for traffic laws, is having to contend with so many different types of vehicle on the same road – 18-wheelers, bicycles, túk-túk (motorised pedicabs) and customised racing bikes. This danger is often compounded by the lack of working lights. In village areas the vehicular traffic is lighter but you have to contend with stray chickens, dogs, water buffaloes and goats. Once you get used to the challenge, driving in Thailand is very entertaining.

HITCHING

Hitchhiking is never entirely safe in any country and we don't recommend it. Travellers who decide to hitch should understand that there's a small but serious risk. However, many people do choose to hitch, and the advice that follows should help to make the journey as fast and safe as possible.

People have mixed success with hitching in Thailand; sometimes it's great and at other times no-one wants to pick you up. It seems easiest in the more touristy areas of the north and south, and most difficult in the central and northeastern regions where tourists are a relatively rare sight. To stand on a road and try to flag every vehicle that passes by is, to the Thais, something only an uneducated village dweller would do.

If you're prepared to face this perception, the first step is to use the correct gesture for flagging a ride – the thumb-out gesture isn't recognised by the average Thai. When Thais want a ride they stretch one arm out with the hand open, palm facing down, and move the hand up and down. This is the same gesture used to flag a taxi or bus, which is why some drivers will stop and point to a bus stop if one is nearby.

In general, hitching isn't worth the hassle as buses are frequent and cheap. However,

there's no need to stand at a bus station – all you have to do is stand on any road going in your direction and flag down a passing bus or *săwngthăew* (pick-up truck).

The exception is in areas where there isn't any bus service, though in such places there's not likely to be very much private vehicle traffic either. If you do manage to get a ride, it's customary to offer food or cigarettes to the driver if you have any.

LOCAL TRANSPORT
Bus
Bangkok has the largest city-bus system in the country. Elsewhere in the country, public transport is typically supplied by săwngthăew that run established routes, although Udon Thani and a few other provincial capitals have city buses. The etiquette for riding public transport is to hail the vehicle by waving your hand palm-side downward; you typically pay the fare once you've taken a seat or when you disembark. Occasionally in tourist centres, drivers operating a săwngthăew intended for shared use will try to convince foreigners to 'charter' the vehicle by quoting a large fare before boarding.

Motorcycle Taxi
Many cities in Thailand also have *mawtoesai ráp jâang*, 100cc to 125cc motorcycles that can be hired, with a driver, for short distances. They're not very suitable if you're carrying more than a backpack or small suitcase, but if you're empty-handed they can't be beaten for quick transport over short distances. In addition to the lack of space for luggage, motorcycle taxis also suffer from lack of shelter from rain or sun. Although most drivers around the country drive at safe, sane speeds, the kamikaze drivers of Bangkok are a major exception.

In most cities you'll find motorcycle taxis clustered near street intersections, rather than cruising the streets looking for fares. Fares tend to run from 10B to 30B, depending on distance. Some motorcycle taxis specialise in regular, short routes, eg from one end of a long street to another. In such cases the fare is usually a fixed 10B.

Săamláw & Túk-túk
Săamláw means 'three wheels' and that's just what they are – three-wheeled vehicles. There are two types of săamláw – motorised and nonmotorised.

You'll find motorised săamláw throughout the country. They're small utility vehicles, powered by horrendously noisy engines (usually LPG-powered); if the noise and vibration don't get you, the fumes will. Tourists commonly know motor săamláw as túk-túk, because of the noise they make. Among themselves, the Thais still call these săamláw – the term túk-túk is strictly foreigner talk but it's what most Thais use when speaking to Western tourists.

The nonmotorised săamláw, ie the bicycle rickshaw or pedicab, is similar to what you may see in other parts of Asia. There are no bicycle săamláw in Bangkok but you will find them elsewhere in the country. With either form of săamláw the fare must be established by bargaining before departure.

Readers interested in pedicab lore and design may want to have a look at Lonely Planet's hardcover pictorial book, *Chasing Rickshaws*, by Lonely Planet founder Tony Wheeler.

Săwngthăew
A săwngthăew (literally, 'two rows') is a small pick-up truck with two rows of bench seats down both sides of the truck bed. They sometimes operate on fixed routes, just like buses, but they may also run a share-taxi type of service or can even be booked individually just like a regular taxi. Săwngthăew are often colour-coded, so that red ones, for example, go to one destination or group of destinations, while blue ones go to another.

Skytrain & Subway
Bangkok is the only city in Thailand to have either an above-ground or underground light-rail public transport system. Known as the Skytrain and the Metro, respectively, both systems have helped to alleviate the capital city's notorious traffic jams. There has been much unfulfilled talk about building a subway in Chiang Mai but little action.

Taxi
Bangkok has the most formal system of metered taxis. In other cities, a taxi can be a private vehicle with negotiable rates. You can also travel between cities by taxi but you'll need to negotiate a price as few taxi drivers will run a meter for intercity travel.

TOURS
Many operators around the world can arrange guided tours of Thailand. Most of them simply

serve as brokers for tour companies based in Thailand; they buy their trips from a wholesaler and resell them under various names in travel markets overseas. Hence, one is much like another and you might as well arrange a tour in Thailand at a lower cost – there are so many available. Long-running, reliable tour wholesalers in Thailand include the following:

Active Thailand (Map pp280-1; ☎ 0 5327 7178; www.activethailand.com; Contact Travel, 73/7 Th Charoen Prathet, Chiang Mai)

Asian Trails (Map pp128-9; ☎ 0 2626 2000; www.asiantrails.net; 9th fl, SG Tower, 161/1 Soi Mahatlek Leung 3, Th Ratchadamri, Bangkok)

Diethelm Travel (Map p127; ☎ 0 2255 9150; www.diethelmtravel.com; Kian Gwan Bldg II, 140/1 Th Withayu, Bangkok) One of the largest tour operators in Bangkok.

World Travel Service (Map pp124-5; ☎ 0 2233 5900; www.wts-thailand.com; 1053 Th Charoen Krung, Bangkok) In business since 1947 and one of the largest tour operators in the city.

Overseas Companies

The better overseas tour companies build their own Thailand itineraries from scratch and choose their local suppliers based on which best serve these itineraries. Of these, several specialise in adventure and/or ecological tours:

Asia Transpacific Journeys (☎ 800-642 2742, 303-443 6789; www.southeastasia.com; 2995 Center Green Dr, Boulder, CO 80301, USA) Northern Thailand trekking to sea canoeing in the Phuket Sea, plus custom tour planning.

Club Adventure (☎ 514-527 0999; www.clubaventure.com; 757 ave du Mont-Royal Est, Montreal, QUE H2J 1W8, Canada) French-language tour operators.

Exodus (☎ 800 228 8747; www.exodustravels.co.uk; 9 Weir Rd, London SW12 0LT) Winner of 2006 British Travel Award for most environmentally responsible tour agency.

Intrepid Travel (☎ 03 9473 2626; www.intrepidtravel.com) Specialises in small-group travel, with dozens of itineraries; check the website for contact details in the USA, UK & Australia.

Hands Up Holidays (☎ 0 776 5601 3631; www.handsupholidays.com; 21 Corayne Rd, Fulham, London SW6 3QA) Volunteer & sightseeing programmes.

Ms Kasma Loha-Unchit (☎ 510 655 8900; www.thaifoodandtravel.com; PO Box 21165, Oakland, CA 94620, USA) This Thai cookbook author offers personalised, 'cultural immersion' tours of Thailand.

TRAIN

The government rail network, the **State Railway of Thailand** (SRT; ☎ 1690; www.railway.co.th), is, on the whole, very well run. The rail network covers four main lines – the northern, southern,

northeastern and eastern lines (see map p762 for major routes). The train is most convenient as an alternative to buses for the long journey north to Chiang Mai or south to Surat Thani. But the emergence of cheap airfares are starting to undermine the 'romance' of the train in favour of time savings. The train is also ideal for trips to Ayuthaya and Lopburi from Bangkok.

Although they take longer (trains generally don't run on time), the trains offer many advantages over buses. To start with, there is more room to move and stretch out than there is on even the best buses. The scenery rolling by the windows is grander from the vantage point of rail than highway and there's usually more local commotion on the trains: hawkers selling food and drinks, babies staring wide-eyed at foreigners, sarong-clad villagers – to name a few.

Main Terminals

Almost all the long-distance trains originate from Bangkok's Hualamphong station. Bangkok Noi station in Thonburi serves the commuter and the short-line trains running to Kanchanaburi/Nam Tok, Suphanburi, Ratchaburi and Nakhon Pathom. You can also get to Ratchaburi and Nakhon Pathom by trains from Hualamphong. Thonburi's Wong Wian Yai station runs a short commuter line to Samut Songkhram.

Classes

The SRT operates passenger trains in three classes – 1st, 2nd and 3rd – but each class varies considerably depending on whether you're on an ordinary, rapid or express train.

THIRD CLASS

A typical 3rd-class carriage consists of two rows of bench seats divided into facing pairs. Each bench seat is designed to seat two or three passengers, but on a crowded rural line nobody seems to care about design considerations. On a rapid train, 3rd-class seats are padded and reasonably comfortable for shorter trips. On ordinary 3rd-class-only trains in the east and northeast, seats are sometimes made of hard wooden slats. Express trains do not carry 3rd-class carriages at all. Commuter trains in the Bangkok area are all 3rd class.

SECOND CLASS

The seating arrangements in a 2nd-class, non-sleeper carriage are similar to those on a bus,

with pairs of padded seats, usually recliners, all facing toward the front of the train.

On 2nd-class sleeper cars, pairs of seats face one another and convert into two fold-down berths, one over the other. Curtains provide a modicum of privacy and the berths are fairly comfortable, with fresh linen for every trip. The lower berth has more headroom than the upper berth and this is reflected in a higher fare (a difference of about 200B). A toilet stall and washbasins are at one end of the carriage.

2nd-class carriages are found only on rapid and express trains. Air-con 2nd class is more common nowadays than ordinary 2nd class (with the latter available only on rapid lines).

FIRST CLASS
Each private cabin in a 1st-class carriage has individually controlled air-con (older trains also have an electric fan), a washbasin and mirror, a small table and long bench seats that convert to beds. Drinking water and soap are provided free of charge. First-class carriages are available only on rapid, express and special-express trains.

Costs
Fares are calculated first by a base price then surcharges are added depending on the train type (special express, express, rapid, ordinary), class and distance. There is an 80B surcharge above the basic fare for *rót dùan* (express trains) and 60B for *rót rew* (rapid trains). These trains are somewhat faster than the ordinary trains, as they make fewer stops. Note that there are no 3rd-class carriages on either rapid or express trains. For the *rót dùan phísèht* (special-express trains) that run between Bangkok and Padang Besar and between Bangkok and Chiang Mai there is a 100B to 120B surcharge. For distances under 500km, the base rate is 50B; over 500km, 70B to 80B.

Some 2nd- and 3rd-class services are air-con, in which case there is a 120B to 140B surcharge. Sleeping berths in 2nd class accrue another 100B to 240B surcharge. There's a choice between upper and lower – the difference being that there is a window next to the lower berth and more head room. No sleepers are available in 3rd class.

All 1st-class cabins come with individually controlled air-con. For a two-bed cabin the surcharge is 400B per person. Single 1st-class

cabins are not available, so if you're travelling alone you may be paired with another passenger, although the SRT takes great care not to mix genders.

Reservations
Advance bookings may be made one to 60 days before your intended date of departure. During holidays – especially around holiday time, eg the middle of April approaching the Songkran Festival, during Chinese New Year and during the peak tourist-season months of December and January – it is advised to book as far in advance as possible as all public transport options become very crowded during this time. You can make bookings from any train station. Throughout Thailand SRT ticket offices are generally open 8.30am to 6pm on weekdays, and 8.30am to noon on weekends and public holidays. Train tickets can also be purchased at certain travel agencies in Bangkok. It is much simpler to book trains through these agencies than to book them at the station; however, they usually add a service charge to the ticket price.

Trains out of Bangkok should be booked as far in advance as possible – a minimum of a week for popular routes such as the northern line to Chiang Mai and the southern line to Hat Yai, especially if you want a sleeper. For the northeastern and eastern lines a few days will suffice. Midweek departures are always easier to book than weekends; during some months of the year you can easily book a sleeper even one day before departure, as long as it's on a Tuesday, Wednesday or Thursday. With the exception of Surat Thani and Chiang Mai, booking trains back to Bangkok is generally not as difficult as booking trains out of Bangkok.

Station Services
You'll find that all train stations in Thailand have baggage-storage services (or 'cloak rooms'). The rates and hours of operation vary from station to station. At Bangkok's Hualamphong station, for example, rates are 20B to 30B per day. Most stations have a ticket window that will open between 15 and 30 minutes before train arrivals. There are also newsagents and small snack vendors, but no full-service restaurants.

Train Dining
Meal service is available in *rót sa-biang* (dining carriages) and at your seat in 2nd- and

1st-class carriages. Menus change as frequently as the SRT changes catering services. All the meals seem a bit overpriced (80B to 200B on average) by Thai standards. Many Thai passengers bring along their own meals and snacks to avoid the relatively high cost of SRT-catered meals.

Train Information

Most train stations have printed timetables in English; although this isn't always the case for smaller stations. Bangkok's Hualamphong station is a good spot to load up on timetables. There are two types of timetable available: four condensed English timetables with fares, schedules and routes for rapid, express and special express trains on the four trunk lines; and four Thai timetables for each trunk line, and side lines. These latter timetables give fares and schedules for all trains – ordinary, rapid and express. The English timetables only display a couple of the ordinary routes; eg they don't show the wealth of ordinary trains that go to Ayuthaya and as far north as Phitsanulok.

Train Passes

The SRT issues a Thailand Rail Pass that may save on fares if you plan to use the trains extensively over a relatively short interval. This pass is only available in Thailand and may be purchased at Hualamphong station.

The cost for 20 days of unlimited 2nd- or 3rd-class train travel is 1500B, or 3000B including all supplementary charges; children aged four to 12 pay half the adult fare. Supplementary charges include all extra charges for rapid, express, special express and air-con. Passes must be validated at a local station before boarding the first train. The price of the pass includes seat reservations that, if required, can be made at any SRT ticket office. The pass is valid until midnight on the last day of the pass, although if the journey is commenced before midnight on the last day of validity, the passenger can use the pass until that train reaches its destination.

Train Routes

Four main rail lines cover 4500km along the northern, southern, northeastern and eastern routes. There are several side routes, notably between Nakhon Pathom and Nam Tok (stopping in Kanchanaburi) in the western central region, and between Thung Song and Kantang (stopping in Trang) in the south. The southern line splits at Hat Yai: one route goes to Sungai Kolok on the Malaysian east-coast border, via Yala; and the other goes to Padang Besar in the west, also on the Malaysian border. A Bangkok–Pattaya spur has not been as popular as expected but is still running.

Health Dr Trish Batchelor

CONTENTS

Health issues and the quality of medical facilities vary enormously depending on where and how you travel in Southeast Asia. Many of the major cities are now very well developed, although travel to rural areas can expose you to a variety of health risks and inadequate medical care.

Travellers tend to worry about contracting infectious diseases when in the tropics, but infections are a rare cause of serious illness or death in travellers. Pre-existing medical conditions such as heart disease, and accidental injury (especially traffic accidents), account for most life-threatening problems. Becoming ill in some way, however, is relatively common. Fortunately most common illnesses can either be prevented with some commonsense behaviour or be treated easily with a well-stocked traveller's medical kit.

The following advice is a general guide only and does not replace the advice of a doctor trained in travel medicine.

BEFORE YOU GO

Pack medications in their original, clearly labelled, containers. A signed and dated letter from your physician describing your medical conditions and medications, including generic names, is also a good idea. If carrying syringes or needles, be sure to have a physician's letter documenting their medical necessity. If you have a heart condition bring a copy of your ECG taken just prior to travelling.

If you happen to take any regular medication bring double your needs in case of loss or theft. In most Southeast Asian countries, except Singapore, you can buy many medications over the counter without a doctor's prescription, but it can be difficult to find some of the newer drugs, particularly the latest antidepressant drugs, blood-pressure medications and contraceptive pills.

INSURANCE

Even if you are fit and healthy, don't travel without health insurance – accidents do happen. Declare any existing medical conditions you have – the insurance company *will* check if your problem is pre-existing and will not cover you if it is undeclared. You may require extra cover for adventure activities such as rock climbing. If your health insurance doesn't cover you for medical expenses abroad, consider getting extra insurance. If you're uninsured, emergency evacuation is expensive; costs of over US$100,000 are not uncommon.

Find out in advance if your insurance plan will make payments directly to providers or reimburse you later for overseas health expenditures. (In many countries doctors expect payment in cash.) Some policies offer lower and higher medical-expense options; the higher ones are chiefly for countries that have extremely high medical costs, such as the USA. You may prefer a policy that pays doctors or hospitals directly rather than having to pay on the spot and claim later. If you have to claim later, make sure you keep all documentation. Some policies ask you to call back (reverse charges) to a centre in your home country where an immediate assessment of your problem is made.

VACCINATIONS

Specialised travel-medicine clinics are your best source of information; they stock all available vaccines and will be able to give specific

recommendations for you and your trip. The doctors will take into account factors such as past vaccination history, the length of your trip, activities you may be undertaking and underlying medical conditions, such as pregnancy.

Most vaccines don't produce immunity until at least two weeks after they're given, so visit a doctor four to eight weeks before departure. Ask your doctor for an International Certificate of Vaccination (otherwise known as the yellow booklet), which will list all the vaccinations you've received.

Recommended Vaccinations

The following vaccinations are those recommended by the World Health Organization (WHO) for travellers to Southeast Asia:

Adult diphtheria and tetanus Single booster recommended if none in the previous 10 years. Side effects include sore arm and fever. There is a new vaccine that includes protection against whooping cough. Ask your doctor if it is recommended for you.

Hepatitis A Provides almost 100% protection for up to a year; a booster after 12 months provides protection for at least another 20 years. Mild side effects such as headache and sore arm occur in 5% to 10% of people.

Hepatitis B Now considered routine for most travellers. Given as three shots over six months. A rapid schedule is also available, as is a combined vaccination with Hepatitis A. Side effects are mild and uncommon, usually headache and sore arm. Lifetime protection occurs in 95% of people.

Measles, mumps and rubella Two doses of MMR required unless you have had the diseases. Occasionally a

---

MEDICAL CHECKLIST

The following are recommended items for a personal medical kit:

- antibacterial cream (eg Muciprocin)
- antibiotics for skin infections (eg Amoxicillin/Clavulanate or Cephalexin)
- antibiotics for diarrhoea (eg Norfloxacin or Ciprofloxacin); for bacterial diarrhoea (eg Azithromycin); for giardiasis or amoebic dysentery (eg Tinidazole)
- anti-diarrhoeal treatments – consider an oral rehydration solution (eg Gastrolyte); diarrhoea 'stopper' (eg Loperamide); and anti-nausea medication (eg Prochlorperazine)
- antifungal cream (eg Clotrimazole)
- antihistamine (eg Cetrizine for daytime and Promethazine for night)
- antiseptic (eg Betadine)
- antispasmodic for stomach cramps (eg Buscopan)
- contraceptives
- decongestant (eg Pseudoephedrine)
- DEET-based insect repellent
- first-aid items such as scissors, Elastoplasts, bandages, gauze, thermometer (but not mercury), sterile needles and syringes, safety pins and tweezers
- Ibuprofen or another anti-inflammatory
- indigestion medication (eg Quick Eze or Mylanta)
- iodine tablets (unless you are pregnant or have a thyroid problem) to purify the water
- laxative (eg Coloxyl)
- paracetamol
- Permethrin to impregnate clothing and mosquito nets
- steroid cream for allergic/itchy rashes (eg 1% to 2% hydrocortisone)
- sunscreen and hat
- throat lozenges
- thrush (vaginal yeast infection) treatment (eg Clotrimazole pessaries or Diflucan tablet)
- Ural or equivalent if you are prone to urine infections

rash and flu-like illness can develop a week after receiving the vaccine. Many young adults require a booster.

Polio In 2006–07, Indonesia was the only Southeast Asian country with reported cases of polio. Only one booster required as an adult for lifetime protection. Inactivated polio vaccine is safe during pregnancy.

Typhoid Recommended unless your trip is less than a week, and only to developed cities. The vaccine offers around 70% protection, lasts for two to three years and comes as a single shot. Tablets are also available, however the injection is usually recommended as it has fewer side effects. Sore arm and fever may occur.

Varicella If you haven't had chickenpox, discuss this vaccination with your doctor.

These immunisations are recommended for long-term travellers (more than one month) or those at special risk:

Japanese B Encephalitis Three injections in all. Booster recommended after two years. Sore arm and headache are the most common side effects. Rarely, an allergic reaction comprising hives and swelling can occur up to 10 days after any of the three doses.

Meningitis Single injection. There are two types of vaccination: the quadrivalent vaccine gives two to three years' protection; meningitis group C vaccine gives around 10 years' protection. Recommended for long-term backpackers aged under 25.

Rabies Three injections in all. A booster after one year will then provide 10 years' protection. Side effects are rare – occasionally headache and sore arm.

Tuberculosis A complex issue. Adult long-term travellers are usually recommended to have a TB skin test before and after travel, rather than vaccination. Only one vaccine given in a lifetime.

Required Vaccinations

The only vaccine required by international regulations is yellow fever. Proof of vaccination will only be required if you have visited a country in the yellow-fever zone within the six days prior to entering Southeast Asia. If you are travelling to Southeast Asia from Africa or South America you should check to see if you require proof of vaccination.

INTERNET RESOURCES

There is a wealth of travel-health advice on the internet. For further information, **Lonely Planet** (www.lonelyplanet.com) is a good place to start. *International Travel & Health* is a superb book published by WHO (www.who.int/ith), which is revised annually and is available online at no cost. Another website of general interest is **MD Travel Health** (www.mdtravelhealth

.com), which provides complete travel-health recommendations for every country and is updated daily. The **Centers for Disease Control and Prevention** (CDC; www.cdc.gov) website also has good general information.

FURTHER READING

Lonely Planet's *Healthy Travel – Asia & India* is a handy pocket-size book that is packed with useful information including pretrip planning, emergency first aid, immunisation and disease information, and what to do if you get sick on the road. Other recommended references include *Traveller's Health* by Dr Richard Dawood and *Travelling Well* by Dr Deborah Mills – check out the website www.travellingwell.com.au.

IN TRANSIT

DEEP VEIN THROMBOSIS (DVT)

Deep vein thrombosis (DVT) occurs when blood clots form in the legs during plane flights, chiefly because of prolonged immobility. The longer the flight, the greater the risk. Though most blood clots are reabsorbed uneventfully, some may break off and travel through the blood vessels to the lungs, where they may cause life-threatening complications.

The chief symptom of DVT is swelling of, or pain in, the foot, ankle or calf – usually, but not always, on just one side. When a blood clot travels to the lungs, it may cause chest pain and difficulty in breathing. Travellers with any of these symptoms should immediately seek medical attention.

To prevent the development of DVT on long flights you should walk about the cabin, perform isometric compressions of the leg muscles (ie contract the leg muscles while sitting), drink plenty of fluids (nonalcoholic) and avoid tobacco.

JET LAG & MOTION SICKNESS

Jet lag is common when crossing more than five time zones; it results in insomnia, fatigue, malaise or nausea. To avoid jet lag try drinking plenty of fluids (nonalcoholic) and eating light meals. Upon arrival, seek exposure to natural sunlight and readjust your schedule (for meals, sleep etc) as soon as possible.

Antihistamines such as dimenhydrinate (Dramamine) and meclizine (Antivert,

HEALTH

Bonine) are usually the first choice for treating motion sickness. Their main side effect is drowsiness. A herbal alternative is ginger, which works like a charm for some people.

IN THAILAND

AVAILABILITY OF HEALTH CARE

Most large cities in Thailand now have clinics catering specifically to travellers and expats. These clinics are usually more expensive than local medical facilities, but are worth using, as they will offer a superior standard of care. Additionally they understand the local system, and are aware of the safest local hospitals and best specialists. They can also liaise with insurance companies should you require evacuation. Clinics are listed under Information in the city sections of this book.

It is difficult to find reliable medical care in rural areas. Your embassy and insurance company are also good contacts.

Self-treatment may be appropriate if your problem is minor (eg traveller's diarrhoea), you are carrying the appropriate medication and you cannot attend a recommended clinic. If you think you may have a serious disease, especially malaria, do not waste time – travel to the nearest quality facility to receive attention. It is always better to be assessed by a doctor than to rely on self-treatment.

Buying medication over the counter is not recommended, because fake medications and poorly stored or out-of-date drugs are common.

INFECTIOUS DISEASES

Avian Influenza

To date Thailand has reported 25 cases of human 'bird flu'. The majority of these occurred in 2004, and at the time of writing there have been no reports in 2007. Transmission from domestic birds to humans is rare and requires close contact with an infected bird or its droppings. Human to human transmission has occurred, but it is even more uncommon. Thus far there have been no cases reported in travellers or expatriates. Avoid live poultry markets, and eating raw or undercooked poultry or eggs; wash your hands frequently and seek medical attention if you develop a fever and respiratory symptoms (cough, shortness of breath etc).

Cutaneous Larva Migrans

This disease, caused by dog hookworm, is particularly common on the beaches of Thailand. The rash starts as a small lump, then slowly spreads in a linear fashion. It is intensely itchy, especially at night. It is easily treated with medications and should not be cut out or frozen.

Dengue Fever

This mosquito-borne disease is becoming increasingly problematic throughout Southeast Asia, especially in the cities. As there is no vaccine available it can only be prevented by avoiding mosquito bites. The mosquito that carries dengue bites day and night, so use insect-avoidance measures at all times. Symptoms include high fever, severe headache and body aches (dengue was previously known as 'breakbone fever'). Some people develop a rash and experience diarrhoea. The southern islands of Thailand are particularly high risk. There is no specific treatment, just rest and paracetamol – do not take aspirin as it increases the likelihood of haemorrhaging. See a doctor to be diagnosed and monitored.

Filariasis

A mosquito-borne disease that is very common in the local population, yet very rare in travellers. Mosquito-avoidance measures are the best way to prevent this disease.

Hepatitis A

A problem throughout the region, this food- and water-borne virus infects the liver, causing jaundice (yellow skin and eyes), nausea and lethargy. There is no specific treatment for hepatitis A, you just need to allow time for the liver to heal. All travellers to Southeast Asia should be vaccinated against hepatitis A.

Hepatitis B

The only sexually transmitted disease (STD) that can be prevented by vaccination, hepatitis B is spread by body fluids, including sexual contact. In some parts of Southeast Asia up to 20% of the population are carriers of hepatitis B, and usually unaware of it. The long-term consequences can include liver cancer and cirrhosis.

Hepatitis E

Hepatitis E is transmitted through contaminated food and water and has similar symp-

toms to hepatitis A, but is far less common. It is a severe problem in pregnant women and can result in the death of both mother and baby. There is currently no vaccine, and prevention is by following safe eating and drinking guidelines.

HIV
HIV is now one of the most common causes of death in people under the age of 50 in Thailand. Heterosexual sex is now the main method of transmission in Thailand.

Influenza
Present year-round in the tropics, influenza (flu) symptoms include high fever, muscle aches, runny nose, cough and sore throat. It can be very severe in people over the age of 65 or in those with underlying medical conditions such as heart disease or diabetes; vaccination is recommended for these individuals. All travellers should consider vaccination as influenza is the most common vaccine-preventable disease to affect travellers. There is no specific treatment, just rest and paracetamol.

Japanese B Encephalitis
While a rare disease in travellers, at least 50,000 locals are infected each year. This viral disease is transmitted by mosquitoes. Most cases occur in rural areas and vaccination is recommended for travellers spending more than one month outside of cities. There is no treatment, and a third of infected people will die while another third will suffer permanent brain damage. Thailand is a high-risk area.

Leptospirosis
Leptospirosis is most often contracted after river rafting or canyoning. Early symptoms are very similar to the flu and include headache and fever. It can vary from a very mild ailment to a fatal disease. Diagnosis is made through blood tests and it is easily treated with Doxycycline.

Malaria
For such a serious and potentially deadly disease, there is an enormous amount of misinformation concerning malaria. You must get expert advice as to whether your trip actually puts you at risk. Many parts of Southeast Asia, particularly city and resort areas, have minimal to no risk of malaria, and the risk of side

> ### AVOIDING MALARIA
> Travellers are advised to prevent mosquito bites by taking these steps:
>
> - use a DEET-containing (ideally 20-30% concentration) insect repellent on exposed skin. Wash this off at night, as long as you are sleeping under a mosquito net. Natural repellents such as citronella can be effective, but must be applied more frequently than products containing DEET.
> - sleep under a mosquito net impregnated with Permethrin.
> - choose accommodation with screens and fans (if not air-conditioned).
> - impregnate clothing with Permethrin in high-risk areas.
> - wear long sleeves and trousers in light colours.
> - use mosquito coils.
> - spray your room with insect repellent before going out for your evening meal.

effects from the tablets may outweigh the risk of getting the disease. For most rural areas, however, the risk of contracting the disease far outweighs the risk of any tablet side effects. Remember that malaria can be fatal. Before you travel, seek medical advice on the right medication and dosage for you.

Malaria is caused by a parasite transmitted by the bite of an infected mosquito. The most important symptom of malaria is fever, but general symptoms such as headache, diarrhoea, cough or chills may also occur. A diagnosis can only be made by taking a blood sample.

Two strategies should be combined to prevent malaria – mosquito avoidance and antimalarial medications. Most people who catch malaria are taking inadequate or no antimalarial medication.

There is a variety of preventive medication available:

Artesunate Derivatives of Artesunate are not suitable as a preventive medication. They are useful treatments under medical supervision.

Chloroquine and Paludrine The effectiveness of this combination is now limited in most of Southeast Asia. Common side effects include nausea (40% of people) and mouth ulcers. Generally not recommended.

Doxycycline This daily tablet is a broad-spectrum antibiotic that has the added benefit of helping to prevent a variety of tropical diseases, including leptospirosis, tick-borne disease, typhus and melioidosis. The potential side effects include photosensitivity (a tendency to sunburn), thrush in women, indigestion, heartburn, nausea and interference with the contraceptive pill. More serious side effects include ulceration of the oesophagus – you can help prevent this by taking your tablet with a meal and a large glass of water, and never lying down within half an hour of taking it. Must be taken for four weeks after leaving the risk area.

Lariam (Mefloquine) Lariam has received much bad press; some of it justified, some not. This weekly tablet suits many people. Serious side effects are rare but include depression, anxiety, psychosis and having fits. Anyone with a history of depression, anxiety, other psychological disorder or epilepsy should not take Lariam. It is considered safe in the second and third trimesters of pregnancy. It is around 90% effective in most parts of Southeast Asia, but there is significant resistance in parts of northern Thailand, Laos and Cambodia. Tablets must be taken for four weeks after leaving the risk area.

Malarone This drug is a combination of Atovaquone and Proguanil. Side effects are uncommon and mild, most commonly nausea and headache. It is the best tablet for scuba divers and for those on short trips to high-risk areas. It must be taken for one week after leaving the risk area.

A final option is to take no preventive medication but to have a supply of emergency medication should you develop the symptoms of malaria. This is less than ideal, and you'll need to get to a good medical facility within 24 hours of developing a fever. If you choose this option the most effective and safest treatment is Malarone (four tablets once daily for three days). Other options include Mefloquine and Quinine but the side effects of these drugs at treatment doses make them less desirable. Fansidar is no longer recommended.

Measles

Measles remains a problem in some parts of Southeast Asia. This highly contagious bacterial infection is spread through coughing and sneezing. Most people born before 1966 are immune as they had the disease in childhood. Measles starts with a high fever and rash, and can be complicated by pneumonia and brain disease. There is no specific treatment.

Meliodosis

This infection is contracted by skin contact with soil. It is rare in travellers, but in some parts of northeast Thailand up to 30% of the local population are infected. The symptoms are very similar to those experienced by tuberculosis (TB) sufferers. There is no vaccine but it can be treated with medications.

Rabies

This uniformly fatal disease is spread by the bite or lick of an infected animal – most commonly a dog or monkey. You should seek medical advice immediately after any animal bite and commence post-exposure treatment. Having a pretravel vaccination means the post-bite treatment is greatly simplified. If an animal bites you, gently wash the wound with soap and water, and apply iodine-based antiseptic. If you are not prevaccinated you will need to receive rabies immunoglobulin as soon as possible.

STDs

Sexually transmitted diseases most common in Thailand include herpes, warts, syphilis, gonorrhoea and chlamydia. People carrying these diseases often have no signs of infection. Condoms will prevent gonorrhoea and chlamydia but not warts or herpes. If after a sexual encounter you develop any rash, lumps, discharge or pain when passing urine seek immediate medical attention. If you have been sexually active during your travels have an STD check on your return home.

Strongyloides

This parasite, also transmitted by skin contact with soil, is common in Thailand but rarely affects travellers. It is characterised by an unusual skin rash called *larva currens* – a linear rash on the trunk which comes and goes. Most people don't have other symptoms until their immune system becomes severely suppressed, when the parasite can cause an overwhelming infection. It can be treated with medications.

Tuberculosis

While rare in travellers, medical and aid workers and long-term travellers who have significant contact with the local population should take precautions. Vaccination is usually only given to children under the age of five, but adults at risk are recommended pre- and post-travel TB testing. The main symptoms are fever, cough, weight loss, night sweats and tiredness.

Typhoid

This serious bacterial infection is spread via food and water. It gives a high and slowly progressive fever, headache and may be accompanied by a dry cough and stomach pain. It is diagnosed by blood tests and treated with antibiotics. Vaccination is recommended for all travellers spending more than a week in Thailand, or travelling outside of the major cities. Be aware that vaccination is not 100% effective so you must still be careful with what you eat and drink.

Typhus

Murine typhus is spread by the bite of a flea whereas scrub typhus is spread via a mite. These diseases are rare in travellers. Symptoms include fever, muscle pains and a rash. You can avoid these diseases by following general insect-avoidance measures. Doxycycline will also prevent them.

TRAVELLER'S DIARRHOEA

Traveller's diarrhoea is by far the most common problem affecting travellers – between 30% and 50% of people will suffer from it within two weeks of starting their trip. In over 80% of cases, traveller's diarrhoea is caused by a bacteria (there are numerous potential culprits), and therefore responds promptly to treatment with antibiotics. Treatment with antibiotics will depend on your situation – how sick you are, how quickly you need to get better, where you are etc.

Traveller's diarrhoea is defined as the passage of more than three watery bowel movements within 24 hours, plus at least one other symptom such as vomiting, fever, cramps, nausea or feeling generally unwell.

Treatment consists of staying well hydrated; rehydration solutions like Gastrolyte are the best for this. Antibiotics such as Norfloxacin, Ciprofloxacin or Azithromycin will kill the bacteria quickly.

Loperamide is just a 'stopper' and doesn't get to the cause of the problem. It can be helpful, for example if you have to go on a long bus ride. Don't take Loperamide if you have a fever, or blood in your stools. Seek medical attention quickly if you do not respond to an appropriate antibiotic.

Amoebic Dysentery

Amoebic dysentery is very rare in travellers but is often misdiagnosed by poor-quality labs in Southeast Asia. Symptoms are similar to bacterial diarrhoea, ie fever, bloody diarrhoea and generally feeling unwell. You should always seek reliable medical care if you have blood in your diarrhoea. Treatment involves two drugs; Tinidazole or Metroniadzole to kill the parasite in your gut and then a second drug to kill the cysts. If left untreated complications such as liver or gut abscesses can occur.

Giardiasis

Giardia lamblia is a parasite that is relatively common in travellers. Symptoms include nausea, bloating, excess gas, fatigue and intermittent diarrhoea. 'Eggy' burps are often attributed solely to giardiasis, but work in Nepal has shown that they are not specific to this infection. The parasite will eventually go away if left untreated but this can take months. The treatment of choice is Tinidazole, with Metronidazole being a second option.

ENVIRONMENTAL HAZARDS
Air Pollution

Air pollution, particularly vehicle pollution, is an increasing problem in most of Southeast Asia's major cities. If you have severe respiratory problems speak with your doctor before travelling to any heavily polluted urban centres. This pollution can also cause minor respiratory problems such as sinusitis, dry throat and irritated eyes. If you are troubled by the pollution leave the city for a few days and get some fresh air.

Diving

Divers and surfers should seek specialised advice before they travel to ensure their medical kit contains treatment for coral cuts and tropical ear infections, as well as treatment for the standard problems.

Divers should also make sure that their insurance covers them for decompression illness – get specialised dive insurance through an organisation such as **Divers Alert Network** (DAN; www.danseap.org). Have a dive medical before you leave your home country – there are certain medical conditions that are incompatible with diving and economic considerations may override health considerations for some dive operators in Thailand.

Food

Eating in restaurants is the biggest risk factor for contracting traveller's diarrhoea. Ways

HEALTH

to avoid it include eating only freshly cooked food, avoiding shellfish, and not eating food that has been sitting around in buffets. Peel all fruit, cook vegetables, and soak salads in iodine water for at least 20 minutes. Eat in busy restaurants with a high turnover of customers.

Heat

Many parts of Thailand are hot and humid throughout the year. For most people it takes at least two weeks to adapt to the hot climate. Swelling of the feet and ankles is common, as are muscle cramps caused by excessive sweating. Prevent these by avoiding dehydration and excessive activity in the heat. Take it easy when you first arrive. Don't eat salt tablets (they aggravate the gut), but drinking rehydration solution or eating salty food helps. Treat cramps by stopping activity, resting, rehydrating with double-strength rehydration solution and gently stretching.

Dehydration is the main contributor to heat exhaustion. Symptoms include feeling weak; headache; irritability; nausea or vomiting; sweaty skin; a fast, weak pulse; and a normal or slightly elevated body temperature. Treatment involves getting out of the heat and/or sun; fanning the victim and applying cool wet cloths to the skin; laying the victim flat with their legs raised; and rehydrating with water containing ¼ teaspoon of salt per litre. Recovery is usually rapid and it is common to feel weak for some days afterwards.

Heat stroke is a serious medical emergency. Symptoms come on suddenly and include weakness, nausea, a hot dry body with a body temperature of over 41°C, dizziness, confusion, loss of coordination, fits and eventually collapse and loss of consciousness. Seek medical help and commence cooling by getting the person out of the heat, removing their clothes, fanning them and applying cool wet cloths or ice to their body, especially to the groin and armpits.

Prickly heat is a common skin rash in the tropics, caused by sweat being trapped under the skin. The result is an itchy rash of tiny lumps. Treat by moving out of the heat and into an air-conditioned area for a few hours and by having cool showers. Creams and ointments clog the skin so they should be avoided. Locally bought prickly-heat powder can be helpful.

Tropical fatigue is common in long-term expats based in the tropics. It's rarely due to disease and is caused by the climate, inadequate mental rest, excessive alcohol intake and the demands of daily work in a different culture.

Insect Bites & Stings

Bedbugs don't carry disease but their bites are very itchy. They live in the cracks of furniture and walls and then migrate to the bed at night to feed on you. You can treat the itch with an antihistamine. Lice inhabit various parts of your body but most commonly your head and pubic area. Transmission is via close contact with an infected person. They can be difficult to treat and you may need numerous applications of an antilice shampoo such as Permethrin. Pubic lice are usually contracted from sexual contact.

Ticks are contracted when walking in rural areas. They're commonly found behind the ears, on the belly and in armpits. If you have had a tick bite and experience symptoms such as a rash at the site of the bite or elsewhere, fever or muscle aches you should see a doctor. Doxycycline prevents tick-borne diseases.

Leeches are found in humid rainforest areas. They do not transmit any disease but their bites are often intensely itchy for weeks afterwards and can easily become infected. Apply an iodine-based antiseptic to any leech bite to help prevent infection.

Bee and wasp stings mainly cause problems for people who are allergic to them. Anyone with a serious bee or wasp allergy should carry an injection of adrenaline (eg an Epipen) for emergency treatment. For others, pain is the main problem – apply ice to the sting and take painkillers.

Most jellyfish in Southeast Asian waters are not dangerous, just irritating. First aid for jellyfish stings involves pouring vinegar onto the affected area to neutralise the poison. Do not rub sand or water onto the stings. Take painkillers, and anyone who feels ill in any way after being stung should seek medical advice. Take local advice if there are dangerous jellyfish around and keep out of the water.

Parasites

Numerous parasites are common in local populations in Southeast Asia, but most of these are rare in travellers. The two rules to follow if you wish to avoid parasitic infections are to wear shoes and to avoid eating raw food, especially fish, pork and vegetables. A number of

parasites, including strongyloides, hookworm and cutaneous *larva migrans*, are transmitted via the skin by walking barefoot.

Skin Problems

Fungal rashes are common in humid climates. Two common fungal rashes affect travellers. The first occurs in moist areas that get less air such as the groin, armpits and between the toes. It starts as a red patch that slowly spreads and is usually itchy. Treatment involves keeping the skin dry, avoiding chafing and using an antifungal cream such as Clotrimazole or Lamisil. *Tinea versicolor* is also common – this fungus causes small and light-coloured patches, most commonly on the back, chest and shoulders. Consult a doctor.

Cuts and scratches become easily infected in humid climates. Take meticulous care of any cuts and scratches to prevent complications such as abscesses. Immediately wash all wounds in clean water and apply antiseptic. If you develop signs of infection (increasing pain and redness) see a doctor. Divers and surfers should be particularly careful with coral cuts as they can easily become infected.

Snakes

Thailand is home to many species of both poisonous and harmless snakes. Assume all snakes are poisonous and never try to catch one. Always wear boots and long pants if walking in an area that may have snakes. First aid in the event of a snake bite involves pressure immobilisation via an elastic bandage firmly wrapped around the affected limb, starting at the bite site and working up towards the chest. The bandage should not be so tight that the circulation is cut off, and the fingers or toes should be kept free so the circulation can be checked. Immobilise the limb with a splint and carry the victim to medical attention. Do not use tourniquets or try to suck the venom out. Antivenin is available for most species.

Sunburn

Even on a cloudy day, sunburn can occur rapidly. Always use a strong sunscreen (at least factor 30), making sure to reapply after a swim, and always wear a wide-brimmed hat and sunglasses outdoors. Avoid lying in the sun during the hottest part of the day (10am to 2pm). If you become sunburnt stay out of the sun until you have recovered, apply cool compresses and take painkillers for the dis-

comfort. One per cent hydrocortisone cream applied twice daily is also helpful.

WOMEN'S HEALTH

Pregnant women should receive specialised advice before travelling. The ideal time to travel is in the second trimester (between 16 weeks and 28 weeks), when the risk of pregnancy-related problems is at its lowest and pregnant women generally feel at their best. During the first trimester there is a risk of miscarriage and in the third trimester complications such as premature labour and high blood pressure are possible. It's wise to travel with a companion. Always carry a list of quality medical facilities available at your destination, and ensure you continue your standard antenatal care at these facilities. Avoid rural travel in areas with poor transportation and medical facilities. Most of all, ensure travel insurance covers all pregnancy-related possibilities, including premature labour.

Malaria is a high-risk disease in pregnancy. Advice from WHO recommends that pregnant women do *not* travel to those areas with Chloroquine-resistant malaria. None of the more effective antimalarial drugs is completely safe in pregnancy.

Traveller's diarrhoea can quickly lead to dehydration and result in inadequate blood flow to the placenta. Many of the drugs used to treat various diarrhoea bugs are not recommended in pregnancy. Azithromycin is considered safe.

In the urban areas of Southeast Asia, supplies of sanitary products are readily available. Birth-control options may be limited so bring adequate supplies of your own form of contraception. Heat, humidity and antibiotics can all contribute to thrush. Treatment of thrush is with antifungal creams and pessaries such as Clotrimazole. A practical alternative is a single tablet of fluconazole (Diflucan). Urinary-tract infections can be precipitated by dehydration or long bus journeys without toilet stops; bring suitable antibiotics.

TRADITIONAL MEDICINE

Traditional medical systems are practised widely throughout Southeast Asia. There is a big difference between these traditional healing systems and 'folk' medicine. Folk remedies should be avoided, as they often involve rather dubious procedures with potential complications. In comparison, traditional healing

HEALTH

systems such as traditional Chinese medicine are well respected, and aspects of them are being increasingly used by Western medical practitioners.

All traditional Asian medical systems identify a vital life force, and see blockage or imbalance as causing disease. Techniques such as herbal medicines, massage and acupuncture are used to bring this vital force back into balance, or to maintain balance. These therapies are best used for treating chronic disease such as chronic fatigue, arthritis, irritable bowel syndrome and some chronic skin conditions. Traditional medicines should be avoided for treating serious acute infections such as malaria.

Be aware that 'natural' doesn't always mean 'safe', and there can be drug interactions between herbal medicines and Western medicines. If you are using both systems ensure you inform both practitioners what the other has prescribed.

Language

CONTENTS

Learning some Thai is indispensable for travel in the kingdom; naturally, the more you pick up, the closer you get to Thailand's culture and people. There are so few foreigners who speak Thai in Thailand that it doesn't take much to impress most Thais with a few words in their own language.

Your first attempts to speak Thai will probably meet with mixed success, but keep trying. Listen closely to the way the Thais themselves use the various tones – you'll catch on quickly. Don't let laughter at your linguistic forays discourage you; this apparent amusement is really an expression of appreciation. Travellers are particularly urged to make the effort to meet Thai college and university students. Thai students are, by and large, eager to meet visitors from other countries. They will often know some English, so communication isn't as difficult as it may be with shop owners, civil servants etc, and they're generally willing to teach you useful Thai words and phrases.

DIALECTS

Thailand's official language is effectively the dialect spoken and written in central

Thailand, which has successfully become the lingua franca of all Thai and non-Thai ethnic groups in the kingdom.

All Thai dialects are members of the Thai half of the Thai-Kadai family of languages. As such, they're closely related to languages spoken in Laos (Lao, northern Thai, Thai Lü), northern Myanmar (Shan, northern Thai), northwestern Vietnam (Nung, Tho), Assam (Ahom) and pockets of south China (Zhuang, Thai Lü). Modern Thai linguists recognise four basic dialects within Thailand: Central Thai (spoken as a first dialect through central Thailand and throughout the country as a second dialect), Northern Thai (spoken from Tak Province north to the Myanmar border), Northeastern Thai (northeastern provinces towards the Lao and Cambodian borders), and Southern Thai (from Chumphon Province south to the Malaysian border). There are also a number of Thai minority dialects such as those spoken by the Phu Thai, Thai Dam, Thai Daeng, Phu Noi, Phuan and other tribal Thai groups, most of whom reside in the north and northeast.

VOCABULARY DIFFERENCES

Like most languages, Thai distinguishes between 'polite' and 'informal' vocabulary, so that *thaan,* for example, is a more polite everyday word for 'eat' than *kin,* and *sĭi-sà* for 'head' is more polite than *hŭa.* When given a choice, it's better to use the polite terms, since these are less likely to lead to unconscious offence.

SCRIPT

The Thai script, a fairly recent development in comparison with the spoken language, consists of 44 consonants (but only 21 separate sounds) and 48 vowel and diphthong possibilities (32 separate signs). Though learning the alphabet is not difficult, the writing system itself is fairly complex, so unless you're planning a lengthy stay in Thailand it should perhaps be foregone in favour of actually learning to speak the language. The names of major places included in this book are given in both Thai and

LANGUAGE

Roman script, so that you can at least 'read' the names of destinations at a pinch, or point to them if necessary.

TONES

In Thai the meaning of a single syllable may be altered by means of different tones – in standard Central Thai there are five: low tone, level or mid tone, falling tone, high tone and rising tone. For example, depending on the tone, the syllable *mai* can mean 'new', 'burn', 'wood', 'not?' or 'not'; ponder the phrase *mái mài mâi mǎi* (New wood doesn't burn, does it?) and you begin to appreciate the importance of tones in spoken Thai. This makes it a rather tricky language to learn at first, especially for those of us unaccustomed to the concept of tones. Even when we 'know' what the correct tone in Thai should be, our tendency to denote emotion, verbal stress, the interrogative etc through tone modulation often interferes with producing the correct tone. Therefore the first rule in learning to speak Thai is to divorce emotions from your speech, at least until you've learned the Thai way to express them without changing essential tone value.

The following is visual representation in chart form to show relative tone values:

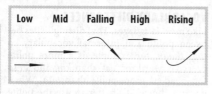

Low	Mid	Falling	High	Rising

Below is a brief attempt to explain the tones. The only way to really understand the differences is by listening to a native or fluent non-native speaker. The range of all five tones is relative to each speaker's vocal range so there is no fixed 'pitch' intrinsic to the language.

low tone – 'flat' like the mid tone, but pronounced at the relative bottom of one's vocal range. It is low, level and with no inflection, eg *bàat* (baht – the Thai currency).

level or mid tone – pronounced 'flat', at the relative middle of the speaker's vocal range, eg *dii* (good); no tone mark is used.

falling tone – sounds as if you are emphasising a word, or calling someone's name from afar, eg *mâi* (no/not).

high tone – usually the most difficult for Westerners. It

is pronounced near the relative top of the vocal range, as level as possible, eg *máa* (horse).

rising tone – sounds like the inflection used by English speakers to imply a question – 'Yes?', eg *sǎam* (three).

PRONUNCIATION

The following is a guide to the phonetic system that's been used for the words and phrases in this chapter (and throughout the rest of the book when transcribing directly from Thai). It's based on the Royal Thai General System (RTGS). The dots indicate syllable breaks within words.

Consonants

The majority of consonants correspond closely to their English counterparts. Here are a few exceptions:

k	as the 'k' in 'skin'; similar to the 'g' in 'good', but unaspirated (ie with no accompanying puff of air); similar to English 'g' but unvoiced (ie with no vibration in the vocal chords)
p	as the 'p' in 'stopper', unvoiced and unaspirated (not like the 'p' in 'put'); actually sounds closer to an English 'b', its voiced equivalent
t	as the 't' in 'forty', unaspirated; similar to 'd' but unvoiced
kh	as the 'k' in 'kite', aspirated (ie with an audible puff of air)
ph	as the 'p' in 'pie', aspirated (not to be confused with the 'ph' in 'phone')
th	as the 't' in 'tie', aspirated
ng	as the 'nging' in 'singing'; can occur as an initial consonant (practise by saying 'singing' without the 'si')
r	similar to the 'r' in 'run' but flapped (ie the tongue touches palate); in everyday speech often pronounced like 'l'

Vowels

i	as the 'i' in 'it'
ii	as the 'ee' in 'feet'
ai	as the 'i' in 'pipe'
aa	as the 'a' in 'father'
a	half as long as **aa**, as the 'a' in 'about'
ae	as the 'a' in 'bat' or 'tab'
e	as the 'e' in 'hen'
eh	as the 'ai' in 'air'
oe	as the 'er' in 'fern' (without the 'r' sound)

u	as the 'u' in 'put'
uu	as the 'oo' in 'food'
eu	as the 'u' in 'fur' (without the 'r' sound)
ao	as the 'ow' in 'now'
aw	as the 'aw' in 'jaw' or 'prawn'
o	as the 'o' in 'bone'
oh	as the 'o' in 'toe'
eua	a combination of **eu** and **a**
ia	as 'ee-ya', or as the 'ie' in French rien
ua	as the 'our' in 'tour'
uay	sounds like 'oo-way'
iu	as the 'ew' in 'new'
iaw	as the 'io' in 'Rio'
aew	like the 'a' in 'cat' followed by a short 'u' as in 'put'
ehw	as 'air-ooh'
awy	as the 'oi' in 'coin'

TRANSLITERATION

Writing Thai in Roman script is a perennial problem – no wholly satisfactory system has yet been devised to assure both consistency and readability. The Thai government uses the RTGS of transcription for official government documents in English and for most highway signs. However, local variations crop up on hotel signs, city street signs, menus and so on in such a way that visitors often become confused. Added to this is the fact that even the government system has its flaws.

Generally, names in this book follow the most common practice or simply copy their Roman script name, no matter what devious process was used in its transliteration! When this transliteration is markedly different from actual pronunciation, the pronunciation is included (according to the system outlined in this chapter) in parentheses after the transliteration. Where no Roman model was available, names have been transliterated phonetically, directly from Thai.

ACCOMMODATION

I'm looking for a ...
phǒm/dì-chǎn kam-lang hǎa ...
ผม/ดิฉันกำลังหา...

guesthouse
bâan phák/ | บ้านพัก/
kèt háo ('guest house') | เกสต์เฮาส์
hotel
rohng raem | โรงแรม

youth hostel
bâan yao·wá·chon | บ้านเยาวชน

Where is a cheap hotel?
rohng raem thîi raa·khaa thùuk yùu thîi nǎi
โรงแรมที่ราคาถูกอยู่ที่ไหน

What is the address?
thîi yùu keu a·rai
ที่อยู่คืออะไร

Could you write the address, please?
khǐan thîi yùu hâi dâi mǎi
เขียนที่อยู่ให้ได้ไหม

Do you have any rooms available?
mii hâwng wâang mǎi?
มีห้องว่างไหม

I'd like (a) ...
tâwng kaan ...
ต้องการ...

bed
tiang nawn | เตียงนอน
single room
hâwng dìaw | ห้องเดี่ยว
double room
hâwng khûu | ห้องคู่
room with two beds
hâwng thîi mii | ห้องที่มีเตียงสองตัว
tiang sǎwng tua
room with a bathroom
hâwng thîi mii | ห้องที่มีห้องน้ำ
hâwng nám
ordinary room (with fan)
hâwng tham·má· | ห้องธรรมดา
daa (mii pát lom) | (มีพัดลม)
to share a dorm
phák nai hǎw phák | พักในหอพัก

How much is it ...? ... thâo rai? | ...เท่าไร?
per night | kheun lá | คืนละ
per person | khon lá | คนละ

May I see the room?
duu hâwng dâi mǎi
ดูห้องได้ไหม

Where is the bathroom?
hâwng nám yùu thîi nǎi
ห้องน้ำอยู่ที่ไหน

I'm/We're leaving today.
chǎn/phûak rao jà àwk wan níi
ฉัน/พวกเราจะออกวันนี้

toilet	hâwng sûam	ห้องส้วม
room	hâwng	ห้อง
hot	ráwn	ร้อน
cold	yen	เย็น
bath/shower	àap nám	อาบน้ำ
towel	phâa chét tua	ผ้าเช็ดตัว

CONVERSATION & ESSENTIALS

When being polite, the speaker ends his or her sentence with khráp (for men) or khà (for women). It is the gender of the speaker that is being expressed here; it is also the common way to answer 'yes' to a question or show agreement.

Hello.
sà-wàt-dii (khráp/khâ)   สวัสดี(ครับ/ค่ะ)
Goodbye.
laa kàwn   ลาก่อน
Yes.
châi   ใช่
No.
mâi châi   ไม่ใช่
Please.
kà-rú-naa   กรุณา
Thank you.
khàwp khun   ขอบคุณ
That's fine. (You're welcome)
mâi pen rai/yin-dii   ไม่เป็นไร/ยินดี
Excuse me.
khǎw à-phai   ขออภัย
Sorry. (forgive me)
khǎw thôht   ขอโทษ
How are you?
sa-bai dii rěu?   สบายดีหรือ?
I'm fine, thanks.
sa-bai dii   สบายดี
What's your name?
khun chêu à-rai?   คุณชื่ออะไร?
My name is ...
phǒm chêu ... (men)   ผมชื่อ...
dì-chǎn chêu ... (women)   ดิฉันชื่อ...
Where are you from?
maa jàak nǎi   มาจากไหน
I'm from ...
maa jàak ...   มาจาก...
See you soon.
dǐaw joe kan ná   เดี๋ยวเจอกันนะ
I like ...
châwp ...   ชอบ...

I don't like ...
mâi châwp ...   ไม่ชอบ...
Just a minute.
raw dǐaw   รอเดี๋ยว
I/me (for men)
phǒm   ผม
I/me (for women)
dì-chǎn   ดิฉัน
I/me (informal, men and women)
chǎn   ฉัน
you (for peers)
khun   คุณ
Do you have ...?
mii ... mǎi?/... mii mǎi?   มี...ไหม/...มีไหม?
(I) would like ... (+ verb)
yàak jà ...   อยากจะ...
(I) would like ... (+ noun)
yàak dâi ...   อยากได้...

DIRECTIONS

Where is (the)...?
... yùu thîi nǎi?   ...อยู่ที่ไหน?
(Go) Straight ahead.
trong pai   ตรงไป
Turn left.
líaw sáai   เลี้ยวซ้าย
Turn right.
líaw khwǎa   เลี้ยวขวา
at the corner
trong mum   ตรงมุม
at the traffic lights
trong fai daeng   ตรงไฟแดง
behind
khâang lǎng   ข้างหลัง

SIGNS

ทางเข้า	Entrance
ทางออก	Exit
ที่ติดต่อสอบถาม	Information
เปิด	Open
ปิด	Closed
ห้าม	Prohibited
มีห้องว่าง	Rooms Available
เต็มแล้ว	Full/No Vacancies
สถานีตำรวจ	Police Station
ห้องน้ำ	Toilets
ชาย	Men
หญิง	Women

in front of	trong nâa	ตรงหน้า
far	klai	ไกล
near	klâi	ใกล้
not far	mâi klai	ไม่ไกล
opposite	trong khâam	ตรงข้าม
left	sáai	ซ้าย
right	khwǎa	ขวา

beach	chaai hàat	ชายหาด
bridge	sà-phaan	สะพาน
canal	khlawng	คลอง
castle	praa-sàat	ปราสาท
church	bòht	โบสถ์
countryside	chon-ná-bòt	ชนบท
hill	khǎo	เขา
island	kàw	เกาะ
lake	thá-leh sàap	ทะเลสาบ
market	ta-làat	ตลาด
mountain	phuu khǎo	ภูเขา
museum	phí-phít-thá-phan	พิพิธภัณฑ์
old city	meuang kào	เมืองเก่า
paddy (field)	(thûng) naa	(ทุ่ง)นา
palace	wang	วัง
pond	nǎwng/beung	หนอง/บึง
river	mâe nám	แม่น้ำ
sea	thá-leh	ทะเล
temple	wát	วัด
tower	hǎw	หอ
town	meuang	เมือง
track	thaang	ทาง
village	(mùu) bâan	(หมู่)บ้าน
waterfall	nám tòk	น้ำตก

HEALTH

I need a (doctor).
 tâwng kaan (mǎw)   ต้องการ(หมอ)
dentist
 mǎw fan   หมอฟัน
hospital
 rohng phá-yaa-baan   โรงพยาบาล
chemist/pharmacy
 ráan khǎi yaa   ร้านขายยา
I'm ill.
 chǎn pùay   ฉันป่วย

It hurts here.
 jèp trong née   เจ็บตรงนี้
I'm pregnant.
 tâng khan láew   ตั้งครรภ์แล้ว
I feel nauseous.
 rúu-sèuk khlêun sâi   รู้สึกคลื่นไส้
I have a fever.
 pen khâi   เป็นไข้
I have diarrhoea.
 tháwng sǐa   ท้องเสีย

I'm ...
 phǒm/dì-chǎn ...
 ผม/ดิฉัน...
  asthmatic
  pen hèut   เป็นหืด
  diabetic
  pen rôhk bao wǎan   เป็นโรคเบาหวาน
  epileptic
  pen rôhk lom bâa mǔu   เป็นโรคลมบ้าหมู

I'm allergic to ...
 phǒm/dì-chǎn pháe ...
 ผม/ดิฉันแพ้...
  antibiotics
  yaa pà-tì-chii-wa-ná   ยาปฏิชีวนะ
  aspirin
  yaa àet-sa-phai-rin   ยาแอสไพริน
  penicillin
  yaa phe-ní-sin-lin   ยาเพนิซิลลิน
  bees
  phêung   ผึ้ง
  peanuts
  thùa lí-sǒng   ถั่วลิสง

antiseptic
 yaa khâa chéua   ยาฆ่าเชื้อ
aspirin
 yaa kâe pùat   ยาแก้ปวด
condoms
 thǔng yaang a-naa-mai   ถุงยางอนามัย
contraceptive
 kaan khum kam-nòet   การคุมกำเนิด
medicine
 yaa   ยา
mosquito coil
 yaa kan yung bàep jùt   ยากันยุงแบบจุด
mosquito repellent
 yaa kan yung   ยากันยุง
painkiller
 yaa kâe pùat   ยาแก้ปวด
sunblock cream
 khriim kan dàet   ครีมกันแดด
tampons
 thaem-phawn   แทมพอน

EMERGENCIES

Help!
  chûay dûay!   ช่วยด้วย
There's been an accident.
  mii ù·bàt·tì·hèt   มีอุบัติเหตุ
I'm lost.
  chǎn lǒng thaang   ฉันหลงทาง
Go away!
  pai sí!   ไปซิ
Stop!
  yùt!   หยุด

Call ...!
  rîak ... nàwy   เรียก...หน่อย
  a doctor   *mǎw*   หมอ
  the police *tam·rùat*   ตำรวจ

LANGUAGE DIFFICULTIES

Do you speak English?
  khun phûut phaa·sǎa ang·krìt dâi mǎi
  คุณพูดภาษาอังกฤษได้ไหม
Does anyone here speak English?
  thîi nîi mii khrai bâang thîi phûut phaa·sǎa ang·krìt dâi mǎi
  ที่นี่มีใครบ้างที่พูดภาษาอังกฤษได้ไหม
How do you say ... in Thai?
  ... wâa yàang rai phaa·sǎa thai
  ...ว่าอย่างไรภาษาไทย
What do you call this in Thai?
  nîi phaa·sǎa thai rîak wâa à·rai?
  นี่ภาษาไทยเรียกว่าอะไร
What does ... mean?
  ... plae wâa à·rai
  ...แปลว่าอะไร
Do you understand?
  khâo jai mǎi?
  เข้าใจไหม
A little.
  nít nàwy
  นิดหน่อย
I understand.
  khâo jai
  เข้าใจ
I don't understand.
  mâi khâo jai
  ไม่เข้าใจ
Please write it down.
  kà·rú·naa khǐan hâi nàwy
  กรุณาเขียนให้หน่อย

Can you show me (on the map)?
  hâi duu (nai phǎen thîi) dâi mǎi
  ให้ดู(ในแผนที่)ได้ไหม

NUMBERS

0	*sǔun*	ศูนย์
1	*nèung*	หนึ่ง
2	*sǎwng*	สอง
3	*sǎam*	สาม
4	*sìi*	สี่
5	*hâa*	ห้า
6	*hòk*	หก
7	*jèt*	เจ็ด
8	*pàet*	แปด
9	*kâo*	เก้า
10	*sìp*	สิบ
11	*sìp-èt*	สิบเอ็ด
12	*sìp-sǎwng*	สิบสอง
13	*sìp-sǎam*	สิบสาม
14	*sìp-sìi*	สิบสี่
15	*sìp-hâa*	สิบห้า
16	*sìp-hòk*	สิบหก
17	*sìp-jèt*	สิบเจ็ด
18	*sìp-pàet*	สิบแปด
19	*sìp-kâo*	สิบเก้า
20	*yîi-sìp*	ยี่สิบ
21	*yîi-sìp-èt*	ยี่สิบเอ็ด
22	*yîi-sìp-sǎwng*	ยี่สิบสอง
30	*sǎam-sìp*	สามสิบ
40	*sìi-sìp*	สี่สิบ
50	*hâa-sìp*	ห้าสิบ
60	*hòk-sìp*	หกสิบ
70	*jèt-sìp*	เจ็ดสิบ
80	*pàet-sìp*	แปดสิบ
90	*kâo-sìp*	เก้าสิบ
100	*nèung ráwy*	หนึ่งร้อย
200	*sǎwng ráwy*	สองร้อย
300	*sǎam ráwy*	สามร้อย
1000	*nèung phan*	หนึ่งพัน
2000	*sǎwng phan*	สองพัน
10,000	*nèung mèun*	หนึ่งหมื่น
100,000	*nèung sǎen*	หนึ่งแสน
one million	*nèung láan*	หนึ่งล้าน
one billion	*phan láan*	พันล้าน

PAPERWORK

name	*chêu*	ชื่อ
nationality	*săn·châat*	สัญชาติ
date of birth	*kòet wan thîi*	เกิดวันที่
place of birth	*kòet thîi*	เกิดที่
sex (gender)	*phêht*	เพศ
passport	*năng·sĕu doen*	หนังสือเดิน
	thaang	ทาง
visa	*wii·sâa*	วีซ่า

SHOPPING & SERVICES

I'd like to buy ...
yàak jà séu ...   อยากจะซื้อ...

How much?
thâo rai?   เท่าไร

How much is this?
nîi thâo rai?/kìi bàat?   นี่เท่าไร/กี่บาท

How much is it?
thâo rai   เท่าไร

I don't like it.
mâi châwp   ไม่ชอบ

May I look at it?
duu dâi măi   ดูได้ไหม

I'm just looking.
duu chŏe chŏe   ดูเฉยๆ

It's cheap.
raa·khaa thùuk   ราคาถูก

It's too expensive.
phaeng koen pai   แพงเกินไป

I'll take it.
ao   เอา

Can you reduce the price a little?
lót raa·khaa nàwy dâi măi
ลดราคาหน่อยได้ไหม

Can you come down just a little more?
lót raa·khaa ìik nít·nèung dâi măi
ลดราคาอีกนิดหนึ่งได้ไหม

Do you have something cheaper?
mii thùuk kwàa nîi măi
มีถูกกว่านี้ไหม

Can you lower it more?
lót ìik dâi măi
ลดอีกได้ไหม

How about ... baht?
... bàat dâi măi
...บาทได้ไหม

I won't give more than ... baht.
jà hâi mâi koen ... bàat
จะให้ไม่เกิน...บาท

Do you accept ...?
ráp ... măi   รับ...ไหม

  credit cards
  bàt khreh·dìt   บัตรเครดิต

  travellers cheques
  chék doen thaang   เช็คเดินทาง

more	*ìik*	อีก
more	*mâak khêun*	มากขึ้น
less	*náwy long*	น้อยลง
smaller	*lék kwàa*	เล็กกว่า
bigger	*yài kwàa*	ใหญ่กว่า
too expensive	*phaeng pai*	แพงไป
inexpensive	*thùuk*	ถูก

I'm looking for ...
phŏm/dì·chăn hăa ...   ผม/ดิฉันหา...

  a bank
  thá·naa·khaan   ธนาคาร

  the church
  bòht khrít   โบสถ์คริสต์

  the city centre
  jai klaang meuang   ใจกลางเมือง

  the ... embassy
  sà·thăan thûut ...   สถานทูต...

  the market
  ta·làat   ตลาด

  the museum
  phí·phít·thá·phan   พิพิธภัณฑ์

  the post office
  prai·sà·nii   ไปรษณีย์

  a public toilet
  hâwng nám   ห้องน้ำสาธารณะ
  săa·thaa·rá·ná

  a restaurant
  ráan aa·hăan   ร้านอาหาร

  the telephone centre
  sŭun thoh·rá·sàp   ศูนย์โทรศัพท์

  the tourist office
  săm·nák ngaan   สำนักงานท่องเที่ยว
  thâwng thîaw

I want to change ...
tâwng kaan lâek ...   ต้องการแลก...

  money
  ngoen   เงิน

  travellers cheques
  chék doen thaang   เช็คเดินทาง

LANGUAGE

Can I/we change money here?
lâek ngoen thîi nîi dâi mǎi
แลกเงินที่นี่ได้ไหม

What time does it open?
ráan pòet kìi mohng
ร้านเปิดกี่โมง

What time does it close?
ráan pìt kìi mohng
ร้านปิดกี่โมง

TIME & DATES

What time is it?
kìi mohng láew?   กี่โมงแล้ว?

It's (8 o'clock).
pàet mohng láew   แปดโมงแล้ว

When?	meua·rai	เมื่อไร
today	wan níi	วันนี้
tomorrow	phrûng níi	พรุ่งนี้
yesterday	mêua waan	เมื่อวาน
Monday	wan jan	วันจันทร์
Tuesday	wan ang·khaan	วันอังคาร
Wednesday	wan phút	วันพุธ
Thursday	wan phá·réu·hàt	วันพฤหัสฯ
Friday	wan sùk	วันศุกร์
Saturday	wan sǎo	วันเสาร์
Sunday	wan aa·thít	วันอาทิตย์
January	má·ka·raa·khom	มกราคม
February	kum·phaa·phan	กุมภาพันธ์
March	mii·naa·khom	มีนาคม
April	meh·sǎa·yon	เมษายน
May	phréut·sà·phaa·khom	พฤษภาคม
June	mí·thù·naa·yon	มิถุนายน
July	ka·rák·ka·daa·khom	กรกฎาคม
August	sǐng·hǎa·khom	สิงหาคม
September	kan·yaa·yon	กันยายน
October	tù·laa·khom	ตุลาคม
November	phréut·sà·jì·kaa·yon	พฤศจิกายน
December	than·waa·khom	ธันวาคม

TRANSPORT
Public Transport

What time does the ... leave?
... jà àwk kìi mohng
...จะออกกี่โมง

What time does the ... arrive?
... jà thěung kìi mohng
...จะถึงกี่โมง

boat	reua	เรือ
bus	rót meh/	รถเมล์/
	rót bát	รถบัส
bus (city)	rót meh	รถเมล์
bus (intercity)	rót thua	รถทัวร์
plane	khrêuang bin	เครื่องบิน
train	rót fai	รถไฟ

I'd like ...
phǒm/dì·chán yàak dâi ...
ผม/ดิฉันอยากได้...

a one-way ticket
tǔa thîaw diaw   ตั๋วเที่ยวเดียว
a return ticket
tǔa pai klàp   ตั๋วไปกลับ
two tickets
tǔa sǎwng bai   ตั๋วสองใบ
1st class
chán nèung   ชั้นหนึ่ง
2nd class
chán sǎwng   ชั้นสอง

I'd like a ticket.
yàak dâi tǔa
อยากได้ตั๋ว

I want to go to ...
yàak jà pai ...
อยากจะไป...

The train has been cancelled.
rót fai thùuk yók lôek láew
รถไฟถูกยกเลิกแล้ว

The train has been delayed.
rót fai jà cháa weh·laa
รถไฟจะช้าเวลา

airport
sa·nǎam bin   สนามบิน
bus station
sa·thǎa·nii khǒn sòng   สถานีขนส่ง
bus stop
pâai rót meh   ป้ายรถเมล์
taxi stand
thîi jàwt rót tháek·sîi   ที่จอดรถแท็กซี่
train station
sa·thǎa·nii rót fai   สถานีรถไฟ
platform number
chaan·chaa·laa thîi   ชานชาลาที่

ticket office
  tûu khǎi tǔa ตู้ขายตั๋ว
timetable
  taa·raang weh·laa ตารางเวลา
the first
  thîi râek ที่แรก
the last
  sùt tháai สุดท้าย

Private Transport
I'd like to hire a/an ...
phǒm/dì·chǎn yàak châo ...
ผม/ดิฉันอยากเช่า...
  car
  rót yon รถยนต์
  4WD
  rót foh wiin รถโฟร์วีล
  motorbike
  rót maw·toe·sai รถมอเตอร์ไซค์
  bicycle
  rót jàk·kà·yaan รถจักรยาน

ROAD SIGNS	
ให้ทาง	Give Way
ทางเบี่ยง	Detour
ห้ามเข้า	No Entry
ห้ามแซง	No Overtaking
ห้ามจอด	No Parking
ทางเข้า	Entrance
ห้ามขวางทาง	Keep Clear
เก็บเงินทางด่วน	Toll
อันตราย	Danger
ขับช้าลง	Slow Down
ทางเดียว	One Way
ทางออก	Exit

Is this the road to ...?
  thaang níi pai ... mǎi
  ทางนี้ไป...ไหม
Where's a service station?
  pâm nám man yùu thîi nǎi
  ปั๊มน้ำมันอยู่ที่ไหน
Please fill it up.
  khǎw toem hâi tem
  ขอเติมให้เต็ม
I'd like (30) litres.
  ao (sǎam sìp) lít
  เอา(สามสิบ)ลิตร

diesel
  nám man soh·lâa
  น้ำมันโซล่า
unleaded petrol
  nám man rái sǎan tà·kùa
  น้ำมันไร้สารตะกั่ว
Can I park here?
  jàwt thîi níi dâi mǎi
  จอดที่นี้ได้ไหม
How long can I park here?
  jàwt thîi níi dâi naan thâo·rai
  จอดที่นี้ได้นานเท่าไร
Where do I pay?
  jàai ngoen thîi nǎi
  จ่ายเงินที่ไหน
I need a mechanic.
  tâwng kaan châang
  ต้องการช่าง
The car/motorbike has broken down (at ...)
  rót/maw·toe·sai sǐa thîi ...
  รถ/มอเตอร์ไซค์เสียที่...
The car/motorbike won't start.
  rót/maw·toe·sai sa·táat mâi tìt
  รถ/มอเตอร์ไซค์สตาร์ดไม่ติด
I have a flat tyre.
  yaang baen
  ยางแบน
I've run out of petrol.
  mòt nám man
  หมดน้ำมัน
I've had an accident.
  mii ù·pàt·tì·hèt
  มีอุบัติเหตุ

TRAVEL WITH CHILDREN
Is there a/an ...
  mii ... mǎi มี...ไหม
I need a/an ...
  tâwng kaan ... ต้องการ...
  baby change room
  hâwng plìan phâa dèk
  ห้องเปลี่ยนผ้าเด็ก
  car baby seat
  bàw nâng nai rót sǎm·ràp dèk
  เบาะนั่งในรถสำหรับเด็ก
  child-minding service
  baw·rí·kaan líang dèk
  บริการเลี้ยงเด็ก

children's menu
raai kaan ah·hǎan sǎm·ràp dèk
รายการอาหารสำหรับเด็ก

(disposable) nappies/diapers
phâa âwm (bàep chái láew tíng)
ผ้าอ้อม(แบบใช้แล้วทิ้ง)

formula (milk)
nom phǒng sǎm·ràp dèk
นมผงสำหรับเด็ก

(English-speaking) babysitter
phîi líang dèk (thîi phûut phaa·sǎa ang·krìt dâi)
พี่เลี้ยงเด็ก(ที่พูดภาษาอังกฤษได้)

highchair
kâo îi sǔung
เก้าอี้สูง

potty
krà·thǒhn
กระโถน

stroller
rót khěn dèk
รถเข็นเด็ก

Do you mind if I breastfeed here?
jà rang·kìat mǎi thâa hâi nom lûuk thîi níi
จะรังเกียจไหมถ้าให้นมลูกที่นี้

Are children allowed?
dèk à·nú·yâht khâo mǎi
เด็กอนุญาตเข้าไหม

Also available from Lonely Planet:
Thai Phrasebook

Glossary

This glossary includes Thai, Pali (P) and Sanskrit (S) words and terms frequently used in this guidebook. For definitions of food and drink terms, see p83.

aahaan – food
aahaan pàa – 'jungle food', usually referring to dishes made with wild game
ajahn – *(aajaan)* respectful title for teacher; from the Sanskrit term *acarya*
amphoe – district, the next subdivision down from province; also written *amphur*
amphoe meuang – provincial capital
ao – bay or gulf
AUA – American University Alumni

bàat – a unit of weight equal to 15g; rounded bowl used by monks for receiving food alms
baht – *(bàat)* the Thai unit of currency
bai sii – sacred thread used by monks or shamans in certain religious ceremonies
ban – *(bâan)* house or village
bàw náam ráwn – hot springs
benjarong – traditional five-coloured Thai ceramics
BKS – Baw Khaw Saw (Thai acronym for the Transport Company)
BMA – Bangkok Metropolitan Authority
bodhisattva (S) – in Theravada Buddhism, the term used to refer to the Buddha during the period before he became the Buddha, including his previous lives
bòt – central sanctuary in a Thai temple used for official business of the Order (Pali: *sangha*) of monks, such as ordinations; from the Pali term *uposatha*; see also *wíhaan*
Brahman – pertaining to Brahmanism, an ancient religious tradition in India and the predecessor of Hinduism; not to be confused with 'Brahmin', the priestly class in India's caste system
BTS – Bangkok Transit System (Skytrain); Thai: *rót fai fáa*

CAT – Communications Authority of Thailand
chao leh – sea gypsies; also *chao náam*
chao naa – farmer
chedi – *stupa*
CPT – Communist Party of Thailand

doi – *(dawy)* the word for mountain in the northern regions

faràng – Western, a Westerner

gopura (S) – entrance pavilion in traditional Hindu temple architecture, often seen in Angkor-period temple complexes

hat – *(hàat)* beach; also *chaihàat*
haw phii – spirit shrine
haw trai – a Tripitaka (Buddhist scripture) hall
hâwng – room; see also *hong*
hâwng thaew – two- or three-storey shophouses arranged side-by-side along a city street
hin – stone
hong – *(hâwng)* room; in southern Thailand this refers to semi-submerged island caves

Isan – *(isaan)* general term used for northeastern Thailand

jâo meuang – political office in traditional Thai societies throughout Southeast Asia; literally 'principality chief'
jataka (P) – *(chaadòk)* stories of the Buddha's previous lives
jiin – Chinese
jiin haw – Yunnanese

kàthoey – lady boys, transvestites and transsexuals
khaen – reed instrument common in northeastern Thailand
khao – hill or mountain
khâo – rice
khlong – *(khlawng)* canal
khohn – masked dance-drama based on stories from the *Ramakian*
khon isaan – the people of northeastern Thailand
KMT – Kuomintang
KNU – Karen National Union
ko – *(kàw)* island; also *koh*
kràbìi-kràbawng – a traditional Thai martial art employing short swords and staves
ku – small *chedi* that is partially hollow and open
kúay hâeng – Chinese-style work shirt
kùtì – meditation hut; a monk's dwelling

laem – cape
làk meuang – city pillar, isthmus
lákhon – classical Thai dance-drama
lâo khao – 'white spirit', an often homemade brew
lâo thèuan – homemade (ie illegal) liquor
lék – little, small (in size); see also *noi*
lí-keh – Thai folk dance-drama
loi krathong – *(lawy kràthong)* the ceremony celebrated on the full moon of the end of the rainy season

longyi – Burmese sarong
lûuk thûng – Thai country music

mâe chii – Thai Buddhist nun
mâe náam – river
Mahanikai – the larger of the two sects of Theravada Buddhism in Thailand
mahathat – (máhaa thâat) common name for temples containing Buddha relics; from the Sanskrit-Pali term mahadhatu
málaeng tháp – collages made from metallic, multicoloured beetle wings
mánohraa – southern Thailand's most popular traditional dance-drama
masjid – (mátsàyít) a mosque
mát-mìi – technique of tie-dyeing silk or cotton threads and then weaving them into complex patterns, similar to Indonesian ikat; the term also refers to the patterns themselves
mâw hâwm – see sêua mâw hâwm
măw lam – an Isan musical tradition
mawn khwaan – wedge-shaped pillow popular in northern and northeastern Thailand
metta (P) – (mêt-taa) Buddhist practice of loving-kindness
meuang – city or principality
mondòp – small square, spired building in a wat; from Sanskrit mandapa
MRTA – Metropolitan Rapid Transit Authority
muay thai – Thai boxing

náam – water
náam tòk – waterfall
naga (P/S) – (nâak) a mythical serpentlike being with magical powers
nákhon – city; from the Sanskrit-Pali nagara
nang – Thai shadow play
něua – north
ngaan thêtsàkaan – festival
nirvana (S) – (Pali: nibbana, Thai: níp-phaan) in Buddhist teachings, the state of enlightenment; escape from the realm of rebirth
noen – hill
noi – (náwy) little, small (amount); also noy; see also lék
nok – (nâwk) outside; outer

paa-té – batik
pàk tâi – southern Thailand
phâa mát-mìi – thick cotton or silk fabric woven from tie-dyed threads
phâakhamáa – piece of cotton cloth worn as a wraparound by men
phâasîn – same as above for women
phansaa – 'rains retreat' or Buddhist Lent; a period of three months during the rainy season that is traditionally a time of stricter moral observance for monks and Buddhist lay followers
phrá phim – magical charm amulets
phii – ghost, spirit
phíksù – a Buddhist monk; from the Sanskrit bhikshu, Pali bhikkhu
phin – small, three-stringed lute played with a large plectrum
phleng khorâat – Khorat folk song
phleng phêua chii-wít – 'songs for life', modern Thai folk music
phrá – an honorific term used for monks, nobility and Buddha images
phrá khrêuang – amulets of monks, Buddhas or deities worn around the neck for spiritual protection; also called phrá phim
phrá phuum – earth spirits
phuu khao – mountain
phûu yài bâan – village chief
pìi-phâat – classical Thai orchestra
PLAT – People's Liberation Army of Thailand
ponglang – (ponglaang) northeastern Thai marimba (percussion instrument) made of short logs
prang – (praang) Khmer-style tower on temples
prasada – blessed food offered to Hindu or Sikh temple attendees
prasat – (praasáat) small ornate building with a cruciform ground plan and needlelike spire, used for religious purposes, located on wat grounds; any of a number of different kinds of hall or residence with religious or royal significance
PULO – Pattani United Liberation Organisation

râi – an area of land measurement equal to 1600 sq metres
reua haang yao – long-tailed boat
reuan thaew – longhouse
reusii – an ascetic, hermit or sage (Hindi: rishi)
rót fai fáa – Skytrain
rót fai tâi din – subway, Metro
rót pràp aakàat – air-con vehicle
rót thammádaa – ordinary bus (non air-con) or ordinary train (not rapid or express)
rót thua – tour bus

săalaa – open-sided, covered meeting hall or resting place; from Portuguese term sala, literally 'room'
sămláw – (also written samlor) three-wheeled pedicab; see also túk-túk
samnák song – monastic centre
samnák wípàtsànaa – meditation centre
samsara (P) – in Buddhist teachings, the realm of rebirth and delusion
sàtàang – A Thai unit of currency; 100 sàtàang equals 1 baht

săwngthăew – (literally 'two rows') common name for small pick-up trucks with two benches in the back, used as buses/taxis; also written *songthaew*
sěmaa – boundary stones used to consecrate ground used for monastic ordinations
serow – Asian mountain goat
sêua mâw hâwm – blue cotton farmer's shirt
soi – *(sawy)* lane or small street
Songkran – *(songkraan)* Thai New Year, held in mid-April
SRT – State Railway of Thailand
stupa – conical Buddhist monument used to inter sacred Buddhist objects
suan aahaan – outdoor restaurant with any bit of foliage nearby; literally 'food garden'
sù-saan – cemetery

tâi – south
tàlàat náam – floating market
tambon – precinct, next subdivision below *amphoe;* also written *tambol*
TAT – Tourism Authority of Thailand
tha – *(thâa)* pier, landing
thâat – four-sided, curvilinear Buddhist reliquary, common in northeastern Thailand; also *that*
thâat kràdùuk – bone reliquary, a small *stupa* containing remains of a Buddhist devotee
THAI – Thai Airways International
thâm – cave
tham bun – to make merit
thammájàk – Buddhist wheel of law; from the Pali *dhammacakka*
Thammayut – one of the two sects of Theravada Buddhism in Thailand; founded by King Rama IV while he was still a monk
thâm reusii – hermit cave
thànon – street

thêtsàbaan – a division in towns or cities much like 'municipality'
thúdong – a series of 13 ascetic practices, for example eating one meal a day, living at the foot of a tree, undertaken by Buddhist monks; a monk who undertakes such practices; a period of wandering on foot from place to place undertaken by monks
tràwk – alley; also *trok*
trimurti – collocation of the three principal Hindu deities, Brahma, Shiva and Vishnu
Tripitaka (S) – Theravada Buddhist scriptures; (Pali: *Tipitaka*)
túk-túk – motorised *săamláw*

ùtsànít – flame-shaped head ornament on a Buddha

Vipassana – *(wípàtsànaa)* Buddhist insight meditation

wâi – palms-together Thai greeting
wan phrá – Buddhist holy days, falling on the days of the main phases of the moon (full, new and half) each month
wang – palace
wat – temple-monastery; from the Pali term *avasa* meaning 'monk's dwelling'
wát pàa – forest monastery
wáthánátham – culture
wíhăn – any large hall in a Thai temple, but not the *bòt;* from the Sanskrit term *vihara,* meaning 'dwelling'; also *wihan* or *viharn*

yâam – shoulder bag
yài – big
Yawi – the traditional language of Java, Sumatra and the Malay Peninsula, widely spoken in the most southern provinces of Thailand; the written form uses the classic Arabic script plus five additional letters

Behind the Scenes

THIS BOOK

This 12th edition of Thailand was researched and written by China Williams (coordinator), Aaron Anderson, Becca Blond, Brett Atkinson, Tim Bewer, Virginia Jealous, Lisa Steer, Trish Batchelor, Joe Cummings and Joel Gershon. This guidebook was commissioned in Lonely Planet's Melbourne office and produced by the following:

Commissioning Editors Carolyn Boicos, Kalya Ryan
Coordinating Editors Shawn Low, Rosie Nicholson
Coordinating Cartographer Malisa Plesa
Coordinating Layout Designer Yvonne Bischofberger
Managing Editors Bruce Evans, Liz Heynes
Managing Cartographer Julie Sheridan
Assisting Editors David Andrew, Maryanne Netto, Kristin Odijk, Stephanie Ong, Dianne Schallmeiner
Assisting Cartographers Anita Bahn, Jessica Deane, Joshua Geoghegan, Erin McManus, Andrew Smith, Jody Whiteoak

Assisting Layout Designer Carol Jackson, Clara Monitto, Jacqui Saunders, Cara Smith, Wibowo Rusli
Cover Designer Jane Hart, Brendan Dempsey
Project Manager Fabrice Rocher
Language Content Coordinator Quentin Frayne

Thanks to Sin Choo, Sally Darmody, Mark Germanchis, Nicole Hansen, Wayne Murphy, Celia Wood

THANKS
CHINA WILLIAMS

Thanks to my usual Bangkok crowd: Mason and Jane, the staff at Bangkok 101, Clay and Jessica, Sarah Wintle, Austin Bush, Ruengsang and Fawn. The international team at the TAT headquarters and the Central Region TAT staff were super-stars. Thanks also to anyone who politely tolerated my cocktail conversations that were really informal interviews. More thanks to my son, Felix, who was a

---

LONELY PLANET: TRAVEL WIDELY, TREAD LIGHTLY, GIVE SUSTAINABLY

The Lonely Planet Story
The story begins with a classic travel adventure: Tony and Maureen Wheeler's 1972 journey across Europe and Asia to Australia. There was no useful information about the overland trail then, so Tony and Maureen published the first Lonely Planet guidebook to meet a growing need.

From a kitchen table, Lonely Planet has grown to become the largest independent travel publisher in the world, with offices in Melbourne (Australia), Oakland (USA) and London (UK). Today Lonely Planet guidebooks cover the globe. There is an ever-growing list of books and information in a variety of media. Some things haven't changed. The main aim is still to make it possible for adventurous individuals to get out there – to explore and better understand the world.

The Lonely Planet Foundation
The Lonely Planet Foundation proudly supports nimble nonprofit institutions working for change in the world. Each year the foundation donates 5% of Lonely Planet company profits to projects selected by staff and authors. Our partners range from Kabissa, which provides small nonprofits across Africa with access to technology, to the Foundation for Developing Cambodian Orphans, which supports girls at risk of falling victim to sex traffickers.

Our nonprofit partners are linked by a grass-roots approach to the areas of health, education or sustainable tourism. Many projects we support – such as one with BaAka (Pygmy) children in the forested areas of Central African Republic – choose to focus on women and children as one of the most effective ways to support the whole community.

Sometimes foundation assistance is as simple as restoring a local ruin like the Minaret of Jam in Afghanistan; this incredible monument now draws intrepid tourists to the area and its restoration has greatly improved options for local people.

Just as travel is often about learning to see with new eyes, so many of the groups we work with aim to change the way people see themselves and the future for their children and communities.

fantastic in-utero companion and to my husband, Matt, who always remembers to pick me up from the airport; also to Kalya Ryan and the LP production team and the dedicated co-authors.

BRETT ATKINSON

Thanks to all the TAT staff especially Khun Pairat in Nakhon Nayok, and Khun Chanyuth in Cha-am. How many other travellers get introduced to the crowd at the Cha-am Feast-Fish-Flock Seafood Festival? Thanks to Chris and Ian on Ko Chang and Dan in Hua Hin for their expat spin. On Ko Mak thanks to flygirl Alexandra for the company and conversation. I told you I'd mention you in the book and I always keep my promises. In LP'ville thanks to Kalya Ryan for the opportunity, and to my coordinating author China Williams for her support. Thanks also to my co-authors Becca Blond, Lisa Steer and Tim Bewer. I hope you had as much fun as I did. In Auckland, thanks to Mum and Dad for their support, and love and special thanks to Carol. Who would have thought two Kiwis meeting in Bangkok in 1991 would have led to this?

VIRGINIA JEALOUS

Thanks to Margie, Kelana, Ali and Kiah for providing my home-away-from-home in Phuket; to Daeng for those complicated phone calls and terrific translations; to Por and Todd for the ride back from Khuraburi (those steamed fishcakes were truly fantastic).

TIM BEWER

A hearty *khàwp jai khráp* to the perpetually friendly people of Isan who never hesitated to answer my endless questions. I owe an extra special thanks to Tommy Manophaiboon, June Niampan, Veena Puntace and Julian Wright who all helped well beyond the call of duty. Also Panleka Suebma, Kejsiri Pongkietkong, Akekapob Polsamart, Noppadol Khayanngan, Bulan Boonphan and Nuan Sarnsorn all provided good help and good company. Finally, special thanks to Yata Saengpromsri for exploring behind closed doors and choosing to be late.

LISA STEER

Huge thanks to Winai Noree for his great driving skills, good company, and getting us out of muddy spots. Don't know what I would have done without the lovely Sonya de Masi who was a great mate, and gave me top tips on Chiang Mai and Mae Sot. Thanks to Kathleen Reen for welcoming me back to Thailand in the first place and letting me crash in her fab Bangkok pad. Much gratitude to the very patient TAT employees I plied with questions, especially those in Phitsanulok and Chiang Rai. Thanks to Gilles Guérard for helping me prepare, doing the Mae Hong Son loop with me, and many other things. Thanks to Kalya Ryan for being an inspirational commissioning editor, and to China Williams for her immense patience and sunny outlook. Last but not least, thanks to the Thais I met along the way who were so generous with their knowledge.

BECCA BLOND & AARON ANDERSON

First off we owe a huge THANK YOU to our friend Laura Clark for watching Duke while we were traipsing around Thailand for this title. Big thanks to Joe Cummings, who offered loads of helpful local advice. In Thailand, we'd like to thank the wonderful staff at the Woraburi Hotel in Phuket for all their fantastic service and willingness to answer our silly demands. In Samui a big thanks goes to Dave and Pete at the Wave and also to Noel at Samui Shamrock. We'd like to thank the folks at Phuket surf for all their advice, and also give a shout out to all the travellers we met on the road who offered super valuable info about where to eat, sleep and drink. In Ko Phi Phi we'd like to thank James Hood at the 007 Bar for his hospitality and also for being so patient with all our questions. In Khao Lak, big thanks to Su for agreeing to talk about her experience in the tsunami on camera. We're rooting that you get a computer soon. Finally, thanks to both our families and friends, without whose support we could never have gotten through this project: David, Patricia, Jessica, Pauline, Uncle Joe, Joyce, Jennie, John, Vera, Natalie, Mike, Danielle, Chris, Russell, Shari and Heather. Last but not least, I owe a big thanks to Kalya Ryan at Lonely Planet for giving me the chance to work on this project and to China Williams and the rest of the author team for being so easy to work with.

JOEL GERSHON

Khàwp khun mâak khráp to those who have made my Thailand years *sanùk mâak*: K Ian, Chris & Pim, Nigel, Fon, May K for the *aahãan jai* and papaya song, Lauruna, Tum, K Megan, Ajarn Chris and my Thammasat *nák sèuksãa*, K Matt, Connery, Poppy, my friends at Yoga Elements and to the many others who brighten my days in so many ways.

OUR READERS

Many thanks to the travellers who used the last edition and wrote to us with helpful hints, useful advice and interesting anecdotes:

A Henrik Ahlen, Laila Alhamad, Dave Allen, Leanne Allen, Luisa Alvarez, Erik Andersson, Biddy Andrews, Patrick Antony, Daci

Armstrong, Katharine Arpagaus, Nick Askew **B** Brant Bady, Sarah Bailey, Renske Bakker, Robert Baldwin, Sylvia Balmer-Bächler, Edwina Barrett, Linda Barrett, Colin & Sally Barrow, Brad Basigin, Sibylle Bauer, R Beck, Jeff Beedie, Siobhan Beirne, Balázs Békeffy, Mylene Belanger, Jinapon & Richard Bell, Josephine Bennett, Dom Bennison, Ebru Berberoglu, Malin Berger, Sharon Betzalel, Nikki Bibring, Jenny & Neil Billig, Rachel Black, Geoffrey Blaisdell, Jarni Blakkarly, Carl-Peter Block, Christel Bockting, Jan Bond, Mike Bond, Martin Boskovic, Harry Bosscha, Marian Bosscha, Winston Boteler, Gonzalo Botija, Jeff Bower, Joanne Boyd, Mark Brennan, Dave Brewer, Suzanne Brierley, Eric Brinkhof, Alexander Brunner, Mike & Theo Bruyns, Peter Buchan, Nikki Buran, Lyndsay Burns, John Bursa, Abdullah Bustani, Yvonne Butler, Gemma Byrne **C** Esly Caldwell, Ellen Campbell, Perego Carlo, Paula Carter, Hayden Cawte, Erik Cempel, Jose Cervera, Chris Chatfield, Jimmy & Madonna Chave, Thomas Christensen, John Christian, Katie Clare, Bornemann Claus, Pieter & Inge Clicteur, Sharon Coates, Giles Colliver, Creighton Connolly, Ben Cooper, Dave Cooper, Mark & Debbie Copple, Charles Cory, Wendell Covalt, Shane Cowlishaw, Matthew Crawford, Sarah Crookshanks, Judi Cunliffe, Jamesj Cunningham, Liz Curran, Natali Cvijeticanin **D** Martin Dahl, Peter Dalby, Josh Damink, Kelly Dare, Robin Davies, Robin & Eileen Davies, Alex & Kate Davis, Stuart & Pam Davis, Tamsin Davis, Chris De Looze, Paul & Ronald De Vries, Mironel De Wilde, Niels Lantz, Linzie Dela Cruz, Regine Denaegel, Guy Denning, Ryan Descoteau, Tina Dietz, Peter Dobo, Laura Dobson, Caitlin Dodd, David Dorey, Robert Downs, Joel Dresen, Lydie Du Basty, Gertjan Duiker, Lliam Dunn, Cyril Duvivier **E** Sjoerd Eckhardt, Christina Eiberg, Sam Elgar, Mougenot Emmanue, Thomas English, Karoly Erdei, Lotta Eriksson, Matt & Eileen Erskine, Eric Eustache, Sam Evans, Naomi Eves **F** Craig Faanes, Eran Farchi, Lucy Farey-Jones, Klaus Federle, Christopher Feierabend, Martin Feix, Anna Fennessy, Paul Ferber, Antoinette Figliola-Kaderli, Alex Findlay, Glyn Fisher, Jennifer Fisher, Stuart Fisher, Susan Fisher, Michelle Fitzpatrick, Klemen Flis, Noel Flor, Esther Forster, Daniel Fraser, E Fup **G** Cheryl Gallagher, Fernando Garcia, Richard Gatward, Louis Gempp, Kay George, Anne Giannini, Karen Ginzburg, Mark Given, Gemma Glanville, Dinah Goebel, Steve Goff, Dersal Goktas, Helen Gratil, Rick Graves, Jenessa Green, Brendan Greenslade, Daniela Grimaldi, Raimke Groothuizen, Dave Gubbins, Clara Guerra, Steve Gunn **H** Craig Hall, Dale Halvorson, Rick Hamann, Monica Hampton, Nina Hansen, Simon Hantly, Vidar Haraldsson, Oliver Harper, Dolev Hasid, K Hecht, Scott Heidecke, Jess Hemmings, Jane Hennessy, Michael Henriksen, Warren Hill, Sarah Hitchcock, Laura Hoar, Ben Hoffman, J Houtman, Tony Howard, Dave Howell, Gerry Howick, Adelle Hutton **I** Amy Igloi, Jackie Irwin, James **J** Jacobs, Ralpha Jacobson, Chris James, Torbjörn Jansson, Craig Jenkins, John & Jasmine Jenks, Rowan Jones, Rowan & Anna Jones, Christine Ju, Eva Jung **K** William Kaderli, Herman Kasper, Monica Kearns, Tong Kelly, Clare Kemp, Louise Kerridge, Nicole Kiefer, Denise Kinghorn, Ryan Kinkade, Jeff Kirschmann, Miriam Kläsener, Alexandra Klier, Else Koefoed, Patrick Kofler, Norbert Kotzan, Miki Koyama, Ben Kraijnbrink, Soeren Kristensen **K** Robert Ladd, Colin Lamont, Nick Lamperd, Simon Lange, Lars Larsen, Louise Larsen, Claus Lauridsen, Otto Lauterbach, Julie Lawson, Charlotte Le

Cornu, M Leach, Thomas Leba, Natalie Lecky, Jaimee Lederman, Che Lee, Lawrence Lee, Raphaela Levy-Moore, Leslie & Robert Lewinter-Suskind, Adam Lewis, Fil Lewitt, Joerg Lietzmann, Bruce Lindsay, Susan Luxford, Eugene Lyttle **M** Hilary Mackay, Patrick Mackenzie, Sandy Mackintosh, Stuart Maclachlan, Grant Mahy, Malcolm Mair, René Malenfant, Ales Markl, Eric Marsman, Peter May, Raleigh Mcclayton, Dan Mcdonald, Thomas Mcghie, Angus Mcintyre, Janet Mease, Amy Merrill, Suzanne Michels, Bernie Miller, Len & Mavis Mills, John Mitchell, Penny Moores, Julie Morgan, Jon Moslet, Bob Mott, Jaromir Mraz, Katrin Müller, Jennifer Mundy, Graham & Beverly Murphy, Caroline Murray **N** Gillian Naghten, Leni Neoptolemos, Nikolaj Nielsen, Aukes Niemer, Ivar Nilsen **O** Jessica Ober, Mike Ober, Rory O'Brien, Nicklas Olsson, Teba Orueta, Eric Owen **P** Ramu Palaniappan, Wendy Palen, Nikolaus Papp, Michael Parasol, Danielle Parsons, Carolina Paulsen, Tippy Payapvattanawong, Darren Pearce, Will Pearce, Helge Peglow, Alexander Vran, Mihaiela Pentuic, Katarina Persson, Rolf Peterson, Stan Petitdemange, Therese Picado, Carol Pimentel, Thomas Pinkowski, Archana Poddar, Peerapong Pongpipat, Ben & Julie Porter, Thornton Price, Paul Primavesi, Ross Pringle, Rebecca Pugh, Robert Purves **R** Brigitte Rahn, Colleen Ramsahoye, Lene Rasmussen, Susie Reddick, Steve Richards, Sarah Riches, Tammo Rieg, Guy Ries, Renault Robert, John Roberts, Alison Robinson, Karen Robinson, Lucy Robson, Andrew Rose, Janne Rueness **S** Leah Salomon, Khemara Samms, Sara Santefort, Megan Savage, Colleen Schamm, Thomas Schelken, John Schilling, David Schindler, Rainer Schmid, Stefan Schneider, Timo Schoch, Carrie Schwender, Gerhard Seidelmann,

Shilts Shah, Bill & Wannee Shaw, Karen Shuan, Luisa Siccia, Neil Silver, Zac Sim, Jamie Simson, Natassja Sinik, Troy & Bonnie Sirett, Tumer Sismanoglu, Dan Slater, Beckie Smith, Laura Smith, Lauren Smith, Michael Smith, Ilana Spector, Arno Spelbos, Robert Stagg, Debra Stanislawski, Dave Stark, Ben Starr, Katie Stewart, Teva Stewart, John Stroobant, Klaus Suemmerer, Attasit Suksomboon, Katy Sullivan, Raweewan Suwanalai, Elena Sving, John & Blanca Swanson, Marian Swart, Bryan Sweeney, Sally Swope, Edward Sylvester **T** Hayley Taylor, Tony Teoh, James Thackray, Jennifer Thomas, Amy Tsai, Anne Tuiskunen **U** Kym Unwin, **V** Jaime Valcarcel, Martijn Van Der Bas, Stefan Van Der Meeren, John Van Der Poel, Craig & Kym Van Straaten, Beata Varju, Monika Vazirani, Thomas Veale, Anthony Vella, Anna Verkade, Roberto Viajero, Chris Voaden, Anja Voigt, Jean Vortkamp **W** Joost Wagenaar, Rebecca Walser, Kathy Walter, Jan Wanetick, Doug Ward, A Watson, Karen Watson, Patsy Way, Lara Weigand, Lindsey Weller, Ros West, Brent Whelan, Natasha Whiting, Simon Wickens, Stefan Wicki, Aron Wilington, Michael Williams, Reg Williams, Barry Wilson, Lorri Wilson, Elke Withalm, Heather Wong, Anthony Wreford **Y** Ron Yaary, Briony Yorke, Lisbet Young, Rodger Young **Z** Celine Zammit, Sven Zimmerman, Mohamad Zolkipli, Nico Zurcher,

ACKNOWLEDGMENTS

Many thanks to the following for the use of their content:
Globe on title page ©Mountain High Maps 1993 Digital Wisdom, Inc.

Index

INDEX

INDEX

000 Map pages
000 Photograph pages

000 Map pages
000 Photograph pages

000 Map pages
000 Photograph pages

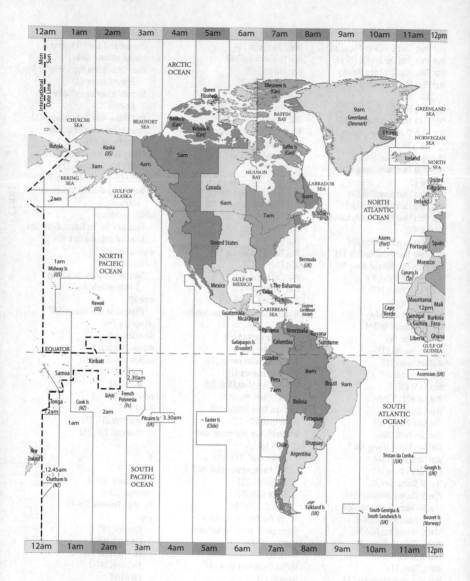